LAW OF ENVIRONMENTAL AND TOXIC TORTS

CASES, MATERIALS AND PROBLEMS

By

Gerald W. Boston
Professor of Law
Thomas M. Cooley Law School

M. Stuart Madden
Charles A. Frueauff Research Professor of Law
Pace University School of Law

AMERICAN CASEBOOK SERIES®

WEST PUBLISHING CO.
ST. PAUL, MINN., 1994

American Casebook Series, the key symbol appearing on the front cover
and the WP symbol are registered trademarks of West Publishing Co.
Registered in the U.S. Patent and Trademark Office.

COPYRIGHT © 1994 By WEST PUBLISHING CO.
          610 Opperman Drive
          P.O. Box 64526
          St. Paul, MN 55164–0526
          1–800–328–9352

Library of Congress Cataloging-in-Publication Data

Boston, Gerald W., 1942–
    Law of environmental and toxic torts : cases, materials, and
problems / Gerald W. Boston, M. Stuart Madden.
          p.   cm.
    Includes index.
    ISBN 0–314–03354–8
    1. Liability for environmental damages—United States—Cases.
2. Toxic torts—United States—Cases. I. Madden, M. Stuart, 1948–
. II. Title.
    KF1298.A7B67   1994
    346.7303'8—dc20
    [347.30638]   93–42310
                                                          CIP

ISBN 0–314–03354–8

 TEXT IS PRINTED ON 10% POST
CONSUMER RECYCLED PAPER    PRINTED WITH
SOY INK

(B. & M.) Environ.Torts ACB

Foreword

To my new wife Susan, who is becoming accustomed to the role of a partner who must live with one who lives to write. I also wish to express my deepest thanks to my assistant, Mary Beth Peranteau, who worked valiantly to meet deadlines and maintained good humor throughout.

G.W.B.

For Mary-Anne O'Donnell Madden, for her love and support, and for Christopher and Michael.

M.S.M.

*

Summary of Contents

	Page
FOREWORD	iii
TABLE OF CASES	xxi
TABLE OF STATUTES AND REGULATIONS	xxxi
TABLE OF RESTATEMENT CITATIONS	xxxvii

Introduction 1

Chapter One. Overview: Conflicting Perspectives on the Adequacy of the Tort System 3
A. Generally 3
B. Special Characteristics of Environmental Tort Claims 6

Chapter Two. Trespass Actions in Environmental Law 21
A. General Principles of Trespass 21
B. Judicial Applications of Trespass 26

Chapter Three. Nuisance: The Comprehensive Environmental Tort Theory 38
A. Nuisance: An Introduction 38
B. Public Nuisance 39
C. Private Nuisance 57
D. Judicial Applications of Private and Public Nuisance Theories ... 78

Chapter Four. Strict Liability for Abnormally Dangerous Activities 94
A. Historical Perspective 94
B. Relationship To Nuisance 96
C. Restatement (Second) of Torts Standard of Liability 97
D. Rationales for Imposing Strict Liability 101
E. Judicial Applications of Strict Liability 106
F. What Constitutes an "Abnormally Dangerous" Activity? 112
G. Note on Emerging Issues in Nuisance and Strict Liability 120

Chapter Five. Remedies and Compensable Interests 140
A. Injunctions: The Comparative Injury Calculus 140
B. Standards for Granting Injunctions: Balancing the Equities 143
C. Damages for Injury to Real Property 153
D. Damages to Persons and Present Liability for Prospective Harm ... 165

Page

**Chapter Six. Environmental Statutory Regulation and the
Common Law: Preemption and Implied Rights** **213**
A. General Principles of Federal Preclusion and Enhancement of
    Private Rights 213
B. State Judicial Considerations of Preemption: A Complementary
    Approach 247
C. Negligence Per Se 251

Chapter Seven. Toxic Products, Processes and Services..... **261**
A. Introduction: Some General Principles 261
B. Toxic Product Claims by Type.................................... 271

Chapter Eight. Causation **339**
A. Causation: Did the Toxic Substance Cause Plaintiff's Harm?.. 339
B. Plaintiff Indeterminacy... 389
C. Did The Defendant Cause Plaintiff's Harm: The Indeterminate
    Defendant Problem 403
D. Apportionment of the Harm or Damage 425

**Chapter Nine. Workplace Injuries and Toxic Substances:
Intersection of Workers' Compensation and Tort Liabil-
ity** **442**
A. Introduction to the Workers' Compensation System............... 442
B. Avoiding The Exclusivity Bar 446
C. Occupational Disease Acts....................................... 457
D. Occupational Safety and Health Requirements 469

**Chapter Ten. CERCLA: Liability and Compensation for
Cleaning up Hazardous Substances** **475**
A. Overview of CERCLA.. 475
B. Government Actions.. 478
C. Parties Liable Under CERCLA 489
D. Private Cost Recovery Actions................................... 496
E. Allocating The Costs: Contribution Actions and Other Devices 503
F. Indemnification Agreements...................................... 518
G. Informational Importance of CERCLA............................. 522

Chapter Eleven. Insurance **527**
A. Introduction 527
B. Insurance Coverage for Environmental and Toxic Torts.......... 529
C. Special Insurance Problems of Environmental Cleanups.......... 542

Chapter Twelve. Defenses.. **567**
A. Introduction 567
B. Statutes of Limitation for Injury to Real Property............. 568
C. Statutes of Limitation in Product and Occupational Exposure
    Cases... 580
D. Successive Actions and Statutes of Limitation.................. 590
E. Statutes of Repose 602

Page
F.   Revival Statutes --- 605
G.   Contributory Fault/Assumption of the Risk in Real Property
        Actions --- 606
H.   Plaintiff's Conduct as a Bar in Toxic Products Cases ------------- 612

**Chapter Thirteen.   Special Problems in Trial Management
    and Settlement of Toxics Litigation** -------------------------- **615**
A.   Class Actions --- 615
B.   Other Aggregative or Disaggregative Procedures ------------------ 620
C.   Asbestos Litigation: Classes, Consolidations, Bifurcations and
        Multidistrict Litigation --- 623
D.   Judicial Case Management --- 637
E.   Settlements -- 648
F.   Choice–of–Law Problems --- 655
G.   Judicial Management of Scientific and Technology Issues -------- 664

Index -- 671

*

Table of Contents

	Page
FOREWORD	iii
TABLE OF CASES	xxi
TABLE OF STATUTES AND REGULATIONS	xxxi
TABLE OF RESTATEMENT CITATIONS	xxxvii
Introduction	1

Chapter One. Overview: Conflicting Perspectives on the Adequacy of the Tort System — **3**

A. Generally	3
1. Tort Goals and Their Application	4
2. Typical Environmental or Toxic Tort Claims	5
B. Special Characteristics of Environmental Tort Claims	6
1. Generally	6
2. Long Latency Periods	7
3. Proof of Causation	7
4. Role of Expert Scientific or Medical Testimony	8
5. Relationship Of Environmental Tort Law to Statutory Environmental Law	9
6. Recurring Themes in Environmental Torts	10
Troyen A. Brennan, Environmental Torts	10
Notes and Questions	13
Michael D. Axline, Navigating the Toxic Bywaters of the Industrial Age	13
Notes and Questions	16
Daniel A. Farber, Toxic Causation	16
Note	20

Chapter Two. Trespass Actions in Environmental Law — **21**

A. General Principles of Trespass	21
1. The Intent Requirement	21
2. Possessory Interest	22
3. Extent of Invasion	23
4. Relationship to Nuisance	23
5. Continuing Trespass	25
6. Damages Recoverable	25
B. Judicial Applications of Trespass	26
Railroad Commission of Texas v. Manziel	26
Notes and Questions	27
Bradley v. American Smelting and Refining Company	28
Notes and Questions	33

Page

Chapter Three. Nuisance: The Comprehensive Environmental Tort Theory.. **38**
A. Nuisance: An Introduction 38
B. Public Nuisance.. 39
    1. Introduction... 39
    2. Unreasonableness of the Interference 39
    3. What Is a "Public Right?"................................. 40
        State of New York v. Schenectady Chemicals, Inc. 41
        Notes and Questions...................................... 44
    4. Private Action for Public Nuisance—The Special Injury
        Rule.. 45
        State of Louisiana, ex rel. William J. Guste, Jr. v. M/V Testbank 47
        Notes and Questions...................................... 51
    5. A Note on Economic Principles 53
    6. Physical Harm as Constituting Special Injury 54
    7. Equitable Actions for Public Nuisance 56
        a. Private Attorneys General............................. 56
        b. Class Actions 56
        c. Associational Standing 57
C. Private Nuisance 57
    1. Generally.. 57
    2. Nature of the Interest Interfered With.................... 58
        Adkins v. Thomas Solvent Company 59
        Notes and Questions...................................... 65
    3. Corrective Justice and Utilitarianism 66
        Bamford v. Turnley...................................... 68
        Notes and Questions...................................... 69
    4. Private Nuisance: The Restatement Position............... 71
    5. Private Nuisance: The Basis of Liability................. 74
        a. Intentional and Unreasonable......................... 74
            (i)   The Intent Requirement 74
            (ii) The Unreasonableness Requirement.............. 75
            (iii) Gravity of the Harm Suffered................. 75
            (iv) Utility of Defendant's Conduct 76
            (v)   Other Considerations on Unreasonableness......... 77
        b. Negligent or Reckless Conduct........................ 77
        Problem 78
D. Judicial Applications of Private and Public Nuisance Theories 78
    The Village of Wilsonville v. SCA Services, Inc............. 78
    Notes and Questions.. 87
    Carpenter v. The Double R Cattle Company, Inc. 89
    Notes and Questions.. 92
    Problem 92

Chapter Four. Strict Liability for Abnormally Dangerous Activities **94**
A. Historical Perspective... 94
B. Relationship To Nuisance 96
C. Restatement (Second) of Torts Standard of Liability............. 97
    1. Relationship to Negligence................................ 98

Page

C. Restatement (Second) of Torts Standard of Liability—Continued
 2. Question of Law _____ 98
 3. Common Usage _____ 99
 4. Locational Appropriateness _____ 99
 5. Value of the Activity to the Community _____ 100
D. Rationales for Imposing Strict Liability _____ 101
 1. Internalization of All Costs: The Enterprise Model _____ 101
 2. Calabresi Model _____ 102
 3. Nonreciprocal Risks Model _____ 103
 4. Epstein's Corrective Justice Model _____ 104
 5. Posner: Reduction in Levels of Activity _____ 105
 6. Proposed Restatement Approach _____ 105
E. Judicial Applications of Strict Liability _____ 106
 State, Department of Environmental Protection v. Ventron Corporation 106
 Notes and Questions _____ 110
F. What Constitutes an "Abnormally Dangerous" Activity? _____ 112
 1. Boundaries to Strict Liability _____ 112
  a. Marketing of Products _____ 112
   Notes and Questions _____ 114
  b. Adequacy of Negligence _____ 114
   Notes and Questions _____ 116
  c. Underground Storage Tanks _____ 117
  d. Disposal of Hazardous Wastes _____ 117
 2. Vicarious Responsibility _____ 119
 3. Causation _____ 119
G. Note on Emerging Issues in Nuisance and Strict Liability _____ 120
 1. Introduction: Setting the Stage _____ 120
 2. Application to Vertical Relationships _____ 121
  Philadelphia Electric Company v. Hercules, Inc. _____ 121
  Notes and Questions _____ 125
  T & E Industries v. Safety Light Corporation _____ 126
  Notes and Questions _____ 131
 3. Knowledge of the Danger as a Prerequisite to Strict Liability _____ 132
  T & E Industries v. Safety Light Corporation _____ 132
  Notes and Questions _____ 135
  Problem _____ 137

Chapter Five. Remedies and Compensable Interests _____ **140**
A. Injunctions: The Comparative Injury Calculus _____ 140
 Notes and Questions _____ 143
B. Standards for Granting Injunctions: Balancing the Equities ____ 143
 Dan B. Dobbs, Law of Remedies § 5.7(2) _____ 144
 Boomer v. Atlantic Cement Company, Inc. _____ 147
 Notes and Questions _____ 151
C. Damages for Injury to Real Property _____ 153
 1. Harm to the Physical Condition of Land _____ 153
  a. The General Rules _____ 153
  b. Other Approaches Limiting Recovery _____ 156
   Notes and Questions _____ 158

Page

C. Damages for Injury to Real Property—Continued
    c. Environmental Damages: An Emerging Approach?.... 159
  2. Loss of Use or Enjoyment ------------------------------------- 162
    Davey Compressor Company v. City of Delray Beach --------------- 162
  3. Personal Discomfort and Annoyance ----------------------- 164
D. Damages to Persons and Present Liability for Prospective
  Harm --- 165
  1. Introduction: The Issues Identified ----------------------- 165
  2. Judicial Treatment of Increased Risks and Medical Moni-
    toring --- 166
    Ayers v. Township of Jackson -------------------------------- 166
    Notes and Questions --- 179
  3. Note on Claims for Enhanced Risk of Future Harm -------- 179
    a. The Prevailing Rule ------------------------------------ 179
    b. Some Contrary Opinions -------------------------------- 181
    c. Autonomy Interests ------------------------------------ 182
  4. Note on Post–Exposure, Pre–Symptom Medical Surveil-
    lance Damages --- 184
    a. Supporting Authority ----------------------------------- 184
    b. Elements of the Surveillance Interest ----------------- 185
    Problem --- 186
    c. The Trend --- 186
    d. ALI Reporters' Study ---------------------------------- 187
    e. Contrary Views --------------------------------------- 188
    f. Generalized Scientific Studies to Determine Increased
      Risk -- 189
    g. Medical Monitoring under CERCLA ------------------- 190
    h. Lump Sum or Periodic Payments --------------------- 191
  5. Judicial Treatment of Fear of Future Disease and Punitive
    Damages -- 191
    Sterling v. Velsicol Chemical Corporation --------------------- 191
    Note and Questions -- 199
  6. Emotional Distress, Fear of Cancer and Enhanced Risk --- 199
    a. Emerging Standards ----------------------------------- 199
    b. Physical Harm Requirements or Surrogates ----------- 201
    c. Some Contrary Views ---------------------------------- 202
    d. Literature -- 203
    Problem --- 203
  7. Note on Punitive Damages ------------------------------- 204
    a. Constitutional Limitations ---------------------------- 205
    b. Punitives in Environmental Tort Cases --------------- 208
    c. Government Suits for Punitive Damages -------------- 209
    d. Some Interpretive Hypotheses ------------------------- 210

Page

Chapter Six. Environmental Statutory Regulation and the Common Law: Preemption and Implied Rights 213

A. General Principles of Federal Preclusion and Enhancement of Private Rights -- 213
    1. Introduction -- 213
    2. Regulation as Enhancing Common Law Rights -------------- 214
    3. Regulation as Precluding Common Law Rights -------------- 215
    4. Supreme Court Decisions Precluding Common Law Rights 216
        Milwaukee v. Illinois -- 216
        Notes and Questions -- 220
        International Paper Co. v. Ouellette --------------------------- 225
        Notes and Questions -- 232
        Cipollone v. Liggett Group ----------------------------------- 232
        Notes and Questions -- 243
        Shaw v. Dow Brands, Inc. -------------------------------------- 244
        Notes and Questions -- 246
B. State Judicial Considerations of Preemption: A Complementary Approach --- 247
C. Negligence Per Se --- 251
    Sheila Bush, Can You Get There From Here? Noncompliance With Environmental Regulation as Negligence Per Se in Tort Cases ------- 252
    Notes and Questions --- 256
    Problem --- 259

Chapter Seven. Toxic Products, Processes and Services ----- 261

A. Introduction: Some General Principles ------------------------------ 261
    1. Negligence -- 262
    2. Breach of Warranty -- 262
        a. Express Warranty -- 262
        b. Implied Warranty of Merchantability ---------------------- 263
        c. Implied Warranty of Fitness for a Particular Purpose 263
        d. Proper Plaintiffs to a Warranty Claim ----------------- 264
        e. Warranty Disclaimers and Limitations ------------------ 264
    3. Strict Liability in Tort --------------------------------------- 265
    4. Misrepresentation --- 267
    5. Restatement (Second) of Torts § 402A: Strict Liability and New Approaches --- 268
B. Toxic Product Claims by Type-- 271
    1. Asbestos --- 271
        a. Liability Standards and Defenses ----------------------- 271
        Borel v. Fibreboard Paper Products Corporation -------------- 271
        Notes and Questions -- 274
        b. Punitive Damages in Asbestos Litigation ------------- 279
        Fischer v. Johns-Manville Corporation --------------------- 280
        Notes and Questions -- 284
    2. Alcohol --- 287
        Notes and Questions -- 291
    3. Prescription Pharmaceuticals, Biological Products and Medical Devices -- 292
        a. Pharmaceuticals and comment k ----------------------- 293
        Brown v. Superior Court ----------------------------------- 293
        Notes and Questions -- 297

Page

B. Toxic Product Claims by Type—Continued
    b. Biological Products: Special Problems of AIDS–Contaminated Blood Products 299
        McKee v. Miles Laboratories 299
        Notes and Questions 302
    c. Medical Devices 305
        Hegna v. E.I. DU Pont de Nemours and Company 305
        Notes and Questions 308
  4. Chemicals 308
    a. Liability Standards for Warnings 308
        Werckenthein v. Bucher Petrochemical Company 308
        Notes and Questions 312
    b. Bulk Suppliers of Chemicals: The Sophisticated User Defense 314
        Swan v. I.P., Inc. 315
        Notes and Questions 324
    c. Foreseeable Users and Uses 324
        High v. Westinghouse Electric Corp. 324
        Notes and Questions 328
  5. Agricultural Chemicals: Use of Express Warranty Theory 328
    Ciba–Geigy Corporation v. Alter 328
    Notes and Questions 334
    Problem 337

Chapter Eight. Causation **339**
A. Causation: Did the Toxic Substance Cause Plaintiff's Harm? .. 339
  1. Introductory Principles 339
    a. Problems With Causation Terminology 340
    b. The Dual Causation Question 342
    c. Early Use of Probabilistic Evidence 345
    Notes and Questions 348
  2. The Scientific Method: Toxicology and Epidemiology 348
    Gerald W. Boston, A Mass Exposure Model of Toxic Causation: The Content of Scientific Proof and the Regulatory Experience 349
  3. Standards of Admissibility of Scientific Evidence 357
    Daubert v. Merrell Dow Pharmaceuticals, Inc. 359
    Notes and Questions 365
    Problem 365
  4. Sufficiency of the Scientific Evidence: Nature and Quantum of Proof 368
    a. Minimalist Requirements 368
        Notes and Questions 369
    b. Rigorous Standards of Sufficiency: The Bendectin Litigation 371
        Brock v. Merrell Dow Pharmaceuticals, Inc. 371
        Notes and Questions 377
        Problem 385
    c. Note on Exposure as an Element of Causation 386
B. Plaintiff Indeterminacy 389
  1. Individualized Model: *Allen v. United States* 389
    Notes and Questions 391

Page

B. Plaintiff Indeterminacy—Continued
    2. The Collective Model: Agent Orange ----------------- 393
        In re Agent Orange Product Liability Litigation ----------- 394
        Notes and Questions ------------------------------ 396
C. Did The Defendant Cause Plaintiff's Harm: The Indeterminate
    Defendant Problem ------------------------------------ 403
    1. Some Devices to Overcome Defendant Indeterminacy ------ 403
        a. Alternative Liability ------------------------- 403
        b. Concert of Action Theory ---------------------- 404
        c. Enterprise or Industry–Wide Liability --------- 404
        d. Market Share Liability ------------------------ 405
            Notes and Questions ------------------------- 406
    2. Market Share at the Boundaries: Factor VIII and Lead
        Paint -- 410
        a. Factor VIII and Contaminated Blood Products --------- 410
            Smith v. Cutter Biological, Inc. ----------- 410
            Notes and Questions ------------------------- 418
            Problem ------------------------------------- 418
        b. Lead Paint Pigments --------------------------- 420
            Notes and Questions ------------------------- 422
        c. Note on Lead Paint and Causation ------------- 423
D. Apportionment of the Harm or Damage ------------------- 425
    1. Apportionment Between Plaintiff and Defendant ------- 425
        Dafler v. Raymark Industries, Inc. -------------- 425
        Notes and Questions ----------------------------- 431
    2. Apportionment or Joint and Several Liability Among Tort-
        feasors -- 434
        Michie v. Great Lakes Steel Division ------------ 434
        Notes and Questions ----------------------------- 437
        Problem --- 439

Chapter Nine. Workplace Injuries and Toxic Substances:
Intersection of Workers' Compensation and Tort Liabil-
ity --- 442
A. Introduction to the Workers' Compensation System -------------- 442
    1. A Bit of History ---------------------------------- 442
    2. Issue Preclusion ---------------------------------- 443
B. Avoiding The Exclusivity Bar -------------------------- 446
    1. The Intentional Tort Exception to Exclusivity -------------- 446
        Notes and Questions ----------------------------- 447
    2. Judicial Rationales for Creating the Exception -------------- 448
        a. The "Nonaccident" Rationale ------------------- 448
        b. Larson's Approach to the Accident Exception ----------- 448
        c. The "Severed" Relationship Rationale -------------- 448
    3. The "Intentional" Tort Standard Used by States ----------- 449
        a. The Majority Rule: Deliberate Intent to Cause Injury 449
        b. "Substantial Certainty" Test of Intent ------------- 449
        c. Wilful, Wanton or Reckless Test --------------- 449
        d. Legislative Standards of Intent --------------- 449

Page

B. Avoiding The Exclusivity Bar—Continued
    4. Toxic Exposure Cases 450
    5. Deceit Exception 451
        Notes and Questions 452
    6. Actions by Spouses or Children Against Employers 453
        a. Claims by Spouses 453
        b. Claims by Children 454
    7. Fetal Protection Policies 455
    8. Take–Home Toxics 456
    9. Aggravation of Injury Exception 456
C. Occupational Disease Acts 457
    1. Introduction 457
    2. Judicial Application of Occupational Disease Acts 458
        Palmer v. Del Webb's High Sierra 459
        Notes and Questions 461
    3. Distinguishing Diseases Incident to One's Employment
        From the Ordinary Diseases of Life 462
    4. Intentional Tort Exception in Occupational Diseases 463
    5. A Note on Environmental Tobacco Smoke 464
        Note and Questions 466
    6. Employees' Actions for Relief 466
        a. Injunctive Relief 466
        b. Claims Based on Workers' Compensation Acts 467
        c. Claims Based on Negligence 468
        d. Miscellaneous Contexts 469
D. Occupational Safety and Health Requirements 469
    1. Toxic and Hazardous Substances 469
    2. OSHA Recordkeeping Requirements 470
    3. Hazardous Chemicals 471
    4. The Role of Noncompliance and Compliance 472

Chapter Ten. CERCLA: Liability and Compensation for Cleaning up Hazardous Substances 475
A. Overview of CERCLA 475
    1. Introduction 475
    2. Principal Statutory Provisions 477
B. Government Actions 478
    1. Release or Threatened Release 479
    2. Hazardous Substance 479
    3. Facility 480
    4. Damages Recoverable by the Government 480
    5. The Government Action: United States v. Monsanto 481
        Notes and Questions 484
    6. Divisibility of Harm 486
        Notes and Questions 488
C. Parties Liable Under CERCLA 489
    1. Owners and Operators 489
        Problem 491
    2. Liability of Parent Corporations and Successors 492

Page

C. Parties Liable Under CERCLA—Continued
 a. Parent Corporations 492
 b. Shareholders 493
 c. Successors 493
 3. Lenders as Owners 494
 4. Liability of Arrangers 495
D. Private Cost Recovery Actions 496
 1. What Are Private Cost Recovery Actions? 496
 2. Plaintiff's Prima Facie Case 497
 3. The Compliance With NCP 498
 4. Proof of Compliance as Affecting Liability or Damages 499
 5. Recovery of Attorneys' Fees 500
 6. Causation in Private Cost Recovery Actions 501
E. Allocating The Costs: Contribution Actions and Other Devices 503
 1. Standards For Obtaining Contribution 503
  United States v. R.W. Meyer, Inc. 505
  Note and Questions 508
 2. Approaches to Allocating Costs 509
  a. Per Capita 509
  b. Comparative Fault 509
  c. Comparative Causation 509
  d. Gore Amendment 510
 3. Causation in Contribution Actions 511
 4. Rights to a Jury Trial 512
 5. Effect of Settlement With the Government 512
  a. Effect of Settlement on Contribution 513
   (i) CERCLA 's Provisions 513
   (ii) Judicial Review of Settlements 514
   (iii) Matters Settled 514
  b. Diversity of Views on Non–Settlor Liability 515
   (i) Dollar Reduction 515
   (ii) Proportionate Reduction 515
   (iii) Settlement Criteria 516
   (iv) Contribution Protection and Notice 517
   (v) Effect of Private Partial Settlements 517
F. Indemnification Agreements 518
 1. The Statutory Provision 518
 2. Are Such Agreements Permitted Under CERCLA? 519
 3. How Should Such Agreements Be Construed? 520
  Problem 521
G. Informational Importance of CERCLA 522
 1. Overview of the ATSDR 522
 2. Health Investigations; Toxicological Profiles 523
 3. Health Assessments 523
  Problem 524

	Page
Chapter Eleven. Insurance	**527**
A. Introduction	527
B. Insurance Coverage for Environmental and Toxic Torts	529
1. Occurrence	529
a. The General Rule	529
b. Differing Views	530
c. Objective versus Subjective Test	531
Problem	532
2. Bodily Injury and Emotional Harm	533
3. Property Damage	534
4. Triggers of Coverage for Bodily Injury	536
a. Exposure	536
b. Manifestation/Discovery	538
c. Injury-in-Fact	538
d. Multiple or Continuous Trigger	539
5. Triggers of Coverage for Property Damage	540
6. Number of Occurrences	541
C. Special Insurance Problems of Environmental Cleanups	542
1. Pay "As Damages" and "Suit" Controversies	542
Coakley v. Maine Bonding and Casualty Company	543
Notes and Questions	551
2. Sudden and Accidental Pollution Exclusion	553
a. Sudden and Accidental Exception to the Pollution Exclusion	554
Problem	557
b. Does the Claim Involve Release of a "Pollutant" into the Atmosphere?	558
3. Absolute Pollution Exclusion	559
4. Personal Injury Endorsement	561
5. Owned Property Exclusion	563
6. Known Risk Limitation	565
Chapter Twelve. Defenses	**567**
A. Introduction	567
B. Statutes of Limitation for Injury to Real Property	568
Mangini v. Aerojet–General Corporation	568
Notes and Questions	574
C. Statutes of Limitation in Product and Occupational Exposure Cases	580
1. Date of the Injury	580
2. Accrual Based on the Discovery Rule	581
Evenson v. Osmose Wood Preserving Company of America, Inc.	582
Notes and Questions	586
Problem	589
D. Successive Actions and Statutes of Limitation	590
Wilson v. Johns-Manville Sales Corporation	591
Notes and Questions	596
E. Statutes of Repose	602
1. How They Differ From Statutes of Limitation	602
2. Constitutional Questions	604

Page

F. Revival Statutes ---- 605
G. Contributory Fault/Assumption of the Risk in Real Property
    Actions ---- 606
    1. Defenses to Nuisance and Real Property Actions ---- 606
    2. Contributory Negligence or Fault ---- 606
    3. Assumption of the Risk ---- 607
    4. Coming to the Nuisance ---- 608
    5. Sale of Property Defense ---- 610
H. Plaintiff's Conduct as a Bar in Toxic Products Cases ---- 612

**Chapter Thirteen. Special Problems in Trial Management
    and Settlement of Toxics Litigation** ---- **615**
A. Class Actions ---- 615
    Notes and Questions ---- 618
B. Other Aggregative or Disaggregative Procedures ---- 620
    1. Consolidation ---- 620
    2. Bifurcation of Claims and Issues ---- 621
    3. Multidistrict Litigation ---- 622
C. Asbestos Litigation: Classes, Consolidations, Bifurcations and
    Multidistrict Litigation ---- 623
    In re Fibreboard Corporation ---- 624
    Notes and Questions ---- 630
D. Judicial Case Management ---- 637
    1. "Lone Pine" Orders ---- 638
       Notes and Questions ---- 640
    2. Protective Orders ---- 643
       a. Nondisclosure Orders ---- 643
       b. Donor Identification ---- 643
       c. Sanctions for Violation of Protective Orders ---- 645
       d. Gag Orders; Sealing of Documents ---- 646
       e. State Statutes ---- 647
E. Settlements ---- 648
    1. General Strategy ---- 648
    2. Releases of Future Injuries ---- 650
    3. Green Cards and Medical Monitoring ---- 651
       a. General Approach ---- 651
       b. Three Mile Island ---- 651
       c. Fernald Litigation ---- 652
    4. Distribution of Settlement Funds ---- 653
    5. Value Protection Programs ---- 653
F. Choice–of–Law Problems ---- 655
    1. Lex Loci Delecti: Vested Rights ---- 656
    2. Most Significant Relationship ---- 656
    3. Strongest Governmental Interest ---- 656
    4. Other Approaches ---- 657
    5. Proposals for Reform ---- 657
       a. Federal Substantive Law ---- 657
       b. Federal Common Law ---- 659
       c. Federalized Choice–of–Law ---- 661

Page

F.   Choice–of–Law Problems—Continued
        Notes and Questions 663
G.   Judicial Management of Scientific and Technology Issues 664
        1. Use of Court–Appointed Experts 665
        2. Special Masters 666
        3. Reasons for Underutilization 667
        4. Recommendations for Change 667
        Notes and Questions 669

INDEX 671

Table of Cases

The principal cases are in bold type. Cases cited or discussed in the text are roman type. References are to pages. Cases cited in principal cases and within other quoted materials are not included.

Abate v. ACHS, Inc., 634
Abel v. Eli Lilly and Co., 407, 408
Abellon v. Hartford Ins. Co., 534
Aceto Agr. Chemicals Corp., United States v., 495, 496
Acevedo v. Consolidated Edison Co. of New York, Inc., 451
Acosta v. Babcock & Wilcox, 432
Acton Corp., United States v., 516
Acushnet River & New Bedford Harbor, In re, 516
Acushnet River & New Bedford Harbor: Proceedings re Alleged PCB Pollution, In re, 512
Adkins v. Thomas Solvent Co., 57, **59,** 66, 69, 157, 654
Aetna Cas. and Sur. Co., Inc. v. Pintlar Corp., 553
Agent Orange Product Liability Litigation, In re, 781 F.Supp. 902, pp. 5, 398
Agent Orange Product Liability Litigation, In re, 611 F.Supp. 1267, p. 398
Agent Orange Product Liability Litigation, In re, 611 F.Supp. 1223, pp. 384, 389, 398
Agent Orange Product Liability Litigation, In re, 597 F.Supp. 740, pp. 393, **394,** 396, 397, 404
Agent Orange Product Liability Litigation, In re, 580 F.Supp. 690, p. 663
Agent Orange Product Liability Litigation, In re, 506 F.Supp. 762, p. 618
Agent Orange Product Liability Litigation, In re, 506 F.Supp. 737, p. 659
Agent Orange Product Liability Litigation, In re, 104 F.R.D. 559, pp. 646, 653
A.H. Robins Co., Inc., In re, 880 F.2d 769, p. 616
A.H. Robins Co., Inc., In re, 880 F.2d 709, p. 619
Aim Ins. Co. v. Culcasi, 533
AIU Ins. Co. v. Superior Court, 552
Akau v. Olohana Corp., 56
Alcan Aluminum Corp., United States v., 990 F.2d 711, pp. 487, 496.

Alcan Aluminum Corp., United States v., 964 F.2d 252, pp. 487, 488, 489, 496, 504
Alexander, United States v., 517
Allen v. A.H. Robins Co., Inc., 587
Allen v. United States, 816 F.2d 1417, pp. 392, 393, 396, 398
Allen v. United States, 588 F.Supp. 247, pp. 389, 392, 586
Allied Corp. v. Acme Solvents Reclaiming, Inc., 812 F.Supp. 124, p. 494
Allied Corp. v. ACME Solvent Reclaiming, Inc., 771 F.Supp. 219, pp. 515, 516, 517
Allied Corp. v. Acme Solvents Reclaiming, Inc., 494
Allied Corp. v. Frola, 125, 515
Allstate Ins. Co. v. Freeman, 531
Alyeska Pipeline Service Co. v. Wilderness Soc., 500, 501
Ambrogi v. Gould, Inc., 190, 499
Amendola v. Kansas City Southern Ry. Co., 180, 201
American Federation of Labor and Congress of Indus. Organizations v. Occupational Safety and Health Admin., 470
American Home Products Corp. v. Liberty Mut. Ins. Co., 748 F.2d 760, p. 539
American Home Products Corp. v. Liberty Mut. Ins. Co., 565 F.Supp. 1485, p. 556
American Motorists Ins. Co. v. E. R. Squibb & Sons, Inc., 538
American Mut. Liability Ins. Co. v. Neville Chemical Co., 530
American Pipe & Const. Co. v. Utah, 616
American Red Cross v. Travelers Indem. Co., 541
AM Intern., Inc. v. International Forging Equipment Corp., 519, 520
Amland Properties Corp. v. Aluminum Co. of America, 808 F.Supp. 1187, pp. 517, 518
Amland Properties Corp. v. Aluminum Co. of America, 711 F.Supp. 784, pp. 125, 480, 498, 499
Ammons v. Wysong & Miles Co., 387
Amorello v. Monsanto Corp., 387

Amphitheaters, Inc. v. Portland Meadows, 36

Anderson v. Eli Lilly & Co., 407

Anderson v. Marathon Petroleum Co., 119

Anderson v. W.R. Grace & Co., 55, 200, 201

Andrulonis v. United States, 303

Appalachian Ins. Co. v. Liberty Mut. Ins. Co., 565

Arcade Water Dist. v. United States, 577

Arlington Forest Associates v. Exxon Corp., 117

Armory Park Neighborhood Ass'n v. Episcopal Community Services in Arizona, 57

Armstrong World Industries, Inc. v. Aetna Casualty & Surety Co., Reliance Insurance Company; Fibreboard Corporation v. Pacific Indemnity Company; GAF Corporation v. Columbia Casualty Company, 540

Arnoldt v. Ashland Oil, Inc., 71, 208

Artesian Water Co. v. Government of New Castle County, 499, 502, 503

Asbestos Litigation, In re, 278

Asbestos Products Liability Litigation (No. VI), In re, 634

Ascon Properties, Inc. v. Illinois Union Ins. Co., 560

Ascon Properties, Inc. v. Mobil Oil Co., 479

Ashland Oil, Inc. v. Sonford Products Corp., 495

Askey v. Occidental Chemical Corp., 176, 187

Ate Fixture Fab v. Wagner, 467

Atlantic Mut. Ins. Co. v. McFadden, 558

Atlas Chemical Industries, Inc. v. Anderson, 524 S.W.2d 681, p. 575

Atlas Chemical Industries, Inc. v. Anderson, 514 S.W.2d 309, p. 102

Atwood v. Warner Elec. Brake and Clutch Co., Inc., 642

Augustine v. A.C. & S. Corp., 389

Ayers v. Township of Jackson, 88, 165, **166,** 179, 180, 184, 185, 186, 187, 188, 199, 201, 596

A.Y. McDonald Industries, Inc. v. Insurance Co. of North America, 536, 552

Ayo v. Johns–Manville Sales Corp., 599

Bagley v. Controlled Environment Corp., 256

Baldwin v. McClendon, 57

Bales v. Gun, 590

Ball v. Joy Technologies, Inc., 188, 203

Bamford v. Turnley, 68, 69, 73

Barber v. Pittsburgh Corning Corp., 463

Barth v. Firestone Tire and Rubber Co., 673 F.Supp. 1466, p. 191

Barth v. Firestone Tire and Rubber Co., 661 F.Supp. 193, p. 189

Bausch & Lomb Inc. v. Utica Mut. Ins. Co., 551, 564

Baxter v. Ford Motor Co., 267

Beauchamp v. Dow Chemical Co., 449, 450

Belik v. Advance Process Supply Co., 314

Bell v. Macy's California, 454, 455

Belle Fourche Pipeline Co. v. Elmore Livestock Co., 158

Bendectin Litigation, In re, 857 F.2d 290, p. 621

Bendectin Litig., In re, M.D.L. No. 486, Doc. No. 1577, 622

Bendectin Litig., In re, M.D.L. No. 486, Doc. No. 3051, 622

Bennett v. Mallinckrodt, Inc., 249

Bergsoe Metal Corp., In re, 494

Berry v. Armstrong Rubber Co., 387

Beshada v. Johns–Manville Products Corp., 151, 277, 278

B.F. Goodrich Co. v. Murtha, 510

Bichler v. Eli Lilly and Co., 404

Blair v. Eagle–Picher Industries, Inc., 388

Blake v. Chemlawn Services Corp., 656

Blankenship v. Cincinnati Milacron Chemicals, Inc., 446, 448, 453

Bloomington, Ind., City of v. Westinghouse Elec. Corp., 112, 114, 115

Bloomquist v. Wapello County, 370

Board of County Com'rs v. Slovek, 154, 156

Boeing Co. v. Aetna Cas. and Sur. Co., 552

Bolin v. The Cessna Aircraft Co., 602

Boomer v. Atlantic Cement Co., 147, 151, 152

Borel v. Fibreboard Paper Products Corp., 271, 274, 275, 279

Borg–Warner Corp. v. Insurance Co. of North America, 555

Borland v. Sanders Lead Co., Inc., 163

Bradley v. American Smelting and Refining Co., 28, 33, 34

Bradley v. American Smelting & Refining Co., 33, 36

Bradway v. American Nat. Red Cross, 992 F.2d 298, p. 304

Bradway v. American Nat. Red Cross, 426 S.E.2d 849, p. 589

Brady v. Safety–Kleen Corp., 447

Branch v. Western Petroleum, Inc., 111, 112, 165

Brewer v. Ravan, 190

Brisboy v. Fibreboard Corp., 432

Briscoe v. Harper Oil Co., 157

Brock v. Merrell Dow Pharmaceuticals, Inc., 371, 378

Broderick Inv. Co. v. The Hartford Acc. & Indem. Co., 531

Brown v. County Com'rs of Scioto Co., 36, 39, 57

Brown v. Dow Chemical Co., 597

Brown v. Superior Court, 293, 297, 298, 299, 304, 405

Buford v. American Tel. & Tel. Co., 463

Burgess v. Eli Lilly & Co., 586

Burgess v. M/V Tamano, 51, 52

Burlington Northern R. Co. v. Time Oil Co., 514

Burns v. Jaquays Min. Corp., 55, 191

Cadillac Fairview/California, Inc. v. Dow Chemical Co., 480, 497

Cain v. Armstrong World Industries, 621
California v. Sierra Club, 220
CAMSI IV v. Hunter Technology Corp., 579
Cannons Engineering Corp., United States v., 513, 515, 516, 517
Capogeannis v. Superior Court, 25, 125, 576, 577
Carlough v. Amchem Products, Inc., 636
Carman v. Steubenville & I. R. R. Co., 96
Carpenter v. The Double R Cattle Co., Inc., 70, **89**
Carroll v. Litton Systems, Inc., 58
Carroll Towing Co., United States v., 77, 262
Case v. Fibreboard Corp., 409
Casey v. Proctor, 650
Celotex Corp. v. Copeland, 409
Central Illinois Public Service Co. v. Industrial Oil Tank & Line Cleaning Service, 515
Chapman v. American Cyanamid Co., 409
Chase v. Cassiar Min. Corp., 580
Chatton v. National Union Fire Ins. Co., 533
Chem–Dyne Corp., United States v., 485
Ciba–Geigy Corp. v. Alter, 328, 335
Cimino v. Raymark Industries, Inc., 631, 634, 666
Cipollone v. Liggett Group, Inc., 112 S.Ct. 2608, pp. 215, **232**, 243, 244, 246, 260, 456, 647.
Cipollone v. Liggett Group, Inc., 893 F.2d 541, p. 263
Cities Service Co. v. State, 111, 112
City of (see name of city)
Cloud v. Olin Corp., 580
Coakley v. Maine Bonding and Cas. Co., 542, **543**, 552, 553
Coleman v. American Red Cross, 645
Collins v. Eli Lilly Co., 407
Colonial Tanning Corp. v. Home Indem. Co., 560
Columbia v. Continental Ins. Co., 563
Commonwealth v. _____ (see opposing party)
Concerned Citizens of Bridesburg v. City of Philadelphia, 251
Conley v. Boyle Drug Co., 408, 410, 418
Connerty v. Metropolitan Dist. Com'n, 52
Conservation Chemical Co., United States v., 504
Continental Cas. Co. v. Rapid–American Corp., 5, 539, 558
Continental Ins. Companies v. Northeastern Pharmaceutical & Chemical Co., Inc., 536, 551, 552
Cook v. Rockwell Intern. Corp., 189
Cooter & Gell v. Hartmarx Corp., 205
Cornell v. Exxon Corp., 607
Cottle v. Superior Court (Oxnard Shores Co.), 640, 641
Coty v. Ramsey Associates, Inc., 164
Coursen v. A.H. Robins Co., Inc., 298
Covalt v. Carey Canada Inc., 601

Cox v. Cambridge Square Towne Houses, Inc., 576
CPC Intern., Inc. v. Aerojet–General Corp., 510
Cremeans v. Willmar Henderson Mfg. Co., a Div. of Waycrosse, Inc., 613
Crown, Cork & Seal Co., Inc. v. Parker, 616
C.R.S. by D.B.S. v. United States, 303
Crushed Stone Co. v. Moore, 58, 70
Cunningham v. Anchor Hocking Corp., 451

Dafler v. Raymark Industries, Inc., **425**, 432
Daigle v. Shell Oil Co., 972 F.2d 1527, p. 117
Daigle v. Shell Oil Co., 133 F.R.D. 600, p. 619
Danella Southwest, Inc. v. Southwestern Bell Telephone Co., 519
Daubert v. Merrell Dow Pharmaceuticals, Inc., 6, **359**, 365, 366, 367, 369, 378
Davenport v. Garcia (Hon. Carolyn), 646
Davey Compressor Co. v. City of Delray Beach, 23, **162**
Dedham Water Co. v. Cumberland Farms Dairy, Inc., 501, 502, 503
DeLuca v. Merrell Dow Pharmaceuticals, Inc., 379, 381, 382
Denoyer v. Lamb, 162
DES Cases, In re, 407
DES Market Share Litigation, Matter of, 427
Desrochers v. New York Casualty Co., 551
Detroit White Lead Works, People v., 87
Diamond Shamrock Chemicals Co., In re, 618
Diamond Shamrock Chemicals Co. v. Aetna, 532
Dimmitt Chevrolet, Inc. v. Southeastern Fidelity Insurance Corporation, 555
Distler, United States v., 494
Dixon v. International Harvester Co., 472
Doe v. American Nat. Red Cross, 589
Doe v. Cutter Biological, 588
Doe v. Miles Laboratories, Inc., 302
Doe v. Puget Sound Blood Center, 644
Dole v. Dow Chemical Co., 314
Donahey v. Bogle, 493, 501
Dougherty v. Hooker Chemical Corp., 312, 313
Downing, United States v., 359, 366
Drayton v. Jiffee Chemical Corp., 334
Dresser Industries, Inc., State ex rel. v. Ruddy, 55, 247
Dunn v. HOVIC, 286
Dunn v. Pacific Employers Ins. Co., 600
Dupont v. Southern Pac. Co., 620
Dykes v. Raymark Industries, Inc., 284

Eagle–Picher Industries, Inc. v. Balbos, 271
Eagle–Picher Industries, Inc. v. Liberty Mut. Ins. Co., 538

Eagle–Picher Industries, Inc. v. United States E.P.A., 479

Eagles Court Condominium Unit Owners Ass'n v. Heatilator, Inc., 603

Earl v. Cryovac, A Div. of W.R. Grace Co., 344

East River S.S. Corp. v. Transamerica Delaval, Inc., 47

East St. Johns Shingle Co. v. City of Portland, 610

Ecodyne Corp. v. Shah, 489

Edgerton, City of v. General Cas. Co. of Wisconsin, 564

Edward Hines Lumber Co. v. Vulcan Materials Co., 491

E.I. du Pont de Nemours & Co. v. Admiral Ins. Co., 560

Eli Lilly and Co. v. Marshall, 643

Ellingwood v. Stevens, 6

Enright v. Eli Lilly & Co., 407

Environmental Transp. Systems, Inc. v. ENSCO, Inc., 510

Erbrich Products Co., Inc. v. Wills, 98, 113

Evenson v. Osmose Wood Preserving Co. of America, Inc., 582, 586

Ewell v. Petro Processors of Louisiana, Inc., 158

Exxon Corp. v. Yarema, 208

Farmland Industries, Inc. v. Morrison–Quirk Grain Corp., 511

Faya v. Almaraz, 6

Federated Dept. Stores, Inc. v. Moitie, 591

Feldman v. Lederle Laboratories, 277, 278

Ferebee v. Chevron Chemical Co., 5, 368, 369, 370, 399

Fernald Litig., In re, 652

Fetter v. De Camp, 611

Fibreboard Corp., In re, 624, 631, 633

Fiffick v. GAF Corp., 388

Filisko v. Bridgeport Hydraulic Co., 165

First United Methodist Church v. United States Gypsum Co., 602, 604

Fischer v. Atlantic Richfield Co., 610

Fischer v. Johns–Manville Corp., 279, **280,** 284

Fleet Factors Corp., United States v., 494, 495

Flue–Cured Tobacco Cooperative Stabilization Corp. v. Environmental Protection Agency, 466

FMC Corp. v. Aero Industries, Inc., 501

Fortier v. Flambeau Plastics Co., 135, 136

Frady v. Portland General Elec. Co., 75

Friedman v. F.E. Myers Co., 202

Friends for All Children, Inc. v. Lockheed Aircraft Corp., 184, 185, 191

Frongillo v. Grimmett, 599

Frye v. United States, 359, 365, 366, 367

Futura Realty v. Lone Star Bldg. Centers (Eastern), Inc., 131

General Elec. Co. v. AAMCO Transmissions, Inc., 496

General Elec. Co. v. Litton Business Systems, Inc., 498

General Elec. Co. v. Litton Indus. Automation Systems, Inc., 498, 500, 501

General Time Corp. v. Bulk Materials, Inc., 517

Gesswin v. Beckwith, 71

Gideon v. Johns–Manville Sales Corp., 591

Glasscock v. Armstrong Cork Co., 284, 286

Globig v. Greene & Gust Co., 512

Gloucester, Township of v. Maryland Cas. Co., 565

Goldman v. Johns–Manville Sales Corp., 409

Goldstein v. Potomac Elec. Power Co., 575

Goodbar v. Whitehead Bros., 324

Gopher Oil Co., Inc. v. Union Oil Co. of California, 501

Gordon Stafford, Inc., United States v., 496

Gould, United States v., 359

Graffagnino v. Fibreboard Corp., 591

Graham v. Pittsburgh Corning Corp., 7

Grant v. E.I. du Pont de Nemours & Co., 638

Grant v. GAF Corp., 444

Green v. Asher Coal Min. Co., 119

Green v. Castle Concrete Co., 87

Greenman v. Yuba Power Products, Inc., 266

Griffin v. Tenneco Resins, Inc., 409

Gulden v. Crown Zellerbach Corp., 450

Gussin Enterprises, Inc. v. Rockola, 498

Habitants Against Landfill Toxicants v. City of York, 191

Haenchen v. Sand Products Co., Inc., 576

Haft v. Lone Palm Hotel, 391

Hagerty v. L & L Marine Services, Inc., 180, 186, 201

Haines v. Liggett Group Inc., 646

Hall v. E. I. Du Pont De Nemours & Co., Inc., 404

Hansen v. Estate of Harvey, 444

Hansen v. Gordon, 462

Hao v. Owens–Illinois, Inc., 432

Hartford Acc. & Indem. Co. v. Aetna Life & Cas. Ins. Co., 538

Hay v. Cohoes Co., 96

Hazen Paper Co. v. United States Fidelity and Guar. Co., 536, 552

Hegna v. E.I. du Pont de Nemours and Co., 305, 314

Helling v. McKinney, 469

Helm v. Helm, 469

Heninger v. Dunn, 156

Herber v. Johns–Manville Corp., 187, 201

Heritage Village Master Ass'n, Inc. v. Heritage Village Water Co., 70, 71

Herman v. Sunshine Chemical Specialties, Inc., 313

Higgins v. E.I. DuPont de Nemours & Co., Inc., 324

High v. Westinghouse Elec. Corp., 324

Hill v. Searle Laboratories, 297, 298

Hill by Hill v. Showa Denko, K.K., 304

Hinman v. Yakima School Dist., 469

Hoemke v. New York Blood Center, 303

Hoffman v. Powell, 604

Holtz v. Holder, 437

Home Ins. Co. v. Stuart–McCorkle, Inc., 580

Hon v. Stroh Brewery Co., 287

Honeycomb Systems, Inc. v. Admiral Ins. Co., 531

Hooker Chemicals & Plastics Corp., United States v., 209

Houston v. Texaco, Inc., 202

Hubbard–Hall Chemical Co. v. Silverman, 334

Hudson v. Peavey Oil Co., 116

Hurt v. Philadelphia Housing Authority, 404, 422

Hymowitz v. Eli Lilly and Co., 404, 405, 406, 407, 418, 429, 605

Idaho, State of v. Bunker Hill Co., 492

Ikonen v. Hartz Mountain Corp., 655

Illinois v. City of Milwaukee, Wis., 220, 225

Illinois v. Milwaukee, 230

Independent Petrochemical Corp. v. Aetna Cas. and Sur. Co., 530

Independent School Dist. No. 197 v. W.R. Grace & Co., 605

Indiana Harbor Belt R. Co. v. American Cyanamid Co., 105, 106, 114, 116, 118

Industrial Union Dept., AFL–CIO v. American Petroleum Institute, 470

In re (see name of party)

Insurance Co. of North America v. Forty–Eight Insulations, Inc., 536, 537

International Paper Co. v. Ouellette, 220, 225

International Union, United Auto. Workers v. Johnson Controls, Inc., 455

Ironbound Health Rights Advisory Com'n v. Diamond Shamrock Chemicals Co., 202

Irwin Memorial Blood Centers v. Falconer, 643, 644

Jackson v. Johns–Manville Sales Corp. (Jackson III), 781 F.2d 394, pp. 201, 284

Jackson v. Johns–Manville Sales Corp., 750 F.2d 1314, pp. 612, 660, 663

Jackson v. Mannesmann Demag Corp., 604

Jackson Lockdown/MCO Cases, In re, 619

Jackson Tp. Municipal Utilities Authority v. Hartford Acc. and Indem. Co., 531, 537

Jacobsen v. Yocum Oil Co., Inc., 22

Jenkins v. Meares, 604

Jenkins v. Raymark Industries, Inc., 782 F.2d 468, pp. 616, 619

Jenkins v. Raymark Industries, Inc., 109 F.R.D. 269, pp. 623, 624, 631

Jensen v. General Elec. Co., 578

J.H. France Refractories Co. v. Allstate Ins. Co., 539

Johannesen v. New York City Dept. of Housing Preservation and Development, 467

Johns–Manville Corp., In re, 634

Johns–Manville Products Corp. v. Contra Costa Superior Court, 453, 456

Johnson v. Clark Equipment Co., 613

Johnson Controls World Services, Inc. v. Barnes, 451

Johnstown, City of v. Bankers Standard Ins. Co., 531

Joint Eastern and Southern Dist. Asbestos Litigation, In re, 635

Joint Eastern and Southern Districts Asbestos Litigation, In re, 634

Joint Eastern Dist. and Southern Dist. Asbestos Litigation, In re, 279

Jones v. Hittle Service, Inc., 314

Jones v. VIP Development Co., 447

Jones–Hamilton Co. v. Beazer Materials & Services, Inc., 496, 520

Joseph v. Hess Oil, 586

Joslyn Mfg. Co. v. T.L. James & Co., Inc., 492

Jost v. Dairyland Power Co-op., 70

Joyce v. A.C. and S., Inc., 591

Joy Technologies, Inc. v. Liberty Mut. Ins. Co., 556

Juzwin v. Amtorg Trading Corp., 285

Kaiser v. Memorial Blood Center of Minneapolis, Inc., 589

Kane v. Johns–Manville Corp., 634

Kayser–Roth Corp., Inc., United States v., 492

Keating v. National Union Fire Ins. Co., 534

Keene Corp. v. Insurance Co. of North America, 539

Kelley v. ARCO Industries Corp., 493

Kelley v. Thomas Solvent Co., 493, 516

Kelly v. Para–Chem Southern, Inc., 23

Kenney v. Scientific, Inc., 118

King v. Armstrong World Industries, Inc., 286

Klaxon Co. v. Stentor Electric Mfg. Co., 656, 664

Knox v. AC & S, Inc., 601

Koch v. Shell Oil Co., 3

Kociemba v. G.D. Searle & Co., 298

Koslowski v. Sanchez, 6

Kozup v. Georgetown University, 303

Kramer v. Scientific Control Corp., 616

Landers v. East Tex. Salt Water Disposal Co., 437

Landrigan v. Celotex Corp., 382

Langan v. Valicopters, Inc., 100, 101

Lansco, Inc. v. Department of Environmental Protection, 554

Lantz v. National Semiconductor Corp., 450

Lavanant v. General Acc. Ins. Co., 533

Leonen v. Johns–Manville Corp., 285

Little Joseph Realty, Inc. v. Town of Babylon, 152

Little Lake Misere Land Co., Inc., United States v., 224

Lloyd E. Mitchell, Inc. v. Maryland Cas. Co., 537
Locke v. Johns–Manville Corp., 580
Lohrmann v. Pittsburgh Corning Corp., 388
Lore v. Lone Pine Corp., 638, 640
Lossee v. Buchanan, 95
Louisiana ex rel. William J. Guste, Jr., State of v. M/V Testbank, 47, 51, 52, 53
Lourdes High School, Inc. v. Sheffield Brick & Tile Co., 604
Lowe v. Sun Refining & Marketing Co., 619
Lumbermens Mut. Cas. Co. v. Belleville Industries, Inc., 555
Lynch v. Merrell–National Laboratories, 383

Mack v. County of Rockland, 467
Maddux v. Donaldson, 437
Madison v. Ducktown Sulphur, Copper & Iron Co., 142
Malcolm v. National Gypsum Co., 621
Mandolidis v. Elkins Industries, Inc., 449
Mangini v. Aerojet–General Corp., 24, 125, **568,** 577, 578
Mardan Corp. v. C.G.C. Music, Ltd., 519
Marinari v. Asbestos Corp., Ltd., 596
Marshall v. Consumers Power Co., 248
Martin v. Abbott Laboratories, 407
Martin v. A & M Insulation Co., 588
Martin v. Johns–Manville Corp., 284
Martin v. Lancaster Battery Co., Inc., 457
Martin v. Owens–Corning Fiberglas Corp., 432
Martin v. Reynolds Metals Co., 33, 34, 35, 36
Martinez v. Humble Sand & Gravel, Inc., 278
Maryland Cas. Co. v. Armco, Inc., 551, 552
Maryland Heights Leasing, Inc. v. Mallinckrodt, Inc., 37
Matter of (see name of party)
Mauro v. Raymark Industries, Inc., 180, 185
McCarthy v. Department of Social and Health Services, 468
McCleery v. Highland Boy Gold Min. Co., 141, 142
McCormack v. Abbott Laboratories, 408
McGuire v. Joseph E. Seagram & Sons, Inc., 291
MCIC, Inc. v. Zenobia, 284
McIntosh v. A & M Insulation Co., 604
McKee v. Miles Laboratories, Inc., 299, 303
McWilliams v. Union Pacific Resources Co., 580
Meadows v. Union Carbide Corp., 580
Mel Foster Co. Properties, Inc. v. American Oil Co., 156
Menne v. Celotex Corp., 603
Merry v. Westinghouse Elec. Corp., 684 F.Supp. 852, p. 6
Merry v. Westinghouse Elec. Corp., 684 F.Supp. 847, p. 202

Mexico Feed and Seed Co., Inc., United States v., 494, 501
Michie v. Great Lakes Steel Div., 434, 437
Michigan Chemical Corp. v. American Home Assur. Co., 541
Middlesex County Sewerage Authority v. National Sea Clammers Ass'n, 214, 222, 224, 225
Miles v. Ashland Chemical Co., 599, 599
Miller v. Armstrong World Industries, Inc., 596
Miller v. Campbell County, 203
Miller v. Cudahy Co., 164, 576
Miller v. Pool and Canfield, Inc., 444
Millison v. E.I. du Pont de Nemours & Co., 457
Milwaukee v. Illinois (Milwaukee II), 216, 220, 221, 224
Mink v. University of Chicago, 180
Minnesota Min. and Mfg. Co. v. Travelers Indem. Co., 552
Miotke v. City of Spokane, 56, 250
Miranda v. Shell Oil Co., 186
Missouri ex rel. Dresser Industries, Inc., State of v. Ruddy, 55, 247
Mobay Corp. v. Allied–Signal, Inc., 520
Monarch Chemicals, Inc., State v., 119
Monsanto Co., United States v., 481, 484, 485, 486, 496, 504, 509
Montana Pole & Treating Plant v. I.F. Laucks and Co., 313
Montrose Chemical Corp. of California v. Superior Court, 536
Moore v. Armour Pharmaceutical Co., 303
Moorenovich, In re, 201
Morris v. Parke, Davis & Co., 409
Morrissy v. Eli Lilly & Co., 180
Morrisville Water & Light Dept., Village of v. United States Fidelity & Guar. Co., 530
Morton Intern., Inc. v. General Acc. Ins. Co. of America, 556
Most v. Tulane Medical Center, 644
Mottolo, United States v., 480
Moy v. Bell, 575
Mulcahy v. Eli Lilly & Co., 407
Murphy v. Taxicabs of Louisville, Inc., 437

National Can Corp. v. Jovanovich, 448, 449
National Steel Corp. v. Great Lakes Towing Co., 164
Neal v. Darby, 88
Nevada v. United States, 591
New Castle County v. Continental Cas. Co., 531
New Castle County v. Hartford Acc. and Indem. Co., 531
New England Legal Foundation v. Costle, 221
New York v. General Elec. Co., 480
New York v. Lead Industries Ass'n, Inc., 336, 423
New York v. SCA Services, Inc., 514

New York v. Shore Realty Corp., 479, 480, 485, 486

New York, State of v. Ferro, 41

New York, State of v. Schenectady Chemicals, Inc., 41, 44, 45

Nissan Motor Corp. in United States A. v. Maryland Shipbuilding and Drydock Co., 37

Northeastern Pharmaceutical and Chemical Co., Inc., United States v., 492

Northeastern Pharmaceutical & Chemical Co., Inc., United States v., 493

Northernaire Plating Co., United States v., 508

Northup v. Eakes, 438

Nurad, Inc. v. William E. Hooper & Sons Co., 490, 491

Nutt v. A.C. & S. Co., Inc., 409

O'Brien v. Eli Lilly & Co., 587

O'Brien v. Ottawa Silica Co., 451

Ohio v. United States Dept. of Interior, 56

Old Island Fumigation, Inc. v. Barbee, 112, 120

Olin Corp. v. Insurance Co. of North America, 530, 558

O'Neil v. Picillo, 485

Ouellette v. International Paper Co., 232

Outboard Marine Corp. v. Liberty Mut. Ins. Co., 554, 565

Owens–Corning Fiberglas Corp., Commonwealth v., 605

Owens–Corning Fiberglas Corp. v. Watson, 433

Owens–Illinois v. Armstrong, 284

Owens–Illinois, Inc. v. Armstrong, 433

Pacific Mut. Life Ins. Co. v. Haslip, 205, 207, 286

Padilla v. Lawrence, 37

Palmer v. Del Webb's High Sierra, 458, **459,** 464

Paoli R.R. Yard PCB Litigation, In re, 3, 186, 187, 188

Park–Ohio Industries, Inc. v. The Home Indem. Co., 556

Patrick v. Sharon Steel Corp., 609

Payton v. Abbott Labs, 201, 420

Pedraza v. Shell Oil Co., 472

Perkins v. Northeastern Log Homes, 605

Peterick v. State, 119

Petersen Sand and Gravel, Inc., United States v., 490

Petriello v. Kalman, 182

Philadelphia, City of v. Lead Industries Ass'n, Inc., 423

Philadelphia Elec. Co. v. Hercules, Inc., 121, 125, 126, 131

Philip Morris, Inc. v. Emerson, 116, 118, 208

Phillips Petroleum Co. v. Hardee, 438

Phillips Petroleum Co. v. Vandergriff, 438

Pierce v. General Motors Corp., 462

Pierce v. Johns–Manville Sales Corp., 596

Pipefitters Welfare Educational Fund v. Westchester Fire Ins. Co., 561

Poole v. Alpha Therapeutic Corp., 410

Potter v. Firestone Tire and Rubber Co., 25 Cal.Rptr.2d 550, p. 187

Potter v. Firestone Tire and Rubber Co., 274 Cal.Rptr. 885, pp. 188, 201

Powell v. Superior Portland Cement, Inc., 610

Pruitt v. Allied Chemical Corp., 52

Public Citizen v. Liggett Group, Inc., 646

Quadion Corp. v. Mache, 493

Queen City Farms, Inc. v. Central Nat. Ins. Co. of Omaha, 531

Racich v. Celotex Corp., 284, 285

Railroad Commission of Tex. v. Manziel, 26, 28

Rassier v. Houim, 609

Ray v. Cutter Laboratories, 754 F.Supp. 193, p. 418

Ray v. Cutter Laboratories, 744 F.Supp. 1124, p. 410

Ray Industries, Inc. v. Liberty Mut. Ins. Co., 540

Readinger v. Gottschall, 448

Reeser v. Weaver Bros., Inc., 156

Renaud v. Martin Marietta Corp., 386, 387, 642

Renaud v. Martin Marietta Corp., Inc., 5, 666

Reynolds Metals Co. v. Lampert, 36

Richardson–Merrell, Inc. Bendectin Products Liability Litigation, In re, 621

Riverside Market Development Corp. v. International Bldg. Products, Inc., 493

Roberts v. Suburban Hosp. Ass'n, Inc., 303

Robertson v. Allied Signal, Inc., 388

Rocco v. Johns–Manville Corp., 438

Rodarte v. Carrier Corp., 605

Rohm & Haas Co., United States v., 515, 516, 517

Rubanick v. Witco Chemical Corp., 358, 367

Runyon v. McCrary, 500, 501

Rushing v. Hooper–McDonald, Inc., 26

Russell v. Ingersoll–Rand Co., 599

Russell–Stanley Corp. v. Plant Industries, Inc., 131

Ruud v. Grimm, 437

R.W. Meyer, Inc., United States v., 504, **505,** 508, 509, 510

Ryan v. Dow Chemical Co., 5, 398

Rylands v. Fletcher, 94, 95, 96, 110, 111, 256

Salazar v. Webb, 119

Sanchez v. Galey, 472

Sanford Street Local Development Corp. v. Textron, Inc., 496

Santiago v. Sherwin–Williams Co., 794 F.Supp. 29, pp. 422, 423

Santiago v. Sherwin–Williams Co., 782 F.Supp. 186, p. 420

Schober v. Mountain Bell Tel., 467
School Asbestos Litigation, In re, 616
Schweitzer v. Consolidated Rail Corp., 181
Scott v. City of Hammond, Ind., 220
Sealey v. Hicks, 604
Sedar v. Knowlton Const. Co., 603, 604, 605
Senn v. Merrell–Dow Pharmaceuticals, Inc., 407, 409
Serafini, United States v., 517
Serota v. M. & M. Utilities, Inc., 22
Serrano–Perez v. FMC Corp., 642
Shackil v. Lederle Laboratories, 408, 409
Shaner, United States v., 512
Shaw v. Dow Brands, Inc., 3, 244
Shilling v. Mobile Analytical Services, Inc., 358
Shimp v. New Jersey Bell Tel. Co., 467
Shockley v. Hoechst Celanese Corp., 996 F.2d 1212, p. 118
Shockley v. Hoechst Celanese Corp., 793 F.Supp. 670, pp. 118, 119
Shorter v. Champion Home Builders Co., 5
Signo Trading Intern., Inc., State v., 563, 564
Silkwood v. Kerr–McGee Corp., 249
Silva v. Southwest Florida Blood Bank, Inc., 589
Simpson v. Pittsburgh Corning Corp., 286, 622
Sindell v. Abbott Laboratories, 339, 367, 391, 405, 406, 407, 408, 418
Slaughter v. Southern Talc Co., 388
Sloggy v. Dilworth, 438
Smallpage v. Turlock Irr. Dist., 576
Smith v. Bethlehem Steel Corp., 596
Smith v. Cutter Biological, Inc., 410
Smith v. Eli Lilly & Co., 407, 408, 418
Smith v. Hughes Aircraft Co. Corp., 560
Smith v. LTV Steel Co., 444
Smith v. Western Elec. Co., 467
Sofie v. Fibreboard Corp., 439
Solid State Circuits, Inc. v. United States E.P.A., 477
Sontag v. Orbit Valve Co., Inc., 448
Southland Corp. v. Ashland Oil, Inc., 520
Spitzfaden v. Dow Corning Corp., 6
Stanton Road Associates v. Lohrey Enterprises, 501
State v. _____ (see opposing party)
State, Dept. of Environmental Protection v. Ventron Corp., 106, 110, 112, 129, 131
State ex rel. v. _____ (see opposing party and relator)
State of (see name of state)
Stenger v. Lehigh Valley Hosp. Center, 644
Sterling v. Velsicol Chemical Corp., 855 F.2d 1188, pp. 5, 88, **191,** 199, 201, 204, 343, 344, 617, 618, 619, 630
Sterling v. Velsicol Chemical Corp., 647 F.Supp. 303, p. 207
Stevenson v. Keene Corp., 439
Stewart v. McLellan's Stores Co., 448
Stites v. Sundstrand Heat Transfer, Inc., 180

Stonewall Ins. Co. v. City of Palos Verdes Estates, 566
Stringfellow, United States v., 489
Strong v. Sullivan, 576
Stubbs v. City of Rochester, 345, 348, 368
Summers v. Tice, 391, 403
Summit Associates, Inc. v. Liberty Mut. Fire Ins. Co., 564
Sundell v. Town of New London, 575
Swan v. I.P., Inc., 315, 324
Swartzbauer v. Lead Industries Ass'n, Inc., 422
Symbula v. Johns–Manville Corp., 599

Taylor v. Celotex Corp., 438
Teal v. E.I. DuPont de Nemours and Co., 472
Techalloy Co., Inc. v. Reliance Ins. Co., 534, 556
Technicon Electronics Corp. v. American Home Assur. Co., 555
T & E Industries, Inc. v. Safety Light Corp., 680 F.Supp. 696, pp. 159, 499
T & E Industries, Inc. v. Safety Light Corp., 587 A.2d 1249, pp. **126,** 131, **132,** 135, 136, 159
Thacker v. UNR Industries, Inc., 389
Theer v. Philip Carey Co., 185, 275
Thiry v. Armstrong World Industries, 284
Thrasher v. B & B Chemical Co., Inc., 313
Three Mile Island Litigation, In re, 651
Tidewater Oil Co. v. Jackson, 28
Tidler v. Eli Lilly and Co., 407
Time Oil Co. v. Cigna Property & Cas. Ins. Co., 565
Titan Holdings Syndicate, Inc. v. City of Keene, N.H., 562
Tomlinson v. Celotex Corp., 604
Tragarz v. Keene Corp., 439
Transtech Industries, Inc. v. A & Z Septic Clean, 514
Trimper v. Porter–Hayden, 599
Tucker v. Nichols, 604
Turpin v. Merrell Dow Pharmaceuticals, Inc., 382
Twitty v. North Carolina, 222
TXO Production Corp. v. Alliance Resources Corp., 5, 206, 286

Union Gas Co., United States v., 743 F.Supp. 1144, p. 514
Union Gas Co., United States v., 586 F.Supp. 1522, p. 479
Union Oil Co. v. Oppen, 53, 103
Uniroyal, Inc. v. Home Ins. Co., 541
United Blood Services v. Quintana, 303
United States v. _____ (see opposing party)
United States Aviex Co. v. Travelers Ins. Co., 552, 564
United States Fidelity and Guar. Co. v. Thomas Solvent Co., 540
United States Fidelity & Guar. Co. v. Wilkin Insulation Co., 529, 534, 558

University of Miami v. Bogorff, 588
Upjohn Co. v. New Hampshire Ins. Co., 555
Urie v. Thompson, 581

Vantage Development Corp., Inc. v. American Environment Technologies Corp., 560
Venie v. South Central Enterprises, Inc., 334
Versatile Metals, Inc. v. Union Corp., 519
Vickridge First & Second Addition Homeowners Ass'n, Inc. v. Catholic Diocese of Wichita, 58
Village of (see name of village)
Voorhees v. Preferred Mut. Ins. Co., 534

Wade, United States v., 479
Walker v. Kerr–McGee Chemical Corp., 444
Warner v. Waste Management, Inc., 619
Watson v. Lowcountry Red Cross, 644
Watson v. Shell Oil Co., 618
Weber v. IMT Ins. Co., 558
Weger v. Shell Oil Co., 588
Welch v. Celotex Corp., 596, 597
Wells v. Ortho Pharmaceutical Corp., 369, 370
Werckenthein v. Bucher Petrochemical Co., 308, 312, 313, 314
Werlein v. United States, 181, 182, 189, 190
Westchester Fire Ins. Co. v. City of Pittsburg, 558
Western Processing Co., Inc., United States v., 504

Western World Ins. Co. v. Dana, 564
Westwood Pharmaceuticals, Inc. v. National Fuel Gas Distribution Corp., 126, 520, 612
Weyerhaeuser Co. v. Koppers Co., Inc., 510
Whalen v. Union Bag & Paper Co., 140, 142, 151
Wheelahan v. G.D. Searle & Co., 298
Wickland Oil Terminals v. Asarco, Inc., 481
Wiegmann & Rose Intern. Corp. v. NL Industries, 520
Wilber v. Owens–Corning Fiberglass Corp., 596
Williams v. Allied Automotive, Autolite Div., 190
Williams v. Monsanto Co., 67
Wilson v. Johns–Manville Sales Corp., 684 F.2d 111, pp. 180, **591,** 596
Wilson v. Johns–Manville Sales Corp., 107 F.R.D. 250, p. 623
Wilson Auto Enterprises, Inc. v. Mobil Oil Corp., 126
Wilsonville v. SCA Services, Inc., 78, 87, 88, 143, 152
Wood v. Picillo, 55
Woodland v. Portneuf Marsh Valley Irr. Co., 438
Woodman v. United States, 190
Woodson v. Rowland, 449

Yommer v. McKenzie, 117

Zelinger v. State Sand & Gravel Co., 657

*

Table of Statutes and Regulations

UNITED STATES

UNITED STATES CONSTITUTION

Amend.	This Work Page
5	604
8	209
14	604

UNITED STATES CODE ANNOTATED

5 U.S.C.A.—Government Organization and Employees

Sec.	This Work Page
8116(c)	454

7 U.S.C.A.—Agriculture

Sec.	This Work Page
136	243
136 et seq.	9
136(q)(1)(G)	243

11 U.S.C.A.—Bankruptcy

Sec.	This Work Page
Ch. 11	635

15 U.S.C.A.—Commerce and Trade

Sec.	This Work Page
1331—1340	234
2601 et seq.	9
2619(c)(3)	225
4401—4408	236

21 U.S.C.A.—Food and Drugs

Sec.	This Work Page
360ee	392

27 U.S.C.A.—Intoxicating Liquors

Sec.	This Work Page
201 et seq.	291

UNITED STATES CODE ANNOTATED

28 U.S.C.A.—Judiciary and Judicial Procedure

Sec.	This Work Page
636(b)(1)(A)	647
1346(b)	393
1407	622
1407(A)	622
2671—2680	454
2671 et seq.	303
2680(a)	393

29 U.S.C.A.—Labor

Sec.	This Work Page
651—678	469
651 et seq.	9
652(8)	470
654(a)(1)	469
657(c)	470
667(a)	472
671(a) et seq.	456

30 U.S.C.A.—Mineral Lands and Mining

Sec.	This Work Page
1201 et seq.	9
1270(e)	225

33 U.S.C.A.—Navigation and Navigable Waters

Sec.	This Work Page
1251 et seq.	9
	222
	225
1321(b)(2)(A)	479
1401 et seq.	222
1515(e)	225

42 U.S.C.A.—The Public Health and Welfare

Sec.	This Work Page
300aa–1 et seq.	409
2001 et seq.	455
2210 et seq.	393
4321 et seq.	9

UNITED STATES CODE ANNOTATED
42 U.S.C.A.—The Public Health and Welfare

Sec.	This Work Page
6901—6987	476
6901 et seq.	9
6921	479
6972(f)	225
7401 et seq.	9
7604(e)	225
9601—9675	120
9601 et seq.	9
	159
	190
	387
	475
9601(8)	601
9601(9)	601
9601(16)	55
9601(33)	601
9604(i)(1)(A)	523
9605(a)(8)(B)	128
9606	553
9607	477
9607(a)(4)	479
9607(f)	56
9613(g)	56
9651(e)(1)	657
9651(e)(3)	657
9658	600
9658(b)	602

STATUTES AT LARGE

Year	This Work Page
1988, Nov. 18, P.L. 100–690, 102 Stat. 4518	259

STATE STATUTES

ALABAMA CODE

Sec.	This Work Page
6–4–121	53
6–4–123	53

ALASKA STATUTES

Sec.	This Work Page
9.45.230	52

ARIZONA REVISED STATUTES

Sec.	This Work Page
23–1022(A)	450
36–601(A)	39

WEST'S ANNOTATED CALIFORNIA CIVIL CODE

Sec.	This Work Page
1542	650
3493	52

WEST'S ANNOTATED CALIFORNIA CODE OF CIVIL PROCEDURE

Sec.	This Work Page
731	125

WEST'S ANNOTATED CALIFORNIA HEALTH AND SAFETY CODE

Sec.	This Work Page
25300–95	9

WEST'S ANNOTATED CALIFORNIA LABOR CODE

Sec.	This Work Page
3682(2)	457

WEST'S FLORIDA STATUTES ANNOTATED

Sec.	This Work Page
Ch. 69.081	647

OFFICIAL CODE OF GEORGIA ANNOTATED

Sec.	This Work Page
72–103	52

HAWAII REVISED STATUTES

Sec.	This Work Page
663–31	607

IDAHO CODE

Sec.	This Work Page
72–438	462

ILLINOIS COMPILED STATUTES

ILCS	This Work Page
735 ILCS 5⁄2–1117	439
735 ILCS 5⁄2–1118	439

KANSAS STATUTES ANNOTATED

Sec.	This Work Page
44–510d(11)	443

MAINE REVISED STATUTES ANNOTATED

Sec.	This Work Page
Tit. 14	607

MARYLAND ANNOTATED CODE

Art.	This Work Page
101, § 36(3)(b)	443

MARYLAND CODE, COURTS AND JUDICIAL PROCEEDINGS

Sec.	This Work Page
5–108	603

CODE OF MASSACHUSETTS REGULATIONS

Tit.	This Work Page
31, § 4.01 et seq.	9

MICHIGAN COMPILED LAWS ANNOTATED

Sec.	This Work Page
299.601 et seq.	9
418.131(1)	450
600.380	53

MINNESOTA STATUTES ANNOTATED

Sec.	This Work Page
604.01	607

NEW HAMPSHIRE REVISED STATUTES ANNOTATED

Sec.	This Work Page
507:7–a	607

NEW JERSEY STATUTES ANNOTATED

Sec.	This Work Page
2A:15–1.1 et seq.	438
2A:15–5.1	438
2A:15–5.3(d)	438
2A:15–5.3(i)	438
2A:58C–1 et seq.	438

NEW JERSEY STATUTES ANNOTATED

Sec.	This Work Page
2A:58C–1(b)(4)	439
58:10–23.11a	110
59:1–3	170
59:9–2(d)	168

NEW YORK, MCKINNEY'S WORKERS' COMPENSATION LAW

Sec.	This Work Page
2(15)	462

NEW YORK COURT RULES

Sec.	This Work Page
Pt. 216	647

NORTH CAROLINA GENERAL STATUTES

Sec.	This Work Page
132–12.2	647

OHIO REVISED CODE

Sec.	This Work Page
2305.131	603
Ch. 4123	462
4123.68	462

OHIO ADMINISTRATIVE CODE

Sec.	This Work Page
3745–15–07(A)	39

OREGON REVISED STATUTES

Sec.	This Work Page
656.156(2)	449

RHODE ISLAND GENERAL LAWS

Sec.	This Work Page
28–34–1(3)	462

TENNESSEE CODE ANNOTATED

Sec.	This Work Page
50–6–204(3)(A)(ii)(q)	443

VERNON'S ANNOTATED RULES OF CIVIL PROCEDURE

Art.	This Work Page
76a	647

UTAH CODE ANNOTATED

Sec.	This Work Page
35–2–107	462

VIRGINIA CODE

Sec.	This Work Page
8.01–42.01	647
8.01–250	603
65.1–46.1	462

WEST'S REVISED CODE OF WASHINGTON ANNOTATED

Sec.	This Work Page
4.22.070	439
51.24.020	450

WASHINGTON LAWS

Year	This Work Page
1993, ch. 4.16	647
1993, ch. 4.24	647

WISCONSIN STATUTES ANNOTATED

Sec.	This Work Page
102.52(3)	443

POPULAR NAME ACTS

CLEAN AIR ACT

Sec.	This Work Page
304(e)	225

COMPREHENSIVE ENVIRONMENTAL RESPONSE, COMPENSATION AND LIABILITY ACT

Sec.	This Work Page
101	485
101(8)	601
101(9)	480
	601
101(14)	479
101(20)	494
101(20)(A)(iii)	493
101(22)	479
101(23)	480
	481
101(25)	480
	500
	501

COMPREHENSIVE ENVIRONMENTAL RESPONSE, COMPENSATION AND LIABILITY ACT

Sec.	This Work Page
101(33)	601
101(35)(C)	490
104	476
104(i)(1)	522
104(i)(3)	523
104(i)(6)(B)	523
105(a)	477
106	477
	503
	518
	553
106(a)	476
106(b)(1)	477
107	477
	481
	498
	499
	511
	518
	519
	525
107(a)	481
	487
	496
	501
	503
107(a)(1)	489
107(a)(2)	490
107(a)(3)	493
	495
107(a)(4)	501
107(a)(4)(A)	480
107(a)(4)(B)	480
	497
	500
	504
107(b)(3)	482
107(c)(3)	477
107(e)	519
107(e)(1)	519
113(f)	484
	504
	509
	512
	515
	517
113(f)(1)	517
	518
113(f)(2)	513
	514
	515
	516
113(f)(3)(B)	517
113(h)	477
122(e)(3)	509
	512
122(f)(4)	513
122(f)(6)(A)	513
301(e)	476
309	600
	601

COMPREHENSIVE ENVIRONMENTAL RESPONSE, COMPENSATION AND LIABILITY ACT

Sec.	This Work Page
309(a)(1)	601
309(b)	602
309(b)(4)(A)	601
310	501
310(f)	501

CIVIL RIGHTS ACT OF 1964

Sec.	This Work Page
Tit. VII, § 703	455

DEEPWATER PORT ACT

Sec.	This Work Page
16(e)	225

FEDERAL WATER POLLUTION CONTROL ACT

Sec.	This Work Page
1321(b)(2)(A)	479

MARINE PROTECTION, RESEARCH AND SANCTUARIES ACT OF 1972

Sec.	This Work Page
105(g)(3)	225

OCCUPATIONAL SAFETY & HEALTH ACT

Sec.	This Work Page
3(8)	470
4(b)(4)	473
18	472

RIVERS AND HARBORS ACT OF 1899

Sec.	This Work Page
10	220

SOLID WASTE DISPOSAL ACT

Sec.	This Work Page
3001	479
7002(f)	225

SURFACE MINING AND RECLAMATION ACT OF 1977

Sec.	This Work Page
520(e)	225

TOXIC SUBSTANCES CONTROL ACT

Sec.	This Work Page
20(c)(3)	225

UNIFORM COMMERCIAL CODE

Sec.	This Work Page
2–313	263
	334
	335
2–314	263
	335
2–315	263
	264
	266
	335
2–316	265
2–318	264
	334
2–719	265
2–719(3)	265

UNIFORM COMPARATIVE FAULT ACT

Sec.	This Work Page
1—10	509
1(b)	509

UNIFORM CONTRIBUTION AMONG TORTFEASORS ACT

Sec.	This Work Page
2	509
4	515

FEDERAL RULES OF CIVIL PROCEDURE

Rule	This Work Page
11	205
	586
16	621
23	616
	631
	635
23(b)	631
23(b)(1)(B)	623
	635
23(b)(3)	616
	623
37	645
42(a)	620
	622
	631
42(b)	621
	622
53	666

FEDERAL RULES OF EVIDENCE

Rule	This Work Page
104(a)	357
401	357
402	357
403	357
	358
407	279
702	358
	365
	369
703	358
	398
706	665
	666
803(18)	366

CODE OF FEDERAL REGULATIONS

Tit.	This Work Page
29, § 1900.1000	470
29, § 1904.2	471
29, § 1904.4	471
29, § 1904.5	471
29, § 1904.6	471

CODE OF FEDERAL REGULATIONS

Tit.	This Work Page
29, § 1910.20	471
29, §§ 1910.1001–1910.1101	469
29, § 1910.1200	614
29, § 1910.1200(a)(1)	471
29, § 1910.1200(b)(2)	471
29, § 1910.1200(c)	471
29, § 1910.1200(d)	471
29, § 1910.1200(e)	471
29, § 1910.1200(g)	471
29, § 1910.1200(h)	472
40, § 156.10(a)(1)	243
40, § 300	498
40, § 300.71(a)(3)	497
40, § 300.1100	495
40, § 302.4	479
40, § 401.15	479
42, § 90.5	524

FEDERAL REGISTER

Vol.	This Work Page
45, pp. 33239–33242	82
54, pp. 2332–2983	470
56, p. 52186	522

Table of Restatement Citations

RESTATEMENT 2ND JUDGMENTS

Sec.	This Work Page
24—26	594
24(1)	591
26(1)(b)	594
26, comment b	594

RESTATEMENT 1ST TORTS

Sec.	This Work Page
519	96
520	96
881	436

RESTATEMENT 2ND TORTS

Sec.	This Work Page
7(1)	174
8A	30
	33
	75
158	29
	33
158, cl. (a), comment	30
158, comment i	21
	23
	26
161, comment b	25
	572
191—211	22
352, reporter's note	122
372	611
373	611
388, comment k	319
388, comment n	320
	321
	322
397A	119
402A	116
	260
	266
	268
	273
	278
	288
	289
	293
	319
	324

RESTATEMENT 2ND TORTS

Sec.	This Work Page
402A (Cont'd)	326
	327
	328
	336
	337
	612
	613
402A, comment i	267
	290
402A, comment j	275
	290
402A, comment k	293
	294
	295
	297
	298
	299
402A, comment n	612
402B	267
	335
	336
	337
402B, comment j	337
427A	118
	119
427B	45
433A	428
	429
	431
	485
433A(1)(b)	428
433A, comment (a)	428
433B(2)	428
	431
	438
433B(3)	404
496	613
496C	613
496D	613
519	17
	94
	97
	114
	119
	132
	136
	256
519—520	109
519(1)	113
519, comment e	120
520	17

RESTATEMENT 2ND TORTS

Sec.	This Work Page
520 (Cont'd)	94
	97
	99
	114
	132
	136
	256
520(c)	105
520(d)	99
520(e)	99
	105
520(f)	105
520, comment c	97
520, comment j	99
520, comment l	98
522	120
523	130
549	336
552	336
821A, comment b	39
821B	50
821B(2)	40
821B, comment g	41
821C	46
	50
821C(1)	39
821C, comment d	54
821D	57
	60
	123
821D—F	61
821F	71
822	72
	74
	94
	606
822, comment g	70
825	75
826	72
	74
	75
826(b)	89

RESTATEMENT 2ND TORTS

Sec.	This Work Page
826(b) (Cont'd)	90
	91
	92
826, comment f	73
827	76
	77
827(d)	76
827, comment g	76
828	76
	77
828(a)	77
828(b)	77
828(c)	77
829	77
829A	77
830	77
832	60
840, comment d	607
840A	58
840A, comment c	611
840B	606
840C	607
840D	608
841	77
851D, comment b	57
875	485
881	485
886A	508
899, comment d	25
912, comment e	174
929	153
	168
	179
929, comment b	154
	155
929, comment e	169
933(1)	85
933, comment b	85
	87
936	144
941	144
941, comment c	144

LAW OF ENVIRONMENTAL AND TOXIC TORTS

CASES, MATERIALS AND PROBLEMS

*

INTRODUCTION

Courts today, federal and state, are increasingly confronted with claims asserted by plaintiffs who have suffered a type of harm which is characterized as "toxic" or "environmental." These materials introduce the student to the complex and recurring issues posed by environmental risk, injury and litigation. In addition, the materials discuss the policy considerations which are important and relevant in resolving disputes among litigants. Policy concerns permeate environmental and toxic tort litigation, and courts regularly enlist them, or refute them, in determining whether to create, expand or modify rules of duty, liability and remedies.

The casebook focuses upon *tort* claims arising from environmental or toxic harm, as well as selected statutory private redress for environmental harm, particularly private actions under the Comprehensive Environmental Response, Compensation and Liability Act ("CERCLA"). The authors do not endeavor to provide comprehensive treatment of the myriad environmental laws and regulations enacted in the last two decades, but do measure the thrust of major federal environmental regulatory initiatives to the extent that a particular statutory scheme directly implicates private rights and remedies.

In environmental and toxic tort law, the plaintiffs are usually private persons or businesses that suffered harm as a result of the exposure to some toxic substance or environmental condition. The claimants are seeking private remedies for that harm—usually money damages for their compensation and occasionally injunctive relief. The most frequent theories of liability are nuisance, trespass, products liability, negligence, strict liability for abnormally dangerous activities, and statutory strict liability.

The term "toxic" is more narrow than the term "environmental," for while many environmental tort cases do involve exposure to toxic substances, certainly many do not. For example, litigation concerning disagreeable odors from a landfill, or airborne ash from an incinerator, may not have toxic implications, although they do represent environmental harm or degradation. To be contrasted, the term "toxic," while lacking a consistent application to all cases, is understood generally to mean substances that by inhalation, ingestion, dermal exposure or otherwise can or do cause personal physical injury or disease. The term toxic is employed in regulatory statutes such as the Toxic Substances Control Act ("TSCA"). It is often used interchangeably with the term "hazardous," but the latter term is also defined by other federal statutes such as CERCLA.

1

Some toxic tort cases relate to substances governed by that statute, but the majority do not. By employing the term "environmental" as embracing any of the surrounding settings in which persons work, live, play, and interact, and all of the conditions and substances to which they are exposed, nearly all toxic cases are comprehended by the phrase environmental torts. Accordingly, the term "environmental" is used whenever the authors intend to embrace the broader range of harms and their causes.

A Note on Style: In the interest of brevity, case and statute citations, as well as footnotes, of courts and commentators have been omitted without so specifying. Numbered footnotes are from the original materials and retain the original numbering; lettered footnotes within the case are those of the authors.

As used throughout this work, "person" means individual persons, business entities, including corporations and public entities. Where person is used in its more individual sense, the text will use the terms "natural", "individual" or "person[s]." The authors employ the third person singular pronouns "he" and "she" interchangeably.

Chapter One

OVERVIEW: CONFLICTING PERSPECTIVES ON THE ADEQUACY OF THE TORT SYSTEM

A. GENERALLY

Environmental and toxic torts comprise harms to persons, to property, or to the environment due to the toxicity of a product, a substance, or a process.[1] In many circumstances, the toxic harm is latent for a period of time, and is not discernible, or in cases of disease, diagnosable, for years, or even decades. As a modern legal term, "tort," derived from the Latin term for "twisted," is a civil, noncontractual wrong for which an injured person may seek a "remedy" in the form of money damages. A tort is a *civil* wrong in the sense that the injured party's remedy is a civil suit for compensatory damages, as distinct from a suit brought by the government for civil or criminal monetary penalties.

Tort law is the cluster of doctrines imposing civil liability, usually in money damages, upon persons or businesses whose substandard conduct causes personal physical or emotional injury to others, or damage to their property.[2] In addition to, or instead of, money damages the environmental tort plaintiff may seek equitable relief in the form of an injunction or order in abatement.

Modern tort law is substantially interwoven with provisions of state and federal statutes pertaining to such subjects as burdens of proof, liability, comparative fault, and statutes of limitation, to name only three. By way of illustration: (1) a business's failure to comply with a

---

1. E.g., Shaw v. Dow Brands, Inc., 994 F.2d 364 (7th Cir.1993) (plaintiff's claims of personal injuries from fumes of defendant's X–14 Instant Mildew Stain Remover); Koch v. Shell Oil Co., 820 F.Supp. 1336 (D.Kan. 1993) (plaintiff's claim of cattle illness and death from ingestion of Rabon Oral Larvacide); In re Paoli Railroad Yard PCB Litigation, 916 F.2d 829 (3d Cir.1990) (PCB contamination of former railroad premises and its environs).

2. An older definition of tort law as comprising liability for civil, noncontractual, nonstatutory harm is, today, somewhat misleading. For example, the remedy for breach of the implied warranty of merchantability, providing money damages for toxic harm, is, by its terms, contractual, but it is often quite tort-like in the proof required and the damages available to the successful litigant.

standard of care established by a labeling regulation might, under state law, be deemed negligence per se; (2) a state or federal environmental statute may vest in individuals or businesses the right to pursue private cost recovery lawsuits against a polluter; or (3) a state statute pertaining to toxic products may provide criteria for evaluation of issues ranging from the hazards posed by a product or substance to the varying burden of proof plaintiffs must sustain against different participants in the chain of manufacture, marketing and distribution.

1. TORT GOALS AND THEIR APPLICATION

Even with the contemporary influence of statutory and warranty law, the goals of tort law remain these: (1) assignment of responsibility, in money damages or equitable relief, to those responsible for creating a risk that produces harm; (2) compensation of persons for loss caused by another's tortious conduct, including concepts of corrective justice or fairness; (3) deterrence of further unreasonably hazardous conduct by the responsible party and others engaged in similar pursuits; and (4) encouragement of innovation, such as changes in process, transportation, disposal, design, formulation, packaging, or labeling that will reduce or eliminate unreasonable hazards.

In a toxic tort suit, most frequently plaintiff sues the responsible party or parties for compensatory damages, i.e., a monetary award calculated to remedy the harm defendant has caused, to the imperfect extent financial relief can, by compensating the injured party for the loss or harm suffered. Where the toxic harm is to property, or to an ongoing business, compensatory damages can be assessed on the basis of diminution in value to a property, or down-time, economic loss, or the costs of clean-up or remediation of the property. In these instances compensatory damages may come close to placing the injured party in the economic position it would have enjoyed but for defendant's conduct, that is, compensation fulfills a restorative objective.

Where, on the other hand, the harm suffered by defendant's wrongdoing is personal physical injury, emotional harm, disease, or death, these losses cannot be truly compensated for, as money damages can cannot restore the plaintiff to her pre-tort condition. Nonetheless, a judge's or a jury's finding of defendant's liability for civil money damages in a toxic tort claim provides the best recompense available through the United States legal system.

There are variations on these themes. Plaintiff may bring a noncompensatory, but remedial, "citizen suit" claim to force compliance with state or federal environmental statutes. In addition, where defendant's injurious conduct is continuing in nature, a court may enjoin further similar conduct. A defendant failing to comply with the requirements of such an injunction or order in abatement may be subject to civil or criminal fines.

Another significant variable is that, in addition to compensatory damages, punitive damages may be awarded upon plaintiff's showing that defendant's conduct was of such a reprehensible nature as to warrant financial punishment in addition to the burden of compensating plaintiff for the injury sustained. See generally TXO Production Corp. v. Alliance Resources Corp., ___ U.S. ___, 113 S.Ct. 2711, 125 L.Ed.2d 366 (1993). Punitive damages are not intended to compensate plaintiff for the harm suffered, but rather to punish a particularly blameworthy defendant who has acted in knowing or reckless disregard of the interests of plaintiff, and to serve to deter that defendant, and others, from engaging in future similar hazardous conduct.

2. TYPICAL ENVIRONMENTAL OR TOXIC TORT CLAIMS

An injury may be personal, physical injury to a worker, a patient, a product user or consumer, or a bystander. It may be damage to property, its breadth ranging from rendering an individual premises uninhabitable to the contamination of a large watershed. E.g., Sterling v. Velsicol Corp., 855 F.2d 1188 (6th Cir.1988) (contamination of 242 acres used as a site for a landfill for by-products of manufacture of chlorinated hydrocarbon pesticides). A person's physical injury may range from nausea to neurological damage or death. See generally In re "Agent Orange" Product Liability Litigation, 781 F.Supp. 902 (E.D.N.Y. 1991), affirmed 996 F.2d 1425 (2d Cir.1993); Shorter v. Champion Home Builders Co., 776 F.Supp. 333 (N.D.Ohio 1991) (claim against homebuilders alleging injurious exposure to formaldehyde vapors, and alleging diverse personal injuries, including lethargy, headaches and emotional harm).

The toxic tort harm may arise from a worker's exposure to hazardous chemicals in the workplace, such as by her inhalation of respirable carcinogens.[3] Contamination of groundwater by waste disposal,[4] by inadequately treated industrial effluent, or by administration of residential or agricultural pesticides may also create toxic tort liability.[5]

Various health procedures may give rise to toxic tort claims, with claims ranging from harmful radiological exposure to x-rays, to treatment with potentially toxic medical devices or implants, to employment of dental surgery products containing paraformaldehyde that plaintiff

---

3. For representative discussion of such claims, in turn, see Comment, Not Just for Doctors: Applying the Informed Intermediary Doctrine to the Relationship Between Chemical Manufacturers, Industrial Employers, and Workers, 85 Nw. U. L. Rev. 562 (1991); Continental Casualty Co. v. Rapid-American Corp., 80 N.Y.2d 640, 593 N.Y.S.2d 966, 609 N.E.2d 506 (1993) (evaluating insurer's duty to defend actions for personal injuries sustained through exposure to asbestos).

4. See, e.g., Renaud v. Martin Marietta Corp., 972 F.2d 304 (10th Cir.1992) (improperly disposed waste water from defendant's missile plant contaminating residential water supply; no liability for insufficient proof of causation).

5. See, e.g., Ferebee v. Chevron Chemical Co., 736 F.2d 1529 (D.C.Cir.1984) (deceased agricultural worker's suit against herbicide manufacturer for pulmonary fibrosis).

claimed had leached into his blood system.[6]

Pharmaceutical and medical products liability is usually considered a matter of products liability, and not toxic torts. Even so, court decisions in pharmaceutical products liability cases often have a bearing on the law of toxic torts. For example, suits against drug manufacturers usually require a judge to evaluate expert testimony bearing on the toxic properties of a chemical, the qualifications of the experts, and the bases for their conclusions. The cutting edge issue in many modern toxic tort suits is the allocation of authority, between the court and the jury, in evaluating expert testimony, and the question of whether experts' methodology, their conclusions, or *both* their methodology *and* conclusions, must reflect the "generally accepted" view within their professional discipline. See Daubert v. Merrell Dow Pharmaceuticals Co., ___ U.S. ___, 113 S.Ct. 2786, 125 L.Ed.2d 469 (1993) (causation testimony of plaintiffs' expert in Bendectin litigation).

Another example of the relationship between toxic torts and pharmaceutical products liability is the developing law permitting, or denying, judgment for plaintiffs claiming long latency injury where plaintiff is unable to identify a particular manufacturer's product, substance, or pharmaceutical as having caused the injury. Some courts have permitted the tortfeasor identification problem to be resolved on a theory of "market-share" liability, or a modification of that theory. Plaintiffs' have sought to apply market share liability to toxic products other than pharmaceuticals, such as HIV-contaminated anti-coagulant blood products, lead paint pigments and asbestos. Accordingly, the casebook does explore drug products liability suits bearing on these and similar subjects.

B. SPECIAL CHARACTERISTICS OF ENVIRONMENTAL TORT CLAIMS

1. GENERALLY

The environmental or toxic tort claimant frequently phrases a complaint in terms of multiple theories of recovery. For example, in the well-water contamination suit of Merry v. Westinghouse Electric Corp., 684 F.Supp. 852 (M.D.Pa.1988), plaintiffs brought suit under theories of negligence, strict liability for abnormally dangerous activities, trespass and nuisance. Even in a modern personal injury action claiming a manufacturer of asbestos products failed to warn adequately, a court will

---

6. See, in turn, Faya v. Almaraz, 329 Md. 435, 620 A.2d 327 (1993) (plaintiff seeking recovery for fear of contracting AIDS following treatment by surgeon infected with the virus); Ellingwood v. Stevens, 564 So.2d 932 (Ala.1990) (claim of inadequate shielding of patient's spinal cord during radiation therapy); Spitzfaden v. Dow Corning Corp., 619 So.2d 795 (La.App. 1993) (silicone breast implant litigation); Koslowski v. Sanchez, 576 So.2d 470 (La. 1991) (root canal filler use of N–2 paste containing 6.5% paraformaldehyde).

turn to the common law negligence standard to find the applicable duty. E.g., Graham v. Pittsburgh Corning Corp., 593 A.2d 567, 568 (Del. Super.1990) ("Delaware law measures the duties owed in terms of reasonableness. One's duty is to act reasonably, as a reasonably prudent [person] (or entity) would.").

2. LONG LATENCY PERIODS

Environmental or toxic torts often involve injury or damage that remains undiscovered for years after the exposure or contamination. A shipyard worker's exposure to respirable asbestos fibers may result in asbestos-related disease only years later. An electroplating plant's contamination of its property, surrounding property, or subterranean aquifers may only be discovered when a successor owner of the property wishes to sell it years later. The Vietnam veteran or the agricultural worker exposed to a chemical herbicide may only be diagnosed with neurological disease or other illness many years thereafter.

Because environmental and toxic tort claims almost always involve injury or damage that has a long latency period before the harm manifests itself, toxic torts are distinguishable from the sporadic accident cases that were the staple of the basic torts course. Due in part to the long latency between exposure to the toxin and claimant's ability to recognize the harm, toxic torts usually involve complex questions of medical or scientific causation. As a consequence, toxic tort litigation will always require the engagement of experts in medicine and other sciences, such as toxicology and epidemiology, to assist counsel and the fact finder alike in determining whether a causal relationship exists between the toxin and the harm. Moreover, the long latency periods create difficult statutes of limitations and repose problems not implicated in accident litigation, as well as problems in developing evidence of the parties' conduct undertaken years earlier.

3. PROOF OF CAUSATION

In claims for environmental or toxic harm, plaintiff must demonstrate that defendant's product or activity was a direct cause of the resulting personal injury or damage to property. Regardless of the theory of liability, defendant's actions must be shown to be the "proximate cause" of the harm. Proximate cause means that the challenged act (1) was a substantial contributing factor in bringing about the injury (or a "but for" cause), that is, it was at least "a" cause in fact of the harm; and (2) that the relationship between defendant's act and the harm is not so remote or attenuated as to suggest that the harm was not foreseeable, rendering it unfair or unreasonable to hold defendant responsible.

Due to the imperfect knowledge of disease etiology, often compounded by the passage of time, the majority of toxic tort claims pose distinctive problems in the proof of proximate cause. In addition, the lapse of time often makes it quite difficult for plaintiff to identify the particular substance involved, and the specific actor who was responsible. Years after exposure to respirable asbestos, a pipe fitter may be unable to identify the particular manufacturer of asbestos products he was exposed to. Even where a particular manufacturer's asbestos products, or chemical solvents, or pesticide can be identified, the passage of time may hinder plaintiff's demonstration of the times, circumstances and degree of exposure suffered.

4. ROLE OF EXPERT SCIENTIFIC OR MEDICAL TESTIMONY

Proof of causation in a toxic tort claim is often more difficult than proof in many conventional personal injury claims. Where, for example, the disease suffered by a toxic tort litigant is cancer of the liver, plaintiff must demonstrate by a preponderance of the evidence that the disease was caused by a toxic exposure for which defendant was responsible, and not simply a "background" case of liver cancer.

Because lay jurors cannot on the basis of common knowledge resolve the causal inquiry, plaintiff must introduce expert scientific or medical evidence that defendant's product or process was a but-for cause or a substantial contributing factor in plaintiff's injury or loss. First, an epidemiologist or toxicologist may have to testify that where a person in plaintiff's circumstance has contracted the disease, it is more likely than not that the disease was capable of being caused by exposure to defendant's toxin. In other words, plaintiff must offer scientific evidence that the toxic substance is known to produce the *kind* of adverse health effect of which plaintiff complains. Second, plaintiff must offer a physician to testify that to a reasonable degree of medical or scientific certainty, defendant's substance caused plaintiff's injury or disease.

Defendant, in turn, will ordinarily counter with experts of its own choosing who have reached conflicting conclusions as to the toxic potential of the substance involved, or who seek to discredit the diagnostic or statistical bases upon which plaintiff's witnesses relied. Accordingly, most toxic tort claims involve complicated, laborious, and expensive litigation preparation.

Moreover, in some contexts, vigorous scientific debate exists as to whether the toxic substance is capable, under any circumstances, of causing the type of injury or disease that plaintiff suffers. As often, and even where defendant concedes that a certain level of exposure to a substance can cause injury, plaintiff must prove that the particular exposure was a producing cause of the injury. Defendant may offer evidence that the injury or disease was caused by (1) exposure to the product of another producer; (2) exposure to a different product or substance altogether, such as alcohol or tobacco products, for which defendant should bear no responsibility; (3) exposure to background levels of toxins in the environment that may affect the health of all persons in the area; or that (4) the disease or injury is simply a background case occurring generally in the population, and for which no known cause has been identified.

Additionally, defendant might argue that plaintiff's exposure to the substance was too remote (i.e., plaintiff was employed at a work station far removed from the location of the toxic substance); or that the form of the toxin was such as to make exposure to it nonharmful (i.e., the asbestos-containing pipe fittings in question were resin-bonded, minimizing the release of respirable asbestos fibers). On all of these issues, both plaintiff and defendant will need to produce expert witnesses to support their allegations or defenses.

5. RELATIONSHIP OF ENVIRONMENTAL TORT LAW TO STATUTORY ENVIRONMENTAL LAW

Manufacturers of a wide array of potentially toxic products are subject to government licensing, regulation, enforcement, and penalties. This licensing may be administered under the Federal Hazardous Substances Act ("FHSA"), the Federal Insecticide, Fungicide and Rodenticide Act ("FIFRA"), or a variety of other laws and associated regulations.

A person's act, or failure to act, regarding a toxic substance may violate an environmental or occupational health statute or regulation. Most regulatory environmental claims involving toxic substances are brought by the government, be it federal, state, or municipal, claiming that defendant's conduct violated a statute or a regulation. A partial list of the sprawling number of statutes that pertain to toxic wrongdoing at the federal level would include the Federal Insecticide, Fungicide and Rodenticide Act ("FIFRA"),[7] the Toxic Substances Control Act ("TSCA"),[8] the Surface Mining Control and Reclamation Act ("SMRCA"),[9] the National Environmental Policy Act ("NEPA"),[10] the Solid Waste Disposal Act ("SWDA"),[11] the Comprehensive Environmental Response, Compensation, and Liability Act ("CERCLA"),[12] the Occupational Safety and Health Act ("OSHA"),[13] the Federal Water Pollution Control Act ("FWPCA"),[14] and the Clean Air Act ("CCA").[15] In addition, the numerous state environmental statutes provide mechanisms for imposing penalties or remediation requirements upon those responsible for environmental harms.[16] That body of law, i.e., public regulation of environmental or toxic harms to persons, property, or the environment, is described as "environmental law."

7. 7 U.S.C.A. § 136 et seq.

8. 15 U.S.C.A. § 2601 et seq.

9. 30 U.S.C.A. § 1201 et seq.

10. 42 U.S.C.A. § 4321 et seq.

11. 42 U.S.C.A. § 6901 et seq.

12. 42 U.S.C.A. § 9601 et seq.

13. 29 U.S.C.A. § 651 et seq.

14. 33 U.S.C.A. § 1251 et seq.

15. 42 U.S.C.A. § 7401 et seq.

16. E.g., Massachusetts Water Quality Standards, codified at 31 Code of Mass. Regs. 4.01 et seq. (1986); Michigan Environmental Response Act, M.C.L.A. § 299.-601 et seq.; California Hazardous Substance Account Act, West's Ann.Cal. Health & Safety Codes § 25300–95.

Most environmental suits brought pursuant to statute by a public body are called "enforcement" or a "penalty" actions, in which the agency might seek civil or criminal monetary penalties. When the government prevails in a penalty or an enforcement action, any moneys recovered devolve to the government's general fund, or to special funds such as the "Superfund" created by CERCLA.

6. RECURRING THEMES IN ENVIRONMENTAL TORTS

Whenever the tort system has been faced with new classes of litigation that raise potentially unique and special problems distinguishable from the traditional tort case, i.e., the automobile or other sporadic accident case, commentators and courts ask whether tort liability rules should be adjusted to accommodate such cases. The overarching question might be phrased: Can the tort system adequately accommodate society's call for providing compensation to individuals suffering from environmental harms consistent with the other objectives of tort law, such as deterrence, economic efficiency, and fairness?

The following articles and materials assume generally divergent views. The materials also serve to set forth a brief overview of coming attractions. When the student has completed all of the cases and comments, he or she can arrive at individual conclusions as to the adequacy and propriety of the tort system's mechanisms for responding to environmental torts.

TROYEN A. BRENNAN, ENVIRONMENTAL TORTS

46 Vanderbilt Law Review 1 (1993).

I. INTRODUCTION

Over the last two decades, a new class of torts has emerged that targets personal injuries caused by toxic substances in the environment. These hybrid environmental torts are quite distinct from the trespass-nuisance precedent that is part of traditional tort theory; nor are environmental torts simply a subset of the mass hazardous substance litigation that has remade product liability law. Environmental torts are informed, in a way product law is not, by environmental regulation. These torts are unique because their deterrent signal is transmitted to producers of hazardous environmental pollutants by litigants who have suffered physical injury or disease.

Environmental tort litigation appears to be burgeoning. While comprehensive evidence on the number and average severity of environmental tort claims nationwide is not available, published cases would suggest both are at unprecedented high levels. Yet the topic is only peripherally discussed in law reviews, and has not penetrated most law school courses on tort law. The academic silence is perhaps understandable, since the subject of environmental torts tends to fall between two relatively well-circumscribed disciplines, tort law and environmental law.

Moreover, the teachers and theoreticians of both subject areas are somewhat introspective at present. Over the past decade, the debate over reforms that would retard the growth of certain kinds of tort claims has preoccupied many tort law professors and some practitioners. Environmental law appears to be experiencing a severe mid-life crisis, as academics struggle to redefine a subject that is increasingly composed of stultifyingly technical statutes. The result of such distractions is that an exciting hybrid of personal injury and environmental law has evolved without much analysis.

This essay develops a theory of environmental torts that has both positive and normative aspects. The positive theory describes why environmental tort litigation occurs. It emphasizes the economic gain, by at least some of the participants, that drives the enterprise. In much of tort law, environmental torts included, the critical economic players are the plaintiffs' attorneys. If the compensation available through contingency fees from personal injury suits is insufficient, attorneys will pursue other kinds of cases. Hence, a positive theory of environmental torts must explain how attorneys are able to gain compensation for their clients, and themselves.

A positive theory of environmental tort litigation is presently unavailable. Much of what has been written about toxic torts, and the little that has addressed environmental torts, suggests that environmental tort suits should be rare because the cases are so difficult to win. The variety of scientific, evidentiary, and tort doctrinal issues would appear to frustrate even the most committed plaintiffs' attorneys. Therefore, the challenge for a positive theory of environmental torts is to explain why and how lawyers are able to obtain fees in the face of such obstacles.

The positive and normative theories are not coincident. For a normative theory of environmental torts, the critical concept is deterrence. Just because a fee mechanism drives attorneys to bring tort suits does not mean these suits will deter high-risk activities. Similarly, while there may be many normative reasons that recommend environmental tort litigation as an effective deterrent, doctrinal or evidentiary issues may yet frustrate successful suits. In the latter situation, a normative theory might recommend law reform that increases economic incentives for attorneys to bring environmental tort claims.

Unlike a positive theory, a normative theory is not neutral. Based on an assessment of the incentives that litigation produces, the normative theory should recommend either more or less environmental tort litigation. With regard to environmental torts, that recommendation likely will remain tentative. While scholars have considered the theoretical deterrence effect of torts suits, they have provided startlingly little evidence that common-law litigation actually prevents injuries in an efficacious manner. From a policy perspective, then, one encourages or discourages any type of tort litigation with great caution and little confidence. Environmental torts are no exception.

Empirical evidence suggests that environmental torts suits currently send a weak deterrent signal. Consider the evidence available concerning the optimal level of environmental tort litigation from a deterrence perspective. Scientists estimate that environmental carcinogens cause at least 10,000 deaths annually in the United States. Also, statistics from 1985–86 indicate that defendants spent a total of $200 million per year on environmental tort litigation, including litigation costs, jury verdicts and settlements. Therefore, each cancer death costs defendants $20,000. In the only other area of tort law where similar figures are readily available, medical malpractice, litigation is estimated to cost defendants $143,000 per death. The environmental litigation deterrence signal is, therefore, relatively weak.

Of course, tort litigation's deterrence effect depends not just on its economic magnitude, but also on the ability of polluters to understand and assess the economic signal. Careful consideration of the circumstances of environmental tort litigants, and of the nature of tort doctrine, might suggest peculiarities that would render the deterrent signal incomprehensible to environmental tort defendants. Nonetheless, the foregoing rudimentary calculations do not provide sufficient basis to conclude that there is too much environmental tort litigation. Therefore, the appropriate normative perspective must be open-minded toward increasing environmental tort litigation, while exploring the nuances of deterrence dynamics.

A critical first step in the development of normative and positive theories of environmental torts is to examine the notion of environmental harm. Torts may target only a subset of the environmental risks that are addressed by environmental law generally. One reason that environmental law seems to be in a state of flux is that the various risks now addressed by environmental law are quite heterogeneous, while the standard assumption in much of the literature is that environmental pollution is homogeneous. Accordingly, [this article] deconstructs environmental pollution and identifies the subset of pollution paradigms, centering on illness caused by toxic substances, that personal injury litigation can profitably address.

The next step is to consider the alternatives to environmental torts that deter these environmental injuries. [The author] suggests that traditional environmental regulation has addressed certain environmental pollution paradigms without much success. Positively, the failure of regulation may explain the persistence of perceived injuries that provide the basis for suits. Normatively, environmental torts may be best characterized as alternative devices for deterrence of environmental injury, again arising because of the failure of conventional regulation. [The article also] discusses how other institutional approaches—the market and criminal law—also fail to deter certain types of environmental injury.

Having suggested that tort law can reasonably deter certain paradigms of environmental injury that other institutions fail to address, [the article then] outlines the distinctive aspects of environmental tort litigation[,] * * * shows how judges have reduced some of the obdurate barriers in traditional personal injury law to help plaintiffs' attorneys bring successful environmental tort claims, thereby providing a positive theory of environmental torts[, and] also examines the efficiency of the deterrence produced by evolving environmental tort litigation.

* * *

Notes and Questions

1. Do Brennan's data (10,000 cancer deaths, $200 million in defense costs, yielding $20,000 per death) sound accurate? Is reliance upon 1985 data simply too inexact given the dynamic growth of environmental tort litigation? Should the relevant data also include how much society expends on preventing the release of toxins into the environment? What reasons might explain the higher per death recovery in the medical malpractice field?

Assuming the validity of 10,000 cancer deaths, how do factors such as lifestyle, dietary habits, or genetic predisposition, influence these data? Are any of these three factors inappropriate for consideration in evaluating the availability of a remedy for a plaintiff's injury or disease?

2. Is Brennan correct in concluding that the environmental law regulatory regime provides little deterrence to conduct producing environmental injuries? Should the analysis incorporate the costs of preventing and remediating property damage, which are the primary objective of CERCLA, which is treated in Chapter 10?

3. For an interesting perspective on the earth's environmental problems, *see* two books authored by James Lovelock. Gaia: A New Look on Earth (Norton, 1979) and The Ages of Gaia: A Biography of the Living Earth (Norton, 1988). Gaia theory posits that the earth is a living organism which acts to preserve itself, where species act in concert and are acted upon, in a manner suitable for the maintenance of life. In speaking out for Gaia, Lovelock often comes into conflict with more conventional views of the environment and environmental laws. He describes various maladies in the environmental movement, such as exploitation of cancer fears by "environmental demagogues" and what he calls the "zero shibboleth;" the contention that a toxic substance that is carcinogenic at any dosage must be completely removed from the environment. He argues that the zero-shibboleth ignores the fact that many potentially harmful substances are essential, in small amounts, to the environment. How would Brennan likely treat this issue?

MICHAEL D. AXLINE, NAVIGATING THE TOXIC BYWATERS OF THE INDUSTRIAL AGE
25 Idaho L. Rev. 459 (1988–1989).

We are in the midst of a revolution in the law of toxic torts. The revolution has been sparked by a social awakening to the hidden costs of the industrial age. Revolutions occur when the costs imposed by one segment of society on another segment of society become greater than the burdened segment is willing to bear. The costs imposed by toxic substances in our environment have assumed proportions that are now impossible to ignore, and those costs continue to increase exponentially. These costs have reached crisis proportions in part because free access to the ambient environment historically made irresponsible disposal of toxic substances economically attractive.

In 1968 Garrett Hardin described the "tragedy of the commons" in the following way:

> Picture a pasture open to all. It is to be expected that each herdsman will try to keep as many cattle as possible on the commons. * * * [T]he rational herdsman concludes that the only sensible course for him to pursue is to add another animal to his herd. * * * But this is the conclusion reached by each and every rational herdsman sharing a commons. Therein is the tragedy. Each man is locked into a system that compels him to increase his herd without limit—in a world that is limited.

Our ambient environment is a shared commons, and the ability to pollute the environment without having to pay for the pollution provides economic benefits as real as those derived from grazing cattle upon the commons. Rational polluters have therefore concluded for some time that the "only sensible course to pursue" is to pollute the environment with toxic substances, rather than pay to dispose of them properly.

The federal and state governments are by now aware of the human health problems caused by rational polluters. They have therefore devised various schemes to address the pollution of our ambient "commons." For example, governments may "sell" access to the environment by charging a fee for pollution or imposing a tax upon polluting activities. Alternatively, governments may demand that polluters pay for and install the technology necessary to prevent the pollution in the first instance. A third solution is to allow the courts to allocate the external costs of pollution through granting damage awards to individuals harmed by the pollution.

The "prevention" approach to the toxics problem is without doubt preferable to compensatory approaches. Preventive measures avoid the transaction costs of reconstructing the chain of events between the generation of a toxic substance and the point at which it causes injury. Preventive measures also avoid the inevitable discrepancy between predicted costs and actual costs (preventive measures too frequently fail to account for Murphy's law). Most importantly, preventive measures avoid the physical and emotional pain that accompanies injuries from exposure to toxic substances.

Rational polluters should realize that it is in their best economic interest to support preventive approaches to toxics problems. The tragic history of human suffering in the asbestos industry provides a valuable lesson for such polluters.

* * *

To convince polluters that the cost of paying damages after the fact will be greater than the cost of paying for prevention before the fact, one must first convince polluters that they are likely eventually to be forced to pay for the damage caused by their pollution. [D]evelopments in the law of toxic torts are moving in the direction of greater liability for the producers, distributors, users, and disposers of toxic substances.

This is not to say that the field of toxic torts is simple or straightforward. The scientific and legal problems swirling in the toxic by-waters of the industrial age are enormously difficult. Those difficulties are principally due to the temporal and spatial dimensions of the risks posed by toxics. It is these dimensions that the field of toxic torts must strive to encompass if it is to influence rational polluters to take steps to prevent toxic pollution.

To illustrate, consider dioxin. One form of dioxin (2,3,7,8–TCDD) is the most toxic synthetic molecule known. It poses serious health risks even in unimaginably small doses. For example, it kills some species of fish when they are exposed to it in the parts-per-quadrillion range (a quadrillionth is one thousandth of a millionth of a millionth). It causes cancer at the lowest levels ever tested. It is an unwanted but unavoidable byproduct of certain types of manufacturing processes. It is also very persistent in the environment.[a]

Such fantastically toxic and persistent molecules, when they become mobile in the environment, have the potential to cause harm in places far removed in time and space from their point of origin. Because these molecules are invisible to the naked eye, it is difficult, and in many cases impossible, to trace the injury causing particle back to its point of origin. Even when the location, time, and cause of exposure can be determined with confidence, it may be difficult to prove that exposure to the substance caused an injury. This difficulty is compounded by the fact that injuries which result from exposure to toxic substances may remain latent for long periods of time. If the source of the contaminant can be located and an injury proven, a statute of limitations or a statute of ultimate repose may still prevent the recovery of damages. In short, the difficulties in defining how and when toxic substances cause injury to human health raise serious barriers to assigning responsibility for those injuries through the legal process.

Despite these barriers, recent innovations in the law of toxic torts provide some hope for fair allocation of at least some of the costs imposed by the use of toxic substances. There are three particularly important aspects of the current revolution in toxic tort law. These are (1) new approaches to proving causation, (2) the collaboration between common law and statutory law, and (3) innovative approaches to defining the nature of damages caused by toxic substances.

* * *

[a]. This is not the form of dioxin which was included in the herbicide Agent Orange which is the subject of litigation covered in Chapter 9. [Eds.]

The toxic risk faced by our generation is the result of mechanisms set in motion long ago. The staggering cost of addressing those risks will be borne by our children and our children's children. It is impossible even to quantify the extent of the risk posed by toxic substances, because until recently, free access to the ambient environment and secrecy about toxic risk were societal norms. Legislators and courts, however, have begun to catch up with those responsible for creating those risks, and legislators and courts have not been sympathetic. The scientific and jurisprudential developments that are briefly described above, and more fully explored in the articles that follow, represent only the first skirmishes of the revolution in the law of toxic torts. Rational polluters should pay close attention to the results of these skirmishes, because they suggest that in the long run an ounce of prevention will be worth a pound of cure.

Notes and Questions

1. What does Professor Axline mean by "hidden costs?" What are the costs? In what respects are they hidden? What is the so-called "tragedy of the commons?" According to the author, why would a "rational" polluter conclude that pollution, rather than proper disposal, is the only sensible course?

2. In his observation on "revolutions," what are the societal "segments" to which Professor Axline refers? According to the author's reasoning, what segment is imposing the burdens? What segment is imposed upon? What are the argued impositions?

3. The author references three potential governmental responses to environmental contamination: (1) the "sale" of access to the environment by means of fees or taxes; (2) standard setting, obliging polluters to pay for pollution-preventing technology; and (3) judicial allocation of the costs of pollution through the mechanism of damage awards. What are the limitations or the inefficiencies of each noted approach? Why does the author state that the "prevention" approach is preferable?

While this casebook is concerned primarily with Professor Axline's alternative (3), are alternative's (1) and (2) of measurable pertinence to issues raised by suits for money damages arising from environmental or toxic harm? On the basis of your reading to this point, what is the basis for Professor Axline's claim that "[r]ational polluters should realize that it is their best interest to support preventative approaches" to toxic problems?

The unique and complex problems which plaintiffs encounter in environmental tort cases, as outlined by Professor Axline, are considered further in the following article.

DANIEL A. FARBER, TOXIC CAUSATION [a]
71 Minnesota Law Review 1219 (1987).

* * *

[a]. Reprinted with permission of Minnesota Law Review; Copyright 1987 by the Minnesota Law Review Foundation; Daniel A. Farber.

A. Toxic Torts in a Nutshell

The plaintiff's first problem is to establish that the defendant's conduct met the requisite liability standard. Although many toxic tort plaintiffs have brought actions under products liability theories holding manufacturers strictly liable for defective products, the liability standard is less clear in cases not involving manufacturers. The generally accepted liability test for hazardous waste releases is stated in the Second Restatement of Torts. Under this test, liability exists despite the exercise of due care if an activity was 'abnormally dangerous.' To determine whether an activity is abnormally dangerous, a court must weigh the probability and severity of foreseeable harm, whether the activity is unusual or is in an inappropriate location, and other factors. Thus, fault plays a role in the Restatement assessment. A few courts have rejected this fault element, however, and have begun to move beyond the abnormally dangerous test. In State v. Ventron Corp.,[b] the New Jersey Supreme Court imposed strict liability for harm caused by toxic substances escaping from a landowner's property.

Even if the defendant's conduct meets the requisite legal standard for liability, several possible barriers may prevent recovery. Statutes of limitations can create major difficulties in some states. For example, a New York trial judge in 1983 dismissed fifty-four of ninety-one personal injury actions by residents of Love Canal. The judge held that the actions were barred by New York's statute of limitations because they were filed more than three years after exposure to the toxic chemicals. The statute of limitations problem has also received great attention in the asbestos cases.

Another problem is establishing a link between the defendant and the release of the substance. For example, many hazardous waste generators may have shipped similar materials to the site in question. It may be quite difficult to establish whose containers leaked or in what quantities. A similar issue can arise in products liability cases. In Sindell v. Abbott Laboratories,[26] the plaintiff's mother was administered the drug diethylstilbestrol (DES) during pregnancy. Although DES was routinely given to prevent miscarriage, it is now known to cause a rare form of cancer in some daughters of women who took the drug. After developing such cancer, the plaintiff sued eleven of the more than two hundred manufacturers of DES. Although the plaintiff was unable to identify the manufacturer of the particular DES which her mother took, the court held that she had stated a cause of action against manufacturers of the drug using an identical formula. Resting this holding on a broad social policy, the court noted that the defendants were 'better able to bear the cost of injury resulting from the manufacture of a defective product.' The Sindell court then adopted a novel theory of liability by making each defendant liable for a share of the plaintiff's damages,

---

[b]. Reprinted infra, Chapter 4.   **26.** 607 P.2d 924 (Cal.1980), cert. denied 449 U.S. 912 (1980).

based on its share of the DES market. Assuming that the *Sindell* theory or one of its variants becomes the norm in products liability litigation, it could be readily adapted to hazardous waste litigation.

B. THE CAUSATION PROBLEM

Sindell and related theories address the problem of linking the defendant to the chemical exposure. An even more difficult problem is that of linking the exposure to the plaintiff's injury. It is a commonplace that toxic chemical regulation involves matters at the boundaries of scientific knowledge. This scientific uncertainty causes severe problems for government regulators, but even more serious problems result for private plaintiffs who must establish a defendant's liability by a preponderance of the evidence.

In considering compensation, it is important to keep in mind that there are really two causation problems. One is the problem of establishing that the chemical involved is capable of causing the type of harm from which the plaintiff suffers. This is often difficult because the causation of diseases like cancer is so poorly understood. For this reason, medical theory is relatively unhelpful in filling in gaps in the factual picture. Facts themselves are hard to come by. Many toxic substances are relatively novel, and, given the long latency periods associated with cancer, sufficient evidence concerning health effects is not likely to be available for the foreseeable future. Animal studies, although useful, generally involve much higher doses that are difficult to extrapolate to low doses over prolonged periods; there is also the question of whether extrapolation of results between species is valid. Epidemiological studies are also helpful but often inconclusive regarding the level of risk created by a toxic substance.

The other problem relating to proof of causation is that of establishing, given that the toxic substance in question can cause harm of the type suffered by the plaintiff, that the plaintiff's harm did in fact result from such exposure. A chemical may increase the prevalence of a disease enough to leave no doubt that some members of the exposed population were injured by that chemical. Others, however, may have suffered injuries from independent sources, and the two groups may be impossible to distinguish. The statistical association between exposure and illness may be too weak to justify a finding that a particular plaintiff's disease is causally linked to an exposure to a hazardous substance.

* * *

2. *Tort Litigation*

Despite the novelty of tort litigation over toxic causation, clear patterns have already evolved in some areas. Swine flu liability is one such area. * * *

Litigation about Agent Orange, a defoliant and herbicide used by American forces in the Vietnam War, has provided the most extensive judicial discussion of toxic causation. Numerous lawsuits were filed against the manufacturers by veterans, their families, and others who contended that Agent Orange had caused various illnesses. Ultimately, the litigation was consolidated in Judge Weinstein's court in the Eastern District of New York.[c] The weakness of the plaintiffs' causation evidence persuaded Judge Weinstein to approve a $180 million settlement, which was considered highly favorable to the defendants.

As Judge Weinstein explained, the evidence concerning the possible dangers from Agent Orange would have been enough for a court to uphold an administrative order limiting its use. Emphasizing the distinction between preventive regulatory measures and compensatory legal actions, however, Judge Weinstein noted that "[i]n the latter [case], a far higher probability (greater than 50%) is required since the law believes it unfair to require an individual to pay for another's tragedy unless it is shown that it is more likely than not that he caused it." The key flaw in the plaintiffs' case was that government epidemiological studies showed no statistical link between Agent Orange exposure and significant health effects. Studies by the Air Force, the CDC, and the Australian government all had concluded that no health effects had been demonstrated. Hence, Judge Weinstein agreed that a settlement was in the best interests of the class.

* * *

Judge Weinstein's stress on the epidemiological data seems consistent with the pattern of rulings in the GBS cases, in which the CDC epidemiological study was the key to recovery.[d] The D.C. Circuit, however, has permitted recovery solely on the basis of expert clinical assessments despite a lack of statistical evidence. In Ferebee v. Chevron Chemical Co.,[78] the court stated:

> Thus, a cause-effect relationship need not be clearly established by animal or epidemiological studies before a doctor can testify that, in his opinion, such a relationship exists. As long as the basic methodology employed to reach such a conclusion is sound, such as use of tissue samples, standard tests, and patient examination, products liability law does not preclude recovery until a 'statistically significant' number of people have been injured or until science has had the time and resources to complete sophisticated laboratory studies of the chemical. In a courtroom, the test for allowing a plaintiff to recover in a tort suit of this type is not scientific certainty but legal sufficiency.

This language, while not inconsistent with Judge Weinstein's rulings, seems more favorable toward the admission of expert testimony.

---

[c]. In re "Agent Orange" Product Liability Litigation, 597 F.Supp. 740 (E.D.N.Y. 1984).

[d]. This refers to the Guillain–Barre Syndrome and litigation arising out of the Swine Flu Vaccine Act's immunization programs in 1976. Epidemiological studies revealed that recipients of the vaccine experienced an increased incidence of GBS for a ten-week period.

78. 736 F.2d 1529 (D.C.Cir.1984).

Although a few courts have followed Ferebee's broader view of admissibility, the law of toxic causation is just beginning to receive judicial attention. Clearly, a 'Restatement of the Law of Toxic Torts' would be premature. It is not too early, however, to look for patterns in the cases and to begin to undertake a theoretical analysis of the causation issue.

* * *

Note

Some commentators have argued that the tort system, even with its difficult causation, statutes of limitation, and indeterminate defendant problems, is an effective and appropriate means for providing compensation to plaintiffs injured by environmental harms. For an article suggesting that conventional tort evidentiary, burden of proof and remedy options present no peculiar obstacles to environmental and toxic tort claimants, see, e.g., Ruhl, Toxic Tort Remedies: The Case Against the "Superduper Fund" and Other Reform Proposals, 38 Baylor L.Rev. 597 (1986), in which the author argues for the retention of the principal tort liability rules. Ruhl's article, unlike that of Professor Axline, concludes that the tort system is an effective and appropriate vehicle for redressing injuries resulting from environmentally related harms. With this background, we now consider each of the common law tort theories.

Chapter Two

TRESPASS ACTIONS IN ENVIRONMENTAL LAW

A. GENERAL PRINCIPLES OF TRESPASS

1. THE INTENT REQUIREMENT

Trespass is classified as one of the "intentional" torts in most casebooks, but in reality could just as logically be classified as a strict liability tort. At common law, the intent element was satisfied by an entry upon the land of another, by a person or thing, as a consequence of a volitional act, regardless of the absence of any "intent" to make an unpermitted entry upon the land of another. In other words, the defendant need not have intended to invade plaintiff's interest in the exclusive possession of land; it was sufficient that such an invasion actually resulted from a volitional act. Moreover, the risk of mistake was borne entirely by the defendant—an honest and reasonable belief that the defendant was on her own property or was not on another's property was not a defense, and neither intent nor negligence by the defendant was an essential element in terms of the fault requirement. The rationale for the strictness of these rules was that a trespass action was a legal means for a lawful possessor to maintain the integrity of her ownership.

To satisfy the "intent" requirement of the prima facie case in trespass, plaintiff need only prove that defendant intended the act that resulted in the trespass, i.e., that defendant's act was volitional, and done with knowledge to a substantial certainty that the act would result in introduction of the substance onto plaintiff's property.[1] For this reason a defendant may not defeat a trespass action by proving that it acted with the mistaken belief that its actions and the invasion were authorized by plaintiff. The inadequacy of mistake as a defense in

---

1. See Restatement (Second) of Torts § 158, comment i: "It is enough that an act is done with knowledge that it will to a substantial certainty result in the entry of a foreign matter."

trespass actions has, curiously, been repeatedly demonstrated in suits involving mistaken deliveries of fuel oil. For example, in Jacobsen v. Yokum Oil Co., Inc., 1993 WL 152313 (Minn.App.1993), the Jacobsens brought an action in trespass and nuisance against Yocum, a fuel oil seller, after Yocum pumped 452 gallons of fuel oil into the basement of their home. Although plaintiffs had converted from oil heating to natural gas and removed the fuel oil tank, they neglected to remove the fill pipe, using it instead as an electrical conduit, and compounded the risk of a mistaken oil delivery by failing to post a street number on their house. Yocum's conceded mistake was no obstacle to the court in sustaining the jury's finding of 75% responsibility for the damage.

In another suit, also involving a fuel-oil distributor's mistaken fuel delivery to a residence and accidental spillage resulting therefrom, the court rejected as a defense defendant's claim that it acted in a reasonable belief that the fuel had been ordered, and stated: "Obviously, the defendant intended to come upon plaintiff's land and make an oil delivery and did not intend to commit a trespass or intentionally to cast oil upon plaintiff's land. His innocence and his mistaken belief that his visit was authorized is of no moment since his intent is clearly shown to have been to deliver oil. This unauthorized act, resulting in whatever damages which may have occurred, rendered him liable." Serota v. M. & M. Utilities, Inc., 55 Misc.2d 286, 285 N.Y.S.2d 121, 124 (1967).

Gradually over the centuries the law came to distinguish between intentional entries upon the land of another (entering another's land with knowledge that it is another's land), and unintentional entries. For *unintentional* entries, modern liability in trespass typically turns on whether the entry is reckless, negligent, or the result of abnormally dangerous activity.

For *intentional* invasions of the land of another, the law of torts still retains most of its strict and inflexible character, except that today a host of privileges may apply to release the defendant from any liability. The Restatement (Second) of Torts recognizes twenty nonconsensual privileges. See Restatement (Second) of Torts §§ 191–211. These privileges embrace such justifications as private necessity (a limited privilege), public necessity (a broad privilege), entry to abate a private nuisance, entry to execute civil process, etc. The most important characteristic of the privileges is that they are very specific and narrow in identifying the factual circumstances which give rise to the privilege to commit what would otherwise constitute an actionable trespass. None of these privileges is so broad as to recognize the reasonableness of the defendant's entry under all the circumstances as an excuse. See Prosser and Keeton on Torts 67–84 (5th ed. 1984); 1 Harper, James & Gray, The Law of Torts §§ 1.11–1.28, 1.22 (2d ed. 1986).

2. POSSESSORY INTEREST

It follows that to maintain an action in trespass, plaintiff must have a contemporaneous legal interest in possession of the property. The consequences of failure to show such a possessory interest was shown in Davey Compressor Co. v. City of Delray Beach, 613 So.2d 60 (Fla.App. 1993), a city's suit in trespass and other claims for toxic contamination beneath its water well field. In that suit, the evidence showed that Delray supplied its citizens with water as permitted by a consumptive use permit issued by the South Florida Water Management District, which was to expire in 1997. From 1981 to 1987, Davey disposed of toxic solvents, used to clean air compressors, onto the ground behind its operating facility. Delray discovered the presence of these solvents in the groundwater, and won a judgment of over $3 million in past damages, and $5.6 million in future damages. On appeal, the Florida court upheld the award of past damages, but reversed the award of future damages on the ground that damages awarded for dates following 1997 were in error, stating: "Since appellant failed to establish its legal interest in the groundwater beneath its well field beyond the expiration date of its water consumptive use permit, appellee cannot recover future damages after the expiration date of its permit."

3. EXTENT OF INVASION

Trespass protects plaintiff's interest in the surface land itself, the earth or other material beneath the surface, and "the air space above it." Restatement (Second) of Torts § 158 comment i. At common law, plaintiff did not have to suffer substantial harm to sue, since many actions were instituted primarily to vindicate an ownership interest, and at least nominal damages were recoverable for any material intrusion. Today, in many jurisdictions the availability of a remedy in trespass may turn upon the seriousness of the contamination of plaintiff's land or of the environment. Where there is an actual invasion, and where the interference is substantial, defendant may be liable in trespass; where the pollution or contamination is of a lesser or a transitory nature, courts in many jurisdictions find the claim to be in nuisance alone. The party prevailing in a trespass action may recover all damages that are the natural and proximate consequence of the trespass. See, e.g., Kelly v. Para–Chem Southern, Inc., 428 S.E.2d 703 (S.C.1993), in which the trespass and nuisance claims of Kelly, the owner of a 330 acre tract contiguous to Para–Chem's property, recovered $14,000 for groundwater contamination.

4. RELATIONSHIP TO NUISANCE

The claim in trespass may be readily confused with that in private nuisance. As explained by a leading authority, "[t]he distinction which is now accepted is that trespass is an invasion of the plaintiff's interest in the exclusive possession of his land, while nuisance is an interference with his use and enjoyment of it." Prosser and Keeton on Torts 622 (5th ed. 1984). In most jurisdictions, invasions of plaintiff's property that amount to trespass may also, if they interfere with plaintiff's use and enjoyment of the property, be actionable in nuisance. In such circumstances, "plaintiff may have his choice" of a claim in trespass or in nuisance, "or may proceed upon both." Mangini v. Aerojet–General Corp., 230 Cal.App.3d 1125, 281 Cal.Rptr. 827 (1991)(quoting Restatement (Second) of Torts § 821D, comment e)(plaintiff's land contamination claim in nuisance, trespass, and other common law causes of action).

The toxic tort claimant will lodge claims against one or more defendants on multiple causes of action. For example, a homeowner claiming that water runoff from a nearby asphalt producing facility has polluted her pond might bring claims in (1) nuisance, alleging that the contamination of the pond interferes with her quiet enjoyment of her home and property; (2) trespass, alleging that the asphalt effluent constituted an actionable invasion of her possessory interest in her property; and (3) negligence, alleging that the asphalt producer failed to exercise due care in conducting its operations so as to prevent, to the extent practicable, the claimed intrusion and contamination.[2]

The *intent* of defendant's conduct that plaintiff must show varies from nuisance to trespass. In trespass, plaintiff does not need to show that defendant *intended* to invade or contaminate plaintiff's land. Regardless of defendant's good faith, or caution, or innocent mistake, a claim for at least nominal damages will be available to a plaintiff suffering toxic contamination of property. This legal solicitude towards the interests protected by the trespass cause of action is due to "the high social value traditionally placed upon the inviolability of a person's real property, and particularly of his home." Christie and Meeks, Cases and Materials on the Law of Torts 52 (2d ed.1990).

A claim in trespass usually requires that plaintiff demonstrate that defendant's pollutant or contaminant have settled on or infiltrated plaintiff's property. The *invasory* (physical interference) requirement of trespass, and absence of that requirement for a private nuisance claim, has greater significance outside of the toxic tort area, for most toxic tort claims arising from contamination or pollution involve a determinable *invasion* of property, even if the substance itself is invisible. For example, contamination by PCBs or by radiation is not visible to the naked eye, but can be considered, nonetheless, a physical invasion of plaintiff's property.

---

2. Environmental tort claims available in other situations might, on these facts, be unavailable to our hypothetical homeowner. A warranty claim might fail for want of a sale; a breach of the implied warranty of habitability might fail for the additional reason that the asphalt producer, unlike the homeowner's direct vendor or building contractor, has warranted nothing concerning the home; a strict tort products liability action might fail because, inter alia, at the time of the damage, the product was not reduced to consumable form, i.e., was not at that time a "product"; and an action claiming liability for an abnormally dangerous activity might fail should it be shown that asphalt production can, with the exercise of reasonable care, avoid the claimed contamination risks and damage. Warranty, strict tort, and abnormally dangerous activity liability claims are discussed at Chapters 4 and 7 respectively.

5. CONTINUING TRESPASS

As in the doctrine of continuing nuisance, a polluter's failure to remove a pollutant or a contaminant from plaintiff's land may represent a "continuing" tort. Plaintiff may frame a claim in *continuing* trespass,[3] which, upon sufficient evidence, "confers on the possessor of the land an option to maintain a succession of actions based on a theory of continuing trespass, or to treat the continuation of the thing on the land as an aggravation of the original trespass." Restatement (Second) of Torts § 899, comment d. The key distinction between a continuing and a permanent trespass is that if a trespass can be discontinued or abated at any time, it is considered a continuing one, and the plaintiff "is permitted to bring successive actions as damages accrue until abatement takes place." Capogeannis v. Superior Court, 12 Cal.App.4th 668, 15 Cal.Rptr. 2d 796, 800 (1993). In contrast, where the trespass is deemed permanent, the land possessor can maintain only one action for the damage sustained and may encounter a statutes of limitation problem if the invasion preceded the prescribed period. The significance of the designation "continuing trespass" is primarily that of relieving some of the strictures of limitations periods within which the possessor would have to bring a toxic tort claim.[4]

6. DAMAGES RECOVERABLE

Although a toxic tort plaintiff will often have a claim in both private nuisance and in trespass, the description and measure of damages plaintiff seeks under each may differ. For private nuisance, plaintiff asks for damages that will compensate for the interference with the use and enjoyment of the land. For example, a property owner's apple orchard mistakenly contaminated by aerial pesticide spraying over nearby land might seek nuisance damages for (1) any period of time the owner had to reside elsewhere in order to permit the contaminant to dissipate; and (2) any economic harm suffered by damage to the apples, or necessary delay in harvesting. The orchard owner's damages in trespass, on the other hand, does not require that he show any actual loss or damage, for he would be entitled to at least nominal damages because defendant's spraying operation technically, although innocuously, invaded the property. Nevertheless, as will be seen below, some courts have required more than a trivial invasion in order to maintain a trespass action.

Moreover, the invasion of plaintiff's property need not be direct, if plaintiff can prove that an intentional act of defendant resulted in the harm. Thus, the causal intervention of natural conditions, such as deterioration, wind, or rain, in initiating or exacerbating the trespass

---

3. "The actor's failure to remove from land in the possession of another a thing he has tortiously * * * placed on the land constitutes a continuing trespass for the entire time which the thing is on the land[.]"

Restatement (Second) of Torts § 899, comment d.

4. Restatement (Second) of Torts § 161, comment b. In Chapter 12 we consider this issue in detail.

will not absolve defendant of liability.[5] It was so held in one action where plaintiff claimed that defendant's dumping of asphalt waste on land contiguous to plaintiff's fish pond eventually resulted in the pollution of the pond. Rushing v. Hooper–McDonald, Inc., 300 So.2d 94 (Ala.1974)("This court holds that it is not necessary that the asphalt or foreign matter be thrown or dumped directly and immediately upon the plaintiff's land but that it is sufficient if the act is done so that it will to a substantial certainty result in the entry of the asphalt or foreign matter onto the real property that the plaintiff possesses.")

As this summary reveals, trespass remains a relatively inflexible concept. Unless an unauthorized entry upon the plaintiff's land has occurred, trespass will not lie no matter how bothersome the defendant's conduct may have been. And whenever an intentional entry is found to have taken place, there is relatively little opportunity for the defendant to talk of justification. Moreover, once a trespass is found to have occurred, the plaintiff may have threatened repetitions enjoined regardless of arguments that to do so would impose a greater hardship on the defendant than would otherwise be suffered by the plaintiff.

B. JUDICIAL APPLICATIONS OF TRESPASS

RAILROAD COMMISSION OF TEXAS v. MANZIEL

Supreme Court of Texas, 1962.
361 S.W.2d 560.

SMITH, JUSTICE.

This direct appeal is the result of a suit filed by the appellees Dorothy N. Manziel et al. in the 126th District Court of Travis County, Texas, to set aside and cancel an order of the Railroad Commission of December 12, 1960, permitting the appellants, the Whelan Brothers, to drill and inject water in their Eldridge # 11 well located at an irregular spacing on the Whelan Brothers–Vickie Lynn unit 206 feet south of the boundary of the Manziel Estate–Mathis lease in the Vickie Lynn Field, Marion County, Texas. The Railroad Commission was the original defendant in this action; the Whelan Brothers intervened and aligned themselves in defense of the Railroad Commission's order. * * *

* * *

After trial, the District Court entered a judgment canceling the order allowing the Whelans to inject water at the irregular location, enjoining its enforcement, and enjoining the Whelans from injecting water in their Eldridge # 11 well under said order. The judgment of the District Court has been brought to this court for review * * *

---

5. Comment i to Restatement (Second) of Torts § 158 gives these examples: "[O]ne who piles sand so close to his boundary that by force of gravity alone it slides down on to his neighbor's land, or who builds an embankment that during ordinary rainfalls the dirt is washed from it upon adjacent lands, becomes a trespasser on the other's land."

The Manziels pleaded that the injection of salt water by the Whelans in the # 11 well will cause damage to their producing wells, and will result in loss and injury to their oil and gas interests due to premature flooding. They assert, and we agree, that under our liberal rules of pleading, this wording is sufficient to give rise to the issue of trespass in considering the status of encroaching secondary recovery waters. * * *

To constitute trespass there must be some physical entry upon the land by some "thing," Gregg v. Delhi–Taylor Oil Corp., Tex., 344 S.W.2d 411 (1961); but is injected water that crosses lease lines from an authorized secondary project the type of "thing" that may be said to render the adjoining operator guilty of trespass? * * *

Secondary recovery operations are carried on to increase the ultimate recovery of oil and gas, and it is established that the pressure maintenance projects will result in more recovery than was obtained by primary methods. It cannot be disputed that such operations should be encouraged, for as the pressure behind the primary production dissipates, the greater is the public necessity for applying secondary recovery forces. It is obvious that secondary recovery programs could not and would not be conducted if any adjoining operator could stop the project on the ground of subsurface trespass. As is pointed out by amicus curiae, if the Manziel's theory of subsurface trespass is accepted, the injection of salt water in the East Texas field has caused subsurface trespass of the greatest magnitude.

The orthodox rules and principles applied by the courts as regards surface invasions of land may not be appropriately applied to subsurface invasions as arise out of the secondary recovery of natural resources. If the intrusions of salt water are to be regarded as trespassory in character, then under common notions of surface invasions, the justifying public policy considerations behind secondary recovery operations could not be reached in considering the validity and reasonableness of such operations. See: Keeton and Jones: "Tort Liability and the Oil and Gas Industry II," 39 Tex.Law.Rev. 253 at p. 268. Certainly, it is relevant to consider and weigh the interests of society and the oil and gas industry as a whole against the interests of the individual operator who is damaged; and if the authorized activities in an adjoining secondary recovery unit are found to be based on some substantial, justifying occasion, then this court should sustain their validity.

We conclude that if, in the valid exercise of its authority to prevent waste, protect correlative rights, or in the exercise of other powers within its jurisdiction, the Commission authorizes secondary recovery projects, a trespass does not occur when the injected, secondary recovery forces move across lease lines, and the operations are not subject to an injunction on that basis. The technical rules of trespass have no place in the consideration of the validity of the orders of the Commission. * * *

Notes and Questions

1. Did the court rule that there was no trespass or did the court rule that the trespass was justified because of a "public necessity," as represented by the actions of the Railroad Commission?

2. Consider the following decision which reached a contrary conclusion. In Tidewater Oil Co. v. Jackson, 320 F.2d 157 (10th Cir.1963), another water injection case, the court found it unnecessary to determine whether recovery would have to be based on a theory of nuisance rather than trespass in view of the trial court's finding that Tidewater had injected water at unreasonable and excessive rates in the wells located along the boundaries of the Barrier lease, "and that such injections at such high rates were especially unreasonable, since the injection wells were deliberately located as close as possible to the boundary line and immediately opposite and within less than 100 feet of two of the plaintiff's wells." Does this language imply that trespassory invasions should be governed by a reasonableness standard, akin to negligence?

3. While *Manziel* arguably did not involve an "environmental" tort, its reasoning could easily be adapted to economic activity that produces subsurface harm to an adjoining landowner. Observe that the court was applying a utilitarian risk versus utility analysis, which was at least partially explainable by the presence of a governmental entity. What considerations was the court weighing on each side of the analysis? Should that make any difference?

BRADLEY v. AMERICAN SMELTING AND REFINING COMPANY

Supreme Court of Washington, 1985.
104 Wash.2d 677, 709 P.2d 782.

Callow, J.

This comes before us on a certification from the United States District Court for the Western District of Washington. Plaintiffs, landowners on Vashon Island, had sued for damages in trespass and nuisance from the deposit on their property of microscopic, airborne particles of heavy metals which came from the American Smelting and Refining Company (ASARCO) copper smelter at Ruston, Washington.

The issues certified for answer are as follows:

(1) Did the defendant have the requisite intent to commit intentional trespass as a matter of law?

(2) Does an intentional deposit of microscopic particulates, undetectable by the human senses, upon a person's property give rise to a cause of action for trespassory invasion of the person's right to exclusive possession of property as well as a claim of nuisance?

(3) Does the cause of action for trespassory invasion require proof of actual damages?

* * *

The parties have stipulated to the facts as follows: Plaintiffs Michael O. Bradley and Marie A. Bradley, husband and wife, are owners and occupiers of real property on the southern end of Vashon Island in

King County, Washington. The Bradleys purchased their property in 1978. * * *

Plaintiffs' property is located some 4 miles north of defendant's smelter. * * * As a part of the industrial process of smelting copper at the Tacoma smelter, various gases such as sulfur dioxide and particulate matter, including arsenic, cadmium and other metals, are emitted. Particulate matter is composed of distinct particles of matter other than water, which cannot be detected by the human senses.

The emissions from the Tacoma smelter are subject to regulation under the Federal Clean Air Act, the Washington Clean Air Act (RCW 70.94) and the Puget Sound Air Pollution Control Agency (PSAPCA). Currently, the Tacoma smelter meets the National Ambient Air Quality Standards (NAAQS), both primary and secondary, for both sulfur dioxide and particulate matter. As a result of the variance granted by PSAPCA, the Tacoma smelter is also in compliance with PSAPCA Regulation I concerning particulate emissions.

* * *

* * * The issues present the conflict in an industrial society between the need of all for the production of goods and the desire of the landowner near the manufacturing plant producing those goods that his use and enjoyment of his land not be diminished by the unpleasant side effects of the manufacturing process. A reconciliation must be found between the interest of the many who are unaffected by the possible poisoning and the few who may be affected.

1.   Did the defendant have the requisite intent to commit intentional trespass as a matter of law?

The parties stipulated that as a part of the smelting process, particulate matter including arsenic and cadmium was emitted, that some of the emissions had been deposited on the plaintiffs' land and that the defendant has been aware since 1905 that the wind, on occasion, caused these emissions to be blown over the plaintiffs' land. The defendant cannot and does not deny that whenever the smelter was in operation the whim of the winds could bring these deleterious substances to the plaintiffs' premises. We are asked if the defendant, knowing what it had to know from the facts it admits, had the legal intent to commit trespass.

The Restatement (Second) of Torts § 158 (1965) states:

["]One is subject to liability to another for trespass, irrespective of whether he thereby causes harm to any legally protected interest of the other, if he intentionally

(a) enters land in the possession of the other, or causes a thing or a third person to do so, or

(b) remains on the land, or

(c) fails to remove from the land a thing which he is under a duty to remove.["]

In the comment on Clause (a) of § 158 at 278 it is stated in part:

["]i. Causing entry of a thing. The actor, without himself entering the land, may invade another's interest in its exclusive possession by throwing, propelling, or placing a thing either on or beneath the surface of the land or in the air space above it. Thus, in the absence of the possessor's consent or other privilege to do so, it is an actionable trespass to throw rubbish on another's land ... In order that there may be a trespass under the rule stated in this Section, it is not necessary that the foreign matter should be thrown directly and immediately upon the other's land. It is enough that an act is done with knowledge that it will to a substantial certainty result in the entry of the foreign matter.["]

Addressing the definition, scope and meaning of "intent", section 8A of the Restatement (Second) of Torts says:

The word "intent" is used ["] ... to denote that the actor desires to cause consequences of his act, or that he believes that the consequences are substantially certain to result from it[.]" * * *

The defendant has known for decades that sulfur dioxide and particulates of arsenic, cadmium and other metals were being emitted from the tall smokestack. It had to know that the solids propelled into the air by the warm gases would settle back to earth somewhere. It had to know that a purpose of the tall stack was to disperse the gas, smoke and minute solids over as large an area as possible and as far away as possible, but that while any resulting contamination would be diminished as to any one area or landowner, that nonetheless contamination, though slight, would follow. * * *

Intent, however, is broader than a desire to bring about physical results. It must extend not only to those consequences which are desired, but also to those which the actor believes are substantially certain to follow from what he does. * * * The practical application of this principle has meant that where a reasonable man in the defendant's position would believe that a particular result was substantially certain to follow, he will be dealt with by the jury, or even by the court, as though he had intended it.

* * *

It is patent that the defendant acted on its own volition and had to appreciate with substantial certainty that the law of gravity would visit the effluence upon someone, somewhere.

We find that the defendant had the requisite intent to commit intentional trespass as a matter of law.

2. Does an intentional deposit of microscopic particulates, undetectable by the human senses, upon a person's property give rise to a cause of action for trespassory invasion of the person's right to exclusive possession of property as well as a claim of nuisance?

The courts have been groping for a reconciliation of the doctrines of trespass and nuisance over a long period of time and, to a great extent, have concluded that little of substance remains to any distinction between the two when air pollution is involved.   * * *

* * *

* * * The principal difference in theories is that the tort of trespass is complete upon a tangible invasion of plaintiff's property, however slight, whereas a nuisance requires proof that the interference with use and enjoyment is "substantial and unreasonable." This burden of proof advantage in a trespass case is accompanied by a slight remedial advantage as well.   Upon proof of a technical trespass plaintiff always is entitled to nominal damages.   It is possible also that a plaintiff could get injunctive relief against a technical trespass—for example, the deposit of particles of air pollutant on his property causing no known adverse effects.   The protection of the integrity of his possessory interests might justify the injunction even without proof of the substantial injury necessary to establish a nuisance.   Of course absent proof of injury, or at least a reasonable suspicion of it, courts are unlikely to invoke their equitable powers to require expensive control efforts.

While the strict liability origins of trespass encourage courts to eschew a balancing test in name, there is authority for denying injunctive relief if defendant has exhausted his technological opportunities for control.   If adopted generally, this principle would result substantially in a coalescence of nuisance and trespass law.   Acknowledging technological or economic justifications for trespassory invasions does away with the historically harsh treatment of conduct interfering with another's possessory interests.

Just as there may be proof advantages in a trespass theory, there may be disadvantages also.   Potential problems lurk in the ancient requirements that a trespassory invasion be "direct or immediate" and that an "object" or "something tangible" be deposited upon plaintiff's land.   * * *

Both of these concepts are nonsensical barriers, although the courts are slow to admit it.   The requirement that the invasion be "direct" is a holdover from the forms of action, and is repudiated by contemporary science of causation.   Atmospheric or hydrologic systems assure that pollutants deposited in one place will end up somewhere else, with no less assurance of causation than the blaster who watches the debris rise from his property and settle on his neighbor's land.   Trespassory consequences today may be no less "direct" even if the mechanism of delivery is viewed as more complex.

The insistence that a trespass involve an invasion by a "thing" or "object" was repudiated in the well known (but not particularly influential) case of Martin v. Reynolds Metals Co., [221 Or. 86, 342 P.2d 790 (1959), cert. denied 362 U.S. 918, 80 S.Ct. 672, 4 L.Ed.2d 739 (1960)], which held that gaseous and particulate fluorides from an aluminum smelter constituted a trespass for purposes of the statute of limitations[.] * * * [:]

"The view recognizing a trespassory invasion where there is no 'thing' which can be seen with the naked eye undoubtedly runs counter to the definition of trespass expressed in some quarters. * * * It is quite possible that in an earlier day when science had not yet peered into the molecular and atomic world of small particles, the courts could not fit an invasion through unseen physical instrumentalities into the requirement that a trespass can result only from a direct invasion. But in this atomic age even the uneducated know the great and awful force contained in the atom and what it can do to a man's property if it is released. In fact, the now famous equation $E = MC^2$ has taught us that mass and energy are equivalents and that our concept of 'things' must be reframed. If these observations on science in relation to the law of trespass should appear theoretical and unreal in the abstract, they become very practical and real to the possessor of land when the unseen force cracks the foundation of his house. The force is just as real if it is chemical in nature and must be awakened by the intervention of another agency before it does harm."[Id.]

[*Martin*] is quite right in hastening the demise of the "direct" and "tangible" limitations on the law of trespass. But any disappearance of these limits on the doctrine is likely to be accompanied by modifications of its strict liability advantages also. While parts per billion of fluorides or rays of light or magnetic invasions may work a trespass as effectively as flying rocks, it would seem that relief (particularly injunctive relief) should not follow without further inquiry into the limits of technology and prevailing land use patterns.

* * *

["]Under the modern theory of trespass, the law presently allows an action to be maintained in trespass for invasions that, at one time, were considered indirect and, hence, only a nuisance. In order to recover in trespass for this type of invasion [i.e., the asphalt piled in such a way as to run onto plaintiff's property, or the pollution emitting from a defendant's smoke stack, such as in the present case], a plaintiff must show 1) an invasion affecting an interest in the exclusive possession of his property; 2) an intentional doing of the act which results in the invasion; 3) reasonable foreseeability that the act done could result in an invasion of plaintiff's possessory interest; and 4) substantial damages to the res. ["][Borland v. Sanders Lead Co., 369 So.2d 523, 529 (Ala. 1979)].

* * *

3. Does the cause of action for trespassory invasion require proof of actual damages?

When airborne particles are transitory or quickly dissipate, they do not interfere with a property owner's possessory rights and, therefore, are properly denominated as nuisances. Born v. Exxon Corp., 388 So.2d

933 (Ala.1980); * * * Amphitheaters, Inc. v. Portland Meadows, [184 Or. 336, 198 P.2d 847 (1948)]. When, however, the particles or substance accumulates on the land and does not pass away, then a trespass has occurred. [Martin v. Reynolds Metals Co., supra.] While at common law any trespass entitled a landowner to recover nominal or punitive damages for the invasion of his property, such a rule is not appropriate under the circumstances before us. No useful purpose would be served by sanctioning actions in trespass by every landowner within a hundred miles of a manufacturing plant. Manufacturers would be harassed and the litigious few would cause the escalation of costs to the detriment of the many. The elements that we have adopted for an action in trespass from Borland require that a plaintiff has suffered actual and substantial damages. Since this is an element of the action, the plaintiff who cannot show that actual and substantial damages have been suffered should be subject to dismissal of his cause upon a motion for summary judgment.

Notes and Questions

1. *Bradley* is important because the court makes several significant changes in the rules usually governing trespass actions. First, it *lowers* the physical invasion requirement by recognizing that increased scientific knowledge enables courts to find as "physical" intrusions, invasions which were previously not observable and, accordingly, not legally cognizable. Indeed, as the court correctly points out, scientific understanding allows us to demonstrate that most interferences are "physical" in the sense that energy, unleashed by a defendant, produces a movement of molecules across land boundaries, in the form of tiny particles, or even noise and light. Second, and closely related, it abolishes the historical distinction between direct and indirect invasions of the landowner's interest. Third, the court *increases* the harm requirement by necessitating that plaintiffs show that the invasion produced substantial harm to their property. Why is this requirement so important?

2. The court's treatment of the intent requirement in trespass actions is important, especially in the environmental area where the defendant will usually not possess any intent or desire to cause harm to the plaintiff. The topic of intent in nuisance cases is addressed in detail in Chapter 3. Under the Restatement (Second) of Torts §§ 8A and 158, the necessary intent is shown if the defendant knew with substantial certainty that an invasion of plaintiff's right to exclusive possession would result from the defendant's activity, i.e., the smelting process.

3. After receiving the answers to the certified questions, the federal district court granted the defendant's motion for summary judgment on both the trespass and nuisance counts. Bradley v. American Smelting & Refining Co., 635 F.Supp. 1154 (W.D.Wash.1986). The court noted that the imperceptible particles did not rise to the level of dangerousness it believed was required by the law of trespass, and that since the plaintiffs had suffered mere anxiety about *possible* health risks, there was no nuisance. Does this result surprise you? Note that the plaintiff would have no opportunity to

obtain review by the state's supreme court because its opinion was on certification, not by review, since the forum of the action was a federal court.

4. In Martin v. Reynolds Metals Co., 221 Or. 86, 342 P.2d 790 (1959), cert. denied 362 U.S. 918, 80 S.Ct. 672, 4 L.Ed.2d 739 (1960), described in *Bradley* as a "well known (but not very influential) case," the "gist" of defendant's argument was that:

> "a trespass arises only when there has been a 'breaking and entering upon real property,' constituting a direct, as distinguished from a consequential, invasion of the possessor's interest in land[.] * * *

* * *

> The defendant asks us to take account of the difference in size of the physical agency through which the intrusion occurs and relegate entirely to the field of nuisance law certain invasions which do not meet the dimensional test, whatever that is. In pressing this argument upon us the defendant must admit that there are cases which have held that a trespass results from the movement or deposit of rather small objects over or upon the surface of the possessor's land.

* * *

> If, then, we must look to the character of the instrumentality which is used in making an intrusion upon another's land we prefer to emphasize the object's energy or force rather than its size. Viewed in this way we may define trespass as any intrusion which invades the possessor's protected interest in exclusive possession, whether that intrusion is by visible or invisible pieces of matter or by energy which can be measured only by the mathematical language of the physicist.

> We are of the opinion, therefore, that the intrusion of the fluoride particulates in the present case constituted a trespass. The defendant argues that our decision in Amphitheaters, Inc. v. Portland Meadows, 1948, 184 Or. 336, 198 P.2d 847, 851, 5 A.L.R.2d 690, requires a contrary conclusion. In discussing the distinction between trespass and nuisance the court referred to a difference between 'a cannon ball and a ray of light' indicating that the former but not the latter could produce a trespassory invasion. * * *"

[In addition to determining that particulates could constitute a trespass, the court also adopted a balancing test for application to this new genre of cases:]

> In every case in which trespass is alleged the court is presented with a problem of deciding whether the defendant's intrusion has violated a legally protected interest of the plaintiff. * * * [W]here neither the defendant's conduct nor the plaintiff's use fall within the familiar trespass pattern of the past the courts are faced with a preliminary inquiry as to whether the plaintiff has a protectible interest under the law of trespass. This in turn calls for the inquiry as to whether the defendant's conduct was such as to constitute an invasion of that interest.

> In some cases the solution can be based upon the ground that the defendant's conduct is not substantial enough to be regarded as a

trespassory intrusion. Thus, the casting of a candle beam upon the screen of a drive-in theater would not constitute an actionable invasion, simply because the intrusion is so trifling that the law will not consider it and the principle de minimis non curat lex is applicable. In some cases the solution may be arrived at by admitting that the intrusion is substantial but refusing to recognize that plaintiff has a legally protected interest in the particular possessory use as against the particular conduct of the defendant. * * *

The Amphitheaters case can be explained in terms of this latter point of view, i. e., that the glare of the defendant's lights could be regarded as an intrusion within the law of trespass, but that the plaintiff had no right to treat the intrusion as actionable in view of the nature of plaintiff's use and the manner in which the defendant interfered with it. Had the defendant purposely, and not as an incidence of his own legitimate use, directed the rays of light against the plaintiff's screen the court might well have taken the position that the plaintiff could have recovered in a trespass action. * * *

* * *

* * * There are adjudicated cases which have refused to find a trespass where the intrusion is clearly established but where the court has felt that the possessor's interest should not be protected. Thus it has been held that the flight of aircraft over the surface of plaintiff's land does not constitute a trespass unless the intrusion interferes with the present enjoyment of property. * * *

The Amphitheaters case may also be viewed as a pronouncement that a possessor's interest is not invaded by an intrusion which is so trifling that it cannot be recognized by the law. Inasmuch as it is not necessary to prove actual damage in trespass the magnitude of the intrusion ordinarily would not be of any consequence. But there is a point where the entry is so lacking in substance that the law will refuse to recognize it, applying the maxim de minimis non curat lex. * * *

* * * Consequently the question as to whether * * * [any other] intrusion is so unsubstantial that it is to be disregarded under the de minimis principle * * * must be evaluated with reference to the nature of the plaintiff's interest. * * * Once recognizing that actual damage need not be shown in making out an actionable invasion, the plaintiff's right to insist upon freedom from interference with his possession seems almost limitless.

5. In *Martin*, the court's refusal to adopt the defendant's argument that there must exist an observable "thing" which intrudes on the land as a predicate to liability for trespass, seems scientifically correct. The court emphasizes "the object's energy or force rather than its size," and defines the trespass as "any intrusion which invades the possessor's protected interest in exclusive possession, whether that intrusion is by visible or invisible pieces of matter or by energy which can be measured only by the mathematical language of the physicist." This approach will, of course, result in recognizing as trespassory invasions many intrusions which were

previously only actionable, if at all, under the law of nuisance. Will this principle necessarily result in more trespass actions?

What is the test for trespass adopted by the court in *Martin*? Does it resemble the balancing test employed in negligence, and some nuisance, cases, or is it a bright line test? What considerations does the court identify as appropriate to this calculation? Is the net result that a jury is free to find a trespass or not as it chooses?

What do you think of the court's treatment of Amphitheaters, Inc. v. Portland Meadows, 184 Or. 336, 198 P.2d 847 (1948), where defendant's lights which cast upon plaintiff's drive-in movie theater were found not to constitute an actionable trespass? Didn't the light constitute energy that emanated from defendant's actions? Does the court distinguish *Amphitheaters* on the basis of the extent of the harm produced by the invasion? On the basis of defendant's conduct? On some other basis? What is the most effective means for limiting the trespass action once it is available for intrusions previously unrecognizable because of advances in science? Or is it on the basis of the defendant's intention? If the invasion is substantial, why might the law nevertheless regard the plaintiff's interest as unprotectable?

6. In *Reynolds Metals Co. v. Lampert*, 324 F.2d 465 (9th Cir.1963), the court, applying Oregon law, dealt with the issue of punitive damages for a fluoride trespass. The trial judge had withdrawn the question of punitive damages from the jury, notwithstanding evidence showing that (1) Reynolds had knowledge that the fluorides caused injury and nonetheless increased production; (2) the plant manager resisted the use of better fluoride controls since it was "cheaper to pay claims than * * * to control fluorides;" and (3) a pollution control device would have removed 98 to 99 percent of the particulate matter. The Court of Appeals reversed and remanded for retrial, holding that the question of punitive damages should have been submitted to the jury. The court reasoned that the jury could reasonably have found that Reynolds acted recklessly, with wanton disregard of the property rights of plaintiffs or with some other improper motive.

7. If the traditional distinction between tangible and intangible invasions has been abolished by *Bradley* and *Martin*, what about odors as constituting a trespass? In Brown v. County Commissioners of Scioto Company, 1993 WL 171493 (Ohio App. 1993), the court considered plaintiffs' allegations that the odors emanating from the sewage treatment plant operated by defendants had been so bad that the "germs and bacteria emitted [had] rotted the ears off of two rabbits that the Browns owned." They further established that the plant had been cited for violations of EPA's standards on bacteria content in its effluent which in turn caused the emission of noxious odors, that its equipment had malfunctioned further exacerbating the odors, and that their home had suffered $25,000 in diminished value. After noting the liberalized trend in trespass cases, the appeals court observed that trespass nevertheless requires at least some interference with the right to the exclusive possession of property. It concluded:

> There is no summary judgment evidence of the polluting substance, i.e., noxious odors, depositing particulate matter on appellant's real property or causing physical damage to it. We are persuaded that under

either the traditional or modern views, since appellant has failed to adduce summary judgment evidence of physical damage to her real property, appellees were entitled to summary judgment on appellant's trespass claim.

8. See also Padilla v. Lawrence, 101 N.M. 556, 685 P.2d 964 (App.1984) (odor, dust and flies caused by manure processing plant did not constitute trespass where there was no proof of settling on and damaging property); Nissan Motor Corp. v. Maryland Shipbuilding and Drydock Co., 544 F.Supp. 1104 (D.Md.1982), affirmed 742 F.2d 1449 (4th Cir.1984) (smoke and soot that landed on new cars constituted neither trespass nor nuisance, since there was no interference with automobile company's exclusive possession and "normal" occupants would not be substantially annoyed or disturbed). But see Maryland Heights Leasing, Inc. v. Mallinckrodt, Inc., 706 S.W.2d 218 (Mo.App. 1985) (complaint alleged cause of action for nuisance and trespass arising out of damage to property caused by low-level radiation emission).

9. For a general treatment of the particulate matter issue, see Annotation, 2 A.L.R. 4th 1054 (1980). See also Robert L. Glicksman, A Guide to Kansas Common Law Actions Against Industrial Pollution Sources, 33 U. Kan. L. Rev. 621 (1985); Warren J. Hurwitz, Environmental Health: An Analysis of Available and Proposed Remedies for Victims of Toxic Waste Contamination, 7 Am. J. L. & Med. 61 (1981); Putt & Bolla, Invasion of Radioactive Particulates as a Common Law Trespass—An Overview, 3 Urb. L. Rev. 206 (1980); Comment, Remedies for Intangible Intrusions: The Distinction Between Trespass and Nuisance Actions Against Lawfully Zoned Businesses in California, 17 U.C. Davis L. Rev. 389 (1983).

Chapter Three

NUISANCE: THE COMPREHEN-
SIVE ENVIRONMENTAL
TORT THEORY

A. NUISANCE: AN INTRODUCTION

Nuisance is a broad and often misunderstood term that is employed to describe a diversity of harms. More than any other tort cause of action, a claim that defendant's actions constitute a nuisance is at the core of environmental law. Professor William H. Rodgers, Jr., 1 Environmental Law: Air and Water § 1.1 at 1 (West 1986), summarizes the significance of the nuisance doctrines in environmental litigation:

> There is simply no common law doctrine that approaches nuisance in comprehensiveness or detail as a regulator of land use and of technological abuse. Nuisance actions have involved pollution of all physical media—air, water, land—by a wide variety of means. * * * Nuisance actions have challenged virtually every major industrial and municipal activity which is today the subject of comprehensive environmental regulation * * * [and] is the common law backbone of modern environmental and energy law.

> * * *

There exists confusion as to what the word "nuisance" describes: is it the nature of the defendant's conduct or defendant's activity? Or is it the nature of the invasion that the plaintiff has experienced? When we describe something as a nuisance are we expressing the legal conclusion that it is an activity for which the actor is liable? Can a nuisance exist without liability?

While many decisions characterize the doctrine inexactly, the term "nuisance" is best understood as the *result* of the activity of an actor which interferes with a landowner's, or an occupant's, right of quiet or profitable enjoyment of property. Activity satisfying this description creates a nuisance whether or not liability attaches. Thus "for a nuisance to exist there must be harm to another or the invasion of an interest, but there need not be liability for it * * *. [N]uisance does not signify any particular kind of conduct on the part of the defendant. Instead the word has reference to two particular kinds of harm—the invasion of two kinds of interests," public nuisance and private nuisance. Restatement (Second) of Torts § 821A, comment b.

B. PUBLIC NUISANCE

1. INTRODUCTION

A public nuisance is an "unreasonable interference with a right common to the general public." Restatement (Second) of Torts § 821B. The origins of the public nuisance doctrines are found in interferences or infringements of the rights of the British Crown, which were applied to any action that produced an inconvenience or some kind of harm to members of the public. A public nuisance was regarded as a crime, and it came to be defined as "any act not warranted by law, or omission to discharge a legal duty, which obstructs or causes inconvenience or damage to the public in the exercise of rights common to all Her Majesty's subjects." Stephen, General View of the Criminal Law of England 105 (1980).

2. UNREASONABLENESS OF THE INTERFERENCE

Today many states have statutes which declare that certain conduct—such as polluting the public waters of the state—constitutes a public nuisance for which the actor is liable for a penalty to the state. E.g., Ariz. Rev. Stat. § 36–601(A), describing specific "conditions" that constitute "public nuisances dangerous to the public health[.]"

Representative of a public nuisance claim predicated on a statute and the difficulties that plaintiffs may encounter is Brown v. County Commissioners of Scioto County, 1993 WL 171493 (Ohio App. 1993), brought by private parties claiming that the county authority had failed to properly maintain and operate a sewage treatment plant. Plaintiff relied upon Ohio Admin. Code 3745–15–07(A), which stated in part: "[T]he emission or escape into the open air from any source or sources whatsoever of smoke, ashes, dust, dirt, grime, acids, fumes, vapors odors, or any other substances, in such a manner or in such amounts as to endanger the health, safety or welfare of the public, or cause unreasonable injury or damage to the health, safety or welfare of the public, or cause unreasonable injury or damage to property, is hereby found and declared to be a public nuisance." Even with such a statutory definition, the Ohio appeals court observed that the public nuisance plaintiffs must show that they suffered a particular harm that is "of a different kind than that suffered by the public in general[,]" citing Restatement (Second) of Torts § 821C(1). Plaintiff satisfied this burden, in the court's view, with her contention that "she lost an opportunity to sell her property and was unable to use and enjoy it." Nonetheless, the court held, where such a waste facility is operated under government authorization, plaintiff's burden of proof in a public nuisance claim is that of showing negligence, an action the court described as one for "qualified public nuisance," as to which claim, and one for qualified private nuisance, the court held, plaintiff merited retrial.

Often plaintiffs, governmental or private, rely on statutory violations by the defendant to support, or compel, the finding of the commission of a public nuisance even though the defendant may have acted unintentionally and non-negligently in interfering with the right common to the public. Pursuant to some statutes, a statutory violation may without more constitute conclusive evidence of the unreasonableness of the interference.[1]

Restatement (Second) of Torts § 821B(2) sets out three criteria for deciding if the interference with the public right is "unreasonable":

(2) Circumstances that may sustain a holding that an interference with a public right is unreasonable include the following:

(a) Whether the conduct involves a significant interference with the public health, the public safety, the public peace, the public comfort or the public convenience, *or*

(b) whether the conduct is proscribed by a statute, ordinance or administrative regulation, *or*

(c) whether the conduct is of a continuing nature or has produced a permanent or long-lasting effect, and, as the actor knows or has reason to know, has a significant effect upon the public right.

Because these three standards are listed in the disjunctive, the presence of any one of them may be sufficient to support a finding of an unreasonable interference with the public right. It is important to observe that only subsection (c) requires, or even assigns relevance to, what the defendant knew or should have known about the extent of the interference. Under subsections (a) and (b) any significant interference with public health or safety or comfort or convenience or statutory breach produces a finding of a public nuisance, without any evidence of the defendant's awareness of the impact its conduct or activity is having upon such public rights. In other words, the liability in strict.

3. WHAT IS A "PUBLIC RIGHT?"

What is a "public right" which the doctrine of public nuisance seeks to protect? The public right is one "common to all members of the general public," such as the right of all members of the public to fish in a navigable stream in the state without an interference in the form of

---

1. The analogy here is unmistakable between the use of statutory authority in this context and the negligence per se doctrine, where a statute or a regulation is sometimes interpreted as establishing the appropriate standard of care. Chapter 6 examines the effects of compliance with, or violation of, pertinent statutes or regulations. As will be seen, where a statute or a regulation is deemed to address the precise risk and the population at risk, defendant's violation may constitute (1) evidence of negligence; (2) a rebuttable presumption of negligence; or (3) negligence per se.

pollution that kills the fish. It is not necessary that all members of the public be adversely affected by the nuisance "so long as the nuisance will interfere with those who come in contact with it in the exercise of a public right or it otherwise affects the interests of the community at large." Restatement (Second) of Torts § 821B, comment g. Moreover, the sometimes close relationship between public and private nuisances can be observed in situations where the nuisance affects a large number of persons in the use and enjoyment of their land, and that condition often accompanies some interference with a public right.[2] Thus, if a defendant's activity interferes with the private interests of a substantial number of individuals, it is quite likely that it will also interfere with a public right. This is often true in the air and water pollution cases, where the private interests and public interests are virtually indistinguishable. See generally William Prosser, Private Actions for Public Nuisance, 52 Va.L.Rev. 997 (1966).

The "public" nature of the harm is often supported by conclusions reached by a state or subdivision therein pursuant to its investigation of environmental concerns. For example, in State of New York v. Ferro, 189 A.D.2d 1018, 592 N.Y.S.2d 516 (1993), the state's Department of Environmental Conservation, investigating the operation of a solid waste management facility, corroborated residents' complaints that the site emitted "high concentrations of hydrogen sulfide * * * which were causing a variety of health problems." The New York appellate court affirmed the trial court's judgment for the state upon evidence of "emissions of hydrogen sulfide gases into the air from defendant's site, which adversely affected the health of area residents exposed to these emissions, and evidence of leachate containing PCBs at the site, which threaten[ed] to contaminate a nearby stream."

STATE OF NEW YORK v. SCHENECTADY CHEMICALS, INC.

Supreme Court, Rensselaer County, 1983.
117 Misc.2d 960, 459 N.Y.S.2d 971, affirmed as modified
103 A.D.2d 33, 479 N.Y.S.2d 1010 (1984).

HUGHES, J.

The court must decide if the State, either by statute or common law, can maintain an action to compel a chemical company to pay the costs of cleaning up a dump site so as to prevent pollution of surface and ground water when the dumping took place between 15 to 30 years ago at a site owned by an independent contractor hired by the chemical company to dispose of the waste material.

* * *

The amended complaint contains the following factual assertions. The action is brought by the State in its role as guardian of the

---

2. Prosser and Keeton state that whether there is an interference with a "public right" is seldom a problem in the litigated cases. Prosser and Keeton on Torts § 90 (5th ed. 1984).

environment against Schenectady Chemicals, Inc., with respect to a chemical dump site [known as the Loeffel site]. Since 1906 Schenectady Chemicals has manufactured paints, alkyl phenols and other chemical products, a by-product of which is waste, including but not limited to phenol, benzene, toluene, xylene, formaldehyde, vinyl chloride, chlorobenzene, 1,2 dichlorobenzene, 1,4 dichlorobenzene, trichloroethylene, chloroform, ethyl benzene, nethylene chloride, 1,1 dichloroethane, 1,2 dichloroethane, trans–1,2 dichloroethylene, lead, copper, chromium, selenium, and arsenic. These chemical wastes are dangerous to human, animal and plant life, and the defendant was so aware. During the 1950's until the mid–1960's the defendant disposed of its chemical wastes by way of contract with Dewey Loeffel, of one of Mr. Loeffel's corporations. Mr. Loeffel made pickups at the defendant's manufacturing plants and disposed of the material by dumping directly into lagoons at the Loeffel site, and in some instances by burying the wastes. It is alleged that with knowledge of the danger of environmental contamination if its wastes were not properly disposed, and knowing of Loeffel's methods, Schenectady Chemicals: (1) hired an incompetent independent contractor to dispose of the wastes; and (2) failed to fully advise Loeffel of the dangerous nature of the waste material and recommend proper disposal methods.

It is alleged that the Loeffel site is approximately 13 acres of low-lying swamp land located in a residential-agricultural area in Rensselaer County with surface soil consisting mainly of gravel and sand. The ground water beneath the site is part of an aquifer which serves as the sole source of water for thousands of area residents and domestic animals. * * *

The complaint alleges that over the years the chemical wastes have migrated into the surrounding air, surface and ground water contaminating at least one area drinking well and so polluting, or threatening to pollute, the area surface and ground water as to constitute an unreasonable threat to the public well-being and a continuing public nuisance. As a result, the Department of Environmental Conservation (DEC) developed a plan to prevent further migration of chemical wastes from the site, and General Electric and Bendix have agreed to pay 82.2% of the costs thereof. Defendant's refusal to pay its portion of the clean-up costs gives rise to this suit.

After alleging the foregoing factual background the State sets forth eight specific causes of action in the amended complaint[.] [In addition to three counts that recited alleged statutory violations, the complaint claimed that:] (4) by permitting the disposal of its waste in the manner described, the defendant has contributed to the creation and maintenance of a public nuisance; (5) the generation and disposal of the chemical wastes described in the complaint constitutes an ultra-hazardous activity rendering defendant strictly liable for the resultant public nuisance; (6) the defendant negligently permitted the creation and maintenance of a dangerous public nuisance by selecting an incompetent contractor and not properly supervising the disposal process or warning of the dangers of the resultant nuisance; (7) through intentional acts and omissions, the defendant contributed to the creation and maintenance of the continuing public nuisance complained of; and (8) failing to abate the nuisance, thus causing DEC to incur $85,087 in investigatory and administrative expenses.

* * *

The fourth through eighth causes of action rely upon a nuisance theory. * * * [Our Court of Appeals has] described a public nuisance as: "A public, or as sometimes termed a common, nuisance is an offense against the State and is subject to abatement or prosecution on application of the proper governmental agency[.] It consists of conduct or omissions which offend, interfere with or cause damage to the public in the exercise of rights common to all in a manner such as to offend public morals, interfere with use by the public of a public place or endanger or injure the property, health, safety or comfort of a considerable number of persons."

* * *

"[W]ith reference to a public nuisance, it is not necessary to show acts of negligence" (42 NY Jur, Nuisances, § 16, p 462), although such a showing is not prohibited. One who creates a nuisance through an inherently dangerous activity or use of an unreasonably dangerous product is absolutely liable for resulting damages, [r]egardless of fault, and despite adhering to the highest standard of care[.] While at first blush this appears a harsh result, Judge Hand explained the basis of the rule in Exner v. Sherman Power Constr. Co. (54 F.2d 510, 514) as follows: "Furthermore, the imposition of absolute liability is not out of accord with any general principles of law. As Professor Holdsworth has said: 'The dominant idea of Anglo–Saxon law' was 'that man acts at his peril' * * * The extent to which one man in the lawful conduct of his business is liable for injuries to another involves an adjustment of conflicting interests. The solution of the problem in each particular case has never been dependent upon any universal criterion of liability [such as 'fault'] applicable to all situations. If damage is inflicted, there ordinarily is liability, in the absence of excuse."

While ordinarily nuisance is an action pursued against the owner of land for some wrongful activity conducted thereon, "everyone who creates a nuisance or participates in the creation or maintenance of a nuisance are liable jointly and severally for the wrong and injury done thereby"[.] Even a nonlandowner can be liable for taking part in the creation of a nuisance upon the property of another. * * * The common law is not static. Society has repeatedly been confronted with new inventions and products that, through foreseen and unforeseen events, have imposed dangers upon society (explosives are an example). The courts have reacted by expanding the common law to meet the challenge, in some instances imposing absolute liability upon the party who, either through manufacture or use, has sought to profit from marketing a new invention or product. The modern chemical industry, and the problems engendered through the disposal of its by-products, is, to a large extent, a creature of the twentieth century. Since the Second World War hundreds of previously unknown chemicals have been created. The wastes produced have been dumped, sometimes openly and sometimes surreptitiously, at thousands of sites across the country. Belatedly it has been discovered that the waste products are polluting the air and water and pose a consequent threat to all life forms. Someone must pay to correct the problem, and the determination of who is essentially a political question to be decided in the legislative arena. As Judge Bergan noted in Boomer v. Atlantic Cement Co. (26 N.Y.2d 219, 222, 223), resolution of the issues raised in society's attempt to ameliorate pollution are to a large extent beyond the ken of the judicial branch. Nonetheless, courts must resolve the issues raised by litigants and, in that vein, this court holds that the fourth through seventh causes of action of the amended complaint state viable causes of action sounding in nuisance.

* * *

Notes and Questions

1. In *Schenectady Chemicals* the state did not have to plead, as it apparently did in an abundance of caution, that the defendant acted intentionally, negligently, or engaged in ultra-hazardous activity. A public nuisance that produces substantial harm is actionable without proof of any specific type of conduct; the "public" nature of the invasion is all that is required. This is explainable by the criminal origins of public nuisance law, where the defendant's conduct would have constituted a criminal offense, which satisfied any fault requirement which the law of torts might otherwise apply.

2. *Liability Under Agency Principles.* It is significant that the defendant is *not* the owner of the waste disposal site, but rather is one of three generators of the hazardous waste. Liability under public nuisance law embraces not only the party responsible for releasing the chemicals in the groundwater, but also the source generator of the waste. Agency law principles are sufficient to regard the site operator or owner as the agent of the defendant, regardless of whether the site operator is an independent contractor. The *Schenectady Chemicals* trial court identified five bases for holding the defendant liable:

> Moreover, defendant could be found liable for Loeffel's acts if: (1) it was negligent in retaining an incompetent contractor; (2) it failed, with knowledge thereof, to remedy or prevent an unlawful act; (3) the work itself was illegal; (4) the work itself was inherently dangerous; or (5) the work involved the creation of a nuisance.

The Appellate Division affirmed, stating:

> The issue of whether Loeffel acted as defendant's agent or as an independent contractor in disposing of the wastes presents a question of fact not to be resolved at this stage of the proceedings. Even the assumption that Loeffel acted as an independent contractor does not

insulate defendant from liability, for an employer may be responsible for the actions of an independent contractor in creating a public nuisance (Restatement, Torts 2d, § 427B; 3 N.Y.Jur.2d, Agency and Independent Contractors, § 353, p. 181). Particularly is this so where the work involved is inherently dangerous, as may reasonably be deemed the case where the disposal of hazardous wastes are involved and the employer has failed to take proper precautions in selecting a competent party with whom to contract.

103 A.D.2d 33, 479 N.Y.S.2d 1010, 1014 (1984).

This form of vicarious liability can be a powerful tool in relying on public nuisance doctrines to challenge environmental harms arising from a waste disposal site. Where the owner of the site is not sufficiently solvent to pay damages, reliance on the *Schenectady Chemicals* approach may be indispensable if the plaintiff is to recover damages, to be reimbursed for clean-up costs, or to compel another to undertake remediation of the site. In Chapter 10 we will consider the principal federal statute which addresses the remediation of hazardous waste sites.

4. PRIVATE ACTION FOR PUBLIC NUISANCE—THE SPECIAL INJURY RULE

Historically the common law has been slow to recognize the right of a private person to maintain an action for a public nuisance. Until 1536 private actions for public nuisance were disallowed on the grounds that "only the King, and certainly no common person" could have a remedy because of a crime. See William Prosser, Private Actions for Public Nuisance, 52 Va.L.Rev. 997, 1005 (1966). In that year a court allowed a private tort action for a public nuisance in a case where the defendant blocked the King's highway and impeded the plaintiff's access "to his close." In the court's language: "Where one man has greater hurt or inconvenience than any other man had * * * then he who had more displeasure or hurt, etc. can have an action to recover his damages that he had by reason of his special hurt." Anonymous, Y.B. 27 Hen. 8 fo. 26, pl. 10 (1536).

This is the origin of the special injury rule which states that a private plaintiff can maintain a suit for a public nuisance only if she can demonstrate a particular, unique damage different from that suffered by the public generally. Three reasons were offered to justify this special injury requirement: (1) that only the sovereign should maintain actions for harm suffered by the public; (2) that courts should protect defendants from a multitude of actions by private parties and from the potential of harassment; and (3) the courts did not wish to be burdened with many suits for trivial damages.

Professor Hodas has argued the impropriety of such a rule today:

These justifications for the special injury rule may have made sense in an era when misuse of existing technology affected only people in the immediate vicinity of the activity and caused only limited harm. However, the concerns of 1536—e.g., a horse falling into a ditch in the road—pale in comparison to modern worries about an accident at a chemical plant that can kill thousands of persons, an oil spill that can spoil thousands of miles of beaches, riverbanks, or underwater areas, or the release of toxic substances that can contaminate the air, water, and land. Although these types of concerns prompted a revolution in statutory environmental law by the early 1970's, the common law public nuisance doctrine remained unchanged.[3]

The Restatement (Second) of Torts reflects a compromise between total abolition and complete retention of the special injury requirement. In § 821C the Restatement addresses the question of *standing*—that is, who can maintain an action, as a consequence of sustaining the type of injury necessary to confer on that person the right to sue:

§ 821C. Who Can Recover for Public Nuisance

(1) In order to recover damages in an individual action for a public nuisance, one must have suffered harm of a kind different from that suffered by other members of the public exercising the right common to the general public that was the subject of interference.

(2) In order to maintain a proceeding to enjoin or abate a public nuisance, one must

(a) have the right to recover damages, as indicated in Subsection (1), or

(b) have authority as a public official or public agency to represent the state or a political subdivision in the matter, or

(c) have standing to sue as a representative of the general public, as a citizen in a citizen's action or as a member of a class in a class action.

Thus, under the Restatement (Second) a private plaintiff who maintains an action for damages must still satisfy the special injury requirement. In contrast a private plaintiff seeking to enjoin or abate a public nuisance is conferred the necessary standing either if acting as a public official or, more importantly, if suing as a representative of the general public, as a citizen in a citizen's action, or as a member in a class action.

What justifications are there for retaining the special injury rule at all? Why should standing requirements in equitable actions seeking injunctive relief be more liberal than standing in private suits for damages?

What have the courts done in the last twenty years to the special injury rule in environmental tort actions for damages? The decisions below all involve some aspect of the special injury rule, but all of them do not specifically label it as such nor do all of the cases necessarily

3. David R. Hodas, Private Actions for Public Nuisance: Common Law Citizen Suits for Relief from Environmental Harm, 16 Ecology L.Q. 833, 884 (1989).

involve public nuisance actions. Closely related to the special injury requirement in public nuisance actions is the requirement of the economic loss doctrine that parties suffering purely economic losses occasioned by the defendant's negligent conduct (e.g., the defendant negligently interferes with contractual relations or prospective economic advantage) cannot maintain an action for such losses, unless the party has also sustained physical harm to person or property, or damage to a proprietary interest, or is otherwise entitled to recover on the basis of a separate tort (e.g., public nuisance). For excellent analyses of the economic loss doctrine, *see* East River Steamship Corp. v. Transamerica Delaval, Inc., 476 U.S. 858, 106 S.Ct. 2295, 90 L.Ed.2d 865 (1986) (holding that under maritime tort law a ship charterer that suffered economic losses because of a defect in the turbines manufactured by defendant could not recover such losses on a products liability or negligence theory); Robert L. Rabin, Tort Recovery for Negligently Inflicted Economic Loss: A Reassessment, 37 Stan.L.Rev. 1513 (1985); Gary T. Schwartz, Economic Loss in American Tort Law: The Examples of J'Aire and Products Liability, 23 San Diego L.Rev. 37 (1986).

The case that follows involves both hurdles which may face a private plaintiff: the recovery for economic losses in the face of the economic loss doctrine and the recovery for private harm on the basis of a public nuisance in the face of the special injury rule.

STATE OF LOUISIANA, EX REL. WILLIAM J. GUSTE, JR. v. M/V TESTBANK

United States Court of Appeals, Fifth Circuit, 1985.
752 F.2d 1019, cert. denied 477 U.S. 903, 106 S.Ct. 3271, 91 L.Ed.2d 562 (1986).

Higginbotham, J.

We are asked to abandon physical damage to a proprietary interest as a prerequisite to recovery for economic loss in cases of unintentional maritime tort. We decline the invitation.

I

In the early evening of July 22, 1980, the M/V SEA DANIEL, an inbound bulk carrier, and the M/V TESTBANK, an outbound container ship, collided at approximately mile forty-one of the Mississippi River Gulf outlet. At impact, a white haze enveloped the ships until carried away by prevailing winds, and containers aboard TESTBANK were damaged and lost overboard. The white haze proved to be hydrobromic acid and the contents of the containers which went overboard proved to be approximately twelve tons of pentachlorophenol, PCP, assertedly the largest such spill in United States history. * * *

Forty-one lawsuits were filed and consolidated before the same judge in the Eastern District of Louisiana. These suits presented claims of shipping interests, marina and boat rental operators, wholesale and retail seafood enterprises not actually engaged in fishing, seafood restaurants, tackle and bait shops, and recreational fishermen. They proffered an assortment of liability theories, including maritime tort [and] private actions pursuant to various sections of [federal and state law].

Defendants moved for summary judgment as to all claims for economic loss unaccompanied by physical damage to property. The district court granted the requested summary judgment as to all such claims except those asserted by commercial oystermen, shrimpers, crabbers and fishermen who had been making a commercial use of embargoed waters. The district court found these commercial fishing interests deserving of a special protection akin to that enjoyed by seamen.

On appeal a panel of this court affirmed, concluding that claims for economic loss unaccompanied by physical damage to a proprietary interest were not recoverable in maritime tort. The panel, as did the district court, pointed to the doctrine of Robins Dry Dock & Repair Co. v. Flint, [275 U.S. 303 (1927)], and its development in this circuit. Judge Wisdom specially concurred, agreeing that the denial of these claims was required by precedent, but urging reexamination en banc. We then took the case en banc for that purpose. After extensive additional briefs and oral argument, we are unpersuaded that we ought to drop physical damage to a proprietary interest as a prerequisite to recovery for economic loss. * * *

* * *

III

The meaning of Robins Dry Dock v. Flint, [275 U.S. 303, 48 S.Ct. 134, 72 L.Ed. 290 (1927)] is the flag all litigants here seek to capture. We turn first to that case and to its historical setting.

Robins broke no new ground but instead applied a principle, then settled both in the United States and England, which refused recovery for negligent interference with "contractual rights." Stated more broadly, the prevailing rule denied a plaintiff recovery for economic loss if that loss resulted from physical damage to property in which he had no proprietary interest. * * * Professor James explains this limitation on recovery of pure economic loss: "The explanation * * * is a pragmatic one: the physical consequences of negligence usually have been limited, but the indirect economic repercussions of negligence may be far wider, indeed virtually open-ended." [Fleming James, Jr., Limitations on Liability for Economic Loss Caused by Negligence: A Pragmatic Appraisal, 25 Vand.L.Rev. 43, 45 (1972)].

In *Robins*, the time charterer of a steamship sued for profits lost when the defendant dry dock negligently damaged the vessel's propeller. The propeller had to be replaced, thus extending by two weeks the time the vessel was laid up in dry dock, and it was for the loss of use of the vessel for that period that the charterer sued. The Supreme Court denied recovery to the charterer[.] * * *

The principle that there could be no recovery for economic loss absent physical injury to a proprietary interest was not only well established when *Robins Dry Dock* was decided, but was remarkably resilient as well. Its strength is demonstrated by the circumstance that *Robins Dry Dock* came ten years after Judge Cardozo's shattering of privity in MacPherson v. Buick Motor Co., 217 N.Y. 382, 111 N.E. 1050 (1916). Indeed this limit on liability stood against a sea of change in the tort law. * * * In sum, it is an old sword that plaintiffs have here picked up.

* * *

Plaintiffs urge that the decisions in Petitions of Kinsman Transit Co., 388 F.2d 821 (2d Cir.1968) (Kinsman II), and Union Oil Co. v. Oppen, 501 F.2d 558 (9th Cir.1974), support their arguments that the *Robins Dry Dock* principle should be abandoned. We disagree. The policy considerations on which both those decisions are bottomed confirm our opinion that pragmatic limitations on the doctrine of foreseeability are both desirable and necessary.

* * *

In *Union Oil*, vast quantities of raw crude were released when the defendant oil company negligently caused an oil spill. The oil was carried by wind, wave, and tidal currents over large stretches of the California coast disrupting, among other things, commercial fishing operations. While conceding that ordinarily there is no recovery for economic losses unaccompanied by physical damage, the court concluded that commercial fishermen were foreseeable plaintiffs whose interests the oil company had a duty to protect when conducting drilling operations. The opinion pointed out that the fishermen's losses were foreseeable and direct consequences of the spill, that fishermen have historically enjoyed a protected position under maritime law, and suggested that economic considerations also supported permitting recovery.

Yet *Union Oil's* holding was carefully limited to commercial fishermen, plaintiffs whose economic losses were characterized as "of a particular and special nature." Union Oil, 501 F.2d at 570. * * *

Review of the foreseeable consequences of the collision of the SEA DANIEL and TESTBANK demonstrates the wave upon wave of successive economic consequences and the managerial role plaintiffs would have us assume. The vessel delayed in St. Louis may be unable to fulfill its obligation to haul from Memphis, to the injury of the shipper, to the injury of the buyers, to the injury of their customers. Plaintiffs concede, as do all who attack the requirement of physical damage, that a line would need to be drawn—somewhere on the other side, each plaintiff would say in turn, of its recovery. Plaintiffs advocate not only that the lines be drawn elsewhere but also that they be drawn on an ad hoc and discrete basis. The result would be that no determinable measure of the limit of foreseeability would precede the decision on liability. We are told that when the claim is too remote, or too tenuous, recovery will be denied. Presumably then, as among all plaintiffs suffering foreseeable economic loss, recovery will turn on a judge or jury's decision. There will be no rationale for the differing results save the "judgment" of the trier of fact. Concededly, it can "decide" all the claims presented, and with comparative if not absolute ease. The point is not that such a process cannot be administered but rather that its judgments would be much less the products of a determinable rule of law. In this important sense, the resulting decisions would be judicial products only in their draw upon judicial resources.

The bright line rule of damage to a proprietary interest, as most, has the virtue of predictability with the vice of creating results in cases at its edge that are said to be "unjust" or "unfair." Plaintiffs point to seemingly perverse results, where claims the rule allows and those it disallows are juxtaposed—such as vessels striking a dock, causing minor but recoverable damage, then lurching athwart a channel causing great but unrecoverable economic loss. The answer is that when lines are drawn sufficiently sharp in their definitional edges to be reasonable and predictable, such differing results are the inevitable result—indeed, decisions are the desired product. But there is more. The line drawing sought by plaintiffs is no less arbitrary because the line drawing appears only in the outcome—as one claimant is found too remote and another is allowed to recover. The true difference is that plaintiff's approach would mask the results. The present rule would be more candid, and in addition, by making results more predictable, serves a normative function. It operates as a rule of law and allows a court to adjudicate rather than manage.

* * *

VI

Plaintiffs argue alternatively that their claims of economic losses are cognizable in maritime tort because the pollution from the collision constituted a public nuisance, and violated the Rivers and Harbors Appropriation Act of 1899 and Louisiana law. We look to each in turn.

1.

Plaintiffs seek to avoid the *Robins* rule by characterizing their claims as damages caused by a public nuisance. They suggest that when a defendant unreasonably interferes with public rights by obstructing navigation or negligently polluting a waterway he creates a public nuisance for which recovery is available to all who have sustained "particular damages." As defined at common law such damages are those which are substantially greater than the presumed-at-law damages suffered by the general public as a result of the nuisance. See generally Restatement (Second) of Torts §§ 821B, 821C (1977); Prosser, Private Action For Public Nuisance, 52 Va.L.Rev. 997 (1966). Characterizing the problem as one of public nuisance, however, does not immediately solve the problems with plaintiffs' damage claims for pure economic losses. * * *

The problem in public nuisance theory of determining when private damages are sufficiently distinct from those suffered by the general public so as to justify recovery is as difficult, if not more so, as determining which foreseeable damages are too remote to justify recovery in negligence. In each case it is a matter of degree, and in each case lines must be drawn. With economic losses such as the ones claimed here the problem is to determine who among an entire community that has been commercially affected by an accident has sustained a pecuniary loss so great as to justify distinguishing his losses from similar losses suffered by others. Given the difficulty of this task, we see no jurisprudential advantage in permitting the use of nuisance theory to skirt the *Robins* rule.

* * *

VII

In conclusion, having reexamined the history and central purpose of the doctrine of *Robins Dry Dock* as developed in this circuit, we remain committed to its teaching. Denying recovery for pure economic losses is a pragmatic limitation on the doctrine of foreseeability, a limitation we find to be both workable and useful. Nor do we find persuasive plaintiffs' arguments that their economic losses are recoverable under a public nuisance theory, as damages for violation of federal statutes, or under state law.

Accordingly, the decision of the district court granting summary judgment to defendants on all claims for economic losses unaccompanied by physical damage to property is AFFIRMED.

* * *

The dissenting opinion of WISDOM, J., joined by RUBIN, J., POLITZ, J., TATE, J. & JOHNSON, J., is omitted.

Notes and Questions

1. The majority opinion deals with the public nuisance special injury question very tersely, stating only that since it concludes that a plaintiff must have suffered some kind of damage to a proprietary interest under its bright line rule, it will not allow that rule to be circumvented by application of a public nuisance theory. Do you agree? Did any of the plaintiffs suffer a loss that might satisfy the special injury requirement? What considerations carried the greatest weight with the majority? How should plaintiffs such as those in *Testbank* protect themselves against business interruption losses?

2. See also, Burgess v. M/V Tamano, 370 F.Supp. 247 (D.Me.1973), where plaintiffs brought class actions seeking damages from an oil spill off the coast of Maine. The federal trial court denied motions to dismiss the claims of the commercial clam diggers and commercial fishermen, but granted the motions as to the owners of motels, trailer parks, campgrounds, restaurants, and grocery stores in the beach area which was affected by the spill. The court stated:

> Since the fishermen and clam diggers have no individual property rights with respect to the waters and marine life allegedly harmed by the oil spill, their right to recover in the present action depends upon whether

they may maintain private actions for damages based upon the alleged tortious invasion of public rights which are held by the State of Maine in trust for the common benefit of all the people. As to this issue, the long standing rule of law is that a private individual can recover in tort for invasion of a public right only if he has suffered damage particular to him—that is, damage different in kind rather than simply in degree from that sustained by the public generally.

* * *

The commercial fishermen and clam diggers in the present cases clearly have a special interest, quite apart from that of the public generally, to take fish and harvest clams from the coastal waters of the State of Maine. The injury of which they complain has resulted from defendants' alleged interference with *their* direct exercise of the public right to fish and dig clams. It would be an incongruous result for the Court to say that a man engaged in commercial fishing or clamming, and dependent thereon for his livelihood, who may have had his business destroyed by the tortious act of another, should be denied any right to recover for his pecuniary loss on the ground that his injury is no different in kind from that sustained by the general public.

The court rejected the claims of those suffering *indirect* injury:

Unlike the commercial fishermen and clam diggers, the Old Orchard Beach businessmen do not assert any interference with *their* direct exercise of the public right. They complain only of loss of customers *indirectly resulting* from alleged pollution of the coastal waters and beaches in which they do not have a property interest. Although in some instances their damage may be greater in degree, the injury of which they complain, which is *derivative* from that of the public at large, is common to all businesses and residents of the Old Orchard Beach area. In such circumstances, the line is drawn and the courts have consistently denied recovery. (emphasis in original).

Is *Burgess* consistent with *Testbank* ? See also Pruitt v. Allied Chemical Corp., 523 F.Supp. 975 (E.D.Va.1981) (reaching the same conclusion as *Testbank* where the chemical Kepone had damaged marine life in Chesapeake Bay and allowing commercial users of the water to recover but not those suffering indirect economic loss). Accord, Connerty v. Metropolitan District Commission, 398 Mass. 140, 495 N.E.2d 840 (1986), which held that a licensed master clam digger could maintain an action on his own behalf and on behalf of other licensed clam diggers for damages to his business caused by the discharge of raw sewage into the harbor by the Metropolitan District Commission. The case was ultimately dismissed on governmental immunity grounds.

3. Many state statutes have codified the special injury requirement in public nuisance actions maintained by private parties. See, e.g., West's Ann.Cal. Civil Code § 3493 (1993) ("A private person may maintain an action for public nuisance, if it is specifically injurious to himself but not otherwise."). See, also, e.g., Alaska Stat. 9.45.230 (private nuisance section extended to public nuisances); Official Ga. Code Ann. § 72–103. Compare the language employed in Alabama: "Nuisances are either public or private. A public nuisance is one which damages all persons which come within the

sphere of its operations * * *. Generally a public nuisance gives no right of action to an individual." "If a public nuisance causes a special damage to an individual in which the public does not participate, such special damage gives a right of action." Ala. Code § 6–5–121; § 6–5–123 (1992); Mich. Comp. Laws Ann. § 600.380.

5. A NOTE ON ECONOMIC PRINCIPLES

Much has been written in recent years regarding the need for tort law to embrace economic efficiency goals in allocating risks of loss among parties. Three individuals have been most influential in bringing about more interest in examining economic considerations in determining legal liability. See Guido Calabresi, The Costs of Accidents (1970); Ronald H. Coase, The Problem of Social Cost, 3 J.Law & Econ. 1 (1960); Richard A. Posner, Economic Analysis of Law (3d ed. 1986). Calabresi has argued that the risks of loss ought to be placed on the party with the lowest avoidance costs so that the aggregate sum of accident costs and avoidance costs are minimized.

Calabresi and Melamed, in a leading article, summarize their view of economic considerations which should be applied in fashioning rules in which the transaction costs are especially high:

> (1) that economic efficiency standing alone would dictate that set of entitlements which favors knowledgeable choices between social benefits and the social costs of obtaining them, and between social costs and the social costs of avoiding them; (2) that this implies, in the absence of certainty as to whether a benefit is worth its costs to society, that the cost should be put on the party or activity best located to make such a cost-benefit analysis; (3) that in particular contexts like accidents or pollution this suggests putting costs on the party or activity which can most cheaply avoid them; (4) that in the absence of certainty as to who that party or activity is, the costs should be put on the party or activity which can with the lowest transaction costs act in the market to correct an error in entitlements by inducing the party who can avoid social costs most cheaply to do so; and (5) that since we are in an area where by hypothesis markets do not work perfectly—there are transaction costs—a decision will often have to be made on whether market transactions or collective fiat is most likely to bring us closer to the Pareto optimal result the "perfect" market would reach.

Guido Calabresi & A. Douglas Melamed, Property Rules, Liability Rules, and Inalienability, 85 Harv.L.Rev. 1089, 1096–97 (1972). See also Richard A. Posner, A Theory of Negligence, 1 J.Legal Stud. 29, 39–40 (1972). An excellent discussion of the economic principles that may be applied in determining liability in cases such as *Testbank* is contained in Union Oil Co. v. Oppen, 501 F.2d 558, 570 (9th Cir.1974), discussed in *Testbank*. In *Oppen*, the court allowed commercial fishermen to recover for losses caused by defendant's oil spill off the coast of California, but did not reach the question of whether others suffering economic losses could recover:

> [O]ur holding * * * does not open the door to claims that may be asserted by those, other than commercial fishermen, whose economic or personal affairs were discommoded by the oil spill * * *. Nothing said in this opinion is intended to suggest * * * that every

decline in the general commercial activity of every business in the
* * * area following the [spill] constitutes a legally cognizable injury
for which the defendants may be responsible.

The Ninth Circuit also concluded that, as between it and the commercial
users of the fish in the ocean, the oil company was the least cost avoider:

The same conclusion is reached when the issue before us is approached from the standpoint of economics. Recently a number of
scholars have suggested that liability for losses occasioned by torts
should be apportioned in a manner that will best contribute to the
achievement of an optimum allocation of resources. This optimum,
in theory, would be that which would be achieved by a perfect
market system. In determining whether the cost of an accident
should be borne by the injured party or be shifted, in whole or in
part, this approach requires the court to fix the identity of the party
who can avoid the costs most cheaply. Once fixed, this determination then controls liability.

It turns out, however, that fixing the identity of the best or
cheapest cost-avoider is more difficult than might be imagined. In
order to facilitate this determination, Calabresi suggests several
helpful guidelines. The first of these would require a rough calculation designed to exclude as potential cost-avoiders those groups/ac-
tivities which could avoid accident costs only at an extremely high
expense. While not easy to apply in any concrete sense, this
guideline does suggest that the imposition of oil spill costs directly
upon such groups as the consumers of staple groceries is not a
sensible solution. Under this guideline, potential liability becomes
resolved into a choice between, on an ultimate level, the consumers
of fish and those products derived from the defendant's total operations.

* * *

[Calabresi's final guideline] unmistakably points to the defendants as the best cost-avoider. Under this guideline, the loss should
be allocated to that party who can best correct any error in allocation, if such there be, by acquiring the activity to which the party
has been made liable. The capacity "to buy out" the plaintiffs if the
burden is too great is, in essence, the real focus of Calabresi's
approach. On this basis there is no contest—the defendant's capacity is superior.

For a fascinating account of Calabresi's principles applied to air
pollution torts, see Frank Michaelman, Pollution as a Tort: A Non–
Accidental Perspective on Calabresi's Costs, 80 Yale L.J. 647 (1971).
See also, William M. Landes and Richard A. Posner, The Economic
Structure of Tort Law 29–53 (1987); Richard A. Posner, Economic
Analysis of Law, 5–9, 42–48, 56–57 (3d ed. 1986); Jeffre G. Murphy and
Jules L. Coleman, The Philosophy of Law 228–34 (1984); A. Mitchell
Polinsky, An Introduction to Law and Economics 11–24 (1983).

6. PHYSICAL HARM AS CONSTITUTING SPECIAL INJURY

The courts generally hold that when a plaintiff has suffered demonstrable physical harm the special injury rule is satisfied. Restatement
(Second) of Torts § 821C, comment d, explicitly provides that personal

injuries are inherently "of a kind different from that suffered by other members of the public."

1. In Anderson v. W.R. Grace & Co., 628 F.Supp. 1219 (D.Mass. 1986), the court considered defendants' alleged contamination of the groundwater in certain areas of Woburn, Massachusetts with chemicals that were capable of causing serious injuries. The plaintiffs consisted of 33 persons: five administrators of estates of children who died of leukemia; allegedly caused by those chemicals; 16 persons who were family members of the decedents; seeking to recover for emotional distress; 3 persons still living but suffering from leukemia; and others living who alleged a variety of physical illnesses or damage to their bodies' systems. This decision is discussed in Chapter 5 (dealing with compensable harms in environmental tort cases); but for current purposes the court denied defendants' motion to dismiss the damages claims but granted the motion as to the claim for injunctive relief. On the special injury requirement it stated:

> The alleged contamination of the groundwater in East Woburn falls into the category of public nuisances. * * *

* * *

> Defendants argue that plaintiffs as private persons, have no standing to bring an action based on the public nuisance of a restriction on use of Woburn's groundwater. The general rule is that the private injury sustained where a common right is impaired is "merged in the common nuisance and injury to all citizens, and the right is to be vindicated [through suit by a public official]." But when a plaintiff has sustained "special or peculiar damage", he or she may maintain an individual action. Injuries to a person's health are by their nature "special and peculiar" and cannot properly be said to be common or public. Restatement (Second) of Torts § 821C, comment d. As plaintiffs allege that they have suffered a variety of illnesses as a result of exposure to the contaminated water, they have standing to maintain this nuisance action.

2. See also, Wood v. Picillo, 443 A.2d 1244 (R.I.1982), allowing an action for public and private nuisance on behalf of individuals living near a "chemical nightmare" who had suffered physical effects from their exposure to the chemicals; Burns v. Jaquays Mining Corp., 156 Ariz. 375, 752 P.2d 28 (1987), holding, inter alia, that plaintiffs who suffered exposure to asbestos tailings which came from the defendants' asbestos mill were entitled to recover on a public or private nuisance theory for discomfort, inconvenience, annoyance and property damage.

3. It has also been held that the state may maintain an action for damages resulting from a public nuisance which causes environmental harm to natural resources. See, e.g., State ex rel. Dresser Industries v. Ruddy, 592 S.W.2d 789 (Mo.1980), for an excellent discussion of the special injury rule in the context of state actions. The potential availability of the public nuisance remedy for damage to natural resources grows in significance. See the natural resource damage provisions of the Comprehensive Environmental Response Compensation and Liability

Act, 42 U.S.C.A. §§ 9601(16), 9607(f), 9613(g); see also, Ohio v. United States Dept. of Interior, 880 F.2d 432 (D.C.Cir.1989).

7. EQUITABLE ACTIONS FOR PUBLIC NUISANCE

As noted above, the Restatement (Second) of Torts dropped the special injury requirement entirely for equitable actions. See § 821C, comment j.

a. Private Attorneys General

In Miotke v. City of Spokane, 101 Wash.2d 307, 678 P.2d 803 (1984), owners of waterfront property and the Lake Spokane Environmental Association sued the City of Spokane and the Washington State Department of Ecology for declaratory, equitable, and monetary relief after the city discharged raw sewage into the Spokane River. The discharge fouled the waters of the river and adjoining Lake Long with fecal matter, solids, toilet paper, prophylactics, and slime; discolored the water; and filled the air with rancid, noxious, and repulsive odors. The trial court enjoined further discharge of raw sewage and awarded the plaintiffs damages, attorneys' fees, and costs. On appeal, the Washington Supreme Court upheld the plaintiffs' right to bring a public nuisance action because they had suffered nausea, headaches, nervousness, and insomnia. Finding that the plaintiffs had incurred considerable expense to effectuate an important public policy that benefitted a large class of people, the court characterized the plaintiffs as common law private attorneys general and upheld the award of the attorneys' fees incurred in seeking the injunction.

Under the test applied in *Miotke*, plaintiffs have standing to sue if they allege exposure to an unpleasant condition and resulting physical symptoms, which may be relatively minor and temporary. The arguable triviality of the personal injuries was counterbalanced by the public interest in preventing the defendants' actions, even where the defendants were public entities. Were you surprised by the award to plaintiffs of attorneys' fees?

b. Class Actions

The Hawaii Supreme Court has adopted the position recognized by the Restatement (Second), and explicitly rejected the special injury rule in a class action suit brought to enforce public rights-of-way along once public trails to a beach. See Akau v. Olohana Corp., 65 Hawaii 383, 652 P.2d 1130 (1982), in which the court found that the trend in the law had turned "away from focusing on whether the injury is shared by the public to whether the plaintiff was in fact injured[,]" and held that a member of the public without special injury has standing to sue to enforce the rights of the public if he can show injury-in-fact and satisfy the court that the concerns of a multiplicity of suits will be satisfied "by any means."

c. *Associational Standing*

The right of a citizen group to seek equitable relief for a public nuisance was specifically recognized in Armory Park Neighborhood Association v. Episcopal Community Services, 148 Ariz. 1, 712 P.2d 914 (1985).

C. PRIVATE NUISANCE

1. GENERALLY

Private nuisance may be described as a "nontrespassory invasion of another's interest in the private use and enjoyment of land." Restatement (Second) of Torts § 821D. The ownership or rightful possession of land carries with it not only the right to exclude other persons and things from gaining entry onto the land, but embraces the right to use and enjoy the land free from significant interferences caused by those outside of the land. The interests protected by the tort of private nuisance are broad and imprecise.[4] Although, in one court's words, "[t]here are countless ways to interfere with the use and enjoyment of land[,] including interference with the physical condition of the land itself, disturbance in the comfort or conveniences of the occupant including his peace of mind, and threat of future injury that is a present menace and interference with enjoyment[,] [t]he essence of private nuisance is the protection of a property owner's or occupier's reasonable comfort[.]"[5]

The distinction between "use" and "enjoyment" is not semantic, as some low level airborne pollution may not altogether prevent an occupant from using his property, but may, nevertheless, interfere with his enjoyment of it, as might a variety of intrusions by odor. It is accepted generally that "smoke, offensive odors, noise or vibrations" that "materially interfere" with the possessor's "ordinary comfort" may constitute a nuisance. E.g., Baldwin v. McClendon, 292 Ala. 43, 288 So.2d 761 (1974) (hog parlor proximate to plaintiff's land); Brown v. County Commissioners of Scioto County, 1993 WL 171493 (Ohio App. 1993) (held: complaint regarding odors emanating from sewage treatment plant stated a claim in qualified private and public nuisance).

A toxic nuisance might take a wide range of forms. The pollution of a residence's well water would interfere both with a resident's use *and*

---

4. "It comprehends not only the interests that a person may have in the actual present use of land for residential, agricultural, commercial, industrial, and other purposes, but also his interests in having the present use value of the land unimpaired by changes in its physical condition. * * * 'Interest in use and enjoyment' also comprehends the pleasure, comfort and enjoyment that a person normally derives from the occupancy of land. Freedom from

discontent and annoyance while using land is often as important to a person as freedom from physical interruption with his use or freedom from detrimental change in the physical condition of the land itself." Restatement (Second) of Torts § 821D, comment b.

5. Adkins v. Thomas Solvent Co., 440 Mich. 293, 487 N.W.2d 715, 720 (1992). *Adkins* is set forth below.

enjoyment of a property. One federal trial court, in a trichloroethylene contamination case, required proof that the presence of the chemical in the water prevented the plaintiffs from indulging in such activities as fishing and swimming. Carroll v. Litton Systems, Inc., 1990 WL 312969 (W.D.N.C.1990). A sulphurous smell emanating from a business in a city's downtown financial district might constitute a nuisance if emitted every morning for several hours, but might not if it were discernable each day only in the two hours before dawn, when the affected office buildings and sidewalks alike were largely empty.

2. NATURE OF THE INTEREST INTERFERED WITH

The particular use to which a property is put and the sensitivities of the persons using the property may be factors in evaluating if defendant's conduct constitutes an unreasonable interference that rises to the level of a private nuisance. For example, if the morning sulphurous smell, described above, enveloped the premises of a nursery school playground, or a retirement residence, the proprietors of either could argue plausibly that the odor interfered substantially with their use of the properties for those purposes. If, on the other hand, the odor affected only adjoining properties engaged in smelting operations, any interference with either use or enjoyment might be too insubstantial to warrant a remedy in private nuisance.

Some decisions distinguish nuisance *per se* from nuisance *per accidens*. A nuisance *per se* would be any act that constitutes a nuisance "at all times and under any circumstances," such as, for example, the permanent or chronic contamination of plaintiff's property. Vickridge 1st and 2nd Addition Homeowners Ass'n v. Catholic Diocese, 212 Kan. 348, 510 P.2d 1296 (1973). Nuisance *per accidens*, on the other hand, requires the fact finder's evaluation of whether, under all the surrounding circumstances defendant's action substantially interferes with plaintiff's comfortable enjoyment. Successful nuisance claims *per accidens* have gained orders in abatement or damages for invasions by particulate matter such as limestone dust.[6]

An owner's or occupier's departure from a premises will not preclude a subsequent action in nuisance where the interference with another's rights of enjoyment of the property is of a continuing nature. A landowner who has polluted or contaminated a property and then sold or leased it to another may remain liable "for the continuation of the nuisance" after the transfer, until the transferee "discovers the condition and has reasonable opportunity to abate it." Restatement (Second) of Torts § 840A ("Continuing Liability After Transfer of Land."). Although the vendor may be liable in nuisance to holders of rights to other property, the vendee cannot himself sue the vendor in nuisance. See discussion of this issue in Chapter 4.

6. E.g., Crushed Stone Co. v. Moore, 369 P.2d 811 (Okla.1962) (the injury claimed by plaintiff included, inter alia, aggravation of allergies and worsening of one resident's nervous condition).

As was pointed out Chapter 2, the interests protected by private nuisance doctrine are distinguishable from trespass, but the two torts may overlap. An invasion of one's possessory interest in land is often accompanied by some interference with the use and enjoyment of land, which is especially likely to occur if the trespass produces actual harm to the land. One factor which distinguishes trespass from private nuisance is that the nuisance action may be maintained only if there is "significant harm", a harm of importance, involving more than a slight inconvenience or petty annoyance. See generally, Page Keeton, Trespass, Nuisance and Strict Liability, 59 Colum.L.Rev. 457 (1959).

Will the plaintiff's apprehension that the defendant's operation will impair the use or enjoyment of property support a claim of private nuisance?

ADKINS v. THOMAS SOLVENT COMPANY

Supreme Court of Michigan, 1992.
440 Mich. 293, 487 N.W.2d 715.

BOYLE, J.

The question before us is whether a claim for relief may be maintained by plaintiffs who claim the right to damages in nuisance for property depreciation caused by environmental contamination of ground water despite testimony by both plaintiffs' and defendants' experts that their properties were not and would never be subject to ground water contamination emanating from the defendants' property.

The trial court dismissed these plaintiffs' claims on the basis that it found no support for recovery in Michigan law. The Court of Appeals reversed the decision of the trial court, rejecting its conclusion that the facts presented no cognizable claim for nuisance.

[We reverse, for we] are persuaded that the boundaries of a traditional nuisance claim should not be relaxed to permit recovery on these facts. Compensation for a decline in property value caused by unfounded perception of underground contamination is inextricably entwined with complex policy questions regarding environmental protection that are more suitably resolved through the legislative process.

* * *

I

In 1984, the plaintiffs sued the Thomas Solvent Company in the Calhoun Circuit Court for damages and injunctive relief from injuries allegedly resulting from the improper handling of chemicals and industrial waste. Claiming that the Thomas Solvent Company's and other defendants' improper handling and storage of toxic chemicals and industrial waste had contaminated the ground water, the plaintiffs brought claims sounding in negligence, continuing nuisance, continuing trespass, strict liability, and ultrahazardous activities.

* * *

[The plaintiffs complained of contaminants emanating from two sites owned or operated by the Thomas Solvent defendants.]

As discovery continued, it became clear that contaminants allegedly discharged into the ground water by the defendants never reached these plaintiffs' property. The plaintiffs' expert, Yaron Sternberg * * * testified that no contaminants from the Thomas Solvent facilities had any effect on the properties of these plaintiffs, which were located south of the divide.

[In responding to defendants' motion to dismiss, plaintiffs] conceded that no contaminants ever reached these twenty-two plaintiffs' property, but urged the court to impose liability on the defendants for any loss in property values due to public concern about the contaminants in the general area. Concluding that any damages that these plaintiffs suffered resulted from unfounded public perception that their ground water was contaminated, the trial court dismissed their claims. * * *

* * * The Court of Appeals reversed the trial court's order and remanded the case to the trial court for further proceedings. * * *

* * *

III

Historically, Michigan has recognized two distinct versions of nuisance, public nuisance and private nuisance. A private nuisance is a nontrespassory invasion of another's interest in the private use and enjoyment of land. 4 Restatement Torts, 2d, § 821D, p. 100. It evolved as a doctrine to resolve conflicts between neighboring land uses. Because nuisance covers so many types of harm, it is difficult to articulate an encompassing definition. Imprecision in defining nuisance leads to confusion regarding the interest it is designed to protect. Nevertheless, the gist of a private nuisance action is an interference with the occupation or use of land or an interference with servitudes relating to land. There are countless ways to interfere with the use and enjoyment of land including interference with the physical condition of the land itself, disturbance in the comfort or conveniences of the occupant including his peace of mind, and threat of future injury that is a present menace and interference with enjoyment. The essence of private nuisance is the protection of a property owner's or occupier's reasonable comfort in occupation of the land in question. It involves "not only a defect, but threatening or impending danger * * * to the property rights or health of persons sustaining peculiar relations to the same * * *." The pollution of ground water may constitute a public or private nuisance. 4 Restatement Torts, 2d, § 832, p. 142.

According to the Restatement, an actor is subject to liability for private nuisance for a nontrespassory invasion of another's interest in the private use and enjoyment of land if (a) the other has property rights and privileges in respect to the use or enjoyment interfered with, (b) the invasion results in significant harm, (c) the actor's conduct is the legal cause of the invasion, and (d) the invasion is either (i) intentional and unreasonable, or (ii) unintentional and otherwise actionable under the rules governing liability for negligent, reckless, or ultrahazardous conduct. 4 Restatement Torts, 2d, §§ 821D–F, 822, pp. 100–115.

Prosser & Keeton's enumeration of the requirements to recover on a private nuisance theory is similar. They set forth the following requirements: "(1) The defendant acted with the intent of interfering with the use and enjoyment of the land by those entitled to the use; (2) There was some interference with the use and enjoyment of the land of the kind intended, although the amount and extent of that interference may not have been anticipated or intended; (3) The interference that resulted and the physical harm, if any, from that interference proved to be substantial. * * * The substantial interference requirement is to satisfy the need for a showing that the land is reduced in value because of the defendant's conduct; (4) The interference that came about under such circumstances was of such a nature, duration or amount as to constitute unreasonable interference with the use and enjoyment of the land. This does not mean that the defendant's conduct must be unreasonable. It only means that the interference must be unreasonable and this requires elaboration." Prosser & Keeton, supra, pp. 622–623.

* * * In this case, the Court considers whether property depreciation based on unfounded fears falls within the boundaries of an action for private nuisance in Michigan.

The plaintiffs alleged that the defendants' improper handling and storage of toxic chemicals and hazardous waste contaminated underground water in the area, thus supporting their recovery of money damages for nuisance. * * *

The Court of Appeals focused upon the lack of any physical intrusion onto plaintiffs' land, stressing that an interference with the use and enjoyment of land need not involve a physical or tangible intrusion. We do not disagree with this rule of law. Nevertheless, we conclude that the trial court properly found that the plaintiffs failed to trace any significant interference with the use and enjoyment of land to an action of the defendants.

The crux of the plaintiffs' complaint is that publicity concerning the contamination of ground water in the area (although concededly not their ground water) caused diminution in the value of the plaintiffs' property. This theory cannot form the basis for recovery because negative publicity resulting in unfounded fear about dangers in the vicinity of the property does not constitute a significant interference with the use and enjoyment of land.

Examination of the historic development of nuisance law helps to clarify the fallacy underlying plaintiffs' theory of recovery. Initially, the assize of novel disseisin was available for a complainant whose enjoyment of his free tenement was disturbed by the defendant. The tort of trespass later developed to remedy this situation in which the defendant interfered with the complainant's interest in land. The source of the injury was always on the complainant's land. Later, the assize of nuisance arose to redress injury due to an act of the defendant that interfered with the complainant's interest, although the injury did not involve an entry onto the complainant's land. Eventually, the action for trespass upon the case for nuisance developed. The appeal of this form of action was its remedy, damages, rather than abatement.

The doctrine of nuisance traditionally encompassed geographic, temporal, and proprietary aspects. In geographic terms, nuisance arose when occupants of neighboring land had a dispute, typically over the proper use of the defendant's land. * * *

In temporal terms, nuisance normally required some degree of permanence. If the asserted interference was "temporary and evanescent," there was no actionable nuisance. This requirement is normally subsumed in the question whether the interference with the use and enjoyment of property is substantial. In proprietary terms, nuisance required that the plaintiff have some interest in the land that was interfered with. Unlike the early assize of novel disseisin, nuisance did not limit suit to freeholders, but permitted lessees and then occupants to sue.

As the doctrine of trespass was gradually transmuted into the action upon the case for nuisance, the requirement that the injury involve entry onto the complainant's land was eliminated. To limit the broader action on the case for nuisance, courts added the requirement that a litigant seeking to recover for nuisance must show a legally cognizable injury, requiring proof of a significant interference with the use and enjoyment of land. Although much confusion has arisen because of the failure to discern that injury and damage are different concepts, an interference that is not substantial and unreasonable does not give rise to an action for damages against the person causing it, damnum absque injuria. Stated otherwise, while nuisance may be predicated on conduct of a defendant that causes mental annoyance, it will not amount to a substantial injury unless the annoyance is significant and the interference is unreasonable in the sense that it would be unreasonable to permit the defendant to cause such an amount of harm without paying for it.

Nuisance on the case thus involved the common law's attempt to ensure accommodation between conflicting uses of adjoining property. * * * Because the doctrine sought to acknowledge the right of both the property owner to carry out a particular use and the neighbor whose property or use and enjoyment of property might be injured by the use, de minimus annoyances were not actionable. Only for a substantial interference with the use and enjoyment of property would an action lie. As a part of this scheme, courts frequently concluded that diminution in property values alone constitutes damnum absque injuria.

The reasoning in Gunther v. E.I. Du Pont De Nemours & Co., 157 F.Supp. 25 (N.D.W.Va., 1957), app. dis. 255 F.2d 710 (CA 4, 1958), exemplifies this reluctance to find a nuisance for mere diminution of property value on the basis of unfounded beliefs or fear of injury. In Gunther, the plaintiffs unsuccessfully sought damages and injunctive relief for claimed injuries to their property and person from test explosions conducted by the defendant in the vicinity of their property. The court refused to find nuisance, reasoning: "The Court believes it a fair inference from the evidence that the Gunthers' enjoyment of their property was lessened because they believed that the test blasting had injured them. If such belief is unfounded, what is left other than depreciation in value? Mere diminution of the value of property because of the use to which adjoining or nearby premises is devoted, if unaccompanied with other ill results, is damnum absque injuria—a loss without an injury, in the legal sense."

That same reasoning applies to this case. Plaintiffs have stipulated the dismissal of all claims except those predicated upon an alleged depreciation in the market value of the property because of the unfounded fears of purchasers. The fact, as the dissent recognizes, that plaintiffs make no claim for relief arising out of their own fears, illustrates the point that defendants' activities have not interfered with their use and enjoyment of property.

This Court has held that property depreciation alone is insufficient to constitute a nuisance. Although there is early authority to the contrary involving circumstances largely subsumed in zoning regulations, most recently this Court has held that a cause of action for nuisance may not be based on unfounded fears. Smith v. Western Wayne Co. Conservation Ass'n., 380 Mich. 526, 543, 158 N.W.2d 463 (1968). In Smith, the plaintiffs sought to have a gun range declared a nuisance, contending that it created fear of injuries, thus decreasing their property values. Adopting the trial court's opinion that "no real or actual danger" existed from the use of the gun range, the Court further held that, even assuming a decrease in property values, this was not "in itself sufficient to constitute a nuisance."

Just as the development of nuisance on the case responded to the limitations of trespass by recognizing a cause of action when there was damage, but not injury amounting to use, the modern formulation of nuisance in fact, acknowledges changing conditions by declining to recognize a cause of action where damage and injury are both predicated on unfounded fear of third parties that depreciates property values. The rationale may be expressed by observing that reasonable minds cannot differ that diminished property value based on unfounded fear is not a substantial interference in and of itself. Thus, in rejecting a claim that tort liability could be based on the creation of fear that depreciates property values, one federal district court observed that the theory was based on "a public reaction which is conjectural, transitory and ephemeral."

This response also corresponds with the historical premise underlying tort liability for nuisance in fact, i.e., that when some significant interference with the use and enjoyment of land causes the property value loss, courts of law accommodate conflicting interests by recognizing claims designed to shift the loss. However, on the present state of the record, plaintiffs do not contend that the condition created by the defendant causes them fear or anxiety. Thus, not only have these plaintiffs not alleged significant interference with their use and enjoyment of property, they do not here posit any interference at all.

Plaintiffs correctly observe that property depreciation is a traditional element of damages in a nuisance action. See, e.g., Prosser, supra, pp. 637–640. We are not persuaded, however, and the dissent has not cited authority to the contrary, that an allegation of property depreciation alone sets forth a cognizable claim in private nuisance of significant interference with the use and enjoyment of a person's property. Diminution in property values caused by negative publicity is, on these facts, damnum absque injuria—a loss without an injury in the legal sense. * * *

* * *

We are thus unpersuaded by the dissent's attempt to avoid the stipulation of the parties by referring throughout the opinion to facts and counts that are not before us. * * * Unlike the dissent, we proceed on the assumption the parties presented to us. We do not know why counsel chose not to assert claims of personal discomfort or annoyance as he did with regard to other plaintiffs, or to appeal from the trial court's order denying leave to amend. These were probably strategy decisions based on his clients' responses in discovery. We are entitled to assume that counsel's present posture is motivated by legitimate interest in securing an appellate court decision that diminution in value is recoverable without a showing of substantial interference with use or enjoyment of property. * * * So viewed, the structuring of this lawsuit involves not a hypertechnical issue, but an issue of considerable significance to these plaintiffs, to litigants similarly situated, and to the jurisprudence.

In short, we do not agree with the dissent's suggestion that wholly unfounded fears of third parties regarding the conduct of a lawful business satisfy the requirement for a legally cognizable injury as long as property values decline. Indeed, we would think it not only "odd," but anachronistic that a claim of nuisance in fact could be based on unfounded fears regarding persons with AIDS moving into a neighborhood, the establishment of otherwise lawful group homes for the disabled, or unrelated persons living together, merely because the fears experienced by third parties would cause a decline in property values.

When appropriate, we have not hesitated to examine common-law doctrines in view of changes in society's mores, institutions, and problems, and to alter those doctrines where necessary. * * *

This case does not present that situation. * * *

The plaintiffs concede that a ground water divide prevented the migration of contaminated water to their property. Nevertheless, the plaintiffs seek to recover for damages because the defendants allegedly contaminated property in the general area. Under such a theory, a cause of action could be stated on behalf of any individual who could demonstrate an effect on property values even if the polluted ground water had neither strayed from defendants' own property, nor disturbed a plaintiff's enjoyment by the fear that it would do so.

If any property owner in the vicinity of the numerous hazardous waste sites that have been identified [37] can advance a claim seeking damages when unfounded public fears of exposure cause property depreciation, the ultimate effect might be a reordering of a polluter's resources for the benefit of persons who have suffered no cognizable harm at the expense of those claimants who have been subjected to a substantial and unreasonable interference in the use and enjoyment of property. Thus, while we acknowledge that the line drawn today is not necessarily dictated by the spectral permutations of nuisance jurisprudence, if the line is to be drawn elsewhere, the significant interests involved appear to be within the realm of those more appropriate for resolution by the Legislature.

IV

For these reasons, we conclude that the Court of Appeals erred when it reversed the trial court's grant of the defendants' summary disposition motion. We reverse the decision of the Court of Appeals, reinstate the trial court's judgment granting summary disposition in favor of the defendants, and remand to the trial court for a continuation of proceedings with regard to the remaining plaintiffs.

GRIFFIN, MALLETT and BRICKLEY J., concur.

Notes and Questions

1. Judge Levin, in dissent, argues, among other things, that the majority misses the mark in characterizing plaintiffs' claims as one based upon "negative publicity resulting in unfounded fear about dangers in the vicinity of the property[.]" To be contrasted, the dissent states, plaintiffs' fear is hardly inchoate, but results from, demonstrable and present economic harm:

> Plaintiffs should, in our opinion be allowed to recover damages in nuisance on proofs introduced at a trial tending to show that the defendants actually contaminated soil and ground water in the neighborhood of plaintiffs' homes with toxic chemicals and industrial wastes, that the market perception of the value of plaintiffs' homes was actually adversely affected by the contamination of the neighborhood, and thus that plaintiffs' loss was causally related to defendants' conduct.

> Preservation of property value is, in itself, a legally cognizable interest in this setting, whether any structure on the land is a home or rental or other commercial or industrial property.

37. Seventy-seven Michigan hazardous waste sites are on the National Priorities List. 56 Fed.Reg. 5606–5627 (February 22, 1991). In addition, the Department of Natural Resources, pursuant to the Environmental Response Act, 1982 P.A. 307, M.C.L. § 299.601 et seq.; M.S.A. § 13.32(1) et seq., has identified approximately 2,837 sites of environmental contamination throughout the state. Department of Natural Resources, Michigan Sites of Environmental Contamination, Act 307 (March, 1991), p. 9.

A condition, tortiously or intentionally created or maintained on neighboring property, that is a substantial and unreasonable nontrespassory interference with the use and enjoyment of property, may constitute a nuisance. Such a condition may cause personal injury, property damage, or a reduction in the market value of property. The condition may be reflected in a reduction of the market value of a home although no personal injury or other property damage is suffered by the homeowner.

We would hold that a homeowner may maintain a nuisance action to recover damages for a decline in the market value of his home that reflects interference with the use and enjoyment of his home by a condition tortiously created or maintained by the defendant on neighboring property, and that the homeowner may do so without demonstrating interference with use or enjoyment that might result in further, separately compensable injuries to persons or property.

2. Why did the majority consider the fears of third parties "unfounded?" Was its conclusion based solely on the hydrogeological fact that contamination from defendants' operations could not reach plaintiffs' property? What rationales did the majority offer to support its conclusion? Was a concern for unlimited or disproportionate liability among the reasons offered? Did the dissent's test of requiring "a condition tortiously created or maintained by the defendant on *neighboring* property" address the widespread liability issue?

3. As in trespass, the plaintiff succeeding in a claim for private nuisance may recover proved damages as measured by the diminution of the property's fair market value. See Chapter 5 for a detailed discussion of the measures of damage available in nuisance and trespass actions. Had plaintiffs in *Adkins* succeeded in "trac[ing] [a] significant interference with the use and enjoyment of the land to an action of the defendants[,]" would the court have treated their claim for property depreciation differently?

4. To the extent that the activities of Thomas Solvent and its co-defendants were continuing at the time plaintiffs began their suit (or if stopped, were capable of resumption) could plaintiffs have succeeded in a petition to enjoin defendants' conduct? Would plaintiffs need to show the likelihood that continuation of defendants' conduct would surely result in contamination of plaintiffs' ground water? That it would probably result? Would plaintiffs' proof be sufficient with evidence of defendants' contamination of property proximate to that of plaintiffs, and defendants' inability to produce positive proof that the contamination would not eventually reach plaintiffs' groundwater?

5. If plaintiffs were successful in securing an injunction, would an accompanying claim for diminished property values have been treated differently by the *Adkins* majority?

3. CORRECTIVE JUSTICE AND UTILITARIANISM

In addressing the law of private nuisance, it is useful to recognize two schools of thought that pull in opposite directions, both of which have influenced the evolution of this tort: the corrective justice view and the utilitarian view. The corrective justice view states that nuisance cases can and should be decided by reference to fairness principles, i.e., that a plaintiff is entitled to redress whenever the defendant's activity has caused an invasion of the plaintiff's property rights, and that in an ideal world all nuisance cases could be adjudicated on that basis. The tort rules relating to battery come very close to achieving that standard. In the law of battery, the plaintiff's interest is in the right to bodily integrity, and it is premised on the individual's ownership of his or her own body. Tort law recognizes that there exists some prior independent method for defining and recognizing property rights both in person and in land and chattels. Once acquired, the "ownership of things is subject to the same entitlements and limitations as the ownership of the person." Professor Epstein, a leading advocate of this theory, offers this illustration rewritten for brevity by your authors:

> C is entitled to make productive use of her land and derive profits therefrom, until in doing so C sets in motion a chain of events (energy and molecules) that produce a substantial invasion of D's land. It is analogous to saying that A's right to swing her arms to enhance the blood circulation is unrestricted until in doing so she unleashes energies that produce a collision with B's chin. In determining whether A is liable to B for battery or negligence, we look at the invasion of B's interest in bodily integrity; we generally take little or no account of how much benefit A derived from her activity, whether the benefit be her physical well-being, pleasure or profits. Corrective justice principles dictate that A compensate B for the invasion of B's interest.
>
> The same principles also dictate that C should compensate D for D's damages, without regard to how much investment C has made, how many she may employ; how important C's activity is to the community, how "locationally appropriate" it is to the surrounding area, or any other utilitarian constraint. There is simply no justification for balancing the so-called "equities" of the situation or performing a balancing of the comparative injuries of the parties. These corrective justice principles seem especially valid in environmental harm nuisance cases where something has invaded D's land—benzene or salt that C has caused to enter the aquifer which contaminated D's well, phosphate particles that settled on D's crops, or chemicals in the air that causes D's emphysema to worsen. These principles, however, work less well in the cases where the interests are more subjective—the placement of a half-way house, funeral parlor, or interference with the flow of light onto D's property.

Richard A. Epstein, Nuisance Law: Corrective Justice and Its Utilitarian Constraints, 8 J. Legal Stud. 49 (1979).

Do you agree with Professor Epstein? Ought locational appropriateness never be a bar to plaintiff's award of compensatory damages? Consider Williams v. Monsanto Co., 856 S.W.2d 338 (Mo.App. 1993), the appeal of a judgment for defendant on plaintiff's claim that his automobile repair business was impaired by regular dusting of particulate STP (tripolyphosphate) from defendant Monsanto's plant, causing, among other problems, the "pitting" of customers' automobiles and the diminution of plaintiff's business. The Missouri appellate court upheld the jury's rejection of plaintiff's nuisance claim on a variety of grounds, but noted pointedly that defendant Monsanto's use was well within the band of reasonableness given its location: "Here no other neighbors complained during the period in question. The area was largely industrial, with a coke plant and a cement plant nearby. * * * The questio[n] of whether a use is "unreasonable * * * [is] particularly fact sensitive and [is] particularly suited to jury resolution."

An early opinion that eloquently sets forth the corrective justice view of private nuisance is Bamford v. Turnley.

BAMFORD v. TURNLEY

Court of Exchequer Chamber, 1886.
3 B. & S. 66.

[A large estate was divided into lots which were sold as building site for houses. Lots were advertised as containing abundant brick clay suitable for building. Plaintiff's house was finished in 1858. In 1860 defendant put up a brick kiln on one of four lots he had bought, and began burning bricks for use in building. Plaintiff brought a nuisance action for damages, complaining of smoke and fumes emitted from the brick kiln some 180 yards from his house. A judgment for defendant was reversed (5–1) on appeal in Exchequer Chamber.]

BRAMWELL, B.— * * * The defendant has done that which, if done wantonly or maliciously would be actionable as being a nuisance to the plaintiff's habitation by causing a sensible diminution of the comfortable enjoyment of it. [This] calls on the defendant to justify or excuse what he has done. And his justification is this: He says that the nuisance is not to the health of the inhabitants of the plaintiff's house, that it is of a temporary character, and is necessary for the beneficial use of his, the defendant's, land, and that the public good requires he should be entitled to do what he claims to do.

[W]hat principle or rule of law can he rely on to defend himself? It is clear to my mind that there is some exception to the general application of the maxim mentioned. The instances put during the argument, of burning weeds, emptying cesspools, making noises during repairs, and other instances which would be nuisances if done wantonly or maliciously, nevertheless may be lawfully done. It cannot be said that such acts are not nuisances, because, by the hypothesis, they are; and it cannot be doubted that, if a person maliciously and without cause made close to a dwelling-house the same offensive smells as may be made in emptying a cesspool, an action would lie. * * * There must be, then, some principle on which such cases must be excepted.

It seems to me that that principle may be deduced from the character of these cases, and is this, viz., that those acts necessary for the common and ordinary use and occupation of land and houses may be done, if conveniently done, without subjecting those who do them to an action. This principle would comprehend all the cases I have mentioned, but would not comprehend the present, where what has been done was not the using of land in a common and ordinary way, but in an exceptional manner—not unnatural nor unusual, but not the common and ordinary use of land. * * * It is as much for the advantage of one owner as of another; for the very nuisance the one complains of, as the result of the ordinary use of his neighbor's land, he himself will create in the ordinary use of his own, and the reciprocal nuisances are of a comparatively trifling character. The convenience of such a rule may be indicated by calling it a rule of give and take, live and let live.

* * *

But it is said that, temporary or permanent, it is lawful because it is for the public benefit. * * * It is for the public benefit there should be railways, but * * * no one thinks it would be right to take an individual's land without compensation to make a railway. It is for the public benefit that trains should run, but not unless they pay their expenses. * * * So in like way in this case a money value indeed cannot easily be put on the plaintiff's loss, but it is equal to some number of pounds or pence, 10*l.*, 50*l.*, or what not: unless the defendant's profits are enough to compensate this, I deny that it is for the public benefit he should do what he has done; if they are, he ought to compensate.

* * *

Notes and Questions

1. When applying corrective justice principles in this context, the liability is *strict* and does not depend on whether the defendant exercised due care under the circumstances.

2. The thrust of the holding in *Bamford* is that corrective justice principles should govern, and any person suffering significant harm should be compensated by the entity which causes the interference and the harm regardless of the worthwhile nature of its activity either to the defendant alone or to segments of society more broadly. In other words, utilitarian values are of no account in determining liability.

3. In *Adkins*, the court's *damnum absque injuria* analysis professes to "acknowledge the right of both the property owner to carry out a particular use and the neighbor whose property or use and enjoyment might be injured by the use[.]" *Bamford* represents one of the oldest examples of the so-called "live and let live" approach in common law nuisance actions. Did the *Adkins* approach track or extend the *Bamford* live and let live analysis?

The live and let live exception posits that certain interferences are so insubstantial and trivial, and so common and inevitable in our society that we all experience them and we all cause them (they are reciprocal nuisances), so that each such interference should not give rise to a cause of action. The Restatement (Second) states the principle in these terms:

> It is an obvious truth that each individual in a community must put up with a certain amount of annoyance, inconvenience, and interference, and must take a certain amount of risk in order that we may all get on together. The very existence of organized society depends on the principle of "give and take, live and let live" and therefore the law of torts does not attempt to impose liability or shift the loss in every case where one person's conduct has some detrimental effect on another. Liability is imposed only in those cases where the harm or risk to one is greater than he ought to be required to bear under the circumstances, at least without compensation.

Restatement (Second) of Torts, § 822, comment g.

4. Where the harm to plaintiff's land is substantial, many courts have declined to permit the defendant to exculpate itself by showing that the value of its conduct outweighed the gravity of any harm to the plaintiff. See e.g., Jost v. Dairyland Power Cooperative, 45 Wis.2d 164, 172 N.W.2d 647 (1969) (sulphur dioxide emissions from power company smokestack). Some courts have adopted a "comparative injury," or utilitarian analysis. For example, in Crushed Stone v. Moore, 369 P.2d 811 (Okl.1962), the court described the process, which it nevertheless rejected: "While we recognize that in proper cases, especially involving businesses upon which the public's interest, or necessity, depends, the matter of 'comparative injury' should be given prominent consideration, this court is among those holding that where damages in an action at law will not give plaintiffs an adequate remedy against a business operated in such a way that it has become a nuisance, and such operation causes plaintiffs substantial and irremediable injury, they are entitled, as a matter of right, to have same abated, by injunction, '* * * notwithstanding the comparative benefits conferred thereby or the comparative injury resulting therefrom.' " See Chapter 5 for a fuller consideration of the balancing of the equities involved in injunctive proceedings.

5. Courts in many cases entertain utilitarian considerations and balance the extent of plaintiff's harm against the utility of the defendant's activity in deciding whether an actionable nuisance exists. The opinion in Carpenter v. Double R Cattle Company, 108 Idaho 602, 701 P.2d 222 (1985), discussed in this Chapter, represents that view in the extreme. Many of the opinions below illustrate the struggle between these two views. As will be seen, in Chapter 5 especially, the willingness of some courts to apply utilitarian principles turns on whether the relief being sought is damages or an injunction. For a discussion of some broad considerations, see Robert C. Ellickson, Alternatives to Zoning: Nuisance Rules and Fines as Land Use Control, 40 U.Chi.L.Rev. 681 (1973).

6. Must the defendant in an action for private nuisance be a land owner or occupier? In Heritage Village Master Association v. Heritage Village Water Company, 30 Conn.App. 693, 622 A.2d 578 (1993), a condominium community's management brought a nuisance claim against its water supplier, alleging that the water's quality accelerated corrosion of the community's copper pipes, causing the need for expensive repair and replacement. As one of alternative grounds for affirming the trial court's judgment

for the supplier, the Connecticut court held that the water supplier enjoyed a relation with neither land nor the plaintiff sufficient to support nuisance liability. In the words of the court: "The evidence was also deficient to permit a jury instruction on the law of nuisance in [the] respect [that] [o]ur case law requires sufficient proof of a defendant's connection to a particular parcel of property and the nature of the defendant's use of his property, before nuisance liability can be imposed." Is the limitation on the nuisance remedy expressed in *Heritage Village* sound? Consider Philadelphia Electric Co. v. Hercules, Inc., 762 F.2d 303 (3d Cir.1985), in which the Third Circuit, denying the nuisance claim of a business purchaser of property, explained: "[T]he historical role of private nuisance law [is] as a means of efficiently resolving conflicts between *neighboring* contemporaneous land uses. * * * Neighbors, unlike purchasers of the land upon which the nuisance exists, have no opportunity to protect themselves through inspection and negotiation."

7. What kind of interest must a plaintiff have in order to have standing to maintain a private nuisance action? The general rule is that the plaintiff must have either an ownership or possessory interest to bring a private nuisance action. Thus, in Arnoldt v. Ashland Oil, Inc., 186 W.Va. 394, 412 S.E.2d 795 (1991). the court held that adult children and non-owners residing with relatives did not have standing because they lacked the requisite ownership or possessory interest. Nevertheless, while nuisance law is designed to protect interests in land "any interest sufficient to be dignified as a property right will support the action." Prosser & Keeton on Torts 621 (5th ed. 1984). In contrast to *Arnoldt*, one court has recognized the standing of a minor child of a tenant to maintain a private nuisance action. Gesswin v. Beckwith, 35 Conn.Sup. 89, 397 A.2d 121 (1978); see also, William H. Rodgers, Jr., Environmental Law: Air and Water § 2.4 at 42 (1986). If a property interest is essential for a private nuisance, how might a student in a school or a worker in a factory who is affected by a nuisance circumvent the standing limitation?

4. PRIVATE NUISANCE: THE RESTATEMENT POSITION

What position does the Restatement (Second) of Torts take on the issue of corrective justice principles versus a utilitarian approach? Does it permit a utilitarian analysis focusing on the benefits conferred by the defendant's enterprise or does it enforce a corrective justice principle that focuses largely on the substantiality of the harm suffered by the plaintiff? The answer is, a bit of both.

First, § 821F only allows a plaintiff to recover damages on a private nuisance theory if she suffers "significant harm," which is defined as harm: "of a kind that would be suffered by a normal person in the community or by property in normal condition and used for a normal purpose." This statement recognizes the "live and let live" rule and precludes recovery for slight inconveniences and petty annoyances. On the other hand, when the invasion involves a detrimental change in the physical condition of land, there is seldom any doubt as to the significance of the harm.

Second, in private nuisance actions for damages—as distinguished from injunction proceedings—§ 822 provides for liability as follows:

§ 822. General Rule

One is subject to liability for a private nuisance if, but only if, his conduct is a legal cause of an invasion of another's interest in the private use and enjoyment of land, and the invasion is either

> (a) intentional and unreasonable, or

> (b) unintentional and otherwise actionable under the rules controlling liability for negligent or reckless conduct, or for abnormally dangerous conditions or activities.

Let us focus first on the meaning of an "intentional and unreasonable" invasion of the plaintiff's interest in the private use and enjoyment of land. What is an "unreasonable" invasion? Does it mean that the courts must consider the utilitarian factors which a defendant would assert? Comment d states:

> For the purpose of determining liability for *damages* for private nuisance an invasion may be regarded as unreasonable even though the utility of the conduct is great and the amount of harm is relatively small. But for the purpose of determining whether the conduct producing the invasion should be enjoined, additional factors must be considered.

Thus, in damages actions the Restatement makes some movement towards applying corrective justice principles and limiting the application of utilitarian constraints. Further support for this treatment exists in § 826, where unreasonableness is defined as follows:

§ 826. Unreasonableness of Intentional Invasion

An intentional invasion of another's interest in the use and enjoyment of land is unreasonable if

> (a) the gravity of the harm outweighs the utility of the actor's conduct, or

> (b) the harm caused by the conduct is serious and the financial burden of compensating for this and similar harm to others would not make the continuation of the conduct not feasible.

It is significant that subsections (a) and (b) are in the disjunctive—either will suffice. Subsection (a) is a utilitarian test that compares the gravity of the actual harm (not the risk of harm as in a negligence case) against the "utility of the actor's conduct." This is precisely the kind of analysis that corrective justice principles resist—examining the effect of the defendant's conduct on its own well being and that of the community.

Subsection (b), however, creates an alternative basis for liability in cases seeking *damages only*. In such cases, the harm must be "serious" and the "financial burden of compensating" the plaintiff (and others similarly situated) must not require that the defendant cease its operations. The careful weighing process between utility and harm applicable to injunction suits gives way to a rule that allows compensatory damages to be awarded, even if the utility of the activity exceeds the harm, so long as the damages are not so great as to become, for practical purposes, an injunction of sorts, shutting down the activity. The objective of the action for damages is not to stop the activity, but rather to require the activity to bear the costs of compensating for the harm it causes to others. This is precisely what the court in *Bamford* expressed and is precisely what corrective justice principles would require. Comment f to § 826 states:

> It may sometimes be reasonable to operate an important activity if payment is made for the harm it is causing, but unreasonable to continue it without paying. The process of weighing the gravity of the harm against the utility of the conduct assesses the social value of the actor's activity in general. * * * The process of comparing the general utility of the activity with the harm suffered as a result is adequate if the suit is for an injunction prohibiting the activity. But it may sometimes be incomplete and therefore inappropriate when the suit is for compensation for the harm imposed. The action for damages does not seek to stop the activity; it seeks instead to place on the activity the cost of compensating for the harm it causes. The financial burden of this cost is therefore a significant factor in determining whether the conduct of causing the harm without paying for it is unreasonable. * * *

> In a damage action for an intentional invasion of another's interest in the use and enjoyment of land, therefore, the invasion is unreasonable not only when the gravity of the harm outweighs the utility of the conduct, but also when the utility outweighs the gravity—provided the financial burden of compensating for the harms caused by the activity would not render it unfeasible to continue conducting the activity. If imposition of this financial burden would make continuation of the activity not feasible, the weighing process for determining unreasonableness is similar to that in a suit for injunction.

Two points are important in applying this rule. First, the court is expected to take into consideration the impact which similar suits by others will have on the defendant's financial ability to continue its operations. If the nuisance consists of the emission of smoke and odors from the factory affecting a significant area, the court might decide (based on the defendant's proofs establishing the factual foundation) that none can recover because the cumulative effect of all obtaining compensatory damages would be to shut down the plant; or, alternatively, it might decide that only those living closest to the plant could recover, even though those farther distant are suffering serious harm. In Bradley v. American Smelting, supra, Chapter 2, the court was obviously concerned about the problem of having hundreds of landowners each suing for a trespass and/or nuisance and for that reason, and others, required that a plaintiff suffer substantial harm as a prerequisite to an action.

Second, there is a certain perversity in this rule created by the fact that the more serious the harms produced and the greater the compensatory damages supported by the evidence, the greater the likelihood that the defendant will not be able to bear the costs without curtailing its operations. At the point of the highest potential damages and the most significant harm, subsection (b) may be defeated by the risk that such damages pose to the defendant's continuing operations. In other words, when the invasion becomes most unreasonable the philosophy of subsection (b) may be displaced.

At that point, the case will be governed, not by subsection (b), but by the pure utility and harm balancing of subsection (a) which characterizes injunctive proceedings. Thus, § 826 does attempt to provide a mechanism for enabling injured private landowners to recover damages whenever the invasion is intentional and serious. The principle here at work is that a business operated for economic gain should internalize the costs of its operations—the harm that it produces is part of the costs of doing business, to be passed along to those to whom it sells or provides services. As you will observe below, some courts have refused to apply subsection (b) and insist on allowing a utility and harm weighing test to be outcome determinative even in cases of a clear and substantial invasion, where the plaintiff is seeking only damages, and where there is no risk that paying such damages would impair the defendant's ability to continue its operations.

5. PRIVATE NUISANCE: THE BASIS OF LIABILITY

As mentioned earlier, the term "nuisance" does not describe a kind of liability-creating conduct but rather describes the nature of the invasion of the plaintiff's interest. Section 822 sets forth the three kinds of conduct by the defendant that can give rise to liability when such invasions do occur.

a. *Intentional and Unreasonable*

(i) The Intent Requirement

The student should see that not all conduct will create liability; there must be some kind of tortious conduct, either intentional, reckless, negligent or abnormally dangerous. Invasions that do not involve some tortious conduct are not actionable as private nuisances. The first kind of invasion that gives rise to liability for a private nuisance are those classified as "intentional and unreasonable." For "intentional and unreasonable" invasions, the threshold inquiry is to determine what constitutes the requisite intent to satisfy subsection (a). Is it the intent to cause harm? The cases have held that it is not necessary to prove that the defendant acted for the purpose of causing or desiring to cause harm to the plaintiff. Rather, it is sufficient if the defendant "knows that [the invasion] is resulting or is substantially certain to result from his conduct." Restatement (Second) of Torts § 825. The defendant's knowledge of the invasion is not the equivalent of its knowledge of *harm* caused by the *invasion*.

Earlier in the trespass area it was pointed out that the necessary intent could be established by showing that the defendant knew with substantial certainty that an invasion of plaintiff's protected interest would result from defendant's activity. The same rule of substantial certainty of the invasion applies to nuisance cases. See Restatement (Second) of Torts § 8A; Frady v. Portland General Electric Co., 55 Or.App. 344, 637 P.2d 1345, 1348 (1981), where the court found that defendant's appearance at trial was sufficient to give it notice that its conduct was producing an invasion of plaintiff's property, stating that "intentional conduct is not limited to activity undertaken for the purpose of damaging another, but includes any act done with the knowledge that damage to another would result."

(ii) The Unreasonableness Requirement

The "unreasonableness" of the invasion, as set forth in Restatement (Second) of Torts § 826, examines the substantiality of the harm—how serious is the invasion—and how the gravity of that harm compares to the utility of the defendant's conduct. In suits seeking damages, however, as discussed above the utility of the defendant's conduct is not weighed, so long as the harm is "serious" (i.e., substantial or significant) and the impact of compensating the plaintiff and others similarly situated will not be so devastating as to require the defendant to cease its operations. In injunctive proceedings that would result in requiring the defendant to cease or curtail its operations, the courts will weigh the utility of the defendant's activities, both to itself and its utility to the public at large—number of employees affected, tax structure and dependence of the community on its operations, the importance of the product or service involved—and determine if the harm suffered by the plaintiff outweighs that utility.

(iii) Gravity of the Harm Suffered

The reasonableness of an invasion is determined from an objective point of view—not whether the plaintiff or the defendant would so regard it, but whether a reasonable person, armed with knowledge of all the surrounding circumstances and utilities, would so regard it. The Restatement sets forth the factors to be considered in the weighing process, which are those frequently encountered in tort law. Section 827 describes the factors involved in determining the gravity of the harm:

§ 827. Gravity of Harm—Factors Involved

In determining the gravity of the harm from an intentional invasion of another's interest in the use and enjoyment of land, the following factors are important:

> (a) the extent of the harm involved;
>
> (b) the character of the harm involved;
>
> (c) the social value which the law attaches to the type of use or enjoyment invaded;
>
> (d) the suitability of the particular use or enjoyment invaded to the character of the locality;
>
> (e) the burden on the person harmed of avoiding the harm.

A few points are noteworthy. Under subsection (a) the degree of the invasion *and* its duration are both relevant. Even minor interferences if extended indefinitely may produce significant harm.

The character of the harm under subsection (b) is obviously important: does it consist of damage to land or buildings or to crops, or is it a personal annoyance or discomfort? Does it raise serious personal safety and health concerns (e.g., carcinogenic chemical wastes)?

The factor in subsection (d) is sometimes referred to as the "locality rule." Comment g to Restatement (Second) of Torts § 827 notes that the harm to a residential plaintiff in a residential area will be considered more serious than the harm to a resident whose home is located in a predominately business or commercial community, not because the harm is less in some objective sense, but because public policy demands that the character of the uses in the area be assigned some weight in the process. For example, zoning ordinances can be relevant in examining this factor. Finally, as subsection (e) recognizes, the plaintiff may easily be able to minimize the effect of the invasion by shutting the windows or taking other simple steps.

(iv) Utility of Defendant's Conduct

The Restatement describes the factors controlling the utility analysis in § 828:

§ 828. Utility of Conduct—Factors Involved

In determining the utility of conduct that causes an intentional invasion of another's interest in the use and enjoyment of land, the following factors are important:

> (a) the social value that the law attaches to the primary purpose of the conduct;
>
> (b) the suitability of the conduct to the character of the locality; and
>
> (c) the impracticality of preventing or avoiding the invasion.

Subsection (a) addresses the usual understanding of the term and requires no special attention, beyond that paid to it in the cases already considered and those below. Subsections (b) and (c) raise the same points as found in assessing the gravity of the harm, asking as to the defendant's activity: how locationally appropriate is the activity and could the defendant have done anything reasonably feasible to reduce or eliminate the invasion?

(v) Other Considerations on Unreasonableness

In addition to the factors in Restatement §§ 827 and 828, the Restatement recognizes that certain kinds of invasions will be regarded as unreasonable. The invasion of the plaintiff's interest will be found to be unreasonable where the defendant's conduct is malicious or indecent (§ 829); where the resulting invasion could have been avoided by the defendant relatively easily ("without undue hardship") (§ 830); where the plaintiff's use of his land is, and the defendant's conduct is not, suited to the locality in which the invasion occurred (§ 841); or where the harm resulting is "severe" and greater than the plaintiff should be required to bear without compensation (§ 829A).

b. Negligent or Reckless Conduct

As the cases below show, there is a lingering confusion about the role of negligence in nuisance law. Some opinions erroneously state that the plaintiff in a private nuisance case must establish negligence. While negligence by the defendant will satisfy the conduct requirement and support liability for nuisance, it is not a necessary element, and, in fact, most private nuisance actions today are predicated upon intentional and unreasonable invasions. Many of the opinions, especially lower courts, contain an alternative finding predicating liability on negligence, as well as intentional or as well as abnormally dangerous activity. While such reliance is superfluous, it is understandable.

As in all negligence or recklessness cases, the defendant must create unreasonable risks of harm. The unreasonableness of the risk of harm is determined by the same risk versus utility analysis undertaken in other negligence or recklessness cases. Note that it is the *risk* of harm that is weighed, not the harm that actually materialized. The same utility considerations discussed above apply to these cases. Restatement (Second) of Torts § 291 essentially incorporates Learned Hand's test of negligence from United States v. Carroll Towing Co., 159 F.2d 169 (2d Cir.1947), by defining the unreasonableness of the actor's conduct by whether the magnitude of the risks created outweighs the utility of the act, where utility includes the extent of the chance that the interest being advanced by the defendant's conduct can be advanced by a less dangerous course of conduct. For criticisms and discussions of the test, see William H. Rodgers, Jr., Negligence Reconsidered: The Role of

Rationality in Tort Theory, 54 S.Cal.L.Rev. 1 (1980); George P. Fletcher, Fairness and Utility in Tort Theory, 85 Harv.L.Rev. 537 (1972).

Problem

Magnum Computer Inc. (Magnum) is a manufacturer of computer hardware. Immediately adjacent and hydrogeologically upgradient to Magnum is a paint and thinner supplier, Thinner Corp. (Thinner). Recently, consumers have returned a large quantity of computer parts manufactured by Magnum, complaining that the parts are defective.

Magnum, which is located in a rural area, uses water from an on-site well in its manufacturing process. While investigating the cause of the defective products, Magnum's quality control personnel discover that the defects are caused by a reaction between a material used in manufacturing the parts and certain toxic chemicals found in the water supplied by Magnum's well. Although Thinner denies any responsibility for the chemicals' presence in the groundwater below Magnum's plant, the toxic chemicals in the water are those that Thinner regularly sells to its customers.

Magnum's attorney is considering a suit against Thinner for costs of removing the toxic contamination from Magnum's property, the economic damages suffered by the company, and for degradation of the groundwater. Magnum, however, is unable to find any direct evidence of spills or careless handling of chemicals by Thinner. It will therefore have difficulty proving that Thinner caused the release of toxic chemicals which seeped into the soil and eventually into the groundwater, or that the Thinner-created contaminant plume subsequently migrated into the groundwater below Magnum's facility.

As Magnum's attorney what evidentiary approach might be considered to overcome the proof problems? What theory of liability is most promising?

D. JUDICIAL APPLICATIONS OF PRIVATE AND PUBLIC NUISANCE THEORIES

THE VILLAGE OF WILSONVILLE v. SCA SERVICES, INC.

Supreme Court of Illinois, 1981.
86 Ill.2d 1, 55 Ill.Dec. 499, 426 N.E.2d 824.

CLARK, J.

On April 18, 1977, the plaintiff village of Wilsonville (the village) filed a complaint seeking injunctive relief in the circuit court of Macoupin County. Plaintiffs Macoupin County and the Macoupin County Farm Bureau were granted leave to intervene[.] * * * The gravamen of the complaints was that the operation of the defendant's chemical-waste-disposal site presents a public nuisance and a hazard to the health of the citizens of the village, the county, and the State. The Attorney General of Illinois filed a complaint on May 26, 1977, seeking an injunction[.] * * * [A 104–day consolidated trial resulted in judgment for the plaintiffs.] The trial court's judgment order concluded that the site constitutes a nuisance and enjoined the defendant from operating its hazard-ous-chemical-waste landfill in Wilsonville. It ordered the defendant to remove all toxic waste buried there, * * * all contaminated soil found at the disposal site[,] * * * [and] to restore and reclaim the site.

The defendant appealed[, and the Appellate Court affirmed.] We affirm.

[SUMMARY OF EVIDENCE]

The defendant has operated a chemical-waste landfill since 1977. The site comprises approximately 130 acres, 90 of which are within the village limits of the plaintiff village. The remaining 40 acres are adjacent to the village. The defendant enters into agreements with generators of toxic chemical waste to haul the waste away from the generators' locations. The defendant then delivers it to the Wilsonville site, tests random samples of chemical waste, and then deposits the waste in trenches. There are seven trenches at the site. Each one is approximately 15 feet deep, 50 feet wide, and 250 to 350 feet long. Approximately 95% of the waste materials were buried in 55–gallon steel drums, and the remainder is contained in double-wall paper bags. After the materials are deposited in the trenches, uncompacted clay is placed between groups of containers and a minimum of one foot of clay is placed between the top drum and the top clay level of the trench.

The site is bordered on the east, west, and south by farmland and on the north by the village. The entire site, the village, and much of the surrounding area is located above the abandoned Superior Coal Mine No. 4, which operated from 1917 to 1954. The No. 6 seam of the mine was exploited in this area at a depth of 312 feet. The mining method used to extract coal was the room-and-panel method, whereby about 50% of the coal is left in pillars which provide some support for the earth above the mine. [Expert testimony at trial indicated] that pillar failure can occur in any mine where there is a readjustment of stress.

* * *

There are 14 monitoring wells along the perimeter of the site. They are designed to detect liquids which seep through the soil and into the wells. They are not designed to contain liquids, however. In fact, monitoring wells Nos. 5 and 6 are 650 feet apart, which would allow many materials to pass between those two wells and not be discovered. The wells are sampled quarterly by a private laboratory, and test results are submitted to the Illinois Environmental Protection Agency (IEPA). Additional water samples are taken from three surface channels and are tested and reported in the same manner as samples taken from the wells. The surface drainage and the ground-water drainage from the site are to the south, away from the village and toward farmland.

The village has no sewage-treatment plant and no municipally owned sewage system. Most homes are served by septic tanks, and some homes and businesses are connected to private sewers. The water-distribution system is centralized, * * * [but] [t]here are still 73 water wells in the village, some of which are used to water gardens or wash cars. At least one well is used to water pets, and another is used for drinking water. * * * Further south are four more springs used to water livestock.

On February 11, 1976, the defendant applied to the IEPA for a permit to develop and operate the hazardous-waste landfill. A developmental permit was issued by the IEPA on May 19, 1976. After a preoperation inspection was conducted by the IEPA, an operational permit was issued to the defendant on September 28, 1976. Each delivery of waste material to the site must be accompanied by a supplemental permit issued by the IEPA. A supplemental permit specifies the chemical nature and quantity of the waste to be deposited at the sites. Between November 12, 1976, and June 7, 1977, the first day of trial, the defendant had obtained 185 such permits.

The materials deposited at the site include polychlorinated biphenyls (PCBs), a neurotoxic, possibly carcinogenic chemical which it has been illegal to produce in this country since 1979. Due to the extensive use of PCBs in electrical equipment such as transformers, capacitors, and heat-transfer systems, and in hydraulic systems, any PCBs that were produced legally now have to be disposed of when they are no longer in use. PCBs have been stored at the site in liquid, solid and semi-solid form. Additionally, there are a number of now-empty drums which had once contained PCBs, which are also buried at the site. Other materials buried at the site in large quantities are solid cyanide, a substance known as C5, 6, paint sludge, asbestos, pesticides, mercury, and arsenic. * * *

* * *

Subsidence of the earth underneath the site is another contention raised by the plaintiffs to support their thesis that the site is unsafe and is therefore an enjoinable nuisance. Dr. Nolan Augenbaugh[, an expert in mining and geological engineering,] testified extensively at trial. Dr. Augenbaugh took pictures of the area from an airplane as well as at ground level. During his testimony, he pointed out where subsidence occurred in the pictures he had taken. Dr. Augenbaugh stated that he had observed subsidence in a wheat field[, and] that a subsidence basin lies to the northeast of the disposal site. The pictures also indicate, according to Dr. Augenbaugh, fractures in the ground. * * * Dr. Augenbaugh testified that, in his opinion, subsidence can and will occur at the disposal site. Further, that ruptures in the earth would occur which, like an open pipe, would act as conduits for artesian water to reach the trenches, thereby contaminating the water.

* * *

[Four of defendant's expert witnesses, including the designer of the site and a consulting engineer for the defendant, an engineer, a geologist with the Illinois State Geological Survey (ISGS), and an engineering geologist with ISGS and coordinator of environmental geology for the

Survey,] testified in summary that there would be subsidence at the site, but that it would not be deep, would close in a short time, and could be repaired by means of engineering techniques.

Another of plaintiffs' witnesses, Dr. Arthur Zahalsky, [a professor of biochemistry and an expert in parasitology,] offered the opinion that an "explosive interaction," resulting in chemical explosions, fires, or emissions of poisonous gases, will occur at the site. * * * He testified in essence that if sufficient oxygen could reach the buried chemicals, and he believed it could, then an explosive interaction of unknown date of occurrence, magnitude, and duration is likely. * * *

* * *

* * * Various residents testified that dust emanating from the site blew toward their houses. Also, odors which caused burning eyes, running noses, headaches, nausea, and shortness of breath were mentioned in testimony. The odors themselves were said to resemble, among other things, fertilizer, insecticide, and burning rubber. There was further testimony that the dust and odors interfered with the witnesses' ability to use their yards for gardening or other recreational uses. The defendant presented witnesses who denied that the disposal site was the source of any odors[.] * * *

* * *

[ISSUES ON APPEAL]

The defendant has raised several issues on appeal: (1) whether the finding of the circuit and appellate courts that the waste-disposal site is a prospective nuisance is contrary to the manifest weight of the evidence; (2) whether those courts applied the wrong legal standard in finding that the waste-disposal site constitutes a prospective nuisance; (3) whether the circuit and appellate courts erred in failing to balance the equities, either in finding a prospective nuisance or in fashioning relief; (4) whether the courts erred in failing to defer to, or to otherwise weigh, the role of the IEPA, the United States Environmental Protection Agency (USEPA), and the Illinois State Geological Survey (ISGS); (5) whether the courts erred in finding that plaintiffs have no adequate remedy at law; (6) whether the courts erred in ordering a mandatory injunction; and, finally, (7) whether the courts' decisions constituted a taking of property without due process of law.

[I]

We conclude that the evidence in this case sufficiently establishes by a preponderance of the evidence that the chemical-waste-disposal site is a nuisance both presently and prospectively. The defendant does not challenge the fact that the spillage from improperly contained chemical waste, the odors, and the dust created by the site constitute a present interference with the right of the plaintiffs to enjoy and use their property. Thus, we will not belabor this point.

The defendant points out three areas where, it argues, the trial court made erroneous findings of fact. The defendant refers to: (1) Dr. Arthur Zahalsky's opinion testimony concerning an explosive interaction and [further expert] testimony which concurred in that opinion; (2) evidence concerning soil permeability; and, (3) infiltration of water into the trenches, and of migration out of the defendant's trenches of chemical waste either through the "bathtub effect" or subsidence.

We have reviewed the extensive record compiled in this case. While it is true that the defendant vigorously challenged the evidence concerning an explosive interaction, permeability, and infiltration and migration due to subsidence, the defendant has not overcome the natural and logical conclusions which could be drawn from the evidence. Findings of fact made by the trial court will not be set aside unless they are contrary to the manifest weight of the evidence.

* * *

[II]

The defendant also contends that the trial court's finding that subsidence warrants closing of the site is erroneous. The defendant argues that, assuming arguendo that subsidence would occur at the site, it could be counteracted by engineering techniques. This issue becomes complicated by the fact that the IEPA adopted a regulation providing that Class I disposal sites (i.e., chemical-waste-disposal sites), must be secure without engineering. The USEPA, however, [has adopted] regulations to require all landfill sites to establish containment-engineering systems to detect and prevent migration of chemicals. [45 Fed. Reg. 33,239–42]. Moreover, the General Assembly has, since the inception of this suit, passed a statute prohibiting the placement of a hazardous-waste-disposal site above a shaft or tunneled mine. Section 21(g) of the Environmental Protection Act provides:

"No person shall:

(g) Locate a hazardous waste disposal site above an active or inactive shaft or tunneled mine or within 2 miles of an active fault in the earth's crust. In counties of population less than 225,000 no hazardous waste disposal site shall be located (1) within 1 1/2 miles of the corporate limits as defined on June 30, 1978, of any municipality without the approval of the governing body of the municipality in an official action; * * *"

The instant disposal site is above an inactive tunneled mine lying partly within the corporate limits of the village of Wilsonville. Without an express statutory provision stating an act is to have retroactive effect, it can only be applied prospectively. [2 A. Sutherland, Statutory Construction sec. 41.04, at 252 (1973).] Thus, the defendant cannot be thought to be in violation of the foregoing provision. The fact remains, however, that the instant site, which is intended to be permanent, is located above an inactive tunneled mine.

* * *

* * * [The defendant argues] that evidence of dust and odors does not justify ordering closure of the site. Less restrictive relief must be ordered instead. We agree, of course, that dust and odors alone do not justify the relief which has been ordered in this case. "Whether smoke, odors, dust or gaseous fumes constitute a[n] [enjoinable] nuisance depends on the peculiar facts presented by each case." (City of Chicago v. Commonwealth Edison Co. (1974), 24 Ill.App.3d 624, 631–32), wherein it was held that "no unreasonable or substantial injury" was established so as to warrant enjoining the defendant from operating its plant[.] But, when the dust and odors the trial court found to be present at the site are considered together with the other evidence indicating that the air, water, and earth in and around the site will become contaminated, the trial court's relief is not excessive.

* * *

[III]

The trial court herein concluded that defendant's chemical-waste-disposal site constitutes both a private and a public nuisance. Professor Prosser has defined a private nuisance as "a civil wrong, based on a disturbance of rights in land" (Prosser, Torts sec. 86, at 572 (4th ed. 1971)), and a public nuisance as "an act or omission 'which obstructs or causes inconvenience or damage to the public in the exercise of rights common to all Her Majesty's subjects.'" (Prosser, Torts sec. 88, at 583 (4th ed. 1971)[.] Prosser has also quoted the following, more precise definition of a public nuisance: "'A common or public nuisance is the doing of or the failure to do something that injuriously affects the safety, health or morals of the public, or works some substantial annoyance, inconvenience or injury to the public.'" (Prosser, Torts sec. 88, at 583 n. 29 (4th ed. 1971))[.] It is generally conceded that a nuisance is remediable by injunction or a suit for damages.

[IV]

* * * The defendant [argues] that the law of Illinois requires that the circuit court engage in a balancing process before reaching a conclusion that the waste disposal site presents a prospective nuisance. The appellate court appears to have agreed with the defendant that the trial court did not engage in a balancing process[.] * * *

We do not agree[.] * * * [This court and other Illinois precedent have held] that where individual rights are unreasonably interfered with, the public benefit from a particular facility will not outweigh the individual right, and the facility's use will be enjoined or curtailed. Such a conclusion presupposes a balancing process with the greater weight being given to the individual's right to use and enjoy property over a public benefit or convenience from having a business operate at a particular location. In such an instance, the individual's right to noninterference takes precedence.

Moreover, the trial court did engage in a balancing process, as is made clear by the following excerpt from the trial court's memorandum opinion[:]

"It is the opinion of the Court that the state of the law is such that nuisance cannot be justified on the ground of necessity, pecuniary interest, convenience or economic advantage.

"The Court understands as does counsel that there is a need for disposal of industrial hazardous wastes. However, where disposal of wastes create a nuisance said disposal site may be closed through legal action.

"Substantial sums of money have been expended by the defendant in developing and operating the Earthline site at Wilsonville. Not only is the site convenient to nearby industries but it is a profit producer for the defendant. All of these elements are relevant to our economic system but notwithstanding the same it is the opinion of the Court that nuisances cannot be justified on such grounds when we have substantial injury to individual rights, community rights, substantial damage to human beings and other living things.

* * *

"Whether or not a business is useful or necessary or whether or not it contributes to the welfare and/or prosperity of the community are elements to be considered in a serious manner but said elements are not determinative as to whether or not the operation is a nuisance.

"The importance of an industry to the wealth and prosperity of an area does not as a matter of law give to it rights superior to the primary or natural rights of citizens who live nearby. However, such matters may be considered and have been in this case.

"It is the opinion of the Court that trifling annoyances or inconveniences of an operation will not give the character of a nuisance to a business that is useful and necessary to society."

* * *

We think the foregoing indicates that the trial court did carefully engage in a balancing process between the site's social utility and the plaintiffs' right to enjoy their property and not suffer deleterious effects from chemical wastes. Accordingly, the defendant's argument that the trial court did not balance the equities in this case is without merit.

[V]

The defendant's next contention is that the courts below were in error when they failed to require a showing of a substantial risk of certain and extreme future harm before enjoining operation of the defendant's site. We deem it necessary to explain that a prospective nuisance is a fit candidate for injunctive relief. Prosser states: "Both public and private nuisances require some substantial interference with the interest involved. Since nuisance is a common subject of equity jurisdiction, the damage against which an injunction is asked is often merely threatened or potential; but even in such cases, there must be at least a threat of a substantial invasion of the plaintiff's interests." (Prosser, Torts sec. 87, at 577 (4th ed. 1971).) The defendant does not dispute this proposition; it does, however, argue that the trial court did not follow the proper standard for determining when a prospective nuisance may be enjoined. The defendant argues that the proper standard to be used is that an injunction is proper only if there is a "dangerous probability" that the threatened or potential injury will occur. (See Restatement (Second) of Torts sec. 933(1), at 561, comment b (1979).) The defendant further argues that the appellate court looked only at the potential consequences of not enjoining the operation of the site as a nuisance and not at the likelihood of whether harm would occur. The defendant assigns error on this basis.

We agree with the defendant's statement of the law, but not with its urged application to the facts of this case. Again, Professor Prosser has offered a concise commentary. He has stated that "[o]ne distinguishing feature of equitable relief is that it may be granted upon the threat of harm which has not yet occurred. The defendant may be restrained from entering upon an activity where it is highly probable that it will lead to a nuisance, although if the possibility is merely uncertain or contingent he may be left to his remedy after the nuisance has occurred." (Prosser, Torts sec. 90, at 603 (4th ed. 1971).) This view is in accord with Illinois law. In Fink [v. Board of Trustees, 71 Ill.App.2d 276, 218 N.E.2d 240 (1966)], the plaintiff sought to enjoin construction of a dam and also the discharge of sewage effluent in a watercourse which flowed past plaintiffs' property. Construction of the dam was not enjoined, but the discharge of effluent was prospectively enjoined. * * *

* * *

In this case there can be no doubt but that it is highly probable that the chemical-waste-disposal site will bring about a substantial injury. Without again reviewing the extensive evidence adduced at trial, we think it is sufficiently clear that it is highly probable that the instant site will constitute a public nuisance[.] * * * That such an event will occur was positively attested to by several expert witnesses. A court does not have to wait for it to happen before it can enjoin such a result. * * *

* * *

[VI]

The next issue we consider is whether the trial court erroneously granted a permanent injunction. The defendant argues first that the courts below granted injunctive relief without proof that the alleged injury is both substantial and certain to occur. We have already addressed this question in discussing whether relief may be granted for a prospective nuisance. We will not unduly prolong this already lengthy opinion with duplicative discussion. The second argument raised is that the courts below did not balance the equities in deciding to enjoin the defendant from continuing to operate the waste-disposal site. * * *

* * *

"Reasonableness is the standard by which the court should fashion its relief in ordinary nuisance cases, Meeks v. Wood, 66 Ind.App. 594, 118 N.E. 591 (1918), and reasonableness is also the appropriate standard for relief from environmental nuisance. Ordinarily a permanent injunction will not lie unless (1) either the polluter seriously and imminently threatens the public health or (2) he causes non-health injuries that are substantial and the business cannot be operated to avoid the injuries apprehended. Thus the particular situation facts of each pollution nuisance case will determine whether a permanent injunction should be issued." [Harrison v. Indiana Auto Shredders, 528 F.2d 1107, 1123 (7th Cir.1975)].

The court concluded in *Harrison* that since the defendant was not in violation of any relevant zoning standards, and since the shredder did not pose an imminent hazard to the public health, the defendant should not be prevented from continuing to operate. The court then ordered that the defendant be permitted a reasonable time to "launder its objectionable features."

This case is readily distinguishable for the reason that the gist of this case is that the defendant is engaged in an extremely hazardous undertaking at an unsuitable location, which seriously and imminently poses a threat to the public health. We are acutely aware that the service provided by the defendant is a valuable and necessary one. We also know that it is preferable to have chemical-waste-disposal sites than to have illegal dumping in rivers, streams, and deserted areas. But a site such as defendant's, if it is to do the job it is intended to do, must be located in a secure place, where it will pose no threat to health or life, now, or in the future. This site was intended to be a permanent disposal site for the deposit of extremely hazardous chemical-waste materials. Yet this site is located above an abandoned tunneled mine where subsidence is occurring several years ahead of when it was anticipated. Also, the permeability-coefficient samples taken by defendant's experts, though not conclusive alone, indicate that the soil is more permeable at the site than expected. Moreover, the spillage, odors, and dust caused by the presence of the disposal site indicate why it was inadvisable to locate the site so near the plaintiff village.

Therefore, we conclude that in fashioning relief in this case the trial court did balance relative hardship to be caused to the plaintiffs and defendant, and did fashion reasonable relief when it ordered the exhumation of all material from the site and the reclamation of the surrounding area. The instant site is akin to Mr. Justice Sutherland's observation that "Nuisance may be merely a right thing in a wrong place—like a pig in the parlor instead of the barnyard." Village of Euclid v. Ambler Realty Co., [272 U.S. 365, 388, 47 S.Ct. 114, 118, 71 L.Ed. 303 (1926).]

* * *

Notes and Questions

1. The plaintiff in *Wilsonville* was a village. What if the plaintiffs consisted of several residents of the village suing on a theory of private nuisance: would the outcome (issuance of a permanent injunction) have been different? Would the court's analysis of the reasonableness of the invasion have been different? Would private persons suing on a public nuisance theory have to satisfy the special injury requirement? Could they have done so? Would it depend on the kind of relief sought—injunctive or damages?

2. At one point, after discussing the substantial investment made by the defendant, the trial court commented:

"All of these [utilitarian] elements are relevant to our economic system but notwithstanding same it is the opinion of the court that nuisances cannot be justified on such grounds when we have substantial injury to individual rights, community rights, substantial damage to human beings and other living things."

Is this a purely corrective justice point of view? To dispel the impression that the outcome in *Wilsonville* is a recent phenomenon, consider the early nuisance decision of the Michigan Supreme Court in People v. Detroit White Lead Works, 82 Mich. 471, 46 N.W. 735 (1890), where the defendant corporation demonstrated both that it conducted its operations "in a careful and prudent manner," and that when it had begun its business, "the lands in the vicinity of its work were open commons." " Whenever such a business becomes a nuisance," the Court stated, "it must give way to the rights of the public, and the owners thereof must either devise some means to avoid the nuisance, or must remove or cease the business."

3. The *Wilsonville* court appeared to follow the usual standards applied in determining whether to grant injunctions: (1) that a tort has been committed or one is threatened; (2) an adequate remedy at law is not available, usually damages; and (3) the balance of equities, including the overall public interest and social utility of the activity, favors the injunction.

Does the Illinois Supreme Court apply this statement of the rule in its opinion? What degree of probability of the threatened harm actually occurring should be required before a permanent injunction issues? The Restatement (Second) of Torts § 933, comment b, states that the appropriateness of injunctive relief for a threatened tort must be influenced by both the *seriousness* and the *imminence* of the threatened harm. How do both of these factors apply in *Wilsonville* ?

4. In *Wilsonville*, the defendant's site was authorized by the Illinois Environmental Protection Agency and the United States EPA. Should that be significant? Does the Court give *any* weight to the regulatory compliance by the defendant? Why doesn't the court address the question of preemption? For a discussion of the preemption of common law remedies by federal statutory regimes, see Chapter 6. For comparison, see Green v. Castle

Concrete Co., 181 Colo. 309, 509 P.2d 588 (1973) (holding that a new limestone quarry was not a nuisance because substantial harm was uncertain and because the site was zoned for quarrying and was in compliance with regulatory requirements). Is *Wilsonville* really a zoning case masquerading as a nuisance case? See discussion of the relationship between zoning laws and nuisance doctrine in 4 William H. Rodgers, Jr., Environmental Law: Hazardous Wastes and Substances § 7.30 (1992). Rodgers points out that in waste disposal nuisance cases the decisions reflect more a pattern of strict liability than nuisance balancing. § 7.30 at 408.

5. In Frederick R. Anderson, Daniel R. Mandelker & A. Dan Tavlock, Environmental Protection: Law and Policy 527 (2d ed. 1990), it is pointed out that the Wilsonville site was one of the most modern and safest chemical disposal facilities in the country, a site to which wastes from other sites were to be transferred. The Illinois Attorney General intervened on the plaintiffs' side of the case (much to the embarrassment of the state EPA) after local citizens' groups made angry demands.

6. Compare the availability of permanent injunctive relief for prospective harm in *Wilsonville*, with the difficulty of recovering damages for prospective physical harm a topic considered later (Chapter 5) in Ayers v. Township of Jackson, 106 N.J. 557, 525 A.2d 287 (1987) and Sterling v. Velsicol Chemical Corp., 855 F.2d 1188 (6th Cir.1988).

7. What about the concept of a *prospective* nuisance? Is it appropriate for a court to enjoin activity that *may* cause harm in the future, if the likelihood is "highly probable"? Would the court have enjoined the activity if there had been no current nuisance? Was such a finding necessary to its sustaining the injunctive relief?

8. Is awarding a permanent injunction—shutting down the operation entirely—based on "a threat to the public health," the best remedy in this case? Is it the *only feasible remedy*? If you were the trial judge, what other alternatives could you devise to remedy this situation?

9. Was it important that the facility in this case came to the village, rather than the village "coming to the nuisance"? Should that be relevant? See Chapter 12.

10. In contrast to *Wilsonville* where the court agonized over the extent of the invasion, present and prospective, caused by the operation of the waste disposal site, in Neal v. Darby, 282 S.C. 277, 318 S.E.2d 18 (App.1984), a South Carolina Court of Appeals found that the defendant's waste disposal site was a public nuisance on the basis of its location. After ruling that the federal and state permits did not preclude a violation of state common law nuisance rules, it concluded:

> To constitute a public nuisance, a nuisance must be in a public place or where the public frequently congregates, or where members of the public are likely to come within the range of its influence * * *. If the use of property is in a remote and infrequented locality, it will not be a nuisance *per se*, or wrong in itself * * *. A public nuisance will be enjoined where injury is inevitable and undoubted * * *.

> The finding that a business operation constitutes a nuisance is one of fact. Based upon our view of the preponderance of evidence previous-

ly discussed, we do not find the landfill is in a remote and infrequented locality. Instead, we find it is a public nuisance by virtue of its location near residential areas and the primary water source as well as its influence on members of the public. In light of this finding, we need not address the question of whether the landfill is also a public nuisance by virtue of its method of operation.

This is a strict liability approach, although the court never addresses the conduct of the owner of the site as relevant to the determination of a public nuisance. Remarkable too is the absence of any focus on whether the site produced an "unreasonable interference" with a public or common right.

CARPENTER v. THE DOUBLE R CATTLE COMPANY, INC.

Supreme Court of Idaho, 1985.
701 P.2d 222.

BAKES, J.

Plaintiffs appealed a district court judgment based upon a court and jury finding that defendant's feedlot did not constitute a nuisance. The Court of Appeals reversed[.] [W]e vacate the decision of the Court of Appeals and affirm the judgment of the district court.

Plaintiff appellants are homeowners who live near a cattle feedlot owned and operated by respondents. Appellants filed a complaint in March, 1978, alleging that the feedlot had been expanded in 1977 to accommodate the feeding of approximately 9,000 cattle. Appellants further alleged that "the spread and accumulation of manure, pollution of river and ground water, odor, insect infestation, increased concentration of birds, * * * dust and noise" allegedly caused by the feedlot constituted a nuisance. After a trial on the merits a jury found that the feedlot did not constitute a nuisance. The trial court then also made findings and conclusions that the feedlot did not constitute a nuisance.

Appellants assigned as error the jury instructions which instructed the jury that in the determination of whether a nuisance exists consideration should be given to such factors as community interest, utility of conduct, business standards and practices, gravity of harm caused, and the circumstances surrounding the parties' movement to their locations. * * *

The case was assigned to the Court of Appeals which reversed and remanded for a new trial. The basis for this reversal was that the trial court did not give a jury instruction based upon subsection (b) of Section 826 of the Restatement (Second) of Torts. That subsection allows for a finding of a nuisance even though the gravity of harm is outweighed by the utility of the conduct if the harm is "serious" and the payment of damages is "feasible" without forcing the business to discontinue.

This Court granted defendant's petition for review. We hold that the instructions which the trial court gave were not erroneous, being consistent with our prior case law and other persuasive authority. We further hold that the trial court did not err in not giving an instruction based on subsection (b) of Section 826 of the Second Restatement, which does not represent the law in the State of Idaho, as pointed out in Part III. Accordingly, the decision of the Court of Appeals is vacated, and the judgment of the district court is affirmed.

* * *

THE LAW OF NUISANCE

The Court of Appeals adopted subsection (b) of Section 826 of the Restatement Second, that a defendant can be held liable for a nuisance regardless of the utility of the conduct if the harm is "serious" and the payment of damages is "feasible" without jeopardizing the continuance of the conduct. We disagree that this is the law in Idaho.

* * *

The Court of Appeals, without being requested by appellant, adopted the new subsection (b) of Section 826 of the Second Restatement partially because of language in Koseris [v. J.R. Simplot Co., 82 Idaho 263, 352 P.2d 235 (1960) (action for injunction only)], which reads:

"We are constrained to hold that the trial court erred in sustaining objections to those offers of proof [evidence of utility of conduct], since they were relevant as bearing upon the issue whether respondents, in seeking injunctive relief, were pursuing the proper remedy; nevertheless, on the theory of damages which respondents had waived, the ruling was correct."

The last phrase of the quote, relied on by the Court of Appeals, is clearly dictum, since the question of utility of conduct in a nuisance action for damages was not at issue in Koseris. It is very doubtful that this Court's dictum in Koseris was intended to make such a substantial change in the nuisance law. When the isolated statement of dictum was made in 1960, there was no persuasive authority for such a proposition. Indeed, no citation of authority was given. The three cases from other jurisdictions which the Court of Appeals relied on for authority did not exist until 1970. See Boomer v. Atlantic Cement Co., 257 N.E.2d 870 (N.Y.1970); Jost v. Dairyland Power Co-op., 172 N.W.2d 647 (Wis.1970). The third case from Oregon, Furrer v. Talent Irr. Dist., 466 P.2d 605 (Or.1970), was not even a nuisance case. Rather, it was an action in "negligence." The Second Restatement, which proposed the change in the law by adding subsection (b) to Section 826, was also not in existence until 1970. Therefore, we greatly discount this Court's dictum in the 1960 Koseris opinion as authority for such a substantial change in the nuisance law. The case of McNichols v. J.R. Simplot Co., 74 Idaho 321, 262 P.2d 1012 (1953) should be viewed as the law in Idaho that in a nuisance action seeking damages the interests of the community, which would include the utility of the conduct, should be considered in the determination of the existence of a nuisance. The trial court's instructions in the present case were entirely consistent with McNichols. A plethora of other modern cases are in accord.

The State of Idaho is sparsely populated and its economy depends largely upon the benefits of agriculture, lumber, mining and industrial development. To eliminate the utility of conduct and other factors listed by the trial court from the criteria to be considered in determining whether a nuisance exists, as the appellant has argued throughout this appeal, would place an unreasonable burden upon these industries. * * * Accordingly, the judgment of the district court is affirmed and the Court of Appeals decision is set aside.

DONALDSON, C.J., and SHEPARD, J., concur.

BISTLINE, J., dissenting.

* * *

I applaud the efforts of the Court of Appeals to modernize the law of nuisance in this state. I am not in the least persuaded to join the majority with its narrow view of nuisance law as expressed in the majority opinion.

The majority today continues to adhere to ideas on the law of nuisance that should have gone out with the use of buffalo chips as fuel. We have before us today homeowners complaining of a nearby feedlot— not a small operation, but rather a feedlot which accommodates 9,000 cattle. The homeowners advanced the theory that after the expansion of the feedlot in 1977, the odor, manure, dust, insect infestation and increased concentration of birds which accompanied all of the foregoing, constituted a nuisance. If the odoriferous quagmire created by 9,000 head of cattle is not a nuisance, it is difficult for me to imagine what is. However, the real question for us today is the legal basis on which a finding of nuisance can be made.

[The majority reasons that] the correct rule of law for Idaho [is that] in a nuisance action seeking damages, the interests of the community, which includes the utility of the conduct, should be considered in determining the existence of a nuisance. I find nothing immediately wrong with this statement of the law and agree wholeheartedly that the interests of the community should be considered in determining the existence of a nuisance. However, where this primitive rule of law fails is in recognizing that in our society, while it may be desirable to have a serious nuisance continue because the utility of the operation causing the nuisance is great, at the same time, those directly impacted by the serious nuisance deserve some compensation for the invasion they suffer as a result of the continuation of the nuisance. This is exactly what the more progressive provisions of § 826(b) of the Restatement (Second) of Torts addresses. * * *

* * *

Notes and Questions

1. What do you suppose is the principal rationale for the majority's refusal to apply Restatement (Second) of Torts § 826(b)? Do you agree or disagree with the dissent's argument (not quoted above) that by refusing to award damages the court is subsidizing the prices of meat (or other products or services) which are not internalizing all the real costs of doing business?

2. Is the court totally rejecting corrective justice principles? One of the often-stated purposes of tort law liability rules is to deter risk-creating conduct by imposing liability on those who create the risks. Does the majority's opinion subvert or advance the deterrence objective of tort law? How about economic efficiency principles?

3. The majority's position is perhaps one of the most extreme in refusing to award damages where plaintiffs have actually suffered substantial harm and where there was no showing that imposing damages on the defendant would have necessitated that it cease operations. Reconsider this decision after Chapter 5.

4. What is the consequence of the majority's holding on future cases involving an alleged private nuisance producing substantial harm to private parties? Can a private party *ever* prevail in an action for damages in Idaho if the defendant's business operation is important to the community?

Problem

The following facts appeared in the November 23, 1992 edition of the National Law Journal, p. 1, under the caption "Toxic Refuge."

The story highlights several families that had moved from New York City to Haverstraw, a sleepy town about 50 miles north, in New York State, and purchased "affordable" middle class homes in a development known as Warren Court. The Warren Court homes cost $161,000, with only a 5% down payment and below-market interest rates offered by the development's manager, the Pension Fund of Carpenters' Union 964. One Warren Court family, the Riveras, had been experiencing a persistent smell of rotten eggs around their home. In January 1992 they discovered the source when the sewer line collapsed beneath their home. When Haverstraw village workers dug into the earth they discovered decomposing gypsum wallboard and an overpowering wave of fumes.

It seems that the homes in Warren Court were built on an industrial landfill consisting of 10,000 cubic yards of gypsum board. Gypsum board, which is not considered hazardous waste, when buried and deprived of oxygen and surrounded by dampness, surrenders to a bacteria that acts upon the harmless material to produce hydrogen sulfide gas. In the late 1960s and 1970s, U.S. Gypsum Company had arranged with village officials to bury its scrap wallboard. The village had been happy to oblige because Haverstraw, once known as "Bricktown," had large unstable underground areas that remained from the clay mining era of the early Twentieth Century. Indeed, the ground was so unstable that in 1906 twenty Haverstraw residents were buried alive when their shanties collapsed into a mine. To reclaim this area, village officials began using the scrap wallboard provided by U.S. Gypsum as clean fill material at many mining sites. By the early

1970s, area residents had discovered that the buried gypsum yielded that terrible rotten egg odor created by hydrogen sulfide gas.

In 1985, the village, which owned the mining areas, rezoned one fill site to residential use. Anchorage Construction Co. ("Anchorage") planned to build twenty-one affordable homes on the site. Anchorage obtained financing from the Carpenters' Pension Fund. However, as construction costs escalated because of the soft ground which made foundations unstable, thereby requiring extra materials and labor, the Pension Fund took over ownership of the project.

The Riveras and others have learned that all state, county, and local permits and environmental audits had been complied with. They also have learned that "high levels" of hydrogen sulfide can be "poisonous."

The village refuses to accept responsibility other than to revoke occupancy permits for the nine unsold homes. The county refuses to permit evacuation of the twelve occupied homes because the gas poses no acute health hazard to the residents. The Pension Fund recommends "neutralizing" the odor, but offers no other relief. The State of New York's Department of Environmental Conservation can't help, because the dumping of wallboard occurred before state law prohibited such disposal. The EPA has agreed to "study" the problem but holds out little opportunity for relief.

Several homeowners, including the Riveras, have filed suit against the Pension Fund, Anchorage, the village, the county, the State of New York, and U.S. Gypsum. What theories of liability may be promising? Drawing on the materials in Chapters 2 and 3 on trespass, negligence, and public and private nuisance describe plaintiffs' claims and defendants' likely responses.

Chapter Four

STRICT LIABILITY FOR ABNORMALLY DANGER-OUS ACTIVITIES

A. HISTORICAL PERSPECTIVE

An increasingly important theory of tort liability in the arsenal of environmental torts is strict liability attaching to injury caused by conducting activities regarded as "abnormally dangerous" or "ultrahazardous." As noted above under the discussions of private nuisance, one type of a defendant's conduct that gives rise to liability under § 822 is engaging in abnormally dangerous activity. Whether the liability of a defendant engaged in abnormally dangerous activity is treated as a private nuisance under § 822, or as a separate strict liability tort under §§ 519 and 520 of the Restatement (Second) of Torts, both avenues are dependent upon establishing the basis for strict liability arising from abnormally dangerous activities.

The common law doctrine of strict liability for abnormally danger-ous activities has taken on heightened significance since the advent of the nation's struggle to clean up the consequences of the disposal of hazardous wastes. As you read this chapter, ask yourself how fairly or efficiently this doctrine, which originated in 1866, can be applied to distribute the costs of remediating land and groundwater from the adverse effects of disposal of hazardous wastes and chemicals. What advantages does the doctrine offer that nuisance or trespass does not? Who can be held liable under this doctrine? Will it include previous owners, operators, or generators of the waste or chemicals? What kinds of activities are properly denominated "abnormally dangerous"? Must a defendant know that its activities are highly dangerous? What role should the doctrine of caveat emptor play in strict liability cases?

The seminal decision is Rylands v. Fletcher, 1 L.R.-Exch. 265 (1866), which involved the flooding of the plaintiff's coal mine by water from the defendant's reservoir which had burst through tunneling. Although the contractors who built the reservoir for defendant were possibly negligent, Judge Blackburn of the Exchequer Chamber, predicated liability on a different theory:

> The question of law therefore arises, what is the obligation which the law casts on a person who, like the defendants, lawfully brings on his land something which, though harmless whilst it remains there, will naturally do mischief if it escape out of his land.

> * * *

> We think that the true rule of law is, that the person who for his own purposes brings on his lands and collects and keeps there anything likely to do mischief if it escapes, must keep it in at his peril, and, if he does not do so, is prima facie answerable for all the damage which is the natural consequence of its escape. * * * [I]t seems but reasonable and just that the neighbour, who has brought something on his own property which was not naturally there, harmless to others so long as it is confined to his own property, but which he knows to be mischievous if it gets on his neighbour's, should be obliged to make good the damage which ensues if he does not succeed in confining it to his own property.

The House of Lords, per Lord Cairns, upheld the Exchequer's decision, but on a slightly narrower ground, stating that liability would turn on whether defendant's use of land was a "natural use of their close," meaning "any purpose for which it might in the ordinary course of the enjoyment of land be used," as opposed to a "nonnatural use." 3 H.L. 330, 339–40 (1868).

Thus, while Judge Blackburn premised strict liability on any nonnatural use of the land, by which he meant any use by the defendant of its land by bringing onto it some "mischief" which by nature was not present, Lord Cairns defined nonnatural in a narrower way, by limiting the concept to activities which are *abnormal*, not ordinary, uses of the land, considering the character and general uses of the surrounding land. What might have caused Lord Cairns to adopt a narrower test of strict liability? For an early analysis of the *Rylands* decision, see Francis H. Bohlen, The Rule in Rylands v. Fletcher, 59 U. Pa. L. Rev. 298 (1911).

In early American decisions the rule of *Rylands* was rejected by courts which regarded it as holding a defendant absolutely liable whenever anything under its control escapes and produces damage without regard to its locational appropriateness or its dangerousness. For example, in the 1873 decision in Lossee v. Buchanan, 51 N.Y. 476, a boiler exploded in defendant's factory, damaging plaintiff's adjacent property. The court refused to impose liability in the absence of negligence:

> We must have factories, machinery, dams, canals and railroads. They are demanded by the manifold wants of mankind, and lay at the basis of all our civilization. [The victim of an accident] receives his compensation * * * by the general good, in which he shares, and the right which he has to place the same things upon his lands.

At about the same time, American courts were generally invoking strict liability on behalf of those injured by explosives—a position that antedated *Rylands* and was accepted as valid in *Lossee*. See, e.g., Hay v. Cohoes Co., 2 N.Y. 159 (1849); Carman v. Steubenville & Ind. R.R., 4 Ohio St. 399 (1854).

However, after an inhospitable beginning, courts began to adopt the narrower rule that the majority of states have embraced in some form, essentially extending it to embrace liability for activities "out of place, the abnormally dangerous condition or activity which is not a "natural" one where it is." Prosser & Keeton, on Torts § 78 at 549, 551 (5th ed. 1984). The First Restatement of Torts accepted the principle of *Rylands*, but specifically limited it to "ultrahazardous activity" of the defendant, which was defined as one which "necessarily involves a risk of serious harm to the person, land or chattels of others which cannot be eliminated by the exercise of the utmost care," and "is not a matter of common usage." Restatement of Torts §§ 519 and 520. This standard goes beyond the narrower interpretation of *Rylands* because it ignores the locational appropriateness of the activity and focuses largely on three factors: (1) the dangerousness of the activity; (2) the impossibility of eliminating the danger with all possible care; and (3) whether the activity is a matter of common usage. Thus, the essence of the First Restatement was to impose strict liability on those activities, however socially desirable, that created in the community an abnormal risk of a serious nature.

B. RELATIONSHIP TO NUISANCE

How do the theories of nuisance and strict liability relate? Prosser & Keeton point out that there is a close identity between the concept of "absolute nuisance" and strict liability:

> Actually even the jurisdictions which reject Rylands v. Fletcher by name have accepted and applied the principle of the case under the cloak of various other theories. Most frequently, in all of the American courts, the same strict liability is imposed upon defendants under the name of nuisance. The "absolute nuisances" for which strict liability is found without intent to do harm or negligence fall into categories already familiar. They include * * * explosives or inflammable liquids stored in quantity in thickly settled communities or in dangerous proximity to valuable property; blasting; * * * oil wells or abnormal mining operations; the accumulation of sewage; * * * and in addition such things as smoke, dust, bad odors, noxious gases and the like from industrial enterprises, all obviously closely related to the cases following Rylands v. Fletcher. There has been general recognition in these nuisance cases that the relation of the activity to its surroundings is the controlling factor; * * * The "non-natural use" becomes an "unreasonable use."

* * *

There is in fact probably no case applying Rylands v. Fletcher which is not duplicated in all essential respects by some American decision which proceeds on the theory of nuisance; and it is quite evident that under that name the principle is in reality universally accepted.

Id. at 552–553. The Restatement (Second) of Torts in comment c to § 520 also recognizes this close relationship between absolute nuisances and strict liability, in stating that strict liability is "applied by many courts under the name of absolute nuisance." For an excellent analysis of the relationship between trespass, nuisance and strict liability, see Page Keeton, Trespass, Nuisance and Strict Liability, 9 Colum. L. Rev. 457 (1959).

C. RESTATEMENT (SECOND) OF TORTS STANDARD OF LIABILITY

When the Second Restatement was published in 1976, it changed the prior label of "ultrahazardous activity" and replaced it with "abnormally dangerous activity." Sections 519 and 520, reproduced below, set forth the governing standards:

§ 519. General Principle

(1) One who carries on an abnormally dangerous activity is subject to liability for harm to the person, land or chattels of another resulting from the activity, although he has exercised the utmost care to prevent the harm.

(2) This strict liability is limited to the kind of harm, the possibility of which makes the activity abnormally dangerous.

§ 520. Abnormally Dangerous Activities

In determining whether an activity is abnormally dangerous, the following factors are to be considered:

(a) existence of a high degree of risk of some harm to the person, land or chattels of others;

(b) likelihood that the harm that results from it will be great;

(c) inability to eliminate the risk by the exercise of reasonable care;

(d) extent to which the activity is not a matter of common usage;

(e) inappropriateness of the activity to the place where it is carried on; and

(f) extent to which its value to the community is outweighed by its dangerous attributes.

1. RELATIONSHIP TO NEGLIGENCE

The Restatement's formulation distinguishes "ordinary" industrial and commercial enterprises, to which strict liability will not be extended, from those that are "abnormally," unusually, or atypically dangerous. The Restatement's six factors can be grouped into two categories: subsections (a) through (c) characterize the abnormally dangerous nature of the activity, which depends on a high degree of risk, the potential of producing significant harm, and the inability to eliminate that risk even by the exercise of great care. Subsections (d) through (f), in contrast, characterize the positive side of the activity, by focusing on its commonness, locational appropriateness, and value to the community. So viewed, the analysis of whether an activity is to be subjected to strict liability, as opposed a negligence test, involves a balancing of these six considerations. That balancing, of course, begins to take on the very trappings of the risk-versus-utility calculus, which is the core of negligence theory. Thus, the strict liability label disguises latent similarities to negligence. For example, drawing on Judge Learned Hand's formula for breach of duty as whether $PL > B$, under § 520, the product of the PL is very high, but the B is virtually infinite because no amount of care is capable of eliminating the risk of harm created by the activity. Therefore, if the B is extremely high liability under negligence principles would be precluded, thereby creating a rationale for imposing strict liability.

An Illinois appellate opinion emphasized the breadth of the judicial inquiry under the Restatement's test:

> When deciding to impose * * * strict liability, we must not look at the abstract propensities of the particular substance involved, but must analyze the defendant's activity as a whole. If the rule were otherwise, virtually every commercial or industrial activity involving substances which are dangerous only in the abstract automatically would be deemed as abnormally dangerous. This result would be intolerable.

Erbrich Products Co. v. Wills, 509 N.E.2d 850, 857 (Ind.App.1987). In *Erbrich*, defendant was a long-time producer of liquid bleach and employed chlorine gas (a well known poison) as integral to the manufacturing process. In 1984, for the first time in over fifty years, chlorine gas escaped from the defendant's plant for reasons unknown and injured nearby residents. The court held that strict liability did not apply because the activity was one where "the exercise of reasonable care would prevent harm of exposure to raw chlorine gas." Id. at 852.

2. QUESTION OF LAW

The application of the factors is to be performed by the court, as a question of law, not by the jury as a factual matter, even though the analysis clearly involves highly fact-specific inquiries. Comment l to § 520 emphasizes this point:

   1. *Function of court.* Whether the activity is an abnormally dangerous one is to be determined by the Court, upon consideration of all the factors listed in this section, and the weight given to each that it merits upon the facts in evidence. In this it differs from questions of negligence. * * * The standard of the hypothetical reasonable [person] is essentially a jury standard, in which the Court interferes only in the clearest cases. * * * The imposition of strict liability, on the other hand, involves a characterization of the defendant's activity or enterprise itself, and a decision as to whether he is free to conduct it at all without becoming subject to liability for the harm that ensues even though he has used all reasonable care. This calls for a decision of the Court; and it is no part of the province of the jury to decide whether an industrial enterprise upon which the community's prosperity might depend is located in the wrong place or whether such an activity as blasting is to be permitted without liability in the center of a large city.

One advantage of the abnormally dangerous doctrine is that it enables the parties to secure a determination of whether it applies at the summary judgment stage of the case. Is the Restatement correct that the balancing under § 520 strict liability is fundamentally different from that involved in negligence? What were the likely motivations for making the finding of whether an activity is abnormally dangerous a function for the court?

   Returning to the chlorine gas example, how would the court apply each of the factors? If you were the judge, how would you have resolved the question, assuming there was no evidence on precisely how or why the gas escaped? If gas had never escaped in over fifty years of operation, does that suggest that defendant *must* have been negligent on this occasion or that even with reasonable care the risk of escape could not be eliminated?

3. COMMON USAGE

   As to matters of common usage, the comments to subsection (d) of Restatement § 520 defines such activities as those engaged in "by the great mass of mankind or by many people in the community." Comment i. To illustrate, the comment states that the use of automobiles is a common usage, whereas the use of explosives, the operation of oil wells, and blasting activities, while of significant social utility, are carried on only by a few persons and are therefore not common usage. What about oil well operations in certain areas of Alaska or Texas? Might they be so prevalent as to constitute a "common usage"?

4. LOCATIONAL APPROPRIATENESS

   Section 520(e) requires the court to assess the activity's appropriateness to the place where it is carried on in deciding whether it is *abnormally* dangerous. As explained in comment j:

If the place is one inappropriate to the particular activity, and other factors are present, the danger created may be regarded as an abnormal one.

Even a magazine of high explosives, capable of destroying everything within a distance of half a mile, does not necessarily create an abnormal danger if it is located in the midst of a desert area, far from human habitation and all property of any considerable value. The same is true of a large storage tank filled with some highly inflammable liquid such as gasoline. Blasting, even with powerful high explosives, is not abnormally dangerous if it is done on an uninhabited mountainside, so far from anything of considerable value likely to be harmed that the risk if it does exist is not a serious one. On the other hand, the same magazine of explosives, the huge storage tank full of gasoline or the blasting operations all become abnormally dangerous if they are carried on in the midst of a city.

* * *

In other words, the fact that the activity is inappropriate to the place where it is carried on is a factor of importance in determining whether the danger is an abnormal one. This is sometimes expressed, particularly in the English cases, by saying there is strict liability for a "non-natural" use of the defendant's land.

5. VALUE OF THE ACTIVITY TO THE COMMUNITY

There exists considerable controversy over whether this factor is an appropriate one for inclusion in the calculus. For example, in Langan v. Valicopters, Inc., 88 Wash.2d 855, 567 P.2d 218 (1977), the Washington Supreme Court, while carefully applying the other five factors, noted the criticism to which this factor had been subjected and refused to apply it to defendant's crop-dusting activities involving the use of pesticides that had damaged the crops of neighboring farmers of organic crops:

As a criterion for determining strict liability, this factor has received some criticism among legal writers. * * *

* * *

There is no doubt that pesticides are socially valuable in the control of insects, weeds and other pests. They may benefit society by increasing production. Whether strict liability or negligence principles should be applied amounts to a balancing of conflicting social interest—the risk of harm versus the utility of the activity. In balancing these interests, we must ask who should bear the loss caused by the pesticides. * * *

In the present case, the Langans were eliminated from the organic food market for 1973 through no fault of their own. If crop dusting continues on the adjoining property, the Langans may never be able to sell their crops to organic food buyers. Appellants, on the other hand, will all profit from the continued application of pesticides. Under these circumstances, there can be an equitable balancing of social interests only if appellants are made to pay for the consequences of their acts.

Accordingly, the Washington Supreme Court discounted the weight of the social utility of crop dusting generally, concluding that once the activity is regarded as abnormally dangerous by applying the other factors, the defendant should absorb the costs in its profit-making enterprise (and thereby distribute those costs across a broad customer base as is typical in the products liability area) as an ordinary cost of doing business.

In 3 Harper, James & Gray, Law of Torts § 14.4 at 214 (1986), the authors challenge the propriety of utilizing value to the community:

> The justification for strict liability, in other words, is that useful but dangerous activities must pay their own way. There is nothing in this reasoning which would exempt *very* useful activities from the rule, as is shown by the granting of compensation even where the activity is of such paramount importance to society that it justifies the exercise of eminent domain. And if the law were to embrace wholly the principle of strict liability and its underlying rationale, there would be no place for the consideration of this factor. But this is not the present case. Tort law today contains two opposing strains or principles, strict liability and liability based on fault. It is not surprising, therefore, that any attempt to draw a line between them (which is being done in § 520) should contain factors which would be irrelevant if one principle or the other alone were being consistently pursued. At any rate this factor will probably continue to influence courts in fact for some time to come.

See also Prosser & Keeton on Torts § 78 at 555 (5th ed. 1984), criticizing the six-factor test as "virtually the same thing as is done with negligence." As you read these cases in this Chapter how have the courts treated the factor of an activity's value to the community?

D. RATIONALES FOR IMPOSING STRICT LIABILITY

1. INTERNALIZATION OF ALL COSTS: THE ENTERPRISE MODEL

As the quotation from the *Langan* case illustrates, one rationale for the imposition of strict liability is that profit-motivated enterprises should pay for all of the losses their activities generate, including so-called "externalities," such as damage from pollution which are external to the enterprise's operations, by incorporating them into the costs of doing business. This rationale states that if an enterprise engages in an activity that is highly dangerous, however socially valuable, and unavoidably exposes others to those risks, then the enterprise should internalize the risk of loss just as product sellers do under § 402A, through adjustments of the price and reallocation of the loss among all consumers of the enterprise's services. The argument has both fairness and efficiency aspects. It is fair to require firms to internalize costs and redistribute losses among all users of the services and not expect innocent persons to bear those losses. It promotes efficiency, the argument continues, for by increasing the costs and prices of those services, it will deter their consumption. For an opinion that contains an eloquent description of this rationale, see Altas Chemical Indus., Inc. v. Anderson, 514 S.W.2d 309, 315–16 (Tex.Civ.App.1974), aff'd in part, rev'd in part 524 S.W.2d 681 (Tex.1975), where the court stated:

> We further believe the public policy of this State to be that however laudable an industry may be, its owners or managers are still subject to the rule that its industry or its property cannot be so used as to inflict injury to the property of its neighbors. * * * The costs of injuries resulting from pollution must be internalized by industry as a cost of production and borne by consumers or shareholders, or both, and not by the injured individual.

Will firms invest more heavily in safety or preventative technology under a strict liability theory than under negligence? Why or why not? Are there justifications for treating product manufacturers differently from those engaged in abnormally dangerous activities in terms of internalizing losses created by their activities? Does strict products liability under Restatement (Second) of Torts § 402A achieve similar fairness and efficiency objectives?

2. CALABRESI MODEL

A second rationale for imposing strict liability derives from the economics of strict liability, which Guido Calabresi first expressed in his classic work, The Costs of Accidents: A Legal and Economic Analysis 26 (1970). Dean Calabresi advocates liability rules that are most likely "to reduce the sum of accident costs and the costs of avoiding accidents":

> This cost, or loss, reduction goal can be divided into three subgoals. The first is reduction of the number and severity of accidents. The second cost reduction subgoal is concerned with * * * reducing societal costs resulting from accidents * * *. The third subgoal * * * involves reducing the costs of administering our treatment of accidents.

Among the criteria that he suggests for determining outcomes in particular cases is to allocate losses to those who can most cheaply reduce the risks of accidents, the so-called "cheapest cost avoider." Calabresi defines the notion of the cheapest cost avoider as the party who can best assess the costs and benefits of the action which caused the harm and can remediate those risks, where appropriate, most effectively and efficiently. This strict liability test does not require a court to evaluate a party's actual or projected costs of avoiding an accident. Instead, the court merely has to choose the party that was in the best position to make that decision. This judicial approach requires no financial acumen per se, just an insight into who had the knowledge and expertise to have made the decision. "[T]he strict liability test would simply require a decision as to whether the injurer or the victim was in the better position both to judge whether the avoidance costs would exceed foreseeable accident costs and to act on that judgment." See Guido Calabresi & Jon T. Hirschoff, Toward a Test for Strict Liability in Tort, 81 Yale L.J. 1055, 1060 (1972).

For example, will it cost less to abate the emissions from the defendant's plant or to install air conditioners on homes of plaintiffs' who are suffering from those emissions? Calabresi would argue that the plant's managers would likely be in the better position to weigh the costs of harm occurring to homeowners and the costs of installing preventative technology, and hence to know which strategy produces lower overall costs. If this weighing is undeterminable or inconclusive, Calabresi then turns to the party that can best correct any error in its entitlements (the best "briber") by purchasing the other parties' interests. Thus, the defendant might occupy the better position to acquire adjoining properties, and therefore, reach an efficient solution. For an opinion applying the "cheapest cost avoider" principle, see Union Oil Co. v. Oppen, 501 F.2d 558, 570 (9th Cir.1974), involving an oil spill.

Under Calabresi's analysis, in most cases involving abnormally dangerous activities the enterprise engaging in the activity would represent the cheaper cost avoider. What problems do you see in this rationale for strict liability?

3. NONRECIPROCAL RISKS MODEL

A third rationale for imposing strict liability is advanced by Professor George Fletcher, in Fairness and Utility in Tort Law, 85 Harv. L. Rev. 537 (1972). He rejects the search for lowest cost avoiders in favor of a search for a rights-based, corrective justice rationale. Professor Fletcher advances a test of fairness that revolves around reciprocal and nonreciprocal risks. Under this paradigm of reciprocity, if the defendant and plaintiff exposed each other to similar degrees of risk (created reciprocal risks), then no strict liability ought to apply. An example of reciprocal risks are those posed by two automobiles converging on a two-lane highway. Even if one vehicle is being operated without due care, as an abstract proposition, each of the two vehicles creates an equivalent or reciprocal risk to the other.

In contrast, if defendant's uncommon activity exposes the plaintiff to a unilateral, nonreciprocal risk, courts should hold the defendant strictly liable:

> Expressing the standard of strict liability as unexcused, nonreciprocal risk-taking provides an account not only of the *Rylands* * * * decision, but of strict liability in general. It is apparent, for example, that the uncommon, ultrahazardous activities pinpointed by the

Restatement are readily subsumed under the rationale of nonreciprocal risk-taking. If uncommon activities are those with few participants, they are likely to be activities generating nonreciprocal risks. Similarly dangerous activities like blasting, fumigating, and crop dusting stand out as distinct, nonreciprocal risks in the community. They represent threats of harm that exceed the level of risk to which all members of the community contribute in roughly equal shares. * * * [A]ccording to the paradigm of reciprocity, the interests of the individual require us to grant compensation whenever this disproportionate distribution of risk injures someone subject to more than his fair share of risk.

George P. Fletcher, Fairness and Utility in Tort Law, 85 Harv. L. Rev. 537, 547, 551 (1972). Copyright ©1972 by the Harvard Law Review Association.

Calabresi criticizes Fletcher's theory of reciprocity as a mere surrogate for which party can better evaluate the costs and benefits of the activity. Do you agree?

4. EPSTEIN'S CORRECTIVE JUSTICE MODEL

Yet another rationale for strict liability is offered by Professor Epstein, who, like Fletcher, rejects an efficiency or utilitarian approach, preferring a concept of fairness. Richard Epstein, A Theory of Strict Liability, 2 J. Legal Stud. 151 (1973). He states that the objective is to develop a normative theory of torts that takes into account common sense notions of individual responsibility and causation. The core of Epstein's position is that individuals possess entitlements to personal bodily integrity (ownership), just as they possess title to land or chattels, that entitle the individual to be free from invasions that cause harm or damage to those interests. He asserts that the concept of causation should be dominant because "it is dominant in the language that people * * * use to describe conduct and to determine responsibility." Id. at 164. While causation may not be necessary to "the development of some theory of tort if the goal of the system is the minimization of the costs of accidents," it is vital to tort law if the system is to "respond to ordinary views on individual blame and accountability." Epstein argues that causation, as in the phrase "A caused harm to B," plays the central role in cases of force (battery), fright (assault), compulsion (false imprisonment), and various instances where A's conduct has created a condition dangerous to B.

In discussing dangerous conditions as a source of harm to others, Epstein contends that a defendant's responsibility depends on a showing that he created the dangerous condition and that the condition "resulted in" (i.e., caused) harm to another. Id. at 177. But once the causation is shown, he argues that affirmative defenses and justifications must be narrowly applied because the focus should be on what the defendant *did*.

As you saw in Chapter 3, Epstein has also spoken of the dominance of corrective justice in nuisance cases and the limited role occupied by utilitarian constraints. Are the two propositions wholly consistent?

5. POSNER: REDUCTION IN LEVELS OF ACTIVITY

Judge Richard Posner, one of the leading legal theoreticians of the last twenty years, raises the proposition in Indiana Harbor Belt Railroad v. American Cyanamid Co., 916 F.2d 1174 (7th Cir.1990) that one purpose of imposing strict liability for high risk activities is to reduce the frequency with which actors choose to engage in such activities. This reduction in activity levels is not explicitly referenced in the Restatement, but represents an incentive that may be created by strict liability. Judge Posner described the points as follows:

> One might for example start with (c) [§ 520], inability to eliminate the risk of accident by the exercise of due care. The baseline common law regime of tort liability is negligence. When it is a workable regime, because the hazards of an activity can be avoided by being careful (which is to say, nonnegligent), there is no need to switch to strict liability. Sometimes, however, a particular type of accident cannot be prevented by taking care but can be avoided, or its consequences minimized, by shifting the activity in which the accident occurs to another locale, where the risk or harm of an accident will be less ((e)), or by reducing the scale of the activity caused by it ((f)). By making the actor strictly liable—by denying him in other words an excuse based on his inability to avoid accidents by being more careful—we give him an incentive, missing in a negligence regime, to experiment with methods of preventing accidents that involve not greater exertions of care, assumed to be futile, but instead relocating, changing, or reducing (perhaps to the vanishing point) the activity giving rise to the accident. The greater the risk of an accident ((a)) and the costs of an accident if one occurs ((b)), the more we want the actor to consider the possibility of making accident-reducing activity changes; the stronger, therefore, is the case for strict liability.

6. PROPOSED RESTATEMENT APPROACH

For a criticism of Posner's analysis, see William K. Jones, Strict Liability for Hazardous Enterprises, 92 Colum. L. Rev. 1705, 1752–54 (1992). Jones proposes a revised Restatement to govern hazardous activities which he formulates as follows:

> (1) An enterprise engaged in a hazardous activity is liable for harm to others resulting from the activity, even though the enterprise has exercised the utmost care to prevent the harm.

> (2) An activity is hazardous if:

> > (a) it poses a risk of loss of life or serious personal injury or substantial property damage; and

> > (b) neither the incidence nor the extent of the harm is subject to significant control by the injured party in the normal course of events.

(B. & M.) Environ.Torts ACB—4

(3) The injured party may be barred from recovery by assumption of risk or other contributory fault, under the doctrine of comparative fault, or because the party is unusually sensitive to the resulting harm; but the injured party is not required to relinquish a property right in order to avoid harm.

(4) This provision does not apply to injuries to persons having a contractual relationship with the enterprise.

Jones briefly describes the advantages of and rationale for his reformulation:

> In brief, the reformulation seeks to compel business enterprises to evaluate the risks posed by their activities; to explore different modes of proceeding, including different locales; and to choose the method of operation most advantageous to the enterprise after considering all benefits and costs (including liabilities to others) of each course of action. The evaluation would consider the possibility of not proceeding at all, if burdens invariably exceeded benefits, or of proceeding at a lower level of production, prompted by higher prices if such were needed to compensate for higher liability claims. Since the benefits and burdens to society are now internalized by the enterprise in the form of costs and prices, the entrepreneurial decision will reflect the appropriate societal decision on the questions: (1) whether to proceed at all; (2) if so, at what level of output; and (3) in what manner, including place and mode of operation and extent of precautions.

William K. Jones, Strict Liability for Hazardous Enterprise, originally appearing in 92 Colum. L. Rev. 1705, 1713 (1992). Reprinted by permission. How does Jones' suggestion modify or deflect the rationale Judge Posner expressed in *Indiana Harbor Belt*? Is Jones' approach essentially that contained in § 402A that governs products liability based on the existence of a defective condition unreasonably dangerous? For another view of strict liability, see Jules Coleman, Risks and Wrongs 219, 221 (1993).

E. JUDICIAL APPLICATIONS OF STRICT LIABILITY

STATE, DEPARTMENT OF ENVIRONMENTAL PROTECTION v. VENTRON CORPORATION

Supreme Court of New Jersey, 1983.
94 N.J. 473, 468 A.2d 150.

POLLOCK, J.

This appeal concerns the responsibility of various corporations for the cost of the cleanup and removal of mercury pollution seeping from a forty-acre tract of land into Berry's Creek[.] The plaintiff is the State of New Jersey, Department of Environmental Protection (DEP); the primary defendants are Velsicol Chemical Corporation (Velsicol), its former subsidiary, Wood Ridge Chemical Corporation (Wood Ridge), and Ventron Corporation (Ventron), into which Wood Ridge was merged and Robert M. and Rita W. Wolf (the Wolfs), who purchased part of the polluted property from Ventron.

Beneath its surface, the tract is saturated by an estimated 268 tons of toxic waste, primarily mercury. For a stretch of several thousand feet, the concentration of mercury in Berry's Creek is the highest found in fresh water sediments in the world. The waters of the creek are contaminated by the compound methyl mercury, which continues to be released as the mercury interacts with other elements. Due to depleted oxygen levels, fish no longer inhabit Berry's Creek, but are present only when swept in by the tide and, thus, irreversibly toxified.

The contamination at Berry's Creek results from mercury processing operations carried on at the site for almost fifty years. In March, 1976, DEP filed a complaint against Ventron, Wood Ridge, Velsicol, Berk, and the Wolfs, charging them with violating the "New Jersey Water Quality Improvement Act of 1971," N.J.S.A. 58:10–23.1 to –23.10, and N.J.S.A. 23:5–28, and further, with creating or maintaining a nuisance. The defendants cross-claimed against each other; Velsicol and Ventron counterclaimed against DEP, which amended its complaint to allege the violation of the "Spill Compensation and Control Act" (Spill Act), N.J.S.A. 58:10–23.11 to –23.11z. The Spill Compensation Fund (Fund), created by the Spill Act to provide funds to abate toxic nuisances, N.J.S.A. 58:10–23.11i, intervened.

* * *

* * * Following the entry of judgment, the trial court entered a "Procedural Order Involving Remedy," which approved for submission to the United States Army Corps of Engineers the DEP plan for the cleanup of Berry's Creek.

* * *

The trial court concluded that the entire tract and Berry's Creek are polluted and that additional mercury from the tract has reached, and may continue to reach, the creek via ground and surface waters. Every operator of the mercury processing plant contributed to the pollution; while the plant was in operation, the discharge of effluent resulted in a dangerous and hazardous mercurial content in Berry's Creek. The trial court found that from 1960–74 the dangers of mercury were becoming better known and that Berk, Wood Ridge, Velsicol, and Ventron knew of those dangers. * * * Based on those findings, the lower courts concluded that Berk, Wood Ridge, Velsicol, and Ventron were liable for damages caused by the creation of a public nuisance and the conduct of an abnormally dangerous activity.

The trial court also determined that the 1977 Spill Act did not impose retroactive liability for discharges of mercury into a waterway of the State. After the entry of the judgment, however, the Legislature amended the act to impose retroactive strict liability on "[a]ny person who has discharged a hazardous substance or is in any way responsible for any hazardous substance" being removed by DEP. See N.J.S.A. 58:10–23.11g(c).

* * *

II

The lower courts imposed strict liability on Wood Ridge under common-law principles for causing a public nuisance and for "unleashing a dangerous substance during non-natural use of the land." In imposing strict liability, those courts relied substantially on the early English decision of Rylands v. Fletcher, L.R. 1 Ex. 265 (1866), aff'd, L.R. 3 H.L. 330 (1868). An early decision of the former Supreme Court, Marshall v. Welwood, 38 N.J.L. 339 (Sup.Ct.1876), however, rejected Rylands v. Fletcher.

Twenty-one years ago, without referring to either Marshall v. Welwood or Rylands v. Fletcher, this Court adopted the proposition that "an ultrahazardous activity which introduces an unusual danger into the community * * * should pay its own way in the event it actually causes damage to others." Berg v. Reaction Motors Div., Thiokol Chem. Corp., 181 A.2d 487 (N.J.1962). Dean Prosser views Berg as accepting a statement of principle derived from Rylands. W. Prosser, Law of Torts s 78 at 509 & n. 7 (4th ed. 1971).

* * *

We believe it is time to recognize expressly that the law of liability has evolved so that a landowner is strictly liable to others for harm caused by toxic wastes that are stored on his property and flow onto the property of others. Therefore, we overrule Marshall v. Welwood and adopt the principle of liability originally declared in Rylands v. Fletcher. The net result is that those who use, or permit others to use, land for the conduct of abnormally dangerous activities are strictly liable for resultant damages. Comprehension of the relevant legal principles, however, requires a more complete explanation of their development.

Even in its nascent stages, the English common law recognized the need to provide a system for redressing unlawful interference with a landowner's right to the possession and quiet enjoyment of his land. Trespass and nuisance developed as the causes of action available to a landowner complaining of an unauthorized intrusion on his lands. * * *

* * *

Early decisions of this State recognized the doctrine of nuisance as a basis for imposing liability for damages. The former New Jersey Supreme Court, however, became one of the first courts to reject the doctrine of Rylands v. Fletcher. See Marshall v. Welwood, 38 N.J.L. 339 (1876). That Court reached this result by referring to the Exchequer Chamber's broad formulation of the rule, which extended liability to anything on the land "likely to cause mischief," rather than the narrowed version affirmed by the House of Lords, which limited liability to "nonnatural" use of the land. Writing for the Court, Chief Justice Beasley refused to adopt Rylands because it did not require the challenged activity to be a nuisance per se. Using the example of an alkalai works, however, he distinguished those situations in which the causes of injury partake "largely of the character of nuisances," even when they "had been erected upon the best scientific principles."

The confusion occasioned by the rejection of the Rylands principle of liability and the continuing adherence to the imposition of liability for a "nuisance" led to divergent results. * * *

* * * Subsequently, in Berg, this Court confirmed strict liability of landowners by noting that it was "primarily concerned with the underlying considerations of reasonableness, fairness and morality rather than with the formulary labels to be attached to the plaintiffs' causes of action or the legalistic classifications in which they are to be placed." 37 N.J. at 405, 181 A.2d 487.

More recently, the Restatement (Second) of Torts reformulated the standard of landowner liability, substituting "abnormally dangerous" for "ultrahazardous" and providing a list of elements to consider in applying the new standard. Id., §§ 519–20. As noted, this standard incorporates the theory developed in Rylands v. Fletcher. Under the Restatement analysis, whether an activity is abnormally dangerous is to be determined on a case-by-case basis, taking all relevant circumstances into consideration. * * *

Pollution from toxic wastes that seeps onto the land of others and into streams necessarily harms the environment. See Special Report to Congress, Injuries and Damages from Hazardous Wastes—Analysis and Improvement of Legal Remedies in Compliance with section 301(e) of the Comprehensive Environmental Response Compensation and Liability Act of 1980 By the "Superfund Section 301(c) Study Group" [hereinafter cited as Special Report]. Determination of the magnitude of the damage includes recognition that the disposal of toxic waste may cause a variety of harms, including ground water contamination via leachate, surface water contamination via runoff or overflow, and poison via the food chain. Special Report, supra, at 27. The lower courts found that each of those hazards was present as a result of the contamination of the entire tract. Further, as was the case here, the waste dumped may react synergistically with elements in the environment, or other waste elements, to form an even more toxic compound. * * *

The disposal of mercury is particularly inappropriate in the Hackensack Meadowlands, an environmentally sensitive area where the arterial waterways will disperse the pollution through the entire ecosystem. Finally, the dumping of untreated hazardous waste is a critical societal problem in New Jersey, which the Environmental Protection Agency estimates is the source of more hazardous waste than any other state. J. Zazzali and F. Grad, "Hazardous Wastes: New Rights and Remedies?," 13 Seton Hall L.Rev. 446, 449 n. 12 (1983). From the foregoing, we conclude that mercury and other toxic wastes are "abnormally dangerous," and the disposal of them, past or present, is an abnormally dangerous activity. We recognize that one engaged in the disposing of toxic waste may be performing an activity that is of some use to society. Nonetheless, "the unavoidable risk of harm that is inherent in it requires that it be carried on at his peril, rather than at the expense of the innocent person who suffers harm as a result of it." Restatement (Second), supra, comment h at 39.

The Spill Act expressly provides that its remedies are in addition to existing common-law or statutory remedies. N.J.S.A. 58:10–23.11v. Our examination leads to the conclusion, consistent with that of the lower courts, that defendants have violated long-standing common-law principles of landowner liability. Wood Ridge and Berk were at all times engaged in an abnormally dangerous activity—dumping toxic mercury. Ventron remains liable because it expressly assumed the liability of Wood Ridge in the merger. After 1967, Velsicol, as an adjacent landowner, permitted Wood Ridge to dump mercury onto its land. That activity has poisoned the land and Berry's Creek. Even if they did not intend to pollute or adhered to the standards of the time, all of these parties remain liable. Those who poison the land must pay for its cure.

We approve the trial court's finding that Berk, Wood Ridge, Velsicol, and Ventron are liable under common-law principles for the abatement of the resulting nuisance and damage. * * *

Notes and Questions

1. Could the court in *Ventron* have reached the same conclusion relying solely on a nuisance theory? The court does appear to base its holding on liability without fault, in the sense that the companies might have used reasonable care and did not know that their activities would harm Berry Creek. This statement in the opinion of the court is quoted frequently:

> We believe it is time to recognize expressly that the law of liability has evolved so that a landowner is strictly liable to others for harm caused by toxic wastes that are stored on his property and flow onto the property of others. Therefore, we * * * adopt the principle of liability originally declared in Rylands v. Fletcher. The net result is that those who use, or permit others to use, land for the conduct of abnormally dangerous activities are strictly liable for resultant damages.

The court's adoption of *Rylands* is certainly a ringing endorsement for the application of strict liability principles to toxic harms. Does the court's application of strict liability seem more like the rule in *Rylands*, or more akin to the Restatement's balancing of factors approach?

2. The court also held that the 1979 Spill Act imposed strict liability on any person "who has discharged a hazardous substance or is in any way responsible for any hazardous substance." The court found that the Spill Act, N.J.S.A. 58:10–23.11a, prohibited both intentional and unintentional discharges of hazardous substances and could be applied retroactively to discharges occurring before its passage in 1977, "if the discharge poses a

substantial risk of imminent damage to the public health or safety or imminent and severe damage to the environment." Given this broad statutory authority to compel defendants to clean up the wastes and pay for clean-up costs, why does the court even establish the strict liability theory?

3. For an opinion that applies strict liability for abnormally dangerous activities to defendant's oil operations where plaintiffs' culinary water wells were contaminated by percolation of waste waters from its oil wells, see Branch v. Western Petroleum, Inc., 657 P.2d 267 (Utah 1982), where the court held:

> [T]he facts of the case support application of the rule of strict liability because the ponding of the toxic formation water in an area adjacent to the Branches' wells constituted an abnormally dangerous and inappropriate use of the land in light of its proximity to the Branches' property and was unduly dangerous to the Branches' use of their water well.

Because the waste waters also flooded onto plaintiffs' land, the court sustained a trespass theory as well.

4. In another frequently cited case, the Florida Court of Appeals in Cities Service Company v. State, 312 So.2d 799 (Fla.App.1975), applied a similar analysis. Cities Service operated a phosphate rock mine and placed one billion gallons of phosphate slimes into settling ponds. When a dam break occurred in one of Cities Service's settling ponds, approximately one billion gallons of slimes escaped into a creek and thence into a major river, killing countless numbers of fish and inflicting other damage. The State of Florida, in an appeal from the lower court's grant of relief, sued for an injunction as well as compensatory and punitive damages. The court considered whether the strict liability doctrine of Rylands v. Fletcher should be applied. After observing that "[i]n early days it was important to encourage persons to use their land by whatever means were available for the purpose of commercial and industrial development. * * * [I]t now seems reasonable that they pay their own way." The court then addressed whether the impounding of phosphate slime was a natural or a non-natural activity to which strict liability would apply:

> In the final analysis, we are impressed by the magnitude of the activity and the attendant risk of enormous damage. The impounding of billions of gallons of phosphatic slimes behind earthen walls which are subject to breaking even with the exercise of the best of care strikes us as being both "ultrahazardous" and "abnormally dangerous," as the case may be.

> This is not clear water which is being impounded. Here, Cities Service introduced water into its mining operation which when combined with phosphatic wastes produced a phosphatic slime which had a high potential for damage to the environment. If a break occurred, it was to be expected that extensive damage would be visited upon property many miles away. In this case, the damage, in fact, extended almost to the mouth of the Peace River, which is far beyond the phosphate mining area described in the Cities Service affidavit. We conclude that the Cities Service slime reservoir constituted a non-natural use of the land such as to invoke the doctrine of strict liability.

5. In another Florida decision, Old Island Fumigation, Inc. v. Barbee, 604 So.2d 1246 (Fla.App.1992), defendant fumigated Buildings A and B of a condominium complex, but not Building C, which was thought to be separated by an impenetrable fire wall. While defendant had the occupants of A and B evacuate during the process, residents of Building C were advised that they could remain. Several residents of C were seriously injured by sulfuryl fluoride poisoning, which came from the fumigation gas used by defendant. Several months after the incident, an architect discovered that the fire wall was defective and contained a four-foot by eighteen-inch open space, that was not visible and had been missed by several building inspectors and defendant. The defendant argued that the architect and contractors of the complex were responsible, but the court upheld a summary judgment in favor of plaintiffs that "fumigation is an ultrahazardous activity," and any alleged negligence of third parties does not free it from strict liability. Should the negligent actions of third parties insulate the defendant from liability? What recourse, if any, does the fumigation company have?

F. WHAT CONSTITUTES AN "ABNORMALLY DANGEROUS" ACTIVITY?

It is not always obvious what activities will be held by a court to be "abnormally dangerous." The decisions in *Branch*, *Cities Service*, and *Ventron* illustrate the kinds of activities that have been classified as abnormally dangerous. The cases in this section all seek to test the boundaries of strict liability in the context of actors or activities as varied as a producer of polychlorinated biphenyls (PCBs), a manufacturer and shipper of liquid acrylonitrile, the maintenance of an underground gasoline storage tank, or the generation of waste dumped at a city-owned landfill.

1. BOUNDARIES TO STRICT LIABILITY

a. *Marketing of Products*

In City of Bloomington v. Westinghouse Electric Corp., 891 F.2d 611 (7th Cir.1989), Bloomington, Indiana sued Westinghouse Electric Corporation for damages and equitable relief, alleging Westinghouse discharged waste containing PCBs into Bloomington's sewers and a sewage treatment plant. Later the city brought in Monsanto Company as a defendant, and added a claim for the presence of PCB waste at a city-owned landfill. After the City settled with Westinghouse, it continued its action against Monsanto, asserting liability under tort theories of public and private nuisance, trespass, abnormally dangerous activity, negligence, and willful and wanton misconduct. The district court dismissed the counts based on nuisance, trespass, and abnormally dangerous activity. The case went to trial on the negligence and willful and wanton misconduct counts, and the jury found in favor of Monsanto. The city appealed on the ground that the trial evidence presented jury issues under the theories of nuisance, abnormally dangerous activity, and trespass. The Court of Appeals affirmed, concluding that the city had no viable claim against Monsanto based on those theories.

PCBs are toxic chemical mixtures which were manufactured by Monsanto and sold for insulation in high voltage electrical equipment such as capacitors and transformers. Monsanto confined its sales of PCBs to sealed containers for electrical uses, informed customers of the latest information on the effects of PCBs, and used warning labels advising customers not to permit PCBs to enter the environment. One of Monsanto's customers, Westinghouse, used them in its Bloomington plant and deposited waste containing PCBs at various Bloomington-area landfills, which permitted concentrations of PCBs to enter the sewer effluent of its plant. The sales agreement between Monsanto and Westinghouse also required Westinghouse to use its best efforts to prevent PCBs from entering the environment and Monsanto instructed Westinghouse how to dispose of PCBs so that they would not enter water systems, including the city's sewer systems.

The court affirmed the dismissal of the nuisance claims on the ground that Monsanto had done nothing to interfere with the city's use and enjoyment of its property, but rather Westinghouse had because it "was in control of the product purchased and was solely responsible for the nuisance it created by not safely disposing of the product." It sustained dismissal of the trespass claim on a similar basis. As to strict liability, the court found that Indiana courts had adopted §§ 519 and 520 of the Restatement and continued:

> Here the harm to the City's sewage and landfill was not caused by any abnormally dangerous activity of Monsanto but by the buyer's failure to safeguard its waste. In denying liability for an ultrahazardous activity here, the district court pointed out that Monsanto did not control the PCBs contained in Westinghouse's waste. This accords with the Restatement view because the Restatement confines strict liability to "[o]ne who carries on an abnormally dangerous activity." Restatement § 519(1). Here that definition would include Westinghouse but not Monsanto.

After discussing *Erbrich Products*, noted earlier, where the Indiana Court of Appeals refused to extend strict liability to the escape of chlorine gas, it continued:

> In addition, the *Erbrich Products* court held that an activity could not be considered abnormally dangerous if the risks therefrom could be limited by the exercise of reasonable care. The risks associated with the disposal of PCBs could have been limited by Westinghouse's exercise of reasonable care.

> * * *

> [W]e are unwilling to extend the doctrine of strict liability for an abnormally dangerous activity to the party whose activity did not cause the injury. * * * Finally, * * * the marketing of the PCBs

was not dangerous itself, and the injury was rather the result of actions taken by a third party.

One judge dissented in *City of Bloomington*, maintaining that Monsanto had "participated to a substantial extent in carrying on the nuisance-creating activity." Conceding that "participation" in abnormally dangerous activity was not the same as control, he expressed this concern with the majority's approach:

> A manufacturer may, however, otherwise "participate" extensively in events subsequent to the sale and could very well incur liability under that test. Here, indeed, there are extensive allegations of the manufacturer's efforts to affect the disposition of the product after sale. * * *
>
> It seems to me that, on the basis of the majority opinion, sellers of toxic chemicals and other dangerous substances, simply by virtue of their commercial status, become insulated from any liability—except that cognizable under a negligence or a products liability theory—beyond the point of sale for any of their activities occurring either before or after the sale. Just because Monsanto's activities here are arguably benign is not a good reason to insulate from liability all manufacturer activity, whether benign or not.

Notes and Questions

With whom do you agree—the majority or the dissent? The decision demonstrates an important limitation on the law of nuisance, trespass, and strict liability for abnormally dangerous activities. In many circumstances a manufacturer of PCB's may not be held liable for nuisance or strict liability because of subsequent disposal activities undertaken by others. The manufacturer was not in a "horizontal" relationship of land ownership usually present in these trespass, nuisance, and strict liability cases.

On the strict liability theory, the court finds that the manufacture of PCB's is not, in itself, an abnormally dangerous activity, and that §§ 519 and 520 of the Restatement were not intended to embrace consumer or industrial product sellers, such as Monsanto. Would the appropriate theory against Monsanto be strict products liability under § 402A of the Restatement? Consider this question after Chapter 7 on toxic products. Note that the activity in which the *defendant* engaged must be abnormally dangerous, and the only activity of Monsanto was in manufacturing and selling PCBs, not in disposing or applying PCBs in a manner that adversely affected others' use and enjoyment of their land.

b. Adequacy of Negligence

Another decision demonstrating that strict liability for abnormally dangerous activities will not be extended where a negligence regime would function effectively is Indiana Harbor Belt Railroad Co. v. American Cyanamid Co., 916 F.2d 1174 (7th Cir.1990). The defendant, Cyanamid, is a manufacturer of acrylonitrile, a chemical used in manufacturing acrylic fibers and other plastic products. Defendant loaded

20,000 gallons of liquid acrylonitrile into a railroad car that it had leased. The railcar was picked up by one railroad line and transported to a railyard operated by plaintiff outside of Chicago. The car developed a leak resulting in the spillage of 4,000 gallons, and because of the chemical's toxicity and flammability local authorities evacuated the homes near the railyard.

The Illinois EPA ordered plaintiff to undertake decontamination measures which cost the Line $981,000. The plaintiff's strict liability claim asserted that the placement of a toxic chemical in a rail shipment that would be transported through a densely populated area is an abnormally dangerous activity. The Seventh Circuit, in an opinion by Judge Richard Posner, dismissed that claim. After tracing the history of strict liability, Judge Posner noted that acrylonitrile is ranked fifty-third on a list of the 125 most hazardous chemicals that are shipped in significant volumes. He characterized extension of strict liability to the shippers of hazardous chemicals as "sweeping," with no direct prior judicial support. In denying strict liability, Judge Posner focused on the plaintiff's failure to demonstrate that "a negligence regime is not perfectly adequate to remedy and deter, at reasonable cost, the accidental spillage" of the chemical. He pointed out that the accident was not caused by the inherent properties of acrylonitrile but by somebody's carelessness, and accordingly, the accident could have been prevented by someone's exercise of reasonable care:

> Accidents that are due to a lack of care can be prevented by taking care; and when a lack of care can be shown in court, such accidents are adequately deterred by the threat of liability for negligence. It is true that the district court purported to find as a fact that there is an inevitable risk of derailment or other calamity in transporting "large quantities of anything." 662 F.Supp. at 642. This is not a finding of fact, but a truism: anything can happen. The question is, how likely is this type of accident if the actor uses due care? For all that appears from the record of the case or any other sources of information that we have found, if a tank car is carefully maintained the danger of a spill of acrylonitrile is negligible. If this is right, there is no compelling reason to move to a regime of strict liability, especially one that might embrace all other hazardous materials shipped by rail as well.

Judge Posner also cited the *City of Bloomington* decision as support for the conclusion that, unlike most strict liability cases, it was not the actors—the transporters of chemicals—who plaintiff sought to hold strictly liable, but rather the manufacturer of the chemical, who had no realistic control regarding transportation routes.

> In emphasizing the flammability and toxicity of acrylonitrile rather than the hazards of transporting it, as in failing to distinguish between the active and the passive shipper, the plaintiff overlooks the fact that ultrahazardousness or abnormal dangerousness is, in the contemplation of the law at least, a property not of

substances, but of activities: not of acrylonitrile, but of the transportation of acrylonitrile by rail through populated areas * * *. Whatever the situation under products liability law (§ 402A of the Restatement), the manufacturer of a product is not considered to be engaged in an abnormally dangerous activity merely because the product becomes dangerous when it is handled or used in some way after it leaves his premises, even if the danger is foreseeable.

Notes and Questions

1. What do you think of Judge Posner's rationale? Central to his analysis is the apprehension that applying strict liability here would imply that all manufacturers and shippers of hazardous chemicals would be liable whenever later events in the distribution of the product resulted in injury. How important is this fact? Judge Posner also emphasized that if the risks can be eliminated by due care there is no occasion to apply strict liability. The plaintiff's negligence count in *Harbor Belt* was permitted to proceed to trial, so the plaintiff was not left without a theory of liability. Could the plaintiff prove negligence on these facts? Assume that a bystander had been injured by the escape of the chemical. Professor William Jones, in an article discussing hazardous activities, points out the following difficulties in Posner's analysis:

> But one of the common deficiencies of the negligence regime is unavailability of proof to the injured party. If a bystander had been injured in *Indiana Harbor*, she would have to trace this carload of acrylonitrile from the supply of the railroad car by North American Car Corporation, to the loading of the car in Louisiana by the American Cynamid Corporation, to the movement of the car to Chicago by the Missouri Pacific Railroad, to the handling of the car in the yard by the switching road, Indiana Harbor. The court was of the opinion that the leak of acrylonitrile was caused by carelessness—whether that of the North American Car Corporation in failing to maintain or inspect the car properly, or that of Cyanamid in failing to maintain or inspect it, or that of the Missouri Pacific when it had custody of the car, or that of the switching line itself in failing to notice the ruptured lid, or some combination of these possible failures of care.

> But the conclusion that negligence is possible or even probable is not the same as identifying or proving negligence in a litigated controversy. By contrast, strict liability assures more certain accountability for accidents, providing appropriate incentives for the control of risk in advance of any mishap. Under Judge Posner's approach, each party has an incentive to point a finger at the others in an effort to shift the blame for an accident. But by then the harm has been done.

William K. Jones, Strict Liability for Hazardous Enterprises, originally appearing in 92 Colum. L. Rev. 1705, 1752–53 (1992). Reprinted by permission.

2. On the point regarding the adequacy of negligence, see also Philip Morris, Inc. v. Emerson, 235 Va. 380, 368 S.E.2d 268 (1988) (holding that strict liability would not apply to the disposal of the highly toxic chemical pentaborane, chiefly because such disposal could have been conducted safely if reasonable precautions had been taken); Hudson v. Peavey Oil Co., 279

Or. 3, 566 P.2d 175 (1977) (no strict liability where evidence did not show that the risk of seepage from underground gasoline tanks could not be eliminated by reasonable care).

c. Underground Storage Tanks

In Arlington Forest Associates v. Exxon Corp., 774 F.Supp. 387 (E.D.Va.1991), involving leakage from an underground storage tank containing gasoline, the court refused to apply strict liability:

> Maintained, monitored, and used with due care, underground gasoline storage tanks present virtually no risk of injury from seepage of their contents. They are not abnormally dangerous. Sound tanks, timely replacement of impaired tanks, modern corrosion control techniques, and adequate testing for leakage can eliminate all but a tolerably small amount of risk. The injury alleged in this case apparently occurred because the tanks fell into a preventable state of disrepair. Only those activities that remain dangerous despite the exercise of all reasonable precautions warrant imposition of strict liability. Here, reasonable precautions would have sufficed to prevent the harm.

Additionally, the court found that the presence of underground storage tanks and the operation of service stations are "so pervasive as reasonably to be considered as matters of common usage," and hence, ineligible for strict liability. Further, as to their locational appropriateness, the court observed that "filling stations are very appropriate in and near residential areas."

The cases involving leaking underground storage tanks are split. In contrast to *Arlington Forest*, in Yommer v. McKenzie, 255 Md. 220, 257 A.2d 138 (1969), the court extended strict liability because "it is proper to surmise that this risk cannot [be] or at least was not, eliminated by the exercise of reasonable care." While acknowledging that not all service stations would create a high degree of risk to others, here a large tank was placed within fifty to sixty feet of plaintiff's water wells; moreover, the court stated that when the operation of such activity involves the placing of a large tank adjacent to a well from which a family must draw its water for drinking, bathing, and laundry, at least that aspect of the activity is inappropriate to the locale, even considering the value of the activity. See generally John Chanin, Comment, LUST on Your Corner: Strict Liability, Victim Compensation, and Leaking Underground Storage Tanks, 62 U. Colo. L. Rev. 365 (1991). For a collection of the cases, see Tort Liability for Pollution from Underground Storage Tanks, 5 ALR 5th 1 (1992).

d. Disposal of Hazardous Wastes

For disposal of hazardous wastes, the cases are unsurprisingly inconsistent. See, e.g., Daigle v. Shell Oil Co., 972 F.2d 1527 (10th Cir.1992) (holding that Shell's use of a basin area leased from the U.S.

Army for impoundment of hazardous wastes generated in its herbicide and pesticide manufacturing operations constituted an ultrahazardous activity); Kenney v. Scientific, Inc., 204 N.J.Super. 228, 497 A.2d 1310 (1985) (imposing strict liability on generators of toxic wastes for damages relating to their disposal); contra, Philip Morris v. Emerson, 235 Va. 380, 368 S.E.2d 268 (1988). In Shockley v. Hoechst Celanese Corp., 793 F.Supp. 670 (D.S.C.1992), plaintiffs sued Hoechst on strict liability when the property they purchased adjacent to defendant's parking lot showed evidence of contamination from hazardous chemicals including carbon tetrachloride, trichloroethylene, and others. Defendant had shipped those chemicals from another location to an independent contractor who operated a chemical reclamation facility. Defendant later purchased that property and turned it into a parking lot for its employees. The court observed that South Carolina had adopted the Restatement § 519 and that cases around the country supported applying strict liability to the use, storage, and disposal of hazardous chemicals. The court also held that Hoechst could not escape liability on the grounds that it had delivered the chemicals to an independent contractor:

> Defendant Hoechst Celanese also contends that the evidence does not support the jury's verdict in Plaintiff's favor on the strict liability cause of action, contending that its only "activity" was to deliver chemicals to [the independent contractor] for reclamation. The use of an independent contractor, however, to handle work involving an abnormally dangerous activity does not insulate Hoechst Celanese from liability. If one "employs an independent contractor to do work which the employer knows or has reason to know involves an abnormally dangerous activity, [he] is subject to liability to the same extent as the contractor for physical harm to others caused by the activity." Restatement (Second) of Torts § 427A. There is ample evidence in the record that Hoechst Celanese knew or had reason to know that the work it employed [the independent contractor] to do involved an abnormally dangerous activity. Moreover, there was testimony at trial that Hoechst Celanese knowingly delivered rusty, aging, and leaking barrels of hazardous chemicals to [the independent contractor's] site where they knew the barrels would be stored for some time before reclamation. Based on this evidence, the jury was justified in finding that Hoechst Celanese itself engaged in the disposal of hazardous chemicals, for which they are strictly liable.

The Fourth Circuit Court of Appeals affirmed on other grounds but disagreed that the disposal of chemical wastes constituted an ultrahazardous activity, observing that the district court had made an unwarranted extension of strict liability theory to embrace such activities even though no South Carolina courts had not done so. Shockley v. Hoechst Celanese Corp., 996 F.2d 1212 (4th Cir.1993). Is the district court opinion consistent with *Indiana Harbor Belt Railroad*? Could the disposal be made safe by the exercise of reasonable care? What are the policy reasons behind the Restatement rule that an employer of an independent contractor cannot escape strict liability?

2. VICARIOUS RESPONSIBILITY

As *Hoechst* illustrates, principals and employers can be held liable for the highly risky activities of their agents. Under the Restatement § 427A, quoted in the opinion, the party who employs an independent contractor to perform abnormally dangerous activities will be subject to the same liability as the contractor. The rationale for doing so is not solely to find a solvent defendant, but to assure that the employer does not intentionally retain judgment-proof contractors to perform danger-ous tasks knowing that the contractors are unable to pay for the costs of injuries and that the employers are not legally obligated to do so. See Anderson v. Marathon Petroleum Co., 801 F.2d 936 (7th Cir.1986), where Judge Posner articulates this rationale. Additionally, as Judge Posner points out, one of the policy objectives identified earlier—that of creating incentives to reduce the frequency or level of the activity—is frustrated if the employer can ignore the accident costs created by the activity by having someone else perform it.

Lessors are generally not liable for the tortious activities of their tenants, unless, at the time the lease was entered, the lessor had knowledge that the tenant's activities would "unavoidably involve * * * unreasonable risk." Restatement (Second) § 397A. For example, in Salazar v. Webb, 44 Colo.App. 429, 618 P.2d 706 (1980), the court held that where plaintiffs were injured by a methane gas explosion on land owned by the defendant, the lessor would be liable if the accident resulted from the dangerous activities of the lessee. But see Peterick v. State, 22 Wash.App. 163, 589 P.2d 250 (1977), holding that employees killed at a plant explosion could not recover from the owner-lessor of the land on which the plant was situated because it did not have control of its operations. The Kentucky Supreme Court has observed that "if potential harm is sufficiently substantial and predictable, it is the duty of the lessor to abate the nuisance created by his lessee." Green v. Asher Coal Mining Co., 377 S.W.2d 68, 71 (Ky. 1964). See also State v. Monarch Chemicals, Inc., 111 Misc.2d 343, 443 N.Y.S.2d 967 (1981), modified 90 A.D.2d 907, 456 N.Y.S.2d 867 (1982), where the court found a triable issue on the lessor's liability where the lessee's storage of toxic chemicals resulted in a public nuisance because they escaped and pollut-ed public water supplies.

Is there a basis for treating lessors differently than employers hiring independent contractors? Return to the rationales for strict liability and assess how they apply to the landlord-tenant relationship.

3. CAUSATION

Section 519 of the Restatement (Second) makes it clear that liability extends only to damages that are "within the scope of the abnormal risk that is the basis of the liability." Comment e. Thus, the enterprise is not liable for every harm that may result from carrying on the activity. For example, in a jurisdiction where crop-dusting by small aircraft has been found to represent an abnormally dangerous activity, the risk to be avoided within the meaning of the doctrine is the erroneous, in content or in target, application of pesticides or herbicides. A mishap of such a nature would be within the contemplation of the abnormally dangerous activities remedy, while an accident involving the crash of the aircraft would not.

On the other hand, the intervening actions of third parties—be they innocent, negligent, or reckless—will not defeat liability. See Restatement (Second) of Torts § 522. For example, in Old Island Fumigation Inc. v. Barbee, 604 So.2d 1246 (Fla.App.1992), it was immaterial that architects and contractors were negligent in building a fire wall that permitted defendant's fumigation gas to enter a building adjacent to the one it was spraying, since the fumigation was an ultrahazardous activity.

G. NOTE ON EMERGING ISSUES IN NUISANCE AND STRICT LIABILITY

1. INTRODUCTION: SETTING THE STAGE

In assessing how relevant and effective the theories of nuisance and strict liability for abnormally dangerous activities are, it is important to know who has standing to assert claims under these theories. The extensive litigation sparked by the nation's commitment to clean up hazardous waste sites in the last fifteen years has brought renewed interest in applying common law theories as part of the legal arsenal of those seeking to distribute those costs among all parties involved with the site. In Chapter 10, we examine the Comprehensive Environmental Response, Compensation and Liability Act, 42 U.S.C.A. §§ 9601–9675 that has stimulated much of the litigation surrounding the remediation of the sites and surrounding properties.

After 1980, CERCLA provided the primary legal framework for resolving whether and to what extent private parties can recover cleanup costs and whether those found liable in government actions can recover from their insurers. State law tort claims played a secondary role. However, CERCLA's predominance over the common law may be subsiding. Common law tort theories of liability in environmental cleanups are resurfacing for several reasons. Many private parties that have cleaned up sites have failed to recover from other parties because they have not fulfilled CERCLA's procedural requirements. Moreover, tort claims may offer plaintiffs certain damages not recoverable under CERCLA, such as emotional distress, medical monitoring and punitive damages. Another reason for its resurgence is that it may permit actions by landowners seeking recovery from predecessors in title, or former tenants or users of the property. Finally, because of changed perceptions, what was once regarded as a normal or routine business practice may be viewed today as an abnormally dangerous activity.

In this section we consider two emerging issues respecting the application of nuisance and strict liability theories. First, do these theories apply to vertical relationships?; and second, what role a defendant's knowledge of the dangers should have in assessing the availability of these doctrines?

2. APPLICATION TO VERTICAL RELATIONSHIPS

In the past few years, one of the battlegrounds which courts have addressed is whether a purchaser or lessee of real property can sue a former owner, lessee or lessor of the same property on a theory of nuisance or strict liability to recover for damages flowing from contamination of the property. In other words, in these cases the relationship between the parties is not that of horizontal, concurrent owners or occupiers of land, but rather vertical relationships between successors in interest. The first decision, Philadelphia Electric Co. v. Hercules, Inc., 762 F.2d 303 (3d Cir.1985), sets forth the traditional rule in nuisance cases, followed by a California opinion that moves in a contrary direction.

PHILADELPHIA ELECTRIC COMPANY
v. HERCULES, INC.

United States Court of Appeals for the Third Circuit, 1985.
762 F.2d 303.

A. Leon Higginbotham, Jr., J.

This is an appeal from a final judgment of the district court in favor of Philadelphia Electric Company ("PECO") and against Hercules, Inc. ("Hercules") in the amount of $394,910.14, and further ordering Hercules to take all appropriate action to eliminate pollution on a property owned by PECO in Chester, Pennsylvania. The case was tried to a jury on theories of public and private nuisance. For the reasons set forth in the opinion that follows, we will reverse the judgment against Hercules on PECO's claims, and vacate the injunction.

I.

Prior to October of 1971, the Pennsylvania Industrial Chemical Corporation ("PICCO") owned a tract of land abutting the Delaware River in Chester, Pennsylvania where it operated a hydrocarbon resin manufacturing plant. At the time PICCO acquired the property ("the Chester site") there was an inlet located at the southern end that opened into the Delaware River. Sometime later PICCO filled in the shoreline at the inlet and thereby created a lake ("the PICCO pond"). PICCO deposited or buried various resins and their by-products in the PICCO pond and possibly other locations.

In 1971 PICCO ceased operations on the Chester site and sold the facility to Gould, Inc. ("Gould"). Gould did not conduct any operations on the Chester site, other than leasing certain tanks to ABM Disposal Services Company ("ABM"), which used them to store large quantities of various waste materials, though apparently not resins or resinous by-products.

In mid–1973, PECO—which operated a plant on an adjoining piece of land—obtained an option to purchase the Chester site from Gould. Prior to exercising its option, a PECO representative inspected the site on more than one occasion, including walking tours along the banks of the Delaware River and the banks of the PICCO pond. PECO learned that Gould's tenant, ABM, had caused a number of spills on the site, including oil spills in the pond area, and was informed that ABM was a "sloppy tenant". ABM was unable to clean up the Chester site in time to meet Gould's original deadline for vacating the premises, a condition of the PECO purchase agreement. PECO exercised its option and acquired the property in March of 1974. * * *

In 1980 the Pennsylvania Department of Environmental Resources ("DER") discovered that resinous materials similar to those once produced by PICCO were seeping from the banks of the Delaware River at the Chester site, and that the PICCO pond was contaminated with the same material [and ordered PECO to clean up the property]. * * *

* * *

* * * PECO produced evidence indicating that it incurred expenses of $338,328.69 in implementing the clean-up [and incurred other losses including lost rentals of the property]. * * *

* * *

* * * PECO instituted suit against Gould and Hercules, which had acquired the remaining assets of PICCO in 1973, in exchange for Hercules stock. * * *

* * *

[T]he district court moulded a verdict and entered judgment for PECO against Hercules in the amount of $394,910.14[.]

* * *

Having determined that Hercules may be liable as PICCO's successor for unknown and contingent liabilities, we must analyze the relationship between Hercules and PECO as that of a vendor and remote vendee of land. Hercules argues that this relationship is governed by the rule of caveat emptor, subject to limited exceptions not applicable here, and that a vendee has no cause of action against a vendor sounding in private nuisance for conditions existing on the land transferred. After carefully considering this question of first impression, we are persuaded that under Pennsylvania law Hercules cannot, as a matter of law, be held liable to PECO on a private nuisance theory. The Reporter's Note to

Restatement (Second) of Torts § 352 (1965) sums up the prevailing view regarding the liability of a vendor of land: Under the ancient doctrine of caveat emptor, the original rule was that, in the absence of express agreement, the vendor of land was not liable to his vendee, or a fortiori to any other person, for the condition of the land existing at the time of transfer. As to sales of land this rule has retained much of its original force, and the implied warranties which have grown up around the sale of chattels never have developed. This is perhaps because great importance always has been attached to the deed of conveyance, which is taken to represent the full agreement of the parties, and to exclude all other terms and liabilities. The vendee is required to make his own inspection of the premises, and the vendor is not responsible to him for their defective condition, existing at the time of transfer. See also M. Friedman, Contracts and Conveyances of Real Property § 1.2(n), at 37 (4th ed. 1984) ("[I]n the sale of realty this doctrine [caveat emptor] not only applies, it flourishes.").

As the Pennsylvania Supreme Court has said: "Generally speaking, the rule is that in the absence of fraud or misrepresentation a vendor is responsible for the quality of property being sold by him only to the extent for which he expressly agrees to be responsible * * *. The theory of the doctrine is that the buyer and seller deal at arm's length, each with an equal means of knowledge concerning the subject of the sale, and that therefore the buyer should be afforded only those protections for which he specifically contracts." Elderkin v. Gaster, 228 A.2d 771, 774–75 (Pa.1972). In Elderkin the court abolished the rule of caveat emptor as to the sale of new homes by a builder-vendor and, in accordance with a national trend, adopted a theory of implied warranties. But the reasoning of the Elderkin opinion leaves us with no doubt that where, as here, corporations of roughly equal resources contract for the sale of an industrial property, and especially where the dispute is over a condition on the land rather than a structure, caveat emptor remains the rule.

* * * PECO's tack has been to cast its cause of action for the condition of the Chester site as one for private nuisance. We, however, do not believe that PECO can escape the rule of caveat emptor by this route.

Restatement (Second) of Torts § 821D defines a "private nuisance" as "a nontrespassory invasion of another's interest in the private use and enjoyment of land." The briefs and arguments, as well as the district court's opinion, give much attention to the questions of whether the condition created by Hercules on the Chester site amounted to a nuisance, and whether Hercules remains liable for the nuisance even after vacating the land. For the purposes of our decision, we may assume that Hercules created a nuisance, and that it remains liable for this condition. See Restatement (Second) of Torts § 840A. The crucial and difficult question for us is to whom Hercules may be liable.

The parties have cited no case from Pennsylvania or any other jurisdiction, and we have found none, that permits a purchaser of real property to recover from the seller on a private nuisance theory for conditions existing on the very land transferred, and thereby to circumvent limitations on vendor liability inherent in the rule of caveat emptor. In a somewhat analogous circumstance, courts have not permitted tenants to circumvent traditional limitations on the liability of lessors by the expedient of casting their cause of action for defective conditions existing on premises (over which they have assumed control) as one for private nuisance. In Harris v. Lewistown Trust Co., 326 Pa. 145, 191 A. 34 (1937), overruled in part on other grounds, Reitmeyer v. Sprecher, 431 Pa. 284, 243 A.2d 395 (1968), the Supreme Court of Pennsylvania held that the doctrine that a landlord not in possession may be liable for injuries resulting from a "condition amounting to a nuisance" is confined to "the owners or occupants of near-by property, persons temporarily on such property, or persons on a neighboring highway or other places." Recovery on this theory was not available to tenants or their invitees: "A breach of duty owed to one class of persons cannot create a cause of action in favor of a person not within the class. A plaintiff must show that as to him there was a breach of duty." Similarly, under the doctrine of caveat emptor Hercules owed only a limited duty to Gould and, in turn, to PECO. PECO concedes that this duty was not violated. PECO cannot recover in private nuisance for the violation of a duty Hercules may have owed to others—namely, its neighbors.

We believe that this result is consonant with the historical role of private nuisance law as a means of efficiently resolving conflicts between neighboring, contemporaneous land uses. All of the very useful and sophisticated economic analyses of private nuisance remedies published in recent years proceed on the basis that the goal of nuisance law is to achieve efficient and equitable solutions to problems created by discordant land uses. In this light nuisance law can be seen as a complement to zoning regulations, * * * and not as an additional type of consumer protection for purchasers of realty. Neighbors, unlike the purchasers of the land upon which a nuisance exists, have no opportunity to protect themselves through inspection and negotiation. The record shows that PECO acted as a sophisticated and responsible purchaser—inquiring into the past use of the Chester site, and inspecting it carefully. We find it inconceivable that the price it offered Gould did not reflect the possibility of environmental risks, even if the exact condition giving rise to this suit was not discovered.

Where, as here, the rule of caveat emptor applies, allowing a vendee a cause of action for private nuisance for conditions existing on the land transferred—where there has been no fraudulent concealment—would in effect negate the market's allocations of resources and risks, and subject vendors who may have originally sold their land at appropriately discounted prices to unbargained-for liability to remote vendees. Such an extension of common law doctrine is particularly hazardous in an area, such as environmental pollution, where Congress and the state legislatures are actively seeking to achieve a socially acceptable definition of rights and liabilities. We conclude that PECO did not have a cause of action against Hercules sounding in private nuisance.

Notes and Questions

1. Do you agree with Judge Higginbotham's analysis? Insofar as private nuisance is relied upon, he accurately portrays the state of the law; that is, the decisions had uniformly disallowed subsequent owners to sue predecessors in title for the costs of remediating the property from the consequences of the predecessor's activities, so long as fraud or misrepresentation in the sale is not shown. See also Amland Properties Corp. v. Aluminum Co. of America, 711 F.Supp. 784, 807–08 (D.N.J.1989) (no vertical actions on a nuisance theory); Allied Corp. v. Frola, 730 F.Supp. 626, 634 (D.N.J.1990). However, two California appellate cases, Mangini v. Aerojet–General Corp., 281 Cal.Rptr. 827, 230 Cal.App.3d 1125 (1991) and Capogeannis v. Superior Court, 12 Cal.App.4th 668, 15 Cal.Rptr. 2d 796 (1993), have broken this rule and authorized vertical actions on a private nuisance theory.

2. In Mangini v. Aeroject–General Corp., property owners sued parties who had leased the land from prior owners and contaminated it with hazardous wastes during the leasehold. According to plaintiffs, defendant had leased the property for ten years pursuant to a lease that required the tenant to surrender the premises in "as good a state and condition as when received by lessee, reasonable use and wear thereof consistent with the business engaged in by lessee * * * excepted"; and that defendant had burned or deposited and failed to remove millions of pounds of waste rocket fuel materials and other hazardous substances. Plaintiffs alleged nine different theories, including public and private nuisance, negligence per se (for violating the state health code and water code), trespass, and strict liability for abnormally dangerous activities. The Court of Appeals reversed the trial court's dismissal of these claims, holding that *Philadelphia Electric* and other general authorities on the law of nuisance "do not correctly reflect California law." It continued:

> In particular, defendant fails to recognize that California nuisance law is a creature of statute. The California nuisance statutes have been construed, according to their broad terms, to allow an owner of property to sue for damages caused by a nuisance created *on* the owner's property. Under California law, it is not necessary that a nuisance have its origin in neighboring property.

It noted that under California statutes, "an action may be brought by any person whose property is injuriously affected, or whose personal enjoyment is lessened by a nuisance." West's Ann.Cal. Code Civil Procedure § 731. Moreover, it also held that it was not necessary that defendant have a possessory interest in the property at the time suit was filed. It acknowledged that consent could be a defense if defendant's use of the property was authorized by the lease, but found the provisions of the lease "patently ambiguous with respect to whether [it] authorized hazardous waste disposal during the term of the lease" and imposed an obligation upon defendant to clean up any hazard before vacating the premises.

3.   How important is it that the defendant was a tenant rather than the owner of the property? In opposing defendant's appeal to the California Supreme Court, plaintiff argued that caveat emptor has no application in this case:

> Caveat emptor means that as between the owner of real property who sells it, and the buyer, there are no implied warranties concerning the property. In this case Aerojet was not the owner or the seller of the property and the Manginis' claims are not for implied warranty. Rather, the Manginis allege that Aerojet was a tenant, that it wrongfully dumped waste on the property (in violation of the lease and the law), and that a trespass and nuisance resulted causing damage to the property which continues to the present time. Aerojet's liability arises not from breach of any implied warranty but from its conduct, done without the consent of the lessor, causing continuing damage to the property.

Hazardous Waste Litigation Reporter, Sept. 9, 1991, at 21450. Do you agree with this rationale for avoiding caveat emptor? At least one court, Wilson Auto Enterprises v. Mobil Oil Corp., 778 F.Supp. 101 (D.R.I.1991), refused to permit a purchaser of real property to sue a former tenant that had operated a service station for damages for loss of property value and mental anguish.

4.   Should the principle of caveat emptor that bars private nuisance claims between those in the chain of title apply with equal force to public nuisance claims? At least one case holds "no". In Westwood Pharmaceuticals, Inc. v. National Fuel Gas Dist. Corp., 737 F.Supp. 1272 (W.D.N.Y.1990) affirmed 964 F.2d 85 (2d Cir.1992) a purchaser of a gas manufacturing facility site was permitted to maintain a public nuisance action to recover the costs of remediating the property against a former operator of the facility. The court distinguished the *Hercules* case on the grounds that New York's law of standing in public nuisance cases was broader than Pennsylvania's, that defendant's release of hazardous substances at the site was a public nuisance, and that plaintiff's incurrence of response costs constituted special injury. However, consistent with *Hercules,* it rejected plaintiff's private nuisance claim as barred by the doctrine of caveat emptor.

In 1991, the New Jersey Supreme Court made an extraordinary and significant departure from the general rule of nonliability in vertical relationships in T & E Industries, Inc. v. Safety Light Corp.

T & E INDUSTRIES v. SAFETY LIGHT CORPORATION

Supreme Court of New Jersey, 1991.
123 N.J. 371, 587 A.2d 1249.

CLIFFORD, J.

This appeal takes us once again over the unsettled waters of toxic-tort litigation. At the storm center of this case is a radium-contaminated site that is now owned by plaintiff, T & E Industries, Inc. (T & E), but was once owned by United States Radium Corporation (USRC), the predecessor corporation of all the defendant corporations. The primary issue is whether an owner of radium-contaminated property can hold a distant predecessor in title that is responsible for the contamination strictly liable for damages caused by its abnormally-dangerous activity. We hold that it can.

I

A

Until 1943 USRC owned an industrial site on Alden Street in Orange. From around 1917 to 1926 it processed radium at that site. USRC sold the radium for medical purposes and also used it to manufacture luminous paint for instrument dials, watches, and other products. It could, however, recover successfully only eighty percent of the radium from the ore. The unextracted radium was contained in "tailings," the solid by-products of the extraction process, which USRC discarded onto the unimproved portions of the Alden Street site.

Carnotite ore consists primarily of Uranium 238, radium, and vanadium. As the nucleus disintegrates, Uranium 238 decays into other elements, one of which is Radium 226. In turn Radium 226 emits gamma rays and decays into Radon 222, which is a naturally-occurring radioactive gas. Radon then decays into radon progeny or radon "daughters," which can adhere to walls, ceilings, dust particles, and, if inhaled, the tissue of the lungs. Gamma-ray exposure can cause bone cancer and leukemia, while radon inhalation can cause lung cancer.

It was not until the mid–1950s, however, that the scientific community engaged in any serious study of the epidemiological risks associated with radon. It did not generally accept the link between radon and lung cancer until the 1960s, and it was not aware of the problems generated by radioactive tailings until the late 1960s. The federal government, reflecting an unfortunate lag time, did not regulate the disposition of tailings until 1978.

Nevertheless, both the scientific community and USRC had suspicions about the hazards of radium at a much earlier date. In 1917 Florence Wall, an employee of USRC, calculated the amount of radium extracted from ore and measured its radioactivity.

* * *

In the early 1920s, USRC acquired still more evidence of the dangers of radium. Some of its employees applied the luminous paint to watch and instrument dials. After dipping their brushes into the paint, the dialpainters often sharpened the tip of the brush in their mouths, thereby ingesting a small amount of radium. Many of those employees eventually developed cancer. After discovering the problems associated with ingesting radium, USRC posted warnings cautioning its employees against sharpening the brushes in that fashion.

Radium processing at the Orange facility ceased in 1926, and USRC vacated the premises. * * * In the mid–1930s USRC leased the premises to various commercial tenants, eventually selling the property to one of those tenants in 1943. During that interim, the risks posed by radium became increasingly apparent.

* * *

In 1941 the U.S. Department of Commerce published a handbook (H–27) entitled "Safe Handling of Radioactive Luminous Compound." That handbook included detailed information on the effects of ingestion or inhalation of solid radioactive luminous compound, * * * [and warned that] "[t]he continued inhalation of radon may produce carcinoma of the lungs."

* * *

In * * * 1943, USRC sold the Orange property to Arpin, a plastics manufacturer. * * *

Arpin, unaware of the potential risks associated with the tailings, added to the plant a new section that rested on the discarded tailings. Since then the property has changed hands several times. Plaintiff, T & E, a manufacturer of electronic components, began leasing the premises in 1969 and purchased it in 1974.

B

The Uranium Mill Tailings Radiation Control Act, 42 U.S.C. § 7901 to § 7942 (1978), calls for the evaluation of inactive mill-tailing sites. In accordance with that Act, * * * the New Jersey Department of Environmental Protection (DEP), visited plaintiff's plant in March 1979 [and] found elevated gamma-radiation levels inside the building, on the vacant property behind the building, and in the parking lot.

Tests on air and soil samples verified that the levels of radon, radon progeny, and gamma radiation exceeded State regulations [and] * * * federal standards as well. The most severe problem existed in the oven room, the portion of the building added by Arpin. DEP instructed plaintiff "to begin immediate remedial action." It also informed plaintiff that such remedial action would serve only as an interim measure. DEP suggested that if funding for a full decontamination of the site could not be found quickly, plaintiff's options would be "limited to undertaking the cost of decontamination or consider[ing] abandoning the site."

In response to DEP's recommendations, plaintiff restricted employee access to the oven room and monitored the use of that room [and] retained a health physicist, Dr. Steidley, as a consultant [who] * * * concluded * * * that decontamination of the site would ultimately require removal of the soil from beneath and around the building. * * *

[I]n 1981 the Environmental Protection Agency (EPA), at DEP's request, placed the property on the National Priorities List, consisting of those sites posing the most significant potential threats to human health because of their known or suspected toxicity. [See 42 U.S.C.A. § 9605(a)(8)(B) (1986)]. Although DEP did not order plaintiff to abandon the site, T & E moved its operations to another building in Orange and closed the Alden Street plant. Under the Environmental Cleanup and Responsibility Act (ECRA), N.J.S.A. 13:1K–6 to –13, T & E cannot sell the property until cleanup has been effected.

C

In March 1981 T & E sued Safety Light Corporation; USR Industries; [and] successor corporations of USRC. The suit is based on nuisance, negligence, misrepresentation and fraud, and strict liability for an abnormally-dangerous activity. * * *

* * *

When plaintiff's case concluded, the court granted defendant's motion to dismiss plaintiff's strict-liability claims. * * *

* * *

II

A

At the outset we must determine whether a property owner can assert against a predecessor in title a cause of action sounding in strict liability for abnormally-dangerous activities. Defendant suggests that only neighboring property owners, not successors in title, can maintain such a suit, and that successors in title must rely on contract law to recover from a prior owner. According to defendant, a wealth of case law, including the Third Circuit decision in Philadelphia Electric Co. v. Hercules, Inc., 762 F.2d 303 (1985), and the historical development of the abnormally-dangerous-activity doctrine support that distinction.

* * *

Drawing from the rationale of the Philadelphia Electric Co. opinion, defendant * * * stresses that a successor in title, unlike an innocent neighbor, could have inspected the property or demanded a warranty deed. We are not persuaded, however, that a landowner who engages in abnormally-dangerous activities should be liable only to neighboring property owners.

We recently chronicled the development of the abnormally-dangerous-activity doctrine in Ventron[.] [*Ventron* appears earlier in this chapter.] * * *

* * *

Although the rule grew out of a need to fill a void in the law governing the rights of adjacent landowners, another thread woven into its rationale justifies much broader application. See Comment, "The Rylands v. Fletcher Doctrine in America: Abnormally Dangerous, Ultrahazardous or Absolute Nuisance?", 1978 Ariz.St.L.J. 99, 105 (doctrine should not be limited to adjacent-landowner situations). The abnormally-dangerous-activity doctrine emphasizes the dangerousness and inappropriateness of the activity. Despite the social utility of the activity, that doctrine imposes liability on those who, for their own benefit, introduce an extraordinary risk of harm into the community.

The rule reflects a policy determination that such "enterprise[s] should bear the costs of accidents attributable to highly dangerous [or unusual activities]." Prosser, supra, at 555. Because some conditions and activities can be so hazardous and of "such relative infrequent occurrence," the risk of loss is justifiably allocated as a cost of business to the enterpriser who engages in such conduct. Although the law will tolerate the hazardous activity, the enterpriser must pay its way.

The rule recognizes an additional policy consideration: such enterprises are in "a better position to administer the unusual risk by passing it onto the public." Prosser, supra, § 75, at 537. Because of that opportunity, the enterprise can better bear the loss.

Neither policy rests on notions of property rights. Rather, the first serves to induce certain businesses to "internalize" the external costs of business, while the second seeks to shift a seemingly-inevitable loss onto the party deemed best able to shoulder it. Because the former owner of the property whose activities caused the hazard might have been in the best position to bear or spread the loss, liability for the harm caused by abnormally-dangerous activities does not necessarily cease with the transfer of property.

* * *

The same rationale is just as, if not more, persuasive when a seller who has engaged in an abnormally-dangerous activity and disposed of the by-products of that activity onto the property markets the land. With knowledge of its activity and of its use of the land, the seller is in a better position to prevent future problems arising from its use of the property. And again, allowing a buyer to recover would place liability on the party responsible for creating the hazardous condition and marketing the contaminated land. Moreover, in many respects that rationale echoes the underlying policy of the abnormally-dangerous-activity doctrine: certain enterprises should bear the costs attributable to their activities.

Defendant complains that holding a predecessor in title strictly liable for its abnormally-dangerous activities "would destroy the real estate market." Not likely. A buyer can assume the risk of harm from an abnormally-dangerous activity. Restatement (Second) of Torts, supra, § 523. To do so, a buyer need only knowingly and voluntarily encounter the risk. "As is" contracts, such as those involved here, do not satisfy that standard. Surely "a party[ ] ignorant of the presence of an abnormally dangerous condition [cannot] be held to have contractually assumed the risk posed by that condition merely by signing an 'as is' purchase contract." Amland Properties Corp. v. Aluminum Co. of Am., 711 F.Supp. 784, 803 n. 20 (D.N.J.1989). A real-estate contract that does not disclose the abnormally-dangerous condition or activity does not shield from liability the seller who created that condition or engaged in that activity.

Notes and Questions

1. Can *T & E Industries* be harmonized with *Philadelphia Electric*? Is there a rationale for allowing vertical actions in cases involving abnormally dangerous activity but not in nuisance cases? What two rationales did the court offer for extending liability to the remote seller? Do those policy objectives, which are relied upon in products liability cases and were discussed earlier in this chapter, have the same force in vertical cases? What may have motivated the court to jettison caveat emptor in *this* case? In hazardous waste cases generally? Why are "as is" contracts insufficient to create an assumption of the risk by the buyer?

2. In Russell–Stanley Corp. v. Plant Industries, 250 N.J.Super. 478, 595 A.2d 534 (1991), a tenant sued a landlord (CPI) asserting claims under a strict liability theory for cleanup costs incurred by the tenant because a former tenant had contaminated the property. Russell–Stanley contended that the landlord was responsible for cleanup costs of all contamination not caused by it, but by the prior tenant based on common law theories of strict liability and landlord-tenant law. The court refused to dismiss the tenant's claims, first pointing out that deposition testimony of an employee of the landlord showed that the landlord may have taken an active role in inspecting the property and the prior tenant's use of it; and that CPI also owned other pieces of industrial property surrounding the same parcels. It emphasized that the same policy reasons which justified the application of strict liability in *Ventron* and *T & E Industries* might well justify it in this case. Moreover, since the state could have ordered CPI to clean up the site rather than ordering the tenant as it did, that supported not allowing CPI to avoid any liability for contribution.

3. A Florida appellate court in Futura Realty v. Lone Star Building Centers (Eastern), Inc., 578 So.2d 363 (Fla.App.1991), refuses to follow New Jersey's lead in strict liability cases and prefers to allow traditional contractual protections between vertically related parties, rather than superimposing tort law:

> In the case at hand, Futura was simply not bringing a claim as an injured adjoining landowner. The commercial property vendor owes no duty for damage to the land to its vendee because the vendee can protect itself in a number of ways, including careful inspection and price negotiation. This is the vital legal and practical distinction between the duty owed a neighbor and the duty owed a successor in title which *T & E Industries* failed to identify.

3. KNOWLEDGE OF THE DANGER AS A PREREQUISITE TO STRICT LIABILITY

T & E INDUSTRIES v. SAFETY LIGHT CORPORATION

Supreme Court of New Jersey, 1991.
123 N.J. 371, 587 A.2d 1249.

[The court now addresses whether the depositing of radium tailings constituted an abnormally dangerous activity. The court quotes the six factors from Restatement (Second) of Torts § 520 and then continues its analysis:]

B

We focus now on the elements of the abnormally-dangerous-activity doctrine. That doctrine is premised on the principle that "one who carries on an abnormally dangerous activity is subject to liability for harm to the person, land or chattels of another resulting from the activity, although he has exercised the utmost care to prevent the harm." Restatement (Second) of Torts § 519. The Restatement sets forth six factors that a court should consider in determining whether an activity is "abnormally dangerous." [Restatement (Second) of Torts, supra, § 520.]

* * * Because of the interplay of [those] factors, it is not possible to reduce abnormally dangerous activities to any definition. Thus, a court must make the determination about the abnormally-dangerous character of an activity one case at a time. The Appellate Division failed to observe that mandate in this case and consequently gave Ventron too broad a reading in concluding that "the processing of radium and the disposal of its waste product is an abnormally dangerous activity as a matter of law."

Defendant does not dispute that liability can be imposed on enterprisers who engage in abnormally-dangerous activities that harm others; but it contends that such liability is contingent on proof that the enterpriser knew or should have known of the "abnormally dangerous character of the activity." According to defendant, absent such knowledge the enterpriser "is in no position to make the cost-benefit calculations that will enable him to spread the risk and engage in the optimal level of activity." Defendant argues that absent such an opportunity, the policy basis for imposing strict liability on those who engage in abnormally-dangerous activities, namely, cost spreading, cannot be realized.

Defendant adds that knowledge, or the ability to acquire such knowledge, must be assessed as of the time the enterpriser engaged in the activity, not at a later time—that is, if the risk of harm from the activity was scientifically unknowable at that time, an enterpriser should not be held liable. Defendant also insists that the inquiry must focus on the enterpriser's ability to learn of the risks inherent in the precise activity that causes harm, not merely of the hazards inherent in the business in general. Thus, defendant stresses that strict liability should be imposed in this case only if USRC knew in 1926 of the specific dangers inherent in the discarded tailings, not simply of those associated with the processing and handling of radium.

Defendant's argument poses an interesting question concerning the availability of a state-of-the-art defense—that is, the risk of the activity was scientifically unknowable at the time—to a strict-liability claim for abnormally-dangerous activities. It is a question we need not resolve here, however, because state-of-the-art becomes an issue only if we agree that knowledge is a prerequisite for strict-liability claims and if we accept defendant's narrow view of the "knowledge" inquiry.

* * *

But requirements such as "knowledge" and "foreseeability" smack of negligence and may be inappropriate in the realm of strict liability.

We need not, however, determine whether knowledge is a requirement in the context of a strict-liability claim predicated on an abnormally-dangerous activity. Even if the law imposes such a requirement, we are convinced, for the reasons set forth more fully below, that defendant should have known about the risks of its activity, and that its constructive knowledge would fully satisfy any such requirement.

C

That brings us to the question of whether defendant's activity was such as to fall within the meaning of "abnormally-dangerous activity." As indicated above, our opinion in Ventron instructs that in making such a determination a court must consider the factors set forth in the Restatement of Torts. As in Ventron, we apply those factors to the circumstances in this case.

Radium has always been and continues to be an extraordinarily-dangerous substance. Although radium processing has never been a common activity, the injudicious handling, processing, and disposal of radium has for decades caused concern; it has long been suspected of posing a serious threat to the health of those who are exposed to it. The harm that can result from excess radium exposure, namely, cancer, is undoubtedly great. In light of those suspicions and the magnitude of the harm, it is not surprising that in the 1930s and 1940s experts concluded that radon exposure should be limited. Wisely, the government now regulates such exposure.

Furthermore, although the risks involved in the processing and disposal of radium might be curtailed, one cannot safely dispose of radium by dumping it onto the vacant portions of an urban lot. Because of the extraordinarily-hazardous nature of radium, the processing and disposal of that substance is particularly inappropriate in an urban setting. We conclude that despite the usefulness of radium, defendant's processing, handling, and disposal of that substance under the facts of this case constituted an abnormally-dangerous activity. * * * Because plaintiff vacated the premises in response to the health concerns posed by the radium-contaminated site and because the danger to health is "the kind of harm, the possibility of which [made defendant's] activity abnormally dangerous," defendant is strictly liable for the resulting harm. Restatement of Torts, supra, § 519. Defendant's asserted lack of knowledge cannot relieve it of that liability.

Recall that defendant argues that the knowledge required is of the precise dangers associated with the disposal of the tailings, not merely those inherent in the processing and handling of radium. Defendant has not, however, cited any authority that supports such a narrow inquiry, nor do we believe that the focus should be that narrow.

Here defendant knew that it was processing radium, a substance concededly fraught with hazardous potential. It knew that its employees who handled radium should wear protective clothing; it knew that some employees who had ingested radium had developed cancer; and prior to the sale of the property, it knew that the inhalation of radon could cause lung cancer. Despite that wealth of knowledge concerning the harmful effects of radium exposure, defendant contends that it could not have known that disposal of the radium-saturated by-products behind the plant would produce a hazard. That contention appears to rest on the idea that somehow the radium's potential for harm miraculously disappeared once the material had been deposited in a vacant corner of an urban lot, or at the least that one might reasonably reach that conclusion—a proposition that we do not accept.

Surely someone engaged in a business as riddled with hazards as defendant's demonstrably was should realize the potential for harm in every aspect of that dangerous business. If knowledge be a requirement, defendant knew enough about the abnormally-dangerous character of radium processing to be charged with knowledge of the dangers of disposal.

* * *

IV

Out of an abundance of caution born of the occasional experience of having our opinions overread, we add a final note about the breadth of our opinion.

By no means do we signal an end to or undermining of that vast body of doctrine by which people regulate their everyday affairs in respect of the conveyancing of land. Today's decision is the proper judicial accommodation of those familiar principles of law to a highly unusual and highly dangerous form of human activity. The law has characterized that activity as "abnormally dangerous." Just as we would not countenance a doctrine of "buyer beware" in the context of fraudulent concealment of infestation of property, we do not wholly countenance a doctrine of "buyer beware" in this rare circumstance of demonstrably-tortious conduct that meets the "abnormally-dangerous" definition of tort liability.

Such conduct bespeaks a qualitative judgment about the way such an actor would expect the societal risks posed by that conduct to be borne. We need not decide today whether the abnormally-dangerous activity presented by this case is in any way comparable to that of, say, the operators of a small general store who, in the 1940s, may have sunk a gas tank on their property. A respectable argument could be made that although a statutory regime of cleanup responsibility, as for example under ECRA or the Spill Fund, might extend to them, it does not follow that that statutory responsibility subsumes in any way the "abnormally dangerous" nature of the activity posed by this case—not because the general store operators are "small fry," but because their activity does not meet the Restatement criteria, particularly factor (d). Their relationships to the intervening title holders may be affected by other principles of law, but not by the principles that apply in this case. We are mindful that what we perceive as a toxic substance today may have been a familiar household commodity in years past.

Notes and Questions

1. The threshold question is whether defendant's knowledge or appreciation of the danger should be a prerequisite to strict liability. What is your opinion? In Chapter 7, we explore that issue as it relates to toxic products where the courts have generally held that a party may defend on the ground that a risk was not scientifically knowable. This defense is sometimes referred to inexactly as the state-of-the-art defense, but is more accurately described as the state-of-knowledge defense. If the state of knowledge is relevant in abnormally dangerous activity cases, should it be plaintiff's burden to establish that the defendant had knowledge of its abnormally dangerous character? Should it be sufficient that reasonable persons in defendant's shoes would have known? Or should any knowledge within the relevant technical, industrial, or scientific communities be sufficient for liability?

Rather than place the burden of proof on plaintiff, should it be considered as an affirmative defense where the defendant bears the burden of pleading and proof on the issue?

2. On the facts in *T & E Industries*, did defendant really have knowledge of the dangerousness of buried *tailings*, as opposed to the dangers associated with use of radium by its employees? Does knowledge of the latter necessarily imply knowledge of the former? Does it matter that other firms similarly situated as USRC in the 1920s and 1930s also buried their tailings? On this point, see Fortier v. Flambeau Plastics Co., 164 Wis.2d 639, 476 N.W.2d 593 (App.1991), where the court held that defendant generators of hazardous waste did not engage in abnormally dangerous activity by depositing such wastes in city-owned landfills because it was a matter of common usage, engaged in by households, municipalities, and private industry, and was entirely lawful when done. Moreover, it concluded that the value to the community of such practices outweighed the dangers,

then perceived, that it created. How might these points bear on the state of knowledge issue?

3. In 1991 the American Law Institute published a Reporters' Study entitled "Enterprise Responsibility for Personal Injury." In the section on standards for environmental liability the authors reviewed Restatement (Second) of Torts §§ 519 and 520 on strict liability for abnormally dangerous activity. Among the issues it addressed were two touched upon in both *T & E Industries* and *Fortier* : Should the state of the defendant's knowledge regarding the abnormally dangerous nature of the activity be relevant and should state-of-the-art be a defense? The discussion of those issues follows:

B. Liability Standards

The common law of environmental liability has always been a mixture of negligence and strict liability. * * *

The primary arguments for imposing strict liability in the kinds of environmental liability claims at the core of the current concern extend a bit beyond the factors set out in the Restatement. To prove negligence plaintiffs must show that the defendant's actions were unreasonable at the time they were taken and that the injury caused was foreseeable. The former requires proof that on balance the costs of precautions would have been foreseeably lower than the cost of the accidents that were risked by the failure to take these precautions. The difficulty of proving these elements of a negligence case when the defendant's activity occurred years before the case is tried is obvious, especially if there is scanty documentation of the character of the activity and the state of the defendant's knowledge at the time. * * *

On the other hand, the courts and the Restatement have always recognized that the decision whether an activity is ultrahazardous or (more recently) abnormally dangerous is context-dependent. Not only the degree of danger posed by the activity, but its location and value to the community must be considered in deciding whether the activity warrants the imposition of strict liability for its consequences. * * *

Nonetheless, we are mindful of the differences between product and environmental injuries. Unlike product liability, in which the price of products may vary with the degree of risk posed, and in which many (though not all) victims are purchasers who may be warned of product risks, virtually all the victims of environmental risk are "strangers" to the enterprise that creates the risk and can do little if anything to protect themselves. It therefore makes good sense that there be greater scope for the imposition of strict liability in the environmental field than in product liability.

The approach we favor would refine the Restatement tradition reflected in Section 520 by making it clear that an environmentally risky activity should not be considered "abnormally dangerous" if the scientific state of knowledge at the time gave no signal that the activity posed a substantial risk to human health. On the other hand, strict liability could be imposed regardless of whether there was technology available at the time that could have avoided or reduced the risk in question. Thus, a limited "state of knowledge" defense would be available even if the other factors set out in the Restatement were satisfied, but a "state of the art" defense would not be available. In many environmental cases a state of knowledge defense probably would have less practical significance than it would in product liability litigation because of general awareness of the risks associated with industrial emissions. The less recent the activity in question, however, the more impact the defense would have. And the defense could play a role in reducing the overdeterrence that some commentators assert stems from the threat of uncompromising strict liability. The availability of the defense might also help to restore the market for insurance against environmental liability, the vehicle that assures compensation to victims who have legally valid claims within the standard of liability we recommend.

2 American Law Institute, Enterprise Responsibility for Personal Injury 365–368 (1991). Copyright 1991 by The American Law Institute. Reprinted with the permission of The American Law Institute.

Do you agree with the Reporters' position of allowing a state-of-knowledge defense, but not a state-of-the-art defense? How should society's ever-increasing understanding of environmental dangers be accounted for in strict liability cases?

Problem

From 1977 to 1987, CHEMCO, Inc. (Chemco) manufactured chlorine using the mercury cell process at its facility on the edge of a riverside industrial park in Newburg, New Union. Louise River bisects Newburg with the industrial park upriver about two miles from the center of town. The manufacturing process produced a waste in the form of a wet, mercury-contaminated sludge.

From 1977 to 1980, prior to the introduction of its state-of-the-art waste handling and disposal process, Chemco placed the sludge into concrete lined basins. The sludge was allowed to settle in the basins, which were separate from the facility's waste water treatment system. During those three years, following the settling process, Chemco separated reusable brine at the top of the basins from the heavy sludge which sank to the bottom of the basins. Mr. David Doubilet managed the Chemco facility throughout 1977–1987.

In 1987, Chemco sold the chlorine facility to Pinatubo Chemical Co. (PCC). PCC retained David Doubilet as plant manager and, under his supervision, made further improvements to its waste handling and disposal process.

In 1992, following an unusual number of neurological disorders and other health problems in the neighborhood, two hundred area residents abutting the industrial park brought a class action against PCC and twenty other manufacturing facilities located in the park, and each of their plant managers. The complaint demanded $100 million in compensatory damages for personal injuries and diminution of property values as a result of chemical contamination of their groundwater, and $200 million in punitive damages for knowing concealment of the contamination. Plaintiffs' class action relied on theories of trespass, public and private nuisance, negligence, and strict liability for abnormally dangerous activities. In their complaint, plaintiffs' alleged that pre-suit hydrogeological studies revealed that traces of mercury threatened the groundwater and were present in the wells of several class members.

After plaintiffs' complaint was filed, Mr. Doubilet informs his counsel (separate from counsel representing PCC), that he is aware of facts that would be prejudicial to both himself and PCC. On three or four different occasions that he can't recall exactly, before Chemco sold the facility to PCC, he observed one of Chemco's officers overseeing several other employees drain the concrete basins into an outflow which flowed through its primary industrial sewer into the Louise River. Doubilet states that he also saw liquid contents at the bottom of the basins seeping into the ground.

Mr. Doubilet tells his lawyer that he does not know whether that drainage or seepage reached the groundwater table eight feet beneath the basins and about three hundred yards to the north of the nearest residential well, but his "guess" is that the mercury-contaminated liquid probably did, or probably will, spill or leak into the groundwater. The facility never has had a permit to dispose of hazardous waste on the ground or into the groundwater, and never has disclosed to any regulatory authority any nonpermitted disposal of hazardous waste. While acknowledging that he is no expert in hydrogeology, he recalls once being advised by the New Union Department of Natural Resources, at the time the industrial park was obtaining the necessary permits, that the area had experienced problems with water wells because the groundwater moved very rapidly through the kind of soil prevalent in that area. Moreover, he recalls being told that anything reaching the Louise River had the potential of contaminating water supplies in the area.

At all times since 1977, federal and New Union laws have prohibited the disposal by any person of hazardous waste (including mercury-contaminated sludge) into the environment (including the groundwater) without a permit. New Union environmental protection statutes, like the federal law, define disposal to mean "the discharge, deposit, injection, dumping, spilling, leaking or placing" of hazardous wastes and defines persons to include "any individual, corporation or other entity who knows or should know of a disposal of hazardous waste." Any violation of these federal and state laws carries civil penalties of $25,000 per day, and constitutes a felony.

Part A

You are counsel for PCC. Among the tasks you need to accomplish is to evaluate plaintiffs' legal theories. You would like to move to dismiss at least a few of the counts based on nuisance, public and private, and trespass, as early in the case as possible. *Assuming* that traces of mercury are found in plaintiffs' wells and in groundwater samples and also assuming that those traces could have (but not necessarily did) originated at PCC's facility, evaluate the public and private nuisance and trespass claims.

Part B

Assume you are counsel for Mr. Doubilet. Your objective is to get your client out of this mess without exposing him to criminal or civil liabilities. Counsel for the class has noticed Doubilet's deposition. Doubilet has shared with you all of the information described above. How do you advise your client to respond to the inevitable questions that will be directed at him regarding his knowledge and participation in the potentially damaging events?

Part C

You are one of the class counsel and have interviewed at least ten residents of the area near the Riverside Industrial Park. Two of your clients were formerly employed by Chemco, but lost their jobs when the plant was sold to PCC. One formerly worked for the cost control manager and he recalls on at least two occasions that the manager had instructed him (and a few others) to drain the contents of the basins into the outflow because they were getting too full. As Chairperson of the Class Coordinating Committee, you know that this newly discovered information is potentially explosive. One threshold question you must resolve is whether to recommend amending the complaint to name Chemco as a defendant. Discuss the strategic concerns relating to instituting suit against Chemco based on the same nuisance and trespass theories and strict liability.

Part D

Assume PCC cleans up the contamination on the property following an EPA or state order to do so. Can PCC sue Chemco on a theory of trespass, nuisance, or strict liability to recover the costs of cleanup?

Alternatively, assume that PCC entered into a settlement agreement with other defendants to pay the class a total of $20 million. If PCC's portion of the settlement is $1 million, can it sue Chemco for recovery of that amount? What tort theories will it rely upon? What other factors might bear upon its ability to recover from Chemco?

Chapter Five

REMEDIES AND COMPENSABLE INTERESTS

Determining that a defendant should be subject to liability under a theory of trespass, nuisance, negligence, or strict liability for an environmental tort is not the end of the inquiry. One of the most troublesome and ancient issues in environmental litigation is the court's determination of the appropriate remedy. This Chapter considers (1) the conflicts between injunctive remedies and damages; and (2) where damages may be appropriate, the types of harms for which they are awardable.

A. INJUNCTIONS: THE COMPARATIVE INJURY CALCULUS

Many of the cases considered in Chapters 3 and 4 have discussed the question of what remedies are appropriate in environmental tort cases. The debate over the appropriate remedies in nuisance suits is not new, and the decisions reveal that the corrective justice view has been in conflict with the utilitarian view for at least a century. Should a plaintiff who has suffered and will continue to suffer substantial harm from a nuisance caused by the defendant's business operations be entitled to injunctive relief to abate the nuisance, when the consequence may be to adversely affect defendant's investment and socially useful operations or shut down such operations entirely? In this section we review briefly three decisions, all nearly ninety years old, which could easily arise today. Each involves paradigmatic claims in nuisance, the staple of environmental torts.

1. First, let us consider two opinions, often cited or quoted, that reflect a strong sense of corrective justice principles. One early case is Whalen v. Union Bag & Paper Co., 208 N.Y. 1, 101 N.E. 805 (1913), where the plaintiff was the owner of a 255–acre farm located on a stream. The defendant's pulp mill, a few miles up the stream, represented a $1 million investment and employed 400 to 500 persons. The mill discharged into the stream large quantities of a liquid effluent

containing sulphuric acid, lime, sulphur and waste material, such as pulp, resins, sawdust, and fiber. At the trial court, the plaintiff secured damages of $312 per year, and an injunction. The decision was reversed by the appellate court. The New York Court of Appeals reinstated the injunction:

> The setting aside of the injunction was apparently induced by a consideration of the great loss likely to be inflicted on the defendant by the granting of the injunction as compared with the small injury done to the plaintiff's land by that portion of the pollution which was regarded as attributable to the defendant. Such a balancing of injuries cannot be justified by the circumstances of this case. * * *

> One of the troublesome phases of this kind of litigation is the difficulty of deciding when an injunction shall issue in a case where the evidence clearly establishes an unlawful invasion of a plaintiff's rights, but his actual injury from the continuance of the alleged wrong will be small as compared with the great loss which will be caused by the issuance of the injunction. * * * Even as reduced at the Appellate Division, the damages to the plaintiff's farm amount to $100 a year. It can hardly be said that this injury is unsubstantial, even if we should leave out of consideration the peculiarly noxious character of the pollution of which the plaintiff complains. The waste from the defendant's mill is very destructive, both to vegetable and animal life, and tends to deprive the waters with which it is mixed of their purifying qualities. It should be borne in mind also that there is no claim on the part of the defendant that the nuisance may become less injurious in the future. Although the damage to the plaintiff may be slight as compared with the defendant's expense of abating the condition, that is not a good reason for refusing an injunction. Neither courts of equity nor law can be guided by such a rule, for if followed to its logical conclusion it would deprive the poor litigant of his little property by giving it to those already rich. * * *

2. A similar position was taken in McCleery v. Highland Boy Gold Mining Co., 140 Fed. 951 (C.C.Utah 1904), in which the plaintiffs were owners of farms located near defendant's mine and smelter, which employed 450 workers. The fumes from defendant's operations containing sulfur dioxide were injurious to the plaintiff's crops and animals. In discussing whether to grant the injunction, the court stated:

> The title of the complainants to their respective farms is admitted. The substantial invasion of their rights to some extent and the purpose to continue this invasion is also admitted. * * * The substantial contention of the defendant is that it is engaged in a business of such extent and involving such a large capital that the value of the plaintiffs' rights sought to be protected is relatively small, and that therefore an injunction, destroying the defendant's business, would inflict a much greater injury on it than it would confer benefit upon the plaintiffs. Under such circumstances, it is

asserted, courts of equity refuse to protect legal rights by injunction and remit the injured party to the partial relief to be obtained in actions at law. * * *

I am unable to accede to this statement of the law. If correct, the property of the poor is held by uncertain tenure, and the constitutional provisions forbidding the taking of property for private use would be of no avail. As a substitute it would be declared that private property is held on the condition that it may be taken by any person who can make a more profitable use of it, provided that such person shall be answerable in damage to the former owner for his injury. * * * Public policy, I think, is more concerned in the protection of individual rights than in the profits to inure to individuals by the invasion of those rights.

* * *

The court, nevertheless, refused an abatement order on the ground that plaintiffs had delayed seeking an injunction until two or three years after the damage had commenced, during which time the defendant had made substantial additional investments in its operation. Permanent damages were, however, awarded. *Whalen* and *McCleery* continue to be relied upon as articulating the rationale for granting an injunction regardless of the comparative "injuries" of the parties. If "damage to the plaintiff [is] slight as compared with defendant's expense of abating the condition," (*Whalen*) what other actions might defendant take? In Chapter 3 you saw that Restatement §§ 822 and 826 (and comments thereto) imply that a "balancing of the equities" is appropriate in injunction cases, but not necessary when damages are sought, so long as the defendant can afford to pay damages without ceasing its operations. Are these cases necessarily inconsistent with that position?

3.   Contrary to McCleery and Whalen, is the decision in Madison v. Ducktown Sulphur, Copper & Iron Co., 113 Tenn. 331, 83 S.W. 658 (1904), where the Tennessee Supreme Court surveyed virtually all of the arguments, pro and con, for granting or denying an injunction. Here the plaintiffs were farmers who suffered crop damage, timber damage, and ill health, who sought to enjoin defendants' copper mining operations using an open air roasting process that produced large volumes of sulfurous smoke. Since roasting was the only known method of ore reduction, an abatement order would terminate their operations, employing 2500 and representing one-half the tax assessment for the county. The lower court granted the injunction, but the Supreme Court held for the defendants. While recognizing that defendants' operations clearly created a nuisance, it also recognized that the availability of injunctive relief is discretionary and relied upon two principles of equity that compelled denial of the injunction.

First, undue delay in seeking an injunction—or laches—was found to be a bar to equitable relief because plaintiffs had waited for ten years before instituting suit. The court developed the second ground for denying the injunction in the following excerpts from the court's opinion, which focus on the comparative injury analysis:

> In order to protect by the injunction several small tracts of land, aggregating in value less than $1,000, we are asked to destroy other property worth nearly $2,000,000, and wreck two great mining and manufacturing enterprises, that are engaged in work of very great importance, not only to their owners, but to the state, and to the whole country as well, to depopulate a large town, and deprive thousands of working people of their homes and livelihood, and scatter them broadcast. The result would be practically a confiscation of the property of the defendants for the benefit of the complainants—an appropriation without compensation. The defendants cannot reduce their ores in a manner different from that they are now employing, and there is no more remote place to which they can remove. The decree asked for would deprive them of all of their rights. * * * [I]n case[s] of conflicting rights, where neither party can enjoy his own without in some measure restricting the liberty of the other in the use of property, the law must make the best arrangement it can between the contending parties, with a view to preserving to each one the largest measure of liberty possible under the circumstances. * * *

Notes and Questions

What "rights" of the defendant is the court referring to? Is the court totally rejecting corrective justice or only insofar as an injunction is concerned? Does an award of damages sufficiently protect the rights of the plaintiffs? Do injunction proceedings necessarily require a balancing process that weighs utilitarian considerations? As these decisions illustrate, the courts often struggle with the propriety of granting injunctive relief where the effect may be to curtail or eliminate the defendant's operations. Injunctions in environmental tort cases can be a powerful remedy and the only remedy that is capable of assuring that the harm will be abated or will not be repeated. Recall that in *Wilsonville v. SCA Services* in Chapter 3, the Illinois Supreme Court enjoined the operation of defendant's hazardous waste site and required it to restore the property to its previous condition. The cases quoted above demonstrate that these issues are not of recent origin, but only the nature of operations have changed.

B. STANDARDS FOR GRANTING INJUNCTIONS: BALANCING THE EQUITIES

An injunction may be "prohibitory," forbidding a defendant from acting in a certain manner; or "mandatory," requiring the defendant to undertake some affirmative action to ameliorate an existing or prospective harm. See generally Dan B. Dobbs, Law of Remedies § 2.9 (2d ed. 1993); reconsider also the discussion of injunctive remedies in *Village of Wilsonville v. SCA Services* in Chapter 3.

Because injunctions are a form of equitable relief and courts possess wide-ranging discretion in determining whether to issue such relief, they vary widely in their terms and application. Restatement (Second) of Torts § 936 sets forth the factors that are relevant when an injunction is sought:

(1) The appropriateness of the remedy of injunction against a tort depends upon a comparative appraisal of all of the factors in the case, including the following primary factors:

(a) the nature of the interest to be protected,

(b) the relative adequacy to the plaintiff of injunction and of other remedies,

(c) any unreasonable delay by the plaintiff in bringing suit,

(d) any related misconduct on the part of the plaintiff,

(e) the relative hardship likely to result to defendant if an injunction is granted and to plaintiff if it is denied,

(f) the interests of third persons and of the public, and

(g) the practicability of framing and enforcing the order of judgment.

These factors usually compel the court to engage in some type of balancing process in deciding whether to issue injunctive relief and the precise nature and terms of the order granting the relief. Section 941 specifically addresses subsection (e), the balancing of the relative hardships which flow if the relief sought is granted or denied, and points out the difficult choices which courts face in making the determination of whether to grant injunctive relief. It provides that courts have at least three possible solutions: (1) holding that there is no actionable nuisance and that the plaintiff must simply bear the harm as a consequence of living in an industrial society; (2) holding that there is a nuisance for purposes of a damage action, but refusing the injunction—that is, the plaintiff must bear the harm, but will receive compensation; and (3) holding that the plaintiff is to be relieved from the harm by an injunction. Restatement (Second) of Torts § 941, comment c.

The following material from the influential work of Professor Dobbs surveys the law respecting the balancing process that occurs in environmental nuisance cases:

DAN B. DOBBS, LAW OF REMEDIES § 5.7(2)
765–70 (2d ed. 1993) (footnotes omitted).

BALANCING HARDSHIPS AND EQUITIES

Threshold, rights, and remedies types of balancing. The discretion in equity to deny, limit or shape relief is reflected in the flexible process of balancing hardships and equities. Relief is limited or expanded in accord with that balance. Balancing occurs in several distinct ways. There is some "threshold balancing," as it has been called, to determine whether the plaintiff has standing in equity in the light of unclean hands, estoppel, laches or the like. Another kind of balancing occurs on the substantive issues themselves in some cases. Nuisance cases, for example, are largely a matter of degree, so a discretionary kind of weighing of relative hardships is almost always involved in such cases. A third level of balancing occurs when the court, having found a nuisance or statutory violation to exist, must determine whether to use a damages remedy or an injunctive remedy. And finally, a similar balancing or discretion is invoked at a fourth stage when the court fixes the exact scope and commands of the injunction issued.

Rights-balancing. In determining whether the defendant's activity is a nuisance at all, courts traditionally balanced the benefits derived from that activity with the harm it caused. A balance of harms, costs, utilities and hardships suggests, for example, that a very valuable industry which is causing annoyance to neighbors might not be a nuisance at all in the light of the relative utilities. In such a case there are no remedial issues at all because there are no rights to be redressed.

The "modern" view taken by the Restatement would hold that some conditions constitute a nuisance even if the nuisance is the result of a socially useful activity. In this view, a balancing of utilities, costs or hardships would be important, but only on the choice of remedies, not on the initial question whether a nuisance existed. The two approaches are quite different, but both recognize that a balancing of utilities or hardships on the remedies issue is distinct from a balancing of utilities on the question whether a nuisance exists at all. The main concern of this text is the balance of utilities or hardships in determining the appropriate remedy and in determining its scope.

Remedies balancing generally. When a nuisance is found to exist, either on the balance of utilities or otherwise, it is still important to balance or re-balance the relative costs and hardships in determining the appropriate remedy. At the remedies stage of the claim, courts routinely reconsider the balance to determine whether an injunction should be granted or whether the plaintiff should be limited to some other remedy such as damages.

Specifically, courts consider the public benefit derived from the defendant's operations, the public benefits that might result from a grant of the injunction, the relative hardships or the economic costs the parties would be likely to suffer if the nuisance is or is not enjoined, and the equities between the parties such as laches, bad faith or misconduct. This new balancing of public and private benefits and harms may lead the court to deny an injunction and leave the plaintiff to a damages remedy on the ground that an injunction would do more harm than good.

* * *

Hardships and economic waste. Courts also take into account the relative hardships of the parties. The hardship that may be worked upon the defendant if the injunction goes is compared to the hardship that may be wreaked upon the plaintiff if it does not. The plaintiff's hardship in nuisance cases is often expressed as an intangible impairment of enjoyment of the quality of living on the property; but this impairment, if substantial, will be reflected in diminished property values as well. In any event, if sufficiently proven, the hardship may outweigh the tangible economic losses the defendant will suffer if its business is enjoined.

The hardship attributed to the defendant is often more frankly economic, and courts often mention the investment that would be lost if the injunction goes. This calls, however, for a practical judgment. If there are reasonable alternatives available to the defendant that will accomplish his goals without causing a nuisance, the supposed hardship counts for little. The same point can be recognized in decisions that grant an injunction against a full-scale operation by the defendant but leave it open to him to operate in ways that cause less harm.

* * *

Public interests against the injunction. A public interest in favor of the defendant and against the injunctive remedy is sometimes found in the fact that the defendant's nuisance is a business or factory that employs individuals and brings economic well-being to the community. Much of what goes under the name of hardship is economic cost. Economic costs, though they do not directly harm the whole community, may do so indirectly. If an injunction closing or limiting the operation of the defendant's business will cause the loss of an investment, courts weigh this factor against the injunction, or at least against it in its broadest and most destructive form.

Public interests favoring the injunction. On the other hand, there may be a public interest in terminating a nuisance causing environmental pollution, even if that nuisance is caused by a conduct that otherwise contributes to the public weal. Poisoning the water supply of a town could hardly be justified even by the most important of industries. Much serious environmental pollution will generate strong public interest reasons in support of an injunction. In less obvious cases, public interest balancing may be controversial and is likely to involve at least some element of political or social decision-making outside the traditional judicial role.

However, the political or social balancing may have been done before trial by the legislature itself. When the defendant's conduct violates a statute, it is possible that the legislature has already weighed the competing interests and has reflected its judgment in the statute. In such a case the court may be willing to discount its own assessment of public interests and issue the injunction authorized by statute.

The judicial decision which is most often cited or relied upon in these disputes over remedies in environmental tort cases is *Boomer v. Atlantic Cement Company.*

BOOMER v. ATLANTIC CEMENT COMPANY, INC.

Court of Appeals of New York, 1970.
26 N.Y.2d 219, 309 N.Y.S.2d 312, 257 N.E.2d 870.

BERGAN, J.

Defendant operates a large cement plant near Albany. These are actions for injunction and damages by neighboring land owners alleging injury to property from dirt, smoke and vibration emanating from the plant. A nuisance has been found after trial, temporary damages have been allowed; but an injunction has been denied.

* * *

But there is now before the court private litigation in which individual property owners have sought specific relief from a single plant operation. The threshold question raised by the division of view on this appeal is whether the court should resolve the litigation between the parties now before it as equitably as seems possible; or whether, seeking promotion of the general public welfare, it should channel private litigation into broad public objectives.

A court performs its essential function when it decides the rights of parties before it. Its decision of private controversies may sometimes greatly affect public issues. Large questions of law are often resolved by the manner in which private litigation is decided. But this is normally an incident to the court's main function to settle controversy. It is a rare exercise of judicial power to use a decision in private litigation as a purposeful mechanism to achieve direct public objectives greatly beyond the rights and interests before the court.

Effective control of air pollution is a problem presently far from solution even with the full public and financial powers of government. In large measure adequate technical procedures are yet to be developed and some that appear possible may be economically impracticable.

It seems apparent that the amelioration of air pollution will depend on technical research in great depth; on a carefully balanced consideration of the economic impact of close regulation; and of the actual effect on public health. It is likely to require massive public expenditure and to demand more than any local community can accomplish and to depend on regional and interstate controls.

A court should not try to do this on its own as a by-product of private litigation, and it seems manifest that the judicial establishment is neither equipped in the limited nature of any judgment it can pronounce nor prepared to lay down and implement an effective policy for the elimination of air pollution. This is an area beyond the circumference of one private lawsuit. It is a direct responsibility for government and should not thus be undertaken as an incident to solving a dispute between property owners and a single cement plant—one of many—in the Hudson River valley.

The cement making operations of defendant have been found by the court at Special Term to have damaged the nearby properties of plaintiffs in these two actions. That court, as it has been noted, accordingly found defendant maintained a nuisance and this has been affirmed at the Appellate Division. The total damage to plaintiffs' properties is, however, relatively small in comparison with the value of defendant's operation and with the consequences of the injunction which plaintiffs seek.

The ground for the denial of injunction, notwithstanding the finding both that there is a nuisance and that plaintiffs have been damaged substantially, is the large disparity in economic consequences of the nuisance and of the injunction. This theory cannot, however, be sustained without overruling a doctrine which has been consistently reaffirmed in several leading cases in this court and which has never been disavowed here, namely that where a nuisance has been found and where there has been any substantial damage shown by the party complaining an injunction will be granted.

The rule in New York has been that such a nuisance will be enjoined although marked disparity be shown in economic consequence between the effect of the injunction and the effect of the nuisance.

The problem of disparity in economic consequence was sharply in focus in Whalen v. Union Bag & Paper Co. (208 N.Y. 1). A pulp mill entailing an investment of more than a million dollars polluted a stream in which plaintiff, who owned a farm, was "a lower riparian owner". The economic loss to plaintiff from this pollution was small. This court, reversing the Appellate Division, reinstated the injunction granted by the Special Term against the argument of the mill owner that in view of "the slight advantage to plaintiff and the great loss that will be inflicted on defendant" an injunction should not be granted. "Such a balancing of injuries cannot be justified by the circumstances of this case." He continued: "Although the damage to the plaintiff may be slight as compared with the defendant's expense of abating the condition, that is not a good reason for refusing an injunction."

* * * This states a rule that had been followed in this court with marked consistency.

* * * Thus if, within Whalen v. Union Bag & Paper Co. which authoritatively states the rule in New York, the damage to plaintiffs in these present cases from defendant's cement plant is "not unsubstantial," an injunction should follow.

Although the court at Special Term and the Appellate Division held that injunction should be denied, it was found that plaintiffs had been damaged in various specific amounts up to the time of the trial and damages to the respective plaintiffs were awarded for those amounts. The effect of this was, injunction having been denied, plaintiffs could maintain successive actions at law for damages thereafter as further damage was incurred.

* * *

This result at Special Term and at the Appellate Division is a departure from a rule that has become settled; but to follow the rule literally in these cases would be to close down the plant at once. This court is fully agreed to avoid that immediately drastic remedy; the difference in view is how best to avoid it.[6]

One alternative is to grant the injunction but postpone its effect to a specified future date to give opportunity for technical advances to permit defendant to eliminate the nuisance; another is to grant the injunction conditioned on the payment of permanent damages to plaintiffs which would compensate them for the total economic loss to their property present and future caused by defendant's operations. For reasons which will be developed the court chooses the latter alternative.

If the injunction were to be granted unless within a short period— e.g., 18 months—the nuisance be abated by improved methods, there would be no assurance that any significant technical improvement would occur.

The parties could settle this private litigation at any time if defendant paid enough money and the imminent threat of closing the plant would build up the pressure on defendant. If there were no improved techniques found, there would inevitably be applications to the court at Special Term for extensions of time to perform on showing of good faith efforts to find such techniques.

Moreover, techniques to eliminate dust and other annoying by-products of cement making are unlikely to be developed by any research the defendant can undertake within any short period, but will depend on the total resources of the cement industry Nationwide and throughout the world. The problem is universal wherever cement is made.

For obvious reasons the rate of the research is beyond control of defendant. If at the end of 18 months the whole industry has not found a technical solution a court would be hard put to close down this one cement plant if due regard be given to equitable principles.

On the other hand, to grant the injunction unless defendant pays plaintiffs such permanent damages as may be fixed by the court seems to do justice between the contending parties. All of the attributions of economic loss to the properties on which plaintiffs' complaints are based will have been redressed.

The nuisance complained of by these plaintiffs may have other public or private consequences, but these particular parties are the only

---

6. Respondent's investment in the plant is in excess of $45,000,000. There are over 300 people employed there.

ones who have sought remedies and the judgment proposed will fully redress them. The limitation of relief granted is a limitation only within the four corners of these actions and does not foreclose public health or other public agencies from seeking proper relief in a proper court.

It seems reasonable to think that the risk of being required to pay permanent damages to injured property owners by cement plant owners would itself be a reasonably effective spur to research for improved techniques to minimize nuisance.

The power of the court to condition on equitable grounds the continuance of an injunction on the payment of permanent damages seems undoubted.

The damage base here suggested is consistent with the general rule in those nuisance cases where damages are allowed. "Where a nuisance is of such a permanent and unabatable character that a single recovery can be had, including the whole damage past and future resulting therefrom, there can be but one recovery" (66 C.J.S., Nuisances § 140, p. 947). * * *

The present cases and the remedy here proposed are in a number of other respects rather similar to Northern Indiana Public Serv. Co. v. Vesey (210 Ind. 338) decided by the Supreme Court of Indiana. The gases, odors, ammonia and smoke from the Northern Indiana company's gas plant damaged the nearby Vesey greenhouse operation. An injunction and damages were sought, but an injunction was denied and the relief granted was limited to permanent damages "present, past, and future."

Denial of injunction was grounded on a public interest in the operation of the gas plant and on the court's conclusion "that less injury would be occasioned by requiring the appellant [Public Service] to pay the appellee [Vesey] all damages suffered by it * * * than by enjoining the operation of the gas plant; and that the maintenance and operation of the gas plant should not be enjoined."

The Indiana Supreme Court opinion continued: "When the trial court refused injunctive relief to the appellee upon the ground of public interest in the continuance of the gas plant, it properly retained jurisdiction of the case and awarded full compensation to the appellee. This is upon the general equitable principle that equity will give full relief in one action and prevent a multiplicity of suits."

It was held that in this type of continuing and recurrent nuisance permanent damages were appropriate. See also City of Amarillo v. Ware (120 Tex. 456) where recurring overflows from a system of storm sewers were treated as the kind of nuisance for which permanent depreciation of value of affected property would be recoverable.

* * *

Thus it seems fair to both sides to grant permanent damages to plaintiffs which will terminate this private litigation. The theory of damage is the "servitude on land" of plaintiffs imposed by defendant's nuisance.

The judgment, by allowance of permanent damages imposing a servitude on land, which is the basis of the actions, would preclude future recovery by plaintiffs or their grantees.

This should be placed beyond debate by a provision of the judgment that the payment by defendant and the acceptance by plaintiffs of permanent damages found by the court shall be in compensation for a servitude on the land.

Although the Trial Term has found permanent damages as a possible basis of settlement of the litigation, on remission the court should be entirely free to re-examine this subject. It may again find the permanent damage already found; or make new findings.

The orders should be reversed, without costs, and the cases remitted to Supreme Court, Albany County to grant an injunction which shall be vacated upon payment by defendant of such amounts of permanent damage to the respective plaintiffs as shall for this purpose be determined by the court.

The dissent by JASEN, J. is omitted.

Notes and Questions

1. Do you agree with the majority? Does the majority's approach create for polluters the power to condemn and appropriate a neighbor's property by paying permanent damages? Did the court overrule *Whalen*? The dissenting opinion labels the effect of the majority's holding as creating an "inverse condemnation" by a private party? Do you agree? For a discussion of *Boomer*, see Comment, Involuntary Sale Damages in Permanent Nuisance Cases: A Bigger Bang From Boomer, 14 B.C. Envtl. Aff. L. Rev. 61 (1986).

2. What do you think of the court's statement that "[f]or obvious reasons the rate of the research is beyond control of defendant"? Consider the comment of the New Jersey Supreme Court in the asbestos products liability personal injury suit Beshada v. Johns–Manville Products Corp., 90 N.J. 191, 447 A.2d 539 (N.J.1982) which is discussed in Chapter 7: "[T]he level of investment in safety research by manufacturers is one determinant of the state-of-the-art at any given time. Fairness suggests that manufacturers not be excused from liability because their prior inadequate investment in safety rendered the hazards of their product unknowable." Are the situations comparable? Are product and nuisance cases, or the role of federal statutory programs, sufficiently different to explain the distinction?

3. The court is visibly concerned with the fact that its role is to adjudicate the dispute before it between two private parties, yet a full resolution of the problem the case presents would require the involvement of numerous public and private groups not before it, such as the legislature,

industry groups, and other experts and affected parties. Do you agree that a court of general jurisdiction should be concerned that the factual and policy record before it does not permit it to resolve systemic issues?

4. The opinion claims that courts are poorly equipped to reach a just solution to the problem of airborne pollution from an industrial enterprise because they lack all of the information needed to devise and implement such a solution. Keeping in mind modern liberal discovery rules and the capacity of federal courts, and many state courts, to appoint their own experts, can you make the opposite argument?

5. Should a comparative injury calculus be the primary determinant in these cases? In what kinds of cases will it be most appropriate to adopt this test as the primary consideration? What if the plaintiff was a representative of a class action of all residences within two miles downwind of the plant? Would the court reach a different conclusion? What might be the consequences of awarding permanent damages to hundreds of residents? Recall that the Illinois Supreme Court in Wilsonville v. SCA Services, 86 Ill.2d 1, 55 Ill.Dec. 499, 426 N.E.2d 824 (1981) was not impressed with such an analysis when it granted full injunctive relief, ordering total restoration of the land to its pre-nuisance condition.

Does it make a difference that in *Wilsonville* the very nature of the defendant's activity was to deal in and dispose of chemical wastes that were harmful, whereas in *Boomer* the pollution was only a necessary incident and by-product of an otherwise "clean" business? Or can the cases be explained by the fact that in *Boomer* the nuisance was not as potentially as harmful to the health of the residents as in *Wilsonville*?

6. In a subsequent decision, the New York Court of Appeals described and distinguished *Boomer* as a case where "no zoning violation, or for that matter, the violation of any other statute, was involved" and, hence, an injunction would issue against an asphalt plant constructed and operated contrary to local zoning ordinances. Little Joseph Realty, Inc. v. Town of Babylon, 395 N.Y.S.2d 428, 363 N.E.2d 1163 (1977). Is that an appropriate and viable basis for distinguishing *Boomer*?

7. While there are many law review articles dealing with the questions raised by these cases, several are especially interesting: John A. Humbach, Evolving Thresholds of Nuisance and the Takings Clause, 18 Colum. J. Envtl. Law 1 (1993); A. Mitchell Polinsky, Resolving Nuisance Disputes: The Simple Economics of Injunctive and Damage Remedies, 32 Stan. L. Rev. 1075 (1980); Robert C. Ellickson, Alternatives to Zoning: Covenants, Nuisance Rules and Fines as Land Use Controls, 40 U. Chi. L. Rev. 681 (1973); Edward Rabin, Nuisance Law: Rethinking Fundamental Assumptions, 63 Va. L. Rev. 1299 (1977); Comment, Internalizing Externalities: Nuisance Law and Economic Efficiency, 53 N.Y.U. L. Rev. 219 (1978); Guido Calabresi & A. Douglas Melamed, Property Rules, Liability Rules and Inalienability: One View of the Cathedral, 85 Harv. L. Rev. 1089 (1972).

C. DAMAGES FOR INJURY TO REAL PROPERTY

1. HARM TO THE PHYSICAL CONDITION OF LAND

a. *The General Rules*

Nuisance, trespass, negligence and strict liability cases often involve some harm to the plaintiff's interests in real property, and in most of the cases considered in Chapters 2, 3 and 4, plaintiffs sustained such damage. The Restatement (Second) of Torts in § 929 sets forth the governing principles for the awarding of damages for injury to real property:

§ 929. Harm to Land From Past Invasions

(1) If one is entitled to a judgment from harm to land resulting from a past invasion and not amounting to a total destruction of value, the damages include compensation for

> (a) the difference between the value of the land before the harm and the value after the harm, or at his election in an appropriate case, the cost of restoration that has been or may be reasonably incurred,

> (b) the loss of use of the land, and

> (c) discomfort and annoyance to him as an occupant.

As a general rule, tort compensation principles endeavor to place the injured party, as best they can, in its pre-tort position—that is, a restorative objective. Therefore, in the ordinary case the general rule permits the plaintiff to recover the difference in the property's value before and after the defendant's tortious acts. Often in nuisance and trespass cases the defendant's acts have permanently adversely affected the value of the land as by pollution, flooding, groundwater contamination, and the like, and the plaintiff is able to establish, usually by introduction of expert testimony, that the price a reasonable purchaser would offer for the land has diminished as a consequence of the resultant harm. However, § 929(1)(a) does not declare that diminution in value is the exclusive remedy; rather, in appropriate cases the plaintiff may be entitled to the costs of restoring the land to its pre-tort condition:

> b. *Restoration.* Even in the absence of value arising from personal use, the reasonable cost of replacing the land in its original position is ordinarily allowable as the measure of recovery. Thus if a ditch is wrongfully dug upon the land of another, the other normally is entitled to damages measured by the expense of filling the ditch, if he wishes it filled. If, however, the cost of replacing the land in its original condition is disproportionate to the diminution in the value of the land caused by the trespass, unless there is a reason personal to the owner for restoring the original condition, damages

are measured only by the difference between the value of the land before and after the harm. This would be true, for example, if in trying the effect of explosives, a person were to create large pits upon the comparatively worthless land of another.

On the other hand, if a building such as a homestead is used for a purpose personal to the owner, the damages ordinarily include an amount for repairs, even though this might be greater than the entire value of the building. § 929, comment b.

As the quotations from the Restatement suggest, controversy may arise where the plaintiff elects to recover the costs of restoration, but such costs exceed the diminution in value to the property. In Board of County Commissioners v. Slovek, 723 P.2d 1309 (Colo.1986), a case involving the county's negligence in allowing river water to enter a gravel pit on its property, overflow from that pit, and inundate much of plaintiffs' property, the Colorado Supreme Court summarized the essential principles and struck the following balance:

In Zwick v. Simpson, 572 P.2d 133 (Colo.1977), a trespass action, we were confronted with an issue concerning the appropriate measure of damages for injury to real property, and we concluded as follows: As the court of appeals noted, market value before and after the injury is ordinarily a rule applied to measure damages to real property. Since the goal of the law of compensatory damages is reimbursement of the plaintiff for the actual loss suffered, there may, of course, be instances in which repair or restoration cost may be a more appropriate measure such as (1) where the property has no market value, or (2) where repairs have already been made, or (3) where the property is a recently acquired private residence and the plaintiff's interest is in having the property restored, repair costs will more effectively return him to the position he was in prior to the injury. The county argues that our discussion in Zwick concerning the exceptions to the "ordinary rule" was dicta, and that when squarely considered we should conclude that any measure of damages other than diminution of market value is inappropriate. We do not agree that damages in the present case must be limited to diminution of market value.

The measure of damages for injury to real property "is not invariable." [I]n justifying the deviation from the market value standard, a Restatement comment relies on such factors as the nature of the owner's use of the property—in particular, whether the owner uses the property as a personal residence, whether the owner has some personal reason for having the property in its original condition, or both—and the nature of the injury—in particular, whether the injury is reparable and at what cost. Restatement (Second) of Torts § 929 comment b. These factors, to varying extents, have also been considered of significance by other commentators and by courts that have considered the issue.

* * *

We agree that the factors enumerated in Restatement (Second) of Torts § 929 comment b are important in determining whether a case is appropriate for application of "cost of restoration" rather than "diminution of market value" as the measure of damages for tortious injury to land. We conclude, however, that the considerations governing what is an "appropriate case" for departure from the market value standard are not susceptible to reduction to a set list and that no formula can be devised that will produce litmus-test certainty and yet retain the flexibility to produce fair results in all cases.

* * *

We prefer to leave the selection of the appropriate measure of damages in each case to the discretion of the trial court, informed by the considerations previously discussed. The trial court must take as its principal guidance the goal of reimbursement of the plaintiff for losses actually suffered, but must be vigilant not to award damages that exceed the goal of compensation and inflict punishment on the defendant or encourage economically wasteful remedial expenditures by the plaintiff.

The county contends that if this court allows the cost of restoration to be considered a proper measure of damages, fairness demands that we place a cap on the recovery of such costs. The county argues that repair costs should not exceed the diminution of the value of the property, or, at least, should not exceed the pre-tort value of the property.

We have no difficulty in rejecting the first limit offered. It is precisely because the reduction in market value is not in many instances an adequate measure of the loss suffered—that is, it is not an amount that most closely approximates what is required to return the property owner to the pre-tort position—that courts allow plaintiffs to recover the costs of restoration in appropriate circumstances. To limit the recovery to an amount that does not exceed the diminution of market value undermines the purpose for allowing the alternative measure of damages.

Although a more compelling case can be made for restricting the award of costs to the pre-tort value of the land—on the theory that defendants should not have to pay more than they would pay for irreparable total damage—we decline to adopt this as an invariable limit either. If the damage is reparable, and the costs, although greater than original value, are not wholly unreasonable in relation to that value, and if the evidence demonstrates that payment of market value likely will not adequately compensate the property owner for some personal or other special reason, we conclude that the selection of the cost of restoration as the proper measure of damages would be within the limits of a trial court's discretion.

Obviously, to the extent that a property owner is allowed to recover costs of restoration that are greater than the diminution in market value, there is the possibility that the owner will receive a monetary windfall by choosing not to restore the property and by selling it instead, profiting to the extent that restoration costs recovered exceed the diminution of market value. The problem is no different, except in degree, if restoration costs are allowed in an amount exceeding the pre-tort value of the property. These possibilities suggest the need for careful evaluation by the trial court to assure that any damages allowed in excess of either of these two measures are truly and reasonably necessary to achieve the cardinal objective of making the plaintiff whole.

Has the court adequately addressed the "windfall" problem? Should a "personal or special reason" ever justify recovering more for restoration costs than the pre-tort value of the land? Will the restoration affect the value of the land? Should the plaintiff "capture" that gain?

The flexible approach adopted in *Slovek* finds support in other modern decisions. See, e.g., Reeser v. Weaver Brothers, Inc., 78 Ohio St.3d 681, 605 N.E.2d 1271 (1992) (pollution of lake and killing of fish as a result of defendant's negligence and nuisance); Heninger v. Dunn, 101 Cal.App.3d 858, 162 Cal.Rptr. 104 (1980).

b. *Other Approaches Limiting Recovery*

Many courts rely on the distinction between permanent and temporary injury, finding that permanent, nonabatable harm to the property is subject to the diminution in value test, and that temporary and abatable harm is properly governed by the costs of restoration measure. For example, in Mel Foster Co. Properties v. American Oil Co., 427 N.W.2d 171, 174 (Iowa 1988), the plaintiff's property was contaminated by gasoline leaking from two defendants' properties. After the sources of the leaks had been corrected, plaintiff sued to recover damages for the lost use of the property. The court described the temporary and permanent nuisance distinction, and its conclusions:

> Chemical contamination of land, such as the gasoline on Foster's property, encompasses aspects of both a temporary and permanent nuisance. This injury is temporary in the sense that the cause of the pollution has been discovered and abated, and the harmful chemicals in the ground will eventually dissipate. This nuisance is permanent in the sense that it constitutes damage to the ground itself and will continue for an indefinite but significant period of time. An attempt to classify chemical pollution as a permanent or temporary nuisance is further complicated by the presence of rapidly changing scientific technology. Scientific knowledge enables society to successfully clean up pollution once thought to be permanent; it also reveals hidden dangers in chemicals once thought to be safe. We agree with one commentator's statement: "The terms 'perma-

nent and 'temporary' are somewhat nebulous in that they have practical meaning only in relation to particular fact situations and can change in characterization from one set of facts to another."

When a nuisance results in contamination of property for an indefinite period of time, the proper measure of damages is the diminution of the market value of the property. This measure of damages is proper even when the source of the contamination or pollution has been abated. Permanent damages may be awarded even if the nuisance is classified as temporary.

The award of permanent damages based on the reduction of market value provides that the plaintiff's remedies stemming from this particular incident will be addressed in one legal action. Successive actions to recover temporary damages stemming from one incident, such as the action currently filed by Foster, are contrary to the goal of efficient legal remedies. * * *

We conclude the proper measure of damages in this nuisance case is the difference between the market value of Foster's property immediately before contamination and the market value of that property after the contamination. The district court erred by establishing the measure of damages as the reduction in the rental value of the property instead of the reduction in the market value of the property caused by the gasoline contamination.

Should the plaintiff be able to treat the nuisance as permanent or temporary at its election? See also Dan B. Dobbs, Law of Remedies § 5.11(1) (2d ed. 1993); Briscoe v. Harper Oil Co., 702 P.2d 33 (Okl. 1985).

On the question of whether an actual physical invasion of the plaintiff's property is necessary in order to recover for diminution in the value of the property, recall Adkins v. Thomas Solvent Co., 440 Mich. 293, 487 N.W.2d 715 (1992) (set forth in Chapter 3), in which the Michigan Supreme Court stated that interference with use and enjoyment of land need not involve a physical or tangible intrusion. Nevertheless, the court held that the plaintiffs who claimed depreciation in value because of public perception that their property had been subject to ground water pollution, even though the properties were not and would never be subject to the ground water contamination emanating from defendants' property, did not show any significant interference with the use and enjoyment of their land based on the action of defendants, and thus could not recover in nuisance; and that publicity concerning contamination of ground water in the area that caused diminution in value of their property could not form the basis for recovery in nuisance.

Despite this evidence of a loosening of the measure of recovery to allow restoration costs even when in excess of the reduction in value, numerous decisions in cases involving environmental harm to property have refused to allow the greater measure of damage.

For a decision that plainly weighs this choice between damage measures in economic terms, see Ewell v. Petro Processors of Louisiana, Inc., 364 So.2d 604 (La.App.1978), writ denied 366 So.2d 575 (La.1979). The plaintiffs in *Ewell* claimed that toxic industrial waste which the defendant had disposed of in pits had leached into their swamp, contaminating the property. Their suit sought damages of over $170 million for the cost of removing the polluted soil and replacing it with clean soil. The trial court held that the plaintiffs could recover only for the diminished value of their property. The jury awarded nearly the full value of their one-eighth interest in the damaged property, which was calculated to be $25,000. On appeal, the court stated that there was no set rule as to which measure should be employed, but that factors to be considered included: (1) the extent of the damage; (2) the use to which the property may be put; (3) the extent of economic loss, both as to value and income; and (4) the cost and practicability of restoration. In this case, because the property was used for cattle grazing and non-commercial hunting and fishing, restoration would be expensive and time consuming. Based on those circumstances, the court affirmed the decision below, holding that diminution in value was the proper measure.

In Belle Fourche Pipeline Co. v. Elmore Livestock Co., 669 P.2d 505 (Wyo.1983), the defendant's high pressure crude oil pipeline ruptured, spilling oil over three acres of Wyoming ranchland owned by the plaintiffs. The jury awarded plaintiffs damages of $40,000 for the harm to the land and $57,250 for costs of cleanup and restoration of groundwater. The Supreme Court of Wyoming reversed, observing that the cost of restoring damaged land cannot exceed its fair market value. Furthermore, it noted, the restoration cost is not to be compared to the fair market value of the land, but to the *depreciation* in fair market value of the whole of the plaintiff's land. The damaged three acres amounted to 1/2600th of the whole ranch. The only evidence, introduced by the defendant, on the depreciation of the market value of the whole ranch indicated that the pre-spill value of the ranch was $4,935,000 and the post-spill value was $4,933,000, for a loss of $2,000, attributable to a loss of hay production capability of the three acres. The plaintiff's expert had testified that cleanup costs would exceed $150,000. The court remanded the case to permit trial of the issue of depreciation in market value. See also Borland v. Sanders Lead Co., 369 So.2d 523, 525 (Ala.1979) (where lead contamination has entered plaintiff's land from defendant's lead recovery process, plaintiff "may be able to recover the cost of restoration if this, plus rental value, is less than diminution in value").

Notes and Questions

1. In your opinion, what should be the proper measure of damages in environmental or toxic tort property cases? Should it turn on the permanent or temporary damage distinction? Should it turn on whether the owner has a personal reason for seeking restoration? Which measure best

restores the plaintiff to her pre-tort condition? If the costs of restoration exceed the reduction in value or the pre-tort value of the land, would a rational person actually expend the judgment to restore the property?

2. In Chapter 10 we consider the Comprehensive Environmental Response, Compensation and Liability Act, 42 U.S.C.A. § 9601 et seq., which is concerned almost exclusively with the costs of remediating the property to its pre-contamination condition, with little regard for the value of the land. What policy considerations might justify departing from the damage principles described above? Should environmental tort law borrow from CERCLA and make restoration the preferred remedy? Will your answer be influenced by the fact that in many areas of the country property may not be transferred without an environmental audit that declares the land free of contamination?

c. *Environmental Damages: An Emerging Approach?*

Some recent decisions are pointing in the direction of permitting restoration and remediation damages, regardless of the value of the land. For example, in T & E Industries, Inc. v. Safety Light Corp., 123 N.J. 371, 587 A.2d 1249 (1991) which is set forth in Chapter 4 on the liability issues, the New Jersey Supreme Court awarded the full range of remediation damages, including future remediation costs and loss of value:

* * *

Finally, we address the issue of damages. At trial plaintiff suggested that damages should include the purchase price of the new building to which it had moved its operations, the cost of specialized improvements, business-interruption expenses, compensation for time that plaintiff's president had spent on the radon problem, and the cost of maintaining the Alden Street site until cleanup. Plaintiff also sought indemnification for future cleanup costs to be assessed by the government.

* * *

Plaintiff's cross-appeal argues that the Appellate Division should have granted indemnification for future cleanup costs as a matter of law. * * * [Defendant] complains that plaintiff's claim for indemnity is premature because the government has not yet compelled cleanup of the site. Moreover, defendant argues that such an award "raises the prospect of a double recovery": first, plaintiff has recovered damages for the diminution in value of the property; then if cleanup costs are awarded, the property will be restored to full value and plaintiff recovers again.

A

On the indemnity issue defendant makes much of the fact that plaintiff has not yet incurred the expense of cleanup. In that connection we note that in February 1988 the United States District Court entered a judgment declaring defendant "liable for any necessary costs of response incurred and to be incurred by T & E." T & E Indus., Inc. v. Safety Light Corp., 680 F.Supp. 696, 709. The fact that plaintiff has not yet incurred cleanup expense, however, is irrelevant when one considers the relief requested. Although plaintiff's claim is couched in terms of indemnification, plaintiff does not argue that it should be indemnified now for unexpended cleanup costs. Rather, plaintiff contends that "if T & E is compelled by a governmental body to clean up the site, [defendant] should indemnify the plaintiff for that cost." In essence plaintiff seeks declaratory relief determining liability for cleanup costs.

* * * We are satisfied that if plaintiff is compelled to clean up the property, it should be indemnified. * * * As between an unsuspecting purchaser and a seller who has engaged in an abnormally-dangerous activity and polluted the property, the polluter should bear the cleanup expense. Because plaintiff would ultimately be entitled to indemnification, it is entitled now to a declaratory judgment holding defendant liable for any necessary cleanup costs. Thus, plaintiff can recover cleanup costs as they are incurred.

Contrary to defendant's assertion, our award of declaratory relief for future cleanup costs does not allow for a double recovery. At trial plaintiff received $225,000, representing the value of the property before the radium contamination rendered it worthless. Plaintiff's real-estate appraiser testified that of that amount, $185,500 reflected the value of the building and lot improvements, while $31,500 represented the value of the land. (The difference between the total of those figures, $217,000, and the appraiser's $225,000 represents appreciation in the value of the property between the time of the appraisal and the time of trial.) With the declaratory judgment, however, plaintiff recovers cleanup costs. When the property has been decontaminated, it will be restored to full value. Plaintiff will then be able to sell the property at market value. Thus, the declaratory judgment precludes plaintiff from recovering the $31,500 awarded for the diminution in the value of the land. However, assuming that the building and improvements will have to be demolished in the cleanup process, plaintiff can recover the $185,500 representing their value.

B

* * * According to defendant, plaintiff was not entitled to recover the cost of specialized improvements, compensation for the president's management time, carrying costs for the new facility, and maintenance costs of the contaminated site. Although at oral argument plaintiff acknowledged that it could not recover the cost of a new facility, it insisted that the other damages should have been submitted to the jury.

A plaintiff should be compensated for those losses or injuries proximately caused by a defendant's acts. Defendant contaminated the property, and as a result plaintiff suffered harm. Plaintiff was compelled to relocate, incurring expenses for specialized improvements. While those improvements were being made, plaintiff bore the carrying costs of the new facility. At the same time State laws barred the sale of the contaminated site. Thus, plaintiff incurred and will continue to incur maintenance expenses for that site until the time of cleanup. All of those losses flowed from defendant's inappropriate disposal of radioactive waste, and all should be considered on remand.

Plaintiff should not, however, be allowed to present a claim for the value of its president's time and services in addressing the contamination problem rather than in handling usual concerns of the corporation. That time does not represent a corporate loss. * * *

Professor Dobbs also considers whether in environmental damage cases the costs of restoration should be the appropriate measure. Dan B. Dobbs, Law of Remedies § 5.2(5) (2d ed. 1993):

> In this situation, damages should not usually be limited to the diminished market value of the land. Instead, the landowner should be permitted to recover full restoration costs and all consequential damages that are properly established, at least if he can give the court assurance that repair, restoration or cleanup will actually take place. Such a scenario gives the landowner no windfall and it entails no waste. Because costs of the pollution affect others, or the public at large, the diminished value of the plaintiff's land is no guide to the actual costs imposed by the pollution. Cost or repair or cleanup are thus appropriate, even if they exceed the diminished value of the land. As indicated below, this result is supported by analogy to environmental laws, even if those laws do not apply to the particular case.

What is the principal rationale for abandoning the common law damage rules in cases of environmental harm? What if a defendant could establish that the contamination created no threats of injury to anyone other than the plaintiff?

Professor Dobbs also discusses CERCLA, and by analogy argues that environmental statutes, which deal with harms to land that produce harm to the public or those outside the land, are relevant authority in crafting private remedies. Id., § 5.2(5) at 725–30. See also Kenneth F. McCallion, A Survey of Approaches to Assessing Damages to Contaminated Private Property, 3 Ford. Envtl. L. Rep. 125 (1992) (advocating that "the full measure of damages should be the sum of the amounts that are or could reasonably be expended for damage assessments, cleanup, and the restoration of the contaminated site, plus the lost use and diminished value of the property prior to 'restoration' and any remaining diminution in value after restoration activities cease. Only through such an analysis can the full extent of losses be determined, which is the goal of both the legal principles of strict liability and theories of economic efficiency. Only by requiring a polluter to pay the true costs of the damage inflicted can society be ensured that the wrongdoer will be properly motivated to internalize the costs of its hazardous activities * * * "); Frank B. Cross, Natural Resources Damage Valuation, 42 Vand.L.Rev. 269 (1989); Denoyer v. Lamb, 22 Ohio App.3d 136, 490 N.E.2d 615 (1984) (owner entitled to restoration expenses where "the owner's use is not * * * measurable by commercial standards, and * * * the trees form a part of an ecological system of personal value to the owner").

2. LOSS OF USE OR ENJOYMENT

In many environmental tort cases—whether predicated on nuisance, trespass, negligence or strict liability theories—the plaintiff has sustained some economic loss because of the inability or diminished ability to make use of the land damaged by pollution or other invasion. In addition to diminished market value (if the land itself is harmed) and the costs of repairs or abatement (to abate the nuisance or trespass and prevent future injury), the loss of rental or use values is an appropriate measure of the damages, covering the rental value of the property for the period that the nuisance has been or will be in existence. Dan B. Dobbs, Law of Remedies § 5.6(2) (2d ed. 1993). The following decision in Davey Compressor Co. v. City of Delray Beach, 613 So.2d 60 (Fla.App.1993) illustrates application of this measure of damages.

DAVEY COMPRESSOR COMPANY v. CITY OF DELRAY BEACH

District Court of Appeal of Florida, 1993.
613 So.2d 60.

DELL, J.

Appellant, the Aero–Dri Division of Davey Compressor Company, appeals an adverse final judgment and 8.7 million dollar damage award in favor of appellee, the City of Delray Beach, Florida, resulting from appellant's toxic contamination of the groundwater beneath appellee's well field. We affirm the final judgment in favor of appellee and the award of past damages; however, we reverse the award of future damages and remand for a new trial on this issue.

Appellee supplies its citizens with potable water pursuant to a water consumptive use permit issued by the South Florida Water Management District (SFWMD). Appellee's use permit expires on December 10, 1997. Appellant operated an industrial facility engaged in the overhauling of air compressors. Appellant operated its plant within approximately one-quarter to one-half mile from appellee's well field. From 1981 to 1987, appellant dumped highly toxic solvents used to clean the air compressors directly onto the ground behind its facility. During this period, it purchased between 5,280 and 6,000 gallons of the toxic solvents. Appellant does not know the amount actually discharged.

In August, 1987, appellee discovered high levels of the toxic solvents in the groundwater beneath its well field. Appellee took corrective action which included the purchase of potable water from neighboring cities and the construction of an interim and a permanent water treatment system to remove the solvents from the groundwater drawn from its wells.

Appellee sued appellant, among other defendants, upon statutory and common law grounds seeking injunctive relief, monetary damages for its response costs, and punitive damages. The case proceeded to trial by jury on the common law claims of negligence, nuisance, trespass and strict liability. The jury found appellant liable on all of the claims and assessed $3,097,488.00 in past damages and $5,600,000.00 in future damages against appellant for a total award of $8,697,488.00. The trial court rendered a final judgment and awarded damages accordingly.

* * * Appellant argues since appellee sued for injury to its real property, its damages cannot exceed the value of its property. We reject this contention. Appellant also argues since appellee only has a limited interest in the groundwater beneath its well field, it cannot recover damages beyond the expiration of its legal interest. We agree. * * *

As a general rule, damages for injury to real property cannot exceed the value of the property. The record, however, shows appellee sought damages for all of its response costs and related expenses as a result of appellant's unlawful disposal practices. Therefore, appellee sued, not for injury to its real property, but rather for injury to its right to the use of the groundwater beneath its real property. * * *

Appellee's damages resulted from foreseeable and direct expenses incurred as a result of appellant's negligent groundwater contamination. In Douglass Fertilizers & Chem., Inc. v. McClung Landscaping, Inc., 459 So.2d 335 (Fla. 5th DCA 1984), the court discussed the proper measure of damages under a negligence theory: In tort cases, the rule, while stated differently, is basically the same, that the plaintiff may recover all damages which are a natural, proximate, probable or direct consequence of the act, but do not include remote consequences. Taylor Imported Motors, Inc. v. Smiley, 143 So.2d 66 (Fla. 2d DCA 1962). Id., 459 So.2d at 336. See also Miller, 592 F.Supp. at 1005 ("It is a general principal that defendants are liable for the actual damages flowing from their negligence.").

Appellee's damages also resulted from costs incurred in abating the nuisance caused by groundwater contamination. In Antun Invs. Corp. v. Ergas, 549 So.2d 706 (Fla. 3d DCA 1989), the court considered the proper measure of damages for costs incurred in abating a nuisance: Antun does not contend that in a nuisance action plaintiffs are not entitled to out-of-pocket costs incurred to abate the nuisance or loss of business during the nuisance. The record supports appellee's claim for damages incurred to abate the nuisance and for damages resulting from appellant's negligence. Therefore, the trial court did not err when it awarded past damages without regard to the value of appellee's property.

* * * The Florida Water Resources Act, in recognizing the need for conservation and control of the waters in the state (Section 373.016, Fla.Stat. (1973)) makes all waters in the state subject to regulation, unless otherwise specifically exempt. § 373.023(1) Fla.Stat. (1973).

The Department of Environmental Regulation and the various water management districts are given the responsibility to accomplish the conservation, protection, management, and control of the waters in the state. § 373.016(3) Fla.Stat. (1973). In order to exercise such controls a permitting system is established which requires permits for consumptive use of water, exempting only "domestic consumption of water by individual users" from the requirements of a permit. § 373.219(1) Fla.Stat. (1973). Appellee, * * * has no right to the groundwater beneath its well field apart from its right pursuant to its water consumptive use permit issued by the SFWMD.

We find merit in appellant's argument that appellee failed to establish its right to the use of the groundwater beneath its well field beyond December 10, 1997, the expiration date of its water consumptive use permit. The record shows the only evidence offered on the permit extension consisted of one witness who could only speculate as to whether the SFWMD governing body will renew appellee's water consumptive use permit when it expires in 1997. * * * The record also shows the SFWMD has previously restricted appellee's use of its eastern well field because of natural salt water intrusion.

Since appellee failed to establish its legal interest in the groundwater beneath its well field beyond the expiration date of its water consumptive use permit, appellee cannot recover future damages after the expiration date of its permit. Therefore, the trial court erred in awarding appellee damages beyond the expiration date of its water consumptive use permit.

Accordingly, we affirm the award of past damages in the amount of $3,097,488.00. We reverse the award of $5,600,000.00 for future damages and remand for a new trial to determine the amount of appellee's future damages up to and including December 10, 1997 and for such further proceedings as may be consistent with this opinion.

————————

Other decisions have also awarded loss of rental or use value resulting from a nuisance or trespass. See, e.g., Miller v. Cudahy Co., 592 F.Supp. 976 (D.Kan.1984), affirmed, 858 F.2d 1449 (10th Cir.1988); Coty v. Ramsey Associates, Inc., 149 Vt. 451, 546 A.2d 196 (1988); National Steel Corp. v. Great Lakes Towing Co., 574 F.2d 339 (6th Cir.1978). For a discussion on the upper limits on recovery of loss of use value, see Dan B. Dobbs, Law of Remedies § 5.6(2), at 755–57.

3. PERSONAL DISCOMFORT AND ANNOYANCE

Section 929 of the Restatement, Second, quoted above, also provides that in addition to damages for diminished value, restoration costs and loss of use, a plaintiff may be entitled to recover for the personal discomfort, annoyance and even for personal injury attributable to the nuisance. See § 929 comment e. Typical of this type of damage is the following description in Filisko v. Bridgeport Hydraulic Co., 176 Conn. 33, 404 A.2d 889, 893–94 (1978), where polluted water from the defendant's refuse dump ran onto plaintiffs' land and into their pond, causing them

> * * * annoyance, discomfort and inconvenience * * * during eight years of continuous pollution to their property. They lost completely the enjoyable uses for which they built the pond. They were subjected to the sight of "big globs of brown-yellow gooey stuff" oozing onto their property, and to the constant odor of "rotten eggs" that was at times so powerful they had difficulty sleeping.

See also Branch v. Western Petroleum Co., 657 P.2d 267, 278 (Utah 1982).

Perhaps the leading case on the recovery of these kinds of damages, often called "quality of life" damages, is Ayers v. Township of Jackson, 106 N.J. 557, 525 A.2d 287 (1987), which is set out in the next section.

D. DAMAGES TO PERSONS AND PRESENT LIABILITY FOR PROSPECTIVE HARM

1. INTRODUCTION: THE ISSUES IDENTIFIED

The diseases and illnesses that form the basis of damage claims in many environmental tort actions develop over long periods, derive from extended periods of exposure to toxic substances, and typically are ones for which the disease processes are not fully understood by medical science, and therefore, pose special problems of proof. Understandably, plaintiffs assert claims for future harms that have not yet, and possibly never will, manifest themselves; or when the disease process is in an early stage and its progression is highly speculative. These claims of prospective harms consist of four kinds:

(1) The plaintiff is suffering an *existing* physical injury that may worsen or develop into or be related to more serious consequences, such as asbestosis and its relation, if any, to lung cancer;

(2) The plaintiff is not suffering any existing injury or disease, but because of the exposure to the toxic substance is at an increased risk of developing a particular disease, often cancer, in the future;

(3) The plaintiff, because of his or her enhanced susceptibility to contracting such a disease, suffers present emotional distress, usually in the form of fear or anxiety about the prospective harm, sometimes accompanied by physical manifestations and sometimes not; and

(4) The plaintiff, again because of the enhanced risk of future serious disease or physical injury, incurs or should incur present and future medical expenses in the nature of surveillance and

monitoring costs to ascertain the presence or development of the disease.

2. JUDICIAL TREATMENT OF INCREASED RISKS AND MEDICAL MONITORING

AYERS v. TOWNSHIP OF JACKSON

Supreme Court of New Jersey, 1987.
106 N.J. 557, 525 A.2d 287.

STEIN, J.

In this case we consider the application of the New Jersey Tort Claims Act (the Act), N.J.S.A. 59:1–1 to 12–3, to the claims asserted by 339 residents of Jackson Township against that municipality.

The litigation involves claims for damages sustained because plaintiffs' well water was contaminated by toxic pollutants leaching into the Cohansey Aquifer from a landfill established and operated by Jackson Township. After an extensive trial, the jury found that the township had created a "nuisance" and a "dangerous condition" by virtue of its operation of the landfill, that its conduct was "palpably unreasonable,"—a prerequisite to recovery under N.J.S.A. 59:4–2—and that it was the proximate cause of the contamination of plaintiffs' water supply. The jury verdict resulted in an aggregate judgment of $15,854,392.78, [which included $2,056,480 for emotional distress, $5,396,940 for deterioration of quality of life, and $8,204,500 for the costs of future medical surveillance]. * * *

The Appellate Division upheld that portion of the judgment awarding plaintiffs damages for impairment of their quality of life. 202 N.J.Super. 106, 120 (1985). It reversed the award for emotional distress, concluding that such damages constituted "pain and suffering" for which recovery is barred by N.J.S.A. 59:9–2(d). Id. at 116. The Appellate Division also set aside the $8,204,500 award for medical surveillance expenses, concluding that it is "impossible to say that defendant has so significantly increased the 'reasonable probability' that any of the plaintiffs will develop cancer so as to justify imposing upon defendant the financial burden of lifetime medical surveillance for early clinical signs of cancer."

In addition, the Appellate Division affirmed the trial court's dismissal of plaintiffs' claim for damages for their enhanced risk of disease, id. at 125–26, and upheld the trial court's reduction of the judgment[.] * * *

* * * We now affirm in part and reverse in part the judgment of the Appellate Division.

I

The evidence at trial provided ample support for the jury's conclusion that the township had operated the Legler landfill in a palpably unreasonable manner, a finding that the township did not contest before the Appellate Division. * * *

At trial plaintiffs offered expert testimony to prove that the chemical contamination of their wells was caused by the township's improper operation of the landfill. The testimony established that, in varying concentrations, the following chemical substances had infiltrated various wells used by plaintiffs as a water source: acetone; benzene; chlorobenzene; chloroform; dichlorofluoromethane; ethylbenzene; methylene chloride; methyl isobutyl ketone; 1,1,2,2–tetrachloroethane; tetrahydrofuran; 1,1,1–trichloroethane; and trichloroethylene. A groundwater expert described the probable movement and concentration of the chemicals as they migrated from the landfill toward plaintiffs' wells. A toxicologist summarized the known hazardous characteristics of the chemical substances. He testified that of the twelve identified chemicals, four were known carcinogens. Other potential toxic effects identified by the toxicologist included liver and kidney damage, mutations and alterations in genetic material, damage to blood and reproductive systems, neurological damage and skin irritations. The toxicologist also testified about differences in the extent of the chemical exposure experienced by various plaintiffs. An expert in the diagnosis and treatment of diseases caused by exposure to toxic substances testified that the plaintiffs required annual medical examinations to afford the earliest possible diagnosis of chemically induced illnesses. * * *

A substantial number—more than 150—of the plaintiffs gave testimony with respect to damages, describing in detail the impairment of their quality of life during the period that they were without running water, and the emotional distress they suffered. * * * Expert psychological testimony was offered to document plaintiffs' claims that they had sustained compensable psychological damage as a result of the contamination of their wells.

We now consider each of the plaintiffs' damage claims. * * *

QUALITY OF LIFE

In November 1978, the residents of the Legler area of Jackson Township were advised by the local Board of Health not to drink their well water, and to limit washing and bathing to avoid prolonged exposure to the water. This warning was issued by the Board after tests disclosed that a number of wells in the Legler area of the township were contaminated by toxic chemicals. Initially, the township provided water to the affected residents in water tanks that were transported by tank trucks to various locations in the neighborhood. Plaintiffs brought their own containers, filled them with water from the tanks, and transported the water to their homes.

This water-supply system was soon discontinued and replaced by a home-delivery system. Residents in need of water tied a white cloth on their mailbox and received a 40 gallon barrel containing a plastic liner filled with water. The filled barrels weighed in excess of 100 pounds and were dropped off, as needed, on the properties of the Legler-area residents. * * *

* * *

The trial court charged the jury that plaintiffs' claim for "quality of life" damages encompassed "inconveniences, aggravation, and unnecessary expenditure of time and effort related to the use of the water hauled to their homes, as well as to other disruption in their lives, including disharmony in the family unit." The aggregate jury verdict on this claim was $5,396,940. This represented an average award of slightly over $16,000 for each plaintiff; thus, a family unit consisting of four plaintiffs received an average award of approximately $64,000.

In the Appellate Division and before this Court, defendant argues that this segment of the verdict is barred by the New Jersey Tort Claims Act, which provides:

> No damages shall be awarded against a public entity or public employee for pain and suffering resulting from any injury; provided, however, that this limitation on the recovery of damages for pain and suffering shall not apply in cases of permanent loss of a bodily function, permanent disfigurement or dismemberment where the medical treatment expenses are in excess of $1,000.00. [N.J.S.A. 59:9–2(d).]

Defendant contends that the legislative intent in restricting damages for "pain and suffering" was to encompass claims for all "non-objective" injuries, unless the statutory threshold of severity of injury or expense of treatment is met. The township asserts that the inconvenience, aggravation, effort and disruption of the family unit that resulted from the loss of plaintiff's water supply was but a form of "pain and suffering" and therefore uncompensable under the Act.

* * *

* * * The Tort Claims Act's ban against recovery of damages for "pain and suffering resulting from any injury" is intended to apply to the intangible, subjective feelings of discomfort that are associated with personal injuries. It was not intended to bar claims for inconvenience associated with the invasion of a property interest. * * * Although the disruption of plaintiffs' water supply is an "injury" under the Act, N.J.S.A. 59:1–3, the interest invaded here, the right to obtain potable running water from plaintiffs' own wells, is qualitatively different from "pain and suffering" related to a personal injury.

As the Appellate Division acknowledged, plaintiffs' claim for quality of life damages is derived from the law of nuisance. 202 N.J.Super. at 117–18. It has long been recognized that damages for inconvenience, annoyance, and discomfort are recoverable in a nuisance action. The Restatement (Second) of Torts § 929 (1977) sets out three distinct categories of compensation with respect to invasions of an interest in land:

(a) the difference between the value of the land before the harm and the value after the harm, or at [plaintiff's] election in an appropriate case, the cost of restoration that has been or may be reasonably incurred;

(b) the loss of use of the land, and

(c) discomfort and annoyance to him as occupant.

While the first two of these components constitute damages for the interference with plaintiff's use and enjoyment of his land, the third category compensates the plaintiff for his personal losses flowing directly from such an invasion. As such, damages for inconvenience, discomfort, and annoyance constitute "distinct grounds of compensation for which in ordinary cases the person in possession is entitled to recover in addition to the harm to his proprietary interests." Restatement (Second) of Torts § 929 comment e (1977).

Accordingly, we conclude that the quality of life damages represent compensation for losses associated with damage to property, and agree with the Appellate Division that they do not constitute pain and suffering under the Tort Claims Act. We therefore sustain the judgment for quality of life damages.

Emotional Distress

The jury verdict awarded plaintiffs damages for emotional distress in the aggregate amount of $2,056,480. The individual verdicts ranged from $40 to $14,000.

Many of the plaintiffs testified about their emotional reactions to the knowledge that their well-water was contaminated. Most of the plaintiffs' testimony on the issue of emotional distress was relatively brief and general. Typically, their testimony did not indicate that the emotional distress resulted in physical symptoms or required medical treatment. No treating physicians testified regarding plaintiffs' emotional distress claims. Nevertheless, the consistent thrust of the testimony offered by numerous witnesses was that they suffered anxiety, stress, fear, and depression, and that these feelings were directly and causally related to the knowledge that they and members of their family had ingested and been exposed to contaminated water for a substantial time period.

* * *

In addition, the township contended that the jury verdict for emotional distress constituted damages for "pain and suffering resulting from any injury," recovery for which is expressly barred by the Tort Claims Act, N.J.S.A. 59:9–2(d). * * *

* * *

* * * Plaintiffs maintain that their emotional distress claims should not be barred by the Act, because they are based on "independent injuries," and do not constitute pain and suffering incidental to a physical injury. They also emphasize that their emotional distress claims are compensable because we have abandoned the requirement of physical impact as a condition to recovery for emotional distress.

We acknowledge that our cases no longer require proof of causally-related physical impact to sustain a recovery for emotional distress. Nevertheless, we reject plaintiffs' assertion that the Tort Claims Act's limitation against recovery for "pain and suffering resulting from any injury" does not apply to claims based on emotional distress.

* * *

Addressing first plaintiffs' contention that emotional distress is not an "injury" as that term is used in the Tort Claims Act, we observe that the Act broadly defines injury to include

> death, injury to a person, damage to or loss of property or any other injury that a person may suffer that would be actionable if inflicted by a private person. [N.J.S.A. 59:1–3.]

The statutory definition is expansive and unqualified and clearly accommodates "emotional distress" as an injury "that a person may suffer that would be actionable if inflicted by a private person." * * * Accordingly, we hold that claims for emotional distress are encompassed by the term "injury" in N.J.S.A. 59:9–2(d).

* * *

Assuming as we do that tortiously-inflicted emotional distress is as much an "injury" under the Act as a broken limb, it is evident that subjective symptoms such as depression, fear, and anxiety—either as a consequence of emotional distress or a broken limb—constitute "pain and suffering" for the purposes of the Tort Claims Act.

* * * Accordingly, we affirm the Appellate Division's reversal of that portion of the jury verdict awarding damages for emotional distress.

CLAIMS FOR ENHANCED RISK AND MEDICAL SURVEILLANCE

No claims were asserted by plaintiffs seeking recovery for specific illnesses caused by their exposure to chemicals. Rather, they claim damages for the enhanced risk of future illness attributable to such exposure. They also seek to recover the expenses of annual medical examinations to monitor their physical health and detect symptoms of disease at the earliest possible opportunity.

Before trial, the trial court granted defendant's motion for summary judgment dismissing the enhanced risk claim. It held that plaintiffs' proofs, with the benefit of all favorable inferences, would not establish a "reasonable probability" that plaintiffs would sustain future injury as a result of chemical contamination of their water supply. The trial court also observed that recognition of the enhanced risk claim would cause the jury to "speculate * * * [as] to the future health of each plaintiff," and raise "the spectre of potential claims * * * increasing in boundless proportion." However, the court specifically noted that future claims for injury attributable to exposure to contaminants in the water supply would not be barred by the statute of limitations. Id. at 568 (citing Lopez v. Sawyer, 62 N.J. 267 (1973), and Lynch v. Rubacky, 85 N.J. 65 (1982)). The Appellate Division affirmed the dismissal of the enhanced risk claim, but characterized the trial court's observation that future claims for physical injury would not be barred by the statute of limitations as "dictum only," having "no controlling significance to the future rights of the parties."

With regard to the claims for medical surveillance expenses, the trial court denied defendant's summary judgment motion, and the jury verdict included damages of $8,204,500 for medical surveillance. The Appellate Division reversed. * * *

* * *

* * * Although we concur with the Appellate Division's refusal to recognize plaintiffs' damage claim based on enhanced risk, we disagree with its conclusion that an award for medical surveillance damages cannot be supported by this record. We also deem it appropriate to clarify the effect of the statute of limitations, N.J.S.A. 2A:14–2, and the single controversy doctrine on future claims for personal injuries.

1.

Our evaluation of the enhanced risk and medical surveillance claims requires that we focus on a critical issue in the management of toxic tort litigation: at what stage in the evolution of a toxic injury should tort law intercede by requiring the responsible party to pay damages?

At the outset, we must recognize that the issues presented by this case and others like it will be recurring. We note the difficulty that both law and science experience in attempting to deal with the emerging complexities of industrialized society and the consequent implications for human health. One facet of that problem is represented here, in the form of years of inadequate and improper waste disposal practices. However dimly or callously the consequences of those waste management practices may have been perceived, those consequences are now upon us. * * *

* * *

In the absence of statutory or administrative mechanisms for processing injury claims resulting from environmental contamination, courts have struggled to accommodate common-law tort doctrines to the peculiar characteristics of toxic-tort litigation. The overwhelming conclusion of the commentators who have evaluated the result is that the accommodation has failed, that common-law tort doctrines are ill-suited to the resolution of such injury claims, and that some form of statutorily-authorized compensation procedure is required if the injuries sustained by victims of chemical contamination are to be fairly redressed.[a]

* * *

[a]. The court's discussion of statutes of limitation problems in toxic tort cases is omitted. That topic is treated in Chapter 12.

By far the most difficult problem for plaintiffs to overcome in toxic tort litigation is the burden of proving causation. In the typical tort case, the plaintiff must prove tortious conduct, injury and proximate cause. Ordinarily, proof of causation requires the establishment of a sufficient nexus between the defendant's conduct and the plaintiff's injury. In toxic tort cases, the task of proving causation is invariably made more complex because of the long latency period of illnesses caused by carcinogens or other toxic chemicals. The fact that ten or twenty years or more may intervene between the exposure and the manifestation of disease highlights the practical difficulties encountered in the effort to prove causation. Moreover, the fact that segments of the entire population are afflicted by cancer and other toxically-induced diseases requires plaintiffs, years after their exposure, to counter the argument that other intervening exposures or forces were the "cause" of their injury. * * *

* * *

Although we acknowledge, as we must, the array of complex practical and doctrinal problems that confound litigants and courts in toxic-tort mass-exposure litigation, we are confronted in this case with fairly narrow and manageable issues. * * * The legal issue we must resolve, in the context of the jury's determination of defendant's liability under the Act, is whether the proof of an unquantified enhanced risk of illness or a need for medical surveillance is sufficient to justify compensation under the Tort Claims Act. In view of the acknowledged difficulties of proving causation once evidence of disease is manifest, a determination of the compensability of post-exposure, pre-symptom injuries is particularly important in assessing the ability of tort law to redress the claims of plaintiffs in toxic-tort litigation.

2.

Much of the same evidence was material to both the enhanced risk and medical surveillance claims. Dr. Dan Raviv, a geohydrologist, testified as to the movements and concentrations of the various chemical substances as they migrated from the landfill toward plaintiffs' wells. Dr. Joseph Highland, a toxicologist, applied Dr. Raviv's data and gave testimony concerning the level of exposure of various plaintiffs. Dr. Highland also compiled toxicity profiles of the chemical substances found in the wells, and testified concerning the health hazards posed by the chemicals and the exposure levels at which adverse health effects had been experimentally observed. According to Dr. Highland, four of the chemicals were known to be carcinogenic, and at least four of the chemicals were capable of adversely affecting the reproductive system or causing birth defects. Most of the chemical substances could produce adverse effects on the liver and kidney, as well as on the nervous system. For at least six of the chemicals, no data was available regarding carcinogenic potential. He also testified that the exposure to multiple chemical substances posed additional hazards to plaintiffs because of the possibility of biological interaction among the chemicals that enhanced the risk to plaintiffs.

Dr. Highland testified that the Legler area residents, because of their exposure to toxic chemicals, had an increased risk of cancer; that unborn children and infants were more susceptible to the disease because of their immature biological defense systems; and that the extent of the risk was variable with the degree of exposure to the chemicals. Dr. Highland testified that he could not quantify the extent of the enhanced risk of cancer because of the lack of scientific information concerning the effect of the interaction of the various chemicals to which plaintiffs were exposed. However, the jury could reasonably have inferred from his testimony that the risk, although unquantified, was medically significant.

* * * Dr. Highland also testified that the exposure to chemicals had already caused actual physical injury to plaintiffs through its adverse effects on the genetic material within their cells.

Dr. Susan Daum, a physician affiliated with the Mount Sinai Hospital in New York and specializing in the diagnosis and treatment of diseases induced by toxic substances, testified that plaintiffs required a program of regular medical surveillance. Acknowledging her reliance on the report of Dr. Highland, Dr. Daum stated that plaintiffs' exposure to chemicals had produced "a reasonable likelihood that they have now or will develop health consequences from this exposure."

She testified that the purpose of the medical surveillance program was to permit the earliest possible diagnosis of illnesses, which could lead to improved prospects for cure, prolongation of life, relief of pain, and minimization of disability. Dr. Daum specified the series of tests and procedure that would constitute an appropriate program, described each procedure and explained its purpose, and estimated the annual cost of each test.

Although both the enhanced risk and medical surveillance claims are based on Dr. Highland's testimony, supplemented by Dr. Daum's testimony in the case of the surveillance claim, these claims seek redress for the invasion of distinct and different interests. The enhanced risk claim seeks a damage award, not because of any expenditure of funds, but because plaintiffs contend that the unquantified injury to their health and life expectancy should be presently compensable, even though no evidence of disease is manifest. Defendant does not dispute the causal relationship between the plaintiffs' exposure to toxic chemicals and the plaintiffs' increased risk of diseases, but contends that the probability that plaintiffs will actually become ill from their exposure to chemicals is too remote to warrant compensation under principles of tort law.

By contrast, the claim for medical surveillance does not seek compensation for an unquantifiable injury, but rather seeks specific monetary damages measured by the cost of periodic medical examinations.

The invasion for which redress is sought is the fact that plaintiffs have been advised to spend money for medical tests, a cost they would not have incurred absent their exposure to toxic chemicals. Defendant contends that the claim for medical surveillance damages cannot be sustained, as a matter of law, if the plaintiffs' enhanced risk of injury is not sufficiently probable to be compensable. In our view, however, recognition of the medical surveillance claim is not necessarily dependent on recognition of the enhanced risk claim.

3.

* * *

A preliminary question is whether a significant exposure to toxic chemicals resulting in an enhanced risk of disease is an "injury" for the purposes of the Tort Claims Act. The Act defines injury to include "damage to or loss of property or any other injury that a person may suffer that would be actionable if inflicted by a private person." N.J.S.A. 59:1–3. We also note that the Restatement defines "injury" as "the invasion of any legally protected interest of another." Restatement (Second) of Torts § 7(1) (1965)[.]

* * *

In our view, an enhanced risk of disease caused by significant exposure to toxic chemicals is clearly an "injury" under the Act. In this case, neither the trial court nor the Appellate Division challenged the contention that the enhanced risk of disease was a tortiously-inflicted injury, but both concluded that the proof quantifying the likelihood of disease was insufficient to submit the issue to the jury. * * *

Among the recent toxic tort cases rejecting liability for damages based on enhanced risk is Anderson v. W.R. Grace & Co., 628 F.Supp. 1219 (D.Mass.1986). That case * * * involved defendants' alleged chemical contamination of the groundwater in areas of Woburn, Massachusetts. See generally P. DiPerna, Cluster Mystery: Epidemic and the Children of Woburn, Mass. (1985) (containing background information on the Woburn case). Plaintiffs alleged that two wells supplying water to the City of Woburn drew upon the contaminated water, and that exposure to the contaminated water caused five deaths and severe personal injuries among plaintiffs. Among the claims for personal injuries dismissed before trial were plaintiff's claims for damages based on enhanced risk. Relying on the Massachusetts rule regarding prospective damages, the Anderson court reasoned that "recovery depends on establishing a 'reasonable probability' that the harm will occur." Id. at 1231 (citing Restatement (Second) of Torts § 912 comment e). However, the Anderson court held that the plaintiffs failed to satisfy this threshold standard. They had not quantified their alleged enhanced risk: "Nothing in the present record indicates the magnitude of the increased risk or the diseases which plaintiffs may suffer." Id.

* * *

The majority of courts that have considered the enhanced risk issue have agreed with the disposition of the District Court in *Anderson*. * * *

Other courts have acknowledged the propriety of the enhanced risk cause of action, but have emphasized the requirement that proof of future injury be reasonably certain. See Hagerty v. L & L Marine Servs., supra, 788 F.2d at 319 ("[A] plaintiff can recover [damages for enhanced risk] only where he can show that the toxic exposure more probably than not will lead to cancer."); * * * Sterling v. Velsicol Chemical Corp., supra, 647 F.Supp. at 321–22, (upholding cause of action for enhanced susceptibility to injury based on chemical contamination of plaintiffs' wells where "reasonable probability" standard is met) * * *.

Additionally, several courts have permitted recovery for increased risk of disease, but only where the plaintiff exhibited some present manifestation of disease. See Jackson v. Johns-Manville Sales Corp., 781 F.2d 394, 412–13 (5th Cir.) (allowing recovery for increased risk of cancer where evidence indicated that due to asbestos exposure, plaintiff had greater than fifty percent chance of contracting cancer; "[o]nce the injury becomes actionable—once some effect appears—then the plaintiff is permitted to recover for all probable future manifestations as well"), cert. denied, ___ U.S. ___, 106 S.Ct. 3339, 92 L.Ed.2d 743 (1986); Brafford v. Susquehanna Corp., 586 F.Supp. 14, 17–18 (D.Colo.1984) (acknowledging that cause of action for increased risk of cancer requires proof of present physical injury, but denying defendant's motion for summary judgment to permit plaintiff to offer proof of present genetic and chromosomal damage due to exposure to radiation) * * *.

* * *

Our disposition of this difficult and important issue requires that we choose between two alternatives, each having a potential for imposing unfair and undesirable consequences on the affected interests. A holding that recognizes a cause of action for unquantified enhanced risk claims exposes the tort system, and the public it serves, to the task of litigating vast numbers of claims for compensation based on threats of injuries that may never occur. It imposes on judges and juries the burden of assessing damages for the risk of potential disease, without clear guidelines to determine what level of compensation may be appropriate. It would undoubtedly increase already escalating insurance rates. It is clear that the recognition of an "enhanced risk" cause of action, particularly when the risk is unquantified, would generate substantial litigation that would be difficult to manage and resolve.

* * *

It may be that this dilemma could be mitigated by a legislative remedy that eases the burden of proving causation in toxic-tort cases where there has been a statistically significant incidence of disease among the exposed population. Other proposals for legislative intervention contemplate a funded source of compensation for persons significantly endangered by exposure to toxic chemicals. We invite the legislature's attention to this perplexing and serious problem.

In deciding between recognition or nonrecognition of plaintiffs' enhanced-risk claim, we feel constrained to choose the alternative that most closely reflects the legislative purpose in enacting the Tort Claims Act. We are conscious of the admonition that in construing the Act courts should "exercise restraint in the acceptance of novel causes of action against public entities." Comment, N.J.S.A. 59:2–1. In our view, the speculative nature of an unquantified enhanced risk claim, the difficulties inherent in adjudicating such claims, and the policies underlying the Tort Claims Act argue persuasively against the recognition of this cause of action. Accordingly, we decline to recognize plaintiffs' cause of action for the unquantified enhanced risk of disease, and affirm the judgment of the Appellate Division dismissing such claims. We need not and do not decide whether a claim based on enhanced risk of disease that is supported by testimony demonstrating that the onset of the disease is reasonably probable, could be maintained under the Torts Claims Act.

4.

The claim for medical surveillance expenses stands on a different footing from the claim based on enhanced risk. It seeks to recover the cost of periodic medical examinations intended to monitor plaintiffs' health and facilitate early diagnosis and treatment of disease caused by plaintiffs' exposure to toxic chemicals. At trial, competent medical testimony was offered to prove that a program of regular medical testing and evaluation was reasonably necessary and consistent with contemporary scientific principles applied by physicians experienced in the diagnosis and treatment of chemically-induced injuries.

The Appellate Division's rejection of the medical surveillance claim is rooted in the premise that even if medical experts testify convincingly that medical surveillance is necessary, the claim for compensation for these costs must fall, as a matter of law, if the risk of injury is not quantified, or, if quantified, is not reasonably probable. This analysis assumes that the reasonableness of medical intervention, and, therefore, its compensability, depends solely on the sufficiency of proof that the occurrence of the disease is probable. We think this formulation unduly impedes the ability of courts to recognize that medical science may necessarily and properly intervene where there is a significant but unquantified risk of serious disease.

* * *

[In Askey v. Occidental Chemical Corp. 102 A.D.2d 130, 477 N.Y.S.2d 242 (1984),] * * * the court affirmed the denial of class certification in a toxic tort suit involving a Niagara, New York, landfill that was the successor to the Love Canal site maintained by defendant. An issue underlying the request for class certification was plaintiffs' contention that persons exposed to the toxic chemicals were entitled to be reimbursed for the cost of medical surveillance out of a fund to be established by defendant. Although denying class certification, the court acknowledged that under New York law plaintiffs could maintain a cause of action to recover the expense of medical surveillance:

> [I]t would appear that under the proof offered here persons exposed to toxic chemicals emanating from the landfill have an increased risk of invisible genetic damage and a present cause of action for their injury, and may recover all "reasonably anticipated" consequential damages. The future expense of medical monitoring, could be a recoverable consequential damage provided that plaintiffs can establish with a reasonable degree of medical certainty that such expenditures are "reasonably anticipated" to be incurred by reason of their exposure. There is no doubt that such a remedy would permit the early detection and treatment of maladies and that as a matter of public policy the tort-feasor should bear its cost.

Compensation for reasonable and necessary medical expenses is consistent with well-accepted legal principles. See C. McCormick, Handbook on the Law of Damages § 90 at 323–27 (1935). It is also consistent with the important public health interest in fostering access to medical testing for individuals whose exposure to toxic chemicals creates an enhanced risk of disease. The value of early diagnosis and treatment for cancer patients is well-documented. * * * An application of tort law that allows post-injury, pre-symptom recovery in toxic tort litigation for reasonable medical surveillance costs is manifestly consistent with the public interest in early detection and treatment of disease.

Recognition of pre-symptom claims for medical surveillance serves other important public interests. The difficulty of proving causation, where the disease is manifested years after exposure, has caused many commentators to suggest that tort law has no capacity to deter polluters, because the costs of proper disposal are often viewed by polluters as exceeding the risk of tort liability. However, permitting recovery for reasonable pre-symptom, medical-surveillance expenses subjects polluters to significant liability when proof of the causal connection between the tortious conduct and the plaintiffs' exposure to chemicals is likely to be most readily available. The availability of a substantial remedy before the consequences of the plaintiffs' exposure are manifest may also have the beneficial effect of preventing or mitigating serious future illnesses and thus reduce the overall costs to the responsible parties.

Other considerations compel recognition of a pre-symptom medical surveillance claim. It is inequitable for an individual, wrongfully exposed to dangerous toxic chemicals but unable to prove that disease is likely, to have to pay his own expenses when medical intervention is clearly reasonable and necessary. * * *

* * *

Accordingly, we hold that the cost of medical surveillance is a compensable item of damages where the proofs demonstrate, through reliable expert testimony predicated upon the significance and extent of exposure to chemicals, the toxicity of the chemicals, the seriousness of the diseases for which individuals are at risk, the relative increase in the chance of onset of disease in those exposed, and the value of early diagnosis, that such surveillance to monitor the effect of exposure to toxic chemicals is reasonable and necessary. * * *

We find that the proofs in this case were sufficient to support the trial court's decision to submit the medical surveillance issue to the jury, and were sufficient to support the jury's verdict.

* * *

5.

The medical surveillance issue was tried as if it were a conventional claim for compensatory damages susceptible to a jury verdict in a lump sum. The jury was so instructed by the trial court, and neither plaintiffs' nor defendant's request to charge on this issue sought a different instruction.

* * *

The indeterminate nature of damage claims in toxic-tort litigation suggests that the use of court-supervised funds to pay medical-surveillance claims as they accrue, rather than lump-sum verdicts, may provide a more efficient mechanism for compensating plaintiffs. A funded settlement was used in the Agent Orange litigation. In re "Agent Orange" Prod. Liab. Litig., 611 F.Supp. 1399 (E.D.N.Y.1985), aff'd, 818 F.2d 194 (2d Cir.1987). The use of insurance to fund future medical claims is frequently recommended by commentators.

* * *

In our view, the use of a court-supervised fund to administer medical-surveillance payments in mass exposure cases, particularly for claims under the Tort Claims Act, is a highly appropriate exercise of the Court's equitable powers. * * *

Although there may be administrative and procedural questions in the establishment and operation of such a fund, we encourage its use by trial courts in managing mass-exposure cases. In litigation involving public-entity defendants, we conclude that the use of a fund to administer medical- surveillance payments should be the general rule, in the absence of factors that render it impractical or inappropriate. This will insure that in future mass-exposure litigation against public entities, medical-surveillance damages will be paid only to compensate for medical examinations and tests actually administered, and will encourage plaintiffs to safeguard their health by not allowing them the option of spending the money for other purposes. The fund mechanism will also foster the legislative objective of limiting the liability of public entities and facilitating the deduction from damage awards of collateral-source benefits.

However, we decline to upset the jury verdict awarding medical-surveillance damages in this case. Such a result would be unfair to these plaintiffs, since the medical surveillance issue was tried conventionally, and neither party requested the trial court to withhold from the jury the power to return a lump-sum verdict for each plaintiff in order that relief by way of a fund could be provided. * * *

Notes and Questions

Quality of Life. *Ayers* is one of the most significant cases on the question of compensable interests in environmental tort cases. It is one of the few that has addressed the array of harms which often are asserted in environmental nuisance cases. The first type of harm it considers is the deprivation of the occupants' quality of life, but as distinct and separate from emotional harm, because it focuses on the *objective* differences in their lifestyle attributable to the nuisance. The Restatement (Second) of Torts § 929, as noted earlier, expressly allows recovery for "discomfort and annoyance to [the] occupant" of the land affected by the nuisance. What are some of the kinds of objective evidence that cases such as *Ayers* may involve? Will it always be feasible to separate emotional distress from "annoyance"? What should the jury instructions provide by way of guidelines so that reasonable jurors can make the distinction?

3. NOTE ON CLAIMS FOR ENHANCED RISK OF FUTURE HARM

The court in *Ayers* asks an overarching question in toxic torts litigation: at what stage in the evolution of toxic injuries should tort law intercede by requiring the responsible party to pay damages?

In discussing the accommodation between traditional tort law doctrines and toxic tort litigation's peculiar problems, the court refers to the view of some commentators, based on numerous published articles, that "the accommodation has failed, that common-law tort doctrines are ill-suited to the resolution of such injury claims." Based on the materials in this and prior chapters, do you agree with that conclusion?

The court's argument that allowing enhanced risk claims will undercompensate those who later do develop cancer and overcompensate those who do not is frequently relied upon in these types of cases. How persuasive is it? The court holds that it will not recognize a cause of action for *unquantified* enhanced risk of disease. How much and how certain must quantification be before it would be compensable under this standard? Would a five percent chance be sufficient? Or would the court require a "reasonable medical certainty," "more probably than not," or similar degree of quantification that exceeds fifty percent? Would a 30% risk be sufficient if the expert stated that she was 90% certain of her opinion?

a. The Prevailing Rule

The general rule today is that the increased risk of developing a future disease, such as cancer, as a consequence of exposure to toxic chemicals is not compensable unless the plaintiff can establish that the probability of the future disease is at least greater than fifty percent. In Wilson v. Johns–Manville Sales Corp., 684 F.2d 111 (D.C.Cir.1982), the D.C. Circuit Court of Appeals offered this statement of the rule:

> The traditional American rule * * * is that recovery of damages based on future consequences may be had only if such consequences are "reasonably certain." Recovery of damages for speculative or conjectural consequences is not permitted. To meet the "reasonably certain" standard, courts have generally required plaintiffs to prove that it is more likely than not (a greater than 50% chance) that the projected consequence will occur. If such proof is made, the alleged future effect may be treated as certain to happen and the injured party may be awarded full compensation for it; if the proof does not establish a greater than 50% chance, the injured party's award must be limited to damages for harm already manifest.

Other recent decisions have essentially arrived at the same conclusion as the courts in *Ayers* and *Wilson* and denied the claim for an increased risk unless the plaintiff offers compelling expert testimony about the substantiality of the increased likelihood of contracting cancer.

In Stites v. Sundstrand Heat Transfer, Inc., 660 F.Supp. 1516 (W.D.Mich.1987), the court granted summary judgment to a defendant whose copper manufacturing plant had improperly disposed of large quantities of trichloroethylene (TCE) which ultimately had entered plaintiffs' water supply because plaintiffs' affidavits had "failed to demonstrate the existence of sufficient facts showing that they could establish at trial a reasonable certainty of acquiring cancer in the future" noting that "none of plaintiffs' experts were able to quantify the enhanced cancer risk plaintiffs face because of their exposure to TCE." Accord, Amendola v. Kansas City Southern Ry. Co. 699 F.Supp. 1401 (W.D.Mo.1988) (denying claims for enhanced risk from asbestos exposure under the Federal Employers Liability Act, after exhaustively considering the reported cases); Hagerty v. L & L Marine Services, Inc., 788 F.2d 315 (5th Cir.1986) (denying enhanced risk of cancer claim under Jones Act for maritime torts because complaint does not allege that "plaintiff will probably develop [cancer] in the future"); Morrissy v. Eli Lilly & Co., 76 Ill.App.3d 753, 32 Ill.Dec. 30, 37, 394 N.E.2d 1369, 1376 (1979); Mink v. University of Chicago, 460 F.Supp. 713, 719 (N.D.Ill.1978).

The New Jersey Supreme Court revisited the increased risk issue a few years after *Ayers* and reaffirmed its holding in Mauro v. Raymark Industries Inc., 116 N.J. 126, 561 A.2d 257 (1989). There it rejected a plaintiff's claim of enhanced risk of cancer attributable to working with asbestos, where the experts testified that there was a "high probability" that the plaintiff had an increased risk of contracting cancer in his lifetime, but they were unable to testify that it was probable that the plaintiff would contract cancer. The opinion contains a thorough discussion of the policy considerations for and against recognizing the enhanced risk claim, and a dissenting opinion that would have permitted the enhanced risk claim, as representing a *more* efficient use of judicial resources and as more attuned to achieving an optimal level of deterrence.

In 2 "Enterprise Responsibility for Personal Injuries, Approaches to Legal and Institutional Change" American Law Institute (1991) the Reporters' Study concludes "We do not advocate reimbursement * * * for increased risk per se."

b. *Some Contrary Opinions*

A few decisions have held to the contrary.

(i) For example, in Werlein v. United States, 746 F.Supp. 887 (D.Minn.1990), persons allegedly exposed to trichloroethylene and other chemicals discharged from the Twin Cities Army Ammunition Plant sought recovery on various theories, including increased risk of future disease. First, the court, in denying defendants' summary judgment motions, held that plaintiffs are not required to rely on epidemiological evidence to support their claim that exposure to these chemicals may cause cancer and other diseases, but may rely on experts' opinions based on animal and in vitro studies. (See Chapter 8 for a thorough treatment of this question.) Second, it refused to dismiss the increased risk claim:

> Here, defendants argue that plaintiffs have not alleged any present harm capable of causing cancer or other diseases in the future. The Court disagrees. Plaintiffs' experts have testified that plaintiffs who have been exposed to contaminated air and drinking water have suffered an actual physical injury in the form of chromosomal breakage, and damage to the cardiovascular and immunal systems. These experts also have testified that the present injuries are the cause of the alleged increased future risk of disease.

> Defendants answer that the injuries identified by plaintiffs' experts are insufficient as a matter of law to support an award of damages for increased risk of future harm because they are primarily subcellular injuries. Based on the record before it, this Court cannot rule as a matter of law that plaintiffs' alleged injuries are not "real" simply because they are subcellular. The effect of volatile organic compounds on the human body is a subtle, complex matter. It is for the trier of fact, aided by expert testimony, to determine whether plaintiffs have suffered present harm.

> Of course, plaintiffs at trial will bear the burden of proof on all damages issues, including present harm and the extent to which that present harm has caused an increased likelihood of future harm. Although the present case involves complicated scientific and medical issues, the damage issues from a legal standpoint turn on basic tort principles.

For a contrary view, that subcellular or subclinical effects should not be sufficient to constitute present injury or a basis for awarding damages for future consequences, see Schweitzer v. Consolidated Rail Corp., 758

F.2d 936 (3d Cir.1985), cert. denied, sub. nom Reading Co. v. Schweitzer, 474 U.S. 864, 106 S.Ct. 183, 88 L.Ed.2d 152 (1985).

(ii) Even more bullish than *Werlein* on allowing compensation for increased risk is Petriello v. Kalman, 215 Conn. 377, 576 A.2d 474 (1990) (not a toxic tort case), where defendant obstetrician negligently performed a procedure on plaintiff, as the result of which plaintiff suffered some immediate injury and also an 8–16 percent chance of specific future injury. The court upheld a jury instruction that permitted an award for the increased risk itself:

> If this increased risk was more likely than not the result of the bowel resection necessitated by the defendant's actions, we conclude that there is no legitimate reason why she should not recover present compensation based upon the likelihood of the risk becoming a reality. When viewed in this manner, the plaintiff was attempting merely to establish the extent of her present injuries. She should not be burdened with proving that the occurrence of a future event is more likely than not, when it is a present risk, rather than a future event for which she claims damages. In our judgment, it was fairer to instruct the jury to compensate the plaintiff for the increased risk * * * rather than to ignore that risk completely.

> [Such a system would also be fairer to a defendant] who should be required to pay damages for a future loss based upon the statistical probability that such a loss will be sustained rather than upon the assumption that the loss is a certainty because it is more likely than not. We hold, therefore, that in a tort action, a plaintiff who has established a breach of duty that was a substantial factor in causing a present injury which has resulted in an increased risk of future harm is entitled to compensation to the extent that the future harm is likely to occur.

Does the rationale of the court in *Petriello* require that a plaintiff be awarded a proportionate recovery when the risk is proved to be greater than 50 percent? Should a plaintiff be able to maintain an action now for proportionate recovery or wait to see if the disease actually develops, at her option? What if a plaintiff had no "present injury"—in other words, a "pure" case of enhanced risk? Would *Petriello* authorize recovery in such a case?

c. Autonomy Interests

The treatment of risk as a compensable injury has stimulated considerable academic ink. See Comment, Toxic Torts and Latent Diseases: The Case for an Increased Risk Cause of Action, 38 U. Kan. L. Rev. 1087 (1990). One of the more interesting and brief treatments is that of Professor Elliott in an article prepared for the Houston Law Review toxic tort symposium. He presents a common sense argument that current tort causation and injury rules unfairly place the entire burden of scientific uncertainty upon the plaintiff and that juries, in making awards in toxic tort cases, bring their own sense of justice into the jury room, including beliefs that enhanced risks of harm for chemical exposure *ought* to be compensable. E. Donald Elliott, The Future of Toxic Torts: Of Chemophobia, Risk as a Compensable Injury and Hybrid Compensation Systems, 25 Houston L. Rev. 781, 783–86 (1988):

> A hypothetical example may help to illustrate why juries are refusing to follow the traditional tort standard in toxics cases. Suppose that before the session today I sneaked into the room and put some white powder from my daughter's chemistry set into the water pitchers from which the audience has been drinking. I then said to you: "I don't know what it was, and I don't know if it will harm you. It's your problem. You prove that whatever I put into our water did something bad to you. If you can't, then I haven't done anything wrong."

> Those of you who have been drinking the water might feel that I had done something wrong, even if no one ever proved that our health had been adversely affected by the incident. You could justifiably feel that your right to bodily autonomy had been violated, and I had turned you into "human guinea pigs" without your consent. As a general matter, if a person's body has been invaded and she has been subjected without her consent to an avoidable and uncompensated risk, including the risk of uncertainty as to what the ultimate consequences to health may be, she has been injured in a way that should be compensated by the legal system where possible. Two distinct harms are involved when people are opposed to chemicals without their consent: (1) the involuntary exposure to risk; and (2) any physical harm to health that may be removable.

> * * *

> My objection is not that juries are compensating plaintiffs for involuntary exposure to risks but that the formal law forces juries to compensate for involuntary exposure to risk under the guise that it is awarding damages for proven bodily harm. This charade serves to reinforce public misperceptions and chemophobia.

> We should purge toxic tort law of the unfortunate and legally anomalous doctrine that no harm is suffered unless the plaintiff can prove that it is more likely than not that involuntary exposure to the chemical caused a recognized disease or other form of physical harm. The violation of a person's bodily autonomy, the affront to one's dignity that occurs when one is assaulted with a potentially hazardous chemical, is also an injury that the law should recognize and compensate.

Do you agree with Elliott's thesis? What problems do you see with allowing recovery in enhanced risk cases? How might one value or measure damages for the violation of autonomy interests caused by the involuntary exposure to toxics? Might there be some way wholly apart from using percentage probabilities of *future* harm?

4. NOTE ON POST–EXPOSURE, PRE–SYMPTOM MEDICAL SURVEILLANCE DAMAGES[1]

a. *Supporting Authority*

The court in *Ayers* concludes that medical surveillance damages claims must be treated differently from the enhanced risk claim. The court rejected the lower court's view that unless the enhanced risk is quantified the medical surveillance claim is not based on a reasonable medical certainty. The court in *Ayers* found that the decision in Friends for All Children v. Lockheed Aircraft Corp., 746 F.2d 816 (D.C.Cir.1984) was a potent authority. In *Friends for All Children*, the legal guardian for Vietnamese orphans who survived an airplane crash alleged that as a result of the decompression of the plane compartment and the crash itself, the children suffered from a neurological disorder called Minimal Brain Dysfunction (MBD). Although this was not a toxic tort case, the court, in determining whether to grant a preliminary injunction, faced many of the same considerations that arise in toxic tort litigation. Plaintiffs requested a preliminary injunction to require the defendant to pay for diagnostic examinations and medical treatment pending the outcome of the trials on the merits, which the district court granted.

The appellate court rejected Lockheed's contention that having to undergo diagnostic examinations does not in itself constitute an injury. The court held that tort law should compensate plaintiffs for diagnostic examination without proof of actual injury:

> A cause of action allowing recovery for the expense of diagnostic examinations * * * will, in theory, deter misconduct. * * * The cause of action also accords with commonly shared intuitions of normative justice which underlie the common law of tort. * * * The [defendant], through his negligence, caused the plaintiff * * * to need specific medical services—at a cost that is neither inconsequential nor of a kind the community generally accepts as part of the wear and tear of daily life.

---

1. Although the terms medical "monitoring" and medical "surveillance" are applied interchangeably by the courts, a medical authority, Ralph E. Yodakin, M.D., in Surveillance, Monitoring and Regulatory Concerns, 78 J. Occup. Med. 569 (1986), defines them differently.

Medical surveillance is a technique used to identify diseases, isolate the first victims, and contain the contacts, in order to ensure that diseases do not claim new victims.

Medical monitoring, in contrast, consists of techniques designed to anticipate any disease before it occurs, avoid pathological consequences, and abort any reversible tissue changes.

Unlike medical surveillance, medical monitoring does not aim to identify or isolate the first case or cases. Medical monitoring is of particular significance where it serves to prevent injury or illness, and thus reduce lost work days and lost wages. Whereas the objective of medical surveillance is that of early detection, identification and isolation, the objective of medical monitoring is disease prevention.

The court also noted that the expense of medical services could deter exposed individuals from seeking treatment when it stated that "medical expenses running into the thousands of dollars would likely constitute a formidable obstacle to families of moderate means."

Identify the policy considerations which the court in *Ayers* regarded as supportive of recognizing a medical monitoring claim? What considerations might argue against awarding monitoring damages? Does *Friends of All Children* suggest any additional arguments supporting medical monitoring?

b. Elements of the Surveillance Interest

Ayers' limitation on the availability of the medical surveillance damages involved five factors. It specifically held that such damages are only available when reliable expert testimony establishes: (1) the significance and extent of exposure to chemicals; (2) the toxicity of the chemicals; (3) the seriousness of the diseases for which individuals are at risk; (4) the increase in the chance of onset of disease in those exposed; and (5) the value of early diagnosis. How often will plaintiffs be able to satisfy these criteria? How large do you suppose the increased risk must be (item 4) to support surveillance? Recall the court stated that plaintiffs did not have to establish "that the occurrence of the disease is probable." Must there be some absolute level of risk?

In a subsequent decision the New Jersey Supreme Court clarified its requirements for awarding medical surveillance damages. In Theer v. Philip Carey Co., 133 N.J. 610, 628 A.2d 724 (1993), the wife of an asbestos fitter who died of lung cancer claimed that her indirect exposure to asbestos by washing her husband's clothes placed her at an increased risk of contracting an asbestos-related disease justifying medical surveillance damages. The court disagreed, pointing out that Mauro v. Raymark Industries, 116 N.J. 126, 561 A.2d 257 (1989):

> extends the *Ayers* cause of action to plaintiffs who have suffered increased risk of cancer when directly exposed to a defective or hazardous product like asbestos, when they have already suffered a manifest injury or condition caused by that exposure, and whose risk of cancer is attributable to the exposure.

* * *

> However, we note that such a cause of action applies only to persons who have been *directly* exposed to hazardous substances. In addition, medical-surveillance damages may be awarded only if a plaintiff reasonably shows that medical surveillance is required because the exposure caused a distinctive increased risk of future injury, and would require a course of medial monitoring independent of any other that the plaintiff would otherwise have to undergo.

Does the holding in *Theer* significantly narrow the requirements set forth in *Ayers*? What might the court mean by a "distinctive increased risk of future injury"?

The Third Circuit recognized a claim for medical monitoring expenses in In re Paoli Railroad Yard PCB Litigation, 916 F.2d 829 (3d Cir.1990) (interpreting Pennsylvania law), where it concluded that in order to establish a claim for medical surveillance costs, the plaintiff would have to prove to a "reasonable degree of medical certainty" the following elements:

(1) Plaintiff was significantly exposed to a proven hazardous substance through the negligent actions of the defendant.

(2) As a proximate result of exposure, plaintiff suffers an increased risk of contracting a serious latent disease.

(3) That increased risk makes periodic diagnostic medical examinations reasonably necessary.

(4) Monitoring and testing procedures exist which make the early detection and treatment of the disease possible and beneficial.

Based on *Paoli* and *Ayers*, what is medical monitoring? Is it a cause of action, a claim, a remedy, a harm or a damage? Must there exist first an underlying cause of action such as nuisance or negligence or strict liability for abnormally dangerous activities? Which do you think is the better approach: to treat medical monitoring as a freestanding cause of action or to treat it as a remedy to be available in some cases where a cause of action on another theory has been established? For a discussion of this issue, see Miranda v. Shell Oil Co., 12 Cal.App.4th 28, 15 Cal.Rptr.2d 569 (1993), review granted 17 Cal.Rptr.2d 608, 847 P.2d 574 (1993). Under *Ayers* or *Paoli* must a plaintiff show *any* physical injury? If not, how does that comport with the principle of negligence requiring that a plaintiff suffer some harm?

Problem

Assume that a community of 10,000 people had been subjected to a contaminated water supply similar to the plaintiffs in *Ayers*. Also assume that the plaintiffs' medical experts testified that the exposure had increased their risk of a particular disease threefold. For example, if the pre-exposure risk of contracting the disease was 10 in 10,000, the post-exposure risk (based on epidemiological studies) was that 30 of the 10,000 would develop the disease. On the basis of this record could any specific plaintiff in a population of 10,000 recover on an enhanced risk claim? Would it fulfill *Ayers'* demand for a "quantified" enhanced risk? What is troubling about doing so? Could the 10,000, as part of a class action, recover medical monitoring expenses? Does it fulfill the criteria in *Ayers*, assuming the disease is serious and one for which early diagnosis is beneficial? Would it be relevant that monitoring would require expensive scanning and laboratory tests?

c. *The Trend*

Several other courts have awarded medical surveillance damages and such awards seem to be the recent trend. See Hagerty v. L & L Marine Services, 788 F.2d 315 (5th Cir.1986); Miranda v. Shell Oil Co.,

12 Cal.App.4th 28, 15 Cal.Rptr.2d 569 (1993), review granted 17 Cal. Rptr.2d 608, 847 P.2d 574 (1993); Potter v. Firestone Tire & Rubber Co., ___ Cal.4th ___, 25 Cal.Rptr.2d 550, 863 P.2d 795 (1993) (Adopting the holding in *Miranda*); Herber v. Johns–Manville Corp., 785 F.2d 79 (3d Cir.1986); Askey v. Occidental Chemical Co., 102 A.D.2d 130, 477 N.Y.S.2d 242 (1984). See also, Note, Medical Surveillance Damages: A Solution to the Inadequate Compensation of Toxic Tort Victims, 63 Ind. L.J. 849 (1989); Leslie S. Gara, Medical Surveillance Damages: Using Common Sense and the Common Law to Mitigate the Dangers Posed by Environmental Hazards, 12 Harv. Envtl. L. Rev. 265 (1988); Allan Kanner, Medical Monitoring: State and Federal Perspectives, 2 Tul. Envtl. L.J. 1 (1989).

d. ALI Reporters' Study

The authors of the American Law Institute Reporters' Study also recommended recognition of medical monitoring awards, but on a more limited basis than expressed in *Ayers* and *Paoli*. See 2 Enterprise Responsibility for Personal Injury, American Law Institute 378–79 (1991), where the study states:

> The kind of medical monitoring that we envision as a prime candidate for a tort award is some form of scientific epidemiological investigation of where and when the disease actually manifests itself among the exposed group. This work would serve both to inform the medical profession about which people are in real need of early treatment and to provide reassurance to people who turn out not to be at risk. We do not favor awarding damages under the label of "medical monitoring" and having the money paid directly to plaintiffs to be spent on additional medical attention only if they are so inclined.

> That position, which reflects our view that tort damages should not be awarded to compensate merely for the *fear* of possible cancer after exposure, dovetails with our proposal in Chapter 6 for a collateral source offset rule. At the present time more than 80 percent of standard medical bills are paid by some form of health care insurance, and there is no strong reason for devising a novel form of early tort intervention to pay for the modest uninsured expenses likely to be incurred by those who were exposed but are not yet diseased. On the other hand, a socially beneficial role for medical monitoring is to finance serious scientific study of the potential impact of health hazards on exposed groups, for which funds are unlikely to be forthcoming from health insurance. Equally if not more important, imposing legal and financial responsibilities for such investigations on the polluting enterprise will facilitate tort litigation that directs a meaningful and timely sanction against hazardous activities.

The Enterprise Responsibility Study also observed that a major advantage of its proposal is that it would "avoid a possible disproportionate financial impact of a tort award covering expensive diagnostic procedures for every member of a large exposed population on the basis of initial evidence of an increase in the modest risk of a disease.''

e. Contrary Views

In contrast to the trend, a California Court of Appeals recently declined to recognize a medical monitoring claim, although it did recognize a claim for cancerphobia. Potter v. Firestone Tire & Rubber Co., 15 Cal.App.4th 490, 274 Cal.Rptr. 885 (1990), reversed in part, affirmed in part, ___ Cal.4th ___, 25 Cal.Rptr.2d 550, 863 P.2d 795 (1953). In *Potter*, four plaintiffs filed suit against Firestone after toxic chemicals from defendant's plant were deposited at the Crazy Horse waste disposal site which contaminated plaintiffs' water supply. While the court found that plaintiffs' actual ingestion of carcinogens created a basis for recognizing the fear of cancer claim, that fact alone was not sufficient to support the medical monitoring claim:

> Although we are sympathetic to the concerns expressed in these cases, we are presently unwilling to create a new cause of action for medical monitoring costs. It may be that our Supreme Court will determine that such a cause of action is permissible, but until that time we decline to create a cause of action for medical monitoring.

The California Supreme Court did indeed reject that conclusion and held that "medical monitoring costs * * * are a compensable item of damages in a negligence action where proofs demonstrate, through reliable medical expert testimony, that the need for future monitoring is a reasonably certain consequence of a plaintiff's toxic exposure and that the recommended monitoring is reasonable.''

Note that neither *Paoli* nor *Ayers* required that the increased risk of disease must reach a level of reasonable certainty to actually occur as a prerequisite to recovery of medical monitoring costs. What do you think of the test used in *Potter*? See also Ball v. Joy Technologies, Inc., 958 F.2d 36 (4th Cir.1991), cert. denied ___ U.S. ___, 112 S.Ct. 876, 116 L.Ed.2d 780 (1992), holding that "a claim for medical surveillance costs is simply a claim for future damages. However, such relief is available only where a plaintiff has sustained a physical injury that was proximately caused by the defendant. Plaintiffs have not demonstrated that they are suffering from a present, physical injury that would entitle them to recover medical surveillance costs under West Virginia or Virginia law.''

While most of the commentary on medical monitoring expenses support recognition of such claims, at least under the conditions specified in *Ayers* and *Paoli*, the theory does have its detractors. See generally Martha Churchill, Medical Monitoring and Cancerphobia—The Rise of Fear Lawsuits, For the Defense (August 1993) at 2.

f. Generalized Scientific Studies to Determine Increased Risk

A series of lawsuits instituted by residents of Colorado living near the Rocky Flats Nuclear Weapons Plant owned by Rockwell International and Dow Chemical sought generalized medical surveillance relief. See Cook v. Rockwell International Corp., 755 F.Supp. 1468, 1477–78 (D.Colo.1991). The plaintiffs sought to have defendants pay the cost to perform population-based epidemiological studies to determine *if* they were at increased risk for contracting disease. The court rejected that request:

> Even assuming that the Colorado Supreme Court would recognize a tort claim for individualized medical monitoring, I do not believe that the Colorado Supreme Court would recognize as cognizable plaintiffs' claim for generalized scientific studies.

> A medical monitoring claim compensates a plaintiff for diagnostic treatment, a tangible and quantifiable item of damage caused by a defendant's tortious conduct. Such relief is akin to future medical expenses. The claim does not compensate a plaintiff for testing others to determine the odds that a particular person might contract a disease. * * *

> Plaintiffs have cited no authority for their common law claims to recover the costs of generalized scientific studies. I discern no basis for such a claim. Thus, I hold that the scientific studies requested by plaintiffs here are not recoverable under a medical monitoring cause of action. * * *

On the other hand, the court did retain plaintiffs' request for a fund that would be used to pool the data derived from the medical tests of the exposed plaintiffs:

> Assuming, as I must at this juncture, that pooling the results of these diagnostic medical examinations is reasonably necessary to detect the onset of disease, I conclude that this relief is cognizable in a medical monitoring cause of action. Pooling the examination results is a reasonable complement to normal diagnostic testing that furthers the objective behind the tort—to assure the early diagnosis of a latent disease.

See Barth v. Firestone Tire & Rubber Co., 661 F.Supp. 193 (N.D.Cal. 1987) (authorizing injunctive relief to establish a medical monitoring fund to pay for medical monitoring and to establish an information-sharing mechanism; to gather and forward to treating physicians information relating to the diagnosis and treatment of diseases which may result from plaintiffs' exposure to toxins); Werlein v. United States, 746 F.Supp. 887, 895 (D.Minn.1990) ("In a case where a number of persons are exposed to a toxin about which little is known, and it is necessary to gather and share information regarding diagnosis and treatment through screening, the court would consider framing a medical monitoring and information-sharing program as injunctive relief.") As quoted above, the authors of the Reporters' Study would favor recognizing medical monitoring *solely* to determine "where and when the disease *actually* manifests itself among the exposed group."

g. Medical Monitoring under CERCLA

Plaintiffs in a substantial number of cases have sought to recover medical monitoring costs under the Comprehensive Environmental Response Compensation and Liability Act, 42 U.S.C.A. § 9601 et seq.. which allows private parties to recover "the necessary costs of response," which are the costs associated with remediation and removal of contamination at various sites around the nation. See Chapter 10 which addresses the CERCLA liability scheme and private actions. An exhaustive consideration of the issue is found in Werlein v. United States, 746 F.Supp. 887, 903–04 (D.Minn.1990), which held that medical surveillance costs are not recoverable under CERCLA because the Act expressly created mechanisms for the Agency of Toxic Substances and Disease Registry to conduct health effects studies to determine the health impact of exposure to toxic chemicals in a community, including providing medical care and testing to exposed individuals but, in the sections dealing with response costs available to private litigants, deleted medical monitoring provisions. Accord, Ambrogi v. Gould, 750 F.Supp. 1233 (M.D.Pa.1990) (costs for medical monitoring, including medical surveillance, health effect studies, and health assessments were not "response costs" recoverable in private plaintiff cost recovery actions brought under CERCLA by neighbors of battery processing plant); Woodman v. United States, 764 F.Supp. 1467 (M.D.Fla.1991) (residents' costs of obtaining medical surveillance due to government's alleged contamination of landfill were not "response costs" under CERCLA; claim for medical monitoring did not relate to public health, but rather related to health of each family member).

A few decisions have reached a contrary conclusion and have allowed generalized medical monitoring claims to proceed as part of CERCLA actions: Brewer v. Ravan, 680 F.Supp. 1176 (M.D.Tenn.1988); Williams v. Allied Automotive, Autolite Div., 704 F.Supp. 782 (N.D.Ohio 1988). In denying a motion to dismiss a claim for medical monitoring under CERCLA, the court in *Brewer* stated, "[T]o the extent that plaintiffs seek to recover the cost of medical testing and screening conducted to assess the effect of the release or discharge on public health or to identify potential public health problems presented by the release, * * * they present a cognizable claim under [CERCLA]." Evidently, the *Brewer* court distinguished medical expenses incurred to treat *personal* injuries from those medical expenses incurred to assess the effect of the release or discharge on the public health. According to the *Brewer* court, the former did not qualify as "necessary costs of response" under CERCLA, but the latter did.

h. *Lump Sum or Periodic Payments*

In *Ayers* the court stated that it believed medical monitoring expenses should be managed through a court-appointed administrator who would distribute funds periodically to individual claimants to cover their medical expenses. What do you think of the fund concept that the court would require in future cases? Why do you think that a court would prefer to have a fund established on which plaintiffs could draw for their medical expenses over many years rather than awarding a one-time lump sum to plaintiffs? What advantages might they provide for plaintiffs? For plaintiffs' lawyers? What ethical considerations are implicated by periodic payments?

While most decisions authorizing medical surveillance have made lump sum awards, a few have acknowledged that periodic payment structure is the preferable method. See Barth v. Firestone Tire & Rubber Co., 673 F.Supp. 1466, 1476 (N.D.Cal.1987); Burns v. Jacquays Min. Corp., 156 Ariz. 375, 752 P.2d 28, 34 (App.1987); Habitants Against Landfill Toxicants v. City of York, 15 Envtl. L. Rep. (Envtl. L. Inst.) 20,937 (Pa.Com.Pl.1985). In Friends for All Children v. Lockheed Aircraft Corp., 746 F.2d 816 (D.C.Cir.1984), the court affirmed the appropriateness of the trust fund mechanism over a lump sum award for medical surveillance.

For a thorough consideration of the period payment alternative, see Amy B. Blumenberg, Medical Monitoring Funds: The Periodic Payment of Future Medical Surveillance Expenses in Toxic Exposure Litigation, 43 Hastings L.J. 661 (1992); see also Roger C. Henderson, Designing a Responsible Periodic–Payment System for Tort Awards: Arizona Enacts a Prototype, 32 Ariz. L. Rev. 21, 25 (1990).

5. JUDICIAL TREATMENT OF FEAR OF FUTURE DISEASE AND PUNITIVE DAMAGES

STERLING v. VELSICOL CHEMICAL CORPORATION

United States Court of Appeals, Sixth Circuit, 1988.
855 F.2d 1188.

GUY, C.J.

A number of persons, including these plaintiffs, who either lived or owned property near defendant's landfill, brought a class action for personal injuries and property damage resulting from hazardous chemicals leaking from the landfill and contaminating the local water supply. The district court held the corporation liable upon legal theories of strict liability, common law negligence, trespass, and nuisance. The court awarded five representative members of the class compensatory damages for their personal injuries, as well as property damages, plus prejudgment interest on the entire award. The district court further held the corporation liable to the class as a whole for punitive damages.

Upon a review of the lengthy record in this difficult case, we find that the district court properly held Velsicol liable to the five representative plaintiffs but erred in the nature and amount of the damage awards. * * *

I.

FACTS

In August, 1964, the defendant, Velsicol Chemical Corporation (Velsicol), acquired 242 acres of rural land in Hardeman County, Tennessee. The defendant used the site as a landfill for by-products from the production of chlorinated hydrocarbon pesticides at its Memphis, Tennessee, chemical manufacturing facility. Before Velsicol purchased the landfill site and commenced depositing any chemicals into the ground, it neither conducted hydrogeological studies to assess the soil composition underneath the site, the water flow direction, and the location of the local water aquifer, nor drilled a monitoring well to detect and record any ongoing contamination. From October, 1964, to June, 1973, the defendant deposited a total of 300,000 55–gallon steel drums containing ultrahazardous liquid chemical waste and hundreds of fiber board cartons containing ultrahazardous dry chemical waste in the landfill.

Shortly after Velsicol began its disposal operations at the landfill site, local residents and county, state, and federal authorities became concerned about the environmental impact of the defendant's activities. As a result of this concern, the United States Geological Survey (USGS), in 1967, prepared the first of several reports on the potential contamination effects of the chemicals deposited into the landfill up to that time. The 1967 report indicated that chlorinated hydrocarbons had migrated down into the subsoil and had contaminated portions of the surface and subsurface environment adjacent to the disposal site. While the chemicals had not reached the local water aquifer, the USGS concluded that both the local and contiguous ground water were in danger of contamination. Subsequent to publication of the 1967 USGS report, Velsicol expanded the size of the landfill disposal site from twenty to forty acres.

State authorities increasingly became concerned about the defendant's disposal of ultrahazardous chemicals at the site. In 1972, the State filed an administrative action to close the landfill because the chlorinated hydrocarbons buried at the site allegedly were contaminating irreparably the subsurface waters. The state ordered Velsicol to cease disposal of all toxic chemicals by August 21, 1972, and all other chemicals by June 1, 1973.

In 1976, three years after the state permanently closed the landfill disposal site, the USGS, in conjunction with state authorities, commenced updating the 1967 USGS report. One major concern, which gave rise to the new USGS study, was the possibility of the chemicals migrating toward wells utilized by local residents. In 1978, the USGS issued a written report detailing the 1976 update of the 1967 report. The 1978 report found that the water table of the local aquifer was highly contaminated. The 1978 USGS report also indicated that the local aquifer moved toward the northwest, north, and northeast, rather than just toward the east as earlier indicated in the 1967 USGS report. Consequently, residents wells, which were previously presumed safe from contamination, were now potentially polluted. In view of the continued complaints by numerous local residents, the Department of Health conducted further well water sampling tests in 1978. These tests revealed the presence of certain chlorinated hydrocarbons in numerous wells. * * *

In 1978, forty-two plaintiffs sued Velsicol in the Circuit Court of Hardeman County, Tennessee, on behalf of themselves and all others similarly situated for damages and injunctive relief. * * *

* * * The district court awarded the five individuals compensatory damages totalling $5,273,492.50 for their respective injuries, plus pre-judgment interest dating back to July, 1965, of $8,964,973.25. All damages, except for $48,492.50 to one plaintiff for property damage claims, were awarded for personal injuries. The district court also awarded $7,500,000 in punitive damages to the class as a whole. * * *

On appeal, * * * the defendant asserts the district court improperly awarded compensatory damages to the plaintiffs for their alleged injuries. Defendant also asserts that prejudgment interest on the compensatory award and punitive damages should not have been awarded. * * *

* * *

[Deleted is that portion of the court's opinion dealing with causation-related issues, which are considered in Chapter 8.]

COMPENSATORY DAMAGES

Velsicol argues that, even assuming proof of a proximate causation, the district court improperly awarded the five representative plaintiffs compensatory damages for their respective injuries and disabilities. The five representative plaintiffs, their exposure to Velsicol's chemicals, and their respective injuries are as follows:

[Court describes each of five plaintiffs' alleged injuries and awards.]

Based upon these findings, the district court awarded the five representative plaintiffs compensatory damages for the following injuries:

	Sterling	Wilbanks	Ivy	Johnson	Maness
Extent of Injury and Disability, Including Increased Risk of Cancer and Disease	$150,000	150,000	75,000	150,000	250,000

	Sterling	Wilbanks	Ivy	Johnson	Maness
Immune System Impairment	75,000	75,000	75,000	75,000	75,000
Post-Traumatic Stress Disorder	50,000	25,000	50,000	250,000	---
Fear of Increased Risk of Cancer and Disease	75,000	100,000	50,000	250,000	250,000
Physical Pain Emotional Suffering	125,000	250,000	50,000	125,000	150,000
Impaired Quality of Life	150,000	75,000	50,000	100,000	500,000
Real Property	48,492.50	---	---	---	---
Lost Wages Earning Capacity	---	---	---	250,000	500,000
Learning Disorders	---	---	---	---	150,000
TOTAL:	$673,492.50	$675,000	$350,000	$1,275,000	$2,300,000

A. Extent of Injury and Disability

Velsicol asserts there was insufficient medical proof of the causal connection between ingestion of contaminated water and certain injuries. First, we focus upon that portion of the award attributed to the plaintiffs' actual physical injuries and then upon the portion of the award attributed to their increased susceptibility to cancer and other diseases.

[The court concludes that some of the plaintiffs offered sufficient medical evidence linking their present injuries to the ingestion of the contaminated water. For example, where the experts testified to a "reasonable medical certainty" that one plaintiff's cancer of the kidney was caused by exposure to carbon tetrachloride, the damage awarded was sustained; in contrast, other plaintiffs failed to prove that their optic atrophy and neuritis were caused by ingesting contaminated water.]

* * *

2. Increased Risk of Cancer and Other Diseases

Plaintiffs sought to recover damages for the prospect that cancer and other diseases may materialize as a result of their exposure.[21] The district court awarded the five representative plaintiffs damages predicated upon their being at risk for, or susceptible to, future disease.

Where the basis for awarding damages is the potential risk of susceptibility to future disease, the predicted future disease must be medically reasonably certain to follow from the existing present injury. While it is unnecessary that the medical evidence conclusively establish with absolute certainty that the future disease or condition will occur, mere conjecture or even possibility does not justify the court awarding damages for a future disability which may never materialize. Tennessee law requires that the plaintiff prove there is a reasonable medical certainty that the anticipated harm will result in order to recover for a future injury. Therefore, the mere increased risk of a future disease or condition resulting from an initial injury is not compensable. While neither the Tennessee courts, nor this court, has specifically addressed damage awards for increased risk or susceptibility to cancer and kidney and liver diseases, numerous courts have denied recovery where plaintiffs alleged they might suffer from these future diseases or conditions as a result of existing injuries.

* * *

In the instant case, the district court found an increased risk for susceptibility to cancer and other diseases of only twenty-five to thirty percent. This does not constitute a reasonable medical certainty, but rather a mere possibility or speculation. Indeed, no expert witnesses ever testified during the course of trial that the five representative plaintiffs had even a probability—i.e., more than a fifty percent chance—of developing cancer and kidney or liver disease as a result of their exposure to defendant's chemicals.

For the foregoing reasons, the district court's award of compensatory damages to each of the five representative plaintiffs is remanded for recalculation to exclude that portion of the damage award attributed to increased susceptibility to cancer and other diseases.

B. Fear of Increased Risk of Cancer and Other Diseases

Velsicol next argues that the district court erroneously awarded the five representative plaintiffs compensatory damages or, in the alterna-

---

21. In awarding damages to the plaintiffs for their increased risk to cancer and other diseases, the court stated in pertinent part:

[I]t must be emphasized that the increased susceptibility to kidney and liver disease and cancer is a presently existing condition in each plaintiff who suffered exposure to the various toxins. Plaintiffs produced scientific experts who testified, that, to a reasonable degree of scientific certainty, each plaintiff now has a presently existing condition known as "enhanced or increased susceptibility" to dis-

ease. Finally, they testified that the condition resulted from consuming the Velsicol chemicals in the water.

* * *

In sum, it is generally recognized that a plaintiff is entitled to damages for an enhanced risk of injury occasioned by a defendant's wrongdoing. There is simply no element of speculation in awarding those damages between the condition and defendant's wrongdoing. 647 F.Supp. at 321–22.

tive, excessive damages for fear of increased risk of contracting cancer and other diseases. Mental distress, which results from fear that an already existent injury will lead to the future onset of an as yet unrealized disease, constitutes an element of recovery only where such distress is either foreseeable or is a natural consequence of, or reasonably expected to flow from, the present injury. See Payton v. Abbott Labs, 386 Mass. 540, 437 N.E.2d 171 (1982) * * *. However damages for mental distress generally are not recoverable where the connection between the anxiety and the existing injury is either too remote or tenuous. While there must be a reasonable connection between the injured plaintiff's mental anguish and the prediction of a future disease, the central focus of a court's inquiry in such a case is not on the underlying odds that the future disease will in fact materialize. To this extent, mental anguish resulting from the chance that an existing injury will lead to the materialization of a future disease may be an element of recovery even though the underlying future prospect for susceptibility to a future disease is not, in and of itself, compensable inasmuch as it is not sufficiently likely to occur. In the context of certain types of injuries and exposures to certain chemicals, cancerphobia has been one basis of claims for mental anguish damages.

In Tennessee, damages for fear arising from an increased risk of disease are recoverable. Laxton v. Orkin Exterminating Co., 639 S.W.2d 431 (Tenn.1982). In *Laxton*, the plaintiffs' water supply was contaminated by the carcinogens chlordane and heptachlor, when defendant serviceman sprayed the exterior of plaintiffs' house for termites. The Department of Water Quality Control told plaintiffs to cease using the water for any purpose and to obtain a new water source. As a result of ingesting the contaminated water for over a period of eight months, the plaintiffs worried about their health and the health of their children. The court awarded the plaintiffs $6,000 each for their mental suffering resulting from their reasonable apprehension of the harmful effects to their own and their children's health due to consuming or otherwise using the contaminated water. The *Laxton* court noted that the period of "mental anguish" deserving compensation was confined to the time between the discovery of ingestion of toxic substances and the determination that puts to rest the fear of future injury.

In the instant case, the plaintiffs' fear clearly constitutes a present injury. Each plaintiff produced evidence that they personally suffered from a reasonable fear of contracting cancer or some other disease in the future as a result of ingesting Velsicol's chemicals. Consistent with the extensive line of authority in both Tennessee and other jurisdictions, we cannot say that the district court erred in awarding the five representative plaintiffs damages for their reasonable fear of increased risk of cancer and other diseases.

In the alternative, Velsicol asserts that the district court awarded excessive damages to the plaintiffs. The amount of the damage award in a personal injury action is for the jury or, in a non-jury case, the trial judge who heard the evidence. Absent a showing of bias, passion, or corruption, excessiveness of a verdict is left to the trial court's discretion. The appellate court will only consider whether the trial court abused that discretion by granting awards so large as to shock the judicial conscience.

The evidence credited by the court shows that each of the plaintiffs suffered from, and should be compensated for, a reasonable fear of contracting cancer or some other diseases in the future. The only issue is the amount of reasonable compensation. In *Laxton*, the court limited the amounts of recovery to $6,000 for each plaintiff's reasonable fear of future disease from ingesting known carcinogens over an extended period of time. In the instant case, the district court awarded plaintiffs damages ranging from $50,000 to $250,000. We find these awards to be excessive, particularly where plaintiffs failed to prove at trial that they have a significant increased risk of contracting cancer and other diseases. Upon a review of the opinion and the adopted findings of fact, we are unable to find any basis upon which the district court differentiated its damage awards to each plaintiff for his or her fear of increased risk of cancer and other diseases. The *Laxton* court awarded each plaintiff $6,000 for his or her fear of increased susceptibility to cancer from consuming known carcinogens for a duration of eight months. Using *Laxton* as a guidepost, we, accordingly, vacate the district court's award and award each of the five representative plaintiffs damages based upon the duration of their exposure to the contaminated water. Plaintiff Johnson, who was exposed to the chemicals for a period of approximately two years, is awarded $18,000 versus the district court's award of $250,000; plaintiff Maness, who was exposed for approximately three years (two years during infancy and approximately one year while his mother was exposed to the chemicals during pregnancy), is awarded $27,000 versus the district court's award of $250,000; plaintiff Ivy, who was exposed for approximately four years, is awarded $36,000 versus the district court's award of $50,000; plaintiff Wilbanks, who was exposed for approximately six years, is awarded $54,000 versus the district court's award of $100,000; and plaintiff Sterling, who was exposed for approximately eight years, is awarded $72,000 versus the district court's award of $75,000.

[The court reversed all awards of compensatory damages for immune system impairment, concluding that such a condition had not been recognized by medical authorities and plaintiffs' experts opinions were insufficient to sustain their burden of proof.]

* * *

VII.

PUNITIVE DAMAGES

Lastly, Velsicol argues that the district court erred in awarding the entire class punitive damages on the grounds of Velsicol's conduct during the course of litigation, upon the baseless conclusion it willfully and wantonly violated state law in disposing its chemicals, and before determining compensatory damages to the entire class.

* * *

In assessing its award of punitive damages, the district court stated:

[V]elsicol's actions in creating, maintaining and operating its chemical waste burial site, with superior knowledge of the highly toxic and harmful nature of the chemical contaminants it disposed of therein, and specifically its failure to immediately cease dumping said toxic chemicals after being warned by several state and federal agencies * * * constituted gross, wilful and wanton disregard for the health and well-being of the plaintiffs, and therefore is supportive of an award of punitive and exemplary damages.

The Court further concludes that Velsicol's attempt to allege that plaintiffs were guilty of assuming the risk, or were guilty of contributory negligence is without factual basis and so outrageous as to subject the defendant to punitive damages.

In addition the Court further finds that Velsicol has also attempted to shift the liability and causation for the psychological disorders suffered by the plaintiffs to the local, state and federal authorities, claiming that the defendant cooperated with them in their attempts to monitor the situation and persuade Velsicol to limit its activities. They contend that news coverage of this case specifically caused the post-traumatic stress disorder. The Court concludes that these attempts by Velsicol are also so outrageous that punitive damages should be imposed.

Punitive damages are allowed under Tennessee law and are given in excess of, and in addition to, compensatory damages. They are awarded in cases involving fraud, malice, gross negligence, or oppression, or where a wrongful act is done with a bad motive or recklessly as to imply a disregard of social obligation, or where there is such willful misconduct as to raise a presumption of conscious indifference. In the state of Tennessee, punitive damages are not recoverable as a matter of right, but are within the sound discretion of the trial judge. We will not reverse an award of punitive damages without proof of an abuse of discretion. Moreover, in reviewing a trial Court's justification for awarding such damages, we view the record in its entirety rather than each particular factor in isolation. The theory behind awarding punitive damages is not to compensate an injured plaintiff for personal injury but to punish a defendant and deter him from committing acts of similar nature.

While the court may award punitive damages when a party's conduct during the course of litigation is either frivolous or in bad faith, a review of the entire record does not suggest that defendant's conduct warranted such punitive sanctions. Unlike *Universal City Studios*, [797 F.2d 70 (2d Cir.1986), cert. denied 479 U.S. 987, 107 S.Ct. 578, 93 L.Ed.2d 581 (1986),] in which the Second Circuit held punitive damages were appropriate where defendant threatened suit alleging trademark infringement despite a prior judicial holding that its trademark was in the public domain, Velsicol's defenses during the course of litigation did not constitute an abuse of process.

There is no evidence that Velsicol's defense was contrived in bad faith. In deciding whether counsel's positions at trial warrants awarding punitive damages, too strict a standard might unduly chill an attorney's advocacy, especially for those advancing unpopular arguments. This determination required sensitivity on the part of the court. Velsicol's conduct in the instant case is an impermissible basis in and of itself for awarding punitive damages.

There is, however, evidence supporting the district court's determination that Velsicol violated state law in establishing, utilizing, and refusing to cease disposal operations at the landfill disposal site. It was within the district court's discretion to consider defendant's disregard of state law in making its award. Lastly, the district court need not defer its award of punitive damages prior to determining compensatory damages for the entire class of 128 individuals. So long as the court determines the defendant's liability and awards representative class members compensatory damages, the district court may in its discretion award punitive damages to the class as a whole at that time. Because the district court erred in awarding punitive damages, in part, upon the positions taken by Velsicol at trial, we remand for recomputation of punitive damages.

Note and Questions

The court rejects as compensable damage the increased risk of cancer and other diseases. It states: "Where the basis for awarding damages is the potential risk of susceptibility to future disease, the predicted future disease *must be medically reasonably certain* to follow from the existing present injury." For this reason, the "mere increased risk of future disease or condition" that might result from an existing condition is not compensable. Is this the same standard as applied in *Ayers*?

6. EMOTIONAL DISTRESS, FEAR OF CANCER AND ENHANCED RISK

a. *Emerging Standards*

In treating the plaintiffs' claims of "cancerphobia," the court in *Sterling* characterized it as "merely a specific type of mental anguish" which is compensable "only where such distress is either foreseeable or is a natural consequence of or reasonably expected to flow from, the present injury. * * * [T]he central focus of a court's inquiry in such a case is not on the underlying odds that the future disease will in fact materialize." What do you think of the court's formulation of the test of liability? Should the plaintiffs' entitlement to emotional distress damages deriving from the future risk of cancer and the claim of increased future risk of cancer be tied together? How would a court judge the reasonableness of the distress without reference to the magnitude of the risk of the disease? Should "fear" be distinguished from "danger"?

A leading case on standards for emotional distress claims is Anderson v. W.R. Grace & Co., 628 F.Supp. 1219 (D.Mass.1986), where the district court considered claims of plaintiffs who consumed water from wells contaminated in Woburn, Massachusetts by chemicals from defendants' operations, including trichloroethylene and tetrachloroethylene which are known carcinogens. The case included wrongful death claims on behalf of decedents' who died of leukemia allegedly caused by exposure to the chemicals. Other family members asserted claims for emotional distress caused by witnessing the deaths of these children, claims of leukemia of individuals who were in remission, and other physical ailments and emotional distress claims.

The defendant contended that those plaintiffs who did not suffer from leukemia should be barred from recovering emotional distress damages because they sustained no physical harm. The court found that some plaintiffs had alleged sufficient physical harm, and objective symptomology, to satisfy the Massachusetts rule that:

> [I]n order for * * * plaintiffs to recover for negligently inflicted emotional distress, [they] must allege and prove [they] suffered physical harm as a result of the conduct which caused the emotional distress. We answer, further, that a plaintiff's physical harm must either cause or be caused by the emotional distress alleged, and that the physical harm must be manifested by objective symptomatology and substantiated by expert medical testimony.

However, the court rejected those claims of emotional distress deriving solely from the defendants' conduct in contributing to the groundwater pollution—"anxiety, fear, depression, anger, hopelessness, and distress"—where these emotional conditions were not directly caused by physical harm that they had allegedly suffered. On the other hand, "elements of plaintiffs' emotional distress [which] stem from the physical harm to their immune systems allegedly caused by defendants' conduct are compensable."

The court also rejected the bystander emotional distress claims asserted by family members who witnessed the deaths from leukemia of five minor children on the grounds that only distress associated with witnessing a dramatic, traumatic shock would be actionable, not that associated with a prolonged illness.

What problems do you foresee courts will experience in applying tort rules, such as those governing emotional distress claims, that were developed in accident and sudden injury cases and applying them to claims in prolonged illness and exposure cases? Should there be separate standards for such cases? What might they consist of?

b. *Physical Harm Requirements or Surrogates*

In toxic tort cases individuals exposed to toxic substances that are known cancer-causing agents may live in fear or dread that cancer will develop in the future. Such claims are asserted in many environmental tort cases, as *Ayers*, *Sterling* and *Anderson* all illustrate, and in many asbestos exposure cases, where plaintiffs are employees who were exposed to asbestos for long periods. Similarly in many DES cases the courts have addressed these claims for cancerphobia, but have generally disallowed recovery for pure emotional distress absent "physical harm manifested by objective symptomatology." See Payton v. Abbott Labs, 386 Mass. 540, 437 N.E.2d 171 (1982). What are the rationales for requiring some physical harm?

Some decisions have recognized the right to recover emotional distress damages based on a fear of contracting cancer in the asbestos context. See, e.g., Jackson v. Johns–Manville Sales Corp., 781 F.2d 394 (5th Cir.1986), cert. denied 478 U.S. 1022, 106 S.Ct. 3339, 92 L.Ed.2d 743 (1986) (applying Mississippi law); Herber v. Johns–Manville Corp., 785 F.2d 79 (3d Cir.1986) (applying New Jersey law). In *Jackson* and *Herber*, however, both plaintiffs were suffering from some physical injuries (asbestosis or pleural thickening) so neither involved "pure" emotional distress. In In re Moorenovich, 634 F.Supp. 634 (D.Me.1986), the court refused to dismiss an allegation of pure emotional distress ("present fear or anxiety he experiences that he will contract cancer in the future"). Contra, Amendola v. Kansas City Southern Ry. Co., 699 F.Supp. 1401 (W.D.Mo.1988).

In Hagerty v. L & L Marine Services, Inc., 788 F.2d 315 (5th Cir.1986), the court recognized a claim for cancerphobia where a seamen had been drenched with toxic chemicals and rejected reliance on the physical manifestation requirement:

> * * * With or without physical injury or impact, a plaintiff is entitled to recover damages for serious mental distress arising from fear of developing cancer where his fear is reasonable and causally related to the defendant's negligence. The circumstances surrounding the fear-inducing occurrence may themselves supply sufficient indicia of genuineness. It is for the jury to decide questions such as the existence, severity and reasonableness of the fear.

The California Court of Appeals, in language similar to that in *Hagerty*, has recognized a cause of action for fear of cancer in Potter v. Firestone Tire & Rubber Co., 15 Cal.App.4th 490, 274 Cal.Rptr. 885 (1990), reversed in part, affirmed in part, ___ Cal.4th ___, 25 Cal.Rptr.2d 550, 863 P.2d 795 (1993). In upholding a $200,000 jury award to each of four plaintiffs, the court held that they did not have to establish a physical injury or a reasonable certainty that cancer will develop in the future in order to recover, so long as the fear is "genuine, serious and reasonable." The court emphasized that its holding was limited to cases in which the plaintiffs "have ingested carcinogens as a result of defendant's conduct and consequently fear that they will develop cancer." The court noted that actual ingestion of carcinogens provided "a certain guarantee that respondents' fears are genuine" and not an attempt to recover for "trivialities." With respect to the requirement that the distress be "serious," the court held that an objective standard should be applied—whether a reasonable person would develop such fear under the circumstances—including evidence regarding the likelihood that cancer will occur; where the likelihood is "remote," a trier of fact might conclude that the fear and distress are unreasonable. The California Supreme Court reversed on that issue, holding that, "in the absence of a present physical injury or illness, recovery of damages for fear of cancer in a negligence action should be allowed only if the plaintiff pleads and proves that the fear stems from a knowledge, corroborated by reliable medical or scientific opinion, that it is more likely than not that the feared cancer will develop in the future due to the toxic exposure."

How about a hospital employee bit on the arm by a patient with AIDS? In order to recover for "AIDS-phobia," must the plaintiff show that bites are capable of transmitting the disease? In Johnson v. West Virginia University Hospitals, Inc., 413 S.E.2d 889 (W.Va.1991), the court implied that exposure to AIDS was sufficient regardless of proof of actual danger. The jury instruction in the *Johnson* trial points out the difference between fear and real danger. The plaintiff was only required to "prove * * * that his fear of contracting the AIDS disease is *reasonable* * * *." Meanwhile, the hospital asked for an alternate instruction based on danger, that the plaintiff "possesses an increased statistical likelihood of developing AIDS and from this knowledge springs a reasonable apprehension * * *." Which do you think is the more appropriate jury instruction?

c. Some Contrary Views

Compare Merry v. Westinghouse Electric Corp., 684 F.Supp. 847 (M.D.Pa.1988) with Friedman v. F.E. Myers Co., 706 F.Supp. 376 (E.D.Pa.1989). In *Merry* the court denied defendant's motion for summary judgment on liability for emotional distress for exposure to chemicals in plaintiffs' wells, and in *Friedman* granted defendant's motion involving PCB contamination of plaintiff's well for emotional distress because of the absence of an identifiable injury, and "mere exposure" was not sufficient. See also Houston v. Texaco, Inc., 371 Pa.Super. 399, 538 A.2d 502 (1988) (overturning award for emotional distress in absence of physical manifestation); Ironbound Health Rights Advisory Comm. v. Diamond Shamrock Chemicals Co., 243 N.J.Super. 170, 578 A.2d 1248 (1990) (exposure of neighborhood residents to dioxin and other toxic chemicals manufactured at nearby plant did not give rise to claim for emotional distress damages absent showing of some physical injury, despite residents' fear that they might some day become seriously ill from previous inhalation and absorption of dioxin; concerns, although understandable, were not compensable where there was no claim of serious mental illness); accord, Ball v. Joy Technologies, Inc., 958 F.2d 36 (4th Cir.1991) (employees exposed to PCBs, dioxins, TCE, and furans could not recover for emotional distress because exposure itself did not constitute a physical injury under Virginia and West Virginia law: "The mere exposure of the plaintiffs to toxic chemicals does not provide the requisite physical injury to entitle the plaintiffs to recover for their emotional distress.") The Wyoming Supreme Court also declined to recognize an emotional distress claim against a county that condemned plaintiffs' property because of methane and hydrogen sulfide gases from a nearby coal mine. Miller v. Campbell County, 854 P.2d 71 (Wyo.1993).

In 2 American Law Institute, Enterprise Responsibility for Personal Injury 380 (1991), the Reporters' Study concluded:

> We do not advocate compensating individuals who are stricken by "cancerphobia." Although some courts have been willing to reimburse individuals for the pain, discomfort, fear, anxiety, annoyance, and emotional distress suffered as a result of exposure to potentially hazardous vapors, this type of reimbursement is highly variable and introduces great uncertainty into hazardous substance litigation. It contrasts sharply with medical monitoring damages, which must be based on expert testimony, perhaps with input from court-appointed experts or science panels regarding the presence of an increased risk of disease. Consequently, we do not advocate reimbursement for emotional damages or for increased risk per se.

Do you agree with the Reporters' conclusions? Is the concern for "variability" and "uncertainty" legitimate? What kind of variability is being referred to?

d. Literature

On these subjects of enhanced risk and emotional distress a number of articles have been written. See Fournier J. Gale III & James L. Goyer III, Recovery for Cancerphobia and Increased Risk of Cancer, 15 Cumb. L. Rev. 723, 741–44 (1985); Note, Increased Risk of Cancer as an Actionable Injury, 18 Ga. L. Rev. 563, 591–92 (1984); Paul R. Lees–Haley & Eric H. Marcus, Litigating Cancerphobia and Toxic Allergy Claims, 57 Defense Coun. J. 377 (1990); Comment, Toxic Torts and Latent Diseases: A Case for an Increased Risk Cause of Action, 38 U. Kan. L. Rev. 1087 (1990); Note, The Inapplicability of Traditional Tort Analysis to Environmental Risks: The Example of Toxic Waste Pollution Victim Compensation, 35 Stan. L. Rev. 575, 618 (1983); Comment, Increased Risk of Disease from Hazardous Waste: Problems with Gideon and a Proposed Solution, 7 Rev. of Litig. 39 (1987) (advocating nonrecognition of cause of action for increased risk of cancer absent proof of medical probability).

Problem

Plaintiffs, Mr. and Mrs. Embry and their two children lived from 1963 to 1986 in a residential neighborhood of Unionville, a moderate size city.

Unionville's residential area abutted an area zoned for light manufacturing. The defendant, Pester–Cide, Inc., a company that has manufactured various types of pesticides (DDT from 1960 until 1975, and chlordane and heptachlor from 1960 until 1980), is located across the street from the plaintiffs' house, a distance of about 800 feet. The plaintiffs allege that pesticides from the defendant's facility drifted across the street and settled in the soil, and also in the dust in their attic where they are found at concentrations in excess of normal "background" levels. The plaintiffs maintain that they have suffered headaches, watery eyes, and asthma due to this continuous exposure during the time defendant's plant was in active production, during which period plaintiffs could also distinctly smell strong odors from the plant. Now, because of their toxic exposures and their demonstrated earlier vulnerability to these poisons, plaintiffs allege further that they live in constant fear of contracting cancer and other serious illnesses.

Plaintiffs demand that defendant Pester–Cide, Inc. pay the costs of monitoring their health to minimize long term effects of exposure to defendant's pesticides by early detection and surveillance. Plaintiffs' plan to offer expert testimony from Dr. Alan Levin concerning the need for medical monitoring, and the damage to plaintiffs' immune systems resulting from alterations to cells in their immune system, which currently leaves them vulnerable to predictable, as well as unpredictable, health problems ranging from allergies to cancer.

You are an associate at the law firm of Grab & Greed that represents Pester–Cide on a number of matters. The partner in charge is concerned that plaintiffs' claims for medical monitoring might fare better than their claims for (1) fear of contracting cancer; and (2) the actual physical symptoms experienced during the plant's operations, as the statute of limitations may have run on any claims for injuries sustained while the plant was actively producing pesticides. The partner acknowledges that he is no expert in toxic tort nuances, but his impression is that some jurisdictions recognizing a claim for medical monitoring have adopted watered-down standards of causality and established elements of the claim that can too easily be satisfied. She asks you to analyze the decisional law in neighboring jurisdictions, since no decided case in Columbia has addressed the question.

Describe for the partner what "medical monitoring" is in terms of a cause of action, a claim for relief, a remedy, or however it may be characterized in legal terms. Analyze the relevant decisional law, and provide the partner with an assessment of what evidence plaintiffs must offer to make out a "claim" for medical monitoring. What underlying causes of action will, or must, plaintiffs assert? How will plaintiffs' claims for emotional distress fare, assuming no statute of limitation problems?

7. NOTE ON PUNITIVE DAMAGES

Awards of punitive damages are increasing in frequency in environmental tort cases. The court in *Sterling* sustains the basis for punitive awards (although it remands for reconsideration of the appropriate amount treating the class as a whole) which are predicated on the defendant's conduct in continuing to dispose of hazardous waste after being warned by governmental officials that it posed a material risk of harm to the community. The court reverses, however, awards of punitive damages based on the defendant's conduct in the trial of the case, specifically the defendant's asserting an assumption of the risk defense and asserting that the government agencies were partially responsible for plaintiffs' damages. This certainly seems to be the proper conclusion; a party should not be at risk for punitive damages just because it raises an unpopular or even inflammatory defense. The proper remedy for raising frivolous claims or defenses is the imposition of sanctions under Federal Rule 11 of the Federal Rules of Civil Procedure. For a discussion of Rule 11, see *Cooter & Gell v. Hartmarx Corp.*, 496 U.S. 384, 110 S.Ct. 2447, 110 L.Ed.2d 359 (1990).

a. Constitutional Limitations

After flirting with constitutional challenges to awards of punitive damages for several years, in 1991 and 1993 the Supreme Court explicitly resolved both procedural and substantive due process challenges to their award. In Pacific Mutual Life Insurance Co. v. Haslip, 499 U.S. 1, 111 S.Ct. 1032, 113 L.Ed.2d 1 (1991), the Court considered an award of $800,000 which had been rendered against an insurance agent and his employer for the agent's fraud in collecting and keeping insurance premiums even after plaintiffs' policies had been cancelled. The Court in *Haslip* addressed the core issue of whether the punitive damages procedures employed in Alabama in this case violated the due process clause. The Court traced the long history of approving the common law approach for determining punitive damages, concluding that "[i]n view of this consistent history we cannot say that the common law method for assessing punitive damages is so inherently unfair as to deny due process and be per se unconstitutional." However, the court proceeded to determine whether the particular award in this case may be "constitutionally unacceptable." Justice Blackmun began the more particularized inquiry by expressing the general constitutional concern:

> One must concede that unlimited jury discretion—or unlimited judicial discretion for that matter—in the fixing of punitive damages may invite extreme results that jar one's constitutional sensibilities. We need not, and indeed we cannot, draw a mathematical bright line between the constitutionally acceptable and the constitutionally unacceptable that would fit every case. We can say, however, that general concerns of reasonableness and adequate guidance from the court when the case is tried to a jury properly enter into the constitutional calculus.

The Court further declared that a "reasonableness" standard respecting the size of awards and "adequate guidance" from the trial courts represent the heart of what constitutional due process demands.

The Court then examined three levels of procedural safeguards: jury instructions, post-verdict review by the trial court, and appellate review, and concluded that Alabama's procedures satisfied procedural due process constraints. The jury's instructions, while affording "significant discretion," were "not unlimited" because they set forth the purposes for such awards—deterrence and punishment. Similarly, it found the post-verdict procedures constitutional because trial courts were required to reflect in the record "the reasons for interfering with a jury verdict, or refusing to do so, on grounds of excessiveness of the damages." Finally, it considered the appellate review which, pursuant to Alabama Supreme Court opinions, required consideration of numerous factors relating to the relationship between compensatory and punitive awards, the reprehensibility of the defendant's conduct, the profitability of the conduct, and the defendant's financial position. The Court concluded that these post-verdict standards created a "sufficiently definite and meaningful constraint on the discretion of Alabama fact finders" that "ensures that punitive damage awards are not grossly out of proportion to the severity of the offense and have some understandable relationship to compensatory damages."

In its discussion of punitive damages procedures, the United States Supreme Court briefly noted that while the award was more than four times the amount of compensatory damages, and 200 times more than out-of-pocket losses, and heavier than any criminal fine that could be imposed on an insurer for fraud, nevertheless, it was not unconstitutionally excessive:

> While the monetary comparisons are wide and, indeed, may be close to the line, the award here did not lack objective criteria. We conclude, after careful consideration, that in this case it does not cross the line into the area of constitutional impropriety.

In TXO Productions Corp. v. Alliance Resources Corp., ___ U.S. ___, 113 S.Ct. 2711, 125 L.Ed.2d 366 (1993), the Supreme Court sustained a $10 million punitive award in the face of both substantive and procedural challenges. The case arose from a dispute over ownership of oil and gas development rights on West Virginia land. Alliance Resources Corp. filed a counterclaim alleging slander of title when TXO sought declaratory judgment on the title issue. The jury found in Alliance's favor, awarding it $19,000 in actual damages and $10 million in punitive damages against TXO. The verdict was affirmed by the West Virginia Supreme Court of Appeals. A plurality of four justices first considered TXO's argument that a $10 million punitive damages award—an award 526 times greater than the actual damages awarded by the jury—is so excessive that it must be deemed an arbitrary deprivation of property denying substantive due process rights.

The plurality was not persuaded by either party's proposed standard of review for such awards. It said that under the respondents' rational basis standard, "apparently any award that would serve the legitimate state interest in deterring or punishing wrongful conduct, no matter how large, would be acceptable." The court also rejected TXO's heightened scrutiny standard, noting there are safeguards in the judicial process and, assuming that fair procedures were followed, "a judgment that is a product of that process is entitled to a strong presumption of validity." With regard to TXO's reliance on objective criteria which calls for an examination of other punitive damage awards and legislative penalties, the plurality said that it questions "the utility of such a comparative approach as a test for assessing whether a particular punitive award is presumptively unconstitutional."

Continuing, the Court said: "Such awards are the product of numerous, and sometimes intangible, factors; a jury imposing a punitive damages award must make a qualitative assessment based on a host of facts and circumstances unique to the particular case before it. Because no two cases are truly identical, meaningful comparisons of such awards are difficult to make."

The Court adopted a "grossly excessive" standard to gauge the size of awards, relying on its language in *Haslip* respecting "reasonableness" of awards. The Court emphasized that it would be inappropriate to look only to the size of actual damages for comparative purposes, and was "appropriate to consider the magnitude of the potential harm that the defendant's conduct would have caused to its intended victim if the wrongful plan had succeeded, as well as the possible harm to other victims that might have resulted if similar future behavior were not deterred." It concluded:

> In sum, we do not consider the dramatic disparity between actual damages and the punitive award controlling in a case of this character. * * * On this record, the jury may reasonably have determined that petitioner set out on a malicious and fraudulent course to win back, either in whole or in part, the lucrative stream of royalties that it had ceded to Alliance. The punitive damages awarded in this case is certainly large, but in light of the amount of money potentially at stake, the bad faith of [TXO], the fact that the scheme employed in this case was part of a larger pattern of fraud, trickery and deceit, and petitioner's wealth, we are not persuaded that the award was so "grossly excessive" as to be beyond the power of the State to allow.

As to procedural due process issues it found that reference to defendant's wealth in the jury's instructions did not violate due process, that the trial judge's failure to articulate reasons for upholding the award was not a constitutional violation, and that the West Virginia Supreme Court of Appeals' review was "thorough." While two Justices, Scalia and Thomas, concurred in the judgment, they would reject any theory of substantive due process rights that an award be "reasonable." Justice Kennedy separately concurred, finding that defendant's malice overcame the inference that the size of the award indicated passion, prejudice and bias by the jury against an out-of-state defendant. Justice O'Connor, joined by Justices White and Souter, dissented.

In Chapter 7 we consider some constitutional issues raised by repetitive awards of punitive damages against the same defendant as a result of the distribution of defective toxic products.

b. *Punitives in Environmental Tort Cases*

The frequency of the award of punitive damages in nuisance, trespass and abnormally dangerous activity cases has grown in the last decade. For a review of the decisions, see Gerald W. Boston, Environmental Torts and Punitive Damages (Two Parts), 14 J. Prod. Liab. 1, 14 J. Prod. Liab. 139 (1992). See, e.g., Philip Morris v. Emerson, 235 Va. 380, 368 S.E.2d 268 (1988) (disposal of pentaborane, a chemical used for executions in gas chambers, not sufficient for punitive liability against original generator or subsequent landowner, but was sufficient against firm hired to remove and dispose of it that exercised no precautions, resulting in serious injuries); Exxon Corp. v. Yarema, 69 Md.App. 124, 516 A.2d 990 (1986) (court sustained a $1 million punitive damages award when defendant's leaking underground storage tanks contaminated the groundwater and jury could have found that it disregarded serious risks by continuing to pump gasoline into the leaking tanks and delayed recovery operations).

A much publicized case that reversed a $9 million punitive damage award is Arnoldt v. Ashland Oil, Inc., 186 W.Va. 394, 412 S.E.2d 795 (1991), where four plaintiffs, drawn randomly from 200, alleged that air emissions from Ashland's oil refinery located in Kentucky interfered with the use and enjoyment of their property in West Virginia, constituting a private nuisance. The punitive damage award was governed by a Kentucky statute which authorized punitives "only upon proving, by clear and convincing evidence, that the defendant * * * acted toward the plaintiff with oppression, fraud or malice." The statute defined malice:

> "Malice" means either conduct which is specifically intended by the defendant to cause tangible or intangible injury to the plaintiff or conduct that is carried out by the defendant both with a flagrant indifference to the rights of the plaintiff and with a subjective awareness that such conduct will result in human death or bodily harm.

Ashland contended that there was no proof of a specific intent to cause injury, although Kentucky decisions had allowed malice to be inferred from "outrageous conduct," if "the conduct is sufficient to evidence conscious wrongdoing." The court reversed the punitive award, stating:

> At first glance, the alternative definition of malice appears to be an exception requiring specific intent to cause injury as an element of recovering punitive damages. However, upon examination, the secondary definition of malice still requires "a subjective awareness that such conduct will result in human death or bodily harm." Even the case law definition that appellees rely upon requires conduct that "is sufficient to evidence conscious wrongdoing." The jury in this case did not have before it any substantial evidence of Ashland's conduct which demonstrated a "conscious wrongdoing"

necessary to award punitive damages under a theory of malice. Because appellees did not introduce evidence which demonstrated a specific intent to cause bodily harm or injury, they likewise failed to demonstrate fraud or oppression toward appellees, the two other bases for awarding punitives under Kentucky law. Accordingly, the punitive damage awards should have been set aside by the trial court.

c. Government Suits for Punitive Damages

In the most infamous of all toxic contaminations—Love Canal— United States v. Hooker Chemical & Plastics Corp., 748 F.Supp. 67 (W.D.N.Y.1990), the State of New York has sought to recover $250 million in punitive damages from Occidental Chemical Corporation (OCC) as a result of the toxic contamination of the "Love Canal" site in New York State. The court rejected the defendant's assertion that the New York common law standard for assessing punitive damages was unconstitutionally vague; rejected the argument that the punitive damages sought by the State were so punitive as to transform them into a criminal penalty requiring proof beyond a reasonable doubt that the State was entitled to recover them; and rejected the assertion that the punitive damages sought would violate the Eighth Amendment's excessive fines clause. OCC's predecessor, Hooker Chemical & Plastics Corporation, buried chemical wastes at the Love Canal site in the 1940s, and then sold the site to the Niagara Falls Board of Education. After an elementary school was built on the site, residential homes were built around the site, until the discovery of groundwater contamination. The United States and the State of New York sought damages on a common law public nuisance theory, and $250 million in punitive damages.

OCC argued that "punitive damages are punishment" and that "New York law does not permit the State to inflict punishment for a public nuisance offense outside of the criminal context." It said that the only punishment authorized for a "public-nuisance offense" of the type involved was that set forth in § 240.45 of the New York Penal Law, which provides that a person is guilty of criminal nuisance when "[b]y conduct either unlawful in itself or unreasonable under all the circumstances, he knowingly or recklessly creates or maintains a condition which endangers the safety or health of a considerable number of persons." Since the maximum fine for such a violation was set at $2000, OCC argued that this amount is the maximum punishment to which it may be exposed. The court held that while the Penal Law is the exclusive *criminal* remedy for public nuisance, punitive damages are not a criminal sanction, and thus the Penal Law does not bar their recovery.

The court said that although there might well be similar purposes served by a punitive damages award and a criminal penalty, that was "simply not enough to compel the conclusion that the two remedies must, for all practical purposes, be equated when the State is the party seeking punitive damages in the context of a public nuisance action." It quoted the Minnesota Supreme Court, which said that "[w]hatever, in legal contemplation, exemplary damages may be, they are not imposed in the sense of or as a substitute for criminal punishment, but rather as enlarged damages for a civil wrong."

OCC's last argument based on state law was that the State's punitive damages claim should be dismissed because it would serve no legitimate purpose. The court noted that one of the purposes served by punitive damages is that of deterrence and that OCC argued that an award of punitive damages would not serve the goal of deterrence in the present case. The court held that while environmental laws, federal and state, do create deterrence incentives, the deterrent effect of a punitive damage award should be regarded not as an alternative, but as cumulative deterrence, and is not superseded by the statutory deterrent effects:

> [I]t makes no sense to weigh the potential deterrent effect of a punitive-damages award *against* that of environmental laws, for any deterrent effect produced by the former would add rather than subtract from any deterrent effect produced by the latter.

d. Some Interpretive Hypotheses

In an article by one of the authors of this casebook, the dozens of environmental tort cases either awarding or refusing to award punitive damages were analyzed, reaching conclusions described below. Gerald W. Boston, Environmental Torts and Punitive Damages (Part One), 14 J. Prod. Liab. 1, 37–38 (1992):

> The cases in these two sections do suggest some unifying principles that may be useful in determining whether a particular business activity in a nuisance-type setting may create liability for punitive damages:
>
> 1. In those exceptional circumstances where an activity is engaged in for a purely improper purpose or motive, liability predicated on the actual or express malice standard is a distinct possibility. If there is no evidence of a viable business justification or commercial advantage, * * * courts will sustain punitive liability on the basis of malice. Moreover, when there exists direct or circumstantial evidence of spite, ill-will, or revenge as the real purpose or motive behind the activity, punitive damage liability reaches its highest probability. In these cases, risk and utility considerations are largely irrelevant because the utility which the defendant gains (satisfaction from seeing harm inflicted) is not a kind of utility that is socially recognizable or legally cognizable. Moreover, in these cases the plaintiff often suffers little compensable harm and punitive damages offers the only method by which the defendant can be punished for its conduct and state of mind and deterred from repeating like behavior in the future.

2. In the decisions in which the punitive damage liability was sustained on the basis of evidence supporting a standard of recklessness, conscious indifferences to the rights of others, or similar standard, there were present several common factual demonstrations.

(1) Defendant possessed a knowledge or awareness that its operations were discharging or emitting some hazardous or harmful substances into the air, water or ground. In many of the cases the defendant was *intentionally* dumping chemicals outside its plant, dumping the salt pans, or dumping the waste water, intending it to percolate into the ground; or intentionally increasing the quantity of emissions or the persistent maintenance of the nuisance. Although all the decisions do not involve this ingredient, many of them do.

(2) Defendant possessed the knowledge of awareness that its activities were producing harm to the plaintiff or invading the plaintiff's rights to the beneficial use of its land. Typically this knowledge or awareness was derived from the occurrence of prior complaints or receipt of statements from neighbors. In some instances defendant did not possess actual knowledge, but was aware of an extremely high risk of harm occurring to the plaintiff or others similarly situated. More troublesome is whether the defendant is under a duty to investigate whether its activities are producing harm to others and is charged with the knowledge that such an investigation would reveal. [One case] holds that the failure to undertake reasonable investigations or studies of the effects of its fluoride emissions supported an award of punitive damages, although that aspect of the decision seems contrary to the overwhelming weight of authority. [In another] the defendant's failure to determine what the legal requirements were respecting the disposal of formation waters falls in the same category. In some cases a governmental agency may have informed the defendant of the harmful effects of its operations which puts it on notice that it is violating the rights of others.

(3) In all of the cases the defendant had knowledge of a means or method by which to reduce or eliminate or abate the risk or harm resulting from its activities. In most of the cases those means were readily available—feasible, known, and usually not terribly costly. Certainly to avoid punitive damage liability there is no demand that the defendant pursue or achieve the state of the art in pollution abatement technology. Other cases involved the failure to take simple precautions or undertake preventative maintenance, as repairing the tin whistle in [one case], or the plant and equipment in another. A few cases suggest that

defendant's failure to install precipitators on its stacks was instrumental in its finding punitive damage liability, but that certainly comes closer to the simple negligence standard.

(4) After the defendant is possessed of the knowledge identified in items (1), (2) and (3) and then fails to act, the risk of punitive liability attaches. It is at this point that the defendant exhibits the conscious indifference to the danger to others, the conscious or flagrant disregard of the rights of others that is instrumental to liability. What is critical is the mental state or attitude of consciously declining to undertake the remedial steps available to abate or reduce or eliminate the harm flowing from its operations. The decision not to maintain or repair the equipment, not to seal the dike, not to install equipment or, not to cease or desist from some aspect of its operations—it is that conscious decision that is the essential ingredient to punitive damages liability that is common to all of these cases. The decision triggers, of course, the risk and utility calculus, because it is the cost, expense, or impairment of the operations which represents the "utility" side of the equation. If the decision not to undertake the remedial steps is a "reasonable" one, or not too unreasonable one—not a reckless one—then liability for punitive damages ought not to attach. The law should only inflict punishment if the actor has refused to take steps that only the most unreasonable actors would refuse—that is, those who deliberately take no such action when the cost of doing so is minimal in comparison to the elimination or reduction in harms to others that would result.

Chapter Six

ENVIRONMENTAL STATUTORY REGULATION AND THE COMMON LAW: PREEMPTION AND IMPLIED RIGHTS

A. GENERAL PRINCIPLES OF FEDERAL PRECLUSION AND ENHANCEMENT OF PRIVATE RIGHTS

1. INTRODUCTION

The law of nuisance, negligence, and strict liability for abnormally dangerous activities is affected today by numerous state and federal environmental statutes, along with volumes of regulations affecting the quality of the air, the purity of the water, control of toxic substances, and disposal of hazardous wastes.

At common law and early in this century, the private rights of action available primarily under nuisance, public or private, trespass, and negligence stood as the sole remedies for environmental or toxic harm. With the adoption of statutory and regulatory schemes, the question arises as to how those statutes and regulations affect the rights and remedies of private parties to maintain tort actions.

There are significant differences between the structure and workings of the common law tort system and the structure and operation of the statutory environmental schemes. Choosing one example, the law of nuisance is thought of as a body of private law, subject to enforcement by private individuals, among others. Environmental regulation, on the other hand, is regarded as public law, with enforcement vested principally in public officials. The law of nuisance consists of general, broad and abstract principles of unreasonable interferences, applicable to any activity. The regulatory structure, in contrast, is highly particularized, detailed and expected to govern well-defined kinds of activity. In nuisance, plaintiff's rights are exclusively determined by courts of gener-

213

al jurisdiction. To be contrasted, the regulatory structure is drafted, enforced and adjudicated within regulatory agencies and under the supervision of officials commanding technical expertise in particular, and often quite specialized, areas of regulation.

While these two systems—one private and one public—can and do operate independently and concurrently, the practical pressure for some level of coordination between the two systems is powerful. The interrelationship between the two is the topic of this Chapter.

2. REGULATION AS ENHANCING COMMON LAW RIGHTS

A statute or regulation may function offensively in private litigation. The private litigant may seek to utilize the statutory mandates by pleading and proving a defendant's violations in the private lawsuit seeking common law remedies of damages or abatement. Alternatively, where the private litigant focuses on obtaining redress for "public" wrongs, she functions as a "private attorney general," supplementing the regulatory machinery in securing compliance.

In addition, the statute and accompanying regulations may themselves expressly provide for citizen actions against violators. Many environmental statutes do so, more often authorizing private actions for equitable relief, as distinct from actions for damages. But even where the legislature is silent about citizen suits, courts may still permit private enforcement actions by one of two means. First, courts may find that a private right of action is implied in the statutory scheme. An implied right to sue is said to turn on whether the would-be plaintiff is one of a class specially benefitted by the statute, and requires an analysis of legislative intent, underlying purposes of the statute, and the likely contribution of private enforcers to fulfillment of the statutory objectives.

Second, courts may view highly specific regulatory standards as an apt way of crystallizing broad common law principles, as in the doctrine of negligence per se. In the latter setting, the private suit retains its common law character, but statutory standards operate within it, in terms of proof or presumptions, to govern or guide decision. One salient difference is that an implied right under a federal statute gives rise to a federal claim, while suits at common law under negligence per se or related principles are normally matters for state courts or federal courts sitting in diversity jurisdiction.

For a survey and analysis of alternatives concerning private enforcement, see Richard B. Stewart and Cass R. Sunstein, Public Programs and Private Rights, 95 Harv. L. Rev. 1195 (1982). See also, Middlesex County Sewerage Authority v. National Sea Clammers Assoc., 453 U.S. 1, 101 S.Ct. 2615, 69 L.Ed.2d 435 (1981), (Stevens, J., on the implied-rights doctrine in the Supreme Court) (portions are reproduced below).

3. REGULATION AS PRECLUDING COMMON LAW RIGHTS

The regulatory scheme may serve defensively as a *shield* against private suits. Instead of recognizing regulatory norms and nuisance principles as complementary bodies of law variously enforced, courts may regard the two as competitive and incompatible, and conclude that systematic regulation within a circumscribed area requires the displacement of nuisance and other common law remedies. When that is true, the common law remedies are precluded from imposing more stringent controls than those prescribed by the regulatory apparatus. The defendant will contend that its compliance with the regulatory scheme should constitute a complete defense, and if the public agency could not secure relief because it is in compliance, then the private party should be disabled from doing so.

Again, the matter may be settled by express legislative provision. A statute may declare that it means to occupy a given field completely and so preclude common law actions. Conversely, the statute may contain a "saving clause"—common in environmental legislation—preserving nonstatutory remedies. But when the legislature is silent about the continuing vitality of the common law, courts may still hold against it under the judicial doctrine of "preemption." Whether a regulatory statute displaces or preempts other law turns on an analysis of legislative intent, the need for uniform or coordinated prescription, and the appropriateness of the subject matter for dual or multiple legal controls. In a federal system, the question is further complicated by the existence of both "vertical" and "horizontal" preemption, each with its distinctive characteristics and effects. Preemption is considered horizontal when it preempts so-called "federal common law" within a given subject matter. Preemption is called vertical when, pursuant to the Supremacy Clause, it preempts state statutes, regulations, or decisional law.

We will consider below decisions of the Supreme Court that (1) grapple with the question of federal preemption and the proper accommodation between federal and state law and common law rights and remedies; and (2) that consider the presence or absence of implied rights of action. Included is the 1992 Supreme Court decision Cipollone v. Liggett Group, Inc., which defines the judicial doctrine of preemption in the context of the 1965 and 1969 federal cigarette labeling acts. As will be seen, the impact of *Cipollone* transcends its smoking subject matter, and affects preemption doctrine under environmental statutes such as the Federal Insecticide, Fungicide and Rodenticide Act ("FIFRA").

4. SUPREME COURT DECISIONS PRECLUDING COMMON LAW RIGHTS

MILWAUKEE v. ILLINOIS

Supreme Court of the United States, 1981.
451 U.S. 304, 101 S.Ct. 1784, 68 L.Ed.2d 114.

* * *

JUSTICE REHNQUIST delivered the opinion of the Court.

When this litigation was first before us we recognized the existence of a federal "common law" which could give rise to a claim for abatement of a nuisance caused by interstate water pollution. Illinois v. Milwaukee, 406 U.S. 91 (1972). Subsequent to our decision, Congress enacted the Federal Water Pollution Control Act Amendments of 1972. We granted certiorari to consider the effect of this legislation on the previously recognized cause of action.

I

Petitioners, the City of Milwaukee, the Sewerage Commission of the City of Milwaukee, and the Metropolitan Sewerage Commission of the County of Milwaukee, are municipal corporations organized under the laws of Wisconsin. Together they construct, operate, and maintain sewer facilities serving Milwaukee County. * * * On occasion, particularly after a spell of wet weather, overflows occur in the system which result in the discharge of sewage directly into Lake Michigan or tributaries leading into Lake Michigan. The overflows occur at discrete discharge points throughout the system.

Respondent Illinois complains that these discharges, as well as the inadequate treatment of sewage at the two treatment plants, constitute a threat to the health of its citizens. Pathogens, disease-causing viruses and bacteria, are allegedly discharged into the lake with the overflows and inadequately treated sewage and then transported by lake currents to Illinois waters. * * *

* * *

On May 19, 1972, Illinois filed a complaint in the United States District Court for the Northern District of Illinois, seeking abatement, under federal common law, of the public nuisance petitioners were allegedly creating by their discharges.

Five months later Congress * * * passed the Federal Water Pollution Control Act Amendments of 1972, * * * Petitioners did not fully comply with the requirements of the permits and, as contemplated by the Act, § 402 (b)(7), 33 U.S.C. § 1342 (b)(7), see Wis. Stat. Ann. § 147.29 (West 1974), the state agency brought an enforcement action in state court. On May 25, 1977, the state court entered a judgment requiring discharges from the treatment plants to meet the effluent limitations set forth in the permits and establishing a detailed timetable for the completion of planning and additional construction to control sewage overflows.

* * * [T]he District Court rendered a decision finding that respondents had proved the existence of a nuisance under federal common law, both in the discharge of inadequately treated sewage from petitioners' plants and in the discharge of untreated sewage from sewer overflows. The court ordered petitioners to eliminate all overflows and to achieve specified effluent limitations on treated sewage. * * *

On appeal, the Court of Appeals for the Seventh Circuit affirmed in part and reversed in part. * * *

II

Federal courts, unlike state courts, are not general common-law courts and do not possess a general power to develop and apply their own rules of decision. Erie R. Co. v. Tompkins, 304 U.S. 64, 78 (1938). The enactment of a federal rule in an area of national concern, and the decision whether to displace state law in doing so, is generally made not by the federal judiciary, purposefully insulated from democratic pressures, but by the people through their elected representatives in Congress. * * *

When Congress has not spoken to a particular issue, * * * and when there exists a "significant conflict between some federal policy or interest and the use of state law," the Court has found it necessary, in a "few and restricted" instances, to develop federal common law. Nothing in this process suggests that courts are better suited to develop national policy in areas governed by federal common law than they are in other areas, or that the usual and important concerns of an appropriate division of functions between the Congress and the federal judiciary are inapplicable. * * *

* * *

III

We conclude that, at least so far as concerns the claims of respondents, Congress has not left the formulation of appropriate federal standards to the courts through application of often vague and indeterminate nuisance concepts and maxims of equity jurisprudence, but rather has occupied the field through the establishment of a comprehensive regulatory program supervised by an expert administrative agency. The 1972 Amendments to the Federal Water Pollution Control Act * * * were viewed by Congress as a "total restructuring" and "complete rewriting" of the existing water pollution legislation considered in that case.

* * * Congress' intent in enacting the Amendments was clearly to establish an all-encompassing program of water pollution regulation. * * * The establishment of such a self-consciously comprehensive program by Congress, which certainly did not exist when Illinois v. Milwau-

kee was decided, strongly suggests that there is no room for courts to attempt to improve on that program with federal common law.[14]

Turning to the particular claims involved in this case, the action of Congress in supplanting the federal common law is perhaps clearest when the question of effluent limitations for discharges from the two treatment plants is considered. The duly issued permits under which the city Commission discharges treated sewage from the Jones Island and South Shore treatment plants incorporate * * * the specific effluent limitations established by EPA regulations pursuant to § 301 of the Act[.] There is thus no question that the problem of effluent limitations has been thoroughly addressed through the administrative scheme established by Congress, as contemplated by Congress. This being so there is no basis for a federal court to impose more stringent limitations than those imposed under the regulatory regime by reference to federal common law, as the District Court did in this case. * * *

Federal courts lack authority to impose more stringent effluent limitations under federal common law than those imposed by the agency charged by Congress with administering this comprehensive scheme.

The overflows do not present a different case. They are point source discharges and, under the Act, are prohibited unless subject to a duly issued permit. As with the discharge of treated sewage, the overflows, through the permit procedure of the Act, are referred to expert administrative agencies for control. All three of the permits issued to petitioners explicitly address the problem of overflows. * * *

* * *

It is quite clear from the foregoing that the state agency duly authorized by the EPA to issue discharge permits under the Act has addressed the problem of overflows from petitioners' sewer system. The agency imposed the conditions it considered best suited to further the goals of the Act, and provided for detailed progress reports so that it could continually monitor the situation. Enforcement action considered appropriate by the state agency was brought, as contemplated by the Act, again specifically addressed to the overflow problem. There is no "interstice" here to be filled by federal common law: overflows are covered by the Act and have been addressed by the regulatory regime established by the Act. Although a federal court may disagree with the regulatory approach taken by the agency with responsibility for issuing permits under the Act, such disagreement alone is no basis for the creation of federal common law.

* * *

The invocation of federal common law by the District Court and the Court of Appeals in the face of congressional legislation supplanting it is

---

14. This conclusion is not undermined by Congress' decision to permit States to establish more stringent standards, see § 510, 33 U.S.C. § 1370. While Congress recognized a role for the States, the comprehensive nature of its action suggests that it was the exclusive source of federal law. * * *

peculiarly inappropriate in areas as complex as water pollution control. * * * Not only are the technical problems difficult—doubtless the reason Congress vested authority to administer the Act in administrative agencies possessing the necessary expertise—but the general area is particularly unsuited to the approach inevitable under a regime of federal common law. Congress criticized past approaches to water pollution control as being "sporadic" and "ad hoc," S. Rep. No. 92–414, p. 95 (1971), 2 Leg. Hist. 1511, apt characterizations of any judicial approach applying federal common law[.]

It is also significant that Congress addressed in the 1972 Amendments one of the major concerns underlying the recognition of federal common law in Illinois v. Milwaukee. We were concerned in that case that Illinois did not have any forum in which to protect its interests unless federal common law were created. In the 1972 Amendments Congress provided ample opportunity for a State affected by decisions of a neighboring State's permit-granting agency to seek redress. Under § 402 (b)(3), a state permit-granting agency must ensure that any State whose waters may be affected by the issuance of a permit receives notice of the permit application and the opportunity to participate in a public hearing. Wisconsin law accordingly guarantees such notice and hearing[.] Respondents received notice of each of the permits involved here, and public hearings were held, but they did not participate in them in any way. Section 402 (b)(5) provides that state permit-granting agencies must ensure that affected States have an opportunity to submit written recommendations concerning the permit applications to the issuing State and the EPA, and both the affected State and the EPA must receive notice and a statement of reasons if any part of the recommendations of the affected State are not accepted. Again respondents did not avail themselves of this statutory opportunity. * * * Under § 402 (d)(4) of the Act, the EPA itself may issue permits if a stalemate between an issuing and objecting State develops. The basic grievance of respondents is that the permits issued to petitioners pursuant to the Act do not impose stringent enough controls on petitioners' discharges. The statutory scheme established by Congress provides a forum for the pursuit of such claims before expert agencies by means of the permit-granting process. It would be quite inconsistent with this scheme if federal courts were in effect to "write their own ticket" under the guise of federal common law after permits have already been issued and permittees have been planning and operating in reliance on them.

* * *

We therefore conclude that no federal common-law remedy was available to respondents in this case. The judgment of the Court of Appeals is therefore vacated, and the case is remanded for proceedings consistent with this opinion.

The dissenting opinion of JUSTICE BLACKMUN, with whom JUSTICE MARSHALL and JUSTICE STEVENS join, is omitted.

Notes and Questions

1.   One of the criteria applied in these types of cases is to determine if the federal statutory scheme left any "gaps" or "interstices" that must be filled by application of federal common law. Should the courts be aggressive or cautious in finding the need to exercise interstitial law-making to occupy such gaps? Does the Supreme Court seem to endorse one approach over the other?

2.   Under the approach followed in *Milwaukee*, the process of deciding whether the court should find horizontal preemption or displacement requires two steps. First, whether the common law claim being asserted is within the regulatory field occupied by the federal statute; and second, whether the regulatory authorities within that broad field have attempted to address the specific subject of the common law claim. The problem is, of course, that the answers to these two questions are usually not clear, especially to the second question, which often is influenced by the existence or perception of inconsistencies between the federal regulatory scheme and the common law remedies sought.

3.   The Court seems to place some significance on the State of Illinois' nonparticipation in the Wisconsin permit process, participation of a type explicitly authorized by the Act. Why do you suppose Illinois chose not to participate in the Wisconsin regulatory proceeding?

4.   What is the source of the federal common law of interstate pollution control? Why is there a need for such a common law? Is there a need for such a law after the 1972 Amendments to the Federal Water Pollution Control Act? Does the federal common law of interstate pollution control always disappear when Congress gets active in the area? Is it necessary that the federal statute explicitly "preempt" federal common law? Or is it sufficient that it merely addresses the same subject matter? Is it simply a matter of Congressional intent? Or is it a matter of legal analysis?

5.   A municipal sewage treatment plant in State A discharges untreated wastes, which foul the beaches of State B. State B brings a *state* nuisance action against the relevant city in State A. Does *Milwaukee II* bar this suit? Cf. Scott v. City of Hammond, 530 F.Supp. 288 (N.D.Ill.1981) rev'd in part, aff'd in part, 741 F.2d 992 (7th Cir.1984). If the suit is not barred, which state's law applies? May State B constitutionally apply its own law? See International Paper Co. v. Ouellette, 479 U.S. 481, 107 S.Ct. 805, 93 L.Ed.2d 883 (1987)(reproduced below); Note, *Milwaukee II*: The Abatement of Federal Common Law Actions for Interstate Pollution, 1982 Utah L.Rev. 401, 416. *See also*, Note, *City of Milwaukee v. Illinois*: The Demise of the Federal Common Law of Water Pollution, 1982 Wis.L.Rev. 627.

6.   The denial of an implied private right of action is consistent with the Supreme Court's recent policy of restricting the availability of such actions. See California v. Sierra Club, 451 U.S. 287, 101 S.Ct. 1775, 68 L.Ed.2d 101 (1981), decided the same day as *Milwaukee*. In that case the plaintiffs claimed that they had an implied private right of action to enjoin violations of section 10 of the Rivers and Harbors Act. The Supreme Court found no Congressional intent to allow a private remedy for violations of the Act and refused to imply the existence of such a remedy.

7. Would any obstacle exist to the application of the law of the state of discharge in order to recover damages, particularly when the harm is accompanied by a violation of state and/or federal permitting requirements? This, of course, assumes that such a state remedy exists and that it applies to harm caused to interests outside the state.

Even if the statutory or common law of the state in which the pollution originates offers some possibility of relief, would a *state* court within that state be an ideal forum to press such a claim by "foreign" interests? How could subject matter jurisdiction exist in federal court?

If suit is brought in state or federal court in the plaintiff's home state, additional problems of obtaining *in personam* jurisdiction might arise. Even under a state long-arm statute, there would be a question of whether a discharger had sufficient minimum contacts within the state where the harm occurred. Would a county or city sewerage authority be likely to have the requisite contacts in the affected state? If the state long-arm statute considers a tort to be sufficient contact, where did the tort occur? Where the pollution was discharged or where it caused the harm?

8. Courts can also conclude that the defendant's compliance with the federal regulatory requirements should preclude its liability under federal common law rules, and this seems especially compelling where the regulatory provisions are technical and the defendant's actions have received express approval by the regulatory agency. In New England Legal Foundation v. Costle, 666 F.2d 30 (2d Cir.1981), the Second Circuit considered whether the plaintiff, a legal foundation, could maintain an action against the Long Island Lighting Company (LILCO), a public utility, and the EPA based on violations of the Clean Air Act and federal common law nuisance. The complaint alleged that LILCO maintained a common law nuisance by burning oil containing 2.8% sulphur at its power plant, which was authorized by the EPA. The Court held that "EPA's approval of LILCO's use of high sulphur fuel precludes [plaintiff] from maintaining a common law nuisance action against LILCO." Relying on the Supreme Court's decision in *Milwaukee II*, the court found that the granting of approval by the EPA must bar a private action:

> Courts traditionally have been reluctant to enjoin as a public nuisance activities which have been considered and specifically authorized by the government. The exercise of such restraint is especially appropriate here where the conduct sought to be enjoined implicates the technically complex area of environmental law and where Congress has vested administrative authority in a federal agency presumably having significant technical expertise. In doing so, Congress has indicated that regulation may be better achieved through a comprehensive statutory approach than through ad hoc common law remedies. The federal courts of course must bow to that expression of congressional intent. *City of Milwaukee* [.] To proceed otherwise by fashioning federal equitable remedies to proscribe the very conduct that the EPA, acting in its regulatory capacity pursuant to its statutory mandate, has specifically approved, as the district court below held, would be both counterproductive and beyond the proper scope of the judicial function.

See, e.g., Twitty v. North Carolina, 527 F.Supp. 778 (E.D.N.C.1981), where property owners brought suit for damages and injunctive relief against the state for storing PCBs in a landfill and the EPA for authorizing the storage under the Toxic Substances Control Act. The court dismissed plaintiffs' claims:

> There is no contention by the plaintiffs that the Toxic Substances Control Act is unconstitutional or that the regulations promulgated thereunder contravene or exceed the authority delegated. This being true, the plaintiff's first [nuisance] and third [violation of a county ordinance] causes of action must fail because courts will not enjoin as a nuisance an action authorized by valid legislative authority and because the Act preempts any local ordinances.

9. In Middlesex County Sewage Authority v. National Sea Clammers Assoc., 453 U.S. 1, 101 S.Ct. 2615, 69 L.Ed.2d 435 (1981), the Supreme Court again visited the issues of damages remedies under either federal common law or under the provisions of two Acts—the Federal Water Pollution Control Act (FWPCA), 33 U.S.C.A. § 1251 et seq., and the Marine Protection, Research, and Sanctuaries Act of 1972 (MPRSA), 33 U.S.C.A. § 1401 et seq. Justice Powell delivered the opinion of the Court:

> * * * We granted [the petitions for certiorari], limiting review to three questions: (i) whether FWPCA and MPRSA imply a private right of action independent of their citizen-suit provisions, (ii) whether all federal common-law nuisance actions concerning ocean pollution now are pre-empted by the legislative scheme contained in the FWPCA and the MPRSA, and (iii) if not, whether a private citizen has standing to sue for damages under the federal common law of nuisance. We hold that there is no implied right of action under these statutes and that the federal common law of nuisance has been fully pre-empted in the area of ocean pollution.

II

A

> It is unnecessary to discuss at length the principles set out in recent decisions concerning the recurring question whether Congress intended to create a private right of action under a federal statute without saying so explicitly. The key to the inquiry is the intent of the Legislature. Texas Industries, Inc. v. Radcliff Materials, Inc., 451 U.S. 630, 639 (1981)[.] We look first, of course, to the statutory language, particularly to the provisions made therein for enforcement and relief. Then we review the legislative history and other traditional aids of statutory interpretation to determine congressional intent.

> These Acts contain unusually elaborate enforcement provisions, conferring authority to sue for this purpose both on government officials and private citizens. * * *

> These enforcement mechanisms * * * are supplemented by the express citizen-suit provisions in § 505 (a) of the FWPCA, 33 U.S.C. § 1365 (a), and § 105 (g) of the MPRSA, 33 U.S.C. § 1415 (g). These citizen-suit provisions authorize private persons to sue for injunctions to enforce these statutes. Plaintiffs invoking these provisions first must

comply with specified procedures—which respondents here ignored—including in most cases 60 days' prior notice to potential defendants.

In view of these elaborate enforcement provisions it cannot be assumed that Congress intended to authorize by implication additional judicial remedies for private citizens suing under MPRSA and FWPCA. * * * In the absence of strong indicia of a contrary congressional intent, we are compelled to conclude that Congress provided precisely the remedies it considered appropriate.

* * *

* * * [Moreover], it is clear that the citizen-suit provisions apply only to persons who can claim some sort of injury and there is, therefore, no reason to infer the existence of a separate right of action for "injured" plaintiffs. * * *

* * *

[T]he structure of the Acts and their legislative history both lead us to conclude that Congress intended that private remedies in addition to those expressly provided should not be implied. Where, as here, Congress has made clear that implied private actions are not contemplated, the courts are not authorized to ignore this legislative judgment.

* * *

III

The remaining two issues on which we granted certiorari relate to respondents' federal claims based on the federal common law of nuisance. * * * The Court has now held that the federal common law of nuisance in the area of water pollution is entirely pre-empted by the more comprehensive scope of the FWPCA, which was completely revised soon after the decision in Illinois v. Milwaukee. See Milwaukee v. Illinois, 451 U.S. 304 (1981).

This decision disposes entirely of respondents' federal common-law claims, since there is no reason to suppose that the pre-emptive effect of the FWPCA is any less when pollution of coastal waters is at issue. To the extent that this litigation involves ocean waters not covered by the FWPCA, and regulated under the MPRSA, we see no cause for different treatment of the pre-emption question. The regulatory scheme of the MPRSA is no less comprehensive, with respect to ocean dumping, than are analogous provisions of the FWPCA.

We therefore must dismiss the federal common-law claims because their underlying legal basis is now pre-empted by statute. As discussed above, we also dismiss the claims under the MPRSA and the FWPCA because respondents lack a right of action under those statutes. We vacate the judgment below with respect to these two claims, and remand for further proceedings.

It is so ordered.

The dissenting opinion of Justice Stevens, with whom Justice Blackmun joined, concurring in the judgment in part, is omitted.

10. Should the court have distinguished *Sea Clammers* from *Milwaukee*? The standard for finding preemption of federal common law which the Court used in *Milwaukee* was whether Congress had spoken directly and comprehensively to the subject matter. While Congress had spoken to the subject of water pollution control, it had not addressed compensation for harm caused by water pollution; nowhere does the Act provide for private damages. Isn't this exactly the type of statutory interstice that federal common law is intended to fill? See United States v. Little Lake Misere Land Co., 412 U.S. 580, 593, 93 S.Ct. 2389, 37 L.Ed.2d 187 (1973), where the Court stated: "The inevitable incompleteness presented by all legislation means that interstitial federal law making is a basic responsibility of the federal courts." In that case, the Court also cited the following language with approval:

> At the very least, effective Constitutionalism requires recognition of power in the federal courts to declare, as a matter of common law or "judicial legislation," rules which may be necessary to fill in interstitially or otherwise effectuate the statutory patterns enacted in the large by Congress. In other words, it must mean recognition of federal judiciary competence to declare the governing law in an area comprising issues substantially related to an established program of government operation.

11. In a situation similar to *Sea Clammers*, where damages were sought and permits were violated, would a court be fulfilling its proper role in awarding damages? William H. Rodgers, Jr., Environmental Law § 2.12 at 47 (1984 Supp.) criticizes the *Sea Clammers* decision because the court seems to find the field occupied and the common law displaced without any detailed analysis, and notes:

> "*Milwaukee v. Illinois* itself requires that the subject of the preempted right be taken up in the administrative process, thus requiring that the common law remedy be displaced and driven out, not merely intimidated into retreat by a potential entry."

12. *Maritime Torts.* The plaintiffs in *Sea Clammers* also asserted a claim based on federal maritime tort. The Circuit Court held that this constituted a valid claim, 616 F.2d 1222, 1236 (3d Cir.1980), but the Supreme Court did not review this issue.

Maritime tort is a part of the body of admiralty law which came to the United States from England along with the concepts of common law and equity. The Constitution has been construed to have incorporated this admiralty law as it then existed as the law of the United States, subject to the power of Congress to alter. Federal courts have exclusive jurisdiction over maritime torts. To invoke that jurisdiction, a plaintiff must show that the tort occurred in a maritime locality (most courts hold that "navigable" waters are sufficient), and that there exists a significant relationship between the tort and a traditional maritime activity (injury to the fishing industry generally meets this requirement). After establishing jurisdiction, a plaintiff must then prove that a tort occurred which caused injury to the plaintiff.

Does the Clean Water Act preempt the field of maritime tort with respect to injuries caused by water pollution?

13. Many federal statutes contain explicit citizen suit provisions. See, e.g., Toxic Substances Control Act, § 20(c)(3), 15 U.S.C.A. § 2619(c)(3); Solid Waste Disposal Act § 7002(f), 42 U.S.C.A. § 6972(f); Surface Mining and Reclamation Act of 1977 § 520(e), 30 U.S.C.A. § 1270(e); Clean Air Act § 304(e); 42 U.S.C.A. § 7604(e); Deepwater Port Act § 16(e), 33 U.S.C.A. § 1515(e); Marine Protection, Research and Sanctuaries Act § 105(g)(5), 33 U.S.C.A. § 1515(e).

14. William H. Rodgers, Jr., Environmental Law § 2.12 at 45–46 (1984 Supp.), points out that the trend set in *Milwaukee* and *Sea Clammers* has been generally followed in later decisions:

> A comparison of the case law before and after *Milwaukee v. Illinois* shows a sharp responsivity to Supreme Court trend-setting. After the decision, courts have embraced the displacement position—by finding a retroactive pre-emption of claims extant before the federal laws were enacted, by turning back the United States' attempts to supplement prescribed remedies, by declining to attach significance to the scaled-down regulatory features of the Clean Air Act and other laws, and even by finding state remedies preempted by the federal choice to have no remedy.

INTERNATIONAL PAPER CO. v. OUELLETTE

Supreme Court of the United States, 1987.
479 U.S. 481, 107 S.Ct. 805, 93 L.Ed.2d 883.

JUSTICE POWELL delivered the opinion of the Court.

This case involves the pre-emptive scope of the Clean Water Act, [33 U.S.C. § 1251 et seq.] (CWA or Act). The question presented is whether the Act pre-empts a common-law nuisance suit filed in a Vermont court under Vermont law, when the source of the alleged injury is located in New York.

I

Lake Champlain forms part of the border between the States of New York and Vermont. Petitioner International Paper Company (IPC) operates a pulp and paper mill on the New York side of the lake. In the course of its business, IPC discharges a variety of effluents into the lake through a diffusion pipe. The pipe runs from the mill through the water toward Vermont, ending a short distance before the state boundary line that divides the lake.

Respondents are a group of property owners who reside or lease land on the Vermont shore. In 1978 the owners filed a class action suit against IPC, claiming, inter alia, that the discharge of effluents constituted a "continuing nuisance" under Vermont common law. Respondents alleged that the pollutants made the water "foul, unhealthy, smelly, and ... unfit for recreational use," thereby diminishing the value of their property. The owners asked for $20 million in compensatory damages, $100 million in punitive damages, and injunctive relief that would require IPC to restructure part of its water treatment system. The action was filed in State Superior Court, and then later removed to Federal District Court for the District of Vermont.

IPC moved for summary judgment and judgment on the pleadings, claiming that the CWA pre-empted respondents' state-law suit. * * *

* * * [The District Court] acknowledged that federal law normally governs interstate water pollution. It found, however, that two sections of the CWA explicitly preserve state-law rights of action. First, § 510 of the Act provides: "Except as expressly provided ..., nothing in this chapter shall ... be construed as impairing or in any manner affecting any right or jurisdiction of the States with respect to the waters (including boundary waters) of such States."

In addition, § 505(e) states: "Nothing in this section shall restrict any right which any person (or class of persons) may have under any statute or common law to seek enforcement of any effluent standard or limitation or to seek any other relief...."

The District Court held that these two provisions (together, "the saving clause") made it clear that federal law did not pre-empt entirely the rights of States to control pollution. * * *

The District Court * * * held that a state action to redress interstate water pollution could be maintained under the law of the State in which the injury occurred. * * *

* * * [T]he Court of Appeals for the Second Circuit affirmed[.] We granted certiorari to resolve the circuit conflict on this important issue of federal pre-emption. We now affirm the denial of IPC's motion to dismiss, but reverse the decision below to the extent it permits the application of Vermont law to this litigation. We hold that when a court considers a state-law claim concerning interstate water pollution that is subject to the CWA, the court must apply the law of the State in which the point source is located.

II

A brief review of the regulatory framework is necessary to set the stage for this case. Until fairly recently, federal common law governed the use and misuse of interstate water. * * *

We had occasion to address this issue in the first of two Supreme Court cases involving the dispute between Illinois and Milwaukee. * * * [Milwaukee I] held that these cases should be resolved by reference to federal common law; the implicit corollary of this ruling was that state common law was preempted. * * *

Congress thereafter adopted comprehensive amendments to the Act. We considered the impact of the new legislation when Illinois and Milwaukee returned to the Court several years later. Milwaukee v. Illinois, 451 U.S. 304 (1981) (Milwaukee II). There the Court noted that the amendments were a " 'complete rewriting' " of the statute considered in Milwaukee I, and that they were " 'the most comprehensive and far reaching' " provisions that Congress ever had passed in this area. Consequently, the Court held that federal legislation now occupied the field, pre-empting all federal common law. The Court left open the question of whether injured parties still had a cause of action under state law.   * * *

One of the primary features of the 1972 amendments is the establishment of the National Pollutant Discharge Elimination System (NPDES), a federal permit program designed to regulate the discharge of polluting effluents.   * * *

The amendments also recognize that the States should have a significant role in protecting their own natural resources. 33 U.S.C. § 1251(b).   * * * Even if the Federal Government administers the permit program, the source State may require discharge limitations more stringent than those required by the Federal Government. See 40 CFR § 122.1(f) (1986). Before the Federal Government may issue an NPDES permit, the Administrator must obtain certification from the source State that the proposed discharge complies with the State's technology-based standards and water-quality-based standards. 33 U.S.C. § 1341(a)(1). The CWA therefore establishes a regulatory "partnership" between the Federal Government and the source State.

While source States have a strong voice in regulating their own pollution, the CWA contemplates a much lesser role for States that share an interstate waterway with the source (the affected States). Even though it may be harmed by the discharges, an affected State only has an advisory role in regulating pollution that originates beyond its borders. Before a federal permit may be issued, each affected State is given notice and the opportunity to object to the proposed standards at a public hearing. An affected State has similar rights to be consulted before the source State issues its own permit; the source State must send notification, and must consider the objections and recommendations submitted by other States before taking action. Significantly, however, an affected State does not have the authority to block the issuance of the permit if it is dissatisfied with the proposed standards. An affected State's only recourse is to apply to the EPA Administrator, who then has the discretion to disapprove the permit if he concludes that the discharges will have an undue impact on interstate waters. Also, an affected State may not establish a separate permit system to regulate an out-of-state source. Thus the Act makes it clear that affected States occupy a subordinate position to source States in the federal regulatory program.

At one point IPC was operating under a federal NPDES permit. A draft of the permit was submitted to Vermont as an affected State, and Vermont as well as other interested parties objected to the proposed discharge standards. Thereafter, New York obtained permitting authority under 33 U.S.C. § 1342(b) and it now administers the permit.

III

With this regulatory framework in mind, we turn to the question presented: whether the Act pre-empts Vermont common law to the extent that law may impose liability on a New York point source.

* * *

A

As we noted in Milwaukee II, Congress intended the 1972 Act amendments to "establish an all-encompassing program of water pollution regulation." 451 U.S., at 318.   * * * The Act applies to all point sources and virtually all bodies of water, and it sets forth the procedures for obtaining a permit in great detail.   The CWA also provides its own remedies, including civil and criminal fines for permit violations, and "citizen suits" that allow individuals (including those from affected States) to sue for injunctions to enforce the statute.   In light of this pervasive regulation and the fact that the control of interstate pollution is primarily a matter of federal law, it is clear that the only state suits that remain available are those specifically preserved by the Act.

Although Congress intended to dominate the field of pollution regulation, the saving clause negates the inference that Congress "left no room" for state causes of action.   Respondents read the language of the saving clause broadly to preserve both a State's right to regulate its waters, 33 U.S.C. § 1370, and an injured party's right to seek relief under "any statute or common law," § 1365(e).   They claim that this language and selected portions of the legislative history compel the inference that Congress intended to preserve the right to bring suit under the law of any affected State.   We cannot accept this reading of the Act.

To begin with, the plain language of the provisions on which respondents rely by no means compels the result they seek.   Section 505(e) merely says that "[n]othing in this section," i.e., the citizen-suit provisions, shall affect an injured party's right to seek relief under state law;   it does not purport to preclude pre-emption of state law by other provisions of the Act.   Section 510, moreover, preserves the authority of a State "with respect to the waters (including boundary waters) of such Stat[e]."   This language arguably limits the effect of the clause to discharges flowing directly into a State's own waters, i.e., discharges from within the State.   The savings clause then, does not preclude pre-emption of the law of an affected State.

Given that the Act itself does not speak directly to the issue, the Court must be guided by the goals and policies of the Act in determining whether it in fact pre-empts an action based on the law of an affected State.   After examining the CWA as a whole, its purposes and its history, we are convinced that if affected States were allowed to impose separate discharge standards on a single point source, the inevitable result would be a serious interference with the achievement of the "full purposes and objectives of Congress."   Because we do not believe Congress intended to undermine this carefully drawn statute through a general saving clause, we conclude that the CWA precludes a court from applying the law of an affected State against an out-of-state source.

* * *

B

In determining whether Vermont nuisance law "stands as an obstacle" to the full implementation of the CWA, it is not enough to say that the ultimate goal of both federal and state law is to eliminate water pollution. A state law also is preempted if it interferes with the methods by which the federal statute was designed to reach this goal. In this case the application of Vermont law against IPC would allow respondents to circumvent the NPDES permit system, thereby upsetting the balance of public and private interests so carefully addressed by the Act.

By establishing a permit system for effluent discharges, Congress implicitly has recognized that the goal of the CWA—elimination of water pollution—cannot be achieved immediately, and that it cannot be realized without incurring costs. The EPA Administrator issues permits according to established effluent standards and water quality standards, that in turn are based upon available technology, 33 U.S.C. § 1314, and competing public and industrial uses, § 1312(a). The Administrator must consider the impact of the discharges on the waterway, the types of effluents, and the schedule for compliance, each of which may vary widely among sources. If a State elects to impose its own standards, it also must consider the technological feasibility of more stringent controls. Given the nature of these complex decisions, it is not surprising that the Act limits the right to administer the permit system to the EPA and the source States.

An interpretation of the saving clause that preserved actions brought under an affected State's law would disrupt this balance of interests. If a New York source were liable for violations of Vermont law, that law could effectively override both the permit requirements and the policy choices made by the source State. The affected State's nuisance laws would subject the point source to the threat of legal and equitable penalties if the permit standards were less stringent than those imposed by the affected State. Such penalties would compel the source to adopt different control standards and a different compliance schedule from those approved by the EPA, even though the affected State had not engaged in the same weighing of the costs and benefits. This case illustrates the problems with such a rule. If the Vermont court ruled that respondents were entitled to the full amount of damages and injunctive relief sought in the complaint, at a minimum IPC would have to change its methods of doing business and controlling pollution to avoid the threat of ongoing liability. In suits such as this, an affected-state court also could require the source to cease operations by ordering immediate abatement. Critically, these liabilities would attach even though the source had complied fully with its state and federal permit obligations. The inevitable result of such suits would be that Vermont and other States could do indirectly what they could not do directly—regulate the conduct of out-of-state sources.

Application of an affected State's law to an out-of-state source also would undermine the important goals of efficiency and predictability in the permit system. The history of the 1972 amendments shows that Congress intended to establish "clear and identifiable" discharge standards. See S. Rep. No. 92–414, p. 81 (1971), 2 Leg. Hist. 1499. As noted above, under the reading of the saving clause proposed by respondents, a source would be subject to a variety of common-law rules established by the different States along the interstate waterways. These nuisance standards often are "vague" and "indeterminate." The application of numerous States' laws would only exacerbate the vagueness and resulting uncertainty. The Court of Appeals in Milwaukee III identified the problem with such an irrational system of regulation: "For a number of different states to have independent and plenary regulatory authority over a single discharge would lead to chaotic confrontation between sovereign states. Dischargers would be forced to meet not only the statutory limitations of all states potentially affected by their discharges but also the common law standards developed through case law of those states. It would be virtually impossible to predict the standard for a lawful discharge into an interstate body of water. Any permit issued under the Act would be rendered meaningless." [Illinois v. Milwaukee, 731 F.2d 403, 414 (7th Cir.1984), cert. denied 469 U.S. 1196, 105 S.Ct. 979, 83 L.Ed.2d 981 (1985)].

It is unlikely—to say the least—that Congress intended to establish such a chaotic regulatory structure.

Nothing in the Act gives each affected State this power to regulate discharges. The CWA carefully defines the role of both the source and affected States, and specifically provides for a process whereby their interests will be considered and balanced by the source State and the EPA. This delineation of authority represents Congress' considered judgment as to the best method of serving the public interest and reconciling the often competing concerns of those affected by the pollution. It would be extraordinary for Congress, after devising an elaborate permit system that sets clear standards, to tolerate common-law suits that have the potential to undermine this regulatory structure.

C

Our conclusion that Vermont nuisance law is inapplicable to a New York point source does not leave respondents without a remedy. The CWA precludes only those suits that may require standards of effluent control that are incompatible with those established by the procedures set forth in the Act. The saving clause specifically preserves other state actions, and therefore nothing in the Act bars aggrieved individuals from bringing a nuisance claim pursuant to the law of the source State. By its terms the CWA allows States such as New York to impose higher standards on their own point sources, and in Milwaukee II we recognized that this authority may include the right to impose higher common-law as well as higher statutory restrictions. 451 U.S., at 328 (suggesting that "States may adopt more stringent limitations ... through state nuisance law, and apply them to in-state dischargers"); see also Committee for Jones Falls Sewage System v. Train, 539 F.2d 1006, 1009, and

n. 9 [4th Cir.1976] (CWA preserves common-law suits filed in source State).

An action brought against IPC under New York nuisance law would not frustrate the goals of the CWA as would a suit governed by Vermont law. First, application of the source State's law does not disturb the balance among federal, source-state, and affected-state interests. Because the Act specifically allows source States to impose stricter standards, the imposition of source-state law does not disrupt the regulatory partnership established by the permit system. Second, the restriction of suits to those brought under source-state nuisance law prevents a source from being subject to an indeterminate number of potential regulations. Although New York nuisance law may impose separate standards and thus create some tension with the permit system, a source only is required to look to a single additional authority, whose rules should be relatively predictable. Moreover, States can be expected to take into account their own nuisance laws in setting permit requirements.[20]

IPC asks the Court to go one step further and hold that all state-law suits also must be brought in source-state courts. As petitioner cites little authority or justification for this position, we find no basis for holding that Vermont is an improper forum. Simply because a cause of action is pre-empted does not mean that judicial jurisdiction over the claim is affected as well; the Act pre-empts laws, not courts. In the absence of statutory authority to the contrary, the rule is settled that a district court sitting in diversity is competent to apply the law of a foreign State.

IV

The District Court correctly denied IPC's motion for summary judgment and judgment on the pleadings. Nothing in the Act prevents a court sitting in an affected State from hearing a common-law nuisance suit, provided that jurisdiction otherwise is proper. Both the District Court and the Court of Appeals erred, however, in concluding that Vermont law governs this litigation.   * * *

The decision of the Court of Appeals is affirmed in part and reversed in part. The case is remanded for further proceedings consistent with this opinion.

The Opinion of JUSTICE BRENNAN, with whom JUSTICE MARSHALL and JUSTICE BLACKMUN join, concurring in part and dissenting in part, is

---

20. Although we conclude that New York law generally controls this suit, we note that the pre-emptive scope of the CWA necessarily includes all laws that are inconsistent with the "full purposes and objectives of Congress." See Hillsborough County v. Automated Medical Laboratories, Inc., 471 U.S. 707, 713 (1985). We therefore do not agree with the dissent that Vermont nuisance law still may apply if the New York choice-of-law doctrine dictates such a result. As we have discussed, supra, the application of affected-state law would frustrate the carefully prescribed CWA regulatory system. This interference would occur, of course, whether affected-state law applies as an original matter, or whether it applies pursuant to the source State's choice-of-law principles. Therefore if, and to the extent, the law of a source State requires the application of affected-state substantive law on this particular issue, it would be pre-empted as well.

omitted. The Opinion of JUSTICE STEVENS, with whom JUSTICE BLACKMUN joins, concurring in part and dissenting in part, is omitted.

Notes and Questions

1.   Under the Court's holding a federal court sitting in Vermont may apply New York common law to a New York point without being barred by the preemption of the Clean Water Act, but that the same court cannot apply Vermont common law to the same activity because it is barred by the preemptive effect of the Clean Water Act. Did you follow the Court's rationale for distinguishing between these two situations? In other words, the Court is finding partial vertical federal preemption, where the state of the source and state of the law are different, e.g., interstate; but no vertical preemption where the state of the source and state of the law are the same, e.g., intrastate.

2.   After the Supreme Court's decision, International Paper Co. moved for the trial court to dismiss the plaintiffs' state common law nuisance claims for the interstate *air* pollution from the mill. Applying the Supreme Court's reasoning on the water claims, the trial court held that plaintiffs' nuisance claim for air pollution was not preempted by the Clean Air Act, insofar as it was based on New York law. Ouellette v. International Paper Co., 666 F.Supp. 58 (D.Vt.1987).

We now turn to further examples of vertical preemption, an analysis that requires evaluation of the relationship between federal statutory law and state common law remedies.

CIPOLLONE v. LIGGETT GROUP

Supreme Court of the United States, 1992.
__ U.S. __, 112 S.Ct. 2608, 120 L.Ed.2d 407.

JUSTICE STEVENS delivered the opinion of the Court, except as to Parts V and VI.

"WARNING: THE SURGEON GENERAL HAS DETERMINED THAT CIGARETTE SMOKING IS DANGEROUS TO YOUR HEALTH." A federal statute enacted in 1969 requires that warning (or a variation thereof) to appear in a conspicuous place on every package of cigarettes sold in the United States.[1] The questions presented to us by this case are whether that statute, or its 1965 predecessor which required a less alarming label, pre-empted petitioner's common law claims against respondent cigarette manufacturers.

Petitioner is the son of Rose Cipollone, who began smoking in 1942 and who died of lung cancer in 1984. He claims that respondents are responsible for Rose Cipollone's death because they breached express warranties contained in their advertising, because they failed to warn

---

1. Public Health Cigarette Smoking Act of 1969, Pub. L. 91–222, 84 Stat. 87, as amended, 15 U.S.C. §§ 1331–1340. In 1984, Congress amended the statute to require four more explicit warnings, used on a rotating basis. See Comprehensive Smoking Education Act, Pub. L. 98–474, 98 Stat. 2201. Because petitioner's claims arose before 1984, neither party relies on this later Act.

consumers about the hazards of smoking, because they fraudulently misrepresented those hazards to consumers, and because they conspired to deprive the public of medical and scientific information about smoking. The [Third Circuit] Court of Appeals held that petitioner's state law claims were pre-empted by federal statutes, and other courts have agreed with that analysis. The highest courts of the states of Minnesota and New Jersey, however, have held that the federal statutes did not pre-empt similar common law claims. Because of the manifest importance of the issue, we granted certiorari to resolve the conflict[.] We now reverse in part and affirm in part.

I

* * *

Petitioner's third amended complaint alleges several different bases of recovery, relying on theories of strict liability, negligence, express warranty, and intentional tort. These claims, all based on New Jersey Law, divided into five categories. The "design defect claims" allege that respondents' cigarettes were defective because respondents failed to use a safer alternative design for their products and because the social value of their product was outweighed by the dangers it created [Count 2]. The "failure to warn claims" allege both that the product was "defective as a result of [respondents'] failure to provide adequate warnings of the health consequences of cigarette smoking" [Count 3], and that respondents "were negligent in the manner [that] they tested, researched, sold, promoted, and advertised" their cigarettes [Count 4]. The "express warranty claims" allege that respondents had "expressly warranted that smoking the cigarettes which they manufactured and sold did not present any significant health consequences" [Count 7]. The "fraudulent misrepresentation claims" allege that respondents had wilfully "through their advertising, attempted to neutralize the [federally mandated] warning" labels [Count 6], and that they had possessed, but had "ignored and failed to act upon" medical and scientific data indicating that "cigarettes were hazardous to the health of consumers" [Count 8]. Finally, the conspiracy to defraud claims "allege that respondents conspired to deprive the public of such medical and scientific data [Count 8].

* * *

* * * We granted the petition for certiorari to consider the pre-emptive effect of the federal statutes.

II

* * *

In 1964, the [Surgeon General's Advisory Committee] issued its Report, which stated as its central conclusion: "Cigarette smoking is a health hazard of sufficient importance in the United States to warrant appropriate remedial action." U.S. Dept. of Health, Education, and Welfare, U.S. Surgeon General's Advisory Committee, Smoking and Health 33 (1964). Relying in part on that report, the Federal Trade

Commission (FTC), which had long regulated unfair and deceptive advertising practices in the cigarette industry, promulgated a new trade regulation rule. That rule, which was to take effect January 1, 1965, established that it would be a violation of the Federal Trade Commission Act to "fail to disclose, clearly and prominently, in all advertising and on every pack, box, carton, or container [of cigarettes] that cigarette smoking is dangerous to health and may cause death from cancer and other diseases." 29 Fed. Reg. 8325 (1964). Several States also moved to regulate the advertising and labeling of cigarettes. Upon a congressional request, the FTC postponed enforcement of its new regulation for six months. In July 1965, Congress enacted the Federal Cigarette Labeling and Advertising Act.[8] The 1965 Act effectively adopted half of the FTC'S Regulation: The Act mandated warnings on cigarette packages (§ 5(A)), but barred the requirement of such warnings in cigarette advertising (§ 5(B)).

Section 2 of the Act declares the Statute's two purposes: (1) adequately informing the public that cigarette smoking may be hazardous to health, and (2) protecting the national economy from the burden imposed by diverse, nonuniform and confusing cigarette labeling and advertising regulations. In furtherance of the first purpose, § 4 of the Act made it unlawful to sell or distribute any cigarettes in the United States unless the package bore a conspicuous label stating: "CAUTION: CIGARETTE SMOKING MAY BE HAZARDOUS TO YOUR HEALTH." In furtherance of the second purpose, § 5, captioned "Preemption," provided in part:

> "(a)No statement relating to smoking and health, other than the statement required by section 4 of this Act, shall be required on any cigarette package.

> "(b) No statement relating to smoking and health shall be required in the advertising of any cigarettes the packages of which are labeled in conformity with the provisions of this Act."

Although the Act took effect January 1, 1966, § 10 of the Act provided that its provisions affecting the regulation of advertising would terminate on July 1, 1969.

As that termination date approached, federal authorities prepared to issue further regulations on cigarette advertising. The FTC announced the reinstitution of its 1964 proceedings concerning a warning requirement for cigarette advertisements. The Federal Communications Commission (FCC) announced that it would consider "a proposed rule which would ban the broadcast of cigarette commercials by radio and television stations." State authorities also prepared to take actions regulating cigarette advertisements.

It was in this context that Congress enacted the Public Health Cigarette Smoking Act of 1969,[12] which amended the 1965 Act in several

---

8. [15 U.S.C.A. §§ 1331–1340].   **12.** [15 U.S.C.A. §§ 1331–1340].

ways. First, the 1969 Act strengthened the warning label, in part by requiring a statement that cigarette smoking "is dangerous" rather than that it "may be hazardous." Second, the 1969 Act banned cigarette advertising in "any medium of electronic communication subject to [FCC] jurisdiction." Third, and related, the 1969 Act modified the pre-emption provision by replacing the original § 5(b) with a provision that reads: "(b) No requirement or prohibition based on smoking and health shall be imposed under State law with respect to the advertising or promotion of any cigarettes the packages of which are labeled in conformity with the provisions of this Act." Although the Act also directed the FTC not to "take any action before July 1, 1971, with respect to its pending trade regulation rule proceeding relating to cigarette advertising", the narrowing of the pre-emption provision to prohibit only restrictions "imposed under State law" cleared the way for the FTC to extend the warning-label requirement to print advertisements for cigarettes. The FTC did so in 1972.

III

Article VI of the Constitution provides that the laws of the United States "shall be the supreme Law of the Land; ... any Thing in the Constitution or Laws of any state to the Contrary notwithstanding." Art. VI, cl. 2. Thus, since our decision in McCulloch v. Maryland, 4 Wheat. 316, 427 (1819), it has been settled that state law that conflicts with federal law is "without effect." Maryland v. Louisiana, 451 U.S. 725, 746 (1981). Consideration of issues arising under the Supremacy Clause "start[s] with the assumption that the historic police powers of the States [are] not to be superseded by ... Federal Act unless that [is] the clear and manifest purpose of Congress." Accordingly, " '[t]he purpose of Congress is the ultimate touchstone' " of pre-emption analysis.

Congress' intent may be "explicitly stated in the statute's language or implicitly contained in its structure and purpose." In the absence of an express congressional command, state law is pre-empted if that law actually conflicts with federal law, or if federal law so thoroughly occupies a legislative field " 'as to make reasonable the inference that Congress left no room for the States to supplement it.' "

* * *

In our opinion, the pre-emptive scope of the 1965 Act and the 1969 Act is governed entirely by the express language in § 5 of each Act. When Congress has considered the issue of pre-emption and has included in the enacted legislation a provision explicitly addressing that issue, and when that provision provides a "reliable indicium of congressional intent with respect to state authority," Malone v. White Motor Corp., 435 U.S., at 505, "there is no need to infer congressional intent to pre-empt state laws from the substantive provisions" of the legislation. California Federal Savings & Loan Assn. v. Guerra, 479 U.S. 272, 282 (1987) (opinion of Marshall, J.). Such reasoning is a variant of the familiar principle of *expressio unius est exclusio alterius* : Congress' enactment of a provision defining the pre-emptive reach of a statute implies that matters beyond that reach are not pre-empted.   In this case, the other provisions of the 1965 and 1969 Acts offer no cause to look beyond § 5 of each Act.   Therefore, we need only identify the domain expressly pre-empted by each of those sections.   As the 1965 and 1969 provisions differ substantially, we consider each in turn.

IV

In the 1965 pre-emption provision regarding advertising (§ 5(b)), Congress spoke precisely and narrowly: "No statement relating to smoking and health shall be required in the advertising of [properly labeled] cigarettes."   Section 5(a) used the same phrase ("No statement relating to smoking and health") with regard to cigarette labeling.   As § 5(a) made clear, that phrase referred to the sort of warning provided for in § 4, which set forth verbatim the warning Congress determined to be appropriate.   Thus, on their face, these provisions merely prohibited state and federal rule-making bodies from mandating particular cautionary statements on cigarette labels (§ 5(a)) or in cigarette advertisements (§ 5(b)).

Beyond the precise words of these provisions, this reading is appropriate for several reasons.   First, as discussed above, we must construe these provisions in light of the presumption against the pre-emption of state police power regulations.   This presumption reinforces the appropriateness of a narrow reading of § 5.   Second, the warning required in § 4 does not by its own effect foreclose additional obligations imposed under state law.   That Congress requires a particular warning label does not automatically pre-empt a regulatory field.   Third, there is no general, inherent conflict between federal pre-emption of state warning requirements and the continued vitality of state common law damages actions.   For example, in the Comprehensive Smokeless Tobacco Health Education Act of 1986,[14] Congress expressly pre-empted State or local imposition of a "statement relating to the use of smokeless tobacco products and health" but, at the same time, preserved state law damages actions based on those products.   See 15 U.S.C. § 4406.   All of these considerations indicate that § 5 is best read as having superseded only positive enactments by legislatures or administrative agencies that mandate particular warning labels.

This reading comports with the 1965 Act's statement of purpose, which expressed an intent to avoid "diverse, nonuniform, and confusing labeling and advertising *regulations* with respect to any relationship between smoking and health."   Read against the backdrop of regulatory activity undertaken by state legislatures and federal agencies in response to the Surgeon General's report, the term "regulation" most naturally refers to positive enactments by those bodies, not to common law damages actions.

---

14.   [15 U.S.C.A. §§ 4401–4408].

The regulatory context of the 1965 Act also supports such a reading. As noted above, a warning requirement promulgated by the FTC and other requirements under consideration by the States were the catalyst for passage of the 1965 Act. These regulatory actions animated the passage of § 5, which reflected Congress' efforts to prevent "a multiplicity of State and local regulations pertaining to labeling of cigarette packages," H.R. Rep. No. 89–449, 89th Cong., 1st Sess., 4 (1965), and to "pre-empt [all] Federal, State, and local authorities from requiring any statement . . . relating to smoking and health in the advertising of cigarettes." Id., at 5 (emphasis supplied).

For these reasons, we conclude that § 5 of the 1965 Act only pre-empted state and federal rulemaking bodies from mandating particular cautionary statements and did not pre-empt state law damages actions.

V

Compared to its predecessor in the 1965 Act, the plain language of the pre-emption provision in the 1969 Act is much broader. First, the later Act bars not simply "statements" but rather "requirement[s] or prohibitions . . . imposed under State law." Second, the later Act reaches beyond statements "in the advertising" to obligations "with respect to the advertising or promotion" of cigarettes.

Notwithstanding these substantial differences in language, both petitioner and respondents contend that the 1969 Act did not materially alter the pre-emptive scope of federal law. Their primary support for this contention is a sentence in a Committee Report which states that the 1969 amendment "clarified" the 1965 version of § 5(b). S. Rep. No. 91–566, p. 12 (1969). We reject the parties' reading as incompatible with the language and origins of the amendments. As we noted in another context, "[i]nferences from legislative history cannot rest on so slender a reed. Moreover, the views of a subsequent Congress form a hazardous basis for inferring the intent of an earlier one." The 1969 Act worked substantial changes in the law: rewriting the label warning, banning broadcast advertising, and allowing the FTC to regulate print advertising. In the context of such revisions and in light of the substantial changes in wording, we cannot accept the parties' claim that the 1969 Act did not alter the reach of § 5(b).

Petitioner next contends that § 5(b), however broadened by the 1969 Act, does not pre-empt *common law* actions. He offers two theories for limiting the reach of the amended § 5(b). First, he argues that common law damages actions do not impose "requirement[s] or prohibition[s]" and that Congress intended only to trump "state statute[s], injunction[s], or executive pronouncement[s]." We disagree; such an analysis is at odds both with the plain words of the 1969 Act and with the general understanding of common law damages actions. The phrase "[n]o requirement or prohibition" sweeps broadly and suggests no distinction between positive enactments and common law; to the contrary, those words easily encompass obligations that take the form of common law rules. As we noted in another context, "[state] regulation can be as effectively exerted through an award of damages as through some form of preventive relief. The obligation to pay compensation can be, indeed is designed to be, a potent method of governing conduct and controlling policy.''

Although portions of the legislative history of the 1969 Act suggest that Congress was primarily concerned with positive enactments by States and localities, see S. Rep. No. 91–566, p. 12, the language of the Act plainly reaches beyond such enactments. "We must give effect to this plain language unless there is good reason to believe Congress intended the language to have some more restrictive meaning." In this case there is no "good reason to believe" that Congress meant less than what it said; indeed, in light of the narrowness of the 1965 Act, there is "good reason to believe" that Congress meant precisely what it said in amending that Act.

Moreover, common law damages actions of the sort raised by petitioner are premised on the existence of a legal duty and it is difficult to say that such actions do not impose "requirements or prohibitions." See W. Prosser, Law of Torts 4 (4th ed. 1971); Black's Law Dictionary 1489 (6th ed. 1990) (defining "tort" as "always [involving] a violation of some duty owing to plaintiff"). It is in this way that the 1969 version of § 5(b) differs from its predecessor: Whereas the common law would not normally require a vendor to use any specific *statement* on its packages or in its advertisements, it is the essence of the common law to enforce duties that are either affirmative *requirements* or negative prohibitions. We therefore reject petitioner's argument that the phrase "requirement or prohibition" limits the 1969 Act's pre-emptive scope to positive enactments by legislatures and agencies.

Petitioner's second argument for excluding common law rules from the reach of § 5(b) hinges on the phrase "imposed under State law." This argument fails as well. At least since Erie R. v. Tompkins, 304 U.S. 64 (1938), we have recognized the phrase "state law" to include common law as well as statutes and regulations. Indeed just last Term, the Court stated that the phrase "all other law, including State and municipal law" "does not admit of [a] distinction ... between positive enactments and common-law rules of liability." Although the presumption against pre-emption might give good reason to construe the phrase "state law" in a pre-emption provision more narrowly than an identical phrase in another context, in this case such a construction is not appropriate. As explained above, the 1965 version of § 5 was precise and narrow on its face; the obviously broader language of the 1969 version extended that section's pre-emptive reach. Moreover, while the version of the 1969 Act passed by the Senate pre-empted "any State *statute or regulation* with respect to ... advertising or promotion," S. Rep. No. 91–566, p. 16, the Conference Committee replaced this language with State *law* with respect to advertising or promotion." In such a situation, § 5(b)'s pre-emption of "state law" cannot fairly be limited to positive enactments.

That the pre-emptive scope of § 5(b) cannot be limited to positive enactments does not mean that that section pre-empts all common law claims. For example, as respondents concede, § 5(b) does not generally pre-empt "state-law obligations to avoid marketing cigarettes with manufacturing defects or to use a demonstrably safer alternative design for cigarettes." For purposes of § 5(b), the common law is not of a piece.

Nor does the statute indicate that any familiar subdivision of common law claims is or is not pre-empted. We therefore cannot follow petitioner's passing suggestion that § 5(b) pre-empts liability for omissions but not for acts, or that § 5(b) pre-empts liability for unintentional torts but not for intentional torts. Instead we must fairly but—in light of the strong presumption against pre-emption—narrowly construe the precise language of § 5(b) and we must look to each of petitioner's common law claims to determine whether it is in fact pre-empted. The central inquiry in each case is straightforward: we ask whether the legal duty that is the predicate of the common law damages action constitutes a "requirement or prohibition based on smoking and health ... imposed under State law with respect to ... advertising or promotion," giving that clause a fair but narrow reading. As discussed below, each phrase within that clause limits the universe of common law claims pre-empted by the statute.

We consider each category of damages actions in turn. In doing so, we express no opinion on whether these actions are viable claims as a matter of state law; we assume *arguendo* that they are.

FAILURE TO WARN

To establish liability for a failure to warn, petitioner must show that "a warning is necessary to make a product ... reasonably safe, suitable and fit for its intended use," that respondents failed to provide such a warning, and that that failure was a proximate cause of petitioner's injury. In this case, petitioner offered two closely related theories concerning the failure to warn: first, that respondents "were negligent in the manner [that] they tested, researched, sold, promoted, and advertised" their cigarettes; and second, that respondents failed to provide "adequate warnings of the health consequences of cigarette smoking." App. 85–86.

Petitioner's claims are pre-empted to the extent that they rely on a state law "requirement or prohibition ... with respect to ... advertising or promotion." Thus, insofar as claims under either failure to warn theory require a showing that respondents' post–1969 advertising or promotions should have included additional, or more clearly stated, warnings, those claims are pre-empted. The Act does not, however, pre-empt petitioner's claims that rely solely on respondents' testing or research practices or other actions unrelated to advertising or promotion.

BREACH OF EXPRESS WARRANTY

Petitioner's claim for breach of an express warranty arises under N.J. Stat. Ann. § 12A:2– 313(1)(a) (West 1991), which provides:

"Any affirmation of fact or promise made by the seller to the buyer which relates to the goods and becomes part of the basis of the bargain creates an express warranty that the goods shall conform to the affirmation or promise."

Petitioner's evidence of an express warranty consists largely of statements made in respondents' advertising. Applying the Court of Appeals' ruling that Congress pre-empted damage[s] actions ... that challenge ... the propriety of a party's actions with respect to the advertising and promotion of cigarettes," the District Court ruled that this claim "inevitably brings into question [respondents'] advertising and promotional activities, and is therefore pre-empted" after 1965. As demonstrated above, however, the 1969 Act does not sweep so broadly: the appropriate inquiry is not whether a claim challenges the "propriety" of advertising and promotion, but whether the claim would require the imposition under state law of a requirement or prohibition based on smoking and health with respect to advertising or promotion.

A manufacturer's liability for breach of an express warranty derives from, and is measured by, the terms of that warranty. Accordingly, the "requirements" imposed by [an] express warranty claim are not "imposed under State law," but rather imposed *by the warrantor*.[23] If, for example, a manufacturer expressly promised to pay a smoker's medical bills if she contracted emphysema, the duty to honor that promise could not fairly be said to be "imposed under state law," but rather is best understood as undertaken by the manufacturer itself. While the general duty not to breach warranties arises under state law, the particular "requirement ... based on smoking and health ... with respect to the advertising or promotion [of] cigarettes" in an express warranty claim arises from the manufacturer's statements in its advertisements. In short, a common law remedy for a contractual commitment voluntarily undertaken should not be regarded as a "requirement ... *imposed under State law* " within the meaning of § 5(b).

That the terms of the warranty may have been set forth in advertisements rather than in separate documents is irrelevant to the pre-emption issue (though possibly not to the state law issue of whether the alleged warranty is valid and enforceable) because although the breach of warranty claim is made "with respect to advertising" it does not rest on a duty imposed under state law. Accordingly, to the extent that petitioner has a viable claim for breach of express warranties made by respondents, that claim is not pre-empted by the 1969 Act.

FRAUDULENT MISREPRESENTATION

Petitioner alleges two theories of fraudulent misrepresentation. First, petitioner alleges that respondents, through their advertising,

---

23. Thus it is that express warranty claims are said to sound in contract rather than in tort. Compare Black's Law Dictionary 1489 (6th ed. 1990) (defining "tort": "There must always be a violation of some duty ... and generally such duty must arise by operation of law and not by mere agreement of the parties") with id., at 322 (defining "contract": "An agreement between two ... persons which creates an obligation").

neutralized the effect of federally mandated warning labels. Such a claim is predicated on a state-law prohibition against statements in advertising and promotional materials that tend to minimize the health hazards associated with smoking. Such a *prohibition*, however, is merely the converse of a state law *requirement* that warnings be included in advertising and promotional materials. Section 5(b) of the 1969 Act preempts both requirements and prohibitions; it therefore supersedes petitioner's first fraudulent misrepresentation theory.

Regulators have long recognized the relationship between prohibitions on advertising that downplays the dangers of smoking and requirements for warnings in advertisements. For example, the FTC, in promulgating its initial trade regulation rule in 1964, criticized advertising that "associated cigarette smoking with such positive attributes as contentment, glamour, romance, youth, happiness . . . at the same time suggesting that smoking is an activity at least consistent with physical health and well-being." The Commission concluded:

"To avoid giving a false impression that smoking [is] innocuous, the cigarette manufacturer who represents the alleged pleasures or satisfactions of cigarette smoking in his advertising must also disclose the serious risks to life that smoking involves." 29 Fed. Reg., at 8356.

Long-standing regulations of the Food and Drug Administration express a similar understanding of the relationship between required warnings and advertising that "negates or disclaims" those warnings: "A hazardous substance shall not be deemed to have met [federal labeling] requirements if there appears in or on the label . . . statements, designs, or other graphic material that in any manner negates or disclaims [the required warning]." 21 CFR § 191.102 (1965). In this light it seems quite clear that petitioner's first theory of fraudulent misrepresentation is inextricably related to petitioner's first failure to warn theory, a theory that we have already concluded is largely preempted by § 5(b).

Petitioner's second theory, as construed by the District Court, alleges intentional fraud and misrepresentation both by "false representation of a material fact [and by] conceal[ment of] a material fact." The predicate of this claim is a state law duty not to make false statements of material fact or to conceal such facts. Our pre-emption analysis requires us to determine whether such a duty is the sort of requirement or prohibition proscribed by § 5(b).

Section 5(b) pre-empts only the imposition of state law obligations "with respect to the advertising or promotion" of cigarettes. Petitioner's claims that respondents concealed material facts are therefore not pre-empted insofar as those claims rely on a state law duty to disclose such facts through channels of communication other than advertising or promotion. Thus, for example, if state law obliged respondents to disclose material facts about smoking and health to an administrative agency, § 5(b) would not pre-empt a state law claim based on a failure to fulfill that obligation.

Moreover, petitioner's fraudulent misrepresentation claims that do arise with respect to advertising and promotions (most notably claims based on allegedly false statements of material fact made in advertisements) are not pre-empted by § 5(b). Such claims are not predicated on a "duty based on smoking and health" but rather on a more general obligation—the duty not to deceive. This understanding of fraud by intentional misstatement is appropriate for several reasons. First, in the 1969 Act, Congress offered no sign that it wished to insulate cigarette manufacturers from longstanding rules governing fraud. To the contrary, both the 1965 and the 1969 Acts explicitly reserved the FTC's authority to identify and punish deceptive advertising practices— an authority that the FTC had long exercised and continues to exercise. See § 5(c) of the 1965 Act; § 7(b) of the 1969 Act[.] This indicates that Congress intended the phrase "relating to smoking and health" (which was essentially unchanged by the 1969 Act) to be construed narrowly, so as not to proscribe the regulation of deceptive advertising.

Moreover, this reading of "based on smoking and health" is wholly consistent with the purposes of the 1969 Act. State law prohibitions on false statements of material fact do not create "diverse, nonuniform, and confusing" standards. Unlike state law obligations concerning the warning necessary to render a product "reasonably safe", state law proscriptions on intentional fraud rely only on a single, uniform standard: falsity. Thus, we conclude that the phrase "based on smoking and health" fairly but narrowly construed does not encompass the more general duty not to make fraudulent statements. Accordingly, petitioner's claim based on allegedly fraudulent statements made in respondents' advertisements are not pre-empted by § 5(b) of the 1969 Act.

Conspiracy to Misrepresent or Conceal Material Facts

Petitioner's final claim alleges a conspiracy among respondents to misrepresent or conceal material facts concerning the health hazards of smoking. The predicate duty underlying this claim is a duty not to conspire to commit fraud. For the reasons stated in our analysis of petitioner's intentional fraud claim, this duty is not pre-empted by § 5(b) for it is not a prohibition "based on smoking and health" as that phrase is properly construed. Accordingly, we conclude that the 1969 Act does not pre-empt petitioner's conspiracy claim.

VI

To summarize our holding: The 1965 Act did not pre-empt state law damages actions; the 1969 Act pre-empts petitioner's claims based on a failure to warn and the neutralization of federally mandated warnings to the extent that those claims rely on omissions or inclusions in respondents' advertising or promotions; the 1969 Act does not pre-empt petitioner's claims based on express warranty, intentional fraud and misrepresentation, or conspiracy.

The judgment of the Court of Appeals is accordingly reversed in part and affirmed in part, and the case is remanded for further proceedings consistent with this opinion.

It is so ordered.

The concurrences and partial concurrences by JUSTICES BLACKMUN, SCALIA, KENNEDY and SOUTER are omitted.

Notes and Questions

1. Justice Steven's opinion commanded a plurality of four Justices. Three Justices, Blackmun, Kennedy and Souter, would have found that no tort actions were preempted by either the 1965 or 1969 Acts. Two Justices, Scalia and Thomas, would have found all claims preempted. According to the Supreme Court in *Cipollone*, in determining if the field is occupied and the common law preempted, should the courts consider whether, in Professor Rodger's words, "the field is occupied by remote sentinel only or must it be seized, tilled and harvested"? William H. Rogers, Jr., Environmental Law, § 2.12 at 46.

2. If preemption is express, not implied, as held by the plurality, what is the logic for construing the language narrowly? Do the same considerations against broad construction of an implied preemption apply with equal force to expressly preempted fields?

3. *Preemption Under FIFRA.* A plaintiff's state law tort claim against the manufacturer of a pesticide for inadequate warning may be preempted by the Federal Insecticide, Fungicide and Rodenticide Act (FIFRA). This act, which is codified at 7 U.S.C.A. § 136, is designed to provide a comprehensive system for the regulation and labeling of pesticides. The EPA is responsible for its enforcement; a pesticide that is duly registered with the EPA must be accompanied by a label that contains EPA-approved warnings that its product is adequate to protect health and environment. 7 U.S.C.A. § 136(q)(1)(G). Moreover, a label cannot contain language that is not approved by the EPA. 40 C.F.R. § 156.10(a)(1).

Following *Cipollone*, the question arises as to the effect of that decision's preemption analysis upon environmental or toxic tort suits involving pesticides, fungicides and rodenticides. Consider the observations of Professor Richard C. Ausness, The Impact of the *Cipollone* case on Federal Preemption Law, 15 J. Prod. & Tox. Liab. 1, 21–22 (1993):

> [FIFRA] gives the EPA the power to oversee most aspects of pesticide development, manufacture, sale, and use. Although the states are given authority to regulate pesticide use to the extent that their activities do not conflict with FIFRA, the EPA retains exclusive control over pesticide labeling. Numerous persons have brought suit against pesticide manufacturers, claiming that EPA-approved warning labels were inadequate. As might be expected, pesticide manufacturers have argued that FIFRA preempts such claims.
>
> [Prior to *Cipollone*,] courts have ruled in favor of the pesticide manufacturers, but a considerable minority have refused to preempt failure to warn claims. Virtually all courts have rejected express preemption and occupation of the field theories, electing instead to ap-

proach the preemption issue in terms of an actual conflict analysis. As in other preemption areas, most of [the pre-*Cipollone*] cases have turned on whether common-law claims are considered to be a form of regulation.

Applying the *Cipollone* Court's preemption analysis to FIFRA, one would start with the statute's preemption provision. This provision does not expressly preempt common-law claims; rather, it prohibits state law "requirements" inconsistent with federal safety standards. FIFRA's legislative history is also silent on the question of whether Congress intended to preempt state law failure to warn claims. Nevertheless, the Court, if it chose, could argue that FIFRA expressly preempts failure to warn claims because they rely on a state requirement with respect to labeling that differs from the requirement imposed by the EPA.

Do you agree with Professor Ausness' prediction? Consider the following opinion in Shaw v. Dow Brands, Inc.

SHAW v. DOW BRANDS, INC.

United States Court of Appeals, Seventh Circuit, 1993.
994 F.2d 364.

CUMMINGS, J.

Billy Joe Shaw claims his lungs were permanently damaged when, on August 12, 1990, he tried to clean his bathroom. Shaw mixed something called "X–14 Instant Mildew Stain Remover" with Dow Bathroom Cleaner, a product manufactured by defendant. Though he opened the windows, set the ceiling fan swirling and let the air conditioner blow, Shaw was twice overcome by the fumes. When an hour later he found it hard to breathe, Shaw went to a doctor and eventually was put in the hospital to treat a lung condition known as Bronchiolitis Obliterans, allegedly caused by exposure to toxic fumes.

Shaw sued a series of companies[.] * * * Shaw filed his suit in Massac County, Illinois; Dow Brands had it removed to federal court in the Southern District of Illinois. The district judge decided that Shaw's state law strict liability and negligence claims for failure to warn were pre-empted by the Federal Insecticide, Fungicide and Rodenticide Act, more commonly and easily referred to as FIFRA, 7 U.S.C. § 136 et seq. Based on a recent Supreme Court decision, we affirm the district court's pre-emption finding.   * * *

* * *

[W]e must decide whether federal pre-emption of an area of regulation also prohibits state common law tort actions. The district judge found that because of FIFRA, the federal law in question, Shaw could not bring a damages action claiming that the label on Dow Bathroom Cleaner was defective because Congress alone may regulate the labels and warnings on such products. FIFRA, enacted in 1947, was originally intended as a licensing and labeling statute for pesticides. Amendments in 1972 strengthened the law, and it became a comprehensive regulation of the sale and use of pesticides and other chemicals including such products as bathroom cleaners. Wisconsin Public Intervenor v. Mortier, 111 S.Ct. 2476 (1991).

* * * Whether a federal statute pre-empts state law turns on congressional intent. That intent may be explicit in the statute itself, Jones v. Rath Packing Co., 430 U.S. 519, 525 [1977]; in this case it is, at least as far as labeling and packaging are concerned. The Act says flatly: "Such State shall not impose or continue in effect any requirements for labeling or packaging in addition to or different from those required under this subchapter." 7 U.S.C. § 136v(b). The Supreme Court recently noted the absolutist nature of FIFRA's pre-emption in the labeling and packaging context even as it held that FIFRA does not pre-empt generalized state regulation of pesticides. Mortier, 111 S.Ct. at 2486. Since the parties do not dispute that Congress has exclusive jurisdiction in labeling and packaging, the only question is: how exclusive is exclusive? Shaw maintains that there is still room for common law tort actions for defective labels.

Shaw's argument is appealing because, unlike federal regulations which firms are required to follow, common law duties may be simply ignored by defendants. See, e.g., Ferebee v. Chevron Chemical Co., 736 F.2d 1529, 1540–1541 (D.C. Cir.), cert. denied, 469 U.S. 1062 (1984) (despite pre-emption under FIFRA, state may decide that manufacturer should bear the risk for compensating losses). Indeed, they are smart to do so if the cost of compensating victims is less than the cost of altering the behavior that gives rise to the suit. On the other hand, damages actions, just like regulatory mandates, cause companies to modify their economic decisions. It would be silly to pretend that federal lawmakers, seeking to occupy a whole field of regulation, wouldn't also be concerned about the distorting effects of tort actions.

In any event, Shaw's argument about common law actions evaporated last summer when the Supreme Court decided Cipollone v. Liggett Group, Inc., 112 S.Ct. 2608 (1992). That opinion held that sweeping congressional efforts to pre-empt state regulation also bar state damages claims. Although the Court said that "there is no general, inherent conflict between federal pre-emption of state warning requirements and the continued vitality of state common law damages actions," it also held that a broad statement in a federal law prohibiting state regulation does, in fact, wipe away common law attempts to impose liability on top of the federal regulation.

The federal laws at issue in Cipollone were the Federal Cigarette Labeling and Advertising Act ("1965 Cigarette Act") and the Public Health Cigarette Smoking Act of 1969 ("1969 Cigarette Act"), 15 U.S.C. §§ 1331–1340. These laws are responsible for, among other things, the surgeon general's warnings that grace the sides of cigarette packages. The pre-emption provision in the 1965 Cigarette Act was quite narrow and said, "No statement relating to smoking and health shall be required in the advertising of [properly labeled] cigarettes." Congress' emphasis on the words "statement" and "advertising" led the Court to conclude that the 1965 Cigarette Act only pre-empted state and federal rules that might require additional warnings, but not state law damages actions. The 1969 Cigarette Act, however, was much broader; it barred not merely "statements" but any "requirement[s] or prohibition[s] * * * imposed under State law." This language, the Court held, signalled legislative intent to ban common law tort actions along with direct state regulation. As Justice Stevens wrote:

> The phrase "[n]o requirement or prohibition" sweeps broadly and suggests no distinction between positive enactments and common law; to the contrary, those words easily encompass obligations that take the form of common law rules. As we noted in another context, "[state] regulation can be as effectively exerted through an award of damages as through some form of preventive relief. The obligation to pay compensation can be, indeed is designed to be, a potent method of governing conduct and controlling policy.

In order to succeed in the wake of Cipollone, then, Shaw would have to show that FIFRA's pre-emption language is less sweeping than the language of the 1969 Cigarette Act. Yet we can discern no significant distinction at all—FIFRA says that "[s]uch State shall not impose * * * any requirements for labeling or packaging in addition to or different from those required * * *," while the cigarette law says "[n]o requirement[s] or prohibition[s] * * * imposed under State law" shall be permitted. Both seem equally emphatic: "[n]o requirements or prohibitions" is just another way of saying a "[s]tate shall not impose * * * any requirements." Not even the most dedicated hair-splitter could distinguish these statements. If common law actions cannot survive under the 1969 cigarette law, then common law actions for labeling and packaging defects cannot survive under FIFRA. The Tenth Circuit recently held the same thing. Arkansas–Platte & Gulf Partnership v. Van Waters & Rogers, Inc., 981 F.2d 1177, 1179 (10th Cir.1993) ("We believe also the prohibition of 'any' requirement is the functional equivalent of 'no' requirement. We see no difference between the operative effect of the two acts"). Because Cipollone destroyed whatever argument Shaw might have had about pre-emption, we are compelled to affirm the district court decision that FIFRA bars this action.

The Dissent by SHADUR, S.D.J., is omitted.

Notes and Questions

1. A further discussion of issues of preemption as it relates to products liability is contained in Chapter 7. See generally Richard C. Ausness, The Impact of *Cipollone* on Federal Preemption Law, 15 J. Prod. & Tox. Liab. 1 (1993); Valle Simms Dutcher, The Malboro Man Meets the Orkin Man: The Effect of Cipollone v. Liggett Group, Inc. on Federal Preemption by the Federal Insecticide, Fungicide and Rodenticide Act of Failure to Warn Claims Brought Under State Tort Law, 15 J. Prod. & Tox. Liab. 29 (1993).

2. In the above article, Dutcher writes:

[After] *Cipollone*, several causes of action relating to failure to warn remain open to plaintiffs [alleging toxic harm caused by products regulated under FIFRA]. First, the Court did not address the issue of whether a manufacturer's failure to submit an adequate label in compliance with federal standards could be held negligence per se. Further, the Court stated that claims based on defendant's negligent testing procedures were not preempted under the 1969 Cigarette Act. Therefore, it could be argued that a pesticide manufacturer is negligent when the label it submits to EPA is inadequate due to insufficient testing. Additionally, the *Cipollone* Court held that breach of warranty actions are not preempted by federal law[.] [Because pesticide manufacturers] submit a label as part of the application for registration under FIFRA, it could be argued that such a submission represents an implied warranty that the product is fit for foreseeable uses in the marketplace.

On the basis of Dutcher's observations, how would you craft additional arguments for Shaw's claim against Dow Brands?

B.   STATE JUDICIAL CONSIDERATIONS OF PREEMPTION: A COMPLEMENTARY APPROACH

1.   In State of Missouri ex rel. Dresser Indus. v. Ruddy, 592 S.W.2d 789 (Mo.1980), the defendant, Dresser, conducted a barite mining operation, which used settling basins with holding ponds which collected waste from the mining activity. A "dam" in the settling basin ruptured, thus polluting the streams, and ultimately a major river, for a period of 200 days. The Missouri Clean Water Commissioner and Department of Natural Resources brought a two-count action, one alleging a violation of clean water law and the other alleging public nuisance, seeking compensatory and punitive damages. Dresser argued that (1) the State could not maintain an action on a nuisance theory, and (2) the Clean Water Act preempted the field, thereby displacing common law nuisance. The court held that the government could maintain a public nuisance action for damages or injunctive relief. A statute provided that "pollution of the waters of this State constitutes a menace ... and creates a public nuisance...." The court found inapplicable authorities declaring that a public entity was barred from recovering damages for the harm to the protectable public interests. On the preemption question it held:

> Did enactment of the Clean Water Law, Chapter 204, pre-empt the field of water pollution "public nuisance" law in Missouri? We have concluded that it did not. Section 204.131, heretofore quoted, in part declares that the Act does not alter or abridge "any right of action" now existing. In so providing, it is apparent that the General Assembly intended to *expand* rather than restrict available remedies. In accordance with the prescriptions of the Federal Water Pollution Control Act, 33 U.S.C. §§ 1251, et seq., § 1253 (1976), the Clean Water Commission was created under the Department of Natural Resources in 1972. §§ 204.021, 204.136, RSMo

Supp. 1975. Eminent among its duties is the development of "comprehensive plans and programs for the prevention, control and abatement of new or existing pollution of the waters of the state." § 204.026.2 * * * [T]he statutory scheme envisions a comprehensive remedial approach to water pollution problems, but preservation of common law remedies is consistent therewith—simply because preservation thereof strengthens and makes cumulative the powers of those charged with taking corrective measures.... Because of the provisions of § 204.131, nothing could be gained by an effort to analyze cases holding otherwise, and we hold that enactment of Chapter 204 did not proscribe common-law nuisance actions for pollution of streams and waterways on behalf of the state or private individuals.

2. It is significant that the last sentence preserves the common law nuisance actions for both public and private parties. Was it critical that the Missouri Clean Water Act contained a savings clause that explicitly preserved "any right of action" now existing? What would have been the outcome if the statute had been silent about the preservation of state common law rights?

In the area of state horizontal preemption (whether a state's regulatory scheme preempts a state's common law) the cases reflect the presumption *against* preemption, and the courts do not usually find a preclusive effect in the absence of explicit legislative intent or an irreconcilable conflict between the statutory objectives and the common law rights.

3. In Marshall v. Consumers Power Co., 65 Mich.App. 237, 237 N.W.2d 266 (1975) a state appellate court considered a vertical preemption question. The plaintiff brought action in state court claiming that defendant's proposed nuclear power plant would constitute a nuisance (a) because its cooling system would create dangerous and annoying "fog and icing" in the vicinity of the plant and (b) because of "the possibility of nuclear accident." The Federal Atomic Energy Commission (AEC) [Now the Nuclear Regulatory Commission] after lengthy hearings had issued a permit authorizing construction of the plant, and a federal appeal from that action was pending. The trial court dismissed plaintiff's nuisance suit on the ground that the federal scheme for regulating atomic energy "preempted the field." But the appellate court disagreed. Federal regulation "preempts state action concerning radiological, but not nonradiological matters." Thus state courts may hear plaintiff's complaint about "effects of steam, fog and icing" and may issue a remedy "founded on common law nuisance theory." The Michigan Court explained:

First, the parties, the rights adjudicated, the interests alleged, and the basic nature of the forum are so different in a state court from what they are in AEC administrative hearings that an adjudication by one should not always prevent the other from deciding a similar question. * * *

* * * A state court must make a case-by-case determination based on a number of factors. * * * In each case, of course, the court is a neutral arbiter. In each case, the only concern is the adjudication of a state common law right.

The AEC, on the other hand, cannot be accurately termed neutral. The agency was established to fulfill the often conflicting goals of both regulating and promoting nuclear energy. * * * The tendency of regulatory agencies to be 'captured' by those whom they regulate is well known. In the agency balancing process, state and local interests will be but one factor, and they will have to compete against concerns vital to national and international policy. Commentators have opined that, in AEC determinations, such Federal concerns as the promotion of nuclear power and the national need for more sources of energy will get greater precedence than such local concerns as icing or fogging.

* * *

Second, without recourse to a state court, * * * a private citizen would be forced to raise the state interest by appealing the AEC ruling. * * * [R]eviewing courts will defer to an agency determination so long as, upon an examination of the whole record, there is substantial evidence upon which the agency could reasonably base its decision. Judicial deference to AEC expertise may make this review a narrow one.

Were you surprised by the court's distinction between "radiological" and "non radiological" matters? Is that a viable and meaningful distinction upon which to circumvent the strong preemption in the nuclear regulatory field?

4. Consider Silkwood v. Kerr-McGee, 464 U.S. 238, 104 S.Ct. 615, 78 L.Ed.2d 443 (1984), where the Supreme Court ruled that the federal statutory scheme did bar the states from regulating the safety aspects of nuclear development and of hazardous nuclear materials, but nevertheless, found ample evidence in the legislative history of the Price-Anderson Act that Congress did not intend to forbid states from providing tort remedies for injuries caused by nuclear radiation. As a result, "[s]tate law remedies, in whatever form they might take, [are] available to those injured by nuclear accidents." Consequently, the mere fact that the federal government has occupied the field of safety does not foreclose state remedies for radiation injuries. Rather, the test for determining preemption in the nuclear energy field is:

[1] whether there is an irreconcilable conflict between the federal and state standards or [2] whether the imposition of a state standard in a damages action would frustrate the objectives of the federal law. See also, Bennett v. Mallinckrodt, Inc., 698 S.W.2d 854

(Mo.App.1985) (no preemption of state law claim for damages from injuries at radiopharmaceutical processing plant).

5.   In some cases the courts find that the federal and state regulatory schemes are not only not irreconcilable, but rather complementary, and apply the statutory objectives and the defendant's breach thereof to support a common law nuisance action.   In Miotke v. City of Spokane, 101 Wash.2d 307, 678 P.2d 803 (1984), private owners of waterfront property sued the City of Spokane for injunctive and monetary relief for discharging raw sewage into the river.   The Washington Supreme Court stated that the fundamental issue was whether "any cause of action lies against governmental units for injuries allegedly caused by their actions taken in violation of various environmental laws."   The court found that discharging raw sewage into the Spokane River in violation of a waste disposal permit to be a wrongful act which gives rise to a public nuisance action.   After the court summarizes the harm suffered by the plaintiffs as a result of defendants' bypassing the ordinary treatment process in order to expedite construction of a new treatment facility, the court concluded that defendant's failure to secure a permit for the bypass was a violation of state and federal water pollution laws.

The court then addressed the question of the availability of a private action based on those violations, since the statutes contained no provisions authorizing a *private* party to sue for damages.   The court considered the state statutes which generally recognize a nuisance cause of action and concluded that a nuisance action could be maintained:

> The October 1975 bypass constituted a nuisance under the statutory definitions.   It was a wrongful act (RCW 7.48.120) because it was conducted in violation of a waste disposal permit and RCW 90.48.   The bypass therefore does not fall within the protection of [the state law] which insulates acts performed under express statutory authority from actions for nuisance.   Moreover, the trial court concluded that the bypass "denied Plaintiffs the full use and enjoyment of their lake front properties and lifestyle."   There is ample support for this conclusion in the record.   This is equivalent to a finding that the bypass "essentially interfere[d] with the comfortable enjoyment of the life and property" of plaintiffs [in violation of the state's nuisance law].

> The bypass, therefore, constituted a nuisance for which an action in damages may be maintained[.] The bypass affected the rights of all members of the community living along the shores of Long Lake.   It therefore comprised a public nuisance[.]

> The plaintiffs are entitled to bring an action for this public nuisance because they can show it is "specially injurious" to themselves.   RCW 7.48.210.   As residents of properties along the waterfront, plaintiffs suffered as a result of the bypass injuries considerably greater than those suffered by the general public.

6. Miotke is important precedent for the proposition that private parties can maintain a private and public nuisance action for violation of the state and federal water pollution laws. The court did not dispense with the special injury requirement for public nuisance actions brought by private parties because it found the nuisance "specially injurious" to plaintiffs. It is also significant that plaintiffs recovered attorneys fees of $88,000 because of the public interest vindicated by their suit. In that sense plaintiffs acted as private attorneys general vindicating a public right that was violated by a public entity.

7. See also, Concerned Citizens of Bridesburg v. City of Philadelphia, 643 F.Supp. 713 (E.D.Pa.1986), affirmed, 843 F.2d 679 (3d Cir. 1988), allowing residents to maintain an action under the citizens' suit provisions of state law against the city for "malodors" emanating from a sewage disposal plant, contrary to the Pennsylvania Air Pollution Control Act and the Philadelphia Air Management Code. The court found that private common law rights were "additional and cumulative remedies to abate pollution of the air," consistent with the statutory scheme. The court allowed an injunction even though plaintiffs had failed to notify the Attorney General as required under the state law; it also disallowed an award of attorneys' fees.

C. NEGLIGENCE PER SE

In some instances a plaintiff may contend that the defendant's violation of a regulatory standard can be utilized to support a private right of action for damages. The contention is that the regulatory standard represents a standard of conduct or standard of care that should be applicable to civil tort cases even though the legislature or administrative agency was silent about the standard's possible application to such civil litigation. The doctrine that incorporates this offensive use of violations of regulatory standards is negligence per se—that is, the defendant's breach of the regulatory requirement is treated as a breach of the standard of conduct that is inferred by the court from the regulatory standard. Where the requisites of the negligence per se doctrine are met, the statute or regulation creates the standard of conduct (or care) that the actor must achieve; the violation of the statute or regulation constitutes the breach of the standard of conduct (or care), and is therefore regarded as conclusive proof of negligence.

In matters of environmental or toxic torts, plaintiffs frequently argue that the breach of the regulatory standard should constitute negligence per se and provide a cause of action, independent of any cause of action for nuisance, strict liability or trespass. As the following article demonstrates, some regulatory standards are appropriate for use in civil litigation as a standard of care, and others are not. It is for the court, not the jury, to decide in individual cases the propriety of applying the regulatory standard to tort cases.

SHEILA BUSH, CAN YOU GET THERE FROM HERE? NONCOMPLIANCE WITH ENVIRONMENTAL REGULATION AS NEGLIGENCE PER SE IN TORT CASES

25 Idaho L.R. 469 (1988–1989).

* * *

[B] THE REQUIREMENT OF A CLEAR STANDARD

The first requirement for application of the negligence per se doctrine is that the statute, ordinance or regulation clearly define the required standard of conduct. If the regulation is clear, a reasonable person presumably can determine and meet the standard of conduct. Despite a well-developed and often well-deserved reputation for unabashed complexity, environmental regulations appear fairly clear in some instances.

An environmental regulation that imposes a specific numerical standard appears definite on its face. For example, the primary and secondary NAAQS for ozone under the Clean Air Act is '0.12 part per million (230 ug/m3)' measured by a designated reference method; 'the standard is attained when the expected number of days per calendar year with maximum hourly average concentrations above 0.12 part per million (235 ug/m3) is equal to or less than one,' as determined by a designated method. If a facility caused a monitoring device to register 0.44 ppm for three days in 1988 under the designated reference method, then it clearly failed to comply with the regulation. In a tort suit, the plaintiff's counsel could argue that the company's conduct fell below the standard established by law or the protection of others against unreasonable risk of harm, i.e., that the company was negligent per se.

However, this superficial analysis of clarity fails to account for the way standards actually are set. For example, in setting the ozone standard, the EPA considered the available scientific information on the effects of ozone on human health and the environment. EPA then exercised its judgment, allowing a margin of safety, and established the number (0.12 ppm) for the standard. Although the numerical standard is certainly clear, the data on which it is based did not lead inexorably to that conclusion. The number was chosen based only on the scientific evidence available at the time it was set, and the agency's best judgment. A violation of the standard therefore may not necessarily signal unreasonable behavior in terms of health or environmental risk.

A violation of a standard later determined scientifically infirm offers the most extreme illustration of this proposition. In fact, the EPA has withdrawn and modified standards based on a better understanding of the scientific evidence. State environmental agencies, lacking the resources of the EPA, often are forced to set standards or regulations based on skimpy records of scientific evidence. * * *

* * *

Many environmental regulations, although complex, apparently meet the clarity requirement of the negligence per se doctrine. However, other factors may militate against using the standard of conduct contained in an environmental regulation. Since a numerical standard is based solely on available scientific evidence and agency judgment, noncompliance with a standard may not necessarily result in unreasonable behavior in terms of health or environmental risk. In addition, the agency may promulgate regulations inconsistent with the enabling statute. The difficulty environmental regulations present in meeting the clarity requirement is echoed in the applicability requirements.

C. CLASS OF PERSONS PROTECTED

* * *

Historically, the negligence per se doctrine has recognized that courts should adopt as the standard of conduct only the requirements of statutes and regulations intended to protect a particular class of individuals, and not the interests of the state or the public at large. * * *

A hypothetical scenario illustrates the issue in the environmental context. A plaintiff who has lived for many years beneath the stack of a smelter now brings suit alleging injury to health caused by exposure to lead and to fine particles. The plaintiff argues that the smelter periodically violated the national ambient standards for lead and particulate matter under the Clean Air Act, and thus was negligent per se. But are the standards 'applicable?' The courts have already agreed that Congress' 'paramount consideration' in enacting the Clean Air Act was protection of public health. While the plaintiff argues that he is a member of the class intended to be protected, the defendant smelter argues that the standards promulgated under the Clean Air Act are not appropriate targets for negligence per se because they are intended to protect the public at large, not a particular class.

When the plaintiff offers an environmental statute or regulation to establish the standard of conduct in a tort case, this issue likely will recur because the purpose Congress advanced in the statutes was protection of the public at large. * * *

D. TYPE OF RISK COVERED

* * *

When an environmental regulation imposes a numerical standard calculated to protect human health and environment, a plaintiff alleging injury to health or property caused by non-compliance with the standard appears to state exactly the harm the regulation was intended to prevent. Because of the different levels of proof required, the courts should hesitate to elevate the regulation to a standard of conduct, whereby the violation of such standard would establish negligence. A plaintiff in a tort case must prove the defendant's breach of duty by a preponderance of the evidence based on adjudicative facts. By contrast, an administrative agency considers legislative facts and exercises its judgment to adopt a regulation setting a numerical standard based on the scientific evidence presented, and incorporating a margin of safety. Unlike the tort case, the 'evidence' in a rulemaking proceeding need not demonstrate the conclusion reached by a preponderance of the evidence.

* * *

Permitting regulations raise equally difficult issues. Traditionally, courts found that the only purpose of a statute imposing an automobile registration requirement was to raise revenue, so the driver of an unlicensed car was not liable to those with whom he collided if he was otherwise exercising proper care. Although resembling a registration requirement, a permit requirement accomplishes more than mere registration because it translates statutory and regulatory requirements into specific obligations for an individual facility.

A key provision of any permitting regulatory scheme is the requirement to obtain a permit in certain instances. For example, a person who discharges a pollutant from a point source into the waters of the United States must obtain an NPDES permit. If a company fails to get a permit when required, and an individual alleges injury from exposure to the unpermitted effluent discharged, courts will have to determine whether failure to obtain a required permit causes harm the regulation was designed to prevent. The court can either allow the plaintiff to establish negligence per se based on the company's failure to get a permit, or allow proof regarding the reasonableness of the company's conduct, or both.

The Fourth Circuit [has] determined * * * that failure to obtain a permit does not constitute negligence per se.[83] Schlitz Brewing Company had violated a city ordinance that required every user of industrial sewers to obtain a discharge permit. The ordinance also limited a user's discharge to wastes containing 2,500 ppm biochemical oxygen demand (BOD) or less, and imposed surcharges for BOD pound loadings caused by concentrations above 300 ppm. Until April of 1971, Schlitz operated without a permit and paid BOD surcharges since its effluent contained more than 2,500 ppm BOD. Land owners along the Yadkin River alleged that the brewery overloaded the city sewage treatment plant, causing it to pollute the river, kill unprecedented numbers of fish, and damage their riverfront property.

The court found that Schlitz's failure to obtain a permit until May, 1971 did not provide the plaintiffs with grounds for recovery. The Fourth Circuit reasoned that the required permit did not protect riparian land owners, but was only an instrument of the city's enforcement program. The absence of a permit, and the failure to comply with the permitting ordinance, did not pollute the river. A logical corollary follows from the court's reasoning: If a company has acted reasonably in controlling pollution, then its failure to obtain a permit should not constitute negligence per se; conversely, if a company has acted unrea-

---

83. Springer v. Joseph Schlitz Brewing   Co., 510 F.2d 468 (4th Cir.1975).

sonably, the company is indeed negligent, but the failure to obtain a permit is independent of the negligence.

[T]he Supreme Court of New Hampshire reached the opposite result in Bagley v. Controlled Environment Corp.[90] The plaintiff alleged that the defendant dumped oil, grease, and other waste materials on its property that contaminated the plaintiff's nearby land and groundwater, and caused her personal injury. The plaintiff alleged generally that the defendant had violated the New Hampshire statutes governing hazardous wastes. One statute required that any person operating a 'hazardous waste facility,' defined as a location where hazardous waste is disposed, obtain a permit. The court noted that the plaintiff's pleading was unclear regarding whether the violation alleged was the failure to obtain a permit, the failure to abide by the terms of a permit, or the failure to conform to the substantive requirements of the statute and regulations.

The court held that both the failure to obtain a permit and the failure to comply with permit terms stated a cause of action based on statutory noncompliance. It reasoned that the legislature regarded the permit process as the essential opportunity to develop detailed substantive standards for a specific facility, so that failure to submit to the permit process could preclude the derivation of standards adequate to protect the public against the dangers posed by hazardous wastes. Given the function of the permitting process, the court reasoned that permit conditions should be accorded the same status as standards contained in a statute or rule.

* * *

IV. WHERE TO GO WHEN YOU CAN'T GET THERE FROM HERE

Noncompliance with environmental regulations does not lead neatly to negligence per se. The folk wisdom 'you can't get there from here' perhaps more accurately describes the relationship. Negligence per se grew up in an era when statutes and regulations more likely reflected a societal consensus on the standard of conduct required in particular situations. Environmental regulations more often reflect an imperfect judgment based on uncertain scientific evidence locked at a point in time already past. * * *

* * *

One possible solution may lie in the treatment accorded statutory and regulatory noncompliance originally rejected by courts in favor of the negligence per se doctrine. The negligence per se doctrine deems negligence to be conclusively shown once the breach of an applicable statute has been proven, and requires the court to so direct the jury. Courts have treated a violation of a statute or regulation differently under the doctrines of negligence per se with excuse, prima facie case of

---

90. 503 A.2d 823 (N.H.1986).

negligence, and mere evidence of negligence, as well as negligence per se.
* * *

The negligence per se with excuse doctrine represents an incremental shift away from the conclusiveness of the strict negligence per se theory by allowing the court to excuse reasonable departures from the regulatory standard. Once the plaintiff has proven noncompliance within an environmental regulation, the burden of proof shifts to the defendant to show sufficient evidence to excuse or justify defeating the presumption. So long as a court maintains flexibility in accepting evidence of excuse, this doctrine appears to provide the defendant with an opportunity to address the noncompliance issue while still providing the plaintiff a hopscotch over the proof of duty and breach.

The prima facie case of negligence theory presents an option one more step removed from negligence per se. The plaintiff's evidence of noncompliance with an environmental regulation under this theory is sufficient to withstand a motion to dismiss. Demonstration of noncompliance with an environmental regulation assures the plaintiff that the jury will consider the case, but the defendant is equally assured of the opportunity to present relevant evidence in rebuttal. * * *

The final option of treating noncompliance with an environmental regulation as 'mere evidence of negligence' may be most appropriate. Jurisdictions that treat noncompliance as mere evidence of negligence attach less significance to noncompliance with a statute or regulation. The 'mere evidence' theory does not shift the burden of proof to the defendant nor give greater weight to evidence of a violation than to any other type of evidence. The rationale for this theory is that the statutes and regulations only represent 'the collective opinion or judgment of the community in the matter.' Since environmental regulations represent only the agency's collective judgment on uncertain science, the reasoning behind the theory applies. Courts therefore should consider foregoing the negligence per se doctrine in favor of the mere evidence negligence treatment.

* * *

Notes and Questions

1. In Bagley v. Controlled Environment Corp., 127 N.H. 556, 503 A.2d 823 (1986), discussed in the Bush article, the plaintiff's suit also contained a count asserting strict liability for abnormally dangerous activities under Restatement (Second) of Torts §§ 519 and 520. The New Hampshire Supreme Court, in an opinion by Judge (now U.S. Supreme Court Justice) Souter, rejected the *Rylands v. Fletcher* doctrine on the ground that in most situations where plaintiffs seek to rely on the doctrine, they can usually establish the defendant's failure to exercise reasonable care, and therefore, prove a negligence cause of action. Do you agree with this conclusion?

The court's consideration of the negligence per se doctrine based on the statutory violation is instructive. The court employs the expression "causal violation" rather than negligence per se, but the analysis is identical:

Souter, J., delivered the opinion of the court.

* * *

While we * * * affirm the dismissal of the count in strict liability, it does not follow that the dangers of hazardous waste will have no particular recognition in the law of the State, because we do hold that the plaintiff has stated a cause of action predicated on a statutory violation. "It is well established law in this State that a causal violation of a statutory standard of conduct constitutes legal fault in the same manner as does the causal violation of a common law standard of due care, that is, causal negligence. In both instances liability is imposed because of the existence of legal fault, that is, a departure from a required standard of conduct." Moulton v. Groveton Papers Co., 112 N.H. 50, 52, 289 A.2d 68, 71 (1972)[.] A causal violation, as that term is used here, is a violation resulting in the damage that the statute was apparently intended to guard against.

* * *

Insofar as the count pleads a violation of RSA chapter 147–A (Supp. 1983), however, it rests on firmer footing. RSA 147–A:4, I (Supp. 1983) requires, inter alia, that any person "operating" a "hazardous waste facility" obtain a permit. An "operator" is "any person who ... operates, or otherwise directs or controls activities at a facility." RSA 147–A:2, XI (Supp. 1983). A "facility" is "a location at which hazardous waste is subjected to ... disposal." RSA 147–A:2, IV (Supp. 1983). "Waste" includes "spent, discarded or abandoned material." RSA 147–A:2, XVIII (Supp. 1983). "Hazardous waste" includes a "liquid ... [w]hich, because of either quantity, concentration, or physical, chemical, or infectious characteristics may ... [p]ose a present or potential threat to human health or the environment when improperly ... disposed of." RSA 147–A:2, VII(a)(2) (Supp. 1983). Such an operator is obligated to conform to the standards set forth in RSA chapter 147–A (Supp. 1983) and in any rules adopted by the office of waste management, and to obey the terms and conditions of any permit issued to him. See RSA 147–A:9,:14, I,:16,:17, I (Supp. 1983).

Turning to the plaintiff's pleadings, the declaration charges that the defendant was an operator of a facility in the sense, at the least, that it disposed of a liquid that was hazardous waste by virtue of its threat to health. It is likewise clear that the declaration charges the defendant with causing contamination and injury by means of disposal of such waste.

The only further allegation necessary to state a claim for causal violation of the statute is the allegation of the violation itself. Although the declaration expressly charges a violation, it does so without specifying whether the violation consisted of a failure to obtain a permit, failure to abide by the terms of a permit or failure to conform to the substantive requirements of the statute or of agency rules. While the courts and parties can reasonably demand more specific pleading than this, under our traditional practice the remedy for undue generality at this stage of a case is normally an order requiring a more definite statement rather than an order of dismissal. We will, therefore, consider the three possible specifications mentioned above, to determine whether the express allegation of one or more of them would complete the statement of a cause of action and withstand a motion to dismiss.

Under the traditional rule, a claim that the defendant had violated a substantive standard imposed by statute or rule would, of course, state a cause of action. Moulton holds that a violation of a statutory "standard of conduct" is equivalent to a violation of the common law duty of care.

It does not, however, follow from our holding in Moulton that the plaintiff would state a claim by alleging only that the defendant's causal violation of the statute consisted of a failure to obtain a necessary permit or a violation of its terms. We nonetheless hold that an allegation of either would be sufficient to state a cause of action. Two considerations lead us to this conclusion. The first is that the permit process itself will be the source of substantive standards. The statute and the rules do not purport to specify all of the circumstances in which the various sorts of hazardous waste should or should not be disposed, and it appears that the legislature regarded the permit process as an essential opportunity for developing standards necessary to protect against the dangers posed by hazardous waste. See, e.g., RSA 147–A:5, I(b) (Supp. 1983) (permits shall be issued only to those with financial responsibility to ensure that "appropriate" measures will be taken to prevent damage to public health and safety and to the environment); N.H. Admin. Rules. The object of the permit process, therefore, is not merely to ensure that an operator will comply with the appropriate statutory or regulatory standards, but to provide the opportunity to devise detailed substantive disposal standards appropriate for the specific case, in light of the statutory objectives.

It follows that the conditions imposed by terms of such a permit should be accorded the same status as substantive standards contained in a statute or rule. It also follows that a failure to comply with, or refusal to submit to, the permit process could preclude the derivation of substantive standards adequate to protect the public. Therefore, such a failure or refusal should itself be treated as causal and as sufficient to establish liability.

The second consideration that supports our holding that the allegation of the causal violation of a permit or of the requirement to obtain a permit states a private cause of action rests by analogy on the provision for a public cause of action found in RSA chapter 147–A. RSA 147–A:9 (Supp. 1983) provides, inter alia, that an operator who disposes of hazardous waste "in violation of RSA 147–A or rules adopted or permits issued under RSA 147–A" shall be "strictly liable" for costs of containment, cleanup and removal of hazardous wastes, and that the attorney general may institute an action to recover these costs.

This is a provision for damages, not a provision for penalty, which is dealt with separately. See RSA 147–A:14,:16,:17 (Supp. 1983). The quoted language makes it clear that such public civil liability for damages is not limited to cases involving violations of substantive statutory or regulatory standards; the statute is explicit in providing that violation of a permit's terms may give rise to a public action for damages, and the further reference to "violation of RSA 147–A" can only mean that disposal without any permit may also be the basis of public liability. (We note in passing that this statute's reference to strict liability is not technically correct; liability is not imposed merely because the operator caused damage, but because he either failed to obtain, or to abide by the terms of, a permit.) Thus, the legislature has evidently assumed that the permit process itself lessens the risk of harm from the disposal of hazardous waste and has therefore provided that disposal without a permit is sufficient to establish legal fault for purposes of an action for damages.

If such a cause of action is appropriate to compensate the general public for the cost of cleanup that it would otherwise bear in the interest of public health and safety, a similar cause of action is appropriate to compensate a private or property-owning plaintiff for the acute damage and injury that can result from unlicensed disposal. Since such a plaintiff, unlike the general public, can suffer personal injury and harm to property, the private right of action should provide compensation for these elements of damage in addition to recoupment of money actually expended on cleanup and containment.

* * *

What did you think of the court's analysis?

2. What are your views regarding the broad question of whether it is appropriate to apply environmental regulations and their breach to tort litigation? The Bush article suggests that the question can only be answered by undertaking a careful analysis of the precise standard, the purpose it was designed to accomplish, the class of persons it was intended to protect, and the harm it was intended to prevent. Further, the article concluded that even in those cases where the regulatory violation should constitute negligence, that the evidentiary effect afforded to that violation should not be conclusive proof of negligence, but rather some lesser level, such as presumptive evidence or merely some evidence of negligence. Do you agree?

Problem

Congress enacted the Alcoholic Beverage Labeling Act of 1988, 102 Stat. 4518, containing the following provisions:

Section 204.(a) On and after the expiration of the 12–month period following the date of enactment of this title, it shall be unlawful for any person to manufacture, import or bottle for sale or distribution in the United States any alcoholic beverage unless the container of such beverage bears the following statement:

GOVERNMENT WARNING: (1) According to the Surgeon General, women should not drink alcoholic beverages during pregnancy because of the risk of birth defects. (2) Consumption of alcoholic beverages impairs your ability to drive a car or operate machinery, and may cause health problems.

Section 205. No statement relating to alcoholic beverages and health, other than the statement required by section 204 of this title, shall be required under state law to be placed on any container of an alcoholic beverage, or on any box, carton, or other package, irrespective of the material from which made, that contains such a container.

What impact will this statute have on tort suits brought under § 402A for failure to warn for actions that accrue after its enactment? Address the impact which the decision in *Cipollone v. Liggett Group* might have on such actions. Will the courts experience the same pre- and post-enactment problems that have been so determinative in cigarette litigation? Describe other causes of action that might survive enactment of the Alcoholic Beverage Labeling Act.

Chapter Seven

TOXIC PRODUCTS, PROCESSES AND SERVICES

A. INTRODUCTION: SOME GENERAL PRINCIPLES

Up to now we have considered liability for environmental harm where the plaintiff and defendant usually stood in a horizontal relationship, typically concurrent adjoining landowners or landowners within the same geographical area, and where the defendant's activity resulted in an invasion of the plaintiff's use and enjoyment of land. Liability was premised on trespass, nuisance, negligence, negligence per se, or strict liability for abnormally dangerous activities. We now turn to vertical relationships between a manufacturer, product seller or service provider, and consumers or users of a product or service down the chain of distribution.

Products liability is best understood by introducing the four major theories of liability: negligence, warranty, strict liability in tort, and misrepresentation.

The factual situations accounting for practically all products liability claims for toxic or environmental injury involve (1) defective design or formulation; (2) the failure to give adequate warnings or instructions for safe use; (3) breach of express or implied warranties; or (4) the failure to truthfully represent a material quality of a product, i.e., safety or performance. The meanings the courts have given to these terms and phrases are described below.

At the outset, it is essential to understand that a single seller dereliction, such as, for example, failure to provide adequate instructions for the application of a herbicide, may give rise to an injured party's cause of action under several legal theories. For example, if presented with facts suggesting a manufacturer's responsibility for a failure to provide information adequate for the safe use of a toxic product, one will necessarily examine the viability of plaintiff's cause of action in each of the available legal theories: negligence, warranty, strict liability in tort, and misrepresentation (including, upon occasion, fraud).

1. NEGLIGENCE

The law of negligence is primarily concerned with the provision of reparations to persons suffering personal injury or property loss due to a failure of others to act with due care under the circumstances. The premises of negligence liability are that (a) the theory is devoted to the protection of persons and property from unreasonable risk of harm; and (b) the actor's liability in tort is limited by concepts of reasonable foreseeability.

From the above, we can state a rule for negligence liability for the sale of an unreasonably dangerous product: A product seller is liable in negligence if he acts or fails to act in such a way as to create an unreasonable risk of harm or loss to the user of a product, or to another who might foreseeably be injured thereby. As in all torts, for plaintiff to prevail in negligence there must be harm to the plaintiff's person or property, and proximate cause between the actor's conduct and the harm suffered.

To locate the line between the reasonable risk and the unreasonable one, most courts use the formulation of Judge Learned Hand, or a comparable risk-benefit model. The Hand formulation states that an actor's conduct creates an unreasonable risk of harm where the burden of taking measures to avoid the harm would be less than the multiple of the likelihood that the harm will occur times the magnitude of the harm should it occur. In formula $(B<(P)(L))$, the actor will be considered negligent when B is less than $(P)(L)$, that is, B (Burden of precautions) is less than P (likelihood, in terms of percentage Probability) times L (magnitude of Loss should the harm occur at all). United States v. Carroll Towing Co., 159 F.2d 169 (2d Cir.1947).

The plaintiff's negligence cause of action in products liability involving toxic harm will be available principally in claims for defective formulation and for failure to provide adequate warnings or instructions. In each instance, a cost benefit analysis will support part or all of the requisite negligence analysis.

2. BREACH OF WARRANTY

There are three primary ways in which the seller may breach its warranty to the purchaser. There may be the breach of an express warranty, the breach of the implied warranty of merchantability, and the breach of the implied warranty of fitness for a particular purpose. In a given factual setting, it is possible for a product to breach one, two, or even all of these warranties.

a. Express Warranty

The express warranty is made when the seller makes a material representation as to the product's composition, durability, performance, or safety. The express warranty may be made by any means of communication, from spoken comment, to leaflets, to product wrappers, to advertisements.

Not every statement from a seller to a buyer creates an express warranty. Where the seller's assurance of qualities in the product pertain to matters equally understandable and observable to the purchaser, the seller's statement will ordinarily not be described as material, and instead is "puffing", which does not create an express warranty.

Prior to the Uniform Commercial Code, to preserve a claim in express warranty the buyer might be required to show that she relied specifically upon the express warranty of the seller. The comments of UCC § 2–313 now provide that the buyer's reliance upon an express warranty will be presumed unless the lack of reliance is proved by the seller. This liberalization of the historical reliance requirement is relevant to the buyer who after the injury or loss may only imperfectly recall (1) the assurances the seller made orally; or (2) which of the seller's written assurances the buyer actually read prior to the mishap. The UCC creates a presumption that the buyer relied upon the seller's warranty in deciding to purchase the product, and the presumption will only be defeated by the seller's affirmative proof to the contrary. For a thorough discussion of the theory of express warranty in the context of tobacco litigation, see Cipollone v. Liggett Group, Inc., 893 F.2d 541 (3d Cir.1990), reversed on other grounds ___ U.S. ___, 112 S.Ct. 2608, 120 L.Ed.2d 407 (1992).

b. Implied Warranty of Merchantability

The implied warranty of merchantability, UCC § 2–314, provides that any seller impliedly warrants that the product sold is fit for its ordinary purposes. This warranty, as its name suggests, conveys with the sale of the product irrespective of the seller's statements or comments. The separate issues of the seller's disclaimer of this and other warranties, or limitation of the remedies available under warranty, are described below.

The threshold issue raised by the implied warranty of merchantability is what is the ordinary purpose of a product. Ordinary purpose is distinguishable from the manufacturer's intended purpose for the product; witness the common use of rubbing alcohol as a cleaning solvent or nail polish remover. Most courts would characterize such use of rubbing alcohol as ordinary, even though admittedly not the use intended by the seller. However, an aerosol tick bomb would not ordinarily be used in a kennel from which the dogs had not first been removed, and injury to animals associated with the latter use would not be redressable in implied warranty of merchantability.

c. Implied Warranty of Fitness for a Particular Purpose

The implied warranty of fitness for a particular purpose, UCC § 2–315, contemplates the buyer's explicit or implicit request that a seller having specialized knowledge of the nature and usage of her products recommend a product suitable for the buyer's goal or project. Where the seller knows of the purchaser's special need, and where the buyer completes the purchase in reliance upon the seller's knowledge and expertise, there arises an implied warranty of fitness for a particular purpose.

The value of this warranty is in providing a remedy to a buyer who has purchased and used an otherwise merchantable product (e.g., housepaint) in a specialized way (to paint a confined area in a home that cannot be effectively ventilated), and has suffered product disappointment, personal injury or property loss resulting from the seller's erroneous advice. Unlike the implied warranty of merchantability, requiring no buyer reliance, and the express warranty, in which there is a rebuttable presumption of reliance, under UCC § 2–315 the buyer must plead and prove reliance upon the seller's knowledge and expertise.

d. *Proper Plaintiffs to a Warranty Claim*

In warranty, the proper plaintiffs are decided by reference to which Alternative to UCC § 2–318 a jurisdiction has selected. The authors of the UCC gave the states three options: Alternative A, the most restrictive, confines the class of plaintiffs along the lines of the common law privity requirement, including members of the buyer's household and guests therein. Alternatives B and C are progressively more liberal in availing the warranty remedy to nonpurchasing users of products and to unrelated bystanders.

In addition to the buyer's cause of action, UCC § 2–318 Alternative A permits a cause of action to "any natural person who is in the family or household of his buyer, or who is a guest in his home, ..." The use of the phrase "natural person" precludes a cause of action to a business or corporation. Alternative B similarly confines the cause of action to natural persons, but extends the class of parties plaintiff to the limits of reasonable foreseeability, i.e., to all natural persons "who may be reasonably expected to use, consume, or be affected by the goods." Alternative C describes a class of permissible plaintiffs coextensive with the liberal class of plaintiffs recognized in the tort remedies of negligence and strict liability. Under Alternative C, plaintiffs are not limited to natural persons, and therefore organizations and businesses may bring an action in warranty. The language of reasonable foreseeability is identical to that of Alternative B.

e. *Warranty Disclaimers and Limitations*

One of the most significant distinctions between products liability remedies in tort and in warranty is that the UCC explicitly grants the seller the ability to disclaim or limit the remedies available to the purchaser. The most straightforward rationale for permitting disclaimers in warranty and not in tort is that the warranty remedies, arising in contract, are said to represent the mutual assent of the buying and selling parties. These parties, given fair and reciprocal disclosure of the terms of the sale, are free to create a contract with any terms not so hidden or oppressive as to be unconscionable in enforcement. A principal goal of tort remedies, on the other hand, is reparations for parties suffering injury or loss caused by the substandard conduct of others. Tort policy generally, and the remedy of strict tort liability specifically, discourages permitting an actor to disclaim or limit damages for injuries caused by his injurious actions.

Where the seller has given an express warranty, a disclaimer of that warranty will not be allowed, as it would be inherently misleading and unfair to permit the seller to give the buyer a remedy with one hand (potential recompense for breach of express warranty) and take that remedy away, by disclaimer, with the other hand.

The seller may, however, disclaim the implied warranty of merchantability or fitness for a particular purpose. UCC § 2–316 provides that the implied warranty of merchantability may be effectively disclaimed if the disclaimer mentions merchantability and is conspicuous. The implied warranty of fitness for a particular purpose, in turn, may be disclaimed where the disclaiming language is "by a writing and conspicuous." The decisions are in substantial agreement that disclaiming language will be considered conspicuous where it is on the face of the controlling document, where it is distinctively displayed by positioning, background, border, type or color, and where the typeface of the disclaimer is at least as large or larger than that used in the balance of the document. M. Stuart Madden, 1 Products Liability 2d §§ 5.17–19 (1988 & 1993 Supp.)

Under all circumstances, UCC § 2–316 states that implied warranties may be excluded "by expressions like 'as is', 'with all faults' or other language which in ordinary understanding calls the buyer's attention to the exclusion of warranties and makes plain that there is no implied warranty[.]"

Pursuant to UCC § 2–719, a seller may limit remedies available under a warranty, such as, for example, limiting the buyer's remedies to return of the goods and repayment of the purchase price or repair. Courts will sustain such limitations unless they operate to deprive the buyer of the remedy's essential purpose, i.e., to receive a fit product or a return of purchase money. In addition, while UCC § 2–719(3) countenances limitation or exclusion of consequential damages, it adds that where the alleged product flaw results in personal injury, limitation of consequential damages for warranties of consumer goods is "prima facie unconscionable."

3. STRICT LIABILITY IN TORT

The limitations inherent in the remedies of negligence and warranty liability encouraged creation of a products liability tort remedy that would alleviate some of the privity and evidentiary burdens placed upon plaintiffs. In negligence the most obvious obstacle to plaintiff's recovery was, and is, the requirement that plaintiff identify and prove that point in the process of manufacture or sale that the seller's conduct fell below the requisite due care under the circumstances. Such proof typically requires plaintiff to not only amass a familiarity with often very complex manufacturing processes, but to be prepared as well to rebut the defendant's claims that its practices, conforming with the actions of other producers in the same industry, did represent due care. In warranty, distinct but equally imposing obstacles to the plaintiff's recovery take the form of the requirement of timely notice to the seller, privity barriers that vary from state to state, and the seller's ability to limit warranty remedies or disclaim warranties altogether.

In 1963 the California Supreme Court in Greenman v. Yuba Power Products, Inc., 59 Cal.2d 57, 27 Cal.Rptr. 697, 377 P.2d 897 (1963) announced a remedy of tort liability without the necessity of proving negligence, that is, strict liability in tort, stating: "A manufacturer is strictly liable in tort when an article he places on the market, knowing that it is to be used without inspection for defects, proves to have a defect that causes injury to a human being."

Prompted by the decision in *Greenman* and the urgings of other courts, in 1965 the American Law Institute (ALI) published Restatement (Second) of Torts § 402A, proposing strict liability in tort for any person "who sells a product in a defective condition unreasonably dangerous to the user or consumer or his property." Since its publication a majority of jurisdictions have adopted § 402A or variations thereon.

The essential distinction between the remedies in negligence and those under § 402A is that in strict liability the focus is on the condition of the product, while in negligence the primary inquiry pertains to the conduct of the seller. In strict liability, liability will be imposed for the sale of a defective, unreasonably dangerous product irrespective of how cautious, circumspect, or reckless the seller has been. Strict liability is liability without regard to fault or negligence for the sale of an unreasonably dangerous product.

As in warranty (except UCC § 2–315), under § 402A the defendant must be a seller of such products in the ordinary course. A growing number of courts have extended the strict liability cause of action to businesses whose position in the stream of commerce resembles that of a product seller in terms of expertise and ability to detect and correct hazards. Thus, many decisions impose strict liability upon product lessors and bailors. 1 Products Liability 2d, supra, §§ 6.17–.18.

Concerning the language "defective condition unreasonably dangerous", most jurisdictions require that the product be in both a defective condition and unreasonably dangerous. Those courts reason that as tort law is primarily concerned with the creation of remedies for conduct and conditions that create an unreasonable risk of injury, a product that is merely defective, but creates no hazard or danger to persons or to other property, is the proper concern of warranty law, but not tort. In a minority of jurisdictions, however, including California, courts have decided that the language "unreasonably dangerous" hints too strongly of a negligence analysis, and induces juries to adopt a higher burden of proof than the language "defective condition." Courts or legislatures in these latter jurisdictions have removed the "unreasonably dangerous" criterion from plaintiff's prima facie case.

Comment i to § 402A states a "consumer expectation" standard for what represents an unreasonably dangerous condition, and provides that evaluation of what is unreasonably dangerous should be had by reference to whether the article sold is "dangerous to an extent beyond that which would be contemplated by the ordinary consumer who purchases it, with the ordinary knowledge common to the community as to its characteristics." More specialized risk/utility evaluations for what constitutes a design defect have been adopted by many courts.

4. MISREPRESENTATION

The remedy of strict liability for misrepresentation, stated in Restatement (Second) of Torts § 402B, was created to afford a tort remedy to one injured in person due to reliance on the product seller's misrepresentation of a material fact. In ways similar to the plaintiff's cause of action in breach of express warranty, § 402B nonetheless differs from warranty in its retention of the requirement that plaintiff prove actual, subjective reliance upon the seller's representations. The section differs from § 402A in that the § 402B misrepresentation remedy does not require that the product be dangerously defective. Under § 402B even the sale of a merchantable product may create a cause of action if the seller's blandishments as to the product's performance or other material qualities, such as safety, are false, and the user is injured in reliance thereon.

A leading case creating the model for the authors of § 402B was Baxter v. Ford Motor Co., 168 Wash. 456, 12 P.2d 409 (1932), affirmed 168 Wash. 456, 15 P.2d 1118 (1932). The Washington Supreme Court therein suggested that where a product's defect was such that "[a]n ordinary person would be unable to discover [it] by the usual and customary examination," liability for misrepresentation without the need to show negligence is appropriate, because placing the product on the market in a condition that does not conform with the advertising or labeling representations in effect breaches the warranty that an article placed in commerce be "safe for the purposes for which the consumer would ordinarily use it."

The plaintiff proceeding under § 402B must show that there has been justifiable reliance upon the misrepresentation, and that personal physical injury resulted. Comment j thereto states that the remedy will not be available "where the misrepresentation is not known [to the buyer], or there is [buyer] indifference to it, and it does not influence the purchase or subsequent conduct."

While the range of products that may be implicated in toxic products suits is unlimited, most litigation has involved workplace injuries from chemical exposures, such as asbestos or Agent Orange, from the consumption of prescription drugs, such as DES and Bendectin, or from the use of tobacco products.

These toxic product cases differ from typical products liability cases in three respects. First, the plaintiffs are seeking compensation for chronic injuries or diseases caused by toxic substances contained in the products, rather than compensation for traumatic injuries involved in sporadic accident cases. The kinds of harms experienced in these cases are different—cancer, birth defects, asbestosis, asthma—rather than the broken bones more typical of products cases. Second, these toxic product claims usually involve long latency periods, and frequently also long periods of exposure to the toxic substance before there exists any objective manifestation of the injury or disease. Asbestos, cigarette and DES-related injuries all illustrate this phenomenon. Third, the number of persons who can suffer harm as a result of exposure to a generic product may be measured in hundreds or thousands, producing a comparable number of individual lawsuits, class actions or multidistrict mass tort proceedings.

5. RESTATEMENT (SECOND) OF TORTS § 402A: STRICT LIABILITY AND NEW APPROACHES

Let us turn to Restatement (Second) of Torts § 402A:

§ 402A. Special Liability of Seller of Product for Physical Harm to User or Consumer

(1) One who sells any product in a defective condition unreasonably dangerous to the user or consumer or to his property is subject to liability for physical harm thereby caused to the ultimate user or consumer, or to his property, if

   (a) the seller is engaged in the business of selling such a product, and

   (b) it is expected to and does reach the user or consumer without substantial change in the condition in which it is sold.

(2) The rule stated in Subsection (1) applies although

   (a) the seller has exercised all possible care in the preparation and sale of his product, and

   (b) the user or consumer has not bought the product from or entered into any contractual relation with the seller.

In May of 1992, the ALI commenced a Restatement (Third) of Torts, and made its first initiative a Restatement of Products Liability. On

April 20, 1993, the Reporters for this project, Professor Aaron D. Twerski and James A. Henderson, Jr., published their "Preliminary Draft Number No. 1." The Reporters' Preliminary Draft [1] sets out standards for product defectiveness. The authors state that "the draft takes no position as to whether liability which meets the requisites of [those sections] should be characterized as strict liability, warranty, or negligence[,]" adding that "[a]s long as the tests for defect are met, how courts decide to label the causes of action is left to the states."

Preliminary Draft § 101 provides:

"(1) One engaged in the business of selling products who sells a product in a defective condition is subject to liability for harm to persons or property caused by the product defect.

"(2) Liability under Subsection (1) may be based on

(a) manufacturing defect in the form of a departure from the product's intended design even though all possible care was exercised in the preparation and marketing of the product;

(b) a design defect if the foreseeable risks of harm presented by the product could have been reduced by the adoption of a reasonable, safer design by the seller or predecessor in the commercial chain of distribution; or

(c) a defect consisting of failure to instruct or warn if the foreseeable risks of harm presented by the product could have been reduced by the adoption of reasonable instructions or warnings by the seller or predecessor in the commercial chain of distribution."

The Reporters' Introductory Note states that "[t]he core of the liability test for design in § 101 is the requirement that the plaintiff establish that a reasonable, safer design could have been adopted by the seller or a predecessor in the distributive chain."

Liability under § 101(2)(c) for failure to provide adequate warnings or instructions, the Reporters comment, "attaches only if the risks presented by the product could have been reduced by the adoption of reasonable instructions or warnings. If the risks of harm against which a seller should have designed, warned or instructed are related to product misuse, alteration or modification, and those risks are either not foreseeable or not reducible by a reasonable safer design or a reasonable instruction or warning, then the product is not defective[.]" Cognizant of the nearly uniform adoption of comment k to Restatement (Second) of Torts § 402A, which preserves a negligence standard for claims involving "unavoidably unsafe" products (most particularly prescription pharma-

---

1. The Preliminary Draft of any potential Restatement is, in every sense, preliminary. It represents the synthesis and approach of the Reporters, and is exclusively the work of its authors. The first of many stages of an eventual Restatement, the ALI's Executive Director, Professor Geof-

frey C. Hazard, Jr., described this Preliminary Draft as a "moving target," and conveyed the caution that concerns or plaudits expressed could be rendered nugatory by revisions prior to consideration by the full Institute.

ceuticals, biological products and medical devices), the Preliminary Draft states that "[t]he rule in Subsection 101(2)(b) does not apply to design defect claims involving prescription drugs."

Sections 106 and 107 of the Preliminary Draft treat affirmative defenses. Section 106, entitled Comparative Responsibility as a Defense, states:

> "When the conduct of the plaintiff combines with a product defect to cause harm to the plaintiff's person or property and the plaintiff's conduct fails to conform to applicable standards of reasonable care, the plaintiff's conduct shall be compared with the product defect pursuant to the applicable general rules of comparative responsibility."

In the final section of this preliminary round of the proposed Products Liability Restatement, the Reporters disavow reliance upon disclaimers and waivers in products liability claims involving personal physical injury. As Preliminary Draft § 107 states: "Disclaimers by product sellers, waivers by product purchasers, or other similar contractual exculpations, oral or written, do not bar or reduce otherwise valid products liability claims for harms to persons."

The prominence of warnings and other informational issues in toxic products litigation warrants these additional observations: The duty of a manufacturer to provide warnings can be understood and justified on grounds of reducing accident costs. See Guido Calabresi, THE COSTS OF ACCIDENTS 26 (1970). Warnings and related product information enhance safety by enabling the user to avoid dangers related to product use which can be averted or reduced when the user is informed of the hazards. Second, warnings promote individual autonomy by informing the user of the risks involved and enabling the individual to make an informed choice of whether to encounter unavoidable risks.

A claim of warning or other informational deficiency may be the only theory available to a plaintiff, in that theories of defective design or formulation usually require the plaintiff to establish an alternative safer design that would have averted or lessened the danger. As the risks of many toxic substances, such as asbestos, prescription drugs and tobacco, are inherent to the formulation of the product and cannot usually be designed out in any meaningful way, the plaintiff's only viable claim may be to assert that the manufacturer did not provide adequate warnings or instructions regarding the risks of harm associated with the use of the product. For differing views on the scope and nature of the obligation to warn consumers and users, compare Aaron Twerski, et al., The Use and Abuse of Warnings in Products Liability—Design Defect Litigation Comes of Age, 61 Cornell L.Rev. 495 (1976), with M. Stuart Madden, The Duty to Warn in Products Liability: Contours and Criticism, 89 W.Va. L. Rev. 221 (1987).

B. TOXIC PRODUCT CLAIMS BY TYPE

1. ASBESTOS

a. *Liability Standards and Defenses*

Judge Alpert of the Court of Special Appeals of Maryland captured in colorful terms the history of asbestos litigation in Eagle–Picher, Inc. v. Balbos, 84 Md.App. 10, 578 A.2d 228, 231 (1990), modified 326 Md. 179, 604 A.2d 445 (1992):

> In this, the last decade of the 20th Century, our judicial system faces an apocalypse in the guise of asbestos cases. As did the "Apocalyptic beast," asbestos rose up "as from the depths of the sea," after having lain dormant for decades, to plague our industries initially and our judicial system consequentially, spreading cancer and asbestosis to thousands of workers along the way.

> This 10–week case is just one of more than 8,000 asbestos cases that have been filed in Maryland since 1980. Although estimates vary, it has been reported that there are as many as 50,000 asbestos cases pending nationally. Quite apart from the sheer magnitude in numbers, asbestos litigation presents features that, unfortunately, are common to complex litigation. Most of the cases are of the multi-litigant variety, averaging as many as twenty defendants. When the multitude of cross-claims between those defendants are factored in, the complex metamorphosizes into the maxi-complex. Thus, it seems quite possible that our dockets shall be visited with asbestos litigation well into the next century, each case presenting its unique yet similar tragic scenario.

Against that vivid backdrop we examine the history of asbestos litigation.

BOREL v. FIBREBOARD PAPER PRODUCTS CORPORATION

United States Court of Appeals, Fifth Circuit, 1973.
493 F.2d 1076, cert. denied 419 U.S. 869, 95 S.Ct. 127, 42 L.Ed.2d 107 (1974).

WISDOM, C.J.:

This product liability case involves the scope of an asbestos manufacturer's duty to warn industrial insulation workers of dangers associated with the use of asbestos.

* * * [Clarence] Borel allege[s] that he had contracted the diseases of asbestosis and mesothelioma as a result of his exposure to the defendants' products over a thirty-three year period beginning in 1936 and ending in 1969. The jury returned a verdict in favor of Borel on the basis of strict liability. We affirm.

I.

* * * Borel's employment necessarily exposed him to heavy concentrations of asbestos dust generated by insulation materials. In his pre-

trial deposition, Borel testified that at the end of a day working with insulation material containing asbestos his clothes were usually so dusty he could "just barely pick them up without shaking them." * * *

Borel said that [although] he had known for years that inhaling asbestos dust "was bad for me"[,] * * * he never realized that it could cause any serious or terminal illness. * * *

[Borel testified that respirators] were not furnished during his early work years. Although respirators were later made available on some jobs, insulation workers usually were not required to wear them and had to make a special request if they wanted one. Borel stated that he and other insulation workers found that the respirators furnished them were uncomfortable, could not be worn in hot weather, and—"you can't breathe with the respirator." * * *

* * *

[In January 1969, Borel was diagnosed with pulmonary asbestosis. In 1970] surgery, the examining doctors determined that Borel had a form of lung cancer known as mesothelioma, which had been caused by asbestosis. As a result of these diseases, Borel later died before the district case reached the trial stage.

* * *

At issue in this case is the extent of the defendants' knowledge of the dangers associated with insulation products containing asbestos. We pause, therefore, to summarize the evidence relevant to this question.

Asbestosis has been recognized as a disease for well over fifty years. The first reported cases of asbestosis were among asbestos textile workers. In 1924, Cooke in England discovered a case of asbestosis in a person who had spent twenty years weaving asbestos textile products. * * *

* * *

Throughout the 1950's and 1960's, further studies and medical reports on asbestosis were published. In 1965, I. J. Selikoff and his colleagues published a study entitled "The Occurrence of Asbestosis Among Insulation Workers in the United States." The authors examined 1,522 members of an insulation workers union in the New York–New Jersey metropolitan area. Evidence of pulmonary asbestosis was found in almost half the men examined. Among those with more than forty years experience, abnormalities were found in over ninety percent. The authors concluded that "asbestosis and its complications are significant hazards among insulation workers". Other studies have since confirmed these findings.

* * *

The plaintiff introduced evidence tending to establish that the defendant manufacturers either were, or should have been, fully aware of the many articles and studies on asbestosis. The evidence also indicated, however, that during Borel's working career no manufacturer ever warned contractors or insulation workers, including Borel, of the dangers associated with inhaling asbestos dust[.] * * *

* * *

II.

* * *

Here, the plaintiff alleged that the defendants' product was unreasonably dangerous because of the failure to give adequate warnings of the known or knowable dangers involved. As explained in comment j to [Restatement (Second) of Torts] section 402A, a seller has a responsibility to inform users and consumers of dangers which the seller either knows or should know at the time the product is sold. The requirement that the danger be reasonably foreseeable, or scientifically discoverable, is an important limitation of the seller's liability. * * * [A] seller is under a duty to warn of only those dangers that are reasonably foreseeable. The requirement of foreseeability coincides with the standard of due care in negligence cases in that a seller must exercise reasonable care and foresight to discover a danger in his product and to warn users and consumers of that danger. * * *

* * *

[I]n cases such as the instant case, the manufacturer is held to the knowledge and skill of an expert. This is relevant in determining (1) whether the manufacturer knew or should have known the danger, and (2) whether the manufacturer was negligent in failing to communicate this superior knowledge to the user or consumer of its product. The manufacturer's status as expert means that at a minimum he must keep abreast of scientific knowledge, discoveries, and advances and is presumed to know what is imparted thereby. But even more importantly, a manufacturer has a duty to test and inspect his product. The extent of research and experiment must be commensurate with the dangers involved. A product must not be made available to the public without disclosure of those dangers that the application of reasonable foresight would reveal. Nor may a manufacturer rely unquestioningly on others to sound the hue and cry concerning a danger in its product. Rather, each manufacturer must bear the burden of showing that its own conduct was proportionate to the scope of its duty.

* * *

[T]he defendants contend that the district court erred in refusing to instruct the jury that a product cannot be unreasonably dangerous if it conforms to the reasonable expectations of the industrial purchasers, here, the insulation contractors. The defendants assert, in effect, that it is the responsibility of the insulation contractors, not the manufacturers, to warn insulation workers of the risk of harm. We reject this argument. We agree with the Restatement: a seller may be liable to the ultimate consumer or user for failure to give adequate warnings. The seller's warning must be reasonably calculated to reach such persons and the presence of an intermediate party will not by itself relieve the seller of this duty. * * *

[We conclude] that the trial court did not err in instructing the jury on strict liability.

* * *

III.

* * *

[The defendants] challenge the jury's finding that their products were unreasonably dangerous for failure to give warnings. * * * They attempt to circumvent this finding by arguing, disingenuously, that the danger was obvious. For present purposes, it is sufficient to note that Borel testified that he did not know that inhaling asbestos dust could cause serious illness until his doctors advised him in 1969 that he had asbestosis. Furthermore, we cannot say that, as a matter of law, the danger was sufficiently obvious to asbestos installation workers to relieve the defendants of the duty to warn.

The jury found that the unreasonably dangerous condition of the defendants' product was the proximate cause of Borel's injury. This necessarily included a finding that, had adequate warnings been provided, Borel would have chosen to avoid the danger. * * *

* * *

IV.

* * *

* * * Under the law of torts, a person has long been liable for the foreseeable harm caused by his own negligence. This principle applies to the manufacture of products as it does to almost every other area of human endeavor. It implies a duty to warn of foreseeable dangers associated with those products. This duty to warn extends to all users and consumers, including the common worker in the shop or in the field. Where the law has imposed a duty, courts stand ready in proper cases to enforce the rights so created. Here, there was a duty to speak, but the defendants remained silent. The district court's judgment does no more than hold the defendants liable for the foreseeable consequences of their own inaction.

For the reasons stated, the decision of the district court is

Affirmed.

Notes and Questions

1. *Borel* is a leading decision in articulating the basis of liability for asbestos producers on a failure to warn theory. The informational defects in this case relate largely to informed choice, and only secondarily to risk

reduction. As the court states elsewhere in its opinion, "the rationale for this rule [requiring disclosure of the risks] is that the user or consumer is entitled to make his own choice as to whether the product's utility or benefits justify exposing himself to the risk of harm." Will employees in the workplace, once informed of the risks, usually make the choice of exposure? See Chapter 9, discussing obligations created by the Occupational Safety and Health Act of 1970, which requires, among other things, that employers provide employees with information regarding the risks of exposure for toxic chemicals.

2. In many toxic tort cases, including asbestos cases, courts have adopted the so-called "heeding presumption." This presumption affects plaintiff's burden of showing that the absence of an adequate warning was a proximate cause of his or her harm by creating a presumption that had an adequate warning been given, plaintiff would have read and heeded it. Cf., Restatement (Second) of Torts § 402A comment j ("Where a warning is given, the seller may reasonably assume that it will be read and heeded[.]"). In Theer v. Philip Carey Co., 133 N.J. 610, 628 A.2d 724 (1993), an action bought on behalf of a deceased asbestos fitter, the New Jersey Supreme Court explained the rationale for the "heeding presumption": "[T]he heeding presumption in failure-to-warn cases serves to ease an injured plaintiff's burden of proof. That objective is especially important because 'in a failure to warn case, establishing that the absence of a warning was a substantial factor in the harm alleged to have resulted from exposure to the product is particularly difficult.' In particular, the heeding presumption serves to eliminate conjecture about whether a given plaintiff would have heeded a hypothetical warning, and discourages determinations that are based on extraneous, speculative considerations and unreliable or self serving evidence."

3. *Borel* is also important because it elaborates the extent of the manufacturer's obligation to become aware of risks inherent in its products: The manufacturer must keep itself informed of the medical and scientific knowledge generally available as well as undertake its own research regarding the dangers that may be associated with the use of its products. The manufacturer will be held to the standard of an expert in the field. It is critical to understand that the duty recognized in *Borel* pertains only to risks that are, in fact, known or knowable. According to the court, and to most courts considering the question, strict liability under comment j of § 402A does not hold a manufacturer strictly liable for failure to warn of risks that are unknown or unknowable.

4. In the Preliminary Draft of the Restatement (Third) of Torts: Products Liability, Reporters Henderson and Twerski propose a conforming position with this comment: "[B]ecause risks of harm arising from the foreseeable consumption of toxics and prescription drugs are sometimes unknowable at the time of sale, it would be inappropriate to attribute knowledge of risks to the seller as a matter of law."

5. *Special Problems of Unknown Risks.* An alternative phrasing of the "unknown and unknowable risk" issue raised in *Borel* is sometimes stated as the availability of the "state of the art" defense to a toxic tort defendant, i.e., can a manufacturer defend a charge that it failed to warn of a danger by

demonstrating that its knowledge and warnings were "state-of-the-art" at the time the product was distributed? The counter argument was best stated in another asbestos personal injury suit, as the following excerpted discussion from Beshada v. Johns–Manville Products Corp., 90 N.J. 191, 447 A.2d 539 (1982) (Pashman, J.) reveals:

[The most important inquiry] is whether imposition of liability for failure to warn of dangers which were undiscoverable at the time of manufacture will advance the goals and policies sought to be achieved by our strict liability rules. We believe that it will.

Risk Spreading. One of the most important arguments generally advanced for imposing strict liability is that the manufacturers and distributors of defective products can best allocate the costs of the injuries resulting from it. The premise is that the price of a product should reflect all of its costs, including the cost of injuries caused by the product. This can best be accomplished by imposing liability on the manufacturer and distributors. Those persons can insure against liability and incorporate the cost of the insurance in the price of the product. In this way, the costs of the product will be borne by those who profit from it[.] * * *

Defendants argue that this policy is not forwarded by imposition of liability for unknowable hazards. Since such hazards by definition are not predicted, the price of the hazardous product will not be adjusted to reflect the costs of the injuries it will produce. Rather, defendants state, the cost "will be borne by the public at large and reflected in a general, across the board increase in premiums to compensate for unanticipated risks." There is some truth in this assertion, but it is not a bad result.

* * * [S]preading the costs of injuries among all those who produce, distribute and purchase manufactured products is far preferable to imposing it on the innocent victims who suffer illnesses and disability from defective products. * * *

Finally, contrary to defendants' assertion, this rule will not cause the price and production level of manufactured products to diverge from the so-called economically efficient level. Rather, the rule will force the price of any particular product to reflect the cost of insuring against the possibility that the product will turn out to be defective.

Accident Avoidance. * * * Defendants urge that this argument has no force as to hazards which by definition were undiscoverable. Defendants have treated the level of technological knowledge at a given time as an independent variable not affected by defendants' conduct. But this view ignores the important role of industry in product safety research. The "state-of-the-art" at a given time is partly determined by how much industry invests in safety research. By imposing on manufacturers the costs of failure to discover hazards, we create an incentive for them to invest more actively in safety research.

Fact finding process. The analysis thus far has assumed that it is possible to define what constitutes "undiscoverable" knowledge and that it will be reasonably possible to determine what knowledge was technologically discoverable at a given time. * * *

Scientific knowability, as we understand it, refers not to what in fact was known at the time, but to what could have been known at the time. In other words, even if no scientist had actually formed the belief that asbestos was dangerous, the hazards would be deemed "knowable" if a scientist could have formed that belief by applying research or performing tests that were available at the time. Proof of what could have been known will inevitably be complicated, costly, confusing and time-consuming. * * * We doubt that juries will be capable of even understanding the concept of scientific knowability, much less be able to resolve such a complex issue. * * *

* * *

In addition, discussion of state-of-the-art could easily confuse juries into believing that blameworthiness is at issue. * * *

What do you think of the court's conclusion that strict liability means that the ability of the manufacturer to know of the danger posed by the product is irrelevant? Should manufacturers of products be held liable for unknown or unknowable risks that materialize? Should only manufacturers of very dangerous products (i.e., asbestos) be held to such as standard? How should such product categories be determined? By a hindsight test of what harm has actually occurred?

6. Not long after its decision in *Beshada* rejecting the state-of-the-art defense in failure to warn cases, the New Jersey Supreme Court considered the same issue in the context of prescription drugs. In Feldman v. Lederle Laboratories, 97 N.J. 429, 479 A.2d 374 (1984), cert. denied 112 S.Ct. 3027, 120 L.Ed.2d 898 (1984), the court concluded that strict liability would apply to prescription drugs, and then considered whether *Beshada* or a state of the art defense should apply, and stated:

[A]s to warnings, generally conduct should be measured by knowledge at the time the manufacturer distributed the product. Did the defendant know, or should he have known, of the danger, given the scientific, technological, and other information available when the product was distributed; or, in other words, did he have actual or constructive knowledge of the danger? * * *

* * *

This test does not conflict with the assumption made in strict liability design defect and warning cases that the defendant knew of the dangerous propensity of the product, if the knowledge that is assumed is reasonably knowable in the sense of actual or constructive knowledge. A warning that a product may have an unknowable danger warns one of nothing. * * *

* * *

* * * The rationale of Beshada is not applicable to this case. We do not overrule Beshada, but restrict Beshada to the circumstances giving rise to its holding. * * *

7. With reference to *Beshada*, compare the following statements by two commentators. Allen Schwartz, Products Liability, Corporate Structure and Bankruptcy: Toxic Substances and the Remote Risk Relationship, 14 J. Legal Stud. 689, 736 (1985):

> Courts should not impose remote risks on firms. A remote risk is a risk whose full extent a cost-justified research program would not reveal. To impose such risks is unfair, for it makes firms responsible for what they would not prevent. Also, firms have incentives to pursue inefficient strategies, such as liquidating when their going concern value exceeds their liquidation value, just to avoid the surprising liability that a remote risk imposition creates.

Joseph Page, Generic Product Risks: The Case Against Comment k and For Strict Liability, 58 N.Y.U.L.Rev. 853, 891 (1983):

> Both the satisfaction of justifiable expectations on the part of product victims and the achievement of modest advances in safety justify the application of strict liability to harm from unknowable generic hazards.

8. *Beshada* was challenged on constitutional equal protection grounds—that is, that the New Jersey Supreme Court had created an irrational classification between asbestos and nonasbestos manufacturers, denying the state of the art defense only to the former. The *Feldman–Beshada* distinction was upheld narrowly in In re Asbestos Litigation, 829 F.2d 1233 (3d Cir.1987), cert. denied 485 U.S. 1029, 108 S.Ct. 1586, 99 L.Ed.2d 901 (1988). Consider the following statement by Judge Weiss:

> In refining and narrowing the § 402A theory, *Beshada* eliminates one more defense to the liability of asbestos defendants. * * * [We cannot] conclude that the state court's position is irrational. The concepts of risk-spreading and compensation for victims by manufacturers of unreasonably dangerous products are cornerstones of § 402A, and they may be consistently applied to asbestos as well as to other products.
>
> Although not in itself a determinative factor in the elimination of a substantive defense, the desirability of simplifying the fact-finding process and thus making it easier for victims to recover has been recognized by the law. Workers' compensation programs and no-fault auto insurance plans share that common goal. * * *
>
> Administrative convenience standing alone is not an adequate ground for the elimination of a substantive defense. However, we cannot help but be conscious of the extraordinary size of the asbestos personal injury litigation. * * * [T]his unprecedented phenomenon in American tort law requires states be given some leeway in devising their own solutions.

9. The symbiosis between worker's compensation claims and the often-later-filed personal injury suits always requires counsel's attention. For example, the issue of when plaintiff's cause of action accrues for limitations purposes was raised in the context of a silicosis claim in Martinez v. Humble Sand and Gravel, 860 S.W.2d 467 (Tex.App.1993), a suit brought by a sandblaster. The Texas appellate court held that the plaintiff's products liability claim accrued on the date that he filed a workers' compensation

claim with the Industrial Accident Board, alleging that he had contracted silicosis as a result of his employment. In Chapter 9 we consider the relationship between the workers compensation system and tort law, and in Chapter 12 the special statutes of limitation concerns are addressed.

10. In toxic torts litigation, as in products liability litigation generally, plaintiff often seeks to introduce evidence that following the injurious exposure or contamination, defendant undertook remedial measures that would permit the inference that defendant's pre-curative conduct was negligent. Federal Rule of Evidence 407 precludes introduction of post-incident remedial measures to show negligence or culpable conduct, on the logic that such evidence is (1) only minimally probative of the care defendant exercised before the mishap; (2) quite prejudicial to defendant; and (3) admission of such evidence would chill the motivation of manufacturers and others to improve their products or processes. See generally M. Stuart Madden, The Admissibility of Post–Incident Remedial Measures, 5. J. Prod. Liab. 1 (1982). In the environmental tort context, consider In re Joint Eastern Dist. and Southern Dist. Asbestos Litigation, 995 F.2d 343 (2d Cir.1993), where the Second Circuit found reversible error in the trial court's admission of evidence that the manufacturer of encapsulated asbestos valve packing placed warnings on its product some time after the last exposure claimed by plaintiff.

11. *Insurance: Liability and Unknowable Risks.* Asbestos liability litigation presents two important issues involving liability insurance. First, can manufacturers adequately insure against risks that are unknown at the time the products are distributed? Second, as of what time does the plaintiff's "bodily injury" (the insured-against event) occur for purposes of determining which of several insurance policies covers the liability in question?

Regarding the first of these issues, a number of commentators have argued that manufacturers cannot, by hypothesis, insure against risks no one knows exist. As a consequence, when liability is later imposed strictly, based on hindsight, all they can do is charge the losses against earnings or capital, or go out of business. Either way, inefficiencies result. See generally, Patricia M. Danzon, Tort Reform and the Role of Government in Private Insurance Markets, 13 J. Legal Stud. 517 (1984). Of course, this answer begs the question of whether efficiency ought to be an overriding consideration. For the argument that fairness reasons do not support hindsight-based strict liability, see generally, James A. Henderson, Jr., Coping with the Time Dimension in Products Liability, 69 Calif. L.Rev. 919 (1981).

As to the issue of which liability policy should cover a risk that took 20 or 30 years (from first distribution to full manifestation of plaintiff's injury) to materialize, courts have disagreed. See discussion of insurance issues in Chapter 11.

b. *Punitive Damages in Asbestos Litigation*

While *Borel* and the early asbestos cases involved only requests for compensatory damages, it wasn't long before plaintiffs began to request and recover punitive damages. The following decision in Fischer v.

Johns–Manville Corp., 103 N.J. 643, 512 A.2d 466 (1986) summarizes the tests for punitive liability that apply in the majority of jurisdictions and the evidence critical to satisfying those tests in the asbestos context.

FISCHER v. JOHNS-MANVILLE CORPORATION

Supreme Court of New Jersey, 1986.
103 N.J. 643, 512 A.2d 466.

CLIFFORD, J.

Plaintiff James Fischer and Geneva Fischer, his wife, brought suit against multiple defendants seeking to recover damages for lung diseases suffered by James Fischer as a result of his exposure to asbestos. The complaint sought compensatory and punitive damages from defendants-suppliers of asbestos under negligence, breach of warranty, and strict products liability theories. Plaintiffs elected to press at trial only the strict liability cause of action for compensatory damages, while at the same time they sought punitive damages. * * *

The case was tried to a jury. At the close of trial, the jury awarded compensatory damages of $86,000 to James Fischer and $5,000 to Geneva Fischer. The jury found Johns–Manville eighty percent liable and Bell twenty percent liable. The jury also awarded James Fischer $300,000 in punitive damages, of which $240,000 was assessed against Johns–Manville and $60,000 against Bell. Both defendants appealed and the Appellate Division affirmed in its entirety the judgment of the trial court.

* * *

* * * Johns–Manville's petition urges that the Appellate Division's determination runs counter to decisions by New Jersey federal district courts and thus requires clarification. As well it repeats the arguments made below, that (1) punitive damages "cannot conceptually flow" from a claim based on strict liability for failure to warn, (2) punitive damages "serve no purpose" in asbestos mass litigation, and (3) the record does not support a finding of punitive damages against Johns–Manville. [We affirm].

I

* * *

* * * [P]laintiffs' punitive damage claim hinged on their contention that "defendants knew of these hazards as early as the 1930's and had made a conscious business decision to withhold this information from the public." * * *

The Appellate Division summarized the evidence in support of those allegations as follows[:]

Johns–Manville, in its answers to interrogatories, which were read to the jury, admitted that

[t]he corporation became aware of the relationship between asbestos and the disease known as asbestosis among workers involved in mining, milling and manufacturing operations and exposed to high levels of virtually 100% raw asbestos fibers over long periods of time by the early 1930s. The corporation has followed and become aware of the general state of the medical art relative to asbestos and its relationship to disease processes, if any.

In response to plaintiffs' requests for admissions, also read to the jury, it admitted that in the early 1940's it knew that asbestos "was dangerous to the health" of those industrial workers who were exposed to excessive amounts of the material. Plaintiffs, moreover, produced as a witness Dr. Daniel C. Braun, president of the Industrial Health Foundation, a research organization which develops, accumulates and disseminates information about occupational diseases. Dr. Braun testified that Johns–Manville has been a member of the Foundation since 1936. He also testified that since 1937 the Foundation has sent to its members a monthly digest of articles appearing in scientific journals which relate to occupational disease. Relevant portions of the digests, which were admitted into evidence, included references to eleven scientific articles published between 1936 and 1941 documenting the grave pulmonary hazards of exposure to asbestos and discussing measures which could be taken to protect workers. * * *

In December of that year high-level representatives of Johns–Manville met with officials of Raybestos–Manhattan, another major asbestos supplier, to discuss steps which the industry as a whole might take to reduce employee risk. It appears, however, that Johns–Manville never did arrange for or participate in any industry-wide meetings on the subject. The minutes of that 1933 meeting also confirm the participants' view that at least for the time being "our past policy of keeping this matter confidential is to be pursued."

Perhaps most damning of all is the so-called Sumner Simpson correspondence of 1935 and 1941. Simpson was president of Raybestos. In October 1935, he received a letter from a Miss Rossiter, editor of the trade periodical Asbestos, suggesting that despite Simpson's earlier requests, made "for certain obvious reasons," that articles relating to asbestosis not be published, perhaps the time had come to print a positive article about industry efforts to reduce the risk in order "to combat some of the rather undesirable publicity given to it [asbestosis] in current newspapers." Simpson thereupon sent a copy of the letter to Johns–Manville's secretary, Vandiver Brown, expressing his opinion that "the less said about asbestos, the better off we are." Brown's reply stated in part: I quite agree with you that our interests are best served by having asbestosis receive the minimum of publicity." * * *

* * *

* * * On this appeal Johns–Manville's position, succinctly stated, is that the punitive damages award against it is legally impermissible, ill-

advised as a matter of public policy in litigation of this nature, and factually unwarranted.

II

The "legally impermissible" argument rests on an asserted theoretical inconsistency between strict liability and punitive damages, which would preclude punitive damage claims when liability for compensatory damages is founded on strict products liability doctrine, if not in all situations at least in asbestos, strict liability lawsuits. We hold that there is no per se legal bar to pursuing a strict liability, failure-to-warn claim and a punitive damage claim in the same case. * * *

* * *

The type of conduct that will warrant an award of punitive damages has been described in various ways. The conduct must be "wantonly reckless or malicious. There must be an intentional wrongdoing in the sense of an 'evil-minded act' or an act accompanied by a wanton and willful disregard of the rights of another." * * *

As should now be apparent, the proofs needed to establish a prima facie case of failure-to-warn, strict products liability differ markedly from the proofs that will support an award of punitive damages. Despite their differences—one going to the theory of liability, the other bearing on the form and extent of relief—they are not mutually exclusive nor even incompatible. There is no reason they cannot be litigated together. * * *

* * *

III

* * *

[One] concern created by the time gap between exposure and litigation is that the corporate personnel who made the decisions at the time of the exposure are no longer with the defendant company, possibly no longer alive. From this fact it is argued that punitive damages are inappropriate because they will not punish the true wrongdoers. But as many courts have observed, this contention ignores the nature of a corporation as a separate legal entity. Although the responsible management personnel may escape punishment, the corporation itself will not. * * * We are reminded that a primary goal of punitive damages is general deterrence—that is, the deterrence of others from engaging in similar conduct. That purpose is, of course, well served regardless of changes in personnel within the offending corporation.

A related argument, which similarly ignores the legal nature of corporations, is that punitive damages unfairly punish innocent shareholders. This argument has been rejected repeatedly. It is the corporation, not the individual shareholders, that is recognized as an ongoing legal entity engaged in manufacturing and distributing products. True, payment of punitive damages claims will deplete corporate assets, which will possibly produce a reduction in net worth and thereby result in a reduction in the value of individual shares. But the same is true of compensatory damages. * * * [W]e would not consider it harmful were shareholders to be encouraged by decisions such as this to give close scrutiny to corporate practices in making investment decisions.

* * *

Defendant argues that the amount of compensatory damages assessed and to be assessed is so great that it will effectively serve the functions of punitive damages—that is, defendants are more than sufficiently punished and deterred. We are not at all satisfied, however, that compensatory damages effectively serve the same functions as punitive damages, even when they amount to staggering sums. Compensatory damages are often foreseeable as to amount, within certain limits difficult to reduce to a formula but nonetheless familiar to the liability insurance industry. * * * The risk and amount of such damages can, and in some cases will, be reflected in the cost of a product, in which event the product will be marketed in its dangerous condition.

Without punitive damages a manufacturer who is aware of a dangerous feature of its product but nevertheless knowingly chooses to market it in that condition, willfully concealing from the public information regarding the dangers of the product, would be far better off than an innocent manufacturer who markets a product later discovered to be dangerous—this, because both will be subjected to the same compensatory damages, but the innocent manufacturer, unable to anticipate those damages, will not have incorporated the cost of those damages into the cost of the product. All else being equal, the law should not place the innocent manufacturer in a worse position than that of a knowing wrongdoer. Punitive damages tend to meet this need.

Defendant argues further that the cumulative effect of punitive damages in mass-tort litigation is "potentially catastrophic." The Johns–Manville bankruptcy is offered as proof of this effect. We fail to see the distinction, in the case of Johns–Manville, between the effect of compensatory damages and that of punitive damages. The amount of punitive damages and the determination that they would cause insolvency that could be avoided in their absence are so speculative as to foreclose any sound basis for judicial decision. * * *

* * *

At the state court level we are powerless to implement solutions to the nationwide problems created by asbestos exposure and litigation arising from that exposure. That does not mean, however, that we cannot institute some controls over runaway punitive damages. * * * [T]here should be some limits placed on the total punishment exacted from a culpable defendant. We conclude that a reasonable imposition of those limits would permit a defendant to introduce evidence of other punitive damage awards already assessed against and paid by it, as well as evidence of its own financial status and the effect a punitive award would have. * * *

We realize that defendants may be reluctant to alert juries to the fact that other courts or juries have assessed punitive damages for conduct similar to that being considered by the jury in a given case. * * * The willingness to accept that risk is a matter of strategy for defendant and its counsel, no different from other strategy choices facing trial lawyers every day.

When evidence of other punitive awards is introduced, trial courts should instruct juries to consider whether the defendant has been sufficiently punished, keeping in mind that punitive damages are meant to punish and deter defendants for the benefit of society, not to compensate individual plaintiffs.

* * *

IV

Defendant argues that even if punitive damages are allowed in strict products liability, mass tort actions, they should not have been assessed against Johns–Manville in this action. We disagree. We hold that punitive damages are available in failure-to-warn, strict products liability actions when a manufacturer is (1) aware of or culpably indifferent to an unnecessary risk of injury, and (2) refuses to take steps to reduce that danger to an acceptable level. This standard can be met by a showing of "a deliberate act or omission with knowledge of a high degree of probability of harm and reckless indifference to consequences." * * *

* * *

Notes and Questions

1. A significant number of decisions have affirmed or authorized awards of punitive damages in asbestos litigation. See Thiry v. Armstrong World Industries, 661 P.2d 515 (Okl.1983) (answering certified questions from United States District Court); Jackson v. Johns–Manville Sales Corp., 781 F.2d 394 (5th Cir.1986) (*Jackson III*), cert. denied 478 U.S. 1022, 106 S.Ct. 3339, 92 L.Ed.2d 743 (1986); Dykes v. Raymark Industries, Inc., 801 F.2d 810 (6th Cir.1986), cert. denied 481 U.S. 1038, 107 S.Ct. 1975, 95 L.Ed.2d 815 (1987); Racich v. Celotex Corp., 887 F.2d 393 (2d Cir.1989); Glasscock v. Armstrong Cork Co., 946 F.2d 1085 (5th Cir.1991), cert. denied ___ U.S. ___, 112 S.Ct. 1778, 118 L.Ed.2d 435 (1992); Owens–Illinois, Inc. v. Armstrong, 87 Md.App. 699, 591 A.2d 544 (1991), modified on other grounds 326 Md. 107, 604 A.2d 47 (1992), cert. denied ___ U.S. ___, 113 S.Ct. 204, 121 L.Ed.2d 145 (1992). But see Martin v. Johns–Manville Corp., 508 Pa. 154, 494 A.2d 1088 (1985); MCIC v. Zenobia, 86 Md.App. 456, 587 A.2d 531 (1991) (vacating one award, affirming one award), reversed 325 Md. 665, 601 A.2d 633 (1992).

2. Decisions such as *Fischer* that reject policy arguments made against the imposition of multiple punitive awards are legion. Defendants have pressed the argument that multiple awards violated constitutional due

process, i.e., the cumulative effect of multiple awards could become so burdensome on a defendant as to constitute a violation of substantive due process protections against grossly excessive punishments. In 1989 one United States District Court ruled that repetitive awards of punitive damages for the same conduct violates a defendant's due process rights. In Juzwin v. Amtorg Trading Corp., 705 F.Supp. 1053 (D.N.J.1989), vacated 718 F.Supp. 1233 (D.N.J.1989), Judge Sarokin wrote:

> subjecting defendants to the possibility of multiple awards of punitive damages for the single course of conduct alleged in this action would deprive defendants of the fundamental fairness required by the Due Process Clause.

After acknowledging the due process problems, Judge Sarokin called for appropriate legislation to address this issue and to set meaningful standards and guidelines. This legislation would include:

> (1) determining initially whether punitive damages should be allowed in mass tort cases, and if so; (2) establish standards for their imposition and for the amounts to be awarded; (3) determine if maximum limits should be imposed and whether they should be fixed by amount or some formula based upon the net worth of the defendant; (4) provide procedures for dealing with successive claims; and (5) determine who shall be entitled to receive and participate in those awards.

In the subsequent vacating opinion, Judge Sarokin expressed concern about the fairness of retroactively applying its ruling "to those adversely affected by this ruling and the court's inability to effectuate its ruling prospectively absent uniformity either through legislation or a Supreme Court determination." The court held that to bar a subsequent claim for punitive damages, the following must be established as having taken place during the first proceeding:

> 1. A full and complete hearing must be held, after adequate time has elapsed to investigate and discover the full scope and consequences of such conduct and during which all relevant evidence is presented regarding the conduct of the defendant against whom the claim is made;
>
> 2. Adequate representation is afforded to the plaintiff, with an opportunity for plaintiffs similarly situated and their counsel to cooperate and contribute towards the presentation of the punitive damages claim, including presentation of the past and probable future consequences of the defendant's wrongful conduct;
>
> 3. An appropriate instruction to the jury that their award will be the one and only award of punitive damages to be rendered against the company for its wrongful conduct;
>
> 4. Such other conditions as will assure a full, fair and complete presentation of all the relevant evidence in support of and in opposition to the claim. 718 F.Supp. 1233 (D.N.J.1989).

In Leonen v. Johns–Manville Corp., 717 F.Supp. 272 (D.N.J.1989), another New Jersey District Court judge reached a contrary conclusion respecting the due process issues inhering in multiple awards.

3. Subsequent to *Juzwin* and *Leonen,* numerous appellate courts have rejected defendants' due process arguments. See, e.g., Racich v. Celotex

Corp., 887 F.2d 393 (2d Cir.1989); Simpson v. Pittsburgh Corning Corp., 901 F.2d 277 (2d Cir.1990), cert. denied 497 U.S. 1057, 111 S.Ct. 27, 111 L.Ed.2d 840 (1990); King v. Armstrong World Industries, 906 F.2d 1022 (5th Cir.1990), cert. denied ___ U.S. ___, 111 S.Ct. 2236, 114 L.Ed.2d 478 (1991); Glasscock v. Armstrong Cork Co., 946 F.2d 1085 (5th Cir.1991), cert. denied ___ U.S. ___, 112 S.Ct. 1778, 118 L.Ed.2d 435 (1992). In Chapter 5 the general due process limitations on punitive damages, both procedural and substantive, were considered. The Supreme Court has not addressed the question of what constitutional constraints, if any, exist on multiple awards arising from a product line or course of conduct.

4. In Dunn v. HOVIC, 1 F.3d 1371 (3d Cir.1993) (en banc), the Third Circuit ruled 8 to 5, that repeated impositions of punitive damages on mass tort defendants is not by itself so unreasonable as to violate substantive due process.

In *Dunn* a jury awarded plaintiff $500,000 in compensatory damages and $25 million in punitive damages against Owens–Corning Fiberglas Corp. The trial court remitted the latter award to $2 million. A panel of the Third Circuit affirmed, but remitted the punitives to $1 million. Owens–Corning sought en banc review to consider its constitutional argument that repetitive impositions of punitive damages arising out of the same course of conduct violated substantive due process. Writing for a majority, Chief Judge Sloviter noted that in Pacific Mutual Life Insurance Co. v. Haslip, 499 U.S. 1, 111 S.Ct. 1032, 113 L.Ed.2d 1 (1991), the Supreme Court approved appellate review of punitive awards to determine if a particular award is greater than is reasonably necessary to punish and deter. After stating that en banc review was justified because of the importance of the question, the court observed that the vast majority of federal and state courts that have addressed the issue have declined to strike punitive awards solely because they constituted repetitive punishments for the same conduct. It commented: "Those courts, and this court, have recognized the arbitrariness of imposing caps on such damages in only one jurisdiction, when what is required is a national, uniform solution to the problem."

Moreover, the court noted that the Supreme Court decision in TXO Production Corp. v. Alliance Resources Corp., ___ U.S. ___, 113 S.Ct. 2711, 125 L.Ed.2d 366 (1993), held only that the enormous award in that case posed no substantive due process violation, and made no reference to the possible impact of repetitive awards. Judge Sloviter continued:

"We would be intrepid indeed were we to use this case to iterate a blanket policy judgment against punitive damages in asbestos cases in light of the Supreme Court's studied silence on the issue."

Nevertheless, the Third Circuit held that a further remittitur was appropriate because the district court gave insufficient consideration to the effect of successive punitive awards in asbestos litigation:

"This factor, above all, leads us to conclude that the maximum amount of punitive damages that could reasonably have been awarded in this case is $1 million."

Judge Joseph Weis dissented from the en banc opinion, and stated that in the unique context of asbestos litigation "punitive awards are not needed for retribution and deterrence. Actually there is little conduct to deter because few asbestos-containing products are still manufactured in the United States." Noting that Owens–Corning stopped manufacturing Kaylo in November 1972 and no longer produces any asbestos-containing products so that there was no conduct to deter in the future, Judge Weis continued: "The avalanche of compensatory claims against asbestos manufacturers has surely served as more of a punishment and deterrent than individual punitive assessments," concluding: There is no compelling reason why injured but fully compensated plaintiffs should receive punitive awards."

Like the majority, Judge Weis acknowledged the need for a national solution, but the immediate need was to "stop the hemorrhaging so as to protect future claimants." He stated that courts should not await congressional or state legislative action, when the courts created the problem. "It is judicial paralysis, not activism, that is the problem ..." Finally, Weis stressed that the available resources of asbestos manufacturers will be exhausted before all deserving claimants are compensated; compensation should rank first, then administrative costs, and far down the list, "if not at the very bottom" should come punitive awards.

Who has the better of the constitutional argument? Are there non-constitutional grounds for refusing to allow repetitive awards of punitive damages? Should asbestos cases have different substantive rules governing punitive damages? What about the concern that future claimants may be denied compensatory damages if punitive damages exhaust defendants' assets?

How might a defendant set out to establish the proposition that resources will be inadequate to compensate future claimants?

2. ALCOHOL

1. Can a manufacturer or distributor of alcohol be liable when a consumer suffers a physical disability or disease from the consumption of moderate quantities of the beverage? A new genre of failure to warn cases is emerging from injuries attributable to moderate use of alcohol, in circumstances where the risks of consumption are not so obvious: pregnant women whose consumption produces fetal injuries and adults whose long-term consumption results in serious conditions, even death.

In Hon v. Stroh Brewery Co., 835 F.2d 510 (3d Cir.1987), we see an early appellate ruling to consider this informational defect claim. *Hon* was a wrongful death action brought by the surviving spouse, whose husband died at age 26 from pancreatitis, allegedly from his consumption of alcohol. Mr. Hon drank Old Milwaukee Beer and Old Milwaukee Light, two to three cans a night, an average of four nights a week. Plaintiff's expert in an affidavit expressed these opinions: (1) the understanding shared by members of the public is that excessive and prolonged use of alcoholic beverages is likely to result in disease, principally of the liver; (2) Mr. Hon's case was not within the risk thus appreciated by the public because (a) his use was prolonged but not excessive and (b) his disease was of the pancreas; and (3) the public's understanding is "archaic" because medical science has now established that either excessive or prolonged, even though moderate, use of alcohol may result in disease of many kinds, including pancreatic disease.

The court then considered the application of Restatement (Second) of Torts § 402A:

"In applying [Restatement (Second) of Torts § 402A], the Supreme Court of Pennsylvania has held that the trial judge must decide a threshold issue as a matter of law: taking the allegations of the complaint to be true, would the social policy considerations underlying strict liability justify recovery under § 402A in this case. The court must thus balance the product's social utility against its unavoidable risks to determine whether the condition of the product could be labeled "unreasonably dangerous" and the risk of loss placed on the manufacturer. Only if the court decides that strict liability would be appropriate does the case go to the jury for a determination regarding the truth of the plaintiff's allegations. * * *

* * *

As one would expect, a manufacturer whose products will enter Pennsylvania may assume that users or consumers will possess the common knowledge of the community. It must therefore warn only of latent risks. If the product's risks "w[ere] known or should have been known to the user, liability cannot be imposed upon the manufacturer merely because the manufacturer allegedly has failed to warn of that propensity." [See also] Restatement (Second) of Torts § 402A comment i ("The article sold must be dangerous to an extent beyond that which would be contemplated by the ordinary knowledge common to the community as its characteristics.").

* * *

Although the district court in this case did not expressly undertake [a] threshold social policy analysis[,] * * * it did suggest that allowing strict liability in this case "could impose an impractical burden on manufacturers of alcoholic beverages to devise warnings suitable for the particular tolerance of each consumer," 665 F.Supp. at 1146. Mrs. Hon does not take issue with this suggestion. Rather, she insists that a general warning of the risk of moderate consumption would suffice, for example, "Alcohol can have adverse effects on your health even when consumed in moderate amounts." If Stroh shows that it is not feasible for it to give an effective warning of the hazard that led to Mr. Hon's death, this case might present a more substantial social policy issue than the typical warning case[.] We do not resolve that issue here because the district court did not fully address it and because we believe the issue would benefit from a more complete development of the record.

The remaining issue under the analysis taught in the Pennsylvania cases is whether, given the common knowledge of the community with respect to the hazards of alcohol consumption, a warning was an "element necessary to make [Stroh's beer] safe for its intended use," namely human consumption. This issue is for the jury unless the record created in response to Stroh's motion for summary judgment reveals no factual basis for an affirmative answer to this crucial question. * * *

The district court granted summary judgment to Stroh because it concluded "as a matter of law that [Mr. Hon] knew or should have known that the amount of beer that he consumed was potentially lethal." 665 F.Supp. at 1146. It erred in reaching this conclusion. On the record before the district court, a trier of fact could properly find that while the amount of beer consumed by Mr. Hon was potentially lethal, that fact was known neither to him nor to the consuming public. For this reason, we conclude that there is a material dispute of fact as to whether Stroh's beer without a warning is safe for its intended purpose and, accordingly, that summary judgment was inappropriate.

Dr. Marks' and Dr. Plotnick's affidavits provide evidence tending to show that beer in the quantity and manner Mr. Hon consumed it can have fatal consequences. Nothing in the record suggests that Mr. Hon was aware of this fact, however. Moreover, Dr. Plotnick's affidavit tends to show that the general public is unaware that consumption at this level and in this manner can have any serious adverse effects. There is no evidence in the record that the public appreciates any hazard that may be associated with this kind of consumption.

In addition, we conclude that the story boards of Stroh's commercials provide additional evidence from which a jury could conclude that the general public is unaware of the hazard that allegedly led to Mr. Hon's death. If a jury finds that Stroh's marketing of its product has effectively taught the consuming public that consumption of beer on the order of eight to twelve cans of beer per week can be a part of the "good life" and is properly associated with healthy, robust activities, this conclusion would be an important consideration for the jury in determining whether an express warning was necessary to make Old Milwaukee beer safe for its intended purpose. Cf., Baldino v. Castagna, [505 Pa. 239, 478 A.2d 807, 810 (1984)] (jury may consider whether a manufacturer has nullified warning that has been given by its promotion of the product); Incollingo v. Ewing, [444 Pa. 263, 282 A.2d 206, 220 (1971)] ("Action designed to stimulate the use of a potentially dangerous product must be considered in testing the adequacy of a warning as to when and how the product should not be used. . . ."). Based on this evidence we believe there is a material dispute of fact as to whether the sale of Stroh's beer products with no warning was safe for its intended purpose.

Stroh's primary argument in response to the evidence presented by Mrs. Hon is that under comment j of § 402A, all that is required to preclude liability is that the consumption of alcohol be "prolonged."[5]

5. Comment j states in relevant part:
"j. Directions or warning. In order to prevent the product from being [in a defective condition] unreasonably dangerous [to the user or consumer], the seller may be required to give directions or warning, on the container, as to its use. The seller may reasonably assume that those with common allergies, as for example to eggs or strawberries, will be aware of them, and he is not required to warn against them. Where, however, the product contains an ingredi-

* * * [Comment j] specifically cites alcohol as an example, states that no warning is needed for products that are made dangerous only "when consumed in excessive quantity, or over a long period of time, *when the danger, or potentiality of danger is generally known and recognized.*" Restatement § 402A comment j (emphasis added).

Stroh interprets comment j to mean that "the dangers of the prolonged consumption of alcohol are well known to the public." But comment j does not say that whenever alcohol is consumed over a long period of time the dangers are necessarily generally known. Rather, it says that when the danger is generally known, no warning is required. * * *[6]

* * *

With one possible exception, all of the cases cited by Stroh presented records from which a trier of fact could conclude only that the consumer of the alcoholic beverages knew or should have known that his or her consumption created a substantial risk of bodily injury. Accordingly, these cases are entirely consistent with Mrs. Hon's theory of liability. * * *

It is true, as Stroh stresses, that Mrs. Hon cites no case holding a brewer strictly liable for a failure to warn. We find this fact neither surprising nor at odds with our analysis, however. So far as we have been able to ascertain, there is no case in which the plaintiff allegedly consumed beer in the quantity and manner reflected in this record. The fact that such a case has not been litigated is explainable on either of two grounds. It may be, as Mrs. Hon contends, that consumers are unaware of the risk created by the consumption of beer in this manner. On the other hand, it may be, as Stroh's answer indicates it will attempt to prove, that Mr. Hon's quantity and manner of beer consumption poses

ent to which a substantial number of the population are allergic, and the ingredient is one whose danger is not generally known, or if known is one which the consumer would reasonably not expect to find in the product, the seller is required to give warning against it, if he has knowledge, or by the application of reasonable, developed human skill and foresight should have knowledge, of the presence of the ingredient and the danger. Likewise in the case of poisonous drugs, or those unduly dangerous for other reasons, warning as to use may be required."

"But a seller is not required to warn with respect to products, or ingredients in them, which are only dangerous, or potentially so, when consumed in excessive quantity, or over a long period of time, when the danger, or potentially of danger, is generally known and recognized. Again the dangers of alcoholic beverages are an example, as are also those of foods containing such substances as saturated fats, which may over a period of time have a deleterious effect upon the human heart."

6. In pertinent part, comment i states:

"Many products cannot possibly be made entirely safe for all consumption, and any food or drug necessarily involves some risk of harm, if only from over consumption. . . . The article sold must be dangerous to an extent beyond that which would be contemplated by the ordinary consumer who purchases it, with the ordinary knowledge common to the community as its characteristics. Good whiskey is not unreasonably dangerous merely because it will make some people drunk, and is especially dangerous to alcoholics. . . ."

Restatement (Second) of Torts § 402A comment i. Thus, although like comment j, comment i cites alcohol as an example, the exception to liability applies only because the dangers of intoxication and alcoholism are within the contemplation of the ordinary consumer.

no significant risk of bodily injury. In this context, the absence of authority for Mrs. Hon's position provides no persuasive reason to depart from the analysis suggested by the Pennsylvania authorities we have discussed above.

III.

We will vacate the summary judgment granted to Stroh and remand the case to the district court for further proceedings consistent with this opinion.

Notes and Questions

1.   What if the record shows that Mr. Hon would not have heeded such a warning as Mrs. Hon argues should have been given?

2.   Congress enacted the Alcoholic Beverage Labeling Act of 1988, 27 U.S.C.A. § 201 et seq., which contains the following provisions:

> Section 204.(a) On and after the expiration of the 12–month period following the date of enactment of this title, it shall be unlawful for any person to manufacture, import or bottle for sale or distribution in the United States any alcoholic beverage unless the container of such beverage bears the following statement:

> **GOVERNMENT WARNING:** (1) According to the Surgeon General, women should not drink alcoholic beverages during pregnancy because of the risk of birth defects. (2) Consumption of alcoholic beverages impairs your ability to drive a car or operate machinery, and may cause health problems.

> Section 205.   No statement relating to alcoholic beverages and health, other than the statement required by section 204 of this title, shall be required under state law to be placed on any container of an alcoholic beverage, or on any box, carton, or other package, irrespective of the material from which made, that contains such a container.

What impact should this statute have on suits brought for actions that accrue after its enactment? Will the courts experience the same pre and post-enactment problems that have been so determinative in cigarette litigation?

3.   The Texas Court of Appeals held in McGuire v. Joseph E. Seagram & Sons, Inc., 790 S.W.2d 842 (Tex.App.1990), reversed 814 S.W.2d 385 (Tex.1991) that alcohol manufacturers, distributors and their trade association have a duty to warn consumers of some of the dangers of alcohol; and that under strict liability when the manufacturer knows or should know of the potential danger to consumers because of the nature of the product and its likelihood of prolonged use, the manufacturer is duty-bound to provide warnings of such dangers. The Texas Supreme Court reversed, 814 S.W.2d 385 (Tex.1991), holding that manufacturers of alcoholic beverages have no duty to warn of the dangers of developing alcoholism from prolonged consumption of their products. This conclusion is consistent with those of many other courts that have held as a matter of law that distilled spirits and other alcoholic beverages are not more dangerous to personal health than would be expected by the ordinary adult consumer.

4. The vitality of a "consumer expectations" approach to evaluating a "defect" in toxic product claims would be affected by its probable abandonment in the expected new Products Liability Restatement. The Preliminary Draft of a Restatement (Third) of Torts: Products Liability, introduced earlier, emphasizes that the classical "consumer expectations" test "is explicitly abandoned as an independent test for determining defect." In its words, the test for design defect properly employs "a risk-utility balancing to determine defectiveness in the context of design." How would you phrase Stroh's risk-utility argument for the acceptable safety of its products? How might a plaintiff argue the case?

The Reporters' proposed liability standards reject the "open and obvious" or "patent danger" rule as a total bar to a design defect claim, and state that "the obviousness of the danger is one factor among many to consider as to whether a product design meets risk-utility norms." In contrast, however, the Reporters state that there is no duty to warn about obvious dangers. Explaining the compatibility between a rule that obviousness is no automatic bar to a design defect claim, and one that preserves obviousness as an exculpatory factor relating to informational obligations, Professors Henderson and Twerski cite their own earlier commentary to this effect:

> "[T]he argument for abandoning the patent danger rule in warning cases, simply because the rule has been abandoned in design cases, makes no sense. In the design case, the obviousness of the danger does not necessarily preclude the possibility that an alternative design could reduce the risk cost- effectively. By contrast, assuming that some risks are patently obvious, the obviousness of a product-related risk invariably serves the same function as a warning that the risk is present. Thus nothing is to be gained by adding a warning of the danger already telegraphed by the product itself."

James Henderson, Jr. & Aaron Twerski, Doctrinal Collapse in Products Liability: The Empty Shell of Failure to Warn, 65 N.Y.U.L. Rev. 265, 282 (1990).

3. PRESCRIPTION PHARMACEUTICALS, BIOLOGICAL PRODUCTS AND MEDICAL DEVICES

A third and principal class of products that may produce exposure to toxic substances is prescription products. Within this general grouping are prescription pharmaceuticals, blood and other biological products, and medical devices. Widely reported personal injury litigation within these categories has involved products ranging from DES, to Bendectin, to contaminated blood or blood derivatives, to silicone breast implants. One similarity between and among most of these categories is the hotly contested issue of causation, a question that is addressed separately in Chapter 8. The second similarity is that each of these products is available only though prescription. The implications of being a prescription product are twofold. The first is that a seller ordinarily discharges its duty to provide adequate warnings, instructions and other information by making that information available to the health provider, most often a physician. The second is that the strict products liability evaluation under Restatement (Second) of Torts § 402A is governed by comment k thereto. The significance of the latter is the subject of the following decision of the California Supreme Court.

a. Pharmaceuticals and comment k

BROWN v. SUPERIOR COURT

Supreme Court of California, 1988.
245 Cal.Rptr. 412, 751 P.2d 470.

MOSK, J.

In current litigation several significant issues have arisen relating to the liability of manufacturers of prescription drugs for injuries caused by their products. Our first and broadest inquiry is whether such a manufacturer may be held strictly liable for a product that is defective in design. * * *

A number of plaintiffs filed actions in the San Francisco Superior Court against numerous drug manufacturers which allegedly produced DES, a substance plaintiffs claimed was used by their mothers to prevent miscarriage. They alleged that the drug was defective and they were injured in utero when their mothers ingested it. * * *

The trial court * * * determined that defendants could not be held strictly liable for the alleged defect in DES but only for their failure to warn of known or knowable side effects of the drug.

* * *

[The Court of Appeal affirmed.] We granted review to examine the conclusions of the Court of Appeal and its potential conflict with Kearl v. Lederle Laboratories [218 Cal.Rptr. 453 (1985)], on the issue of strict liability of a drug manufacturer for a defect in the design of a prescription drug.

I. STRICT LIABILITY

* * *

B. Strict Liability and Prescription Drugs

* * *

[Restatement (Second) of Torts § 402A comment k] provides that the producer of a properly manufactured prescription drug may be held liable for injuries caused by the product only if it was not accompanied by a warning of dangers that the manufacturer knew or should have known about. It declares:

k. Unavoidably unsafe products. There are some products which, in the present state of human knowledge, are quite incapable of being made safe for their intended and ordinary use. These are especially common in the field of drugs. An outstanding example is the vaccine for the Pasteur treatment of rabies, which not uncommonly leads to very serious and damaging consequences when it is injected.   Since the disease itself invariably leads to a dreadful death, both the marketing and use of the vaccine are fully justified, notwithstanding the unavoidable high degree of risk which they involve.   Such a product, properly prepared, and accompanied by proper directions and warning, is not defective, nor is it unreasonably dangerous.   The same is true of many other drugs, vaccines, and the like, many of which for this very reason cannot legally be sold except to physicians, or under the prescription of a physician.   It is also true in particular of many new or experimental drugs as to which, because of lack of time and opportunity for sufficient medical experience, there can be no assurance of safety, or perhaps even of purity of ingredients, but such experience as there is justifies the marketing and use of the drug notwithstanding a medically recognizable risk.   The seller of such products, again with the qualification that they are properly prepared and marketed, and proper warning is given, where the situation calls for it, is not to be held to strict liability for unfortunate consequences attending their use, merely because he has undertaken to supply the public with an apparently useful and desirable product, attended with a known but apparently reasonable risk.

Comment k has been analyzed and criticized by numerous commentators.   While there is some disagreement as to its scope and meaning, there is a general consensus that, although it purports to explain the strict liability doctrine, in fact the principle it states is based on negligence.   * * *

Comment k has been adopted in the overwhelming majority of jurisdictions that have considered the matter.

* * *

* * * Most cases have embraced the rule of comment k without detailed analysis of its language.   A few, notably Kearl v. Lederle Laboratories, supra, 172 Cal.App.3d 812 (hereafter Kearl), have conditioned application of the exemption stated therein on a finding that the drug involved is in fact 'unavoidably dangerous,' reasoning that the comment was intended to exempt only such drugs from strict liability.   (Accord, Toner v. Lederle Laboratories (1987) 112 Idaho 328 [732 P.2d 297, 303–309]; see also Feldman v. Lederle Laboratories (1984) 97 N.J. 429 [479 A.2d 374, 382–383] [involving allegations of a failure to warn, but stating that "whether a drug is unavoidably unsafe should be decided on a case-by-case basis."].)   * * *

We appear, then, to have three distinct choices: (1) to hold that the manufacturer of a prescription drug is strictly liable for a defect in its product because it was defectively designed, as that term is defined in Barker[v. Lull Engineering Co., 573 P.2d 443 (Cal.1978)], or because of a failure to warn of its dangerous propensities even though such dangers were neither known nor scientifically knowable at the time of distribution; (2) to determine that liability attaches only if a manufacturer fails to warn of dangerous propensities of which it was or should have been aware, in conformity with comment k; or (3) to decide, * * * that strict liability for design defects should apply to prescription drugs unless the particular drug which caused the injury is found to be "unavoidably dangerous."

We shall conclude that (1) a drug manufacturer's liability for a defectively designed drug should not be measured by the standards of strict liability; (2) because of the public interest in the development, availability, and reasonable price of drugs, the appropriate test for determining responsibility is the test stated in comment k; and (3) for these same reasons of policy, we disapprove the holding of Kearl that only those prescription drugs found to be "unavoidably dangerous" should be measured by the comment k standard and that strict liability should apply to drugs that do not meet that description.

1. Design Defect

[Barker] set forth two alternative tests to measure a design defect: first, whether the product performed as safely as the ordinary consumer would expect when used in an intended and reasonably foreseeable manner, and second, whether, on balance, the benefits of the challenged design outweighed the risk of danger inherent in the design. In making the latter determination, the jury may consider these factors: "the gravity of the danger posed by the challenged design, the likelihood that such danger would occur, the mechanical feasibility of a safer alternative design, the financial cost of an improved design, and the adverse consequences to the product and to the consumer that would result from an alternative design."

Defendants assert that neither of these tests is applicable to a prescription drug like DES. As to the 'consumer expectation' standard, they claim, the 'consumer' is not the plaintiff but the physician who prescribes the drug, and it is to him that the manufacturer's warnings are directed. A physician appreciates the fact that all prescription drugs involve inherent risks, known and unknown, and he does not expect that the drug is without such risks. We agree that the 'consumer expectation' aspect of the Barker test is inappropriate to prescription drugs. While the 'ordinary consumer' may have a reasonable expectation that a product such as a machine he purchases will operate safely when used as intended, a patient's expectations regarding the effects of such a drug are those related to him by his physician, to whom the manufacturer directs the warnings regarding the drug's properties. The manufacturer cannot be held liable if it has provided appropriate warnings and the doctor fails in his duty to transmit these warnings to the patient or if the patient relies on inaccurate information from others regarding side effects of the drug.

The second test, which calls for the balancing of risks and benefits, is inapposite to prescription drugs, according to defendants, because it contemplates that a safer alternative design is feasible. * * *

We agree with defendants that Barker contemplates a safer alternative design is possible, but we seriously doubt their claim that a drug like DES cannot be "redesigned" to make it safer. For example, plaintiff might be able to demonstrate at trial that a particular component of DES rendered it unsafe as a miscarriage preventative and that removal of that component would not have affected the efficacy of the drug. Even if the resulting product, without the damaging component, would bear a name other than DES, it would do no violence to semantics to view it as a "redesign" of DES.

* * *

Of course, the fact that a drug with dangerous side effects may be characterized as containing a defect in design does not necessarily mean that its producer is to be held strictly liable for the defect. The determination of that issue depends on whether the public interest would be served by the imposition of such liability. As we have seen, the fundamental reasons underlying the imposition of strict liability are to deter manufacturers from marketing products that are unsafe, and to spread the cost of injury from the plaintiff to the consuming public, which will pay a higher price for the product to reflect the increased expense of insurance to the manufacturer resulting from its greater exposure to liability.

These reasons could justify application of the doctrine to the manufacturers of prescription drugs. It is indisputable, as plaintiff contends, that the risk of injury from such drugs is unavoidable, that a consumer may be helpless to protect himself from serious harm caused by them, and that, like other products, the cost of insuring against strict liability can be passed on by the producer to the consumer who buys the item. Moreover, as we observe below, in some cases additional testing of drugs before they are marketed might reveal dangerous side effects, resulting in a safer product.

But there is an important distinction between prescription drugs and other products such as construction machinery * * * Moreover, unlike other important medical products (wheelchairs, for example), harm to some users from prescription drugs is unavoidable. Because of these distinctions, the broader public interest in the availability of drugs at an affordable price must be considered in deciding the appropriate standard of liability for injuries resulting from their use.

Perhaps a drug might be made safer if it was withheld from the market until scientific skill and knowledge advanced to the point at which additional dangerous side effects would be revealed. But in most cases such a delay in marketing new drugs—added to the delay required to obtain approval for release of the product from the [FDA]—would not serve the public welfare. Public policy favors the development and marketing of beneficial new drugs, even though some risks, perhaps serious ones, might accompany their introduction, because drugs can save lives and reduce pain and suffering.

If drug manufacturers were subject to strict liability, they might be reluctant to undertake research programs to develop some pharmaceuticals that would prove beneficial or to distribute others that are available to be marketed, because of the fear of large adverse monetary judgments. Further, the additional expense of insuring against such liability—assuming insurance would be available—and of research programs to reveal possible dangers not detectable by available scientific methods could place the cost of medication beyond the reach of those who need it most.

* * *

The possibility that the cost of insurance and of defending against lawsuits will diminish the availability and increase the price of pharmaceuticals is far from theoretical. Defendants cite a host of examples of products which have greatly increased in price or have been withdrawn or withheld from the market because of the fear that their producers would be held liable for large judgments.

* * *

There is no doubt that, from the public's standpoint, these are unfortunate consequences. And they occurred even though almost all jurisdictions follow the negligence standard of comment k. It is not unreasonable to conclude in these circumstances that the imposition of a harsher test for liability would not further the public interest in the development and availability of these important products.

We decline to hold, therefore, that a drug manufacturer's liability for injuries caused by the defective design of a prescription drug should be measured by the standard set forth in Barker.

* * *

Notes and Questions

1. *Brown* applies comment k to *all* prescription drugs as a class without requiring a case by case determination of whether the conditions described in comment k should apply to a particular drug. The court justifies this blanket immunity from strict liability on the basis that failure to provide it would retard the development, introduction and availability of new drugs. Do you agree? How does one test the validity of such a proposition?

2. Some courts have held that comment k should be applied on a case-by-case adjudication. For example, in Hill v. Searle Laboratories, 884 F.2d 1064 (8th Cir.1989), a case involving the CU–7 intrauterine device, the Eighth Circuit found that Arkansas would adopt comment k, but would treat it as a qualified affirmative defense with the burden on the defendant to establish that the drug involved was incapable of being made safe and filled an exceptional social need, which it concluded the CU–7 did not:

> The drafters of comment k did not intend to grant all manufacturers of prescription drugs a blanket exception to strict liability. Such an exception was proposed at the American Law Institute meeting where

section 402A and comment k were adopted, but this proposal was defeated. 38 ALI Proc. 19, 90–98 (1961). The language of comment k suggests that only exceptional products, albeit such exceptional products are more likely to be found in the field of prescription drug products, should be excluded from the strict liability provisions. But more importantly, the example given, the vaccine for the Pasteur treatment of rabies—suggests that only special products, those with exceptional social need, fall within the gamut of comment k.

* * *

With which court do you agree, *Brown* or *Hill*? A significant number of those decisions, such as *Hill*, that have treated comment k as a limited affirmative defense have involved contraceptive devices. See, e.g., Kociemba v. G.D. Searle & Co., 680 F.Supp. 1293, 1301 (D.Minn.1988); Wheelahan v. G.D. Searle & Co., 814 F.2d 655 (4th Cir.1987); Coursen v. A.H. Robins & Co., 764 F.2d 1329, 1337 (9th Cir.1985). Should manufacturers of such devices be treated less favorably than manufacturers of other prescription drugs?

3. Section 103 of the Preliminary Draft of the Restatement (Third) of Torts: Products Liability (ALI 1993) pertains to liability for sale of prescription drugs or medical devices, and posits that plaintiff should only prevail if there was (1) a "manufacturing defect;" (2) "reasonable instructions or warnings ... were not provided to those medical providers, including prescribing providers;" or (3) "the foreseeable risks of harm presented by the drug or medical device could have been reduced by the adoption of a reasonable safer design that would have provided the same, or greater therapeutic benefits at substantially reduced risks." Preliminary Draft § 103(1)(a)-(c). The Reporters' vision of liability associated with pharmaceuticals or medical devices continues with the statement that retail sellers of prescription drugs or devices, i.e., pharmacists, will incur liability only upon sale of a product containing a manufacturing defect, or where the retail seller has "failed to exercise reasonable care in the preparing, packaging, labeling or marketing [of] the drug or medical device." Preliminary Draft § 103(2)(a)-(b).

With regard to both manufacturer and downstream seller liability for pharmaceuticals, vaccines and medical devices, it is seen that the Reporters preserve the orthodox rule that the informational obligation is satisfied ordinarily by providing adequate warnings to the medical profession (Reporters' Notes, Preliminary Draft at 116), as well as strict liability for manufacturing defects (Reporters' Notes, Preliminary Draft at 116–17).

4. Comment k does not, even when applied as in *Brown*, create a safe harbor from all liability. In two locations within comment k the protection afforded is explicitly qualified: "such a product, properly prepared, and accompanied by proper directions and warnings, is not defective nor is it unreasonably dangerous ... The seller of such products, again with the qualification that they are properly prepared and marketed, and proper warnings given, where the situation calls for it, is not to be held strictly liable ..." Thus, a manufacturer may be held liable for failure to provide sufficient information about the risks attending use of the product or the means of avoiding or reducing those risks; the liability, however, is not

strict: the product seller is liable only if it fails to warn of dangers of which it knew or should have known. There is no liability for failing to warn about the unknown or unknowable risks. The comment k test essentially amounts to a negligence standard.

5. While the court in *Brown* declines to apply strict liability for defective formulation to prescription drugs, it does point out that in its view such a defect theory could conceptually apply; that is, a drug might have an alternative safer design or formulation that could create a standard for measuring the defectiveness of the formulation present in the drug. What about a manufacturer's *negligence* in formulating a drug? Does the opinion preclude a plaintiff from advancing such a theory? Does comment k? Or, as a practical matter, does the court's conclusion that a risk/utility evaluation under Barker v. Lull Engineering Co. is inappropriate in a pharmaceuticals case effectively bar plaintiffs from winning on a theory of defective formulation?

b. Biological Products: Special Problems of AIDS–Contaminated Blood Products

McKEE v. MILES LABORATORIES

United States District Court, Eastern District of Kentucky 1987.
675 F.Supp. 1060, affirmed 866 F.2d 219 (6th Cir.1989).

SILER, J.

This matter is before the Court on the motion by defendant Miles Laboratories, Inc. and its division, Cutter Laboratories, for summary judgment. * * *

This action arose from the circumstances surrounding the blood transfusion of plaintiff's decedent, David Allen McKee. David McKee suffered from Hemophilia A, which meant he lacked a protein necessary for the normal coagulation of his blood. That missing protein is called Factor VIII. A method used by pharmaceutical companies for the treatment of hemophiliacs involved producing Factor VIII by combining (or pooling) plasma collected from thousands of individuals all over the United States. The Factor VIII is precipitated out of the combined plasma and then it is lyophilized (or freeze dried). David McKee used defendant's concentrated Factor VIII Product by the pooled lyophilized method. As a result of its use he contracted acquired immune deficiency syndrome ("AIDS"). Decedent was so diagnosed as having AIDS in October 1983 and subsequently died in 1984. His Administratrix and wife, Stella Mae McKee, brought this action for damages as representative of his estate and on her own behalf.

Defendants move for summary judgment as to plaintiff's strict liability claims, contending that these claims are barred by Kentucky's Blood Shield statute, K.R.S. 139.125. Defendants also move for summary judgment as to the merits of the case, contending that at the time plaintiff's decedent contracted AIDS there was no test which would have revealed the presence of this dreaded disease. In opposition to the motion for summary judgment, plaintiff argues that there is a genuine issue of material fact as to whether an alternative testing method was available in 1983 when decedent contracted AIDS. Plaintiff also asserts that Kentucky's blood shield statute did not bar product liability claims and that, in any event, the statute is not applicable to this situation, but, if applicable, then unconstitutional.

The two central issues before the Court are: (1) whether strict liability applies to defendant's conduct; and (2) whether there existed, at the time plaintiff's decedent contracted the disease, a plausible alternative testing for determining the AIDS virus.

* * *

The relevant statute in question provides:

Procurement, processing or distribution of blood or human tissue deemed service and not sale.

The procurement, processing, distribution or use of whole blood, plasma, blood products, blood derivatives and other human tissues such as corneas, bones or organs for the purpose of injecting, transfusing or transplanting any of them into the human body is declared to be, for all purposes, the rendition of a service by every person participating therein and, whether or not any remuneration is paid therefor, is declared not to be a sale of such whole blood, plasma, blood products, blood derivatives or other tissues, for any purpose, subsequent to enactment of this section.

K.R.S. 139.125.

[The Court is guided] by defendants' authority under Coffee v. Cutter Biological and Miles Laboratories, Inc., 809 F.2d 191 (2d Cir. 1987). In that case the Court analyzed a blood shield statute similar to Kentucky's blood shield statute. Based upon the analysis of that opinion and the plain language of the statute, this Court concludes that Kentucky's blood shield statute was intended to preclude the assertion of product liability claims arising out the sale of blood components. The plain and unambiguous words of the statute clearly state that supplying blood or blood derivatives is to be considered a service by every person participating therein. Only four jurisdictions in the nation have not legislatively barred the application of products liability theories to blood and blood products. Kentucky is not [one] of those four states. Because transactions involving blood and blood components are to be considered services, as opposed to sales, they are outside the purview of Kentucky's product liability statute. K.R.S. 411.300; 411.320; 411.340[.]

* * * [B]lood shield statutes in other states uniformly have been interpreted as barring strict liability claims. To permit the plaintiff to circumvent the exemption of blood and blood derivatives by pursuing claims under the product liability statute would defeat the obvious legislative intent of K.R.S. 139.125. Consequently, plaintiff's claims against defendants arising under strict liability should be dismissed.

The Court now turns its attention to the second issue, that is, whether at the time plaintiff's decedent contracted the AIDS virus a plausible alternative testing method existed to detect its presence within the blood derivatives. In reaching this answer, the Court is guided by the well-reasoned decision in Kozup v. Georgetown University, 663 F.Supp. 1048 (D.D.C.1987), which analyzed existing methods available for the testing of AIDS during the early 1980s. Kozup involved a newborn receiving a blood transfusion for hypovolemia, a condition associated with premature birth, in January 1983. The child received three transfusions which were contaminated with the virus now known to transmit AIDS. The contaminated blood was supplied by the American Red Cross, which received it from an individual in 1982, and was administered by the Georgetown University Hospital. The child subsequently died from complications related to the AIDS infection.

In its analysis, the District Court reviewed the medical chronology of the AIDS virus to determine exactly what was known about AIDS by the scientific and medical communities and when. As in the present case, much of what the plaintiffs claimed in Kozup turned on allegations that defendants knew or should have known certain facts related to AIDS. This Court needs not rehash the same chronology medical history of AIDS which the Kozup Court so methodically composed. It is suffice to conclude that it was not until 1984 that the medical community reached a consensus as to the proposition that AIDS was transmittable by blood. In April, 1984, scientists identified the virus HTLV–III as the cause of AIDS. By May, 1985, an enzyme-linked immunosorbent assay (ELISA) test was made available, which screens for the antibodies sensitive to HTVL–III. Once it was available, the Center for Disease Control issued guidelines for implementing the ELISA test. This laboratory test has proven 98.6 percent effective in detecting exposure to AIDS. When coupled with a second test, the Western Blot Analysis, the rate of detection for exposure to AIDS rises to 100 percent. However, there is still no test for presence for the virus itself, nor is there a cure for the disease. As no recent breakthrough has been cited to the Court for the diagnosis, testing or treatment of AIDS, it can rely upon the Court's analysis and conclusions in Kozup.

As in Kozup, plaintiff alleges negligence as a basis for recovery from defendant. In short, plaintiff alleges that Cutter was negligent in failing to take measures designed to protect her husband from being infected with AIDS. Specifically, plaintiff contends that alternatives existed for the testing of the AIDS virus in defendant's product, citing the procedure of heat treatment. However, a review of the medical chronology set forth in Kozup reveals this contention inaccurate. As of 1983, no pharmaceutical company, blood bank, hospital or federal health care regulator in the United States took special AIDS-related measures in connection with transfusions. Doctors diagnosed plaintiff's decedent with AIDS in the Fall of 1983 before any specialized measures existed. Furthermore, plaintiff can point to no organization, government entity or medical association within the United States which advocated the use of plaintiff's alternative testing as a means of screening defendant's product for AIDS. Instead, plaintiff offers testimony of an expert whose current opinion is that pharmaceutical companies should have used a heat treating method to exclude viruses such as AIDS. This expert cannot alone create a standard of care or a prima facie case of negligence, where he is entirely in opposition to the standard prevailing in 1982–83. His opinion cannot be permitted to supplant the standard of care as established by the conduct of the pharmaceutical community which plaintiff's expert criticizes. * * *

It is clear that in order to prevail on the theory of negligence, plaintiff must show that defendant, Cutter Laboratories, violated a standard of care. That standard is established by looking to the conduct of the industry or profession in similar circumstances as of that date. Ulrich v. Kasco Abrasives Co., 532 S.W.2d 197 (Ky. 1976). The standard of care for pharmaceutical companies at the time of decedent's transfusions did not require defendant to screen or perform plaintiff's suggested alternative testing to eliminate the risk of AIDS contamination. Consequently, no negligence occurred as defendants met the standard of care as then existed within the industry.

As stated in Kozup, this Court is mindful of the terrible personal tragedy that David McKee's struggle with AIDS must have been for the McKee family, especially in light of the recent breakthroughs in AIDS research. However, because plaintiff fails to make out a prima facie case of negligence, summary judgment for defendant on the issue of negligence is proper as well. An appropriate Order shall be entered.

Notes and Questions

1. Most states have enacted statutes which expressly shield manufacturers or suppliers of blood products from strict liability. For example, prior to 1986, Maryland's statute was limited to serum hepatitis, but was later broadened to treat the supplying of blood products as the rendering of a service, and not the sale of a product, thereby requiring proof of negligence to establish liability.

In Doe v. Miles Laboratories, 675 F.Supp. 1466, 1479–80 (D.Md.1987), affirmed 927 F.2d 187 (4th Cir.1991), the plaintiff contracted AIDS from a blood transfusion in 1983 when the statute was confined to hepatitis. The court, therefore, was faced with a purely common law question of whether strict liability rules should apply to blood products contaminated with AIDS virus, at a time when the risk was allegedly unknown, unknowable, and beyond the state of scientific art. The court held that comment k should not apply because the comment relates only to drugs involving a "reasonable danger," which AIDS contaminated blood exceeds, especially considering the needs of hemophiliacs for blood products and the inevitably fatal nature of the disease for those who develop it. The court rejected the state of the art defense stating: "The fact that the virus was undetectable prior to 1985 is not a mitigating factor. The best view is to consider blood containing undetectable diseases to be a defective product and therefore that strict liability is applicable ... The arguments in favor of strict liability apply persuasively to blood and blood products as they do to any other product."

Do you agree with the court's conclusion? See Kozup v. Georgetown University, 663 F.Supp. 1048 (D.D.C.1987), reversed on other grounds 851 F.2d 437 (D.C.Cir.1988) (discussing the developments in AIDS research and relied upon by the court in *McKee*); Roberts v. Suburban Hospital Assn., 73 Md.App. 1, 532 A.2d 1081, 1086 n. 3 (1987) (involving AIDS, listing the 48 states that have blood shield statutes; only New Jersey, Vermont, and the District of Columbia did not at that time).

2. On liability for transfused blood containing the HIV virus, consider Hoemke v. New York Blood Center, 912 F.2d 550 (2d Cir.1990), which held that a blood center could not be held negligent for failing to screen out gay male donors in 1981, before AIDS had been discovered to be blood-borne disease, or for not having administered alanine aminotransferase (ALT) test on its blood supply. But see Morre v. Armour Pharmaceutical Co., [Not Reported in F.Supp.], Prod. Liab. Rep.(CCH) ¶ 12,665 (M.D. Fla.1990) (rejecting Armour's argument that it was not obligated to warn hemophiliacs that they could contract HIV virus through blood products until medical community reached a consensus that the disease was transmittable by blood products).

3. Another related issue that has arisen in contaminated blood products litigation is whether the standard of care is to be measured against a professional standard—such as that applicable to physicians and hospitals—or against that of the ordinary reasonable person. For a defendant such as blood bank, the advantage of the professional standard is that there can be no finding of negligence if its practices conformed to the industry standard in terms of screening and blood gathering procedures. In United Blood Services v. Quintana, 827 P.2d 509 (Colo.1992), the Colorado Supreme Court found a middle ground, concluding that while the professional standard of care was applicable to blood product suppliers, a plaintiff would be permitted to challenge that standard. Specifically, a plaintiff could overcome the rebuttable presumption that adherence to the standard of care adopted by profession is due care by offering expert testimony that the profession's standard is "unreasonably deficient by not incorporating readily available practices and procedures more protective of the harm suffered by the plaintiff."

4. What of actions brought against governmental blood providers, such as the armed forces? The effect of the discretionary function exemption to the Federal Tort Claims Act (FTCA), 28 U.S.C.A. § 2671 et seq., was considered by the federal trial court in C.R.S. by D.B.S v. United States, 820 F.Supp. 449 (D.Minn.1993), a suit brought by a serviceman who contracted the AIDS virus following a blood transfusion administered at a military hospital. The court held that the armed forces' adherence to FDA and American Association of Blood Banks screening and recipient notification guidelines rather than development of their own, was within the discretionary function exemption to the FTCA. Compare Andrulonis v. United States, 924 F.2d 1210 (2d Cir.1991), cert. granted and judgment vacated __ U.S. __, 112 S.Ct. 39, 116 L.Ed.2d 18 (1991), previous decision reinstated 952 F.2d 652 (2d Cir.1991), cert. denied __ U.S. __, 112 S.Ct. 2992, 120 L.Ed.2d 869 (1992)(discretionary function exemption of the FTCA did not apply because decision of a government scientist not to warn a laboratory worker of dangerous laboratory conditions "did not lend itself to policy balancing,

[nor] is there any indication that [the scientist] considered the policy implications or the pros and cons of allowing the experiment to proceed.").

5. The potentially harsh operation of a statute of repose is revealed in Bradway v. American Nat. Red Cross, 992 F.2d 298 (11th Cir.1993), an action brought by a patient against a blood bank, and alleging that she had contracted AIDS during a transfusion administered following surgery. Under Georgia's five-year statute of repose governing medical malpractice actions, the court held that her cause of action accrued upon the blood bank's actions or omissions that caused contaminated blood to be released to the hospital, rather than at the later time when plaintiff became infected with the virus. Adoption of the earlier accrual date, the court held, necessitated dismissal of plaintiff's claim as untimely. See Chapter 12 for further consideration of the statutes of limitation and repose problems in contaminated blood products litigation.

6. Should strict liability apply only to some products—those possibly most dangerous—such as asbestos and tobacco? Or, alternatively, should it apply to all products, except those of the greatest social need such as prescription drugs as *Brown* held? Or apply to all products and some prescription drugs, but not to the most beneficial within that class, as *Feldman* held? Who should decide whether a product is entitled to "special" treatment—either placed in the strict liability class or placed in the protected class?

7. *L–Tryptophan.* As of 1993, hundreds of lawsuits were pending in federal and state courts arising out of the use of L-tryptophan, an amino acid supplement used to treat insomnia, depression and premenstrual syndrome. The FDA recalled L-tryptophan products in March 1990 and in April announced that its use was linked to eosinophilia-myalgia syndrome (EMS), a rare blood disorder which produces muscle and joint pain, hair loss, swelling and numbness of hands and feet, walking difficulties, rashes, fever, and shortness of breath. The FDA also announced that the outbreak of EMS was linked to a single manufacturer, Showa Denko KK, a Japanese producer of the raw product. While Showa Denko is a defendant in most of the litigation, other defendants include its American subsidiary and wholesalers, distributors, retailers, and packagers. The Center for Disease Control stated that as of November 15, 1990, there were 1,539 reported cases of EMS, including 27 deaths. The investigation by the CDC and FDA has found that the L-tryptophan amino acid tablets were contaminated with a bacteria used in an "untested" and "experimental" generic manufacturing process.

In Hill by Hill v. Showa Denko, K.K., 188 W.Va. 654, 425 S.E.2d 609 (1992), cert. denied ___ U.S. ___, 113 S.Ct. 2338, 124 L.Ed.2d 249 (1993), the West Virginia Supreme Court of Appeals affirmed a lower court's assertion of personal jurisdiction over the Japanese manufacturing parent of L–Tryptophan, whose wholly-owned subsidiary, the parent's sole U.S. distributor, upon a showing, inter alia, that the subsidiary had solicited business in West Virginia.

What theories of liability would be asserted in these cases? Will comment k possibly be available as a defense or qualified defense? Why or why not? What factors would influence the potential liability of U.S. firms involved in the distribution of the product? Will class actions be appropriate? How about consolidated trials? What are the likely common questions of fact or law in these cases? What factual and legal questions will necessitate individual resolution?

c. *Medical Devices*

HEGNA v. E.I. DU PONT de NEMOURS AND COMPANY

United States District Court District of Minnesota, 1993.
825 F.Supp. 880.

DOTY, J.

This matter is before the court on defendant E.I. DuPont de Nemours and Company's ("DuPont") motion for summary judgment on plaintiff Marilyn Hegna's ("Hegna") negligence and strict liability claims. In the alternative, DuPont requests that the court reconsider its prior ruling on Hegna's negligence and strict liability claims in light of the more fully developed factual record now before the court. Based on a review of the file, record and proceedings herein, the court grants DuPont's request for reconsideration and determines that summary judgment in favor of DuPont on Hegna's negligence and strict liability claims is appropriate.

BACKGROUND

* * *

The present action arises from alleged defects in implants ("TMJ implants") that Hegna received during surgery on her temporomandibular joints ("TMJ"). Vitek, Inc. ("Vitek") made the implants out of Proplast, a porous and fibrous compound made in an eight-step process in which polytetraflouroethylene ("PTFE") is mixed with other materials. Vitek purchased its PTFE from DuPont.

Hegna alleges that her implants disintegrated, that PTFE particles from the disintegrated implants caused her injury and that Dupont is liable for those injuries. Hegna claims that DuPont knew of studies questioning the propriety of using PTFE in medical implants and that Vitek was using PTFE to make the TMJ implants. Hegna thus claims that DuPont had a duty to warn her or her physician of the risks involved in using PTFE-based implants, that DuPont failed to provide any warning and that if DuPont had provided a warning, she could have avoided her injuries. * * *

DuPont previously moved for summary judgment on Hegna's negligence and strict liability claims. DuPont argued that Hegna's negligence claim fails because it merely supplied Vitek with raw materials and played no role in the design, manufacture or sale of the TMJ implants. DuPont argued that it was a bulk supplier and, as such, had no legal duty either to ascertain whether Vitek's specialized use of PTFE was safe or to warn Hegna or her physician of any potential dangers associated with the use of PTFE in implants. In the alternative, DuPont argued that even if it had a duty to warn as a bulk supplier, it satisfied that duty by warning Vitek that PTFE was not made for medical purposes, that it had conducted no tests to determine the efficacy of using PTFE for medical purposes and that Vitek would have to rely on its own medical and legal judgment if it chose to use PTFE to make implants. With respect to the strict liability claim, DuPont argued that Hegna's claim fails because Vitek's Proplast manufacturing process altered the chemistry, composition and mechanical properties of the raw PTFE.

The court denied DuPont's motion for summary judgment on Hegna's negligence claim. The court, relying in part on Forest v. E.I. DuPont de Nemours & Co., 791 F.Supp. 1460 (D.Nev.1992) and Hill v. Wilmington Chem. Corp., 156 N.W.2d 898 (Minn.1968), determined that DuPont, as a bulk supplier, had a duty to warn at least Vitek of the possible dangers of using PTFE to make TMJ implants and that material fact disputes concerning the sufficiency of DuPont's warning precluded summary judgment.   * * *

* * *

The court also denied DuPont's motion for summary judgment on Hegna's strict liability claim. In making that determination, the court noted that: [t]he distinction between strict liability and negligence in ... failure to warn cases is that in strict liability, knowledge of the condition of the product and the risks involved in that condition will be imputed to the manufacturer, whereas in negligence these elements must be proven. The court concluded that: "[i]f Hegna is unable to support her negligence claim at trial by presenting sufficient evidence of DuPont's knowledge, the court will then determine whether such knowledge should be imputed to DuPont."

DuPont now asks the court to reconsider its prior ruling and grant its motion for summary judgment. DuPont renews its argument that as a bulk supplier to Vitek it had no duty to warn Hegna or her physician and had no duty to assure the safety of Vitek's specialized use of PTFE. * * * In the alternative, DuPont raises two new arguments in support of its summary judgment motion. First, DuPont contends that Hegna's claims are preempted by 21 U.S.C. § 360k of the Medical Device Amendments. Second, DuPont contends that the applicable statute of limitations bars Hegna's strict liability claim.

DISCUSSION

* * *

1. Hegna's Negligence Claim

In its previous order, the court found that under Minnesota law, DuPont, as a bulk supplier, had a duty to at least warn Vitek of the potential danger of using PTFE to make TMJ implants. Hegna, 806 F.Supp. at 826 ("The court thus concludes that if faced with the present situation, a Minnesota court would find that DuPont had a duty to warn at least Vitek of the possible dangers of using PTFE for jaw implants.''). The court adopted the test set forth in Forest, 791 F.Supp. 1460, another case involving DuPont's liability for alleged injuries stemming from disintegrated TMJ implants, to determine whether DuPont discharged its duty to warn.

The relevant question in bulk supplier cases is whether the bulk supplier was objectively reasonable in relying on a knowledgeable intermediary to provide a warning to ultimate users. This involves proof of two elements: 1) that the bulk supplier was reasonable in believing that the intermediary knew of the dangers associated with the bulk product, and 2) that the bulk supplier was reasonable in relying on the intermediary to warn the ultimate user of such dangers. . . . [F]or [d]efendant DuPont to succeed with its bulk supplier doctrine defense in the instant case, it will have to show that it reasonably relied upon Vitek's knowledge of the risks involved with using PTFE in medical implants and that it also reasonably relied upon Vitek to warn implant patients of those dangers. To do this, DuPont must show that it took some reasonable, affirmative steps to ascertain that Vitek was a knowledgeable intermediary. Such steps must rise above the level of a mere disclaimer but need not go so far as to have required DuPont to second-guess Vitek's actions in carrying-out its own duty to warn.

The factual record before the court has been supplemented since DuPont filed its previous summary judgment motion. It is now undisputed that Vitek knew both the properties of DuPont's PTFE and the scientific community's concerns regarding the use of PTFE-based materials to make implants such as the TMJ implant. Moreover, it is undisputed that DuPont informed Vitek of its concerns regarding the use of PTFE-based materials to make implants, that it had little overall knowledge concerning the efficacy of using PTFE-based materials to make implants, that it performed no testing to determine whether use of PTFE in implants is appropriate and that Vitek would have to rely on its own medical and legal judgment if it chose to use PTFE to make implants. Finally, it is undisputed that the FDA regulated the sale of the TMJ implants. Applying the standard set forth above to the supplemented factual record now before it, the court finds that DuPont reasonably believed that Vitek knew of the dangers associated with using PTFE-based materials to make implants and that DuPont reasonably relied on Vitek to warn the ultimate users of such dangers. Accordingly, the court concludes that, as a matter of law, DuPont discharged its duty to warn. Hegna cannot support one of the essential elements of her negligence claim and the court concludes that summary judgment in favor of DuPont on the negligence claim is appropriate.

2. Hegna's Strict Liability Claim

The court finds that its ruling with respect to Hegna's negligence claim is applicable to Hegna's strict liability claim because the limited distinction between negligent failure to warn and strict liability failure to warn claims is not outcome determinative in this case. In Minnesota, "[t]he distinction between strict liability and negligence in . . . failure to warn cases is that in strict liability, knowledge of the condition of the product and the risks involved in that condition will be imputed to the manufacturer, whereas in negligence these elements must be proven." Bilotta [v. Kelley Co., Inc., 346 N.W.2d 616, 622 (Minn.1984)].

It is undisputed that DuPont had knowledge of the risks involved with using PTFE-based materials to make implants. Even with that knowledge, DuPont nevertheless satisfied its duty to warn and, therefore, Hegna cannot support one of the elements of her strict liability claim. Accordingly, the court concludes that summary judgment in favor of DuPont on Hegna's strict liability claim is appropriate. Because it concludes that DuPont, as a bulk supplier, satisfied its duty to warn and, therefore, Hegna can maintain no negligence or strict liability claim against DuPont, the court determines that it need not consider DuPont's other bases for summary judgment.

* * *

Notes and Questions

1. In the principal case, the court notes, at footnote 4: "DuPont also argued that it had no duty to warn, because the [FDA] approved the use of PTFE for TMJ implants and regulated their sale. In addition, DuPont claimed that Vitek was obligated under federal law and FDA regulations to both develop appropriate warnings and ensure that Hegna's physician received those warnings. Based on those arguments, DuPont argued that it would be superfluous to impose on it a second duty to warn. The court rejected those arguments[.]" On what rationale would the court reject DuPont's assertions?

4. CHEMICALS

a. *Liability Standards for Warnings*

WERCKENTHEIN v. BUCHER PETROCHEMICAL COMPANY

Appellate Court of Illinois, 1993.
248 Ill.App.3d 282, 188 Ill.Dec. 332, 618 N.E.2d 902.

DiVito, J.

Plaintiff Charles Werckenthein (plaintiff) filed this negligence and strict liability action against, among others, defendants Bucher Petroleum Chemical Company; PPG Industries, Inc.; Shell Oil Company; Sun Refining and Marketing Company; Dow Chemical Company; and Technical Petroleum (collectively, defendants), which supplied chemical products in bulk to his employer. He claimed that he had been injured as a result of their failure to warn him adequately of the dangers arising from his quality control analysis of the chemicals. Plaintiff's wife, Grace, added a count for loss of consortium; she was subsequently declared his guardian. The circuit court granted partial summary judgment for defendants on certain claims as untimely, and it later granted defendants summary judgment on the remaining claims against them. Plaintiff and his wife appeal both orders, asserting that the circuit court incorrectly determined that some claims were time-barred and that the circuit court erred in finding that as a matter of law, defendants had no duty to warn against using a particular testing procedure. We affirm.

In his complaint, plaintiff alleged that among his duties as chief chemist for Ashland was a routine company procedure requiring him to sniff, evaluate, and record the odors of the chemicals defendants supplied to his employer. He contended that as a result of the exposure from this procedure, he suffered a number of health problems, including cancers and fibrillation that resulted in a stroke. Although the exposure occurred between February 1969 and March 1983, plaintiff and his wife further alleged that they neither knew nor had reason to know of the causal link between his injuries and defendants' conduct until consultation with medical experts in industrial injuries, which did not occur until April 1986. Plaintiff filed his complaint shortly after this consultation.

* * *

[The court's discussion of the statute of limitations issue is deleted]

Defendants then moved jointly for summary judgment on the remaining claims against them. They raised five independent grounds: (1) as bulk suppliers, their duty to warn extended only to their purchaser, Ashland, not to plaintiff; (2) Ashland was a sophisticated user and as such, needed no warning and could be relied upon to warn and protect its employees; (3) even if they did owe plaintiff a duty to warn, he had received the warnings and they were adequate; (4) the dangerous properties of the chemicals were obvious and well- known to both Ashland and plaintiff; and (5) even if the warnings were inadequate, their inadequacy was not the cause of plaintiff's injuries. In support of their motion, defendants attached a number of documents, including material safety data sheets (MSDS's) for the chemicals in question and an affidavit from Ashland's Director of Health and Safety since 1978. In that affidavit, Dr. Toeniskoetter stated that his department maintained a library with these sheets and other information on the safe handling of chemicals and that Ashland's policy was to make the MSDS's available to employees. Also attached were portions of depositions from two of plaintiff's former assistants and an article by plaintiff about printing solvents, which stressed the need for ventilation during use. In addition, through discovery, defendants obtained from plaintiff's home library many of the challenged warnings, indicating his awareness of the chemical's properties.

Plaintiff replied that (1) the bulk supplier and sophisticated user doctrines did not apply in Illinois; (2) whether warnings were given to him and the sufficiency thereof were fact questions precluding summary judgment; and (3) he had presented enough facts to support a reasonable inference that exposure to defendants' chemicals had caused his injuries. In his supporting affidavit, he explained that he or his assistant tested a sample from every bulk delivery during his tenure, that a 55–gallon drum of waste chemicals was kept open at all times in a storeroom adjacent to the lab, that the lab was inadequately ventilated, that he was not given any breathing apparatus, and that he was told that use of a fume hood was generally unnecessary. He commented in his deposition, however, that "we never inhaled over the TLV [threshold limit value] in sniff testing the samples." According to the other attached documents, defendants' representatives never reviewed the lab's procedures for quality control testing. In addition, an affidavit from plaintiff's assistant challenges Dr. Toeniskoetter's on a number of grounds: the assistant had never seen or heard of Dr. Toeniskoetter or his department; he had never been told of the TLV's of the chemicals he worked with and had not even heard the term "Threshold Limit Value" until he left Ashland; no MSDS's were kept on hand or made accessible to him; and few of Ashland's high-ranking employees had any knowledge of the products at issue, much less of their effects on health. In a 1982 memo, a manager commented that the vapor level in the laboratory had never been measured, commenting that "this might be in order sometime in the future."

At an interim hearing, the court asked for supplemental submissions on the issue of industry custom and practice for testing for odor by briefly inhaling the chemicals directly from an open container (the sniff test). The court wondered whether, if testing in the industry was performed in violation of the warnings given, manufacturers who knew this should have a duty to give express warnings against such testing methods. It then framed the issue for summary judgment as follows: if the industry custom was to test without exceeding TLV's (threshold limit values), the warnings defendants gave were adequate as a matter of law; if not, defendants would have had a duty to warn against the dangerous testing technique because they knew or should have known that quality control staff would misuse the products. Defendants' documents showed that the American Society for Testing and Materials (ASTM) recommended that testing be done by dipping filter paper into the chemical and then smelling the filter paper; plaintiff's expert opined that the only way to test for bulk odor was through direct inhalation, which he described as an "extremely dangerous" test albeit "widely used in industry." He opined that six minutes of this type of testing would be equivalent to six hours of deliberate solvent abuse, such as sniffing paint thinner.

The court granted summary judgment for defendants. * * *

* * *

III.

For injuries caused by defective products, a plaintiff may have four theories of recovery available: express warranty, implied warranty, negligence, and strict liability. Negligence, of course, concerns injuries arising from a defendant's breach of the duty of reasonable care; strict liability addresses injuries resulting from a product that was in an unreasonably dangerous condition when it left a defendant's control. The two theories are not identical, however: strict liability for failure to warn requires evidence of the industry's knowledge of the product's dangerous propensity, and it turns on the nature of the product and the adequacy of the warning; negligence focuses on the particular defendant's knowledge and conduct. * * *[3] Plaintiff grounded his complaint in both theories of recovery, alleging that defendants' breach of their duty to warn him against directly sniffing the chemicals while testing them caused his fibrillation and resultant stroke. For the purposes of this appeal, we assume without deciding that defendants had a duty to warn plaintiff as well as Ashland, so we address only whether defendants demonstrated as a matter of law that their warnings were not so inadequate as to render the chemicals "unreasonably dangerous."

The purpose of warnings is to reduce the risk of harm. This may be accomplished either by shifting or by reducing the risk of injury. Thus, if warnings are adequate, users proceed at their own risk. Examples of inadequate warnings include those that do not specify the risk, are inconsistent with use of the product, provide no reason for the warning, or do not reach the user. Adequacy of warnings generally is a question of fact. Accordingly, it is an issue inappropriate for summary judgment unless the movant demonstrates conclusively that there remains no triable question.

Here, the circuit court determined that defendants' warnings were adequate as a matter of law, reasoning that "because there was a safe method of doing this type of odor test, * * * the defendants were under [no] duty to warn of Ashland's particular method of doing this test." Plaintiff contends that the adequacy of these warnings is a question of fact not suitable for summary judgment and that, in particular, the warnings on the MSDS's or on the specifications sheet accompanying each shipment should have included quality control testing instructions, not just general warnings against exceeding TLV's and improper ventilation.

We cannot agree. Defendants' submissions made plain that dire consequences would flow from prolonged or intensive exposure to these products. For example, one document initialed by plaintiff in March 1979 contained the following safety rules for handlers of chlorinated solvents:

> "Always wear protective garments and use safety equipment when exposure to chlorinated solvents cannot be avoided.

* * *

3. Some jurisdictions view these two causes of action as identical for all practical purposes. (Note, Failures to Warn and the Sophisticated User Defense, 74 Va.L.Rev. 579, 583; Forest v. E.I. Du Pont de Nemours & Co. (Nev.1992), 791 F.Supp. 1460, 1463.) Not so Illinois. Hunt v. Blasius (1978), 74 Ill.2d 203, 210, 23 Ill.Dec. 574, 578, 384 N.E.2d 368, 372 ("The elements of a cause of action in strict products liability, of course, differ markedly from their counterparts in negligence.").

Do not use solvents in open containers unless ventilation is adequate to draw the vapors away from the work area.

* * *

Do not tolerate a continuing strong or objectionable solvent odor. It is an indication of excessive vapor in the air."

The document also warned that "[r]epeated and prolonged (chronic) exposure to organic solvents at or above levels producing beginning anesthetic effects, such as dizziness or light-headedness, should be considered a health hazard." In Illinois, manufacturers are entitled to assume that such warnings, if communicated, will be heeded. Furthermore, the standard testing procedure in the industry, as demonstrated by the ASTM recommendations, was to conduct the tests in a different, safer manner, which plaintiff elected not to follow. As to the alleged lack of warning against plaintiff's injury, the document further states that "concentrations of chlorinated solvents that produce 'drunkenness' or unconsciousness may sensitize the heart to [certain drugs]. This high exposure may result in cardiac arrhythmia, including ventricular fibrillation (a particular and serious kind of irregular heartbeat)." We also note that plaintiff presented no facts demonstrating that his injuries were caused by defendants' failure to warn him not to inhale the chemicals directly rather than by the chemicals themselves. Indeed, plaintiff himself said during his deposition that "the sniff test was not the problem."

In sum, defendants did not breach their duty, if any, to warn plaintiff, and their product was not unreasonably dangerous because the warnings did not need to include specific cautions against plaintiff's testing procedure to be adequate as a matter of law. Consequently, although adequacy of warnings is generally a fact question reserved for the jury, under the circumstances here the circuit court correctly held that defendants were entitled to summary judgment.

Affirmed.

Notes and Questions

1. The Material Safety Data Sheets (MSDS) which the court referred to are federally-mandated communications that require employers and suppliers to describe the toxic properties of chemicals and the means necessary to eliminate risks of injury. See Chapter 9 for a fuller discussion of MSDS and other requirements under the Occupational Safety & Health Act. What if the evidence in *Bucher* revealed that the defendants knew that plaintiff's employer was permitting employees to conduct sniff tests rather than following the prescribed procedure?

2. With *Bucher* compare Dougherty v. Hooker Chemical Co., 540 F.2d 174 (3d Cir.1976), where evidence showed that workers used defendant's industrial solvent, trichloroethylene, which posed a latent, potentially lethal hazard; that no warnings of this risk were communicated by the employer, or by the manufacturer, to the workers who were being exposed; and that there was no reasonable basis on which the manufacturer could rely upon

the employer-purchaser to give "appropriate information to the employees of all the hazards of working with [the product]." In determining whether a manufacturer of a toxic product had a duty to provide warnings to persons other than the immediate purchaser, the court in *Dougherty* called for balancing of these considerations: "the dangerous nature of the product, the form in which the product is used, the intensity and the form of the warnings given, and the likelihood that the particular warning will be adequately communicated to those who will foreseeably use the product. * * * " How would the court in *Dougherty* have considered and decided *Bucher*?

3. Should improper packaging that leads to the injurious dispersal of a chemical create a claim in products liability? Consider Thrasher v. B & B Chemical Co., 2 F.3d 995 (10th Cir.1993), the appeal from a grant of summary judgment for a manufacturer of paint stripper in a suit brought by an airline employee. Plaintiff suffered physical injury when paint thinner erupted from a valve in its container. The manufacturer of the paint thinner brought in the manufacturer of the drum as a third party defendant.

How might the following facts affect your answer:

(a) Neither the valve nor the drum could be located, but plaintiff testified that in his six months working as a paint stripper for the airline he only saw thinner barrels stenciled "B & B," and no invoices produced by the airline showed thinner other than that produced by "B & B" were purchased during the six months of plaintiff's employment.

(b) Testimony suggested that the barrel might have been improperly stored in sunlight, which could create abnormally high pressure.

4. In Herman v. Sunshine Chemical Specialties, Inc., 133 N.J. 329, 627 A.2d 1081 (1993), the New Jersey Supreme Court confirmed the availability, upon proper proof, of punitive damages in a chemical personal injury failure to warn case. In that case, plaintiff, an independent contractor who conducted demonstrations of the efficacy of defendant's product, developed "occupational asthma" from incidental inhalation of defendant's "Sun–Clean" all-purpose cleaner, which contained a caustic, sodium-hydroxide. The product's label stated that the product contained no caustics and contained no warnings against breathing its vapors. The court further endorsed the approach, adopted in most jurisdictions, of permitting jury consideration of the defendant's wealth in the course of weighing punitive damages.

5. Chemical contamination cases may lose the benefit of longer limitations periods under the theory of continuing nuisance or continuing injury where the contamination has abated, and thus be governed by the limitations period for ordinary torts. E.g., Montana Pole and Treating Plant v. I. F. Laucks & Co., 993 F.2d 676 (9th Cir.1993), in which the claims by operators of a wood treatment facility against the manufacturers of the preservative pentachlorophenol ("penta") were found barred under the state's two-year limitations period. A theory of continuing nuisance would not operate to toll the prescriptive period, the court held, as the injury had been abated upon cessation of plaintiff's operations two years before.

6. In Chapter 9 we examine the workers' compensation bar to employee claims against employers, and the limited exceptions to that bar, including the intentional misconduct exception. Should there exist an intentional tort exception that would permit a manufacturer to sue an employer where the manufacturer claims that the products liability suit it must now defend against, brought by an injured employee, was caused by the employer's fraudulent misrepresentation? Consider the following two treatments:

a. In Belik v. Advance Process Supply Co., 822 F.Supp. 1184 (E.D.Pa. 1993), the trial court disallowed a manufacturing defendant's third-party claim against plaintiff's employer in which the third-party plaintiff claimed that the employee's injury from exposure to toxic chemicals was caused by the manufacturer's fraudulent misrepresentation. Acknowledging that the exclusivity of Pennsylvania workers' compensation law had countenanced a narrow exception permitting employee suits upon a showing of an employer's intentional misconduct, the court held that the narrow exception should not be enlarged to permit an intentional tort rationale for manufacturer claims against employers.

b. In Dole v. Dow Chemical Co., 30 N.Y.2d 143, 331 N.Y.S.2d 382, 282 N.E.2d 288 (1972), the underlying injury was the death of an employee who, at the direction of his employer, used the manufacturer's hazardous fumigant on a storage bin, in which he was overcome by fumes. The employer countered the manufacturer's action in indemnification with the defense that the manufacturer's failure to warn constituted active negligence, barring indemnification. On appeal, the New York Court of Appeals held that the relative liabilities of employer and manufacturer were properly apportionable according to their respective degrees of fault.

b. Bulk Suppliers of Chemicals: The Sophisticated User Defense

Hegna and *Bucher* establish that in evaluating the bulk supplier's informational obligation, the court may properly take into account the purchaser's superior knowledge of the end uses of the product and the hazards posed to those who will come into contact with it. The issue requires resolution of whether the bulk seller for resale discharges its duty by conveying adequate information to the distributor intermediary. It also extends to the question of what circumstances represent adequate assurance to the initial seller that the intermediary is likely to pass along such product information to the latter's customers or employees.

The question has been treated in actions on claims involving chemicals and natural gas, with a resolution that can be stated generally as providing that for products sold in bulk, the wholesaler discharges its duty to warn by conveying adequate warning to the immediate purchaser. If, on the other hand, the products sold by the bulk seller are already packaged, "ordinary prudence may require the manufacturer to put his warning on the package where it is available to all who handle it." Jones v. Hittle Service, Inc., 219 Kan. 627, 549 P.2d 1383 (1976).

SWAN v. I.P., INC.

Supreme Court of Mississippi, 1993.
613 So.2d 846 (en banc).

HAWKINS, C.J.:

Nancy Swan, a former teacher at Long Beach Junior High School, filed this action on January 7, 1986, in the Circuit Court of Harrison County, First Judicial District, alleging injury as a result of exposure to fumes and spray of polyurethane roofing materials being used to re-roof Long Beach Junior High School in October, 1985. Initially named as defendants were I.P., Inc. (I.P.), the manufacturer of the polyurethane foam used during the roofing project, and Miri, Inc. (Miri), the local polyurethane roofing contractor which applied the roofing materials to the school. In her First Amended Complaint, Swan added Carboline Company (Carboline), the manufacturer of the polyurethane coating used during the roofing project, as a defendant. In her Second Amended Complaint, Swan added as a defendant James C. English, the president of Miri, alleging that at all material times he was engaged in a joint venture with Miri. Swan's allegations against I.P. and Carboline were based on negligence, strict liability and breach of warranty. Her allegations against Miri and English were based solely on negligence.

On January 10, 1989, one week prior to trial, the trial court granted summary judgment in favor of I.P., Carboline and English. The next day Miri filed its motion for summary judgment and the trial court granted summary judgment in favor of Miri on October 11, 1989. The trial court denied Swan's motion to reconsider, and Swan now appeals.
* * *

We reverse [.]

FACTS

On August 21, 1985, the Long Beach Municipal Separate School District entered into a contract with Miri, Inc. for the reroofing of the Long Beach schools. [Swan alleges that James C. English was also a party to the contract.] The roofing system consisted of a sprayed polyurethane foam, manufactured by I.P., which provided insulation, and a polyurethane coating, manufactured by Carboline, which created the necessary waterproofing for the roof. The polyurethane foam manufactured by I.P. is known by the trade name "Isofoam SS- 0658" and contains the toxic ingredient methylene diphenyl isocyanate, or MDI. The color of the foam is beige when it is sprayed and it turns yellow as it begins to harden. The coating manufactured by Carboline is known by the trade name "Chem–Elast 2819S" and contains the toxic ingredient toluene diisocyanate, or TDI. The color of the coating is light gray.

Miri began working on the roof of Long Beach Junior High in early October, 1985. * * * Swan alleged that she was first exposed to the chemicals around noon on October 8, 1985, when she was accompanying her class to the cafeteria. She saw a yellow mist coming from the roof of a nearby building and she was soon in the middle of the mist, which had a strong, nauseating odor. She continued walking with the children to the cafeteria where she left them for the remainder of the lunch period, while she went to the teachers' lounge and to the women's restroom. In the restroom she observed that Miri's workers had removed the turbine on the roof and had sprayed the foam into the restroom. She left because the odor of the foam was too strong. * * *

Shortly after Swan arrived at her classroom the next morning, she noticed that Miri's workers were spraying foam on the roof of the building which contained her classroom. The fumes from the foam were strong and nauseating. She opened the windows for approximately ten minutes which only made the smell worse. * * * According to her, the spraying continued on her building all day except for one hour at lunch. During the lunch period, Swan and her class again had to walk through a cloud of spray on the way to the cafeteria. In addition to the nausea, the fumes also caused Swan's eyes to sting and burn. She opened her windows again that afternoon for about three hours because of the heat.

Other teachers and students complained to the school's administration about the physical effects of the spraying, and that afternoon the subject was discussed at a faculty meeting. Marlin Roger Ladner, the principal, told the teachers that from what he had read in a letter written by the architect who was handling the roofing project and other information he had received, the spray was not dangerous and would only cause mild irritation of the eyes. Ladner instructed the teachers to keep their classroom windows closed. * * *

Swan testified that her physical condition worsened that night. She experienced "[b]urning, sharp pains" in her chest and shoulders and her eyes continued to burn and sting. She also discovered that she was suddenly extremely hoarse and unable to project her voice. She testified that her throat hurt when she spoke. She also experienced frequent, painful headaches. * * *

Spraying operations continued on October 10, 1985. Miri's employees were spraying the roof of a building adjacent to her classroom and at times the mist drifted into Swan's classroom. She opened the windows several times because her students complained about the heat. When she took her students to the cafeteria during lunch period, they had to walk through a cloud of the spray and the particles got on Swan. Swan testified that water blisters developed on her arm either that afternoon or on Friday, October 11. After October 10 Miri no longer conducted spraying operations during school hours.

In addition to the physical problems described above, Swan testified that after her exposure to the spray, she often had problems maintaining her balance while walking. The right side of her body also became extremely weak, particularly her right arm and leg, and she suffered memory loss.

Two physicians by deposition testified that Swan's exposure to the chemical had caused serious throat and lung problems, and permanent brain damage.

* * *

In its study entitled "Criteria for a Recommended Standard—Occupational Exposure to Diisocyanates", The National Institute of Occupational Safety and Health (NIOSH) found that exposure to TDI and MDI can cause irritation to the respiratory tract and reduced pulmonary function which can lead to a condition resembling asthma or chronic bronchitis. Diisocyanates are also skin irritants and can cause irritation to the eyes. NIOSH also noted that studies have indicated that exposure to TDI can have neurological effects. I.P.'s material data safety sheet for its foam stated that with overexposure, it was an irritant to the eyes and respiratory tract and may cause headaches, nausea, coughing, shortness of breath, chest pains and respiratory distress. Similarly, Carboline's material data safety sheet lists several effects of overexposure including respiratory tract irritation, headaches, dizziness and nausea.

In its study, NIOSH recommended establishment of a threshold level value, or acceptable concentration level, of exposure to isocyanates for employees at five parts per billion for a ten-hour work shift. NIOSH also defined this level as 35 micrograms per cubic meter for TDI and 50 micrograms per cubic meter for MDI. NIOSH recommended a ceiling limit of twenty parts per billion (or .02 parts per million) for a ten-minute period which should never be exceeded. Frank Livingston, I.P.'s designee, testified that I.P. had conducted studies which measured the concentration of MDI when sprayed in confined areas and in these studies, the concentration had never exceeded .02 parts per million. John Montle, Carboline's technical representative, testified that if Carboline 2819–S is sprayed outdoors, the level of the isocyanate in the vapor could exceed the threshold limit value in the immediate area between the spray gun and the surface of the roof. However, according to Montle, the probability of the level of isocyanate in the vapor exceeding the threshold level even a "few feet away" from the immediate area being sprayed is extremely low. The defendants produced several experts who specialized in isocyanate chemistry who also testified that the concentration of the isocyanate once it leaves the nozzle spray would be below the threshold limit value. Dr. Frisch testified that isocyanates are very reactive chemicals, and when the spray hits the surface of the roof, the isocyanates in the foam react immediately and form the polyurethane, leaving only trace amounts of isocyanates behind. The reaction process in the coating is slower, however. The isocyanates in any overspray would immediately react with the moisture in the air to form the harmless material polyurea.

In his first deposition, English stated that he had not been informed by either I.P. or Carboline prior to the spraying operations of any hazard associated with the inhalation of either the foam or coating. In his second deposition, English testified that sometime after October 8, 1985, he had seen a brochure which I.P. provided Dr. Bob Ferguson, the superintendent of the Long Beach schools, which described the foam and its physical properties. According to English, he had not been provided any information directly from I.P. concerning possible hazards of the foam. Also, his second deposition, English said that Carboline did provide him with a technical data sheet for the coating sometime before October 8, 1985. He also had seen a Carboline brochure or catalog entitled "Chem–Elast Lasts" at some time but he was not sure when. Robert English, James English's son who was Miri's foreman and one of its principal sprayers, testified that to his knowledge, Miri had not received any documents from either I.P. or Carboline setting forth any hazards associated with the use of the foam and coating.

Frank E. Livingston testified that I.P. did not send Miri, James English or the Long Beach school system any material data safety sheets for the foam or any other warnings at any time prior to Swan's exposure. The material data safety sheets were sent to Long Beach Junior High School afterwards. In 1984, I.P. distributed copies of the Upjohn Technical Bulletin (recognized as the most complete compilation of information on polyurethane products and their safe application) to its distributors, including North Brothers, Inc. of Atlanta, whose Jackson office distributed the foam to Miri. Livingston had no knowledge as to whether the Upjohn Bulletin was ever distributed to Miri. John Montle and Van Rusling, Carboline's sales representative for the Gulf Coast, testified that Carboline provided material data safety sheets for its polyurethane coating to its customers upon request. Neither knew whether Miri ever requested a material data safety sheet.

James English testified that he and the other sprayers wore respirators when spraying the foam. He and Robert English both testified that before they began spraying on the roofs, they always instructed the school administration to make an announcement to the teachers instructing them to close the windows. If the teachers did not close the windows one of the Englishes or another employee of Miri would close the windows themselves. They also placed rope barricades around their work areas, although this was mainly done for the purpose of keeping the children away from the equipment. According to James English, representatives of both I.P. and Carboline visited the job site while the work was in progress and witnessed Miri's spraying procedures. None of the representatives expressed any concern about these procedures to Miri.

LAW

The Court Erred in Granting Summary Judgment in Favor of Defendants I.P. and Carboline.

* * *

The trial court granted summary judgment in favor of I.P. and Carboline based on the "learned intermediary" defense to products liability actions which provides that a manufacturer's duty to warn may be discharged by providing information to a third person upon whom it can reasonably rely to communicate the information to the ultimate users of the product or those who will be exposed to its hazardous effects.   * * *

Swan's claims against I.P. and Carboline are based on negligent failure to warn and strict liability. [After quoting Restatement (Second) of Torts § 402A, the court continues:]

Lack of an adequate warning is a defect which makes a product unreasonably dangerous for strict liability purposes. This Court has extended this duty to bystanders, holding that the duty imposed by § 402A "exists in favor of anyone who may reasonably be expected to be in the vicinity of the product's probable use and to be endangered by it if it is defective." Coca Cola Bottling Co., Inc. v. Reeves, 486 So.2d 374, 378 (Miss.1986).

I.P. and Carboline contend that they had no duty to warn Miri or Swan about any possible hazards associated with their products because Miri was an experienced, knowledgeable applicator of these products and is therefore charged with knowledge of the properties of the products. This argument stems from § 388 of the Restatement (Second) of Torts and comment "k" under § 388. This section provides:

> One who supplies directly or through a third person a chattel for another to use is subject to liability to those whom the supplier should expect to use the chattel with the consent of the other or to be endangered by its probable use, for physical harm caused by the use of the chattel in the manner for which and by a person for whose use it is supplied, if the supplier (a) knows or has reason to know that the chattel is or is likely to be dangerous for the use for which it is supplied, and (b) has no reason to believe that those for whose use the chattel is supplied will realize its dangerous condition, and (c) fails to exercise reasonable care to inform them of its dangerous condition or of the facts which make it likely to be dangerous.

Comment "k" to § 388 provides in part:

> k. When warning of defects unnecessary. One who supplies a chattel to others to use for any purpose is under a duty to exercise reasonable care to inform them of its dangerous character in so far as it is known to him, or of facts which to his knowledge make it likely to be dangerous, if, but only if, he has no reason to expect that those for whose use the chattel is supplied will discover its condition and realize the danger involved. . . .

The learned intermediary theory developed in cases involving prescription drugs.   * * * This Court has applied the learned intermediary theory in prescription drug cases. Generally, the cases discussing the learned intermediary theory which do not involve prescription drugs involve products which have injured employees on the job and the manufacturer's reliance on the employer to warn the employee of the dangers of the product. I.P. and Carboline rely on several cases. In Martinez v. Dixie Carriers, Inc., 529 F.2d 457 (5th Cir.1976), the widow of a worker, who died when he was overcome by noxious fumes while cleaning the tank of a barge which had been carrying a petrochemical mixture, filed suit against the owner of the barge and the manufacturer of the mixture alleging inadequate warning. The manufacturer had placed a warning card on the main deck of the barge which set out the hazards associated with the chemicals. The court held that the manufacturer was not liable for negligent failure to warn or strict liability. The court noted that the manufacturer marketed the chemical mixture only to industrial users and not to the general public, and the manufacturer could reasonably anticipate that only professionals familiar with the precautions necessary for the safe handling of the chemicals would come into contact with the chemicals. The card placed on the barge was an adequate warning to the limited class of professionals, of which the plaintiff's husband was a member, who were experienced in the stripping and cleaning of chemical storage tanks.

In Adams v. Union Carbide Corp., 737 F.2d 1453 (6th Cir.1984), the plaintiff, an employee of General Motors, filed suit against Union Carbide alleging that she suffered respiratory problems as a result of Union Carbide's failure to adequately warn the employees of General Motors of the hazards associated with toluene diisocyanate (TDI), which Union Carbide manufactured and supplied to General Motors for use in the automotive assembly process. Union Carbide had prepared a manual for General Motors which addressed the hazards associated with exposure to TDI and also included information on the safe use and handling of TDI and a chemical safety data sheet. Officials from Union Carbide and General Motors had also met to discuss the handling of TDI to minimize personnel exposure. The trial court granted summary judgment in favor of Union Carbide, and the Sixth Circuit affirmed. The court relied on Comment "n" to Restatement (Second) of Torts § 388 which states that the manufacturer's duty to warn may be discharged by providing information of the dangerous propensities of the product to a third person upon whom it can reasonably rely to communicate the information to the ultimate users of the product or those who will be exposed to its hazardous effects. The court held that the fact that General Motors repeatedly updated its information about TDI from Union Carbide, along with the fact that General Motors itself had a duty to its employees to provide them with a safe place to work, supported the conclusion that it was reasonable for Union Carbide to rely upon General Motors to convey the information about TDI to its employees.

In Smith v. Walter C. Best, Inc., 927 F.2d 736 (3rd Cir.1990), the plaintiff was injured as a result of his inhalation of silica dust contained in sand supplied by various parties to his employer. He claimed that the suppliers had a duty to warn him directly about the hazards of the dust. The court affirmed the trial court's entry of summary judgment in favor of the suppliers, finding that the plaintiff's employer was a knowledgeable industrial purchaser of silica sand familiar with its dangers. The court analyzed whether it was reasonable for the suppliers of the sand to rely on the plaintiff's employer to warn its employees about the hazards of the sand under the factors set out in Comment "n" to § 388 of the Restatement: (1) the dangerous condition of the product; (2) the purpose for which the product is used; (3) the form of any warnings given; (4) the reliability of the third party as a conduit of necessary information about the product; (5) the magnitude of the risk involved; and (6) the burdens imposed on the supplier by requiring that he directly warn all users. The court held that it was reasonable for the sand suppliers to rely on the plaintiff's employer to warn the plaintiff of the dangers. The court listed several facts which led it to this conclusion: (1) common medical knowledge of the hazards; (2) there were various statutes and regulations governing silica; (3) the employer was a member of a non-profit foundation which provided information to its members relative to occupational diseases, including silicosis, and their prevention; and (4) the duty of the employer to provide its employees a safe working environment. The court therefore held that the suppliers did not have a duty to warn the plaintiff directly of any hazards associated with the sand.

In its ruling on the motion for summary judgment, the trial court referred to Helene Curtis Industries, Inc. v. Pruitt, 385 F.2d 841 (5th Cir.1967). In Helene Curtis, the plaintiff's scalp and ears were burned by a mixture of two bleaching products purchased from a beauty parlor and applied to the plaintiff's hair by a friend. The plaintiff alleged that she was not adequately warned. The label on the Helene Curtis product stated: "FOR PROFESSIONAL USE ONLY—NOT FOR PUBLIC SALE." It also warned against mixing the product with any products other than one recommended by Helene Curtis. The 5th Circuit Court held that Helene Curtis was not liable, and that the warning was sufficient because it need only be reasonably calculated to reach and be understood by the person likely to use the product, the professional beautician. The sale of the product by the beauty parlor to the plaintiff's friend was an intervening cause of the plaintiff's injuries, as was the mixing of the two bleaching products by the plaintiff's friend.

These cases are distinguishable. Unlike Helene Curtis, the polyurethane foam and coating were applied by an intended, professional user. In Martinez, the manufacturer of the chemicals placed a warning on the barge and it was unlikely that anyone but professional tank cleaners would come into contact with the chemicals. Swan received no warnings concerning the hazards associated with the chemicals and it is not certain that Miri received warnings from the manufacturers. Also, the likelihood that someone not knowledgeable about the hazards of the chemicals would come into contact with the chemicals was more likely in this case because the chemicals were being sprayed at a school. In Adams and Smith, the plaintiffs' employers had knowledge of the hazards associated with TDI and the silica dust. Here, although James English and Miri had much experience spraying polyurethane foam and coating, they both testified that they were not aware of any hazards associated with the spraying.

In other cases, courts have held that the presence of an intermediary did not relieve the manufacturer of its duty to warn. In Borel v. Fibreboard Paper Products Corp., 493 F.2d 1076 (5th Cir.1973), an insulation worker brought an action against the manufacturers of insulation which contained asbestos. The court rejected the manufacturers' argument that it was the responsibility of the insulation contractors to warn the insulation workers of the risk of harm. The court noted that under the Restatement, a seller may be liable to the ultimate user or consumer for failure to give adequate warnings. The seller's warning must be reasonably calculated to reach such persons and the presence of an intermediary party will not by itself relieve the seller of this duty.

In Hall v. Ashland Oil Co., 625 F.Supp. 1515 (D.Conn.1986), a widow brought suit against a manufacturer of benzene who sold benzene to her deceased husband's employer. The manufacturer filed a motion for summary judgment based on the learned intermediary theory, arguing that when a product is sold in bulk to an industrial user for use by its employees, the supplier's duty to warn extends only to the employer as a learned intermediary. Further, that a supplier's duty to warn an industrial purchaser is excused where the purchaser is held to know of the risks independently. The court held that even if the learned intermediary theory were to be applied to cases involving the sale of chemicals in the industrial workplace, that theory alone would not relieve the supplier of a duty to warn. The court noted that the prescription drug cases which apply the learned intermediary theory merely shift the direction that such a warning must take, by requiring the manufacturer to provide an adequate warning to the intermediary. The court held that the facts were disputed as to whether the manufacturer supplied any warnings to the deceased's employer and as to whether the deceased's employer could be considered knowledgeable of the health risks associated with benzene.

In Adkins v. GAF Corp., 923 F.2d 1225 (6th Cir.1991), the supplier contended that § 388 of the Restatement relieved it of its duty to warn since it sold the asbestos to a "sophisticated user," the plaintiff's employer, which had full knowledge of the hazards associated with the use of asbestos and which could be relied upon to take the appropriate precautions. The court stated that the pivotal inquiry in determining whether this defense is available is a fact-specific evaluation of the reasonableness of the supplier's reliance on the intermediary to provide the warning. In a similar case, the Fourth Circuit stated that Comment "n" to § 388 of the Restatement clearly focuses on what the product manufacturer knew and the reasonableness of its reliance on the intermediary to and during the time the plaintiff was exposed. Willis v. Raymark Industries, Inc., 905 F.2d 793, 797 (4th Cir.1990)[.] In Little v. Liquid Air Corp., 952 F.2d 841 (5th Cir.1992), the Court of Appeals held that * * * (t)he bulk seller may rely on an informed distributor to pass information concerning the dangers of the product to the consumer.

However, the bulk seller's reliance upon the intermediate distributor must be reasonable, and it fulfills its duty to the ultimate consumer only if it ascertains (1) that the distributor to which it sells is adequately trained, (2) that the distributor is familiar with the properties of the product and the safe methods of handling it, and (3) that the distributor is capable of passing this knowledge to the consumer.

I.P. and Carboline contend that because they sold the foam and coating to Miri, a professional applicator chargeable with knowledge of the properties of the products, they had no duty to warn. Miri and James English indeed are experienced applicators of polyurethane roofing products. Miri's primary business was insulation and polyurethane roofing and the company had been involved in this business since 1977.
* * *

* * *

The learned intermediary defense does not relieve the manufacturer of its duty to warn, however, unless the manufacturer's reliance on the intermediary is reasonable. Material issues of fact exist in this case as to whether I.P.'s and Carboline's reliance on Miri was reasonable. From this record we do not know whether James and Robert English, the principal sprayers of the foam and coating, had knowledge of the hazards associated with the foam and coating. James English testified that had he known of any hazards associated with the products, he would not have sprayed them while school was in session. Robert English testified that at the time the foam and coating were sprayed on the roof of the school, he had no knowledge of any hazards associated with the foam or the coating.

From this record we cannot know whether it was reasonable for I.P. and Carboline to assume that Miri was knowledgeable about the hazards because the facts are in dispute as to whether I.P. and Carboline ever sent Miri any information concerning the chemical properties of the products and the hazards associated with them.

Frank E. Livingston testified that I.P. did not send Miri, James English or the Long Beach school system any material data safety sheets for the foam or any other warnings at any time prior to Swan's alleged exposure.

Also, because the evidence was insufficient to conclude that Miri was a sophisticated user, the learned intermediary doctrine still required I.P. and Carboline to furnish information and warnings to Miri. The trial court recognized this in its ruling: "[T]his manufacturer is not required to go further than to furnish information to the applicator or the professional who is going to use the product itself." Because of these disputed material issues of fact, the trial court erred in granting summary judgment in favor of I.P. and Carboline.

* * *

Notes and Questions

1. In cases where the bulk supplier asserts a sophisticated or knowledgeable user defense, should it make any difference whether the plaintiffs are proceeding under § 402A or under a negligence theory?

2. Many of the decisions discussed in *Swan* focused on the reasonableness of the supplier's reliance on the employer to furnish necessary warnings and instructions. Consider how the following factors might influence a court or jury in deciding the reasonableness question: (1) identification of the actual users would require monitoring of the employer's workforce; (2) the manner in which the products are actually delivered to the purchaser—i.e., unpackaged railroad car lots, barrels, or small containers; (3) the manner in which the product is maintained or stored by the purchaser; (4) who is in the best position to provide training, housekeeping measures, and warnings on a continuous and systematic basis; (5) the possible confusion arising from having different suppliers of the same or similar products; and (6) the ability of a supplier to exert pressure on a customer to insist that certain procedures be followed.

3. How does the fact that many states' laws and the federal Occupational Safety and Health Act, discussed in Chapter 9, require employers to provide a safe working environment bear on the sophisticated user defense?

4. In addition to the decisions referred to in *Swan*, other decisions have also addressed the bulk supplier—sophisticated user issue. See Goodbar v. Whitehead Bros., 591 F.Supp. 552 (W.D.Va.1984), affirmed sub. nom. Beale v. Hardy, 769 F.2d 213 (4th Cir.1985); Higgins v. E.I. DuPont de Nemours & Co., 671 Supp. 1055 (D.Md.1987).

c. *Foreseeable Users and Uses*

HIGH v. WESTINGHOUSE ELECTRIC CORP.

Supreme Court of Florida, 1992.
610 So.2d 1259.

OVERTON, J.

We have for review [an appellate affirmance of] the trial court summary judgment, holding that Westinghouse, as the manufacturer of electrical transformers, is not liable to an employee of a scrap metal salvage business for injuries allegedly sustained from a hazardous fluid that was released in dismantling transformers in the scrapping process. * * * While we approve the district court's decision on the question of strict liability, we find that there remains an issue of fact on the question of negligence. Consequently, we quash in part the decision of the district court of appeal and remand this case for further proceedings.

The relevant facts in the record are as follows. Westinghouse manufactured electrical transformers and sold them to Florida Power and Light Company (FPL). From 1967 to 1983, FPL sold its electrical transformers for junk to Pepper's Steel and Alloys (Pepper's), a scrap metal salvage business. To manufacture the electrical transformers sold to FPL, Westinghouse purchased products from Monsanto, a manufacturer of polychlorinated biphenyls (PCBs). In a January 15, 1972, letter and indemnification agreement from Westinghouse to Monsanto, Westinghouse acknowledged that Monsanto had notified Westinghouse that the PCBs used in its products tended to persist in the environment; that care was required in their handling, possession, use, and disposition; and that tolerance limits had been or were being established for PCBs in various food products.[2] In 1976, Westinghouse wrote a letter to its utility company customers, including FPL, disclosing the potential existence of PCBs in their transformers. In that letter, Westinghouse informed them that some oil- filled transformers had been contaminated with PCBs in the manufacturing process. Westinghouse's letter suggested that when performing repairs, routine maintenance, or disposal, all oil-filled transformers should be checked for the presence of PCBs.[3]

Studies of humans exposed to PCBs have shown numerous adverse effects, including but not limited to chloracne and other epidermal disorders, digestive disturbances, jaundice, impotence, throat and respiratory irritations, and severe headaches. It is undisputed that none of the junk transformers that FPL sold to Pepper's contained any labels, markings, or warnings of any kind[.] * * *

Willie J. High was the main truck driver for Pepper's from 1965 to 1983. As part of his duties, he picked up aluminum wire, cable, and other scrap metal. He also picked up transformers from FPL in Miami and other cities around Florida. * * * During this process, he came into contact with the PCB-contaminated transformer oil.

* * * [O]n July 9, 1983, High brought this action under strict liability and negligence theories.

The trial court granted Westinghouse's motion for summary judgment, holding as a matter of law that the ultimate disposal of the transformer was not foreseeable to the manufacturer as a reasonably intended "use." On appeal, the district court of appeal, in a split decision, affirmed. In explaining why strict liability under section 402A of the Restatement (Second) of Torts (1965) is not applicable, the district court stated: "The dismantling and recycling of products after they have been destroyed have been held to be product uses not reasonably foreseeable to manufacturers....

... Westinghouse's transformers were destroyed prior to the alleged injuries. While the transformers were sealed and intact there was no harm. Rather, the alleged damage occurred after the contents of the devices were exposed through the dismantling process. * * *

2. In the letter and indemnity agreement, Westinghouse agreed to indemnify and hold harmless Monsanto from Westinghouse's use of PCBs purchased from Monsanto. * * *

3. The pertinent portion of the letter read as follows: "In addition, when performing repair, routine maintenance or disposal, oil-filled transformers should be checked for the presence of PCBs. We also suggest that you check your own transformer oil storage and handling systems for possible presence of PCBs."

Here, the determination of no liability is based upon a substantial change in the product from the time it left the manufacturer's control to the time of the subject incident[.]" * * *

The district court concluded that the actual products supplied by Westinghouse were the electrical transformers, not the contaminated dielectric fluid. As a matter of law, the unsealing, stripping, and dumping of the contents of Westinghouse's product in order to salvage junk components were not reasonably foreseeable "uses" of the product nor was Willie High an intended "user" within the meaning of section 402A.

There are two questions we must address. The first is whether strict liability applies under section 402A of the Restatement (Second) of Torts for injuries that occur in dismantling an item. The second is whether the manufacturer, Westinghouse, in this instance was negligent in failing to timely warn of dangerous contents in its product that could cause injuries in its alteration and dismantling.

While these are questions of first impression in this state, other courts have addressed similar issues. In Kalik v. Allis–Chalmers Corp., 658 F.Supp. 631 (W.D.Pa.1987), the owners of a scrap metal business that had been contaminated by PCBs sued the manufacturers and suppliers of the products containing the PCBs to recover cleanup costs and damages incurred under [CERCLA]. In that case, the scrap metal business had purchased junk electrical components as scrap. The electrical components contained, as they did in this instance, PCBs. During the course of dismantling, handling, and storing the junk electrical components, PCB-contaminated oil leaked or spilled onto the site. A furnace used in dismantling and processing the components caused PCBs in the components to allegedly produce dioxins, which also polluted the site. Plaintiff's damage claims were based upon a negligent failure to warn and strict liability in tort. The United States District Court in Pennsylvania considered whether plaintiff's use of the product was reasonably foreseeable to the manufacturer. Although the court agreed that this was ordinarily a question of fact, it held as a matter of law that the recycling of a product after it had been destroyed and the destruction of a product were not reasonably foreseeable uses to the manufacturer. * * * [Similarly], in Johnson v. Murph Metals, Inc., 562 F.Supp. 246 (N.D.Tex.1983), a United States District Court in Texas granted a summary judgment and held that fumes and particulates from smelting lead from scrap batteries were not created from a "use" of the batteries. In that case, the employees of various lead-smelting companies who had sued certain automotive battery manufacturers stipulated that their injuries did not result from working with intact batteries or from the destruction of batteries to obtain the lead for smelting. The lead fumes and dust that allegedly injured them were created only after the lead was extracted from the destroyed batteries and used in the smelting process. In determining that the plaintiffs were not "users" of defendants' products, the court held that "the defendants' product had ceased to exist."

With regard to the first question and the applicability of strict liability under section 402A of the Restatement (Second) of Torts, we find that strict liability is not applicable. [In Florida] for strict liability to apply to the manufacturer, the transformers in this instance must have been used for the purpose intended. In the instant case, High's injury resulted from dismantling the transformers and coming into contact with the PCBs as a result of this process. We agree with the district court that section 402A does not apply because of the substantial alteration of the product when High came into contact with the contaminated oil. Secondly, section 402A applies to intended uses of products for which they were produced. When an injury occurs under those circumstances, the manufacturer is strictly liable. We find, under the circumstances in the instant case, that dismantling a product is not an intended use as prescribed by section 402A. Therefore, we find, under these facts, that strict liability does not apply.

The second question we must address concerns liability based on negligence. We find that a manufacturer has a duty to warn of dangerous contents in its product which could damage or injure even when the product is not used for its intended purpose. This issue, which is not directly addressed by the district court of appeal, is whether Westinghouse was negligent in warning FPL of the possible danger of PCB contamination.

We find that Westinghouse had a duty to timely notify the entity to whom it sold the electrical transformers, FPL in the instant case, once it was advised of the PCB contamination. The record reflects that Monsanto, the PCB manufacturer, notified Westinghouse sometime between 1970 and 1972, of the dangerous toxic propensities of PCBs used by Westinghouse. We find that Westinghouse's November 22, 1976, letter to its utility customers, including FPL, relaying PCB information was adequate notice. However, whether or not the letter was timely is a question of fact that has not been resolved by this record. As stated earlier, Monsanto informed Westinghouse sometime between 1970 and 1972 of the dangers regarding PCB contamination, and in 1976, Westinghouse informed FPL that some products were contaminated. If Westinghouse knew or should have known from its early 1970s communications with Monsanto that some mineral oil transformers contained PCBs, then it is clear from the record that Westinghouse delayed in warning FPL of the contamination of these transformers. Although we hold that Westinghouse's letter to FPL was adequate notice, we find that Westinghouse had a duty to timely notify FPL so that FPL could timely notify Pepper's of the possible danger that could occur in dismantling the transformers so that it could proceed in the prescribed manner. If this notice was not timely, then the next question is whether the lack of timely notice by Westinghouse was the proximate cause of High's injury. Given the circumstances, we find the knowledge by Westinghouse of the PCB contamination in its transformers and the timeliness of Westinghouse's notice to FPL of that contamination are issues of fact that must be resolved in this case and are not proper for summary judgment.

For the reasons expressed, we approve in part and quash in part the decision of the district court of appeal and remand for further proceedings consistent with this opinion.

It is so ordered.

The partial concurrences and dissents of Barkett, J. and Kogan, J. are omitted.

Notes and Questions

1. In a partial concurrence and partial dissent, Justice Barkett wrote:

[I] agree with the majority's disposition of the duty-to- warn issue but also find the case presents a valid claim for strict liability.

The majority is correct in stating that section 402A of the Restatement (Second) of Torts "applies to intended uses of products for which they were produced." The majority's deficiency, however, is in failing to define "intended uses." The prevailing view recognizes that an "intended use" includes unintended uses of a product if they were reasonably foreseeable by the defendant. See, e.g., Bloxom v. Bloxom, 512 So.2d 839, 843 (La.1987) (" 'Normal use' is a term of art that includes all intended uses, as well as all foreseeable uses and misuses of the product."); J.I. Case Co. v. McCartin–McAuliffe Plumbing, [516 N.E.2d 260, 266 (Ill.1987)] ("Misuse is the use of a product 'for a purpose neither intended nor "foreseeable" (objectively reasonable) by the defendant' and may defeat a cause of action."); see also M. Stuart Madden, Products Liability § 13.9, at 20 (1988) (and cases cited therein) ("[A] use of the product for a purpose, or in a manner neither intended nor reasonably foreseeable will bar recovery. However, some abnormal, or unintended uses will not constitute a legal misuse of the product, if they are reasonably foreseeable.").

As the majority apparently recognizes, foreseeability is usually a jury question. Neither the majority opinion nor the cases cited therein explain why * * * the manufacturer would not have reasonably foreseen that its product would be dismantled.

Are Justice Barkell's additional observations more readily harmonized with the principle of actor liability for foreseeable harm than is the conclusion reached by the majority?

5. AGRICULTURAL CHEMICALS: USE OF EXPRESS WARRANTY THEORY

CIBA–GEIGY CORPORATION v. ALTER

Supreme Court of Arkansas, 1992.
309 Ark. 426, 834 S.W.2d 136, 1992.

Newbern, J.

John Alter sustained severe injury to his corn crop allegedly as the result of his use of Dual 8E, a herbicide manufactured by Ciba–Geigy, Inc. Alter sued Ciba–Geigy asserting theories of strict liability, negligence, breach of warranty, misrepresentation, and breach of a settlement contract. The jury returned a general verdict of $100,410.51 in Alter's favor. Ciba–Geigy argues the Trial Court abused its discretion by refusing to bifurcate the trial, separating the breach of settlement contract claim from the remaining claims. Ciba–Geigy contends the failure to bifurcate resulted in inadmissible evidence of settlement negotiations coming before the jury. We agree and reverse and remand on this point. Other issues which may arise on retrial will also be addressed. Dual is a herbicide registered with the [EPA], and it is widely used by farmers to control weeds and grass. The herbicide was advertised as giving farmers longer control over weeds and grass for a lower price than competitive products. It was "the longer lasting grass herbicide." The advertising materials which were distributed to farmers by Ciba–Geigy also stated, "Crop injury? You don't have to worry when you use Dual. Gives you peace of mind. That's worth a lot." Dual was accompanied by a "label," consisting of several printed pages, which contained the following language at page five:

> Conditions of Sale and Warranty[:] CIBA–GEIGY warrants that this product conforms to the chemical description on the label and is reasonably fit for the purposes referred to in the Directions for Use subject to the inherent risks referred to above. CIBA–GEIGY makes no other express or implied warranty of fitness or merchantability or any other express or implied warranty. In no case shall CIBA–GEIGY or the Seller be liable for consequential, special, or indirect damages resulting from the use or handling of this product.

> Directions for Use[:] FAILURE TO FOLLOW ALL PRECAUTIONS ON THIS LABEL MAY RESULT IN POOR WEED CONTROL, CROP INJURY, OR ILLEGAL RESIDUES.

The following warning is found in the label in a box at page six:

> Precaution: Injury may occur following the use of Dual BE under abnormally high soil moisture conditions during early development of the crop.

In early 1985, Ron Wulfkuhle and John McLeod, two Ciba–Geigy sales representatives, met with several Arkansas County farmers to promote the use of Dual. Alter was present at the meeting. Alter testified the salesmen told him Dual would control weeds longer at a cheaper price than other herbicides. They also said Dual was safe and would not injure a corn crop. Although Wulfkuhle knew that Dual could damage a corn crop if the crop received heavy moisture after planting, he did not tell Alter about that possibility. Hazards associated with Dual use were not mentioned. Alter testified he generally read the labels accompanying herbicides, but he could not recall whether he read the precautionary language on the Dual label. Alter did not read the Dual advertising materials, but purchased Dual in reliance on the representations made by the salesmen. He began planting his 997.8 acre corn crop on March 19th. A week and a half later Alter applied Dual to the crop. Midway through the Dual application, a heavy rain fell.

Alter noticed severe injury to his corn crop in early May. The greatest injury occurred in the field referred to as Pittman # 3. Some corn was simply not coming up, and other plants looked twisted and "buggywhipped." The crops treated with Dual nearest the time of the rainfall were severely injured, but those treated with Dual after the rainfall were not injured.

Alter immediately reported the problem to his herbicide supplier, Martin Gilbert. Gilbert then called Wulfkuhle who came to the Alter farm. Wulfkuhle determined the percentages of injury of the crop in the various fields. He noticed that some fields were 100% injured, and there were others with less than 2% crop injury. Wulfkuhle admitted the damage looked like it had been caused by Dual. Wulfkuhle told Alter to replant his crop and that Ciba–Geigy would pay him $25.00 an acre for replanting costs. Alter replanted 139 acres. On May 30th, Alter's counsel sent a letter to Ciba–Geigy's main office in Greensboro, North Carolina. Counsel informed Ciba–Geigy of the injury to Alter's crop and demanded compensation for loss of crop yield resulting from the Dual application, as well as replanting costs.

* * *

Harper Grimes, a former trouble shooter for Ciba–Geigy, testified that Dual caused the damage in Alter's field. He stated Dual frequently caused damage when the soil was extremely wet or when a substantial rain occurred in a short period of time during or just after application. The critical point for Dual damage was from the time of germination. Grimes did not believe that the precautionary language on the Dual label adequately informed farmers about the risks of rainfall. The warning should have been placed in two locations, and it should have described the conditions of danger more adequately.

Dr. Everett Cowlett, director of technical services for Ciba–Geigy, stated there was a potential for crop injury resulting from Dual use when high moisture conditions occurred within seven days to a month after the seed was planted. Dr. Cowlett admitted a farmer could not determine whether it was safe to apply Dual after planting. The farmer will not know whether there will be an abnormally high moisture condition within seven days to a month after planting. For this reason, Ciba–Geigy put the precautionary language on the label. Dr. Cowlett further stated that the Dual label was approved by the EPA. Dr. Edward Higgins, an employee of the agricultural division at Ciba–Geigy, stated Dual was safe to use on corn. He stated Ciba–Geigy had conducted several studies and tests on Dual. The tests showed that the type of crop damage Alter experienced occurred in only one-tenth of one percent of cases.

Dr. Higgins said the warnings on the Dual label were adequate, and they were like those commonly used in the herbicide industry. Placing the warnings in two places on the label would be burdensome.

The jury returned a general verdict in Alter's favor for $100,410.51 in compensatory damages and no punitive damages.

* * *

I. Bifurcation

[In this part of the court's opinion, it examines defendant's claim that the trial court abused its discretion in declining to bifurcate defendant's breach of settlement contract claim from plaintiff's claims in strict liability, negligence, breach of warranty and misrepresentation. Holding that failure to bifurcate had resulted in prejudice to defendant, the court reversed and ordered a retrial. It thereupon stated its expectations as to the issues and legal standards upon retrial:]

II. Issues on Retrial

A. FIFRA preemption

[In this part of its opinion, entered before the Supreme Court's decision in Cipollone v. Liggett Group, the court concludes that FIFRA neither expressly nor impliedly preempts plaintiff's common law claims in tort or warranty]

* * *

C. Breach of warranty

Ciba–Geigy also asserts a directed verdict should have been granted in its favor on the breach of express and implied warranty claims because the Dual label effectively disclaimed all warranties, and the label prohibited recovery for consequential damages in the form of lost profits.

To exclude the implied warranty of merchantability, the disclaimer must mention merchantability and be conspicuous. Ark. Code Ann. § 4–2–316(2) (Repl.1991). To exclude the implied warranty of fitness, the exclusion must be in writing and conspicuous. § 4–2–316(2). Words or conduct relevant to the creation of an express warranty and words or conduct tending to negate or limit the warranty shall be construed wherever reasonable as consistent with each other; but negation or limitation is inoperative to the extent that such construction is unreasonable. § 4–2–316(1). Consequential damages may be limited or excluded unless the limitation or exclusion is unconscionable, or the limited remedy fails of its essential purpose. Ark.Code Ann. § 4–2–719(2) and (3) (Repl.1991).

1. Disclaimer of warranties

We do not decide the question, but we note a factual issue with respect to the implied warranties claim. The language on the Ciba–Geigy label could have been effective to disclaim all implied warranties under § 4–2–316(2). The disclaimer was in bold type on page five of the label and clearly mentioned merchantability. The Uniform Commercial Code defines "conspicuous" as being "written in that a reasonable person against whom it is to operate ought to have noticed it. Language in the body of a form is conspicuous if it is in larger or other contrasting type or color." Ark.Code Ann. § 4–12–201(10) (Repl.1991)[.]

The next question is whether Ciba–Geigy's express warranties and the disclaimer of all express warranties can be reasonably construed as consistent with each other under § 4–2–316(1). If they cannot, the disclaimer is ineffective. First to be examined is the nature of the express warranties Ciba–Geigy made to Alter. "Any affirmation of fact or promise made by the seller to the buyer which relates to the goods and becomes part of the basis of the bargain creates an express warranty that the goods shall conform to the affirmation or promise." Ark.Code Ann. § 4–2–313(1)(a) (Repl.1991). An affirmation of the seller's opinion or commendation does not create an express warranty. Ark.Code Ann. § 4–2–313(2) (Repl.1991).

The advertising materials distributed to farmers by Ciba–Geigy contained an express warranty that a farmer need not worry about crop injury when using Dual. Alter, however, did not recall reading any of the advertising materials. An affirmation of fact must be part of the basis of the parties, bargain to be an express warranty. See Currier v. Spencer, 299 Ark. 182, 772 S.W.2d 309 (1989). When a buyer is not influenced by the statement in making his or her purchase, the statement is not a basis of the bargain. See generally American Law of Warranties § 2:7 (1991). Clearly, Alter was not influenced by the advertising materials when purchasing Dual, and hence they were not a basis of the bargain.

There was testimony that Wulfkuhle and McLeod told Alter during the sales meeting that Dual was safe and would not injure a corn crop. The question is whether this was a mere statement of opinion. In the misrepresentation context, we indicated "an opinion is merely an assertion of one man's belief as to a fact." Grendell v. Kiehl, 291 Ark. 228, 723 S.W.2d 830 (1987), citing Prosser & Keeton on Torts (5th Ed.),Ch. 19 § 109 (1984). There are no set criteria to help ascertain opinion from affirmation of fact, and the determination must be made on a case-by-case basis. Williston on Sales, § 17–6 (4th ed.1974).

The evidence before the Trial Court supported the conclusion that Ciba–Geigy's statements that Dual was safe and would not injure a corn crop were affirmations of fact and not mere opinions or commendations. The jury had sufficient evidence to conclude the statements were not "sales puffing" and constituted specific express warranties that the goods would conform to the affirmations. See, e.g., Pritchard v. Liggett & Myers Tobacco Co., 295 F.2d 292 (3rd Cir.1961) (if a manufacturer assures the public that his product is safe when in fact it is harmful, he can "no doubt" be held liable for breach of warranty)[;] American Law of Warranties § 2:57 (1991) (a statement that a product is safe is generally an absolute undertaking that it is so). Again, we do not decide the issue, but we note that if the evidence is the same on retrial, a jury could conclude the disclaimer ineffective.

2. Limitation of remedies

A seller of goods may limit the buyer's remedies for breach of warranty pursuant to Ark.Code Ann. § 4–2–719(1)(a) (Repl.1991). A limitation of remedies provision restricts the remedies available to the buyer once a breach of warranty is established. An otherwise valid limitation of remedy is avoided by the buyer if the limitation fails of its essential purpose, or is unconscionable. § 4–2–719(3).

The "failure of essential purpose" exception is most commonly applied when the buyer's remedy is exclusively limited to repair or replacement of defective goods, and the seller is unable to repair or replace the goods to conform to the warranty. In this case, we are not dealing with a seller who failed to correct a defect after being asked to do so by the buyer, and the failure of essential purpose exception is not applicable. See Hill v. BASF Wyandotte Corp., 696 F.2d 287 (4th Cir.1982). Ciba–Geigy has not limited or substituted Alter's remedy to repair or replacement of the defective goods and has only limited its liability for consequential damages.

While we cannot definitely resolve the issue, some comment on whether the limitation on consequential damages was unconscionable and unenforceable under § 4–2–719(3) is appropriate. Unconscionability must be determined in light of general commercial background, commercial needs in the trade or the particular case, the relative bargaining positions of the parties, and other circumstances existing when the contract was made. The commentary to § 4–2–719 states "it is of the very essence of a sales contract that at least minimum adequate remedies be available."

In Dessert Seed Co. v. Drew Farmers Supply, 248 Ark. 858, 454 S.W.2d 307 (1970), we held a limitation of liability clause unreasonable, unconscionable, and against public policy when negligence of the seller was clearly established, and the buyer was unable to discover the defect in the goods. See also Latimer v. William Mueller & Son, Inc., 149 Mich.App. 620, 386 N.W.2d 618 (1986) (limitation of remedy unconscionable when the defect could not be discovered); Majors v. Kalo Laboratories, Inc., 407 F.Supp. 20 (M.D.Ala.1975) (limitation of remedy unconscionable when a latent defect is involved). Because other evidence might be presented on this issue on retrial, we cannot pass on the unconscionability question on this appeal.

D. Punitive damages

Ciba–Geigy argues that, although no liability for punitive damages was imposed, the issue of punitive damages and evidence of financial condition should not have been submitted to the jury. Ciba–Geigy fails to mention that the jury was instructed on the tort of deceit. Although we do not know the basis of the general verdict in this case, punitive damages are available in cases of misrepresentation or deceit. Stein v. Lukas, 308 Ark. 74, 823 S.W.2d 832 (1992); Thomas Auto Co. v. Craft, 297 Ark. 492, 763 S.W.2d 651 (1989). If there is substantial evidence to show deliberate misrepresentation or deceit the issue of punitive damages may be submitted to the jury.

* * *

Reversed and remanded.

Notes and Questions

1. The manufacturer of agricultural chemicals may be required to take into account the fact that a sizeable proportion of the agricultural workforce speaks English as a second language. Some decisions suggest a manufacturer's duty to present warnings that go beyond English description to include as well international symbols of risk and means of avoidance. For example, in Hubbard–Hall Chemical Co. v. Silverman, 340 F.2d 402 (1st Cir.1965), the court held that the manufacturer of a pesticide might properly prepare warnings including international symbols of toxicity, such as the skull and crossbones, where the evidence showed that the product was applied by semi-English literate farm employees.

2. While a thorough discussion of the law governing liability under an express warranty theory is beyond the scope of this casebook, certain points should be recognized when considering the possible application of UCC § 2–313 to toxic product claims. First, the absence of manufacturer-buyer privity is not a bar to recovery, so that the express warranty runs directly to the ultimate purchaser of the product. See UCC § 2–318. Alternatives A, B and C ("Third Party Beneficiaries of Warranties—Express or Implied.) Second, the breach of an express warranty requires no showing of fault— that is, liability is strict, and the plaintiff need not establish negligence or intent on the part of the seller. Accordingly, the defendant need not be aware of the toxic characteristic of the product, nor have acted unreasonably in failing to learn or warn of it, so long as it warranted that it was not toxic.

Third, it is not necessary to prove the presence of a defective or unreasonably dangerous condition as it is under § 402A. The nonconformance of the product to the warranty constitutes the breach of the warranty and supports a finding of liability. E.g., Venie v. South Central Enterprises, 401 S.W.2d 495 (Mo.App.1966)(manufacturer's statements to the buyer that 2,4,5–t, a hormone herbicide, was "perfectly safe for strawberries" was actionable in breach of express warranty when, following application of the product in a normal manner, it killed not only the target weeds but the strawberries as well).

Fourth, state of the art is not a defense. Thus, even if the manufacturer made the product as safe as was possible under the state of the art existing at the time the warranty was made, it is not excused from liability so long as the warranty that the product would perform as represented was breached. Accordingly, even if it was not scientifically possible to make the product as safe as warranted, the manufacturer is liable.

Fifth, a general representation that a product is "safe" is ordinarily sufficient to support an express warranty action when the plaintiff or the plaintiff's property is injured or damaged by use of the product. E.g., Drayton v. Jiffee Chemical Corp., 395 F.Supp. 1081 (N.D.Ohio 1975), modified on other grounds 571 F.2d 352 (6th Cir.1978) (advertising claims that a particularly caustic drain cleaner was safe for household use held to be express warranty).

3. Another reason that dependence on express warranty theory is common is cases such as *Alter* is because of the economic loss doctrine. If a plaintiff suffers only an economic loss such as the costs of repair or replacement and consequential damages including lost profits—negligence and strict products liability are not ordinarily available because of the absence of personal injury or property damage. In other words, where a toxic product has not produced any safety-related harm, a plaintiff may have to rely on contractual warranties as a basis for compensation for economic losses.

4. *Note on Misrepresentation and Fraud.* While an action under UCC §§ 2–313, 2–314 or 2–315 may implicate seller misrepresentations, or fraud, plaintiffs may also evaluate potential separate claims in misrepresentation or fraud. Such claims may enjoy congruence with claims in warranty, but are not dependent upon them, *i.e.*, a seller's silence, while not constituting a statement of material fact for warranty purposes, may constitute a misrepresentation.

A.   *Strict Liability for Innocent Misrepresentation Under Restatement (Second) of Torts § 402B*

The Restatement (Second) recitation of strict liability for innocent misrepresentation provides:

Section 402B: Misrepresentation by Seller of Chattels to Consumers

One engaged in the business of selling chattels who, by advertising, labels, or otherwise, makes to the public a misrepresentation of a material fact concerning the character or quality of a chattel sold by him is subject to liability for physical harm to a consumer of the chattel caused by justifiable reliance upon the misrepresentation, even though

(a) it is not made fraudulently or negligently, and

(b) the consumer has not bought the chattel from or entered into any contractual relation with the seller.

This section derives from the outgrowth of the legal principles governing fraudulent and negligent misrepresentations, most of which involved non-product cases. While it is beyond the purpose of this book to address liability rules for fraud and negligent misrepresentation, a defendant in a toxic product case could be held liable under those theories, which require more stringent tests than those under § 402B. But a plaintiff proving fraud or negligent misrepresentation does have an advantage which may be relevant: he can recover not only for physical harm, but also for economic damages alone which are generally unrecoverable in product cases grounded in strict liability and negligence theory. A plaintiff seeking to recover only intangible economic losses must usually have to rely on its contractual and UCC remedies, unless an action for fraud or negligent misrepresentation can be established.

B. *Negligent Misrepresentation and Fraud*

Many of the rules governing innocent misrepresentation under § 402B are transplanted from the fraud and negligent misrepresentation torts. See generally, Michael Green, Strict Liability under Sections 402A and 402B: A Decade of Litigation, 54 Tex.L.Rev. 1185 (1976).

2. Fraud

To establish an action for fraud, the plaintiff must prove these elements:

(a) Defendant made a false representation;

(b) of an existing material fact;

(c) defendant knew the statement was false, or had no knowledge of its truth or falsity, or acted recklessly as to its truth or falsity;

(d) defendant intended the plaintiff to rely on the statement;

(e) the plaintiff did rely on the statement and the reliance was justifiable; and

(f) the plaintiff suffered damage.

To prove fraud, the plaintiff must essentially prove that the defendant intentionally or recklessly deceived him; in negligent misrepresentation, he must prove that the defendant negligently deceived him. Under § 402B no such proof of intentional or negligent deception is necessary: the liability is *strict*.

Allegations of fraud formed a basis for the suit brought by the City of New York against a lead-based paint trade association in New York v. Lead Industries Association, Inc., 190 A.D.2d 173, 597 N.Y.S.2d 698 (1993). In that suit, the New York appellate court affirmed the trial court's denial of defendants' motion to dismiss, and explained:

According to the complaint, defendants have known for years, from their own privately financed studies, that lead-based interior house paint presented a health threat, putting children particularly at risk. Despite their decision not to use such paint on toys and childrens' furniture, they nevertheless not only continued to manufacture lead-based paint for interior surfaces, but also concealed their knowledge of the hazard, suppressed its dissemination, and lobbied against governmental regulation that would have required appropriate warnings to the public. Indeed, well into the 1950s, having known of the hazard for three decades, defendants continued to advertise and promote their lead-based product as appropriate for uses which might result in exposure to young children through inhalation, ingestion or absorption. Armed with such knowledge, which was clearly superior to that of the consuming public, defendants' actions cannot be protected as mere statements of opinion in an action for fraud and misrepresentation.

The scope of liability for fraud is generally broader than for negligence—under fraud it extends to anyone whom the defendant had "reason to know" might rely, and under negligence extends to only those foreseeable persons within a class defendant actually knew would rely. See Restatement (Second) of Torts § 552. The recoverable damages are also broader for fraud under § 549, with the plaintiff having the option of choosing between the out-of-pocket measure of damages or the benefit-of-the-bargain measure plus consequential economic losses, whereas under negligent misrepresentation in § 552B the plaintiff must settle for out-of-pocket losses and consequential economic losses.

The requirement that the defendant make a false representation of a material fact is the same under fraudulent, negligent or innocent misrepresentation. The representation must relate to a *material* fact. The usual test of materiality is whether the information would be regarded as important to a reasonable person in making a choice of action. Therefore, trivial or unimportant false statements are not actionable. In the toxic torts area, courts should properly regard as material any information about the safety, risks, or the harmful effects of the product. Any fact or risk sufficiently material to create an obligation to warn of it under § 402A would also be material if the defendant misrepresented that fact or risk under § 402B. Further, a statement would be material if it significantly affects the manner in which the plaintiff uses the product, thereby increasing its danger.

According to comment j of § 402B, liability will not be found "where the misrepresentation is not known, or there is indifference to it, and it does not influence the purchase or subsequent conduct." The representation need not, however, be the "sole inducement to purchase or to use the chattel, and it is sufficient that it has been a substantial factor in that inducement." In most product cases involving toxic products one would expect that the plaintiff's alleged reliance would relate to some representation about the safe use of the product or the absence of harmful effects, which might be one factor in inducing a consumer to purchase or use the product.

A plaintiff who is aware of the falsity of the representation is generally precluded from recovery. Moreover, some courts have held that if a reasonably prudent person would have been aware of the facts or would have investigated further, the plaintiff will be deemed to have knowledge of those facts which such an investigation would reveal and cannot recover for the misrepresentation.

Problem

In 1986, before Dr. James and Rhonda Conant moved into their newly constructed Pomeroy, South Hampshire home, the builder contracted with pesticide applicator Swat Terminating Co. ("Swat") to pre-treat the home for insects and termites. In 1987, soon after the family moved in, Swat applied 400 gallons of Chemco's Gold Crest C–100 termiticide to the basement walls and soil around the home. The chlordane-based product was applied through holes drilled into concrete blocks. Standard practice required that the holes be filled in afterward, but this did not occur.

Consequently, chlordane seeped into the living areas, and emitted toxic fumes throughout the house. The Conants and their three children began to experience illnesses, including headaches, nausea, and diarrhea. The couple's 15–month–old baby has been hospitalized and the family cat died. In November 1990, after an autopsy showed chlordane in the cat's liver, the family left the house.

The plaintiffs sued Chemco and Swat for personal injuries and property damage. They maintain that the house has been rendered uninhabitable, and the family's exposure to chlordane over a three-year period left them

with severe permanent illnesses, including blood irregularities, liver problems, and immune system dysfunction.

There is evidence that Chemco's Gold Crest C–100 used by Swat carried
labels on the canisters that stated that "independent studies reveal no
evidence of any long-term latent health effects." Chemco maintains that
these labels were intended solely as information to professional applicators,
not for consumers.

After Swat settled with the plaintiffs, Chemco moved to dismiss all
claims. The claims against Chemco, based on § 402A of the Restatement
(Second) of Torts, contend that Chemco's Gold Crest C–100 was unreasonably dangerous to consumers and property. Specifically, plaintiffs contend
that the product was unreasonably dangerous under the consumer expectation test of § 402A comment (i) and, alternatively, under a risk-utility test
for design defect. In addition, they assert an informational defect related to
the failure of the labels to inform consumers of the risks of short-term and
long-term exposure. Finally, they assert express warranty claims predicated
on the contents of the label.

A 1990 EPA study revealed that the use of chlordane-based termiticides
on subterranean termites does create low-level risks of adverse health effects
to those exposed, especially headaches, watery eyes, nausea, and similar
symptomology. Additionally, the EPA recommended chemical alternatives
to the ingredients in Gold Crest C–100 and other manufacturers' products,
but those alternatives were not generally available in 1986 and 1987.

The county Board of Revisers lowered the appraised value of the
Conants' property from $136,600 to $22,680. The arrived-at value was
based on the land beneath the house, the pool, and the garage. The home
itself was found to have no value because of the contamination.

Evaluate the plaintiffs' claims under § 402A and express warranty
theory.

Chapter Eight

CAUSATION

INTRODUCTION

This Chapter deals with the broad topic of causation, which consists of several discrete elements, each of which is treated separately, but which are closely related: (1) Was the harm suffered by the plaintiff—usually a disease or illness which occurs generally in the population as integral to a background risk—caused by the exposure to the toxic substance? This raises the traditional question of cause-in-fact that is the focus of the basic torts course, but puts the inquiry into a different setting. (2) While some people may have experienced a harm caused by the defendant, is this plaintiff among that class of people? This is referred to in the literature as the indeterminate plaintiff or plaintiff identification problem. (3) Is the defendant the one who is responsible for the substance that produced the alleged harm—did the defendant cause the harm plaintiff allegedly suffered? This is the question which cases such as *Sindell v. Abbott Laboratories* wrestle with, which is often labeled the indeterminate defendant or indeterminate source problem.

A. CAUSATION: DID THE TOXIC SUBSTANCE CAUSE PLAINTIFF'S HARM?

1. INTRODUCTORY PRINCIPLES

No issue is more difficult in environmental tort litigation than resolving the question of whether the exposure to the toxic substance was the cause in fact of the plaintiff's harm. The special problems of causation in environmental torts are summarized by Professor Ora Fred Harris in an article, Toxic Tort Litigation and the Causation Element: Is There Any Hope of Reconciliation, 40 S.W.L.J. 909, 911–912 (1986):

> Causation problems are greatly compounded when applied to the field of toxic or hazardous exposure injury. A common, generally accurate, evaluation of humankind's understanding of the behavior of hazardous or toxic wastes and the effect of exposure on humans points to a vast amount of scientific uncertainty. This

uncertainty is understandable given that many of these issues are at the very frontiers of science. Thus, a plaintiff attempting to establish that exposure to a particular substance has in fact caused his or her injury may face a dubious court or jury because of the lack of scientific certainty. Moreover, because this "new" tort injury can have a latency period of up to as many as twenty to thirty years, it may be, as a practical matter, virtually impossible to establish the requisite causal relationship between an exposure that may have taken place many decades ago and a recently manifested injury now claimed to be the consequence of that exposure. Not only does this long latency period stymie the toxic or hazardous exposure victim's ability to isolate the alleged substance that precipitated the injury, it also diminishes the chances of identifying the responsible parties. These two requirements are critical if an injured plaintiff is to establish causation successfully in a toxic tort case. * * *

a. *Problems With Causation Terminology*

But what is meant by "cause" in the context of toxic torts? How does "cause" in law relate to the meaning of "cause" in science?

Causation in science finds its origins in Newtonian physics, with its emphasis on the laws of motion and acceleration, and a simplistic vision of mechanistic cause and effect—objects or particles changing direction following collisions with other objects or particles. Professor Troyen Brennan identifies this characterization of causation as "corpuscularian," and as requiring the presence of "causal chains." Troyen Brennan, Causal Chains and Statistical Links: The Role of Scientific Uncertainty in Hazardous–Substance Litigation, 75 Cornell L. Rev. 469 (1988). This mechanistic model of cause and effect has dominated the discourse on legal cause-in-fact, and has worked reasonably well in resolving causation in sporadic accident and intentional tort cases for hundreds of years. With toxic torts, however, new wrinkles arise because the mechanistic or corpuscularian model does not conform to the evolutions in science toward deeper dependence on probabilistic and statistical evidence to establish causal relationships. Brennan continues his analysis by relating tort law's dependency on mechanistic causation to the corrective justice rationale for tort liability, and how that model is strained by toxic tort litigation:

> In summary, legal notions of causation reflect a complex interplay of several concepts. But for causation or cause in fact, which reflects commonly held assumptions about causation as well as certain moral and political notions of responsibility, tends to dominate the disposition of tort claims. Moreover, this rendition of but for causation coincides neatly with that of corpuscularian science. Probabilistic linkage is distinguished from but for cause, but has a nebulous role in Anglo–American legal reasoning. Probabilistic causal notions correspond to the causal notions that modern science

employs in that they are based on probabilistic evidence rather than simply deductively derived causal chains. * * *

From this discussion of competing notions of causation in law and science emerges a hypothesis that explains why courts have so much trouble with causation issues in toxic tort litigation. The scientific association between a toxic substance and injury to a person relies on probabilistic evidence: epidemiological studies and statistical associations. Philosophers of science readily accept such evidence and, indeed, acknowledge that probabilistic reasoning dominates much of physics and medicine. In corpuscularian writing, probabilistic evidence is second best, if acceptable at all, and corpuscularian notions of causation coincide with but for concepts of causation in tort law. Both rely heavily on causal chain analyses and individual actions. Corrective justice aspects of tort law assume the existence of traceable causal chains leading from actor to harm. As a result, tort law tends to induce a corpuscularian approach to scientific evidence. Litigants bringing scientific issues to court are expected to show causes in fact or but for causes, with minimal support from the policies of proximate cause.

A corpuscularian judge would not want to deal with probabilistic notions, as he would regard these as inferior methods of reasoning. Rather than accept probabilistic statements, a corpuscularian judge would delay a decision until deductive, mechanistic, but for causes are available. Nor would a corpuscularian judge welcome uncertainty in a scientific issue—uncertainty will be overcome according to positivism, and it is best to wait until this occurs. In addition, tort law's corrective justice aspects would not permit uncertainty in the causal assignment of responsibility.

In this regard, common law courts are neither unscientific nor ignorant. Rather, they cling to conceptions of individual responsibility that coincide neatly with eighteenth century science's notions of causation. Thus, it is not enough simply to say that courts should adopt probabilistic reasoning. They must be instructed. But given the importance of the moral concept of individual responsibility in tort law, we can expect courts to accommodate only so much probabilistic reasoning.

Unfortunately, toxic substance injury cases cannot produce mechanistic, deductively-derived causal evidence, and a corpuscularian judge cannot process the available probabilistic evidence. Thus, the causation problem in toxic tort litigation could result from an epistemological quandary. Judges, using but for causation when analyzing tort claims, may slip into corpuscularian reasoning about scientific evidence, even when that evidence is primarily probabilistic.

1. Why do corrective justice and notions of individual accountability require a mechanistic or causal chains treatment of cause-in-fact? Would the same be true if tort law's rationale rests or should rest on

deterrence and efficiency considerations? Are there other reasons why science has moved inexorably toward probabilistic evidence while legal institutions have been more hesitant to do so?

2. On the philosophy of cause and effect, many writers have had influence over the centuries. For example, John Stuart Mill in 1862 defined the concept in these words: "The cause, then, philosophically speaking, is the sum total of the conditions positive and negative taken together; the whole of the contingencies of every description, which being realized, the consequent invariably follows." John Stuart Mill, 3 A System of Logic, Ratiocinative and Inductive, ch. V, § 3, ch. VIII, §§ 1–4 in 7 The Collected Works of J.S. Mill (J. Robson, ed. 1973). It is interesting that Mill's definition is empirical because it does not require an understanding of how or why the relationship exists; only that if certain conditions do exist, then certain consequences follow. Understanding the mechanisms or instrumentalities that may explain these relationships among conditions and consequences is not a necessary part of the analysis. David Hume likewise observed that "we are never able, in a single instance, to discover any power or necessary connection, any quality which binds the effect to the cause, and renders the one the infallible consequence of the other. We only find that one does actually, in fact, follow the other." David Hume, 1 Treatise on Human Nature, Pt. III, §§ 14–15 (Selby-Bigge Rev. ed., P. Nidditch 1978); see also T. Beauchamp & A. Rosenberg, The Problem of Causation 284–300 (1981).

3. Based on the writings of Hume and Mill and others, it appears that the effort in law and science to define "cause" is not to identify a single, exclusive and unitary cause, but rather to identify or isolate some of the "contingencies" or "conditions" which are part of the causal web. Dr. Kenneth Rothman, one of the nation's leading epidemiologists, has described this same idea of a constellation of causes producing a disease. He notes that while "a cause which inevitably produces the effect is sufficient, * * * most causes that are of interest in the health field are components of sufficient causes, but are not sufficient in themselves." Kenneth J. Rothman, Causes, 104 Am.J.Epidem. 587, 588 (1976); see also Kenneth J. Rothman, Modern Epidemiology 11–12 (1986); Richard W. Wright, Causation, Responsibility, Risk, Probability, Naked Statistics and Proof: Pruning the Bramble Bush by Clarifying Concepts, 73 Iowa L.Rev. 1788 (1986) (explaining Wright's necessary element of sufficient set (NESS) test, which captures the idea that an entire spectrum of causal contributions is necessary for the caused condition without any one causal contribution being indispensable).

b. The Dual Causation Question

In determining whether a plaintiff can establish that the toxic substance and exposure to it was the cause in fact of the harm suffered, the inquiry can be analyzed as two separate inquiries: (1) Was the toxic substance *capable* of causing the *kind* of harm of which the plaintiff complains? This is a generic question since it focuses not on the particulars of the plaintiff's experience regarding the extent and duration of exposure, but on the general questions about propensities of the chemical agents to cause the kind of harm plaintiff alleges. The Bendectin cases set forth below address largely this question, which rely heavily upon epidemiological and other scientific studies and that are not dependent on the particulars of plaintiff's case. (2) Was *this plaintiff's* harm actually caused by the exposure to the defendant's chemical rather than being attributable to some other source? The answer to this question typically focuses on the testimony of medical doctors who have examined the plaintiff or his medical records, or conducted other tests specifically relating to the plaintiff.

In Sterling v. Velsicol Chemical Corp., 855 F.2d 1188 (6th Cir. 1988)(set forth in Chapter 5), the Sixth Circuit considered the claims of various resident groups for enhanced risk of cancer, cancerphobia, and immune system dysfunction arising from defendant's hazardous waste which had contaminated plaintiffs' water supply. The trial court had certified a class action and had relied on the proofs of five representative plaintiffs to establish causation for the class. The Sixth Circuit's discussion of causation is extremely important because the court recognized that these causation-in-fact issues must usually be divided into two discrete analyses:

> [T]he [trial] court, as is appropriate in this type of mass tort class action litigation, divided its causation analysis into two parts. It was first established that Velsicol was responsible for the contamination and that the particular contaminants were capable of producing injuries of the types allegedly suffered by the plaintiffs. Up to this point in the proceedings, the five representative plaintiffs were acting primarily in their representative capacity to the class as a whole. This enabled the court to determine a kind of generic causation—whether the combination of the chemical contaminants and the plaintiffs' exposure to them had the capacity to cause the harm alleged. This still left the matter of individual proximate cause to be determined. Although such generic and individual causation may appear to be inextricably intertwined, the procedural device of the class action permitted the court initially to assess the defendant's potential liability for its conduct without regard to the individual components of each plaintiff's injuries. However, from this point forward, it became the responsibility of each individual plaintiff to show that his or her specific injuries or damages were proximately caused by ingestion or otherwise using the contaminated water. We cannot emphasize this point strongly enough because generalized proofs will not suffice to prove individual damages. The main problem on review stems from a failure to differentiate between the general and the particular. This is an understandably easy trap to fall into in mass tort litigation. Although many common issues of fact and law will be capable of resolution on a group basis, individual particularized damages still must be proved on an individual basis.

Where the damages involve bodily injuries, it must be shown to a reasonable medical certainty that the contaminated water was the cause of the injury. * * * This standard implicates the qualifications of the witnesses testifying, the acceptance of the scientific community of their theories, and the degree of certainty as to their conclusions. This is particularly true when dealing with injuries or diseases of a type that may be the product of a variety of causes and inflict society at random, often with no known specific origin. * * *

It is important to recognize the relationship between the legal question to be resolved and the propriety of applying class action procedures: aggregative approaches work effectively in resolving the generic causation question but are of lesser utility in answering the individual causation question. (Chapter 13 contains a fuller discussion of these issues). The court identified the appropriate standard as that of a "reasonable medical certainty," which requires more than speculation or conjecture based on probability, likelihood, an educated guess, or an opinion that something is "more likely than not."

What do you think of the test of a "reasonable medical certainty" for determining whether the plaintiff's illness or disease was caused by exposure to the toxic substance? How high is a reasonable medical certainty? Is it like proof beyond a reasonable doubt?

In *Sterling* the court reviewed the causation evidence in each of the five individual cases point by point. It rejected as insufficient testimony regarding one plaintiff's kidney cancer:

Plaintiff's testifying physician, Dr. Rhamy, stated that while "it's more likely it was caused by the chemicals, * * * [it] is difficult to determine." Dr. Rhamy further stated that "[n]o one knows what causes cancer of the kidney." Dr. Rhamy's conclusions that Wilbanks' environmental exposure to carbon tetrachloride was a "reasonable cause" for his kidney cancer and a statement by another testifying physician, Dr. Rodericks, that Wilbank's cancer was "consistent" with the exposure do not constitute sufficient medical proof of causation.

Why is the testimony of Dr. Rhamy deficient? The court also rejected such testimony as "most probably secondary to chemical exposure;" "probably due to exposure to toxic chemicals;" "most probable cause;" and "most likely reason." Four of the five cases were remanded for recalculation of damages to account for the exclusion of those items for which the court found there was insufficient proof of causation.

For another opinion discussing the nature of the dual causation inquiry, but rejecting the "reasonable medical certainty" standard in favor of the more typical "more probable than not" test, see Earl v. Cryovac, A Division of W.R. Grace & Co., 115 Idaho 1087, 772 P.2d 725 (1989), in which the court reversed a summary judgment for the defendant where a meatpacker had alleged that his obstructive pulmonary disease was caused by exposure to chemicals in defendant's plastic film used to wrap meat products.

This Chapter seeks to address the causation in fact question in some depth. Because environmental torts necessarily involve subtle and complex scientific and medical questions, this Chapter explores the subjects of toxicology and epidemiology in sufficient depth (it is hoped) to permit the student to intelligently assess what rules of causality courts are in fact applying to these questions and to evaluate for yourself what standards should be applied. These questions also require an examination of evidentiary issues and consideration of the standards for admissibility of scientific evidence, which have evolved in the last decade.

c. Early Use of Probabilistic Evidence

One early case to raise difficult issues of causality is Stubbs v. City of Rochester, 226 N.Y. 516, 124 N.E. 137 (1919) in which the New York Court of Appeals addressed the causation-in-fact question between a contaminated city water supply and the plaintiff's typhoid fever. The City had two water systems, one called the Holley Water System which contained sewage from the Genesee River, and the other the Hemlock Water System, which provided drinking water to the residents in sections of the City. After complaints were received in June of 1910 the city health officers tested the water at several homes and discovered a "serious condition of contamination," whereupon the City notified the public not to drink the water without boiling it. An investigation lasting several months revealed the source of the contamination to be discharges from the Holley System into the Hemlock System because of a malfunctioning check valve between the two.

The plaintiff contended that the City was negligent in permitting poisonous and polluted water from the Genesee River to flow into the Holley System pipes and into the Hemlock Water System, contaminating the water and making it dangerous to the life and health of city residents. The plaintiff recovered a judgment at the trial court which the appellate division had reversed. The court framed the issue as whether the "plaintiff produced evidence from which inference might reasonably be drawn that the cause of his illness was due to the use of contaminated water furnished by the defendant." The defendant contended that plaintiff's evidence was deficient because (1) it failed to establish that he contracted typhoid fever by drinking contaminated water, and (2) it was incumbent on plaintiff to establish that his illness was not due to any other cause to which typhoid fever may be attributed. The expert testimony revealed *eight* other possible causes including impure raw fruits and vegetables, infected milk, certain flies, contact with an infected person, and other known and unknown causes. The court's discussion is instructive:

> * * * [T]he source of contamination having been discovered, the doctor made an investigation as to the reported cases of typhoid fever in the city in the months of August, September, and October, for the purpose of determining the number of cases, where the cases came from, what gave rise to it, and he stated that in his opinion the

outbreak of typhoid was due to polluted water, contaminated as he discovered afterwards by sewage. In answer to a hypothetical question embracing generally the facts asserted by plaintiff the witness testified that he had an opinion as to the cause of the infection of plaintiff, and such opinion was that it was due to contaminated water.

Dr. Dodge, of the faculty of the University of Rochester, a professor of biology, also bacteriologist of the city of Rochester, about October 1st made an analysis of samples of water taken from No. 58 Warehouse street, and from the Holley system, corner of Oak and Platt streets. The analysis of the water from Warehouse street disclosed the number of bacteria to be 880 cubic centimeter. The analysis of the Holley water disclosed 4,000 bacteria cubic centimeter. An analysis of the Hemlock water at the University disclosed approximately 150 to 200. While his examination did not disclose any colon bacillus, it did disclose some evidence of the same. Dr. Brady, the physician who attended the plaintiff, and Dr. Culkin both testified that in their opinion the plaintiff contracted typhoid fever from drinking polluted water.

Plaintiff called a witness who resided on Brown street, about two minutes' walk from the bridge, and proved by her that she drank water from the Hemlock mains in the fall of 1910 and was ill with typhoid fever. Thereupon counsel for defendant stipulated that 57 witnesses which the plaintiff proposed to call will testify that they drank water from the Hemlock taps in the vicinity of the district west of the Genesee river and north of Allen street in the summer and fall of 1910, and during said summer and fall suffered from typhoid fever, that in view of the stipulation such witnesses need not be called by plaintiff, and the stipulation shall have the same force and effect as though the witnesses had been called and testified to the facts.

* * *

A table of statistics as to typhoid fever in the city of Rochester for the years 1901–1910, inclusive, was produced by the health officer and received in evidence. That exhibit was the subject of comment in the opinion of Justice Foote upon the first appeal. The fact is evident from a perusal of his opinion that upon the first trial plaintiff did not undertake to establish the number of cases of typhoid fever in the district where the water was contaminated as compared with the total number of cases in the city in 1910, which evidence was supplied upon this trial. The statistics disclose that the number of typhoid cases in the city in 1910 was 223, an excess of 50 cases of any year of the nine years preceding. Recalling that complaints as to water commenced in the summer of 1910, and as shown by the evidence that typhoid fever does not develop until two or three weeks after the bacilli have been taken into the system, in connection with the fact that the source of contamination was not discovered until October, the statistics disclose that of the 223 cases of typhoid in the city in the year 1910, 180 cases appear during the months of August, September, October, and November as against 43 cases during the remaining eight months, 35 of which were prior to August and 8 in the month of December, two months after the source of contamination of the water was discovered.

The evidence on the trial discloses that at least 58 witnesses, residents of the district, drank the contaminated water and suffered from typhoid fever in addition to plaintiff; thus one-third of the 180 cases during the months stated were shown to exist in that district.

Counsel for respondent asserts that there was a failure of proof on the part of plaintiff, in that he did not establish that he contracted disease by drinking contaminated water, and in support of his argument cites a rule of law that when there are several possible causes of injury for one or more of which a defendant is not responsible, plaintiff cannot recover without proving that the injury was sustained wholly or in part by a cause for which defendant was responsible. He submits that it was essential for plaintiff to eliminate all other of seven causes from which the disease might have been contracted. If the argument should prevail and the rule of law stated is not subject to any limitation, the present case illustrates the impossibility of a recovery in any case based upon like facts. One cause of the disease is stated by counsel to be 'personal contact with typhoid carriers or other persons suffering with the disease, whereby bacilli are received and accidentally transferred by the hands or some other portion of the person or clothes to the mouth.' Concededly a person is affected with typhoid some weeks before the disease develops. The plaintiff here resided three miles distant from his place of employment, and traveled to and from his work upon the street car. To prove the time when he was attacked with typhoid, then find every individual who traveled on the same car with him, and establish by each one of them that he or she was free from the disease even to his or her clothing is impossible. Again, the evidence disclosed that typhoid fever was caused by sources unknown to medical science. If the word of the rule stated is to prevail plaintiff would be required to eliminate sources which had not yet been determined or ascertained. I do not believe the rule stated to be as inflexible as claimed for. If two or more possible causes exist, for only one of which a defendant may be liable, and a party injured established facts from which it can be said with reasonable certainty that the direct cause of the injury was the one for which the defendant was liable, the party has complied with the spirit of the rule.

The plaintiff was employed in the immediate locality where the water was contaminated. He drank the water daily. The consumption of contaminated water is a very frequent cause of typhoid fever. In the locality there were a large number of cases of typhoid fever, and near to 60 individuals who drank the water and had suffered from typhoid fever in that neighborhood appeared as witnesses on behalf of plaintiff. The plaintiff gave evidence of his habits, his home surroundings, and his method of living, and the medical testimony indicated that his illness was caused by drinking contaminated water. Without reiteration of the facts disclosed on the trial I do not believe that the case on the part of plaintiff was so lacking in proof as matter of law that his complaint should be dismissed. On the contrary, the most favorable inferences deducible from the plaintiff were such as would justify a submission of the facts to a jury as to the reasonable inferences to be drawn therefrom, and a verdict rendered thereon for either party would rest, not in conjecture, but upon reasonable possibilities.

Notes and Questions

1. The opinion is remarkable for the sophistication it brings to the complex causation question over 70 years ago. The court employed a "reasonable certainty" test of causation. Do you think the evidence satisfied that standard of proof? Or did the court simply rule that there existed sufficient evidence to justify submitting the question to the jury, that is, the evidence of causation was not insufficient as a matter of law? What about the burden of eliminating other possible causes for the plaintiff's typhoid—how strongly must plaintiff's evidence exclude those other potential causes?

2. The role of expert witnesses was pervasive. Plaintiff obtained a favorable opinion from Dr. Goler, the health officer of the City, that the typhoid was caused by the contaminated water, and two other physicians similarly concluded that the typhoid was attributable to the contaminated water. The parties' use of statistical evidence was significant in demonstrating the substantial increase in the incidence of typhoid in 1910 over prior years, and the concentration of cases in the four months during which the contamination was discovered.

In a recent article, Professor Walker has reanalyzed the data from *Stubbs*, added population data and applied contemporary epidemiological methodologies to arrive at a relative risk of 2.5, meaning that for Stubbs and other persons similarly situated, the risk of contracting typhoid was two and one-half times greater for those who ingested the contaminated water than for those who did not. In this next section we explore those principles of epidemiology which enable such a comparison to be made and to draw causal inferences. Intuitively, should a 2 1/2 times greater incidence suffice to establish causation in a toxic tort case? See Vern R. Walker, The Concept of Baseline Risk in Tort Litigation, 80 Ky. L.J. 631 (1992).

2. THE SCIENTIFIC METHOD: TOXICOLOGY AND EPIDEMIOLOGY

Because toxic and environmental harms involve complex and often elusive questions of science and medicine, it is necessary to develop some understanding of the basic concepts of toxicology and epidemiology. The outcome of many cases which are considered in this Chapter are, to a considerable extent, controlled by the quality of the scientific evidence which the parties introduce to the fact finder.

GERALD W. BOSTON, A MASS EXPOSURE MODEL OF
TOXIC CAUSATION: THE CONTENT OF SCIENTIFIC
PROOF AND THE REGULATORY EXPERIENCE

18 Colum. J. Envtl. L. 181, 213–25, 231–40 (1993).

B. TOXICOLOGY AND RISK

Toxicology and toxicologists are primarily concerned with the capacity of chemicals or environmental agents to produce harmful effects in living organisms. Toxicologists study the interactions between chemicals and biological systems, attempt to identify the mechanism of action and attempt to assess quantitatively the relationship between doses of chemicals and responses in living systems.

* * *

For the most part, toxicologists conduct investigations of toxicity using exposed living animals, typically rats and mice (in vivo studies), or by studying cultures or treating isolated tissues or cells (in vitro and short term studies). The objectives of these studies are two-fold: (1) to examine the nature of the adverse effects produced by the chemical agent, and (2) to assess the probability and cause of their occurrence. The primary method by which the toxicologist accomplishes both tasks is the development and use of dose-response relationships or gradients.

All chemicals are toxic at some dose. An expression that captures this idea is that "there are no harmless substances—there are only harmless ways of using substances." This statement serves to emphasize the second basic function of toxicology, risk assessment, which is an evaluation of the conditions under which an adverse effect can be produced or is likely to have occurred.

* * *

To answer the questions of what level of exposure is sufficient to produce harm and what is the expected harm for that level of exposure necessitates development of dose-response relationships. Toxicologists state that a response exhibits a dose-response relationship when a consistent, mathematical relationship describes the proportion of individuals responding for a given dosage interval for a given exposure period. For example, the risk of contracting lung cancer from exposure to asbestos particles increases one percent for each fiber per cubic centimeter year of exposure.

* * *

C. TOXICOLOGIC STUDIES

The principal types of toxicologic studies are: (1) short term screening assays (such as in vitro laboratory experiments that examine bacteria or cells); (2) animal bioassays that involve exposure of groups of animals, usually rodents, to the chemical under investigation to test for the onset of various adverse effects; and (3) epidemiologic studies that compare populations of exposed and non-exposed humans in order to draw inferences respecting possible causal associations. * * *

1. Short Term Assays

Short term in vitro (i.e., test-tube) tests are used to identify various kinds of toxins by examining the biochemical effects of substances on cells, bacteria, organs, or embryos. For example, * * * [i]n vitro testing for teratogens involves transplanting animal fetal cells, organs, or embryos into a medium where they are subjected to the chemical under investigation in order to examine the effects on the transplanted tissues. Another form of toxicity study is the examination and comparison of the molecular structures of the agent under investigation with that of known toxins. It is believed that if the structures are similar, then the toxic effects produced may also be similar.

All of these forms of short term and in vitro assays focus on the biochemical mechanisms. They examine the smallest building blocks of life and subject them to intensive investigation and experimentation in hopes of developing data useful in understanding the cellular mechanics of the disease process in humans. Yet, despite their increasing sophistication, the value of such tests in establishing causal relationships in humans is problematic. * * *

2. Animal Toxicity Studies

a. Basic Objectives

The intermediate step in the hierarchy of toxicological evidence in support of causal relationships between a chemical and human pathology is animal toxicity studies. * * * As with all toxicity studies, the objective is to identify the nature of the adverse health effect produced by a chemical agent and the range of doses over which such effects are observed. * * * The beginning point for toxicity animal studies is to investigate the acute, single-dose toxicity of a chemical. * * * Toxicologists determine the lethal properties of a chemical and estimate its LD_{50} dose, which is defined as that dose which on average is lethal for fifty percent of the animals tested. * * *

Once acute toxicity data is arrived at, subchronic and chronic studies may be undertaken, which involve repeated or continuous exposures for several weeks or months or the full lifetime of the animal. These studies identify the specific organs or body systems that may be damaged and the conditions of exposure and dose that are required to produce such an effect and the exposure level at which no adverse effects are observed. * * *

* * *

b. Designs of Toxicity Animal Studies

Rats and mice are the favorite species among toxicologists because of cost and handling considerations as well as a greater understanding of their genetic background and disease susceptibility. Moreover, because their lifespans are short, toxicologists can perform lifetime studies within a reasonable period. * * *

Two important considerations in test design involve the magnitude of the doses administered and the duration of exposure. Beginning with the LD_{50} dose, investigators study the effects of lower doses administered over longer periods of time. * * * The selection of the dose range is controversial because the * * * doses administered are proportionally much higher than the levels to which humans are exposed. However, such high doses are essential because of the relatively short life spans of the bioassay tests and the practical limit on the number of animals that can be tested. * * *

c. Interpretation of Animal Studies

The single largest purpose for undertaking animal bioassays is to enable regulatory agencies to determine what substances to regulate and to set permissible exposure levels, including possibly zero, for such substances. * * *

d. Extrapolative Models

Critical to the risk assessment process is the selection of an extrapolative model that takes data from the bioassays and predicts the level of risk in humans. * * * Risk assessments must extrapolate from results in high-dosage animal tests to low-dose animal risks and then to long-term human hazards at significantly lower doses.[159] Scientists have

159. The graph in Section III illustrates the problem of extrapolating from animal data at the top ranges of the dose level to human exposures at lower dose levels.

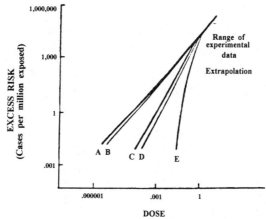

DOSE

Figure 3A. Low-dose extrapolation for a carcinogen under several mathematical models: A, B, C, D, and E.   [G12423]

Logically, these are the two distinct routes to follow in the extrapolation, since there are logically two distinct dose-response curves involved. One can extrapolate from high dose to low dose using the animal dose-response curve, and then extrapolate to humans, or extrapolate to humans at high doses and then use a human dose-response curve to extrapolate to low doses. See Alan Rosenthal et al., Legislating Ac-

developed a number of competing extrapolative models during the past two decades, but none has achieved general acceptance. * * *

* * *

III. EPIDEMIOLOGY

A. *Introduction*

Epidemiology is the study of the distribution and determinants of disease in human populations. Epidemiologists test biological inferences by combining the disciplines of statistics (biostatistics more precisely), sociology, and demography; they look for unusual incidences of human disease and endeavor to identify those factors which distinguish the affected population group from other groups. Epidemiologic studies can be either experimental or observational. In experimental studies one group is deliberately exposed to a carefully controlled amount of a chemical and compared to another equivalent but non-exposed group, as in the case of clinical trials of pharmaceutical products. However, society's ethical and practical constraints would not accept taking a putative carcinogen and experimentally subjecting it to one group of persons in order to assess whether they contracted cancer. Therefore, in the context of pollutants and the kinds of toxic substances involved in most toxic tort litigation, observational studies are the norm. These studies are made possible because of "unplanned experiments" in which certain persons have already been exposed to a chemical agent (e.g., persons voluntarily choosing to smoke cigarettes; or non-smoking persons choosing to live with persons who smoke), while others have not been so exposed, enabling investigators to compare the incidence of a particular disease among the two groups.

B. *Study Designs and Objectives*

1. Types of Study Designs

There are at least five kinds of epidemiological studies, although only the last two are the focus of much of this article. * * *

* * *

4. Case-control studies compare individuals with the disease (cases) to persons who do not have the disease (controls) in an attempt to retrospectively determine commonalities within the diseased group which may reveal a relationship to an exposure to a chemical agent. For example, if an investigator were interested in whether exposure to environmental tobacco smoke ("ETS") may be related to lung cancer in non-smokers, she could take non-smokers who contract the disease (cases) and compare them to those non-smokers without lung cancer (controls) in terms of whether they

ceptable Cancer Risk from Exposure to Tox-   (1992).
ic Chemicals, 19 Ecology L.Q. 269, 282

had lived with a smoking spouse. One would expect that if there is an association between lung cancer and exposure to environmental tobacco smoke, a greater proportion of cases than of controls would have a history of exposure to ETS. This one example reveals a number of potential problems that affect the validity of the association. First, it is essential to obtain accurate information about past exposures—i.e., were the cases actually exposed to ETS? When and for how long? Where did the exposures take place? And did the cases actually smoke themselves (were they ex-smokers or never-smokers)? Second is the problem of recall bias respecting past exposures in which it is possible that those with the disease (cases) are more likely to recall exposures than those without the disease (controls). Third, in selecting the control group care must be taken to assure that persons exposed are not artificially excluded; that is, the cases and controls should be comparable in all respects except their disease status. If there are some exposed persons in the cases but none in the controls, it will likely increase the proportion of cases with the exposure and yield misleading proportional data.

The case-control study methodology is reflected diagrammatically as follows:

CASE-CONTROL (RETROSPECTIVE) STUDY

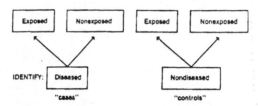

Viewed retrospectively, this study will compare the ratio of cases that were exposed to the ratio of controls that were exposed, and if exposure is a factor in the disease, the study should show a higher ratio of exposure status among cases than controls.

5. The cohort or follow-up study is regarded as the most powerful of the observational types in terms of its ability to identify causal associations. These studies begin with a group of exposed persons and compare them to a group of individuals who were not exposed and tracks them prospectively to determine the incidence over time within the two groups of a specific disease being investigated. In a prospective study, the objective is to determine if the risk of developing the disease is greater in exposed individuals than in non-exposed individuals. The cohort study alleviates one of the major problems of the case-control study—that of memory bias—because the exposure is the starting point for constructing the study.

The cohort study can be represented diagrammatically as follows:

<u>DESIGN OF A PROSPECTIVE STUDY</u>

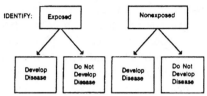

2. Measurement of Risks

The cohort study enables the investigator to calculate the comparative rates of disease within the exposed and non-exposed groups and to compare those two rates. This comparison of rates is the relative risk: The risk in the exposed population relative to the risk in the non-exposed population and may be expressed as:

$$\text{Relative Risk (RR)} = \frac{R_1}{R_2},$$

where R_1 = the risk of disease in the exposed population and R_2 = the risk of disease in a non-exposed population.

If the relative risk equals one (i.e., the numerator is the same as the denominator), the risk in the exposed group is the same as the risk in the nonexposed group, and there is no suggestion of any association between the factor and the disease in question. If the relative risk is greater than one, the risk in the exposed group is greater than in the non-exposed group, and there is a positive association between the exposure and the disease. Conversely, if the relative risk is less than one, then the risk in exposed individuals is less than the risk in non-exposed individuals, suggesting a protective effect. A study of workers exposed to asbestos in connection with their employment by asbestos product manufacturers revealed that they were dying from lung cancer at a rate of 64 per 100,000 per year, whereas in the general population of males during the same period and at the same ages the death rate from lung cancer was only 31 per 100,000 per year. The relative risk for this study would be expressed as: $RR = \dfrac{64}{31} = 2.06$.

In epidemiology the probability of causation is determined by the attributable risk ("AR"), which is defined as the difference between the risk in the exposed and the risk in the non-exposed, and is expressed as: $AR = \dfrac{P(RR - 1)}{P(RR - 1) + 1}$,

where P = proportion exposed in the study group and R = relative risk of the study group. If the entire group is exposed, $P = 1$ and $AR = \dfrac{RR - 1}{RR}$.

Based on the above study on asbestos workers the $AR = \dfrac{2.06 - 1.00}{2.06}$, or 51% which means that the probability that a given case of lung cancer in the exposed group was attributable to the asbestos exposure would be about even, or 51 percent. This percent is sometimes referred to as the etiologic probability or etiologic fraction.

Of course, not all cases of lung cancer are caused by asbestos exposure; that is, lung cancer has many causes, some known, such as smoking, and some unknown. Therefore within the exposed group there will be "background" cases of lung cancer which are not attributable to the exposure to asbestos. Additionally, the relative risks will vary according to occupational groups because of the different exposure levels and duration of the exposure to asbestos. Finally, note that if the RR for a certain exposure is 1 or less, the corresponding AR is 0; no etiologic probability can be attributed to that exposure and the cancer (or other disease) is simply a background case.

3. Criteria for Determining Causal Relationships

Epidemiological evidence which reveals that exposure to a chemical creates a relative risk greater than one does not end the inquiry into causality. The enhanced relative risk reveals only an association between two factors—the exposure and the disease. The association is not necessarily a causal relationship because other factors may be at work. For example, one major study revealed an association between coffee consumption and the development of pancreatic cancer. How should such an association be interpreted? Does coffee drinking actually cause pancreatic cancer or is coffee consumption associated with an increased risk of pancreatic cancer because of confounding by smoking? Smoking is known to increase the risk of pancreatic cancer and people who smoke often drink coffee. Thus, the association could be causal or could be explained by the association of smoking with both coffee drinking and pancreatic cancer.

To determine if an association is causal, epidemiologists have developed criteria that treat the statistical association as the starting point of the analysis. Because the associational data alone do not permit biological inferences, scientists apply additional, more particularistic, analytic and biologic tests before reaching a conclusion respecting a causal relationship. * * *

The criteria are:

1. *The strength of the association.* The greater the relative risk, the more likely it is that the association is causal. For example, Hill observed that the mortality rates for lung cancer among heavy cigarette smokers (those who smoked more than one pack per day) ranged from twenty to thirty times the normal rates of lung cancer across a large number of epidemiologic studies. The stronger the relative risks, the less likely it is that the association is explainable by confounding factors, bias, or other factors. On the

other hand, smaller relative risks may be explainable on the basis of other factors, although the smallness of the risk does not rule out causal relationships.

2. *Consistency.* The presence of repeatedly consistent observations made in different populations over differing observation periods, utilizing different study designs and under different circumstances implies that the associations are causal. The chance that all of the associations are the result of error or fallacy is simply too remote. Again, however, inconsistent associations across studies do not rule out a causal relationship, since differing study methodologies might produce varying relative risks.

3. *Specificity.* This criterion refers to the correspondence of exposure to a specific disease. Is the exposure associated with a specific disease and vice versa? Is the association restricted to specific workers and to a specific disease (specific cancer site or specific histological type)? The argument for a causal relationship is weakened if the relationship is nonspecific. However, this criterion has been de-emphasized in recent years because many causes have multiple effects and many diseases have multiple causes. For example, cigarette smoking can cause malignancies other than lung cancer and some lung cancer patients never smoke. In short, the presence of specificity adds to the cogency of the inference of a causal relationship, but its absence does not preclude such an inference.

4. *Temporality.* This seemingly simple criterion refers to the requirement that exposure to the causal factor must precede disease in order to support a causal association. This criterion is particularly important for chronic diseases with long latency periods (time between onset of exposure and diagnosis) and for study factors which change over time.

5. *Biologic gradient (dose-response relationship).* A dose-response relationship refers to the severity or frequency of disease increasing with the level or duration of exposure. If the association reveals such a dose-response relationship or biologic gradient, the argument for causal association becomes very persuasive. For example, the observation that lung cancer risk increases with the amount of cigarettes smoked lends great support to the argument that smoking is a causal factor of lung cancer. A dose-response relationship allows a simple and intuitive explanation, and obviously enhances the causal interpretation. Unfortunately, in many epidemiological studies, precise exposure data are absent, making it difficult or impossible to calculate dose-response relationships. The existence of a dose-response curve does not invariably suggest causality because there may be a confounding factor that also yields a separate gradient.

6. *Biologic plausibility.* This criterion looks to how compatible is the association with the biologic knowledge then known,

including information from animal studies, pharmacokinetics, geno-toxicity, and in vitro studies. However, given the constant flux in the state of knowledge respecting biology with new theories frequently advanced, rejected, and modified to fit new evidence, too much reliance on consistency with existing knowledge would run counter to more basic exploratory and creative scientific principles.

7. *Coherence.* This criterion, closely related to plausibility, considers whether the associational data seriously conflicts with the natural history and biology of the disease. For example, do animal studies, histopathological studies, or other evidence cohere with the epidemiologic findings? However, the absence of coherent information, as distinguished from the presence of conflicting evidence, should not be taken as proof that the association is not causal.

———

For further study on these topics, the following sources are suggested: Austin B. Hill, The Environment and Disease: Association or Causation?, 58 Proc. Royal Soc'y Med. 295 (1965); U.S. Environmental Protection Agency, Guidelines for Carcinogen Assessment, 51 Fed. Reg. 33,992 (1986); James Huff, et al., Scientific Concepts: Value and Significance of Chemical Carcinogenesis Studies, 31 Annals Rev. of Pharm. & Toxic. 621 (1991); Kenneth J. Rothman, Modern Epidemiology (1st ed. 1986); Ellen K. Silbergeld, The Role of Toxicology in Causation: A Scientific Perspective, 1 Courts, Health Science and the Law 374 (1991); Elements of Toxicology and Chemical Risk Assessment, Handbook for Nonscientists, Attorneys and Decisionmakers (Environ 1986); Chris F. Wilkinson, Toxicology and the Law, in The Role of Science in Toxic Tort Litigation, Evaluating Causation and Risk, ABA Torts and Insurance Practice Section (1988); Ernest Hodgson & Patricia Levi, Modern Toxicology (Elsevier Science Publ. 1987); Michael A. Kamrin, Toxicology (Lewis 1988).

3. STANDARDS OF ADMISSIBILITY OF SCIENTIFIC EVIDENCE

Because toxic tort cases necessarily implicate the scientific principles described above, a critical and controversial concern in the litigated cases is the admissibility of the expert opinions offered by the parties to establish the ultimate factual issue of causation. Whether an expert's opinion is admissible is governed by several sections of the Federal Rules of Evidence or state evidentiary counterparts. Rule 104(a) authorizes the trial court to make preliminary determinations "concerning the qualifications of a person to be a witness" and the "admissibility of evidence." The Rules of Evidence 401, 402 and 403 are also pertinent in determining the admissibility of expert testimony. Rule 401 defines "relevant evidence," Rule 402 declares that "all relevant evidence is admissible, except as otherwise provided by the Constitution, by Act of

Congress or by these rules," and Rule 403 allows the exclusion of relevant evidence when "its probative value is substantially outweighed by the danger of unfair prejudice, confusion of issues or misleading the jury * * * " Finally, Rules 702 and 703 directly address the admissibility of expert testimony:

Rule 702—Testimony by Experts

If scientific, technical, or other specialized knowledge will assist the trier of fact to understand the evidence or to determine a fact in issue, a witness qualified as an expert by knowledge, skill, experience, training, or education, may testify thereto in the form of an opinion or otherwise.

Rule 703—Bases of Opinion Testimony by Experts

The facts or data in the particular case upon which an expert bases an opinion or inference may be those perceived by or made known to the expert at or before the hearing. If of a type reasonably relied upon by experts in the particular field in forming opinions or inferences upon the subject, the facts or data need not be admissible in evidence.

The credentials or qualifications of the proposed expert are relevant under Rule 702. The party calling the expert must satisfy the requirement by showing that the expert is qualified based on his or her knowledge, skill, experience, training, or education. Rule 702 does not require any specific degree, certification, or membership in particular societies or associations. Generally, the courts take a flexible and liberal attitude toward the sufficiency of the proposed experts' qualifications. See The National Institute for Trial Advocacy, Evidence: Text, Rules, Problems and Illustrations 250–52 (2d ed., rev. 1989) (hereafter NITA) for a description of the governing principles.

Courts in toxic tort cases have demonstrated considerable flexibility in allowing experts to render opinions as to the cause of plaintiff's injury, even though they were not medical doctors. For example, in Rubanick v. Witco Chemical Corp., 125 N.J. 421, 593 A.2d 733 (1991), the New Jersey Supreme Court held that an expert who possessed a doctorate in biochemistry, was a primary cancer researcher at the Sloan–Kettering Cancer Institute, and had published numerous articles on colon cancer, could testify that plaintiff's workplace exposure to PCBs had caused his colon cancer. Similarly, in Shilling v. Mobile Analytical Services, Inc., 65 Ohio St.3d 252, 602 N.E.2d 1154 (1993), the Ohio Supreme Court held that a Ph.D. specializing in neurotoxicology was qualified to render an opinion that the ingestion of gasoline injured the plaintiff's brain and nervous system.

The critical objective of Rule 702 is to enable expert testimony where it will assist the court and jury to understand the evidence introduced or to determine a fact, such as causation, in issue. In order for such expert testimony to be of assistance to the court or jury it must be predicated on a sufficiently reliable body of scientific, technical or other specialized knowledge. NITA identifies six factors which influence the reliability of the evidence derived from a scientific principle:

> (1) the validity of the underlying scientific principle; (2) the validity of the technique or process that applies the principle; (3) the condition of any instrumentation used in the process; (4) adherence to proper procedures; (5) the qualifications of the person who performs the test; and (6) the qualifications of the person who interprets the results.

The test articulated in Frye v. United States, 293 Fed. 1013, 1014 (D.C.Cir.1923) has been applied by many courts to determine the validity of the scientific principle and the technique applying it, measured by whether they "have gained general acceptance in the particular field in which [they] belong." The student is aware of the considerable diversity of views regarding the *Frye* standard. See Charles T. McCormick, Evidence § 203 at 608 (3d ed. 1984); United States v. Gould, 741 F.2d 45, 49 (4th Cir.1984); Graham C. Lilly, Introduction to the Law of Evidence 494–95 (2d ed. 1987). See the thorough discussion of the *Frye* standard, a rationale for its rejection, and related evidentiary issues in United States v. Downing, 753 F.2d 1224, 1232–1243 (3d Cir.1985). On this topic generally, which has stimulated considerable law review comment, see Paul C. Giannelli & Edmund J. Imwinkelried, Scientific Evidence ch.1 (1986 & Supp. 1991); Edmund J. Imwinkelried, The Standard for Admitting Scientific Evidence: A Critique from the Perspective of Juror Psychology, 28 Vill. L. Rev. 554 (1983).

In Daubert v. Merrell Dow Pharmaceuticals, Inc., __ U.S. __, 113 S.Ct. 2786, 125 L.Ed.2d 469 (1993), the Supreme Court unanimously laid the *Frye* test to rest and articulated a set of standards for federal courts to apply in determining the admissibility of expert testimony.

DAUBERT v. MERRELL DOW PHARMACEUTICALS, INC.

Supreme Court of the United States, 1993.
__ U.S. __, 113 S.Ct. 2786, 125 L.Ed.2d 469.

JUSTICE BLACKMUN delivered the opinion of the Court.

In this case we are called upon to determine the standard for admitting expert scientific testimony in a federal trial.

I

Petitioners Jason Daubert and Eric Schuller are minor children born with serious birth defects. They and their parents sued respondent in California state court, alleging that the birth defects had been caused by the mothers' ingestion of Bendectin, a prescription anti-nausea drug marketed by respondent. Respondent removed the suits to federal court on diversity grounds.

After extensive discovery, respondent moved for summary judgment, contending that Bendectin does not cause birth defects in humans and that petitioners would be unable to come forward with any admissible evidence that it does. In support of its motion, respondent submitted an affidavit of Steven H. Lamm, physician and epidemiologist, who is a well-credentialed expert on the risks from exposure to various chemical substances. Doctor Lamm stated that he had reviewed all the literature on Bendectin and human birth defects—more than 30 published studies involving over 130,000 patients. No study had found Bendectin to be a human teratogen (i.e., a substance capable of causing malformations in fetuses). On the basis of this review, Doctor Lamm concluded that maternal use of Bendectin during the first trimester of pregnancy has not been shown to be a risk factor for human birth defects.

Petitioners did not (and do not) contest this characterization of the published record regarding Bendectin. Instead, they responded to respondent's motion with the testimony of eight experts of their own, each of whom also possessed impressive credentials. These experts had concluded that Bendectin can cause birth defects. Their conclusions were based upon "in vitro" (test tube) and "in vivo" (live) animal studies that found a link between Bendectin and malformations; pharmacological studies of the chemical structure of Bendectin that purported to show similarities between the structure of the drug and that of other substances known to cause birth defects; and the "reanalysis" of previously published epidemiological (human statistical) studies.

The District Court granted respondent's motion for summary judgment. The court stated that scientific evidence is admissible only if the principle upon which it is based is " 'sufficiently established to have general acceptance in the field to which it belongs.' " The court concluded that petitioners' evidence did not meet this standard. Given the vast body of epidemiological data concerning Bendectin, the court held, expert opinion which is not based on epidemiological evidence is not admissible to establish causation. Thus, the animal-cell studies, live-animal studies, and chemical-structure analyses on which petitioners had relied could not raise by themselves a reasonably disputable jury issue regarding causation. Petitioners' epidemiological analyses, based as they were on recalculations of data in previously published studies that had found no causal link between the drug and birth defects, were ruled to be inadmissible because they had not been published or subjected to peer review.

The United States Court of Appeals for the Ninth Circuit affirmed. 951 F.2d 1128 (1991). Citing Frye v. United States, 293 F. 1013, 1014 (1923), the court stated that expert opinion based on a scientific technique is inadmissible unless the technique is "generally accepted" as reliable in the relevant scientific community.

* * *

We granted certiorari, 113 S.Ct. 320 (1992), in light of sharp divisions among the courts regarding the proper standard for the admission of expert testimony.

II

A

In the 70 years since its formulation in the Frye case, the "general acceptance" test has been the dominant standard for determining the admissibility of novel scientific evidence at trial. Although under increasing attack of late, the rule continues to be followed by a majority of courts, including the Ninth Circuit.

The Frye test has its origin in a short and citation-free 1923 decision concerning the admissibility of evidence derived from a systolic blood pressure deception test, a crude precursor to the polygraph machine. In what has become a famous (perhaps infamous) passage, the then Court of Appeals for the District of Columbia described the device and its operation and declared: "Just when a scientific principle or discovery crosses the line between the experimental and demonstrable stages is difficult to define. Somewhere in this twilight zone the evidential force of the principle must be recognized, and while courts will go a long way in admitting expert testimony deduced from a well-recognized scientific principle or discovery, the thing from which the deduction is made must be sufficiently established to have gained general acceptance in the particular field in which it belongs." 293 F., at 1014. Because the deception test had "not yet gained such standing and scientific recognition among physiological and psychological authorities as would justify the courts in admitting expert testimony deduced from the discovery, development, and experiments thus far made," evidence of its results was ruled inadmissible.

The merits of the Frye test have been much debated, and scholarship on its proper scope and application is legion.[4] Petitioners' primary attack, however, is not on the content but on the continuing authority of the rule. They contend that the Frye test was superseded by the adoption of the Federal Rules of Evidence. We agree.

We interpret the legislatively-enacted Federal Rules of Evidence as we would any statute. * * *

Frye, of course, predated the Rules by half a century. In United States v. Abel, 469 U.S. 45, 105 S.Ct. 465, 83 L.Ed.2d 450 (1984), we considered the pertinence of background common law in interpreting the Rules of Evidence. We noted that the Rules occupy the field, 105 S.Ct., at 467, but, quoting Professor Cleary, the Reporter explained that the common law nevertheless could serve as an aid to their application: "In principle, under the Federal Rules no common law of evidence remains. 'All relevant evidence is admissible, except as otherwise provided * * *.' In reality, of course, the body of common law knowledge continues to exist, though in the somewhat altered form of a source of guidance in the exercise of delegated powers." 105 S.Ct., at 469.

4. See, e.g., Green, Expert Witnesses and Sufficiency of Evidence in Toxic Substances Litigation: The Legacy of Agent Orange and Bendectin Litigation, 86 Nw. U.L.Rev. 643 (1992) (hereinafter Green); [other citations omitted].

Here there is a specific Rule that speaks to the contested issue. Rule 702, governing expert testimony, provides: "If scientific, technical, or other specialized knowledge will assist the trier of fact to understand the evidence or to determine a fact in issue, a witness qualified as an expert by knowledge, skill, experience, training, or education, may testify thereto in the form of an opinion or otherwise." Nothing in the text of this Rule establishes "general acceptance" as an absolute prerequisite to admissibility. Nor does respondent present any clear indication that Rule 702 or the Rules as a whole were intended to incorporate a "general acceptance" standard. The drafting history makes no mention of Frye, and a rigid "general acceptance" requirement would be at odds with the "liberal thrust" of the Federal Rules and their "general approach of relaxing the traditional barriers to 'opinion' testimony." Given the Rules' permissive backdrop and their inclusion of a specific rule on expert testimony that does not mention "general acceptance," the assertion that the Rules somehow assimilated Frye is unconvincing. Frye made "general acceptance" the exclusive test for admitting expert scientific testimony. That austere standard, absent from and incompatible with the Federal Rules of Evidence, should not be applied in federal trials.

B

That the Frye test was displaced by the Rules of Evidence does not mean, however, that the Rules themselves place no limits on the admissibility of purportedly scientific evidence. Nor is the trial judge disabled from screening such evidence. To the contrary, under the Rules the trial judge must ensure that any and all scientific testimony or evidence admitted is not only relevant, but reliable.

The primary locus of this obligation is Rule 702, which clearly contemplates some degree of regulation of the subjects and theories about which an expert may testify. "If scientific, technical, or other specialized knowledge will assist the trier of fact to understand the evidence or to determine a fact in issue" an expert "may testify thereto." The subject of an expert's testimony must be "scientific * * * knowledge." The adjective "scientific" implies a grounding in the methods and procedures of science. Similarly, the word "knowledge" connotes more than subjective belief or unsupported speculation. The term "applies to any body of known facts or to any body of ideas inferred from such facts or accepted as truths on good grounds." Webster's Third New International Dictionary 1252 (1986). Of course, it would be unreasonable to conclude that the subject of scientific testimony must be "known" to a certainty; arguably, there are no certainties in science. See, e.g., Brief for Nicolaas Bloembergen et al. as Amici Curiae 9 ("Indeed, scientists do not assert that they know what is immutably 'true'—they are committed to searching for new, temporary theories to explain, as best they can, phenomena"); Brief for American Association for the Advancement of Science and the National Academy of Sciences as Amici Curiae 7–8 ("Science is not an encyclopedic body of knowledge about the universe. Instead, it represents a *process* for proposing and refining theoretical explanations about the world that are subject to further testing and refinement") (emphasis in original). But, in order to qualify as "scientific knowledge," an inference or assertion must be derived by the scientific method. Proposed testimony must be supported by appropriate validation—i.e., "good grounds," based on what is known. In short, the requirement that an expert's testimony pertain to "scientific knowledge" establishes a standard of evidentiary reliability.

Rule 702 further requires that the evidence or testimony "assist the trier of fact to understand the evidence or to determine a fact in issue." This condition goes primarily to relevance. "Expert testimony which does not relate to any issue in the case is not relevant and, ergo, non-helpful." 3 Weinstein & Berger ¶ 702[02], p. 702–18. See also United States v. Downing, 753 F.2d 1224, 1242 (CA3 1985) ("An additional consideration under Rule 702—and another aspect of relevancy—is whether expert testimony proffered in the case is sufficiently tied to the facts of the case that it will aid the jury in resolving a factual dispute").

C

Faced with a proffer of expert scientific testimony, then, the trial judge must determine at the outset, pursuant to Rule 104(a), whether the expert is proposing to testify to (1) scientific knowledge that (2) will assist the trier of fact to understand or determine a fact in issue. This entails a preliminary assessment of whether the reasoning or methodology underlying the testimony is scientifically valid and of whether that reasoning or methodology properly can be applied to the facts in issue. We are confident that federal judges possess the capacity to undertake this review. Many factors will bear on the inquiry, and we do not presume to set out a definitive checklist or test. But some general observations are appropriate.

Ordinarily, a key question to be answered in determining whether a theory or technique is scientific knowledge that will assist the trier of fact will be whether it can be (and has been) tested. "Scientific methodology today is based on generating hypotheses and testing them to see if they can be falsified; indeed, this methodology is what distinguishes science from other fields of human inquiry." Green, at 645. See also C. Hempel, Philosophy of Natural Science 49 (1966) ("[T]he statements constituting a scientific explanation must be capable of empirical test"); K. Popper, Conjectures and Refutations: The Growth of Scientific Knowledge 37 (5th ed. 1989) ("[T]he criterion of the scientific status of a theory is its falsifiability, or refutability, or testability").

Another pertinent consideration is whether the theory or technique has been subjected to peer review and publication. Publication (which is but one element of peer review) is not a sine qua non of admissibility; it does not necessarily correlate with reliability and in some instances well-grounded but innovative theories will not have been published. Some propositions, moreover, are too particular, too new, or of too limited interest to be published. But submission to the scrutiny of the scientific community is a component of "good science," in part because it increases the likelihood that substantive flaws in methodology will be detected. The fact of publication (or lack thereof) in a peer-reviewed journal thus will be a relevant, though not dispositive, consideration in assessing the scientific validity of a particular technique or methodology on which an opinion is premised.

Additionally, in the case of a particular scientific technique, the court ordinarily should consider the known or potential rate of error, see, e.g., United States v. Smith, 869 F.2d 348, 353–354 (CA7 1989) (surveying studies of the error rate of spectrographic voice identification technique), and the existence and maintenance of standards controlling the technique's operation.

Finally, "general acceptance" can yet have a bearing on the inquiry. A "reliability assessment does not require, although it does permit, explicit identification of a relevant scientific community and an express determination of a particular degree of acceptance within that community." United States v. Downing, 753 F.2d, at 1238. Widespread acceptance can be an important factor in ruling particular evidence admissible, and "a known technique that has been able to attract only minimal support within the community," Downing, supra, at 1238, may properly be viewed with skepticism.

The inquiry envisioned by Rule 702 is, we emphasize, a flexible one. Its overarching subject is the scientific validity—and thus the evidentiary relevance and reliability—of the principles that underlie a proposed submission. The focus, of course, must be solely on principles and methodology, not on the conclusions that they generate.

Throughout, a judge assessing a proffer of expert scientific testimony under Rule 702 should also be mindful of other applicable rules. Rule 703 provides that expert opinions based on otherwise inadmissible hearsay are to be admitted only if the facts or data are "of a type reasonably relied upon by experts in the particular field in forming opinions or inferences upon the subject." Rule 706 allows the court at its discretion to procure the assistance of an expert of its own choosing. Finally, Rule 403 permits the exclusion of relevant evidence "if its probative value is substantially outweighed by the danger of unfair prejudice, confusion of the issues, or misleading the jury * * *." Judge Weinstein has explained: "Expert evidence can be both powerful and quite misleading because of the difficulty in evaluating it. Because of this risk, the judge in weighing possible prejudice against probative force under Rule 403 of the present rules exercises more control over experts than over lay witnesses." Weinstein, 138 F.R.D., at 632.

Accordingly, the judgment of the Court of Appeals is vacated and the case is remanded for further proceedings consistent with this opinion.

It is so ordered.

The opinion of CHIEF JUSTICE REHNQUIST, with whom JUSTICE STEVENS joins, concurring in part and dissenting in part, is omitted.

Notes and Questions

1. Deleted in the editing of Justice Blackmun's opinion were extensive citations to scientific and legal articles bearing on the nature of scientific proof and the scientific method. Students interested in these topics should consult the opinion for a virtual bibliography of relevant materials.

2. Based on Justice Blackmun's description of the qualifications and methodology of plaintiffs' experts, how is the trial court likely to rule on the admissibility issue on remand?

Problem

Plaintiff seeks damages for a condition or disease allegedly caused by defendant's drug or chemical. The disease, like cancer, provides no physical evidence of the inducing agent and the etiology of the illness is unknown. All relevant epidemiological studies to date conclude that there is no "statistically significant" link between exposure to defendant's product and the type of illness or injury suffered by plaintiff. The current scientific consensus is that it is impossible to conclude that a cause-and-effect relationship exists. Nevertheless, plaintiff's qualified expert is prepared to testify that it is more probable than not that causation exists. Her opinion is based upon chemical structure activity analysis, animal studies, in vivo and in vitro, and the patient's history. These sources, from which she reasoned to a conclusion favoring plaintiff, would be considered by many scientists. However, most would find this data inadequate to support a finding of causation in the absence of positive epidemiological studies. Plaintiff's expert has either rejected the epidemiological data as a basis for her opinion or has reinterpreted the data underlying these negative studies to reach a contrary conclusion. Based on *Daubert*, can this opinion be admitted?

3. Justice Blackmun states that scientific evidence must "not only [be] relevant, but reliable," and declares that reliability is part of "scientific * * * knowledge" that is allowed under Rule 702 because "scientific knowledge" must be "derived by the scientific method" and "supported by appropriate validation." The term "reliable" does not appear in the text of Rule 702; from what source does Justice Blackmun derive his requirement of reliability?

Interestingly, a proposed amendment to Rule 702 of the Federal Rules of Evidence would require that "testimony providing scientific * * * information, in the form of an opinion or otherwise, may be received if (1) [it] is *reasonably reliable* and will, if credited, *substantially* assist the trier of fact * * * and (2) the witness is qualified as an expert. * * * " Jud. Conf. of the U.S., Comm. on Rules of Prac. and Proc., Preliminary Draft of Proposed Amendments to the Federal Rules of Civil Procedure 83 (Law. Co-op., Aug. 15, 1991). The proposed committee notes indicate that while the revisions are intended to tighten the admissibility standards for expert testimony, the language is not intended to resolve the debate over the "general acceptance" test set forth in *Frye*. Assuming the desirability of such an amendment, does *Daubert* eliminate the need for it?

4. Did the Court offer sufficient guidance to the district court judges as to the considerations that should bear on whether the "reasoning or methodology underlying the testimony is scientifically valid"? What does the Court mean when it states that the theory or technique should be testable or falsifiable? Were you surprised that the Court gave importance to the peer review and publication process? It was the Ninth Circuit's emphasis on a requirement for peer review that drew an avalanche of criticism, much of it from the scientific community. What matters respecting peer review: that the expert's theory has been reviewed or that it has been reviewed *favorably*? What does the Court mean by the consideration of the "known or potential rate of error" of a particular scientific technique? What does that mean in the sciences of epidemiology and toxicology?

Finally, were you surprised that the Court resuscitated the "general acceptance" standard as part of the reliability calculus? The Court relies heavily on the Third Circuit's opinion in United States v. Downing, 753 F.2d 1224 (3d Cir.1985), which had rejected *Frye*, but allowed some inquiry into the "degree of acceptance within" the scientific community.

5. How would you characterize the role of district court judges in assessing admissibility after *Daubert*?—a strict scrutiny or "hard look" approach, moderate scrutiny, or deferential? What does the Court mean when it states that the "focus * * * must be solely on the principles and methodology, not on the conclusions that they generate"? Under the *Frye* test, the trial court would assess the proposed expert testimony against the consensus of the relevant scientific community; the former could be presented by affidavit, whereas the latter could be determined largely through judicial notice and the use of learned treatises under Rule 803(18). By contrast, *Daubert* will require district judges to make findings on a number of issues, and to weigh those findings in order to reach their ultimate conclusions. How demanding is this procedure likely to be on federal district judges? If you are plaintiff's counsel, what kind of record must you be prepared to offer to address the *Daubert* reliability criteria? What will defense counsel likely offer?

6. What standard of review will courts of appeal apply to district court admissibility determinations? Although evidentiary rulings are generally reviewed for abuse of discretion, district court determinations of general acceptance generally have been reviewed de novo because that conclusion does not vary according to the circumstances of each case, and because virtually all the materials needed to reach that conclusion are equally available to the courts of appeals. Will appellate courts under the *Daubert* multi-factor balancing test use the abuse of discretion standard? Consider these possibilities: In one case, a federal district judge determines that a proffered scientific technique or theory is testable but not peer-reviewed, with a low rate of error but not generally accepted across its scientific field— in other words, two positive findings against two negative ones. On balance, the judge concludes that the testimony is admissible. Assuming none of the underlying findings is clearly erroneous, is the judge's striking of the balance going to be disturbed on appeal?

In case two, another district judge in the same district, in an identical case, makes the same underlying findings, but concludes on balance that the evidence should not be admitted. Would that conclusion be an abuse of that judge's discretion, even if the affirmance of the first judge's decision had resulted in a published opinion?

7. In a portion of the opinion that was deleted, Justice Blackmun states that a trial court also retains the authority to direct a verdict when it concludes that a party has failed to offer sufficient evidence to reach a jury on causation or to grant summary judgment based on the insufficiency of plaintiff's evidence. In the next section we will focus on that aspect of the causation inquiry.

8. In Rubanick v. Witco Chemical Corp., 125 N.J. 421, 593 A.2d 733 (1991), the New Jersey Supreme Court, under state evidentiary rules similar to the Federal Rules, also overturned the *Frye* standard specifically for toxic tort cases. After discussing the special causation problems which plaintiffs encounter in toxics cases and the "undeniable indications that persons do suffer grave and lethal injury as a result of the wrongful and tortious exposure to toxic substances," it stated a new test:

> Accordingly, we hold that in toxic-tort litigation, a scientific theory of causation that has not yet reached general acceptance may be found to be sufficiently reliable if it is based on a sound, adequately-founded scientific methodology involving data and information of the type reasonably relied on by experts in the scientific field. The evidence of such scientific knowledge must be proffered by an expert who is sufficiently qualified by education, knowledge, training, and experience in the specific field of science. The expert must possess a demonstrated professional capability to assess the scientific significance of the underlying data and information, to apply the scientific methodology, and to explain the bases for the opinion reached.

Is there a difference between the scientific *method* (referred to in *Daubert*) and scientific "methodology" (also referred to in *Daubert*)? The answer is clarified in *Rubanick* itself when the court unequivocally rejected the scientific method as a standard of admissibility, stating that "the scientific method fails to address or accommodate the needs and goals of the tort system." Is this true? Does the "methodology" standard include not only the types of data and information relied upon, but also embrace the reasoning process of getting from the data to the conclusions?

9. Justice Alan B. Handler, who authored the opinion in *Rubanick*, authored an article entitled, The Judicial Pursuit of Knowledge: Truth and/or Justice, 41 Rutgers L. Rev. 1 (1988), in which he recognized the important role which scientific evidence and theory play in civil and criminal litigation. He advocates an enhanced judicial role in scientific fact-finding and recommends that such enhanced participation occur in certain classes of cases, including "those where critically relevant scientific knowledge is controversial and experts are polarized, yet the decisional result hangs in the balance; or where there are serious litigational imbalances that realistically will impugn the integrity and soundness of the final determination; or where the public importance of the case eclipses the private interests of the individual litigants, implicating significant concerns of public policy." Was *Rubanick* such a case? Did the opinion reflect Handler's position?

4. SUFFICIENCY OF THE SCIENTIFIC EVIDENCE: NATURE AND QUANTUM OF PROOF

a. *Minimalist Requirements*

We turn now to the issue first raised in *Stubbs* at this Chapter's beginning: How much evidence of causation is enough? A closely related, indeed inseparable, issue is what *kind* of evidence must the plaintiff offer? Often the question turns on whether epidemiological studies supporting the causal association is indispensably necessary or merely desirable. The opinion which has come to stand most starkly for the proposition that supportive epidemiological studies are not an essential component of a plaintiff's prima facie case is Ferebee v. Chevron Chemical Company, 736 F.2d 1529 (D.C.Cir.1984). In *Ferebee* the plaintiff's decedent, an agricultural worker for the United States Department of Agriculture, alleged that he had contracted pulmonary fibrosis, from which he ultimately died, as a result of long-term dermal exposure to dilute solutions of paraquat, an herbicide distributed by defendant. The jury had rendered a verdict for the plaintiff and on appeal defendant argued that plaintiff's experts' opinions were insufficient, standing alone, to make out a submissible case on causation. Plaintiff offered two pulmonary experts who testified, based on their examination of the decedent and medical studies which they reviewed, that dermal absorption of paraquat could cause pulmonary abnormalities and that, in this case, did cause the decedent's. The court first declared that the issue of weighing the experts' conflicting opinions is appropriate for jury determination, especially in cases such as this:

> These admonitions apply with special force in the context of the present action, in which an admittedly dangerous chemical is alleged through long-term exposure to have caused disease. Judges, both trial and appellate, have no special competence to resolve the complex and refractory causal issues raised by the attempt to link low-level exposure to toxic chemicals with human disease. On questions such as these, which stand at the frontier of current medical and epidemiological inquiry, if experts are willing to testify that such a link exists, it is for the jury to decide whether to credit the testimony.

Although no epidemiological data was introduced suggesting that long-term exposure to paraquat could cause pulmonary fibrosis, the court relied on the two experts' contrary conclusions as sufficient to sustain the jury's verdict:

> Thus, a cause-effect relationship need not be clearly established by animal or epidemiological studies before a doctor can testify that, in his opinion, such a relationship exists. As long as the basic methodology employed to reach such a conclusion is sound, such as use of tissue samples, standard tests, and patient examination, products liability law does not preclude recovery until a "statistically signifi-

cant" number of people have been injured or until science has had the time and resources to complete sophisticated laboratory studies of the chemical. In a courtroom, the test for allowing a plaintiff to recover in a tort suit of this type is not scientific certainty but legal sufficiency; if reasonable jurors could conclude from the expert testimony that paraquat more likely than not caused Ferebee's injury, the fact that another jury might reach the opposite conclusion or that science would require more evidence before conclusively considering the causation question resolved is irrelevant. That Ferebee's case may have been the first of its exact type, or that his doctors may have been the first alert enough to recognize such a case, does not mean that the testimony of those doctors, who are concededly well qualified in their fields, should not have been admitted.

Notes and Questions

1. The court in *Ferebee* seems to be applying a "willing testifier" standard for the admissibility and reliability of expert testimony in emerging areas of scientific knowledge—if an expert is willing to testify and meets the qualification requirement of Rule 702—they are the only criteria which must be satisfied before a jury is permitted to weigh the credibility and persuasiveness of the testimony. Do you agree with this standard? Federal Rule of Evidence 702 quoted earlier sets forth the requirement that the expert testimony be able to "assist the trier of fact;" is that what Judge Mikva is expressing in his "willing testifier" rule? Is the underlying premise of such a rule that courts are institutions established for resolution of disputes, not arbiters of scientific truth? Can courts ever be expected to seek to resolve the question of whether novel scientific theories are valid? Would the experts' opinions be admissible after *Daubert*?

2. Why did the court refuse to place reliance on epidemiological studies? Does the court make any minimum requirements on the nature of the proof necessary to make out a submissible case?

3. Wells v. Ortho Pharmaceutical Corp., 615 F.Supp. 262 (N.D.Ga. 1985), affirmed 788 F.2d 741 (11th Cir.1986) (reducing plaintiff's verdict from $5.1 million to $4.7 million), cert. denied 479 U.S. 950, 107 S.Ct. 437, 93 L.Ed.2d 386 (1986), demonstrates a reliance on the *Ferebee* reasoning. In *Wells*, the parents of a child born with multiple birth defects brought a products liability action on behalf of the child against the manufacturer of a spermicide used by the child's mother before and after conception. The trial court, which tried the case without a jury, began its opinion by declaring what its scientific demands were:

> The Court emphasizes, however, that plaintiffs' ultimate burden was not to produce an unassailable scientific study which proves that spermicides have caused birth defects in rats, rabbits, or members of a large group health plan, but rather to show from *all* the evidence presented, to a reasonable degree of medical certainty, that the spermicide caused some or all of *Katie Well's* birth defects (emphasis in original).

Then, the court placed minimal weight on defendant's evidence showing that no statistical association had been shown to exist between use of the product and the kind of injury suffered. The court noted simply that "[a]lthough the studies on which defendant relied failed to detect an association between spermicides and birth defects, some of the defendants' own experts testified that these studies do not rule out all possibility that spermicides can cause birth defects." Does this indicate that negative epidemiological studies will not be persuasive in disproving generic causation? Is the court ignoring that the burden of proof is on the plaintiff?

Second, the court relied on testimony concerning "mechanisms" or theories to demonstrate causation. Specifically, experts testified about an amniotic-band syndrome and vascular-disruption hypotheses to explain the plaintiff's injury. This testimony influenced the court largely because it was based on examination of the plaintiff. The court pointed out that it was concerned only with "this plaintiff's injury." The court's opinion asserts that when epidemiological evidence shows no association between the product and the disease, but hypothesized " 'mechanisms' of causation" appear to support an association, a fact finder may find causation.

On appeal, Ortho Pharmaceutical argued that the trial court had failed to consider adequately the epidemiological evidence of no association. The Circuit Court rejected this argument, and after quoting *Ferebee*, continued: "As the D.C. Circuit noted in *Ferebee*, a distinction exists between legal sufficiency and scientific certainty."

The decision in *Wells* was roundly criticized by the medical community. In an article in the New England Journal of Medicine, two physicians from the National Institute of Child Health and Human Development noted that *Wells* took the medical community by surprise, because the overwhelming body of evidence indicates that spermicides are not teratogenic. James L. Mills & Duane Alexander, Teratogens and "Litogens," 315 New. Eng. J. Med. 1234, 1235 (1986). They further wrote that plaintiff had won "despite testimony citing the considerable medical evidence that spermicides do not cause birth defects," and despite the United States Food and Drug Administration's decision that warnings about birth defects were not warranted. Should the civil justice system care about these criticisms?

4. Brennan criticizes the *Ferebee* and *Wells* decisions. (Troyen Brennan, Causal Chains and Statistical Links: The Role of Scientific Uncertainty in Hazardous Substance Litigation, 73 Cornell L. Rev. 469, 497–499 (1988)) on the grounds that the court reversed the scientific method by finding an association even though the epidemiological evidence failed to show an association.

Some state courts have also concluded that supportive epidemiological evidence should not be required in order to reach a jury on the issue of causation. See Bloomquist v. Wapello County, 500 N.W.2d 1 (Iowa 1993) (relying on *Ferebee*, and concluding that "we reject the reasoning of *Brock*", set forth in the next section).

b. Rigorous Standards of Sufficiency: The Bendectin Litigation

BROCK v. MERRELL DOW PHARMACEUTICALS, INC.

United States Court of Appeals, Fifth Circuit, 1989.
874 F.2d 307.

GARZA, J.

Mr. & Mrs. Floyd Brock filed suit in federal district court on behalf of their minor child, Rachel Brock, to recover damages for birth defects that allegedly resulted from Mrs. Brock's ingestion during her pregnancy of the anti-nausea drug Bendectin, which is manufactured by Merrell–Dow Pharmaceuticals, Inc. ("Merrell–Dow"). The Brocks obtained a jury verdict in the amount of $550,000 against Merrell–Dow, representing $240,000 in compensatory damages and $310,000 in punitive damages. Merrell–Dow appeals that verdict here, arguing that the Brocks did not present sufficient evidence to allow the jury to conclude that Bendectin caused Rachel Brock's birth defect. After reviewing the record and decisions of other courts confronted with similar suits regarding Bendectin, we hold that Merrell–Dow was entitled to judgment notwithstanding the verdict, and the judgment in favor of the Brocks is therefore reversed and the case will be dismissed.

BACKGROUND

Mrs. Brock conceived Rachel Brock on or around July 2, 1981. On July 28, 1981, Mrs. Brock began to experience morning sickness, and she began to take Bendectin, a prescription drug manufactured by Defendant, Merrell–Dow. Rachel Brock was born on March 19, 1982 with a limb reduction defect known as Poland's Syndrome, which is recognized by a shortening or absence of fingers with a decrease in the corresponding pectoralis muscle on one side.

Mr. and Mrs. Brock filed a diversity suit against Merrell–Dow on behalf of their daughter in the U.S. District Court for the Eastern District of Texas. The complaint alleged theories of improper inspection, design defect, and failure to warn. Causation was a hotly contested issue, with both sides presenting expert testimony and studies regarding the possible teratogenicity [2] of Bendectin. At the end of trial, Merrell–Dow moved for a directed verdict, arguing that there was no credible evidence tending to show that Bendectin causes birth defects. Merrell–Dow's motion was denied, and the issue of whether Bendectin caused Rachel Brock's birth defect was given to the jury. The jury found for the Brocks, and awarded both compensatory and punitive damages. Merrell–Dow then moved for judgment notwithstanding the verdict, and that motion was denied. Merrell–Dow here appeals the denial of its

2. A teratogen is a substance that causes birth defects.

motions for directed verdict and for judgment notwithstanding the verdict.

STANDARD FOR DETERMINING SUFFICIENCY OF THE EVIDENCE

The standard for granting a judgment notwithstanding the verdict is the same as that governing rulings on directed verdicts: judgment notwithstanding the verdict is proper only when there can be only one reasonable conclusion drawn from the evidence. * * * Viewing the evidence in the light most favorable to the party against whom the motion is made, the court must give that party the benefit of all reasonable inferences from the evidence.

These general and abstract formulations lose much of their usefulness, however, when we attempt to apply them to the concrete factual situation at hand. One certainly might infer from the evidence in the case that Bendectin causes birth defects, and further that Bendectin caused Rachel Brock's limb reduction defect—in fact, the jury concluded that this very thing occurred. However, the court must determine whether this is a reasonable inference to be drawn from the evidence presented, and the formulae provide us with little guidance as to what constitutes a reasonable, as opposed to unreasonable, inference that a jury could draw from the evidence. Ultimately, the "correctness" of our decision that there was insufficient evidence presented by plaintiff on the issue of whether Bendectin caused Rachel Brock's limb reduction defect to enable a jury to draw a reasonable inference may be just a matter of opinion, but hopefully the reasoning below will persuade others of the insights of our perspective.

The first problem is that there is often no consensus in the medical community regarding whether a given substance is teratogenic; this is the case with Bendectin. Moreover, while we now recognize some of the many factors which can cause birth defects, medical science is now unable, and will undoubtedly remain unable for the foreseeable future, to trace a known birth defect back to its precipitating cause. The second problem, in addition to the problem of unknowability, is that juries are asked to resolve these questions, upon which even our brightest medical minds disagree, in order to resolve the case at hand and decide whether the plaintiff is entitled to recovery, and in so doing must necessarily resort to speculation.

Under the traditional approach to scientific evidence, courts would not peer beneath the reasoning of medical experts to question their reasoning. Confronted, as we now are, with difficult medical questions, courts must critically evaluate the reasoning process by which the experts connect data to their conclusions in order for courts to consistently and rationally resolve the disputes before them. Moreover, in mass torts the same issue is often presented over and over to juries in different cases, and the juries often split both ways on the issue. The effect of this is to create a state of uncertainty among manufacturers contemplating the research and development of new, and potentially lifesaving drugs. Appellate courts, if they take the lead in resolving those questions upon which juries will go both ways, can reduce some of the uncertainty which can tend to produce a sub-optimal amount of new drug development.

We are not without precedent in our approach to this problem. The case before us parallels in many respects the recently conducted Agent Orange Litigation. In those cases, plaintiffs attempted to prove that exposure to Agent Orange, a defoliant used during the Vietnam War, had caused them adverse health effects. Judge Weinstein granted summary judgment against opt-out plaintiffs on the basis that they had been unable to prove that exposure to low levels of dioxin caused their health problems. Although plaintiffs had provided the affidavits of experts indicating that exposure to Agent Orange had caused their health problems, the court attacked the reasoning of the experts and found it to be inadequate.

Courts have not always been so willing to analyze the reasoning employed by experts to reach their conclusions. [The court describes *Ferebee*].

The District of Columbia Circuit retreated from this approach recently when it considered, in a Bendectin case, the very same issue we are addressing here. In Richardson by Richardson v. Richardson–Merrell, Inc., 857 F.2d 823 (D.C.Cir.1988), the D.C. Circuit affirmed the lower court's grant of judgment notwithstanding the verdict to defendant. In its discussion of its approach to resolving the conflicting expert testimony in favor of defendant, the court opined that "[e]xpert witnesses are indispensible in a case such as this. But that is not to say that the court's hands are inexorably tied, or that it must accept uncritically any sort of opinion espoused by an expert merely because his credentials render him qualified to testify." The court then proceeded to look behind the conclusion of plaintiff's expert and found his reasoning inadequate. In distinguishing *Ferebee*, the court narrowly interpreted the case to apply only where the causation issue is novel and "stands at the frontier of current medical and epidemilogical inquiry." The Bendectin cases are different, opined the D.C. Circuit, in that there is a wealth of published epidemiological data, none of which has concluded that the drug is teratogenic. Thus, in *Richardson*, the court affirmed its willingness to look behind the conclusions of experts, at least in cases which are not at the frontier of epidemiological inquiry. We too, have chosen to take the same approach as the *Richardson* court, and in the next section we will present our analysis of the reasoning employed by the expert witnesses in this case.

SUFFICIENCY OF THE EVIDENCE PRESENTED

Undoubtedly, the most useful and conclusive type of evidence in a case such as this is epidemiological studies. Epidemiology attempts to define a relationship between a disease and a factor suspected of causing it—in this case, ingestion of Bendectin during pregnancy. To define that relationship, the epidemiologist examines the general population, comparing the incidence of the disease among those people exposed to the factor in question to those not exposed. The epidemiologist then uses statistical methods and reasoning to allow her to draw a biological inference between the factor being studied and the disease's etiology.

One difficulty with epidemiologic studies is that often several factors can cause the same disease. Birth defects are known to be caused by mercury, nicotine, alcohol, radiation, and viruses, among other factors. When epidemiologists compare the birth defect rates for women who took Bendectin during pregnancy against those who did not take Bendectin during pregnancy, there is a chance that the distribution of the other causal factors may not be even between the two groups. Usually, the larger the size of the sample, the more likely that random chance will lead to an even distribution of these factors among the two comparison groups, unless there is a dependence between some of the other factors and the factor being studied. For example, there would be a dependence between variables if women who took Bendectin during pregnancy were more or less likely to smoke than women who did not take Bendectin. Another source of error in epidemiological studies is selective recall—i.e., women who have children with birth defects may be more likely to remember taking Bendectin during pregnancy than those women with normal children. Fortunately, we do not have to resolve any of the above questions, since the studies presented to us incorporate the possibility of these factors by use of a confidence interval. The purpose of our mentioning these sources of error is to provide some background regarding the importance of confidence intervals.

In this case, the parties described the results of epidemiologic studies in terms of two numbers: a relative risk and a confidence interval. The relative risk is a number which describes the increased or decreased incidence of the disease in question in the population exposed to the factor as compared to the control population not exposed to the factor. In this case, the relative risk describes the increased or decreased incidence of birth defects in the group of women who took Bendectin versus women who did not take Bendectin. A relative risk of 1.0 means that the incidence of birth defects in the two groups were the same. A relative risk greater than 1.0 means that there were more birth defects in the group of women who took Bendectin.

Just because an epidemiological study concludes that a relative risk is greater than 1.0 does not establish that the factor caused the disease. If the confidence interval is so great that it includes the number 1.0, then the study will be said to show no statistically significant association between the factor and the disease. For example, if a study concluded that the relative risk for Bendectin was 1.30, which is consistent with a 30% elevated risk of harm, but the confidence interval was from 0.95 to 1.82, then no statistically significant conclusions could be drawn from this study because the relative risk, when adjusted by the confidence interval, includes 1.0. Again, it is important to remember that the confidence interval attempts to express mathematically the magnitude of possible error, due to the above mentioned sources as well as others, and therefore a study with a relative risk of greater than 1.0 must always be considered in light of its confidence interval before one can draw conclusions from it.

The Brocks relied on a reanalysis conducted by Dr. Jay Glasser of the previously conducted Heinonen study. The Heinonen study, which was conducted by Professor O.P. Heinonen under the auspices of the U.S. National Institute of Neurological and Communicative Disorders, was based on over 50,000 pregnancy records collected in the United States. Dr. Heinonen, in analyzing these records, found that approximately 1,000 women had taken Bendectin during the first four months of their pregnancies. 63 of those women had infants with malformations as opposed to 3,200 out of 49,000 who had not taken Bendectin. This yielded a relative risk of 0.97 with confidence limits from 0.75 to 1.26. Therefore, this study does not support the proposition that Bendectin causes birth defects.

The Heinonen study considered as birth defects all malformations, of which limb reduction defects of the type experienced by Rachel Brock are a subset. Dr. Glasser's reanalysis of the data used in the Heinonen study only considered limb reduction defects. That study found a relative risk of 1.49. However, Dr. Glasser admits that the confidence interval was from 0.17 to 3; this renders the study statistically insignificant. The plaintiffs did not offer one statistically significant (one whose confidence interval did not include 1.0) study that concludes that Bendectin is a human teratogen. No published epidemiological study has found a statistically significant increased risk between exposure to Bendectin and birth defects. One of plaintiff's experts, Dr. Snodgrass, conceded that he was not aware of any such studies. Transcript at 198–99. Nor have any such studies been presented to the other two federal appeals courts which have considered this matter.

Although we find Dr. Glasser's results inconclusive due to the fact that the confidence intervals include 1.0, we further note that Dr. Glasser has not published his study or conclusions for the purposes of peer review. While we do not hold that this failure, in and of itself, renders his conclusions inadmissible, courts must nonetheless be especially skeptical of medical and other scientific evidence that has not been subjected to thorough peer review. Clearly, "the examination of a scientific study by a cadre of lawyers is not the same as its examination by others trained in the field of science or medicine."

We find, in this case, the lack of *conclusive* epidemiological proof to be fatal to the Brock's case. While we do not hold that epidemiologic proof is a necessary element in all toxic tort cases, it is certainly a very important element. This is especially true when the only other evidence is in the form of animal studies of questionable applicability to humans.
* * *

The Brocks have also introduced animal studies in order to prove that Bendectin is a teratogen.

* * *

We need not address at length the animal studies presented by plaintiffs below, except to note several of the more important studies and their methodological flaws. The plaintiffs presented an in vitro study conducted by Drs. Hassell and Horigan. This study used cells cut from the limbs of mice and chickens which were then exposed to various test compounds, including Bendectin. According to plaintiff's experts, limb bud cells which normally form in six days were reduced if those cells were exposed to Bendectin; these limb bud cells ultimately form the arms and legs. However, Dr. Hassell himself cautioned that the body may break down doxylamine, the active ingredient in Bendectin, into a metabolic product which may differ from the pure test compound. Thus, human limb bud cells in a fetus may not be exposed to doxylamine, but rather the metabolic product of doxylamine. Moreover, extrapolation of these findings to humans cannot be done without knowing the dosage level and the corresponding drug level in the bloodstream of the mother. Taking the concept of metabolic products one step further, the plaintiff introduced the testimony of Drs. Snodgrass and Newman, who hypothesized that the human body breaks down doxylamine into less complex molecules called metabolites. These metabolites, some of which are negatively charged, are attracted to the relatively alkaline embryotic fluids, and ultimately bond with the cells in the embryo, producing tissue damage. However, both experts admitted that different species of animals metabolize chemicals differently, and that there are no studies which show that doxylamine is broken down by humans into toxic metabolites. Thus, we must view the limb bud tests as quite speculative.

* * *

Dr. McBride, another expert called by plaintiffs, conducted research in Australia, exposing white rabbits and marmosets to high doses of doxylamine—up to 500 times the normal human dose. Thirteen of 18 of the rabbits died due to either the toxic effects of doxylamine or the improper insertion of gavage tubes which were used to administer the doxylamine to the rabbits. Of the marmosets, all four which were given high doses of doxylamine (500 times the human dosage) aborted their fetuses, and it was impossible to tell if those fetuses were malformed since the aborted fetus is generally eaten by the mother. Dr. McBride hypothesized that the abortions were the result of the teratogenic effect of doxylamine, rather than the high dosage. However, the fifth marmoset was given a lesser dose (100 times the human dosage), and two of the three fetuses later examined lacked a hind leg. On the basis of this, Dr. McBride concluded that doxylamine is a teratogen. He hypothesized that Bendectin, an anticholinergic drug, reduces the amount of acetylcholine, a neurotransmitter released by nerve cells, in the embryo. If the amount of acetylcholine in the embryo is diminished, the trophic effect on body growth is interfered with. Essentially, Dr. McBride speculated that the development of body tissue depends on the initial development of the nervous system. He cited another hypothesis, that of Professor Alexander Karczman, as supporting his theory of the anticholinergic action of doxylamine. However, the theory regarding the effects of doxylamine on acetylcholine, the nervous system and, ultimately, tissue development is nothing more than unproven medical speculation lacking any sort of consensus. Assuredly, one day in the future, medical science may have a clearer understanding of the mechanics of tissue development in the fetus. However, that is not the case today, and speculation unconfirmed by epidemiologic proof cannot form the basis for causation in a court of law.

In light of the evidence presented, we are convinced that the Brocks did not present sufficient evidence regarding causation to allow a trier of fact to make a reasonable inference that Bendectin caused Rachel Brock's limb reduction defect. We expect that our decision here will have a precedential effect on other cases pending in this circuit which allege Bendectin as the cause of birth defects. Hopefully, our decision will have the effect of encouraging district judges faced with medical and epidemiologic proof in subsequent toxic tort cases to be especially vigilant in scrutinizing the basis, reasoning, and *conclusiveness* of studies presented by both sides. However, we do not wish this case to stand as a bar to future Bendectin cases in the event that new and *conclusive* studies emerge which would give a jury a firmer basis on which to determine the issue of causation.

Reversed.

Notes and Questions

1. The subsequent history of *Brock* is fascinating. On a motion for rehearing en banc, the same panel, treating it as a motion for rehearing by the panel, modified its opinion in two respects. See 884 F.2d 166 (5th Cir.1989). The *underscored* language in the last paragraph of the opinion and on the prior page originally appeared as "the lack of *conclusive* epidemiological proof," but was modified to read "statistically significant epidemiological proof." What is the importance of the court's replacing references to "conclusive epidemiological proof," with "statistically significant epidemiological proof?"

2. The Fifth Circuit then considered a rehearing en banc, with the court deciding 8 to 6 to deny the rehearing. 884 F.2d 167 (5th Cir.1989). Judge Reavley in his dissent from the denial of the rehearing makes the following statement:

Six highly qualified and experienced experts testified that Bendectin is a human teratogen, i.e. capable of causing human birth defects. Three of them testified to the opinion that Bendectin was a cause of Rachel Brock's deformation. Their opinions of causation were not the product of faulty syllogisms but were predicated upon medical study and research and upon their explanation of the process by which the doxylamine element in Bendectin can interfere with the development of nerve cells in an embryo. The panel picks at details in the testimony lacking expert consensus, but its characterization of this voluminous expert proof as "speculation" could just as well doom virtually all expert testimony. The panel reaches its climax with the novel declaration that only epidemiological studies can prove causal relation between Bendectin and birth defects, and it enters into the debate with Dr. Glasser on the statistical significance of the Heinonen study. In the absence of expert consensus must we now always await populations studies before a jury verdict may be based upon medical opinion? So says the panel, at least for Bendectin cases. This, despite the testimony here that case reports and laboratory research reveal teratogens and that no epidemiological study has ever discovered a teratogen.

Judge Reavley also commented that the holding calls into question the "Seventh Amendment right to trial by jury." What is the Seventh Amendment argument? Does *Brock* survive *Daubert*? Apparently so, because Justice Blackmun cited it with approval for the proposition that trial judges retain the power to dispose of cases on the basis of the insufficiency of the plaintiff's evidence.

3. Michael Green, Expert Witnesses and Sufficiency of Evidence in Toxic Substances Litigation: The Legacy of Agent Orange and Bendectin Litigation, 86 Nw. L. Rev. 643, 680–82 (1992) offers the following criticism of *Brock*, and its requirement for statistically significant epidemiological studies:

> For most potentially toxic substances, there will not be a solid body of epidemiological evidence on which to rely. Epidemiology is expensive and time consuming, even ethically proscribed in certain contexts. There are thousands upon thousands of synthetic agents being used in the United States that might pose toxic risks, yet only a tiny fraction have been the subject of any epidemiologic inquiry. * * * Imposing a burden of production that includes an epidemiologic threshold will screen out all of these cases, but at a cost of precluding more refined attempts, based on animal studies, structure analysis, available knowledge about biological mechanisms and related evidence, to make an assessment of whether there exists a causal relationship.

> Toxic causation must be assessed with due regard for the available evidence. Where the epidemiologic record is substantial, reliable, and consistent, the saliency of animal studies or other evidence of toxicity is quite low. However, when epidemiologic evidence is lacking, thin, of questionable validity and ultimately inconclusive, dismissing other toxicological evidence is unjustifiable. The point is that plaintiffs should be required to prove causation by a preponderance of the *available evidence*, not by some predetermined standard that may require nonexistent studies. This means that in every case involving an alleged toxic agent for which a mature epidemiologic record does not exist, analysis of the sufficiency of plaintiff's evidence would begin by considering the universe of available evidence of toxicity. * * * No doubt, opening the courthouse doors to plaintiffs entering with such thin and attenuated evidence and rendering a decision on such a record is discomfiting and unfortunate. But the reality is that stronger and better evidence is unavailable through no fault of anyone and a decision based on the preponderance of the available evidence, rather than imposing an evidentiary threshold, would seem in keeping with the role of the civil justice system.

Even in those instances where a modicum of epidemiologic evidence exists, serious judicial scrutiny of the sort advocated and employed by Judge Weinstein [in the *Agent Orange* litigation discussed below] would require an appreciation for methodological errors and inadequacies in those studies, an ability to assess the validity of a reanalysis of those studies, an understanding of the biological record on mechanisms associated with the disease in question, and a firm grounding in the concept of relative risk, statistical significance and confidence intervals, and their relationship to the preponderance of the evidence standard. One must doubt that a judge will have sufficient expertise to make or review those judgments, especially when ruling on a motion for summary judgment without the benefit of a full hearing to explain these matters.

The *Brock* decision, in ascribing wondrous powers to the concept of statistical significance, contributes to doubts that these matters are ones that reasonably can be mastered by generalist judges. Statistical significance addresses only random error due to the sampling inherent in any epidemiologic study. It cannot and does not speak to systematic error, which requires an informed review of the methodology employed in conducting the study. Moreover, statistical significance is merely an instrument for assisting in evaluating a study, not a truth serum that can be simplistically prescribed. (emphasis in original).

Do you agree with Professor Green's arguments? Is his "preponderance of the *available* evidence" consistent with "role of the civil justice system"? How does he consider plaintiff's burden of proving that defendant did in fact cause the injury? For a contrary view, that requiring statistically significant supportive studies is appropriate, see Bert Black, A Unified Theory of Scientific Evidence, 56 Ford. L. Rev. 595 (1988).

4. *Statistical Significance and Hypothesis Testing.* *Brock* contained only a cursory reference to the principles of hypothesis testing, by which scientists attempt to "disprove" the null hypothesis that no relationship exists between the chemical studied and the effect observed. Albert Einstein observed that "no amount of experimentation can ever prove me right; a single experiment can prove me wrong." In DeLuca v. Merrell Dow Pharmaceuticals, Inc., 911 F.2d 941 (3d Cir.1990), another Bendectin case, the court describes hypothesis testing and the role of statistical significance in greater detail:

* * * Epidemiological studies do not provide direct evidence that a particular plaintiff was injured by exposure to a substance. Such studies have the potential, however, of generating circumstantial evidence of cause and effect through a process known as hypothesis testing, a process which "amounts to an attempt to falsify the null hypothesis and by exclusion accept the alternative." K.J. Rothman, Modern Epidemiology 116 (1986) ("Rothman"). The null hypothesis is the hypothesis that there is no association between two studied variables, id.; in this case the key null hypothesis would be that there is no association between Bendectin exposure and an increase in limb reduction defects. The important alternative hypothesis in this case is that Bendectin use is associated with an increased incidence of limb reduction defects.

* * *

Epidemiological studies, of necessity, look to the experience of sample groups as indicative of the experience of a far larger population. Epidemiologists recognize, however, that the experience of the sample groups may vary from that of the larger population by chance. Thus, a showing of increased risk for birth defects among women using Bendectin in a particular study does not automatically prove that Bendectin use creates a higher risk of having a child with birth defects because the discrepancy between the exposed and unexposed groups could be the product of chance resulting from the use of only a small sample of the relevant populations. As a result of the acknowledged risk of this so-called "sampling error," researchers typically have rejected the associations suggested by epidemiological data unless those associations survive the rigors of "significance testing." This practice has also found favor in the legal context. A number of judicial opinions, discussed infra, have found Bendectin plaintiffs' causation evidence inadmissible because every published epidemiological study of the relationship of Bendectin exposure to the incidence of birth defects has concluded that there is not a "statistically significant" relationship between these two events.

Significance testing has a "P value" focus; the P value "indicates the probability, assuming the null hypothesis is true, that the observed data will depart from the absence of association to the extent that they actually do, or to a greater extent, by actual chance." Rothman, supra, at 116. If P is less than .05 (or 5%) a study's finding of a relationship supportive of the alternative hypothesis is considered statistically significant, if P is greater than 5% the relationship is rejected as insignificant. Accordingly, the results of a particular study are reported as simply "significant" or "not significant" or as P<.05 or P>.05.

Use of a .05 P value to determine whether to accept or reject the null hypothesis necessarily enhances one of two types of possible error. Type one error is when the null hypothesis is rejected when it is in fact true. Type two error is when the null hypothesis is in fact false but is not rejected. Rothman notes that at .05, the null hypothesis will "be rejected about 5 per cent of the time when it is true," a relatively small risk of type one error. Unfortunately, the relationship between type one error and type two error is not simple; however, one study in the context of an employment discrimination case concluded that when the risk of type one error equalled 5%, the risk of type two error was 50%. Cohen, Confidence in Probability: Burdens of Persuasion in a World of Imperfect Knowledge, 60 N.Y.U.L.Rev. 329, 411 & n. 116 (1985) (citing Dawson, Investigation of Fact—The Role of the Statistician, 11 Forum 896, 907–08 (1976)). Type one error may be viewed here as the risk of concluding that Bendectin is a teratogen when it is not. Type two error is the risk of concluding that Bendectin is not a teratogen, when it in fact is.

Rothman contends that there is nothing magical or inherently important about .05 significance; rather this is just a common value on the tables scholars use to calculate significance. Rothman, supra, at 117; see also Cohen, supra, at 412 (noting that the .05 level of significance used in the social and physical sciences is a conservative and arbitrary value choice not necessarily valuable in the legal setting). He stresses that the data in a certain study may indicate a strong relationship between two variables but still not be "statistically significant" and that the level of significance which should be required depends on the type of decision being made and the relative values placed on avoiding the two types of risk.

* * *

A confidence interval is a way of graphically representing the probability that the relative risk figure or any other relationship between two studied variables is the actual relationship. The interval is a range of sets of possible values for the true parameter that is consistent with the observed data within specified limits. Rothman, supra, at 119. A 95% confidence interval is constructed with enough width so that one can be confident that it is only 5% likely that the relative risk attained would have occurred if the true parameter, i.e., the actual unknown relationship between the two studied variables, were outside the confidence interval. If a 95% confidence interval thus contains "1", or the null hypothesis, then a researcher cannot say that the results are "statistically significant," that is, that the null hypothesis has been disproved at a .05 level of significance. Kaye, Is Proof of Statistical Significance Relevant? [61 Wash.L.Rev.] at 1348.

The result of a study should be reported, in Rothman's view, by reference to the confidence intervals at various confidence levels, e.g., 90%, 95%, 99%. The inclusion of confidence intervals of a variety of levels reflects Rothman's view that the predominating choice of a 95% confidence level is but an arbitrarily selected convention of his discipline. More importantly, however, Rothman insists that the precise locations of the boundaries of the confidence intervals, the all important focus of "significance testing," are far less important than their size and location. According to Rothman, statistical theory suggests that it is "much more likely that the [true] parameter [i.e., the true relationship between the studied variables] is located centrally within an interval than it is that the parameter is located near the limits of the interval." Rothman, supra, at 124. As such, the primary focus should not be on the ends of an interval but rather on the "approximate position of the interval as a whole on its scale of measurement * * *." Id.

The court in *DeLuca* remanded the case for the district court to reevaluate its ruling on the admissibility of plaintiffs' expert's testimony, including whether significance testing "should be a threshold requirement" for any study purporting to find that Bendectin is a teratogen, and observing that "the root issue it poses is what risk of what type of error the judicial system is willing to tolerate."[1] The relationship between type I and II

---

1. This reference to type I and type II error in *DeLuca* is best illustrated by an example from the criminal law, where the jury is being asked to decide between H_0, the null hypothesis that the defendant is innocent, and the alternative H_A, that the defendant is guilty. A type I error results if an innocent person is convicted, while a type II error results if a guilty person is acquitted. The jury instruction that "guilt must be proved beyond a reasonable doubt" means that type II is kept very small.

The reciprocal nature of the type I and type II errors is shown by efforts to reduce type I error by use of the exclusionary rule preventing the admission of unfairly prejudicial evidence. This reduces the probabili-

errors and hypothesis testing is demonstrated in the following tables where type I error and the probability of committing it is designated by the Greek letter α (alpha); type II error and its probability is designated by the Greek letter β (beta).

FOUR POSSIBLE RESULTS OF AN HYPOTHESIS TEST

State of Reality as to Causation	Decision	
	H_0 Acceptable	H_0 Rejected
If H_0 is true	Correct decision. Probability = $1-\alpha$ = confidence level	Type I error. Probability = α
If H_0 is false	Type II error. Probability = β	Correct decision. Probability = $1-\beta$

How would you describe the meaning of type I error in a civil tort case? How does it relate to the plaintiff's burden of proof? What does type II error mean? Are the concerns in civil cases equivalent to those in criminal cases?

In remanding the case, the court in *DeLuca* pointed out that even if plaintiffs' expert's testimony is admitted, summary judgment might nevertheless be appropriate if the *only* evidence plaintiffs offered established a relative risk of 2.0 or less, and noted also that statistical significance "may appropriately play some role in deciding" the sufficiency of the evidence. *DeLuca*'s suggestion (in applying New Jersey tort law) that a relative risk greater than 2.0 is essential has been undercut by the New Jersey Supreme Court in Landrigan v. Celotex Corp., 127 N.J. 404, 605 A.2d 1079 (1992).

5. For another Bendectin decision that adopts the insufficiency of the evidence rationale in dismissing plaintiff's claim, see Turpin v. Merrell Dow Pharmaceuticals, 959 F.2d 1349 (6th Cir.1992). In *Turpin,* the court expressed concern with special problems of inconsistency in the mass tort setting:

> For a judicial system founded on the premise that justice and consistency are related ideas, the inconsistent results reached by courts and juries nationwide on the question of causation in Bendectin birth defect cases are of serious concern.

The court stressed the duty of courts to inspect the reasoning of qualified scientific experts before permitting a case to reach the jury and declared flatly that whether Bendectin causes birth defects is "not capable of being proved to the requisite degree of legal probability based on the scientific evidence currently available." It described the inconsistency of outcomes as resulting from two factors: (1) the difficulty of scientists, judges, lawyers, and jurors in knowing what inferences to draw from toxicologic and epidemiologic evidence; and (2) the uncertainty of judges in knowing how far to

ty that an innocent person will be convicted but increases the likelihood that a guilty person will go free. The only way type I can be reduced without increasing type II errors is to obtain more evidence (i.e., a larger sample), which makes the distributions more accurate. What are the comparable statements in a civil trial?

intrude into the underlying reasoning and methodology adopted by experts. Choosing to pursue a "hard look" doctrine and perform a "close judicial analysis * * * of technical and specialized" proofs, the court exhaustively reviewed a "sampling" of six of the thirty-five epidemiological studies which have failed to find a statistically significant association between Bendectin and birth defects. In a balanced analysis, it identified a number of grounds for attacking the validity of the studies offered by defendant, observing that "Merrell Dow overstates the persuasive power of these statistical studies." Nevertheless, in examining the plaintiff's proofs, the court found that the animal and in vitro studies, while "capable" of showing Bendectin as a "possible" teratogen, failed to meet the plaintiffs' burden of proof:

> The decisive weakness in the plaintiffs' animal studies is that the factual and theoretical bases articulated for the scientific opinions stated will not support a finding that Bendectin more probably than not caused the birth defects here. * * * Here, except for Dr. Palmer's testimony discussed below, the plaintiffs' experts stop short of testifying that Bendectin more probably than not caused the birth defects in babies. They stop short because they have no factual or theoretical basis for a stronger hypothesis. They testify that the animal studies show that Bendectin is "capable of causing," "could cause" or its effects are "consistent with causing" birth defects, not that it probably causes birth defects in general or that it did in this case. In short, they testify to a possibility rather than a probability.

6. *Animal Studies.* What of animal studies referred to in the above cases? Other courts have also questioned the efficacy of relying on animal studies to prove causation. See, e.g., Lynch v. Merrell-National Labs., 830 F.2d 1190 (1st Cir.1987) (animal bioassays "do not have the capability of proving causation in human beings in the absence of confirmatory epidemiological data"). There exists a vigorous debate within the scientific community as to the efficacy of such studies in serving to predict the effects of chemicals on humans. Dr. Ellen Silbergeld has described the refusal of some courts to consider animal studies in determining the potential of toxic chemicals on human health as the equivalent of placing creationism over Darwinism. She argues that toxicological studies of animals are indispensable because of the paucity of direct data of chemicals on humans, the thousands of untested chemicals entering our environment, the importance of prevention of damage to human health, and the ethical and practical limitations on obtaining causation data from human research:

> Because of the essentiality of toxicology in understanding and preventing human disease, it is unreasonable and inefficient to exclude toxicology from legal decision making. It would separate causation as understood in medicine from causation as understood in law. The rejection of any and all toxicological data from legal decision making merely because it is derived from nonhuman organisms is scientifically unreasonable because of two powerful concepts in biology, Darwinism and cell theory.... To refuse to consider toxicology would be to consider rational the decision by a mother to allow her child to drink a substance that had just killed her cat on the grounds that no human had yet been harmed by it.

She points out further that "excluding toxicology [in making judicial decisions on human causality] has the effect of removing much of the scientifically relevant and useful information from consideration by a court." See Ellen K. Silbergeld, The Role of Toxicology in Causation: A Scientific Perspective, 1 Courts, Health Science and the Law 374 (1991); see also, for similar statements, James Huff et al., Scientific Concepts: Value and Significance of Chemical Carcinogenesis Studies, 31 Ann. Rev. Pharm. Toxicol. 621, 622 (1991). For a view that animal studies are of limited utility in identifying human carcinogens, see Bruce Ames & Lois Swirsky Gold, Too Many Rodent Carcinogens: Mitogenesis Increases Mutagenesis, 249 Sci. 970 (1990); C. Jelleff Carr & Albert C. Kolbye, A Critique of the Use of the Maximum Tolerated Dose in Bioassays to Assess Cancer Risk from Chemicals, 14 Reg. Toxicol. & Pharmacol. 78 (1991).

7. Finally, perhaps the most ringing endorsement of treating supportive epidemiology as an indispensable element of a plaintiff's causation evidence comes from Judge Weinstein in In re Agent Orange Product Liability Litigation, 611 F.Supp. 1223, 1231 (E.D.N.Y.1985), where he dismisses a veteran's suit:

> A number of sound epidemiological studies have been conducted on the health effects of exposure to Agent Orange. These are the only useful studies having any bearing on causation.

> All the other data supplied by the parties rests on surmise and inapposite extrapolations from animal studies and industrial accidents. It is hypothesized that, predicated on this experience, adverse effects of Agent Orange on plaintiffs might at some time in the future be shown to some degree of probability.

> The available relevant studies have addressed the direct effects of exposure on servicepersons and the indirect effects of exposure on spouses and children of servicepersons. No acceptable study to date of Vietnam veterans and their families concludes that there is a causal connection between exposure to Agent Orange and the serious adverse health effects claimed by plaintiffs.

Has Judge Weinstein overstated the case for epidemiology? How relevant is it that epidemiological studies of Vietnam servicepersons revealed no higher incidences of certain diseases associated with exposure to dioxin?

8. *Some Literature.* There are a number of articles that deal specifically with the role of epidemiological proof in environmental tort litigation which were cited or quoted in the above opinions. See, e.g., Bert Black, A Unified Theory of Scientific Evidence, 56 Fordham L. Rev. 595 (1988); Bert Black and David E. Lilienfeld, Epidemiological Proof in Toxic Tort Litigation, 52 Fordham L. Rev. 732 (1984); Susan R. Poulter, Science and Toxic Torts: Is There a Rational Solution to the Problem of Causation?, 7 High Tech. L. J. 1 (1993); Phantom Risk: Scientific Inference and the Law (Kenneth R. Foster, David E. Bernstein & Peter W. Huber eds. 1993). Michael Dore, A Commentary on the Use of Epidemiological Evidence in Demonstrating Cause-in-fact, 7 Harv. Envtl. L. Rev. 429 (1983); Khristine L. Hall & Ellen K. Sibergeld, Reappraising Epidemiology: A Response to Mr. Dore, 7 Harv. Envtl. L. Rev. 441 (1983); Daniel S. Farber, Toxic Causation, 71 Minn. L. Rev. 1219 (1987); Troyen Brennan, Helping Courts With Toxic

Torts: Some Proposals Regarding Alternative Methods for Presenting and Assessing Scientific Evidence in Common Law Courts, 51 U. Pitt. L. Rev. 1 (1989).

On the application of statistical evidence to litigation more generally, including topics such as statistical significance, standard deviations, "P" values and confidence intervals, see Neil B. Cohen, Conceptualizing Proof and Calculating Probabilities: A Response to Professor Kaye, 73 Cornell L. Rev. 78 (1987); David H. Kaye, Apples and Oranges: Confidence Coefficients and Burdens of Persuasion, 73 Cornell L. Rev. 54 (1987); D. Barnes & J. Conley, Statistical Evidence in Litigation (1986 & 1991 Supp.); Neil B. Cohen, Confidence in Probability: Burdens of Persuasion in a World of Imperfect Knowledge, 60 N.Y.U. L. Rev. 329 (1985); David H. Kaye, Is Proof of Statistical Significance Relevant? 61 Wash. L. Rev. 1833 (1986); 1 Steven M. Crafton, Quantitative Methods for Lawyers (1992).

Problem

A jury awarded Willie Earl Davis $676,000 in damages in a case alleging that his rare kidney disease resulted from exposure to solvents aboard defendants' oil rigs. At issue in the post-trial motion is a jury award to the former oil rig worker, who claimed he contracted Goodpasture's Syndrome from workplace exposure to hydrocarbon solvents aboard rigs owned and operated by Odeco Inc. Davis, a roustabout employed by Odeco, worked aboard 13 different offshore oil rigs between 1980 and 1990. His duties included spray-painting drilling vessels with solvent-based paints. The jury found Odeco liable under the Jones Act for negligence and negligence per se, determining that unseaworthy conditions on seven of the eleven Odeco vessels caused Davis' illness.

Evidence at trial showed the following: Davis began spitting up blood in November 1989, but had no other symptoms of illness. A diagnostic test at the time revealed excess protein and blood in his urine. In February 1990, Davis collapsed while working aboard another oil rig. He was diagnosed to be suffering from respiratory failure attributable to declining kidney function, with the illness diagnosed as Goodpasture's Syndrome, a rare autoimmune disease of the kidneys in which membrane inflammation is accompanied by pulmonary hemorrhaging. There have only been about 500 reported cases since the disease was first diagnosed in 1919.

Davis was discharged from the hospital in March 1990, but suffers permanent kidney damage and residual scarring of the lungs. At trial, Davis contended that Odeco failed "to institute adequate safety measures" to protect workers from hydrocarbon exposure, and failed to comply with regulations, pursuant to a state occupational safety statute, requiring the company to implement and enforce a comprehensive respiratory protection program for employees. Plaintiff's causation experts testified that seven of eight epidemiologic studies on the association between hydrocarbons and Goodpasture's Syndrome "revealed a statistically significant increased risk of contracting the disease" among individuals exposed to hydrocarbons. Those studies showed a relative risk elevation of between 1.09 and 1.47.

Defense causation experts testified that the association between the hydrocarbons and the illness was insufficient to establish a causal relationship. They also testified that the lack of any confirmatory animal data on the alleged relationship further strained the validity of the epidemiologic studies. The defense contended that Davis was the first employee in the company's 39–year history to allege he had the disease. Furthermore, the defense contended, the causes of Goodpasture's Syndrome are primarily hereditary. The defense maintains additionally that Davis' prior work at an auto body repair shop and his cigarette smoking—1 1/2 packs per day for ten years—also could have been a significant contributing cause of the illness.

Based on this record, the defense counsel has filed a motion for a judgment n.o.v. You are the law clerk for the trial judge who has received the motion. How would you rule on the motion? Prepare a memorandum setting forth your ruling and rationale.

c. *Note on Exposure as an Element of Causation*

1. In proving that substance X caused plaintiff's harm, the plaintiff must prove that he or she was sufficiently exposed to the toxic substance that its harmful characteristics had the opportunity to produce the injuries which plaintiff alleges. In cases involving the nuisance-type model—one landowner discharging a harmful substance and other land-owners, usually residential, suffering some type of illness which they attribute to the discharge—proof of actual exposure to the toxic substance can often prove difficult, as the following case illustrates.

2. *Exposure in Nuisance–Model Cases*: A decision that demonstrates the difficulties plaintiffs may experience in proving exposure as integral to the causation question even where their injuries are uncontested and defendants' contamination unquestioned, is Renaud v. Martin Marietta Corp., 749 F.Supp. 1545 (D.Colo.1990), affirmed, 972 F.2d 304 (10th Cir.1992). In granting defendants' motion for summary judgment the court stated: "[P]roof that Martin committed reprehensible acts coupled with evidence of injury is not enough to prevail on a tort claim. * * * Plaintiffs must prove that the reprehensible acts caused, or increased the likelihood of, the alleged injuries."

In *Renaud*, the plaintiffs were residents of an area that drew its water supply from a water treatment plant, one of whose sources was contaminated by defendant's missile operations. Plaintiff's evidence on causation consisted of experts' postulations that waste water containing a concentration of hydrazines and other contaminants had been discharged by Martin Marietta into a creek on a regular basis over an 11–year period and that these contaminants in smaller percentages arrived at the water treatment plant and were thereafter delivered in measurable quantities to the residents' neighborhood. This 11–year postulation by plaintiffs was extrapolated back by their experts from a single water sample, taken from Martin's waste water pond in 1985, two years *after* plaintiffs had received their water from the water treatment plant. The trial court concluded that an 11–year fate and transport model, supported by only a single data point, would not suffice to support a jury finding that contaminated water from Martin's plant had probably reached plaintiffs' taps over critical periods at levels sufficient to cause their injuries. The Tenth Circuit concurred that the trial court's refusal to infer exposure on the basis of a single water sample taken from defendant's pond was correct.

To overcome the nearly insurmountable difficulties in proving directly that they had been exposed to sufficient quantities of hydrazines to cause their injuries, the district court had stated that plaintiffs could also have offered circumstantial evidence in the form of epidemiological studies. The idea is that if an epidemiologic study of the residents living in a community reflects a significantly higher incidence of particular disease over the expected rates occurring in the general population, then it is possible to infer that they were exposed to the toxic chemicals. Plaintiffs argued that they should not be required to introduce epidemiologic evidence. However, this placed them in an untenable position because they needed such studies to serve as circumstantial evidence of exposure. Indeed, they sought to criticize the one study that had been performed showing a twofold higher rate of childhood cancer because the expert who performed it found it to be inconclusive due to the small sample involved. Finally, plaintiffs did not attempt their own epidemiological study because they thought it would be "futile," hence destroying any opportunity of circumstantially establishing exposure and causation.

It is important to understand that epidemiology would not be used here to establish a causal association between chemical hyrazines and cancer, which was not a seriously contested issue in the case; but rather to show a sufficiently greater incidence of cancer above expected rates to create circumstantial evidence that the residents of the area were in fact exposed to hydrazines.

Renaud stands as cogent evidence that nuisance model cases are extremely difficult for plaintiffs because of the multi-layered causation steps that must be overcome. *Renaud* illustrates that plaintiffs must be able to demonstrate actual exposure and dose at levels sufficient to cause the kinds of injuries alleged, and that such proof may be extremely difficult to develop.

How should plaintiffs go about proving exposure in nuisance model cases long after the alleged exposure occurred? In many cases the release of an exposure to toxic substances is documented by governmental agencies at the time it is occurring, making proof of this element more manageable. In Chapter 10 we consider The Agency for Toxic Substances and Disease Registry, created by the Comprehensive Environmental Response, Compensation and Liability Act, 42 U.S.C.A § 9601 et seq., which is designed to help address this very problem where hazardous waste sites are involved. See Ammons v. Wysong & Miles Co, 110 N.C.App. 739, 431 S.E.2d 524 (1993) (plaintiffs' strict liability action dismissed because they could not prove contaminants in their wells had migrated from leaks in nearby chemical storage tanks); Berry v. Armstrong Rubber Co., 780 F.Supp. 1097 (S.D.Miss.1991); Amorello v. Monsanto Corp., 186 Mich.App. 324, 463 N.W.2d 487 (1990).

3. *The Frequency, Regularity and Proximity Test.* In asbestos litigation, an increasingly contested issue is whether the plaintiff was actually and significantly exposed to the defendants' asbestos-containing products in the workplace. The courts have developed a three-pronged "frequency, regularity and proximity" test, first articulated in Lohrmann v. Pittsburgh Corning Corp., 782 F.2d 1156 (4th Cir.1986), which requires that the plaintiff offer "evidence of exposure to a specific product on a regular basis over some extended period of time in proximity to where plaintiff actually worked." For example, in Fiffick v. GAF Corp., 412 Pa.Super. 261, 603 A.2d 208 (1992), the defendant Owens–Corning Fiberglass (OCF) manufactured Kaylo insulation. After 1972, OCF stopped using asbestos in the production of Kaylo. From 1947 until 1985, Fiffick worked at a steel plant where Kaylo was allegedly used. He sued OCF, among others, alleging that he had suffered injury from workplace exposure to airborne asbestos fibers. During discovery, plaintiff was unable to demonstrate how often he was exposed to Kaylo before the late 1970s. The trial court entered summary judgment in favor of OCF.

The Superior Court affirmed, holding that proof of frequent, regular work at a site near a defendant's asbestos-containing product is necessary to defeat a summary judgment motion on a claim alleging workplace exposure to asbestos. The court rejected plaintiff's argument that a jury could infer his exposure to Kaylo before 1972 based on expert testimony that asbestos fibers drift after they are released into the air. Although fiber drift testimony is valuable in meeting the proximity prong of the frequency-regularity-proximity test, it does not show how often a particular product was used or how often a worker was present where fibers may have drifted. Such evidence must be produced first in order to lay a proper foundation for introduction of expert testimony on fiber drift. Here, plaintiff had failed to show when, where, and how frequently asbestos-containing Kaylo had been used or that he had worked near it.

In contrast, in Slaughter v. Southern Talc Co., 949 F.2d 167 (5th Cir.1991), several hundred tire plant workers sued Owens–Corning Fiberglass Corporation (OCF), alleging workplace exposure to Kaylo. The trial court granted OCF summary judgment on the ground that plaintiffs had presented no eyewitness testimony that they had worked near Kaylo insulation.

The Fifth Circuit Court of Appeals reversed, acknowledging that the appropriate test for a minimum showing of exposure in asbestos cases is the "frequency-regularity-proximity test." However, it found sufficient, evidence showing that (1) Kaylo had been delivered to the plant, (2) Kaylo had been installed all over pipes in the plant, and (3) all plaintiffs had worked near the plant's insulated pipes. Thus, if a jury believed plaintiffs' circumstantial evidence, it could reasonably infer sufficient proximity to OCF's asbestos product to establish causation. See also, applying this theory, Blair v. Eagle–Picher Industries, 962 F.2d 1492 (10th Cir.1992); Robertson v. Allied Signal, Inc., 914 F.2d 360 (3d Cir.1990) (fiber drift may satisfy the proximity requirement, but not the regularity and frequency requirements); Thacker v. UNR Industries, 151 Ill.2d 343, 177 Ill.Dec. 379, 603 N.E.2d 449 (1992) (upholding a verdict against Manville which had supplied 3 percent of the asbestos material used at the plant, concluding that 3 percent of total dust was not insignificant as a matter of law, in light of medical evidence indicating that even a slight exposure could cause cancer, and in light of the total volume of asbestos at the UNR plant). Should expert testimony be required to show that asbestos fibers could have drifted from one section of a plant to the area where plaintiff worked regularly? How best can a defendant rebut the fiber drift hypothesis? Will evidence that plaintiff worked at job sites where other employees handled asbestos-containing insulation products be sufficient? See Augustine v. A.C. & S. Corp., 971 F.2d 129 (8th Cir.1992).

B.   PLAINTIFF INDETERMINACY

In many respects, the question of whether the substance was capable of producing plaintiff's injury and whether we can differentiate the plaintiff from the background population that would have otherwise contracted the disease are closely related. Nevertheless, the focus of the Bendectin litigation was less on differentiating plaintiffs from all of the children suffering birth defects and more on whether the drug was or was not a teratogen. In this section our focus is on how the courts perform the function of differentiating between background cases of the disease and those attributable to the toxic exposure and what devices courts might use to facilitate the process and yet preserve the basic goals of tort liability rules. The first approach, as to which *Allen v. United States* is the paradigm, seeks to solve the indeterminate plaintiff problem by combining three evidentiary forms: (1) burden shifting; (2) strong probabilistic proof; and (3) an overlay of relevant particularistic or anecdotal proof. The second approach, described in the *Agent Orange* litigation, rejects the possibility of individualized proof and relies solely on classwide proportional causation proofs.

1.   *INDIVIDUALIZED MODEL: ALLEN v. UNITED STATES*

Allen v. United States, 588 F.Supp. 247 (D.Utah 1984), reversed on other grounds 816 F.2d 1417 (10th Cir.1987), cert. denied 484 U.S. 1004, 108 S.Ct. 694, 98 L.Ed.2d 647 (1988) was an action brought against the United States government under the Federal Tort Claims Act (FTCA) by approximately 1200 named plaintiffs, alleging some 500 deaths and injuries as a result of radioactive fallout from open air atomic bomb tests held in Nevada in the 1950s and early 1960s. The district court selected twenty-four "bellwether" claims and held a full trial on those claims to develop a framework for managing the remainder of the claims. The court entered final judgment in favor of the government on fourteen of the claims, against the government on nine, and left one unresolved. Portions of the court's opinion (the entire opinion is 230 pages) address the complex questions of causation raised by the court's determination of whether the ionized radiation from the nuclear tests was the cause in fact of the variety of physical injuries and illnesses, including death, suffered by the twenty-four selected individual plaintiffs.

First, relevant for our purposes, was the court's description of what it meant by the statement that "radiation causes cancer": "We simply mean that a population exposed to a certain dose of radiation will show a greater incidence of cancer than the same population would have shown in the absence of the added radiation." Second, the court pointed out several reasons why causation is more problematic in these mass exposure cases, including the long latency periods, the possible involvement of "intervening causes," and the "non-specific nature" of the injury. Relying on J. Gofman, Radiation and Human Health (1981), Judge Jenkins found that radiation-induced cancer cannot be distinguished from cancer in the same organs attributable to natural, unknown, or "spontaneous" causes or sources. To overcome these difficulties, the court seeks to establish "exclusive factual connections"; for example, that the defendant engaged in particular risk-creating conduct by the manner in which it conducted the tests and its failure to provide either warnings to or monitoring of exposed persons and that the plaintiffs' injuries are consistent with the kind of harm that one would predict and observe as one of the risks created. The court adopted this test of establishing the necessary legal connection:

> Where the defendant who negligently creates a radiological hazard which puts an identifiable population group at increased risk, a member of that group at risk develops a biological condition which is consistent with having been caused by the hazard to which he has been negligently subjected, such consistency having been demonstrated by substantial, appropriate, persuasive, and connecting factors, a fact finder may reasonably conclude that the hazard caused the condition absent persuasive proof to the contrary offered by the defendant.

How would you interpret this test? Does it mean that once the plaintiff establishes generic causation by the appropriate factors, the burden shifts to the defendant to disprove individual causation? Among the connecting factors it included: (1) the probability that the plaintiff was exposed to ionizing radiation from the Nevada Test Site (NTS) at rates in excess of the natural background radiation; (2) that the plaintiff's injury is of the type consistent with those known to be caused by radiation exposure; and (3) that the plaintiff resided in proximity to the NTS during the relevant period.

In addition, the court identified other relevant factors such as the time and extent of exposure, radiation sensitive factors such as age, sensitivity of certain organs or tissues to radiation, estimation of doses of radiation, consistency between latency period and known cancer etiology, and statistical incidence of the injury greater than that which would be expected in the population group. Further, the court applied a "substantial factor" test of causation, relying upon Restatement (Second) of Torts § 433 and treated its legal connecting factors approach as satisfying a substantial factor causation test. With such a test the plaintiff need not conclusively eliminate all other possible causes of the harm.

In a section entitled "problems with mathematical proof," Judge Jenkins rejected a reliance solely on statistical proof, even if such proof suggests that a particular plaintiff's disease is more likely than not to have been caused by the defendant's conduct, criticizing such an approach as reincarnating the "but for" test, which he explicitly rejected.

Judge Jenkins then explored the dose-response relationships between exposure to ionized radiation and the kind of plaintiffs' injuries, finding the following factors relevant: (1) type of radiation; (2) type of cancer; (3) personal variables of the individual exposed—age, sex, and physical characteristics; and (4) interactions with other stimuli and environmental factors. Unlike some chemical agents, medical scientists have not established any "safe" or threshold level of exposure for radiation; therefore cases could not simply be dismissed on the basis that the plaintiff's dose of the chemical or agent was below that threshold level. Despite the application of a substantial factor test, the consideration of multiple factors, the refusal to rely solely on statistical proof, and an obvious distaste for the government's role in conducting the tests without adequate precautions to the affected populations, it denied recovery to the majority of the twenty-four claimants.

The court treated each claimant individually and the reasons given for rejecting their claims varied; some claimants did not suffer the type of cancer which was shown to be caused by radiation exposure; one did not die from a provable cancer at all. Indeed, the rejection of ten of the fourteen claimants denied recovery were largely attributable to their inability to show an increased incidence of their specific type of cancers in the exposed population above the background level based on population studies.

For example, one man was denied recovery because the evidence showed an increase of stomach cancer among women from radiation exposure, but not among men; and the existence of a strong correlation among men between stomach cancer and other factors, such as diet and age, which contraindicated radiation as the cause. In contrast, the evidence supporting recovery for one woman, Peggy Orton, seemed overwhelming—a 240 to 340 percent increase in childhood leukemia in certain counties and age groups, a consistent latency period, and close proximity to the testing site.

Notes and Questions

1. What judicial support exists for the court's burden shifting in this case? Are the defendant identification cases such as Summers v. Tice, 33 Cal.2d 80, 199 P.2d 1 (1948) (the two hunters case), and Sindell v. Abbott Laboratories, 26 Cal.3d 588, 607 P.2d 924 (1980) relevant? The court also relied upon Haft v. Lone Palm Hotel, 3 Cal.3d 576, 91 Cal.Rptr. 745, 478 P.2d 465 (1970), in which a father and son drowned at a motel where

defendant, contrary to local ordinance, failed to provide a lifeguard or warnings; the California Supreme Court shifted the burden to defendant on the ground that the reason the causes of death were unknown was precisely because of defendant's negligence in not having a lifeguard present. Can you analogize the motel to the United States government in *Allen* ?

2. In determining that the government's testing program was a substantial factor in several of the leukemia cases, the court did not make any finding with respect to the degree of radiation exposure suffered by each of the plaintiffs. There was little evidence on this subject and, not surprisingly, a wide divergence in expert opinion. In Peggy Orton's case, for example, plaintiffs' expert testified that the absorbed dose of her bone marrow was 14.1 rads, while the government expert estimated 0.5 rads. Differences of this magnitude are important. The radioepidemiologic tables prepared by a National Institute of Health Ad Hoc Working Group estimated that the likelihood of developing leukemia by age 13 for a female exposed at age 0 is 4.6% for 1 rad, 34% for 10 rads, and 90% for 100 rads.

The Orphan Drug Act, 21 U.S.C.A. § 360ee, directed the U.S. Department of Health and Human Resources to construct radioepidemiologic tables to show the probabilities that various dosages of radiation caused various types of cancer. See Report of the National Institutes of Health Ad Hoc Working Group to Develop Radioepidemiologic Tables, NIH Pub. No. 85–2748 (1985). The tables include a recommendation that where the government's "assigned share" of the risk is more than 50% full recovery be allowed; where the assigned share is between 10–50% recovery be proportional; and where less than 10% there be no recovery.

3. The case is additionally noteworthy because the indeterminate causation problems did not overwhelm the court. Judge Jenkins held a three-month trial at which both sides introduced a significant volume of testimonial and documentary evidence, much of it highly sophisticated, which he was able to comprehend, digest and apply. Apparently the Judge did not alter his calendar significantly or even employ special masters. See Howard Ball, The Problems and Prospects of Fashioning a Remedy for Radiation Injury Plaintiffs in Federal District Court: Examining Allen v. United States, 1985 Utah L. Rev. 267, 302 n.147; see also Robert L. Rabin, Environmental Liability and the Tort System, 24 Houston L. Rev. 36–39 (1987). Would a jury have been as capable of resolving the causation questions? How would a jury trial have altered the nature of the evidence? The length of trial? Professor Rabin is critical of the decision and finds that it "engenders deep pessimism about the efficacy of tort [law] for multi-party cases," because of the long delay in reaching dispositive results. Of course, that is not peculiar to such cases and even no-fault systems, such as workers' compensation, involve long periods between injury and recovery (or denial).

4. The district court's rulings were reversed by the Court of Appeals, Allen v. United States, 816 F.2d 1417 (10th Cir.1987), cert. denied 484 U.S. 1004, 108 S.Ct. 694, 98 L.Ed.2d 647 (1988), on the grounds that the Atomic Energy Commission, in planning, conducting and monitoring the open air atomic bomb tests held in Nevada was engaged in policy judgments and

discretionary-decisional activities exempting the government from liability under the FTCA, 28 U.S.C.A. §§ 1346(b), 2680(a). The Court of Appeals did not consider the causation issues which were the focus of the district court opinion. The story of the "downwinders," the medical controversy surrounding the issue of causation, and legal battle for compensation is chronicled in H. Bull, Justice Downwind (1986).

For the conflicting statistical studies at issue in the *Allen* case, compare Lyon, et al., Childhood Leukemias Associated with Fallout from Nuclear Testing, 300 New Eng. J. Med. 397 (1979) (concluding that the data show an excess of leukemia) with Land, et al., Childhood Leukemia and Fallout from the Nevada Nuclear Tests, 223 Science 139 (1984) (concluding that the data are not sufficient to support the finding of such an excess). See also Hamilton, Alternative Interpretations of Statistics on Health Effects of Low–Level Radiation (with comments and rejoinder), 37 The Am. Statistician 442 (1983).

5. *Legislative Remedy*. The victims of the Nevada nuclear testing have been recently provided a legislative solution. Congress has enacted the Radiation Exposure Compensation Act of 1990 at 42 U.S.C.A. § 2210 et seq., which offers compensation to those exposed to radiation from nuclear testing and from uranium mining. The Act establishes a trust fund of $100 million and specifies an individual's recovery of $50,000 if the disease is one specified by the Act, (e.g., childhood leukemia, female breast cancer), the exposure occurred at prescribed ages, the claimants resided in a specified area, and other requirements are satisfied, such as not being a heavy smoker.

2. THE COLLECTIVE MODEL: AGENT ORANGE

In contrast to *Allen*, in the Agent Orange settlement opinion, In re Agent Orange Products Liability Litigation, 597 F.Supp. 740 (E.D.N.Y. 1984), affirmed 818 F.2d 145 (2d Cir.1987),cert. denied sub nom. Pickney v. Dow Chemical Co., 484 U.S. 1004, 108 S.Ct. 695, 98 L.Ed.2d 648 (1988), Judge Weinstein eschewed any attempt to make individualized determinations of causality and instead opted for a collective, proportional basis of liability. In approving a $180 million settlement which he was instrumental in crafting, he emphasized the need to view the indeterminate plaintiff problem in the aggregate rather than individually. He pointed out that the DES and asbestos litigation largely involved injuries that did not occur generally at background levels, so that the indeterminate plaintiff problem was not substantial. Further, even in *Allen*, he stated, the cancers attributable to ionized radiation did have some unusual characteristics that served to help differentiate among plaintiffs. Here, however, no such factors were present. Moreover, if plaintiffs were viewed individually, no single plaintiff could overcome the more probable than not standard and all would be denied recovery. His analysis and proposed solution continue:

IN RE AGENT ORANGE PRODUCT
LIABILITY LITIGATION

United States District Court, Eastern District of New York, 1984.
597 F.Supp. 740.

* * *

(a) Application of the Preponderance Rule to Mass Exposure Cases

Conventional application of the "weak" version of the preponderance rule would dictate that, if the toxic substance caused the incidence of the injury to rise more than 100% above the "background" level, each plaintiff exposed to the substance could recover if he or she is suffering from that type of injury. If, however, to put it in somewhat graphic, albeit artificial terms, the incidence rose only 100% or less, no plaintiff could recover—i.e., the probability of specific causation would not be more than 50%.

Where a plaintiff's injuries result from a series of unrelated sporadic accidents, this "all-or-nothing" rule is justifiably rationalized on the ground that it is the fairest and most efficient result. In mass exposure cases, however, this all-or-nothing rule results in either a tortious defendant being relieved of all liability or overcompensation to many plaintiffs and a crushing liability on the defendant. These results are especially troublesome because, unlike the sporadic accident cases, it may be possible to ascertain with a fair degree of assurance that the defendant did cause damage, and, albeit with somewhat less certainty, the total amount of that damage.

* * *

Under the traditional application of the preponderance rule, whether individual plaintiffs recover will depend on where the probability percentage line is drawn despite the fact that a reasonable trier would conclude that a large proportion of the plaintiffs were injured by the defendant and a large number were not. Even if the statistical increase attributed to the substance in question is just a few percentage points, if statistical theory supports a finding of correlation there is no reason why the industry as a whole should not pay for the damages it probably caused.

A simple hypothetical will illustrate why too heavy a burden should not be placed on plaintiffs by requiring a high percentage or incidence of a disease to be attributable to a particular product. Let us assume that there are 10 manufacturers and a population of 10 million persons exposed to their product. Assume that among this population 1,000 cancers of a certain type could be expected, but that 1,100 exist, and that this increase is "statistically significant," permitting a reasonable conclusion that 100 cancers are due to the product of the manufacturers. In the absence of other evidence, it might be argued that as to any one of the 1100 there is only a chance of about 9% ($^{100}/_{1100}$) that the product caused the cancer. Under traditional tort principles no plaintiff could recover.

(b) Inadequacy of Individualized Solutions

Any attempt to resolve the problem on a plaintiff-by-plaintiff basis cannot be fully satisfactory. The solution that would most readily suggest itself is a burden shifting approach, analogous to that used in the indeterminate defendant situation already discussed. *Allen v. United States* provides a good example of how burden-shifting would be applied in an indeterminate plaintiff case. A plaintiff must show that the defendant, in that case the United States, negligently put "an identifiable population group" of which he was a member at "increased risk" and that his injury is

> consistent with having been caused by the hazard to which he has been negligently subjected, such consistency having been demonstrated by substantial, appropriate, persuasive and connecting factors. * * *

Allen, 588 F.Supp. at 415. At that point, the burden shifts to the defendant which will be held liable unless it can offer "persuasive proof" of noncausation. *Id.*

Generally courts have shifted the burden to the defendant to prove that it was not responsible for plaintiff's injury only in sporadic accident cases where it was certain that one of a very limited number of defendants injured the plaintiff, *see, e.g., Summers v. Tice,* 33 Cal.2d 80, 199 P.2d 1 (1948); *Ybarra v. Spangard,* 25 Cal.2d 486, 154 P.2d 687 (1944), or in mass exposure cases where general causation was certain and liability was apportioned in accordance with some market-share theory.

Shifting the burden of proof in such cases will, at least theoretically, not result in crushing liability for the defendant either because the litigation only involves a sporadic accident, as in *Summers* and *Ybarra,* or because the defendant will only be held liable for the amount of damage it caused based on market share—although * * *, there may be practical problems in defining market share. By contrast, shifting the burden of proof in the indeterminate plaintiff situation could result in liability far out of proportion to damage caused. It is not helpful in most situations to say that the defendant will not be liable for "those harms which [he] can reasonably prove were *not* in fact a consequence of his risk-creating, negligent conduct," *Allen,* 588 F.Supp. at 415, since, were such individualized proof available, there would have been no need to shift the burden.

(3) POSSIBLE SOLUTION IN CLASS ACTION

Since the problem results from a plaintiff-by-plaintiff method of adjudication, one solution is to try all plaintiffs' claims together in a class action thereby arriving at a single, class-wide determination of the total harm to the community of plaintiffs. Given the necessarily heavy reliance on statistical evidence in mass exposure cases, such a determination seems feasible. The defendant would then be liable to each exposed plaintiff for a pro rata share of that plaintiff's injuries.

This approach can be illustrated using the hypothetical given above. Suppose all 1,100 of those who were exposed to the harmful substance and who developed the cancer in the example join in a class action against all 10 manufacturers. Let us say that damages average $1,000,-000 per cancer. A recovery of $100,000,000 (100 × $1,000,000) in favor of the class would be allowed with the percentage of the award to be paid by each manufacturer depending on the toxicity of its product. For example, if a company produced only 20% of the substance in question but, because of the greater toxicity of its product, likely caused 60% of the harm, it would contribute 60% of the total amount. If accurate records are available on the composition of each defendant's product, that analysis should be possible.

Since no plaintiff can show that his or her cancer was caused by any one of the defendants, they should divide the $100,000,000 by 1,100, giving each a recovery of about $90,000. While any plaintiff might feel that his or her recovery denigrated the degree of harm, the alternative of receiving nothing is far worse. The latter is, of course, the necessary result in any plaintiff's individual suit. Moreover, the deterrent effect of this result on producers would be significant.

* * *

Notes and Questions

1. *Preponderance of the Evidence and Particularistic Proof.* Judge Weinstein makes clear the recurrent problem in mass exposure cases—that it is extremely difficult for individual plaintiffs to establish causation under what he calls the "strong version" of the preponderance of the evidence rule because two conditions must exist: epidemiological studies which show that the add-on risk is 100% above the background risk (i.e., the relative risk must exceed 2.0) *and* "particularistic" proof which supports causation. Which version of the preponderance rule do you favor in sporadic accident cases, the weak version, which dispenses with the requirement of particularistic proof and allows recovery solely on the basis of probabilistic evidence, or the strong version? Which do you favor in mass exposure cases? What might justify the difference?

What kind of "particularistic" proof might exist in mass exposure cases like *Agent Orange* connecting plaintiff's injuries to the defendant's wrongful conduct and serve to distinguish plaintiffs from the "background" population? Are they precisely the same kinds of proof Judge Jenkins concentrated upon in *Allen*, such as the details of exposure and data on the dose-response relationships? Other factors could include any unique characteristics of the disease or plaintiff's condition that is medically remarkable; or the absence of other common causes (e.g. a non-smoker, no family history of the disease, little or no alcohol consumption) that would often be present for others suffering the disease. But how should a court address these particularistic proofs where there exist hundreds or thousands of plaintiffs? One approach, applied in some asbestos litigation, is described in Chapter 13.

2. Consider the following statement:

In mass tort cases, the problem of reliance on "bare" statistics for an affirmative case is likely to be more hypothetical than real. When there is a causal mechanism that produces a strong statistical association, the epidemiologic data will generally be incorporated into a body of professional opinion that relies on a variety of biological as well as statistical evidence. To require such other evidence in a legal context is not unreasonable; epidemiologists themselves would generally insist on it before drawing a causal inference from the data. Michael O. Finkelstein & Bruce Levin, Statistics for Lawyers 21 (1990).

Does this undercut Judge Weinstein's approach?

3. *Multiple Studies.* Most complex cases will not involve a single reliable study that reveals a statistically significant increase in the relative risk that is accepted by all of the parties and the court. In *Agent Orange* none of the epidemiological studies of Vietnam veterans showed any increase in any identifiable serious illness that was attributable to exposure to Agent Orange. In fact, in *Agent Orange* there were epidemiological studies performed of workers involved in industrial accidents that exposed them to large concentrations of dioxin that did reveal positive associations between dioxin and certain diseases. Why weren't these admissible? What if there are two epidemiological studies with differing results—one showing a positive correlation between a disease and the toxic substance and the other showing no correlation? How does the fact finder decide which is "correct" or "more likely than not" to be correct?

4. *"Signature" Diseases.* Judge Weinstein pointed out that the indeterminate plaintiff problem is especially intractable in cases where the disease is one that occurs generally in the population. But that is not always true. Some diseases are rare and are manifested *only* in persons exposed to a particular toxic substance. Professor Brennan describes these diseases in Troyen Brennan, Helping Courts With Toxic Torts: Some Proposals Regarding Alternative Methods for Presenting and Assessing Scientific Evidence in Common Law Courts, 51 U. Pitt. L. Rev. 1, 21, 22 (1989):

> Much of the impetus to develop alternatives to litigation, or modifications of existing tort doctrine, is informed by what Abraham and Merrill have termed signature diseases. Signature diseases are those diseases which are most often discovered through cluster analysis; they are rare and often associated with a specific exposure. For example, clear cell adenocarcinoma is a rare tumor, and it is frequently associated with maternal exposure to DES. The DES/clear cell causal connection, as well as that between asbestos and mesothelioma, has informed much of the discussion about alternative methods for deciding causal issues in courtrooms.

> Signature diseases are not the rule in toxicology. Much more frequently, hazardous substances cause diseases that can occur sporadically without exposure. In most cases, the fraction of the overall incidence of a disease that can be attributed to the hazardous substance is small. In addition, many people who are exposed to one hazardous

substance are also exposed to others. This makes the causation issue even more difficult.[101]

Judge Weinstein seems to suggest that some of the cancers in *Allen* were "signature" diseases, or at least ones rarely occurring in the absence of ionizing radiation. Is that true?

5. Judge Weinstein's commitment to rejecting individualized solutions was demonstrated in his dismissal of claims brought by "opt-out" plaintiffs. See In re Agent Orange Product Liability Litigation, 611 F.Supp. 1223 (E.D.N.Y.1985), affirmed 818 F.2d 187 (2d Cir.1987), cert. denied sub. nom.; Lombardi v. Dow Chemical Co., 487 U.S. 1234, 108 S.Ct. 2898, 101 L.Ed.2d 932 (1988); Lilley v. Dow Chemical Co., 611 F.Supp. 1267 (E.D.N.Y.1985). He granted defendants' summary judgment motions because of plaintiff's reliance on expert opinions that were not founded on epidemiological studies, but on animal studies and industrial accidents. In addition, his treatment of the individual plaintiffs was greatly influenced by his commitment to achieve a classwide settlement of the controversy and his refusal to differentiate among individual plaintiffs in any manner that might undermine the class-wide settlement.

More recently, Judge Weinstein continued to preclude individual law-suits against the Agent Orange manufacturers when he dismissed actions brought by thirty-seven Texas veterans and their families. See Ryan v. Dow Chemical Co., 781 F.Supp. 902 (E.D.N.Y.1991), affirmed 996 F.2d 1425 (2d Cir.1993). Judge Weinstein rejected the plaintiffs' arguments that they were not class members because their injuries did not manifest themselves until after the opt-out deadline for the $180 million settlement. The plaintiffs contended their claims should have been treated as an ordinary toxic tort action in the Texas court where they were filed. In contrast, he did remand to Texas courts two suits brought by Vietnam *civilians* who were not members of the class. Ivy v. Diamond Shamrock Co., 781 F.Supp. 934 (E.D.N.Y.1992).

The outcome of the opt-out litigation and the separate suit by Lilley are criticized by Professor Charles Nesson, Agent Orange Meets the Blue Bus: Factfinding at the Frontier of Knowledge, 66 Boston U. L. Rev. 521, 522–29 (1986). Professor Nesson, who had two years earlier challenged the propriety of relying on statistical proof to establish whether an event had occurred, argues that Judge Weinstein should not have dismissed the Lilley case (and presumably the other opt-out cases) because he was usurping a function that properly belonged to the jury by holding expert testimony inadmissible under Rule 703 and by finding that *only* epidemiological studies are relevant in such litigation; indeed, his arguments respecting the sufficiency of a

---

101. The concept of a signature disease is deceptively simple. Clear cell adenocarcinoma is considered a signature disease of DES exposure. Recent research suggests that this disease is relatively common in the absence of DES exposure. The effect which this information may have on DES litigation is unclear. The signature disease of asbestos is mesothelioma, but it also causes lung cancer and a variety of other pulmonary diseases. See Becklake, Asbestos–Re-lated Diseases of the Lung and Other Organs: Their Epidemiology and Implications for Clinical Practice, 114 Am. Rev. Respiratory Disease 187, 211 (1976). Many of the most recently filed asbestos claims are based on these diseases other than mesothelioma, and a new flood of litigation has swamped the Wellington groups. See Williger, Asbestos Litigation in the Federal Courts (1986). Thus, the signature disease paradigm is of limited use.

plaintiff's proof of causation closely mirror those set forth in *Ferebee*, discussed earlier in this chapter.

5. *Proportionality proposals.* Professor Rosenberg, whose article was frequently quoted by Judge Weinstein, recommends the application of proportionality rules, rather than preponderance rules (even the weak version), as producing fairer outcomes in a system where corrective justice principles should predominate, compatible with goals of deterrence and compensation. His defense of the proportionality rule is contained in the following article.

DAVID ROSENBERG, CAUSAL CONNECTION IN MASS EXPOSURE CASES: A "PUBLIC LAW" VISION OF THE TORT SYSTEM

97 Harv. L. Rev. 849, 868–77 (1984).

* * * Rarely, if ever, are courts able to conclude with certainty in the case of a particular victim that the disease resulted from the defendant's use of the toxic agent in question, rather than from any one of the independent factors comprising the "background" risk. This is especially true when dealing with moderate to low level exposures. The most that can be said about what happened to the particular victim is a statement of causal probabilities derived from epidemiological and other scientific studies finding a statistically identifiable "excess" incidence of the particular disease, and associating it with the defendant's hazardous activities. The probability that any particular claimant's disease was caused by the defendant's toxic activity is computed, all else being equal, by dividing the total risk into the excess risk of the particular disease in the exposed population.

In the view of many commentators, the problem of causal indeterminacy can be effectively dealt with by replacing the traditional common-law preponderance of the evidence rule with proportional liability. Proportional liability holds the defendant liable for the losses of each victim of disease in the exposed population discounted by the probability that the defendant's hazardous activity was the cause. All disease victims in the exposed population would be compensated for a fraction of their losses equal to the ratio in the whole population of excess disease incidence to total disease incidence.

Given conditions of causal indeterminacy, proportional liability appeals to both intuitions of fairness and the pragmatic need for the tort system's measure of deterrence. Proportional liability allays fairness concerns because defendants only pay for the loss their hazardous activity has caused. While the actual if unidentifiable victims of the defendant's activity receive less than full compensation, the deficit is not unfair. * * *

* * *

Essentially, in rejecting an all-or-nothing approach, proportional liability recognizes the competing, irreconcilable chances that each claimant was the victim of either the excess risk attributed to the defendant or the background risk. In effect, the compensation awarded to all disease victims under the proportional liability rule represents the proceeds of a hypothetical insurance policy purchased by the defendant on behalf of the exposed population, covering only the excess risk attributed to the toxic agent hazard.

The system's deterrence objectives would also be well served by proportional liability. No longer would it be possible for industry and government to misuse toxic agents, even in the most heedless fashion, and still expect to be exempted from tort liability for the harm they cause. Since deterrence objectives are concerned with controlling the aggregate risk created by an activity or class of activities, it is immaterial that the probability of causation for any given claimant fails to exceed fifty percent. As such, the deterrence rationale argues strongly for adopting the "pure" form of proportional liability with no threshold probability. Finally, it should be clear that there is no threat of overdeterrence from liability tailored strictly to the loss caused by the defendant's activity.

6. The emergence of proportional causation as a doctrine has gained respectability among a wide cross-section of scholars and is endorsed in 2 Reporters' Study, "Enterprise Responsibility for Personal Injury: Approaches to Legal and Institutional Change" (American Law Institute 1991). Chapter 12 of the Reporters' Study entitled "Standards of Environmental Liability" contains a number of proposals for improving the adjudication of toxic tort claims, including the adoption of proportionate compensation. The following is from pages 369–75:

IV. Proportionate Compensation

* * *

Consider a group of 1,000 people in an area surrounding an industrial plant that uses several carcinogens in its manufacturing process. When one of the chemicals escapes from a holding tank, all 1,000 neighbors are exposed. The escaped substance can cause hepatic carcinoma, or liver cancer. Suppose that 20 individuals out of the original 1,000 would have been expected to develop liver cancer in the absence of any exposure, but that 42 individuals rather than 20 actually develop hepatic cancer. This means that 22 out of the 40 cancers are attributable to the exposure, and an attributable fraction of 53 percent (22/40) would be applicable to each individual case. For each individual it is more probable than not that the cancer is a result of exposure to the hazardous substances. Under current rules all of the plaintiffs with hepatic cancer could prove that their disease is more probably than not the result of exposure to the hazardous substance.

In most environmental injury tort actions, however, exposure levels are usually relatively low; as a result, the increased risks are relatively small. Suppose that exposure to the substance leaking from the plant increased the risk of hepatic cancer by a factor of 1.5. This means that 30 individuals develop liver cancer. Since only 20 such cancers would be expected, the attributable fraction is 33 percent (10/30). None of these plaintiffs would be able to prove that their disease was caused more probably than not by exposure to the substance. * * *

One way to avoid these problems would be to provide compensation on the basis of attributable fractions of causation. The use of proportionate compensation based on the attributable fraction of disease would lower both the burden of proof on plaintiffs and the threshold for bringing environmental injury tort cases. Plaintiffs would be compensated for that fraction of their damages from a particular disease which is attributable to the environmental exposure in question. For example, in the cases cited above each of the individuals afflicted with hepatic cancer would receive some compensation. The compensation would, however, be only a portion of the total damages suffered, calculated using the attributable fraction derived from epidemiological evidence. In the first example each person afflicted with hepatic carcinoma would receive 53 percent of his or her damages as an award. In the second example the proportionate compensation would be 33 percent.

* * *

In the version in which it is sometimes proposed, probabilistic causation and proportionate liability are subject to this criticism, because liability would be imposed whenever the probability of future harm can be quantified. In such a setting liability would be imposed ex ante—that is, before the occurrence of injury. We believe that this legal step is premature at best.

Instead, we advocate only ex post use of probabilistic causation and proportionate liability. We propose that a trier of fact assess the probability of causation and impose proportionate liability only after epidemiological evidence has matured and the actual victims of disease are known. Probabilistic causation would then be used only to overcome the problems associated with indeterminate attribution, not the problems that arise when a party is put at risk of disease. Ours is a more conservative use of proportionate liability and is highly dependent on the use of medical monitoring during the latency period (see below).

We would further limit the scope of our proposal by cautioning against across-the-board use of attributable fractions of any and every size. Many exposures to environmental toxins will cause only slight increases in the risk of disease, sometimes on the order of 2 or 3 percent. If large enough groups of plaintiffs were exposed to such toxins, it could make economic sense for plaintiffs' attorneys to file claims if proportionate compensation were available. This would vastly expand the scope of environmental tort litigation, causing a great deal of legal and economic disruption. A major theme of this Report is the need to increase the predictability of litigation and to facilitate insurance for environmental liability. Allowing litigation no matter how low the attributable fraction would frustrate these efforts. This is not to say that society should attempt to eliminate these exposures. Efforts to eliminate environmental hazards that create a small risk to any single individual but nonetheless create a large disease burden for society should fall mainly within the purview of state and federal environmental regulation.

As a result, we must propose some threshold for the use of attributable fractions and proportionate compensation. The twin demands of fairness to defendants and a commitment to some economic liability require that the threshold represent a substantial increase above the background risk of disease. An attributable fraction of roughly 20 percent would, we believe, accomplish this goal. On the other hand, such a threshold would significantly lower the barrier now set by the "more probable than not" standard.

In summary a proportionate compensation scheme could operate in the following manner. The exposed population would be certified as a class. The class would include all individuals with a disease potentially associated with the exposure. A science panel or a court-appointed expert would estimate the attributable fraction of each disease at various levels of exposure. Once the attributable fractions dropped below 20 percent, the assumption would be that there was no causation of injury. For exposures causing an attributable fraction greater than 20 percent, each individual harmed would receive a fraction of his or her total damages, equal to the attributable fraction. To create symmetry and fairness, any injuries that involved an attributable fraction greater than 80 percent would be compensated at a level of 100 percent. In this way proportionate compensation based on attributable fractions drawn from epidemiological data would both create rational awards to environmental tort litigants and lower the threshold for bringing such cases.

The Reporters' Study, the conclusions of which were neither approved nor disapproved by its sponsor, The American Law Institute, also advocated extensive use of class actions as integral to the application of proportional liability, and greater availability of the medical monitoring remedy.

Do you agree with the exclusion of proportionate liability for attributable fractions less than 20 percent? What purposes does such a threshold serve? Does it eliminate all deterrence against creating such "small" risks? The ALI Reporters' Study relied on several law review articles as the primary authority for its recommendations, including the following: Glen O. Robinson, Multiple Causation in Tort Law: Reflections on the DES Cases, 68 Va. L. Rev. 713 (1982) (advocating expanding the market share analysis into a causal apportionment scheme in which each defendant would pay the proportion of the plaintiff's damages represented by that defendant's contribution to the risk of harm); Richard Delgado, Beyond *Sindell* : Relaxation of Cause–In–Fact Rules for Indeterminate Plaintiffs, 70 Calif. L. Rev. 881 (1982); Glen O. Robinson, Probabilistic Causation and Compensation for Tortious Risk, 14 J. Legal Stud. 779, 783–91 (1985); Joseph H. King, Jr., Causation, Valuation, and Chance in Personal Injury Torts Involving Pre–Existing Conditions and Future Consequences, 90 Yale L.J. 1353 (1981); Steven Shavell, Uncertainty Over Causation and the Determination of Civil Liability, 19 J. L. & Econ. 587 (1985).

C. DID THE DEFENDANT CAUSE PLAINTIFF'S HARM: THE INDETERMINATE DEFENDANT PROBLEM

1. SOME DEVICES TO OVERCOME DEFENDANT INDETERMINACY

Environmental tort litigation often reveals causal indeterminacy on both sides of the caption: indeterminate plaintiffs and indeterminate defendants. A cardinal tenet of traditional tort law liability rules is that the plaintiff must prove that the defendant's conduct was a producing cause of the harm suffered. In the conventional sporadic accident case identifying the responsible defendant is usually not difficult because of the availability of physical or direct evidence that implicates a particular defendant. In toxic and environmental harm cases, however, the chemical agent or polluting source often does not come branded or trademarked with the defendant's name. While defendant or source indeterminacy arose occasionally in products liability cases and accident cases, the frequency and difficulty of source indeterminacy in environmental and toxic torts creates new demands on the courts to develop rules that continue to fulfill the objectives of tort law.

To date, the judicial response to this problem of source indeterminacy has been the creation of mechanisms to ease the plaintiff's burden, most commonly the shifting of the burden of proof to establish noncausation on the shoulders of the defendant. Much of the law in this area has developed in the DES cases. Their origin is found in a simple hunting accident.

a. Alternative Liability

The modern origin of the burden-shifting approach to tortfeasor indeterminacy is found in Summers v. Tice, 33 Cal.2d 80, 199 P.2d 1 (1948), an accident case with an unusual twist. The plaintiff was shot in the eye and in the lip from either of two guns fired by two negligent hunters, but the plaintiff could not prove which one fired the shot that struck his eye by a preponderance of the evidence because it was equally likely that each was the source of that bullet. The California Supreme Court, instilled with a corrective justice view of the situation and the dilemma faced by the plaintiff, held that the burden of proof as to which defendant caused his injury was shifted to the defendants for each to exculpate himself and to apportion damages, with the practical effect of making the defendants jointly and severally liable. See 2 M. Stuart Madden, Products Liability 2d § 15.2 at 88, 89 (1988) for a fuller description of the decision.

The alternative liability theory of *Summers* has considerable appeal to plaintiffs because of the ameliorative impact it has on the onus of causation. However, its principal limitations are that courts are reluctant to apply it in the absence of clear evidence that all or at least one of the defendants are at fault and all of the possible responsible parties are defendants before the court. See Restatement (Second) of Torts § 433B(3) (all actors' conduct must be negligent). What impediments do you see to applying alternative liability in toxic tort cases? For a modified version of alternative liability in the Agent Orange cases, see In re Agent Orange Prod. Liab. Litig., 597 F.Supp. 740, 826–32 (E.D.N.Y. 1984); for a decision declining to apply the alternative liability theory in the lead-based paint litigation, see Hurt v. Philadelphia Housing Authority, 806 F.Supp. 515 (E.D.Pa. 1992).

b. Concert of Action Theory

Concert of action theory posits that a group of actors jointly carried on an activity in a consciously parallel manner, similar to two drivers engaging in a race on city streets. The idea is that they have implicitly agreed to follow a similar pattern of conduct, usually in research, manufacturing or marketing methods, that justifies treating them as jointly and severally liable, and allowing a plaintiff to sue one of the group and hold it liable for all of the damages suffered. While the theory is obviously attractive to plaintiffs, it is of minimal utility in toxic or environmental harm litigation because rarely can a plaintiff establish, by sufficient evidence, the presence of consciously parallel behavior together with proof of an implicit agreement. One opinion of the New York Court of Appeals utilized the theory in an early DES case, Bichler v. Eli Lilly & Co., 55 N.Y.2d 571, 450 N.Y.S.2d 776, 436 N.E.2d 182 (1982), but has been since rejected, in favor of a market share liability mechanism. Hymowitz v. Eli Lilly & Co., 73 N.Y.2d 487, 541 N.Y.S.2d 941, 539 N.E.2d 1069 (1989).

c. Enterprise or Industry–Wide Liability

Courts have occasionally used the novel approach of enterprise liability in an effort to help plaintiffs meet the causation burden of proof. The pioneer case in this area is Hall v. E.I. Du Pont De Nemours & Co., 345 F.Supp. 353 (E.D.N.Y.1972). In *Hall*, some exploding blasting caps injured a group of children, who sued several manufacturers of the blasting caps but could not identify the manufacturer of the blasting caps that actually caused them harm. As a consequence, the plaintiffs sued a limited number of defendants who manufactured blasting caps and their trade association, relying on "substantially similar industry-imposed safety standards," where the defendants had jointly rejected certain safety measures and had jointly lobbied against labeling regulation. Under the enterprise liability theory espoused in *Hall*, the industry-wide standard caused the injury by "joint or group control of risk," so that each defendant that used the standard contributed to and was liable for the plaintiffs' injuries. Enterprise liability thus is a hybrid theory combining elements of alternative liability and concert of action.

See 2 M. Stuart Madden, Products Liability 2d § 15.3 at 93, 94 (1988). To date, the courts have not specifically embraced enterprise liability in an environmental tort case.

d. Market Share Liability

The seminal decision to apply a market share liability theory was Sindell v. Abbott Laboratories, 26 Cal.3d 588, 163 Cal.Rptr. 132, 607 P.2d 924 (1980), cert. denied 449 U.S. 912, 101 S.Ct. 285, 66 L.Ed.2d 140 (1980). The plaintiffs in these DES cases are often unable to identify which producer of the generic drug made the DES which their mothers ingested during pregnancy to minimize risks of miscarriages for several reasons: (1) the passage of many years since the ingestion of the drug (plaintiffs' exposure to the toxic substance in utero); (2) the long latency period before the adverse effects on the female children of the mothers were manifested; (3) the destruction or loss of marketing and manufacturing records of the producers; and (4) the significant number of firms producing the drug (several hundred companies produced or distributed DES in the United States between 1947 and 1962).

Assuming that the plaintiffs could prove negligence or the necessary elements of strict products liability, the court held that if the plaintiff could successfully sue firms which, in the aggregate represented a "substantial share" of the market for DES, the burden would shift to each named defendant to exculpate itself, i.e. to prove that it could not have caused plaintiff's harm because it did not market the kind of DES that her mother took, or did not market DES during the year(s) or in the location where it was purchased. For those defendants failing to carry that burden, each would be held liable for a percentage of plaintiff's damages corresponding to its market share. In a later decision, Brown v. Superior Court (Abbott Laboratories), 44 Cal.3d 1049, 245 Cal.Rptr. 412, 751 P.2d 470 (1988), the California Supreme Court determined that liability would be proportionate only.

There are two principal rationales for applying market share liability. The first, adopted in *Sindell*, is that a firm's share of the market (say 20%) represents the probability that it *actually caused* the individual plaintiff's harm, and imposing liability for 20% of the damages represents a judgment that it should be liable to that extent for the chance that it did in fact cause her damages. Indeed, in mass tort cases if courts in all states followed the identical approach, the theory goes, a manufacturer's damages under the market share analysis will converge with the actual harm it caused to all plaintiffs.

A second rationale, merging concepts of risk contribution with those of market share, was adopted in Hymowitz v. Eli Lilly & Co., 73 N.Y.2d 487, 541 N.Y.S.2d 941, 539 N.E.2d 1069 (1989), decided nine years after *Sindell*. In *Hymowitz* the court found the administrative difficulties engendered by local markets required a different approach. The New York Court of Appeals described the reasoning and structure of its modified market share liability as follows:

Consequently, for essentially practical reasons, we adopt a market share theory using a national market. We are aware that the adoption of a national market will likely result in a disproportion between the liability of individual manufacturers and the actual injuries each manufacturer caused in this State. Thus our market share theory cannot be founded upon the belief that, over the run of cases, liability will approximate causation in this State (see Sindell v. Abbott Labs). Nor does the use of a national market provide a reasonable link between liability and the risk created by a defendant to a particular plaintiff. Instead, we choose to apportion liability so as to correspond to the over-all culpability of each defendant, measured by the amount of risk of injury each defendant created to the public-at-large. Use of a national market is a fair method, we believe, of apportioning defendants' liabilities according to their total culpability in marketing DES for use during pregnancy. Under the circumstances, this is an equitable way to provide plaintiffs with the relief they deserve, while also rationally distributing the responsibility for plaintiffs' injuries among defendants.

To be sure, a defendant cannot be held liable if it did not participate in the marketing of DES for pregnancy use; if a DES producer satisfies its burden of proof of showing that it was not a member of the market of DES sold for pregnancy use, disallowing exculpation would be unfair and unjust. Nevertheless, because liability here is based on the over-all risk produced, and not causation in a single case, there should be no exculpation of a defendant who, although a member of the market producing DES for pregnancy use, appears not to have caused a particular plaintiff's injury. It is merely a windfall for a producer to escape liability solely because it manufactured a more identifiable pill, or sold only to certain drugstores. These fortuities in no way diminish the culpability of a defendant for marketing the product, which is the basis of liability here.

Finally, we hold that the liability of DES producers is several only, and should not be inflated when all participants in the market are not before the court in a particular case. * * *

Which rationale, *Sindell* or *Hymowitz*, do you find more convincing from a fairness perspective? From a deterrence standpoint?

Notes and Questions

1. *Limits of Decision.* The court in *Hymowitz* was concerned that its opinion not be read overly broad to extend to non-comparable circumstances. For example, it described the DES situation as a "singular case, [1] with manufacturers acting in a parallel manner, [2] to produce an identical, generically marketed product, [3] which causes injury many years later * * * " Can you think of any other circumstances where these three factors exist? Asbestos? Cigarettes? Lead paint? What do you think of the court's reasoning? Does it seem more consistent and more readily justiciable than local market share liability or individual risk contribution?

2. a. Following its decision in *Hymowitz*, the New York Court of Appeals has answered three questions about the scope of its risk contribution market share theory. First, in Enright v. Eli Lilly & Co., 77 N.Y.2d 377, 568 N.Y.S.2d 550, 570 N.E.2d 198 (1991), the court refused to extend liability of DES manufacturers to third generation plaintiffs, whose grandmothers consumed DES and whose mothers are the "DES daughters" typically suing in these cases for injuries to their reproductive systems. Drawing on an earlier medical malpractice decision that refused to extend a physician's duty to a child who was not yet conceived at the time of his negligence, the court declined to extend a DES manufacturer's duty to such children, observing that DES claimants were not "a favored class for whose benefit all traditional limitations on tort liability must give way," and citing the need to "confine liability within manageable limits," and the prospect of overdeterrence of the development of beneficial drugs.

b. Second, in Anderson v. Eli Lilly & Co., 79 N.Y.2d 797, 580 N.Y.S.2d 168, 588 N.E.2d 66 (1991), it held that a plaintiff-husband, whose wife suffered from DES-related injuries, could not recover for loss of consortium because the tortious conduct and resultant injuries occurred prior to the marriage.

c. Finally, in In the Matter of DES Market Share Litigation, 79 N.Y.2d 299, 582 N.Y.S.2d 377, 591 N.E.2d 226 (1992), the court held that the plaintiffs in the DES litigation are entitled to a jury trial on the issue of the respective market shares of the defendants, rejecting the view of defendants that *Hymowitz* established an equitable proceeding to which no jury trial rights attached.

d. In perhaps the most extraordinary fallout of the *Hymowitz* decision, the federal district court in New York held that manufacturers of DES that had never sold their product in New York State are subject to the personal jurisdiction of the court under New York's long arm statute. Ashley v. Abbott Laboratories, 789 F.Supp. 552 (E.D.N.Y.1992). In that action Judge Weinstein held that jurisdiction could be exercised over such manufacturers that did not sell DES in New York and were not present in that state by virtue of the manufacturers' engagement in the national DES industry, on the rationale that the producers had marketed a generic drug in one part of the country that produced economic and trade consequences in other parts, including New York.

3. Market share has received a mixed reaction in the courts, a number of which have refused to adopt the doctrine. See, e.g., Mulcahy v. Eli Lilly & Co., 386 N.W.2d 67 (Iowa 1986); Senn v. Merrell–Dow Pharmaceuticals, Inc., 305 Or. 256, 751 P.2d 215 (1988); Tidler v. Eli Lilly & Co., 851 F.2d 418 (D.C.Cir.1988); Smith v. Eli Lilly & Co., 137 Ill.2d 222, 148 Ill.Dec. 22, 560 N.E.2d 324 (1990). However, several decisions while rejecting certain aspects of the *Sindell* market share approach, provide plaintiffs with somewhat similar "solutions" to the defendant identification problems in the DES cases. See, e.g., Abel v. Eli Lilly & Co., 418 Mich. 311, 343 N.W.2d 164 (1984), cert. denied 469 U.S. 833, 105 S.Ct. 123, 83 L.Ed.2d 65 (1984) (concerted action, or modified alternative liability); Martin v. Abbott Laboratories, 102 Wash.2d 581, 689 P.2d 368 (1984) (modified market share); and Collins v. Eli Lilly Co., 116 Wis.2d 166, 342 N.W.2d 37 (1984), cert.

denied, 469 U.S. 826, 105 S.Ct. 107, 83 L.Ed.2d 51 (1984) (individual risk contribution applying comparative fault statute). Conley v. Boyle Drug Co., 570 So.2d 275 (Fla.1990) applies an actual causation rationale, adopting an intensively local market definition including, where possible, identification of individual pharmacies. *Conley* further stated a rule that would require a showing of due diligence by plaintiffs to identify the actual producer, impose proportionate liability, and assign equal market shares to nonexculpating defendants who failed to establish their actual share.

4. Should a plaintiff seeking to utilize a market share (or similar) theory in a DES case be required to make a genuine effort first to identify the manufacturer that supplied her mother's DES? Compare Abel v. Eli Lilly & Co., 418 Mich. 311, 343 N.W.2d 164 (1984) (yes), with McCormack v. Abbott Laboratories, 617 F.Supp. 1521 (D.Mass.1985) (no).

If the plaintiff does have some, but not conclusive, identification evidence, should she be entitled to have both the individual and the market share claims submitted to the jury?

If a plaintiff establishes that a particular defendant's relevant market share was 51% (or higher), should she be entitled to recover 100% of her damages from the defendant on the grounds that it is more likely than not that the defendant was the cause-in-fact of her harm?

5. In Smith v. Eli Lilly & Co., 137 Ill.2d 222, 148 Ill.Dec. 22, 560 N.E.2d 324 (1990), the Illinois Supreme Court declined to adopt market share liability in a DES case, concluding (1) that the *Sindell-Hymowitz* line of cases resulted in overdeterrence of useful activity that would be deterred by excessive liability; (2) that because reliable market share data is rarely available, the courts would be imprudently bogged down in an almost "futile endeavor" that would "create a tremendous cost in terms of workload on the court system and litigants"; (3) that the inconsistency of verdicts in different cases when juries would apportion damages based on market share data that may be different or unavailable; (4) that the likelihood that the defendant who actually sold the product to the plaintiff would not be before the court, so none of the remaining defendants actually caused the harm, and imposing liability would be unfair and too speculative; (5) that market share liability might result in plaintiffs who cannot identify the manufacturer of the DES receiving a larger recovery than those who can, because the latter group of plaintiffs' recoveries will be dependent on the continued existence and solvency of that firm, whereas the former will be able to turn to many companies, some of whom are certain to remain viable and solvent.

Which of the rationales offered seems most persuasive? Does the *Hymowitz* approach solve the administrative-related concerns? The Illinois Supreme Court quoted heavily from an article by Professor Fischer. See David A. Fischer, Products Liability—An Analysis of Market Share Liability, 34 Vand. L. Rev. 1623, 1657 (1981) ("The legal fees and administrative costs arising from litigation of this magnitude easily could rival the cost of the plaintiff's judgment").

6. a. *Vaccines*. Plaintiffs have pursued the application of market share liability with minimal success in areas other than DES cases. The plaintiff in Shackil v. Lederle Laboratories, 116 N.J. 155, 561 A.2d 511 (1989) became severely retarded as a result of diphtheria, pertussis and

tetanus (DPT) vaccine. Unable to identify the specific manufacturer, plaintiff sued a number of manufacturers who potentially could have produced the vaccine she was given and argued for adoption of a market share liability theory. The court determined that (1) to adopt market share liability in a DPT case "would frustrate overarching public-policy and public-health considerations by threatening the continued availability of needed drugs and impairing the prospects of the development of safer vaccines"; (2) that another remedy was available to the plaintiff under the National Childhood Vaccine Injury Compensation Act of 1986, 42 U.S.C.A. § 300aa–1 et seq. (1993); and (3) that the absence of a generically identical product produced a major distinction between the vaccine in *Shackil* and DES because the DPT vaccine contained a defective batch, but was not generically defective. Accord, Senn v. Merrell–Dow Pharmaceuticals, Inc., 305 Or. 256, 751 P.2d 215 (1988); Chapman v. American Cyanamid Co., 861 F.2d 1515 (11th Cir.1988) (child died after receiving a DPT vaccine; parents could not proceed against three manufacturers on an alternative liability theory); Griffin v. Tenneco Resins, Inc., 648 F.Supp. 964 (W.D.N.C.1986) (court determined that producers of dyes could not be held liable based on market share theory); but see Morris v. Parke, Davis & Co., 667 F.Supp. 1332 (C.D.Cal.1987) (applying market share liability against manufacturers of DPT based on allegations of industry-wide manufacturing defects).

b. *Asbestos Litigation.* In asbestos cases, most courts hold that market share liability should not be recognized. See Goldman v. Johns–Manville Sales Corp., 33 Ohio St.3d 40, 514 N.E.2d 691 (1987) in which the Ohio Supreme Court rejected its application in an action against suppliers and manufacturers of products containing asbestos. The court reasoned that market share liability is inappropriate "where it cannot be shown that all the products to which the injured party was exposed are completely fungible." Moreover, the court held that the risk the manufacturer created is not accurately reflected in its market share because many products contain different degrees of asbestos, and the largest asbestos supplier, Johns–Manville, was not amenable to suit.

Accord, Case v. Fibreboard Corp., 743 P.2d 1062, 1067 (Okl.1987) ("the public policy favoring recovery on the part of an innocent plaintiff does not justify the abrogation of the rights of a potential defendant to have a causative link proven between the defendant's specific tortious acts and the plaintiff's injuries"); Nutt v. A.C. & S. Co., 517 A.2d 690, 694 (Del.Super.1986) (rejecting market share liability and recognizing that such a change in tort law should be left to the legislature); Celotex Corp. v. Copeland, 471 So.2d 533 (Fla.1985), reversing 447 So.2d 908 (Fla.App.1984) rejecting application of market share theory on the facts before it because plaintiff was able to identify some of the specific products, and their manufacturers, to which he had been exposed, and because asbestos products contain a divergence of toxicity depending on several factors, including friability (the extent to which the fibers are released from the product into the air), the specific type (among six) of asbestos fiber used in the product, and the amount of asbestos used in the product).

2. MARKET SHARE AT THE BOUNDARIES: FACTOR VIII AND LEAD PAINT

a. *Factor VIII and Contaminated Blood Products*

One product line that has resulted in several opinions considering the application and scope of market share principles is blood products. Several recent opinions have considered whether producers of Factor VIII, an anti-coagulant taken by hemophiliacs, may be subjected to market share analysis when an HIV-contaminated batch of the product results in the transmission of HIV and the recipient plaintiffs are incapable of identifying the producer of the Factor VIII which was infected. Prior to the decision of the Florida Supreme Court in Conley v. Boyle Drug Co., 570 So.2d 275 (Fla.1990), a Florida federal district court refused to apply a market share liability theory to three brothers who alleged that they contracted the AIDS virus from contaminated blood products and were unable to identify the manufacturer of the product which was the source of the virus. Ray v. Cutter Laboratories, Inc., 744 F.Supp. 1124 (M.D.Fla.1990). See also Poole v. Alpha Therapeutic Corp., 696 F.Supp. 351 (N.D.Ill.1988). The following decision points in the other direction.

SMITH v. CUTTER BIOLOGICAL, INC.

Supreme Court of Hawaii, 1991.
72 Hawaii 416, 823 P.2d 717.

Lum, C.J.

This court has accepted a request to address certified questions from the Ninth Circuit Court of Appeals. Smith v. Cutter Biological, Inc., 911 F.2d 374 (9th Cir.1990).

I.

Certified Questions of Law

1. Does Hawaii's Blood Shield Law, Haw.Rev.Stat. § 327–51, preclude Smith from bringing a strict liability claim? 2. Does Hawaii's Blood Shield Law, Haw.Rev.Stat. § 327–51, preclude Smith from bringing a negligence claim? 3. Would Hawaii allow recovery in this case when the identity of the actual tortfeasor cannot be proven? If Hawaii would allow recovery, what theory (i.e. burden-shifting, enterprise liability, market share or other) would the Hawaii Supreme Court adopt? In considering our response to the questions, we note that the issue as to questions two and three concerns the causation factor in negligence. The instant problem is that the plaintiff cannot identify which particular defendant caused his injury.

Our consideration of the issues is limited to the facts as stated in this record. Procedurally, this case reached the Ninth Circuit Court on a summary judgment motion. The order granting summary judgment did not rule on duty and breach as to the manufacturers; summary judgment was granted on the basis that plaintiff failed to prove causation.

The other elements of negligence, i.e., duty, breach and damages, are not at issue here. We note that at least two courts have determined, in cases similar to the instant action, that there was no breach of duty. Jones v. Miles Laboratories, Inc., 887 F.2d 1576 (11th Cir.1989); McKee v. Cutter Laboratories, Inc., 866 F.2d 219 (6th Cir.1989). However, those cases are distinguishable. We do not render an opinion as to whether appellant here will overcome the obstacles met by plaintiffs in those cases; the duty and breach issue here has not only not been decided, it is not before this court on the certified questions. Therefore, we do not deal with the viability of those questions.

Our conclusions deal only with this case—as it comes to us. Therefore, on our reading of the record as it stands, the relevant statutes, and the relevant case law, we answer "yes" to question one, and "no" to question two. Our answer to question three is "yes," using the alternative market share theory of recovery, as defined herein.

II.

Appellant is a hemophiliac who has tested HIV-positive with the AIDS virus. He claims that his exposure to the AIDS virus occurred in 1983 or 1984, through injections of the Antihemophilic Factor Concentrate (Factor VIII or AHF). Factor VIII, is a blood protein which enables the blood to properly coagulate when a hemophiliac suffers a bleeding episode. The original source of the Factor VIII is through blood donors.

* * * Upon appellant's first being tested for HIV antibodies in 1986, the results were positive.

* * *

III.

The first question asks whether the Hawaii Blood Shield Law precludes a strict liability claim. The blood shield statute reads as follows: *Exemption from strict liability.* No physician, surgeon, hospital, blood bank, tissue bank, or other person or entity who donates, obtains, prepares, transplants, injects, transfuses, or otherwise transfers, or who assists or participates in obtaining, preparing, transplanting, injecting, transfusing, or otherwise transferring any tissue, organ, blood or component thereof, from one or more persons, living or dead, to another person, shall be liable as a result of any such activity, save and except that each such person or entity shall remain liable for the person's or *its own negligence* or wilful misconduct. Hawaii Revised Statutes (HRS) § 327–51 (1985) (emphasis added). The answer to this question then depends on whether Factor VIII can be categorized as a "blood component." Appellant argues that the legislature was merely referring to blood or blood plasma for the definition of blood component. The legislative history does not appear to us to be that narrow. * * *

* * *

Therefore, we believe that Factor VIII is a component prepared from blood. With that finding, we answer the first question in the affirmative; Hawaii's blood shield statute precludes a strict liability claim.

IV.

The second question is tied to the third question. It requires that this court decide what the Hawaii blood shield statute means by the phrase "its own negligence." Appellees argument is that the phrase bars a lawsuit where the tortfeasor cannot be positively identified. In other words, the question is virtually identical to the first query in the third certified question. The distinction is, in the first instance, whether the legislature, by means of the blood shield statute, allows a claim against an unidentified tortfeasor, and in the second instance, whether this court would allow such an action based on the general development of Hawaii tort law. If "its own negligence" literally means the negligence must be of that particular defendant and have caused the damage to the plaintiff, then there would be no room to consider any of the various multi-tortfeasor theories of liability.

Looking at the legislative history behind the blood shield statute, we note that it merely states that excluding strict liability does not "affect remedies based upon other legal theories, such as negligence or willful misconduct." Sen.Conf.Comm.Rep. No. 773, in 1971 Senate Journal, at 1135. The wording on which appellees rely so heavily, "own negligence," is conspicuously absent from the history. Lacking that wording, or any other wording giving such an indication, we believe that the legislature has not spoken on this issue. We believe a lacuna exists, and we are free to use our own determination to explain pertinent words in the blood shield statute. Therefore, the second question is answered in the negative.

V.

The final question posed to this court comes in two parts. The first part asks whether this court would allow recovery in negligence when the actual tortfeasor cannot be proven. We concluded, in Part IV, that the Hawaii blood shield statute does not mandate specific identification of the tortfeasor. We now consider whether general Hawaii tort law would allow the action.

The reason this case is before this court is because the legislature has not fully legislated in the field of torts. When the occasion arises for which there is no specific rule to apply, "we are free to fashion an appropriate rule of law."

Appellees take issue with applying theories which were developed, in a large part, for remedies in the field of diethylstilbestrol (DES) drug litigation and the inherent problems associated with those actions.

Their strongest argument against using these theories is the lack of comparison of DES to Factor VIII as a fungible product. DES was produced by more than 200 different companies, some of which are defunct, but the identical formula was used universally in a highly regulated industry. With Factor VIII, there are only a handful of manufacturers, and although the product is fungible insofar as it can be used interchangeably, it does not have the constant quality of DES. The reason is obvious—the donor source of the plasma is not a constant. Therefore, Factor VIII is only harmful if the donor was infected; DES is inherently harmful. As we see that the lack of screening of donors and failure to warn are the breaches alleged, appellee's argument for not using DES theories is not convincing. We find consideration of the theories discussed in the DES cases to be helpful, as we strive to find an equitable and fair solution to the case at bar.

* * *

Our initial reference is to the reasoning of the Supreme Court of California, in Sindell v. Abbott Laboratories, 607 P.2d 924, cert. denied, 449 U.S. 912 (1980). We subscribe to the policy reasons propounded in Sindell * * * for by-passing the identification requirement.

In addition, we note that tort law is a continually expanding field. As discussed in the American Law Institute Enterprise Responsibility for Personal Injuries—Reporter's Study (1991) (ALI Study), the field of torts has now expanded to include personal injury actions described in three tiers of actions. * * * [T]he third tier includes "mass" torts where toxic exposure to many plaintiffs may, many years later, cause cancer or other illness. It is this final tier with which this case deals. It necessitates considering how to fairly deal with the plight of plaintiffs unable to identify, for no fault of their own, the person or entity who should bear the liability for their injury.

No longer can we apply traditional rules of negligence, such as those used in individual and low level negligence to mass tort cases, especially here, where we are dealing with a pharmaceutical industry that dispenses drugs on a wide scale that could cause massive injuries to the public, and where fungibility makes the strict requirements difficult to meet. The problem calls for adopting new rules of causation, for otherwise innocent plaintiffs would be left without a remedy. * * *

The policies in Sindell convince us that it is appropriate to consider a negligence action where the actual tortfeasor cannot be proven. Therefore, although inherent in the proof of negligence is proof of causation, we believe that this state is amenable to consideration of group theories of liability.

VI.

The second part of the third certified question asks what theory or theories this court might adopt where the tortfeasor cannot be proven. There are several theories which have evolved in the last several years. The genesis of these theories comes from Sindell v. Abbott Laboratories,

607 P.2d 924 (Cal.1980). The theories are generally described as: alternative liability, concert of action, enterprise or industry-wide liability, and market share liability. In the evolution of the DES cases, the market share theory has undergone various modifications, to suit the policies and needs of the particular courts.

* * *

D. Market Share Liability & Its Progeny

This theory has been most susceptible to variations and refinements, especially in DES litigation, but also in line with the law of the state in which it has been applied. It was first defined in Sindell, 607 P.2d 924 (1980). * * * We expand on those policies to acknowledge that defendants may bear the loss by passing that cost of doing business on to consumers. In addition, we feel that equity and fairness calls for using the market share approach. Another justification is that where many drugs can be lethal, and it is difficult for the consumer to identify the source of the product, the burden should shift. The concept itself meets the objectives of tort law, both by providing plaintiffs a remedy, but also by deterring defendants from negligent acts.

* * * We feel that this basic theory, with modifications and distinctions to suit the policies of this state, discussed infra, provides an appropriate modem for appellant's case. The relevant considerations are: 1. defining the market, 2. identification and joint and several liability, and finally 3. exculpatory allowances.

1. Defining the Market

Criticisms of Sindell include the need for a definition of "substantial share" of the market, in order not to distort the share of liability. Martin v. Abbott Laboratories, 689 P.2d 368, 381 (1984). The Martin court adopted a narrow definition of the market, that being the plaintiff's particular geographic market. * * *

Another court has specifically adopted the national market as the best option. Hymowitz v. Eli Lilly and Co., 73 N.Y.2d 487, 511, 539 N.E.2d 1069, 1077 (1989). Several premises supported this holding: 1. it was difficult to reliably determine any market smaller than the national one, 2. it avoided the need to establish separate matrices as to market share, and 3. it avoided an unfair burden on litigants. The national market was intended to "apportion liability so as to correspond to the over-all culpability of each defendant, measured by the amount of risk of injury each defendant created to the public-at-large." This provides equitable relief for plaintiffs, and a rational distribution of responsibility among defendants. It also avoids a windfall escape to the producer who happens to sell only to certain distributors. The culpability, therefore, is for marketing the product.

As we are faced here with a minimal number of manufacturers of the product, we believe that culpability for marketing the product is a better policy. Should the issue arise under different circumstances at some point, we may find it appropriate to narrow the definition. For this case, however, we believe the national market is the more equitable consideration.

2. *Identification and Joint and Several Liability*

Courts differ on their requirements of an assertive effort on the part of plaintiffs to identify the actual manufacturer of the specific product which caused the harm. We take another approach to this concern. Whereas manufacturers here argue that appellant should have kept a log of which manufacturer's product he was using, we fail to see how such failure affects the viability of appellant's suit in view of our adoption of the theory of market share liability.

Plaintiffs should use due diligence to join all manufacturers, but failure to do so is not a defense. Failure to do so may affect the percentage of recovery, discussed infra. However, manufacturers are permitted to implead other manufacturers. But, in this case, all manufacturers are joined, so the issue is not before us. However, we note in passing that the conditions of the Martin court, which would allow plaintiffs to initiate suit against only one defendant, and of Sindell, which would require plaintiffs to join a "substantial" number of defendants, are immaterial as long as plaintiffs realize their recovery will depend on joining as many manufacturers as they can; plaintiffs will endeavor to join all manufacturers.

We have already discussed our feeling that this action should not be subject to joint liability. * * * Therefore, we advocate several liability.

We define the rules of distribution as to market share for this case as was done in Martin, that is: "The defendants that are unable to exculpate themselves from potential liability are designated members of the plaintiffs' * * * market[ ] * * *. These defendants are initially presumed to have equal shares of the market and are liable for only the percentage of plaintiff's judgment that represents their presumptive share of the market. These defendants are entitled to rebut this presumption and thereby reduce their potential liability by establishing their respective market share of [Factor VIII] in the ... market." Martin, 689 P.2d 368, 383 (1984). As to several liability, we adopt the theory that a particular defendant is only liable for its market share. Defendants failing to establish their proportionate share of the market will be liable for the difference in the judgment to 100 percent of the market. However, should plaintiff fail to name all members of the market, the plaintiff will not recover 100 percent of the judgment if the named defendants prove an aggregate share of less than 100 percent.

3. *Exculpatory Allowances*

As a result of our determination that a national market is appropriate, as long as defendant is actually one of the producers of Factor VIII, there is little to justify exculpation of defendant. However, the exception would occur where defendant could prove that it had no product on the market at the time of the injury. As far as the defendants in this suit are concerned, it appears that none of them would be able to escape liability on that basis.

VII.

In conclusion, we will recognize the basic market share theory of multi-tortfeasor liability, as defined herein. Acknowledging that this could open a Pandora's box of questions, we believe that we have defined at least a starting point as to appropriately responding to the certified questions. However, as we are deciding issues in a virtual factual vacuum, we recognize that our opinion is limited to the facts presented to us, and we reserve the right to modify or amend our answers to these questions.

MOON, J. concurring and dissenting.

I concur in the majority's decision that Hawaii's blood shield statute precludes plaintiff's claim for strict liability. I also concur in the majority's opinion to the extent that it rejects the alternative liability, concert of action, and enterprise liability theories of causation. However, as to the majority's decision to adopt the market share theory of liability, I respectfully dissent.

* * *

I. STATUTORY CONSTRUCTION

* * * Eliminating causation as an element of proof and shifting the burden to the defendant is not only a radical departure from traditional negligence law, but is inconsistent with Hawaii's blood shield statute.

* * *

The statute is plain and unambiguous. It protects manufacturers of blood products from all liability, with one exception: "save and except that each * * * entity shall remain liable for * * * *its own negligence* * * *" (emphasis added). In other words, the statute requires proof of all elements of a negligence action, including causation.

* * *

Hawaii's blood shield statute is similar to blood statutes enacted in virtually all states. Even in the absence of legislative history, the underlying purpose of such statutes is obvious. * * * These statutes reflect a legislative judgment that to require providers to serve as insurers of the safety of these materials might impose such an overwhelming burden as to discourage the gathering and distribution of blood.

In 1988, the American Medical Association reported that "in the pharmaceutical industry, meaningful product liability insurance has all but disappeared." A.M.A., Report of the Board of Trustees on Impact of Product Liability on the Development of New Medical Technologies 2 (1988). This lack of insurance is largely due to the development of non-identification theories of liability.

The application of the market share liability theory may result in liability being placed on defendants bearing no responsibility for the defective product and may create unpredictable costs to innocent parties. In enacting HRS § 327–51, the Hawaii legislature unquestionably sought to guard against the risk of adversely affecting the supply of blood and blood components. However, the majority's decision imposes that very risk and may not only jeopardize the supply of blood products which protect the "health * * * of the people of Hawaii," but may also "restrict the availability of important scientific knowledge and skills."

II. DES CASE LAW

The primary authority cited by the majority in support of its position is the DES case of Sindell v. Abbott Laboratories, * * * The court determined that two essential factual elements, fungibility and the inability to identify specific producers, must be present in order for the market share liability theory to be appropriate. Both elements are glaringly absent in the Factor VIII case before us.

A. Fungibility

* * *

Unlike DES, Factor VIII is not a generic, fungible drug. Each processor prepares its Factor VIII concentrate by its own proprietary processes using plasma collected from its own sources. Each firm's Factor VIII concentrate is clearly distinguishable by brand name, package color, lot number, and number of units of Factor VIII per vial; each firm's Factor VIII concentrate is separately licensed by the Food and Drug Administration. There is no evidence that all Factor VIII products caused or were equally capable of causing HIV infection. Thus, the risk posed by the different brands of Factor VIII is not identical.

The majority here admits that Factor VIII is not fungible, that is, it does not pose the same risk of harm to users because, as the majority states, "[t]he reason is obvious—the donor source of the plasma is not constant. Therefore, Factor VIII is only harmful if the donor was infected; DES is inherently harmful." However, having conceded that Factor VIII is not fungible, the majority disregards the fungibility requirement, which under Sindell renders market share inapplicable.

* * *

B. Inability to Identify Specific Producers

The second prerequisite of applying market share liability is that the product "cannot be traced to any specific producer." Sindell, 607 P.2d at 936. * * * Here, the majority dilutes the second prerequisite by merely requiring a showing that "it is difficult for the consumer to identify the source of the product * * *." Difficulty in identifying a wrongdoer is clearly an insufficient and unreasonable basis to distort Hawaii's tort law and adopt the market share liability theory.

Unlike the DES situation, this is not a case where product identification, and thus proof of causation, is impossible because a generation has lapsed between exposure and injury. * * * Here, the period of time from plaintiff's claimed exposure to the HIV virus, between 1983 and 1984, to the time he tested positive for HIV antibodies, in 1986, was no more than two to three years. Also, unlike the DES plaintiffs who were in utero and could not identify the source of DES used by their mothers, plaintiff here could have identified the Factor VIII he used. Unfortunately, through no fault of the defendant processors, plaintiff failed to observe and record the name and lot numbers of the Factor VIII he used and the dates he used them.

As noted by defendant Armour Pharmaceutical Company (Armour) in its answering brief, most hospitals and pharmacies maintain records of therapeutic materials purchased and dispensed. The fact that the particular pharmacy where Smith received his Factor VIII did not keep such records long enough or in a form appropriate to meet Smith's litigation requirements is not an inherent circumstance of all AIDS cases involving hemophiliacs which would justify a new rule of law.

Based on the foregoing discussion, I submit that the majority's reliance on DES cases to support its decision to adopt the market share theory of liability is misplaced.

* * *

Notes and Questions

1. With whom do you agree—the majority or the dissent—on the propriety of applying market share liability to Factor VIII? On what basis did the majority avoid the generic defect or fungibility problem? What is the role of the generic product requirement as originally described in the DES cases? Is Factor VIII more like DES or asbestos in terms of its similarity? Should plaintiffs in these cases argue that what is generic is that all firms employed similar screening procedures to obtain their blood products and therefore whether a particular firm's batch is tainted is a fortuity?

2. How about the inability to identify the tortfeasor requirement—should plaintiffs or defendants bear that burden on these facts? Are the DES cases distinguishable? As a matter of fairness, which so strongly motivated the courts in *Sindell* and *Hymowitz*, who can better maintain the records of what product and lots a particular hemophiliac purchased? Which way does the fact that the industry is comprised of only four firms cut? One of the decisions referred to in *Smith* was Ray v. Cutter Laboratories, 754 F.Supp. 193 (M.D.Fla.1991), decided after *Conley*, which also held that Florida's version of market share liability could be applied to Factor VIII.

Problem

Harrison H. Schmidt and Ellen Schmidt purchased a parcel of land in 1961, in the town of Salmon, which they owned outright until 1976. In 1972, after highway improvements had resulted in their parcel facing a busy intersection, the Schmidts began operating a gasoline service station at that location. In 1975 the Schmidts decided to lease the gas station to Mayfair and Martha Gooding. The Goodings maintained the lease and operated the station until 1979.

The station ceased operations in 1979. However, the Schmidts sold the underlying title in 1976 to Fal Allen, who owned it until 1978, and who sold it to Maurice and Katia Kraft who owned the property until 1980. In 1980 the Krafts sold the property to Roger Ressmeyer.

Thus, diagrammatically, the title to and operation of the property appear as follows:

	Owners
1961–1976	Schmidts
1978	Allen
1980	Krafts
	Ressmeyer

	Operators
1972–1975	Schmidts
1979	Goodings

In 1980, the Salmon Fire Department informed Ressmeyer that the underground gasoline tanks had to be removed to comply with the Uniform Fire Code. When the tanks were removed, the soil was tested for contamination and substantial deposits of hydrocarbons were discovered. Ressmeyer retained an expert who is of the opinion that between 30,000 to 40,000 gallons of gasoline contamination had occurred. Roger Ressmeyer is required to clean up the property before he can resell it and has expended $350,000 in that effort. In 1983 Ressmeyer sues all prior owners and operators for recovery of his losses. The plaintiff maintains that he never used the gasoline station and that the tanks were empty when he purchased the land. However, defendants have one witness who will testify that she saw plaintiff place a gasoline hose from the site in his car a few years ago.

As defendants, the Krafts assert that the gasoline pumps and tanks on the property had been abandoned and were no longer in use at the time they sold the property to Ressmeyer. In Ressmeyer's tort action against the defendants he moves for summary judgment on the ground that there is no genuine issue of material fact in dispute as to the contamination occurring during defendants' ownership and operation of the site. Defendants also move for summary judgment on the grounds that plaintiff must identify which defendant(s) was (were) the cause of the contamination, and has failed to offer any proof to show how or when any particular defendant was responsible for the contamination.

As the law clerk to the trial judge presented with these cross motions for summary judgment, prepare a memorandum addressing how the motions should be resolved. Please address how the question of causal responsibility should be managed at trial if the motions are denied.

b. *Lead Paint Pigments*

The last Section addressing the scope of market share liability involve allegations that manufacturers of lead pigments incorporated into indoor paints applied in apartments and other buildings are liable on various products liability theories to occupants suffering injuries as a result of lead exposure and consumption. Here too the plaintiffs are unable to identify the manufacturers of the pigment that they ingested and have sought to rely on market share theory to overcome that difficulty. In Santiago v. Sherwin–Williams Co., 782 F.Supp. 186 (D.Mass.1992), affirmed 3 F.3d 546 (1st Cir.1993), the United States District Court in Massachusetts rejected application of the theory. Because the court was bound by Massachusetts law, it relied on Payton v. Abbott Labs, 386 Mass. 540, 437 N.E.2d 171 (1982) in which the Massachusetts Supreme Judicial Court had rejected the theory on the facts of that case. In *Payton* the court had stated that two purposes are served by requiring defendant and product identification: "it separates wrongdoers from innocent actors, and also ensures that wrongdoers are held liable only for the harm that they have caused." It then applied those principles in declining to apply the theory to the pigment manufacturers:

A. *Absence of a Unique Injury*

In DES cases, the market share theory succeeded in separating wrongdoers from innocent actors, because DES plaintiffs suffered from a signature DES injury—a rare form of cancer, adenocarcinoma, that was directly attributable to exposure to DES. * * * In contrast, defendants here assert that heredity, social and environmental factors, or lead in other products, could have caused, or at least contributed to, Santiago's injuries. In other words, defendants argue that Santiago does not suffer from a signature lead paint injury.

Santiago claims that lead poisoning retarded her "educational, social, vocational and intellectual development." Plaintiff's injury is manifested by "difficulties in spelling/language arts, in organization, in requiring extra time and effort to check her work, and with frustration in learning to type." Defendants counter that none of the deficits associated with Santiago "can ever be attributed solely or primarily to lead," and that such "injuries" have been "strongly associated in the vast literature on childhood development with a large variety of factors including heredity, child-rearing techniques, mental and physical health of the parents, and other factors in the social and educational setting in which children develop." * * *

Moreover, even if all of Santiago's injuries could be attributed to lead poisoning, she cannot prove that defendant's lead pigment was the cause of her lead poisoning. Defendants have shown that lead is widespread in many different forms, and that more than 90 percent of lead used in this country during the relevant period was contained in products other than paint. They further show that the air and water in and around Santiago's home during the relevant period may have contained lead that contributed to her blood levels. In addition, the City of Boston identified Santiago's neighborhood in Dorchester as a "hot spot" in soil lead contamination requiring attention by the Environmental Protection Agency. Defendants' expert asserts, as well, that vehicular traffic is a major source of elevated soil lead levels.

* * *

Defendants have produced evidence to show that factors other than lead pigment in paint were adequate producing causes of Santiago's injuries. The jury in this case, therefore, could only speculate as to the degree to which, if at all, the defendants' conduct caused her harm.

B. *Defendant's Market Share*

Market share liability holds defendants responsible only to the extent that their product has contributed to the risk of injury to the public. Presumably, defendants can calculate this risk by determining the percentage of the market that their product occupied during the relevant period. If factors significantly skewing this calculation exist, then Massachusetts would not apply market share, because of the danger that defendants could be held liable for harm "exceeding their responsibility."

1. Scope of the Market

In *Payton*, the SJC indicated that, in order to hold defendants liable, each had to have been "actively in the DES market during all or a substantial part of the relevant period of time in which the mothers of the plaintiffs ingested DES." There, the market was limited to the year in which the named plaintiff's mother ingested DES. Here, the market spans five decades. Santiago contends that the house was first painted around 1917, and that the walls inside the house contain five layers of paint, with the last layer having been applied between 1955 and 1969.

Defendants show that, by 1954, three of the five defendants had ceased producing white lead pigments. In addition, defendant Glidden did not begin producing white lead pigment until 1924, and it stopped in the late 1950's. Defendant Sherwin–Williams has shown, moreover, that by the mid–1930's its lead pigment was used primarily for commercial and industrial applications. Finally, defendants contend that, given the fifty-four year window here, there is insufficient data to establish to what degree each defendant's product was used in lead-based paint.

* * *

This court concludes that there is insufficient evidence that would warrant a jury in finding that all the defendants, or any of them, actively participated in the lead pigment market for lead based paint during the fifty-four year period involved here.

2. Defendants as Bulk Suppliers

Of particular significance as well is the fact that defendants here supplied lead pigment in bulk to paint manufacturers. They are not being sued as manufacturers or marketers of the allegedly offending paint. They, therefore, could not control all of the risks that their products may have presented to the public.

* * *

No court has applied market share theory to a defendant that supplies an ingredient for a product packaged and sold by others. The facts of this case do not warrant a different result.

* * *

Notes and Questions

1. How convincing is the court's analysis? What about the "signature injury" point that at least in DES cases there was no question that plaintiffs' injuries were caused by the DES, and not some other toxic exposure? In other words in lead paint cases plaintiffs have not satisfied the causation in fact issue addressed in the first portion of this chapter. How about the Factor VIII cases—could plaintiffs have contracted AIDS from other sources? Who should bear the burden on this issue?

2. How would a court define the market in these lead pigment cases? Would records be more likely available than in the DES cases? Would national market definitions help? How would you account for the fact that defendants' product was incorporated into another product—paints?

3. In a later opinion, the same court declined to apply a concert of action theory on these facts and held that Massachusetts did not recognize enterprise theory. Santiago v. Sherwin–Williams Co., 794 F.Supp. 29 (D.Mass.1992), affirmed 3 F.3d 546 (1st Cir.1993).

In Swartzbauer v. Lead Industries Association, 794 F.Supp. 142 (E.D.Pa. 1992), a class action on behalf of house painters, the court rejected the whole array of alternative liability theories. It found that the plaintiffs did not sufficiently allege a conspiracy among the industry trade association, paint and pigment manufacturers. It rejected enterprise theory because Pennsylvania courts had not yet accepted the theory. Third, it rejected market share and alternative liability theories because plaintiffs could identify some of the paint and pigment manufacturers of the products to which they were exposed. Accord Hurt v. Philadelphia Housing Authority, 806 F.Supp. 515 (E.D.Pa. 1992).

Most recently, the Third Circuit affirmed the dismissal of a class action brought by the City of Philadelphia and its public housing authority to recover the costs of abatement, concluding that none of the plaintiffs' theories to circumvent the defendant identification causation requirement were recognized by Pennsylvania courts or were applicable on these facts. See City of Philadelphia v. Lead Industries Association, 994 F.2d 112 (3d Cir.1993). But see New York v. Lead Industries Association, 190 A.D.2d 173, 597 N.Y.S.2d 698 (1993) (complaint stated cause of action based on concert of action and fraud).

c. *Note on Lead Paint and Causation*

While the major lead paint litigation against the pigment manufacturers may have fallen on the defendant identification prong of causation, lead paint litigation also presents the extremely difficult questions of linking plaintiff's injuries to the lead exposure. As we saw in *Santiago*, the court actually used that point to buttress its rejection of market share liability. Lead has been recognized as poisonous for millennia, as evidenced by Hippocrates' diagnosis of a metal extractor as suffering from lead poisoning. However, not until the 1970s did the U.S. government take strong action against lead paint, banning it in government-controlled buildings accessible to children and banning the sale of lead-based paint; and banning lead in gasoline in the 1970s. For children, the most vulnerable population group, the exposure to lead is typically caused by ingestion of paint chips or the consumption of the lead chalk or dust. See Hearings Before the U.S. Senate Subcomm. on Toxic Substances, Environmental Oversight, Research and Development, March 8 and 9, 1990 (statements of Kathryn Mahalley, Ph.D., National Institutes of Health; Dr. Ellen K. Silbergeld).

The Centers for Disease Control has published extensive data on the exposure levels that represent a "level of concern." See CDC, Preventing Lead Poisoning in Young Children (Oct. 1991). Typically measured in micrograms per deciliter (μg/dL), the federally-defined threshold of "level of concern" has been lowered from 60 μg/dL to 15 μg/dL in 1991. By comparison, the average lead level in children under two years of age is 4.2 to 5.2 μg/dL and has been declining in recent years largely because of the ban on leaded gasoline. As noted in *Santiago*, a primary problem with lead poisoning is that it produces asymptomatic effects: cognitive difficulties by blocking neuroreceptors in the brain. Acute encephalopathy, usually associated with blood levels of 100 μg/dL, is the most serious condition, producing coma, seizures, ataxia, loss of coordination, vomiting, altered states of consciousness, and loss of recently acquired skills. Less severe symptoms, including decreases in play activity, anorexia, lethargy, abdominal pain and constipation are associated with levels as low as 50 μg/dL.

While there exists little dispute among medical scientists regarding the adverse effects of high blood levels, there is, unsurprisingly, considerable divergence of opinion respecting the effect of low-level lead exposures in children's learning skills and cognitive development. One study, by Dr. Herbert Needleman, suggests that exposed children are: (1) seven times more likely to drop out of high school; (2) six times more likely to have a reading disability; and (3) more likely to have decreased hand-eye coordination, reaction time, and finger tapping. See, e.g., Needleman, et al., The Long–Term Effects of Exposure to Low Doses of Lead in Childhood: An 11–Year Follow–Up Report, 322 New Eng. J. Med. 83 (1990). Another study, of children living near a lead smelter in Australia, is cited for the proposition that three to four IQ points are lost for every 10 µg/dL of exposure over 10 µg/dL.

As indicated, this research is hotly contested. Some scientists believe that the human research to date has not adequately controlled for the myriad of factors known to affect child development. Other researchers point out that the vast majority of children who sustain lead poisoning are from underprivileged socio-economic backgrounds and question whether the presence of such factors may provide an explanation for observed IQ variances and learning problems in the studied population. See, e.g., Ernhart, et al., Subclinical Lead Level & Developmental Deficit: Reanalysis of Data, 18 J. of Learning Disabilities 475 (1985). The debate includes hypotheses that children who are likely to eat paint chips are those already hyperactive, impulsive, or intellectually slower, which is what causes them to eat more paint, or are children of less attentive parents, which makes the children more likely to engage in thumb-sucking or other behaviors that may elevate blood lead levels. See, e.g., Ruff & Bijur, The Effects of Low to Moderate Lead Levels on Neurobehavioral Functioning in Children: Toward a Conceptual Model, 10:2 Developmental & Behavioral Pediatrics 103–09 (1989).

Moreover, as was stressed in the material on epidemiology earlier in this Chapter, causal inferences are undermined by the absence of proper controls for confounding social, economic, nutritional, familial and physical factors which may influence the cognitive and behavioral effects being investigated. Further, the study results have not been consistent regarding the presence of a specific pattern of cognitive deficits associated with lead poisoning. Faust & Brown, Moderately Elevated Blood Lead Levels: Effects on Neuropsychologic Functioning in Children, 80:5 Pediatrics 623–29 (1987). See studies collected in David A. Carter, Lead Poisoning Litigation: Causes of Action, Defenses and Challenging Causation, 7 Toxics L. Rptr. 1539, 1542 (5/26/93).

Assuming plaintiffs' counsel can sufficiently establish generic causation, what theories of liability are most promising in the lead paint cases? What about premises liability actions against landlords or property owners? What difficulties will such theories face? Would a private nuisance theory work in premises cases?

What defenses would be likely asserted in lead paint litigation? How about the bar of statutes of limitations? What about the landlord's lack of notice respecting the problem? How about exculpatory clauses in the tenants' leases? How will plaintiffs sufficiently eliminate other possible sources of lead—leaded gasoline (still available for older vehicles), plumbing fixtures, dust and soil, and industrial emissions? How will plaintiffs sufficiently establish that other factors did not cause or explain the cognitive or behavioral conditions, such as heredity, parental behavior, other health problems, poor nutrition, and other toxins?

D. APPORTIONMENT OF THE HARM OR DAMAGE

1. APPORTIONMENT BETWEEN PLAINTIFF AND DEFENDANT

Closely related to the issue of causal indeterminacy is the issue of the apportionment of damages. In some environmental tort cases—as in other tort cases—the harm which the plaintiff experienced can be attributable to both the defendant's activity and that of the plaintiff, as the *Dafler* case below demonstrates. The problem is to apportion that harm for which the defendant should be responsible and respond in damages, and that portion of the harm for which the plaintiff must accept responsibility.

DAFLER v. RAYMARK INDUSTRIES, INC.

Superior Court of New Jersey, Appellate Division, 1992.
259 N.J.Super. 17, 611 A.2d 136.

The opinion of the court was delivered by

KING, J.

I

This appeal and cross-appeal are taken from a verdict in plaintiff's favor and a jury's apportionment of responsibility between plaintiff and defendant in an asbestos product liability case. The case presents a question of first impression in this State concerning apportionment of damages for lung cancer between an asbestos producer and a cigarette smoker. The jury found that plaintiff contributed 70% to his lung cancer by cigarette smoking and that defendant Keene Corporation (Keene) contributed 30% to plaintiff's lung cancer by its asbestos products used in shipbuilding. The damage verdict for lung cancer was molded to reflect this apportionment. We conclude that both the apportionment by the jury and the general verdict in plaintiff's favor find reasonable factual support in the record and we affirm.

II

This is the procedural background. On October 10, 1986 plaintiff sued 11 defendants, all manufacturers or distributors of asbestos products. At the jury trial in May 1991 the only remaining defendant was Keene. Plaintiff claimed that he developed asbestosis and lung cancer as a result of occupational exposure to asbestos during his six-year employment at the New York Shipyard in Camden, from 1939 to 1945.

On May 21, 1991 the jury returned liability and damage verdicts in plaintiff's favor. The jury found unanimously that "asbestos exposure was a substantial contributing cause of Mr. Dafler's lung cancer." The jury found Keene, through its predecessors, a substantial contributing cause and 95% responsible. The jury found Garlock, Inc., a defendant who had settled for $2,500 before trial, 5% responsible. The monetary awards were: for asbestosis, $60,000; for lung cancer, $140,000—an aggregate of $200,000. * * *

* * *

Both plaintiff and Keene appeal. In this appeal plaintiff raises these claims of error: (1) there was insufficient evidence to allow the jury to apportion damages for plaintiff's lung cancer; (2) the judge improperly influenced the jury's apportionment decision. * * *

III

These are the facts presented at trial. Plaintiff, Frank Dafler, age 70, worked as a shipfitter at the New York Shipyard in Camden from 1939 to 1945. During the World War II era New York Shipyard was one of the world's busiest ship building facilities, employing 36,000 men. During this period plaintiff worked on 12 to 13 ships. * * *

Dafler spent all of his time at the Shipyard working on board these ships. He spent about 70% of his time working in engine rooms and boiler rooms in very close proximity to the pipefitters who used asbestos and asbestos-containing products to cover the numerous pipes housed in those areas. Dafler himself did not work with asbestos, but he said it was all around him. The pipefitters and pipe coverers worked continuously, cutting and cementing pipes. No masks were used or provided. He did recall that the pipefitters' use of asbestos made the air very dusty. There was no ventilation in the boiler or engine rooms during construction.

* * *

The plaintiff began experiencing shortness of breath in the 1970s. In 1984 he went to the hospital for breathing problems. The diagnosis in 1984 was asbestosis. He then decreased the time that he worked between 1984 and 1989 because of his breathing problem. In 1984 he began seeing Dr. Agia, a pulmonary specialist, twice a year for x-rays and pulmonary function tests. In 1989 the doctors found a cancerous tumor in plaintiff's lung and surgery ensued. Plaintiff said that he smoked cigarettes for almost 45 years, since age 18. He had a pack-a-day habit until his diagnosis of asbestosis in 1984 when he quit.

The plaintiff presented two medical experts: Dr. Guidice, a pulmonary specialist, and Dr. Stone, a pathologist. * * *

The experts also testified on the epidemiological aspects of asbestosis and cigarette smoking. Dr. Guidice explained that there is a "base line" relative risk of 11 cases of lung cancer per 100,000 persons in the general population per year. This "base line" is for people in the general population who do not smoke and are not exposed to asbestos. The relative risk of lung cancer with industrial exposure to asbestos, like plaintiff's occupational exposure, increases five-fold (5:1), or to 55 cases per 100,000 of population per year. The relative risk with cigarette smoking increases ten-fold (10:1), or to 110 cases per 100,000 of population per year. The relative risk of exposure to asbestos plus cigarette smoking is not additive, i.e., 10 + 5 or 15–fold, but becomes what Dr. Guidice described as "multiplicative or synergistic," or 50 times (50:1) the "base line," i.e., 550 cases per 100,000 of population per year.

Dr. Guidice could not apportion the causation of plaintiff's lung cancer between his asbestosis and his long-term cigarette smoking. He said when asked about apportionment: "No, and I don't know anybody that's able to do that. That's not possible. This relationship is synergistic and multiplicative between those two cancer causing agents. It's not possible to distinguish which contribution is caused by asbestos and which is caused by cigarette smoking." He conceded that the major cause of lung cancer in the United States is cigarette smoking.

Dr. Stone essentially agreed with Dr. Guidice on the epidemiological data. He thought the relative risk for cigarette smoking alone was about 10 to 12:1 above the "base line," the relative risk for asbestosis alone was about 6 to 7:1 above the "base line." He said that "the lung cancer was caused by the synergistic interaction of his cigarette smoking and asbestos exposure." He also agreed that cigarette smoking was by far the greatest cause of all lung cancers in the United States. He did not attempt to apportion responsibility, saying that "both were significant contributory causes." Both doctors agreed that the relative risk of smoking was twice as great as the relative risk for asbestos with respect to cancer.

As noted, the defendant's expert, Dr. DeMopolous, completely discounted any role for asbestos in causing the plaintiff's lung cancer. He emphasized the role of cigarette smoking as solely causative in this case and in lung cancer in general. * * * He recognized the theoretical synergistic effect of two causative factors but denied any role for asbestos in plaintiff's lung cancer. Dr. DeMopolous did not speak to apportionment.

The jury seemed to have apportioned the damages for plaintiff's lung cancer according to the relative risk factors for asbestos (5:1 or 30%) and cigarette smoking (10:1 or 70%), roughly one-third to two-thirds. The judge molded the jury's monetary verdict on the lung cancer aspect, $140,000, accordingly.

IV

Plaintiff's principal claim on this appeal is that the judge erred in submitting the issue of apportionment to the jury in the first place. Plaintiff contends that there was insufficient evidence in the record to provide any basis for apportionment. Judge Weinberg thought this case presented enough evidence to justify allowing the issue to go to the jury. * * * Although the issue is novel in this jurisdiction, we agree with the trial judge and affirm on this point.

Plaintiff asserts that the lung cancer was an indivisible harm with indivisible damages, that the defendant failed to meet its burden of showing that there was a reasonable basis for apportionment, and that the percentages found by the jury, 30%–70%, were against the weight of the evidence. Defendant Keene contends that the use of apportionment in this case was consistent with the evidence and the development of the law in this State.

Apportionment of damages among multiple causes is a well-recognized tort principle. The Restatement (Second) of Torts § 433A, at 434 (1965), regarding apportionment of harm to causes, states: "(1) Damages for harm are to be apportioned among two or more causes where (a) there are distinct harms, or (b) there is a reasonable basis for determining the contribution of each cause to a single harm. (2) Damages for any other harm cannot be apportioned among two or more causes." Comment (a) to the Restatement indicates that "[t]he rules stated apply also where one of the causes in question is the conduct of the plaintiff himself, whether it be negligent or innocent." Restatement (Second) of Torts § 433A, Comment (a), at 435. Prosser and Keeton, Law of Torts § 52, at 345 (5th ed. 1984), states the problem this way: "Once it is determined that the defendant's conduct has been a cause of some damage suffered by the plaintiff, a further question may arise as to the portion of the total damage sustained which may properly be assigned to the defendant, as distinguished from other causes. The question is primarily not one of the fact of causation, but of the feasibility and practical convenience of splitting up the total harm into separate parts which may be attributed to each of two or more causes. * * *" The Restatement and Prosser both recognize that the concern in apportioning responsibility is more practical than theoretical: is there "a reasonable basis for determining the contribution of each cause to a single harm?" Restatement, supra, § 433A(1)(b) at 434. Here the single harm to the plaintiff was his lung cancer. The two causes were his six-year occupational exposure to asbestos and his 45–year cigarette smoking habit. The trial judge had to determine, as a matter of law in the first instance, whether the harm was capable of apportionment. See Martin v. Owens–Corning Fiberglas Corp., 528 A.2d 947, 949 (Pa.1987). The burden of proving that the harm is capable of apportionment is on the party seeking it, here defendant Keene. Restatement, supra, § 433B(2), at 441.

Several state and federal courts have considered the apportionment issue in similar occupational asbestos-smoking cases. The Pennsylvania Supreme Court addressed the apportionment issue in Martin v. Owens–Corning Fiberglas Corp., supra. The plaintiff, a former insulation worker, brought suit against various asbestos manufacturers seeking damages for asbestosis and lung impairment. Plaintiff worked with asbestos for about 39 years, and smoked for about 37 years. At trial, plaintiff's experts testified that his lung impairment was due to the combined effect of emphysema, caused by cigarette smoking, and asbestosis, from occupational asbestos exposure. They said that it was impossible to apportion the lung impairment between the two causes. Defendant's expert testified that the lung impairment was caused solely by plaintiff's cigarette smoking. The question presented on appeal was whether the trial judge erred in instructing the jury that it could apportion damages between the asbestos exposure and smoking. There were no epidemiological data or relative risk factors before the jury in Martin.

A plurality of the Pennsylvania Supreme Court applied § 433A of the Restatement and held that it was error for the trial judge to instruct the jury on apportionment since the evidence failed to establish a reasonable basis on which to apportion. The court commented: "The jury, although presented with a great deal of testimony concerning appellant's history and physical condition, was provided no guidance in determining the relative contributions of asbestos exposure and cigarette smoking to appellant's disability. In fact, two experts testified that such a determination was not possible.

* * *

Here, the jury cannot be expected to draw conclusions which medical experts, relying on the same evidence, could not draw. The causes of disability in this case do not lend themselves to separation by lay-persons on any reasonable basis. Thus, common sense and common experience possessed by a jury do not serve as substitutes for expert guidance, and it follows that any apportionment by the jury in this case was a result of speculation and conjecture and hence, improper. "Rough approximation" is no substitute for justice."

In his concurring opinion, Justice McDermott said that he would limit the holding of the three-judge plurality to a single proposition, that "under the facts and circumstances of this case there was not enough evidence to submit the issue of apportionment to the jury." Thus, the Pennsylvania Supreme Court did not rule out apportionment in cases where the evidence in fact supports a reasonable basis upon which to divide the harm.

In strong, separate dissents, both Chief Justice Nix, joined by Justice Zappala, and Justice Hutchinson criticized the plurality for overstepping its bounds and usurping the jury's fact-finding function. They emphasized that a jury should be allowed to make "rough approximations" where there is a reasonable basis to apportion, especially where the plaintiff's own conduct is a substantial factor in bringing about the harm. Justice Hutchinson, in his dissent, made these thoughtful comments in expressing his view that the jury should enjoy considerable latitude and employ common sense in its apportionment task: "I am at a loss to imagine what additional testimony would satisfy the majority. Requiring the experts to speak in terms of numerical percentages introduces a false precision into the evidence. Mathematical exactitude is not found in the real world of medicine. We should not mislead lay jurors by requiring experts to falsely imply its existence. Honest, but more flexible, words such as "substantial factor," "major contribution" or "significant cause" are more suitable to the proper jury function of justly and fairly resolving uncertainties. It is unfair and unjust to place on appellee the whole burden of supporting appellant for a disability his own experts admit he himself substantially caused."

* * *

Some other jurisdictions have permitted apportionment in these cases. In Brisboy v. Fibreboard Corp., 418 N.W.2d 650 (Mich.1988), the Supreme Court of Michigan upheld a jury finding that plaintiff's smoking contributed 55% to his lung cancer while 45% was attributable to his asbestos exposure, apparently without the benefit of epidemiological testimony. See Jenkins v. Halstead Indus., 706 S.W.2d 191 (1986) (92% of worker's chronic obstructive pulmonary disease apportioned to lifelong cigarette smoking in workers' compensation case). See also Gideon v. Johns–Manville Sales Corp., 761 F.2d 1129, 1138–1140 (5th Cir.1985) (under Texas law, determination is for the jury); Fulgium v. Armstrong World Indus., Inc., 645 F.Supp. 761, 763 (W.D.La.1986) (apportionment allowed under Louisiana law); Champagne v. Raybestos–Manhattan, Inc., 562 A.2d 1100, 1118 (Conn.1989) (plaintiff's smoking found 75% contributory to his lung cancer, citing Michigan's Brisboy v. Fibreboard Corp., supra); Hao v. Owens–Illinois, Inc., 69 Haw. 231, 738 P.2d 416 (1987) (51% smoking; 49% asbestos exposure ratio of apportionment affirmed).

No New Jersey cases have specifically addressed the issue of apportionment of civil law damages in an asbestos-exposure cigarette smoking context. * * * However, the concept of apportionment of damages is not alien to this jurisdiction. The theory of § 433A of the Restatement (Second) of Torts has been applied in varied circumstances. See Scafidi v. Seiler, 574 A.2d 398 (N.J.1990) ("increased risk" and "lost chance" concepts in medical malpractice); Waterson v. General Motors Corp., 544 A.2d 357 (N.J.1988) (automobile "crashworthiness" case); Fosgate v. Corona, 66 N.J. 268, 330 A.2d 355 (1974) (medical malpractice aggravating tuberculosis)[.] These cases involve pre-existing or concurrent injuries; apportionment was limited to instances of distinct injuries or to circumstances when a reasonable basis existed to determine the contribution of each cause. The burden with respect to proof of apportionment rested, of course, with the party seeking it. Restatement (Second) of Torts § 433B(2).

* * *

As we well know, apportionment is also consistent with the principles of the Comparative Negligence Act, N.J.S.A. 2A:15–5.1 to –5.3, and the Contribution Among Tortfeasors Act, N.J.S.A. 2A:53A–1 to –5. See also Feldman v. Lederle Lab., 608 A.2d 356 (App.Div.1992) (apportionment of damages for incremental injury approved).

We conclude that there was ample basis in the record of this trial to submit the issue of apportionment to the jury. The extant legal precedent supports rational efforts to apportion responsibility in such circumstances rather than require one party to absorb the entire burden. The jury obviously accepted the epidemiological testimony based on relative risk factors, the smoking history over 45 years, and the substantial occupational exposure over six years. The synergistically resultant disease, lung cancer, was produced by a relative risk factor of 10:1 contributed by plaintiff and 5:1 contributed by defendant. The jury probably shaded the apportionment slightly in defendant's favor, 70% instead of two-thirds, because of the strong emphasis on cigarette smoking as the greatly predominant overall cause of lung cancer in this country.

The result was rational and fair. We can ask no more. This is fairer than requiring defendant to shoulder the entire causative burden where its contribution in fact was not likely even close to 100%. Or fairer, for certain, than no recovery at all for plaintiff who, while a victim of the disease of asbestosis which probably led in part to the lung cancer, confronts a reluctant jury which might not want to saddle a defendant with a 100% verdict in the circumstances of a particular case.

We conclude that our Supreme Court's recent decision in Landrigan v. Celotex Corp., 605 A.2d 1079 (N.J.1992), a colon cancer asbestos claim, supports the result we reach in relying on the epidemiological data for apportionment. This discipline of epidemiology "studies the relationship between a disease and a factor suspected of causing the disease, using statistical methods * * *." The Supreme Court recognized that "proof of causation in toxic-tort cases depends largely on inferences derived from statistics about groups," and conceded that plaintiffs in toxic-tort cases "may be compelled to resort to more general evidence, such as that provided by epidemiological studies."

* * *

Affirmed.

Notes and Questions

1. Do you agree with the court's analysis? The Restatement (Second) of Torts § 433A quoted by the court is the primary authority relied upon to justify apportionment in these cases, and requires only a "reasonable basis" for the apportionment. If no apportionment can be made, what is the effect? As the court also observed, Restatement § 433B also places the burden of proving apportionment on the party seeking it—here the defendant Keene. Once the plaintiff succeeds in demonstrating that a defendant's tortious conduct is a cause of the harm, the burden shifts to the defendant to limit its liability. See § 433B(2).

2. Were you impressed by the sophistication of the experts' testimony on relative risks? Did plaintiff undermine her case by having her experts provide the numerical basis for making the apportionment? Why didn't Dr. Guidice's statement that it is "not possible" to apportion causes of lung cancer preclude the jury findings on apportionment? What was the strategy of defendant's expert in testifying that cigarette smoking was the sole cause?

Why didn't defendant's expert explicitly support the relative risk analysis of plaintiffs' experts?

3. In Martin v. Owens–Corning Fiberglas Corp., 515 Pa. 377, 528 A.2d 947 (1987), quoted and distinguished by the court in *Dafler*, the Pennsylvania Supreme Court refused to allow apportionment on comparable facts except the experts offered no epidemiological data demonstrating the relative risks of asbestos exposure and smoking. The experts in *Martin* testified identically to Dr. Guidice—both asbestos exposure and smoking were "contributory causes," but "it is not possible to apportion them." Why the different outcome? The dissenting opinions in *Martin* criticize the majority for demanding precise percentages before apportionment would be permissible, because "mathematical exactitude is not found in the real world of medicine." Do the relative risks provide mathematical exactitude?

4. As stated in *Dafler*, medical studies demonstrate the synergistic effect of smoking and asbestos exposure in causing lung cancer. One important study found that the relative risk (ratio of occurrence of disease in exposed group to occurrence in general population) of lung cancer for nonsmoking insulation industry workers exposed to asbestos was 5.17; for smokers not exposed to asbestos—10.85; but for exposed smokers—and for exposed heavy smokers—87.36. See Surgeon General of the United States, The Health Consequences of Smoking: Cancer and Chronic Lung Disease in the Workplace 213–20 (1986); United States Dep't of Labor, Disability Compensation for Asbestos–Associated Disease in the United States 335 (1981).

5. *Comparative Fault.* In comparative fault jurisdictions, juries may be required to apportion damages if they find that the plaintiff's smoking constituted contributory fault. In Brisboy v. Fibreboard Corp., 429 Mich. 540, 418 N.W.2d 650 (1988), cited in *Dafler*, the court upheld a jury's finding that decedent's smoking was contributorily negligent and that the smoking contributed 55 percent to his lung cancer. Addressing the quality of evidence on the apportionment question, the court stated: "We reject plaintiff's claim that there is no rational basis for the jury's apportionment of fault and note that juries are frequently called upon to make such judgments." See also Hao v. Owens–Illinois, Inc., 69 Hawaii 231, 738 P.2d 416 (1987) (applying pure comparative fault to apportion plaintiff's negligence in smoking and defendant's responsibility for providing asbestos products).

6. An interesting contrast to *Dafler* is found in Acosta v. Babcock & Wilcox, 961 F.2d 533 (5th Cir.1992). In *Acosta*, the jury rendered a verdict for defendant, which the appeals court reversed because the jury instruction improperly barred three plaintiffs from arguing that cigarette smoking and workplace exposure to asbestos may have combined to cause plaintiffs' cancer. The court held that the instruction by a federal trial court wrongly required the plaintiffs to prove that "but for" workplace exposure to asbestos, the long-term smokers would not have developed lung cancer. The court said it was medically impossible "to determine whether cigarettes alone or asbestos alone" caused the workers' cancer and remanded the cases for a new trial. One of the plaintiffs' medical experts testified that asbestos exposure was a "substantial contributing factor" to a worker's interstitial

fibrosis and asbestosis. The expert also testified that smoking could have played a part in the development of the cancer. Another plaintiffs' expert contended that asbestos exposure was a causal factor of the cancer and that the two causes multiplied the risks.

The trial judge instructed the jury that the law recognizes that there may be more than one cause of an injury, but "each may be the cause, so long as it can reasonably be said that, except for asbestos exposure, the injury complained of would not have occurred." The appeals court explained:

> The testimony of the plaintiffs' witnesses was to the effect that the asbestos exposure "played a substantial part in bringing about or actually causing the injury." That the jury was not informed that this testimony could have been sufficient to establish legal causation * * * constitutes reversible error. In today's world of carcinogens, a conscientious jury would be hard pressed to state unequivocally that a person would not get cancer absent exposure to asbestos.

Would apportionment be possible in this case? If not, what will the defendants' liability be in the event the jury finds that asbestos was a contributing cause of the cancer? Should defendant use different tactics for its experts' testimony?

7. In several asbestos cases, defendants have sought to introduce plaintiffs' smoking history in order to demonstrate that plaintiffs would not have heeded any warnings on asbestos products even if they had been provided, and hence the defendants' failure to warn of the dangers of asbestos exposure was not the cause of their injuries. In other words, if plaintiffs ignored the warnings on cigarette packages, which contributed to lung cancer, they would have been unlikely to heed any warnings on asbestos containers. See Owens–Corning Fiberglas Corp. v. Watson, 243 Va. 128, 413 S.E.2d 630 (1992) (evidence that plaintiff did not heed warnings on cigarette carton was properly excluded by trial court; fact that plaintiff disregarded warnings on cigarette packages, without more, was not probative of whether he would have heeded any warnings that might have been affixed to packages of insulation products); Owens–Illinois v. Armstrong, 326 Md. 107, 604 A.2d 47 (1992) (same).

8. See Lewis A. Kornhauser & Richard L. Revesz, Sharing Damages Among Multiple Tortfeasors, 98 Yale L.J. 831 (1989); Mario J. Rizzo & Frank S. Arnold, Causal Apportionment in the Law of Torts: An Economic Theory, 80 Colum. L. Rev. 1399 (1980); William M. Landes & Richard A. Posner, Joint and Multiple Tortfeasors: An Economic Analysis, 9 J. Legal Stud. 517 (1980). Rizzo and Arnold's proposal and methodology are criticized in David Kaye & Michael Aickin, A Comment on Causal Apportionment, 13 J. Legal Stud. 191 (1984), and in Mark Kelman, The Necessary Myth of Objective Causation Judgments in Liberal Political Theory, 63 Chi.-Kent L. Rev. 579, 611–17 (1987).

2. APPORTIONMENT OR JOINT AND SEVERAL LIABILITY AMONG TORTFEASORS

If the plaintiff is entirely innocent—without fault and without making any contribution to the injury—how should the courts allocate the harm among two or more defendants? The decision that follows answers that question in the nuisance setting.

MICHIE v. GREAT LAKES STEEL DIVISION

United States Court of Appeals, Sixth Circuit, 1974.
495 F.2d 213.

EDWARDS, C.J.

This is an interlocutory appeal from a District Judge's denial of a motion to dismiss filed by three corporations which are defendants-appellants herein. The District Court certified that the appeal presented a controlling issue of law and this court granted leave to appeal under 28 U.S.C. § 1292(b) (1970).

Appellants' motion to dismiss was based upon the contention that each plaintiff individually had failed to meet the requirement of a $10,000 amount in controversy for diversity jurisdiction set forth in 28 U.S.C. § 1332 (1970).

The facts in this matter, as alleged in the pleadings, are somewhat unique. Thirty-seven persons, members of thirteen families residing near LaSalle, Ontario, Canada, have filed a complaint against three corporations which operate seven plants in the United States immediately across the Detroit River from Canada. Plaintiffs claim that pollutants emitted by plants of defendants are noxious in character and that their discharge in the ambient air violates various municipal and state ordinances and laws. They assert that the discharges represent a nuisance and that the pollutants are carried by air currents onto their premises in Canada, thereby damaging their persons and property. Each plaintiff individually claims damages ranging from $11,000 to $35,000 from all three corporate defendants jointly and severally. There is, however, no assertion of joint action or conspiracy on the part of defendants.

* * *

We believe the principal question presented by this appeal may be phrased thus: Under the law of the State of Michigan, may multiple defendants, whose independent actions of allegedly discharging pollutants into the ambient air thereby allegedly create a nuisance be jointly and severally liable to multiple plaintiffs for numerous individual injuries which plaintiffs claim to have sustained as a result of said actions, where said pollutants mix in the air so that their separate effects in creating the individual injuries are impossible to analyze.

Appellants argue that the law applicable is that of the State of Michigan and that Michigan law does not allow for joint and several liability on the part of persons charged with maintaining a nuisance. They cite and rely on an old Michigan case. Robinson v. Baugh, 31 Mich. 290 (1875). They also quote and rely upon Restatement of Torts (First) 881:

> "Where two or more persons, each acting independently, create or maintain a situation which is a tortious invasion of a landowner's interest in the use and enjoyment of land by interfering with his quiet, light, air or flowing water, each is liable only for such proportion of the harm caused to the land or of the loss of enjoyment of it by the owner as his contribution to the harm bears to the total harm."

* * *

Appellees rely strongly upon the opinion of the District Judge in denying the motion to dismiss:

> "This court is of the view that this is not the state of the law in Michigan with respect to air pollution. In the absence of any Michigan cases on point, analogous Michigan cases in the automobile negligence area involving questions of joint liability after the simultaneous impact of vehicles and resultant injuries, are instructive."

In Watts v. Smith, 375 Mich. 120, 134 N.W.2d 194, the Michigan Supreme Court said:

> "Although it is not always definitely so stated the rule seems to have become generally established that, although there is no concert of action between tort feasors, if the cumulative effects of their acts is a single indivisible injury which it cannot certainly be said would have resulted but for the concurrence of such acts, the actors are to be held liable as joint tort feasors."

In Maddux v. Donaldson, 362 Mich. 425, 108 N.W.2d 33, the Michigan Supreme Court * * * indicated that

> " * * * it is clear that there is a manifest unfairness in 'putting on the injured party the impossible burden of proving the specific shares of harm done by each * * *. Such results are simply the law's callous dullness to innocent sufferers. One would think that the obvious meanness of letting wrongdoers go scot free in such cases would cause the courts to think twice and to suspect some fallacy in their rule of law.' "

Plaintiffs contend that the Maddux, id., and Watts, supra, language applies here since there is no possibility of dividing the injuries herein alleged to have occurred and that it is impossible to judge which of the alleged tortfeasors caused what harm.

It is the opinion of this court that the rule of Maddux, supra, and Landers, supra, cited therein is the better, and applicable rule in this air pollution case.

On this point we affirm the decision of the District Judge. This complaint appears to have been filed under the diversity jurisdiction of the federal courts. All parties have agreed that Michigan law alone controls.

Like most jurisdictions, Michigan has had great difficulty with the problems posed in tort cases by multiple causes for single or indivisible injuries. Compare Watts v. Smith, 375 Mich. 120, 134 N.W.2d 194 (1965); Maddux v. Donaldson, 362 Mich. 425, 108 N.W.2d 33 (1961).

* * *

We believe that the issue was decided in the lengthy consideration given by the Michigan court in the Maddux case. There Justice Talbot Smith in an opinion for the court majority held:

It is our conclusion that if there is competent testimony, adduced either by plaintiff or defendant, that the injuries are factually and medically separable, and that the liability for all such injuries and damages, or parts thereof, may be allocated with reasonable certainty to the impacts in turn, the jury will be instructed accordingly and mere difficulty in so doing will not relieve the triers of the facts of this responsibility. This merely follows the general rule that "where the independent concurring acts have caused distinct and separate injuries to the plaintiff, or where some reasonable means of apportioning the damages is evident, the courts generally will not hold the tort-feasors jointly and severally liable."

But if, on the other hand, the triers of the facts conclude that they cannot reasonably make the division of liability between the tortfeasors, this is the point where the road of authority divides. Much ancient authority, not in truth precedent, would say that the case is now over, and that plaintiff shall take nothing. Some modern courts, as well, hold that his is merely the case of the marauding dogs and the helpless sheep relitigated in the setting of a modern highway. The conclusion is erroneous. Such precedents are not apt. When the triers of the facts decide that they cannot make a division of injuries we have, by their own finding, nothing more or less than an indivisible injury, and the precedents as to indivisible injuries will control. * * * Maddux v. Donaldson, 362 Mich. 425, 432–433, 108 N.W.2d 33, 36 (1961).

* * *

* * * [A]ppellants call our attention to what appears to be a contrary rule applicable to nuisance cases referred to in the Maddux opinion. Restatement of Torts (First) 881.

In the latest Restatement, however, both the old and the newer rule are recognized and as the Michigan court held in Maddux, the question of whether liability of alleged polluters is joint or several is left to the trier of the facts. Where the injury itself is indivisible, the judge or jury must determine whether or not it is practicable to apportion the harm among the tortfeasors. If not, the entire liability may be imposed upon one (or several) tortfeasors subject, of course, to subsequent right of contribution among the joint offenders.

* * *

Assuming plaintiffs in this case prove injury and liability as to several tort-feasors, the net effect of Michigan's new rule is to shift the burden of proof as to which one was responsible and to what degree from the injured party to the wrongdoers.

* * *

Since our instant case has not been tried, we do not speculate about what the facts may show, either as to injury or liability. But it is obvious from the briefs that appellant corporations intend to make the defense that if there was injury, other corporations, persons and instrumentalities contributed to the pollution of the ambient air so as to make it impossible to prove whose emissions did what damage to plaintiffs' persons or homes. Like the District Judge, we see a close analogy between this situation and the Maddux case. We believe the Michigan Supreme Court would do so likewise.

* * *

As modified, the judgment of the District Court is affirmed.

Notes and Questions

1. Would the rule of the *Michie* case apply to most nuisance cases where there are multiple tortfeasors, each making some contribution to the total harm suffered by the plaintiffs? The synergistic nature of many toxic chemical agents could be relevant to such cases because it is the combined impact of the chemicals which caused the harm to the nearby residents and there would not appear to exist any feasible means for the plaintiff to apportion the damages or apportion the causation. In Chapter 10 we consider this same question in allocating the harm among potentially responsible parties in suits brought under the Comprehensive Environmental Response, Compensation and Liability Act.

2. Is the situation of the successive (and simultaneous) automobile collisions relied on in *Michie* analogous to the air or water pollution or waste site disposal situation?

3. *Michie* indicates the attitude of many of the more recent decisions in finding the defendants each liable for the total damage. Two different legal means are used to accomplish this result: (a) to find that the injury is indivisible and therefore not apportionable as a matter of substantive law, and (b) to hold that the burden of proof is upon the defendants to show factual basis for apportionment, with the result that apportionment is unavailable as a practical matter. Illustrations of the first approach are Holtz v. Holder, 101 Ariz. 217, 418 P.2d 584 (1966) (chain collision); Ruud v. Grimm, 252 Iowa 1266, 110 N.W.2d 321 (1961) (same); Landers v. East Texas Salt Water Disposal Co., 151 Tex. 251, 248 S.W.2d 731 (1952) (pollution). Illustrations of the second approach are Murphy v. Taxicabs of Louisville, 330 S.W.2d 395 (Ky. 1959) (chain collision); Maddux v. Donald-

son, 362 Mich. 425, 108 N.W.2d 33 (1961) (same); Phillips Petroleum Co. v. Hardee, 189 F.2d 205 (5th Cir.1951) (pollution); see Restatement (Second) of Torts § 433B(2). Is there any significant difference between these two ideas?

4. Suppose twenty-six defendants discharge waste into a stream; no one of them discharges enough to pollute the stream, but the combined discharge does pollute it. Is the plaintiff entitled to damages, and if so, how much from each defendant? Does it make any difference that the defendants, although not acting in concert, each knows what the others are doing? See Woodland v. Portneuf Marsh Valley Irr. Co., 26 Idaho 789, 146 P. 1106 (1915); Sloggy v. Dilworth, 38 Minn. 179, 36 N.W. 451 (1888).

Two defendants independently pollute a stream by discharging oil into it. The oil on the surface catches fire, and the fire burns the plaintiff's barn. Can the damages be apportioned? Northup v. Eakes, 72 Okl. 66, 178 P. 266 (1918); Phillips Petroleum Co. v. Vandergriff, 190 Okl. 280, 122 P.2d 1020 (1942).

5. In apportioning the damages among joint tortfeasors the courts have taken a variety of approaches. Some courts have relied upon the comparative fault statutes and allocated liability based on each defendant's share of fault, as determined by the jury. See, e.g., Taylor v. Celotex Corp., 393 Pa.Super. 566, 574 A.2d 1084 (1990) (applying New Jersey law, allocated according to each defendant's causal fault under New Jersey Comparative Negligence Act, 2A:15–5.1); Rocco v. Johns–Manville Corp., 754 F.2d 110 (3d Cir.1985) (applying Pennsylvania Joint Tortfeasors Act, which is based on the Uniform Contribution Among Tortfeasors Act, each defendant is assigned a pro-rata share, one-ninth in this case).

6. *Effect of Comparative Fault on Joint and Several Liability.* Some states, as part of their enactment of comparative fault systems, have modified or abolished joint and several liability. For example, the New Jersey Comparative Negligence Act, N.J.S.A. 2A:15–1.1 et seq., altered joint and several liability so that only defendants determined to be 60% or more responsible for damages would be liable for the total amount of an award. A defendant found to be more than 20% but less than 60% responsible for the damages would be liable for the entire amount of economic loss, but only for that percentage of non-economic loss directly attributable to his fault. A defendant found to be responsible for 20% or less of any damages would be liable only for the percentage of the award directly attributable to his fault.

Consequently, defendants found only 1% responsible can no longer be held liable for the entire amount of an award. This demonstration is significant in toxic tort and environmental claims, where the value of damages can be enormous. The statute, however, contains an exception for environmental tort actions: "With regard to environmental tort actions the party so recovering may recover the full amount of the damage award from any party determined to be liable." N.J.S.A. 2A:15–5.3(d). An "environmental tort action" is defined as "a civil action seeking damages for personal injuries or death where the cause of the damages is the negligent manufacture, use, disposal, handling, storage or treatment of hazardous or toxic substances." N.J.S.A. 2A:15–5.3(i). New Jersey's Product Liability Act, N.J.S.A. 2A:58C–1 et seq., enacted at the same time as the Comparative

Negligence Act, similarly exempted environmental tort actions. In that act, an "environmental tort action" is defined as "a civil action seeking damages for harm where the cause of the harm is exposure to toxic chemicals or substances, but * * * not * * * actions involving drugs or products intended for personal consumption or use." N.J.S.A. 2A:58C–1(b)(4).

In Stevenson v. Keene Corp., 254 N.J.Super. 310, 603 A.2d 521 (1992), affirmed 131 N.J. 393, 620 A.2d 1047 (1993), the appellate division held that asbestos cases did constitute "environmental tort actions" and hence the defendants were not entitled to the abolition of joint and several liability. The court emphasized that asbestos was regulated by a variety of state and federal environmental statutes. The New Jersey Supreme Court in a per curiam affirmance observed, however, that the "environmental tort action exception" should not be enlarged to include every conceivable injury involving a toxic product.

In Tragarz v. Keene Corp., 980 F.2d 411 (7th Cir.1992), the Seventh Circuit interpreted the Illinois exception to its elimination of joint and several liability (Ill.—S.H.A. 735 ILCS 5/2–1117; and 5/2–1118) which provides:

> notwithstanding the provisions of Section 2–1117 in any action in which the trier of fact determines that the injury or damage for which recovery is sought was caused by an act involving the discharge into the environment of any pollutant, including any waste, hazardous substance, irritant, or contaminant, including, but not limited to smoke, vapor, soot, fumes, acids, alkalis, asbestos, toxic or corrosive chemicals * * * any defendants found liable shall be jointly and severally liable for such damage.

The court held that the discharge of asbestos fibers into the internal environment of a building constituted "the discharge into the environment of any pollutant."

Other courts have reached similar conclusions. See, e.g., Sofie v. Fibreboard Corp., 112 Wash.2d 636, 771 P.2d 711 (1989), amended ___ Wash. ___, 780 P.2d 260 (1989) (as amended holding that Wash. Rev. Code Ann. 4.22.070 providing exception for "hazardous waste or substances" encompassed asbestos litigation).

What is the rationale for creating environmental tort exceptions, allowing joint and several liability to apply to such cases?

Problem

Buy–Products, Inc. operated a chemical research plant on Main and Third streets in Anytown, State from 1945 to 1979, when the plant was closed. Buy–Products' operations focused on research related to potential commercial uses or recycling of chemical by-products and wastes. These chemicals were purchased from other chemical manufacturers.

Although successful in part, Buy–Products could not find commercial uses for all of the chemical by-products and wastes which were shipped to its plant. From 1945 to 1968, unusable materials were dumped into several unlined open pits located near the back of the plant property. These pits were within ten yards of the Chem Creek which ran through the back of the property and through several surrounding neighborhoods.

When Buy–Products stopped pouring materials into the pits in 1968, it leveled a small storage building which had served as a transfer center for the disposal of chemicals. Several leaking barrels were left within the building rubble. In 1978, the pits were dug up and covered over with top soil. For a short period of time until the plant closed, Buy–Products poured some of its wastes into a sewer grate located near the plant entrance.

In 1979, the State Department of the Environment (DE) began its initial investigation of the site. The DE discovered that wastes from metal degreasing operations and byproducts from pesticide manufacture were the main source of material dumped into the pits. Of particular concern to DE were the relatively high concentrations of trichlorethylene and polychlorinated dibenzodioxins, which included 2, 3, 7, 8 tetrachlorodibenzodioxin (TCDD). Experts have estimated that 10,000 gallons of these wastes and byproducts were dumped into the pits over a 40–year period.

The DE also learned that byproducts from pesticide manufacture had been mixed with other chemicals and then spread over the plant property in the 1940s and 1950s for dust control. Periodically, the plant grounds would be plowed by bulldozers and the soil would be stored in a pile near the creek. Subsequently, this soil was sold to a developer and was used for landscaping the lawns of surrounding homes. Preliminary sampling by DE in 1985 indicated very localized "hot spots" of TCDD contamination in some yards, up to 20 ppb (parts per billion). All identified hot spots were excavated down to 12 inches and removed. Some residents refused DE access to their yards.

In 1987, DE, while digging up the property, discovered three leaking underground storage tanks containing gasoline. These tanks were all located on the western edge of the plant property. The gasoline had been used in the operation of Buy–Products' chemical trucking operation. It is believed that more than 500 gallons of gasoline had leaked into the soil over 15 years.

The Pure Water Aquifer, which is 100 feet below the surface, runs directly below the Buy–Products plant site and provides well water for some of the Anytown residents. Other Anytown residents receive municipal water from the Sparkle Reservoir five miles to the north. There is also a shallow aquifer 20 feet below the surface which is not used for drinking water. Trichloroethylene and other compounds at high levels (up to 1,000 ppm) have been found in the shallow aquifer. The Anytown sewer system runs through the plant property and down Main Street. When the storage building was leveled in 1968, local residents noted a strange odor, and releases of dust which settled on their houses and yards.

Main Street is an east/west street located on the south border of the site. Third Street forms the eastern border of the plant. Chem Creek runs along the northern boundary. The Jones family resides on the corner of Main and Fourth Streets on the western border of the property. The Smith family resides on Fourth Street on the western border of the plant along Chem Creek. The Lowe family resides across Fourth Street from the Smith family, and Mrs. High resides across Main Street from the plant entrance.

The following is known with regard to each family member:

Mr. Fred Jones: 60 years old; steel worker; moved into new home in 1954; Smoker; Mother had breast cancer; in 1990, was diagnosed with acute myelogenous leukemia; Of all plaintiffs, the Joneses live closest to site.

Mrs. Ethel Jones: 58 years old; Town Librarian; moved into new home in 1954; non-smoker; no history of cancer; frequently complained of "gasoline" odors in basement; doctor diagnoses immune system dysfunction manifested in frequent illnesses.

Ms. Judy Jones: daughter; born 1958; as child, waded in Chem Creek; now lives on Seventh Street; insurance broker; complains of frequent headaches and anxiety.

Mr. Sam Smith: 58 years old; steel worker; moved into new home in 1954; non-smoker; notes yard soil is discolored in areas and nothing grows.

Mrs. Shirley Smith: 57 years old; school teacher who left job because of claimed illness; non-smoker; had vegetable garden along west fence line of Buy-Products plant from 1955–1980; reveals elevated blood levels of TCDD.

Mr. Steve Smith: son; born 1956; had frequent skin rashes which have now ceased; married with one child; lives on Tenth Street; school teacher; as child, swam in Chem Creek.

Mr. John Lowe: 50 years old; banker; moved into home in 1989; non-smoker; recent tests indicate some liver dysfunction, but no overt disease.

Mrs. Jane Lowe: 50 years old; not employed; non-smoker.

Mrs. High: 68 years old; moved into home 1945; husband was plant foreman for Buy–Products from 1945–1975 and he died of a heart attack in 1975.

Ms. Lee High: daughter; born 1953

You are a private attorney in Anytown. You are visited by Sam Smith, who provides to you the above information. Speaking on behalf of his family, the Jones and the Lowes, he asks you to advise him of any potential legal claims the family members might pursue, individually or collectively. Please advise him, providing him as well with your evaluation of the likely legal responses of any parties against whom liability may be sought. In particular you are concerned respecting the possible causation problems which these clients may encounter in establishing the relationship between their injuries and the exposures.

Chapter Nine

WORKPLACE INJURIES AND TOXIC SUBSTANCES: INTERSECTION OF WORKERS' COMPENSATION AND TORT LIABILITY

A. INTRODUCTION TO THE WORKERS' COMPENSATION SYSTEM

1. A BIT OF HISTORY

Many of the cases in earlier chapters illustrate that employees may suffer physical harm or emotional distress as a result of exposure to toxic substances or chemicals in the workplace. The decisions we have previously considered are actions by the injured employee usually against third party product manufacturers, not against the employer. The rights and remedies which an employee may have against the employer are generally governed by workers' compensation and occupational disease statutes, whereas the rights against a third party manufacturer are governed by common law tort rules.

Under the law of virtually every state, an employee who is injured in a work-related capacity is barred from instituting a tort suit against her employer, provided that the employee is entitled to seek workers' compensation benefits from the employer's insurer. At the same time, the employee is not barred from suing a third party who causes or contributes to the injury. Workers' compensation protection does not affect the action against the third party, but the employer (or its carrier) usually is subrogated to the extent of benefits paid. Prior to the widespread enactment of the workers' compensation systems, an injured employee could institute a tort suit against her employer, but substantial obstacles hampered the injured employee's success in such common law actions. The employee had to establish the employer's negligence, a difficult task in most industrial accidents, and the employer was allowed to assert the defenses of contributory negligence, assumption of the risk, or the fellow servant doctrine—Dean Prosser's "unholy trinity." Prosser & Keeton on Torts § 80 at 569 (5th ed. 1984).

By the early twentieth century, workers' compensation statutes began to sweep the country. Almost universally these statutes provide for recovery of determinate amounts from the employer upon proof that the injury was one "arising out of and in the course of employment," without regard to fault. Thus, negligence of the employer or its agents, or of the injured employee, is irrelevant. At the same time, all workers' compensation statutes bar the injured employee from suing his employer in most cases, even when the employer would otherwise have been liable under common law doctrine. This exclusive remedy provision constitutes the core political trade-off. The employee receives defined compensation under a strict liability regime without the need to invest time, cost and uncertainty of litigation. The employer, in turn, is afforded immunity from tort suits. Third parties, such as product manufacturers, were not included in the trade-off barring the injured employee's common law suit.

As courts and juries in tort cases moved much more rapidly to increase the dollar amounts awarded than did legislatures and administrative boards in control of the workers' compensation system, injured workers and their lawyers found an increasing incentive to avoid the exclusive remedy provision and the accompanying damage limitation. While product liability suits are often available in workplace injuries, as the asbestos litigation demonstrates vividly, often the employee's injury did not involve the use of a product manufactured by a third party. Therefore, injured workers have sought to find gaps in the exclusivity bar that would free them to sue their employers in a tort suit.

The quest for tort liability against employers is also stimulated by the tremendous variation among state systems in the dollar amounts awarded for a given injury or disability. For example, an employee who loses a hand in Kansas receives benefits computed at 150 weeks, see Kan. Stat. Ann. 44–510d(11), while in Wisconsin, the loss of a hand is computed at 400 weeks, Wis. Stat. Ann. 102.52(3). An employee in Tennessee who loses an eye receives compensation computed at 100 weeks, Tenn. Code Ann. § 50–6–207(3)(A)(ii)(q), but in Maryland, receives 250 weeks, Md. Code Art. 101, § 36(3)(b) (1990).

2. ISSUE PRECLUSION

One issue bearing on the relationship between tort actions and workers' compensation claims is whether an adverse finding in a compensation proceeding will be given collateral estoppel effect in a subsequent tort suit against a third party, such as a product manufacturer or supplier. For example, if the compensation board determines that the claimant's injury or disease was not causally linked to her employment, will a court be bound by that adverse factual finding in a subsequent tort suit?

While the decisions are split, the weight of authority seems to answer the inquiry affirmatively, holding that the requirements for issue preclusion may be satisfied by the prior proceeding. In Grant v. GAF Corp., 415 Pa.Super. 137, 608 A.2d 1047 (1992), three widows brought wrongful death actions against various manufacturers of asbestos products, alleging that the decedents had developed asbestosis and carcinoma from workplace exposure to asbestos products. Prior to filing the civil action the plaintiffs had filed for workers' compensation/occupational disease benefits under Pennsylvania law. A workers' compensation referee determined that each "decedent's cancer and subsequent death were not a result of any occupational exposure," and that the widows had not met their "burden of proving that Decedent's lifetime disability or death [were] occupationally related." Those determinations were upheld on appeal. After reviewing the four essentials of issue preclusion: (1) the issue decided in the prior action was identical with the one presented in the later action; (2) there was a final judgment on the merits; (3) the party against whom the plea is asserted was a party or in privity with a party to the prior adjudication; and (4) the party against whom the plea is asserted has had a full and fair opportunity to litigate the issue in question in a prior action, the court held:

> The preclusive effect of this determination in a subsequent tort action is clear; the element of causation is necessary to recovery in a tort action against the defendants/manufacturers. * * * The issue of causation, injury as a result of exposure in the workplace, was decided adversely to the plaintiffs in the workmen's compensation proceeding and thus recovery in a subsequent tort action is precluded.

* * *

> * * * Here, the referees' findings that the decedents' carcinoma was not related to occupational exposure were determined on appeal to be supported by sufficient competent evidence. The doctrine of collateral estoppel is not unavailable simply because administrative procedures are involved; where the agency is acting in a judicial capacity and resolves disputed issues of fact which the parties had an opportunity to litigate, the courts will not hesitate to apply preclusion principles.

See also Miller v. Pool and Canfield, Inc., 800 S.W.2d 120 (Mo.App.1990) (recognizing the applicability of issue preclusion, but refusing to apply it because the compensation determination was not a final judgment); Smith v. LTV Corp., 1992 WL 316324 (Ohio App. 1992); Hansen v. Estate of Harvey, 119 Idaho 333, 806 P.2d 426 (1991). But see Walker v. Kerr–McGee Chem. Corp., 793 F.Supp. 688 (N.D. Miss.1992) (refusing to apply issue preclusion because under Mississippi law strict mutuality is required between the parties in the two actions).

One of the casebook authors has offered these observations on dissimilarities between workers' compensation proceedings and ordinary civil trials. M. Stuart Madden, Issue Preclusion in Products Liability, 11 Pace L. Rev. 87, 131–133 (1990):

Although workers' compensation boards are court-like "in legal effect," to accomplish the principal goal of compensation, administrative procedures in workers' compensation make substantial accommodations to economy and celerity.   The jurisdiction of the workers' compensation tribunal is limited to findings of fact and conclusions of law pertaining to whether the claim arose "out of and in the course of employment."   Explicit limitations are placed upon the appellate review of board findings of fact.   In the proceedings themselves, a "rule of informality" obtains, and thus, compared with proceedings before courts of general jurisdiction, workers' compensation boards employ generally relaxed rules of notice and pleading.

Hearsay and even incompetent evidence is admissible, and indeed, the rules of evidence are so relaxed that workers' compensation findings are more likely to be reversed for failure to admit evidence than for denying admission to evidence.   Employee claimants frequently appear on their own behalf, without counsel.

The specialized role of workers' compensation as a compensation system administered by agencies in a quasi-judicial capacity should disable any issue preclusive effect of such judgments in later tort actions against the manufacturer or other third parties.   Agency findings and appellate affirmations that an injury was, or was not, sustained in the course of employment, merit conclusive effect, as ceding to compensation panels finality in deciding this issue is integral to the bargained-for exchange between employee and employer to forego tort remedies in return for expedited compensation for work-related injuries.   However, grave fairness questions arise from giving preclusive effect to any other holdings a board may consider within its ancillary jurisdiction.   In deciding the work-relatedness of an injury, for example, a board may have to reach conclusions on issues such as identification of the product or instrumentality causing claimant's injury, or the claimant's incautious conduct short of intentional misconduct.   It does not, however, follow that findings on such ancillary matters should be accorded preclusive effect in later tort actions, for given the primary purpose, the limited parties, and the informality of workers' compensation proceedings, it would be quite unlikely for a claimant to anticipate and assert or defend fact issues solely because of the potential relevance of such issues in a later tort action against third parties.

In light of these considerations, what would you advise a client who may have sustained a work-related toxic injury or disease but who also has a potential tort claim against a third party?   What are the strategic considerations which you must evaluate?   What do you tell your client about the odds of risking an adverse impact on a tort suit?

B. AVOIDING THE EXCLUSIVITY BAR

Unsurprisingly, the efforts to avoid the exclusivity bar have yielded some success as the courts and some legislatures have engrafted exceptions to the basic employer immunity from tort suit.

1. THE INTENTIONAL TORT EXCEPTION TO EXCLUSIVITY

A major and expanding exception to the workers' compensation exclusivity provisions barring the employee's suit for tort liability is the intentional tort exception. Essentially, a recent line of cases has held that if an employee can establish that the employer committed an intentional tort, the employee can sue the employer directly and recover tort damages. In the landmark case of Blankenship v. Cincinnati Milacron Chemicals, Inc., 69 Ohio St.2d 608, 433 N.E.2d 572 (1982), cert. denied 459 U.S. 857, 103 S.Ct. 127, 74 L.Ed.2d 110 (1982), the Ohio Supreme Court held that employees could sue their employers for exposure to toxic chemicals under narrowly defined circumstances.

In *Blankenship*, eight employees alleged that they were exposed to fumes and noxious chemicals within the scope of their employment which rendered them "sick, poisoned, and chemically intoxicated, causing them pain, discomfort, and emotional distress * * * causing suffering and permanent disability." They further alleged that knowing that such conditions existed, the employer failed to take any corrective action, failed to warn employees of the dangers that existed, and failed to report the conditions to various state and federal agencies. The Ohio workers' compensation statute provided:

> Employers * * * shall not be liable to respond in damages at common law or by statute for any injury, or occupational disease, or bodily condition, received or contracted by any employee in the course of or arising out of his employment * * * whether or not such injury, occupational disease [or] bodily condition * * * is [otherwise] compensable under the Revised Code.

The court, in recognizing the intentional tort exception, reasoned:

> [W]here an employee asserts in his complaint a claim for damages based on an intentional tort, " * * * the substance of the claim is not an 'injury * * * received or contracted by any employee in the course of or arising out of his employment' within the meaning of R.C. 4123.74 * * *." No reasonable individual would equate intentional and unintentional conduct in terms of the degree of risk which faces an employee nor would such individual contemplate the risk of an intentional tort as a natural risk of employment. Since an employer's intentional conduct does not arise out of employment, R.C. 4123.74 does not bestow upon employers immunity from civil liability for their intentional torts and an employee may resort to a civil suit for damages.

* * *

* * * [T]he protection afforded by the Act has always been for negligent acts and not for intentional tortious conduct. Indeed, workers' compensation acts were designed to improve the plight of the injured worker, and to hold that intentional torts are covered under the Act would be tantamount to encouraging such conduct, and this clearly cannot be reconciled with the motivating spirit and purpose of the Act.

It must also be remembered that the compensation scheme was specifically designed to provide less than full compensation for injured employees. Damages such as pain and suffering and loss of services on the part of a spouse are unavailable remedies to the injured employee. Punitive damages cannot be obtained. Yet, these damages are available to individuals who have been injured by intentional tortious conduct of third parties, and there is no legitimate reason why an employer should be able to escape from such damages simply because he committed an intentional tort against his employee.

In addition, one of the avowed purposes of the Act is to promote a safe and injury-free work environment. Affording an employer immunity for his intentional behavior would not promote such an environment, for an employer could commit intentional acts with impunity with the knowledge that, at the very most, his workers' compensation premiums may rise slightly.

Moreover, as this court noted, workers' compensation " * * * is founded upon the principle of insurance * * *." An insurance policy does not protect the policyholder from the consequences of his intentional tortious act. Indeed, it would be against public policy to permit insurance against the intentional tort.

Notes and Questions

1. Which, if any, of the court's rationales do you find most convincing? Is the court correct that failure to recognize an intentional tort exception would "be tantamount to encouraging such conduct"? How about the concern with denying employees damages for pain and suffering and punitive damages? Employees injured by negligent or reckless acts are denied such damages under the Act. Is it unfair to deny such kinds of recovery to those intentionally injured?

2. The Ohio Supreme Court in subsequent decisions has broadened the intentional tort exception to embrace egregious negligence and, more surprisingly, has held that the employee's filing for and receiving a workers' compensation benefit does not preclude a separate tort action and, most surprisingly, the employer receives no set-off against the tort judgment for the amount of benefits awarded. See Jones v. VIP Development Co., 15 Ohio St.3d 90, 472 N.E.2d 1046 (1984). Finally, when the Ohio legislature sought to bring some rationality to this scheme, the Ohio Supreme Court struck down the statutory amendments as unconstitutional. See Brady v. Safety–Kleen Corp., 61 Ohio St.3d 624, 576 N.E.2d 722 (1991). For a

criticism of the Ohio court's actions, see 2A Arthur Larson, Workmen's Compensation Law § 68.15 at 13–15 (1990) & Supp. at 13–16 (1993).

3. A majority of states maintain that employers' intentional torts are outside the exclusive coverage of the workers' compensation system. States have recognized such an exception by judicial, as well as legislative, action and have imposed varying standards to satisfy the "intentional tort" exception. For a listing of states recognizing the intentional tort exception, see 2A A. Larson, *id*, § 68.13 at 13–10 (1990) & Supp. (1993).

2. JUDICIAL RATIONALES FOR CREATING THE EXCEPTION

In addition to rationales catalogued in *Blankenship*, others have been offered to justify the intentional tort exception.

a. The "Nonaccident" Rationale

One theory applied by many courts is that an employer is prevented from claiming its own intentional acts were "accidental" because the employer should be estopped from relying on the limited accident-based recovery once its conduct is intentional and blameworthy. See, e.g., Stewart v. McLellan's Stores Co., 194 S.C. 50, 9 S.E.2d 35 (1940); Readinger v. Gottschall, 201 Pa.Super. 134, 191 A.2d 694, 696 (1963); National Can Corp. v. Jovanovich, 503 N.E.2d 1224 (Ind.App.1987).

b. Larson's Approach to the Accident Exception

Larson suggests that viewing whether an incident is an "accident" should be determined from the viewpoint of the person seeking protection under the exclusive remedy of the act. 2A Larson § 68.12, at 13–9. Difficulty arose because courts, by viewing the affair from the viewpoint of the victim, found deliberate assaults to be "accidents" under the acts. Larson recommends that when the employer is pleading the exclusive remedy provision as a defense to a tort suit, whether the incident is considered an accident would be determined from its perspective.

c. The "Severed" Relationship Rationale

Another theory advanced by some courts is that the employment relationship is "severed" by an employer's act of violence. Although this theory is criticized as being fictitious, it has been accepted and followed by several courts. See, e.g., Sontag v. Orbit Valve Co., 283 Ark. 191, 672 S.W.2d 50, 51 (1984) ("Whenever an employee is injured by the willful and malicious acts of the employer he may treat the acts of the employer as a breach of the employer-employee relationship and seek full damages in a common law action.").

3. THE "INTENTIONAL" TORT STANDARD USED BY STATES

Courts recognizing the intentional tort exception have developed different standards relating to the employer's state of mind.

a. The Majority Rule: Deliberate Intent to Cause Injury

As a rule, "the common law liability of the employer cannot be stretched to include * * * injuries caused by gross, wanton, wilful, deliberate, intentional, reckless, culpable or malicious negligence, or other misconduct of the employer short of genuine intent to cause injury." 2A Larson § 68.13, at 13–4. Most states limit the recovery under the intentional tort exception by implementing the "true intentional tort" or "actual, specific, and deliberate" intent standard. Under this view, the employer must have intended the specific injury as well as the act. See, e.g., National Can Corp. v. Jovanovich, 503 N.E.2d 1224 (Ind.App.1987) ("In light of the quid pro quo underlying * * * Indiana's Workmen's Compensation Act, we believe a stringent standard of specific intent is necessary to avoid the workmen's compensation scheme from being 'swallowed up' by a glut of common law suits outside the Act.").

b. "Substantial Certainty" Test of Intent

A few states utilize the broader Restatement (Second) of Torts definition of "intent." Restatement (Second) of Torts § 8A (1965); "The word 'intent' is used * * * to denote that the actor desires to cause consequences of his act, or that he believes that the consequences are substantially certain to result from it." Under this definition, the employer must have only intended the act that caused the injury, with knowledge that the injury was substantially certain to follow. See, e.g., Beauchamp v. Dow Chem. Co., 427 Mich. 1, 398 N.W.2d 882 (1986) (superseded by statute); Woodson v. Rowland, 329 N.C. 330, 407 S.E.2d 222 (1991).

c. Wilful, Wanton or Reckless Test

At least one state has applied a lesser standard of "wilful, wanton or reckless" conduct for the intentional act exception. Under this view the employer must have a subjective awareness of a substantial risk of bodily injury resulting from the activity. See Mandolidis v. Elkins Indus., Inc., 161 W.Va. 695, 246 S.E.2d 907 (1978). See Note, Workers' Compensation: Expanding the Intentional Tort Exception to Include Willful, Wanton, and Reckless Employer Misconduct, 58 Notre Dame L. Rev. 890 (1983).

d. Legislative Standards of Intent

Most state legislatures which have addressed the issue have opted for the narrow "true" intentional tort standard. See, e.g., Or. Rev. Stat.

656.156(2) ("If injury or death results to a worker from the deliberate intention of the employer of the worker to produce such injury or death"); Wash. Rev. Code Ann. 51.24.020 ("If injury results to a worker from the deliberate intention of his or her employer to produce such injury"); but see Ariz. Rev. Stat. § 23–1022(A) ("if the injury is caused by the employer's willful misconduct, * * * and the act causing the injury is the personal act of the employer * * * and the act indicates a willful disregard of the life, limb or bodily safety of employees").

After the Michigan Supreme Court had adopted the Restatement's substantial certainty test of intent in Beauchamp v. Dow Chemical Co., 427 Mich. 1, 398 N.W.2d 882 (1986), a case involving a chemist's exposures to dioxin, the legislature overruled the decision by expressly recognizing an intentional tort exception but adopting a "specific intent" test:

> An intentional tort shall exist only when an employee is injured as a result of a deliberate act of the employer and the employer specifically intended an injury. An employer shall be deemed to have intended to injure if the employer had actual knowledge that an injury was certain to occur and willfully disregarded that knowledge. The issue of whether an act was an intentional tort shall be a question of law for the court.

M.C.L.A. § 418.131(1).

What is the principal motivation for legislatures in defining "intentional tort" narrowly?

4. TOXIC EXPOSURE CASES

For examples of decisions applying the intentional tort exception in toxic exposure cases, see Gulden v. Crown Zellerbach Corp., 890 F.2d 195 (9th Cir.1989), where an employer had required employees to clean up spilled PCBs on their hands and knees for five days, with PCB levels in which they were in contact were 500 times greater than EPA allowable levels. The district court granted the defendant's motion for summary judgment based on the Oregon workers' compensation scheme's exclusive remedy provision. The court of appeals reversed and remanded, holding that "a jury could conclude that the intention to injure—in this case, to expose [plaintiffs] Gulden and Steele to toxic levels of PCB—was deliberate where the employer had an opportunity to weigh the consequences and to make a conscious choice among possible courses of action." To be contrasted is Lantz v. National Semiconductor Corp., 775 P.2d 937 (Utah App.1989), where a former employee sued his supervisor and employer for injuries received from toxic fumes after the supervisor denied him permission to evacuate the work area following a chemical spill. The Utah Supreme Court left stand the trial court's dismissal, finding that the plaintiff failed to establish that the supervisor had actual, deliberate intent to injure the employee, so the employer was immune from any tort action.

Also illustrative is Acevedo v. Consolidated Edison Co. of New York, 189 A.D.2d 497, 596 N.Y.S.2d 68 (1993), holding that New York's workers' compensation act barred claims brought by utility workers who contended that they were intentionally exposed to friable asbestos when they were assigned to clean up debris from an explosion of asbestos-insulated steam pipes. The workers claimed that their employer had fraudulently concealed the danger of the asbestos. Relying upon the workers' compensation statute, the court also rejected their nuisance and medical monitoring claims, even though damages for such claims are not available in workers' compensation. The court explained: "[the] exclusive reach [of the Act] does not depend on compensability."

5. DECEIT EXCEPTION

A few courts have recognized what might be termed a "deceit" exception to the bar. For example, in O'Brien v. Ottawa Silica Co., 656 F.Supp. 610, 611–12 (E.D.Mich.1987), the federal district court, applying Michigan law, relieved a worker from the operation of the exclusivity doctrine when evidence showed that his employer was aware that its employees were suffering from asbestos-related disease but concealed that information. This withholding of specific medical information regarding the worker's personal health condition, the court concluded, constituted sufficient intentional fraud to fall outside of the exclusivity doctrine. Similarly, a Florida appellate court held that an employer's alleged deceit in exposing employees to toxic substances without warnings or appropriate safety measures constituted intentional conduct that brought the action outside the state workers' compensation scheme. Cunningham v. Anchor Hocking Corp., 558 So.2d 93 (Fla.App.1990).

However, a New Mexico decision, Johnson Controls World Services v. Barnes, 115 N.M. 114, 847 P.2d 761 (App.1993), explicitly rejected such an exception as part of the broader intentional tort exception. In *Johnson Controls*, the plaintiff was directed to remove underground storage tanks that his employer had allegedly falsely represented were "properly and completely drained of hazardous liquid." He further alleged that he was splashed with toxic liquid which caused him injury, and that the employer had "deliberately and intentionally failed to warn him of the dangers involved." In rejecting plaintiff's attempt to assert a tort claim, the court first stated a test of intent that required "an actual intent * * * to injure the worker," rather than the "substantial certainty" test of the Restatement. It continued:

> Plaintiff also argues that since the allegations of his complaint alleged that Johnson engaged in fraudulent conduct, these acts rendered its conduct so egregious that it knew the injury that resulted was substantially certain to occur. Plaintiff reasons that his allegations of fraud distinguish this case from factual situations existing in earlier decisions of both our Supreme Court and this Court, and necessitate an expanded interpretation of the common-law exception to our exclusivity statute. We think the answer to

this argument is governed by the plain language of Section 52–1–9. The words "accidentally sustained," as used in Section 52–1–9, refer to injury or death arising from an unintended or unexpected event.

Additionally, the inquiry is not whether the employer had an intent to deceive or misrepresent the facts, see § 52–1–9 (all injuries "accidentally" sustained are subject to the exclusivity provision of the Act), but rather whether the employer had an intent to injure the worker. An injury may unintentionally result even though an employer set the stage for the injury by deceiving or misrepresenting facts to the worker.

The majority of jurisdictions that have considered the question appear to agree that a mere showing of misrepresentation or deceit is insufficient to defeat the exclusivity provisions of their respective worker's compensation statutes. See generally Larson, supra, § 68.-32(a). Instead, the intent issue should involve two steps. First, did the employer intend to commit the alleged act? Second, do the circumstances support a reasonable inference that the employer directly intended to harm the worker? The latter question involves the "true intent" requirement discussed above. Under this analysis, fraudulent misrepresentation, like any other act by the employer, may or may not remove an action from the exclusivity provision of the Act.

Applying this two-step analysis to the complaint, * * * [p]laintiff has satisfied the first prong of the test. We therefore look to Plaintiff's description of the incident to see whether it was an "accident" or whether it may be characterized as a deliberate consequence of Johnson's behavior. The complaint states that Plaintiff picked up a pipe with the trackhoe and the pipe "flew up, hit the trackhoe and sprayed a gasoline-benzene liquid all over [Plaintiff]." Based on this description of how Plaintiff was injured, we do not believe that it is reasonable to infer that Johnson truly intended this series of events to occur. Therefore, even if we assume as true Plaintiff's allegation that Johnson's conduct fraudulently misrepresented the hazard to Plaintiff, the facts do not show that Johnson's conduct was equivalent to a "left jab to the chin."

Notes and Questions

a. What explains the real resistance to enlargement of the exception to embrace substantially certain injuries or fraudulent concealment? Why do legislatures nearly unanimously reject anything other than a true intentional tort standard?

b. The decisions creating exceptions to the exclusivity provision of workers' compensation are roundly denounced by Professor Epstein. See Richard A. Epstein, The Historical Origins and Economic Structure for Workers' Compensation Law, 16 Ga. L. Rev. 775 (1982). For a different perspective, see Robert L. Rabin, The Historical Development of the Fault Principle: A Reinterpretation, 15 Ga. L. Rev. 925 (1981). Epstein argues that the workers' compensation system represents a voluntary bargain between employers and employees intended by both to substitute for a tort system that was perceived as unfair and cumbersome. For Epstein, "workers' compensation rules are in most instances a closer approximation to the consensual ideal than the negligence rules to which they are opposed." Moreover, the fact that the employer (but not the employee) knows that injury is likely to occur as a by-product of productive activity in the workplace does not justify breaching the exclusivity provision of the workers' compensation bargain. Epstein concludes that had the workers' compensation systems developed contractually by voluntary means, rather than statutorily, it would be inconceivable that exceptions to exclusivity such as *Blankenship* and *Johns–Manville Products* (p. 457, infra) would have resulted. For a different analysis on the historical development of workers' compensation and tort laws, see Gary T. Schwartz, Tort Law and the Economy in Nineteenth Century America: A Reinterpretation, 90 Yale L.J. 1717, 1769 nn.389–390 (1980).

6. ACTIONS BY SPOUSES OR CHILDREN AGAINST EMPLOYERS

In some instances a spouse or child may sustain an injury as a result of events which the other spouse or parent experienced in the workplace. See Jean Macchiaroli Eggen, Toxic Reproductive and Genetic Hazards in the Workplace: Challenging the Myths of the Tort and Workers' Compensation Systems, 60 Ford. L. Rev. 843, 878–79 (1992), for a thorough discussion of the cases.

a. *Claims by Spouses*

Claims by spouses arising out of the workers' occupational exposure generally fall into two categories: (1) those that are derivative, exemplified by suits for loss of consortium; and (2) those suits for spouses' direct personal injuries. Loss-of-consortium claims typically are barred by the workers' compensation exclusivity doctrine. However, as described by Eggen, the direct injury claim may be sustainable:

> In contrast, when spouses suffer independent injuries arising from the breach of an independent duty owed to the spouse by the employer, the exclusivity doctrine may be circumvented. To bring a personal injury action, however, a spouse must distinguish between the original injury to the worker and the independent injury to the spouse. * * *

* * *

One federal appellate case may shed some light on future judicial analysis of this problem. In Woerth v. United States [714 F.2d 648, 649 (6th Cir.1983)], the spouse of a federal employee contracted hepatitis from the employee. The employee, a nurse at a Veteran's Administration hospital, had contracted the disease in the course of her employment. When the spouse commenced an action against the United States pursuant to the Federal Tort Claims Act

[28 U.S.C.A. §§ 2671–2680], the government argued that the action was barred by the exclusivity provision of the Federal Employee's Compensation Act [5 U.S.C.A. § 8116(c) ("FECA")], a federal scheme analogous to state workers' compensation statutes. The district court concluded that the FECA exclusivity provision barred the spouse's action because the employee was subject to the FECA provisions.

The United States Court of Appeals for the Sixth Circuit reversed, distinguishing the independent injury suffered by Mr. Woerth from the loss-of-consortium claims that typically would be barred by the FECA exclusivity provision. The court stated:

> The proper inquiry * * * is whether the claim is "with respect to the injury or death of an employee." While Woerth's hepatitis may derive from his wife as a matter of proximate cause, his cause of action does not. His right to recover for the negligence of the United States is based upon his own personal injury, not a right of "husband and wife." The fact that the disease was transmitted through his spouse does not place Woerth in a position different from that of any other unrelated, but similarly injured tort victim.

Accordingly, the court readily recognized that the spouse could maintain this action for personal injuries regardless of the fact that his immediate exposure was through the employee who was covered by FECA. This simple approach opts to draw the exclusivity line along the traditional boundary between derivative claims and individual claims rather than construct a more complicated distinction related to proximate cause.

b. Claims by Children

Children also may suffer a variety of injuries from either parents' exposure to workplace toxins. Like spouses, children bringing tort actions for injuries against a parent's employer must make the threshold showing of an independent injury.

One court has limited a child to the parent's workers' compensation benefits. In Bell v. Macy's California, 212 Cal.App.3d 1442, 261 Cal. Rptr. 447, 453 (1989), the injuries to a pregnant worker's fetus resulting in the death of the offspring at approximately two years of age were deemed to be covered by the California workers' compensation statute. However, the child recovered no benefits because the California workers' compensation statute failed to provide any actual compensation for the child's medical and other expenses. It held that the injury to the fetus "was derived from the compensable injury" to the worker and, therefore, was collateral to the covered injury. The court reasoned:

> * * * [W]ere the fetus of a pregnant worker to retain a separate tort cause of action for injury to it, the employer would face a serious risk. * * * The range of common workplace injury that could result

in injury or death to a fetus needs little exposition. Trips and falls, car accidents, explosions, fires, and other unfortunate but not unheard-of incidents of employment all may cause serious injury or death to the unborn as well as its parent. Less obvious are cases of subtle poisoning by exposure to toxic substances, genetic damage caused by radiation, and the other numerous and cautionary byproducts of the Industrial Revolution.

The court expressed concern that allowing liability could lead to the unacceptable result that employers would exclude women from the workplace to avoid the liability from such accidents and exposures.

Why do courts, such as the California court in *Bell v. Macy's California*, opt for an analysis that limits the employer's exposure by treating the child's action as within the compensation system? Do the same considerations that have resulted in confining the intentional tort exception within narrow limits also explain the judicial reluctance to allow spouses and children to sue the employer in a tort action? Can you identify any policy justifications for treating the two situations differently?

7. FETAL PROTECTION POLICIES

In International Union, United Auto Workers v. Johnson Controls, Inc., 499 U.S. 187, 111 S.Ct. 1196, 113 L.Ed.2d 158 (1991), a class action was brought challenging an employer's policy of barring all women, except those whose infertility was medically documented, from holding jobs involving actual or potential exposure to lead at defendant's battery manufacturing plant because of its concern that the exposure created a risk of harm to any fetus carried by a female employee. The Supreme Court held that the employer's fetal protection policy violated the antisex discrimination provisions of the Civil Rights Act of 1964 and the Pregnancy Discrimination Act, 42 U.S.C.A. § 2001 et seq., § 703 of Title VII. Although the Court acknowledged the concern of the employer that it could be subjected to tort liability for prenatal injuries suffered by the children whose mothers may choose to work in the lead-exposed job positions, it discounted the potential tort liability exposure:

> According to Johnson Controls, however, the company complies with the lead standard developed by OSHA and warns its female employees about the damaging effects of lead. It is worth noting that OSHA gave the problem of lead lengthy consideration and concluded that "there is no basis whatsoever for the claim that women of childbearing age should be excluded from the workplace in order to protect the fetus or the course of pregnancy." 43 Fed. Reg. 52952, 52966 (1978). Instead, OSHA established a series of mandatory protections which, taken together, "should effectively minimize any risk to the fetus and newborn child." Without negligence, it would be difficult for a court to find liability on the part of the employer. If, under general tort principles, Title VII bans sex-specific fetalprotection policies, the employer fully informs the woman of the

risk, and the employer has not acted negligently, the basis for holding an employer liable seems remote at best.

Justice White, in a concurring opinion, was not so sanguine about the remoteness of the tort liability:

> The Court dismisses the possibility of tort liability by no more than speculating. * * * Such speculation will be small comfort to employers. First, it is far from clear that compliance with Title VII will pre-empt state tort liability, and the Court offers no support for that proposition. Second, although warnings may preclude claims by injured *employees*, they will not preclude claims by injured children because the general rule is that parents cannot waive causes of action on behalf of their children, and the parents' negligence will not be imputed to the children. Finally, although state tort liability for prenatal injuries generally requires negligence, it will be difficult for employers to determine in advance what will constitute negligence. Compliance with OSHA standards, for example, has been held not to be a defense to state tort or criminal liability. * * * Moreover, it is possible that employers will be held strictly liable, if, for example, their manufacturing process is considered "abnormally dangerous." See Restatement (Second) of Torts § 869, comment b (1979). (White, J., concurring) (emphasis in original)

Who, in your opinion, has the better of the argument on the prospects for tort liability? What effect will state courts in tort suits likely give to the employer's defense that it complied with OSHA regulations? Would a court, federal or state, conclude that OSHA preempts state tort actions? Recall the material in Chapter Six on preemption, and the Supreme Court's holding in *Cipollone v. Liggett Group, Inc.*

8. TAKE–HOME TOXICS

Congress has recognized the problem of workers in industrial settings inadvertently tracking toxic chemicals from the workplace to their homes and contaminating family members. The Fire Administration Authorization Act of 1992, as amended with the Workers' Family Protection Act, 29 U.S.C.A. § 671(a) et seq., calls for the National Institute for Occupational Safety and Health as the lead agency to work with OSHA, the Environmental Protection Agency, the Agency for Toxic Substances and Disease Registry, and the Department of Energy in order to gather information and share data with experts in professions ranging from medicine to industrial hygiene to develop a strategy to combat the problem. The Act does not grant authority to federal agencies to issue regulations.

9. AGGRAVATION OF INJURY EXCEPTION

An aggravation of injury exception has been applied in a few states. In Johns–Manville Products Corp. v. Contra Costa Superior Court, 27

Cal.3d 465, 165 Cal.Rptr. 858, 612 P.2d 948 (1980), the California Supreme Court allowed a tort action brought by a worker against his employer on the basis of asbestos exposure in the workplace. The gravamen of the suit was that the employer had knowingly concealed the hazards of the occupational exposure from the worker, thus causing an aggravation of the physical condition of the employee. While the court refused to recognize a broad fraudulent concealment or deceit exception as it related to the employee's initially contracting the disease, it recognized a narrower exception for the aggravation of injury. Addressing the legal system's concerns that recognition of such an exception would invite a flood of litigation, the court stated:

> We conclude the policy of exclusivity of workers' compensation as a remedy for injuries in the employment [setting] would not be seriously undermined [by this exception], since we cannot believe that many employers will aggravate the effects of an industrial injury by not only deliberately concealing the existence but also its connection with the employment. Nor can we believe that the Legislature in enacting the workers' compensation law intended to insulate such flagrant conduct from tort liability.

The decision places the burden of showing how much harm was caused by the initial contraction of the disease, rather than by its subsequent aggravation, upon the defendant, as the problem of apportionment emanated from the defendant's wrongful acts. The holding led to the amendment of the California workers' compensation statute that includes an express exception to exclusivity for aggravation of injury, but limits the tort recovery to damages for aggravation only. See West's Ann. Cal. Lab. Code § 3682(2). Accord, Millison v. E.I. du Pont de Nemours & Co., 101 N.J. 161, 501 A.2d 505 (1985); Martin v. Lancaster Battery Co., Inc., 530 Pa. 11, 606 A.2d 444 (1992).

C. OCCUPATIONAL DISEASE ACTS

1. INTRODUCTION

Some states have enacted statutes which specifically address employers' liability for occupational diseases contracted by employees as a result of exposure to harmful substances in the workplace environment. Concerns with asbestos-related diseases were a major impetus for such legislation, which generally contain the same exclusivity provisions as the workers' compensation acts. 2A A. Larson, Workmen's Compensation Law § 41.00 at 7–94 (1992) summarizes the state of the law:

> All states now provide general compensation coverage for occupational diseases. For the purpose of defining the affirmative inclusion of diseases within this term, the older definition distinguishing occupational disease from accident has been largely abandoned, with its stress on gradualness and on prevalence of the disease in the particular industry. Jurisdictions having general coverage of occu-

pational disease now usually define the term to include any disease arising out of exposure to harmful conditions of the employment, when those conditions are present in a peculiar or increased degree by comparison with employment generally. Thus, even a disease which is rare and which is due to the claimant's individual allergy or weakness combining with employment conditions will usually be held to be an occupational disease if the increased exposure occasioned by employment in fact brought on the disease.

2. JUDICIAL APPLICATION OF OCCUPATIONAL DISEASE ACTS

The following decision, Palmer v. Del Webb's High Sierra, 108 Nev. 673, 838 P.2d 435 (1992), places the Occupational Disease Acts in the contemporary context of environmental tobacco smoke (ETS). Before turning to the majority opinion, which does not recite the facts, the following description is drawn from a separate concurrence:

> For over twenty years, Palmer was employed at Del Webb's High Sierra Casino ("High Sierra") as a "pit boss." His job required that he supervise gaming tables from an area in the casino referred to as the "pit." The pit area had noticeably high levels of secondhand tobacco smoke. During most of Palmer's years at High Sierra, the casino encouraged smoking by providing free cigarettes and numerous ashtrays. * * *

> In Spring 1988, at the age of fifty-eight, Palmer experienced coughing and breathing problems. He curtailed his outdoor activities but continued working until August 1, 1988, when, following doctors' orders, he took a medical leave of absence. Although Palmer was not a smoker, several doctors diagnosed him as suffering from reactive airways disease, severe bronchitis and asthma. They concluded that Palmer's condition was caused by, or substantially aggravated by, the smoke-filled environment at High Sierra. His doctors ordered that he not return to work unless he could do so in a smoke-free environment.

* * *

[Despite uncontested medical testimony connecting Palmer's condition with his exposure to ETS, High Sierra and a hearings officer both denied his claim because he did not suffer a compensable occupational disease because lung diseases, under the Nevada Act, were restricted to firemen and police officers.]

The appeals officer reversed the decision of the hearings officer, finding that: "The evidence presented by testimony and by documents establish[es] a direct causal connection between Palmer's work in an enclosed area containing smoke in the air he breathed and his occupational disease of chronic pulmonary dysfunction. * * * His employment is the proximate cause of his occupational disease since he was not exposed to [secondhand tobacco] smoke in a greater amount than other workers. His chronic pulmonary disorder is incidental to the character of being a pit boss in a gaming establishment since he was required to be in a smokey area in order to perform his job duties.''

The district court reversed the decision of the appeals officer, summarily concluding that the disease was not incidental to the character of the business.

The Nevada Occupational Disease Act (NODA) which is the subject of *Palmer* provides:

1. An occupational disease defined in this chapter shall be deemed to arise out of and in the course of the employment if:

(a) There is a direct causal connection between the conditions under which the work is performed and the occupational disease;

(b) It can be seen to have followed as a natural incident of the work as a result of the exposure occasioned by the nature of the employment;

(c) It can be fairly traced to the employment as the proximate cause; and

(d) It does not come from a hazard to which workmen would have been equally exposed outside of the employment.

2. The disease must be incidental to the character of the business and not independent of the relation of the employer and employee.

3. The disease need not have been foreseen or expected, but after its contraction must appear to have had its origin in a risk connected with the employment, and to have flowed from that source as a natural consequence.

PALMER v. DEL WEBB'S HIGH SIERRA

Supreme Court of Nevada, 1992.
108 Nev. 673, 838 P.2d 435.

SPRINGER, J.:

The issue in this case is whether a worker who claims to suffer from a disease caused by inhaling tobacco smoke exhaled by others in the work place is eligible for compensation under the Nevada Occupational Disease Act (NODA). Appellant Palmer filed a claim for occupational disease compensation, claiming that his lung disease was caused by environmental tobacco smoke present at his place of employment. The trial court, in reversing an appeals officers' adjudication in favor of Palmer, ruled that "[u]ntil such time as the Legislature so decides, the claim must fail." We agree with the trial court that until the legislature so decides, occupational disease claims based on inhalation of environmental smoke in the work place must fail. Specifically, we agree that environmental smoke, although usually present in a casino, is not uniquely "incidental to the character" of that business. Further, we conclude that secondary smoke is a hazard to which workers, as a class, may be "equally exposed outside of the employment." Therefore, we affirm the judgment of the trial court.

In reading the occupational disease statute one learns that an occupational disease must arise out of the employment, that is to say, it must be related to the nature of the employment at hand. The definitional statute, NRS 617.440, requires an occupational disease to be an incident of the employment and not merely an accidental consequence that is not related to the nature of the employment. Specifically, NRS 617.440(1) provides that the disease must be a *"natural incident* of the work as a result of the exposure occasioned by the *nature* of the employment." (Our emphasis.)

What this language means is that the disease must arise out of job conditions, specifically, the "nature of the employment." With regard to this requirement, that the disease-causing conditions must be "incidental to the character of the business," it is apparent that the legislature intended that there must be a connection between the kind of job and the kind of disease. Mere causation is not enough. One could easily say that going to work caused a person to develop ulcers; but the "nature of the employment" is, in most cases, not inherently ulcerogenic; and ulcers are not in all probability a "natural incident of the work" claimed to be the cause of the disease.

We are, then, talking about a special kind of cause, "work-related" cause; and where, as appears to be the case here, disease is not related to the nature of the job, the disease cannot properly be called "occupational." It is apparent to us that despite its common presence in bars and casinos, environmental tobacco smoke is not incidental to the character of these businesses, is not a natural incident of these businesses.

The trial court disallowed Palmer's claim, stating that it "must fail under NRS 617.440(2)." We agree with this conclusion. Under NRS 617.440(2), an occupational "disease must be incidental to the character of the business and not independent of the relation of the employer and employee." Again, contracting the disease must be part of the actual job. Unless the disease is a part of the job, unless it is "incidental" to the character of the business, a disease cannot be said to have the necessary "direct causal relation" to the employment. NRS 617.-440(1)(a). To illustrate: breathing in coal dust is certainly incidental to the character of coal mining work. Whereas coal dust, the cause of "black lung" disease, is certainly incidental to the character of coal mining (mining coal necessarily creates coal dust), tobacco smoke is not part of the nature or character of a bar or casino business. Tobacco smoke is not a "natural incident" of Palmer's employment nor is exposure to smoke "occasioned by the nature of the employment." NRS 617.440(1)(b). It is probably true that more environmental smoke is associated with the casino and bar businesses than with other business-es; still, the amount and density of such tobacco smoke is highly inconstant and may range from none to quite dense, depending on the particular bar or casino and depending on the air filtration systems and other variables that vary from business to business.

Of course, any individual business establishment might be shown to have an excessive amount of secondary smoke in the work place. Until fairly recently, many office environments were so filled with smoke that they were virtually intolerable to nonsmokers. Still, there is nothing in the "nature" of office work that would make stale tobacco smoke a "natural incident of the work." A nonsmoker unfortunate enough to contract some disease because of the excessive smoke rather clearly would not be entitled to compensation, because "environmental smoke disease" is not an occupational disease of office work. The legislature, of course, is free to declare that any person who contracts some secondary smoke-related disease at work is eligible for occupational disease compensation. The courts, we believe, do not have this power.

What we must not lose sight of is the reality that occupational disease coverage is designed to protect those who suffer illness because of the special nature of their occupation, those who suffer from an occupational disease. That is why words like "natural incident" of the employment and "occasioned by the nature of the employment" are used in NRS 617.440. In NRS 617.450, the statutory schedule of occupational diseases, we find further indication of the legislature's intention that occupational diseases be incidental to the character of the business and occasioned by the nature of the employment. The diseases listed in the statute are quite job-specific and are closely related to the nature of the particular occupation, diseases such as "brass and zinc poisoning" or "chrome ulceration of the skin or nasal passages." In addition, NRS 617.450 provides a description of the specific processes by which the listed diseases are contracted. The statutory purpose is clearly to provide protection for people who have diseases that are related to their particular jobs. If the disease is not related to the character of the particular business and not proximately caused by the "conditions under which the work is performed," it is not an occupational disease.

* * *

Based on the statutory provisions and on our case law, we hold as a matter of law that diseases claimed to be caused by environmental tobacco smoke present in the work place are not covered by the Nevada Occupational Disease Act. We therefore affirm the judgment of the trial court.

Notes and Questions

1. Is the court correct that environmental tobacco smoke (ETS) is not related to the nature of the job as a "pit boss"? What might be the court's unstated rationale for rejecting this claim? In a separate concurring opinion one justice concluded that the exposure to ETS was work-related, but that

the Nevada Occupational Disease Act covered only those diseases specifically listed in the statute, and diseases from exposure to ETS were not listed. The majority opinion, by implication, concludes that nonlisted diseases and exposures may be covered if they satisfy the rigorous "nature of the employment" test. Another justice separately opined that had the legislature sought to limit coverage to the twenty-two tested diseases, that "the results of such a scheme would be unfair, discriminatory, and most probably lacking in a rational basis." Does this mean the Act is unconstitutional?

2. Some jurisdictions, unlike Nevada, list specific diseases, but include a savings clause to capture non-listed conditions. See Idaho Code § 72–438 (Supp. 1991) ("Recognizing that additional toxic or harmful substances or matter are continually being discovered and used or misused, the above enumerated occupational diseases [the scheduled diseases] are not to be taken as exclusive. * * * "); Ohio Rev. Code § 4123.68 (Anderson 1991) ("A disease which meets the definition of an occupational disease is compensable pursuant to Chapter 4123 of the Revised Code though it is not specifically listed in this section.").

3. Other jurisdictions do not list specific diseases, but contain instead generalized descriptions of the diseases covered by their respective acts. See, e.g., N.Y.—McKinney's Work. Comp. Law § 2(15) (occupational disease defined as "a disease resulting from the nature of employment and contracted therein"); R.I. Gen. Laws § 28–34–1(3) (1993) (occupational disease means "a disease which is due to causes and conditions which are characteristic of and peculiar to a particular trade, occupation, process or employment"); Utah Code Ann. 35–2–107 (Supp. 1991) (a compensable occupational disease "is defined as any disease or illness which arises out of and in the course of employment").

3. DISTINGUISHING DISEASES INCIDENT TO ONE'S EMPLOYMENT FROM THE ORDINARY DISEASES OF LIFE

a. All jurisdictions' statutes attempt to differentiate between the so-called "ordinary diseases of life" and occupational diseases. If you were drafting a statute, how might you attempt to make the distinction? Virginia's Code § 65.1–46.1 provides in part:

> An ordinary disease of life to which the general public is exposed outside of the employment may be treated as an occupational disease for purposes of this Act if it is established by clear and convincing evidence, to a reasonable medical certainty, that it arose out of and in the course of employment as provided in § 65.46 with respect to occupational diseases and did not result from causes outside of the employment. * * *

Is this a sensible approach to the problem? How about alcoholism? Can an employee maintain that the disease of alcoholism resulted from stress in the workplace or other workplace conditions? See Pierce v. General Motors Corp., 443 Mich. 137, 504 N.W.2d 648 (1993) (court declines to extend workers' compensation benefits to cover diseases of addiction).

b. A Connecticut case illustrates how some courts attempt to address the occupational disease problem. In Hansen v. Gordon, 221

Conn. 29, 602 A.2d 560 (1992), plaintiff worked as a dental hygienist. In 1984 she began to wear a mask and gloves because of increased awareness of communicable diseases, and received precautionary vaccinations against hepatitis. In 1986 claimant's husband was diagnosed as having hepatitis B (HBV). Claimant was tested, and it was determined that she was a carrier. She ceased employment with her employer because she posed a threat to the patients. The commissioner determined that it was more likely than not that claimant's condition arose out of and in the course of her employment. Defendant contended, however, that claimant had not established that HBV was an occupational disease because diseases which occur broadly within the general public cannot be characterized as occupational. The Connecticut Supreme Court disagreed. References in case law that the disease must be a "natural" incident of the employment cannot be construed so as to hold the disease must be peculiar or unique to the employment. Moreover, the facts fulfilled all the requirements of an occupational disease because dental hygienists are at increased risk because of their contact with blood and other secretions.

4. INTENTIONAL TORT EXCEPTION IN OCCUPATIONAL DISEASES

Courts have been extremely reluctant to extend the intentional tort exception as applied in injury cases to the contracting of occupational diseases. For example, in Barber v. Pittsburgh Corning Corp., 555 A.2d 766 (Pa.1989), the Pennsylvania Supreme Court considered whether employees could maintain a tort action outside the exclusivity of the ODA where they alleged exposure to asbestos dust in a defendant's thermal insulation manufacturing plant. Plaintiffs alleged that the employer knew of the danger of asbestos and did nothing to protect the workers from the danger; allowed levels of asbestos dust to exceed safe levels; failed to implement controls to reduce airborne levels of asbestos dust; failed to warn employees of the health hazards created by exposure to the asbestos; and that defendant knew to a substantial certainty that harm would result to its employees. The court held that it would not recognize an intentional tort exception to the ODA, relying on the statutory language of the Pennsylvania ODA which stated that the exclusivity agreement "shall operate as a surrender by the parties thereto of their rights to any form or amount of compensation or damages for any disability or death resulting from occupational disease * * * other than as provided in [this Act]." Holding that this language "operates as a forfeiture by the employee of any and all common law causes of action," it refused to even recognize an intentional tort exception.

Why might occupational diseases be less susceptible to an intentional tort exclusion than are workplace injuries? See Buford v. American Telephone & Telegraph Co., 881 F.2d 432 (7th Cir.1989).

5. A NOTE ON ENVIRONMENTAL TOBACCO SMOKE

The facts in *Palmer* are not unique. No doubt millions of American workers have been subjected to ETS in the workplaces and many may have experienced resulting injury or aggravation of pre-existing conditions. Until recently, there has been some debate respecting whether ETS can be established as the cause (or "a" cause) of various conditions, including lung cancer. That debate, however, seems to have reached a scientific resolution as evidenced by an EPA report, Office of Health and Environmental Assessment, Respiratory Health Effects of Passive Smoking: Lung Cancer and Other Disorders (December 1992) (the Report), which concludes:

> Based on the assessment of all the evidence considered in * * * this report and in accordance with the EPA *Guidelines* and the causality criteria above for interpretation of human data, this report concludes that ETS is a Group A human carcinogen, the EPA classification "used only when there is sufficient evidence from epidemiologic studies to support a causal association between exposure to the agents and cancer."

The Report estimates that approximately 3,000 lung cancer deaths per year among nonsmokers (never-smokers and former smokers) of both sexes are attributable to ETS in the United States. It points out that while smoking is responsible for more than one of every six deaths in the United States, smokers are not the only ones exposed to tobacco smoke. Moreover, an excess cancer risk is biologically plausible because sidestream smoke emitted from a smoldering cigarette between puffs (the main component of ETS) contains virtually all of the same carcinogenic compounds (known or suspected human and animal carcinogens) that have been identified in the mainstream smoke (MS) inhaled by smokers. The Report reviewed thirty epidemiologic studies of effects from normally occurring environmental levels of ETS. It continues:

> Because there is widespread exposure and it is difficult to construct a truly unexposed subgroup of the general population, these studies attempt to compare individuals with higher ETS exposure to those with lower exposures. Typically, female never-smokers who are married to a smoker are compared with female never-smokers who are married to a nonsmoker. * * * Use of the female never-smoker studies provides the largest, most homogeneous database for analysis to determine whether an ETS effect on lung cancer is present.

> * * *

> Results from all of the analyses described above strongly support a causal association between lung cancer ETS exposure. The overall proportion (9/30) of individual studies found to show an association between lung cancer and spousal ETS exposure at all levels combined is unlikely to occur by chance [less than one chance in 10,000]. When the analysis focuses on higher levels of spousal

exposure, every one of the 17 studies with exposure-level data shows increased risk in the highest exposure group; 9 of these are significant at the $p < 0.05$ level, * * * another result highly unlikely to occur by chance [one chance in 1,000,000]. Similarly, the proportion (10/14); showing a statistically significant exposure-response trend is highly supportive of a causal association.

The Report's conclusions rest on a variety of separate indicia of causation:

[a] Biological plausibility. * * *

[b] Supporting evidence from animal bioassays and genotoxicity experiments. * * *

[c] Consistency of response. 4 of the cohort studies and 20 of the 26 case-control studies observed a higher risk of lung cancer among the female never-smokers classified as ever exposed to any level of spousal ETS. Furthermore, every one of the 17 studies with response categorized by exposure level demonstrated increased risk for the highest exposure group. * * * Evaluation of the total study evidence from several perspectives leads to the conclusion that the observed association between ETS exposure and increased lung cancer occurrence is not attributable to chance.

[d] Broad-based evidence. These 30 studies provide data from 8 different countries, employ a wide variety of study designs and protocols, and are conducted by many different research teams. * * * No alternative explanatory variables for the observed association between ETS and lung cancer have been indicated that would be broadly applicable across studies.

[e] Upward trend in exposure-response. Both of the largest of the cohort studies * * * demonstrate a strong exposure-related statistical association between passive smoking and lung cancer. * * *

* * *

[f] Effects remain after adjustment for potential upward bias. Current and ex-smokers may be misreported as never-smokers, thus inflating the apparent cancer risk for ETS exposure. The evidence remains statistically significant and conclusive, however, after adjustments for smoker misclassification. For the United States, the summary estimate of relative risk from nine case-control plus two cohort studies is 1.19 (90% confidence interval [C.I.] = 1.04, 1.35; $p < 0.05$) after adjustment for smoker misclassification. For Greece, 2.00 (1.42, 2.83), Hong Kong, 1.61 (1.25, 2.06), and Japan, 1.44 (1.13, 1.85), the estimated relative risks are higher than those of the United States and more highly significant after adjusting for the potential bias.

[g] Strong associations for highest exposure groups. Examining the groups with the highest exposure levels increases the ability to detect an effect, if it exists. * * * The overall pooled estimate of [relative risk of] 1.81 for the highest exposure groups is highly statistically significant (90% C.I. = 1.60, 2.05). For the United States, the overall pooled estimate of 1.38 (seven studies, corrected for smoker misclassification bias) is also highly statistically significant (90% C.I. = 1.13, 1.70; p = 0.005).

The EPA Report has stimulated considerable response. The cigarette manufacturers filed suit against the EPA seeking to have the Report declared "null and void." The suit contends that EPA went beyond its statutory authority in preparing its risk assessment, failed to follow its own guidelines for conducting such cancer-risk studies, and made numerous mistakes in its assessment, which were compounded by "data manipulations." It also alleged that the EPA resorted to "manipulating and cherry picking" the data to "falsely disparage" cigarettes. The tobacco groups want the court to declare that EPA's classification of ETS as a Group A carcinogen and the ETS Risk Assessment violate the due process guarantee of the U.S. Constitution. See Flue–Cured Tobacco Cooperative Stabilization Corp. v. Environmental Protection Agency, U.S. Dist. Ct. N.C., No. 6:93CV00370 (1993).

Note and Questions

Consider whether a personal injury toxic tort action could be maintained on the basis of exposure to ETS. Might products liability attorneys who have been unsuccessful in suits on behalf of smokers be more successful on behalf of nonsmokers who suffer injury as a result of exposure to ETS? A major difference between an ETS claim brought by a nonsmoker and the many claims that have been litigated by smokers is that this new class of potential plaintiffs has not voluntarily chosen to expose themselves to the well-recognized dangers of smoking, and thus may represent a more sympathetic group to jurors and courts. What do you foresee as the primary problem facing plaintiffs in such suits? What about the effect of living in a home where the plaintiff's spouse or other family member smoked? Given the kinds of relative risks identified above, and assuming no other impediments to a tort suit, will they be sufficient to satisfy the requirements of causation as described in Chapter 8? What other particularistic evidence might a plaintiff offer to supplement the epidemiological studies?

6. EMPLOYEES' ACTIONS FOR RELIEF

a. Injunctive Relief

One method by which employees may seek relief from environmental tobacco smoke is through an injunction requiring an employer to provide employees with a smoke-free work environment. As an injunction provides equitable relief, rather than monetary relief, any court with equitable powers can grant an order requiring an employer to provide a smoke-free working environment. If monetary relief is requested, then the plaintiff must seek relief through the workers' compensation system.

Two cases in which state courts have granted injunctions requiring employers to ban smoking in work areas are relatively old: Shimp v. New Jersey Bell Telephone Co., 145 N.J.Super. 516, 368 A.2d 408 (1976) and Smith v. Western Electric Co., 643 S.W.2d 10 (Mo.App.1982). In *Shimp*, the plaintiff, who was allergic to ETS, worked in an area where the employer permitted employees to smoke. After a grievance procedure and requests to her employer failed to eliminate the employee's exposure to her co-workers' tobacco smoke, the employee requested an injunction requiring the employer to institute a no-smoking policy in the work areas. In granting the injunction, the court recognized that an employer is under an affirmative duty to provide a safe work area for its employees. After taking judicial notice of the "toxic nature of cigarette smoke and its well-known association with emphysema, lung cancer and heart disease," the court pointed out that cigarette smoke is not a necessary by-product of any business or manufacturing process, and that plaintiff, therefore, had not voluntarily assumed the risk of exposure to ETS in pursuing her career.

b. Claims Based on Workers' Compensation Acts

A few decisions have granted compensation benefits to employees asserting claims under workers' compensation acts. In Johannesen v. New York City Dept. of Housing Preservation & Development, 154 A.D.2d 753, 546 N.Y.S.2d 40 (1989), an employee worked in an office in which co-workers smoked. As a result of exposure to ETS over a period of years, the compensation claim alleged, the employee suffered from bronchial asthma. The administrative law judge granted benefits after finding that the "claimant had suffered from a compensable *occupational disease*." The Workers' Compensation Board rescinded that decision, but granted benefits by determining that the "claimant had sustained an *accidental injury* as a result of the repeated trauma of exposure to cigarette smoke." The New York Appellate Division affirmed the Board's decision, stating that the "Board could properly find that the concentration of smoke at claimant's work station constituted an unusual environmental hazard."

Which is the better argument: that injury from ETS is an "occupational disease" or that it is an "accidental injury?" See also Schober v. Mountain Bell Telephone Co., 96 N.M. 376, 630 P.2d 1231 (App.1980) (collapse in workplace from ETS is an accident). In contrast, see Ate Fixture Fab v. Wagner, 559 So.2d 635 (Fla.App.1990), where the state compensation board awarded claimant "permanent total disability benefits for acceleration and aggravation of obstructive lung disease due to inhalation" of ETS, only to be reversed by the Florida Court of Appeals which remanded for further evidence on causation between the worker's condition and the exposure to ETS. Cf. Mack v. County of Rockland, 71

N.Y.2d 1008, 530 N.Y.S.2d 98, 525 N.E.2d 744 (1988), in which the court rejected a claim of aggravation of a pre-existing eye disorder from exposure to ETS on the basis of its conclusion that the claimant's injury was not an occupational disease under New York's Workers' Compensation Act.

c. Claims Based on Negligence

A final theory of liability that has appeared in the cases is predicated on the employer's negligence, where the facts permitted the employee to circumvent the exclusivity provisions of the workers' compensation system. In McCarthy v. Department of Social & Health Services, 110 Wash.2d 812, 759 P.2d 351 (1988), an employee complained to her employer regarding the adverse health consequences of exposure to ETS in the office, but the employer took no remedial action. The employee developed chronic obstructive pulmonary disease with diminished pulmonary function which she claimed was a result of sensitivity to ETS. The employee's workers' compensation benefit claim was denied because the Board concluded that her pulmonary lung disease was not the result of an industrial injury and did not constitute an occupational disease within the Washington Industrial Insurance Act. Because she was denied her workers' compensation claim she filed a civil tort suit alleging that the employer had negligently failed to provide her a tobacco smoke-free working environment. On appeal, the Supreme Court of Washington first determined that denying a remedy for exposure to ETS through the Industrial Insurance Act, without allowing for a common law remedy, would disrupt the quid pro quo relationship between the employer and the employee that is the basis of the workers' compensation system. As a result, the court held that the employee could sustain a common law negligence action because the Workers' Compensation Board found that the employee's injury was not within the scope of the Industrial Insurance Act.

Second, the court stated that because the "hazardous nature of cigarette smoke to non-smokers is well established, * * * [the] employer's common law duty to provide a safe workplace includes the duty to provide a work environment reasonably free of tobacco smoke pollution." Moreover, the employer's failure to protect this employee from tobacco smoke, after receiving notice by the employee, could be a breach of the employer's common law duty. As a result, the court determined that the facts supported a prima facie case of negligence and remanded the case for trial.

What problems do you foresee from decisions such as McCarthy ? Does denial of a workers' compensation claim on its merits form the basis of a negligence action? Must the denial be jurisdictional in order to avoid the exclusivity bar? How would you argue the reverse, i.e., that permitting the common law claim disrupts the quid pro quo relationship between the employer and employee that is the basis of the workers' compensation system?

d. Miscellaneous Contexts

That the impact of passive smoke can no longer be doubted is attested to by the variety of settings, outside of tort law, in which claims are brought based on exposure to passive smoke. Compare Hinman v. Yakima School District, 69 Wash.App. 445, 850 P.2d 536 (1993) (an asthmatic teacher's exposure to passive smoke due to her classroom's proximity to the smoking-permissive teachers' lounge, and not reassigning her until she was hospitalized, stated a cause of action under state's law requiring employers to provide reasonable accommodations to handicapped workers), with Helm v. Helm, 1993 WL 21983 (Tenn.App.1993) (father who smoked and exposed his child to passive smoke not denied custody on that ground). In Helling v. McKinney, ___ U.S. ___, 113 S.Ct. 2475, 125 L.Ed.2d 22 (1993), the Supreme Court held that prisoners have a constitutional right not to be exposed to cellmates' cigarette smoke if such exposure creates an extreme health risk. In addition to proving an "unreasonable" health risk, a prisoner would have to show that "society considers the risk so grave that it violates contemporary standards of decency to expose anyone unwillingly to such a risk." Moreover, the court stated, the prisoner would have to show that prison officials were "deliberately indifferent" to the health risk.

D. OCCUPATIONAL SAFETY AND HEALTH REQUIREMENTS

The relationship between toxic tort litigation and the workplace would be incomplete if it did not include some appreciation of one federal regulatory program that has considerable relevance in this field. The Occupational Safety and Health Administration (OSHA) administers the Occupational Safety and Health Act, 29 U.S.C.A. §§ 651–678 (OSH Act or Act), and the regulations promulgated pursuant to that statute. The Act contains a general duty clause which requires employers to provide "a place of employment which [is] free from recognized hazards that are causing or are likely to cause death or serious physical harm to his employees." 29 U.S.C.A. § 654(a)(1). In addition, certain rules and standards have been promulgated for regulating specific hazards in the workplace.

1. TOXIC AND HAZARDOUS SUBSTANCES

For most industrial facilities, the number one OSHA concern is workers' contact with toxic and hazardous substances. The Code of Federal Regulations has 25 separate standards for such substances, which include asbestos, coal tar pitch, vinyl chloride, arsenic, lead, benzene, cotton dust, and formaldehyde. See 29 C.F.R. §§ 1910.1001–1910.1101, which specify in great detail requirements concerning exposure levels, training requirements, warning signs, and medical surveillance.

OSHA also has issued permissible exposure limits for 376 air contaminants. See the tables at 29 C.F.R. § 1900.1000; "Air Contaminants–Permissible Exposure Limits," OSHA Pub. No. 3112. Employees who work in proximity to these toxic substances must use engineering controls and personal protection equipment to assure that the level of air contamination is within the permissible exposure limit. The regulations also provide short-term exposure limits, ceiling limits, and skin protection designations.

OSHA's promulgation of substance-specific health standards which establish the permissible exposure limits ("PELs") reflect the maximum amount of contaminants to which workers may be exposed over a given time period. After promulgating 425 initial PELs in 1971, by 1988 OSHA had issued only 24 new or updated substance-specific standards. In 1988 OSHA proposed over 400 new or revised PELs in one generic rulemaking. 54 Fed. Reg. 2332–2983 (Jan. 19, 1989). In AFL–CIO v. OSHA, 965 F.2d 962 (11th Cir.1992), the court of appeals held that OSHA's procedures in adopting these standards failed to comply with the Act. Specifically, the Act requires in § 3(8) (29 U.S.C.A. § 652(8)) that OSHA establish that the standards are "reasonably necessary or appropriate to provide safe or healthful employment or places of employment." The Supreme Court in Industrial Union Dept., AFL–CIO v. American Petroleum Inst., 448 U.S. 607, 100 S.Ct. 2844, 65 L.Ed.2d 1010 (1980) had previously interpreted this provision to require that before promulgating any permanent health standard, OSHA must make a threshold finding that a significant risk of material health impairment exists at the current levels of exposure to the toxic substance in question "and that a new, lower standard is therefore 'reasonably necessary or appropriate to provide safe or healthful employment and places of employment.'" Thus, OSHA is entitled to regulate only those risks which present a "significant" risk of "material" health impairment. Moreover, OSHA ultimately bears the burden of proving by substantial evidence that such a risk exists and that the proposed standard is necessary; and must provide at least an estimate of the actual risk associated with a particular toxic substance and explain why that risk is significant. Because OSHA had failed to estimate the risk that workers would contract various adverse health effects associated with each of the over 400 substances, the court held that the rulemaking was defective.

2. OSHA RECORDKEEPING REQUIREMENTS

Most employers are governed by OSHA's general recordkeeping rules. See 29 U.S.C.A. § 657(c). OSHA has been vigorously enforcing its injury reporting requirements, imposing a $10,000 fine per misrecorded or nonreported injury. The Budget Reconciliation Act of 1990 increased the maximum fine to $70,000 for each incorrectly recorded injury.

Except for certain exempt industries where the risk of physical injury is slight (e.g., banking), all employers (with 10 or more employees) must keep records of workplace injury. An employer must maintain a log and summary of all occupational illnesses, fatalities, and any workplace injury which causes a loss of a work-day, work restrictions, transfers to another job, loss of consciousness, or requires medical treatment, and complete this recordation within six working days of the injury. 29 C.F.R. §§ 1904.2, 1904.4; OSHA Forms Nos. 200, 101. A summary of occupational injuries and illnesses must be posted annually, and the records must be retained for five years and be available to employees. 29 C.F.R. §§ 1904.5, 1904.6.

An employer must maintain, for workers exposed to toxic substances or harmful physical agents, any medical records, exposure records, and analyses of such records which the employer has created. Moreover, given the long latency of many diseases, these records must be retained for thirty years after the employee leaves the workplace. 29 C.F.R. § 1910.20.

All occupational diseases must be recorded and placed into the following categories: occupational skin diseases or disorders, dust diseases of the lungs (pneumoconiosis), respiratory conditions due to toxic agents, poisoning, disorders due to physical agents, and disorders associated with repetitive trauma.

3. HAZARDOUS CHEMICALS

The hazard communication standard was written to ensure two goals: (1) that the hazards of all chemicals produced or imported by chemical manufacturers or importers are evaluated; and (2) that information concerning chemical hazards is transmitted to affected employers and employees. 29 C.F.R. § 1910.1200(a)(1). The key to compliance with the requirements of the standard is maintenance of a complete set of Material Safety Data Sheets (MSDS), a written hazardous communication program, and mandated training programs for all affected workers.

The standard requires that certain information and training be given to employees who handle any chemical "which is a physical hazard or health hazard." 29 C.F.R. § 1910.1200(c). Manufacturers and importers must provide MSDS for all hazardous chemicals. Employers can rely on the manufacturer's hazard determination and the manufacturer's Material Safety Data Sheets which it prepared. 29 C.F.R. § 1910.-1200(d), and 1910.1200(g). In any event, the employer must obtain MSDS for all hazardous chemicals his "employees may be exposed [to] under normal conditions of use or in a foreseeable emergency." 29 C.F.R. §§ 1910.1200(b)(2), 1910.1200(g).

In accordance with 29 C.F.R. § 1910.1200(e), all employers must develop and implement a written hazard communication program which includes the following:

(1) A list of hazardous chemicals known to be present in the workplace;

(2) The methods the employer will use to inform employees [and exposed independent contractors] of the hazards associated with such chemicals; and

(3) The procedures to be followed with respect to labeling, MSDS and employee information and training.

Employers must ensure that each container of hazardous chemicals in the workplace is labeled, tagged, or marked with the identity of the hazardous chemicals contained therein and appropriate hazard warnings.

Information and training on hazardous chemicals in the employer's workplace must be provided to employees. They must be informed of the OSHA requirements, any operations in their work area where hazardous chemicals are present, and the location and availability of the written hazard communication program. 29 C.F.R. § 1910.1200(h).

4. THE ROLE OF NONCOMPLIANCE AND COMPLIANCE

OSHA and its regulations only govern the employer-employee relationship. Its jurisdiction is limited to the control of how employers treat their workers. Thus, OSHA cannot directly control environmental exposure to toxic substances. However, the standards set by OSHA are generally recognized as the minimum acceptable for reasonable conduct; hence, failure to meet the OSHA standards can indirectly result in nonstatutory toxic tort liability based on a breach of the standard of reasonableness.

For example, an agricultural worker injured by exposure to toxins subject to OSHA standards was able to successfully argue that his employer's violation of various OSHA regulations constituted negligence per se. Sanchez v. Galey, 112 Idaho 609, 733 P.2d 1234 (1986). Accord, Dixon v. International Harvester Co., 754 F.2d 573, 581 (5th Cir.1985); Teal v. E.I. DuPont de Nemours & Co., 728 F.2d 799 (6th Cir.1984). However, the converse is not true—if an employer complies with all of the OSHA requirements, it will not necessarily escape liability. In egregious situations, the injured employee may be allowed to sue outside the workers' compensation system, and even criminal responsibility can attach based on willful and wanton disregard for a worker's safety.

In Pedraza v. Shell Oil Co., 942 F.2d 48 (1st Cir.1991), the plaintiff commenced a civil action alleging that he developed respiratory ailments from workplace exposure to Epichlorohydrin ("ECH"), a toxic chemical manufactured by the defendant Shell. The district court dismissed the action on the ground that the OSH Act preempted state tort law. Section 18 of the OSH Act, 29 U.S.C.A. § 667(a), provides that:

(a) Nothing in this Act shall prevent any State agency or court from asserting jurisdiction under State law over any occupational safety or health issue with respect to which no standard is in effect under section 655 of this title.

(b) Any State which, at any time, desires to assume responsibility for development and enforcement therein of occupational safety and health standards relating to any occupational safety or health issue with respect to which a Federal standard has been promulgated under section 655 of this title shall submit a State plan for the development of such standards and their enforcement.

Shell contended that the Act preempted all the state-created rights since the adjudication of private rights arising under state law would result in the imposition of "prospective normative constraints on the manufacture and distribution of ECH." The court observed that substantial authority exists for the view that this section preempts the unapproved establishment of state standards and regulatory schemes in competition with OSHA, but that there is no authority for the view that OSHA preempts provisions of state law of the sort relied upon by Pedraza.

It continued:

We are aware of no case which holds that OSHA preempts state tort law. Rather, most courts have been concerned with how OSHA affects tort actions, not with whether it preempts state tort law. Thus, every court faced with the issue has held that OSHA creates no private right of action. We have embraced the majority view that the regulations promulgated under OSHA prescribe standards of care relevant in common law negligence actions.

While we discern in OSHA's language, structure and context a clear congressional signal that section 18 preempts unapproved assertions of state jurisdiction in the development and enforcement of standards relating to occupational health and safety issues in competition with federal standards, we find no warrant whatever for an interpretation which would preempt enforcement in the workplace of private rights and remedies traditionally afforded by state laws of general application. Connecticut's accustomed maintenance of judicial fora for the enforcement of private rights in the workplace, under State laws of general application, seems to us a function far less prophylactic than reactive; less normative than compensatory; and less an arrogation of regulatory jurisdiction over an "occupational safety or health issue" than a neutral forum for the orderly adjustment of private disputes between, among others, the users and suppliers of toxic substances.

Additionally, the court drew on § 4(b)(4) of the Act which contains a savings clause explicitly stating that OSH Act shall not "affect any workmen's compensation law or affect in any other manner the common law or statutory rights, duties, or liabilities of any employers and employees * * * "

As a matter of fairness, should compliance with OSHA regulations constitute a defense to a toxic tort action based on an exposure entirely legal under applicable federal law?

Are the Hazard Communication Standard and related OSHA requirements likely to prove more advantageous to plaintiffs or to defendants? For a discussion of that question, see, Michael D. Green, When Toxic Worlds Collide: Regulatory and Common Law Prescriptions for Risk Communication, 13 Harv. Envtl. L. Rev. 209 (1989).

Chapter Ten

CERCLA: LIABILITY AND COMPENSATION FOR CLEANING UP HAZARDOUS SUBSTANCES

A. OVERVIEW OF CERCLA

1. INTRODUCTION

The Comprehensive Environmental Response, Compensation and Liability Act of 1980 ("CERCLA"), 42 U.S.C.A. § 9601 et seq., is broadly concerned with the clean-up of hazardous substances that may be present in the environment. Its principal focus, however, is on the removal of hazardous waste and the remediation of waste sites. Unlike most of the other major environmental statutes, its objective is not largely regulatory in the sense of command and control regulations although CERCLA does contain some regulatory provisions. It is designed instead to establish rules of liability upon certain classes of actors for the necessary costs of undertaking cleanups, and to establish measures of compensation for those who have in fact undertaken the cleanups of sites where hazardous substances have been released or are threatened to be released. Because CERCLA concentrates on liability and compensation, it becomes complementary to the law of toxic torts. As you review these materials, compare and contrast how the theories of liability and compensable interests described in the earlier chapters are similar to or different from the liability and compensation principles governing CERCLA litigation.

CERCLA was enacted as a last-minute compromise in the closing days of the Carter Administration in December 1980. Although the legislative history of CERCLA (which is also known as the "Superfund" Act because of the fund created to pay for some of the cleanups) is not a paragon of clarity, it is nonetheless clear that one of Congress' primary objectives was "assuring that those responsible for any damage, environmental harm, or injury from chemical poison bear the costs of their actions." See S. Rep. No. 848 at 13, to S. 1480, 96th Cong., 2d Sess. (1980). The objective of providing toxic tort compensation contained in earlier versions of the bill was deleted as part of last-minute compromises, in exchange for the establishment of a study group, known as the Section 301 Study Group, to examine toxic tort laws and determine if a federal tort compensation system was justified. CERCLA § 301(e). The Study Group's report is described in Chapter 13. On the legislative history of CERCLA, see Alfred R. Light, The Importance of "Being Taken": To Clarify and Confirm the Legislative Reconstruction of CERCLA's Text, 18 B.C. Envtl. Affrs. L. Rev. 1 (1990); Frank P. Grad, A Legislative History of the Comprehensive Environmental Response, Compensation and Liability ("Superfund") Act of 1980, 8 Colum. J. Envtl. L. 1 (1982).

Congress concluded that the states, including state common law tort liability principles, were unable to respond adequately to the distinctly national problem of mitigating the consequences of hazardous substance releases, and that a uniformly administered federal program that imposed a single liability standard would be more effective than a patchwork of differing state laws. Congress had previously enacted the Resource Conservation and Recovery Act (RCRA) of 1976, which established a prospective "cradle-to-grave" system for tracking hazardous wastes from their generation, through their transport, storage, and treatment, and to their disposal at permitted facilities. See 42 U.S.C.A. §§ 6901–6987. RCRA, however, did not give the EPA the tools to address the retrospective problem of cleaning up abandoned hazardous waste sites, and hence, CERCLA was designed to focus on remediating the harm already visited on the environment.

CERCLA created the Hazardous Substances Response Trust Fund, the "Superfund," a $1.6–billion fund with a life span of five years, to cover the costs of government responses at hazardous waste sites. In 1986, Congress passed the Superfund Amendments and Reauthorization Act (SARA), which replenished the fund with $8.5 billion and addressed many of the problems identified since 1980 in securing prompt and effective cleanups of hazardous substances. In order to preserve the Superfund's resources, liable parties are required to reimburse the fund for the government's cleanup expenditures and private parties are encouraged to initiate and pay for cleanups that the fund otherwise would finance.

The central objective of CERCLA is to place ultimate responsibility for cleaning up sites of hazardous waste upon the parties that were responsible for placing them at the sites. CERCLA addresses both short-term or emergency responses to spills or discharges of hazardous substances (so-called "removal costs"), and permanent responses to long-term releases of hazardous substances into the environment (known as "remedial" costs). See CERCLA § 104. CERCLA also authorizes the Attorney General to institute an action for abatement or other immediate relief when there exists "an imminent and substantial endangerment to the public health or welfare or the environment because of the actual or threatened release of a hazardous substance." CERCLA § 106(a).

Because of the thousands of hazardous sites existing throughout the country, the EPA is required to establish a National Contingency Plan which includes "criteria for determining priorities among releases or threatened releases throughout the United States for the purpose of taking remedial action." CERCLA § 105(a). The most significant component of the EPA's power to force remediation of waste sites is contained in CERCLA § 106 which empowers the agency to issue administrative orders or seek a court order requiring a responsible party to undertake response activities. Moreover, under § 106, the recipient of the administrative order may not challenge its issuance or its terms unless and until the EPA initiates an enforcement proceeding in federal court (§ 113(h), no pre-enforcement review), at which time the PRP may be subject to civil penalties of $25,000 per day (CERCLA § 106(b)(1)) and treble damages of the EPA's expended remediation costs unless the potentially responsible party (PRP) can affirmatively establish that it had "sufficient cause" for not complying with the order (CERCLA § 107(c)(3)). See Solid State Circuits, Inc. v. U.S. EPA, 812 F.2d 383 (8th Cir.1987) for a thorough treatment of the EPA's power under CERCLA § 106.

2. PRINCIPAL STATUTORY PROVISIONS

The basic principles of liability are set forth in CERCLA § 107, 42 U.S.C.A. § 9607:

Liability (a) * * * Notwithstanding any other provision or rule of law, and subject only to the defenses set forth in subsection (b) of this section—

(1) the owner and operator of a vessel or a facility,

(2) any person who at the time of disposal of any hazardous substance owned or operated any facility at which such hazardous substances were disposed of,

(3) any person who by contract, agreement, or otherwise arranged for disposal or treatment, or arranged with a transporter for transport for disposal or treatment, of hazardous substances owned or possessed by such person, by any other party or entity, at any facility or incineration vessel owned or operated by another party or entity and containing such hazardous substances, and

(4) any person who accepts or accepted any hazardous substances for transport to disposal or treatment facilities, incineration vessels or sites selected by such person, from which there is a release, or a threatened release which causes the incurrence of response costs, of a hazardous substance, shall be liable for—

(A) all costs of removal or remedial action incurred by the United States Government or a State or an Indian tribe not inconsistent with the national contingency plan;

(B) any other necessary costs of response incurred by any other person consistent with the national contingency plan;

(C) damages for injury to, destruction of, or loss of natural resources, including the reasonable costs of assessing such injury, destruction, or loss resulting from such a release; and

(D) the costs of any health assessment or health effects study carried out under section 9604(i) of this title.   * * *

(b) *Defenses.*   There shall be no liability under subsection (a) of this section for a person otherwise liable who can establish by a preponderance of the evidence that the release or threat of release of a hazardous substance and the damages resulting therefrom were caused solely by—

(1) an act of God;

(2) an act of war;

(3) an act or omission of a third party other than an employee or agent of the defendant, or than one whose act or omission occurs in connection with a contractual relationship, existing directly or indirectly, with the defendant * * *, if the defendant establishes by a preponderance of the evidence that (a) he exercised due care with respect to the hazardous substance concerned, taking into consideration the characteristics of such hazardous substance, in light of all relevant facts and circumstances, and (b) he took precautions against foreseeable acts or omissions of any such third party and the consequences that could foreseeably result from such acts or omissions; or

(4) any combination of the foregoing paragraphs * * *.

Thus, the statute specifies the classes of persons who may be held liable (potentially responsible parties, or PRPs), given the congressional intent to allocate the financial burden of cleaning up contaminated sites broadly among parties who may be responsible for causing contamination. Potentially responsible parties include (1) the current owner or operator of the site; (2) any person who owned or operated the site at the time hazardous substances were disposed of; (3) any person who arranged to have its waste taken to the site for disposal or treatment, usually referred to as generators or arrangers; and (4) any person who transported waste for disposal or treatment to a site it selected.

B. GOVERNMENT ACTIONS

While the focus of this Chapter is on private actions under CERCLA, the elements of a government action must first be understood because the government action often precedes private litigation and influences the liability and damage phase of the private actions.

1. RELEASE OR THREATENED RELEASE

In addition to establishing that a defendant satisfies one of the categories of PRPs, the government must also prove that there was a "release or threatened release * * * of a hazardous substance." 42 U.S.C.A. § 9607(a)(4). CERCLA § 101(22) defines release as "any spilling, leaking, pumping, pouring, emitting, emptying, discharging, injecting, escaping, leaching, dumping, or disposing into the environment (including the abandonment or discarding of barrels, containers, and other closed receptacles containing any hazardous substance or pollutant or contaminant). * * * "

In New York v. Shore Realty Corporation, 759 F.2d 1032 (2d Cir.1985), the Second Circuit held that "leaking tanks and pipelines," "continuing leaching and seepage," and "leaking drums" of hazardous materials all constituted releases. However, more than the act of disposal is required to constitute a release; there must be some evidence that the waste has affected or come into contact with the environment. When a contaminant is found near a disposal site, one may conclude that a release has occurred even though no proof exists that the particular contaminant actually flowed from the site. See United States v. Wade, 577 F.Supp. 1326 (E.D.Pa.1983). In addition, the Ninth Circuit has held that a plaintiff need not allege the particular manner in which a release, or threatened release, occurred in order to make out a prima facie case. Ascon Properties, Inc. v. Mobil Oil Co., 866 F.2d 1149 (9th Cir.1989).

What constitutes a threatened release is more problematic. In *Shore Realty*, supra, the Second Circuit stated that "corroding and deteriorating tanks, [the defendant's] lack of expertise in handling hazardous waste, and even the failure to license the facility, amount to a threat of release." This language suggests that the harm from a threatened release need not be imminent.

2. HAZARDOUS SUBSTANCE

To trigger liability under CERCLA, the release or threatened release must involve a "hazardous substance." The statute defines "hazardous substance" in CERCLA § 101(14) primarily by reference to designations made in other environmental statutes, such as § 3001 of the Solid Waste Disposal Act, 42 U.S.C.A. § 6921, and § 1321(b)(2)(A) of the Federal Water Pollution Control Act, 33 U.S.C.A. § 1321(b)(2)(A). For a list of some of these substances, see 40 C.F.R. § 302.4 (1992); 40 C.F.R. § 401.15 (1989). The definition is noteworthy for its exclusions, which include petroleum, petroleum derivatives and natural gas. For cases interpreting these provisions, see Eagle–Picher Indus. v. U.S. EPA, 759 F.2d 922 (D.C.Cir.1985); United States v. Union Gas Co., 586 F. Supp 1522 (E.D.Pa.1984), affirmed 792 F.2d 372 (3d Cir.1986), vacated and remanded on other grounds 479 U.S. 1025, 107 S.Ct. 865, 93 L.Ed.2d 821 (1987).

3. FACILITY

The next question is where must the waste be located in order for liability to attach. Not surprisingly, the courts have interpreted the statutory language very broadly. See CERCLA § 101(9); New York v. Shore Realty Corp., 759 F.2d 1032, 1043 n.15 (2d Cir.1985) ("CERCLA defines the term 'facility' broadly to include any property at which hazardous substances have come to be located"); Amland Properties Corp. v. Aluminum Co. of America, 711 F.Supp. 784 (D.N.J.1989) (facility includes enclosed manufacturing plants and warehouses); United States v. Mottolo, 695 F.Supp. 615, 622 (D.N.H.1988) ("a 'facility' is essentially any site where a hazardous substance is located").

The statute contains an exclusion from "facility" for "consumer products in consumer use." This provision helps define the overall scope of CERCLA by excluding consumer or household use of consumer products.

4. DAMAGES RECOVERABLE BY THE GOVERNMENT

What damages may be recovered by the government under CERCLA? CERCLA § 107(a)(4)(A) permits the recovery of "all costs of removal or remedial action incurred by the U.S. Government * * * not inconsistent with the national contingency plan." For government actions "all costs of removal or remediation action" affords compensation to the EPA for virtually all expenses in any way related to its efforts to secure cleanup of the area. The double negative "not inconsistent" with the national contingency plan (NCP) also has the practical effect of placing the burden on the defendant of proving such inconsistency.

A clue to the meaning of "response costs" as used in CERCLA § 107(a)(4)(B) comes from CERCLA's definition of the terms "respond" and "response." CERCLA § 101(25) states: "The terms 'respond' or 'response' means remove, removal, remedy, and remedial action; all such terms (including the terms 'removal' and 'remedial action') include enforcement activities related thereto." In short, "response costs," means at a minimum all of the costs relating to the cleanup of the site.

A significant amount of litigation has addressed the issue of whether "response costs" include costs of investigating or monitoring a site as a prelude to or as part of actual cleanup operations. These costs generally involve determining the existence of the environmental problem, conducting tests and chemical analyses, and drilling or monitoring wells to determine the nature and extent of the problem. A majority of cases have held that these costs are recoverable. See New York v. General Electric Co., 592 F.Supp. 291, 298 (N.D.N.Y.1984) ("removal" action is defined under CERCLA § 101(23) to embrace "such actions as may be necessary to monitor, assess and evaluate the release or threat of release of hazardous substances".) See also Cadillac Fairview/California, Inc. v. Dow Chemical Co., 840 F.2d 691 (9th Cir.1988) (testing and security expenditures available under CERCLA § 101(23)); Wickland Oil Terminals v. Asarco, Inc., 792 F.2d 887, 892 (9th Cir.1986) (testing expenses considered "cost of response").

5. THE GOVERNMENT ACTION: UNITED STATES v. MONSANTO

One of the major decisions which has spelled out the scope of liability to the EPA or the United States is United States v. Monsanto Co., 858 F.2d 160 (4th Cir.1988), cert. denied 490 U.S. 1106, 109 S.Ct. 3156, 104 L.Ed.2d 1019 (1989). In these so-called Tier One actions, the government is suing one or more of the potentially responsible parties identified in CERCLA § 107 to recover for the response costs that it has or will incur in connection with the property.

In *Monsanto* Seidenberg and Hutchinson entered a 1972 lease, under a verbal, month-to-month arrangement, for a four-acre tract of land they owned to the Columbia Organic Chemical Company (COCC), a chemical manufacturing corporation. Thereafter, COCC expanded its business to include the brokering and recycling of chemical waste generated by third parties and used the site as a waste storage and disposal facility for its new operations. In 1976, COCC's principals incorporated South Carolina Recycling and Disposal Inc. (SCRDI), for the purpose of assuming COCC's waste-handling business, and the site-owners began accepting lease payments from SCRDI.

SCRDI contracted with numerous off-site waste producers for the transport, recycling, and disposal of their chemical and other wastes, including Monsanto, Allied Chemical and EM Industries (the non-settling generators). Between 1976 and 1980, SCRDI haphazardly deposited more that 7,000 fifty-five gallon drums of chemical waste on the site. Over time, many of the drums rusted and deteriorated, permitting hazardous substances to leak from the decaying drums and ooze into the ground. The substances commingled with incompatible chemicals that had escaped from other containers, generating noxious fumes, fires, and explosions. After several fires and explosions occurred at the site, and after expending approximately $1.8 million in a partial cleanup, the United States sued all of the identified owners and operators of the site and generators of waste at the site, most of whom settled with the EPA.

The district court granted the government's motion for summary judgment on liability against the owners and non-settling generators. First, the Fourth Circuit held, consistent with various district court holdings, that CERCLA § 107(a) "established a strict liability scheme." The court's holdings and rationale are set forth in these excerpts from its opinion, beginning with the liability of the two owners of the site:

> In light of the strict liability imposed by section 107(a), we cannot agree with the site-owners' contention that they are not within the class of owners Congress intended to hold liable. The traditional elements of tort culpability on which the site-owners rely

simply are absent from the statute. The plain language of section 107(a)(2) extends liability to owners of waste facilities regardless of their degree of participation in the subsequent disposal of hazardous waste.

Under section 107(a)(2), *any* person who owned a facility at a time when hazardous substances were deposited there may be held liable for all costs of removal or remedial action if a release or threatened release of a hazardous substance occurs. The site-owners do not dispute their ownership of the Bluff Road facility, or the fact that releases occurred there during their period of owner-ship. Under these circumstances, all the prerequisites to section 107(a) liability have been satisfied.

The court also rejected the owners' affirmative defenses under CERCLA § 107(b)(3), which permit exculpation only upon proof of a complete absence of causation based on the actions of third parties not in a "contractual relationship," together with a showing that the defendants "took precautions" against the foreseeable actions of such parties:

First, the site-owners could not establish the absence of a direct or indirect contractual relationship necessary to maintain the affir-mative defense. They concede they entered into a lease agreement with COCC. They accepted rent from COCC, and after SCRDI was incorporated, they accepted rent from SCRDI. Second, the site-owners presented no evidence that they took precautionary action against the foreseeable conduct of COCC or SCRDI. They argued to the trial court that, although they were aware COCC was a chemical manufacturing company, they were completely ignorant of all waste disposal activities at Bluff Road before 1977. They maintained that they never inspected the site prior to that time. In our view, the statute does not sanction such willful or negligent blindness on the part of absentee owners. The district court committed no error in entering summary judgment against the site-owners.

Next the Fourth Circuit considered the more complicated liability status of the three generator defendants:

The generator defendants first contend that the district court misinterpreted section 107(a)(3) because it failed to read into the statute a requirement that the governments prove a nexus between the waste they sent to the site and the resulting environmental harm. They maintain that the statutory phrase "containing such hazardous substances" requires proof that the specific substances they generated and sent to the site were present at the facility at the time of release.   * * *

Reduced of surplus language, sections 107(a)(3) and (4) impose liability on off-site waste generators who:

arranged for disposal * * * of hazardous substances * * * at any facility * * *containing such hazardous substances * * * from which there is a release * * * of a hazardous substance.

In our view, the plain meaning of the adjective "such" in the phrase "containing such hazardous substances" is "[a]like, similar, of the like kind." Black's Law Dictionary 1284 (5th ed. 1979). As used in the statute, the phrase "such hazardous substances" denotes hazardous substances alike, similar, or of a like kind to those that were present in a generator defendant's waste or that could have been produced by the mixture of the defendant's waste with other waste present at the site. It does not mean that the plaintiff must trace the ownership of each generic chemical compound found at a site. Absent proof that a generator defendant's specific waste remained at a facility at the time of release, a showing of chemical similarity between hazardous substances is sufficient.

The overall structure of CERCLA's liability provisions also militates against the generator defendants' "proof of ownership" argument. * * * As the statute provides—"[n]otwithstanding any other provision or rule of law"—liability under section 107(a) is "subject *only* to the defenses set forth" in section 107(b). Each of the three defenses established in section 107(b) "carves out from liability an exception based on causation." Congress, has, therefore, allocated the burden of disproving causation to the defendant who profited from the generation and inexpensive disposal of hazardous waste. We decline to interpret the statute in a way that would neutralize the force of Congress' intent.

The court also concluded that defendants had failed to establish that all of their waste had been removed from the site prior to the commencement of cleanup operations.

Finally, the court rejected defendants' arguments that the district court had erroneously held them jointly and severally liable because their respective responsibilities were "divisible":

The [trial] court concluded that joint and several liability was appropriate because the environmental harm at Bluff Road was "indivisible" and the appellants had "failed to meet their burden of proving otherwise." We agree with its conclusion.

While CERCLA does not mandate the imposition of joint and several liability, it permits it in cases of indivisible harm. In each case, the court must consider traditional and evolving principles of federal common law, which Congress has left to the courts to supply interstitially.

Under common law rules, when two or more persons act independently to cause a single harm for which there is a reasonable basis of apportionment according to the contribution of each, each is held liable only for the portion of harm that he causes. When such persons cause a single and indivisible harm, however, they are held liable jointly and severally for the entire harm. Restatement (Second) of Torts § 433A (1965). We think these principles, as reflected in the Restatement (Second) of Torts, represent the correct and uniform federal rules applicable to CERCLA cases.

* * *

Placing their arguments into the Restatement framework, the generator defendants concede that the environmental damage at Bluff Road constituted a "single harm," but contend that there was a reasonable basis for apportioning the harm. They observe that each of the off-site generators with whom SCRDI contracted sent a potentially identifiable volume of waste to the Bluff Road site, and they maintain that liability should have been apportioned according to the volume they deposited as compared to the total volume disposed of there by all parties. In light of the conditions at Bluff Road, we cannot accept this method as a basis for apportionment.

The generator defendants bore the burden of establishing a reasonable basis for apportioning liability among responsible parties. To meet this burden, the generator defendants had to establish that the environmental harm at Bluff Road was divisible among responsible parties. They presented no evidence, however, showing a relationship between waste volume, the release of hazardous substances, and the harm at the site. Further, in light of the commingling of hazardous substances, the district court could not have reasonably apportioned liability without some evidence disclosing the individual and interactive qualities of the substances deposited there. Common sense counsels that a million gallons of certain substances could be mixed together without significant consequences, whereas a few pints of others improperly mixed could result in disastrous consequences. Under other circumstances proportionate volumes of hazardous substances may well be probative of contributory harm. In this case, however, volume could not establish the effective contribution of each waste generator to the harm at the Bluff Road site.

Finally, the *Monsanto* court held that the district court acted within its discretion in refusing to apportion liability among all the defendants pursuant to the contribution provisions of CERCLA § 113(f), and instead choosing to defer the contribution action until "the plaintiff has been made whole." Judge Widener dissented on that aspect of the court's holding, arguing that once any defendant to the government's action requests it, the court must incorporate the contribution phases into the main action.

Notes and Questions

1. *Strict Liability*. As *Monsanto* makes clear, the courts have uniformly interpreted CERCLA as providing for a strict liability standard, despite the congressional silence on this critical point. CERCLA's legislative history suggests that Congress intended to leave to the judiciary the task of developing the appropriate liability standard rather than requiring the courts to impose a potentially inflexible or inequitable standard. Moreover,

CERCLA § 101, the definition section, states that liability under CERCLA "shall be construed to be the standard of liability which obtains under § 311 of the Federal Water Pollution Control Act." Although the FWPCA is similarly silent on the liability standard, Congress was aware that courts had interpreted it to be a strict liability standard. In enacting the SARA amendments in 1986, Congress reaffirmed its intention that courts impose a strict liability standard on PRPs under CERCLA. See H.R. Rep. No. 253, 99th Cong., 2d Sess., pt. 1, at 74 (1986), reprinted in 1986 U.S. Code Cong. & Admin. News 2835, 2856. Why not apply a negligence standard? A nuisance standard?

2. *Joint and Several Liability.* Congress also chose to delete from the final legislation any reference to joint and several liability contained in earlier versions. Nonetheless, as *Monsanto* illustrates, the courts have generally interpreted CERCLA as inviting the application of a joint and several liability rule. See United States v. Chem–Dyne Corp., 572 F.Supp. 802 (S.D.Ohio 1983); O'Neil v. Picillo, 883 F.2d 176, (1st Cir. 1989), cert. denied 493 U.S. 1071, 110 S.Ct. 1115, 107 L.Ed.2d 1022 (1990); New York v. Shore Realty Corp., 759 F.2d 1032 (2d Cir.1985).

Monsanto applied the Restatement (Second) of Torts as the source of the rules governing joint liability. A law review Note describes the Restatement approach and attempts to explain why courts have defaulted to its use. Elizabeth F. Mason, Contribution, Contribution Protection and Non–Settlor Liability Under CERCLA, 19 B.C. Envtl. Aff. L. Rev. 73, 83–85 (1991):

> According to the Restatement approach, CERCLA section 9607(a) defines the scope of a PRP's liability pursuant to a strict interpretation of §§ 433A, 875, and 881 of the Restatement (Second) of Torts. Under this interpretation, once a court has established that a group of PRPs is liable under CERCLA, it may impose joint and several liability, rendering each PRP individually liable for the full amount of the cleanup costs; in the alternative, the court may hold each PRP liable only for that party's portion of the costs. To determine which option to select, a court must undertake a factual inquiry into whether the harm at a site is divisible.

> Following Restatement § 875, courts will apply the joint and several liability standard when confronted with joint tortfeasors that have caused a single and indivisible harm. Conversely, as §§ 433A and 881 of the Restatement suggest, a court may apportion liability among tortfeasors where two or more tortfeasors acting independently have combined to bring about a harm; in this circumstance, each joint tortfeasor is liable only for the part of the harm that it caused. Such an apportionment is appropriate when the court can either distinguish the causes from one another or find a reasonable basis for determining how much harm each cause contributed to the total harm.

> Courts allocating liability under CERCLA are more likely to impose joint and several liability on PRPs than to attempt to divide cleanup costs among all of them for two reasons. It is very difficult to distinguish among the causes of the overall harm at hazardous waste sites. At the typical site, disparate amounts of various wastes, which differ in makeup and degrees of toxicity, have commingled and begun to migrate.

Moreover, generator and transporter records of the types and quantities of wastes sent to a site are often incomplete or missing altogether. Most courts thus have rejected theories of apportionment based solely on volume of waste contributed as inappropriate.

One commentator has suggested another reason that courts have tended to interpret CERCLA so that apportionment is the exception rather than the rule. Such an approach facilitates cleanups by enabling the government to recover the entire cost of a cleanup from one PRP without suing all of the liable parties at a site. According to this view, identifying and joining all the PRPs at a site and proving the contribution of each PRP to the harm would be a lengthy, expensive, and often impossible endeavor that would delay cleanups.

We will address later in greater detail the battle over apportionment in the context of contribution actions. For more on the question of divisibility, see Note, Divisibility of Injury Under CERCLA: Reaching for the Unreachable Goal, 5 B.Y.U. J. Pub. L. 195 (1991); Lewis A. Kornhauser & Richard L. Revesz, Sharing Damages Among Multiple Tortfeasors, 98 Yale L.J. 831 (1989).

3. *Causation.* As *Monsanto* demonstrates, the requirement of a causal link between the actions of the PRPs and the incurrence of response costs by the government is not a rigorous test. The original version of the legislation in the House of Representatives contained a causation requirement imposing liability upon "any person who caused or contributed to the release or threatened release" of a hazardous substance. The House Report was explained:

> [T]he usual common law principles of causation, including those of proximate causation, should govern the determination of whether a defendant "caused or contributed" to a release or threatened release. * * * Thus, for instance, the mere act of generation or transportation of hazardous waste or the mere existence of a generator's or transporter's waste in a site with respect to which cleanup costs are incurred would not, in and of itself, result in liability. * * * [F]or liability to attach under this section, the plaintiff must demonstrate a causal or contributory nexus between the acts of the defendant and the conditions which necessitated response action.

H.R. Rep. No. 1016, 96th Cong., 2d Sess., pt. 1, at 33–34, reprinted in 1980 U.S. Code Cong. & Admin. News 6119, 6136–37. See New York v. Shore Realty Corp., 759 F.2d 1032, 1044 (2d Cir.1985). However, the final version deleted that explicit requirement and instead contains no express causation requirement. Why would Congress have preferred silence?

6. DIVISIBILITY OF HARM

Despite the stringent holdings in *Monsanto* on causation and joint and several liability, a few more recent cases have suggested that occasionally responsible parties may be able to limit their liability. In two opinions, both as a result of Alcan Aluminum's determination to fight liability, the Third and Second Circuit Courts of Appeal have recognized a narrow channel through which a PRP must sail to avoid joint liability for the full costs of remediation. United States v. Alcan Aluminum Corp., 964 F.2d 252 (3d Cir.1992) (referred to as *Alcan–Butler*); United States v. Alcan Aluminum Corp., 990 F.2d 711 (2d Cir.1993).

In the Second Circuit's *Alcan* opinion, defendant argued that trace amounts of hazardous substances such as the amounts in "breakfast cereal" and "nearly everything else on which life depends" should not be a basis of CERCLA liability. However, the court rejected that argument because of its concern that "each potential defendant in a multi-defendant CERCLA case would be able to escape liability simply by relying on the low concentration of hazardous substances in its wastes, and the government would be left to absorb the cleanup costs." Moreover, the court noted that "the statute on its face applies to 'any' hazardous substance, and it does not impose quantitative requirements." As to the causation requirement, it held:

> The plain meaning of [of CERCLA § 107(a)] dictates that the government need only prove: (1) there was a release or threatened release, which (2) caused incurrence of response costs, and (3) that the defendant generated hazardous waste at the clean-up site. What is not required is that the government show that a specific defendant's waste caused incurrence of cleanup costs.

However, the court then recognized that a defendant could escape joint and several liability by demonstrating the divisibility of harm:

> Based on these common law principles, Alcan may escape any liability for response costs if it either succeeds in proving that its oil emulsion, when mixed with other hazardous wastes, did not contribute to the release and the clean-up costs that followed, or contributed at most to only a divisible portion of the harm. See Alcan–Butler, 964 F.2d at 270. Alcan as the polluter bears the ultimate burden of establishing a reasonable basis for apportioning liability. The government has no burden of proof with respect to what caused the release of hazardous waste and triggered response costs. It is the defendant that bears that burden. To defeat the government's motion for summary judgment on the issue of divisibility, Alcan need only show that there are genuine issues of material fact regarding a reasonable basis for apportionment of liability. As other courts have noted, apportionment itself is an intensely factual determination.

> In so ruling we candidly admit that causation is being brought back into the case—through the backdoor, after being denied entry at the frontdoor—at the apportionment stage. We hasten to add nonetheless that causation—with the burden on defendant—is reintroduced only to permit a defendant to escape payment where its pollutants did not contribute more than background contamination and also cannot concentrate. To state this standard in other words, we adopt a special exception to the usual absence of a causation requirement, but the exception is applicable only to claims, like

Alcan's, where background levels are not exceeded. And, we recognize this limited exception only in the absence of any EPA thresholds.

Contrary to the government's position, commingling is not synonymous with indivisible harm, and Alcan should have the opportunity to show that the harm caused at [the site] was capable of reasonable apportionment. It may present evidence relevant to establishing divisibility of harm, such as, proof disclosing the relative toxicity, migratory potential, degree of migration, and synergistic capacities of the hazardous substances at the site.

Alcan declares that the response actions at [the site] were attributable to substances such as PCB's, nitro benzene, phenol, dichlonoethone, toluene, and benzene. It contends that no soil contamination due to heavy metals was found there, and insists that the metallic constituents of its oil emulsion are insoluble compounds, submitting an affidavit supporting this theory of divisibility. The government submitted a declaration stating that metal contaminants like those found in Alcan's waste emulsion were present in environmental media at [the site], that the commingling of metallic and organic hazardous substances resulted in indivisible harm, and that though some forms of lead, cadmium and chromium are insoluble, they may chemically react with other substances and become water-soluble. These differing contentions supported by expert affidavits raise sufficient questions of fact to preclude the granting of summary judgment on the divisibility issue.

Finally, the court disagreed with the Third Circuit on the timing of the divisibility determination. In *Alcan–Butler* the Third Circuit held that the divisibility inquiry is one "best resolved at the initial liability phase" because it involves "relative degrees of liability." See *Alcan–Butler*, 964 F.2d at 270, n.29. The Second Circuit, while stating that "we prefer this common sense approach," concluded that the "statutory dictates of CERCLA" were to the contrary:

> Consequently, the language of CERCLA and SARA and their legislative histories appear to demonstrate the following chronology: liability is fixed first and immediately for enforcement purposes; litigation later to sort out what contribution is owed and by whom as a result of the remediation effort. But we do not rule that this chronology be followed or that the *Alcan–Butler* approach of deciding divisibility at the initial liability phase of the case is the best way for the district court to proceed. Instead, the choice as to when to address divisibility and apportionment are questions best left to the sound discretion of the trial court in the handling of an individual case.

Notes and Questions

1. How much benefit do you suppose Alcan will derive from the court's recognition of an affirmative defense? How often will defendants to a

government action be able to sustain the rigorous burden which the Second Circuit placed on those seeking to avoid joint and several liability? Is the court correct on the timing of the divisibility issue? On the timing issue, what in fact *did* the court hold? Why would defendants prefer the *Alcan–Butler* chronology? Is the court confusing the contribution action, which is concerned with apportionment, with the divisibility issue, which goes to the heart of the initial proceeding with the government?

2. Some important issues were not touched upon in this decision. For example, how does a remaining PRP such as Alcan attack the government's tendency to leave everyone who does not settle with the remainder of the costs? Will a showing of the level of contribution to the release or response costs be an "all or nothing" proposition that results in either total vindication or total responsibility or can such a judicial skirmish result in diminished levels of responsibility? Some courts have allowed "remainder" PRPs to attack the share of costs levied by the government, while other courts have allowed disproportionate allocations as the price for not settling.

3. What does the court's reference to concentrations above background mean? Is it the typical background levels found in soil and water? Would this approach bar its use by any PRP whose substances are not naturally occurring? Is the measurement to be taken at the disposal site? In the neighborhood of the generator? In the area surrounding the site, but not at the site itself? Further, when can it be determined that pollutants have "concentrated"?

4. In *Alcan–Butler*, the Third Circuit did not include language linking the affirmative defense to situations where hazardous substances are at levels below background levels. Under *Alcan–Butler* so long as the defendant's substances "did not or could not, when mixed with other hazardous substances, contribute to the release and the resultant response costs, [the defendant] should not be responsible for any response costs." 964 F.2d at 270. How significant is this difference?

C. PARTIES LIABLE UNDER CERCLA

As was observed above, the categories of parties that may be liable as PRPs include the present and past owners and operators of the site, generators of waste that is deposited at the site, and transporters of the waste.

1. OWNERS AND OPERATORS

CERCLA's focus on the status of parties, and not on their actual conduct or activities at a site, is reflected in the decisions interpreting what constitutes an "owner" or "operator." In United States v. Stringfellow, 661 F.Supp. 1053, 1063 (C.D.Cal.1987), the court imposed liability on the current owner of a waste disposal site, finding that proof of ownership of the facility is sufficient, and noting that CERCLA § 107(a)(1) "does not require that the present owner [of a facility] contribute to the release." See also Ecodyne Corp. v. Shah, 718 F.Supp. 1454, 1457 (N.D.Cal.1989).

In Nurad Inc. v. William E. Hooper and Sons Co., 966 F.2d 837 (4th Cir.1992), the Fourth Circuit held that "passive owners could be held liable * * * [for] simply owning property when hazardous waste leaked from storage tanks on the premises." The court reasoned that to premise CERCLA liability on affirmative human conduct would frustrate the goal of encouraging voluntary cleanups because owners could avoid liability by standing idle. The court concluded, therefore, that § 107(a)(2) "imposes liability, not only for active involvement in the 'dumping' or 'placing' of hazardous waste at a facility, but for ownership of the facility at the time that hazardous waste was 'spilling' or 'leaking.'" The duration of a party's ownership and its affirmative or passive conduct would be relevant, however, on the issue of allocating costs among the liable parties. As to the burden of proof, the Fourth Circuit held that "we do not think in such circumstances that Congress intended to impose on a CERCLA plaintiff the onerous burden of pinpointing at what precise point a leakage may have begun." Thus, the CERCLA defendant who is an owner in the chain of title must demonstrate that no disposal of hazardous substances occurred during its period of ownership in order to escape liability. With potentially continuously leaking barrels or underground tanks, could an interim owner ever satisfy such a burden of proof? Under this ruling, interim owners of a facility will face CERCLA liability, even if they did not participate in the disposal, did not own at the time others actively disposed, and did not know that hazardous substances were ever stored or disposed of on the property.

Might the most significant impact of the *Nurad* decision be exactly the opposite of the result that the Fourth Circuit intended? Isn't the problem about which the court was concerned covered in CERCLA § 101(35)(C), the so-called "innocent purchaser" defense? That section reads:

> (C) * * * Notwithstanding this paragraph, if the defendant obtained actual knowledge of the release or threatened release of a hazardous substance at such facility when the defendant owned the real property and then subsequently transferred ownership to another person without disclosing such knowledge, such defendant shall be treated as liable under section 9607(a)(1) of this title and no defense under section 9607(b)(3) of this title shall be available to such defendant.

Might the *Nurad* decision have the effect of making such interim owners liable even if they do disclose, thereby minimizing incentives for disclosure by an interim owner to its purchaser?

At least one federal district court has rejected the passive disposal theory adopted in *Nurad*. United States v. Petersen Sand & Gravel, Inc., 806 F.Supp. 1346 (N.D.Ill.1992).

As to operator liability, an operator certainly includes one who personally supervises and controls hazardous substance disposal activities at a site. "Only those who actually operate or exercise control over the facility that creates an environmental risk can be held liable under

CERCLA for the costs of reducing that risk." Edward Hines Lumber Co. v. Vulcan Materials Co., 685 F.Supp. 651, 657 (N.D.Ill.1988), affirmed 861 F.2d 155 (7th Cir.1988).

In *Nurad*, however, the court held that the actual exercise of control was not the proper standard, but rather "that authority to control * * * was the appropriate standard." In concluding that tenants of portions of property where underground tanks had leaked were not liable as "operators," it stated:

> [The rule] is one which properly declines to absolve from CERCLA liability a party who possessed the authority to abate the damage caused by the disposal of hazardous substances but who declined to actually exercise that authority by undertaking efforts at a cleanup.

Which do you think is the preferable test of "operator" status—actual exercise of control or authority to control? Which test finds greater support in tort law? Which might Congress have intended? Does "authority" to control imply actual knowledge of the disposal activities?

Problem

In 1979 Bartlesville Electric Co. (Bartlesville) acquired from Galvins Consolidated Properties (Galvins) a parcel of land on the outskirts of Bartlesville on which it intended to construct a retail consumer relations office. However, because of an economic downturn in 1980 it postponed construction until 1986, when it began excavations only to discover hazardous chemicals and wastes buried below the surface of the undeveloped property. In fact, the property had been used as a wood treatment facility from 1948 until 1978, when the facility was torn down.

Galvins had acquired the property in 1978 from Columbia State University, which held title by virtue of a 1960 bequest made to the University. In that year J. Renald Morrison III passed away, leaving most of his estate to Columbia State, his alma mater. Morrison had founded a wood treatment operation in the 1940s and acquired the subject property in 1948 to build a "state-of-the-art" plant to process wood for home construction purposes by applying various chemical substances. The operation was financially successful, but yielded a high volume of liquid wastes, some of which Morrison had simply disposed of on the property. In 1959, when Morrison became terminally ill, he decided to bequeath all of his stock to Columbia. His bequest provided instructions that Columbia retain John Astorhurst, Morrison's trusted manager for 15 years, to manage the operation under a long term contract. Following his death, Columbia complied with the bequest by giving Astorhurst a ten-year employment contract, but the University retained overall authority for the operation by appointment of a three-person Board of Directors, consisting of two persons selected by the University and Astorhurst. Astorhurst provided reports to the Board respecting major operational matters, and at one point sent a letter to the Board that stated: "We continue to be troubled by our waste disposal practices, which consist of hiring haulers to take for a fee about 75% of our toxic treatment chemicals, with the remainder being handled on the property. While I have endeavored to reuse some chemicals as a cost savings matter, the results have been of questionable value. I would appreciate the Board's advice on this issue.

Perhaps the University has some professor who can think of a cost-effective means to dispose of used chemicals."

In 1978, Astorhurst resigned from the business, and Columbia decided to sell the property to Galvins, a real estate developer. Galvins proceeded to tear down the plant and advertise the property for sale as suitable for light commercial or retail purposes. Bartlesville acquired it in 1979.

The Columbia Department of Environmental Quality (CDEQ) has recently examined the property and issued orders mandating its cleanup because of the extremely hazardous nature of the chemicals Morrison and Astorhurst had applied in their processes and disposed of on the property.

Bartlesville is interested in bringing an action against Columbia University who, in a moment of soul searching, unearthed the above-quoted letter and provided it to the CDEQ. What prospects does Bartlesville have to successfully maintain a cost recovery action against the University?

2. LIABILITY OF PARENT CORPORATIONS AND SUCCESSORS

a. *Parent Corporations*

CERCLA has been applied by some courts to permit the imposition on parent companies of liability as "operators" or "owners" under circumstances departing from these traditional rules. A few courts have applied a "capacity to control" test of parental liability. See, e.g., United States v. Northeastern Pharmaceutical & Chemical Co., 579 F.Supp. 823 (W.D.Mo.1984), reversed in part on other grounds and affirmed in part 810 F.2d 726 (8th Cir.1986), cert. denied 484 U.S. 848, 108 S.Ct. 146, 98 L.Ed.2d 102 (1987) (those who have the capacity and power to control the pollution-causing activities, to discover discharges when they occur, and to prevent and abate damage, are uniquely qualified to answer for their actions that result in CERCLA cleanup costs); Idaho v. Bunker Hill Co., 635 F.Supp. 665, 670–71 (D.Idaho 1986) (invoked the "capacity to control" test and found sufficient the "capacity, if not total reserved authority" of a parent corporation "to make decisions and implement actions and mechanisms to prevent and abate" hazardous substance contamination). Other courts have applied a narrower test, epitomized by United States v. Kayser–Roth Corp., 910 F.2d 24 (1st Cir.1990), cert. denied 498 U.S. 1084, 111 S.Ct. 957, 112 L.Ed.2d 1045 (1991) (imposing "operator" liability on the basis of the parent entity's actual participation in, or control of, the management of the facility that released the hazardous substances).

Not all courts have accepted these expansive approaches to liability of parent corporations. See Joslyn Manufacturing Co. v. T.L. James & Co., 893 F.2d 80 (5th Cir.1990), cert. denied 498 U.S. 1108, 111 S.Ct. 1017, 112 L.Ed.2d 1098 (1991), where the Fifth Circuit held that CERCLA does not impose liability on parent corporations. It noted that "CERCLA does not define 'owners' or 'operators' as including the parent company of offending wholly-owned subsidiaries." Moreover, the legislative history revealed that where Congress was silent it expected traditional and evolving principles of common law would govern. Further, in another definition section of CERCLA § 101(20)(A)(iii), Congress had expressly incorporated a control concept in the definition, but failed to do so in the definition of "owner" or "operator."

b. Shareholders

As to shareholder liability, some courts apply analyses similar to the corporate parent cases. See Donahey v. Bogle, 987 F.2d 1250 (6th Cir.1993) (holding that a sole shareholder of a corporation is a responsible party "as a matter of law" under CERCLA where the evidence showed that he "had the authority to prevent the contamination of the property of the corporation."). See also Kelley v. Thomas Solvent Co., 727 F.Supp. 1532 (W.D.Mich.1989); Riverside Market Development Corp. v. International Building Prods. Inc., 931 F.2d 327 (5th Cir.1991), cert. denied ___ U.S. ___, 112 S.Ct. 636, 116 L.Ed.2d 654 (1991) (majority shareholder not an owner under facts of that case); United States v. Northeastern Pharmaceutical & Chemical Co., 810 F.2d 726 (8th Cir. 1986) (shareholder and officer liable under § 107(a)(3) because he arranged personally for the disposal of hazardous waste).

Should courts take a different approach to shareholders than to parents and subsidiary relationships? How about officers or directors? At least two courts have adopted a "prevention test" that imposes operator liability on an officer if the individual officer "could have prevented or significantly abated" the waste activity. Kelley v. ARCO Industries Corp., 723 F.Supp. 1214, 1217 (W.D.Mich.1989); Quadion Corp. v. Mache, 738 F.Supp. 270 (N.D.Ill.1990). What incentives does such a rule create?

See Frank H. Easterbrook & Daniel R. Fischel, Limited Liability and the Corporation, 52 U. Chi. L. Rev. 89 (1985) (arguing in favor of strict preservation of corporate identities); Lynda J. Oswald, Strict Liability of Individuals under CERCLA, 20 B.C. Envtl. Aff. L. Rev. 579 (1993).

c. Successors

Closely related to shareholder and parent corporation liability is the liability of successor entities, which have acquired the equity or assets of an entity that would otherwise have been a PRP. Some courts have adopted a "continuity of enterprise" theory or a "substantial continuation" theory of successor liability in determining that a firm which purchased most of the assets and retained most of the employees was subject to CERCLA liability. Some of the factors that are considered include whether: (1) the business of both the old and new companies are the same; (2) the employees of the new company are doing the same jobs under the same conditions and supervisors; (3) the new entity has the same production process, manufactures the same product, and has the same customers; and (4) the transfer to the new company was part of an effort to avoid existing or potential environmental liability. See, e.g., United States v. Mexico Feed & Seed Co., 980 F.2d 478 (8th Cir.1992) (adopting the "substantial continuation" test of successor liability, but finding that defendant asset purchaser was not liable as a successor because it purchased assets without knowledge of the seller's potential CERCLA liability). See also Allied Corp. v. Acme Solvents Reclaiming, Inc., 812 F.Supp. 124 (N.D.Ill.1993) (stating that the "substantial continuity" or "continuity of the enterprise" exception "only applies when it has been shown that the asset purchaser has knowledge of the potential liability and responsibility for that liability"); United States v. Distler, 741 F.Supp. 637 (W.D.Ky.1990) (liability premised on a "mere continuation" theory where there was substantial continuity between the two companies).

What role should a purchaser's knowledge of the seller's potential environmental liability have on the successor liability question? Is there a due diligence duty on purchasers? If actual knowledge increases the likelihood of CERCLA liability on purchasers, what incentives does such a rule create? See Allen Kezsbon & Alan Goldman, Corporate Successor Liability for CERCLA Cleanup Costs: Recent Developments, 7 Toxics L. Rptr. 1156 (March 3, 1993) (drawing a distinction between the objective and subjective approaches to successor liability and criticizing the subjective knowledge test). See Michael D. Green, Successors and CERCLA: The Imperfect Analogy to Products Liability and an Alternative Proposal, 87 Nw. L. Rev. 897 (1993).

3. LENDERS AS OWNERS

Not surprisingly, the government has looked to lenders as a source of resources to fund cleanups. When lenders make loans to owners or operators of facilities and the borrower encounters financial difficulties, the lender may attempt to salvage its commitment by exercising some influence over the operations of the debtor's business. CERCLA § 101(20) does create a limited exemption for lenders by defining "owner" as "not includ[ing] a person, who, without participation in the management of a vessel or facility, holds indicia of ownership primarily to protect his security interest in the vessel or facility."

In 1990, two courts of appeal reached arguably conflicting conclusions with respect to the liability of lenders. In United States v. Fleet Factors Corp., 901 F.2d 1550 (11th Cir.1990), the court held:

[A] secured creditor may incur section 9607(a)(2) liability, without being an operator, by participating in the financial management of a facility to a degree indicating a capacity to influence the corporation's treatment of hazardous wastes. It is not necessary for the secured creditor actually to involve itself in the day-to-day operations of the facility in order to be liable. * * *

Shortly after the decision in *Fleet Factors*, the Ninth Circuit in In re Bergsoe Metal Corp., 910 F.2d 668 (9th Cir.1990), held that "[i]t is clear from the statute that, whatever the precise parameters of 'participation,' there must be *some* actual management of the facility before a secured creditor will fall outside the exception," while "[h]ere there was none."

In 1992 the EPA promulgated a final rule on lender liability that is designed to broaden lenders' exemptions from liability beyond the holding in *Fleet Factors*. 40 C.F.R. § 300.1100 "Security Interest Exception" (April 29, 1992). The rule sets forth various actions by the holder of a security interest that will constitute "participation in management," and thereby lose the exemption from CERCLA liability. See Ashland Oil, Inc. v. Sonford Products Corp., 810 F.Supp. 1057 (D.Minn.1993) (finding lender qualified for "safe harbor" from CERCLA liability and new EPA lender liability rule was consistent with the statutory language and entitled to deference).

4. LIABILITY OF ARRANGERS

CERCLA § 107(a)(3) provides that "any person who * * * *arranged for* disposal or treatment * * * of hazardous substances owned or possessed by such person" may be liable as a PRP. In United States v. Aceto Agricultural Chemicals Corp., 872 F.2d 1373 (8th Cir.1989), affirming in part 699 F.Supp. 1384 (S.D.Iowa 1988), the Eighth Circuit Court of Appeals held that manufacturers could be liable for releases caused by the operations of a third party—the manufacturer's independent contractor—on land owned by the third party under the ambiguous "arranged for" liability provision in CERCLA § 107(a)(3). In *Aceto*, the EPA and the State of Iowa sought to recover $10 million in response costs from eight pesticide manufacturers who contracted with Aidex to formulate their technical-grade pesticides into commercial-grade pesticides. It is a common industry practice for pesticide manufacturers to contract with a pesticide formulator, such as Aidex, to mix active pesticides with inert ingredients pursuant to specifications provided by the manufacturer. After mixing, the formulator packages the commercial product and ships it back to the manufacturer or sells it directly to farmers. The EPA and the State of Iowa alleged that the generation of pesticide-containing wastes was an "inherent" part of the formulation process because of inevitable spills, cleaning of equipment, mixing and grinding operations, and production of batches that do not meet specifications. The government asserted that the manufacturers were liable under CERCLA "because [the manufacturers] arranged for Aidex to formulate and package their pesticides through processes that necessarily result in the generation of wastes."

The defendants argued that the contract was for the performance of services on a valuable product, which left responsibility for the control and disposal of any resulting hazardous wastes with Aidex. The Eighth Circuit concluded that Congress had intended to impose liability under CERCLA on parties responsible for harmful conditions created by hazardous waste, and this responsibility could not be avoided by parties claiming they only had intended that the formulator produce useful products and never intended disposal. The *Aceto* court reasoned that the defendants had never transferred ownership and that common law tort principles supported imposition of liability. To reach its holding, the appellate court distinguished *Aceto* from cases that have held that liability cannot be imposed when a useful substance is sold to another party who incorporates it into a product and then disposes of it.

In Sanford Street Local Development Corp. v. Textron Corp., 768 F.Supp. 1218 (W.D.Mich.1991), vacated on other grounds 805 F.Supp. 29 (W.D.Mich.1992), the district court ruled that under CERCLA, the below-market-value sale of a property that contained PCB-laden electrical transformers could constitute "arranging for disposal" of a hazardous substance, so as to render the seller of the property liable for the costs of cleaning up the PCBs. It applied this reasoning not only to the company which originally used the transformers, but to a company which bought the site for a reduced price and later sold it for a further reduced price.

The decision in *Aceto* has been followed in the Ninth Circuit in Jones–Hamilton Co. v. Beazer Materials & Services, Inc., 973 F.2d 688 (9th Cir.1992) (imposing liability upon owner of raw hazardous substances formulated into wood preservation compounds by independent formulator under an agreement allowing loss of up to 2% through spillage). However, the Second Circuit refused to extend arranger liability to petroleum companies whose service stations had disposed of hazardous waste products that contaminated a waste site. The fact that the oil firms sold oil products and leased underground storage tanks to the independent dealers did not create arranger liability because they did not have an "obligation to exercise control over [their] hazardous waste disposal." General Electric Co. v. AAMCO Transmissions, Inc., 962 F.2d 281 (2d Cir.1992). See also United States v. Gordon Stafford, Inc., 810 F.Supp. 182 (N.D.W.Va.1993) (sale of PCB-containing transformers in working condition to a dealer in used mining equipment did not constitute "arranging" for disposal).

D. PRIVATE COST RECOVERY ACTIONS

1. WHAT ARE PRIVATE COST RECOVERY ACTIONS?

Private cost recovery actions are indispensable to the achievement of CERCLA's objectives of obtaining efficient and effective cleanups of contaminated sites and distributing the costs of such cleanups among responsible parties. The material above, as illustrated by the *Monsanto* and *Alcan Aluminum* cases, demonstrates that frequently the United States and state governments will institute actions against a few or only one party, often the current site owner. In order to undertake remedial action, the involvement of the current owner is indispensable even though the owner is not necessarily a responsible party within CERCLA § 107(a). However, because the cleanups of real property contaminated by hazardous waste can be quite costly, owners of such property face difficult choices about how to remedy that contamination in the most cost-effective manner. As part of their strategy to recover the costs associated with cleanup, many landowners institute private cost recovery actions under the provisions of CERCLA to help them obtain contribution or a total shifting of those costs from a variety of parties who were responsible for the contamination.

CERCLA § 107(a)(4)(B) provides that "any other necessary costs of response incurred by *any other person* consistent with the national contingency plan" may be recovered from those who qualify as PRPs. It is also equally clear that no prior government action or approval is necessary before such an action can be maintained. See 40 C.F.R. § 300.71(a)(3); Cadillac Fairview/Calif., Inc. v. Dow Chem. Co., 840 F.2d 691 (9th Cir.1988). To protect against reimbursing inadequate or ill-conceived cleanups, the court in *Cadillac Fairview* identified two safeguards: (1) the party undertaking the response action must prove that the costs it incurred were "necessary," and (2) it incurred those costs in a manner "consistent with the National Contingency Plan." These cost recovery actions commonly arise in three situations:

a. Where innocent current owners of contaminated property are held liable to a state or federal government for all costs of cleaning up hazardous waste and, to avoid the cost and uncertainty of litigating the issue of liability, choose instead to clean up the property themselves and then sue other potentially responsible parties under CERCLA or state and common law theories of liability;

b. Where a property owner may be under no immediate threat of liability or enforcement order from any governmental entity, but finds the presence of contamination incompatible with its intended use of the property, and chooses to voluntarily clean up the contamination and then sue any PRPs to recover the full cost of the cleanup;

c. Where owners of adjacent property that is not itself contaminated but which is adversely affected by threatened releases of hazardous substances from nearby property attempt to clean up the threatened pollution to abate or avoid damage to their property.

2. PLAINTIFF'S PRIMA FACIE CASE

In the private cost recovery suit the plaintiff must prove the five elements required in all CERCLA actions: (1) the site in question must be a "facility"; (2) the defendant is a liable party under CERCLA § 107(a); (3) a release or threatened release; (4) of a hazardous substance has occurred; (5) which has caused the plaintiff to incur response costs. In many cases, these elements may be fairly easy to establish.

But CERCLA § 107(a)(4)(B) also states that private plaintiffs may only recover the "necessary costs of response incurred * * * consistent with the national contingency plan." The NCP is a document that sets forth procedures and standards for waste site cleanups and is designed to ensure that cleanups proceed in a consistent and orderly fashion. The

EPA revised the NCP in 1990. See 40 C.F.R. § 300 (1990). How the requirement of "consistency" with the NCP fits into the plaintiff's prima facie case or whose burden it is to prove or disprove such consistency is a matter of considerable importance and difficulty.

One of the factors that influences the requirements of compliance with the NCP is whether the cleanup performed on the property is characterized as a "remedial" action, which results in the application of stringent standards, or as a "removal" action, where the NCP only prescribes minimal requirements.

In general, courts characterizing a cleanup as a removal action often find that plaintiff's costs are consistent with the NCP. See, e.g., General Electric v. Litton Business Systems, Inc., 715 F.Supp. 949 (W.D.Mo. 1989), affirmed 920 F.2d 1415 (8th Cir.1990). On the other hand, courts characterizing a cleanup as a remedial action are less inclined to find that cleanup costs incurred are consistent with the NCP. See, e.g., Amland Properties Corp. v. Aluminum Co. of America, 711 F.Supp. 784, (D.N.J.1989); Gussin Enterprises, Inc. v. Rockola, 1993 WL 114643 (N.D.Ill.1993).

3. THE COMPLIANCE WITH NCP

General Electric Co. v. Litton Industrial Automation Systems, Inc., 920 F.2d 1415 (8th Cir.1990), cert. denied 499 U.S. 937, 111 S.Ct. 1390, 113 L.Ed.2d 446 (1991), is a leading case on consistency with the NCP. From 1959 to 1962, during the occupancy of the company taken over by defendant Litton, improper disposal of cyanide-based electroplating wastes and other pollutants had occurred on the parcel. In the early 1980s, GE, which later acquired the property, and the Missouri Department of Natural Resources (MDNR) investigated the site and decided that no cleanup was necessary. In 1984, GE sold the site to a commercial real estate developer. Shortly thereafter, the MDNR changed its position on the need for a cleanup, and, threatened with CERCLA lawsuits by both its vendee and MDNR, GE agreed to clean up the site. GE then brought a cost recovery action against Litton under CERCLA § 107, which defended on the ground that the cleanup was not consistent with the NCP.

In reviewing the critical finding that the costs incurred were consistent with the NCP despite having omitted some detailed requirements mentioned in the NCP, the Eighth Circuit Court of Appeals wrote:

> We are satisfied that the thorough evaluation that was performed here is consistent with the NCP, specifically with 40 CFR § 300.-65(b)(2). The site evaluation does not have to comply strictly with the letter of the NCP, *but only must be consistent with its requirements*. It is not necessary that every factor mentioned by the NCP be dealt with explicitly; thus, for instance, a failure to consider explicitly the weather conditions factor is not fatal to an evaluation's consistency with the NCP. (emphasis in original).

The 1990 revisions of the NCP generally relax the standard of NCP compliance by permitting private parties to recover their cleanup costs based upon a dual showing that they have (1) substantially complied with the requirements of the NCP and (2) performed a CERCLA-quality cleanup.

4. PROOF OF COMPLIANCE AS AFFECTING LIABILITY OR DAMAGES

One major disagreement revolves around whether a showing of consistency with the NCP goes to the issue of liability, or whether liability can be determined independently of compliance with the NCP, with consistency bearing only on the amount of damages eligible for recovery.

One line of cases holds that consistency with the NCP is an element of a private plaintiff's prima facie case on liability. Artesian Water Company v. Government of New Castle County, 659 F.Supp. 1269, (D.Del.1987), affirmed 851 F.2d 643 (3d Cir.1988) so held, noting that the NCP plays a central role in the CERCLA scheme in that it establishes a standard against which response actions are judged appropriate or inappropriate in the first instance, not merely a limit on the amount of damages recoverable from liable parties.

In Amland Properties Corporation v. Aluminum Company of America, 711 F.Supp. 784, (D.N.J.1989), the district court stated that "the weight of recent authority in cases * * * of private party recovery actions holds that response costs incurred consistent with the NCP is an element of a CERCLA plaintiff's case on liability." In *Amland*, the determination of consistency was made after a full record had been developed. Accordingly, the *Amland* court stated that it must address consistency with the NCP in order to determine whether a plaintiff is entitled to recover *any* of its response costs and to avoid the risk of a pointless trial at some later date. Accord Ambrogi v. Gould, Inc., 750 F.Supp. 1233 (M.D.Pa.1990).

Another line of cases has differed with the above rationale and permitted a ruling on liability independent of a ruling on the specific amount of costs that a party may recover. In T & E Industries, Inc. v. Safety Light Corp., 680 F.Supp. 696, 709 (D.N.J.1988), the district court held that a plaintiff may establish liability under CERCLA § 107 by establishing that a "covered person" caused a "release" or "threatened release" of a "hazardous substance" from a "facility" which caused the plaintiff to incur "response costs." The court held that if undisputed facts establish each of these elements, the plaintiff is entitled to a summary judgment declaring the defendant liable. With regard to costs, the decision held:

> While the determination of whether such costs were "necessary" and "consistent with the National Contingency Plan" does preclude this Court from entering summary judgment as to specific amounts

of the costs, the question of amount can be dealt with at a later date. For now, it is clear that certain items which T & E seeks to recover are included within the meaning of response costs under CERCLA.

What are the strategic consequences of how the courts treat the issue of NCP compliance affecting damages or liability? Which rule is more likely to expedite cleanups? If a plaintiff fails to establish NCP consistency, could a common law tort theory rescue the case? Which of the basic theories considered in Chapters 2, 3 and 4 is most likely to offer assistance?

5. RECOVERY OF ATTORNEYS' FEES

In Alyeska Pipeline Service Co. v. Wilderness Society, 421 U.S. 240, 247, 95 S.Ct. 1612, 1616, 44 L.Ed.2d 141 (1985), the Supreme Court held that under the "American Rule" litigants must pay their own costs and "the prevailing litigant is ordinarily not entitled to collect a reasonable attorney's fee from the loser." In Runyon v. McCrary, 427 U.S. 160, 96 S.Ct. 2586, 49 L.Ed.2d 415 (1976), the Court stated that without explicit congressional authorization, attorney fees are not recoverable as a cost of litigation under federal statutes. With these principles in mind, the courts are surprisingly divided on whether attorneys' fees are recoverable as a "necessary cost of response" under CERCLA § 107(a)(4)(B).

In General Electric Co. v. Litton Industries Automation Systems, Inc., 920 F.2d 1415 (8th Cir.1990), cert. denied 499 U.S. 937, 111 S.Ct. 1390, 113 L.Ed.2d 446 (1991) (the same opinion in which the court adopted a liberal view of NCP consistency), the Eighth Circuit determined that the statutory language in CERCLA was explicit enough to permit GE to recover attorneys' fees in a private cost recovery action. The court looked for guidance in CERCLA § 107(a)(4)(B) which allows private parties to recover "necessary costs of response * * * consistent with the national contingency plan." "Response" is defined in § 101(25) as "remove, removal, remedy, and remedial action; all such terms (including the terms 'removal' and 'remedial action') include enforcement activities thereto." The court determined that a private party cost recovery action "such as this one is an enforcement activity within the meaning of the statute." The court continued:

> Attorney fees and expenses necessarily are incurred in this kind of enforcement activity and it would strain the statutory language to the breaking point to read them out of the "necessary costs" that Section 9607(a)(4)(B) allows private parties to recover. We therefore conclude that CERCLA authorizes, with a sufficient degree of explicitness, the recovery by private parties of attorney fees and expenses. This conclusion based on the statutory language is consistent with two of the main purposes of CERCLA—prompt cleanup of hazardous waste sites and imposition of all cleanup costs on the responsible party. These purposes would be undermined if a nonpolluter (such as GE) were forced to absorb the litigation costs of recovering its response costs from the polluter. The litigation costs

could easily approach or even exceed the response costs, thereby serving as a disincentive to clean the site.

The Sixth Circuit in Donahey v. Bogle, 987 F.2d 1250 (6th Cir.1993) and two Eighth Circuit decisions, Gopher Oil Co. v. Union Oil Co. of California, 955 F.2d 519 (8th Cir.1992) and United States v. Mexico Feed & Seed Co., 980 F.2d 478 (8th Cir.1992), have followed *Litton*.

In Stanton Road Associates v. Lohrey Enterprises, 984 F.2d 1015 (9th Cir.1993), the Ninth Circuit's response to the Eighth Circuit was quite direct: "We are unpersuaded by the Eighth Circuit's explanation of its holding. The words "enforcement activities" used in CERCLA § 101(25) "do not explicitly authorize the payment of attorneys fees," because "Congress has repeatedly demonstrated that it knows how to express its intention to create an exception to the American Rule." For example, in § 310(f) of CERCLA, Congress authorized courts "to award costs of litigation (including reasonable attorneys' fees and expert witness fees) to the prevailing party or the substantially prevailing party whenever the court determines such an award is appropriate in citizen suit actions."

The Ninth Circuit also disagreed that "necessary costs of response" is explicit enough to authorize the awarding of attorney fees. Rather than reading attorney fees out of § 107(a)(4) of CERCLA, which the Eighth Circuit said it feared doing, the Ninth Circuit felt that under *Aleyska* and *Runyon* it could not justify reading attorney fees into the statute. Finally, it rejected the public policy argument that Congress must have intended for private litigants to recover attorney fees to effectuate the rapid cleanup policy supposedly underlying CERCLA because *Aleyska* specifically rejected such an approach.

Which court has the stronger of the arguments? How do you answer the argument that Congress did not include attorneys' fees explicitly in § 107(a), but did do so in § 310, governing citizen suits? Which viewpoint facilitates more expeditious cleanups of contaminated property? Is that last question even relevant? Will disallowance of attorneys' fees create a disincentive for voluntary cleanups? The Tenth Circuit Court of Appeals has weighed in on the side of disallowing attorneys' fees that pertain to the cost recovery litigation itself, while authorizing non-litigation related fees. FMC Corp. v. Aero Industries, Inc., 998 F.2d 842 (10th Cir.1993).

6. CAUSATION IN PRIVATE COST RECOVERY ACTIONS

Does the private party suing to recover its costs secure the same advantages of watered-down causation standards, strict, joint and several liability? In Dedham Water Co. v. Cumberland Farms Dairy, Inc., 889 F.2d 1146 (1st Cir.1989), the court phrased the causation issue as follows:

> The central question on appeal is whether, under CERCLA, the plaintiff must prove that a hazardous substance released by the

defendant's facility physically migrated onto the plaintiff's property, causing contamination of the well field, or whether it is sufficient for the plaintiff to prove that there were releases or threatened releases of a hazardous substance from defendant's facility which caused the plaintiff reasonably to incur response costs, regardless of whether physical migration actually occurred.

The court answered the inquiry:

CERCLA states: "the owner and operator * * * of a facility * * * from which there is a release or a threatened release of a hazardous substance, which causes the incurrence of response costs, shall be liable * * *." 42 U.S.C.A. § 9607(a). A literal reading of the statute imposes liability if releases or threatened releases from defendant's facility cause the plaintiff to incur response costs; it does *not* say that liability is imposed only if the defendant causes actual contamination of the plaintiff's property.

To our knowledge, every court that has addressed this issue, with the exception of the district court in the instant case, has held that it is not necessary to prove actual contamination of plaintiff's property by defendant's waste in order to establish liability under CERCLA. There is nothing in the statute, its legislative history, or the case law, which requires proof that the defendant's hazardous waste actually have migrated to plaintiff's property, causing contamination of plaintiff's property, before CERCLA liability is triggered. Nor is there anything in the statute suggesting that a "two-site" case be treated differently than a one-site case, where the issue is whether a release or threat of release caused "response costs."

On remand, Dedham Water Co. v. Cumberland Farms Dairy, Inc., 770 F.Supp. 41 (D.Mass.1991), the district court held that plaintiffs' expenditure of funds for building and operating a water treatment plant was not related to any perceived threat of contamination of plaintiffs' well field by the defendant's facility, and thus that the plaintiffs could not recover from the defendant for those costs. The court concluded that from the record in this case, "the response for which the plaintiffs seek reimbursement was not related to the 'potential threat.'"

Although the court said that the defendant appeared to be "a blatant polluter" and that it "would be gratifying to exact reimbursement from the defendant for the benefit of the plaintiffs," it concluded that "[a]s long as causation is a necessary element of liability * * * I cannot do so on this record." Are you surprised by this outcome? The court of appeals affirmed, 972 F.2d 453 (1st Cir.1992).

In cases such as *Dedham Water* the site of the release is different from the site on which response costs are incurred. The courts have shown more diversity in developing causation standards in these two site cases. The Third Circuit discussed the causation question in Artesian Water Co. v. Government of New Castle County, 659 F.Supp. 1269 (D.Del.1981), affirmed 851 F.2d 643 (3d Cir.1988), where a water company sought recovery for its response costs in monitoring and evaluating the impact on its wells of leachate from an adjacent landfill. Applying a substantial factor rule of causation, the court found the plaintiff entitled to relief. The court stated first that CERCLA's strict liability scheme requires that a plaintiff demonstrate a causal connection between the defendant's released substance and the response costs incurred. However, the court rejected a "but-for" causation test because more than two causes had acted concurrently to bring about the harm, including pollutants from another landfill, saltwater intrusion, and the state's aquifer management policy. The court ruled that if the release or threatened release of contaminants from the defendant's site is a substantial factor in causing a plaintiff to incur response costs, then the court will hold the defendant liable under CERCLA.

Does *Dedham Water* adopt a substantial factor test of causation? The district court had required that defendant's hazardous substances have actually migrated to and contaminated plaintiff's property; in other words, the critical issue was "whether contaminants from the Cumberland Farms site ever reached the groundwater and thereafter found their way to WL–3." What, if anything, is objectionable respecting the district court's test? What disadvantages and advantages do you see in applying watered-down causation standards in private cost recovery actions? Is the substantial factor test of *Artesian Water* a logical approach?

E. ALLOCATING THE COSTS: CONTRIBUTION ACTIONS AND OTHER DEVICES

1. STANDARDS FOR OBTAINING CONTRIBUTION

The contribution action is brought by one or more PRPs against other PRPs for the purpose of distributing the costs of cleanup among many parties. It is this area of CERCLA law that is most influenced by the law of torts and where nuisance and strict liability tort actions are often involved. Under tort law, the right of contribution enables one joint tortfeasor that has paid more than its fair share in resolving a tort claim to sue other joint tortfeasors to recover the amount that it has paid in excess of that fair share. This principle helps to soften the harsh effects of joint and several liability by allowing the contribution plaintiff to recoup some of the losses it incurred in paying the original plaintiff (either the government or a private cost recovery plaintiff). Thus, even though the harm was indivisible for purposes of a government or private cost recovery action, nevertheless the damages are allocable among many PRPs for contribution purposes.

Under CERCLA, an action for contribution usually arises in one of three situations: (1) the EPA has sued fewer than all the PRPs at a site under CERCLA § 106 or 107(a), and those "named" parties seek contribution against the other, unnamed PRPs at the site; (2) a PRP that has financed the cleanup at a site has brought a cost recovery action under CERCLA § 107(a)(4)(B) against fewer than all of the other PRPs at the site, and those named parties bring actions for contribution against the unnamed PRPs at the site, as well as counter-claims for contribution against the PRP originally seeking to recover its costs; or (3) a PRP brings an action to recover its response costs from another PRP at a site. This last situation is not technically a contribution action, but rather a cost recovery action, discussed above. A PRP's liability in a contribution action is not joint and several; rather it is proportionate liability only, which differentiates it from the cost recovery action which may result in the imposition of joint and several liability.

Recall that the issue of divisibility of harm (or costs) may arise at the initial stage of a government-instituted action. In this phase a court must determine the allocation of liability among PRPs according to principles of joint and several liability; this phase, as illustrated in *Monsanto* and *Alcan Aluminum*, focuses on the divisibility or indivisibility of the harm at the site. See United States v. Western Processing Co., 734 F.Supp. 930, 938 (W.D.Wash.1990) for an excellent discussion of this process. However, the question of divisibility of harm for purposes of defeating joint and several liability is not the same as apportioning costs among joint tortfeasors. Once the court has determined which PRPs are jointly and severally liable to the government, then these PRPs attempt to limit the amount of damages they must pay by securing contribution from other PRPs. As initially enacted in 1980, CERCLA contained no explicit right to contribution, although a few courts implied such a right. See, e.g., United States v. Conservation Chem. Co., 619 F.Supp. 162, 228 (W.D.Mo.1985). However, in 1986, Congress enacted an explicit contribution action provision in CERCLA § 113(f), which provides:

> (1) *Contribution.* Any person may seek contribution from any other person who is liable or potentially liable under section 9607(a) of this title, during or following any civil action under section 9606 of this title or under section 9607(a) of this title. Such claims shall be brought in accordance with this section and the Federal Rules of Civil Procedure, and shall be governed by Federal law. In resolving contribution claims, the court may allocate response costs among liable parties using such equitable factors as the court determines are appropriate. Nothing in this subsection shall diminish the right of any person to bring an action for contribution in the absence of a civil action under section 9606 of this title or section 9607 of this title.

The following decision in United States v. R.W. Meyer, Inc., 932 F.2d 568 (6th Cir.1991) demonstrates many of the considerations that may influence the apportionment of liability in contribution actions under CERCLA § 113(f).

UNITED STATES v. R.W. MEYER, INC.

United States Court of Appeals, Sixth Circuit, 1991.
932 F.2d 568.

Before GUY and BOGGS, Circuit Judges, and BERTELSMAN, District Judge.

BERTELSMAN, D.J.

This appeal involved the construction of the provisions of the Comprehensive Environmental Response, Compensation, and Liability Act (CERCLA) governing contribution actions among responsible parties following a cleanup of a hazardous waste site and an Immediate Removal Action by the Environmental Protection Agency (EPA). 42 U.S.C. §§ 9607, 9613(f)(1).

BACKGROUND

The facts and background necessary to place this opinion in context were well stated by Chief Judge Hillman in his unpublished opinion awarding contribution, as follows: "This matter stems from a suit brought by the United States against Northernaire Plating Company ('Northernaire') for recovery of its costs in conducting an 'Immediate Removal Action' pursuant to CERCLA. Northernaire owned and operated a metal electroplating business in Cadillac, Michigan. Beginning in 1972, it operated under a 10–year lease on property owned by R.W. Meyer, Inc. ('Meyer'). Northernaire continued operations until mid–1981 when its assets were sold to Toplocker Enterprises, Inc. ('Toplocker'). From July of 1975 until this sale, Willard S. Garwood was the president and sole shareholder of Northernaire. He personally oversaw and managed the day-to-day operations of the company. Acting upon inspection reports from the Michigan Department of Natural Resources ('MDNR'), the United States Environmental Protection Agency ('EPA') conducted an Immediate Removal Action at the Northernaire site from July 5 until August 3, 1983. Cleanup of the site required neutralization of caustic acids, bulking and shipment of liquid acids, neutralization of caustic and acid sludges, excavation and removal of a contaminated sewer line, and decontamination of the inside of the building. All of the hazardous substances found at the site were chemicals and by-products of metal electro-plating operations. In an earlier opinion and order this court found the defendants Garwood, Northernaire, and Meyer jointly and severally liable to plaintiff for the costs of the Immediate Removal Action under Section 107(a) of CERCLA. 42 U.S.C. § 9607(a). The court awarded plaintiff $268,818.25 plus prejudgment interest. The court later determined the prejudgment interest. Each defendant, (Northernaire and Garwood moving together) has brought cross-claims for contribution against the other. Currently before the court are the summary judgment motions on these cross-claims." CERCLA specifically allows actions for contribution among parties who have been held jointly and severally liable: [court quotes § 113(f)].

Apparently, the parties allowed the building to degenerate into a true environmental disaster area. As this court observed in the former appeal: "* * * State tests on samples of the soil, sludge, and drum contents disclosed the presence of significant amounts of caustic and corrosive materials. During their examination of the site, EPA and MDNR officials observed drums and tanks housing cyanide littered among disarray outside the facility. Based on their observations outside the building, the officials determined that Northernaire had discharged its electroplating waste into a 'catch' basin and that the waste had seeped into the ground from the bottom of the basin. The waste then entered a pipe that drained into a sewer line that discharged into the sewage treatment plant for the city of Cadillac." Meyer, 889 F.2d at 1498–99.

In the former appeal, this court affirmed the decision of the trial court finding that the damage to the site had been "indivisible" and imposing joint and several liability on the present parties to reimburse the EPA for the removal costs for the cleanup of the building.

* * * In this subsequent contribution action, the trial court held that two-thirds of the liability should be borne by Northernaire and its principal shareholder, each contributing one-third each. But the court held that the remaining one-third ($114,274.41) should be borne by the appellant property owner.

The appellant attacks this apportionment, arguing strenuously that its responsibility should be limited to an amount apportioned according to the degree that the sewer line mentioned in the above quote contributed to the cleanup costs. Applying this approach, the appellant generously offers to pay $1,709.03. Appellees accept the trial court's apportionment.

* * *

ANALYSIS

The trial court held that it was within its discretion to apply certain factors found in the legislative history of CERCLA in making its contribution apportionment. Although these factors were originally intended as criteria for deciding whether a party could establish a right to an apportionment of several liability in the EPA's initial removal action, the trial court found "these criteria useful in determining the proportionate share each party is entitled to in contribution from the other."

The criteria mentioned are: (1) the ability of the parties to demonstrate that their contribution to a discharge release or disposal of a hazardous waste can be distinguished; (2) the amount of the hazardous waste involved; (3) the degree of toxicity of the hazardous waste involved; (4) the degree of involvement by the parties in the generation, transportation, treatment, storage, or disposal of the hazardous waste; (5) the degree of care exercised by the parties with respect to the hazardous waste concerned, taking into account the characteristics of such hazardous waste; and (6) the degree of cooperation by the parties with Federal, State, or local officials to prevent any harm to the public health or the environment.

The trial court recognized that the lessee was the primary actor in allowing this site to become contaminated. (Appellant argues that the lessee was the only actor.) The trial court found, however, that in addition to constructing the defective sewer line which contributed to the contamination, appellant bore significant responsibility "simply by virtue of being the landowner." The trial court observed further that appellant "neither assisted nor cooperated with the EPA officials during their investigation and eventual cleanup of the * * * site."

Chief Judge Hillman concluded, "As it is well within the province of this court, I have balanced each of the defendants' behavior with respect to the equitable guidelines discussed." As a result of the balancing, he made the apportionment described above.

The trial judge was well within the broad discretion afforded by the statute in making the apportionment he did.

Congress intended to invest the district courts with this discretion in making CERCLA contribution allocations when it provided, "the court may allocate response costs among the liable parties using such equitable factors as the *court determines are appropriate*." 42 U.S.C. § 9613(f)(1) (emphasis added)

Essentially, appellant argues here that a narrow, technical construction must be given to the term "contribution," so that, as in common law contribution, contribution under the statute is limited to the percentage a party's improper conduct causally contributed to the toxicity of the site in a physical sense. This argument is without merit. On the contrary, by using the term "equitable factors" Congress intended to invoke the tradition of equity under which the court must construct a flexible decree balancing all the equities in the light of the totality of the circumstances.

* * *

[U]nder § 9613(f)(1) the court may consider any factor it deems in the interest of justice in allocating contribution recovery. Certainly, the several factors listed by the trial court are appropriate, but as it recognized, it was not limited to them. No exhaustive list of criteria need or should be formulated. However, in addition to the criteria listed above, the court may consider the state of mind of the parties, their economic status, any contracts between them bearing on the subject, any traditional equitable defenses as mitigating factors and any other factors deemed appropriate to balance the equities in the totality of the circumstances.

Therefore, the trial court quite properly considered here not only the appellant's contribution to the toxic slough described above in a technical causative sense, but also its moral contribution as the owner of the site. Review of the trial court's equitable balancing process is limited to a review for "abuse of discretion." This is in accord with the principle of equity that the chancellor has broad discretion to frame a decree.

This case, even though it involves over $300,000, is but a pimple on the elephantine carcass of the CERCLA litigation now making its way through the court system. Some of these cases involve millions or even billions of dollars in cleanup costs and hundreds or even thousands of potentially responsible parties.

I do not believe Congress intended to require meticulous findings of the precise causative contribution each of several hundred parties made to a hazardous site. In many cases, this would be literally impossible. Rather, by the expansive language used in § 9613(f)(1) Congress intended the court to deal with these situations by creative means, considering all the equities and balancing them in the interests of justice. * * *

Although such an approach "cannot be applied with mathematical precision," it is the fairest and most workable approach for apportioning CERCLA liability. Such an approach furthers the legislative intent of encouraging the prompt cleanup of hazardous sites by those equitably responsible. The parties actually performing the cleanup can look for reimbursement from other potentially responsible parties without fear that their contribution actions will be bogged down by the impossibility of making meticulous factual determinations as to the causal contribution of each party. Chief Judge Hillman was well within the equitable discretion afforded him by Congress in the way he handled this CERCLA contribution action.

Affirmed.

Note and Questions

Meyer is atypical in terms of the small number of parties and the relatively simple facts. For prior history in the *Meyer* case, see United States v. Northernaire Plating Co., 670 F.Supp. 742 (W.D.Mich.1987), affirmed sub nom. United States v. R.W. Meyer, Inc., 889 F.2d 1487 (6th Cir.1989), cert. denied 494 U.S. 1057, 110 S.Ct. 1527, 108 L.Ed.2d 767 (1990). Judge Guy in *Meyer* wrote a concurring opinion joined in by the third member of the panel. In it he concludes that the trial court had erroneously found that defects in the sewer line had contributed to Northernaire's inability to remove hazardous waste from the building because it was the city's revocation of Northernaire's permit, not Meyer's faulty sewer line, that contributed to its failure to properly dispose of its wastes. Nevertheless, he agreed with the trial court's allocation because Meyer was not in reality an "absentee" landlord but had involved itself in assuring that Northernaire could undertake its operations. Judge Guy also relies on Restatement (Second) of Torts § 886A, which provides that "no tortfeasor can be required to make contribution beyond his own equitable share of the liability." Finding that the facts revealed "that Meyer was instrumental in efforts to bring Northernaire to Cadillac, was fully aware of the nature of the manufacturing to be conducted on the site, built the building that housed the facility, and failed to construct or maintain an adequate sewer line," he concluded that Meyer's relative culpability justified the trial court's allocation.

2. APPROACHES TO ALLOCATING COSTS

Meyer illustrates that there are various methods which a court might adopt for allocating damages that satisfy the statutory requirement of applying "equitable factors." The following represent the major alternatives:

a. *Per Capita*

This approach is the simplest and requires only the division of damages by the number of PRPs, with each paying an equal share. This method finds support in the Uniform Contribution Among Tortfeasors Act § 2, 12 U.L.A. 87 (1975) (UCATA) which was adopted in 1955, before most states enacted comparative fault statutes. Does this approach fulfill Congress' objectives under CERCLA § 113(f)?

b. *Comparative Fault*

This method requires a court to distribute liability among PRPs in accordance with each PRP's relative degree of fault in causing harm at the site. This method is reflected in the 1977 Uniform Comparative Fault Act §§ 1–10, 12 U.L.A. 39 (Supp. 1990) (UCFA). While this approach has obvious appeal from the perspective of fairness, it places an administrative burden on courts because of the necessity of examining each party's conduct. The UCFA scheme is not limited to negligence or reckless conduct, but also includes as "fault" acts or omissions which subject a party to strict liability. UCFA § 1(b), 12 U.L.A. 41. If a PRP is insolvent or absent from the action, the UCFA requires that its share be redistributed among all of the remaining PRPs according to their degrees of fault, rather than requiring the contribution plaintiff to bear all of that loss.

c. *Comparative Causation*

This method allocates damages by looking to the amount and characteristics of hazardous substances each party has contributed to the site. Under this approach the court must analyze largely technical and scientific information on volume, toxicity, interaction among chemical substances, and the like. Recall that in *Monsanto*, the Fourth Circuit observed how difficult and unnecessary it was for the district court to attempt to make an allocation on that basis. However, CERCLA § 122(e)(3) of CERCLA, which relates to settlement procedures and the EPA's development of non-binding allocations of responsibility (NBARs), does provide some support for use of this methodology.

d. *Gore Amendment*

Quoted in *Meyer*, this proposed amendment to CERCLA sponsored by then Representative Albert Gore (D. Tenn.) (Vice President) would have required the application of six criteria in determining the divisibility of response costs: (1) a PRP's ability to demonstrate that its contribution to the harm at a site can be distinguished from that of other PRPs; (2) the amount of hazardous waste attributable to the PRP; (3) the toxicity of that waste; (4) the PRP's involvement in the generation, transportation, treatment, storage, or disposal of the waste; (5) the degree of care that the PRP exercised with respect to the waste; and (6) the extent to which the PRP cooperated with government officials in preventing further harm. The Gore Amendment approach combines the comparative causation method (three technical factors that look only to the characteristics of the waste) with the comparative fault method (three conduct factors that look to the defendant's fault).

What other factors did *Meyer* add to these six? What other factors might be appropriate? Despite the fact that Congress did not enact the Amendment, it has received some acknowledgement in judicial opinions as evidenced by *Meyer*. Consistent with *Meyer*, the courts have repeatedly held that they are not bound to any particular set of factors, nor must they apply any particular test in allocating response costs. In Environmental Transp. Systems, Inc. v. ENSCO, Inc., 969 F.2d 503 (7th Cir.1992), the court stated that the "Gore factors are neither an exhaustive nor exclusive list," and pointed out that they had been originally proposed as elements bearing on divisibility of harm so as to defeat joint and several liability to the government, not for the purpose of allocating costs among those determined to be jointly and severally liable. The court in *ENSCO* also explicitly rejected applying a pro rata test in favor of a case-by-case approach that would "weigh and consider relevant factors, including fault, in order to effectuate Congress' intent." Nevertheless, it observed that "there may be cases in which a pro rata apportionment in a contribution action is appropriate."

Other examples of equitable factors identified by courts in interpreting § 113(f) include: B.F. Goodrich Co. v. Murtha, 958 F.2d 1192 (2d Cir.1992) (court may consider an array of factors including the financial resources of the parties involved); CPC Int'l, Inc. v. Aerojet–General Corp., 777 F.Supp. 549 (W.D.Mich.1991) (listing responsible party's degree of involvement in disposal of hazardous waste, amount of hazardous waste involved, and degree of care exercised by the parties); Weyerhaeuser Co. v. Koppers Co., 771 F.Supp. 1420, 1426 (D.Md.1991) (indicating as important factors the benefits received by the parties from contaminating activities and the knowledge and/or acquiescence of the parties in the contaminating activities). For further exploration of these issues of allocation, see Note, Contribution Under CERCLA, 14 Colum. J. Envtl. L. 267 (1990) (quoted in *Meyer*); Ellen J. Garber, Federal Common Law of Contribution Under the 1986 CERCLA Amendments,

14 Ecology L.Q. 365, 366 (1987); Elizabeth F. Mason, Note, Contribution Protection and Non–Settlor Liability Under CERCLA, 19 B.C. Envtl. Aff. L. Rev. 73 (1991).

3. CAUSATION IN CONTRIBUTION ACTIONS

The causation question in private actions was considered in Farmland Industries, Inc. v. Morrison–Quirk Grain Corp., 987 F.2d 1335 (8th Cir.1993).   In *Farmland*, the EPA had originally sued Morrison for response costs, in which action the district court found it to be a PRP as an owner during the time that a disposal of hazardous substances had occurred on the site, but had not made any determination that it had caused the contamination.   Farmland and Morrison subsequently filed cross actions for indemnity or contribution for response costs already incurred and any future response costs.   Morrison had owned and used the site for a grain storage and liquid fumigant facility, which Farmland later acquired.   Sometime during the Morrison's and Farmland's respective periods of ownership, 2500 gallons of the fumigants had been released.   In its private cross action Farmland had sought an issue preclusion ruling on Morrison's liability based on the EPA's successful suit.   The court of appeals rejected that argument by pointing out that liability in the government action is strict and does not depend on any showing of causation or fault, and therefore, the EPA's action did not determine that Morrison had caused the contamination at the site.

The court stated that the issue of whether Morrison should be liable to Farmland for any expenses incurred as a result of contamination at the subsite is inextricably linked to causation.   The district court, however, had specifically refused to consider issues of causation in the EPA's suit, but had ruled that Morrison was a responsible party under CERCLA § 107.   The court of appeals concluded that the jury instructions were erroneous because they incorrectly stated the law governing the allocation of costs between private parties.   The trial court instructed the jury on Morrison's claim against Farmland by defining the elements in terms of the causation of "response costs," when the proper inquiry was the causation of the contamination at the site:

> Reading these instructions together, we are forced to conclude that the district court's instructions were, at least, incomplete.   The second paragraph of this counterclaim instruction, read in conjunction with the previous case instruction, made it difficult, if not impossible, for the jury to find for Morrison.   The court had already told the jury that as a matter of law Morrison "caused the United States to incur response costs," and that Morrison was "a person responsible" for those costs.   Therefore, without further explanation of the CERCLA statutory scheme, the jury may have had difficulty concluding that Farmland was "the sole cause of the incurrence of response costs by Morrison–Quirk."   Had the district court given more detailed instructions on the various facets of CERCLA liability, or had it explained the difference between the standards for liability

to the government under section 9607 and for liability to a third party under section 9613, these instructions might have been a harmless error. In the absence of further direction, these instructions tended to be confusing, and, therefore, could have resulted in prejudice to Morrison.

The court also found objectionable the trial court's use of the term "person responsible" without explaining that in CERCLA lexicon its meaning differs from common parlance.

4. RIGHTS TO A JURY TRIAL

While there is no guarantee of a right to a jury trial in a CERCLA cost recovery case, at least one court has held that there is a right to jury trial in contribution actions under CERCLA § 113(f). In United States v. Shaner, 23 Envtl. L. Rep. 20, 236, 1992 WL 154618 (E.D.Pa.1992), the court stated that use of the term "equitable factors" in § 113(f) did not convert the action to one in equity because the essence of the contribution action is a tort action for damages. Accord In re Acushnet River & New Bedford Harbor, 712 F.Supp. 994 (D.Mass.1989) (holding that jury trial rights exist for natural resource damage actions because they are legal in nature, but not for cost recovery actions because they seek restitution). Is it relevant that contribution actions under the Federal Tort Claims Act against the United States permit jury trials? See Globig v. Greene & Gust Co., 184 F.Supp. 530 (E.D.Wis.1960) (contribution actions are legal not equitable in nature, and rights to a jury trial attach to such actions). Why should parties to cost recovery actions not have a right to a jury trial, but parties in a contribution action have such rights?

5. EFFECT OF SETTLEMENT WITH THE GOVERNMENT

In 1986 Congress added settlement provisions expressly authorizing EPA to enter into settlement agreements with PRPs to clean up sites if it is in the public interest. If the EPA can obtain all or nearly all of the cleanup costs without resorting to protracted litigation it may expedite remedial actions and minimize transaction costs. CERCLA encourages private parties to settle in five ways: (1) by allocating response costs among the PRPs, which avoids joint and several liability; (2) making partial settlements available in some circumstances; (3) releasing settling parties by giving covenants not to sue; (4) creating protection from contribution actions; and (5) giving de minimis contributors favorable treatment.

To help achieve settlement, CERCLA § 122(e)(3) authorizes the EPA to prepare non-binding allocations of responsibility (NBARs) which allocate 100 percent of the response costs among PRPs. In making allocations, the EPA is not limited by so-called "indivisible" harm (which it advances in litigation) but rather is permitted to allocate costs among classes of PRPs by applying various factors including: volume, toxicity, mobility, strength of evidence, ability to pay, litigative risks, public interest considerations, precedential value, inequities, and aggravating factors. In addressing classes of PRPs, it allocates first among generators based on volume; it then adjusts those allocations based on the equitable criteria above; it then factors in transporter, owner and operator participation. For owners and generators, EPA examines the length of time of ownership or operation and the degree of involvement and knowledge of the disposal of hazardous substances. Lastly, EPA reallocates the shares of "orphans," insolvent or absent PRPs among the remaining solvent parties. See Daniel R. Hansen, CERCLA Cost Allocation and Nonparties Responsibility: Who Bears the Orphan Shares, 91 J. Envtl. L. 37 (1992).

If a settlement is reached, the EPA may grant a release from present and future liability, if such a covenant not to sue is in the "public interest," a term defined in the statute. See CERCLA § 122(f)(4). However, releases are required to contain a "reopener" provision, except under "extraordinary circumstances." CERCLA § 122(f)(6)(A).

Of special relevance for our purposes is the effect which settlement with the government may have on a private party's exposure to future contribution actions.

a. Effect of Settlement on Contribution

(i) CERCLA 's Provisions

CERCLA's settlement provisions influence contribution in two ways: (1) those PRPs who settle are immune from contribution actions by nonsettling PRPs who litigate with the EPA and end up paying more than their "equitable" share of the cleanup costs; and (2) the amount which the settling PRPs pay will be applied to reduce the liability of the nonsettlors. These points are explicitly covered in CERCLA § 113(f)(2) which states:

> A person who has resolved its liability to the United States or a State in an administrative or judicially approved settlement shall not be liable for claims for contribution regarding matters addressed in the settlement. Such settlement does not discharge any of the other potentially liable persons unless its terms so provide, but it reduces the potential liability of the others by the amount of the settlement.

In United States v. Cannons Engineering Corp., 899 F.2d 79 (1st Cir.1990), the court held that the language "amount of the settlement" requires only a dollar-for-dollar reduction. Is the language capable of any other interpretation? See *Cannons Engineering* for a thorough discussion of settlement procedures.

(ii)   Judicial Review of Settlements

Settlements are not always approved by the courts precisely because they are found to unfairly allocate the costs of cleanups. For example, in New York v. SCA Services, 36 ERC 1439, 1993 WL 59407 (S.D.N.Y. 1993), the court considered the government's request to enter a consent judgment settling CERCLA claims with third-party waste generators. The site also involved a transporter that had borne the bulk of the cleanup costs, and the court stressed that private parties would not accept such responsibility if they confronted the risk of such an unfair settlement. In reviewing the standards for approval of the consent judgment, the court reviewed the fairness of its terms, including fairness to non-settling parties. The court found the settlement terms unfair, noting that the "settling third-party defendants comprise 20 out of the 24 known generators of hazardous waste materials disposed at the site, and over 90% of the hazardous waste materials."

While SCA bears a "major responsibility" for the site problems, the court continued, "it is also significant that the hazardous materials generated and disposed of by the settling third-party defendants would have been disposed of at some site and required response costs in that event." The consent judgment "does not come close to reflecting this division of responsibility for pollution at the site." The generators of more than 90% of the waste would be excused for less than one-third of the past costs of response, leaving the few non-settling third-party defendants the remaining two thirds. Although SCA may seek contribution from the settling defendants for certain future RI/FS costs, this fact did not reduce the "gross inequity of the proposed settlement's distribution of past costs and [natural resource damage] liability."

(iii)   Matters Settled

Another question respecting the effect of a settlement is determining what "matters" are settled. CERCLA § 113(f)(2) states that settling PRPs are not liable for contribution to non-settlors regarding "matters addressed in the settlement." The matters addressed would seem to necessarily include: the hazardous substance(s) at the site; the particular site involved; the time period covered by the settlement; and the costs of the cleanup. Consequently, a non-settlor may not be precluded from pursuing a contribution action if it can establish that the settlement did not cover the subject matter of the contribution action. See, e.g., United States v. Union Gas Co., 743 F.Supp. 1144 (E.D.Pa.1990); Burlington Northern R. Co. v. Time Oil Co., 738 F.Supp. 1339 (W.D.Wash.1990).

For example, in Transtech Industries, Inc. v. A & Z Septic Clean, 798 F.Supp. 1079 (D.N.J.1992), the 221 contribution defendants had entered into a consent decree with the United States paying $4.9 million which covered the government's claims "for Past Response Costs and Past Response Actions and for any administrative costs and civil penalties which may have accrued prior to April 30, 1987 * * *." The court held that the plaintiff, who had paid $13 million to clean up the site, which included costs not accrued at the date in the decree, could maintain the contribution action under § 113(f) against the settling parties.

While non-settlors lose their right to contribution, settling PRPs retain their contribution rights and may sue non-settlors to distribute some of the damages they paid.

b.   Diversity of Views on Non–settlor Liability

(i) Dollar Reduction

Cannons Engineering, supra, held what represents the majority view that CERCLA § 113(f)(2) reduces non-settlors liability by the dollar amount of the settlement. This view incorporates the principles of the UCATA § 4, which prescribes a dollar-for-dollar reduction, which may result in non-settlors bearing a disproportionate share of the cost of cleanup. In United States v. Rohm & Haas Co., 721 F.Supp. 666 (D.N.J.1989), the district court, in approving a partial settlement, concluded that Congress had purposefully incorporated UCATA § 4 into CERCLA, mandating that courts bar non-settlors' claims for contribution and credit non-settlors "with the amount of the settlement and nothing more," notwithstanding that non-settlors would be stuck bearing more than their equitable share of the costs. In *Rohm & Haas*, the court also rejected application of the UCFA method of crediting non-settlors a proportionate reduction because it found that Congress had expressly chosen language more closely tracking the UCATA. Moreover, it believed that the UCFA method would disserve CERCLA's goals of minimizing litigation and promoting voluntary settlements because it would compel the government to litigate with non-settlors the issue of whether the settlors had paid their proportionate share. Do you understand why this would discourage settlements? What might be the consequence on the recovery of all cleanup costs if a court later held that settling PRPs had paid less than their equitable shares? Is the non-settlor any worse off than it would be if the government had sued it initially and sought complete cleanup costs under the rule of joint and several liability? See Central Illinois Public Service Co. v. Industrial Oil Tank & Line Cleaning Service, 730 F.Supp. 1498 (W.D.Mo.1990) (suggesting that it is not); Allied Corp. v. Frola, 730 F.Supp. 626, 638 (D.N.J.1990) ("Since the non-settlors remain jointly and severally liable, they must make good the balance regardless of whether the settlor pays less than its proportionate share of liability.").

(ii) Proportionate Reduction

A few courts have declined to adopt the UCATA-based analysis and instead give the non-settlors the benefit of a proportionate share reduction in their potential liability. Illustrating that approach is Allied Corp.

v. ACME Solvent Reclaiming, Inc., 771 F.Supp. 219 (N.D.Ill.1991), where the court ruled that when some defendants in a private CERCLA cost-recovery action settle their liability to the plaintiffs, they are entitled to protection from contribution claims of any other defendants, and that the liability of the non-settling defendants is reduced by the equitable share of liability attributable to the settling defendants, as later determined at the trial of the non-settlors, rather than by the dollar amount of the settlement. In so ruling, the court adopted the approach of the UCFA rather than that of the UCATA.

Although CERCLA § 113(f)(2) is modeled on the UCATA, the court said that this applied only to settlements with the federal or state government and not to private party actions. The court stressed that CERCLA's contribution protection provision "expressly applies to settlements with the federal or state government, and the statute is silent as to its applicability to private party settlements." It said that a uniform federal rule of contribution should be developed independently of state contribution and settlement law. The court chose to follow those cases that viewed the UCFA, rather than the UCATA, as being more consistent with CERCLA. Moreover, it observed that applying the comparative fault approach would eliminate the necessity of holding a hearing to determine the fairness of the initial settlement, since a non-settling party will only be held liable for its equitable share, not the entire amount not paid in the settlement.

Which approach do you find more persuasive—*Cannons Engineering* and *Rohm & Haas*, or *ACME Solvent*? Does it make sense to have one rule for government settlements and a different one for private settlements?

(iii) Settlement Criteria

The courts evaluate the overall procedural and substantive fairness and reasonableness of the consent decrees that embody the settlements. See *Cannons Engineering* for a discussion of this process. Courts typically evaluate these decrees according to a set of criteria which include the following: (1) the relative costs and benefits of litigating the case; (2) the strength of the government's case against the settling PRPs; (3) the degree to which the bargain between the government and PRP negotiators was conducted in good faith, at arm's-length, and with candor and openness; (4) the rational relationship of the settlement amount to a plausible, if inaccurate, estimate of the settlors' volumetric contribution of wastes to the site; (5) the ability of the settlors to satisfy an even larger judgment; and (6) finally, the degree to which the settlement serves the public interest. See *Rohm & Haas*, supra; United States v. Acton Corp., 733 F.Supp. 869 (D.N.J.1990); In re Acushnet River & New Bedford Harbor, 712 F.Supp. 1019, (D.Mass.1989) (proposing settlement criteria); Kelley v. Thomas Solvent Co., 717 F.Supp. 507 (W.D.Mich.1989) (proposing settlement criteria).

(iv) Contribution Protection and Notice

On the point also considered in *Cannons Engineering, Rohm & Haas*, and *Acme Solvent* respecting contribution protection afforded to settling PRPs, the courts have held that the protection against future contribution action applies to later claims brought by non-settling PRPs even though the non-settlors had no actual notice of the settlement. In United States v. Serafini, 781 F.Supp. 336 (M.D.Pa.1992), the court ruled that the contribution protection accorded settling parties by CERCLA section 113(f) extends even to such claims brought by parties who had no actual notice of the settlement or of the fact that they might be potentially responsible parties. The court also held that the cross-claim plaintiffs' rights to due process and equal protection were not violated. But see, General Time Corp. v. Bulk Materials, Inc., 826 F.Supp. 471 (M.D.Ga.1993) (holding non-settlor could pursue contribution action against settling PRP when it was given no notice or opportunity to comment on an administrative settlement).

It has also been held that the contribution protection afforded by CERCLA § 113(f) extends not only to contribution suits brought under CERCLA, but also to claims based on *state* law. See United States v. Alexander, 771 F.Supp. 830 (S.D.Tex.1991), vacated on other grounds 981 F.2d 250 (5th Cir.1993). Thus, state law contribution claims based on nuisance, negligence or strict liability will be barred against any PRP that has entered a settlement agreement with the government. Would that bar personal injury claims? Why or why not?

(v) Effect of Private Partial Settlements

Can a private party that has settled with a private plaintiff, but has not reimbursed all of the plaintiff's cleanup costs, maintain a contribution action against third parties? In Amland Properties Corp. v. Aluminum Co. of America, 808 F.Supp. 1187 (D.N.J.1992), the court answered in the negative. It observed that CERCLA § 113(f)(3)(B) expressly authorizes those who settle their liability to the United States or a State to seek contribution from persons not party to the settlement "for some or all of a response action * * * or for some or all of the costs of such action * * *." Thus, when a settlement with the government precedes the contribution action, the settlor's right to contribution does not depend on whether it had extinguished all claims the government may have against other parties. However, the court said § 113(f)(1) is silent as to the settling party's right to seek contribution against defendants whose liability has not been extinguished. It continued:

> In contrast, Congress created a general right of contribution in private party actions but declined to include a provision which would secure that right for settlements of less than the entire action. This is particularly important in light of the fact that the great weight of common law and statutory authority prior to the Superfund amend-

ments adhered to the requirement that a settling party must have at least extinguished the plaintiff's claims against the party from whom contribution is sought. See, e.g., Restatement (Second) of Torts § 886A(2) ("The right of contribution exists only in favor of a tortfeasor who has discharged the entire claim for the harm by paying more than his equitable share of the common liability * * * "); Uniform Contribution Among Tortfeasors Act § 1(d), 12 U.L.A. 63 (1975) ("A tortfeasor who enters into a settlement with a claimant is not entitled to recover contribution from another tortfeasor whose liability for the injury or wrongful death is not extinguished by the settlement nor in respect to any amount paid in a settlement which is in excess of what was reasonable."); Uniform Comparative Fault Act § 4(b), 12 U.L.A. 53 (Supp. 1992) ("Contribution is available to a person who enters a settlement with a claimant only (1) if the liability of the person against whom contribution is sought has been extinguished and (2) to the extent that the amount paid in settlement was reasonable."). The clear implication to be drawn is that Congress did not intend to alter these clear and ringing principles of contribution in actions between private parties.

What rationale, apart from Congressional silence, might support the court's rule? Later in its opinion the court observed that allowing such contribution actions "could spawn even more litigation, as parties scramble to redistribute liability in any number of directions." Why might more litigation ensue? The one underlying rationale for the court's approach is that of prohibiting a party that has settled for no more than its appropriate equitable share of liability from seeking contribution from other parties who might yet be found to be liable to the original plaintiff, thereby exposing such third-party defendants to a disproportionate share of liability.

What if the statute of limitations has already run against the third parties so that they could not be sued by the original plaintiff? In fact, in *Amland* that was true, but the court found it immaterial. Does the court's opinion conflict with the language of CERCLA § 113(f)(1), which allows "any person" to seek contribution from "any other person who is liable or potentially liable" under CERCLA § 107, "during or following" any CERCLA action under § 106 or § 107? If such a claim may be brought *during* the action against the original defendant, how could that defendant have already resolved the entire claim of the plaintiff, so as to have completely extinguished any liability that might exist on the part of the third-party defendants?

F. INDEMNIFICATION AGREEMENTS

1. THE STATUTORY PROVISION

Indemnification provisions are often used in transactions involving the acquisition of property to address unknown environmental and other liabilities relating to the assets and business transferred. Two key issues are raised by CERCLA's statutory language and decisions concerning the enforceability of indemnification agreements. First, are indemnification agreements barred by the language of CERCLA § 107(e)? Second, if CERCLA does not bar such agreements, should they, nonetheless, be construed narrowly?

CERCLA § 107(e)(1) provides:

> No indemnification, hold harmless, or similar agreement or conveyance shall be effective to transfer from the owner or operator of any vessel or facility or from any person who may be liable for a release or threat of release under this section, to any other person the liability imposed under this section. Nothing in this subsection shall bar any agreement to insure, hold harmless, or indemnify a party to such agreement for any liability under this section.

2. ARE SUCH AGREEMENTS PERMITTED UNDER CERCLA?

A majority of federal courts interpret § 107(e) as allowing indemnity agreements. Thus, as a consequence, indemnity agreements have become an integral part of real estate transactions. For example, in Mardan Corp. v. C.G.C. Music, Ltd., 804 F.2d 1454 (9th Cir.1986), a seller sold real property on which it had manufactured musical instruments and deposited waste. As part of the sale the purchaser agreed to release the seller from undisclosed environmental liabilities. After the EPA brought an enforcement action against the purchaser (which had also deposited waste on the property), the purchaser sued the seller under § 107 of CERCLA for recovery of its cleanup costs. The court of appeals affirmed a summary judgment for the seller:

> Contractual arrangements apportioning CERCLA liabilities between private "responsible parties" are essentially tangential to the enforcement of CERCLA's liability provisions. Such agreements cannot alter or excuse the underlying liability, but can only change who ultimately pays that liability.

Since the *Mardan* decision, most federal district courts to discuss the indemnity issue under CERCLA § 107 have accepted the *Mardan* rationale. See, e.g., Danella Southwest v. Southwestern Bell Telephone Co., 775 F.Supp. 1227 (E.D.Mo.1991); Versatile Metals, Inc. v. Union Corp., 693 F.Supp. 1563 (E.D.Pa.1988).

In AM International v. International Forging Equip. Corp., 982 F.2d 989 (6th Cir.1993) the Court of Appeals for the Sixth Circuit joined the chorus of those courts holding that § 107(e) does not bar indemnification agreements:

> The underlying purpose of the statutory language under scrutiny is to ensure that responsible parties will pay for the cleanup and that they may not avoid liability to the government by transferring this liability to another. However, this purpose is not inconsistent with parties responsible for the cleanup transferring or allocating among themselves the cost associated with this liability, so long as they

remain liable to the third party who can demand the cleanup. This is what is permitted by the second sentence—the shifting or allocation of the risk of the cost of liability between potentially responsible persons, without diluting CERCLA liability for the cleanup itself.

The Ninth Circuit reached the same conclusion in Jones–Hamilton Co. v. Beazer Materials & Services, Inc., 973 F.2d 688 (9th Cir.1992).

3. HOW SHOULD SUCH AGREEMENTS BE CONSTRUED?

Most of the courts that have considered the application of indemnification have applied, either explicitly or implicitly, a rule that such arrangements can stand as a bar to CERCLA liability only in the presence of clear language in the agreement anticipating and requiring such a result.

Judicial reluctance to release parties from hazardous waste liability is reflected in the Sixth Circuit's decision in *AM International*. In that case, plaintiff AMI, which had leased a manufacturing facility, sold its assets "as is" to defendants in 1982, and in 1984 provided defendants a release of all claims "of every kind and description, known or unknown" in settlement of various outstanding disputes in return for a payment of $2 to $3 million. AMI later agreed to perform a cleanup of the facility and sued defendants for contribution. The Sixth Circuit held that even though the release was not barred under CERCLA, it may not be effective as to unanticipated environmental claims:

> Under Ohio case law, even where a release contains unambiguous language that purports to bar claims based on unknown future causes, the release will not be effective where evidence clearly indicates that, at the time they signed the release, the parties had neither foreseen nor considered the specific cause which later gave rise to the claim.

The court stated further, "the fact that events causing the harm upon which liability is predicated has not occurred at the time of the signing of a release is strong evidence that the parties did not intend the release to bar such liability."

In interpreting release and indemnification agreements, courts have been reluctant to apply those agreements to CERCLA liability absent a finding that the agreement expressly provided for a release of such liabilities or, at a minimum, of "CERCLA-like" environmental liabilities. See Mobay Corp. v. Allied-Signal Inc., 761 F.Supp. 345 (D.N.J.1991); Southland Corp. v. Ashland Oil Inc., 696 F.Supp. 994 (D.N.J.1988). This is a particular concern in cases in which the agreement at issue was entered into before enactment of CERCLA and in the absence of knowledge of the potential for CERCLA-like liabilities. See Westwood Pharmaceuticals, Inc. v. National Fuel Gas Dist. Corp., 737 F.Supp. 1272 (W.D.N.Y.1990), affirmed 964 F.2d 85 (2d Cir.1992); Wiegmann & Rose Int'l v. NL Industries, 735 F.Supp. 957 (N.D.Cal.1990).

How narrowly should courts construe such indemnification agreements? If CERCLA is not interpreted to preclude the private allocations of cleanup expenses, what limitations should courts place on their enforcement? If an indemnity agreement is negotiated after CERCLA's enactment and with the explicit transference of CERCLA-like liabilities, how will the seller actually "pay" for its pollution? Should bargaining power be treated as a factor in enforcing indemnity agreements between liable parties? What if the language of the agreement mentions CERCLA-type liabilities, but in fact neither party was aware of any facts—i.e., the existence of contamination—that might trigger liability? See Thaddeus Bereday, Contractual Transfers of Liability Under CERCLA Section 107(e)(1): For Enforcement of Private Risk Allocation in Real Property Transactions, 43 Case W. Res. L. Rev. 161 (1993).

Problem

In 1985 Carey Recycling Products (CRP) acquired some of the business assets of Western Metals Co. (Western), which related to buying and reselling scrap metals and used batteries. As part of the purchase CRP agreed to "assume all liabilities for or arising from claims related to the assets to be acquired, their condition and/or the processing of inventory from any and all sources whether related to events, conditions occurrences arising or accruing before or after closing and regardless of whether based on statute, regulatory or common law."

Three years after the sale, Western was targeted as a potentially responsible party under Superfund for a battery recycling site in Richmond, Columbia. Western seeks indemnification from CRP. The latter refuses, and both parties have filed actions in United States District Court seeking declaratory judgments of non-liability.

CRP argues that the "processing of inventory" phrase only requires CRP to indemnify Western for acts done to prepare the inventory for sale. Because the environmental liabilities at issue resulted from Western's sale of inventory to contaminated facilities, the express terms of the indemnification provision exclude such liabilities.

CRP points out that the liability for which Western seeks indemnity does not stem from the sale of inventory, but rather from Western's arranging for the disposal of hazardous substances (i.e., inventory) at contaminated off-site facilities.

Facts also show that CRP was eager to buy Western without much negotiation, and was confident that its knowledge of Western's operations would protect it from any unforeseen liabilities.

Who has the better of the argument? Should a court enforce an indemnification agreement on these facts? What considerations are most important in resolving that question?

G. INFORMATIONAL IMPORTANCE OF CERCLA

One of the most significant impacts of CERCLA on toxic tort litigation is the Act's creation of the Agency for Toxic Substances and Disease Registry, which is established under CERCLA § 104(i)(1).

1. OVERVIEW OF THE ATSDR

The ATSDR, a federal public health agency, is part of the Public Health Service within the United States Department of Health and Human Services and was created to address Congress' concern respecting the adverse health consequences of hazardous waste sites. The ATSDR is required to maintain a registry of persons who have been exposed to hazardous substances and have serious illnesses, conduct studies on the health effects of toxic substances found at waste sites, and conduct periodic screening programs to determine the relationship between exposure to these substances and human illnesses.

The ATSDR evaluates data and information on the release of hazardous substances to assess the impact on the public health, and identifies studies or actions needed to evaluate or prevent human health effects. To carry out that objective, the ATSDR is mandated to work with the EPA to develop and place, in priority order, a list of hazardous substances found at National Priorities List (NPL) sites. In developing this hazardous substance priority list, the ATSDR and the EPA use the following criteria to rank the substances by potential human health risk: (1) frequency of occurrence at NPL sites; (2) toxicity; and (3)potential for human exposure to the substance. See 56 Fed. Reg. 52168, No. 201 (Oct. 17, 1991). Because these criteria define human health risk of the substance in terms of its toxicity and human exposure potential, they have significance for toxic tort litigation since those substances which have been most frequently the subject of litigation will be the ones of highest priority to the ATSDR.

The ATSDR is also required to conduct health assessments for all waste sites on the NPL. One example of a recent health assessment that illustrates the potential utility of the ATSDR activities to toxic tort cases is the ATSDR investigation of the radiological and chemical hazards associated with the Navajo–Brown Vanderer uranium mines in New Mexico. After the preliminary investigation, the ATSDR prepared a public health advisory to inform the EPA, the Navajo Nation, the Indian Health Service (IHS), the Bureau of Indian Affairs, the State of New Mexico, and the public of the potential environmental health hazards associated with radioactive materials, heavy metal soil contamination, and varied physical hazards. The ATSDR recommended that further studies be undertaken to determine the extent of the radioactive contamination and that residents be provided with personal radiation dosimeters and radon detection devices to begin estimating external radiation exposure. See U.S. Dept. of Health & Human Services, Agency for Toxic Substances and Disease Registry, Biennial Report 1989–1990 at 37–38.

2. HEALTH INVESTIGATIONS; TOXICOLOGICAL PROFILES

Under CERCLA, the administrator of the ATSDR is required to prepare and submit a report to Congress and the EPA describing the results of Agency activities regarding: (1) health assessments and pilot health effect studies; (2) epidemiological studies; and (3) hazardous substances listed, toxicological profiles developed and toxicological testing conducted or being conducted. This third item is extremely significant because the ATSDR is mandated to prepare toxicological profiles of all ATSDR priority substances and to assure that a research program is initiated to fill identified needs for information associated with these substances. CERCLA § 104(i)(3) requires that each toxicological profile include an examination, summary, and interpretation of available toxicological information and epidemiologic evaluations. The profiles must also include a determination of whether adequate information on the health effects of each substance is available and, if not, the ATSDR, in cooperation with the National Toxicology Program (NTP), is required to assure the initiation of research to determine these health effects.

By 1992 the EPA had completed over 130 of the toxicological profiles required under the 1986 CERCLA amendments. The profiles include an array of data relevant to toxic tort litigation, including the physical and chemical properties of the substance in the air, water, and soil media, the pharmacokinetics of the substance, its toxicity to humans and animals, and a bibliography of important studies. These toxicologic profiles may be of tremendous long-term significance to toxic tort litigation of all kinds—mass and isolated cases, nuisance and occupational exposures, and even product liability cases. In addition, the ATSDR establishes and maintains a registry of persons exposed to hazardous substances and a registry of serious diseases and illnesses which such persons contract (§ 9604(i)(1)(A)). This information may also be important in toxic tort litigation to verify a plaintiff's exposure and illness.

Finally, the ATSDR is to report any assessments of increased incidence of adverse health effects that may be associated with released hazardous substances. Thus, through epidemiologic, surveillance, and toxicologic studies of toxic substances and their effects, the ATSDR will increase the understanding of the relationship between exposure to hazardous substances and adverse human health effects.

3. HEALTH ASSESSMENTS

The ATSDR is required to perform public health assessments of sites listed on the EPA's National Priorities List (NPL). CERCLA § 104(i)(6)(B) authorizes the Administrator of ATSDR to perform public health assessments of releases for which it receives information that individuals have been exposed to a hazardous substance, and for which the probable source of such exposure is a release, as defined under CERCLA. On the basis of a health assessment, the ATSDR may decide to conduct a pilot study to determine the desirability of conducting a full-scale epidemiological or other health effects study.

When a petition is received, a team of scientists gathers environmental and health information from local, state, and federal agencies. The information is presented to a screening committee which ascertains whether there is a reasonable basis for conducting a health assessment. To determine if there is such a reasonable basis, the ATSDR considers the following factors: (1) whether individuals have been exposed to hazardous substances; (2) the location, concentration, and toxicity of the hazardous substances; (3) the potential for further human exposure; (4) the recommendations of other governmental agencies; and (5) the ATSDR resources available and other ATSDR priorities. See 42 C.F.R. § 90.5. The first three factors dovetail with the needs of litigants because the existence of these factors strongly suggests that toxic tort litigation is a distinct possibility arising from the release of hazardous substances to which humans have been exposed. For further analysis of the role of the ATSDR in toxic tort litigation, see James A. Rogers, The Potential Role of Superfund in Toxic Tort Litigation, in The Environmental Law Manual, American Bar Association (Theodore Garrett ed., 1992) at 486–95; Gerald W. Boston, A Mass Exposure Model of Toxic Causation: The Content of Scientific Proof and the Regulatory Experience, 18 Colum. J. Envtl. L. 181 (1993).

Problem

Waste Managers, Inc. (WMI) owns and operates a hazardous waste disposal site on land which it acquired in 1970. WMI contracts with generators of hazardous waste to manage the disposal of their wastes at its site. WMI disposes of both liquid and solid wastes, with the liquid wastes contained in 55–gallon metal drums and the solid wastes in specially designed plastic bags and liners. The site also contains a double layer of plastic liners that are installed below the surface that creates an additional barrier between the liquid and solid wastes and the ground and groundwater below. WMI utilizes an inventory tracking system to track the contents of the generators' wastes that relies on the information furnished by the generator in the manifests which they prepare pursuant to federal and state hazardous waste acts, which set forth the quantity and identity of the wastes. WMI does not perform any tests of its own to verify the statements in the manifests respecting the content of the shipments.

WMI's principal customers and their wastes are as follows: Pestercides, Inc. ships primarily liquid hazardous wastes containing 2,3,4–T (trichlorophenoxy acetic acid), 2,3,7,8—TCDD (tetrachloro-p-dibenzodioxin (dioxin); Agrigro Inc. ships the same two wastes as Pestercides. Chemsanto Corp., ships wastes that are comprised of mercury, asbestos, trichloroethylene (TCE) and benzene. Bank Rupts, Inc. (BRI) has shipped a wide variety of wastes including dioxin and mercury, and has gone out of business in the past year. Cutting Edge Inc. (CEI) has shipped 2,3,4–T, dioxin, lead, and radium by-products, which are contained in specialized containers to assure that the by-products will not be released into the environment.   Before shipping its wastes to WMI, CEI conducted inspections of the site to assure itself of the safety and integrity of WMI's operations and procedures. Together, Pestercides, Agrigro, and Chemsanto account for 80 percent of the total volume of wastes at the site, and CEI and BRI account for most of the remainder.

Prior to WMI's acquisition of the land in 1970, the property was vacant. However, from 1930 to 1947 the property was part of a much larger parcel that contained a large aircraft parts manufacturing facility that produced precision parts for cockpits, including radium dials, instruments and instrument covering materials, such as asbestos.   That facility, owned by Air Parts Company, was acquired in 1947 by what has become a large conglomerate, United Instruments Co. (UIC).   UIC gradually phased out the instruments manufacturing business at that location, but continues to operate a large aircraft parts manufacturing division at other locations nationwide.   UIC converted the facility to a warehouse where it stored automobile and aircraft parts for shipment to locations throughout the country.   UIC sold the property in 1968 to a developer who envisaged the site as ideal for upscale residential housing because of its proximity to attractive streams and wooded hills.   UIC, as part of the sale, demolished and removed the warehouse.

By 1970, the developer had soured on building homes because of high mortgage interest rates and declining demand, and sold portions of the property to WMI.

In 1990, when WMI was expanding its operations, it unearthed radium tailings, lead and asbestos materials which had apparently been disposed of by Air Parts Co. When WMI acquired the property in 1970 it conducted only superficial inspections and testing of the land which did not reveal any of the recently discovered hazardous wastes.   The recent discoveries caused WMI to check more thoroughly into the history of the property and the nature of Air Part Co.'s usage.

In 1992 dioxin and lead has been found in soil in a new residential area adjacent to the site and in one of the nearby streams.   In addition, soil studies indicate that a number of toxic wastes including radium tailings, asbestos and TCE, have migrated from the WMI site to the neighboring properties.   TCE and lead wastes have been detected in wells used for drinking water as much as a mile away.

PART A

A neighborhood group is concerned about the potential for personal injury and property damage (including reduced property values) created by the WMI's site.   You are counsel for the neighborhood association.   Should you recommend to the association that it petition the EPA or state DNR to take some remedial action to clean up the site?

PART B

If the EPA decides that remediation is necessary and pays for the cleanup from the Superfund, from whom can it recoup these costs under § 107 of CERCLA?   From WMI?   From BRI?   From Agrigo, Pestercides, Chemsanto, and CEI?   What defenses will each assert?

PART C

Assume that the EPA has expended $3.5 million of Superfund moneys in the cleanup and the WMI has contributed, as a result of a settlement with the EPA, $2.5 million of that amount. WMI now wants to recoup that amount and any future amounts it may pay, since the settlement agreement with the EPA contains a "reopener" clause. Should WMI pursue a cost recovery action? Should it pursue a contribution action? What is the difference? Against whom? For how much? How successful is it likely to be?

PART D

Assume that the EPA has instituted an action against BRI, Chemsanto, Agrigo, and Pestercides to recover $1 million of the cleanup costs. How should they attempt to defend themselves against the action? Will they succeed? Can they obtain contribution? From whom?

Chapter Eleven

INSURANCE

A. INTRODUCTION

While questions regarding the nature and scope of insurance coverage are important in all tort contexts, insurance issues occupy center stage in toxic tort and environmental remediation litigation. As this Chapter will reveal, such litigation, involving billions of dollars in claims, has produced a wealth of disputes between insureds and insurers, implicating virtually every major aspect of the insurance contract. This Chapter identifies the principal areas of controversy that are engendered by at least three major types of underlying litigation: (1) tort suits involving defective or dangerous toxic products resulting in bodily injury or property damage, of which asbestos is the primary exemplar; (2) tort suits of the nuisance, trespass, or strict liability model involving the disposal of hazardous or toxic wastes or substances producing bodily injury or property damage; and (3) CERCLA actions, initiated by the government or a private party, involving the remediation of property that has been contaminated by release of hazardous wastes or substances.

When the insured becomes a defendant or party in one of these three genres of litigation, it seeks to shift all or part of the cost of defending the action and the payments of settlements or judgments to the insurer. This is typically done pursuant to comprehensive general liability (CGL) policies, which were renamed commercial general liability policies in the mid 1980s. These CGL policies were first introduced in the United States in the early 1940s, and have become the predominant source of insurance protection in three categories of coverage. The first category provides for the protection of the insured because of an injury or a loss suffered by a third party while an activity of the insured is in progress, and prior to the completion thereof, as the result of an act of negligence or an omission by the insured. Such an activity might be the disposal of hazardous waste as part of a manufacturing process. The second category, commonly referred to as "completed operations" coverage, deals with situations involving operations of the insured which have been completed, such as the installation of PCB-containing transformers or the construction of a landfill, and liability results thereafter either by reason of a defect in merchandise or improper workmanship. The third category is "products" coverage which pertains to products distributed in commerce where liability results from defects in the products causing bodily injury or property damage.

Early general liability policies used an accident-based insuring agreement whereby the insurer agreed to pay damages because of bodily injury or property damage "caused by an accident." In 1966, most insurers changed to an occurrence-based general liability form which read:

> [The insurer] hereby agrees to pay on behalf of the insured all sums which the insured shall become legally obligated to pay as damages because of (A.) bodily injury or (B.) property damage to which this insurance applies caused by an occurrence, and the [insurer] shall have the right and duty to defend any suit against the insured seeking damages on account of such bodily injury or property damage.

The typical grant of coverage provision was simplified in 1985 to read:

> [The insurer] hereby agrees to pay on behalf of the insured all sums which the insured shall become legally obligated to pay as damages because of bodily injury or property damage, to which the policy applies, caused by an occurrence.

As a general rule of insurance law, the insurer's duty to defend is broader than the duty to indemnify because the latter depends on the applicable law giving rise to a claim under the policy. The typical CGL policy provides that "the company shall have the right and duty to defend any suit against the insured seeking damages on account of bodily injury or property damage, even if any of the allegations of the suit are groundless, false or fraudulent * * *." Generally, courts determine the obligation of the insurer to defend by comparing the allegations of the underlying complaint with the terms of the insurance policy, and if any allegations (regardless of their frivolousness or falsity) are embraced by the coverage provided, the insurer must defend the action. Moreover, any ambiguity in the factual allegations of the complaint is resolved in favor of the duty to defend because there exists a potential claim under the policy. Finally, it is immaterial that the underlying complaint also alleges matters that are outside of the policy's coverage, until such time as those allegations within the policy are stricken or eliminated. See generally Robert Keeton & Alan Widiss, Insurance Law § 9.1(b) (1988).

B. INSURANCE COVERAGE
FOR ENVIRONMENTAL
AND TOXIC TORTS

In these insurance coverage cases the insured is seeking to be indemnified against bodily injury or property damage claims brought by third parties arising out of its release or use of hazardous substances. Among the issues that have engendered considerable controversy among insureds and insurers is what constitutes an "occurrence" triggering coverage.

1. OCCURRENCE

The definition of what constitutes an "occurrence" has been the source of considerable dispute. Prior to 1966, the terms of the CGL policy typically required the insurer to respond to claims resulting from an "accident." In 1966 the policy language changed from "accident" to "occurrence," which typically is defined to mean:

> an accident, including a continuous or repeated exposure to conditions, which results, during the policy period, in bodily injury or property damage neither expected nor intended from the standpoint of the insured.

Although the language change broadened coverage to reach beyond the common understanding of the term "accident" to include continuous or repeated exposure to conditions, not all damages from long-term exposure to conditions or substances are recoverable under the CGL policy. This is so because by the terms of the "occurrence" definition, the damage must be "neither expected nor intended from the standpoint of the insured."

Insurers take the position that this issue can be resolved in their favor as a matter of law when the insured engages in an intentional act, such as the discharge of waste as a part of its business, i.e., where the discharge is known, routine, and repeated. In contrast, insureds argue that it is the *damage*, not the discharge, which must be expected or intended. They contend that they are covered in so far as they do not subjectively desire or know to a substantial certainty that damage will result from the discharge. The majority of courts have adopted the insureds' perspective which focuses on the intent to cause damage.

a. The General Rule

In the asbestos case of United States Fidelity & Guaranty Co. v. Wilkin Insulation Co., 144 Ill.2d 64, 161 Ill.Dec. 280, 578 N.E.2d 926 (1991), the Supreme Court of Illinois rejected the insurers' argument that the alleged damage was expected or intended because the underlying complaints alleged that the insured intentionally installed asbestos-containing products in the buildings "with knowledge of the products' threat to human health." The court stated: "it is the contamination of the buildings and their contents that must be neither expected nor intended from the standpoint of the insured." Based on its review of the underlying complaints the court found no allegations that the insured expected or intended "to contaminate the buildings and the contents therein with toxic asbestos fibers." Thus, the court concluded that the complaint alleged potential coverage for "property damage" caused by an "occurrence" sufficient to trigger the insurers' duty to defend. See also Village of Morrisville Water & Light Dept. v. U.S. Fidelity & Guaranty Co., 775 F.Supp. 718 (D.Vt.1991), holding that where the insured city sent hazardous PCB-laden materials to another's site where the harm occurred, that intentional act did not negate coverage "because Morrisville neither expected nor intended to damage the site."

In Olin Corporation v. Insurance Company of North America, 762 F.Supp. 548 (S.D.N.Y.1991), the district court denied the insurers' motion for summary judgment based on the argument that the insured manufacturer expected or intended the damages that resulted from its continuous release of DDT over a sixteen-year period. Although the court acknowledged that strong evidence had been presented to show that Olin should have known that damages would result from its release of DDT, the court concluded that the evidence "permitted the inference that Olin did not 'intend' to cause the damages" based on the standard of review previously set forth by the Second Circuit. As explained by that court:

> In general, what makes injuries or damages expected or intended rather than accidental are the knowledge and intent of the insured. It is not enough that an insured was warned that damages might ensue from its actions, or that, once warned, an insured decided to take a calculated risk and proceed as before. Recovery will be barred only if it can be said that the damages were, in a broader sense, "intended" by the insured because the insured knew that the damages would flow directly and immediately from its intentional act. City of Johnstown v. Bankers Standard Ins. Co., 877 F.2d 1146, 1150 (2d Cir.1989).

b. Differing Views

Not all courts agree, with some entering a finding of no coverage upon the lesser showing that the insured knew of the likelihood or the substantial probability of the resultant harm. See American Mutual Liability Ins. Co. v. Neville Chemical Co., 650 F.Supp. 929 (W.D.Pa.1987) (where insured continued its disposal of hazardous wastes despite knowledge that it was contaminating nearby wells, court granted insurer's motion for summary judgment because the insured knew or should have known that there was a substantial probability that the contamination would result); Independent Petrochemical Corp. v. Aetna Casualty & Sur. Co., 654 F.Supp. 1334, 1360 (D.D.C.1986) (in case involving personal injury claims arising out of exposure to dioxin, court concluded that there would be no coverage if facts show that insured "was aware of the likely results of its acts in disposing of the waste materials"), affirmed in part, rev'd in part, 944 F.2d 940 (D.C.Cir.1991); Jackson Township Mun. Utils. Auth. v. Hartford Accident & Indem. Co., 186 N.J.Super. 156, 451 A.2d 990, 993–94 (1982) (where residents alleged personal injury and property damage resulting from exposure to water contaminated by insured's landfill operations, court stated that manufacturer "who discharges * * * waste material knowingly, or who may have been expected to know, that it would pollute, will be excluded from coverage by the clause. The industry, for example, which is put on notice that its emissions are a potential hazard to the environment and who continues those emissions is an active polluter excluded from coverage by the clause.").

c. Objective versus Subjective Test

Another issue sometimes raised in determining whether an event was "expected or intended" is the state of mind and/or degree of foreseeability necessary to trigger this clause. The provision typically states that the event or damage must be expected or intended "from the standpoint of the insured." Insurers argue that the test for meeting this requirement is *objective*: if a reasonable insured should have foreseen the event/harm, it was "expected or intended." Insureds argue that the test is *subjective*: the insurer must prove that the event or injury was "subjectively foreseen as practically certain," *by the insured*.

Most courts reject a purely objective "reasonably foreseeable" test because such a test would deny coverage for simple negligence—a result which most courts find a reasonable insured would not expect. See, e.g., Queen City Farms, Inc. v. Central Nat'l Ins. Co. of Omaha, 64 Wash. App. 838, 827 P.2d 1024 (1992) (trial court erred by instructing the jury that the insured's expectation was to be determined on a reasonable person basis); Broderick Investment Co. v. The Hartford Accident & Indem. Co., 954 F.2d 601 (10th Cir.1992) (applying Colorado law) (jury properly instructed to apply subjective standards). At the opposite end of the spectrum, some courts go so far as to find that the test is wholly subjective, and/or an occurrence is not expected or intended unless the resultant injury is a "substantial certainty." See, e.g., City of Johnstown, New York v. Bankers Standard Ins. Co., 877 F.2d 1146, 1150 (2d Cir.1989); Honeycomb System Inc. v. Admiral Ins. Co., 567 F.Supp. 1400 (D.Me.1983). Other courts take the middle road, finding that the operative degree of expectation is "substantial probability"—higher than reasonable foreseeability, but lower than a more subjective, substantial certainty. See, e.g., New Castle County v. Hartford Accident and Indem. Co., 685 F.Supp. 1321, 1330, 1331 (D.Del.1988) and New Castle County v. Continental Casualty Co., 725 F.Supp. 800, 813 (D.Del.1989) (companion case). Cf. Allstate Ins. Co. v. Freeman, 432 Mich. 656, 443 N.W.2d

734, 743 (1989) (substantial probability test applied, but from subjective viewpoint of insured).

Application of the subjective test generally increases the burden on the insurer. However, in Diamond Shamrock Chemicals v. Aetna, 258 N.J.Super. 167, 609 A.2d 440 (1992), the insured still lost the battle of whether there had been an occurrence. The court affirmed the trial judge's finding that the insured subjectively knew the waste that it discharged would cause harm where the insurers proved that Diamond Shamrock knew that it was discharging a hazardous substance and that some employees had contracted skin diseases from contact with its product. Despite this knowledge, the insured purposefully discharged waste water containing contaminants onto the ground and into a nearby river. Furthermore, the insured rejected a process which would have lowered the level of dioxin in its product since it would have decreased production efficiency. Based on this evidence, the court found that Diamond Shamrock subjectively expected or intended the injury which occurred: "Diamond did know the nature of the chemicals it was handling, it did know that they were being continuously discharged into the environment, and it did know they were doing at least some harm. * * * [W]e cannot ignore reality by accepting the blithe assurance of Diamond that it did not intend to injure others. The evidence abounds the other way. * * * Instead we are convinced that subjective knowledge of harm was proven as a matter of fact."

Problem

Larco Inc., sought insurance coverage with respect to an action brought by the Columbia Department of Natural Resources ("CDNR") for remediation of chemical contamination at Larco's plant in Big Rapids, Columbia. The CDNR filed its action against Larco in 1990. The trial court granted Larco's motion for summary disposition on the issue of the duty to defend and issued an order requiring American Insurance Co. to indemnify plaintiff for 68% of the remediation costs.

On appeal, American Insurance argued that the trial court clearly erred in finding that the plaintiff had not "intended or expected" volatile organic compounds ("VOCs") to disperse into the groundwater.

The trial record consisted of testimony of numerous former Larco employees who testified that they intentionally dumped VOCs into the drains that led to an unlined seepage lagoon in back of the plant over a 15 year period from 1964 to 1979. Several of these former employees also testified that they had observed other Larco employees doing the same. One of the witnesses testified that he observed a Larco employee deliberately dump about 150 gallons of VOCs directly onto the bare ground behind the plant and another employee deliberately dump VOCs into the drains. Former Larco employees also testified that VOCs were used to mop the plant floor from at least 1964 to 1979, which mopping was often performed on and around the drains which led directly to the lagoon, and that some of the VOCs would invariably go into the drains and be washed into the lagoon. Larco's expert witness testified that during the manufacturing process, VOCs were discharged into the lagoon, and Larco's plant chemist testified that he knew as early as 1972 that VOCs should not be discharged into the unlined lagoon because they would degrade the environment. Nevertheless, Larco's corporate policy had been to require its employees to comply with environmental laws and regulations and notices were posted commencing in 1980 advising employees not to discard chemicals into the drains or on the ground. Further beginning in 1978 Larco had hired a reputable waste hauler to remove all VOCs created in the manufacturing process.

Based on this record, Larco argues that it did not know with substantial certainty that the acts of its employees would result in contamination of the groundwater, and that had it not "intended" or "expected" such contamination to result from its employees' activities.

As a law clerk for an appeals court judge, resolve the question of whether the actions of Larco and its employees constitute an exception to the definition of an occurrence within the standard CGL policy.

2. BODILY INJURY AND EMOTIONAL HARM

What constitutes "bodily injury" within the scope of CGL policies in the toxic tort context raises important coverage questions. The typical policy defines "bodily injury" as "bodily injury, sickness or disease sustained by any person which occurs during the policy period." While insureds generally will take the position that all toxic tort-related damages fall within the bodily injury definition, insurers oppose judicial expansion of the meaning of the term, arguing that the policy language is unambiguous and that its plain meaning is limited to physical injury alone.

A few courts that have addressed the issue of whether claims for emotional distress or mental anguish fall within the bodily injury definition have concluded that they do not. A California appellate court, reading the policy language in its "ordinary sense," held that the term "bodily injury" is unambiguous and, based on various dictionary definitions of the word "bodily," concluded that the term "does not reasonably encompass, and in fact suggests a contrast with, the purely mental, emotional and spiritual." Aim Ins. Co. v. Culcasi, 229 Cal.App.3d 209, 280 Cal.Rptr. 766, 772 (1991); accord Chatton v. Nat'l Union Fire Ins. Co., 10 Cal.App.4th 846, 13 Cal.Rptr.2d 318 (1992).

A few courts, however, have concluded that the term "bodily injury" should be construed in its broad sense to encompass claims for emotional distress. For example, the New York Court of Appeals in Lavanant v. General Accident Ins. Co., 79 N.Y.2d 623, 584 N.Y.S.2d 744, 595 N.E.2d 819 (1992) addressed the issue in the context of a ceiling collapse case and concluded that mental injury alone is recoverable. The underlying claimants did not allege any physical injury or property damage based on the insured building owner's alleged tortious acts. The policy at issue defined bodily injury as "bodily injury, sickness or disease." Finding the policy language ambiguous, the court observed that "[t]he categories 'sickness' and 'disease' in the insurer's definition not only enlarge the term 'bodily injury', but also, to the average reader, may include mental as well as physical sickness." Moreover, the insurer could have limited bodily injury by providing for "bodily sickness" or "bodily disease" but did not do so. The court also relied on its analysis of recent case law in New York that allowed recovery for pure emotional distress in other contexts. In light of that development, the court looked to the reasonable expectations of the insured and concluded that:

> the reasonable expectation of property owners purchasing a comprehensive policy such as plaintiffs' would be that their liability for purely mental injury would fall within their insurance coverage.

See also Voorhees v. Preferred Mut. Ins. Co., 246 N.J.Super. 564, 588 A.2d 417, 422 (1991) ("mental anguish qualifies as 'bodily injury' at least to the extent that emotional distress alleged does not constitute 'parasitic' damages attached to an independent cause of action").

Still other courts have acknowledged the difficulty in distinguishing between physical and emotional injuries because "there is no bright line separating them." Keating v. National Union Fire Ins. Co., 754 F.Supp. 1431, 1438 (C.D.Cal.1990); See Abellon v. Hartford Ins. Co., 167 Cal. App.3d 21, 212 Cal.Rptr. 852, 855–57 (1985). How would you resolve the question of whether purely emotional distress should be embraced within the "bodily injury" category? What if a state only allows recovery for negligently inflicted distress if it is accompanied by objective physical manifestations? Should cancerphobia be treated differently than other forms of mental distress or anguish? See Techalloy Co. v. Reliance Ins. Co., 338 Pa.Super. 1, 487 A.2d 820 (1984) ("[A]t a minimum, personal injury encompasses allegations of exposure to a hazardous substance, increased risk of injury, anxiety, various internal disorders and tissue damage. * * * "). How should courts analyze claims for increased risk of future disease if that state's courts would recognize such a claim?

3. PROPERTY DAMAGE

In the asbestos context, much litigation has resulted from the costs of removing asbestos-containing materials from the interior of buildings because of the owners' concerns that such materials may pose a risk to the health of occupants. A leading decision that considers whether an insured, who must respond to such claims brought by building owners, can be indemnified under CGL policies on the basis of the property damage clause, is United States Fidelity & Guaranty Co. v. Wilkin Insulation Co., 144 Ill.2d 64, 161 Ill.Dec. 280, 578 N.E.2d 926 (1991). The Illinois Supreme Court's resolution of that issue follows:

> We have reviewed each of the nine underlying complaints pursuant to the liberal duty to defend standard set forth above. Each complaint alleges that asbestos-containing products were installed in the buildings. The complaints further allege that, upon deterioration of the asbestos-containing product itself or upon disturbance from an outside force, asbestos fibers are released into the air.

These fibers are extremely durable and lasting. * * * [T]he buildings and their contents (e.g., carpets, upholstery, drapery, etc.) are virtually contaminated or impregnated with asbestos fibers, the presence of which poses a serious health hazard to the human occupants. Finally, under various theories of recovery, the underlying complaints seek damages in the form of the costs of inspecting their buildings and the contents therein for the presence of asbestos fibers. The complaints further seek to recover from all defendants, including Wilkin, any costs associated with the containment, removal and/or replacement of the asbestos-containing products.

Turning to the definitions of property damage[,] * * * [t]he post–1973 standard form policy * * * defines property damage as:

(1) physical injury to or destruction of tangible property, which occurs during the policy period, including the loss of use thereof at any time resulting therefrom.

All plaintiffs essentially argue that the underlying complaints do not allege physical injury to tangible property. Rather, plaintiffs contend that the presence of health-threatening, asbestos-containing products results only in intangible economic loss in the form of diminished market values of the buildings.

This court, however, has already found that asbestos fiber contamination constitutes physical injury to tangible property, i.e., the buildings and their contents. (Board of Education v. A.C. & S., Inc., 546 N.E.2d 580 (Ill.1989)). In *Board of Education*, * * * this court found:

[I]t would be incongruous to argue there is no damage to other property when a harmful element exists throughout a building or an area of a building which by law must be corrected * * *. The view that asbestos fibers may contaminate a building sufficiently to allege damage to property has been recently adopted in a number of cases.

* * *

The essence of the allegations [of the complaints] is that the buildings have been contaminated by asbestos to the point where corrective action, under the law, must be taken. Thus, the buildings have been damaged.

In the instant action, the underlying complaints allege that the buildings and the contents therein were contaminated by toxic asbestos fibers. Therefore, the underlying complaints allege physical injury to tangible property. Thus, we find that the underlying complaints allege potentially covered property damage.

Do you agree that property damage existed in these cases? What might motivate the court to find property damage in these asbestos removal cases? How does the threat of bodily injury bear on the resolution of this issue? Does the court sufficiently dispose of the economic loss argument?

A number of decisions that have considered the question have held that contamination of the environment constitutes "property damage" as that term is used in the CGL policies. See A.Y. McDonald Industries, Inc. v. Ins. Co. of North America, 475 N.W.2d 607 (Iowa 1991); Montrose Chem. Corp. of California v. Superior Court, 18 Cal.App.4th 1386, 10 Cal.Rptr.2d 687 (1992), affirmed 6 Cal.4th 287, 24 Cal.Rptr.2d 467, 861 P.2d 1153 (1993) (natural resource damages for injuries to land, water and wildlife sought by CERCLA complaint, as well as response costs, are forms of property damage); Hazen Paper Co. v. U.S. Fidelity & Guaranty Co., 407 Mass. 689, 555 N.E.2d 576 (1990) (contamination of soil and groundwater is "property damage"); Continental Ins. Cos. v. Northeastern Pharmaceutical & Chem. Co., 842 F.2d 977 (8th Cir.1988), cert. denied 488 U.S. 821, 109 S.Ct. 66, 102 L.Ed.2d 43 (1988).

4. TRIGGERS OF COVERAGE FOR BODILY INJURY

In determining whether a particular CGL policy will respond to a given claim requires an initial determination of whether the policy has been "triggered" by the occurrence of an event or loss within the period covered by the policy. Toxic tort and remediation cases present difficult issues of triggering because contamination may go undetected for long periods or diseases characterized by long latency periods may not manifest themselves until long after the defendant's conduct, whether it involved installation of a defective product or the disposal of hazardous substances.

Various theories on how to pinpoint the date or time of an occurrence are currently in debate, including: (1) exposure; (2) injury-in-fact; (3) manifestation or discovery; and (4) triple or continuous trigger. The trigger theory selected can have a significant impact on what policies may cover the loss. For example, over a twenty-five year period an insured might have various carriers, changing each year; if carriers learn, years later, of claims lodged against insureds for their activities undertaken years or decades earlier, one issue will be whether the policy's coverage had been triggered during the finite term of their coverage. As a general rule, carriers on the risk early, but who did not write insurance in the later years, will favor a manifestation theory. Conversely, those who wrote the later years' policies will favor an exposure theory. The respective theories are briefly described below:

a. Exposure

Under this theory, the trigger is the date of the first injurious exposure. The leading case adopting the exposure theory is Insurance Company of North America v. Forty–Eight Insulations, Inc., 633 F.2d 1212, 1217–22 (6th Cir.1980), modified on other grounds 657 F.2d 814 (6th Cir.1981) (en banc), cert. denied 454 U.S. 1109, 102 S.Ct. 686, 70

L.Ed.2d 650 (1981) (applying Illinois and New Jersey law). There, the court rejected the manifestation theory, noting that although keying the ripeness of a claim to the manifestation of diagnosable symptoms of disease may be appropriate for the purposes of statute of limitations questions and protecting the injured claimant, the same policy considerations are not present with regard to the coverage issue:

> A manifestation rule would deny coverage to the insured manufacturer. Moreover, it is the injury and not its discovery that makes the manufacturer liable in the underlying tort suit. As noted above, such underlying liability should also trigger insurance coverage * * *. Statutes of limitations are meant to protect defendants against stale claims, not bar injured plaintiffs who have acted in good faith. Insurance contracts are meant to cover the insured.

In addition, the *Forty–Eight Insulations* court held that liability should be pro-rated among the various insurers on the risk during the exposure period.

Many other courts have adopted the exposure theory, as illustrated by Jackson Township Municipal Utilities Authority v. American Home Insurance Co., 451 A.2d 990 (N.J.Super.1982) where it was alleged that the township was negligent in its design and maintenance of a hazardous waste site and residential plaintiffs were exposed to chemicals through ingestion and showering, causing sub-clinical injury and a risk of future disease. The court stated:

> The policy insures against an injury; sub-clinical body or tissue change caused by chemicals is an injury, even though nonobservable. This exposure theory is more easily and equitably applied to a groundwater contamination than manifestation, since plaintiffs here receive money damages for emotional distress, medical surveillance for potential disease, and not the disease itself. Since the disease may never manifest itself, it should be the sub-clinical injury which triggers coverage. Moreover, if we applied the manifestation theory, coverage would be triggered by the fortuitous event of disclosure of the condition, which may depend upon many factors unrelated to the contamination process.

In Lloyd E. Mitchell v. Maryland Casualty Co., 324 Md. 44, 595 A.2d 469 (1991), in a case where the insured was liable for asbestos-related bodily injuries, the Maryland Court of Appeals traced the nature of the asbestos-related diseases. In opting for the exposure theory, and rejecting the manifestation theory which would have resulted in no coverage, the court stressed that "the exposure to asbestos fibers and the inflammatory response of the body to those fibers constitute sub-clinical injuries and disease processes which would be detectable by a pathologist if he could examine the bodily tissue prior to the manifestation of the asbestos related disease." The insurer argued that microscopic subclinical alterations which produce no functional impairment are not bodily injury. The court concluded:

Considering the plain meaning of the term "bodily injury," as used in the policy, and in light of the medical evidence concerning the development of asbestos-related diseases, we align ourselves with the overwhelming weight of authority in the country and conclude that "bodily injury" occurs when asbestos is inhaled and retained in the lungs. In this regard, for purposes of policy coverage, it is not important that [the experts] may disagree as to the time when the changes in the lungs may be classified as a disease. On the record developed in this case, we conclude that, at a minimum, coverage under the policy to provide a defense and indemnification of the insured is triggered upon exposure to the insured's asbestos products during the policy period by a person who suffers bodily injury as a result of that exposure. Accordingly, we hold that the trial judge erred in adopting, as the sole trigger of coverage, the "manifestation" theory of coverage, namely, that coverage is not afforded until harm actually becomes manifest.

Would these results be unique to asbestos-related diseases?

b. *Manifestation/Discovery*

Under the manifestation theory, the occurrence is deemed to take place at the time when the illness or disease is reasonably capable of medical diagnosis i.e., when it manifests itself in diagnosable symptoms of disease. The manifestation theory was applied in an asbestos personal injury action in Eagle–Picher Industries, Inc. v. Liberty Mutual Insurance Co., 829 F.2d 227 (1st Cir.1987). There, the court affirmed the district court's ruling that coverage is triggered "when the asbestos-related disease becomes manifest, as measured by the date of actual diagnosis or, with respect to those cases in which no diagnosis was made prior to death, the date of death." The court concluded that the date of manifestation is when the disease is "reasonably capable of medical diagnosis." The court approved the district court's adoption of a six-year "rollback" theory under which the date of diagnosability is presumed to precede actual diagnosis by six years. The court further noted that the rollback presumption was rebuttable and could be overcome by the insurer's clear and convincing medical evidence that the asbestosis was first reasonably capable of diagnosis at some time outside of the insurer's policy periods. See also Hartford Accident & Indem. Co. v. Aetna Life & Cas. Ins. Co., 98 N.J. 18, 483 A.2d 402 (1984) (ingestion of drug by child); American Motorists Ins. Co. v. E.R. Squibb & Sons, Inc., 95 Misc.2d 222, 406 N.Y.S.2d 658 (1978) (manifestation trigger theory applied in the DES context).

c. *Injury-in-Fact*

Another theory, although adopted by few courts, is that of injury-in-fact which comes close to the manifestation theory. This theory holds the insurer on the risk when bodily injury first occurs to be liable for coverage, without regard to when the victim may have been exposed or when the disease was first diagnosed. In Continental Casualty Company v. Rapid–American Corporation, 80 N.Y.2d 640, 593 N.Y.S.2d 966, 609 N.E.2d 506 (1993), the New York Court of Appeals impliedly adopted an injury-in-fact rule, describing it as "when the injury, sickness, disease or disability actually began," the "onset of disease, whether discovered or not."

In American Home Products Corporation v. Liberty Mutual Insurance Company, 748 F.2d 760, 764 (2d Cir.1984), another bodily injury asbestos case, the court held that coverage is triggered when real personal injury first occurs. The Second Circuit affirmed a lower court decision that the trigger-of-coverage clause in a general liability policy unambiguously provides for coverage based upon "the occurrence during the policy period of an injury in fact. We reject only so much of the [lower] court's decision as holds that 'injury in fact' means an injury was 'diagnosable' or 'compensable' during the policy period."

d. Multiple or Continuous Trigger

Under the multiple or continuous trigger theory, any policies in effect from the time of initial exposure to the time of manifestation are on the risk in terms of the duty to defend and indemnify the insured. Because this theory maximizes coverage, it is generally the most favored by insureds. In the landmark case of Keene Corp. v. Insurance Co. of North America, 667 F.2d 1034 (D.C.Cir.1981), cert. denied 455 U.S. 1007, 102 S.Ct. 1645, 71 L.Ed.2d 875 (1982), the court held coverage in bodily injury continuous tort cases is triggered in a manner such that insurance policies in effect during the entire period from first exposure to disease onset had defense and indemnification duties. Coverage was triggered, *Keene* held, throughout the period from the injured person's first exposure to the insured's asbestos, through the period of residence *in situ* of the asbestos fibers, until the asbestos-related disease was diagnosed.

The Pennsylvania Supreme Court in J.H. France Refractories Company v. Allstate Insurance Company, 626 A.2d 502 (Pa.1993) adopted the multiple trigger approach whereby each insurance policy in force during the course of a continuous injury—from the first exposure to a toxic substance through manifestation of disease symptoms—is triggered and must indemnify the policyholder for any damages caused by the injury. The court said asbestos-related disease is a continuous injury because the fibers begin to harm human tissue upon first exposure, and then cause progressive harm. The court reversed a lower court ruling that held policyholders were required to share indemnity costs for periods of time they were uninsured, finding that such a pro rata apportionment would be inconsistent with the multiple-trigger theory.

Additionally, the court held that once the policy limits of a given insurer are exhausted, the policyholder is free to seek coverage from any of the remaining insurers. The court noted that the insurers are free to seek contribution from each other. Finally, a California appeals court adopted the continuous trigger rule in Armstrong World Industries, Inc. v. Aetna Cas. & Sur. Co., 20 Cal.App.4th 296, 26 Cal.Rptr.2d 35 (1993).

What benefit might *insurers* derive from the continuous trigger approach? Will it depend on how many different insurers wrote policies during the continuous period? How should damages be allocated among different insurers? Is it fair to let the insured select from which insurer it will seek indemnity?

5. TRIGGERS OF COVERAGE FOR PROPERTY DAMAGE

The trigger of coverage in continuing bodily injury cases is not, however, necessarily the trigger in continuing property damage cases. Although several property damage decisions have adopted a continuous trigger theory, great controversy exists as to whether the continuous trigger approach is correct in property damage cases. For example, in United States Fidelity & Guaranty Co. v. Thomas Solvent Co., 683 F.Supp. 1139, 1163 (E.D.Mich.1988), a case involving property damage from industrial contamination, the court adopted a hybrid continuous trigger, observing:

> There is no reason why some variation of the "continuous trigger" theory should not be seen as applicable here—at least at this juncture where the facts are quite complex and the issue of precisely when the so-called "continuous occurrences" should be "fixed" is so hotly disputed. Such a "hybrid" continuous trigger theory would clearly require all the insurers to defend where the date upon which the "continuous" damage first occurred has not been settled and/or where continuing exposure (damage) is also alleged. Under such a theory every policy in effect at any time during the (continuous) injury process—from the initial exposure(s) until the last manifest development of bodily injury or property damage would be triggered for coverage.

Ray Industries, Inc. v. Liberty Mutual Insurance Co., 974 F.2d 754 (6th Cir.1992) also rejected uniform application of the manifestation rule. The insured in that case had disposed of some of its waste by trucking it to independently owned landfills. The insured was subsequently named as a potentially responsible party for the cleanup of one of these sites. The court found that, because the insured's waste was "constantly dumped" at the landfill between 1966 and 1979, the insured could look to every policy written during those years for coverage. The court specifically refrained, however, from establishing continuous trigger as a general rule in environmental pollution insurance cases.

What rule makes the most sense in these environmental contamination cases? Should the courts follow the continuous versus permanent nuisance or trespass theory that applied in the statutes of limitation context, using a manifestation or discovery trigger rule in cases of permanent damage, but a continuing trigger in continuing damage cases?

6. NUMBER OF OCCURRENCES

Because waste discharge may occur repeatedly or continuously, a question arises whether one or multiple occurrences have taken place. This distinction becomes important when there is a dollar limit for each occurrence, a deductible for each occurrence, or coverage is provided by more than one policy. See, e.g., Uniroyal Inc. v. Home Ins. Co., 707 F.Supp. 1368, 1382 (E.D.N.Y.1988). *Uniroyal* involved the spraying of Agent Orange herbicide in Vietnam. The insurer argued that each of tens of thousands of sprayings was a separate occurrence, requiring a separate deductible. The insured argued (and the court found) that there had been only one occurrence with one deductible. The decision includes a thorough survey of the one/multiple occurrence case law.

Most courts determining this issue in a nonenvironmental context agree that the focus should be on the causal event or underlying circumstances, not the number of injuries or claims arising from the event or circumstances. On the other hand, a few courts have calculated the number of occurrences on the basis of *effects*, particularly when the cause has been interrupted.

Applying even the majority test, moreover, can be difficult and lead to apparently inconsistent results. For example, in Michigan Chemical Corp. v. American Home Assurance Co., 728 F.2d 374 (6th Cir.1984), the court found that various shipments of the allegedly defective goods constituted several occurrences; in contrast, separate shipments of Agent Orange were deemed one occurrence in *Uniroyal*, 707 F.Supp. at 1386. In *Uniroyal*, Judge Weinstein tried to reconcile the apparently disparate results in the case law by stating that courts are more likely to find multiple occurrences when there is a small number of events—as opposed to when hundreds or thousands of events are involved.

For an interesting case involving HIV-contaminated blood products, see American Red Cross v. Travelers Indem. Co., 816 F.Supp. 755 (D.D.C.1993), where the insured had been subjected to numerous claims by donees of its blood products. Travelers argued that all the claims combined constituted a single "occurrence," and therefore, fell within the $1 million "per occurrence" liability limit for the policies at issue. The parties agreed that the court should examine the circumstances underlying the claims, rather than the effect of each claimant's injury, to define a single occurrence. Under this analysis, a court asks if there was but one proximate, uninterrupted, and continuing cause that resulted in all of the injuries and damages.

The court held that the facts do not support the suggestion that the Red Cross engaged in a single, negligent practice that could be considered "one cause." Rather, the Red Cross made many decisions regarding its handling of the blood—whether to screen donors, test blood, and provide warnings to recipient hospitals. Therefore, each of these decisions independently may have affected whether bodily injury would result from a given transfusion. Moreover, negligence regarding screening, testing, or notification could not result in injury until a particular unit of contaminated blood was provided to a facility that would administer the transfusion. The court concluded that the proximate cause of the injuries was the distribution of the HIV-tainted blood and that each act of distribution constituted an "occurrence" for purposes of applying the $1 million per occurrence limit.

C. SPECIAL INSURANCE PROBLEMS OF ENVIRONMENTAL CLEANUPS

Most of the insurance questions focused on above arose out of toxic tort bodily injury or property damage claims. Here, in contrast, we focus on insurance problems that are directly related to governmental action, federal or state, pursuant to CERCLA or state-law counterparts. Typically, the insured is required to expend resources remediating a contaminated site, either voluntarily in anticipation of a government mandate that it do so, or in response to a letter or suit from the EPA making such a demand. The property contaminated can be insured's own or, as is required under nearly all CGL policies, that of third parties where the hazardous waste has caused environmental harm.

1. PAY "AS DAMAGES" AND "SUIT" CONTROVERSIES

The "as damages" controversy relates to property damage claims resulting from the release of hazardous substances on property owned by third parties. As noted above, the post–1966 language requires the insurer to pay on behalf of its insured "all sums which the insured shall become legally obligated to pay as damages * * *." Insurers have argued that the term "as damages" means legal damages only and does not include expenses connected with equitable remedies or statutorily-mandated environmental cleanup activities. The issue arises in connection with governmentally-mandated environmental remediation such as orders or actions brought under CERCLA.

Closely related is whether the administrative process pursued by the EPA or an equivalent state environmental agency against an insured qualifies as a "suit" against an insured within the meaning of the CGL policy in which the insurer agrees to indemnify against and defend "any *suit* against the insured seeking damages on account of bodily injury or property damage."

The following decision, Coakley v. Maine Bonding & Casualty Co., 136 N.H. 402, 618 A.2d 777 (1993) represents the trend and majority view on both issues.

COAKLEY v. MAINE BONDING AND CASUALTY COMPANY

Supreme Court of New Hampshire, 1993.
618 A.2d 777.

JOHNSON, J.

The central issue in this appeal is whether the defendants, Maine Bonding and Casualty Company (Maine Bonding) and St. Paul Fire and Marine Insurance Company (St. Paul), must indemnify the plaintiffs, Ronald C. Coakley and Coakley Landfill, Inc. (collectively, the Coakleys), for environmental "response" costs imposed or likely to be imposed by the United States Environmental Protection Agency (EPA) and the New Hampshire Department of Environmental Services (NHDES) pursuant to the Comprehensive Environmental Response, Compensation, and Liability Act, 42 U.S.C.A. §§ 9601 et seq. (CERCLA), and comparable State statutes, RSA chapter 147–B (1990 & Supp.1991). The Superior Court granted the defendants' motion for summary judgment below, ruling that the word "damages," found in the granting clause of the defendants' comprehensive general liability policies, does not include these response costs. In addition, the court ruled that the EPA and NHDES demands concerning Coakley Landfill, contained in "notices of potential responsibility" and other letters, are not "suits," and that therefore the defendants are not bound to defend the Coakleys. The Coakleys appeal both rulings and we reverse.

Coakley Landfill, the focal point of this dispute, straddles the border of Greenland and North Hampton. For many years, it accepted municipal and industrial waste from the Portsmouth area, as well as incinerator residue from the Pease Air Force Base. In 1984, the Coakleys were forced to close the landfill after the NHDES discovered contaminants in the area's groundwater and in the wells of neighboring properties. The contamination also forced surrounding municipalities to extend water supply distribution lines to service the residents who had depended on the well-water.

In 1984, the environmental protection division of the State Attorney General's office notified Ronald Coakley that he was "potentially responsible" for the contamination at the Coakley Landfill and asked him to fund and help conduct a "Remedial Investigation/Feasibility Study" (RI/FS) of the site, at an expected cost of at least $500,000. The division warned that "EPA is prepared to initiate the RI/FS process whenever it appears that our cooperative effort will not succeed." It appears that the Coakleys chose not to heed this warning because the EPA eventually conducted an RI/FS itself. The cost of the RI/FS and other landfill-related investigations exceeded $1,225,000.

In September 1987, the EPA sent Ronald Coakley a "Request for Information" about the landfill. The letter stated that compliance with the request was mandatory, and subject to a $25,000 penalty for each day of noncompliance. The record does not disclose whether the Coakleys complied with this "request." * * *

[I]n February 1990, the EPA sent Coakley Landfill, Inc. a "Notice of Potential Liability." The notice warned that, under CERCLA, a potentially responsible party (PRP) could be obligated to (1) "implement relief actions deemed necessary by EPA to protect the public health, welfare or environment"; (2) pay "for all costs incurred by the government in responding to any release or threatened release at the [landfill]"; and (3) "pay damages for injury to, destruction of, or loss of natural resources." * * *

The "response activities" referenced in the EPA's PRP notice consist of "[d]esign and implementation of the Remedial Action selected and approved by EPA for the [landfill]" and "[o]peration, maintenance and monitoring necessary at the [landfill]." As of February 1990, the EPA's proposed "Remedial Action," or "Preferred Alternative," included "placing a cap over the landfill to minimize the migration of contaminants from the landfill" and "collection and treatment of groundwater to remove and prevent further migration of contaminants." This containment and cleanup plan, bearing an estimated cost of $20,200,000, represents a compromise between less expensive, less environmentally protective plans and more costly, more protective ones.

* * *

In the midst of all this agency activity, the Coakleys contacted two of their insurance carriers, Maine Bonding and St. Paul, and requested coverage for any costs they might be forced to bear in connection with the EPA and NHDES demands. The relevant portion of the carriers' comprehensive general liability policies, purchased by the Coakleys, reads as follows: "The Company will pay on behalf of the insured all sums which the insured shall become legally obligated to pay as damages because of A. bodily injury or B. property damage to which this insurance applies, caused by an occurrence, and the Company shall have the right and duty to defend any suit against the insured seeking damages on account of such bodily injury or property damage, even if any of the allegations of the suit are groundless, false or fraudulent, and may make such investigation and settlement of any claim or suit as it deems expedient * * *."

* * *

Maine Bonding and St. Paul each filed motions for summary judgment. St. Paul's motion was confined solely to the two main questions we address here on appeal—the interpretation of the words "damages" and "suit"—and explicitly reserved other, more fact-based coverage issues. The Coakleys objected to both motions on the grounds "that there are genuine issues of material fact as to whether [the carriers] must provide insurance coverage to [the Coakleys] under the terms of its insurance policies and, therefore, [the carriers are] not entitled to judgment as a matter of law." * * * Relying on Desrochers v. Casualty

Co., 99 N.H. 129, 106 A.2d 196 (1954), and on dictionary definitions, the superior court granted the carriers' motions for summary judgment and denied the Coakleys' motions. This appeal followed.

The issues presented by the parties on appeal are narrow and limited: 1. Are response costs, including the costs of complying with an injunction and reimbursing the EPA for its expenditures, covered as "damages" by the carriers' insurance policies? 2. Are the EPA's and NHDES's demands "suits" for purposes of triggering the carriers' duty to defend the Coakleys? * * *

Preliminarily to the "damages" issue, we note that the parties and amici curiae have deluged the court with arguments, citations, references, and exhibits. No small forest fell to deliver their contentions to our steps. In particular, counsel have consumed reams of paper in an effort to focus our attention on the workings of the numerous other jurisdictions forced to interpret the term "damages" in the CERCLA context. Neither side of the issue appears to enjoy a clear majority, although state adjudicators evidently tend towards granting coverage. See AIU Ins. Co. v. FMC Corp., 51 Cal.3d 807, 274 Cal.Rptr. 820, 829–30, 799 P.2d 1253, 1262–63 (1990) (citing cases). We acknowledge that the issue before us is in many ways identical to the one decided by these foreign courts, but emphasize that, like those courts, we must decide our case on the basis of State law and State rules of construction. We therefore eschew a detailed survey of out-of-state decisions and instead center our inquiry on our own precedent, using the arguments of other courts only as occasional guides.

The "damages" issue presents a question of contract interpretation, and "[i]n general, the rules governing the construction and interpretation of written contracts apply with equal force to insurance policies. Thus, in interpreting contracts, the fundamental inquiry centers on determining the intent of the parties at the time of agreement. Any determination of intent is generally made by this court." Trombly v. Blue Cross/Blue Shield, 120 N.H. 764, 770, 423 A.2d 980, 984 (1980) (citations omitted). The burden of proof here is on the insurance carrier. RSA 491:22–a.

An insurance contract is interpreted according to state law, and where judicial precedent clearly defines a term at issue, we need look no further than that definition. Cf. 13 J. Appleman & J. Appleman, Insurance Law and Practice § 7404, at 339 (1976) (if policy terms have clear meaning by judicial decision, they are not ambiguous). If no such definition exists and the contract itself contains no explanation of the term, we construe the policy "in the light of what a more than casual reading of the policy would reveal to an ordinarily intelligent insured."

Where the policy's terms are unambiguous, the language "must be accorded its natural and ordinary meaning." Trombly, 423 A.2d at 984. But where the language is ambiguous, and one possible interpretation favors coverage, we resolve the ambiguity in favor of the insured. 423 A.2d at 985. * * *

The reasons for the ambiguity rule are two-fold. First, "it is the insurer who controls the language of the policy and, therefore, any resulting ambiguity should be resolved in favor of the insured." Trombly. Second, "since the object of the contract is to provide protection for the insured, the construction that best achieves this purpose should be adopted." Trombly. The one exception to the rule is that a term in a contract already clearly defined by judicial decision cannot be considered ambiguous. 13 Appleman, supra § 7404, at 339.

Armed with these standards of construction, we proceed with our analysis. We look first to the seminal case of Desrochers v. Casualty Co., 99 N.H. 129, 106 A.2d 196 (1954), as both parties argue that it dispositively defines "damages" in their favor. Desrochers involved an insurance policy with language similar to that at issue here. The underlying dispute arose when the plaintiffs blocked a town culvert, causing the neighboring property to flood. The neighbors sued the plaintiffs, and the plaintiffs were ordered to remove the obstruction and to pay $200 for injury to the flooded property. Although the plaintiffs' insurance carrier agreed to indemnify them for the $200, it refused to pay for the costs of complying with the injunction.

The court decided the case in favor of the insurance carrier, holding that the costs of complying with the injunction did not constitute "damages." "Damages," the court stated, "are recompense for injuries sustained." Desrochers. "They are remedial rather than preventive, and in the usual sense are pecuniary in nature. The expense of restoring the plaintiff's property to its former state will not remedy the injury previously done, nor will it be paid to the injured parties." Furthermore, the court reasoned, "the cost of removing the obstruction has no relation to the amount of damages which might result to adjoining premises if the obstruction should not be removed."

The court also rejected an argument that the injunction was a substitute for future damages, for which the plaintiffs would be liable every time the neighbors' land flooded. "The defendant's [insurance carrier's] liability under [the policy]," the court explained, "is limited to the payment of sums which the plaintiffs became legally obligated to pay while the policy was in effect * * *. Consequently the affirmative relief could not be a 'substitute' for any monetary damages for which the defendant was liable." Desrochers. Based in part on this policy limitation, the court denied coverage.

We find the Desrochers case, a pre-Trombly decision in which the question of ambiguity is never addressed, to be inconclusive authority for the issue before us. Desrochers' definition of "damages" as "recompense for injuries sustained" is far from clear in the context of CERCLA and RSA chapter 147–B response costs. See 13 Appleman, supra § 7404, at 339. Moreover, while some of the statements explaining that definition help the Coakleys' case, others hurt it. For example, the cost of cleaning up the contaminated groundwater is undoubtedly "remedial rather than preventive," Desrochers, as is reimbursement of that portion of the EPA's investigatory costs necessary to a cleanup. The same cannot be said, however, of the proposed containment cap, a predominantly preventive measure, and those investigatory costs related to the cap. Moreover, while reimbursement of response costs is directly "pecuniary in nature," Desrochers, an injunction is not.

In the Coakleys' favor, we note that neither insurance carrier has argued that a policy limitation such as the one used by the Desrochers court could be used here to dispel the argument that the injunction was a substitute for a future damages action. The substitution argument is persuasive here: an EPA injunction to clean up the groundwater is an alternative to a monetary damages action for injury to the groundwater, see 42 U.S.C.A. § 9607(a)(4) (Supp.1992); Desrochers, 106 A.2d at 198–99, the measure of which would likely be the cost of cleaning up the contamination, see 42 U.S.C.A. § 9607(f)(1) (Supp.1992); Ohio v. United States Dept. of Interior, 880 F.2d 432, 446 (D.C.Cir.1989) (42 U.S.C.A. § 9607(f)(1) "carries in it an implicit assumption that restoration cost will serve as the basic measure of damages in many if not most CERCLA cases").

Similarly, the cost of cleaning up the contamination, including related investigatory costs, is directly related "to the amount of damages which might result" to the groundwater if the groundwater is not cleaned up. Desrochers, 106 A.2d at 199. The damage has already been done to the groundwater, and thus the cost of cleaning it up would likely be the same as the amount of "damages" which have resulted. See 42 U.S.C.A. § 9607(f)(1) (Supp.1992); Ohio v. United States Dept. of Interior, 880 F.2d at 446. The cost of constructing the preventive containment cap and related investigatory costs, however, are not related to the amount of "damages" which have resulted and thus do not easily fit into the Desrochers definition of "damages."

* * *

* * * State v. Charpentier "involve[d] the liability of a landowner * * * for the cost of cleaning a hazardous waste dump located on her property * * *." State v. Charpentier, 126 N.H. 56, 58, 489 A.2d 594, 596 (1985). We stated that "[t]he present action was brought by the State * * * to recover damages for the cost of cleaning up the Gilson Road dump site, which now contains large quantities of hazardous chemical wastes." Throughout the opinion, we referred to the action as one for "damages."

* * *

From the foregoing, it appears that, but for the non-pecuniary nature of an injunction, Desrochers and Charpentier would support coverage for the cost of cleaning up the contaminated groundwater and related investigations, although not for the cost of building the containment cap and its related investigations. See Desrochers, 106 A.2d at 198 ("damages" are "pecuniary in nature"; plaintiffs' injunction not "damages" in part because costs of compliance will not "be paid to the injured parties"). The Desrochers "pecuniary in nature" limitation apparently would allow coverage only if the EPA cleaned up the contaminated groundwater itself and demanded reimbursement from the Coakleys. If the Coakleys, and not the EPA, perform the cleanup, they would pay the costs of the cleanup directly to an engineering firm, instead of indirectly, through the federal and State governments.

We reject as specious this distinction between direct and indirect payment. It should make no difference in terms of insurance coverage whether the engineering firms hired to clean up the polluted groundwater receive their money from the Coakleys or from the federal or State government. Direct payment is in a "real sense equivalent" to indirect payment, see Desrochers, 106 A.2d at 199, because either way, the damage to the groundwater is repaired. Moreover, if we were to allow coverage only when the EPA performs the cleanup, we would encourage parties such as the Coakleys to ignore EPA cleanup demands and court injunctions, at an added cost to the environment, the insurance companies, and the public. See, e.g., AIU, 274 Cal.Rptr. at 845, 799 P.2d at 1278.

We disapprove the apparent distinction found in Desrochers between direct and indirect payment, and find that the case, along with Charpentier, otherwise supports coverage of remedial, though not preventive, response costs, including reimbursement of investigatory costs related to the cleanup. We acknowledge that Desrochers does not clearly define the terms at issue, however. Cf. 13 Appleman, supra § 7404, at 339. We therefore proceed for additional support to examine the insurance policies, which themselves contain no definition of "damages," for the term's plain and ordinary meaning. See Trombly, 423 A.2d at 984.

The insurance carriers, Maine Bonding and St. Paul, insist that the plain and ordinary meaning of the word "damages," as found in their insurance policies, includes neither injunctive relief nor restitution, such as reimbursement of the money spent on investigative costs. We disagree. As Maine Bonding argues in its brief, the distinctions among "legal damages," "injunctive relief," and "restitution" are alive and well in the legal field, and are probably still taught in remedies courses in most American law schools. The average insured, however, has not attended law school, much less a law school remedies class. To discover the plain and ordinary meaning of "damages" in the absence of a clear definition from Desrochers or the insurance policies, we turn not to the distillation of a law student after a semester's worth of course work, but to the word's plain and ordinary meaning as understood by a layperson of average intelligence. See Trombly, 423 A.2d at 984.

Webster's defines "damages" as "the estimated reparation in money for detriment or injury sustained: compensation or satisfaction imposed by law for a wrong or injury caused by a violation of a legal right." Webster's Third New International Dictionary 571 (unabridged ed. 1961) (Webster's). This definition is similar to the one found in Desrochers, 106 A.2d at 198 ("recompense for injuries sustained"), and is just as unhelpful in the CERCLA and RSA chapter 147–B context. The distinctions among injunctive relief, restitution, and traditional legal damages that the carriers insist are so obvious here elude us. * * *

* * * The first part of the dictionary definition of "damages," "reparation in money," excludes injunctive relief by its very terms, but the second part does not. Webster's, supra at 571. To the extent there is any conflict between the two or ambiguity, we must of course accept the interpretation that affords coverage. Consequently, we focus our attention on the second part of the definition—compensation or satisfaction imposed by law for a legal injury.

An EPA-ordered cleanup injunction, as well as reimbursement of related investigatory costs, easily fit this second part of the definition. They both qualify as the discharge of a legal obligation, and they both make up, or make good, for the legal injury the Coakleys are accused of committing—the contamination of the groundwater. If an administrative order requires the Coakleys to both comply with such an injunction and reimburse the EPA for its investigatory costs, the order will be "compensation or satisfaction imposed by law."

It follows then that cleanup costs and reimbursement for related investigatory costs satisfy the plain and ordinary definition of "damages." If insurance carriers wish to limit coverage to non-injunctive, non-restitutionary costs, they are free to do so in plain, intelligible language.

On the other hand, containment costs, including related investigatory costs, do not fit the definition because they are not "compensation or satisfaction imposed by law for a wrong or injury caused by a violation of a legal right." The hazardous waste sought to be contained within the landfill has not yet injured the groundwater. The containment plan is thus essentially preventive and, as Desrochers explained, "damages" are "remedial rather than preventive," Desrochers, 106 A.2d at 198.

The carriers argue that our interpretation of "damages" in essence reads the word right out of the insurance policy, making it mere surplusage. Our resolution of the issue, they insist, makes an insurance carrier responsible for payment of all sums an insured is legally obligated to pay, not just those which the insured is obligated to pay as "damages." We disagree. Our determination does not strip the word "damages" of all meaning; to the contrary, it refines the definition to include only those costs which are remedial, not preventive. Moreover, we have already stated in the insurance context that "damages" may exclude interest. * * *

The carriers also contend that CERCLA itself distinguishes between "damages" and injunctive relief or restitution, thus supporting the argument that the word "damages" excludes the costs of complying with an injunction or reimbursing the EPA. See, e.g., 42 U.S.C.A. §§ 9607(i), 9613(a) (1983 & Supp.1992). We reject this contention for two reasons. First, assuming arguendo that the parties could have foreseen the passage of CERCLA, we cannot believe that any of them divined the wording of the statute at the time they signed the insurance policy. Second, we decide an insurance dispute on the basis of State law, and State rules of construction, not on the basis of federal law. CERCLA may be the immediate source of this controversy, but its use of the word "damages" has nothing to do with our interpretation of the word found in the insurance policies at issue here.

We next turn to the question whether Maine Bonding and St. Paul must defend the Coakleys against the actions of the EPA and NHDES. The carriers argue that there is no duty to defend because none of the agency actions to date initiated a "suit" within the meaning of the word as it appears in the insurance policies. There are no cases in New Hampshire in point, and therefore we turn to the language of the policy to determine its plain and ordinary meaning. As the carriers point out, while the policies do not define "suit," they do distinguish between "claim" and "suit," requiring a defense only in the case of a "suit." Therefore, their argument goes, a "suit" must be more than a "claim." We have no quarrel with this reasoning, but cannot agree that the agency actions here are necessarily merely "claims" and, thus, not subject to the defense requirement.

To determine the plain and ordinary meaning of the word "suit," as understood by a layperson of average intelligence, we look again to the dictionary. Webster's gives several definitions for the word, the two most relevant being: (1) "the attempt to gain an end by legal process: prosecution of a right before any tribunal"; and (2) "an action or process in a court for the recovery of a right or claim: a legal application to a court for justice." Webster's, supra at 2286. If the agency actions fit either of these definitions, then our ambiguity rule requires that we hold in favor of the Coakleys.

A close look at the EPA's PRP notice, as well as relevant portions of CERCLA, reveals an agency action that fits the first definition above. The PRP notice, like a civil complaint, alerted the Coakleys that the EPA had begun a legal process to conclusively and legally determine, subject only to review for abuse of discretion, see 42 U.S.C.A. §§ 9604(c)(4), 9613(j)(2), 9621 (Supp.1992), the appropriate "response activities" liable parties must perform or pay for to abate the pollution at Coakley Landfill. This determination is akin to the determination of "damages" in a tort suit.

While it is true that the PRP notice does not purport to establish the Coakleys' liability for the pollution, CERCLA liability is strict and has few exceptions. See 42 U.S.C.A. § 9607 (Supp.1992). The predominant question under CERCLA is not whether a PRP is liable, but rather for how much. One would not expect a traditional tort defendant to concede the "damages" portion of a case, and it likewise would be myopic to conclude that the Coakleys' rights are not substantially determined by the administrative process described in the PRP notice. See id. We therefore find that the EPA's action fits the first definition of "suit" listed above. As the process falls within one possible meaning of the word "suit," we interpret it as such and need not examine the second definition described above.

The NHDES administrative order, compelling Ronald Coakley to perform certain remedial tasks, also satisfies the "suit" requirement. It hardly needs saying that an administrative order manifests an "attempt to gain an end by legal process." Webster's, supra at 2286. Administrative proceedings are the equivalent of court proceedings for purposes of the "suit" requirement, see 7C J. Appleman, Insurance Law and Practice § 4682, at 25 (W. Berdal ed., 1979), and an administrative order quite obviously indicates that an administrative proceeding is under way.

* * *

For the foregoing reasons, we hold that remedial, "response" costs, imposed by the EPA under CERCLA and by the NHDES under RSA chapter 147–B (1990 & Supp.1991), including the costs of complying with a cleanup injunction and reimbursing the EPA for related investigatory costs, are "damages" for purposes of coverage under the carriers' comprehensive general liability and excess liability policies. Although it appears from the record before us that certain costs, such as the cost of constructing the containment cap, do not fall within the definition of "damages," while other costs do, we recognize that these issues were not directly argued or decided in the superior court. Given the procedural posture of this case, we do not here finally determine whether any particular cost constitutes "damages" as we have defined them in this opinion; we leave such disputes to be resolved in the first instance by the superior court. Further, we hold that the EPA's PRP notice and the NHDES's administrative order satisfied the policies' "suit" requirement. We remand for proceedings consistent with this opinion.

Reversed and remanded.

Opinion of BROCK, C.J., dissenting is omitted.

Notes and Questions

1. Many of the decisions which have held against the insured on the "as damages" question have relied upon *Desrochers*, which the New Hampshire Supreme Court has now distinguished. The leading decisions finding remediation costs are not covered come from two federal appellate courts interpreting state law: Continental Ins. Cos. v. Northeastern Pharmaceutical and Chemical Co., 842 F.2d 977 (8th Cir.1988), cert. denied 488 U.S. 821, 109 S.Ct. 66, 102 L.Ed.2d 43 (1989) (*"NEPACCO "*); Maryland Casualty Co. v. Armco, Inc., 643 F.Supp. 430, 434 (D.Md.1986), affirmed 822 F.2d 1348 (4th Cir.1987), cert. denied 489 U.S. 1008, 108 S.Ct. 703, 98 L.Ed.2d 654 (1988). The *Armco* decision has been repudiated by the Court of Appeals of Maryland, Bausch & Lomb v. Utica Mutual Ins. Co., 330 Md. 758, 625 A.2d 1021 (1993). What about the court's distinction between remediation costs, which are covered, and preventative or containment costs, which are not? Is that a logical basis upon which to allocate total costs associated with environmental cleanups?

2. A substantial and growing body of law supports the view taken in *Coakley* that cleanup costs are within the ambit of the CGL's policy "pay as damages" provision. The California Supreme Court unanimously held that government-ordered cleanup costs are "damages" covered by CGL insurance policies. AIU Insurance Co. v. Superior Court, 51 Cal.3d 807, 274 Cal.Rptr. 820, 799 P.2d 1253 (1990). The court ruled that policy language should be construed according to the mutual intentions of the parties and its plain and ordinary meaning, explicitly rejecting the holdings in *Armco* and *NEPACCO* and also agreed with *Coakley* that the costs of preventative actions were not covered. The earliest and most influential of the pro-insurance decisions was United States Aviex Co. v. Travelers Insurance Co., 125 Mich.App. 579, 336 N.W.2d 838 (1983).

3. The decisions in *Armco* and *NEPACCO* involve federal courts interpreting *state* law; the construction of insurance contracts is governed by state law, not the federal law which controls in CERCLA cases. Although state supreme courts did not decide the "damages" issue during the 1980s, eight have done so between 1990 and 1993. These state decisions stand in contrast to the more closely divided prior predictions of state law outcomes as they emerged from the federal circuits that have ruled on the question. Seven of the first eight supreme courts to decide the damages issue have ruled in favor of policyholders. In addition to *Coakley* and *AIU*, see, e.g., A.Y. McDonald Ind., Inc. v. Insurance Co. of North America, 475 N.W.2d 607 (Iowa 1991); Boeing Co. v. Aetna Casualty & Surety Co., 113 Wash.2d 869, 784 P.2d 507 (1990) (en banc); Hazen Paper Co. v. U.S. Fidelity & Guaranty Co., 407 Mass. 689, 555 N.E.2d 576 (1990); Minnesota Mining & Mfg. Co. v. Travelers Indem. Co., 457 N.W.2d 175 (Minn.1990).

4. See Stephen Mountainspring, Insurance Coverage of CERCLA Response Costs: The Limits of "Damages" in Comprehensive General Liability Policies, 16 Ecology L.Q. 755, 801 (1989), where the author supports the outcomes finding "damages" by focusing on market principles:

> In balancing the social usefulness of a strong insurance industry against the interests of insured parties in receiving the (unanticipated) benefits of their policies, the judicial view sees each insurance contract as an isolated transaction, and from this perspective, law and equity favor the insured. From a societal viewpoint, insurance companies are independent enterprises performing a valuable function. While we might think of insurance companies as free market entities, in reality because of extensive government regulation, coverage is assured even if the insurance company becomes bankrupt. As a societal issue, insurance coverage of CERCLA response cost claims should not be seen as an impediment to the industry's vitality. Rather, coverage will lead to more expensive insurance, to the bankruptcy of inefficient or unfortunate companies, and perhaps to some extent to the government subsidization of involuntary insurance guaranty associations. These phenomena are part of a free market, of evolution toward greater economic efficiency. Concerns that insurance industry vitality will be diminished are inconsistent with a free market viewpoint, even if it leads us to new vistas of self-insurance, risk retention mechanisms, or government insurance agencies. To this extent, the argument that the narrow definition of damages is necessary to maintain the position of the insurance

industry is founded on specious premises, for it assumes a superior right of economic existence of insurance companies over other enterprises. Thus, in balancing the insured's interests against the insurer's on this issue, societal interests are best served by focusing on the insurance contract's legal implication per se, without additionally considering the impact on the social functions of the present insurance system.

Do you agree with the author?

5. *What is a "Suit"?* The holding in *Coakley* on the "suit" issue also seems to be the emerging view favoring insureds. Should a PRP letter be treated differently than a § 106 order?[1] Must the PRP letter contain an immediate threat of liability?

If the § 106 proceeding is adjudicatory, seeks damages, or affects the conduct of the insured, should the duty to defend be triggered? How about if the insured voluntarily agrees to participate in a remediation investigation and feasibility study?

If voluntary actions result in a determination of no "suit," does that encourage insureds to "fight" rather than settle? See Aetna Cas. & Sur. Co. v. Pintlar Corp., Gulf Resources & Chem. Corp., 948 F.2d 1507 (9th Cir. 1991), concluding that because a PRP's substantive rights and ultimate liability are affected from the start of the administrative process, and the ordinary person receiving such a notice would believe that it was the commencement of a suit, coverage was triggered.

2. SUDDEN AND ACCIDENTAL POLLUTION EXCLUSION

The insurance industry first inserted a pollution exclusion into the standard CGL policy in 1970. This exclusion is known as the "standard" or "sudden and accidental" exclusion and was used until 1985. The exclusion provides:

> This policy does not apply to bodily injury or property damage arising out of the discharge, dispersal, release or escape of smoke, vapors, soot, fumes, acids, alkalines, toxic chemicals, liquids or gases, waste materials, or other irritants, contaminants or pollutants into or upon land, the atmosphere or any water course or body of water; but this exclusion does not apply if such discharge, dispersal, release or escape is sudden and accidental.

This exclusion has given rise to at least three interpretative issues in toxic tort and remediation litigation: (1) whether the dispersal, release or escape of pollutants was "sudden and accidental"; (2) whether the substance released was a "pollutant" within the clause; and (3) whether the substance was released "into or upon land [or] the atmosphere."

---

1. A § 106 order is an administrative order issued by the EPA pursuant to CERCLA § 106, 42 U.S.C.A. § 9606, following an administrative proceeding and may require the policyholder to conduct a cleanup or require other remedial steps. Failure to comply may result in liability for EPA's costs of cleanup, plus treble damages.

a.   *Sudden and Accidental Exception to the Pollution Exclusion*

Courts addressing the so-called sudden and accidental pollution exclusion have been required to determine whether the discharge, dispersal, release or escape is sudden and accidental, and therefore, not excluded from coverage. Most of the decisional law addressing this question has arisen in the context of environmental insurance coverage litigation involving property damage. The courts are split on the meaning of the "sudden and accidental" clause. Some courts, finding the clause to be clear and unambiguous, have concluded that for coverage to exist, the discharge, dispersal or release must be both sudden, defined in the temporal sense meaning instantaneous or abrupt, and accidental, defined as unexpected and unintended. Thus, according to these courts, no coverage exists for gradual releases.

Other courts, finding the clause to be ambiguous because the term "sudden" is susceptible to more than one reasonable interpretation, have concluded that the "sudden and accidental" language is merely a restatement of the occurrence definition and means only "unexpected and unintended." Many early cases construed this exclusion to be co-extensive with the definition of "occurrence" so that, in practice, the exclusion excluded few pollution-related claims. This trend began with the New Jersey decision of Lansco v. Department of Environmental Protection, 138 N.J.Super. 275, 350 A.2d 520, 524 (1975), affirmed 145 N.J.Super. 433, 368 A.2d 363 (1976), cert. denied 73 N.J. 57, 372 A.2d 322 (1977).

An Illinois Supreme Court decision summarizes the logic of the interpretation favoring insureds. In Outboard Marine Corp. v. Liberty Mutual Insurance Co., 154 Ill.2d 90, 180 Ill.Dec. 691, 607 N.E.2d 1204 (1992), the court, in reversing a lower court, held that the pollution exclusion for costs of responding to pollution that is not "sudden and accidental" is ambiguous, and thus that coverage exists even for pollution that occurs in a gradual fashion. In that action, the EPA and the State of Illinois brought suit against Outboard Marine for the discharge of toxic PCBs into Lake Michigan during the period from 1959 until 1972. As to the issue of the pollution exclusion, the Illinois Supreme Court stated:

> We find that the term "sudden" as used in the pollution exclusion exception contained in these * * * policies is ambiguous * * *.
>
>   Numerous dictionaries define "sudden" as happening unexpectedly, without notice or warning, or unforeseen. These same dictionaries also define "sudden" as abrupt, rapid, or swift. * * * Courts throughout the country are divided on the meaning of "sudden" within the instant context. * * * We conclude that the two definitions of "sudden" as set forth above are both reasonable interpretations of this term in the context in which it appears. Therefore, sudden is, at a minimum, ambiguous as used in these policies. In Illinois, ambiguities and doubts in insurance policies are resolved in favor of the insured, especially those that appear in exclusionary clauses. * * * Consequently, in this particular context, we construe

"sudden" in favor of OMC and find it to mean unexpected or unintended. * * *

In addition, * * * construing "sudden" to mean "abrupt" creates a contradiction within this particular clause and the policy as a whole.

* * * The pollution exclusion retriggers coverage for toxic releases which are "sudden and accidental." The policy defines "accident" to include "continuous or repeated exposure to conditions." * * * To construe "sudden" to mean "abrupt" results in a contradiction if one accepts the insurers' own definition of the term "accident." * * * Such a construction would result in the pollution exception clause retriggering coverage for toxic releases which are "abrupt" *and* gradual or "continuous and repeated" releases. Clearly, under such a construction this clause would be rendered absurd.

Other courts have interpreted "sudden" differently and have found that, for a release or discharge of hazardous waste to be sudden within the meaning of the pollution exclusion, it must occur abruptly or quickly or over a short period of time. They have given "sudden" a temporal meaning, rather than interpreting it as "unexpected" and found the term "sudden" to be unambiguous. See, e.g., Borg–Warner Corp. v. Insurance Co. of North America, 174 A.D.2d 24, 577 N.Y.S.2d 953 (1992); Technicon Electronics Corp. v. American Home Assurance Co., 141 A.D.2d 124, 533 N.Y.S.2d 91 (1988); Upjohn Co. v. New Hampshire Ins. Co., 438 Mich. 197, 476 N.W.2d 392, 397 (1991) ("The term 'sudden,' when considered in its plain and easily understood sense, is defined with a temporal element that joins together conceptually the immediate and unexpected; the common everyday understanding of the term 'sudden' is happening, coming, made or done quickly without warning or unexpectedly, abrupt; and 'accidental' means occurring unexpectedly and unintentionally, by chance."); Lumbermens Mut. Cas. Co. v. Belleville Indus., Inc., 407 Mass. 675, 555 N.E.2d 568 (1990). Dimmitt Chevrolet Inc. v. Southeastern Fidelity Ins. Corp., ___ So.2d ___, 1993 WL 241520 (Fla.1993) (court holds 5 to 4 that the drafting history of the sudden and accidental exception is immaterial because the language is clear; while "sudden" standing alone could connote unexpected, when it is joined by the conjunctive with "accidental," it would be redundant to give it the same meaning).

Does the nearly even split in decisions itself constitute proof of the existence of ambiguity?

Several courts have focused on the drafting history of the sudden and accidental clause. The definition of "occurrence" was added in 1966 to include unexpected and unintended damage, and explicitly provided that occurrence includes "continuous or repeated exposure to conditions." The pollution exclusion was designed to re-emphasize that distinction by eliminating coverage for deliberate and intentional pollution, but continuing to cover damage from gradual, unintended, "accidental" pollution. See American Home Prods. Corp. v. Liberty Mut. Ins. Co., 565 F.Supp. 1485, 1500–03 (S.D.N.Y.1983), affirmed as modified 748 F.2d 760 (2d Cir.1984) (discussing drafting history and background of the standard CGL policy); Joy Technologies Inc. v. Liberty Mut. Ins. Co., 187 W.Va. 742, 421 S.E.2d 493 (1992). For example, the New Jersey Supreme Court has ruled that insurers are estopped from arguing that the qualified pollution exclusion clause bars costs for cleaning up gradual environmental contamination because the industry should not be rewarded for "misrepresentation and nondisclosure" to state regulatory authorities. Morton International, Inc., v. General Accident Ins. Co. of America, 134 N.J. 1, 629 A.2d 831 (1993). The court found that the insurance industry "knowingly misstated [the exclusion's] intended effect" in 1970 when it sought to have state insurance regulators approve the new policy language. It concluded:

> We hold that notwithstanding the literal terms of the standard pollution-exclusion clause, that clause will be construed to provide coverage identical with that provided under the prior occurrence-based policy, except that the clause will be interpreted to preclude coverage in cases in which the *insured* intentionally discharges a known pollutant, irrespective of whether the resulting property damage was intended or expected. (emphasis in original).

See generally 10A Couch, Couch on Insurance 2d § 42:396 (rev. ed. 1983).

The exclusion has also been applied in toxic tort and product cases. See, for example, Techalloy Co. v. Reliance Ins. Co., 338 Pa.Super. 1, 487 A.2d 820, 827 (1984) in which the court found no duty to defend where the claimant's injuries resulted from exposure to toxic substances that the insured sporadically discharged over a 25–year period. The court concluded that the "allegations disclosing the circumstances and nature of the chemical discharge explicitly negate any potential for finding a sudden event in order to render the exclusion inapplicable."

Park–Ohio Industries Inc. v. The Home Indemnity Co., 975 F.2d 1215 (6th Cir.1992) held that the pollution exclusion could operate to bar coverage for injuries caused by allegedly defective products. In *Park–Ohio* the insured sought coverage for claims arising from the manufacture of induction furnaces, an allegedly defective product. The furnaces allegedly released rubber combustion products which were inhaled by workers and caused bodily injury. The insured argued that the pollution exclusion should not apply in products liability cases where the insured was not actively engaged in the discharge of the pollutants at issue or did not discharge the pollutants on its premises. The Sixth Circuit rejected these arguments: "The 'discharge' applies to any discharge, and there is nothing in the facts of this case which bring into question the meaning of 'the discharge' or who must make the discharge. In a sense, the pollution exclusion follows the product, as do all the terms of the policy."

Problem

In 1965, the Ciamarataro Brothers (the Brothers) established an open dump at the East Columbia landfill site in Tonka County. At that time, the Brothers believed the soil underlying a dump or landfill would act as a filter to prevent pollutants from migrating into and contaminating the groundwater. The landfill, as an open dump, received film and photo processing chemicals, oil filters containing waste oil, asphalt and solvents, paint, ink, liquid ether, foundry slag, asphalt tar, roofing materials, waste ash, kerosene, oil-soaked rags, cleaning solvents and dry cleaning solvents.

In 1970, because of the potential for causing groundwater problems, both the Columbia Pollution Control Agency (CPCA) and Tonka County adopted regulations prohibiting the acceptance of toxic and hazardous waste by landfills. Following promulgation of these regulations, the Brothers operated the East Columbia site as one of the state's first sanitary landfills. In 1974, East Columbia became a "modified sanitary" landfill, accepting only demolition fill, certain waste generated by companies involved in the construction industry, and municipal solid waste brought by individuals living in the area. The landfill is currently operated as a modified sanitary/demolition landfill.

In 1980, Tonka County hired an engineering firm to evaluate data collected from the testing of groundwater at four of the county's landfill sites. The firm's evaluation concluded that there existed extensive groundwater contamination at East Columbia. The CPCA notified the Brothers that they would be regarded as a potentially responsible party for purpose of studying and remediating the groundwater contamination. In 1985, the Brothers and the CPCA entered into a consent decree which made them responsible for all costs involved in the investigation and cleanup of groundwater contamination at East Columbia. The Brothers have instituted a declaratory judgment action against their insurers under policies which contain the standard pollution exclusion with the "sudden and accidental" exception to the exclusion. The Brothers maintain that the exception is satisfied because, by looking at individual releases, by each chemical, they are sudden, not gradual. The State of Columbia Supreme Court has previously held that "sudden" has a temporal meaning, implying "abrupt, quickly or over a short period of time."

The defendant insurers move for summary judgment on the grounds that no genuine factual issue exists as to the gradual nature of the contamination, and that they are therefore entitled to a judgment in their favor as a matter of law. An affidavit from one of the plaintiff's experts counters that there are, indeed, triable issues of fact, for it may be feasible to determine for many of the chemicals the proximity of the releases in time and space, the number of releases and the mechanism of the release, thus enabling a jury to determine if individual releases were "sudden." For the landfill's later period of operation commencing in 1974 during which the waste was limited to the sanitary landfill, another of plaintiffs' experts has given an affidavit stating that it is "normally possible to make an estimate of the timing of the discharge, at least for certain substances." The affidavit states further that the contamination that continues to the present time is caused by materials that were disposed of at the landfill over 20 years ago.

Based upon this record, can the insurers motion be granted?

b. Does the Claim Involve Release of a "Pollutant" into the Atmosphere?

In Olin Corp. v. Insurance Co. of North America, 762 F.Supp. 548 (S.D.N.Y.1991), the court rejected the insured's argument that the exclusion did not apply because the alleged pollutant, DDT, was its own "product." The court concluded that "the same substance may be a useful product when employed for its intended purpose and yet still be a pollutant when inappropriately introduced into the environment." See also Weber v. IMT Ins. Co., 462 N.W.2d 283 (Iowa 1990) (hog manure "unambiguously constitutes waste" when it is spilled on the road).

However, numerous other decisions have declined to apply the exclusion in the toxic products setting. In Continental Casualty Co. v. Rapid–American Corp., 80 N.Y.2d 640, 593 N.Y.S.2d 966, 609 N.E.2d 506 (1993), the New York Court of Appeals held that the clause "is ambiguous with regard to whether the asbestos fibers at issue—fibers inhaled by persons working closely with or suffering long term exposure to asbestos products—were discharged into the 'atmosphere' as contemplated by the exclusion." It observed that the terms "discharge" and "dispersal" coupled with the three places of discharge—into or upon land, the atmosphere, and bodies of water—"support the conclusion that the clause was meant to deal with broadly dispersed environmental pollution * * * not the confined environs of the present complaints." Accord, U.S. Fidelity & Guaranty Corp. v. Wilkin Insulation Co., 144 Ill.2d 64, 161 Ill.Dec. 280, 578 N.E.2d 926 (1991) (asbestos exposure); Atlantic Mut. Ins. Co. v. McFadden, 413 Mass. 90, 595 N.E.2d 762 (1992) (rejecting application of exclusion where underlying complaint alleged bodily injuries caused by exposure to lead paint because the term "pollutant" did not embrace such products, nor was the product dispersed into the atmosphere).

In a case involving injuries from inhalation of a sprayed insecticide, one federal trial court declined to apply the exclusion and drew a distinction between pollutants and products:

> [T]here is virtually no substance or chemical in existence that would not irritate or damage some person or property. The terms "irritant" or "contaminant," however, cannot be read in isolation, but must be construed as substances generally recognized as polluting the environment. In other words, a "pollutant" is not merely any substance that may cause harm to the "egg shell plaintiff," but rather it is a toxic or particularly harmful material which is recognized as such in industry or by governmental regulators.

Westchester Fire Ins. Co. v. City of Pittsburg, 768 F.Supp. 1463 (D.Kan. 1991). Which is the better interpretation of pollutant—to include otherwise useful products or to apply the *Westchester* analysis? See generally

Seth A. Ribner, Modern Environmental Insurance Law: "Sudden and Accidental", 63 St. John's L. Rev. 755 (1989), which concluded:

> The contract analysis that judges perform in insurance coverage disputes is familiar and routine. However, in high-stakes, highly charged environmental coverage litigation, courts applying the same general principles often do not agree. At best, the disagreements reflect legitimate differences of opinion. At worst, as in New York and Illinois, competing courts ignore the precedents that supposedly bind them. One immediate result of all this was that in 1986 ISO (the Insurance Services Office) extensively revised the standard CGL policy, which among other changes, includes a sweeping pollution exclusion that eliminates the "sudden and accidental" exception. However, because pollution damage frequently happens over long periods of time and is often not discovered until long after the pollution begins, pre–1986 policies will be litigated well into the next century. In the end, if things continue as they are, the process of case-by-case adjudication will yield a rough justice with insurers and industry each paying a share of the daunting tab for cleaning up the environment.

> For the present, the disarray in the judiciary, which makes every case a potential winner, only encourages more litigation. But before they enter the fray both insurers and insureds should take pause. Only fools fight in a burning house.

3. ABSOLUTE POLLUTION EXCLUSION

In 1986 the insurance industry expanded the pollution exclusion as part of an overall revision of the CGL policy. The 1986 standard policy excludes from coverage:

(1) "Bodily injury" or "property damage" arising out of the actual, alleged or threatened discharge, dispersal, release or escape of pollutants:

    (a) At or from premises you own, rent or occupy;

    (b) At or from any site or location used by or for you or others for the handling, storage, disposal, processing or treatment of waste;

    (c) Which are at any time transported, handled, stored, treated, disposed of, or processed as waste by or for you or any person or organization for whom you may be legally responsible;

* * *

(2) Any loss, cost, or expense arising out of any governmental direction or request that you test for, monitor, clean up, remove, contain, treat, detoxify or neutralize pollutants.

Pollutants mean any solid, liquid, gaseous or thermal irritant or contaminant, including smoke, vapor, soot, fumes, acids, alkalis, chemicals and waste. Waste includes materials to be recycled, reconditioned or reclaimed.

In sum, the revised provision excludes coverage of injury or damage *arising from* an actual or threatened release of "pollutants" (a) at or from the policyholder's owned premises or site of ongoing operations using the pollutants, or (b) from the policyholder's "waste" (wherever it is located). The exclusion also precludes coverage of any expenses arising out of governmental requests to monitor or clean up "pollutants." Virtually every court which has addressed the meaning of the "absolute" pollution exclusion has held, on summary judgment, that the exclusion was clear and unambiguous, and thus, precluded insurance coverage. See, e.g., Smith v. Hughes Aircraft Co. Corp., 783 F.Supp. 1222 (D.Ariz.1991); Ascon Properties, Inc. v. Illinois Union Ins. Co., 908 F.2d 976 (9th Cir.1990), opinion at 1990 WL 98860 (interpreting California law); E.I. du Pont de Nemours & Co. v. Admiral Ins. Co., 1990 WL 140100 (Del. Super. 1990); Vantage Development Corp. v. American Envt. Technologies Corp., 251 N.J.Super. 516, 598 A.2d 948 (1991); Colonial Tanning Corp. v. Home Indem. Co., 780 F.Supp. 906 (N.D.N.Y. 1991).

Despite the seeming clarity of the exclusion, one author has concluded that one may anticipate courts finding coverage. See generally Burke, Pollution Exclusion Clauses: The Agony, the Ecstasy, and the Irony for Insurance Companies, 17 N. Ky. L. Rev. 443, 471 (1990), where the writer states:

> The history of pollution insurance has been marked with attempts to provide coverage, and then repeated attempts to severely limit that coverage. The 1973 pollution exclusion succeeded somewhat in restricting pollution coverage, but not until after 13 years of judicial interpretation did its restrictions begin to have some effect. The irony for the insurance industry is that it had ditched the 1973 pollution exclusion by the time most courts had begun giving it at least some of the force and effect that the insurers had sought from the beginning.
>
> That effect, of course, had been mixed. Federal courts are much more likely to restrict coverage and a duty to defend under the 1973 pollution exclusion, but they also are following the majority rule of a fact-specific analysis of what the insured business intended or expected, or knew or should have known. The result has been cases almost evenly split regarding landfills, underground pipes and storage tanks, and pollution that was a continuous part of regular business practices. Coverage and a duty to defend are less likely to be granted for continuous industrial pollution, while insurers are more likely to lose cases involving leaks from underground tanks and pipes.

Given the millions of dollars at stake in hundreds of pollution cases across the country, it is uncertain whether the courts will give a restrictive reading to the 1985 pollution exclusion. Ample evidence exists, however, to support the thesis that insurance companies and their clients will endure the same sorting-out period with the next exclusion as they had to experience with the old one. The new exclusion proscribes many types of coverage, but enough ambiguities exist to provide at least several instances of coverage that the insurers may never have intended.

What kinds of contamination-related injuries can you identify that would not be within the scope of the exclusion? See Pipefitters Welfare Educational Fund v. Westchester Fire Ins. Co., 976 F.2d 1037 (7th Cir.1992), where insured was sued in a toxic tort suit arising from PCB-laden oils that injured an employee of a scrap metal dealer who received electrical transformers from the insured. The court held that an insurer with an absolute pollution exclusion clause had no duty to defend or indemnify because the transfer of the transformer for scrap was "waste" and the discharge of eighty gallons of PCB oil onto land was "pollution."

4. PERSONAL INJURY ENDORSEMENT

In an attempt to avoid some of the limitations on coverage under the terms, conditions and exclusions of the CGL policy, insureds have sought new approaches to obtaining coverage for toxic tort and environmental claims. One approach has been to invoke an endorsement sometimes found in CGL policies known as the "personal injury and advertising liability" endorsement, which provides coverage for "damages because of personal injury or advertising injury." Personal injury typically is defined in the policy to mean:

(1) false arrest, detention, imprisonment, or malicious prosecution;

(2) wrongful entry or eviction or other invasion of the right of private occupancy;

(3) a publication or utterance

    (a) of a libel or slander or other defamatory or disparaging material, or

    (b) in violation of an individual's right of privacy.

It would seem at first reading that coverage for personal injury under the endorsement is precisely limited to damages resulting from one of the specifically enumerated torts. Nevertheless, in Pipefitters Welfare Educational Fund v. Westchester Fire Insurance Co., 976 F.2d 1037 (7th Cir.1992), the Seventh Circuit found a duty to defend under the personal injury endorsement in a case involving the release of PCBs. Evidence showed that a spill of eighty gallons of oil laden with PCBs took place while the claimant in the underlying action was preparing a transformer purchased from the insured for resale as scrap. The claimant alleged that the insured had disposed of the transformer unlawfully by failing to warn that it contained PCBs, and sought damages arising out of the spill, including cleanup costs, diminution of property value, imposition of a reclamation lien by the government and restricted access as a result of the government's actions.

In the coverage action, the insured argued that the underlying claim alleged a "wrongful entry or eviction or other invasion of the right to private occupancy" within the meaning of the personal injury endorsement. The insurer, on the other hand, argued that coverage under the endorsement is limited to conduct that is: (1) undertaken by one claiming an interest in property; and (2) intended to deprive the injured party of its right to privately occupy that property. The court observed that the term "other invasion of the right to private occupancy" has "less than a precise meaning" and encompassed the conduct alleged in the underlying claim.

The court found that the underlying claim did not allege an "eviction" because, by its plain and ordinary meaning, that term refers to the landlord/tenant context, but nevertheless, observed that the term "wrongful entry" is substantially similar to trespass. Moreover, "to commit a trespass, one need not intend to take possession of the encroached-upon premises, or to deprive occupants of their right to possess those premises." Thus, the court concluded that the underlying complaint "arguably alleges an 'other invasion'" sufficient to trigger the insurer's duty to defend.

See also Titan Holdings Syndicate v. City of Keene, 898 F.2d 265 (1st Cir.1990), where the underlying claim against the insured city alleged that as a result of the city's operation of a sewage treatment plant claimants were "continuously bombarded by and exposed to noxious, fetid and putrid odors, gases and particulates, to loud and disturbing noises during the night, and to unduly bright night lighting." In the coverage action, although the court agreed with the insured's argument that the pollution exclusion clause did not apply to coverage under the personal injury endorsement, it determined that, with one possible exception, the underlying claims did not fall within the scope of the personal injury coverage. The court stated: "[t]o come within the personal injury coverage, a suit must be based upon allegations of an offense to which the City might become liable." The court noted that New Hampshire law does not define the tort of "wrongful entry" as used in the personal injury endorsement and, thus, turned to the law on trespass. It concluded that the sewage plant's emissions did not reach the level of "intentional invasion" necessary to be actionable under New Hampshire law and, thus, did not constitute "wrongful entry" within the meaning of the personal injury endorsement.

However, the court then focused on a term contained in the personal injury endorsement of only one of the policies before it, which provided coverage for liability arising out of any "other invasion of the right of private occupancy." Because under New Hampshire law an invasion of the right of private occupancy need not involve a "physical invasion," the court concluded that the underlying allegations relating to the treatment plant's noxious odors, noise and light fell within the meaning of the personal injury endorsement and thus, triggered the insurer's duty to defend.

Can trespass and nuisance-like claims be reasonably interpreted as within the scope of the "right of occupancy" coverage? What might the insurers have intended in these clauses? See Columbia v. Continental Ins. Co., 189 A.D.2d 391, 595 N.Y.S.2d 988 (1993) (the wrongful entry, eviction or invasion of private occupancy was directed at liability for purposeful acts aimed at dispossession of real property by someone asserting an interest therein, not leachate contaminations, regardless of whether the legal theory is trespass or nuisance).

5. OWNED PROPERTY EXCLUSION

CGL policies are third party policies which provide coverage only for damages to such third parties, not for first party losses of the insured. This is reflected in the standard CGL's "owned property exclusion" which typically states:

This insurance does not apply to property damage to

(1) property owned or occupied by or rented to the insured.

(2) property used by the insured, or

(3) property in the care, custody or control of the insured or as to which the insured is for any purpose exercising physical control.

For example, a policyholder defending a CERCLA suit often seeks to recover from its insurer the costs of cleaning up its own property or the underlying groundwater. Policyholders often argue that these costs are covered despite the owned property exclusion because the cleanup prevents damages to the property of others or, under the common law, the policyholder does not "own" the groundwater.

Of the few that have considered the issue, the most significant case is the New Jersey Supreme Court opinion in State, Dept. of Environmental Protection v. Signo Trading Int'l, Inc., 130 N.J. 51, 612 A.2d 932 (1992). In a 4–3 decision, the court held that the owned property exclusion precludes coverage when there is only a "threat" of damage to the property of a third party, even if that threat is "imminent" and "immediate." Despite public policy which strongly favors a finding of coverage, the court stated the clear language of the policy must govern:

[T]hus, under its clear terms, the policy does not cover the costs of cleanup performed by or on behalf of an insured on its own property when those costs are incurred to alleviate damage to the insured's own property and not to the property of a third party.

In *Signo Trading*, a chemical fire occurred at the insured's warehouse. After the fire, the New Jersey Department of Environmental Protection and Energy discovered hazardous waste in the warehouse and filed suit to have the property cleaned. The issue presented was whether the imminent or immediate threat of damage to properties adjacent to the warehouse from the leaking hazardous wastes would be sufficient to trigger coverage under the policies despite the owned property exclusion. The trial court had previously found that while potential damages to adjacent properties were imminent, no actual damages to third parties had occurred.

The court rejected the holding of the appellate division in *Signo Trading* as well as the logic of another case, Summit Associates, Inc. v. Liberty Mutual Fire Insurance Co., 229 N.J.Super. 56, 550 A.2d 1235 (1988), which had held that an insured may recover the cost of measures intended to prevent future injury to a third party, if the threat of such injury appears to be "imminent" or "immediate." Instead, the court held that the "plain language" of the policy whose "definition of property damage does not encompass 'threatened harm' even if that threat is 'imminent' and 'immediate' " governed.

Do you agree with the majority here? The dissent argues that unless these costs are expended on the insured's property, damage to third parties will occur, and therefore, they are not within the exclusion.

In contrast, a Wisconsin appeals court in City of Edgerton v. General Casualty Co. of Wisconsin, 172 Wis.2d 518, 493 N.W.2d 768 (App.1992) held that the owned property exclusion would not bar coverage where there was ongoing groundwater contamination. The court concluded that "repairs to the site itself, when made as an element of a comprehensive cleanup and remediation plan designed to repair the environment, are not excluded from coverage by an owned-property exclusion." See also, United States Aviex Co. v. Travelers Ins. Co., 125 Mich.App. 579, 336 N.W.2d 838 (1983) (under Michigan law, groundwater was not "owned" by the surface landowner, and therefore, groundwater was outside the exclusion for property owned by the insured). But cleanup costs for soil contamination or exclusively on-site contamination may invite a different coverage result from groundwater contamination. See Western World Ins. Co. v. Dana, 765 F.Supp. 1011 (E.D.Cal. 1991) (coverage for removal of hazardous materials from policyholder's soil before materials reached adjacent land or groundwater barred by owned property exclusion).

What do you think regarding the treatment of groundwater? How about an aquifer partially situated under the insured's land?

In an unusual twist, the Maryland Court of Appeals in Bausch & Lomb v. Utica Mutual Insurance Co., 330 Md. 758, 625 A.2d 1021 (1993) held that insured's cleanup of groundwater contamination was not covered because the state's interest in the groundwater did not constitute a property interest sufficient to make the insured's pollution a damage to a third party's property.

6. KNOWN RISK LIMITATION

Related but not identical to the "expected or intended" issue is the insurer's argument that an event or harm is not covered because it was a "known risk" at the time the insured entered into its CGL policy. It is generally accepted in insurance law that one cannot obtain insurance for a risk that has already transpired or for damage that was known prior to the effective date of an insurance contract. See, e.g., Appalachian Ins. Co. v. Liberty Mut. Ins. Co., 676 F.2d 56 (3d Cir.1982). In other words, once the risk of loss is a certainty, it is no longer an insurable interest.

Insurers argue that when a policy period commenced at a time when an insured already had been discharging waste for a considerable time, or worse, had known that a site was contaminated, the loss was already in progress, so that the "known risk" doctrine should apply and preclude coverage. In response, insureds argue that there is a difference between a "known risk" and a "known loss": insureds obtain insurance for known *risks* ; only prior knowledge of actual *loss* should make the risk uninsurable. Consequently, they argue, it is not enough to show that the insured knew that a site was contaminated; instead the determinative fact is whether the insured knew that it was going to be liable for damage resulting from the discharge of toxic substances. See Outboard Marine Corp. v. Liberty Mut. Ins. Co., 607 N.E.2d 1204 (Ill.1992) in which the court held that proof that a policyholder knew it was discharging pollution did not make any resulting loss a "known risk" sufficient to defeat coverage. To preclude coverage, the court held that a carrier must show the policyholder also knew or should have known the pollution would lead to a loss or liability.

Some cases do hold that once an insured receives a notification from a governmental agency that it is responsible for contamination of property, it becomes a known loss and is uninsurable. For example, in Township of Gloucester v. Maryland Casualty Co., 668 F.Supp. 394, 403 (D.N.J.1987), Home Insurance Co. moved for summary judgment on the grounds that its coverage commenced after the New Jersey Department of Environmental Protection filed a complaint against the township. Sustaining the insurer's denial of coverage, the court stated:

> It is clear, based on the record before the court, that the township had actual knowledge of the occurrence prior to The Home's policy period. In the case of The Home policy, this is not a situation where the township could have reasonably expected that it "was free of the risk of becoming liable for injuries of which it could not have been aware prior to its purchase of insurance." * * * One cannot obtain insurance for a risk that the insured knows has already transpired.

If the insured obtains a policy without disclosing receipt of a PRP letter or receipt of other notice that it may be liable for cleanup costs, does that constitute fraud? See, e.g., Time Oil Inc. v. Cigna Property & Casualty Ins. Co., 743 F.Supp. 1400 (W.D.Wash.1990) (discussing the duty of the insured to act in good faith and make disclosure to the insurer of information revealing a "substantial probability" that it would be liable).

What if the insured is named as a potentially responsible party by the EPA for remediating a site, then acquires insurance which disclosed the proceeding, and later is sued by private parties arising out of the migration of the wastes beyond the site? See Stonewall Ins. Co. v. City of Palos Verdes Estates, 18 Cal.App.4th 1234, 9 Cal.Rptr.2d 663 (1992), review granted and limited by ___ Cal. ___, 13 Cal.Rptr.2d 724, 840 P.2d 266 (1992). Should it make a difference whether the loss arises out of first party coverage i.e., the site is owned by the insured, or out of third party liability coverage?

Chapter Twelve

DEFENSES

A. INTRODUCTION

This Chapter brings together the defenses commonly asserted in toxic tort litigation. In prior Chapters we considered some issues that may be asserted by a defendant, such as the absence of proof of injury, uncertainty as to causation, superseding causes, and the bulk supplier/knowledgeable purchaser defense. Here the primary focus will be on statutes of limitation, statutes of repose, contributory negligence or fault, and assumption of the risk—most of which are affected by the plaintiff's conduct, be it action or the failure to act.

As we briefly mentioned in Chapter 1, toxic tort litigation presents special statutes of limitation problems which distinguish such cases from sporadic accident cases. The difficulties posed for plaintiffs derive from factors which have been explored in earlier chapters: (1) the long latency periods between exposure to a toxic substance and manifestation of the disease or condition which may have resulted from the exposure; (2) the uncertainty as to the causal relationships between the exposure and the harm suffered by the plaintiff; (3) the physiological evolution in the nature of the harm itself—for example, from a plaintiff developing pleural thickening at one stage in the exposure/manifestation process, to symptoms of asbestosis at a later stage, to finally developing lung cancer or mesothelioma at an even later stage; and (4) the problem of whether a plaintiff will be permitted to split her causes of action as her physical conditions evolve, or whether she must assert all her claims in one unitary proceeding.

Because of these time-based problems which a plaintiff may experience, some state legislatures have enacted special statutes reviving toxic tort claims that would have otherwise lapsed. Other states have enacted so-called "discovery" statutes of limitation. All of these discovery statutes prevent a plaintiff's cause of action from accruing until such time as a reasonable person would have discovered the injury, and some delaying accrual until both the injury and defendant's contribution to it could reasonably be discovered. Still other states have enacted statutes of repose which grant defendants immunity after a prescribed number of years from a particular event, such as the construction of a building or sale of a product.

Another important dichotomy respecting statutes of limitation is the influence which plaintiff's theory of the case has on the selection of the appropriate statute. Nuisance and trespass cases have special statute of limitation conundra rarely present in products liability, strict liability or negligence cases—that of the "continuing" versus permanent invasion, a distinction which has spawned a body of often abstruse opinions seeking to apply them. For that reason, we have divided the discussion between "land-based" theories of liability from product and occupational cases.

B. STATUTES OF LIMITATION FOR INJURY TO REAL PROPERTY

It can be extremely important in cases based on theories of nuisance, trespass, and strict liability to understand the special problems posed by statutes of limitation. As the cases below demonstrate, resolution of statutes of limitation issues will turn on whether the nuisance or trespass is characterized as "continuing" or "permanent." First, we consider Mangini v. Aerojet–General Corp., 230 Cal.App.3d 1125, 281 Cal.Rptr. 827 (1991). In *Mangini*, the plaintiffs were current landowners who were suing lessees of a prior owner of the property for contamination that occurred during the lessees' occupancy and as a result of their industrial uses of the land. The material below is the appellate court's determination of whether each of plaintiffs' claims can survive statutes of limitation challenges.

MANGINI v. AEROJET–GENERAL CORPORATION

California Court of Appeals, 1991.
230 Cal.App.3d 1125, 281 Cal.Rptr. 827.

SIMS, J.

* * *

Defendant leased the property in question from its former owners, the Cavitts, from 1960 to 1970. Plaintiffs acquired the property pursuant to an exchange of other real property from the executor and administrator of the Cavitts' estate, codefendant James H. Cavitt, in 1975.

Defendant's lease (attached to the complaint as an exhibit) provided, "The term of this lease is for a period of ten (10) years, commencing [in 1960] and ending [in 1970] * * *." The lease also stated, among other things, "Upon termination of this lease, Lessee shall surrender the premises in as good state and condition as when received by Lessee, reasonable use and wear thereof consistent with the business engaged in by Lessee * * * excepted." Despite this provision, defendant failed to remove millions of pounds of waste rocket fuel materials and other hazardous substances which it burned, buried, or otherwise disposed of on the property during the term of its lease, creating hazardous conditions which remain on the property.

Plaintiffs have been compelled by the Sacramento County Air Pollution Control District to undertake testing of the property and may be required under state and federal law to abate the hazardous conditions created by defendant.

Plaintiffs did not learn of the hazardous conditions until "recently."

* * *

III

Plaintiffs Should Be Allowed to Amend Their Complaint to Allege Facts Showing Continuing Nuisance and Trespass

Defendant contends all of plaintiffs' counts are barred by the statute of limitations and that plaintiffs cannot escape this bar by any amendment to their complaint.

A.   *A Claim for Damages for a Permanent Public Nuisance is Subject to the Three-Year Statute of Limitations in Code of Civil Procedure Section 338, Subdivision (b)*

Plaintiffs assert their count based upon public nuisance is not barred by the statute of limitations because in their view a claim based on public nuisance is never barred by the statute of limitations. This argument is not well taken.

Plaintiffs assert there is no statute of limitations running on their claim for public nuisance because section 3490 provides: "No lapse of time can legalize a public nuisance, amounting to an actual obstruction of public right."

Section 3490 has been construed to mean that the statute of limitations is no defense to an action brought by a public entity to abate a public nuisance. However, where private citizens have sued for damages for special injury based on public nuisance, our Supreme Court has characterized the nuisance as either "continuing" or "permanent" and has used the characterization to determine whether the suit is subject to the statute of limitations.   * * *

Thus, for example, in Phillips v. City of Pasadena [162 P.2d 625 (Cal.1945)], plaintiff sued for damages for the unlawful obstruction of a public road.   * * *

Addressing defendant's contention that plaintiff's claim was barred by the statute of limitations, the Phillips court concluded, "Where a nuisance is of such character that it will presumably continue indefinitely it is considered permanent, and the limitations period runs from the time the nuisance is created. On the other hand, if the nuisance may be discontinued at any time it is considered continuing in character. Every repetition of a continuing nuisance is a separate wrong for which the person may bring successive actions for damages until the nuisance is abated, even though an action based on the original wrong may be barred."

Our Supreme Court recently applied Phillips's rule in Baker v. Burbank–Glendale–Pasadena Airport Authority [705 P.2d 866 (Cal. 1985)]. There, plaintiffs sued for (among other things) nuisance caused by noise, smoke, and vibrations from flights over their homes. The trial court ruled the action was barred by the statute of limitations. In reversing the trial court, our Supreme Court framed the issue as whether the nuisance was permanent or continuing: "Two distinct classifications have emerged in nuisance law which determine the remedies available to injured parties and the applicable statute of limitations. On the one hand, permanent nuisances are of a type where ' "by one act a permanent injury is done, [and] damages are assessed once for all." ' * * * In such cases, plaintiffs ordinarily are required to bring one action for all past, present and future damage within three years after the permanent nuisance is erected * * *. Damages are not dependent upon any subsequent use of the property but are complete when the nuisance comes into existence * * *.

"On the other hand, if a nuisance is a use which may be discontinued at any time, it is considered continuing in character and persons harmed by it may bring successive actions for damages until the nuisance is abated * * *. Recovery is limited, however, to actual injury suffered prior to commencement of each action. Prospective damages are unavailable."

* * * We therefore conclude the continuing/permanent nuisance distinction drawn by Phillips and Baker applies to private suits for damages based upon public nuisances.

* * *

Thus, where a private citizen sues for damages to real property caused by a public nuisance, and the nuisance is permanent, the three year statute of limitations in Code of Civil Procedure section 338, subdivision (b) (for trespass or injury to real property), begins to run when the permanent nuisance is created.

B. *Plaintiffs May Amend Their Complaint to Plead Facts Showing a Continuing Nuisance*

This leaves the question whether the nuisance alleged in the instant case is permanent or continuing. "In case of doubt as to the permanency of the injury the plaintiff may elect whether to treat a particular nuisance as permanent or continuing." Baker v. Burbank–Glendale–Pasadena Airport Authority, supra[.]

Defendant argues that plaintiffs' complaint manifests an election of permanent nuisance. Defendant points out that plaintiffs have alleged their property is "unusable and extremely difficult to market for an indefinite period of time" and there is "little likelihood that the Subject Property will ever be as valuable as it would have been if not contaminated." Moreover, defendant notes that plaintiffs seek to recover all diminution in the market value of their property by seeking an injunction that would make defendant buy the property from plaintiffs at its market value unaffected by contamination. This form of relief is incompatible with a claim based on injuries caused by continuing nuisance.

On the other hand, plaintiffs allege they can amend their complaint to allege facts showing a continuing nuisance, i.e., the contamination can be abated and defendant has entered into a federal consent decree agreeing to clean up the property. The question is whether these proposed averments sufficiently allege a continuing nuisance.

"The cases finding the nuisance complained of to be unquestionably permanent in nature have involved solid structures, such as a building encroaching upon the plaintiff's land, a steam railroad operating over plaintiff's land, or regrade of a street for a rail system.

"The classic example of a continuing nuisance is an ongoing * * * disturbance, caused by noise, vibration or foul odor [and] * * * the distinction to be drawn is between encroachments of a permanent nature erected upon one's lands, and a complaint made, not of the location of the offending structures, but of the continuing use of such structures." Baker v. Burbank–Glendale–Pasadena Airport Authority, supra.

Here, according to plaintiffs, no structures are involved and the nuisance consists of the offensive chemical pollution which can be abated. In the decisions of our Supreme Court, the crucial distinction between a permanent and continuing nuisance is whether the nuisance may be discontinued or abated. * * *

Plaintiffs' proposed pleading therefore meets the crucial test of a continuing nuisance: that the offensive condition is abatable.

We note plaintiffs' land may be subject to a continuing nuisance even though defendant's offensive conduct ended years ago. That is because the "continuing" nature of the nuisance refers to the continuing damage caused by the offensive condition, not to the acts causing the offensive condition to occur.

* * *

In cases of doubt respecting the permanency of an injury caused by a nuisance, courts are inclined to favor the right to successive actions. * * * Whether contamination by toxic waste is a permanent or continuing injury is ordinarily a question of fact turning on the nature and extent of the contamination. We therefore conclude plaintiffs should be allowed to amend their complaint to state their proposed facts so as to aver a theory of continuing nuisance and to seek damages caused them within three years of the date of filing the complaint.

C. Plaintiffs May Amend Their Complaint to Allege a Continuing Trespass

Historically, the application of the statute of limitations for trespass has been the same as for nuisance and has depended on whether the trespass has been continuing or permanent. As we have recounted, the crucial test of the permanency of a trespass or nuisance is whether the trespass or nuisance can be discontinued or abated. We have already seen how plaintiffs' proposed amendments to their complaint meet this test.

We note that plaintiffs' theory of continuing trespass is sanctioned by the Restatement (Second) of Torts, which states: "(b) Continuing trespass. The actor's failure to remove from land in the possession of another a thing which he has tortiously * * * placed on the land constitutes a continuing trespass for the entire time during which the thing is on the land and * * * confers on the possessor of the land an option to maintain a succession of actions based on a theory of continuing trespass or to treat the continuance of the thing on the land as an aggravation of the original trespass." (Id. at § 161, comm. b.)

We therefore conclude plaintiffs should be afforded the opportunity to amend their complaint clearly to allege facts that show a continuing trespass.

IV

PLAINTIFFS' COUNTS FOR NEGLIGENCE, NEGLIGENCE PER SE, AND STRICT LIABILITY ARE BARRED BY THE STATUTE OF LIMITATIONS

We have no occasion to determine whether plaintiffs' counts for negligence, negligence per se, or strict liability state facts sufficient to constitute a cause of action because, assuming they do, each is barred by the statute of limitations. The parties agree each of these counts is subject to the three-year statute of limitations. As we shall explain, plaintiffs had good reason to inquire about (and therefore learn about) these matters more than three years before their complaint was filed.

In the third count, the complaint avers defendant was negligent by selecting the subject property as a site for disposing of hazardous substance disposal, improper disposing of hazardous substances, failing to determine the nature and extent of the contamination, failing to contain or remedy the contamination, and failing to inform plaintiffs of the contamination.

The fourth count, for negligence per se, is premised on defendant's alleged violation of statutes and regulations by their discharge of hazardous waste on the property and into the waters of the state.

The sixth count, for strict liability, is premised on defendant's alleged use, disposal, storage and maintenance of hazardous substances on the subject property.

The traditional rule is that a statute of limitations begins to run upon the occurrence of the last element essential to the cause of action, even if the plaintiff is unaware of his cause of action. The harshness of that rule has been ameliorated in cases where it would be manifestly unjust to deprive a plaintiff of a cause of action before he is aware he has been injured. A cause of action under this discovery rule accrues when " 'plaintiff either (1) actually discovered his injury and its negligent cause or (2) could have discovered injury and cause through the exercise of reasonable diligence.' " The limitations period begins once the plaintiff has notice or information of circumstances to put a reasonable person on inquiry. Subjective suspicion is not required. If a person becomes aware of facts which would make a reasonably prudent person suspicious, he or she has a duty to investigate further and is charged with knowledge of matters which would have been revealed by such an investigation.

* * *

Here, the complaint alleges that defendant released toxic substances on the property from 1960 to 1970. Plaintiffs acquired their interests in the property between 1975 and 1983. The lawsuit was filed on January 14, 1988, and alleges that plaintiffs did not learn of the hazardous conditions until "recently." The complaint fails to allege when plaintiffs made the discovery, the circumstances of the discovery and why, in the exercise of reasonable diligence, they could not have made the discovery sooner.

The question then becomes whether the defect can be cured by amendment.

Plaintiffs set forth the following additional facts which they intend to plead if allowed to do so:

"In late 1979, the Manginis were contacted by an investigator for the California Department of Justice, who informed the Manginis that he was conducting an investigation of [defendant's] hazardous waste disposal practices and was interviewing people who owned land near [defendant's] Sacramento facilities. The investigator asked the Manginis whether they had any knowledge of [defendant's] waste disposal practices in the area. The Manginis told him that they did not. He informed them that there was no reason for them to be concerned about any environmental problems on their property."

"On or about April 24, 1984, more than four years later, the Manginis received a letter from [defendant] asking for permission to inspect the property. For the next two years, [defendant] discussed with the Manginis its plans for inspecting and conducting tests on the property. Never during that period of time did [defendant] tell the Manginis anything about the nature of [defendant's] activities while it had leased the property." * * *

* * *

At some undisclosed time, defendant took soil samples and plaintiffs hired an independent laboratory. In January 1987, defendant gave plaintiffs its laboratory test results, which appeared to show chemical contamination in the soil, but told plaintiffs this was laboratory error. In April 1987, the Sacramento Air Pollution Control District informed plaintiffs their property was contaminated with hazardous substances.

In mid–1987, plaintiffs retained an attorney and obtained [EPA] records, including 1979–1980 Department of Justice investigative reports.

Plaintiffs state, "Those reports disclosed for the first time to the Manginis the nature of [defendant's] activities while it had leased the property from 1960 to 1970. The reports showed that [defendant] had disposed of thousands of pounds of trichloroethylene (TCE), ammonium perchlorate rocket fuel and other chemical contaminants on the property. The reports also showed that the California Attorney General's Office and the EPA had filed lawsuits against [defendant] to compel it to clean up contamination on property which [defendant] owned or leased in the Sacramento area." Plaintiffs filed their complaint on January 14, 1988.

* * *

Thus, in 1984, more than three years before filing the complaint, plaintiffs knew the following facts: (1) the recorded lease gave notice that defendant had engaged in activities of a potentially hazardous nature on their land; (2) the Department of Justice investigated defendant's practices regarding disposal of hazardous waste in the area; and (3) defendant asked plaintiffs for permission to inspect their property.

Whether any of these three facts in isolation would be sufficient to impart notice is open to dispute. However, the combination of these facts together establish as a matter of law that, when defendant contacted plaintiffs in 1984, plaintiffs had sufficient information to put them on notice of the possibility that defendant had dumped hazardous waste on their land.

That defendant gave evasive, or even untruthful, reasons for the inspection did not relieve plaintiffs of their duty of inquiry once they had sufficient facts to suspect the cause of action. Indeed, the evasiveness gave further reason for suspicion.

Here, had plaintiffs investigated in a timely fashion, they would have discovered the Department of Justice reports, which they admittedly received shortly after requesting them from the EPA in 1987. Plaintiffs are charged with knowledge of the information in those reports.
* * *

We therefore conclude the statute of limitations on plaintiffs' claims for negligence, negligence per se, and strict liability began to run no later than April 24, 1984, when plaintiffs received defendant's letter asking to inspect the property. These claims, asserted in the complaint filed January 14, 1988, are barred by the three-year statute of limitations.

Notes and Questions

1. The distinction between permanent or continuing nuisances and trespasses, which sometimes are described as permanent or temporary for damage purposes, is well described in William H. Rodgers, Jr., Environmental Law § 2.9 at 29–30 (Supp. 1984):

Statutory limitation periods, adding the weight of legislative opinion to arguments for respecting the status quo, are of some importance in nuisance cases. The key distinction that emerges here is that insufferable one between a permanent and a temporary nuisance. With due respect for the obscurity of the differences, a permanent nuisance describes those continuous polluters with odds-on prospects of conducting business as usual in the years ahead. For these offenders, the expectation is that permanent damages will be recovered in a single lawsuit. The damage action accrues for limitation purposes when the first actionable injury occurs, which usually is when the polluting business commences operations.

The classical understanding of a temporary nuisance is the occasional invasion dependent upon contingencies such as wind and rain. The definition is usually extended to include all nuisances with prospects of being controlled, so that anything not a permanent nuisance is temporary. If the nuisance is temporary, the plaintiff is entitled to have it abated and may recover for all injury sustained during the statutory period.

The permanent/temporary nuisance classification has troubling features. As an abstract matter, there are obvious transaction costs in encouraging repeated lawsuits (by invoking the temporary category) and obvious risks of error in attempting to effectuate a final accounting of a social conflict with high uncertainties (by invoking the permanent category). Enhancing a money judgment if a nuisance is "uncontrollable" skews incentives for plaintiffs who are expected to be pressing for controls to the limits of technology. Giving defendants advantages for demonstrating that their spillovers are "uncontrollable" relieves them of the obligation to develop imaginative new abatement strategies.

Perhaps the best way out of this difficulty is to allow plaintiffs to make an election, typically after discovery, between the permanent or temporary characterization. Presumably in most cases the prospects of a "bigger" judgment for a permanent nuisance would be overcome by plaintiff's fears of no compensation for injuries not discovered or hopes that the future will bring some corrective technology or practice. * * *

2. For a comprehensive analysis of the permanent and temporary distinction, see Goldstein v. Potomac Electric Power Company, 285 Md. 673, 404 A.2d 1064 (1979), where the Maryland Court of Appeals held that plaintiffs' action for the diminution in value to their land was barred by a three-year statute because the injury occurred at the time the public utility's pollution commenced to invade plaintiffs' land and constituted a permanent nuisance. The court was influenced by the fact that it could not order the utility to cease operations, and hence, the nuisance was not abatable.

Some other examples of courts' treatment of this issue include: Atlas Chemical Industries v. Anderson, 524 S.W.2d 681 (Tex.1975) (longstanding air pollution is a permanent nuisance); Sundell v. Town of New London, 119 N.H. 839, 409 A.2d 1315 (1979) (longstanding water pollution is a temporary nuisance); Moy v. Bell, 46 Md.App. 364, 416 A.2d 289, 294 (1980) ("Recognizing * * * that any nuisance man creates, man can abate, it seems that the question * * * is not the possibility of abatement but rather its likelihood").

For an extensive discussion of temporary versus permanent damages where defendant's salt plant damaged the aquifer, which in turn, harmed plaintiffs' agricultural operations and land values, see Miller v. Cudahy Company, 592 F.Supp. 976 (D.Kan.1984), affirmed 858 F.2d 1449 (10th Cir.1988). Defendants often argue that the nuisance *is permanent* so that all actions are time-barred. Rejecting this argument, see Haenchen v. Sands Products Co., 626 P.2d 332, 334 (Okl.App.1981); Cox v. Cambridge Square Towne Houses, Inc., 239 Ga. 127, 236 S.E.2d 73 (1977). See Annot., Statute of Limitations for Nuisance Based on Air Pollution, 19 A.L.R. 4th 442 (1979); Application of Statute of Limitations in Private Tort Actions Based on Injury to Persons or Property Caused by Underground Flow of Contaminants, 11 ALR 5th 438 (1993).

One likely inference of adopting the continuing nuisance analysis is that it undermines a defendant's argument that it has obtained prescriptive rights to pollute plaintiff's property. See Miller v. Cudahy Company, 592 F.Supp. 976 (D.Kan.1984), affirmed 858 F.2d 1449 (10th Cir.1988). This is especially so for public nuisances. See also Smallpage v. Turlock Irrigation District, 26 Cal.App.2d 538, 79 P.2d 752 (1938) ("One may not acquire an easement by prescription to maintain a public nuisance, and there can be no prescriptive right to pollute a stream to the detriment of the public"); and Strong v. Sullivan, 180 Cal. 331, 181 P. 59 (1919) ("No lapse of time can legalize a public nuisance * * * No right by prescription may be acquired to obstruct a sidewalk. Nor to maintain any other sort of nuisance.").

3. Another recent California case, Capogeannis v. Superior Court (Spence), 12 Cal.App.4th 668, 15 Cal.Rptr.2d 796 (1993), sets forth a rationale for classifying most nuisances as continuing. In *Capogeannis*, plaintiffs, who acquired the property in 1984, sued the prior owner and one of its tenants for leaking underground storage tanks that had contaminated the property during the 1970s. Plaintiffs first learned of the tanks in 1986 and of the contamination in early 1987, but did not sue until December 1990. To overcome the three-year statute, plaintiffs offered affidavits of a registered geologist and an environmental assessor who opined that the contamination from the petroleum products was "abatable through environmental remediation," whereas defendant's experts opined that the contamination would not be "entirely abatable because there will always be some residual contamination regardless of the technology or combination of [remediation] technologies used." Finding for the plaintiffs on this issue, the court articulated the rationale for its holding:

> The Capogeannises do not quarrel with the defendants' two factual premises. They acknowledge in essence that they may be unable to prove the contamination can be wholly removed from the soil and groundwater. And although they assert (and the Spences' expert cannot deny) that they can reduce contamination to officially acceptable levels, it may be inferred from the record as a whole that the reduction will be a slow and uncertain process, in some measure dependent on variables such as climatic conditions.

But the Capogeannises assert, and we conclude as a matter of law, that the defendants' premises do not compel a conclusion that the nuisance was permanent. At the very least the question whether this was a permanent or continuing nuisance was so close or doubtful as to empower the Capogeannises to proceed on a theory of continuing nuisance.

Our conclusion is influenced primarily by policy considerations * * *. First and foremost, today's environmental awareness establishes beyond argument that there is simply no legitimate interest to be served by permitting this contamination to persist. Conversely, the well-documented tendency of such contamination to migrate, particularly in groundwater, strongly supports a conclusion that the contamination should be cleaned up as promptly and thoroughly as possible. Both considerations support application, in this case, of the courts' general preference for a finding of continuing nuisance (or, at least, of a question close enough to empower the Capogeannises to proceed upon that theory). Such a finding will tend to encourage private abatement, and perhaps monetary cooperation in abatement efforts, if only to limit successive lawsuits. On the other hand a finding that the nuisance is permanent would leave the Capogeannises with private recourse barred, and with no practical motivation to proceed promptly and efficiently beyond that provided by the enforcement practices of governmental agencies acting at public expense. * * * That in this case abatement efforts may take considerable time and may never be wholly successful should not be permitted to dictate a result that would lessen incentives to proceed as promptly and effectively as possible to abate the contamination.

4. Do you agree with the court's rationales for construing the permanent/continuing distinction in a manner that facilitates the cleanup of properties? Why shouldn't plaintiffs be bound by whatever contractual or warranty rights that they may have against the prior owners? See also Arcade Water District v. United States, 940 F.2d 1265 (9th Cir.1991), applying continuing nuisance to contamination of wells caused by a military laundry that had closed thirteen years prior to suit.

Interestingly, after the appellate decisions in *Mangini* and *Capogeannis*, the court that tried *Mangini* on remand vacated a jury award of $13.2 million based on the continuing nuisance and trespass theories. The court concluded that the "jury's finding that the trespass and nuisance are abatable is contrary to the weight of the evidence," because the nature and extent of the contamination was not established, nor did the evidence support the technical feasibility of remediating the property, particularly in light of plaintiffs' expectation that the land be rendered useful for residential development considering its current use of grazing land for cattle.

Moreover, the court found that the $13.2 million award, which represented the "taint" placed on the entire 2400–acre parcel, even though the contamination was largely confined to 125 acres, was more consistent with a permanent nuisance, not a continuing one. While acknowledging that some federal cases allow nuisances to be classified as continuing for statutes of limitation purposes and permanent for assessing damages, it could find no support in California law for doing so. Mangini v. Aerojet–General Corp., Superior Court Calif., Case No. 500170, Feb. 3, 1993, Hazardous Waste Litig. Rptr., March 3, 1993.

5. The significance of the continuing nuisance doctrine is illustrated by the New York case of Jensen v. General Electric Co., 182 A.D.2d 903, 581 N.Y.S.2d 917 (1992), where a special statute of limitations had been enacted which provided:

> The three-year period within which an action to recover damages for * * * injury to property caused by the latent effects of exposure to any substance or combination of substances * * * upon or within property must be commenced shall be computed from the date of discovery of the injury by the plaintiff or from the date when through the exercise of reasonable diligence such injury should have been discovered by the plaintiff, whichever is earlier.

The court held that

> Although these causes of action do qualify as actions "to recover damages for * * * injury to property caused by the latent effects of exposure" to the toxic chemicals present on plaintiffs' property, being recurring wrongs they are not subject to any Statute of Limitations because they constantly accrue, thus giving rise to successive causes of action. As a consequence they are unaffected by the enactment of CPLR 214–c(2), which is aimed at providing "relief to injured New Yorkers whose claims would otherwise be dismissed for untimeliness simply because they were unaware of the latent injuries until after the limitation period had expired."

The Court of Appeals, 4–3, reversed the Appellate Division, 82 N.Y.2d 77, 603 N.Y.S.2d 420, 623 N.E.2d 547 (1993), stating that the 1986 law had an "all-encompassing sweep" and left "no room for judicial insertion of qualification or exceptions by interpretation." The court said with the passage of the 1986 law, the Legislature intended to alter the accrual date for "all property damage actions caused by all substances."

According to the opinion, "If no statute of limitations at all was to apply, as the Appellate Division found, then the provision for a three-year period from discovery of the act of wrongdoing would be rendered a theoretical and superfluous appendage to the state statute with no practical vitality."

In addition, the court said the result of exempting continuing trespass and nuisance claims in many cases would be to eliminate any repose, "even against parties who choose to sit interminably on known rights before bringing suit."

However, the majority preserved plaintiffs' actions for injunctive relief because the statute by its terms applied only to damages actions.

Why were the continuing damage approaches unavailable to the Manginis on the negligence and strict liability claims? What is the fundamental distinction between nuisances and negligence so far as applying statutes of limitation?

6. As *Mangini* demonstrated, actions based on negligence or strict liability for abnormally dangerous activity are subjected to a firmer limita-

tions period. The point is illustrated dramatically by yet another California decision, CAMSI IV v. Hunter Technology Corp., 230 Cal.App.3d 1525, 282 Cal.Rptr. 80 (1991). Monsanto owned a parcel of land and conducted manufacturing operations from 1950 to 1983 and disposed of liquid and solid wastes. It leased a portion of the property to Hunter, which, until 1983, manufactured printed circuit boards. In its manufacturing process, Hunter discharged volatile organic chemicals (VOCs) and TCE. In 1983, Monsanto sold the parcel to third parties who sold it to KSP in October 1984. In 1985, KSP sold it to CAMSI IV, a partnership. In July 1985, the San Francisco Bay Regional Water Quality Control Board issued an order naming Monsanto and KSP as dischargers of TCE and VOCs on the land. In 1986, CAMSI IV sold an uncontaminated portion of the property. In 1987, the Regional Board issued a tentative cleanup order and in 1988 a final order naming Monsanto, Hunter, and CAMSI IV as parties responsible for the cleanup of the site.

The court held that for injury to real property the cause of action accrues with the last act causing the injury. The fact that CAMSI IV asserted that it didn't suffer any harm until it acquired the property didn't toll the statute:

> [I]t is apparent as an abstract proposition, and has been assumed in a number of cases, that for limitations purposes the harm implicit in a tortious injury to property is harm to the property itself, and thus to any owner of the property once the property has been injured and not necessarily to a particular owner. Thus once the sewer line has been improperly located on the property, or the lot preparation and foundation construction have been improperly done, or the encroaching buildings are constructed, the tort is complete and the statute of limitations (unless forestalled by the "discovery rule" or some other special doctrine) begins to run: An owner must bring its claim to court within the statutory period or the claim will be barred for that and all subsequent owners. Normally a subsequent owner will not be personally harmed by the tort until he or she becomes the owner, but no case has held that each new owner thus becomes entitled to a new statute of limitations against the tortfeasor. Such a rule would wholly disregard the repose function of statutes of limitations.

The court also held that CAMSI could not rely on the discovery rule because the court concluded that it should have discovered the contamination, and was put on notice of the problem, by the Regional Board's July 1985 order which it received more than three years before suit was filed.

Why do you suppose that plaintiff didn't allege a continuing nuisance count? If it had, would the outcome been different? Why is a subsequent owner of the property better off, for statutes of limitation purposes, relying on a nuisance theory rather than a strict liability or negligence theory? Recall that in most jurisdictions a nuisance theory would only extend to horizontally related parties and would not grant standing to those in a vertical relationship as to the same parcel of land. What is a buyer's best protection against acquiring property that is subsequently subjected to a government-mandated remediation order?

7. It is important to identify the relevant statutes of limitation that may be implicated by one set of facts. In the toxic tort field typical

possibilities to investigate include statutes applicable to personal injury, trespass to personal or real property, special statutes for products liability and special statutes for exposure to toxic substances.

C. STATUTES OF LIMITATION IN PRODUCT AND OCCUPATIONAL EXPOSURE CASES

Many toxic tort cases arise because a consumer or user of a product or an employee in a workplace has sustained injury as a result of exposure to a toxic substance. As a general rule, the date of accrual of a cause of action is either one of two dates: the date when all elements necessary to the tort are first completed; or the date when the plaintiff knew or should have known of the cause of action.

1. DATE OF THE INJURY

In the absence of judicial precedent to the contrary, the common law rule is that a cause of action accrues, and the statute of limitation begins to run, on the date of the injury to plaintiff. As interpreted originally, plaintiff's claim would be deemed to have arisen irrespective of whether the plaintiff knew or even could know of the nature or extent of his injuries. See, e.g., McWilliams v. Union Pac. Resources Co., 569 So.2d 702, 703–04 (Ala.1990) (citing Home Ins. Co. v. Stuart–McCorkle, Inc., 291 Ala. 601, 608, 285 So.2d 468, 473 (1973)). For causes of action based on negligence or strict liability, damage to the plaintiff is a necessary element of the cause of action. A few courts have extended this proposition to mean that a substantial injury is necessary, based on the principal of de minimis non curat lex. See, e.g., Cloud v. Olin Corp., 552 F.Supp. 528 (N.D.Ala.1982); Locke v. Johns–Manville Corp., 221 Va. 951, 275 S.E.2d 900, 905 (1981) (asbestos statute begins running from date cancer or lung impairment begins).

One familiar variation on this theme states that injury occurs on the date of last exposure to the offending substance. See, e.g., Meadows v. Union Carbide Corp., 710 F.Supp. 1163, 1166 (N.D.Ill.1989) (applying Illinois law). Such a rule is understandable if it is assumed that exposure equals injury. Under this view, each exposure to an offending substance creates an injury at that time. Thus, continuing exposures lead to continuing injuries, similar to the continuing nuisance rule discussed earlier, and plaintiff's claims concerning all of the exposures which occur within the statute of limitation will escape the bar. On the other hand, if all of the exposures take place outside of the limitation period, the cause of action will be held to be time-barred. When exposures take place both inside and outside of the limitation period, there is a split of authority as to whether the exposures outside of the limitation period will be time-barred. Compare *Cloud* (exposures outside limitation period are barred) with Chase v. Cassiar Mining Corp., 622 F.Supp. 1027 (N.D.N.Y.1985) (in personal injury action, plaintiff is not limited to damages caused by exposure to asbestos within the statute of limitation period and is instead entitled to recover for 25–year cumulative effect).

2. ACCRUAL BASED ON THE DISCOVERY RULE

Either as a result of judicial decision or statutory enactment, most jurisdictions have adopted a discovery rule for determining when a cause of action accrues. Under the discovery rule, a cause of action accrues on either of two dates: on the date that the plaintiff first knew or should have known of the injury *or* on the date when the plaintiff first knew or should have known of the injury *and* of the causal link to the defendant. One of the earliest recognitions of the fundamental fairness of adopting a discovery rule in a toxic tort case is found in Urie v. Thompson, 337 U.S. 163, 69 S.Ct. 1018, 93 L.Ed. 1282 (1949), in which the Supreme Court interpreted the Federal Employers' Liability Act to sustain a railroad employee's action for disability caused by the inhalation of silica dust. Urie became permanently disabled in 1940 and filed suit on November 25, 1941; FELA cases were subject to a three-year limitation period. Defendant railroad argued that because he had been exposed to silica dust since 1910, he must have contracted silicosis long before 1938, and hence, the action accrued before 1938. Alternatively, defendant argued that if each inhalation of silica dust was a separate tort, Urie was limited to that injury occasioned by his exposures between 1938 and when he last worked in 1940.

The Court rejected both arguments, and instead, adopted a discovery rule:

> [I]f we assume that Congress intended to include occupational diseases in the category of injuries compensable under the Federal Employers' Liability and Boiler Inspection Acts, such mechanical analysis of the "accrual" of petitioner's injury—whether breath by breath, or at one unrecorded moment in the progress of the disease—can only serve to thwart the congressional purpose.

> If Urie were held barred from prosecuting this action because he must be said, as a matter of law, to have contracted silicosis prior to November 25, 1938, it would be clear that the federal legislation afforded Urie only a delusive remedy. It would mean that at some past moment in time, unknown and inherently unknowable even in retrospect, Urie was charged with knowledge of the slow and tragic disintegration of his lungs; under this view Urie's failure to diagnose within the applicable statute of limitations a disease whose symptoms had not yet obtruded on his consciousness would constitute waiver of his right to compensation at the ultimate day of discovery and disability.

> Nor can we accept the theory that each intake of dusty breath is a fresh "cause of action." In the present case, for example, application of such a rule would, arguably, limit petitioner's damages to that aggravation of his progressive injury traceable to the last

eighteen months of his employment. Moreover petitioner would have been wholly barred from suit had he left the railroad, or merely been transferred to work involving no exposure to silica dust, more than three years before discovering the disease with which he was afflicted.

We do not think the humane legislative plan intended such consequences to attach to blameless ignorance. * * * There is no suggestion that Urie should have known he had silicosis at any earlier date. It follows that no specific date of contact with the substance can be charged with being the date of injury, inasmuch as the injurious consequences of the exposure are the product of a period of time rather than a point of time; consequently the afflicted employee can be held to be "injured" only when the accumulated effects of the deleterious substance manifest themselves * * *.

The following decision illustrates how the discovery rule has evolved and applies in close cases.

EVENSON v. OSMOSE WOOD PRESERVING COMPANY OF AMERICA, INC.

United States Court of Appeals, Seventh Circuit, 1990.
899 F.2d 701.

Wood, Jr., C.J.

This products liability action arises from injuries allegedly caused by the plaintiff's exposure to wood-treating chemicals. Gary E. Evenson appeals from the district court's grant of summary judgment for defendants Osmose Wood Preserving, Inc. ("Osmose"), Mineral Research & Development Corporation, Inc. ("Mineral Research"), and American Wood Preservers Institute ("American Wood"), on the ground that the district court erred in holding that the Indiana statute of limitations barred his action. [W]e reverse and remand.

I. Factual Background

The defendants are parties to this suit because of their involvement with chromated copper arsenate ("CCA"). Osmose and Mineral Research manufacture a wood preservative that contains CCA. Osmose prepared a "Material Safety Data Sheet" and wrote the label used on CCA containers. American Wood represented the interests of the CCA industry before the federal [EPA] during that agency's regulatory investigation of the arsenic used in treating wood. Indiana Wood Preserving, Inc. ("Indiana Wood") purchased CCA from Osmose and Mineral Research to treat lumber. Indiana Wood then sold the treated lumber. Evenson worked at Indiana Wood as a wood treatment worker where he was exposed to CCA while carrying out his duties.

The events of this case are best understood chronologically: Late summer-early fall 1983: Dr. Dean Felker, Evenson's general practitioner, diagnoses hay fever, nasal polyps, asthma, and allergic rhinitis. Dr. Felker makes no causal diagnosis except to say that severe allergies are the usual cause of nasal polyps. He refers Evenson to Dr. Steven Isenberg, an ear, nose, and throat specialist, for treatment of the nasal polyps in August 1983. April 1984: Dr. Steven Isenberg refers Evenson to Dr. Paul Isenberg, an asthma specialist. Dr. Paul Isenberg diagnoses Evenson as having an asthma triad (asthma, nasal polyps, and aspirin sensitivity) as well as certain other allergies. February 20, 1985: Because he is concerned that CCA may be causing his medical problems, Evenson asks Dr. Felker to run tests for CCA in his urine. March 20, 1985: The urine test is completed and shows normal levels of the chemicals that make up CCA. Because of the test results, Dr. Felker believes that CCA is not causing Evenson's symptoms. April 1985: For the second time, Dr. Steven Isenberg removes Evenson's nasal polyps. Evenson requests that the polyps be checked for CCA. Dr. Steven Isenberg sends out a sample for testing but never receives the results and is unable to identify the cause of the polyps. Evenson also asks Dr. Paul Isenberg if CCA might be related to his problems but receives no affirmative response. December 3, 1986: Evenson first speaks with attorney David McCrea, who is involved in other CCA litigation. January 1987: On McCrea's referral, Evenson sees Dr. Henry Peters, [who] tells Evenson that exposure to CCA for any length of time is extremely hazardous. March 13, 1987: Evenson files his complaint in state court. April 1987: Dr. Daniel Teitelbaum, examines Evenson after McCrea arranges an appointment. Dr. Teitelbaum confirms Evenson's suspicions that CCA is the cause of his injuries.

Evenson sought recovery on theories of strict liability in tort, negligence, wilful misconduct for failure to warn of the dangers associated with CCA exposure, and for fraudulent concealment of such dangers.

The district court granted the defendants' motions for summary judgment, holding that the two-year Indiana statute of limitations barred Evenson's product liability action as well as his fraudulent concealment and failure-to-warn claims. * * *

II. DISCUSSION

In the context of a summary judgment motion based on the statute of limitations, we must find (1) that the statute of limitations has run and (2) there exists no genuine issue of material fact as to when the plaintiff's cause of action accrued. * * *

Indiana's applicable statute of limitations provides: "[A]ny product liability action in which the theory of liability is negligence or strict liability in tort must be commenced within two (2) years after the cause of action accrues * * *." Ind.Code § 33–1–1.5–5. Because chemicals and products are capable of causing injuries that often do not become evident until well after a plaintiff's last exposure to them, Indiana, like many other states, has adopted a discovery rule. Under this rule, the Indiana statute of limitations begins to run from the date that the plaintiff knew or should have discovered (1) that the plaintiff suffered an injury or impingement and (2) that the injury or impingement was caused by the product or act of another. Thus, the Indiana discovery rule has both an injury and a causation prong.

Evenson was aware that he was experiencing medical problems in the latter part of 1983, well over two years before he filed his complaint. The focus is therefore on the causation prong—when Evenson knew or should have discovered that his injuries were caused by his exposure to CCA.

The district court observed that the Indiana discovery rule emphasizes knowledge of a potential rather than an actual link. Citing Miller v. A.H. Robins Co., 766 F.2d 1102 (7th Cir.1985), the district court stated that the causation prong of the discovery rule "is satisfied if the plaintiff is informed of a 'possible causal connection' between the foreign substance and the injury of which he complains." Again relying on Miller, the district court noted that having a fair opportunity to investigate available sources of information does not require possessing irrefutable proof of causation. The district court believed it was enough that Evenson himself suspected that CCA may have been causing his injuries. The court therefore held that the statute of limitations began to run on February 20, 1985, when Evenson requested Dr. Felker to order tests that might substantiate Evenson's theory about CCA being a possible cause of his medical problems. Because Evenson did not file his complaint until March 13, 1987, the district court concluded that the statute of limitations barred his action.

The district court's conclusion was clearly reasonable. We would agree with the court's holding except we believe that the court, in applying the Indiana discovery rule, did not give sufficient weight to an unusual factor in this case. Evenson, despite his diligent efforts, received no indication anytime prior to the two-year period before he filed his complaint that his suspicion as to the cause of his injuries might be correct. * * *

Evenson, a mere layperson, only suspected that CCA was causing his medical problems. Although Evenson asked various doctors over the course of his continuous medical treatment if CCA could be the cause of his injuries, no doctor, prior to the two-year period before he filed his complaint, confirmed his suspicions that CCA might be the cause. Evenson, because of his suspicions, also requested appropriate tests to substantiate his theory; yet the urine test done under Dr. Felker's direction came back negative and Dr. Steven Isenberg never received the results of the tests done on the polyp sample following Evenson's second surgery.

On appeal, Evenson argues that a layperson's mere suspicion is not sufficient to trigger the statute of limitations under Indiana's discovery rule. He contends that information as to the probable, not possible, cause of the injury is required before the statute will begin to run. Evenson urges this court to construe the causation prong to require actually finding a doctor willing to testify, based on medical probability, that the defendant's product caused the injury. Evenson asserts that the statute began to run on December 3, 1986, because it was then that he first spoke with his attorney, David McCrea. McCrea knew Dr. Teitelbaum through other CCA litigation and was aware of Dr. Teitelbaum's belief that a causal link existed between CCA and the type of injuries exhibited by Evenson. Because he filed his complaint within two years of his first conversation with McCrea, Evenson argues his action is not time barred.

Although we agree locating a doctor willing to testify that a particular product is the probable cause of the plaintiff's injuries would trigger the statute of limitations, we disagree with Evenson that this is the only event capable of doing so. Defendants correctly point out that the cases cited by Evenson applying the Indiana discovery rule establish only that a medical diagnosis causally connecting a plaintiff's exposure to a product and his injuries is sufficient to start the statute running, not that such a diagnosis is necessary. At the same time, we disagree with defendants that a layperson's mere suspicion, even when coupled with the start of an investigation, automatically triggers the statute. Fed. R.Civ.P. 11 would arguably require sanctions against a party who files suit based on nothing more than the kind of suspicions Evenson had in the present case.

While we are aware of the value of bright lines in rules of procedure, it is futile to try to draw firm lines in the context of the discovery rule in these circumstances. We can be no more specific than to say that where knowledge of causation is at issue, a person knows or should have discovered the cause of his injury when he has or should have discovered some evidence that there was a reasonable possibility that his injury was caused by the act or product of another. A reasonable possibility, while less than a probability, requires more than the mere suspicion possessed by Evenson, a layperson without technical or medical knowledge. In applying this rule, district courts will necessarily be bound to a fact-specific inquiry.

In the present case, the evidence on the record does not show that as of February 20, 1985, Evenson had or should have discovered some evidence that there was a reasonable possibility that his CCA exposure was the cause of his injuries. Although Evenson himself suspected at this time that CCA was the culprit, his attempts to determine the actual cause were rebuffed by his doctors in whom he could place some reliance. What Evenson had on February 20, 1985, was not some evidence of a reasonable possibility that CCA was the cause but only a layman's mere suspicion to this effect.

Events short of a doctor's diagnosis can provide a plaintiff with evidence of a reasonable possibility that another's act or product caused his injuries. Nevertheless, there must be something more than a plaintiff's mere suspicion or speculation—a reasonable, not a mere, possibility is required to trigger the statute.

Evenson filed his complaint on March 13, 1987, and we have concluded that the statute had not begun to run as of February 20, 1985. Evenson's claim, therefore, will be barred by the two-year statute of limitations only if, between February 20, 1985 and March 13, 1985, Evenson knew or should have discovered some evidence that there was a reasonable possibility that CCA was the cause of his injuries. Although we ordinarily would remand to the district court to determine when the statute of limitations began to run, we need not burden the district court in this case. We have the complete record before us and our review of the record reveals that nothing happened during that critical three-week period to satisfy this test. We therefore conclude that Evenson's suit is not barred by Indiana's statute of limitations.

* * *

[The dissent of MANION, J. is omitted].

Notes and Questions

1. The court finds plaintiff's "mere suspicion" insufficient to trigger the statute. Do you agree with the court's adoption of the reasonable possibility test? What if plaintiff had not received negative or equivocal responses from his doctors? What if he never saw any doctors until after he visited the attorney? What if he knew several co-workers had confirmed diagnoses of CCA-related injuries similar to Evenson's injuries? Perhaps the court's most telling criticism of the mere suspicion test is the statement that suits filed on such a basis would "arguably require sanctions" under Rule 11 of the Federal Rules of Civil Procedure. Does this sound reasonable? In a dissenting opinion in *Evenson*, Judge Manion observes that plaintiff would obviously need an expert to testify as to causation at trial, but it is not essential to have a physician confirm plaintiff's belief in order to file suit, to establish accrual of the cause of action, or to avoid Rule 11 sanctions. With whom do you agree? One court has held that a special statute of limitation that it interpreted as triggering the running of the limitation period based on a "mere possibility" was unconstitutional under the right to a remedy and due process clauses of the Ohio Constitution. See Burgess v. Eli Lilly & Co., 66 Ohio St.3d 59, 609 N.E.2d 140 (1993).

2. *Community Knowledge.* Should a general knowledge in the community about the risks posed by certain toxic exposures be sufficient to satisfy the discovery rule? One court's treatment of this issue is found in Allen v. United States, 588 F.Supp. 247 (D.Utah 1984), reversed on other grounds 816 F.2d 1417 (10th Cir.1987), cert. denied 484 U.S. 1004, 108 S.Ct. 694, 98 L.Ed.2d 647 (1988), where the district court held that knowledge of the general hazards associated with radiation, and knowledge of the fact that defendant had been exploding nuclear devices, did not constitute discovery until plaintiff became aware of the precise risks of particular diseases. In Joseph v. Hess Oil, 867 F.2d 179, 184 (3d Cir.1989), in reversing the trial court's order for summary judgment, the appeals court noted that the plaintiff knew that he was sick and knew that exposure to asbestos, a substance with which he worked, could be harmful was not enough to demonstrate that the plaintiff knew or should have known that his injury was asbestos-related.

In order to prove when a plaintiff should have known of the injury and the causal link to defendant's product, the defendant frequently will attempt to demonstrate community awareness of the harm or potential for harm. Defendant may adduce proof that a plaintiff knew of the hazard, for example, by showing that the plaintiff had actually read articles describing the harm and its cause. See O'Brien v. Eli Lilly & Co., 668 F.2d 704, 707–10 (3d Cir.1981) (accrual if and when the plaintiff actually read articles linking DES and her disease). In most instances, however, proving a general community awareness of the causal linkage and of the likelihood of injury may be the defendant's only way to pinpoint the accrual date. In Allen v. A.H. Robins Co., 752 F.2d 1365 (9th Cir.1985), the manufacturer of the Dalkon shield attempted to show that a statute of limitations began to run when defendant sent out over two hundred thousand "Dear Doctor" letters informing *doctors* of the medical risks associated with the Dalkon shield. The court rejected this argument, holding that such awareness in the medical community was insufficient to cause the statute of limitations to begin to run. The court commented that the plaintiff could not be considered to have been aware of the causal connection between the defendant's product and her ailment until she had watched a televised report on the subject by *60 Minutes.*

3. *Level of Medical Knowledge Required.* Consider the following testimony from the plaintiff on deposition:

Plaintiff remembered that his family physician had informed him that he had "bad lungs" and should change jobs so that plaintiff's "lungs don't get worse." Plaintiff gave the following deposition testimony during examination by defense counsel:

Q. "What did [the family physician] tell you about why you should quit?"

A. "So it doesn't get worse."

Q. "So what is 'it'?"

A. "Whatever it is. My lungs don't get worse. I don't know which way he meant it." * * *

Q. "[The family physician] told you at that time you had a lung problem from your work?"

A. "Right. He didn't say from the work. He just says, 'You have a lung problem.' He must have meant from work, because he says 'You have worked with asbestos. It must be from work,' is what he told me."

* * *

Q. "Did [the family physician] describe your lung problem with any kind of word?"

A. "Word, no, he just said, 'You have bad lungs,' that's all."

Reversing the trial court, an appeals court held that it was a jury question of whether the plaintiff possessed sufficient information to cause him to inquire further in order to determine whether a legal wrong had occurred from occupational exposure to asbestos. Martin v. A & M Insulation Co., 207 Ill.App.3d 706, 152 Ill.Dec. 688, 566 N.E.2d 375 (1990).

In contrast, in Weger v. Shell Oil Co., 966 F.2d 216 (7th Cir.1992), Weger was a sheet metal worker for fourteen years, until he was forced to leave his job in 1982 because of kidney problems. He sued defendants in 1986, alleging his kidney problems were caused by exposure to solvents produced by the defendants. In December 1982, he suffered renal failure, and he and his wife began to investigate the cause of his kidney problems. In November 1983, Marilyn Weger read an article in the *International Association of Machinists and Aerospace Workers Journal* on the long-term negative health effects of workplace exposure to solvents. Marilyn Weger wrote George Robinson, the article's author, stating, "I feel solvents are directly related to his [Mr. Weger's] medical problems." Robinson responded, advising the couple to seek medical advice and referring them to a specialist, Dr. Samuel Epstein. On January 12, 1984, Marilyn Weger wrote to Epstein, saying her husband was exposed to chemicals at work. The doctor replied July 30, 1984, recommending that the couple contact a lawyer. In August 1984, attorney Robert Douglas filed a workers' compensation claim on Weger's behalf. The claim stated, "As a result of exposure to chemicals, Petitioner has liver and kidney disease." On July 16, 1985, Dr. David Main examined Weger and reported to Douglas that it was not clear what caused Weger's illness.

In finding the action barred, according to the court, it was apparent that the Wegers understood that someone might be responsible for Roger Weger's kidney condition. As the court summarized: "Mrs. Weger expressed that belief in a letter to Robinson which he, in turn, confirmed. They were advised to contact a lawyer to pursue the matter and did so, showing that they possessed sufficient information that caused them to inquire further."

For another illustrative case about the level of medical knowledge sufficient to trigger the running of the statute of limitations, see University of Miami v. Bogorff, 583 So.2d 1000 (Fla.1991) (where plaintiff's 3–year–old son with leukemia received injection of defendant's drug and later developed quadriplegia, statute began to run when parents were aware of child's dramatically changed condition after last injection and had constructive knowledge of medical opinion that the drug may have contributed to the injuries).

4. *AIDS-Related Issues.* Suits filed by hemophiliacs against the suppliers of blood clotting agents for transmission of the HIV virus raise varied issues of when a claim was reasonably discoverable. In Doe v. Cutter Biological, 813 F.Supp. 1547 (M.D.Fla.1993), the plaintiff received a memorandum from the defendant, a blood bank in 1983 that enclosed a letter notifying that certain lot numbers of KOATE were being withdrawn because they contained plasma whose donor was diagnosed as having AIDS. Plaintiff actually returned six vials to the blood bank. In 1985, plaintiff tested positive for HIV, and his physician told him he had a 50/50 chance of developing AIDS. During this time, however, the National Hemophilia Information Foundation published pamphlets read by plaintiff stating that many hemophiliacs exposed to the HIV virus had not developed full-blown AIDS.

In 1988, Doe, after hearing about a suit brought by another family, spoke with a physician who worked with the Florida Hemophilia Association, who told him that the other family was wrong to sue, claiming that because, as the makers of the agents, they did everything possible to make their product safe, it would be "asinine" to sue because it would force the producers out of business. In 1989, the same physician consulted for Cutter on another case. In 1990, Doe developed AIDS and sued Cutter. Rejecting Doe's argument that he suffered no injury until he developed symptoms of AIDS in 1990, the court held the action was time-barred under a four-year statute. The court held that although the receipt of the tainted blood constituted injury, the statute wasn't triggered until 1985 when he tested positive for HIV and was informed that he had a 50/50 chance of developing AIDS, a disease he knew would result in death. The court also held that the physician's statements to Doe in 1988 did not constitute fraudulent concealment because Doe already knew he had a cause of action by 1985.

At least one court has held that a plaintiff is on notice that he was injured when the blood supplier recalled some of its factor concentrate in 1983. Doe v. American National Red Cross, 796 F.Supp. 395 (W.D.Wis. 1992).

At least two state supreme courts have held that shorter statutes of limitation applicable to physicians and hospitals in some states do not apply to actions against blood product suppliers, which are governed by the longer general statutes. See Silva v. Southwest Florida Blood Bank, 601 So.2d 1184 (Fla.1992) (blood bank did not render diagnosis, treatment or care to hospital patients, and thus suits governed by the four-year negligence statute of limitations, not the shorter two-year statute for malpractice actions); Kaiser v. Memorial Blood Center of Minneapolis, Inc., 486 N.W.2d 762 (Minn.1992); contra Bradway v. American National Red Cross, 263 Ga. 19, 426 S.E.2d 849 (1993).

Problem

Diana Krause filed suit in 1987 against Feldman Laboratories, Inc. (Feldman), the manufacturer of a medication used to treat blood clots, Coumadin. Krause was treated with Coumadin in February 1981 for blood clots in her legs. The prescribing physician told Diana not to get pregnant and to stop taking Coumadin if she did. Additionally, the doctor wrote her a letter repeating his instructions to stop the medication if she became pregnant. Krause stated on deposition that she stopped using the drug as soon as she learned of her pregnancy in June or July of 1981. David P. Krause, Jr. was born prematurely on December 6, 1981. He had problems immediately, including birth trauma, blood clots, respiratory difficulties, and cerebral palsy.

In February 1985, Diana was treated again for blood clots and resumed taking Coumadin. While in the hospital for this course of treatment, she received and kept two Feldman pamphlets regarding Coumadin. She stated on deposition that she read the information but was not immediately concerned about the contents because she and her husband had no plans to conceive additional children. However, she said the pamphlets made her begin to think it was dangerous to take Coumadin during pregnancy. She further testified that when David was born, no one specifically told her the child's birth problems might have been caused by the child's exposure in utero to Coumadin. While David's medical records documented Coumadin-related malformities, she never had access to these records.

A trial court granted Feldman's motion for dismissal on grounds that the suit, filed in March 1987, was time-barred under the applicable two-year discovery rule statute of limitations. The court held that her doctor's directive that she stop using the drug Coumadin if she became pregnant, the fact she did stop the medication when she suspected pregnancy, her child's severe birth defects, and informational pamphlets she received during the second course of treatment several years after the birth all combined to put her on notice of injury and causation no later than February 1985.

In the trial court's view, the fact that neither the manufacturer nor the plaintiff's treating physician told her specifically that the drug caused her son's problems did not defeat the statute of limitations defense. The trial court emphasized that though the pamphlets Diana received during the 1984 or 1985 hospitalization might not be sufficient information by itself to put her on notice of the cause of her son's problems, the information "did not come to her in a vacuum." In combination with Diana's other experiences, the court held, the pamphlets were sufficient to trigger the limitations statute.

Plaintiff appeals the dismissal of her case, contending she did not know and could not reasonably have discovered that her son's problems were related to prenatal exposure to Coumadin more than two years before she filed suit. Specifically, she contends that no doctor ever told her that David's problems were caused by the drug, that she had no medical training that would have allowed her to come to this conclusion on her own, and that she did not have access to her son's medical records that could have indicated his condition was related to the drug. She emphasizes further that at the time of the pregnancy and birth, she was not given any warning information from Feldman concerning Coumadin.

These events occurred in the State of Southshire, where in Bales v. Gun, 85 S.S. 2d 146 (1981), the Southshire Supreme Court said the limitations period starts "when a person knows or reasonably should know of his or her injury and also knows or reasonably should know that it was wrongfully caused."

Decide the appeal. Will you affirm or reverse the trial court? Why? Prepare a brief opinion.

D. SUCCESSIVE ACTIONS AND STATUTES OF LIMITATION

Plaintiffs in toxic tort cases may face the problem that the toxic exposures produce multiple kinds of harm which are manifested at different points in time. This paradigm is illustrated by asbestos cases where the worker first may sustain damage in the form of pleural thickening of the lung walls, later experiences asbestosis, and still later may develop lung cancer or mesothelioma. If plaintiff sues for asbestosis, is he barred by the doctrine of claim preclusion (res judicata) if ten years later he sues for mesothelioma? If he waits to file suit until he develops mesothelioma, has the statute expired because his cause accrued when he learned of the asbestosis but chose not to sue? The tension between these two issues focuses on how the "cause of action" is defined for each purpose, and whether it is appropriate to make the definition turn on the purpose for which the inquiry is made. To enhance judicial efficiency and discourage piecemeal litigation, courts have adopted a broad "transactional" approach in determining if a second suit is barred by a judgment in the first. See Restatement (Second) of Judgments § 24(1) (1982); Nevada v. United States, 463 U.S. 110, 130 n.12, 103 S.Ct. 2906, 2918 n.12, 77 L.Ed.2d 509 (1983); Federated Department Stores v. Moitie, 452 U.S. 394, 101 S.Ct. 2424, 69 L.Ed.2d 103 (1981).

Some courts have held the second suit to be barred because of the importance placed on the policy reasons for the claim preclusion doctrine. See, e.g., Graffagnino v. Fibreboard Corp., 776 F.2d 1307, 1308 (5th Cir.1985) ("[E]xposure to asbestos can give rise to only a single cause of action for all injuries that are caused by that exposure, whether or not all the injuries have become manifest at the time the cause of action accrues."); Gideon v. Johns–Manville Sales Corp., 761 F.2d 1129, 1137 (5th Cir.1985) ("Gideon could not split his cause of action and recover damages for asbestosis, then later sue for damages caused by such other pulmonary disease as might develop, then still later sue for cancer should cancer appear."); Joyce v. A.C. & S., Inc., 785 F.2d 1200 (4th Cir.1986) (applying Virginia law).

In the statutes of limitation context, even if courts define the cause of action more narrowly in order to preserve a plaintiff's ability to sue for subsequently acquired harm, the tension and risk are not entirely eliminated. The case that follows attempts to resolve this difficulty.

WILSON v. JOHNS-MANVILLE SALES CORPORATION

United States Court of Appeals, District of Columbia Circuit, 1982.
684 F.2d 111.

GINSBURG, J.

This case presents a novel and difficult legal issue in the context of the mounting volume of litigation relating to deaths or injuries caused by exposure to asbestos products. We are asked to decide whether manifestation of any asbestos-related disease (in this case, asbestosis) triggers the running of the statute of limitations on all separate, distinct, and later-manifested diseases (here, malignant mesothelioma, an extremely lethal form of cancer) engendered by the same asbestos exposure. We hold that time to commence litigation does not begin to run on a separate and distinct disease until that disease becomes manifest.

I. INTRODUCTION

A. *The Facts*

Beginning in 1941, Henry J. Wilson was steadily employed as an insulation worker at various construction sites in the metropolitan Washington, D.C. area. As an integral element of this employment, Wilson regularly handled and was otherwise exposed to asbestos and asbestos products.

On February 14, 1973, Wilson was x-rayed as part of his local union's routine program instituted to determine which workers, if any, had contracted asbestosis. Evaluation of these x-rays revealed that Wilson was indeed suffering from "mild asbestosis." Following his receipt of this diagnosis, Wilson began a new job, still in the insulation trade, but involving little, if any, exposure to asbestos.

Subsequent to 1973, Wilson's health rapidly deteriorated. He suffered two heart attacks in June 1974 and a collapsed lung in February 1975, and was hospitalized on each occasion. Because of these episodes and on the advice of his physician, Wilson retired.

Complaining of sharp pains in his chest, Wilson was again hospitalized in February 1978. On this occasion, Wilson was diagnosed as having mesothelioma, a cancer of the mesothelial cells with a poor prognosis for recovery. Wilson died on May 17, 1978.

B. *The District Court Proceedings*

On May 16, 1979, just short of one year after Wilson's death, his widow, Blannie S. Wilson ("Appellant"), instituted the instant diversity action. Named as defendants (collectively "Johns–Manville") were designers, manufacturers, and distributors of asbestos and asbestos products. * * * Appellant asserted that Johns–Manville's actions were the direct and proximate cause of her husband's pulmonary illnesses and death. * * *

After extensive discovery by the parties, Johns–Manville moved for summary judgment on both statutory counts. Johns–Manville asserted that Henry Wilson had one, and only one, indivisible cause of action for all past, present, and future injuries resulting from his exposure to asbestos products. This cause of action, Johns–Manville claimed, accrued, at the latest, when Wilson first knew or should have known that he was suffering from any asbestos-related disease, i.e., in February 1973, when Wilson was diagnosed as suffering from asbestosis. Therefore, Johns–Manville concluded, the applicable three-year statute of limitations barred the 1979 Survival action. Furthermore, Johns–Manville argued, Appellant's Wrongful Death action was also time-barred; as a wholly derivative claim, Johns–Manville maintained, a Wrongful Death action may not proceed unless the decedent at the time of his death could have initiated a timely action for personal injuries had he lived.

[T]he district court granted Johns–Manville's motion and dismissed Appellant's complaint with prejudice. This appeal followed.

II. Analysis

The applicable statute of limitations, D.C.Code § 12–301(8), provides that a Survival claim "may not be brought after (3 years) from the time the right to maintain the action accrues." Appellant's Survival claim, therefore, is timely only if Henry Wilson had a right of action which "accrued" after May 17, 1976.

A. The Discovery Rule

The accrual date of a claim for relief based on a disease with a long incubation period, such as asbestosis or mesothelioma, is an issue on which judicial opinion is in flux. Some courts adhere to the traditional view that " 'the cause of action accrues at the time of invasion of (plaintiff's) body.' " Steinhardt v. Johns–Manville Corp., 446 N.Y.S.2d 244, 246 (N.Y.1981). Other courts employ the "discovery" rule under which a "cause of action accrues when the plaintiff knows or through the exercise of due diligence should have known of the injury." See Burns v. Bell, 409 A.2d 614, 617 (D.C.App.1979). Johns–Manville points out that to date "the District of Columbia Court of Appeals has not extended the 'discovery' rule to cases beyond the area of professional malpractice." We are persuaded, however, that, if faced with the issue, the District of Columbia courts would apply the discovery rule to latent disease cases.

* * *

Johns–Manville principally argues, however, that even if the discovery rule is applicable to the instant case, Appellant's claim is nonetheless barred by the three-year limitations period. Henry Wilson, Johns–Manville urges most strenuously, had only one indivisible cause of action for asbestos-related injuries and that cause of action accrued five years before he "discovered" that he had cancer; it accrued in 1973 when Wilson "discovered" he was suffering from "mild asbestosis." We now turn to that central contention.

B. Distinct Illnesses as Separate Causes of Action

Johns–Manville focuses on the alleged wrongful conduct and asserts that once some harm is apparent, a claim accrues not only for harm then manifest, but for all harm that may eventuate in the future as a result of the same conduct. Johns–Manville's theory is that Henry Wilson's claim ripened no later than February 1973 when he was diagnosed as having "mild asbestosis." Within three years of that diagnosis, Johns–Manville reasons, Wilson could have instituted a personal injury action seeking damages, not only for asbestosis, but for consequences that might develop later, including separate and distinct illnesses such as mesothelioma[33] or another form of cancer. Had Wilson sued between 1973 and 1976, and then attempted to return to court after the February 1978

---

33. Johns–Manville concedes that asbestosis and mesothelioma are separate and distinct diseases, and that mesothelioma is not a complication of the former. Johns–Manville does maintain that both diseases "had the same precise cause," i.e., "(Wilson's) years of exposure to asbestos."

malignant mesothelioma diagnosis, he would have been blocked, Johns–Manville asserts, by the well-established rule that a claim or cause of action may not be split. See generally Restatement (Second) of Judgments §§ 24–26 (1982). It follows, Johns–Manville concludes, that Wilson's mesothelioma claim is similarly barred when, as occurred here, he simply sat on his right to sue and did not institute any tort action between February 1973 and February 1976. In essence, Johns–Manville argues, Wilson did not have the option to waive tort recovery for asbestosis, and sue for a lethal cancer if and when such a condition developed. We disagree.

Preliminarily, we note that we need not and do not decide whether Johns–Manville's initial premise is correct, i.e., whether judgment on a claim for asbestosis pursued between 1973 and 1976 would have precluded a subsequent claim based on the 1978 mesothelioma diagnosis.[34] It suffices to point out that res judicata (claim preclusion) doctrine and policy would control the decision of that question. * * * This case requires us to focus, not on judgments and their preclusive effects, but on statutes of limitations and the policies they implicate in personal injury actions. We therefore consider below the appropriate delineation of the claim or cause of action in suit in the relevant context.

"Statutes of limitation find their justification in necessity and convenience rather than in logic. They represent expedients, rather than principles." Chase Securities Corp. v. Donaldson, 325 U.S. 304 (1945). Two considerations, particularly, motivate legislation placing time limitations on the commencement of litigation. The first, which may be designated evidentiary, relates to "the search for truth (which) may be seriously impaired by the loss of evidence, whether by death or disappearance of witnesses, fading memories, disappearance of documents, or otherwise." The second, repose, concerns the potential defendant's interests in security against stale claims and in planning for the future without the uncertainty inherent in potential liability.

In the case at hand, these considerations pull in opposite directions. Repose, beyond question, is best served by Johns–Manville's broad definition of the "cause of action" at stake. But in situations involving the risk of manifestation of a latent disease, unlike the mine run of litigation, the evidentiary consideration counsels narrower delineation of the dimensions of a claim. Key issues to be litigated in a latent disease case are the existence of the disease, its proximate cause, and the resultant damage. Evidence relating to these issues tends to develop, rather than disappear, as time passes.

Looking beyond repose and evidentiary considerations, we take into account the interests generally involved in personal injury and death cases: plaintiff's in obtaining at least adequate compensation, defendant's in paying no more than that. Integrating these two, the community seeks to advance, through the system of adjudication, relief that will

---

34. But cf. Restatement (Second) of Judgments, supra, § 26(1)(b) & comment b   (court in first action may expressly reserve plaintiff's right to maintain second action).

sufficiently, but not excessively, compensate persons for injuries occasioned by the tortious acts of others. In latent disease cases, this community interest would be significantly undermined by a judge-made rule that upon manifestation of any harm, the injured party must then, if ever, sue for all harms the same exposure may (or may not) occasion some time in the future.

The traditional American rule, adopted in the District of Columbia, is that recovery of damages based on future consequences may be had only if such consequences are "reasonably certain." Recovery of damages for speculative or conjectural future consequences is not permitted. To meet the "reasonably certain" standard, courts have generally required plaintiffs to prove that it is more likely than not (a greater than 50% chance) that the projected consequence will occur. If such proof is made, the alleged future effect may be treated as certain to happen and the injured party may be awarded full compensation for it; if the proof does not establish a greater than 50% chance, the injured party's award must be limited to damages for harm already manifest.

In view of the "reasonably certain" standard, it appears that Johns–Manville is urging for cases of this sort (in which cancer is diagnosed years after asbestosis becomes manifest) more than a time-bar; it is urging, in essence, that there can never be a recovery for cancer unless (1) a lawsuit is filed within three years of the asbestosis diagnosis, and (2) cancer becomes manifest during the course of that lawsuit. For it is altogether likely that had Wilson, upon receiving the "mild asbestosis" diagnosis, sought to recover for a cancer which might (or might not) develop, Johns–Manville would have argued forcibly that the probability of such a development was far less than 50%, and was therefore too speculative, conjectural, uncertain to support a damage award.

Concern for judicial economy also influences our decision. Upon diagnosis of an initial illness, such as asbestosis, the injured party may not need or desire judicial relief. Other sources, such as workers' compensation or private insurance, may provide adequate recompense for the initial ailment. If no further disease ensues, the injured party would have no cause to litigate. However, if such a person is told that another, more serious disease may manifest itself later on, and that a remedy in court will be barred unless an anticipatory action is filed currently, there will be a powerful incentive to go to court, for the consequence of a wait-and-see approach to the commencement of litigation may be too severe to risk. Moreover, a plaintiff's representative in such a case may be motivated to protract and delay once in court so that the full story of his client's condition will be known before the case is set for trial.

* * * With respect to the statute of limitations issue before us, we conclude that a potential defendant's interest in repose is counterbalanced and outweighed by other factors, including evidentiary considerations, securing fair compensation for serious harm, and deterring uneconomical anticipatory lawsuits. We therefore hold that the diagno-

sis of "mild asbestosis" received by Henry Wilson in February 1973 did not start the clock on his right to sue for the separate and distinct disease, mesothelioma, attributable to the same asbestos exposure, but not manifest until February 1978. Blannie Wilson's action, we decide, to the extent that it seeks recovery based on mesothelioma, from which her husband suffered and died, was timely filed.

* * *

It is so ordered.

Notes and Questions

1. Although not the first case to reach the same holding, *Wilson* is the decision most frequently cited for the proposition that in toxic tort cases involving multiple stages of disease, each is a separate cause of action for statutes of limitation purposes. See also Pierce v. Johns–Manville Sales Corp., 296 Md. 656, 464 A.2d 1020 (1983); Wilber v. Owens–Corning Fiberglass Corp., 476 N.W.2d 74 (Iowa 1991); Marinari v. Asbestos Corp., Ltd., 417 Pa.Super. 440, 612 A.2d 1021 (1992); Miller v. Armstrong World Industries, Inc., 817 P.2d 111 (Colo.1991). Do these cases turn on the medical fact that each of the asbestos-related diseases is separate and independent? What if they were stages of a single disease process that always resulted in cancer?

2. *Claim Preclusion.* The court declines to resolve the issue preclusion question of what happens if the plaintiff does file an earlier action for asbestosis or pleural thickening and then files a later action for cancer or mesothelioma. How would the court have resolved it if Wilson had instituted an earlier action for asbestosis? See Smith v. Bethlehem Steel Corp., 303 Md. 213, 492 A.2d 1286, 1296 (1985); Ayers v. Township of Jackson, 106 N.J. 557, 525 A.2d 287 (1987) (explicitly reserving plaintiffs' right to bring a second action for cancer should it develop after declining to recognize a cause of action for increased risk of future disease). The discussion in Chapter 5 on the availability of present compensation for future consequences necessarily implies some recognition of the claim or issue preclusion problem. Can you see why?

3. *Filing Workers' Compensation Claims.* The decisions are split on whether the filing of a workers' compensation claim starts the running of the limitations period for a later-filed tort suit. In Welch v. Celotex Corp., 951 F.2d 1235 (11th Cir.1992), Welch, an insulator, began to experience shortness of breath and became concerned that he was developing an asbestos-related disease. He filed a workers' compensation claim against his employer in 1984. In 1987, Welch was diagnosed as having asbestosis and filed a tort action against several manufacturers and distributors of asbestos products. The trial court granted defendants' summary judgment on the ground that Georgia's two-year statute of limitations for personal injury actions had already run. The Eleventh Circuit reversed, stating that the limitations period does not begin to run until a plaintiff reasonably should have known the causal connection between the injury and a defendant's allegedly negligent conduct. In the court's view, while plaintiff may have known that asbestos had caused his injury when he filed his workers' compensation action, the filing did not show that plaintiff had reason to

know that defendants' conduct had caused his injury. The court noted that the only evidence showing the extent of plaintiff's knowledge of defendants' conduct was that he had (1) worked with asbestos products for many years; and (2) given a sworn affidavit that he had been unaware of any wrongdoing by defendants until he consulted an attorney about the present action.

In Brown v. Dow Chemical Co., 875 F.2d 197 (8th Cir.1989), the court held that plaintiff's workers' compensation claim alleging that his sterility was caused by exposure to dibromochloropropane (DBCP) was sufficient to trigger the statute against his later filed tort action.

Should there be a presumption that a compensation claim demonstrates sufficient knowledge of injury and causation to start the limitations period? Given the knowledge of asbestos-related diseases, is it likely that the plaintiff in *Welch* did not know that the producers of the product were responsible? How about the lawyer who handled the compensation claim? What are some of the strategy considerations which might influence an employee in deciding whether or not to file a claim against his employer? How about issue preclusion (collateral estoppel) if a substantive issue, such as causation, is determined adversely to the claimant? In *Brown*, the court also held that the finding by the Compensation Commission that plaintiff did not establish by a preponderance of the evidence that exposure to DBCP had caused his sterility was entitled to preclusive effect in the tort action.

4. A proposal directed at the claim preclusion-statute of limitations tension appears in Note, Claim Preclusion in Modern Latent Disease Cases: A Proposal for Allowing Second Suits, 103 Harv. L. Rev. 1989 (1990). The Note argues that application of the claim preclusion rule ignores the unique situation of the victim of a double-harm toxic tort. If the development of the latent injury is unforeseeable to both the plaintiff and the court at the time of the first action, inclusion of a claim for that second injury—even an increased risk claim—is impossible. Even if epidemiological studies or other medical knowledge alert the plaintiff to the risk of a second disease, the court will reject the demand for immediate compensation unless the court determines that it is probable that the plaintiff will actually contract the second disease. The Note argues that a narrower definition of the cause of action—which separates the immediate disease or injury and the latent disease—would permit compensation for victims' later developing harm. The Note proposes a limited second suit, consisting of four components: (1) adoption of a definition of a cause of action consistent with the discovery rule; (2) elimination of pain and suffering damages from the second suit; (3) suspension of the collateral source rule in those jurisdictions where it would otherwise apply; and (4) an application of attorney's fee shifting:

A. *Definition of the Cause of Action*

* * * This Note does not propose allowing a plaintiff to bring a separate suit for each distinct disease, because that would virtually defeat all the beneficial effects of claim preclusion and would simply replace the problem currently plaguing plaintiffs with potentially greater problems for the legal system and defendants. Instead, courts should adopt an approach similar to the "entire controversy doctrine" currently in effect in New Jersey. Under this doctrine, the plaintiff must consolidate in a single suit all related claims, even if each claim can be supported by a

separate cause of action. The unit of litigation is the "entire controversy" rather than its constituent claims or causes of action. Therefore, the "entire controversy" rule should be modified to exclude claims for unknown or speculative harms, thereby permitting plaintiffs to bring a second suit for those distinct harms that subsequently materialize.

B. *Pain and Suffering Damages*

Disallowing pain and suffering is a key element of the proposed intermediate solution. Eliminating pain and suffering damages in the second suit would preserve some measure of protection to defendants and would encourage settlement by making the amount of damages more predictable. Although pain and suffering damages may be warranted for many suits, they cannot be justified for the second suits allowed under this proposal on the basis of the tort system's two primary goals—deterrence and compensation. Deterring the tortfeasor justifies pain and suffering damages for the first suit but not the second, while simply compensating the plaintiff never justifies such damages.

* * *

C. *The Collateral Source Rule*

The collateral source rule allows plaintiffs to recover economic losses even when those losses are already covered by insurance. Although this rule often results in windfalls to plaintiffs, it is nevertheless generally allowed because it enhances the deterrence value of the suits. The deterrence factor in the second suits, however, is indeterminate and thus cannot support the collateral source rule. Therefore, under the proposal advanced here, courts should not apply the collateral source rule in the second suits.

After the simultaneous elimination of pain and suffering damages and the collateral source rule, pecuniary losses would be the only possible recovery. Because most people are covered by workers' compensation or some other form of first-party insurance and would thus receive compensation for their pecuniary losses through insurance awards, disallowing both the collateral source rule and pain and suffering damages would eliminate the incentive to sue for all plaintiffs except those few not covered by insurance. Thus, the proposed scheme would preclude the possibility of duplicative compensation and would minimize the incentive for lawyers to bring suits that are not necessary for compensatory purposes.

D. *Attorney Fee–Shifting*

The elimination of both pain and suffering damages and the collateral source rule from the second suits risks leaving plaintiffs no recovery from which to pay their lawyers. The second suits would only compensate plaintiffs for their pecuniary losses, and plaintiffs would be left to pay their lawyers out of their own pockets or out of awards that may not even cover the lawyer's bill. That outcome might inhibit even those few suits that plaintiffs could bring under the proposed exception to claim preclusion. * * * Under this arrangement, if the plaintiff wins, the defendant would pay the plaintiff's reasonable legal fees. This result makes sense intuitively and is economically justified, because the plaintiff's legal fees are both a loss that the defendant imposes on the plaintiff by committing the tort and a loss that is "economic"—the loss increases the plaintiff's marginal utility of money and can be replaced by a monetary payment. * * *

Note, Claim Preclusion in Modern Latent Disease Cases: A Proposal for Allowing Second Suits, 103 Harv. L. Rev. 1989, 1998, 1999, 2002–03 (1990). Copyright ©1990 by the Harvard Law Review Association. What do you think of this proposal? How might the plaintiffs' bar view it? The defense bar?

5. *Wrongful Death and Survival Actions.* Some courts hold that the limitations period is derivative of the decedent's claim had he or she lived to bring a personal injury action. For example, in Russell v. Ingersoll-Rand Co., 795 S.W.2d 243 (Tex.App.1990), the plaintiff's survivors brought an action against a company that supplied the decedent with equipment for his sandblasting career. In 1981 the decedent discovered that he had silicosis and commenced suit against several suppliers but not against the current defendant. Following his January 1988 death, the decedent's survivors brought suit in March 1988 against the current defendant, only to have the court grant summary judgment for the defendant, reasoning that had the decedent not perished, his action against the current defendant would have been time barred as the injury was discovered in 1981.

In other jurisdictions, however, a survivor's legal right to recover is considered independent from any claim that might have vested in the decedent prior to his death. Decisions following this rule hold that the statute of limitations for wrongful death actions begins to run upon the death of the decedent, not the time that the injury was discovered. Frongillo v. Grimmett, 163 Ariz. 369, 788 P.2d 102 (App.1989) (held: wrongful death action accrued on the date of the husband's death even though the statute of limitations on the husband's personal injury action had expired before his death).

The Georgia Supreme Court held that the discovery rule did not apply in wrongful death actions. Miles v. Ashland Chemical Co., 261 Ga. 726, 410 S.E.2d 290 (1991) (answering certified questions from the Court of Appeals for the Eleventh Circuit). Many states agree and refuse to apply the discovery rule in wrongful death or survival actions. See, e.g., Ayo v. Johns–Manville Sales Corp., 771 F.2d 902 (5th Cir.1985) (discovery rule unavailable in survival action); Trimper v. Porter–Hayden, 305 Md. 31, 501 A.2d 446 (1985) (discovery rule unavailable in wrongful death or survival action); Symbula v. Johns–Manville Corp., 514 Pa. 527, 526 A.2d 328 (1987) (discovery rule may not be employed to extend the time for filing wrongful death or survival action).

In *Miles*, three decedents, all of whom worked for the same firm, had died from cancer, two in 1984 and one in 1979. In 1987 plaintiffs learned that their decedent's deaths may have been caused by occupational exposure to methylene chloride and sued the manufacturers of a product containing that chemical. The Georgia statute provided for a two-year limitations period. The court acknowledged that if the cause of their injuries had been discovered during their lifetimes, they would have derived the benefit of the discovery rule, but because the wrongful death action accrues at death, not when an injury or cause is discovered, the actions were barred:

> Under OCGA § 9–3–33, the defendants' liability extended two years from the date of death. To prolong the running of this period would be to subject the defendants to potentially infinite liability and is counter to the policy underlying statutes of limitation. We decline to extend the statute of limitation by adopting the discovery rule in wrongful death cases.

The dissent was harsh:

> The majority opinion causes the wrongful death statutes to become a "delusive remedy" for those who cannot detect a causal link between the decedent's death and the tortfeasor's acts within two years of the decedent's death. See Urie v. Thompson, 337 U.S. 163, 69 S.Ct. 1018, 93 L.Ed. 1282 (1949). "We do not think the humane legislative plan intended such consequences to attach to blameless ignorance."

> The legislature granted us the flexibility to punish wrongdoers and meet social and economic needs by allowing us to determine when an action "accrues." The Eleventh Circuit offered us the opportunity to use our flexibility; the majority of this Court prefers rigidity without rationale.

> * * *

> The majority's obdurate opinion fails to scrutinize the policy considerations that underlie the wrongful death statutes.

> * * *

> The majority opinion has brought the evolution of the wrongful death statutes to an abrupt halt; the ability to punish wrongdoers and meet the social and economic needs of our citizens has ended. * * *

> The danger we face today comes in a far more furtive manner through toxins and carcinogens that do not instantly maim or kill, but that destroy life cell by cell, slowly, painfully, and as finally as any major physical trauma. The people who commit homicide with these toxins and carcinogens are just as culpable as those who commit homicide with exploding boilers. Our public policy requires that these people be punished and the survivors be compensated. Those goals can only be achieved by tolling the statutes until the causal link and the tortfeasor are discovered.

With whom do you agree? Is there a rational basis for not applying the discovery rule to extend wrongful death limitations statutes? The North Carolina Supreme Court has held that a wrongful death claim filed more than three years after diagnosis of a fatal disease, but within two years of death, is not barred. Dunn v. Pacific Employers Ins. Co., 332 N.C. 129, 418 S.E.2d 645 (1992).

6. *Federally–Mandated Statute of Limitation for Toxic Harms.* A provision of CERCLA § 309, as amended by SARA 42 U.S.C. § 9658, actually preempts state statutes of limitation for personal injury or property

damage actions arising from exposure to hazardous substances when the state provisions are more restrictive than the federally mandated limitations periods. The federal statute creates a federally required commencement date which is defined as "The date the plaintiff knew (or reasonably should have known) that the personal injury or property damage * * * were caused or contributed to by the hazardous substance or pollutant or contaminant concerned." CERCLA § 309(b)(4)(A). The federal statute governs whenever "the applicable limitations period for such action (as specified in the state statute of limitations or under common law) provides a commencement date which is earlier than the federally-required commencement date." CERCLA § 309(a)(1).

The language of the statute may be expansive enough to encompass products liability actions based on occupational exposure to toxic substances, as well as land-based trespass/ nuisance/strict liability suits. Section 9658 applies to actions meeting the following conditions: (1) "any action brought under state law for personal injury, or property damage"; (2) caused by exposure to any "hazardous substance, or pollutant or contaminant"; (3) which substances are "released into the environment"; (4) "from a facility." A toxic substance products liability claim would, by its very nature, satisfy the first condition. In regard to the second condition, the definition of "pollutant or contaminant" includes all agents that upon release into the environment cause "death, disease, cancer, and physiological malfunctions." See CERCLA § 101(33), 42 U.S.C.A. § 9601(33) (West 1994). Finally, the definition of "facility" in CERCLA § 101(9), 42 U.S.C.A. § 9601(9) includes any "building, structure, [or] installation * * *" and the definition of "environment" in CERCLA § 101(8), 42 U.S.C.A. § 9601(8) includes "any * * * land surface or subsurface strata, or ambient air within the United States." Thus, the nub of the interpretation question is whether the sale of a toxic product by a manufacturer or distributor constitutes a "release" of the toxin into the "environment." The definition of "facility" does contain an exception for "any consumer product in consumer use," which suggests that the federally-mandated statute of limitation provision would not apply to exposure to consumer toxic products. For a discussion of cases addressing the definition of "release," see Elizabeth Ann Glass, Superfund and SARA: Are There Any Defenses Left?, 12 Harv. Envtl. L. Rev. 385, 400–402 (1988).

At least some legislative history suggests that this limitation provision was primarily concerned with hazardous waste litigation, which would not encompass products liability claims. See Superfund § 301(e) Study Group, Injuries and Damages from Hazardous Wastes—Analysis and Improvement of Legal Remedies, Serial No. 97–12, 97th Cong. 2d Sess. 26027 (Comm. Print 1982). Two cases addressing this issue are Covalt v. Carey Canada Inc., 860 F.2d 1434 (7th Cir.1988), and Knox v. AC & S, Inc., 690 F.Supp. 752 (S.D.Ind.1988). Both courts agreed that although asbestos is a "hazardous substance" that came from a "facility," it was not "released into the environment." Hence, the applicable state statutes of limitation and repose were not preempted by CERCLA § 309.

For those states which have not adopted a discovery rule, this federal law now mandates that statutes of limitation not begin to run until the plaintiff knows or should have known that the injury or property damage was caused by the hazardous substance. Thus, the prerequisites for the running of the statute of limitations in all such actions are an awareness of the injury and a recognition of the causal connection between the injury and exposure to a hazardous substance.

Significantly, the statute appears broad enough to delay the commencement of the statutes of limitation in death cases until the administrator of the estate knows of the toxic agent's causal contribution to the decedent's disease. Even among those states that have adopted a discovery rule for injury cases, a number have refused to apply it to death cases, as noted above. The statute also contains a retroactivity provision which provides that the federally mandated discovery rule is applicable to all cases brought after December 11, 1980. This provision thus revives claims that would have been barred by existing state statute of limitations provisions. CERCLA § 309(b), 42 U.S.C.A. § 9658(b). See also Michael Green, When Toxic Worlds Collide: Regulatory and Common Law Prescriptions for Risk Communication, 13 Harv. Envtl. L. Rep. 209, 229–31 (1989). Regarding the constitutionality of this federal statute of limitations as applied to state law nuisance claims that would otherwise have been barred, the United States District Court in Bolin v. The Cessna Aircraft Co., 759 F.Supp. 692 (D.Kan. 1991), upheld the law in the face of Tenth Amendment and Commerce Clause challenges.

E. STATUTES OF REPOSE

1. HOW THEY DIFFER FROM STATUTES OF LIMITATION

In contrast to statutes of limitation, which bar actions at a specified time period *after* the cause accrued, statutes of repose bar the institution of an action a specified number of years after a particular event, such as the date of first sale of a product or the date of improvements to real property. After that time, no action can be brought, even though the elements of a claim may not have all yet occurred and only occur years after the period has run. Thus, a cause of action may be extinguished before it ever accrues, with the repose conferring an immunity upon the defendant. The difference is illustrated by the fact that while fraudulent concealment can toll the running of a statute of limitations, it has no such effect upon the repose statute. See First United Methodist Church v. U.S. Gypsum Co., 882 F.2d 862, 866 (4th Cir.1989), cert. denied 493 U.S. 1070, 110 S.Ct. 1113, 107 L.Ed.2d 1020 (1990):

> Statutes of repose are based on considerations of the economic best interests of the public as a whole and are substantive grants of immunity based on a legislative balance of the respective rights of potential plaintiffs and defendants struck by determining a time limit beyond which liability no longer exists. * * * [A]s a general rule, a statute of limitations is tolled by a defendant's fraudulent concealment of a plaintiff's injury because it would be inequitable to allow a defendant to use a statute intended as a device of fairness to perpetrate a fraud. Conversely, a statute of repose is typically an absolute time limit beyond which liability no longer exists and is not

tolled for any reason because to do so would upset the economic balance struck by the legislative body.

In other words, while statutes of limitation are procedural in nature, repose statutes are substantive because they confer a vested, substantive right on the defendant. See Menne v. Celotex Corp., 722 F.Supp. 662 (D.Kan.1989), where the court described the differences between limitations and repose in determining whether a statute was procedural or substantive.

A statute of repose does not have to specifically refer to toxic torts in order to be applicable. For example, if a manufacturer of asbestos or other allegedly toxic building material is sued in a state with a construction no-action statute, and the manufacturer supplied the material for use in the construction of an improvement to real property, the statute of repose may bar an action for personal injury or wrongful death. To utilize this defense, the manufacturer must demonstrate that it comes within the statute's protection, as a supplier of a good for use in construction. The wording of the particular statute involved is dispositive. The version in effect in Ohio reads as follows:

> No action to recover damages for any injury to property, real or personal, or for bodily injury or wrongful death, arising out of the defective and unsafe condition of an improvement to real property * * * shall be brought against any person performing services for or furnishing the design, planning, supervision of construction, or construction of such improvement to real property, more than ten years after the performance or furnishing of such services and construction.

Ohio Rev. Code Ann. § 2305.131 (Anderson 1989).

The Ohio Supreme Court found that "the statute * * * does not apply to any person who supplies materials, rather than services, to be used in the construction of an improvement to real property, as they may be liable for damages caused by defects in the materials under Section 402A of the Restatement (Second) of Torts (1965)." Sedar v. Knowlton Constr. Co., 49 Ohio St.3d 193, 551 N.E.2d 938, 942 (1990). Thus, asbestos manufacturers in Ohio would be unable to avail themselves of this statute of repose in suits premised on products liability. See also Eagles Court Condominium Unit Owners Ass'n v. Heatilator, Inc., 239 Va. 325, 389 S.E.2d 304 (1990) (interpreting Va. Code § 8.01–250 (1973) as applying only to manufacturers or suppliers of machinery or equipment).

However, the same is not true in all jurisdictions. In Maryland, a statute of repose simply bars any action based on injury caused by an improvement to real property after the period has run, without regard to the parties protected. Md. Code Ann., Cts. & Jud. Proc. § 5–108 (1989). The Fourth Circuit has interpreted the statute very broadly:

> This statute unequivocally states that "no cause of action for damages accrues" after the 20-year time limit. And, it is comple-

ly silent as to any limitation on the class of persons it protects. To remove manufacturers from the ambit of § 5–108(a) as First United suggests, would be flatly inconsistent with this language's plain mandate.

First United Methodist Church v. United States Gypsum Co., 882 F.2d 862, 865 (4th Cir.1989), cert. denied 493 U.S. 1070, 110 S.Ct. 1113, 107 L.Ed.2d 1020 (1990); accord McIntosh v. A & M Insulation Co., 244 Ill.App.3d 247, 185 Ill.Dec. 69, 614 N.E.2d 203 (1993) (Illinois statute of repose applies to latent disease claims).

2. CONSTITUTIONAL QUESTIONS

Federal constitutional attacks on statutes of repose have recently been brought in a number of jurisdictions, including Minnesota (Lourdes High School, Inc. v. Sheffield Brick & Tile Co., 870 F.2d 443 (8th Cir.1989)), Kansas (Tomlinson v. Celotex Corp., 244 Kan. 474, 770 P.2d 825 (1989), reversed on other grounds sub nom. Gilger v. Lee Constr., Inc., 249 Kan. 307, 820 P.2d 390 (1991)), South Carolina (Jenkins v. Meares, 302 S.C. 142, 394 S.E.2d 317 (1990), Hoffman v. Powell, 298 S.C. 338, 380 S.E.2d 821 (1989)), and Ohio (Sedar v. Knowlton Constr. Co., 49 Ohio St.3d 193, 551 N.E.2d 938 (1990)). In each of these cases, statutes of repose barring actions based on injuries caused by improvements to real property, wrongful death, or damage to real or personal property withstood constitutional challenge under the Fifth and Fourteenth Amendments. Each court noted that it was neither a due process violation nor a violation of the Equal Protection clause to hold that certain types of causes of action were time-barred before they ever actually arose.

Differing results have been reached when interpreting state constitutions. In Alabama, a state constitutional provision that "all courts shall be open; and that every person, for any injury done to him, in his lands, goods, person or reputation, shall have a remedy by due process of law; and right and justice shall be administered without sale, denial, or delay," was interpreted to mean that a statute of repose could not completely bar an action for personal injury before it ever arose. Instead, a limited period of time would have to be made available during which personal injury plaintiffs could bring an action. See Jackson v. Mannesmann Demag Corp., 435 So.2d 725 (Ala.1983) (invalidating statute of repose relating to improvements to real estate); see also Tucker v. Nichols, 431 So.2d 1263 (Ala.1983) (medical malpractice statute of repose upheld, with six months "saving provision").

The primary difference between federal and state constitutional attacks is that many state constitutions contain a "right to a remedy" clause similar to the Alabama constitution excerpted above, whereas no such provision is found in the United States Constitution. Nevertheless, a few courts which have recently considered the question have found statutes of repose to be consistent with such clauses. Sealey v. Hicks,

309 Or. 387, 788 P.2d 435 (1990), cert. denied 498 U.S. 819, 111 S.Ct. 65, 112 L.Ed.2d 39 (1990); Sedar v. Knowlton Constr. Co., 49 Ohio St.3d 193, 551 N.E.2d 938 (1990); Rodarte v. Carrier Corp., 786 S.W.2d 94 (Tex.App.1990); Commonwealth v. Owens–Corning Fiberglas Corp., 283 Va. 595, 385 S.E.2d 865 (1989).

But see Perkins v. Northeastern Log Homes, 808 S.W.2d 809 (Ky. 1991), where the Kentucky Supreme Court held unconstitutional a seven-year statute of repose (although it was entitled a statute of limitations), which required tort actions involving real property to be filed within seven years of any improvement, on the grounds that it violated protections against legislative interference guaranteed by the Kentucky Constitution of 1891. The statute gave plaintiff only until 1982 to file suit, even though she did not realize until 1989 that pentachlorophenol in the log home kit she purchased in 1977 may have caused her disease, non-Hodgkins lymphoma.

F. REVIVAL STATUTES

Some states have enacted special statutes that are targeted at resuscitating claims that had previously expired because of the statute of limitations bar. For example, the New York legislature in 1986 enacted a statute to revise claims related to exposure to certain identified toxic substances—DES, asbestos, chlordane, and polyvinylchloride—for one year which had previously expired. In Hymowitz v. Eli Lilly & Co., 73 N.Y.2d 487, 541 N.Y.S.2d 941, 539 N.E.2d 1069 (1989), the New York Court of Appeals upheld the statute as not transgressing any constitutional right of the defendants because it did not create new substantive rights, but rather was a procedural device:

> The Federal Due Process Clause provides very little barrier to a State Legislature's revival of time-barred actions (see Chase Sec. Corp. v. Donaldson, 325 U.S. 304, 65 S.Ct. 1137 (1945). In *Chase*, the United States Supreme Court upheld the revival of a time-barred action, stating that Statutes of Limitation "represent a public policy about the privilege to litigate * * * the history of pleas of limitation show them to be good only by legislative grace and to be subject to a relatively large degree of legislative control. [T]he Legislature may constitutionally revive a personal cause of action where the circumstances are exceptional and are such as to satisfy the court that serious injustice would result to plaintiffs not guilty of any fault if the intention of the Legislature were not effectuated."

Thus, if revival statutes are viewed as retroactive modifications to the statute of limitations, they are deemed procedural, and hence, subject to legislative modification without violating vested rights of defendants. See also Independent School District No. 197 v. W.R. Grace & Co., 752 F.Supp. 286 (D.Minn.1990) (asbestos).

G. CONTRIBUTORY FAULT/ASSUMPTION OF THE RISK IN REAL PROPERTY ACTIONS

1. DEFENSES TO NUISANCE AND REAL PROPERTY ACTIONS

William H. Rodgers, Environmental Law § 2.9 at 31 (Supp. 1984) summarizes the defenses predicated on a plaintiff's conduct as it relates to nuisance cases:

> Plaintiff misconduct defenses are theoretically significant and practically confusing. Contributory negligence is not a defense in those nuisance cases where liability is strict, either on an intentional tort or abnormally dangerous activity theory. Contributory negligence is a defense where the nuisance rests upon negligence, which makes the choice of theory highly important in a practical way. The New York Court of Appeals recently adopted this negligence/contributory negligence model in a nuisance case of pollution exposure over time, despite a strong dissent that the case deserved a strict liability analysis. The conflict did present cause-in-fact doubts and involved two commercial establishments (an automobile servicing business complaining about damage to cars from a power plant), not the starkly non-reciprocal interactions of a power plant and a home owner. Despite this, it appears that the better analysis would be to call this an instance of strict liability, allowing as a defense a showing of bargained-for risk acceptance which would be called assumption of risk.

> For the record, however, it must be noted that assumption of risk is a defense essentially unrecognized in nuisance law. The defenses that can be called plaintiff misconduct or risk acceptance are described as either contributory negligence or discussed under the heading of coming to the nuisance.

2. CONTRIBUTORY NEGLIGENCE OR FAULT

The Restatement (Second) of Torts addresses the defenses of contributory fault and assumption of the risk. Section 840B makes the availability of the plaintiff's fault as a defense turn on the kind of conduct engaged in by the defendant which gave rise to the nuisance. Because § 822, discussed in Chapter 3, recognizes that negligent, reckless, intentional, and abnormally dangerous activity can be the basis for a nuisance, the availability of contributory fault is controlled by whether the nuisance is created by negligent conduct.

§ 840B. Contributory Negligence

(1) When a nuisance results from negligent conduct of the defendant, the contributory negligence of the plaintiff is a defense to the same extent as in other actions founded on negligence.

(2) When the harm is intentional or the result of recklessness, contributory negligence is not a defense.

(3) When the nuisance results from an abnormally dangerous condition or activity, contributory negligence is a defense only if the plaintiff has voluntarily and unreasonably subjected himself to the risk of harm.

Therefore, when negligent conduct creates the nuisance, contributory negligence of the plaintiff is available as a defense as fully and under the same rules and conditions as in any other case predicated on negligence. See § 840, comment d. If defendant's conduct is reckless, then plaintiff's fault must be contributory recklessness in order to constitute a defense; and if intentional, as in fact most nuisances are because the defendant knows that its conduct is causing a nuisance or is substantially certain to do so and continues its action in the face of such knowledge, then contributory fault is not a defense.

As the student learned in the first-year torts course, states have enacted or judicially adopted a potpourri of comparative fault approaches. The UCFA adopts a "pure" comparative fault system under which, conceptually at least, a 99 percent at-fault plaintiff still recovers 1 percent of its damages. In contrast to the "pure" comparative negligence rule is the "modified" rule under which the plaintiff who is less than 100 percent at fault may, because of his negligence, be precluded from recovering, depending upon whether the jurisdiction follows the "50 percent bar" or the "51 percent bar." For example, in Maine and Minnesota, which adopted the "50 percent bar," a plaintiff to whom is attributed less than 50 percent of the total fault may recover damages reduced by his share of the negligence. See Me. Rev. Stat. Ann. tit. 14 and Minn. Stat. Ann. § 604.01. The States of Hawaii and New Hampshire, for example, in adopting the "51 percent bar," allow the plaintiff to recover so long as his negligence does not exceed that of the others who have caused him harm. See Hawaii Rev. Stat. § 663–31 and also N.H. Rev. Stat. Ann. 507:7–a.

3. ASSUMPTION OF THE RISK

The Restatement (Second) of Torts § 840C provides that assumption of the risk is a defense to an action for nuisance to the same extent as in other tort actions. The burden rests with the defendant who must show (a) the plaintiff knew that the exposure was dangerous; (b) the plaintiff appreciated the nature or extent of the danger; and (c) the plaintiff voluntarily exposed himself to the danger. A mere showing of negligence in failing to discover risks associated with an exposure, for example, would not constitute an adequate defense. Professor Rodgers' statements to the contrary notwithstanding, assumption of the risk is asserted in nuisance-type cases. For example, in Cornell v. Exxon Corp., 162 A.D.2d 892, 558 N.Y.S.2d 647 (1990), plaintiffs, who relied upon a well on their property for drinking and other purposes, sued in nuisance, trespass, and negligence to recover for physical injuries suffered as a result of contamination traceable to defendants' underground storage tanks.

Following an investigation by the State Department of Transportation revealing that the water was contaminated with gasoline traced to underground storage tanks, DOT installed the first of several double charcoal filters on plaintiffs' well. The filters were routinely replaced through December 1982. At the time the initial filter was installed, DOT indicated to plaintiffs that the filter "should deal with [their] problem" and that "[i]t should filter out most of it." However, plaintiffs were also advised at that time not to drink the water. Although plaintiffs subsequently attempted to abstain from drinking the water, the record indicates that they continued to use it for bathing, cooking and cleaning purposes.

The appeals court held that assumption of the risk may be a complete bar to recovery if the evidence showed that plaintiffs had knowledge of the risk and voluntarily chose to encounter it. The court, in remanding for trial on the issue, commented:

> Here, there is an absence of evidence indicating that plaintiffs were instructed not to use the well water for purposes other than drinking or that they were aware, at that time, of the potential health risk. While there is evidence in the record that after the filters were installed plaintiffs were told not to drink the water, there is also evidence that they were told that the filters "should deal with [their] problem." Thus, factual questions are present requiring jury resolution.

What if plaintiffs were unequivocally instructed not to use the well water? What if they were so instructed, but replacement water was expensive or hard to obtain?

4. COMING TO THE NUISANCE

Closely related to assumption of the risk is the defense of coming to the nuisance, where the plaintiff has acquired or improved her property after a nuisance interfering with its use and enjoyment has come into existence. See Restatement (Second) of Torts § 840D. However, § 840D also states that proof of the defense does not bar an action but is "a factor to be considered in determining whether the nuisance is actionable." The principal policy considerations involved in assigning weight to the defendant's priority in time has been summarized as follows:

> In addressing this question, courts have considered two views which two views which lead in opposite directions. On the one hand, it seems inequitable for a plaintiff to be able to come into an area where the defendant has long operated and force the defendant out. This is especially so in light of the likelihood that the plaintiff obtained his interest in his own land at a price discounted to reflect any inconvenience caused by the defendant's operations. Granting such a plaintiff relief results in a windfall for the plaintiff at the defendant's expense.
>
> On the other hand, allowing this defense may effectively grant the defendant an easement free of charge with which it can burden

its neighbors' land. Plaintiffs could then argue that this too is inequitable, in that it amounts to a windfall for the defendant and might encourage people entering a low density area to impose the maximum burdens upon the surrounding area and thereby gain rights to continue doing so indefinitely.

The majority rule in this area is that each purchaser of land is entitled to use it in the same degree as any prior purchaser. Therefore, generally there is no coming to the nuisance defense.

See Ernest Getto & James Arnone, Nuisance Law in a Modern Industrial Setting: Confusion, Misinformation Can Be Dangerous, 6 Toxics L. Rptr. 1122–23 (Feb. 6, 1991).

A recent North Dakota decision, Rassier v. Houim, 488 N.W.2d 635 (N.D.1992), demonstrates that the doctrine still carries some weight. In *Rassier*, the plaintiff sued to abate a private nuisance created by a neighboring defendant's use of a wind generator in a residential area. Defendant erected a tower and installed a wind generator on his residential lot in 1986. In October 1988, Rassier and her family purchased the adjoining lot and moved a mobile home onto the lot. Two years later, in November 1990, she sued Houim, claiming that his wind generator was a private nuisance. After a bench trial, the trial court dismissed her claim.

In affirming the trial court, the Supreme Court emphasized that "the basic criterion of the whole law of private nuisance is reasonable conduct" and the plaintiff's coming to the nuisance bears directly on the reasonableness of the defendant's use of its own property and the reasonableness of the interference with plaintiff's use and enjoyment. It found that the trial court had engaged in a weighing of the circumstances.

Stating that the basis for denying plaintiff's claim was the fact that she "came to the nuisance," the Court observed that "anyone who comes to a nuisance has a heavy burden to establish liability." This holding was reached despite the fact that the generator was located only 40 feet from her house, that the noise levels as measured by the State Department of Public Health were between 50 and 69 decibels, that most communities (but not this one) had ordinances prohibiting noise exceeding 55 decibels, and that evidence that the noise was irritating, stressful, and interfered with plaintiffs' sleep. One justice dissented.

Most courts, however, have rejected the defense. See, for example, Patrick v. Sharon Steel Corp., 549 F.Supp. 1259, 1267 (N.D. W.Va. 1982), where West Virginia residents sought damages from pollution from Sharon Steel's coke works. The coke works were in operation at the time plaintiffs moved into their residences, and Sharon argued that by such conduct they "assumed the risk of living near a nuisance." The court disagreed:

> This argument is untenable. Sharon relies upon an outdated
> doctrine that has never been recognized in West Virginia and which

has been rejected by the majority of jurisdictions in which it had been previously adopted. * * * Support for the majority view is found in the argument that the doctrine is out of place in modern society where people often have no real choice as to whether or not they will reside in an area adulterated by air pollution. In addition, the doctrine is contrary to public policy in the sense that it permits a defendant to condemn surrounding land to endure a perpetual nuisance simply because he was in the area first. Another reason given for rejecting the doctrine is that the owner of land subject to a nuisance will either have to bring suit before selling his land in order to attempt to receive the full value of the land or reconcile himself to accepting a depreciated price for the land since no purchaser would be willing to pay full value for land subject to a nuisance against which he is barred from bringing an action.

There are some courts, however, that take a contrary position. These cases have arisen in instances where a plaintiff knowingly and voluntarily chose to locate near a defendant in whose operations the public has an important interest. One such case is East St. Johns Shingle Co. v. City of Portland, 195 Or. 505, 246 P.2d 554 (1952). There the plaintiff, a shingle mill company, moved onto land knowing that the city was disposing of sewage in a slough running through the land. The court held that by knowingly locating near a nuisance in which the public has a substantial interest, the plaintiff was estopped from suing for damages from the nuisance. See also Powell v. Superior Portland Cement, 15 Wash.2d 14, 129 P.2d 536 (1942). The concept of "coming to the nuisance" which effectively barred equitable relief to persons who intentionally placed themselves in a position to be interfered with has also been rationalized by notions of protecting the reasonable investment expectations of the existing industry. See Fischer v. Atlantic Richfield, 774 F.Supp. 616, 619 (W.D.Okl.1989) (coming to nuisance doctrine applies only where the injury caused is permanent). See also Donald Wittman, First Come, First Served: An Economic Analysis of "Coming to the Nuisance," 9 J. Legal Stud. 557 (1980).

5. SALE OF PROPERTY DEFENSE

Another defense, rarely invoked, to nuisance liability is that asserted by a defendant who has disposed of the property causing the nuisance prior to the institution of suit. Restatement (Second) of Torts § 840A provides:

(1) A vendor or lessor of land upon which there is a condition involving a nuisance for which he would be subject to liability if he continued in possession remains subject to liability for the continuation of the nuisance after he transfers the land.

(2) If the vendor or lessor has created the condition or has actively concealed it from the vendee or lessee the liability stated in Subsection (1) continues until the vendee or lessee discovers the

condition and has reasonable opportunity to abate it. Otherwise the liability continues only until the vendee or lessee has had reasonable opportunity to discover the condition and abate it.

The rationale for continuing to impose liability on the seller of property who was responsible for creating the nuisance is straight forward: it would be unfair to allow those who had created tortious conditions to walk away from their liability by disposing of the property. However, if the buyer was aware of the condition or has sufficient opportunity to discover and abate the condition, then liability of the seller ends. Comment c to § 840A states that the best rationale for imposing continuing liability is that "his responsibility toward those outside of his land is such that he is not free to terminate his liability to them for the condition that he himself caused or concealed, by passing the land itself on to a third person. The effect of the rule is to require vendors and lessors in order to avoid liability to take reasonable steps to abate existing conditions involving any nuisance before they transfer the land." See also Restatement (Second) of Torts § 373 which supplies the same principles to dangerous conditions created on the land prior to sale which involves an unreasonable risk of harm to those outside the land.

In Fetter v. De Camp, ___ A.D.2d ___, 600 N.Y.S.2d 340 (1993) plaintiffs sued the former owner of a neighboring home, alleging that the defendants' repair of their septic system had caused the contamination of their water wells with fecal matter. Defendants moved for summary judgment on the grounds that any liability they may have had ended with their sale of the property, and alternatively, they had no actual or constructive knowledge of the defect in the septic system. The trial court denied the motion, but the appeals court reversed. First, the court observed that while the general rule under the Restatement (Second) of Torts § 372 terminated liability for conditions on land upon the transfer of the property, an exception is recognized under § 373. It continued:

Because it is obvious that an improperly designed and installed septic system can present an unreasonable risk of harm to others, especially where the water source for the properties in the immediate area are private wells which draw from subterranean streams or percolating water, there can be little doubt that to the extent plaintiffs can prove that defendants' actions relative to the septic system were negligent or satisfied the requisite elements of a nuisance, they can recover against defendants.

However, the court said, "because of the often unknown course of subterranean streams or the channel of percolating water, the rule has evolved that for negligence liability to ensue in cases involving the pollution of underground waters, the plaintiff must demonstrate that the defendant failed to exercise due care in conducting the allegedly polluting activity or in installing the allegedly polluting device, and that he or she know or should have known that such conduct could result in the contamination of the plaintiff's well." Here, because plaintiffs offered no evidence to establish that the septic system was defective or that defendants knew or should have known of any defect, summary judgment was granted.

For another decision addressing the sale of property defense where a purchaser of a manufacturing site sued a former operator of the site for the costs of cleaning up the property, see Westwood Pharmaceuticals, Inc. v. Natural Fuel Gas Distribution Corp., 737 F.Supp. 1272 (W.D.N.Y. 1990), affirmed 964 F.2d 85 (2d Cir.1992).

CERCLA, which was considered in Chapter 10, will trump these Restatement rules in cases where remediation is undertaken in response to actual or possible governmental action.

H. PLAINTIFF'S CONDUCT AS A BAR IN TOXIC PRODUCTS CASES

The doctrine of assumption of risk acts to bar or reduce a plaintiff's recovery for any harm caused him due to a risk which he or she knowingly accepts. In toxic products cases the key issue is typically whether the proof demonstrates that a particular toxic risk was a known or appreciated risk. In cases brought under Restatement (Second) of Torts § 402A, governing strict products liability, two provisions are especially relevant. First, as noted in comment j, if directions or warnings are given which would keep a product from being unreasonably dangerous, "the seller may reasonably assume that [the warning] will be read and heeded; and a product bearing such a warning which is safe for use if it is followed, is not in a defective condition, nor is it unreasonably dangerous." Thus, if instructions are given as to the use of a potentially hazardous product which will minimize exposure to the risk, and the *specific danger* associated with the product is pointed out, a seller may avoid liability under § 402A. See Jackson v. Johns–Manville Corp., 750 F.2d 1314, 1320 (5th Cir.1985) ("Because one of the purposes of the warning is to allow the user to make his own decision whether to expose himself to the risks of harm, a manufacturer fulfills its duty to warn * * * only if it warns of all dangers associated with its product of which it has actual or constructive knowledge."). On the other hand, if the precise toxic risk is not warned against, or if the warning provided is not calculated to reach the ultimate user, the doctrine of assumption of the risk will not function as a bar.

Secondly, comment n to § 402A explicitly recognizes assumption of the risk as a separate defense to strict liability:

n. Contributory negligence. Since the liability with which this Section deals is not based upon negligence of the seller, but is strict liability, the rule applied to strict liability cases applies. Contributory negligence of the plaintiff is not a defense when such negligence consists merely in a failure to discover the defect in the product, or to guard against the possibility of its existence. On the other hand the form of contributory negligence which consists in voluntarily and unreasonably proceeding to encounter a known danger, and commonly passes under the name assumption of the risk, is a defense under this Section as in other cases of strict liability. If the user or consumer discovers the defect and is aware of the danger, and nevertheless proceeds unreasonably to make use of the product and is injured by it, he is barred from recovery.

Additionally, § 496 repeats the same principle more broadly to embrace risks beyond those satisfying the narrower product requirements of § 402A:

> A plaintiff who voluntarily assumes a risk of harm arising from the negligent or reckless conduct of the defendant cannot recover for such harm.

Section 496C explains further:

> [A] plaintiff who fully understands a risk of harm to himself or his things caused by defendant's conduct or by the condition of defendant's land or chattels, and who nevertheless voluntarily chooses to enter or remain, or to permit his things to enter or to remain within the area of that risk, under circumstances that manifest his willingness to accept it, is not entitled to recover for harm within that risk.

Section 496D emphasizes that a plaintiff does not assume the risk "unless he then knows of the existence of the risk and appreciates its unreasonable character."

Assumption of the risk does not meet with general approval in the toxic tort or hazardous waste disposal situation, particularly where there are long latency periods associated with injuries or disease or deaths related to exposure. From the defense perspective, frequently, the defendant does not have access to sources of proof dating back to a person's first exposure to the hazardous substance, and therefore, the defense cannot counter plaintiff's claim that he was unaware of the risks associated with the toxic or hazardous substance when he was allegedly first exposed to it. Furthermore, in toxic tort cases where plaintiff's theory is generally defendant's failure to warn, it will, as a practical matter, be difficult for a defendant, who has allegedly failed to warn of the health hazards associated with the exposure, to convince court or jury that the plaintiff, nevertheless, knew of the alleged hazard and chose to encounter it voluntarily.

From the standpoint that the assumption of the risk defense can operate unfairly to bar a plaintiff's claim, some courts have declined to apply the doctrine in the employment relationship on the theory that exposure to a known danger in the course of one's job is not truly voluntary, or that the encounter with the danger was not unreasonable. See, e.g., Johnson v. Clark Equipment Co., 274 Or. 403, 547 P.2d 132 (1976) (design defect case); Cremeans v. Willmar Henderson Mfg. Co., 57 Ohio St.3d 145, 566 N.E.2d 1203 (1991). However, as was noted in Chapter 9 on the workplace, federal laws are increasingly requiring the disclosure of hazard-related information to employees whose jobs necessitate exposure to or use of toxic substances. Statutes such as the OSH

Act mandate that employees be provided training respecting the safe use of toxic materials and that employers post detailed information describing the health risks posed by and instructions for the safe use of toxic chemicals. See 29 C.F.R. § 1910.1200. An assumption of the risk defense might be implicated if the employee were to ignore the training and instructions and act in a manner that causes a harmful exposure. See James T. O'Reilly, Risks of Assumptions: Impact of Regulatory Label Warnings Upon Industrial Products Liability, 37 Cath. U. L. Rev. 85 (1987).

Chapter Thirteen

SPECIAL PROBLEMS IN TRIAL MANAGEMENT AND SETTLEMENT OF TOXICS LITIGATION

This Chapter addresses a collection of issues that have emerged from the legal system's effort to manage the increasing volume and complexity of toxic tort litigation, especially those that are assigned the label "mass" tort. While there exists no uniform definition of what constitutes "mass" toxic tort litigation, it is clear that it contemplates hundreds or thousands of claimants, all of whom were exposed to the same or similar toxic substances either simultaneously, as in an explosion at a chemical plant or a chemical spill precipitated by a tank car derailment, or by gradual, separately occurring events, as in occupational exposure to asbestos or consumption of a prescription drug, or ingestion of contaminated water by a community.

We first focus on the aggregative mechanisms that are available for the trial of mass tort litigation, with emphasis on class action devices, consolidation and multidistrict litigation procedures. Second, we consider some of the controls which trial courts have exercised to manage toxic tort cases more effectively and to protect the basic rights of the litigants, such as case management orders, protective orders, and special discovery orders. Third, we examine settlement procedures and look at least one creative approach to the resolution of a toxic tort dispute. And finally, because mass toxic torts implicate intractable choice-of-law problems, we examine some of the proposals that have been advanced to federalize either the substantive tort law or the choice-of-law rules.

A. CLASS ACTIONS

One of the most profound and controversial developments in the law of federal civil procedure is the growth of the class action, spawned by the 1966 amendments to Rule 23 of the Federal Rules of Civil Procedure. A class action provides a means by which one or more may sue or be sued as representatives of a class without the necessity of joining every member of the group of persons interested in a matter. See generally 7B Charles A. Wright, Arthur Miller, & Mary K. Kane, Federal Practice and Procedure § 1785 (2d ed. 1986).

Class actions serve two essential purposes. First, a class action achieves judicial economy by avoiding multiple suits. See Crown, Cork & Seal Co. v. Parker, 462 U.S. 345, 103 S.Ct. 2392, 76 L.Ed.2d 628 (1983); American Pipe & Constr. Co. v. Utah, 414 U.S. 538, 553, 94 S.Ct. 756, 766, 38 L.Ed.2d 713 (1974); In re A.H. Robins Co., 880 F.2d 769 (4th Cir.1989); Jenkins v. Raymark Indus., Inc., 782 F.2d 468, 471 (5th Cir.1986). Second, a class action can protect the rights of those who for practical reasons such as cost, temerity or ignorance would not press claims individually. See Kramer v. Scientific Control Corp., 534 F.2d 1085, 1091 (3d Cir.1976), cert. denied 429 U.S. 830, 97 S.Ct. 90, 50 L.Ed.2d 94 (1976).

Upon promulgation of the current rule, however, the Federal Rules of Civil Procedure Advisory Committee expressed a restrictive view of the applicability of Rule 23 class actions in mass tort litigations:

> A "mass accident" resulting in injuries to numerous persons is ordinarily not appropriate for a class action because of the likelihood that significant questions, not only of damages but of liability and defenses to liability, would be present, affecting the individuals in different ways. In these circumstances an action conducted nominally as a class action would degenerate in practice into multiple lawsuits separately tried.

Fed. R. Civ. P. 23(b)(3) Advisory Committee's Notes, reprinted in 39 F.R.D. 69, 103 (1966).

On the use of class actions generally, see Williams, Mass Tort Class Actions: Going, Going, Gone?, 98 F.R.D. 323, 329 (1983) (Judge Williams suggests there exists an "unarticulated antipathy and aversion that appellate courts display toward class action use in the mass tort context."); Linda S. Mullenix, Class Resolution of Mass Tort Cases: A Proposed Federal Procedure Act, 64 Tex. L. Rev. 1039 (1986). For an article debunking some of the myths about the individualized relationship between attorney and client which is often proffered as a reason for denying class certification, see Deborah Hensler, Resolving Mass Toxic Torts: Myths and Realities, 1989 U. Ill. L. Rev. 89.

There is, however, a growing trend toward accepting class actions as a viable and helpful procedure for handling mass tort claims and especially mass toxic tort cases. In In re School Asbestos Litigation, 789 F.2d 996, 1008 (3d Cir.1986), cert. denied 479 U.S. 915, 107 S.Ct. 318, 93 L.Ed.2d 291 (1986), the Court of Appeals for the Third Circuit stated:

> [T]here is a growing acceptance of the notion that some mass accident situations may be good candidates for class action treat-

ment. * * * Determination of the liability issues in one suit may represent a substantial savings in time and resources. Even if the action thereafter "degenerates" into a series of individual damage suits, the result nevertheless works an improvement over the situation in which the same separate suits require adjudication on liability using the same evidence over and over again.

The prerequisites and rationale for class certification are briefly summarized in a toxic tort case involving personal injury and property damage claims brought against a chemical company which had disposed of hazardous waste at a site in proximity to plaintiffs' homes. Sterling v. Velsicol Chemical Corp., 855 F.2d 1188 (6th Cir.1988), affirming in part, reversing in part 647 F.Supp. 303 (W.D.Tenn.1986). In the appeal of that suit, the Sixth Circuit affirmed the district court's order to certify as a class all of their claims, despite the individual nature of the causation and damage issues:

> Velsicol argues that the district court improperly certified this case as a Fed.R.Civ.P. 23(b)(3) class action because common questions of law or fact did not predominate over individual questions. As to the requirements necessary for certification of a Rule 23(b)(3) class action, the district court held * * * that (1) the class was so large that joinder of all members was impractical (Rule 23(a)(1)), (2) there were questions of law or fact common to the class (Rule 23(a)(2)), (3) representative claims were typical of the claims of the class (Rule 23(a)(3)), and (4) the representative parties would fairly and adequately protect the interests of the class (Rule 23(a)(4)). The court further found that questions of law or fact common to the members of the class predominated over any questions affecting only individual members and that a class action would be superior to other available methods for the fair and efficient adjudication of the controversy (Rule 23(b)(3)).[7]

> The procedural device of a Rule 23(b)(3) class action was designed not solely as a means for assuring legal assistance in the vindication of small claims but, rather, to achieve the economies of time, effort, and expense. However, the problem of individualization of issues often is cited as a justification for denying class action treatment in mass tort accidents. While some courts have adopted this justification in refusing to certify such accidents as class actions, numerous other courts have recognized the increasingly insistent need for a more efficient method of disposing of a large number of lawsuits arising out of a single disaster or a single course of conduct. In mass tort accidents, the factual and legal issues of a defendant's

---

7. In its September 29, 1986 order, the court stated in pertinent part: Early on in this case, because of the sheer magnitude of this litigation, the claims of five representative plaintiffs, whose claims are fairly representative of the claims of the class as a whole, were selected for trial. It was decided all claims would be tried by the court in this phase of the trial and final judgment entered on all of the claims of the five representative plaintiffs * * *. This approach was adopted by the Court as the only reasonable way for the Trial Court to manage in an efficient way the complex factual and legal issues presented by this mind-boggling class action lawsuit.

liability do not differ dramatically from one plaintiff to the next. No matter how individualized the issue of damages may be, these issues may be reserved for individual treatment with the question of liability tried as a class action. Consequently, the mere fact that questions peculiar to each individual member of the class remain after the common questions of the defendant's liability have been resolved does not dictate the conclusion that a class action is impermissible.

The district court retains broad discretion in determining whether an action should be certified as a class action, and its decision, based upon the particular facts of the case, should not be overturned absent a showing of abuse of discretion. In complex, mass, toxic tort accidents, where no one set of operative facts establishes liability, no single proximate cause equally applies to each potential class member and each defendant, and individual issues outnumber common issues, the district court should properly question the appropriateness of a class action for resolving the controversy. However, where the defendant's liability can be determined on a class-wide basis because the cause of the disaster is a single course of conduct which is identical for each of the plaintiffs, a class action may be the best suited vehicle to resolve such a controversy.

In the instant case, each class member lived in the vicinity of the landfill and allegedly suffered damages as a result of ingesting or otherwise using the contaminated water. Almost identical evidence would be required to establish the level and duration of chemical contamination, the causal connection, if any, between the plaintiffs' consumption of the contaminated water and the type of injuries allegedly suffered, and the defendant's liability. The single major issue distinguishing the class members is the nature and amount of damages, if any, that each sustained. To this extent, a class action in the instant case avoided duplication of judicial effort and prevented separate actions from reaching inconsistent results with similar, if not identical, facts. The district court clearly did not abuse its discretion in certifying this action as a Rule 23(b)(3) class action. However, individual members of the class still will be required to submit evidence concerning their particularized damage claims in subsequent proceedings.

Notes and Questions

1. The conclusion reached in *Sterling* is shared increasingly by other courts faced with the prospect of trying hundreds or thousands of individual cases. See, e.g., Watson v. Shell Oil Co., 979 F.2d 1014 (5th Cir.1992) (over 18,000 class members in mass tort litigation arising out of an explosion at an oil refinery); In re Agent Orange Product Liability Litigation, 506 F.Supp. 762 (E.D.N.Y.1980), modified 100 F.R.D. 718 (E.D.N.Y.1983), mandamus denied sub nom. In re Diamond Shamrock Chem. Co., 725 F.2d 858 (2d

Cir.1984), cert. denied 465 U.S. 1067, 104 S.Ct. 1417, 79 L.Ed.2d 743 (1984); Jenkins v. Raymark Indus., Inc., 782 F.2d 468, 473 (5th Cir.1986) ("Courts have usually avoided class actions in the mass accident or tort setting. Because of differences between individual plaintiffs on issues of liability and defenses of liability, as well as damages, it has been feared that separate trials would overshadow the common disposition for the class. The courts are now being forced to rethink the alternatives and priorities by the current volume of litigation and more frequent mass disasters."); accord In re A.H. Robins Co., 880 F.2d 709 (4th Cir.1989) ("Many courts are now abandoning their historical reluctance to certify mass tort class actions in light of what is often an overwhelming need to create an orderly, efficient means for adjudicating hundreds of thousands of related claims."). Moreover, where the defendant's assets are limited and the prospect exists that many later claimants will face empty coffers, class treatment is increasingly recognized as a viable means to equitably distribute those assets.

See also In re Jackson Lockdown/MCO Cases, 107 F.R.D. 703, 712 (E.D.Mich.1985) ("Where a limited fund exists in a particular litigation and the projected number of claims would exceed the amount of that fund, it is both equitable and reasonable that the mere fortuitousness of one party filing before another should not be the deciding factor in determining the availability of recompense.").

2. Observe that the court in *Sterling* employed class representatives whose causation and damages factual issues were thought to be typical of others in the class. In the asbestos litigation, discussed below, you will observe how some courts have utilized this procedure, coupled with statistical methods, to arrive at class-wide damages. What Constitutional concerns are implicated by using class representatives whose outcomes are applied to other class members?

3. Federal courts are not alone in utilizing class action procedures. See, e.g., Warner v. Waste Management, Inc., 36 Ohio St.3d 91, 521 N.E.2d 1091 (1988) (court affirms class certification with modifications to the definition of the class limited to all those "who live or owned real property within a five mile radius of the * * * hazardous waste site."); Lowe v. Sun Refining & Mktg. Co., 73 Ohio App.3d 563, 597 N.E.2d 1189 (1992) (class of residents and businesses in Sandusky River Watershed was not identifiable, precluding certification in action alleging negligence, nuisance, and strict liability, because the geographic parameters of class were imprecise; requirement that there be questions of law or fact common to class was satisfied; and common questions predominated over questions affecting individual members in action arising out of spill of toluene in creek). Some courts have concluded that the purported class is insufficiently defined and refused certification on that basis. See, e.g., Daigle v. Shell Oil Co., 133 F.R.D. 600 (D.Colo.1990). For a view that class actions are of limited utility, see Marjorie H. Mintzer & Yasmin Daley-Duncan, Mass Tort Litigation: Why Class Action Suits Are Not the Answer, *For the Def.,* Fall 1992, at 25.

B. OTHER AGGREGATIVE OR DISAGGREGATIVE PROCEDURES

1. CONSOLIDATION

Consolidation of individual actions against a single defendant or multiple defendants is a valuable procedural tool, especially in the context of mass toxic torts. Joint trials or hearings may prevent needless repetition of discovery and presentations of evidence. The text of Rule 42(a) provides:

> When actions involving a common question of law or fact are pending before the court, it may order a joint hearing or trial of any or all the matters in issue in the actions; it may order all the actions consolidated; and it may make such orders concerning proceedings therein as may tend to avoid unnecessary costs or delay. Fed. R. Civ. P. 42(a).

The term consolidation has been used to denote two different situations. 7B Charles A. Wright, Arthur Miller & Mary K. Kane, Federal Practice and Procedure § 2382 at 254 (2d ed. 1986). In the first situation, several actions are combined into one and each loses its separate identity, thereby returning a single judgment. In the second situation, several actions are tried together at the same trial, but each case retains its separate character as an individual cause of action and a separate judgment is entered for each case.

Although the plain language of Rule 42(a) refers to both joint trials and hearings and to consolidations, courts have interpreted the rule as providing only for the second of these procedures, where individual identities are retained. 9B Charles A. Wright, Arthur Miller & Mary K. Kane, Federal Practice and Procedure § 2382 at 255 (2d ed. 1986).

The chief prerequisite for consolidation is a common question of law or fact. A plaintiff is not entitled to have his action consolidated with another action pending in the same court, even though some of the same parties are involved, if the questions of law and fact in the two actions are not the same. The court is given broad discretion in deciding the existence of common issues of law or fact and in deciding the general propriety of consolidation. Additionally, the principal consideration for the court beyond common issues of law or fact is whether consolidation promotes convenience and judicial economy, and accordingly, the court may order consolidation without the consent of the parties. Further, Rule 42(a) is permissive, and a court is under little obligation to order consolidation. However, consolidation is impermissible if a party is aligned with another party with whom the first party has a conflicting interest in another portion of the consolidated cases. Dupont v. Southern Pac. Co., 366 F.2d 193 (5th Cir.1966) (consolidation of conflicting interests was reversible error), cert. denied 386 U.S. 958, 87 S.Ct. 1027, 18 L.Ed.2d 106 (1967).

In Malcolm v. National Gypsum Co., 995 F.2d 346 (2d Cir.1993), the Second Circuit held that a trial court had abused its discretion in consolidating 48 asbestos cases for trial; it noted that the goals of "convenience and economy must yield to a paramount concern for a fair and impartial trial." The court identified a number of criteria that district courts had applied as guidelines in determining the propriety of consolidation. Here the fact that 48 plaintiffs had worked in 250 different work sites where they were exposed to asbestos, each for different periods of time, in a period ranging from the 1940s to the 1970s, and suffered from different diseases (asbestosis, lung cancer and mesothelioma), and some were deceased but others survived, in the aggregate made consolidation unfair. Accord Cain v. Armstrong World Industries, 785 F.Supp. 1448 (S.D.Ala.1992).

Individual suits may be consolidated in the pretrial stage, thereby enabling common discovery and pretrial conferences which can often prove economically and administratively desirable. 9B Charles A. Wright, Arthur Miller & Mary K. Kane, Federal Practice and Procedure § 2382 at 257 (2d ed. 1986).

2. BIFURCATION OF CLAIMS AND ISSUES

Closely related to consolidation is the procedure of bifurcation or separating particular claims and issues. Judicial economy and prevention of jury confusion or prejudice provide the primary rationale for allowing separate trials of various issues or claims. Rule 42(b) provides:

> SEPARATE TRIALS. The court, in furtherance of convenience or to avoid prejudice, or when separate trials will be conducive to expedition or economy, may order a separate trial of any claim, cross-claim, counterclaim, or third-party claim, or of any separate issue or of any number of claims, cross-claims, counterclaims, third-party claims, or issues, always preserving inviolate the right of trial by jury as declared by the Seventh Amendment to the Constitution or as given by a statute of the United States.

Bifurcation has proven to be an especially fertile procedural device in toxic tort cases, usually involving the separation of the issue of liability from damages. Ordering bifurcation is discretionary with the trial court and will not be reversed in the absence of an abuse of discretion. See In re Bendectin Litig., 857 F.2d 290 (6th Cir.1988), cert. denied 488 U.S. 1006, 109 S.Ct. 788, 102 L.Ed.2d 779 (1989). Bifurcation may take several forms. In the first, the judge will sequence the presentation of evidence so that the weakest portion of a plaintiff's case (as determined perhaps at pretrial conference under Rule 16) is heard first. If plaintiff is unable to make out a prima facie case on this essential element, the judge will direct a verdict or otherwise dismiss the complaint. In the second type of bifurcation, the jury is asked to return a verdict on the first essential issue or claim to be tried; if this verdict is dispositive of other issues or claims to be tried, then the trial is terminated and the jury never hears evidence on the other issues or claims.

Given the critical importance and difficulty of the proof of the causation element of a plaintiff's case, it is not surprising that some courts have bifurcated causation and liability. In the Bendectin class action products liability litigation, Chief Judge Carl B. Rubin ordered the jury to return a verdict on the issue of whether Bendectin causes birth defects. In re Bendectin Litig., M.D.L. No. 486, Doc. No. 1577 (S.D.Ohio April 12, 1984). See 624 F.Supp. 1212 (S.D.Ohio 1985). Under the terms of the order, if plaintiffs prevailed in this first phase, the jury would then be asked to decide whether the manufacturer was negligent in failing to test the drug adequately and warn users of potential side effects. If the plaintiffs were to prevail on the liability issue, they would pursue damages individually in the district courts in which their cases were filed originally. This resolution is an interesting synthesis of consolidation, bifurcation, and multidistrict consolidation under Rules 42(a) and (b) and 28 U.S.C.A. § 1407 (1976). However, the jury returned a verdict for defendants on the causation issue, which was affirmed. In re Bendectin Litig., M.D.L. No. 486, Doc. No. 3051 (S.D.Ohio March 12, 1985), modified 857 F.2d 290 (6th Cir.1988).

Which party is most likely to prefer bifurcation? Won't a defendant *always* prefer to isolate the damages issue from the question of liability? What types of prejudice might a defendant assert from the jury hearing the damages evidence before it renders a verdict on liability? Defendants are especially eager to obtain bifurcation of plaintiff's claim, if any, for punitive damages because in most jurisdictions evidence of defendant's wealth and income are relevant and admissible to enable the jury to assess the amount of the award. Simpson v. Pittsburgh Corning Corp., 901 F.2d 277 (2d Cir.1990) (describing bifurcation as the "preferred method" of trying punitive damages issues, but deferring to trial court's discretion in denying bifurcation in this case). See generally Gerald W. Boston, Punitive Damages in Tort Law §§ 32.14–32.18 (1993).

3. MULTIDISTRICT LITIGATION

The last of the devices that are available to assist courts in the management of mass toxic tort cases is the employment of multidistrict consolidations of cases pending in various federal districts. Section 1407 of the Judicial Code, 28 U.S.C.A. § 1407, authorizes the temporary transfer of multidistrict litigation to a single district for coordinated pretrial proceedings. The statute establishes a special Judicial Panel on Multidistrict Litigation to determine whether transfer is appropriate in a particular case and what district should be denominated the transferee forum. While the statute does not set forth any particular genre of litigation to which consolidated pretrial transfers should be applied, the House Report accompanying the legislation provides that products liability actions and "common disasters" litigation are contemplated by the Act. See 1968 U.S. Code Cong. & Admin. News 1898–1900. Section 1407 contains no explicit limitations on the designations of the transferee forum, as the Panel is permitted to transfer actions "to any district." 28 U.S.C.A. § 1407(A).

C. ASBESTOS LITIGATION: CLASSES, CONSOLIDATIONS, BIFURCATIONS AND MULTIDISTRICT LITIGATION

The asbestos litigation—by any numerical criterion one might apply—is the most significant mass tort litigation in the nation's history. As one author stated:

> The large number of claims, the severity of injuries, the financial stakes involved, the social issues raised by the past behavior of asbestos manufacturers, and the possibility that the available resources for compensation will be insufficient have led many observers to view asbestos litigation as a test of the civil justice system's ability to efficiently and equitably compensate injured parties while deterring future injurious behavior.

Deborah R. Hensler et al., Asbestos in the Courts: The Challenge of Mass Toxic Torts v (1985).

One of the earliest asbestos cases to apply an aggregative approach was Wilson v. Johns–Manville Sales Corp., 107 F.R.D. 250 (S.D.Tex. 1985), in which the federal district court consolidated 50 of 150 pending cases for a single trial on two issues: product defectiveness and punitive damages, both of which turned on the state of the art evidence—*what* the defendants knew or should have known respecting the dangers posed by exposure to asbestos and *when* they knew or should have known such knowledge and informed users of those risks. That same year, Judge Robert Parker in Jenkins v. Raymark Industries, Inc., 109 F.R.D. 269 (E.D.Tex.1985), affirmed, 782 F.2d 468 (5th Cir.1986) went beyond *Wilson* and considered whether to certify a class under Rule 23(b)(1)(B) of the Federal Rules of Civil Procedure. First, he found that a class consisting of 893 cases, with over 1000 plaintiffs, satisfied the Rule 23 requirements of numerosity, commonality, typicality, and adequate representation. Judge Parker granted plaintiffs' motion to certify the class under Rule 23(b)(3) relating to situations where the common questions of law and fact predominate over individual questions. The court concluded, as in *Wilson*, that the predominant common question was state of the art, which would be determinative of both underlying liability for failure to warn and punitive damages liability. The Fifth Circuit Court of Appeals affirmed *Jenkins*, 782 F.2d 468 (5th Cir.1986):

> [T]he decision at hand is driven in one direction by all the circumstances. Judge Parker's plan is clearly superior to the alternative of repeating, hundreds of times over, the litigation of the state of the art issues with, as that experienced judge says, "days of the same witnesses, exhibits and issues from trial to trial."
>
> This assumes plaintiffs win on the critical issues of the class trial. To the extent defendants win, the elimination of issues and docket will mean a far greater saving of judicial resources. Further-

more, attorneys' fees for all parties will be greatly reduced under this plan, not only because of the elimination of so much trial time but also because the fees collected from all members of the plaintiff class will be controlled by the judge. From our view it seems that the defendants enjoy all of the advantages, and the plaintiffs incur the disadvantages, of the class action—with one exception: the cases are to be brought to trial. That counsel for plaintiffs would urge the class action under these circumstances is significant support for the district judge's decision.

After *Jenkins*, Judge Parker sought to employ the class action mechanisms to get beyond the common issues of state of the art and gross negligence, which focused exclusively on the conduct and knowledge of the defendants, and sought to try the plaintiff-specific factual questions of causation and damages.

In In re Fibreboard Corporation, 893 F.2d 706 (5th Cir.1990), the Fifth Circuit, in the opinion that follows, held that Judge Parker had exceeded the authority granted in Rule 23 and implemented a procedure that raised constitutional and other concerns.

IN RE FIBREBOARD CORPORATION
United States Court of Appeals, Fifth Circuit, 1990.
893 F.2d 706.

HIGGINBOTHAM, J.

Defendants Fibreboard Corporation and Pittsburgh Corning Corporation, joined by other defendants, petition for writ of mandamus, asking that we vacate pretrial orders consolidating 3,031 asbestos cases for trial entered by Judge Robert Parker, Eastern District of Texas.

In 1986 there were at least 5,000 asbestos-related cases pending in this circuit. We then observed that "because asbestos-related diseases will continue to manifest themselves for the next fifteen years, filings will continue at a steady rate until the year 2000." [1] Id. at 470. That observation is proving to be accurate. In Jenkins v. Raymark, we affirmed Judge Parker's certification of a class of some 900 asbestos claimants, persuaded that the requirements of Rule 23(b)(3) were met for the trial of certain common questions including the "state of the art" defense. After that order and certain settlements, approximately 3,031 asbestos personal injury cases accumulated in the Eastern District of Texas.

The petitions for mandamus attack the district court's effort to try these cases in a common trial.

The standard of review is familiar. We are to issue a writ of mandamus only "to remedy a clear usurpation of power or abuse of discretion" when "no other adequate means of obtaining relief is available." As we stated in In re Willy, 831 F.2d 545, 549 (5th Cir.1987):

---

1. See Jenkins v. Raymark Industries, Inc., 782 F.2d 468, 470 (5th Cir.1986).

"Mandamus cannot be used as a substitute for appeal even when hardship may result from delay or from an unnecessary trial. Mandamus is an extraordinary remedy that should be granted only in the clearest and most compelling cases. [M]andamus relief is ordinarily inappropriate when review is obtainable on direct appeal." After a brief look at the background of these cases, we will return to the question of whether petitioners have met this extraordinary burden.

I

On September 20, 1989, Professor Jack Ratliff of the University of Texas Law School filed his special master's report in Cimino v. Raymark. The special master concluded that it was "self-evident that the use of one-by-one individual trials is not an option in the asbestos cases." On October 26, the district court entered the first of the orders now at issue. The district court concluded that the trial of these cases in groups of 10 would take all of the Eastern District's trial time for the next three years, explaining that it was persuaded that "to apply traditional methodology to these cases is to admit failure of the federal court system to perform one of its vital roles in our society * * * an efficient, cost-effective dispute resolution process that is fair to the parties." The district court then consolidated 3,031 cases under Fed.R.Civ.P. 42(a) "for a single trial on the issues of state of the art and punitive damages and certified a class action under rule 23(b)(3) for the remaining issues of exposure and actual damages." The consolidation and certification included all pending suits in the Beaumont Division of the Eastern District of Texas filed as of February 1, 1989, by insulation workers and construction workers, survivors of deceased workers, and household members of asbestos workers who were seeking money damages for asbestos-related injury, disease, or death

Phase I is to be a single consolidated trial proceeding under Rule 42(a). It will decide the state of the art and punitive damages issues. The district court explained that: "the jury will be asked to decide issues such as (a) which products, if any, were asbestos-containing insulation products capable of producing dust that contained asbestos fibers sufficient to cause harm in its application, use, or removal; (b) which of the Defendants' products, if any, were defective as marketed and unreasonably dangerous; (c) when each Defendant knew or should have known that insulators or construction workers and their household members were at risk of contracting an asbestos-related injury or disease from the application, use, or removal of asbestos-containing insulation products; and (d) whether each Defendant's marketing of a defective and unreasonably dangerous product constituted gross negligence. In answering issue (d), the Jury will hear evidence of punitive conduct including any conspiracy among the Defendants to conceal the dangers (if any) of asbestos. The wording of issues (c) and (d) will depend on the applicability of the 1987 Texas Tort Reform legislation to a particular class member's individual case. By its order of December 29, 1989, the district court explained that "the jury may be allowed to formulate a multiplier for each defendant for which the jury returns an affirmative finding on the issue of gross negligence."

The district court also described the proceedings for Phase II in its October 26 order. In Phase II the jury is to decide the percentage of plaintiffs exposed to each defendant's products, the percentage of claims barred by statutes of limitation, adequate warnings, and other affirmative defenses. The jury is to determine actual damages in a lump sum for each disease category for all plaintiffs in the class. Phase II will include a full trial of liability and damages for 11 class representatives and such evidence as the parties wish to offer from 30 illustrative plaintiffs. Defendants will choose 15 and plaintiffs will choose 15 illustrative plaintiffs, for a total of 41 plaintiffs. The jury will hear opinions of experts from plaintiffs and defendants regarding the total damage award. The basis for the jury's judgment is said to be the 41 cases plus the data supporting the calculation of the experts regarding total damages suffered by the remaining 2,990 class members.

Class members have answered questionnaires and are testifying in scheduled oral depositions now in progress. Petitioners attack the limits of discovery from the class members, but we will not reach this issue. It is sufficient to explain that defendants are allowed a total of 45 minutes to interrogate each class member in an oral deposition. These depositions will not be directly used at the trial in Phase II. Rather, the oral depositions, with the other discovery from class members, provide information for experts engaged to measure the damages suffered by the class.

II

Defendants find numerous flaws in the procedures set for Phase II of the trial. They argue with considerable force that such a trial would effectively deny defendants' rights to a jury under the seventh amendment, would work an impermissible change in the controlling substantive law of Texas, would deny procedural due process under the fifth amendment of the United States Constitution, and would effectively amend the rules of civil procedure contrary to the strictures of the enabling acts.

A

The contentions that due process would be denied, the purposes of Erie would be frustrated, and the seventh amendment circumvented are variations of a common concern of defendants. Defendants insist that one-to-one adversarial engagement or its proximate, the traditional trial, is secured by the seventh amendment and certainly contemplated by Article III of the Constitution itself. Defendants point out, and plaintiffs quickly concede, that under Phase II there will inevitably be individual class members whose recovery will be greater or lesser than it would have been if tried alone. Indeed, with the focus in Phase II upon the "total picture", with arrays of data that will attend the statistical presentation, persons who would have had their claims rejected may recover. Plaintiffs say that "such discontinuities" would be reflected in the overall omnibus figure. Stated another way, plaintiffs say that so long as their mode of proof enables the jury to decide the total liability of defendants with reasonable accuracy, the loss of one-to-one engagement infringes no right of defendants. Such unevenness, plaintiffs say, will be visited upon them, not the defendants.

With the procedures described at such a level of abstraction, it is difficult to describe concretely any deprivation of defendants' rights. Of course, there will be a jury, and each plaintiff will be present in a theoretical, if not practical, sense. Having said this, however, we are left with a profound disquiet. First, the assumption of plaintiffs' argument is that its proof of omnibus damages is in fact achievable; that statistical measures of representativeness and commonality will be sufficient for the jury to make informed judgments concerning damages. It is true that there is considerable judicial experience with such techniques, but it is also true we have remained cautious in their use. Indeed, as the district court stated in one massive Title VII case resting on math models: "[I]t has to judicial eyes a surrealistic cast, mirroring the techniques used in its trial. Excursions into the new and sometimes arcane corners of different disciplines is a familiar task of American trial lawyers and its generalist judges. But more is afoot here, and this court is uncomfortable with its implications. This concern has grown with the realization that the esoterics of econometrics and statistics which both parties have required this court to judge have a centripetal dynamic of their own. They push from the outside roles of tools for 'judicial' decisions toward the core of decision making itself. Stated more concretely: the precision-like mesh of numbers tends to make fits of social problems when I intuitively doubt such fits. I remain wary of the siren call of the numerical display" * * *.[2]

This concern is particularly strong in this case, where there are such disparities among "class" members.

The plaintiffs' answers to interrogatories and the depositions already conducted have provided enough information to show that if, as plaintiffs contend, the representative plaintiffs accurately reflect the class, it is a diverse group. The plaintiffs' "class" consists of persons claiming different diseases, different exposure periods, and different occupations. The depositions of ten tentative class representatives indicate that their diseases break down into three categories: asbestosis (plural and pulmonary)—eight representatives; lung cancer—three representatives; and Mesothelioma—one representative. The class breaks down as follows:

2. Vuyanich v. Republic Nat. Bank of Dallas, 505 F.Supp. 224, 394 (N.D.Tex. 1980).

Disease	#	%
Pleural cases	907	37.2%
Asbestosis cases	1184	48.6%
Lung cancer cases	219	9.0%
Other cancer cases	92	3.8%
Mesothelioma cases	33	1.4%

In addition, plaintiffs' admissions of fact show the following disparities among class members. a. The class includes persons who do not have legal claims against Defendant ACandS, Inc. b. One or more members of the class may be barred from prosecuting claims against ACandS by virtue of their prior employment with ACandS. c. The severity and type of physical or mental injuries varies among class members. d. The nature and type of damage varies among class members. e. Not all of the Plaintiffs have been injured by the acts, omissions, conduct or fault of all of the Defendants. f. The dates of exposure to asbestos-containing products varies among class members. g. The types of products to which class members were exposed varies among class members. h. The dates that class members knew or should have known of their exposure to asbestos-containing products is not identical among class members.

We are also uncomfortable with the suggestion that a move from one-on-one "traditional" modes is little more than a move to modernity. Such traditional ways of proceeding reflect far more than habit. They reflect the very culture of the jury trial and the case and controversy requirement of Article III. It is suggested that the litigating unit is the class and, hence, we have the adversarial engagement or that all are present in a "consolidated" proceeding. But, this begs the very question of whether these 3,031 claimants are sufficiently situated for class treatment; it equally begs the question of whether they are actually before the court under Fed.R.Civ.Proc.Rules 23 and 42(b) in any more than a fictional sense. Ultimately, these concerns find expression in defendants' right to due process.

B

These concerns are little more than different ways of looking at a core problem. The core problem is that Phase II, while offering an innovative answer to an admitted crisis in the judicial system, is unfortunately beyond the scope of federal judicial authority. It infringes upon the dictates of Erie that we remain faithful to the law of Texas, and upon the separation of powers between the judicial and legislative branches.

Texas has made its policy choices in defining the duty owed by manufacturers and suppliers of products to consumers. These choices are reflected in the requirement that a plaintiff prove both causation and damage. In Texas, it is a "fundamental principle of traditional products liability law ... that the plaintiffs must prove that the defendant supplied the product which caused the injury." [4] These elements focus upon individuals, not groups. The same may be said, and with even greater confidence, of wage losses, pain and suffering, and other ele-

---

4. Gaulding v. Celotex Corp., 772 S.W.2d 66, 77 (Tex.1989).

ments of compensation. These requirements of proof define the duty of the manufacturers.

Plaintiffs say, of course, that these requirements will be met by the proposed procedures. This proof for 2,990 class members will be supplied by expert opinion regarding their similarity to 41 representative plaintiffs. Plaintiffs deny that they will be extrapolating a total universe from a sample. While we are skeptical of this assertion, plaintiffs' characterization is of little moment. The inescapable fact is that the individual claims of 2,990 persons will not be presented. Rather, the claim of a unit of 2,990 persons will be presented. Given the unevenness of the individual claims, this Phase II process inevitably restates the dimensions of tort liability. Under the proposed procedure, manufacturers and suppliers are exposed to liability not only in 41 cases actually tried with success to the jury, but in 2,990 additional cases whose claims are indexed to those tried.

Texas has made its policy choices in its substantive tort rules against the backdrop of a trial. Trials can vary greatly in their procedures, such as numbers of jurors, the method of jury instruction, and a large number of other ways. There is a point, however, where cumulative changes in procedure work a change in the very character of a trial. Significantly, changes in "procedure" involving the mode of proof may alter the liability of the defendants in fundamental ways. We do not suggest that procedure becomes substance whenever outcomes are changed. Rather, we suggest that changes in substantive duty can come dressed as a change in procedure. We are persuaded that Phase II would work such a change.

The basic changes in the dynamics of trial caused by the rules of evidence and procedure have been particularly noted with respect to the use of expert testimony. A contemplated "trial" of the 2,990 class members without discrete focus can be no more than the testimony of experts regarding their claims, as a group, compared to the claims actually tried to the jury. That procedure cannot focus upon such issues as individual causation, but ultimately must accept general causation as sufficient, contrary to Texas law. It is evident that these statistical estimates deal only with general causation, for "population-based probability estimates do not speak to a probability of causation in any one case; the estimate of relative risk is a property of the studied population, not of an individual's case." This type of procedure does not allow proof that a particular defendant's asbestos "really" caused a particular plaintiff's disease; the only "fact" that can be proved is that in most cases the defendant's asbestos would have been the cause. This is the inevitable consequence of treating discrete claims as fungible claims. Commonality among class members on issues of causation and damages can be achieved only by lifting the description of the claims to a level of generality that tears them from their substantively required moorings to actual causation and discrete injury. Procedures can be devised to implement such generalizations, but not without alteration of substantive principle.

We are told that Phase II is the only realistic way of trying these cases; that the difficulties faced by the courts as well as the rights of the class members to have their cases tried cry powerfully for innovation and judicial creativity. The arguments are compelling, but they are better addressed to the representative branches—Congress and the State Legislature. The Judicial Branch can offer the trial of lawsuits. It has no power or competence to do more. We are persuaded on reflection that the procedures here called for comprise something other than a trial within our authority. It is called a trial, but it is not.

The 2,990 class members cannot be certified for trial as proposed under Rule 23(b)(3), Fed.R.Civ.Pro.Rule 23(b)(3) requires that "the questions of law or fact common to the members of the class predominate over any questions affecting individual members." There are too many disparities among the various plaintiffs for their common concerns to predominate. The plaintiffs suffer from different diseases, some of which are more likely to have been caused by asbestos than others. The plaintiffs were exposed to asbestos in various manners and to varying degrees. The plaintiffs' lifestyles differed in material respects. To create the requisite commonality for trial, the discrete components of the class members' claims and the asbestos manufacturers' defenses must be submerged. The procedures for Phase II do precisely that, but, as we have explained, do so only by reworking the substantive duty owed by the manufacturers. At the least, the enabling acts prevent that reading.

Finally, it is questionable whether defendants' right to trial by jury is being faithfully honored, but we need not explore this issue. It is sufficient now to conclude that Phase II cannot go forward without changing Texas law and usurping legislative prerogatives, a step federal courts lack authority to take.

We admire the work of our colleague, Judge Robert Parker, and are sympathetic with the difficulties he faces. This grant of the petition for writ of mandamus should not be taken as a rebuke of an able judge, but rather as another chapter in an ongoing struggle with the problems presented by the phenomenon of mass torts. The petitions for writ of mandamus are granted.

Notes and Questions

1. Was causation or damages the more intractable problem according to Judge Higginbotham? Can causation ever be established on an aggregative or representative basis? Refer back to the material in Chapter 8 and the dual nature of the causation question. In *Sterling v. Velsicol Chemical Corp.*, discussed supra, while the Sixth Circuit approved the certification of the class action, it also held that *only* the generic causation issue could be resolved on a class-wide basis—i.e., whether the kinds of harm suffered by plaintiffs could have been produced by exposure to the chemicals released, whereas the individual causation inquiry must be resolved on a plaintiff-by-plaintiff basis. If that is true, how can a class action ever resolve all of the elements of the plaintiffs' prima facie case? Was it the Judge's hope that

resolution of the representative plaintiffs' causation elements (if favorable) would have resulted in some global settlement?

2. In *Fibreboard* isn't it "obvious" that most of the plaintiffs' injuries were caused by exposure to asbestos? For mesothelioma the relative risk for asbestos exposure is extremely high, meaning that few people ever contract that disease unless exposed to asbestos. Why not apply epidemiological data and the principle of proportionality discussed in Chapter 8 to arrive at a total value to the class for each disease category?

3. Is Texas' substantive tort law on causation unique? Was Judge Higginbotham concluding that the proportionality principle has no basis in Texas tort law? Is there any jurisdiction referred to in Chapters 5 or 8 that might find the approach advocated by Judge Parker acceptable?

4. What were the defendants' motivations for seeking a writ of mandamus? Wouldn't they save substantial litigation expenses under Judge Parker's proposed methods?

5. Of at least four separate rationales advanced by Judge Higginbotham to justify granting the writ of mandamus, which seemed the most persuasive? Why didn't he simply hold that the Phase II class failed to satisfy the requirements of Rule 23(b) that common questions predominate? Was the remainder of the opinion dicta? How compelling is the argument (which the court declined to reach) that defendants are denied their right to a jury trial guaranteed by the Seventh Amendment? Don't class actions under Rule 23 necessarily place some constraint on individual jury trials?

6. Judge Parker applied reverse bifurcation in *Jenkins* and *Fibreboard* by first trying common defenses and punitive damages *before* trying causation and compensatory damages. What is the rationale for applying reverse bifurcation?

7. Observe that Judge Parker sought to utilize both consolidation under Rule 42(a) for the common issues (defenses and punitive damages), as he had done successfully in *Jenkins*, and a class action under Rule 23(b) for the individual issues of causation and damages. Judge Higginbotham, in a deleted segment of the opinion, praised Judge Parker for his imaginative and innovative approaches and encouraged him to seek to find other techniques to manage these cases.

8. In Cimino v. Raymark Industries, 751 F.Supp. 649 (E.D.Tex.1990), Judge Parker sought to steer between the success of *Jenkins* and the failure of *Fibreboard*.

a. Judge Parker describes the Phases of the trial as follows:

Phase I would involve trial of the common questions of product defectiveness under § 402A, adequacy of the warnings, the state of the art defense and punitive damages liability.

Phase II required a jury finding for each of nineteen worksites during certain time periods regarding which asbestos containing insulation products were used, which crafts were sufficiently exposed to asbestos fibers from those products for such exposure to be a producing cause of an asbestos-related injury or disease and an apportionment of causation among defendants, settling and non-settling.

In other words, the exposure questions to be submitted would be specific as to time, place, craft, and amounts of exposure.

He then described the stipulation to which the parties had agreed on Phase II pertaining to exposure and causation:

The Court first compiled a list of worksites, various locations consisting mostly of oil and chemical refineries, where the majority of the plaintiffs allegedly were occupationally exposed to asbestos in the course of their employment. The Court next compiled a list of job classifications, or crafts, which the plaintiffs worked in during their employment at the worksites. It was contemplated that any plaintiff whose work history did not include a threshold amount of time in any of the worksites would have the exposure issue tried in an individual mini-trial.

Prior to the Court drafting a verdict form for Phase II, the parties agreed to stipulate as to what the jury findings would have been had the Phase II been tried to a jury. The parties stipulated that the jury would have apportioned causation among the defendants in the amounts of 10% causation for each of the non-settling defendants and 13% causation for the settling defendant Johns–Manville Corporation.

The verdict form for Phase II would have been worksites. For each worksite there would have been two interrogatories. The first interrogatory would have asked whether or not each of the various crafts at a worksite was sufficiently exposed to asbestos for that exposure to be a producing cause of the disease of asbestosis during successive time periods. The second interrogatory then would have requested the jury to determine, for each craft and each time period answered affirmatively in the first interrogatory, the percentage of comparative causation, if any, that each defendant's products contributed to the exposure.

Why do you suppose the defendants agreed to stipulate causation on this basis? If there had not been agreement would this approach have satisfied the concerns of Judge Higginbotham? What central fact made Phase II a workable approach?

b. Phase III dealt with damages:

The 2,298 class members were divided into five disease categories based on the plaintiff's injury claims. The Court selected a random sample from each disease category as follows:

	SAMPLE SIZE	DISEASE CATEGORY POPULATION
Mesothelioma	15	32
Lung Cancer	25	186
Other Cancer	20	58
Asbestosis	50	1,050
Pleural Disease	50	972
TOTAL	160	2,228

The damage case of each trial sample class member randomly drawn was then submitted to a jury. Each plaintiff whose damage case was submitted to the jury is to be awarded his individual verdict for

each disease category will constitute the damage award for each non-sample class member.

Plaintiffs have agreed to the procedure, thereby waiving their rights to individual damage determinations.

In addition, Phase III addressed any contributory negligence by the representative plaintiffs, including smoking, if the evidence showed that a plaintiff had subjective knowledge of the synergistic relationship between the asbestos-related disease and smoking and appreciated the danger of continued smoking. These elements of contributory negligence were also applied to the failure of a plaintiff to wear a respirator and the failure to follow a doctor's advice. In cases where there was no evidence of smoking constituting contributory negligence, evidence of a plaintiff's smoking was allowed on the issue of damages to show quality of life and life expectancy.

The damage Phase depended on the application of statistical methods. Judge Parker described those methods and explained why they satisfied the defendants' constitutional rights:

The Court finds no persuasive evidence why the average damage verdicts in each disease category should not be applied to the non-sample members. The averages are calculated after remittitur and take into consideration those cases where plaintiffs failed to prove the existence of an asbestos-related injury or disease resulting in a zero verdict. Individual members of a disease category who will receive an award that might be different from one they would have received had their individual case been decided by a jury have waived any objections, and the defendants cannot show that the total amount of damages would be greater under the Court's method compared to individual trials of these cases. Indeed, the millions of dollars saved in reduced transaction costs inure to defendants' benefit.

* * *

The 160 damage cases tried with all the variables inherent in such cases produced a result to a 99% confidence level the average of which would be comparable to the average result if all cases were tried. If the existence of variables are the driving force behind defendants' due process argument, then due process has been served.

However, a due process concern remains that is very troubling to the Court. It is apparent from the effort and time required to try these 160 cases, that unless this plan or some other procedure that permits damages to be adjudicated in the aggregate is approved, these cases cannot be tried. Defendants complain about the 1% likelihood that the result would be significantly different. However, plaintiffs are facing a 100% confidence level of being denied access to the courts. The Court will leave it to the academicians and legal scholars to debate whether our notion of due process has room for balancing these competing interests.

Judge Parker also held that these procedures satisfied any requirements set forth in the *Fibreboard* opinion. In your opinion, do they deny defendants any constitutional rights of due process? Any seventh amendment rights to jury trial? Any other rights? For an excellent discussion of the constitutional and practical propriety of the *Cimino* methodology, see Glen O. Robinson & Kenneth S. Abraham, Collective Justice in Tort Law, 78 Va. L. Rev. 1481 (1992).

9. Judge Parker is not the only one applying aggregative mechanisms to resolve asbestos litigation. In one suit, the state circuit court in Baltimore, Maryland consolidated 8,550 plaintiffs. The court first submitted to a jury the common issues of state of the art and product defectiveness and then applied "mini-trials" on compensatory and punitive damages. See Abate v. ACHS, Inc., Md. Cir. Ct., Baltimore City, No. 89236704 (Dec. 12, 1992), 6 Toxics L. Rptr. 863 (12–23–92). The jury awarded $11.2 million in compensatory damages to three plaintiffs, and zero to three others; it also established punitive damage multipliers for each of six defendants, ranging from a low of .35 for each $1 of compensatory damages to a high of $2.50. The trial judge, fearing that the punitive awards would deplete the assets of defendants to pay future compensatory awards, held that all punitive awards made in the mini-trials would be delayed until all compensatory damages are paid.

10. In 1991, the Judicial Panel on Multi-District Litigation in In re Asbestos Products Liability Litigation, 771 F.Supp. 415 (Jud. Pan. Mult. Lit. 1991) ordered the pretrial consolidation of 26,639 cases pending in 87 federal districts.

11. *Bankruptcy of Manville.* The asbestos litigation was further complicated by the 1982 bankruptcy filing of Johns-Manville Corporation, the largest of the asbestos producers. Johns-Manville, faced with claims from current and future victims of asbestos exposure estimated to total $2 billion, filed a voluntary petition in bankruptcy under chapter 11 on August 26, 1982. The reorganization proceeding involved both "present claimants," those who had developed an asbestos-related disease, and "future claimants," those who had been exposed to Manville asbestos but had not yet shown any signs of disease. After four years of negotiation, a Plan of Reorganization ("The Plan") was confirmed in 1986, In re Johns-Manville Corp., 68 B.R. 618 (Bkrtcy.N.Y.1986). The cornerstone of the plan was the Manville Personal Injury Settlement Trust ("The Trust"), a mechanism designed to satisfy the claims of all asbestos health claimants and which required all claimants to proceed only against the Trust, not against Manville. If a settlement could not be reached with the Trust, the claimant could elect mediation, binding arbitration, or traditional tort litigation in state or federal court, including trial by jury. The claimant could collect from the Trust the full amount of whatever compensatory damages are awarded, but punitive damages were prohibited. Another provision called for the settlement of claims against the Trust on a first in, first out basis.

The plan was approved by the Second Circuit. Kane v. Johns–Manville Corp., 843 F.2d 636 (2d Cir.1988). Pursuant to the Plan, the Trust received $909 million in cash, two bonds with an aggregate value of $1.8 billion, 24 million shares of Manville common stock, and 7.2 million shares of Manville convertible preferred stock, aggregating 80 percent of the stock of the reorganized Manville. See In re Joint Eastern & Southern Districts Asbestos Litigation, 120 B.R. 648, 652 (Bkrtcy.N.Y.1990). Despite this funding, it was apparent by 1990 that the liquidation of the claims of thousands of asbestos victims was substantially depleting the Trust's cash. By March 30, 1990, the Trust had received more than 150,000 claims, 50 percent above the highest number estimated when the Plan was approved. The Trust had settled 22,386 of those claims at an average liquidated value of $42,000.

In 1990, Judge Jack Weinstein of the Eastern District of New York was given supervisory authority over the Plan because he was separately handling the trials of hundreds of asbestos cases pending in that court. Judge Weinstein appointed a special master in response to a motion by the Trust for a determination that its assets constituted a limited fund within the meaning of Rule 23(b)(1)(B). The Special Master's report concluded that the Trust was "deeply insolvent." In November 1990, beneficiaries under the Trust filed a class action on behalf of all beneficiaries which Judge Weinstein and Bankruptcy Judge Lifland certified. A proposed settlement reordered the priorities of the Trust by dividing all claimants into two levels: those most severely injured, which included cancer, other serious conditions, and death claims; and all others. In addition, it set payment levels ranging from a maximum of $350,000 for mesothelioma to $30,000 for pleural disease. Secondly, Level One would receive up to 45 percent of their claims in the first two years, but Level Two recipients would be deferred until the third year.

Some personal injury claimants and co-defendant manufacturers opposed the settlement. The health claimants challenged the accord on several fronts, arguing that it violated procedural due process, Rule 23 requirements, and violated the Bankruptcy Code. In In re Joint Eastern and Southern District Asbestos Litigation, 982 F.2d 721 (2d Cir.1992), the Second Circuit (2–1) overturned portions of the Plan.

The Second Circuit held that the orders and procedures embodied in Judge Weinstein's efforts to control the disposition of the Trust assets and dispose of pending asbestos claims were not authorized under Rule 23(b)(1)(B) (a limited fund class) and violated provisions of the Bankruptcy Code. Essentially, combining co-defendant manufacturers (other than Manville) and all health claimants into a single class transgressed the requirements of Rule 23 that those with adverse interests cannot have the same representatives. Similarly, treating all health claimants as a class, when the Proposed Settlement would significantly alter priorities that existed under the original Manville Plan, was improper because consent to the settlement was given by representatives who purported to represent an undifferentiated class of claimants, rather than the interests of the subclasses whose rights were altered. Further, it held that the Plan was an impermissible modification of a confirmed and substantially consummated plan of reorganization without complying with all of the requirements of the Bankruptcy Code.

Six months later, in response to a motion for reconsideration, the Second Circuit reversed itself and held that separate subclasses of claimants were not necessary. 993 F.2d 7 (2d Cir.1993). For a proposal that would permit modifications of a mass tort debtor's Chapter 11 plan to ensure compensation for mass tort victims, see Comment, Modifications of a Chapter 11 Plan in the Mass Tort Context, 92 Col. L. Rev. 192 (1992).

12. *Innovative Settlement Proposal.* In 1993, the Center for Claims Resolution (CCR) in Princeton, New Jersey, which represents twenty asbes-

tos companies, announced a $1 billion class-wide settlement that would avoid court litigation. The details of the compensation program, including exposure requirements, medical criteria, payment schedules, and dispute resolution procedures, are spelled out in a 106–page stipulation of settlement filed in the U.S. District Court for the Eastern District of Pennsylvania (Carlough v. Amchem Products Inc., 834 F.Supp. 1437 (E.D.Pa.1993), complaint, third-party complaint, and stipulated settlement filed 1/15/93). The voluntary agreement would settle a putative class action filed the same day against the defendants. The third party complaint is against eighty insurance companies that underwrite policies for the twenty firms that seek a declaration that the settlement not jeopardize their coverage.

a. Under the proposed settlement, the defendants will provide $1 billion during the next ten years to settle an average of 10,000 claims a year by workers who contract mesothelioma, lung cancer, other cancers, and non-malignant conditions related to their asbestos exposure. The court will conduct a series of fairness hearings to review the terms of the settlement. Most claims will be processed and paid within one to six months of filing.

The proposed settlement agreement sets up a "flow rate" calling for settlement of 700 mesothelioma claims, 700 lung cancer claims, 200 other cancer claims, and 13,500 claims for nonmalignant conditions in the first year, with the numbers gradually declining in the final year. The flow rate numbers represent the maximum number of claims that can be settled in a particular year. If more people file, their claims will be pushed into the following year. The settlement covers a ten-year period. After ten years, the defendant companies may choose to continue, and make another round of contributions. If they do not, the settlement is over, and claimants would go back to the tort system.

b. The compensation schedule provides for payments ranging from $20,000 to $200,000 and averaging between $37,000 and $60,000 for mesothelioma. Qualifying claims for nonmalignant conditions are compensable at the rate of $2,500 to $30,000, with the average payment to be maintained between $5,800 and $7,500. The payment schedule is based on average jury awards and settlements during the past four years, according to the CCR's summary of the agreement.

A total of 1 percent of qualifying claims for non-malignant conditions and 3 percent of other qualifying claims will be eligible each year for higher payments—averaging $300,000 for mesothelioma claims; $125,000 for lung cancer; $50,000 for other cancers; and $50,000 for nonmalignant conditions—when the claims involve extraordinary circumstances.

An independent panel will determine if a claim meets the "extraordinary claims" criteria, which include a combination of age, number and age of dependents, relevant economic factors, exposure to only the CCR defendants' asbestos products, and other similar factors. Extraordinary claims must be nominated for panel review. The panel reviews submitted claims each year to determine those eligible for extraordinary treatment compensation, up to the 1 percent and 3 percent caps.

c. Additionally, each year, up to 1 percent of people with qualifying claims may turn down the CCR's settlement offer and resolve their claims through the courts or through binding arbitration. However, only limited issues may be resolved through the tort system and do not include claims for increased risk of cancer or punitive damages. The refusal option is on a first-come, first-served basis and claims exceeding the 1–percent maximum would receive priority in the next settlement year. The agreement caps attorneys' fees at 25 percent of the amount of any award.

d.   The CCR settlement contains another interesting twist in dealing with claimants who may have minimal injuries at present, but develop cancer, say, eight years later. The statute of limitations conundrum discussed in Chapter 12 on defenses is avoided. Claimants who fail to meet court-approved medical criteria for impairment may resubmit their claims if impairment develops. Claimants compensated for a nonmalignant condition will be eligible for supplemental compensation if a malignant condition later develops.

e.   The settlement also eliminates joint and several liability because each of the twenty firms is allocated a specific percentage of every compensation payment, regardless of whose products the claimant was exposed to. If a participating firm goes bankrupt or defaults, only that share of each compensation payment will remain unpaid.

f.   Finally, if a claimant was also exposed to asbestos products of nonparticipants, such claims may be pursued against such firms in court. See ABA Journal, April 1993, p. 22–23; 7 Toxics L. Rptr. 1018–20 (Feb. 3, 1993).

If you were representing a group of plaintiffs who received notice of the proposed settlement, would you recommend that your clients participate? What advantages do you see accruing to your clients? What disadvantages? Would you opt out of the class? For a debate on the merits of this proposal, see John D. Aldock, Carlough v. Amchem: A Fair and Lawful Solution to the Asbestos Crisis, 8 Toxics L. Rptr. 58 (June 16, 1993); Frederick M. Baron, Carlough v. Amchem: Prepackaged Future Claimants Class and Article III, 8 Toxics L. Rptr. 24 (June 9, 1993).

D.   JUDICIAL CASE MANAGEMENT

After a court has resolved the manner in which the litigation is to be structured—class action, consolidations, or individual trials—most courts in toxic tort cases use pretrial orders or other orders that organize the sequence of litigation milestones. Plaintiffs' counsel will typically prefer parallel track discovery procedures that permit each side to conduct depositions, request documents, and propound interrogatories. Defense counsel, on the other hand, will strongly prefer that plaintiffs be required to prepare their cases first. The defendants will, therefore, attempt to obtain a court order requiring the plaintiffs to disclose their experts and set forth individualized statements establishing a connection between the alleged toxic exposure and each plaintiff's medical complaints. Some courts are persuaded to follow this approach when convinced that it will save judicial resources and provide an opportunity for a prompt resolution of the entire case.

1. "LONE PINE" ORDERS

a. The expression "Lone Pine" order has become a term of art in toxic tort litigation and refers to orders that require plaintiffs to submit at the pretrial stage, supporting proofs, including expert opinions, to establish causation and injury. The term derived from the case of Lore v. Lone Pine Corp., No. L–03306–85, slip op. (N.J. Sup. Ct., Law Div., Nov. 18, 1986). The case management order in that case, which ultimately resulted in the dismissal of plaintiff's action for failure to comply with its terms, was as follows:

Order * * * that on or before June 1, 1987: (1) plaintiffs would provide the following documentation with respect to each claim for personal injuries: (a) facts of each individual plaintiff's exposure to alleged toxic substances at or from the Lone Pine landfill; (b) reports of treating physicians and medical or other experts, supporting each individual plaintiff's claim of injury and causation by substances from Lone Pine landfill; (2) plaintiffs would provide the following with respect to each individual plaintiff's claims for diminution of property value: (c) each individual plaintiff's address, including tax block and lot number, for the property alleged to have declined in value; (d) reports of real estate or other experts supporting each individual plaintiff's claim of diminution of property values, including the timing and degree of such diminution and the causation of same. These were considered to be the basic facts plaintiff must furnish in order to support their claim of injury and property damage.

Interrogatories to be propounded that would support a *Lone Pine* order would request the plaintiffs to list every chemical they were exposed to, to list every injury caused by the chemical, to list the name of every doctor who says the injury was caused by the chemical, and to list the evidence that they have that each defendant is responsible for the injury caused by the chemical.

b. Illustrative of such an order, but more comprehensive in its coverage, was that issued recently in Grant v. E.I. Du Pont de Nemours & Co., 1993 WL 146634, U.S. Dist. Ct., E.D.N.C., Feb. 17, 1993. The litigation involved twelve separate civil actions brought against du Pont by twenty-two residents who alleged that Du Pont had contaminated their homes and personally injured them through the release of certain chemicals into the air and groundwater. The total amount in controversy, including punitive damages claims of $500 million, exceeded $1.3 billion.

With some deletions, the court's order included the following provisions:

1. Plaintiffs are to complete the scientific testing of their properties, including soil, groundwater, surface water, and air, by May 31, 1993. On or before June 15, 1993, Plaintiffs are to provide

Du Pont with all testing results, analyses and other data, and file with the Court and provide Du Pont with the affidavit of a competent expert witness, specifying the nature, duration, and level of contamination of each Plaintiff's property. The expert's affidavit must specify each chemical substance by name, the date of testing, the level and concentration of the substance detected as of the testing date, the testing methodology, the detection limits of the methodology, the connection of the chemical to Kentec Inc. and Du Pont, and the path and route of the chemical from Kentec to the Plaintiff's property. The failure of any Plaintiff to comply with this paragraph may result in his or her action being dismissed.

2. Du Pont shall have from July 1, 1993 through September 30, 1993 to complete its scientific testing of the properties, including soil, groundwater, surface water, and air, of all Plaintiffs who have demonstrated their interest in continuing in this litigation by their compliance with the preceding paragraph. The failure of any Plaintiff to cooperate with Du Pont's efforts to comply with this paragraph may result in his or her action being dismissed. * * * The failure of Du Pont to comply with this paragraph may result in its being precluded from introducing evidence on this issue at trial.

3. Plaintiffs are to complete all appraisals of their properties by April 30, 1993. On or before May 15, 1993, Plaintiffs are to provide Du Pont with all such appraisals, and file with the Court and provide Du Pont with the affidavit of each qualified real estate appraiser, specifying the value of each Plaintiff's property, the comparables upon which such value is based, whether the property has been in any way impaired, and the reason for the impairment. * * * The failure of any Plaintiff to comply with this paragraph may result in his or her claims for injury to property being dismissed.

4. Du Pont is to have from June 1, 1993 through July 31, 1993 to complete its appraisals of the properties of all Plaintiffs * * *

5. Plaintiffs are to have until July 31, 1993 to consult with competent expert witnesses and conduct scientific testing to determine the costs of cleaning up their properties or otherwise restoring the properties' value. On or before August 15, 1993, Plaintiffs are to provide Du Pont with all results, analyses, conclusions, and other data, and file with the Court and provide Du Pont with the affidavit of a competent expert witness specifying the actions each Plaintiff intends to conduct to clean up his property. The affidavit must specify a timetable for completion of the cleanup, an estimate of the costs of the cleanup, and the methodology for calculating the cleanup costs. The failure of any Plaintiff to comply with this paragraph may result in his or her claims for recovery of cleanup costs being dismissed.

6. [Sets forth Du Pont's obligations respecting the determination of clean up costs]

7. Plaintiffs are to have until May 31, 1993 to consult with and be examined by physicians, psychiatrists, psychologists, and any other health care providers regarding Plaintiffs' claims of potential future harm to their health, fear of harm to their health, stress, anxiety, or other emotional harm, or any other personal injury. On or before June 15, 1993, Plaintiffs are to provide Du Pont with all results, analyses and other data, and file with the Court and provide Du Pont with a physician's affidavit specifying the nature, duration, and amount of exposure (including blood levels) each Plaintiff has had to chemical contamination, when such exposure occurred, and the nature and extent of each such Plaintiff's personal injury. The physician's affidavit may be supplemented with the affidavits of other competent expert witnesses, but submission of such supplementary affidavits will not excuse the failure to submit the physician's affidavit, including the required contents, described in this paragraph. The physician's affidavit shall state his or her opinion, based on a reasonable degree of medical certainty, that the particular Plaintiff has suffered injuries as a result of exposure to chemicals from Kentec Inc.; shall specify any and every injury, illness or condition suffered by the Plaintiff that, in the opinion of the physician, caused each and every specific injury, illness, and condition listed; shall include differential diagnoses which rule out alternative possible causes of Plaintiffs' injuries; and shall state the scientific and medical bases for the physician's opinions. With regard to future personal injury, the affidavit shall state the physician's opinion, based upon a reasonable degree of medical certainty, that the particular Plaintiff is more likely than not to suffer a particular injury in the future; shall identify such specific injury; shall state the time at which such future injury shall manifest itself; and shall comply with the remaining requirements of this paragraph as if the injury currently existed. The failure of any Plaintiff to comply with this paragraph may result in his or her claims for personal injury being dismissed.

Notes and Questions

1. The effect of noncompliance with such orders is dismissal, which is recited in each paragraph. What is the justification for dismissals on that basis? Is that too drastic a sanction? Does it deprive plaintiffs of those protections that summary judgment procedures would afford? In Cottle v. Superior Court (Oxnard Shores Co.), 3 Cal.App. 4th 1367, 5 Cal.Rptr. 2d 882 (1992), a California appeals court, in affirming dismissal of plaintiff's claims for failing to comply with a series of case management orders, sustained orders (which were similar to those in *Lone Pine*) requiring "statements establishing a prima facie claim for personal injury or property damage" and excluding plaintiffs' causation evidence for failure to comply. The court first held that in complex litigation courts have broad inherent powers to control the management of such cases:

The extent of the trial court's inherent managerial power in complex civil litigation has not yet been delineated by this state's reviewing courts. However, federal courts have long recognized that active and effective judicial management of such litigation is crucial. One federal court has explained, "Managerial power is not merely desirable. It is a critical necessity. * * * We face the hard necessity that, within proper limits, judges must be permitted to bring management power to bear upon massive and complex litigation to prevent it from monopolizing the services of the court to the exclusion of other litigants."

In view of all these authorities, most of which were relied upon by the trial court, it is apparent that courts have the power to fashion a new procedure in a complex litigation case to manage and control the case before it. Although it is not possible to set forth precise guidelines as to when such an order can be issued or what other kinds of procedure can be used, we conclude that a court should consider the totality of the circumstances of the particular case in deciding how to manage a complex litigation case.

We conclude that Judge Johnson properly used the court's inherent powers to manage the complex litigation case before her and hold that in a complex litigation case which has been assigned to a judge for all purposes, a court may order the exclusion of evidence if the plaintiffs are unable to establish a prima facie claim prior to the start of trial.

Second, the court held that the exclusion orders were valid, given the extensive, repeated opportunities afforded to plaintiffs to comply. Third, the court held that such orders did not deprive plaintiffs of any due process rights nor rights to a jury trial. Although plaintiffs had argued that the "cauldron of chemicals" present on their properties made precise exposure and causation testimony impossible, the court emphasized that the trial court indicated its willingness to accept "a synergistic cause and effect linkage between exposure and symptoms" which they had not provided. The dissenting opinion in *Cottle* argued that the judiciary lacks the kind of sweeping inherent powers relied upon by the majority and designation of the case as "complex" or "toxic tort" does not create special powers:

> [U]nder the authority of this section and similar provisions in the Code of Civil Procedure (§ 128(a), § 177), courts have devised various procedural rules to fairly and expeditiously handle litigation before them which presented procedural problems not otherwise covered in the statutes or rules.

> However, appellate decisions construing these provisions indicate resort to a trial court's inherent authority to craft new rules of civil procedure is only a proper exercise of inherent powers when made necessary because of the *absence* of any statute or rule governing the situation. Thus, the rationale for devising new rules of procedure has historically been one of necessity. In other words, to fill a void in the statutory scheme, a court had a duty to create a new rule of procedure in the interests of justice and in order to exercise its jurisdiction. However, unlike the "procedure" employed in the case at bar, none of the judicially created procedures involved a ruling to decide the merits of a cause of action and, on that basis, to remove that cause of action from jury consideration.

In the instant case, there was not statutory void which required the court's "inherent power" to fill. To the contrary, the trial court's case management order was the substantial equivalent of a mechanism the Legislature has long provided—the motion for summary judgment. The Legislature, however, has surrounded this mechanism with procedural protections it considers essential to fairness and justice. These procedural protections were not afforded plaintiffs in this case.

Plaintiffs were ordered to present evidence of physical injury from exposure to the toxic substances through medical records, physician affidavits and the like. When the trial court deemed this evidence insufficient it terminated plaintiffs' causes of action, preventing them from being considered by the jury. As a consequence, the case management order in this case changed the legislatively established procedure of Code of Civil Procedure section 437c. Had the procedural guidelines for summary judgment been followed, the defendants would have had to have initiated the process and have supplied evidence causation could *not* be proved. Strictly construing these moving papers and liberally construing plaintiffs' documents in opposition to the motion, the court would have then decided whether there remained any triable issues of material fact as to causation. However, the trial court here did not employ the statutory provision for summary judgment with its built-in procedural safeguards. In its place the trial court substituted a bastardized process which had the purpose and effect of summary judgment but avoided the very procedures and protections the Legislature deemed essential.

The Legislature has provided a pretrial procedure for terminating a cause of action because the plaintiff has insufficient evidence to warrant a jury trial of the claim. That procedure is summary judgment. Consequently, trial courts lack "inherent power" to do the same thing under another name, especially one which omits vital procedural protections the Legislature guaranteed in its summary judgment statute. This attempt to grant the functional equivalent of a summary judgment in the guise of a case management order impinges on a litigant's constitutional right to have material issues of fact decided by a jury without affording the procedural protections the Legislature deemed essential before this drastic step would be allowed.

With whom do you agree: the majority or the dissent? Do complex cases justify more extreme controls? What about plaintiffs' argument that they were denied a right to a jury trial? Doesn't a grant of a summary judgment motion have the same effect? While the Federal Rules of Civil Procedure authorize courts to issue pretrial and discovery orders, and to issue sanctions for noncompliance, the Rules do not explicitly refer to case management orders as such. Some federal courts have linked noncompliance with CMOs with the summary judgment procedure. See Serrano–Perez v. FMC Corp., 985 F.2d 625 (1st Cir.1993); Renaud v. Martin Marietta Corp., 749 F.Supp. 1545 (D.Colo.1990), affirmed, 972 F.2d 304 (10th Cir. 1992). See also Atwood v. Warner Electric Brake & Clutch Co., 239 Ill.App.3d 81, 179 Ill.Dec. 18, 605 N.E.2d 1032 (1992) (trial court required plaintiffs to certify their personal injury claims and causation; on appeal held that trial court possessed authority to bar noncertified claims and use of partial summary judgment, rather than discovery sanctions, was permissible).

2. PROTECTIVE ORDERS

a. Nondisclosure Orders

Courts have issued a wide range of orders designed to protect a party or witness from disclosing information which courts find unnecessarily injurious to a person's legitimate interests. For example, in Eli Lilly & Co. v. Marshall (Hon. John), 850 S.W.2d 155 (Tex.1993) (see also dissenting opinion at 1993 WL 82683 (1993)), the Texas Supreme Court ruled that Eli Lilly did not have to disclose the identities of health care providers such as hospitals and physicians, which had reported adverse reactions in patients using the antidepressant drug Prozac. The decision arose in a products liability case filed against Lilly by the estate of Michael Hays Biffle, who committed suicide six days after he began using Prozac. The court ruled that the Texas District Court abused its discretion by ordering Lilly to disclose the provider names or face a default judgment on the Biffles' $25 million complaint without requiring the plaintiffs to show "particularized relevance and need" for the information.

Doctors voluntarily report adverse drug reactions to pharmaceutical companies, which are then required to provide the information to the Food and Drug Administration. The reports are available from the FDA, but only after the names of the patient and health care provider are redacted. The Texas Supreme Court stressed the public policy behind confidentiality because disclosure of provider names would jeopardize the voluntary reporting system because doctors would fear being pulled into litigation or violating physician/patient confidentiality. It stated:

"To the extent that Lilly has been ordered to act in a manner inconsistent with the public interest concerns manifested by federal law, and without due consideration having been given to those concerns, that order is erroneous as a matter of law."

b. Donor Identification

A frequently debated issue is whether the identities of blood donors, who may have transmitted the HIV or AIDS virus to recipients of blood products, may be subject to protective orders. In Irwin Memorial Blood Centers v. Falconer, 229 Cal.App.3d 151, 279 Cal.Rptr. 911 (1991), plaintiff had received blood products during her heart transplant therapy, and subsequently, tested positive for the AIDS virus. The trial court issued discovery orders that would authorize a referee to conduct depositions of donors of defendant's blood products behind a screen. A California statute provides:

To protect the privacy of individuals who are the subject of blood testing for antibodies to the probable causative agent of acquired immune deficiency syndrome (AIDS) * * * no person shall be compelled in any state, county, city or other local civil, criminal, administrative, legislative, or other proceedings to identify or provide identifying characteristics which would identify any individual who is the subject of a blood test to detect antibodies to the probable causative agent of AIDS. (§ 199.20.)

The court held that the trial court's order violated the statute:

> Real parties contend that the orders challenged do not violate section 199.20 because the identity of the donor is completely protected, or can be completely protected if petitioner will cooperate in having the deposition at the blood bank and behind a screen. We cannot agree. The donor will be seen or heard during the deposition by at least the referee and the reporter. The appearance and the voice of a person are obviously identifying characteristics.

> More fundamentally, however, the production of the donor for deposition is in itself an identification within the meaning of the statute. * * * Until the time that the donor appears for deposition, the donor is a number unconnected to a person. Once the person is required to step forth, the connection between the number and the person is made. The donor has been identified. The *extent* to which that identification is made known to third parties will depend upon the care taken at the deposition but the identification in a civil proceeding has been made. This the statute prohibits. (emphasis in original).

Is the court's reading of the statute too restrictive? How should courts balance the privacy rights of donors and plaintiff's right to develop her case?

In contrast to *Irwin Memorial Blood Centers*, the Supreme Court of Louisiana in Most v. Tulane Medical Center, 576 So.2d 1387 (La.1991) held that the need of a patient at a medical center to discover the identity of the donor of blood which infected the patient with the HIV virus outweighed the privacy interests of the donor and public policy considerations favoring nondisclosure. The patient sought only the identity of the donor of one specific unit of blood, and sought to question the donor about the screening process he went through when donating blood, rather than the details of his personal life. Accord Stenger v. Lehigh Valley Hosp. Ctr., 530 Pa. 426, 609 A.2d 796 (1992); Doe v. Puget Sound Blood Center, 117 Wash.2d 772, 819 P.2d 370 (1991). The relevance of the donor's testimony is to establish whether the blood bank used reasonable care in screening donors by asking donors what questions were asked and what procedures were utilized in selecting the donor.

Some courts are inclined to reject the defendant's and donors' interests in favor of disclosure by questioning the validity of their premises. In Watson v. Lowcountry Red Cross, 974 F.2d 482 (4th Cir.1992), the appeals court upheld a lower court order allowing the plaintiff to prepare confidential questions for approval by the defendant.

The donor's identity, already known to the Red Cross, would be revealed only to the court and to the court-appointed lawyer. All answers were to be maintained in a sealed envelope marked "confidential," and the answers provided by the donor must have the signature redacted prior to filing. The donor's answers would exclude all references to identity.

The Fourth Circuit held that the district court did not abuse its discretion or violate the donor's privacy rights by ordering discovery. The court remarked that acceptance of defendant's position that even limited discovery would threaten the U.S. blood supply "would amount to a grant of virtual blanket immunity from donation-related liability." The court determined that "there is not one shred of tangible evidence in the nature of hard statistical data to substantiate an otherwise speculative claim that the blood supply will be jeopardized." The dissenting opinion said the public interest in maintaining a safe and adequate blood supply and the blood donor's privacy interest outweigh the plaintiff's interest in deposing the donor and that even the restricted discovery does not adequately protect these important interests.

How would you balance the interests of donors in preserving their privacy and the needs of plaintiffs to develop evidence supportive of their theory of the case?

c. Sanctions for Violation of Protective Orders

Plaintiffs and their counsel must be exceedingly careful not to violate a protective order preserving the confidentiality of a blood donor's identity. For example, in Coleman v. American Red Cross, 145 F.R.D. 422 (E.D.Mich.1993), the federal district judge dismissed plaintiffs' suit against the Red Cross after their attorney hired a private investigator to find out the name and location of the donor whose social security number had been inadvertently disclosed during discovery. Earlier in the case, the district court issued a protective order that was affirmed on appeal restricting the plaintiffs' access to the identity of the donor of the infected blood. After discovering the donor's name and address through a private investigator, plaintiffs' attorney conveyed this information to the plaintiffs and informed defense counsel they had learned the donor's name. The defendants filed an emergency motion for a second protective order.

Treating the question as a motion under Fed. R. Civ. P. 37, which authorizes sanctions for discovery abuse, the district court found four factors relevant to the motion: prejudice to the defendants, warning of probable dismissal for violation of the order, the parties' blameworthiness, and consideration of less drastic sanctions. The prejudice to defendants was based on evidence showing a 13 percent drop in blood donations after a 1992 Detroit Free Press article headlined "Pair Can Sue Donor of AIDS Blood":

> Plaintiffs' violation went to the very heart of the protective order: the perceived need to protect the privacy of the implicated donor and

the Southeastern Michigan blood supply. * * * [A]ny party who has complied with a court order to produce is necessarily prejudiced when another party abuses this judicial process to discover protected information. If the case against defendants is not dismissed, plaintiffs will benefit substantially from the deliberate violation by being able to bring suit against both defendants and the donor. This court can find no excuse or mitigating circumstances to explain the flagrant disregard of the court's order and the bad faith and egregious conduct exemplified by plaintiffs and their counsel.

Turning to the parties' blameworthiness, the court observed that the flagrant and deliberate violation of plaintiffs' counsel is imputable to the clients. The court noted that the plaintiffs were not left without a remedy, for they could sue their attorney for malpractice based on his "inexcusable error in judgment." Finally, the court said, "no sanction less drastic than dismissal would suffice to cure the harm suffered by the defendants." Do you agree with the severity of this sanction? What about the court's comment—most unusual—that the clients sue their attorney for malpractice? Is that the best remedy?

d. Gag Orders; Sealing of Documents

Orders that require the parties or their counsel not to discuss the case with the media or third parties have been issued in toxic tort litigation. In Davenport v. Garcia (Hon. Carolyn), 834 S.W.2d 4 (Tex. 1992), the Texas Supreme Court overruled a gag order that had prohibited a guardian ad litem of children exposed to chemicals from a dump site from speaking in public about the case or in private to the children that she represented, relying on the Texas Constitution's free speech clause.

Orders sealing documents that defendants produced in discovery have been subject to challenge, especially after the case has been concluded. In In re Agent Orange Product Liability Litigation, 104 F.R.D. 559 (E.D.N.Y.1985), affirmed, 821 F.2d 139 (2d Cir.1987), a protective order was entered during the discovery and settlement phases of the case protecting some of defendants' documents against disclosure. The Second Circuit recognized that the settlement would not end the public debate about what should be done with respect to veterans exposed to phenoxy herbicides. The court found that the reasons for secrecy had changed since the pretrial phase of the case. The *Agent Orange* protective order was entered as a way to move the complex case to trial. But once it settled, other factors, such as the public interest in the underlying controversy, required that nonconfidential discovery materials be available to the public.

The tobacco litigation has been a fertile source of controversy respecting the sealing of documents. In Public Citizen v. Liggett Group, Inc., 858 F.2d 775 (1st Cir.1988), the Court of Appeals agreed with arguments by Public Citizen and other health organizations that important public health concerns about tobacco products warranted disclosure of sealed data. In Haines v. Liggett Group Inc., 975 F.2d 81 (3d

Cir.1992), Third Circuit vacated an order of a district court judge that had reversed a magistrate's finding that 1500 documents were entitled to protection from disclosure based on the attorney-client privilege. Judge H. Lee Sarokin had ordered the disclosure because based on his review (and the review of materials in the *Cipollone* case, discussed in Chapter 6), the documents revealed that defendants and their research association, the Council for Tobacco Research, had concealed evidence on the health risks related to smoking. Judge Sarokin, in reversing the magistrate, found that the fraud exception to the attorney-client privilege vitiated their protection, and made this stinging rebuke of the industry:

> In light of the current controversy surrounding breast implants, one wonders when all industries will recognize their obligation to voluntarily disclose risks from the use of their products. All too often in the choice between the physical health of consumers and the financial well-being of businesses, concealment is chosen over disclosure, sales over safety, and money over morality. Who are these persons who knowingly and secretly decide to put the buying public at risk solely for the purpose of making profits and who believe that illness and death of consumers is an appropriate cost of their own prosperity! * * * As the following facts disclose, despite some rising pretenders, the tobacco industry may be the king of concealment and disinformation.

The defendants filed a writ of mandamus to the Third Circuit, which it granted. The Third Circuit held that the quoted statements and others justified removal of Judge Sarokin from trial of the case and reversed his order vacating the magistrate because he (1) considered the record in *Cipollone*, which the magistrate did not have before him; (2) incorrectly applied the Federal Magistrates Act, 28 U.S.C.A. § 636(b)(1)(A); and (3) had not "zealously protected" the attorney-client privilege.

e. State Statutes

In the last few years several states have enacted statutes or court rules that seek to limit a party's ability to seal court documents and to narrow the circumstances under which a trial court may grant protective orders for discovery materials after the litigation has settled or concluded. See Florida Sunshine in Litigation Act, West's Fla.Stat.Ann. ch. 69.081 (1992); Vernon's Ann.Tex.R.Civ.P., Rule 76a; Va. Code Ann. § 8.01–42.01 (Michie 1989) (banning unwarranted protective orders that prevent information sharing among attorneys in similar personal injury or wrongful death cases); N.C. Gen. Stat. § 132–12.2 (prohibiting confidential settlements in suits relating to duties of state officials and employees); Act of April 12, 1993, ch. 4.16 and 4.24, West's Rev.Code Wash.Ann. (adding sections similar to Florida's Sunshine in Litigation Act); N.Y. Ct. R. Rev. Part 216 (1991) (prohibits sealing court records without a finding of good cause and consideration of public interest).

For a thorough discussion of these subjects, see Arthur R. Miller, Confidentiality, Protective Orders, and Public Access to the Courts, 105 Harv.L.Rev. 428 (1991).

E. SETTLEMENTS

It is well recognized that most lawsuits are resolved by a settlement between the parties, rather than by a dismissal or plaintiffs' judgment. Toxic tort litigation is no different in this regard, but mass toxics cases present particularly difficult issues that may distinguish them from catastrophic mass accident cases.

1. GENERAL STRATEGY

The following statement, authored by a defense counsel, summarizes some of the principal issues through the eyes of the defense:

A defendant facing a toxic tort lawsuit is confronted with divergent choices for handling such litigation. On the one hand, there is a desire to pursue an aggressive defense all the way through to trial because the plaintiffs are not believed to be injured and to do otherwise would only encourage the filing of more cases. An aggressive defense dictates high transactional costs in the short run, but hopefully lower transactional costs over the long term.

On the other hand, a defendant may seek to buy its way out as early as possible in order to reduce litigation costs at a particular toxic site. When to settle is a difficult question, the answer to which will vary from site to site.

In approaching toxic tort litigation, it is difficult to prescribe a blueprint to be used for each and every toxic substance or site. The identity of the defendants, the identity of the toxic substance and the client's role changes with each site. However, a basic framework for preparing and resolving your case in your client's best interests can be suggested.

The cost of a trial is significant, but it is only when plaintiffs know that you are willing to "go to the mat" that settlement demands plummet and new case filings decline. The trick is knowing which cases to settle and which to try because if you try the "wrong one" (and lose), then settlement demands and new filings will increase.

There are disadvantages to settlement. It fuels the plaintiffs' war chest against the nonsettling defendants, thereby causing feelings of mistrust between your client and the nonsettling defendants and enhancing a "soft touch" image among other plaintiffs' attorneys. Nonsettling defendants may distrust such a defendant because it did not share in defense costs (thereby reducing their transactional costs) and became a "traitor" to the cause—the cause being to fight the battle through trial to dissuade the filing of meritless cases.

However, sometimes the plaintiffs have a good medical case, i.e., toxin did cause severe physical injury or death. These cases must be taken seriously in today's proenvironmental society and an early assessment of your client's liability should be made. If an opportunity for settlement presents itself, only an unsophisticated defendant would fail to realize that your client had made a "good deal."

Even in non-medically serious cases, if you can pay low value settlements to resolve a large volume of cases, then the resultant savings in transactional costs may be worth it. There is a cost/benefit analysis that must be considered at each site. This analysis can only be made after the facts as to medical causation, damages and liability have been fully developed.

For example, in a recent asbestos "single" case the jury awarded $2.5 million in compensatory damages and $4.5 million in punitive damages. In hindsight, the defendant is surely second guessing itself for not accepting the pretrial demand and settling the case; such a decision would have saved millions. At that point you can't afford to think about how settlement may appear to nonsettling defendants. Experience shows that in toxic tort cases plaintiffs will often only settle with only one or two defendants. Thus it is not only sometimes wise to settle, but often becomes a race to settle.

Judging from experience in toxic tort litigation, it is difficult for a company to be both an "appeaser" (i.e., one who will pay money in virtually any case simply to keep litigation costs down) and a "fighter" (i.e., one who will aggressively litigate every case). In my experience, most plaintiffs' attorneys will not settle with a defendant at a low price early in the litigation unless the attorney is convinced that the settling defendant is a marginal or peripherally involved player.

It may therefore be difficult, if not impossible, for a defendant to buy its way out of cases cheaply unless and until the plaintiffs' attorney has identified a sufficient critical mass of "big players." Plaintiffs do not want to risk finding that an early settlement was grossly disproportionate to the settling party's actual liability.

Reprinted with permission from N. Kathleen Strickland, Reducing Costs in Toxic Tort Litigation with Case Management and Defense Cooperation, 7 Toxics Law Reporter 1189–1190 (March 10, 1993). Copyright 1993 by the Bureau of National Affairs, Inc. (800–372–1033). How would you articulate the plaintiffs' viewpoint on each of the concerns that she identifies? Do plaintiffs actually share some of the same problems? For whom are transactional costs typically the greater barrier?

2. RELEASES OF FUTURE INJURIES

As we have seen, toxic exposure may produce immediate and manifested injuries or it may produce latent harms that are not manifested for many years, even decades. As a general practice, parties to a settlement execute a general release that settles all liabilities that arise from a particular occurrence. Such general releases, however, may not work in toxic tort settlements because releases purporting to discharge liability for unknown injuries often conflict with state statutory law imposing limitations on such releases.

In California, for example, West's Ann.Cal. Civil Code § 1542 provides that a "general release does not extend to claims which the creditor does not know or suspect to exist * * * at the time of executing the release, which if known by him would have materially affected his settlement. * * * " Therefore, such statutory public policy will prevail over generalized releases of future injuries in the absence of a clear expression of the parties' intent. California courts have interpreted Civil Code § 1542 as precluding the application of a release to unknown claims in the absence of a showing, apart from the words of the release, of an intent to include such claims. See, e.g., Casey v. Proctor, 59 Cal.2d 97, 28 Cal.Rptr. 307, 378 P.2d 579 (1963).

Even though a release may set forth the statutory language, evidencing plaintiffs' intent to waive rights to sue for future injuries, plaintiffs may nevertheless later argue mistake as to the nature and extent of the injuries which are the subject of the release. Therefore, an enforceable release agreement will require that plaintiffs know they are releasing *all* future injuries resulting from the alleged exposure, whether presently known or suspected, including cancer and death.

What steps would you take to insure that your client fully comprehends a release applying to latent injuries? Should you list all of those conditions for which there exist some epidemiological or toxicological evidence connecting them to the kind of exposure involved? How about future fear of cancer? What risks might such a list create? What steps should defense counsel take to insure that claims for future unknown injuries are released? How would the parties value the consideration for the release of future injuries? In an asbestos exposure case, if the plaintiff currently manifested asbestosis, how would you value the risk of lung cancer or mesothelioma? Defendant will not pay a settlement equivalent to the value of actually contracting cancer, so each party will be assuming some risk—plaintiff will be overcompensated if he never develops the disease, but undercompensated if he does.

3. GREEN CARDS AND MEDICAL MONITORING

a. *General Approach*

One solution to the problems created by efforts to settle future and unknown injuries is to explicitly preserve the plaintiff's right to seek redress for subsequently-manifested injuries. Such a provision authorizing later claims should conditions warrant is called a "green card" and is becoming increasingly common in toxic tort litigation. Green card settlements typically require considerable specificity in identifying both the claims released by the settlement and those preserved for future assertion. A green card provision normally incorporates a waiver of the defendant's right to assert a statute of limitations defense as to the claims being preserved. The defendant will obviously prefer not to have a wholly open-ended exposure to liability and will seek provisions requiring plaintiff to assert a claim at the time of earliest manifestation of the condition.

Settlements involving the preservation of future claims are often accompanied by defendant's agreement to fund medical monitoring expenses for some specified period or until the preserved condition manifests itself. If the condition is one for which early detection and treatment are especially beneficial, both parties may reap some economic benefit from the monitoring program. What disagreement are the parties likely to have regarding the funding of monitoring expenses? Must the agreement identify precisely what kinds of tests and examinations are covered? Will negotiations over medical monitoring expenses be influenced by the state's recognition or non-recognition of monitoring costs as compensable damages?

A few examples of settlements involving monitoring may be suggestive of the variety of ways in which that remedy may be implemented.

b. *Three Mile Island*

For example in the *Three Mile Island* (TMI) litigation arising of the 1979 accident at a nuclear facility near Harrisburg, Pennsylvania, thousands of individual plaintiffs' actions were consolidated into three classes, two seeking economic losses and a third, Class III, requesting the costs of obtaining medical detection services for those residing within 25 miles of TMI. See In re Three Mile Island, 557 F.Supp. 96 (M.D.Pa. 1982). The stipulation and agreement of settlement called for the creation of $5 million fund, the Public Health Fund, to finance studies of the long term health effects relating to the accident; including:

> (b) funding of studies or analyses relating to the possible health related effects (and related studies and analyses) resulting from the TMI Accident and related events and approved, now or hereafter, by the TMI Advisory Board on Health Research Studies * * *

> (c) funding of public education programs involving the general public residing or working within twenty-five miles of TMI or the

medical community within or serving that region on the subjects of [cancer and cancer detection; evacuation procedures; or public education of any nature to reduce stress];

* * *

(e) funding general research into the effects of low level radiation on human health and related studies and analyses.

The results of the epidemiological studies performed pursuant to the settlement may be found in Hatch, et al., Cancer Near The Three Mile Island Nuclear Plant: Radiation Emissions, 132 Am. J. Epidemiol. 397 (1990). See also Three Mile Island Public Health Fund, 1989–1990 Annual Report (1991). What considerations might have resulted in a settlement providing for generalized epidemiological studies, but not including individual plaintiff medical monitoring?

c. Fernald Litigation

A comprehensive medical surveillance program resulted from the settlement of the Fernald Litigation which arose out of the release of uranium and other hazardous substances from National Lead's operation of U.S. Department of Energy's Feed Material Production Center in Fernald, Ohio. See, In re Fernald Litig., No. C–1–85–0149 (S.D.Ohio 1985), opinion and order approving settlement, 1989 WL 267039. The settlement is described in Amy B. Blumenberg, Medical Monitoring Funds: The Periodic Payment of Future Medical Surveillance Expenses in Toxic Exposure Litigation, 43 Hastings L. J. 661, 706–708 (1992):

> Plaintiffs sought an order requiring the defendants to establish a fund to pay the medical monitoring costs of all class members and to fund epidemiological studies to determine the adverse health effects of the radiation exposure. An advisory summary jury trial was conducted in 1989 to facilitate pretrial settlement. The summary jury returned a nonbinding verdict in favor of the plaintiffs, awarding them a total of one hundred thirty-six million dollars, including eighty million dollars for a medical monitoring fund.
>
> Under the terms of a settlement agreement which the parties reached subsequent to the summary jury trial, the defendants agreed to pay a total of seventy-three million dollars to the plaintiff class. The court appointed three special masters, or trustees, to receive and manage all of the settlement proceeds that formed the Fernald Settlement Fund. The trustees were authorized to develop and administer a medical monitoring program to provide class members with medical examinations and to conduct epidemiological studies.
>
> Pursuant to a court-approved agreement between the Fernald Settlement Fund trustees and the University of Cincinnati, a pilot medical monitoring program was conducted in September and Octo-

ber 1990. Shortly after completion of the pilot program, the *Fernald* Medical Monitoring Program was fully implemented.

The Program provides uniform diagnostic examinations to *Fernald* Settlement Fund claimants at the *Fernald* Program Facility at Mercy Hospital, a Fernald area hospital. Child and adolescent medical examinations are provided pursuant to a contract with Children's Hospital Medical Center of Cincinnati. The Program director provides the *Fernald* Settlement Fund trustees with monthly reports and quarterly summaries. Because the health of thousands of Fernald area residents will be monitored at the same medical facility by the same staff and with the same procedures, the information gathered may paint a useful picture of the specific health consequences, if any, that result from the plaintiffs' exposure to uranium and other toxic substances.

As of June 1991, the trustees had received more that 5600 applications to participate in the Medical Monitoring Program. As of May 1991, 1175 class members had received medical examinations.

4. DISTRIBUTION OF SETTLEMENT FUNDS

As the material on the asbestos litigation illustrated, there are a variety of distribution formulae that have been applied. For example, the proposed agreement set forth in the asbestos section, supra, used a sliding scale of payments depending on which of certain conditions a claimant manifested.

In the *Agent Orange* litigation discussed in Chapter 8, Judge Jack B. Weinstein extracted a $180 million settlement from the producers of the herbicide to the Vietnam veterans. The plan called for awards in varying amounts up to $13,800, based on the severity of injuries. To qualify for payment, claimants needed to show only: (1) service in areas where the spraying of Agent Orange was conducted; (2) disability as defined in the Social Security Act; and (3) that their injuries were not accidental, traumatic, or self-inflicted. This type of settlement minimizes battles over the intractable causation issue by establishing criteria that do not require a claimant to offer even colorable evidence of causation. This approach has the principal advantage of lowering transactional costs by simplifying the administration of the settlement proceeds.

5. VALUE PROTECTION PROGRAMS

Many of the toxic tort cases described in this casebook resulted in claims that defendant's release of toxic substances has adversely affected the value of plaintiffs' property, especially in residential areas. Residential homeowners represent special settlement concerns because the value of their properties is typically their most important asset. Of course, property values are influenced by many variables, one of which is the fear that contamination of their properties poses a health risk to the occupants. (But see the discussion in Chapter 3 of Adkins v. Thomas Solvent Co., 440 Mich. 293, 487 N.W.2d 715 (1992), where the Michigan Supreme Court held that plaintiffs who alleged diminution in property values could not maintain a nuisance action where the actual contamination of their properties had not occurred). Media publicity and governmental reports can have an extraordinary impact on a neighborhood's property values. One of the innovations that has evolved in recent years to settle toxic tort claims is the value protection program. The elements of such a program may include:

1. Guarantees against loss of property value.

2. Low interest mortgage subsidies.

3. Below–market financing for new buyers.

4. Grants and low interest home improvement loans.

5. Reimbursement of relocation expenses for residents choosing to move.

6. Temporary relocation costs.

Du Pont's Value Protection Programs

In 1990, Du Pont learned that lead and mercury were released from its Pompton Lakes Works facility in northern New Jersey into a creek which fed a flood plain in which over 100 homes with market values between $125,000 and $180,000 were situated. Pursuant to a New Jersey Spill Act Consent Order, Du Pont agreed to remediate the site and affected portions of the community within the flood plain. Du Pont was required to move heavy earth moving equipment and backhoes into the community and remove elevated levels of lead and mercury from homeowners' yards. After Du Pont signed an administrative consent order with the New Jersey Department of Environmental Protection that required it to conduct tests of the water quality in the Brook, it communicated to both the DEP and area residents that the soil in the flood plain was contaminated with metals. To address concerns for potential health consequences from the contamination, Du Pont undertook to test the fish in the Acid Brook and the vegetables in homeowners' gardens. Based upon the results of those tests, Du Pont announced, in conjunction with local public health officials and retained outside experts, that garden vegetables and fish did not create a pathway of exposure that could cause a health problem. The health advisory issued by Du Pont was issued jointly by Du Pont and local health officers.

Du Pont also followed a program of ringing doorbells and dealing with individual community members one on one. The results of soil and vegetable sampling and an analysis explaining the significance of these results were discussed with each individual family in terms of how these results affected that particular family. Du Pont then offered a Value

Protection Program which was developed on the basis of discussions with homeowners and experts. Du Pont offered Level I benefits to 135 homeowners which included the following:

1. property value protection for three years;

2. guaranty of the appreciation rate of property for three years;

3. low interest mortgage financing of first or second mortgages or refinancing of existing mortgages, at approximately 3 percent below existing market rates;

4. a home improvement restoration benefit for each property for three years pursuant to which Du Pont would pay 75 percent of up to $6,000 of approved costs (25 percent of approved costs are paid by the homeowner. The maximum Du Pont payment is $4,500).

In addition, Du Pont offered benefits to Level I homeowners who left the neighborhood, including property value and appreciation protection, as well as payment of an additional incentive commission to the selling broker equal to 1.5 percent of the sale price at the time of closing and an interest-free bridge loan up to the value of the owner's equity in the affected neighborhood to purchase new property, and relocation expenses.

Level II benefits were offered to 49 homeowners who resided next to Level I beneficiaries but whose property revealed no contamination. They received no value guarantee, but were eligible for home improvement grants.

F. CHOICE–OF–LAW PROBLEMS

Mass tort cases generally, and mass toxic tort cases more particularly, generate complex choice-of-law issues. Judges and practitioners have recognized the problematic choice-of-law problems dogging their mass tort cases. Many of the cases considered in this casebook have involved multiple plaintiffs dispersed across state lines or even if all plaintiffs were situated in one state, defendants or defendants' activities implicating many jurisdictions, with the result that courts have struggled to determine which state's substantive tort law should govern the controversy. As the section on class actions and other aggregative approaches revealed, mass tort cases are often perceived as poor candidates for class treatment because common factual or legal questions may not predominate over individualized questions of causation and damages. The choice-of-law problems provide an additional dimension of difficulty for courts struggling to resolve the "common" versus "individualized" balancing, with the result that many courts have cited choice-of-law problems as a reason for denying class certification. See, e.g., Ikonen v. Hartz Mountain Corp., 122 F.R.D. 258, 265 (S.D.Cal.1988) (denying class certification after holding that the law of the states of the various plaintiffs would need to be separately analyzed and applied to each class member, creating a situation in which common issues of law and fact would not predominate over individual ones); Blake v. Chemlawn Serv. Corp., 1988 WL 6151 (E.D. Pa., 1988) (denying class certification, in part because "choice of law problems would be unmanageable"); Linda S. Mullenix, Resolution of the Mass–Tort Case: A Proposed Federal Procedure Act, 64 Texas L. Rev. 1039, 1057 (1986); David F. Boyle, Note, Mass Accident Class Actions, 60 Cal. L. Rev. 1615, 1622 (1972).

Under current law, a federal court exercising diversity jurisdiction will apply the conflicts rules of the forum state based on the Supreme Court's decision in Klaxon Co. v. Stentor Electric Manufacturing Co., 313 U.S. 487, 61 S.Ct. 1020, 85 L.Ed. 1477 (1941). Thus, depending on which of the alternative conflicts approaches the forum state adopts, the federal court analysis will vary from state to state. State courts have adopted four basic approaches to conflicts resolution:

1. LEX LOCI DELECTI: VESTED RIGHTS

A substantial number of jurisdictions apply the choice-of-law principle that looks to the place of the wrong—the state where the plaintiff's legal interest has been invaded as a result of defendant's tortious act. The Restatement of Conflict of Laws § 377 (1934) adopted the lex loci or vested rights approach, which offered a moderately simple, consistent, or predictable standard for resolving conflicts issues in tort litigation.

2. MOST SIGNIFICANT RELATIONSHIP

The Restatement (Second) of Conflicts of Law abandoned the vested rights approach in favor of a more complex balancing approach which seeks to identify which state has the "most significant relationship to the occurrence and the parties." Under this approach the courts are expected to examine four kinds of "contacts" by applying seven different principles. According to § 145, the four contacts to be examined are: (1) the place where the injury occurred; (2) the place where the conduct causing the injury occurred; (3) the places of domicile, residence, nationality, incorporation, and business of the parties; and (4) the place where the relationship, if any, between the parties is centered. Moreover, the Second Restatement in § 145(1) does not seek to determine the law to apply to the entire cause of action but rather is addressed to which state has the most significant relationship to "that issue." Hence it is possible for a court to conclude that one state's law is more significantly related to liability questions and another state's law more significantly related to the damages issues.

3. STRONGEST GOVERNMENTAL INTEREST

This approach looks less to the interests of the parties involved and more to the interests of the competing jurisdictions. This "interest analysis" as it is sometimes labeled necessitates the identification and analysis of the policies which underlie each state's law and a determination of whether those policies would result in the state's having an "interest" in seeing its substantive law applied to the controversy. Because the forum state will often possess a strong interest in applying its own law, this approach tends to favor the forum jurisdiction, in the absence of a compelling competing state's interest.

4. OTHER APPROACHES

Finally, at least one state has adopted what is known as the "better law" approach, derived from Professor Leflar's work on conflicts of law. Robert A. Leflar, American Conflicts of Law § 110 (1968); Zelinger v. State Sand & Gravel Co., 38 Wis.2d 98, 156 N.W.2d 466 (1968). This approach focuses on five separate concerns which emphasize judicial administration and the "better" rule of law: (1) predictability of results; (2) maintenance of interstate and international order; (3) simplification of the judicial task; (4) the advancement of the forum's governmental interest; and (5) the application of the better rule of law.

5. PROPOSALS FOR REFORM

Consequently, in dispersed mass tort cases the potential number of applicable state laws is extraordinary, given the interstate nature of many claims relating to Agent Orange, asbestos, DES, Bendectin, breast implants, lead paint, and others.

Faced with these difficulties in resolving mass tort litigation choice-of-law problems, it is not surprising that various proposals have surfaced that would attempt to simplify and unify their resolution. There are at least three basic models that reformers have advanced to manage choice-of-law rules in mass tort cases. See Linda S. Mullenix, Federalizing Choice of Law for Mass–Tort Litigation, 70 Tex. L. Rev. 1623 (1992) for a thoughtful description of the alternative approaches.

a. Federal Substantive Law

The first and most dramatic would be for Congress to enact, under its plenary commerce powers, federal substantive tort and products liability legislation that would embrace substantive legal standards, jurisdictional requisites, statutes of limitation, and damages. One of the provisions of CERCLA, 42 U.S.C.A. § 9651(e)(1) as enacted in 1980, called for the establishment of a study group to make recommendations as to the need for and content of a federal toxic tort compensation program. The study group was instructed to "determine the adequacy of existing common law and statutory remedies in providing legal redress for harm to man and the environment caused by the release of hazardous substances into the environment."

Section 9651(e)(3) specified in greater detail that among the issues which the study group should address were "the nature of barriers to recovery (particularly with respect to burdens of going forward and of proof and relevancy)," the "scope of evidentiary burdens placed on the plaintiff," including the impact of scientific uncertainty over causation regarding "carcinogens, mutagens and teratogens" and the effects of low doses of hazardous substances, and barriers to recovery posed by existing statutes of limitation. The internal workings of the study group are described by two members of the group in James R. Zazzali & Frank P. Grad, Hazardous Wastes: New Rights and Remedies? The Report and Recommendations of the Superfund Study Group, 13 Seton Hall L. Rev. 446 (1983).

The study group concluded that the recurring problems encountered by plaintiffs in recovering for physical harm to person or property primarily centered on the statutes of limitation problems, the joinder and combination of parties, and the proof of causation. See Zazzali & Grad, supra, at 454–458 for a fuller explanation of these problems.

The study group issued a two-tiered remedial proposal. The Tier One proposal called for a no-fault compensation system for personal injury resulting from hazardous waste, to be managed by the states but under a federal legislative program. This compensation plan, functioning analogously to a workers' compensation program, would provide full recovery for medical expenses and two-thirds recovery of lost earnings. Under Tier One, "[t]o establish a claim, the claimants must offer proof of exposure, proof of disease or injury, and proof of causation." However, proof of causation would be eased considerably by reliance on appropriate rebuttable presumptions:

> The first rebuttable presumption requires a showing that: (1) the defendant was engaged in a waste activity; (2) the claimant was exposed to such waste; and (3) the claimant suffered resulting injury. Upon proof that the claimant was exposed to waste and suffered injury which is known to result from such exposure, the rebuttable presumption then arises that the exposure proximately caused the death, injury, or disease, and that the source of such exposure was responsible.

In addition, an injured party could pursue a Tier Two tort remedy in state court, but states would be encouraged to adopt five unifying principles to govern such cases:

> (a) The unified adoption of a broad discovery rule, i.e., that the cause of action accrues from the time the plaintiff discovers or should have discovered the injury and its cause;
>
> (b) the adoption of liberal joinder rules to allow complex issues of causation and liability to be tried together, leaving individual damages to a separate trial if necessary;
>
> (c) substantive and procedural rules to shift the burden of damage apportionment to the defendants proven to have contributed to the risk or injury;
>
> (d) the adoption of the rule of joint and several liability; and

      (e) application of strict liability which would focus on the nature of the hazardous waste activity and the magnitude of the risk of injury.

The Report, however, rejected use of Tier One rebuttable presumptions and class suits in a Tier Two personal injury claim.

      Shortly after the issuance of the Study Group Report, two bills were introduced in Congress, each containing some of the recommendations contained in the report but also with substantial differences. Senator Mitchell (D–Maine) and Senator Stafford (R–Vermont) introduced the Environmental Poisoning Compensation Act, as an amendment to the Federal Insecticide, Fungicide and Rodenticide Act (FIFRA) (S.1486, 97th Cong., 1st Sess., 127 Cong. Rec. S 7694), which would create a private right of action but not include the Tier One compensation plan. Congressman LaFalce (D–New York) introduced a Toxic Victims Compensation Act, which would establish a compensation board similar to the Tier One recommendations. H.R. 7300, 97th Cong., 2d Sess., 128 Cong. Rec. H 8490 (Oct. 1, 1982). When CERCLA was amended in 1986 only the recommendation for a discovery rule was enacted, which is discussed in Chapter 12.

      One of the most expansive administrative reform proposals, in the form of a model statute, is authored by Professor Trauberman, entitled Compensating Victims of Toxic Substances Pollutions: A Proposed Model Statute, contained in an article written in 1983. See Jeffrey Trauberman, Statutory Reform of "Toxic Torts": Relieving Legal, Scientific and Economic Burdens of the Chemical Victim, 7 Harv. Envtl. L. Rev. 177 (1983). See also Mullenix, supra, at 1631–33, bemoaning the lack of any serious substantive legislative effort.

b. Federal Common Law

      What some have labeled as the first truly mass toxic tort case, In re Agent Orange Product Liability Litigation, 506 F.Supp. 737 (E.D.N.Y. 1979), reversed 635 F.2d 987 (2d Cir.1980), the federal district judge who initially was assigned the case held that federal common law should govern the controversy. Judge Pratt ruled that federal question subject matter jurisdiction applied because federal common law should apply to mass tort claims brought by Vietnam veterans and their families. The court identified three analytical factors in deciding whether to allow the common law tort theories to be governed by a uniform federal approach: "(1) the existence of a substantial federal interest in the outcome of [the] litigation; (2) the effect on this federal interest should state law be applied; and (3) the effect on state interests should state law be displaced by federal common law." Applying these considerations, the court found significant federal interests at stake in the litigation because of (1) the rights of soldiers to be compensated for their harms; (2) the potentially "broad questions about the conduct of military operations"; (3) the legal uncertainty engendered for both war veterans and contractors by the prospect of applying different state laws; and (4) the unfairness of according different legal treatment to litigants who, in all relevant respects, had similar claims. See earlier discussion of federal common law at Chapter 6.

The Court of Appeals for the Second Circuit reversed Judge Pratt. Judge Kearse held that there was no "identifiable federal policy at stake in this litigation that warrants the creation of federal common 'law rules." Therefore, the cases would be controlled by assorted state substantive law rules relating to statutes of limitation, products liability rules, causation standards, and damages.

As discussed by Professor Peter Schuck, the Second Circuit decision represents "a classic example of the perils of treating [a toxic tort dispute like] Agent Orange as a larger version of a conventional tort dispute. [This] approach, perfectly defensible in the ordinary case in which one or a few soldiers sue concerning a discrete incident, made no sense at all in a mass action going to the heart of a broad federal policy." Peter H. Schuck, Agent Orange on Trial: Mass Toxic Disasters in the Courts 67 (1986).

Five years later, the Fifth Circuit in Jackson v. Johns–Manville Sales Corp., 750 F.2d 1314 (5th Cir.1985), cert. denied 478 U.S. 1022, 106 S.Ct. 3339, 92 L.Ed.2d 743 (1986), in an en banc opinion, similarly rejected the position that the volume, nationwide distribution and complexity of asbestos litigation warranted the adoption of federal common law rules, rather than various state law rules under diversity requirements, to resolve these cases. While acknowledging the "unique nature" of asbestos litigation, the court rejected fashioning a federal common law in asbestos cases and concluded that "ensuring the availability of compensation for injured [asbestos] plaintiffs is predominantly a matter of state concern and, in the absence of congressional enactments, state law, both as to the extent of compensation available and punitive damages, must apply." Moreover, the court articulated a policy reason to support its condition, namely that if it were applied in asbestos cases, "there would be no principled means of restricting the application of federal common law to other matters, either in the context of asbestos litigation or in relation to similar legal problems."

Five judges on the court of appeals dissented from the *Jackson* en banc decision. The dissenters viewed the problems of mass toxic tort suits as a threat to the continued functioning of the federal judiciary. They observed: "[W]e confront a sequence of massive tort claims that has unparalleled geographic and financial dimensions. We confront cases where the application of divergent governing principles can destroy the rights of similarly situated claimants. We confront no less than a challenge to our purpose as courts." For an analysis of the broader area of federal common law, see generally Martha A. Field, Sources of Law: The Scope of Federal Common Law, 99 Harv. L. Rev. 881 (1986). See also Robert Blomquist, American Toxic Tort Law: An Historical Background 1979–1987, 10 Pace Envtl. L. Rev. 85, 88–89, 123–24 (1992), tracing the history and rejection of federal common law in toxic tort cases.

c. *Federalized Choice–of–Law*

The bulk of recent proposals focus on the adoption of a federalized choice-of-law approach. The House, in the Multiparty, Multijurisdiction Reform Act of 1991, H.R. 2450, 102d Cong., 2d Sess. (1991), proposed the creation of criteria that a federal judge would apply in determining which states' substantive law should govern the controversy. See also Multiparty, Multiforum Jurisdiction Act of 1990, H.R. 3406, 101st Cong., 2d Sess. (1990) (also providing for a federalized choice-of-law rule). This latter legislation was passed by the House of Representatives under a suspension of the rules by a two-thirds vote on June 5, 1990 and referred to the Senate Judiciary Committee on June 11, 1990. The legislation died in committee through inaction. Professor Mullenix critically describes this legislation:

> Reviewing each scholar's list of relevant preference factors for a federalized, mass-tort choice-of-law scheme tends to induce intellectual vertigo. The apotheosis of this process was epitomized by Congress's first draft version of its Multiparty, Multiforum Jurisdiction Act of 1991, which inadvertently parodied the worst excesses of conflicts law. In this version, Congress would have had a transferee federal judge in a consolidated mass-tort case determine the source of applicable federal law according to the following factors:
>
> (1) the law that might have governed if the jurisdiction created * * * by this title did not exist;
>
> (2) the forums in which the claims were or might have been brought;
>
> (3) the location of the accident on which the action is based and the location of related transactions among the parties;
>
> (4) the place where the parties reside or do business;
>
> (5) the desirability of applying uniform law to some or all aspects of the action;
>
> (6) whether a change in applicable law in connection with removal or transfer of the action would cause unfairness;
>
> (7) the danger of creating unnecessary incentives for forum shopping;
>
> (8) the interest of any jurisdiction in having its law applied;
>
> (9) any reasonable expectation of a party or parties that the law of a particular jurisdiction would apply or not apply; and
>
> (10) any agreement or stipulation of the parties concerning the applicable law.

Clearly, Congress had serious second thoughts about its federalized choice-of-law rules, because it went back to the drawing board and reported new draft legislation six months later in November 1991. This version of the bill would have a transferee federal judge determine applicable law in consolidated mass-tort cases according to the following considerably pared-down list:

(1) the principal place of injury;

(2) the place of the conduct causing the injury;

(3) the principal places of business or domiciles of the parties;

(4) The danger of creating unnecessary incentives for forum shopping; and

(5) whether choice of law would be reasonably foreseeable to the parties.

Congress then instructs that "[t]he factors set forth in paragraphs (1) through (5) shall be evaluated according to their relative importance with respect to the particular actions."

Congress's revised approach is a highly distilled pastiche of conflicts concerns: territorialism, contacts, and *Erie* jurisprudence, with the policy value of foreseeability thrown in for good measure. It is a kind of essence of conflicts law. Congress's latest approach is, more importantly, a fascinating variation on Professor Juenger's proposed rules for mass-tort cases (Friedrich K. Juenger, Mass Disasters and Conflicts of Law, 1989 U. Ill. L. Rev. 105, 121–22, 126), which would reduce the choice-of-law inquiry to what are essentially Congress's first three concerns. Professor Juenger said it first, though. Thus, Professor Juenger would resolve mass-tort choice-of-law problems as follows:

> In selecting the rule of decision applicable to any issue in a mass disaster case, the court will take into account the laws of the following jurisdictions:
>
> (a) the place of the tortfeasor's conduct;
>
> (b) the place of injury;
>
> (c) the home state of each party.
>
> As to each issue, the court shall select from the laws of these jurisdictions the most suitable rule of decision.

* * *

The problems with Congress's original ten-factor choice-of-law scheme are evident, and Congress abandoned that idea. Congress's revised five-factor scheme reflects an interesting conflicts triage, but why these factors made the short list can only be subject to speculation and forthcoming legislative history, if the legislators choose to enlighten the citizenry concerning their own conflicts preferences. But if Congress's proposed five-factor list is an improvement over its earlier version, then why is Professor Juenger's three-factor list not an even further improvement? And if Professor Juenger is *conceptually* correct in suggesting that his list merely embodies the old notion of federal common law, then why not simply go all the way and authorize federal common law?

Published originally in 70 Texas Law Review 1623, 1658–60 (1992). Copyright 1992 by the Texas Law Review Association. Reprinted by permission.

Professors Robert Sedler and Aaron Twerski have prepared a thoughtful critique of this proposed legislation as well as a Mass Torts Proposal of the American Bar Association. See Robert Sedler & Aaron Twerski, The Case Against All–Encompassing Federal Mass Tort Legislation: Sacrifice Without Gain, 73 Marq. L. Rev. 76 (1990).

Notes and Questions

1. The intuitive appeal for federal substantive law is considerable, particularly when one observes the tremendous judicial management problems engendered by the asbestos litigation catalogued earlier in this chapter. Why has Congress not enacted substantive law to govern mass tort controversies? What interest groups are likely to favor such legislation? What groups are likely to oppose it? Why might Congress be reluctant to federalize tort law? Are there any constitutional impediments?

The Section 301 Study Group recommendations never got beyond the introduction stage in Congress. Why? What is the "conservative" position on these issues—states' rights or pro-business? How might those views differ? What is the "liberal" position—federal government programs or consumer rights?

2. Why have the federal courts been so reluctant to find a sufficient federal interest in mass tort litigation to justify a federal common law? What federal or national interests can you identify that support a federal common law approach? What states' interests cut in the other direction? In *Jackson*, quoted earlier, the majority refers to the line-drawing problem— if we adopt federal common law in asbestos litigation there is no principled stopping point. How persuasive is this? Is the federal interest in the efficient operation and administration of justice in the federal judiciary a significant factor favoring national common law?

Judge Weinstein, who inherited the Agent Orange litigation from Judge Pratt, proposed a "national consensus law" to govern the litigation. In re Agent Orange Prod. Liab. Litig., 580 F.Supp. 690 (E.D.N.Y.1984). Is that a workable compromise in mass tort litigation?

3. Are any equal protection problems implied by two plaintiffs injured by the same toxic exposure being subjected to differing states' laws, one recognizing cancerphobia, medical monitoring, and increased risks claims and the other rejecting such remedies? The Second Circuit in *Agent Orange* dismissed such concerns cavalierly: "The fact that application of state law may produce a variety of results is of no moment. It is the nature of a federal system that differing states will apply different rules of law." 635 F.2d 987, 994 (2d Cir.1980). Is that a satisfactory response to the question?

4. What is your assessment of the proposed federal legislation that would in effect create a statutory Restatement of Conflicts multiple-factor approach? Why hasn't this proposal generated more political support?

The American Bar Association also offered a Federal Mass Tort Jurisdiction Reform Act. See ABA Mass Tort Report (1989). The proposed Act, which is directed at mass toxic tort litigation, and cites the asbestos, Bendectin, Agent Orange, vaccine, and DES litigations, calls for the establishment of a federal judicial panel for mass tort litigation. Whenever at least 100 civil tort actions, claiming damages in excess of $50,000 arising from a single accident, or use of or exposure to the same product or substance, are pending in state or federal courts, the panel may declare the cases "mass tort litigation" and transfer some or all of the actions to a federal court authorized to resolve all issues, including liability and damages. The transferee court may decide which issues should be tried on a consolidated basis, and which issues it wishes to remand for individualized resolution. Acting pursuant to the interstate commerce clause, the legislation sets forth federal question jurisdiction as the grounds for asserting removal power over pending state and federal actions.

However, the ABA-proposed statute does *not* adopt federal substantive law, nor does it call for the judicial creation of a federal common law for mass torts. Instead, it seeks to empower federal courts to develop their own choice-of-law rules for mass tort cases. In calling for legislative overruling of *Klaxon Co. v. Stentor Electric Manufacturing Co.* in mass tort cases, the ABA proposal seeks the application of the law of a single state to govern the mass tort claim. The only statutory guideline provided to the court is that it makes its determination "in light of reason and experience as to which State(s) rule(s) shall apply to some or all of the actions, parties or issues." Does this represent a better approach?

G. JUDICIAL MANAGEMENT OF SCIENTIFIC AND TECHNOLOGY ISSUES

In Chapter 8, the role of scientific and technological evidence was center stage in resolving seemingly intractable causation questions implicated in much toxic tort litigation. As the opinions in this casebook, especially those in the causation and remedies Chapters, demonstrate, the parties engage in an intensive struggle to obtain expert testimony sufficiently powerful to persuade judge and jury. Moreover, the fact finder's conclusions can have extraordinary impact upon plaintiffs, industries, and government.

A recent study entitled, "Science and Technology in Judicial Decision Making: Creating Opportunities and Meeting Challenges," A Report of the Carnegie Commission (1993) at 12–13, describes the situation facing the judiciary:

> Recent developments in both law and science have conspired to bring increasingly complex scientific issues before the courts for resolution. In particular, the dramatic growth in toxic torts and environmental litigation has put new pressure on the legal system,

which is simultaneously being asked to adjudicate issues on the cutting edge of science and to develop theories of substantive law. This pressure is intense because of the large numbers of people that are involved and the profound social, economic, and public policy concerns that these new legal claims raise.

The growing prominence of science in the courtroom has exacerbated criticism of the courts' management and adjudication of S & T issues. Some allege that "junk science" is flooding the courtroom through the testimony of "experts," whose primary qualification is their willingness to testify in support of their client's position. As a result of these and similar concerns, there have been calls to remove certain categories of cases from the judicial system altogether. While some commentators believe that current legal procedures must be overhauled to deal with these abuses, others go even further in suggesting that the courts, dependent as they are on lay judges and juries, are incapable of properly resolving issues that turn on abstruse principles of epidemiology, toxicology, or statistics. Still others claim that the volume of litigation, as for instance in the cases arising from the use of asbestos, threatens the traditional model of individualized decision making. Given our judicial resources, it may be impossible to treat each case separately.

1. USE OF COURT–APPOINTED EXPERTS

Judges and juries are expected to evaluate complex technological evidence and scientific theories on the basis of the parties' diametrically opposed testimony. One increasingly employed means to assist the court (and often juries) is for the judge to appoint scientific experts who can perform a variety of functions. A recent study concluded that when experts had been appointed, it was either because of "a thorough disagreement among the parties' experts over interpretation of technical evidence, or when one or more of the parties failed to present expert testimony on a critical issue and the judge perceived an extraordinary need to protect minors or the public health." Joe S. Cecil & Thomas E. Willging, Defining a Role for Court Appointed Experts, Federal Judicial Center Directions, No. 4 at 9 (1992).

Interestingly, however, the same study found that while 87 percent of the federal judges surveyed thought appointment of experts were likely to be helpful in some cases, only 20 percent had ever appointed one under Rule 706 of the Federal Rules of Evidence. Rule 706, Court Appointed Experts, provides in part:

(a) Appointment. The court may on its own motion or on the motion of any party enter an order to show cause why expert witnesses should not be appointed, and may request the parties to submit nominations. The court may appoint any expert witnesses agreed upon by the parties, and may appoint expert witnesses of its own selection. * * * A witness so appointed shall advise the parties of his findings, if any; his deposition may be taken by any party;

and he may be called to testify by the court or any party. He shall be subject to cross-examination by each party, including a party calling him as a witness.

Thus, the court-appointed expert can be used for testimonial purposes and be subject to cross-examination by the parties. In that sense, such experts are more aligned with the adversarial process. The objective of the Rule, as described in the Advisory Committee notes, is that the use of court-appointed experts will exert a "sobering effect" on the *parties'* experts. Moreover, Rule 706 allows the court to inform the jury that the expert is court-appointed which, according to the same study, found a strong correlation between those experts' testimony and the outcomes of the cases in which they testified. Cecil & Willging, supra, at 14.

In Cimino v. Raymark Industries, Inc., 751 F.Supp. 649 (E.D.Tex. 1990), Judge Robert Parker, whose innovative approaches in applying aggregative mechanisms in asbestos litigation are described earlier in this Chapter, appointed an expert in statistics and quantitative methods to determine if the damages phase of the trial, which involved determining category-wide damages from sample plaintiffs in each category, would yield accurate results sufficient to satisfy defendants' due process objections. The expert concluded, and the judge adopted as a finding, that the results would be within a 99 percent level of confidence.

Similarly, a recent toxic tort case, Renaud v. Martin Marietta Corp., 972 F.2d 304 (10th Cir.1992), affirming 749 F.Supp. 1545 (D.Colo.1990), illustrates the impact of a court-appointed expert. The federal district judge's expert critiqued the methodology of plaintiff's expert for determining the amount of toxic substances that had reached plaintiff's drinking water by relying on a single data point (water sample) to extrapolate contamination over a large geographic area for an eleven-year period. The court-appointed expert opined that plaintiff's expert's methodology was deficient and "inappropriate," resulting in summary judgment for defendants.

2. SPECIAL MASTERS

In addition, judges may appoint special masters pursuant to Federal Rule of Civil Procedure 53. Such masters can perform a variety of non-testimonial functions, including pretrial tasks such as investigating factual issues; examining and evaluating physical, documentary and oral evidence and issuing a report thereon; administering pretrial tests; and promoting or evaluating settlements. Unlike under Rule 706, the parties do not possess any discovery rights to the work product of the masters. See generally Wayne D. Brazil, Special Masters in Complex Cases: Extending the Judiciary or Reshaping Adjudication, 53 U. Chi. L. Rev. 394, 413–14 (1986); Linda S. Mullenix, Beyond Consolidation: Post–Aggregative Procedure in Asbestos Mass Tort Litigation, 32 Wm. & Mary L. Rev. 475, 547 (1991) ("Mass tort litigation repeatedly demonstrates that the parties need assistance in presenting technical testimony because their own experts are not always sufficient").

3. REASONS FOR UNDERUTILIZATION

Despite their utility, Cecil & Willging identify numerous reasons why judges are reluctant to appoint their own experts, observing that "judges acknowledged that relying only on parties' experts * * * may hinder a reasoned solution to the conflict, but found such concerns to be outweighed by the importance of maintaining the adversarial system and the control exercised by the parties in the presentation of evidence." Cecil & Willging at 8. The study revealed that each of these reasons plays some part in the underutilization of court-appointed experts:

    (1) Lawyers' antipathy toward court-appointed experts because of their lack of control over and inability to conduct ex parte communications with such experts.

    (2) The lack of an effective referral system from which courts can select an expert.

    (3) Reputable scientists may be reluctant to serve as expert witnesses.

    (4) The difficulty in structuring compensation even though Rule 706 and Rule 53 explicitly provide for the parties to bear the cost.

    (5) The existence of ex parte communications between the judge and the expert causes the parties to object to appointment of such experts, especially Rule 53 masters, who bring knowledge and background to the task that may influence his or her conclusions.

4. RECOMMENDATIONS FOR CHANGE

The Carnegie Commission Report made some findings that were intuitive and interesting:

    a. Federal judges have adequate authority under the present Federal Rules of Civil Procedure and of Evidence to manage S & T issues effectively, and the rules of many state judicial systems are modeled on the federal rules.

    b. Increased attention to S & T issues at the pretrial stage makes cases more amenable to disposition by summary judgment, facilitates settlement, and leads to more focused, speedier trials.

    c. Expert testimony can be made more comprehensible to jurors.

    d. Judges and jurors may need information or assistance in handling S & T information that the parties cannot furnish because of insufficient expertise, mismatched resources, or excessive partisanship.

The Report made the following recommendations for addressing these problems (at 16–18):

a. *Judges should take an active role in managing the presentation of science and technology issues in litigation whenever appropriate.*

Many tools are available to state and federal judges to manage the presentation of S & T issues in litigation. The judicial reference manual and protocols, which are being developed by the Task Force in collaboration with the Federal Judicial Center, are two key elements of the effort to facilitate greater use of these tools.

The reference manual outlines the wide range of techniques that judges have used to manage S & T issues in litigation. It focuses on process and on the encouragement of judicial control. The manual presents judges with a range of options available to resolve a given issue and refers judges to S & T cases where those options have been used; it does not suggest substantive outcomes on contested science and technology issues.

Using the protocols, which are being developed jointly with members of the S & T community, will enable judges to identify and employ techniques that will permit quicker and more effective rulings on challenges to expert testimony, whether those challenges are based on the qualifications of experts, the validity of the theory on which the expert is relying, the reliability of the data underlying the theory, or the sufficiency of the expert's opinion to sustain a verdict.

* * *

b. *Scientific and technical issues should be integrated into traditional judicial education programs, "modules" should be developed that can be appended to existing programs, and intensive programs should be supported.*

Judicial education programs play an important role in introducing judges to scientific methodology, which is an essential element in reducing misunderstandings about S & T evidence and in increasing judicial willingness to take an active role in managing that evidence. * * * These programs offer the greatest opportunity to give judges extensive, hands-on experience in dealing with the difficult S & T issues they may encounter in court.

c. *Institutional linkages between the judicial and scientific communities should be developed.*

Sustained improvement of judicial decision making on matters of science and technology requires the establishment of institutional ties to encourage greater dialogue and cooperation between the judicial and scientific communities.

(i) The federal and state judiciaries should create S & T resource centers to provide judges with access to the collective experience of their colleagues in case management techniques for S & T issues and to educate judges on scientific methodology. Each resource center would also act as a clearinghouse for substantive scientific information compiled by the scientific community, monitor the impact of S & T issues on the courts, and serve as a bridge for cooperation with the scientific community. * * *

(ii) The scientific community should create a resource center as a counterpart to the proposed judicial S & T resource centers in order to facilitate cooperation among the professional societies and to explore the benefits of continued interaction between the judicial and scientific communities.

(iii) A judicial S & T education clearinghouse should be established to collect and distribute curricula and other materials on science education for judges.

d. *An independent nongovernmental Science and Justice Council of lawyers, scientists, and others outside the judiciary should be established to monitor changes that may have an impact on the ability of the courts to manage and adjudicate S & T issues; it should also initiate improvements in the courts' access to and understanding of S & T information, including judicial education and communication between the judicial and scientific communities.*

Notes and Questions

1. Why do the parties' counsel resist court-appointed experts, apart from the reasons identified above (lack of control and ex parte communications with the court)? Do the materials raise questions respecting the efficacy of the adversarial system in dispensing justice? Do toxic and environmental tort cases raise scientific and technological issues absent from other major categories of litigation? Absent from other kinds of tort cases?

2. Which of the Carnegie Commission recommendations appear most feasible? Which are likely to engender the greatest opposition from trial lawyer associations—defense or plaintiff? How about the appointment of scientific panels to adumbrate or decide the scientific issues which are then only for use by courts? Could a federal judge appoint three experts and authorize them to reach "consensus" on scientific issues before the court?

*

Index

References are to page numbers.

ABNORMALLY DANGEROUS ACTIVITIES
Activities constituting, 108, 112–119
  Crop dusting, 100
  Disposal of hazardous chemicals, 108, 117–118
  Fumigation, 112
  Impoundment of slimes, 111–112
  Marketing of products, 112–114
  Oil wells, 111
  Radium tailings, 132–134
  Transportation of chemicals, 114–116
  Underground storage tanks, 117
Basis for private nuisance, 72
Causation, 119–120
Caveat emptor, 126–131
Common usage, 99
Historical perspective, 94–96
Knowledge as element, 132–136
Locational appropriateness, 95, 99–100
Non-natural use, 95
Question of law, 98–99
Rationales for, 101–106, 108–109, 130
  Cheapest cost avoider, 102–103
  Internalization of costs, 101–102
  Non-reciprocal risks, 103–104
  Posner's, 105
  Proposed approach, 105–106
Relationship to negligence, 98, 105, 114–116
Relationship to nuisance, 96–97, 110, 114
Reporter's Study, 136–138
Restatement test for, 97, 98–101, 101, 105, 109–110, 113–114
Rylands v. Fletcher, 94–96, 108, 256
Ultrahazardous activity, 96
Value of activity, 100
Vertical relationships, application to, 126–131
  Landlord—tenant, 131
Vicarious liability for, 119

AGENT ORANGE, 19–20, 373, 393–397
Choice-of-law, 659–661, 663
Opt-out cases, 398

AGGREGATIVE AND DISAGGREGATIVE PROCEDURES
Asbestos litigation, 623–637
Bifurcation, 621–622
Class actions, 623–624
Consolidation, 620–621, 624–630

AGGREGATIVE AND DISAGGREGATIVE PROCEDURES—Cont'd
Constitutional issues, 626–629, 633–634
Multidistrict litigation, 622, 634

AIDS OR HIV
  See also, Blood Products; Case Management; Private Nuisance; Products Liability; Statutes of Limitation.
Blood products, 299–305
Donor identification, 643–645
Factor VIII and market share, 299–302, 410–418
Protective orders, 643
Standard of care, 300–303
State-of-the-art, 302
Statutes of limitation, 588–589
Statutes of repose, 304
Strict liability for, 302

AIR POLLUTION
Apportionment of damage, 434–438
Trespass, 28–35

ALCOHOL
Failure to warn of moderate use, 287–291
Products liability for, 287–292
Restatement, comment i, j, 288–290

ALCOHOL LABELING ACT, 259–260, 291

ALTERNATIVE LIABILITY
See, Causation

ANIMAL BIOASSAYS OR STUDIES
See, Causation; Toxicology

APPORTIONMENT, 425–439
Allocation under CERCLA, 503–511
Between parties, 425–433
Comparative fault, 430, 432, 438–439
Divisibility under CERCLA, 483–484, 486–489
Environmental tort exception, 438–439
Joint and several liability, 434–439
Nuisance cases, 434–438
Reasonable basis, 428–429, 430–431
Restatement rule, 425–432
Smoking and asbestos, 425–432

ASBESTOS
Apportionment, 425–432
Bankruptcies, 634–635
Class actions, 615–621, 623–632
Emotional distress, 201
Frequency, regularity and proximity, 388–389
Increased risk claims, 180–181
Medical monitoring, 185
Products liability, 165, 271–287
Punitive damages, 279–287
Settlement of, 635–637

ASSUMPTION OF THE RISK
Products liability cases, 612–614
Real property actions, 606–608
Relation to coming to the nuisance, 88, 608–610

ATTORNEYS' FEES, 251
Under CERCLA, 500–501

AUSNESS, RICHARD C.
Preemption, 243–244

AXLINE, MICHAEL D.
Toxic Age, 13–16

BALANCING OF EQUITIES AND INTERESTS
See, Equitable Relief and Injunctions
Abnormally dangerous activity, 97–98, 105, 110
Hardships and equities, 143–146, 152
Harm and utility, 72–73, 75–77
Injunction actions, 87–88, 142–146
Private nuisance, 70

BANKRUPTCY
See, Asbestos

BENDECTIN, 359–364, 381–384, 621–622

BIFURCATION
See, Aggregative Procedures; Class Actions

BLOOD PRODUCTS
See, AIDS or HIV
AIDS–Contaminated blood, 299–305
Blood shield statutes, 300–301, 410–418
Factor VIII anticoagulant, 299–302, 410–418
Standard of care, 301–302, 303

BLUMENGERG, AMY B.
Medical monitoring funds, 652–653

BOSTON, GERALD W.
Punitive damages, 210–212
Toxicology and Epidemiology, 349–357

BRENNAN, TROYEN
Causal chains, 340–341
Environmental torts, 10–13
Signature diseases, 397–398

BULK SUPPLIER, 305–324
Adequacy of warnings, 310–312

BULK SUPPLIER—Cont'd
Knowledgeable intermediary, 422
Restatement § 388, comments k and n, 319–323
Sophisticated user, 308–324

BUSH, SHEILA
Negligence per se, 252–256

CALABRESI, GUIDO
Application to abnormally dangerous activity, 102
Cheapest cost avoider, 54, 102–103
Economic principles in public nuisance, 53

CANCER
Asbestos litigation, 623–636
Cancer deaths, 13
Carcinogens, 5, 353–356
Fear of,
See, Damages and Compensable Interests, Emotional distress
Increased risk for, 179–181
Settlements, 651–653

CANCERPHOBIA
See, Damages and Compensable Interests, Emotional distress

CASE MANAGEMENT, 637–648
Donor identification, 643–644
Lone Pine orders, 638–639
Non-disclosure orders, 643
Protective orders, 643–648
Sanctions for violating, 645–646
Scientific and Technology issues, 664–669
Sealing documents, 646–648
Sunshine statutes, 647–648

CAUSATION
Admissibility of Scientific Evidence, 357–367
Federal Rules of Evidence, 357–359
Frye rule, 359–365
General acceptance test, 359–365
Scientific knowledge, 362–364
Scientific method, 362–366
Willing testifier, 369
Animal studies, 350–352, 376–377, 383–386
Apportionment
See, Apportionment
Asbestos class actions, 631–632
Bifurcation, 621–622
But For, 390, 432
Case Management orders, 638–642
Causal chains, 340–341
CERCLA, 482–483, 486, 501, 502, 511–512
Defendant Indeterminacy, 403–423
Alternative liability, 403–404
Concert of action, 404
Enterprise liability, 404–405
Market share liability, 405–418
Asbestos, 409–410
Exculpation, 415–416
Factor VIII, 410–418
Fungibility, 417

CAUSATION—Cont'd
Defendant Indeterminacy—Cont'd
   Market share liability—Cont'd
      Identification, 408, 417–418
      Joint and Several, 415
      Jury Trial, 407
      Lead paint pigments, 420–423
      National market share, 406, 414–415
      Rationales, 405–406, 408
      Risk contribution, 406
      Vaccines, 408–409
  Dual question, 342–344
  Epidemiology, 352–357
    Causal criteria, 355–357
    Necessity for, 371–379, 384
    Relative risks, 354–355
    Unnecessary, 368–370
  Exposure, 386–389
    Epidemiology to prove, 386–387
    Frequency, Regularity and Proximity, 388–389
  Issue Preclusion, 444
  Lead and causation, 423–425
  Lone Pine orders, 638–642
  Plaintiff Indeterminacy, 389–402
    Burden shifting, 390–392
    Class actions, 395–397
    Collective model, 393–397
    Inadequacy of individual solutions, 395
    Individualized model, 389–393
    Particularistic proof, 396–397
  Probabilistic evidence—early use of, 340–341, 345–348
  Proportionality proposals, 399–402
  Signature diseases, 397–398
  Sufficiency of evidence, 368–389
    Animal studies, 383–386
    Epidemiology necessary 371–379, 384
    Epidemiology unnecessary, 368–370
    Rigorous standards, 371–385
  Terminology, 340–342
  Toxic substance causation, 339–389
  Toxicologic studies, 349–352

CAVEAT EMPTOR
Abnormally dangerous activity, 126–131
Nuisance, 123–126

CHEMICALS
  See, Products liability, Agricultural products, Chemical products, Failure to warn
Bulk supplier and sophisticated users, 304–325
Disposal of hazardous chemicals, 106–110, 112–119, 125
Foreseeable users and uses, 324–328
Hazardous chemicals, 42
Punitive damages for, 197–199, 208–210

CHOICE–OF–LAW
Interstate water pollution, 231
Lex Loci Delecti, 656
Reform proposals, 657–664
  Federal common law, 659–661

CHOICE–OF–LAW—Cont'd
Reform proposals—Cont'd
  Federal statutes, 661–662
  Federal substantive law, 657–659
  Federalized choice-of-law, 661–663
Significant relationship test, 656
Strongest government interest, 656–657

CIGARETTE LABELING ACT, 232–244
See, Preemption

CIGARETTES, 232–244
Protective orders, 646–647

CITIZENS SUITS
Public nuisance actions, 56
Statutes allowing, 4
Water Pollution Control Act, 222–223, 228

CLASS ACTIONS
  See, Aggregative procedures
Advisory committee, 616
Asbestos litigation, 623–632
Constitutional issues, 626–629, 633–634
Dual causation, 343–344
Examples of, 615–621
Hazardous wastes, 191–192
Public nuisance, 56–57
Rule 23(b) requirements for, 615–618
Statistical methods, 628–629, 633

COMING TO THE NUISANCE
Defense to nuisance action, 608–610
Private nuisance, 88
Relation to assumption of risk, 607–608

COMMON LAW RIGHTS
  See, Preemption; Implied rights of action
  Generally, 214–217
Regulation enhancing, 214–215
Regulation precluding, 215–216

COMPARATIVE FAULT OR NEGLIGENCE
Apportionment, as affecting, 432, 438–439
Asbestos litigation, 633
Products cases, 612–614
Real property actions, 606–607
Relation to joint and several liability, 430, 432, 438–439

COMPREHENSIVE ENVIRONMENTAL, RE-SPONSE, COMPENSATION AND LIA-BILITY ACT (CERCLA)
Agency for Toxic Substances and Disease Registry, 522–524
  Health assessments, 523–524
  Health investigations, 523
  National priorities list, 522
  Purpose, 522–523
  Toxicologic profiles, 523
  Use in tort suits, 522–524
Contribution actions, 503–518
  Allocation standards, 503–512
  Approaches to allocation, 509–511
    Comparative causation, 509

COMPREHENSIVE ENVIRONMENTAL, RE-SPONSE, COMPENSATION AND LIABILITY ACT (CERCLA)—Cont'd
Contribution actions—Cont'd
  Approaches to allocation—Cont'd
    Comparative fault, 509
    Gore factors, 510–511
    Per Capita, 509
Costs of remediation, 159
Divisibility of harm, 483–484, 486–489
Government actions, 478–489
  Causation, 482–483, 486
  Damages recoverable, 480
  Facility, 480
  Generators liability, 482–484
  Hazardous substance, 479
  Joint and several liability, 485–486
  Owners liability, 481–482
  Release, 479
  Remedial action, 480
  Response costs, 480
  Strict liability, 481, 484–485
History and purpose, 9, 415–417
Indemnity, 518–521
  Construction of arguments, 520–521
  Permissibility, 519–520
  Statutory provision for, 518–519
Medical monitoring, 190–191
National priorities list, 65, 128, 523
Nuisance suits, impact on, 120–121, 522–524
Parties liable (PRP's), 489–496
  Arrangers, 495–496
  EPA lender rule, 495
  Innocent purchaser, 490
  Lenders, 494–495
  Owners and operators, 489–494
  Parent corporations, 492–493
  Passive owners, 490
  Shareholders and officers, 493
  Successors, 493–494
Principal statutory provisions, 477–478
  Defenses, 478
  Liability, 477–478
Private response cost recovery actions, 496–503
  Attorneys' fees, 500–501
  Causation, 501–502
  Compliance affecting damages, 499–500
  Compliance affecting liability, 499–500
  Compliance with NCP, 498–499
  Defined, 496–497
  National contingency plan, 497–499
  Prima facie case, 497–500
Section 301(e) study group, 109, 601, 658–659, 663
Statutes of limitation, 600–602

CONCERT OF ACTION
See, Causation

CONSOLIDATION
See, Aggregative and Disaggregative Procedures, asbestos litigation, Class actions

CONTRIBUTION
See, Comprehensive Environmental Response, Compensation and Liability Act (CERCLA)

COURT–APPOINTED EXPERTS
Reasons for underutilization of, 667
Recommendation for, 667–669
Use of, 665–666

DAMAGES AND COMPENSABLE INTERESTS
Case management and Lone Pine orders, 638–642
CERCLA actions recoverable by government, 480–481
Class actions, 623–636
Economic loss rule, 47, 48, 335, 535–536
Emotional distress, 165, 169–170, 199–203
  AIDS-phobia, 202
  Bystander, 200
  Exposure, 203–204
  Fear of cancer (and cancerphobia), 195–197, 199–203
  Physical harm as a requirement, 201–202
Immune system impairment, 194
Increased or enhanced risk of disease or cancer, 165, 170–176, 179– 184, 195
  Autonomy interests, 182–184
  Prevailing rule, 179–181
  Proportionate recovery, 181
  Subcellular injury, 181
Inverse condemnation, 151
Lone Pine orders, 638–642
Loss of use or enjoyment, 162–164
Medical monitoring and surveillance, 165–166, 172, 176–179, 184–191
  CERCLA, 190–191
  Contrary views, 188–189
  Lump sum or periodic payment, 178–179, 191
  Scientific studies, 189–190
  Settlements, 651–653
  Standards for, 177–178, 185–186
  Support for, 184–185
Nuisance actions, 72–74, 91, 121–122, 147–151
Permanent damages or injunction, 147–151
Permanent or temporary damages, 147–151, 156–157, 158–159, 574–580
Personal discomfort and annoyance, 164–166, 167–169, 179, 194
  Restatement view, 169
Post traumatic stress, 194
Property damage, insurability, 534–536
Punitive damages, 5, 36, 197–199, 204–212
  Asbestos, 279–287, 623, 625–626
  Conduct for, 199, 210–212, 284
  Constitutional limitations, 205–207, 284–287
  Discretion in awarding, 206
  Environmental torts, 208–212
  Express warranty liability, 333–334

DAMAGES AND COMPENSABLE INTER-ESTS—Cont'd
Punitive damages—Cont'd
Governmental suits, 209–210
Love canal, 209–210
Multiple awards of, 284–287
Permissibility in strict liability, 282–284
Relation to compensatory, 207
Wealth as a factor, 207
Real Property, injury to,
Cleanup costs, 159–161, 638
Declaratory relief, 160
Diminution of value, 153–159, 638
Environmental damages, 161
Future cleanup costs, 160
Natural resources, 161
Restatement rule, 153, 154
Restoration costs, 153–159
Trespass, 25–26, 32–33

DEFENSES
See, Assumption of the Risk; Comparative Fault or Negligence; Statutes of Limitation; Statutes of Repose
Laches, 142

DES, 405–408

DOBBS, DAN D.
Balancing hardships and equities, 144–146
Environmental damages, 161

DOSE-RESPONSE CURVES
Epidemiology, 355
Radiation, 391
Toxicology, 349

DUTCHER, VALLE SIMMS
Preemption, 246–247

ECONOMIC ANALYSIS
Applied to public nuisance, 53–54
Cheapest cost avoider, 54, 102–103

EGGEN, JEAN MACCHIAROLI
Genetic injuries, 453–454

ELLIOTT, E. DONALD
Chemophobia and increased risk, 182–183

EMOTIONAL DISTRESS
See, Damages and Compensable Interests

ENVIRONMENTAL TOBACCO SMOKE
Causal criteria, 465–466
Employee actions, 466–468
EPA study, 464–466
Occupational disease acts, 458–462

EPIDEMIOLOGY
Apportionment, 425–432
Asbestos relative risks, 425–432
Attributable risk, 354
Causal criteria, 355–357
Causal terminology, 342
Confidence intervals, 374–375, 380–382
Definition, 352

EPIDEMIOLOGY—Cont'd
Environmental tobacco smoke, 464–466
Expert testimony, 358, 360, 371–379
Health assessments, 523–524
Hypothesis testing, 379–382
Indispensability to prove causation, 368–370, 371–379
Lead paint, 423–424
Measurement and relative risks, 354–355, 374–375, 426–427, 431
Medical monitoring, 189
Multiple studies, 397
P-values, 380
Signature diseases, 397–398
Smoking relative risks, 425–432
Statistical significance, 375, 377, 379–382
Study designs, 352–354
Case-control, 352–353
Cohort, 353–354
Types I and II error, 381–382

EPSTEIN, RICHARD
Dangerous activities and corrective justice, 104
Private nuisance, corrective justice and utilitarianism, 67

EQUITABLE RELIEF AND INJUNCTIONS
Balancing of equities and hardships, 142, 143, 148
Comparative injury calculus, 140–143
Corrective justice, 142, 143
Permanent damages or injunction, 147–151
Private nuisance, 66, 72, 75–77, 85–87, 140–142, 143–146
Public nuisance, private actions for, 56–57
Restatement factors, 144
Utilitarianism, 140

EXPERT TESTIMONY
Admissibility, 357–367
Damages to real property, 153
Daubert standards, 362–367
Early use, 344–348
Epidemiologists, 360
General acceptance test, 360–367
"Hard look" standard, 366, 383
Judicial management of scientific issues, 663–669
Judicial review of, 366–367
Role in proof of causation, 8–9, 348
Scientific evidence admissibility, 357–367
Scientific method or methodology, 362–366, 367
Sufficiency of testimony, 368–389
Toxicologists, 167, 172, 173

FARBER, DANIEL A.
Toxic Causation, 16–20

FEAR OF CANCER
See, Damages and Compensable Interests, Emotional distress

FEDERAL COMMON LAW
Generally, 216–219

FEDERAL COMMON LAW—Cont'd
Gaps or interstices, 220, 224

FEDERAL TORT CLAIMS ACT
AIDS contaminated blood, 303
Discretionary function exemption, 303–304,
   392–393
Nuclear testing, 389–392

FETAL PROTECTION POLICY
See, Workers' Compensation and Workplace

FISCHER, DAVID
Market share, 408

FLETCHER, GEORGE
Abnormally dangerous activity, 103–104

GREEN, MICHAEL D.
Epidemiology, 378–379

HAND, LEARNED, 77, 98, 262

HARPER, JAMES & GRAY
Abnormally dangerous activity, 101

HAZARDOUS SUBSTANCES
See, Chemicals; Comprehensive Environ-
   mental, Response, Compensation and
   Liability Act (CERCLA)

HAZARDOUS WASTE
See, Chemicals

HAZARDS COMMUNICATION, 470–473
Material safety data sheet, 309–312,
   471–472
National Institute of Occupational Safety &
   Health, 317
Permissible exposure limits, 470–471
Threshold limit values, 310

**HENDERSON, JAMES A. JR. & TWERSKI,
   AARON D.**
Patent dangers, 292
Proposed Restatement Third, 269–270, 275

HODAS, DAVID R.
Public nuisance, 45–46

IMPLIED RIGHTS OF ACTION, 220
Marine Protection Research and Sanctuar-
   ies Act, 222–223
Water Pollution Control Act, 222–223

INCREASED RISK OF CANCER
See, Damages and Compensable Interests

INDEMNIFICATION
See, Comprehensive Environmental, Re-
   sponse, Compensation and Liability
   Act (CERCLA)

INJUNCTIONS
See, Equitable actions

INNOCENT PURCHASERS
See, Comprehensive Environmental, Re-
   sponse, Compensation and Liability
   Act (CERCLA)

INSURANCE, 527–566
Commercial General Liability (CGL) histo-
   ry, 527–528
Environmental cleanups coverage, 542–566
   Absolute pollution exclusion, 559–561
   "As Damages" Issue, 542–553
   Known risk limitation, 565–566
   Owned property exclusion, 563–564
   Personal injury endorsement, 561–563
   Sudden and accidental exception,
      553–559
      History, 553
      "Pollutant", 558–559
      Products liability, 556
      Relation to occurrence, 555–556
   "Suit" issue, 542–553
Environmental tort coverage, 529–542
   Economic loss, relation to, 535–536
   Emotional harm as bodily injury,
      533–534
   Intended or expected exception, 529
      Differing views, 530–531
      General rule, 529–530
      Objective test, 531–532
      Subjective test, 531–532
   Number of occurrences, 541–542
   Occurrence, 529–532
   Property damage, 534–536
   Triggers of coverage, 536–541
      Exposure, 536–538
      Injury-in-fact, 538–539
      Manifestation, 538
      Multiple or continuous, 539–540
      Property damage, 540–541
Products liability, 279, 297, 528

INTENT
Private nuisance, 74–75

INTENTIONAL TORT
See, Workers' Compensation and Workplace, Intentional tort exception

INTERSTATE WATER POLLUTION,
   225–232

**ISSUE PRECLUSION (COLLATERAL ES-
   TOPPEL)**
Statutes of limitation, 597–598
Workers' compensation, 443–445

JOINT AND SEVERAL LIABILITY
Apportionment, 434–439
Divisibility of harm, 483–484, 486–489
For nuisance, 44–45
Under CERCLA, 481, 485–486

JONES, WILLIAM K.
Hazardous activities, 105–106, 116

LARSON, A.
Occupational disease acts, 457–458
Workers' compensation, 448–449

LEAD BASED PAINT
Causation, 420–425

LEAD BASED PAINT—Cont'd
Market share liability, 420–423
Products, 336

LENDER LIABILITY
See, Comprehensive Environmental, Response, Compensation and Liability Act (CERCLA)

MADDEN, M. STUART
Issue preclusion, 444–445

MARITIME TORTS, 224

MARKET SHARE LIABILITY
See, Causation

MASON, ELIZABETH F.
Joint and several liability, 485–486

MASS TORTS, 615–621
See, Aggregative and Disaggregative Procedures; Class Actions; Asbestos Litigation; Settlements

MEDICAL MONITORING
See, Damages and Compensable Interests

MILL, JOHN STUART
Causation, 342

MISREPRESENTATION AND FRAUD
Deceit exception, 452
Fraud, 336–337
Inducement, 337
Materiality, 337
Negligent, 336–337
Preemption, 240–243
Products liability, 267–268
Restatement 402B, 335

MOUNTAINSPRING, STEPHEN
As damages in insurance coverage, 552–553

MULLENIX, LINDA S.
Choice-of-law, 657, 661–663

MULTIDISTRICT LITIGATION
See, Aggregative and Disaggregative Procedures

NATIONAL CONTINGENCY PLAN
See, Comprehensive Environmental, Response, Compensation and Liability Act (CERCLA)

NATIONAL INSTITUTE OF OCCUPATIONAL SAFETY & HEALTH, 317

NATIONAL PRIORITIES LIST
See, Comprehensive Environmental, Response, Compensation and Liability Act (CERCLA)

NEGLIGENCE
Abnormally dangerous activity, relation to, 98–105, 114–116
AIDS-contaminated blood, 300–303
Blood shield statutes, 410–418

NEGLIGENCE—Cont'd
Employee actions for ETS, 468
Failure to warn, 272–275
Formulation of drugs, 299
Medical devices, 305–308
Private nuisance based on, 77–78
Products liability, 262
Statutes of limitation, 572–574, 578–579

NEGLIGENCE PER SE, 4, 40, 214, 251–260
Causal violation, 257–259
Class protected, 253
Clear standard, 252–253
Compliance or non-compliance with regulation, 214
Effects given to, 255–256
OSHA regulations, 472
Risks covered, 253–254
Statutes of limitation, 572–574, 578–579

NUISANCE
See, Assumption of the Risk; Comparative Fault; Private Nuisance; Public Nuisance; Statutes of Limitation
Generally, 38–93
Apportionment, 434–437
Continuing or temporary nuisance, 313, 568–580
Interests protected, 38–39
Joint and several liability, 434–437
Relation to trespass, 23–24, 28

OCCUPATIONAL DISEASE ACTS
See, Workers' Compensation and Workplace

OCCUPATIONAL HEALTH AND SAFETY ACT
Bulk suppliers, 324
Compliance and non-compliance, 472–474
Fetal protection, 456
Hazard communications, 470–471
Hazardous chemicals, 469–470
Material safety data sheet, 471–472
Preemption of tort law, 472–473
Recordkeeping requirements, 470–471
Take home toxics, 456

PAGE, JOSEPH
Products risks, 278

PARENT CORPORATION
See, Comprehensive Environmental, Response, Compensation and Liability Act (CERCLA)

PHARMACEUTICAL PRODUCTS, 6, 293–299
Comment k, 293–299
Design defect, 295–297

POSNER, RICHARD
Abnormally dangerous activity, 105, 114–116
Economic analysis, 53
Vicarious liability, 119

PREEMPTION, 213–251
Cigarette labeling act, 232–243
Conspiracy to misrepresent, 240–242
Constitution, 235
Express warranty, 239–240
Failure to warn claims, 239
Federal common law, 216–220
Federal Insecticide, Fungicide & Rodenticide Act, 243–247
Fraudulent misrepresentation, 240–242
OSHA, 472–473
Products liability actions, 232–243
Radiological hazards, 248–250
Savings clauses, 215
State common law nuisance, 225–232, 250–251
Vertical or horizontal, 215, 232, 247–251

PRIVATE ATTORNEYS–GENERAL
Common law rights, 214
Equitable actions for public nuisance, 56

PRIVATE NUISANCE
See, Damages and Compensable Interests; Equitable Relief and Injunctions; Public Nuisance; Statutes of Limitation
Caveat emptor, 123–126
Coming to the nuisance, 88
Comparative injury, 70
Corrective justice, 66–70, 72, 73, 87
Damages for, 165–169
Defenses to, 606–612
    Assumption of the risk, 607–608
    Coming to the nuisance, 608–610
    Contributory fault, 606–607
    Sale of property defense, 610–612
Diminution of property values, 59–65
Groundwater contamination, 59–60
Injunctions against, 66, 85–87, 144–146
Intentional and unreasonable, 72–77
    Balancing harm and utility, 72–74, 75, 83–85
    Gravity of harm, 76
    Intent requirement, 74
    Restatement view, 72–74
    Unreasonableness, 72–74
    Utility of conduct, 76–77
Interests protected, 57–65
Negligent or reckless conduct, 77–78
Nuisance per se, 58
Per accidens, 58
Permanent damages, 147–151
Permanent nuisance, 150
Prospective nuisance, 81, 82, 85–86, 88
Standing to assert, 70–71, 121–126
Unfounded fears, 58–61
Utilitarianism, 66–70, 89–91
Vertical relationships vendor—vendee, 121–126

PRODUCTS LIABILITY, 261–338
Agricultural products, 328–335
    Express warranty, 328–335
Alcohol, 287–292

PRODUCTS LIABILITY—Cont'd
Asbestos, 271–287
Biological products; AIDS contaminated, 299–305
Bulk supplier, 305–308
Chemical products, 308–328
Comment k, 293–299
Consumer expectations test, 292, 295
Defenses to, 612–614
    Assumption of the risk, 612–614
    Contributory negligence, 612–613
Design defect, 295–297
Express warranty, 262–263, 328–335
Failure to warn, 271–279
    Adequacy, 311–312, 313
    Alcohol, 287–292
    Asbestos, 271–287
    Chemical warnings, 308–314
    Constitutional issues, 278
        Foreseeability, 273–274
    Heeding presumption, 275
    Proposed restatement, 275
    Standard of expert, 273–274, 275
    Unknown risks and state-of-the-art, 275–278
Foreseeable users and uses, 324–328
    Dismantling and recycling, 324–328
    Misuse, 328
General principles, 261–270
Implied warranty, 263–265
Insurance, 279
Learned intermediary, 295
L-tryptophan, 304–305
Medical devices TMJ implants, 305–308
Misrepresentation, 267–268
Negligence, 262
Open and obvious dangers, 288, 292
Patent danger rule, 292
Pharmaceutical products, 293–299
Proposed restatement, 298–299
Remedial measures, 279
Strict liability in tort, 265–267
    Proposed restatement, 269–270
    Restatement view, 266–267, 268
Unavoidably unsafe products, 293–299

PROSSER, WILLIAM J. & KEETON, PAGE
Abnormally dangerous activity, 96–97
Trespass, 23

PUBLIC NUISANCE
See, Damages and Compensable Interests; Private Nuisance; Statutes of Limitation
Agency, vicarious liability, 44–45
Equitable action for, 56–57
    Associational standing, 57
    Class actions, 56
    Private attorney general, 56
Negligence not necessary, 43
Preemption, 250–251
Private action for, 45–47
Public right, 39, 40–41, 44
Punitive damages for, 209–210

PUBLIC NUISANCE—Cont'd
Relation to private nuisance, 41
Special injury requirement, 45–47, 50–51
    Cheapest cost avoider, 54
    Economic loss doctrine, 47–48
    Fishermen cases, 51–52
    Physical injury as, 54–55
    Rationales for, 45
    Robins rule, 50
Statutes of limitation, 569–570
Unreasonableness of interference, 39–40
Vertical relationships, 125–126

PUNITIVE DAMAGES
See, Damages and Compensable Interests

QUALITY OF LIFE DAMAGES
See, Damages and Compensable Interests,
    Personal discomfort and annoyance

RADIOLOGICAL HAZARDS, 248–250

REGULATION
CERCLA, 475
Compliance as barring private actions, 221
Enhancing common law, 214–215
Negligence per se, 251–260
Precluding common law, 215–216
Violation, public nuisance, 40

RELEASE OF HAZARDOUS SUBSTANCE
See, Comprehensive, Environmental, Re-
    sponse, Compensation and Liability
    Act (CERCLA)

REPORTERS' STUDY (ALI)
Abnormally dangerous activity, 135–138
Fear of cancer, 203
Increased risk of disease, 181
Medical monitoring, 187–188
Proportionate compensation, 400–402
State-of-knowledge, State-of-the-art,
    135–138

**RESOURCE CONSERVATION AND RE-
COVERY ACT**
Relation to CERCLA, 476

RIBNER, SETH A.
Sudden and accidental, 558–559

RISK–UTILITY ANALYSIS
See, Balancing of Equities and Interests,
    Private nuisance

RODGERS, WILLIAM, JR.
Nuisance, 38
Permanent or continuing nuisances,
    574–575
Preemption of common law, 224–225

ROSENBERG, DAVID
Proportionality proposal, 399–400

RYLANDS V. FLETCHER
See, Abnormally Dangerous Activities

SCHWARTZ, ALLEN
Remote risks, 278

SELIKOFF, IRVING J.
Asbestos, 272

SETTLEMENTS
CERCLA, 512–518
Distribution of funds, 653
Future injuries, 650–651
Green cards, 651
Medical monitoring, 651–653
Special problems in toxics, 648–655
Strategy, 648–649
Three Mile Island, 651–652
Value protection program, 653–655

SILBERGELD, ELLEN, DR.
Animal studies, 383–384

SMOKING
    See, Environmental Tobacco Smoke
Apportionment, 425–532
Asbestos litigation, 425–432, 633

SPECIAL MASTERS, 666–667

SPERMICIDES, 369–370

STANDING
See, Private Nuisance; Public Nuisance

STATE–OF–KNOWLEDGE
Abnormally dangerous activity, 132–138
Reporters' study, 136–138

STATE–OF–THE–ART
Abnormally dangerous activity, 135–138
AIDS-contaminated blood, 302
Express warranty, 334
Nuisance, 151
Products liability, unknown risks, 275–278

STATUTES OF LIMITATION, 568–602
CERCLA-mandated, 600–602
Products and occupational, 580–602
    AIDS-related issues, 588–589
    Community knowledge, 586–587
    Date of injury, 580–581
    Discovery rule, 581–589
    Medical knowledge, 587–588
    Mere suspicion test, 584–586
    Reasonable possibility test, 584–588
Rationales for, 594
Real property, 568–580
    Abatability, 571, 576–577
    Continuing or permanent nuisance,
        568–580
    Continuing trespass, 571–572
    Discovery rule, 578–580
    Negligence, 572–574, 578–579
    Negligence per se, 572–574
    Public nuisance, 569–570
    Special statutes, 578
    Strict liability, 572–574, 578–579
Repose different, 602–604
Revival statutes, 605

STATUTES OF LIMITATION—Cont'd
Successive actions as affecting, 590–602
    Attorneys' fees, 598–599
    Claim preclusion, 596
    Collateral source rule 598
    Discovery rule, 593
    Issue preclusion, 597–598
    Rationales, 594
    Separate causes of action, 593
    Workers' compensation, 596
Wrongful death and survival, 599–600

STATUTES OF REPOSE
AIDS-contaminated blood, 304
Constitutional issues affecting, 604–605
Difference from limitations, 602–604

STATUTES OF REVIVAL, 605

STRICKLAND, N. KATHLEEN
Settlement strategy, 648–649

STRICT LIABILITY
See, Abnormally Dangerous Activity; Products Liability

SUCCESSOR LIABILITY
See, Comprehensive Environmental, Response, Compensation and Liability Act (CERCLA)

TAKE HOME TOXICS
See, Workers' Compensation and Workplace

THREE MILE ISLAND
See, Settlements

TORT LAW
    See, Economic Analysis; Private Nuisance, Corrective justice
Goals of, 4–5, 14–16
Normative theory, 10–13
Positive theory, 10–13

TOXICOLOGY
Animal studies, 350–352
    Extrapolations, 351–352
    Insufficiency to prove causation, 376–377
    LD50, 351
    Proof of causation, 383–384
    Study designs, 350–351
Toxicologic studies, 349–352
Toxicological profiles, 523
Toxicology and risk, 349

TRESPASS, 21–37
    See, Air Pollution; Damages and Compensable Interests; Statutes of Limitation
Balancing test, 34–35
Continuing, 25, 571–572
Damages, 25–26, 32–33
Extent of invasion, 23, 30–32, 34–35
Injection wells, 26–28
Intent, 21–22, 29–30, 33

TRESPASS—Cont'd
Odors, 36–37
Possessory interest, 22–23
Punitive damages, 36
Relation to nuisance, 23–24, 28

ULTRAHAZARDOUS ACTIVITY
See, Abnormally Dangerous Activity

UNDERGROUND STORAGE TANKS, 117
    See, Abnormally Dangerous Activity
Punitive damages for, 208

UNIFORM COMMERCIAL CODE
Express warranty, 330–334
Warranty liability, 262–267

VALUE PROTECTION PROGRAM
See, Settlements

VERTICAL LIABILITY
Abnormally dangerous activity, 126–131
Nuisance, 121–126

VICARIOUS LIABILITY
Abnormally dangerous activity, 119
Nuisance, public, 44

WARRANTY
Agricultural products, 328–334
Disclaimers and limitations, 264–265, 331–332
Economic loss doctrine, 335
Express warranty, products liability, 262–263
Express warranty preemption, 239–240
Failure of essential purpose, 333
Implied warranty of fitness, 263–264
Implied warranty of merchantability, 263, 331
Opinions and puffing, 332
Proper plaintiffs, 264
Unconscionability, 333

WATER POLLUTION
Federal Water Pollution Control Act, 216–219, 222–223
Interstate water pollution, 225–231
NPDES, 227

WORKERS' COMPENSATION AND WORKPLACE
Aggravation of injury exception, 456–457
Childrens' claims, 454–455
Deceit exception, 451–452
Exclusivity bar, 446–457
Employee actions for environmental tobacco smoke, 466–468
    Injunction, 466–467
    Negligence, 468
    Workers' compensation, 467–468
Fetal protection, 455–456
History, 442–443
Intentional tort exception, 446–452
    Intent standard, 449–450
    Occupational diseases, 463
    Rationales for, 447–448

References are to page numbers.

WORKERS' COMPENSATION AND WORK-PLACE—Cont'd
Issue preclusion, 443–445
Occupational Disease Acts, 457–469
    Environmental tobacco smoke, 459–463, 464–466
    Natural incident, 460–461
    Nature of employment, 460–461
    Nevada ODA, 458–462
    Ordinary diseases of life, 462–463

WORKERS' COMPENSATION AND WORK-PLACE—Cont'd
Occupational Disease Acts—Cont'd
Occupational health & safety requirements, 469–474
Spouses' claims, 453–454
Take home toxics, 456
Toxic exposures, 450–451

WRONGFUL DEATH AND SURVIVAL
Statutes of limitation, 599–600

†